R. Gupta's®

POPULAR MASTER GUIDE

HTET

HARYANA TEACHER ELIGIBILITY TEST

LEVEL–2

Trained Graduate Teacher **(TGT)**

(For Classes VI to VIII)

ENGLISH

by

RPH Editorial Board

RAMESH PUBLISHING HOUSE, NEW DELHI

Published by

O.P. Gupta *for* Ramesh Publishing House

Admin. Office

12-H, New Daryaganj Road, Opp. Officers' Mess,
New Delhi-110002 ✆ 23275224, 23245124

E-mail: info@rameshpublishinghouse.com
For Online Shopping: www.rameshpublishinghouse.com

Showroom

• Balaji Market, Nai Sarak, Delhi-110006 ✆ 23282525 📱 9354373464
• 4457, Nai Sarak, Delhi-110006

Book Code: R-1933

ISBN: 978-93-86845-61-0

Price: ₹ 490

Printed at: B.K. Offset, Delhi

CONTENTS

LANGUAGES

GENERAL STUDIES

Scheme of Exam

Level-2: Trained Graduate Teacher (TGT) English

There shall be only one paper. All questions will be Multiple Choice Questions (MCQs) each carrying one mark with four alternatives out of which one answer will be correct.

S.No.	Subjects	No. of Questions	Marks
1.	Child Development and Pedagogy	30	30
2.	**Languages** (Hindi 15 MCQs and English 15 MCQs)	30	30
3.	**General Studies** (Quantitative Aptitude 10 MCQs, Reasoning Ability 10 MCQs and Haryana G.K. and Awareness 10 MCQs)	30	30
4.	Subject Specific (English)	60	60
	Total	**150**	**150**

NATURE AND STANDARD OF QUESTIONS

- The test items on Child Development and Pedagogy will focus on educational psychology of teaching and learning, relevant to the age group of 11-16 years. They will focus on understanding the characteristics, needs and psychology of diverse learners, interaction with learners and the attributes and qualities of a good facilitator of learning.
- The test items for Languages (Hindi & English) will focus on the proficiencies related to the medium of instruction relevant to the age group of 11-16 years.
- The test items for Quantitative Aptitude, Reasoning Ability and Haryana G.K. and Awareness will focus on the elements of Mental and Reasoning ability and General Knowledge regarding Haryana State.
- The test items in subject specific will focus on the concepts, problem solving abilities and pedagogical understanding of the subjects. The test items shall be evenly distributed over different divisions of the syllabus of that subject as prescribed for classes VI-X by the Board of School Education Haryana.

NEGATIVE MARKING

- There shall be no negative marking.

LANGUAGE OF QUESTION PAPERS

- All questions except those concerning language subjects, will be bilingual *i.e.* Hindi and English.

Previous Years' Paper

Haryana Teacher Eligibility Test (HTET)

TGT English (Level-2), Exam 2024

(Exam held on 31-07-2025)

PART-I : CHILD DEVELOPMENT AND PEDAGOGY

1. The most appropriate group of qualities in reference of adolescent boys and girls is:

1. Ideal, Good adjustment, Self-respect
2. Abstract thinking, Reasoning, Decision-making
3. Observation, Feeling of revolt, Habit of repetition
4. Philosophy, Good adjustment, Feeling of social service

2. Who experimented on 'cat' with reference to trial and error theory of learning?

1. Pavlov 2. Skinner
3. Thorndike 4. Guilford

3. Heredity plays the greatest role in the:

1. Social Development 2. Spiritual Development
3. Physical Development 4. Cultural Development

4. Which of the following is **not** a projective method of personality measurement?

1. Association technique 2. Construction technique
3. Case study 4. Completion technique

5. Who was the exponent of the method of Insight learning?

1. Thorndike 2. Kohler
3. Davis 4. Skinner

6. "Learning takes place through a process of need reduction." The learning theory related to the statement is:

1. Insight theory
2. Operant conditioned theory
3. Conditioned response theory
4. Reinforcement theory

7. "Anything can be taught at any stage of development." Expressed by:

1. Ausubel 2. Bruner
3. Piaget 4. Gagne

8. Who postulated the Brain Storming Method for fostering and boosting creativity?

1. Myres 2. Torance
3. Osborn 4. Gordon

9. Plateau in the learning curve indicates:

1. Working conditions are favourable
2. No fatigue
3. Task is simple
4. Loss of interest

10. According to a traditional saying, 'when the fox could not reach the grapes despite all it's efforts, it said that the grapes are sour'. This is an example of:

1. Withdrawal 2. Rationalization
3. Projection 4. Regression

11. Conditioned Response Theory is given by:

1. Pavlov 2. Skinner
3. Thorndike 4. Kohler

12. ______ is **not** necessary for the education of visually impaired students.

1. Books in small letters
2. Audio cassette
3. Brail text material on the paper
4. Abacus for teaching of Mathematics

13. The concept of reformatory school is:

1. for mentally retarded children
2. for gifted children
3. for juvenile delinquent children
4. for normal children

14. Theory of Intelligence given by Spearman is:

1. One factor theory 2. Two factor theory
3. Three factor theory 4. Multi-factor theory

1. 2	**2.** 3	**3.** 3	**4.** 3	**5.** 2	**6.** 4	**7.** 2
8. 3	**9.** 4	**10.** 2	**11.** 1	**12.** 1	**13.** 3	**14.** 2

15. Tolman's theory is related to:
1. Energy system 2. Cathexes
3. Topology 4. Development stages

16. According to the need hierarchy theory of Maslow, basic need at bottom level's is considered:
1. Belongingness
2. Physiological Need
3. Self-Actualization
4. Security

17. Agraphia is:
1. In this the patient loses the ability to read.
2. In this the patient does not have the ability to express his thoughts in writing.
3. In this the patient does not have the ability to do simple addition and subtraction.
4. In this the patient is found to be unable to name the objects.

18. Kohler proved that learning is:
1. bonding of stimulus and responses.
2. the perception of different part of situation.
3. an autonomous random activity.
4. the whole situation perception.

19. The concept of 'emotional intelligence' was given by:
1. Dan Golman
2. Peter Salovay and John Mayer
3. Tolman
4. Terman

20. Following are the stages of Kohlberg's theory **except** ________.
1. Conventional 2. Pre-conventional
3. Sensori Motor 4. Post-conventional

21. "The development of child starts from the head and moves towards the feet." The given statement is related to which theory of development?
1. Principle of Development Direction
2. Principle of Development Sequence
3. Principle of Continuous Development
4. Principle of Interrelation

22. Which is **not** an appropriate statement regarding learning?
1. Learning is universal process.
2. Learning is not the change in behaviour.
3. Learning helps in adjustment.
4. Learning is transferable from one situation to another.

23. Teacher needs to create an inclusive environment in the classroom:
1. special children should be kept away from educational activities.
2. the rights and dignity of special children should be protected.
3. special children should be considered as inferior to normal children.
4. special children should be looked down upon among normal students.

24. According to Piaget, concrete operational stage is:
1. 0 to 2 years 2. 7 to 11 years
3. 11 to 12 years 4. above 12 years

25. In continuous and comprehensive evaluation, 'comprehensive' means:
1. by evaluation of all subjects
2. by evaluation of only educational field
3. by homework evaluation
4. by evaluating the development of educational and co-educational field

26. "You can make a student to sit in the class but can't force him to acquire knowledge." This statement is confirmed by which law of learning?
1. by the law of Readiness
2. by the law of Exercise
3. by the law of Disuse
4. by the law of Effect

27. Which out of the following is the process of arousing, sustaining and regulating activity?
1. Interest 2. Opinion
3. Attitude 4. Motivation

28. In which of the following, instinct does **not** match with related emotion?
1. Laughter – Amusement
2. Self-Abasement – Feeling of superiority
3. Gregariousness – Feeling of loneliness
4. Repulsion – Disgust

29. In the following who is related to modeling concept?
1. Sigmund Freud 2. Thorndike
3. Albert Bandura 4. Guilford

30. The mental age of a 6 (six) years old girl is 7.5 (seven years six months) years, her I.Q. will be:
1. 125 2. 90
3. 75 4. 140

15. 3	**16.** 2	**17.** 2	**18.** 4	**19.** 2	**20.** 3	**21.** 1	**22.** 2
23. 2	**24.** 2	**25.** 4	**26.** 1	**27.** 4	**28.** 2	**29.** 3	**30.** 1

PART-II : भाषा – हिन्दी

31. तत्सम-तद्भव शब्दों के संदर्भ में अनुपयुक्त विकल्प चुनिए :
1. गर्त - गड्ढा 2. जृम्भिका - जवाँई
3. चर्मचटक - चमगादड़ 4. परिकूट परकोटा

32. निम्न में से 'शिक्षण-सूत्र' **नहीं** है :
1. पूर्ण से अंश की ओर 2. प्रेरणा से तर्क की ओर
3. स्थूल से सूक्ष्म की ओर 4. उपर्युक्त सभी

33. निम्न में से **असंगत** को चुनिए :
1. अं, अः – अयोगवाह ध्वनियाँ
2. ड़, ढ़ – उत्क्षिप्त ध्वनियाँ
3. श, ष, स – स्पर्श संघर्षी
4. ऐ, औ – अर्ध संवृत

34. निम्न में से प्रक्षेपित शिक्षण सहायक सामग्री **नहीं** है :
1. दूरदर्शन 2. फिल्म स्ट्रीप
3. ओवरहेड प्रोजेक्टर 4. फिल्म

35. समस्तपद एवं समास विग्रह की दृष्टि से **असंगत** विकल्प चुनिए:
1. लोकप्रिय - अधिकरण तत्पुरुष
2. पवन से चलने वाली चक्की - पनचक्की
3. नवयुवक - नव है जो युवक
4. परीक्षाभवन - परीक्षा के लिए भवन

36. किस विकल्प में विलोम-युग्म सही **नहीं** है?
1. वैमनस्य - सौमनस्य 2. अभिमानी - निरभिमानी
3. अभ्यर्थी - प्रत्यर्थी 4. स्वार्थी - निस्स्वार्थ

37. प्रत्यय की दृष्टि से **असंगत** विकल्प चुनिए :
1. ई - द्रौपदी, जानकी, वाल्मीकि
2. य - माहात्म्य, वैधव्य, पौलस्त्य
3. तर - महत्तर, वृहत्तर, दृढ़तर
4. एय - भागिनेय, पाथेय, वैनतेय

38. 'पर्यायवाची' की दृष्टि से **असुमेलित** को चुनिए:
1. तरंग - ऊर्मि, वीचि, कल्लोल
2. तरणि - नौका, द्रोणी, करवाल
3. तोता - रक्ततुंड, कीर, सुग्गा
4. योनि - अपत्यपथ, जन्मवर्त्म, रतिकुहर

39. **असंगत** विकल्प चुनिए :
1. समुद्र में लगने वाली आग - दावानल
2. लोक-प्रचलित बात, जिसके वक्ता का पता न हो - किंवदन्ती
3. पशुओं द्वारा जुगाली करने की प्रक्रिया - पागुर
4. जिसके पति ने दूसरा विवाह कर लिया हो - अध्यूढा

40. किस शब्द में 'कु' उपसर्ग का प्रयोग **नहीं** हुआ है
1. कुज 2. कुमार 3. कुचो 4. कुमति

41. समश्रुत भिन्नार्थक शब्द 'मनुजात - मनुजाद' का क्रमशः **सही** अर्थ चुनिए:
1. मनुष्य को खाने वाला, मनुष्य से पैदा हुआ
2. मनु उत्पन्न हुआ, अफ्रीकी निवासी
3. मनु उत्पन्न, मनुष्य को खाने वाला
4. मनुज का पुत्र, मनुज से संबंध रखने वाला

42. यण् संधि दृष्टि से **संगत** विकल्प चुनिए :
1. जात्यर्मान = जाती + अभिमान
2. पर्युषण = परि + ऊषण
3. वध्विच्छा = वधु + इच्छा
4. महैन्द्रजालिक = महा + ऐन्द्रजालिक

निर्देश (प्र.सं. 43 से 45 तक): *अधोलिखित गद्यांश को पढ़कर उत्तर दीजिए :*

हमें इस बात को समझना होगा कि युद्ध की अनुपस्थिति ही शांति की परिभाषा नहीं है। बुद्ध ने जिस शांतिपूर्ण समाज की परिकल्पना की थी, उसमें समानता का वह संदेश भी शामिल था, जो हमें इस बात का अहसास कराता है कि मनुष्य को मनुष्य से पृथक् दिखाने का हर प्रयास मनुष्यता का शत्रु है। ऐसे प्रत्येक प्रयास को विफल बनाना मनुष्योचित है, एक शर्त भी है मनुष्य के रूप में जीने की। हमारी चिंता यह होनी चाहिए कि हमें स्वयं को मनुष्य कैसे बनाएँ एवं कैसे मनुष्य बनाए रखें। मनुष्य बनने का अर्थ है - अपने भीतर दूसरे की पीड़ा को समझने का अहसास जगाना, अपने भीतर करुणा का वह भाव जगाना, जो हमें दूसरे से जोड़ता है। छोटे-छोटे पुल बनाने होंगे हमें दूसरे से जुड़ने के लिए—करुणा का पुल, मैत्री का पुल, समानता का पुल, विषमता मिटाने वाला पुल ____। ऐसा समझकर ही हम मानवोचित आचरण का मंत्र अपना सकते हैं, प्रबुद्ध बन सकते हैं।

43. लेखक के अनुसार शांति की परिभाषा **नहीं** है :
1. युद्ध की अनुपस्थिति।
2. शांतिपूर्ण समाज की परिकल्पना।
3. जिसमें समानता का संदेश सम्मिलित हो।
4. स्वयं को मनुष्य बनाना।

44. लेखक के अनुसार मनुष्य बनने का क्या अर्थ है?
1. बुद्धोपदिष्ट राह का अनुगामी।
2. मनुष्य को मनुष्य से पृथक दिखाना।
3. दूसरे की पीड़ा को समझने का भाव जगाना।
4. प्रबुद्ध मानवोचित आचरण।

45. गद्यांश में प्रयुक्त पदों की व्याकरणिक विवेचना के संदर्भ में **असंगत** कथन चुनिए।
1. अनुपस्थिति - दो उपसर्ग 2. मनुष्यता - जातिवाचक संज्ञा
3. प्रत्येक - अव्ययीभाव समास 4. विषमता - व्यंजन संधि

31. 2	**32.** 2	**33.** 4	**34.** 1	**35.** 2	**36.** 3	**37.** 1	**38.** 2
39. 1	**40.** 2	**41.** 3	**42.** 2	**43.** 1	**44.** 3	**45.** 4	

PART-II : LANGUAGE – ENGLISH

46. Fill in the blank with the **correct** option:
Stress, intonation and rhythm can be taught through _______.
1. skimming 2. scanning
3. drills of various types 4. transcription

47. Which one of the following is **not** a teaching aid in developing listening skills?
1. Use of phonetic dictionary
2. Gramophones
3. Television
4. Film & film strips

48. Fill in the blank with the **correct** option:
Multimedia materials for teaching _______ are.
1. LSRW lesson
2. grammar, syntax and lexicon
3. text, image, audio, video and animation
4. phonetic, phonemic lessons

49. Complete the sentence with the **correct** option:
Multilinguistic resource _______.
1. will increase the level of learner participation
2. will decrease the level of learner participation
3. is poor compared to any standardized text-book
4. deprives the teacher's role as a facilitator

Directions (Qs. No. 50 to 59): *Read the following passage and answer the questions that follow:*

I worked for a brief while in a college in Delhi, and among my more uncomfortable memories is a language exercise, I gave a group of eight undergraduates: I asked them to imagine that they had already graduated and wanted them to write an application for a suitable job. Seven of the eight students wrote applications for the jobs of clerks. Even in one of the good universities, and in a college that had a reputation for it academic standard, the system has snuffed out all youthful ambition.

Even the highest youthful ambition in the prestigious colleges is to pass the competitive examination for appointments in the administrative services, and there are colleges that are more proud of the bureaucrats among their alumni than of any scholars, scientists or leaders of opinion. And these latter, understandably, are a small number. Students derive the meanness of their ambitions from the meanness of the goals that the colleges propose to themselves. And of the most ambitious, as well as of the least, among the students, it could be said that they think more of what society will do to or for them, than of what they would be able to do for and to society. This is an excellent apprenticeship for joining the ranks of hirelings or of the unemployed.

50. How long did the author work in a Delhi College?
1. long time 2. short time
3. three years 4. seven years

51. What exercise did the author give the students?
1. a comprehension passage
2. precis writing
3. expansion of a poem
4. a language exercise

52. Seven out of the eight students wanted to become _______.
1. scholars 2. bureaucrats
3. clerks 4. scientists

53. What according to the author is the highest ambition of students in good colleges?
1. to qualify for administrative services
2. to become leaders of opinion
3. to teach
4. to practice medicine

54. In the sentence "And these latter understandably are a small number", what does "these latter" refer to?
1. clerks, doctors & engineers
2. bureaucrats, scholars and clerks
3. scholars, scientists and leaders of opinion
4. only administrators

55. Fill in the blank with the **correct** option:
The thinking of the most ambitious and the least ambitious is _______.
1. uncommon 2. alike
3. dissimilar 4. for the society

56. Identify the statement which is **true**:
1. The college where the author worked in Delhi had a reputation for its academic standards.
2. The students, who were asked to do the language exercise were graduates.
3. All colleges produce scientists, scholars and leaders of opinion.
4. The language exercise is stored in the author's less comfortable memories.

46. 3	**47.** 1	**48.** 3	**49.** 1	**50.** 2	**51.** 4
52. 3	**53.** 1	**54.** 3	**55.** 2	**56.** 1	

57. Fill in the blank with the **correct** option:
Another word for "snuffed out" is ______.
1. smelled
2. instilled
3. encouraged
4. killed

58. Choose the opposite of "former" from the passage:
1. least 2. latter
3. already 4. most

59. Fill in the blank with the **correct** option:
"Alumni" in the passage means ______.
1. unsuccessful students 2. successful students
3. bureaucrats 4. old students

60. Which one of the following is the first step in teaching formal grammar?
1. comparison & generalization
2. collection and presentation of examples
3. application of rules
4. motivation and testing of previous knowledge

PART-III : GENERAL STUDIES

Quantitative Aptitude, Reasoning Ability and GK & Awareness

61. The square root of $\dfrac{\left(1\frac{3}{4}\right)^4-\left(2\frac{1}{3}\right)^4}{\left(1\frac{3}{4}\right)^2-\left(2\frac{1}{3}\right)^2}$ is equal to:
1. $2\frac{11}{12}$ 2. $2\frac{1}{12}$
3. $3\frac{11}{12}$ 4. $3\frac{1}{12}$

62. X can do a work in 6 days and Y can do same work in 8 days. With the help of Z, all three finished the work in 3 days. If they altogether got ₹ 2000 after completing the work, then Z gets:
1. ₹ 200 2. ₹ 250
3. ₹ 400 4. ₹ 500

63. Find the **odd** one:
1. Rectangle 2. Square
3. Cube 4. Triangle

64. By selling an item for ₹ 153, a man gets loss of 10%. For how much should he sell them to get profit of 20%?
1. ₹ 204 2. ₹ 214
3. ₹ 220 4. ₹ 170

65. A, B, C, D and E are sitting around a circular table facing the centre. Only A is between E and B. D is to the immediate left of B. Who is to the immediate left of C?
1. E 2. D
3. B 4. A

66. Shekhar walks 10 metres towards North. Then he walks 6 metres towards South. Then he walks 3 metres towards East. How far is he from his starting point?
1. 7 metres 2. 6 metres
3. 5 metres 4. 4 metres

67. Next term of the following number series will be:
5, 6, 9, 15, 25, ?
1. 35 2. 377
3. 40 4. 411

68. If the letters in the word CYBERNETICS are rearranged in the alphabetical order, which letter will be in the middle in order after rearrangement?
1. E 2. I 3. N 4. R

69. P is Q's sister. R is Q's mother. S is R's father. T is S's mother. How is P related to S?
1. Daughter 2. Sister
3. Grandmother 4. Granddaughter

70. If ZIP = 300 and ZAN = 400, then ZOO = ?
1. 250 2. 350 3. 200 4. 500

71. Find the missing term in the following letter series:
AYD, BVF, DRH, ?, KGL
1. FMJ 2. GMJ
3. GNJ 4. FNK

72. Sachin is shorter than Kamal, but taller than Ram. Mohan is the tallest. Arun is a little shorter than Kamal and a little taller than Sachin. Who is the second tallest among these five persons?
1. Sachin 2. Arun
3. Ram 4. Kamal

57. 4	**58.** 2	**59.** 4	**60.** 4	**61.** 1	**62.** 2	**63.** 3	**64.** 1
65. 1	**66.** 3	**67.** 3	**68.** 2	**69.** 4	**70.** 1	**71.** 2	**72.** 4

73. The diameter of a sphere whose volume is $113\frac{1}{7}$ cubic metres is:

1. 3 metres 2. 6 metres
3. 7 metres 4. 14 metres

74. If the diameter of a right circular cylinder is 28 cm and its height is 20 cm, then the total surface area is equal to:

1. 1760 cm^2 2. 1232 cm^2
3. 1496 cm^2 4. 2992 cm^2

75. The perimeter of the rhombus is 52 cm. If one of the diagonal is 24 cm, the area of the rhombus is equal to:

1. 240 cm^2 2. 120 cm^2
3. 180 cm^2 4. 90 cm^2

76. The radius and the height of right circular cone are in the ratio 5 : 12. If its volume is 314 $metre^3$, the diameter of its base is equal to ($\pi = 3.14$):

1. 10 metres 2. 5 metres
3. 20 metres 4. 15 metres

77. The value of $\sec(90°-A) - \cot A\cos(90°-A)\tan(90°-A)$ is:

1. tan A 2. cot A
3. cos A 4. sin A

78. If the height of a tower is $2\sqrt{3}$ metres and the length of its shadow is 2 metres, then the angle of elevation of sun is equal to:

1. 30° 2. 45°
3. 60° 4. 75°

79. The least number of complete years, in which a sum of money put at 20% compound interest will be more than doubled, is:

1. 2 2. 3
3. 4 4. 5

80. How many numbers from 11 to 50 are there which are exactly divisible by 7 but not by 3?

1. 3 2. 4
3. 5 4. 7

81. Who among the following received Arjuna Award of 2023?

1. Diksha Dagar 2. Vinesh Phogat
3. Babita Kumari 4. Reetika Hooda

82. Which of the following Wild Life Sanctuary is located in Panchkula?

1. Chhilchhila Sanctuary
2. Bir Shikargarh Sanctuary
3. Nahar Sanctuary
4. Kaparwas Sanctuary

83. Which of the following districts does **not** come under the Shivalik Development Agency?

1. Ambala 2. Panchkula
3. Yamuna Nagar 4. Kurukshetra

84. Per capita income of Haryana during 2023-24 on constant prices is:

1. ₹ 3,25,759 2. ₹ 1,85,490
3. ₹ 1,63,285 4. ₹ 1,04,550

85. The Chief Justice of Punjab and Haryana High Court is:

1. Justice Sheel Nagu 2. Justice Ravishankar Jha
3. Justice Ritu Bahri 4. Justice Krishna Murari

86. Identify the composition of Haryana Public Service Commission:

1. Chairman and four members
2. Chairman and three members
3. Chairman and five members
4. Chairman and six members

87. Read the following statements about Bhadanakas:
(*a*) During 12th century they were ruling over the area of Gurugram & Rewari
(*b*) They defeated Chauhan ruler Prithviraj-III.
Choose the **correct** code:

1. Only statement (*a*) is true.
2. Only statement (*b*) is true.
3. Neither statement (*a*) nor statement (*b*) is true.
4. Both the statements are true.

88. As per Mahabharata, who among the following led an expedition to Rohtak?

1. Bhishma 2. Arjuna
3. Bhim 4. Nakul

89. Which district of Haryana shares its boundaries with Seven districts of Haryana?

1. Ambala 2. Panchkula
3. Kurukshetra 4. Jind

90. The Sikh Chieftain of Ladawa who fought against British during the First-Anglo-Maratha war:

1. Gurdit Singh 2. Lal Singh
3. Bhoj Singh 4. Manohar Singh

73. 2	**74.** 4	**75.** 2	**76.** 1	**77.** 4	**78.** 3	**79.** 3	**80.** 2	**81.** 1
82. 2	**83.** 4	**84.** 2	**85.** 1	**86.** 3	**87.** 1	**88.** 4	**89.** 4	**90.** 1

PART-IV : SUBJECT KNOWLEDGE—ENGLISH

91. When is beauty heard according to the poem "Beauty" by Shure?

1. in the sunlight
2. in the farms
3. in the night
4. in trees & birds

92. Choose the **correct** option to fill in the blank:

I .... a letter to him yesterday.

1. wrote
2. have written
3. have been writing
4. had wrote

93. Choose the **correct** option to fill in the blank:

To blow one's own trumpet means ....

1. to make music
2. to reveal something
3. speak aloud
4. to boast

94. Fill in the blank with the **correct** option:

In the sentence "This is his book."

"his" is a/an ....

1. pronoun
2. noun
3. adjective
4. adverb

95. Fill in the blank with the **correct** option:

Please write .... ink. Don't use a pencil.

1. in
2. by
3. with
4. on

96. Fill in the blank with the **correct** option:

Gessler died of ....

1. starvation
2. sorrow
3. shocked at his brother's death
4. the new shopkeeper's cruelty

97. In the fight between the snake and the mongoose which of these hurled themselves at the cobra?

1. the crow and the myna
2. the squirrel
3. only the crow
4. only the myna

98. Who is Kalua in the story "Chandni"?

1. another name for Chandni
2. Chandni's sister
3. the wolf's name
4. name of the wise old bard

99. Fill in the blank with the **correct** option:

She is .... than stupid.

1. lazier
2. more lazier
3. lazy
4. more lazy

100. Which of the following is a collective noun?

1. women
2. parliament
3. childhood
4. hatred

Directions (Qs. No. 101-105): *Read the following passage and answer the questions that follow.*

Let me turn to a brief discussion on some basic aspects of the philosophy of non-violence.

First, it must be emphasized that non-violent resistance is not a method for cowards; it does resist. If one uses this method because he is afraid or merely because he lacks the instruments of violence, he is not truly non-violent. This is why Gandhi often said that if cowardice is the only alternative to violence, it is better to fight. He made this statement conscious of the fact that there is always another alternative : no individual or group need submit to any wrong, nor need they use violence to right the wrong; there is the way of non-violent resistance. This is ultimately the way of the strong man. The mathod is passive physically, but strongly active spiritually. It is not passive non-resistance to evil, it is active non-violent resistance to evil.

A second basic fact that characterizes non-violence is that it does not seek to defeat or humiliate the opponent, but to win his friendship and understanding. The non-violent resister must often express his protest through non-cooperation or boycotts, but he realizes that these are not ends themselves; they are merely means to awaken a sense of moral shame in the opponent. The end is redemption and reconciliation.

101. Which one of the following is **correct** according to your reading of the passage?

1. The non-violent resistance is not a method for the brave.
2. It is better to fight rather than being non-violent.
3. The discussion in the passage is about the socio-psycho aspects of violence.
4. Cowards cannot go for non-violent resistance.

91. 3	**92.** 1	**93.** 4	**94.** 3	**95.** 1	**96.** 1
97. 1	**98.** 2	**99.** 4	**100.** 2	**101.** 4	

102. Fill in the blank with the **correct** option:

According to the passage, the non-violent method is ....

1. active violent fight against evil.
2. passive brutal fight against evil.
3. passive physically but active spiritually.
4. passive non-resistance to evil.

103. Which one of the following is a characteristic of non-violence?

1. it aims to defeat and insult the opponent.
2. it seeks to win over the opponent's friendship and understanding.
3. it doesn't seek to redeem or reconcile.
4. rejection of boycotts and non-cooperation.

104. Find the word from the passage which means "lower the self-dignity or self-respect of":

1. humiliate 2. defeat
3. moral shame 4. reconciliation

105. Pick the word from the passage which means "goals or desired results":

1. aspects 2. ends
3. protests 4. means

106. Why did the king send messengers throughout the kingdom in the story "Three Questions"?

1. to look for the wise hermit.
2. to fetch wise men
3. to announce a reward for anyone who would answer the questions
4. to catch the bearded man

107. Which are the old methods of teaching English?

1. the bilingual method.
2. the substitution table method.
3. Dr. West's new method.
4. translation-cum-grammar and direct method.

108. Who was in charge of all deserts?

1. The Camel 2. Man
3. The Djinn 4. The horse and the dog

109. Fill in the blank with the **correct** option:

The unhappy school boy compares himself to the ....

1. caged bird & the withered plant
2. singing skylarks
3. summer fruits
4. huntsman

110. Fill in the blank with the **correct** option:

In the sentence "She gave him a present," 'him' is the:

1. direct object 2. indirect object
3. subject 4. predicate

111. Which plan succeed in spite of a final problem in "Dad and the Cat and the Tree"?

1. Plan B 2. Plan A
3. Plan D 4. Plan C

112. Which one of the following is **true** of the Translation-cum-grammar method?

1. It lacks conversation practice.
2. Comprehension is not easily tested.
3. Grammar is ignored.
4. Students' vocabulary remains limited.

113. How much time does the elephant take to learn the master call?

1. one year 2. a few hours
3. five years 4. a day

114. Choose the option that can meaningfully replace, the underlined part of the sentence:

The firemen <u>extinguished</u> the fire.

1. put down 2. put out
3. put off 4. put on

115. To whom did Algu sell his bullock?

1. Jumman 2. Samjhu Sahu
3. Jumman's aunt 4. No one

116. Identify the sentence which contains a *gerund*:

1. He is fond of riding.
2. Riding along the road, he fell down.
3. He rode a horse.
4. She wanted to ride a horse.

117. Which one of the following sentences has a noun clause?

1. Wait, until I come.
2. Where the piper went the children followed.
3. The pen that I bought is lost.
4. Where he lives is not known to anyone.

118. Fill in the blank with the **correct** option:

In the sentence "We had a lovely time with them," "lovely" is a/an ....

1. adverb 2. verb
3. adjective 4. participle

102. 3	**103.** 2	**104.** 1	**105.** 2	**106.** 3	**107.** 4	**108.** 3	**109.** 1	**110.** 2
111. 4	**112.** 1	**113.** 3	**114.** 2	**115.** 2	**116.** 1	**117.** 4	**118.** 3	

119. Fill in the blank with the **correct** option:

The shepherd hadn't been to school because ....

1. he wasn't interested in studies
2. he couldn't afford the fees
3. no school would admit him
4. there were few schools in those days

120. Which one of the following sentences has the given pattern?

Subject + Verb + Subject Complement

1. I know his address.
2. She wants to go.
3. This is a pen.
4. The bell has rung.

121. Fill in the blank with the **correct** option:

When she heard the little orphan crying .... mother in her was roused.

1. a 2. an
3. zero article 4. the

122. What happened to Jody's father?

1. he was attacked by a doe
2. he was bitten by a rattlesnake
3. he was stung by bees
4. he was dying

123. Who is the father of rays in "A Pact with the Sun"?

1. cloud 2. the Sun
3. light 4. the earth

124. Which one of the following is the **correct** transcription of the word "record" as a noun?

1. /rikɔ:d/ 2. /rekɔ:d/
3. /rikɔ:rd/ 4. /rə:kDd/

125. Identify the **correct** sentence out of the following:

1. He had scarcely reached the station than it began to rain.
2. He not only visited Mumbai, but also Pune.
3. Neither he is a rogue nor a mad man.
4. No sooner did the bell ring than the boys rushed out of their class.

126. Choose the option that **correctly** expresses the concept stated in the brackets:

She .... sit for hours in the garden and knit. (past habit)

1. would 2. might
3. dare 4. ought to

127. Choose the **correct** passive of the given sentence from the options that follow:

The mason is building the wall.

1. The wall is built by the mason.
2. The wall was being built by the mason.
3. The wall is being built by the mason.
4. The wall has been built by the mason.

128. Substitute the underlined part of the sentence with the **correct** option:

There was <u>hardly any</u> food in the house.

1. little 2. a little
3. the little 4. few

129. Who is the poet of "The Rebel"?

1. John Galsworthy 2. Mildred Armstrong
3. D.J. Enright 4. Shirley Bauer

130. Choose the option that **correctly** expresses the concept stated in the brackets:

It .... rain tomorrow. (possibility)

1. must 2. should
3. may 4. shall

131. Which one of the following **false**?

1. content words are nouns and pronouns.
2. form words are conjunctions and prepositions.
3. content words are not structural words.
4. form words are not structural or functional words.

132. What jobs did Macpherson and Wolf have when they were not soldiers?

1. Macpherson was a cello player, Wolf, a teacher.
2. Wolf was a Football coach and Macpherson a Cricket trainer.
3. Both of them were unemployed.
4. Macpherson was a school teacher, Wolf a cello player.

133. Match the following correctly.

A. Communicative approach	(*i*) Gradation of structure
B. Structural approach	(*ii*) Language item and real situation
C. Situational approach	(*iii*) C.J. Dodson
D. Bilingual method	(*iv*) Less stress on grammar

The correct answer is:

1. A-(*i*), B-(*ii*), C-(*iii*), D-(*iv*)
2. A-(*ii*), B-(*i*), C-(*iv*), D-(*iii*)
3. A-(*iv*), B-(*i*), C-(*ii*), D-(*iii*)
4. A-(*iii*), B-(*iv*), C-(*i*), D-(*ii*)

119. 4	**120.** 3	**121.** 4	**122.** 2	**123.** 2	**124.** 2	**125.** 4	**126.** 1
127. 3	**128.** 1	**129.** 3	**130.** 3	**131.** 4	**132.** 4	**133.** 3	

134. Choose the **correct** option:

"They give it its body and swing

And everyone today is longing to hear

Some fresh and beautiful thing."

The above lines occur in:

1. The Wonderful Words
2. Vocation
3. A House, A Home
4. Beauty

135. Choose the **correct** *assertive form* of the following sentence from the options given:

Shall I ever forget those happy days?

1. I shall not never forget those happy days.
2. I shall never forget those happy days.
3. I should never ever forget those happy days.
4. I can never forget those happy days.

136. Who adopted the substitution table method?

1. Dr. West 2. D.J. Dodson
3. H.E. Palmer 4. Piaget

137. The dog in search of a new master found the masters in which order?

1. bear, wolf, lion, man.
2. man, lion, bear, wolf.
3. wolf, lion, bear, man.
4. wolf, bear, lion, man.

138. Which one of the following is a fable?

1. On the grasshopper and the Cricket
2. The Ant and the Cricket
3. This is Jody's fawn
4. Children at work

139. Which one of the following is **false**?

1. Velu ran away from home to escape his father's beating.
2. The girl Velu met was a ragpicker.
3. Her name was Jaya.
4. Jam Bazaar Jaggi, never bought any thing from the ragpickers.

140. Who sings the songs that symbolise the poetry of the earth?

1. the grasshopper & the cricket
2. the birds
3. the frost
4. only the grasshopper

Directions (Qs. No. 141-150): *Read the following poem and answer the questions that follow.*

Love came to Flora asking for a flower
That would of flowers be undisputed queen,
The lily and the rose, long, long had been
Rivals for that high honour, Bards of power
Had sung their claims, "The rose can never tower
Like the pale lily with her Juno Mien"—
"But is the lily lovelier?" Thus between
Flower factions rang the strile in Psyche's bower.
Give me a flower delicious as the rose
And stately as the lily in her pride"—
"But of what colour?"—"Rose-red", Love first chose.
Then prayed,—"No, lily-white, – or, both provide:"
And Flora gave the lotus, "rose-red" dyed.
And "lily-white",–the queenliest flower that blows.

141. Who came to Flora for choosing the queen of flowers?

1. The Rose 2. Love
3. The Lily 4. The Bards

142. Who were the rivals for the queenship?

1. The rose and the lily
2. The flower factions
3. Juno and Psyche
4. The lotus and the lily

143. Fill in the blank with the **correct** option:

The beauty and stateliness of the lily is similar to that of ……….. .

1. The Rose 2. Flora
3. Juno 4. Lotus

144. "But of what colour?" These lines are spoken by:

1. The Bards to Love
2. Love to Flora
3. Rose to Lily
4. Flora to Love

145. What kind of flower did Love want?

It wanted a flower ……………

1. red as a rose
2. white as a lily
3. red as a rose and white as a lily
4. delicious as a rose

134. 1	**135.** 2	**136.** 3	**137.** 4	**138.** 2	**139.** 4
140. 1	**141.** 2	**142.** 1	**143.** 3	**144.** 4	**145.** 3

146. Pick a word from the poem which means "poets"?
1. Bards 2. Juno
3. Psyche 4. None of these

147. Fill in the blank with the **correct** option:
"The lily and the rose long, long had been". This line is an example of ....
1. simile 2. metaphor
3. oxymoron 4. alliteration

148. Which word in the poem is closest in meaning to the word "conflict"?
1. rivals 2. strife
3. undisputed 4. claims

149. Fill in the blank with the **correct** option:
"delicious as the rose/And stately as the lily" is an example of ....
1. simile 2. metaphor
3. hyperbole 4. onomatopoeia

150. Choose the **correct** option:
A. "Rose-red"
B. "No, lily white,–"
C. "Or, both provide"
1. A is spoken by Love; B, C by Flora
2. B is spoken by Love, A, by Flora C by the Bards
3. A, B, C are all spoken by Love
4. A, B, C are all spoken by Flora

EXPLANATORY ANSWERS

1. During adolescence, the cognitive abilities of boys and girls develop rapidly. They begin to move beyond concrete experiences to develop abstract thinking. They use reasoning to analyze situations and gradually acquire the ability of independent decision-making. These qualities are considered most appropriate for this stage.

2. Edward Lee Thorndike conducted experiments on cats and propounded the "Trial and Error Learning Theory". In his puzzle-box experiments, he showed how the cat, after several trials and errors, learned the correct way to escape, establishing the basis of trial-and-error learning.

3. Heredity plays its greatest role in physical development. Traits such as height, weight, body structure, complexion, and other physical characteristics are largely determined by genetic factors. While environment influences social or cultural development, heredity is dominant in shaping physical growth.

4. Projective methods of personality assessment include Association techniques, Construction techniques, and Completion techniques, as they reveal unconscious aspects of personality. The Case study method, however, is a descriptive and observational method, not a projective one. Hence, this option is correct.

5. German psychologist Wolfgang Köhler was the exponent of the theory of Insight Learning. Through experiments on chimpanzees, he demonstrated that animals often solve problems suddenly by perceiving the relationships among elements in a situation, leading to the so-called "Aha experience". This approach was different from Thorndike's trial-and-error learning.

6. The statement "Learning takes place through a process of need reduction" relates to reinforcement theory. According to this view, learning occurs when a response reduces a need or drive, such as hunger or thirst. The reduction of need works as reinforcement, strengthening the behaviour and making it more likely to occur again.

7. Jerome Bruner emphasized that "anything can be taught at any stage of development, provided it is presented in an intellectually honest form". He advocated the spiral curriculum, where complex ideas can be introduced at a simple level and revisited at more advanced levels as the learner develops.

8. Alex Osborn, an advertising executive, postulated the brainstorming method as a group creativity technique. It encourages generating a large number of ideas without immediate criticism, thus fostering originality and boosting creative thinking.

9. A plateau in the learning curve indicates that progress in learning has temporarily stopped. This often happens due to loss of interest, mental fatigue, or lack of motivation, even though the learner may have the ability to progress further with renewed effort.

10. The saying about the fox and the grapes (from Aesop's fable) is an example of rationalization, a defense mechanism where an individual justifies failure or inability by giving acceptable but false reasons. The fox, unable to get the grapes, rationalized the situation by claiming the grapes were sour.

11. The Conditioned Response Theory was given by Ivan Pavlov. Through his classical conditioning experiments with dogs, Pavlov demonstrated how a neutral stimulus (like a bell) could become associated with an unconditioned stimulus (food) to produce a conditioned response (salivation).

12. For the education of visually impaired students, small-letter books are not useful. Instead, aids such as audio cassettes, Braille text material, and mathematical tools like the abacus are essential for effective learning.

146. 1	**147.** 4	**148.** 2	**149.** 1	**150.** 3

13. Reformatory schools are specially designed for juvenile delinquents, i.e., children who are involved in crimes or socially unacceptable behaviour. These schools focus on rehabilitation, moral development, and social adjustment.

14. Charles Spearman gave the Two-Factor Theory of Intelligence. According to him, intelligence is based on a general factor (g) that influences overall mental performance and specific factors (s) related to particular abilities or tasks.

15. Edward Tolman's theory, known as purposive behaviorism, emphasized that learning is purposeful and goal-directed. He is most famously associated with the concept of cognitive maps, where rats in mazes learned to form spatial representations of their environment. This idea links his work to **topology**, i.e., the mapping of paths, routes, and spatial relations.

At the same time, Tolman also described six types of learning, one of which was **cathexis**, the learned tendency to connect specific objects with the satisfaction (or frustration) of a drive. For example, a hungry rat developing a preference for a path leading to food (positive cathexis) or avoiding a path linked to shock (negative cathexis).

Thus, while his broader system included cathexis, equivalence beliefs, field expectancies, and others, the most widely recognized and exam-relevant link is with **topology** because of his cognitive map experiments.

16. In Maslow's hierarchy of needs, the most basic level is physiological needs. These include food, water, air, shelter, sleep, and other essentials for survival. Only when these are fulfilled can individuals move upward to higher needs like safety, belongingness, esteem, and finally self-actualization.

17. Agraphia is a neurological disorder where an individual loses the ability to write, despite having intact motor skills and understanding. It is usually caused by damage to specific areas of the brain such as the left parietal lobe.

18. Kohler, in his experiments with chimpanzees, showed that learning occurs through sudden insight, not mere trial-and-error. He emphasized perceiving the entire situation as a whole, leading to the sudden "Aha" moment of problem-solving.

19. The concept of emotional intelligence was first introduced by Peter Salovey and John Mayer in 1990, describing the ability to understand and manage one's own emotions as well as those of others. Daniel Goleman later popularized the term through his book in 1995, but he was not the originator.

20. Kohlberg's theory of moral development has three main levels—pre-conventional, conventional, and post-conventional—each with two stages. The *sensorimotor stage*, however, is part of Piaget's cognitive development theory, not Kohlberg's moral theory.

21. The statement "the development of a child starts from the head and moves towards the feet" explains the *cephalocaudal principle*, which is part of the principle of development direction. It shows that growth and motor control first appear in the head region and then progress downward to the arms, trunk, and legs.

22. This is not an appropriate statement. Learning is in fact defined as a relatively permanent change in behaviour or knowledge resulting from experience and practice. The other statements—universality of learning, its role in adjustment, and transferability—are correct features of learning.

23. An inclusive classroom ensures that children with special needs are given equal opportunities, respect, and dignity. They should participate in educational activities with others, without being treated as inferior or separated from normal students.

24. According to Jean Piaget's stages of cognitive development, the *concrete operational stage* spans from 7 to 11 years. During this stage, children develop logical thinking, understand concepts of conservation, and can classify and organize objects, though abstract reasoning is still limited.

25. In Continuous and Comprehensive Evaluation (CCE), "comprehensive" refers to assessing both scholastic (educational/academic) and co-scholastic (non-academic such as attitudes, values, life skills, arts, sports) aspects of development to ensure holistic evaluation of a child's progress.

26. Thorndike's law of readiness states that learning becomes effective only when a learner is mentally and physically ready to learn. The statement that one can make a student sit in the class but not force knowledge into him reflects this law—unless the child is prepared, real learning cannot take place.

27. Motivation is the process of arousing, sustaining, and regulating activity. It energizes behaviour, directs it toward a goal, and maintains it until the goal is achieved. Interest, opinion, and attitude influence learning, but motivation is the direct driving force.

28. This pair does not match correctly. Self-abasement is linked with feelings of inferiority, humility, or shame, not superiority. The other instincts and related emotions—laughter with amusement, gregariousness with loneliness, and repulsion with disgust—are properly matched.

29. The concept of modeling is associated with Albert Bandura's Social Learning Theory. He emphasized that individuals, especially children, learn by observing and imitating the behaviours of role models in their environment.

30. Intelligence Quotient (IQ) is calculated as:

$$IQ = \frac{\text{Mental Age}}{\text{Chronological Age}} \times 100$$

Here, Mental Age = 7.5 years,

Chronological Age = 6 years.

$$IQ = \frac{7.5}{6} \times 100 = 125$$

Thus, the girl's IQ is 125.

31. जृम्भिका - जवाँई अनुपयुक्त है। जृम्भिका (तत्सम) का तद्भव रूप जँभाई या जम्हाई है, जबकि जवाँई का तत्सम रूप जामातृ है। अतः यह युग्म गलत है। गर्त-गड्ढा, चर्मचटक-चमगादड़ और परिकूट-परकोटा सही मेल हैं।

32. प्रेरणा से तर्क की ओर शिक्षण-सूत्र नहीं है। शिक्षण-सूत्र जैसे "पूर्ण से अंश की ओर" और "स्थूल से सूक्ष्म की ओर" स्थापित हैं, लेकिन 'प्रेरणा से तर्क की ओर' कोई मान्य सूत्र नहीं है।

33. ऐ, औ - अर्ध संवृत असंगत है। स्वर वर्गीकरण में ऐ और औ अर्ध विवृत स्वर हैं, अर्ध संवृत नहीं। अन्य विकल्प जैसे अं, अः (अयोगवाह), ड़, ढ़ (उत्क्षिप्त), और श, ष, स (संघर्षी) संगत हैं।

34. दूरदर्शन प्रक्षेपित शिक्षण सहायक सामग्री नहीं है।

प्रक्षेपित शिक्षण सहायक सामग्री वे होती हैं जिन्हें किसी स्क्रीन पर प्रकाश स्रोत या प्रोजेक्टर की सहायता से प्रदर्शित किया जाता है। दूरदर्शन एक इलेक्ट्रॉनिक उपकरण है जो सीधे प्रसारण (Broadcast) के आधार पर चित्र और ध्वनि प्रस्तुत करता है। यह प्रक्षेपण उपकरण नहीं है, बल्कि स्वयं में दृश्य-श्रव्य सामग्री का प्रसारण माध्यम है।

- **फिल्म स्ट्रीप :** इसमें स्थिर छवियाँ होती हैं जिन्हें प्रोजेक्टर द्वारा स्क्रीन पर प्रक्षेपित किया जाता है।
- **ओवरहेड प्रोजेक्टर :** यह पारदर्शी शीट पर लिखी या छपी सामग्री को स्क्रीन पर प्रक्षेपित करता है।
- **फिल्म :** यह चलचित्र है जिसे प्रोजेक्टर की सहायता से परदे पर दिखाया जाता है।

अतः स्पष्ट है कि दिए गए विकल्पों में केवल **दूरदर्शन** अप्रक्षेपित सामग्री है।

35. पवन से चलने वाली चक्की - पनचक्की असंगत है। वास्तव में 'पनचक्की' का समास विग्रह "पानी से चलने वाली चक्की" है, न कि "पवन से चलने वाली चक्की"। अन्य विकल्प सही हैं—लोकप्रिय (लोक में प्रिय, अधिकरण तत्पुरुष), नवयुवक (नव है जो युवक, कर्मधारय), परीक्षाभवन (परीक्षा के लिए भवन, सम्प्रदान तत्पुरुष)।

36. अभ्यर्थी - प्रत्यर्थी सही विलोम-युग्म नहीं है।

'अभ्यर्थी' का अर्थ है याचक या उम्मीदवार, जो किसी पद या अवसर के लिए निवेदन करता है। 'प्रत्यर्थी' का अर्थ है—प्रतिद्वंदी या विरोधी, जो उसी अवसर पर प्रतिस्पर्धा में खड़ा होता है। दोनों शब्द एक ही संदर्भ में प्रयुक्त होते हैं, पर अर्थ की दृष्टि से एक-दूसरे के विपरीत नहीं हैं, इसलिए इन्हें विलोम नहीं कहा जा सकता।

- **वैमनस्य - सौमनस्य :** वैरभाव और सद्भाव के लिए यह सही विलोम है।
- **अभिमानी - निरभिमानी :** अभिमान से युक्त और अभिमान रहित - यह भी विलोम है।
- **स्वार्थी - निस्स्वार्थ :** स्वार्थ में लिप्त और स्वार्थ से रहित - यह भी उपयुक्त विलोम है।

अतः दिए गए विकल्पों में अनुपयुक्त विलोम-युग्म **अभ्यर्थी - प्रत्यर्थी** है।

37. ई - द्रौपदी, जानकी, वाल्मीकि असंगत है। 'ई' प्रत्यय से स्त्रीलिंग सूचक शब्द बनते हैं, जैसे द्रौपदी, जानकी। लेकिन 'वाल्मीकि' इसमें नहीं आता, क्योंकि यह ई प्रत्यय से नहीं बना है। बाकी विकल्प - 'य', 'तर' और 'एय' - सही उदाहरणों के साथ संगत हैं।

38. तरणि - नौका, द्रोणी, करवाल असुमेलित है। 'तरणि' का अर्थ सूर्य होता है, इसका पर्यायवाची आदित्य, भानु, भास्कर आदि हैं। नौका, द्रोणी और करवाल 'नाव' के पर्याय हैं, अतः यह युग्म असंगत है।

39. समुद्र में लगने वाली आग - दावानल असंगत है। दावानल का अर्थ है वन में लगने वाली अग्नि, न कि समुद्र में। समुद्र में लगने वाली आग को 'बड़वानल' कहा जाता है। शेष विकल्प सही हैं - लोक-प्रचलित बात जिसके वक्ता का पता न हो = किंवदन्ती, पशुओं की जुगाली = पागुर, और जिसके पति ने दूरारा विवाह कर लिया हो – अध्यूढा।

40. कुमार में 'कु' उपसर्ग का प्रयोग नहीं हुआ है। कुमार शब्द संस्कृत धातु से बना है और इसमें 'कु' उपसर्ग नहीं है। जबकि कुज, कुचो और कुमति में 'कु' उपसर्ग के प्रयोग से ही शब्द निर्मित हुए हैं।

41. मनुजात का अर्थ है मनु से उत्पन्न, अर्थात् मनुष्य या मानव। मनुजाद का अर्थ है मनुष्य को खाने वाला। इसमें 'आद' प्रत्यय का अर्थ है खाने वाला। इसलिए यह युग्म सही है।

42. पर्युषण = परि + ऊषण : यह यण संधि दृष्टि से संगत विकल्प है। यहाँ 'परि + ऊषण' में 'इ + ऊ = यू' होता है, जो यण संधि का नियम है। इस प्रकार 'परि + ऊषण → पर्युषण' बनता है।

- जाती + अभिमान → जात्यभिमान (यह यण संधि है, लेकिन विकल्प में 'जार्त्यामान' लिखा है, जो गलत रूप है)।
- वधु + इच्छा → वध्विच्छा (यह यण संधि है, पर विकल्प में आधार शब्द 'वधु' को सही रूप में नहीं दिया गया है)।
- महा + ऐन्द्रजालिक → महेन्द्रजालिक (यह वृद्धि संधि है, यण संधि नहीं)।

अतः सही उत्तर है **पर्युषण = परि + ऊषण।**

43. लेखक के अनुसार शांति की परिभाषा केवल युद्ध की अनुपस्थिति नहीं है। गद्यांश में स्पष्ट कहा गया है कि बुद्ध की परिकल्पना के अनुसार शांति का अर्थ समानता के संदेश से युक्त शांतिपूर्ण समाज है। इसलिए युद्ध का न होना मात्र शांति नहीं माना जा सकता।

44. मनुष्य बनने का अर्थ है अपने भीतर करुणा और संवेदनशीलता को विकसित करना, जिससे हम दूसरों की पीड़ा को समझ सकें और उनसे जुड़ सकें।

45. विषमता - व्यंजन संधि : यह असंगत है। 'विषमता' शब्द 'विषम' + 'ता' से बना है, जो प्रत्यय की प्रक्रिया है, संधि नहीं। शेष विकल्प - 'अनुपस्थिति' (दो उपसर्ग), 'मनुष्यता' (जातिवाचक आधार से बना भाववाचक), और 'प्रत्येक' (अव्ययीभाव समास) - सही हैं।

46. The most suitable way to teach stress, intonation, and rhythm is through different types of drills. Drills give students repeated opportunities to practice pronunciation, intonation, and rhythm, which helps them achieve naturalness in speaking.

47. A phonetic dictionary does not help in developing listening skills. It helps in understanding pronunciation and knowing the correct phonetic transcription of words, but it does not directly develop listening ability. On the other hand, gramophones, television, and films/film strips engage both listening and viewing, thereby developing listening skills.

48. The use of multimedia materials in teaching involves various media such as text, pictures, sound, video, and animation. This integrated approach makes teaching more effective, attractive, and participatory.

49. The use of multilingual resources increases student participation. When various linguistic resources are used, learners feel connected to their mother tongue and other languages, which enhances their active participation and strengthens the learning process.

50. The author worked for a short time (a brief while) in a college in Delhi. Therefore, the correct answer is *short time*.

51. The author assigned the task of writing an application for a job after graduation as a *language exercise* for students.

52. Seven out of eight students wrote job applications for the position of *clerks*.

53. According to the author, the highest ambition of students in good colleges is to pass the competitive examination for appointment to the *Administrative Services*.

54. In the sentence "And these latter, understandably, are a small number," the phrase "these latter" refers to *scholars, scientists, and leaders of opinion*, whose number is very small.

55. According to the author, the thinking of the most ambitious and the least ambitious students is *alike*.

56. The college where the author worked in Delhi had a reputation for its academic standards: This statement is true. The passage clearly mentions that the college was well-known for its academic standards.

57. "Snuffed out" means to end or to *kill*. Therefore, the correct meaning is *killed*.

58. The antonym of "former" is "latter," and this is the word used in the passage.

59. "Alumni" means *former students* or old students of an educational institution.

60. The first stage in teaching any lesson, including formal grammar, is to prepare students and connect the new topic with their prior knowledge. This stage is called *Motivation* and *Testing of Previous Knowledge*.

- **Motivation:** Creates interest and curiosity among students about the topic.
- **Testing of Previous Knowledge:** Helps the teacher find out what the students already know, so new knowledge can be built on that foundation.

After this, the sequence of the teaching process includes:

- Collection and presentation of examples,
- Comparison and generalization,
- And finally, application of rules.

Hence, the first stage is *Motivation and Testing of Previous Knowledge*.

61. The given expression is

$$= \sqrt{\frac{\left(\frac{7}{4}\right)^4 - \left(\frac{7}{3}\right)^4}{\left(\frac{7}{4}\right)^2 - \left(\frac{7}{3}\right)^2}}$$

Using the identity $a^4 - b^4 = (a^2 - b^2)(a^2 + b^2)$, the fraction reduces to $a^2 + b^2$. Substituting $a = 7/4$, $b = 7/3$:

$$a^2 + b^2 = \left(\frac{7}{4}\right)^2 + \left(\frac{7}{3}\right)^2 = \frac{49}{16} + \frac{49}{9}$$

$$\text{Taking LCM} = \frac{441}{144} + \frac{784}{144} = \frac{1225}{144}$$

$$\text{Now, } \sqrt{\frac{1225}{144}} = \frac{\sqrt{1225}}{\sqrt{144}} = \frac{35}{12} = 2\frac{11}{12}$$

62. Rates: $X = \frac{1}{6}$, $Y = \frac{1}{8}$ (work/day).

Together finish in 3 days $\Rightarrow$ rate $= 1/3$.

$$Z = \frac{1}{3} - \left(\frac{1}{6} + \frac{1}{8}\right) = \frac{1}{24}$$

In 3 days, Z does $3 \times \frac{1}{24} = \frac{1}{8}$ of work

$$\Rightarrow \quad Z \text{ share} = \frac{1}{8} \times 2000 = ₹\, 250$$

63. Cube : It's the only 3-D solid, the others (rectangle, square, triangle) are 2-D figures.

64. SP $= 153$ at 10% loss

$$\Rightarrow CP = \frac{153}{0.9} = 170.$$

For 20% profit: SP $= 1.2 \times 170 =$ ₹ 204.

65. Around the circle (facing center):

"Only A is between E and B" $\Rightarrow$ order E – A – B.

"D is to the immediate left of B"

$\Rightarrow$ clockwise after B is D.

Arrangement: E $\rightarrow$ A $\rightarrow$ B $\rightarrow$ D $\rightarrow$ C (clockwise).

Immediate left of C (clockwise neighbour) is E.

66. Shekhar walks 10 m north, then 6 m south $\rightarrow$ net movement $= 4$ m north. Next, he walks 3 m east. His position forms a right triangle with sides 4 m (north) and 3 m (east). Distance from the start

$$= \sqrt{4^2 + 3^2} = \sqrt{25} = 5\text{ m}.$$

67. Series: 5, 6, 9, 15, 25, ?

Differences: +1, +3, +6, +10. These are triangular numbers T_1, T_2, T_3, T_4. The next triangular number is 15. Therefore, next term = 25 + 15 = 40.

68. Rearranging "CYBERNETICS" alphabetically gives: B, C, C, E, E, I, N, R, S, T, Y.

The word has 11 letters, so the 6th letter is the middle. The 6th letter is **I**.

69. R is Q's mother. Since P is Q's sister, R is also P's mother. S is R's father, meaning S is P's grandfather. Thus, P is related to S as his granddaughter.

70. Rule → Each letter value = 27 − (alphabetical position), then sum × 10.

- ZIP: Z = 1, I = 18, P = 11
  → total 30 → 30 × 10 = 300.
- ZAN: Z = 1, A = 26, N = 13
  → total 40 → 40 × 10 = 400.
- ZOO: Z = 1, O = 12, O = 12
  → total 25 → 25 × 10 = 250.

71. The series is AYD, BVF, DRH, ?, KGL. Each letter follows its own independent sequence.

- **First letters (A, B, D, ?, K):**
  Positions → A(1), B(2), D(4), ? , K(11).
  Differences: +1, +2, +3, +4.
  So, after D(4), we get G(7).
- **Second letters (Y, V, R, ?, G):**
  Positions → Y(25), V(22), R(18), ?, G(7).
  Differences: −3, −4, −5, −6.
  After R(18), we get M(13).
- **Third letters (D, F, H, ?, L):**
  Positions → D(4), F(6), H(8), ?, L(12).
  Differences: +2 consistently.
  After H(8), we get J(10).

Thus, the missing term is GMJ.

72. We arrange the five persons by height step by step.

- Given: Sachin is shorter than Kamal but taller than Ram ⇒ order so far: Ram < Sachin < Kamal.
- Mohan is the tallest ⇒ Mohan > Kamal.
- Arun is shorter than Kamal but taller than Sachin ⇒ Ram < Sachin < Arun < Kamal < Mohan.

From this order, Mohan is the tallest and Kamal is the **second tallest**.

73. Formula for the volume of a sphere:

$$V = \frac{4}{3}\pi r^3$$

It is given that the volume corresponds to a sphere of radius 3 m.

So, diameter = $2r$ = 6 m.

Thus, the correct diameter is **6 metres**.

74. Given: Diameter = 28 cm

⇒ Radius = 14 cm.; Height = 20 cm.

Total surface area of cylinder:

$$TSA = 2\pi r(h + r)$$

Substitute values:

$$\begin{aligned} TSA &= 2 \times \pi \times 14 \times (20 + 14) \\ &= 2 \times \pi \times 14 \times 34 \\ &= 952\pi \\ &= 952 \times \frac{22}{7} \\ &= 2992 \text{ cm}^2 \end{aligned}$$

So, the total surface area = 2992 cm^2.

75. Perimeter of rhombus = 52 cm

⇒ Side = 52 ÷ 4 = 13.

One diagonal = 24 cm ⇒ half of it = 12 cm.

Using Pythagoras in right triangle:

$$\left(\frac{d_2}{2}\right)^2 + 12^2 = 13^2$$

$$\left(\frac{d_2}{2}\right)^2 + 144 = 169$$

$$\left(\frac{d_2}{2}\right)^2 = 25$$

$$\Rightarrow \quad \frac{d_2}{2} = 5$$

$$\Rightarrow \quad d_2 = 10$$

$$\text{Area of rhombus} = \frac{d_1 \times d_2}{2} = \frac{24 \times 10}{2} = 120 \text{ cm}^2.$$

So, the required area is **120 cm^2**.

76. Let the radius of the cone be r and the height be h.

Given ratio, $r : h = 5 : 12$

⇒ $r = 5x$, $h = 12x$.

Volume of cone: $V = \frac{1}{3}\pi r^2 h$

Substituting, $V = 314$, $\pi = 3.14$:

$$\begin{aligned} 314 &= 1/3 \times 3.14 \times (5x)^2 \times 12x \\ 314 &= 1/3 \times 3.14 \times 25x^2 \times 12x \\ 314 &= 314x^3 \end{aligned}$$

⇒ $x^3 = 1 \Rightarrow x = 1$

So, $r = 5x = 5$ m.

Diameter = $2r$ = 10 m.

77. Expression:

$$E = \sec(90° - A) - \cot A \cdot \cos(90° - A) \cdot \tan(90° - A)$$

Use identities:

$\sec(90° - A) = \text{cosec } A$,

$\cos(90° - A) = \sin A$, $\tan(90° - A) = \cot A$.

So,

$$\begin{aligned} E &= \text{cosec } A - \cot A \cdot \sin A \cdot \cot A \\ &= \text{cosec } A - \cot^2 A \sin A \end{aligned}$$

Now, $\operatorname{cosec} A = \frac{1}{\sin A}$

$\cot^2 A = \frac{\cos^2 A}{\sin^2 A}$

$$E = \frac{1}{\sin A} - \frac{\cos^2 A}{\sin^2 A} . \sin A$$

$$= \frac{1}{\sin A} - \frac{\cos^2 A}{\sin A}$$

$$= \frac{1-\cos^2 A}{\sin A} = \frac{\sin^2 A}{\sin A} = \sin A.$$

78. Height of tower $= 2\sqrt{3}$ m,

Shadow = 2 m.

$$\tan\theta = \frac{\text{heigth}}{\text{shadow}}$$

$$= \frac{2\sqrt{3}}{2} = \sqrt{3}$$

So, $\theta = 60°$.

79. Compound interest formula:

$$A = P\left(1+\frac{r}{100}\right)^n$$

Here, $r = 20\%$.

For doubling: $(1.2)^n > 2$

Check values:

$(1.2)^2 = 1.44$

$(1.2)^3 = 1.728$

$(1.2)^4 = 2.0736 > 2$

So, least $n = 4$.

80. Numbers between 11 and 50 divisible by 7:

14, 21, 28, 35, 42, 49.

Exclude those divisible by 3 also: 21, 42.

Remaining: 14, 28, 35, 49.

Count = 4.

81. Diksha Dagar, the professional golfer from Haryana, was one of the 26 athletes honoured with the Arjuna Award in 2023. This recognition was for her achievements and contributions to golf at both national and international levels. The other names listed are prominent wrestlers, but they were not in the final Arjuna Award list for 2023.

82. Bir Shikargarh Wildlife Sanctuary is situated in Panchkula district, Haryana. It is notable for its Vulture Conservation and Breeding Centre at Pinjore. By contrast, Chhilchhila Sanctuary lies in Kurukshetra, Nahar in Rewari, and Kaparwas in Jhajjar. Hence, only Bir Shikargarh matches Panchkula.

83. The Shivalik Development Agency covers the districts that fall under the Shivalik range: Ambala, Panchkula, and Yamuna Nagar. Kurukshetra lies in the plains and is not included under the Agency's jurisdiction.

84. According to Haryana's economic survey and budget estimates for 2023–24 at constant (2011–12) prices, the state's per capita income is around ₹ 1,85,490. This figure reflects income growth adjusted for inflation.

85. Justice Sheel Nagu is the present Chief Justice of the Punjab and Haryana High Court. He assumed office in July 2024 and continues to serve as the head of the High Court, which has jurisdiction over Punjab, Haryana, and Chandigarh.

86. The Haryana Public Service Commission (HPSC) is constituted with one Chairman and five Members. While the State Government has the authority to vary the strength, the most recognized and cited composition is six in total (1 Chairman + 5 Members).

87. (*a*) **True** → In the 12th century, the Bhadanakas ruled over the area around Gurugram and Rewari. Their domain extended into regions of present-day Haryana, including parts of Delhi and Bayana.

(*b*) **False** → The Bhadanakas did not defeat Prithviraj Chauhan. On the contrary, Prithviraj-III destroyed their power around 1182 CE, leading to their decline.

88. In the Mahabharata's Sabha Parva, Nakul, the Pandava prince, led the western Digvijaya campaign. He conquered Rohitaka (identified with present-day Rohtak), which was then a prosperous cattle-rich region and a center of Karttikeya worship. Hence, Nakul is credited with leading the expedition to Rohtak.

89. Jind district, often called the "Heart of Haryana" because of its central location, uniquely shares borders with seven districts: Fatehabad, Hisar, Rohtak, Sonipat, Panipat, Karnal, and Kaithal. This makes Jind the only district in Haryana with such extensive adjacency.

90. The Sikh chieftain of Ladawa who resisted the British during the First Anglo-Maratha War was **Gurdit Singh**. Historical and regional records mention Gurdit Singh as a prominent leader from Ladawa (in present-day Haryana) who stood against British forces during the late 18th century conflict. His opposition formed part of the broader resistance by local Sikh sardars against the growing influence of the East India Company in North India.

91. In the poem "Beauty" by E-Yeh-Shure, beauty is described as being seen in sunlight, heard in the night, and felt in dreams and deeds. The poet says beauty is heard in the night when wind sighs, rain sings, and people dance joyfully to songs. Hence, beauty is heard in the night.

92. The action "writing a letter" took place yesterday, which indicates the simple past tense. The correct sentence is "I wrote a letter to him yesterday."

93. The idiom "to blow one's own trumpet" means to praise oneself or to boast about one's own achievements. It refers to self-glorification or talking proudly about oneself.

94. In the sentence "This is his book," the word 'his' describes ownership of the noun 'book.' Hence, it is a possessive adjective, as it qualifies a noun by showing possession.

95. The correct preposition to use is 'in ink' when referring to the medium of writing. Therefore, the correct sentence is "Please write in ink. Don't use a pencil."

96. In the story "Quality" by John Galsworthy, Gessler, the devoted shoemaker, died of starvation. He worked so hard to maintain the quality of his boots that he neglected his health and could not earn enough to live. His dedication to perfection ultimately led to his death from starvation.

97. In the story "The Snake and the Mongoose" from The Jungle Book by Rudyard Kipling, both the crow and the myna joined the fight and hurled themselves at the cobra to attack it. However, their involvement was brief, and only the mongoose fought bravely till the end.

98. In Zakir Hussain's story "Chandni", Kalua is described as Chandni's sister, who was about the size of a big deer. Abbu Khan, the caretaker of the goats, tells Chandni the story of Kalua to caution her against venturing into the hills, where a dangerous wolf lives. Kalua once tried to enjoy her freedom in the hills but was attacked and killed by the wolf after fighting bravely all night. Through this story, Abbu Khan warns Chandni about the deadly risk of leaving the safety of her pen.

99. The correct comparative form of "lazy" is more lazy (though "lazier" is preferred in common usage). As per the sentence pattern, "She is more lazy than stupid" is grammatically correct.

100. A collective noun denotes a group of individuals considered as a single entity. "Parliament" represents a group of lawmakers functioning as one body, hence it is a collective noun.

101. The passage clearly emphasizes that non-violent resistance is not a method for cowards. It requires courage, strength, and spiritual power. Gandhi believed that if cowardice was the only alternative to violence, it was better to fight, because non-violence is the way of the strong man, not the weak or fearful.

102. The author points out that non-violent resistance is physically passive but spiritually strong and active. This means that though it avoids physical aggression, it requires deep inner strength and active moral courage to resist evil non-violently.

103. A key characteristic of non-violence, as explained in the passage, is that it aims not to defeat or humiliate the opponent, but to win his friendship and moral understanding through peaceful resistance and awakening of conscience.

104. The word "humiliate" in the passage means to lower someone's self-respect or dignity. It appears in the line that non-violence does not seek to "defeat or humiliate the opponent."

105. The word "ends" in the passage means goals or desired results. It is used in the context where boycotts and non-cooperation are described as means to achieve higher moral ends such as redemption and reconciliation.

106. In Leo Tolstoy's story "Three Questions", the king wanted to find answers to three important questions about the right time to begin something, the right people to listen to, and the most important thing to do. To get correct answers, he sent messengers throughout the kingdom to announce a reward for anyone who could answer these questions satisfactorily.

107. The old methods of teaching English include the Translation-cum-Grammar Method and the Direct Method. These methods emphasize memorization of grammar rules and vocabulary through translation, and sometimes conversation practice, but without much focus on real-life communication skills.

108. In Rudyard Kipling's story "How the Camel Got His Hump", the Djinn (the spirit of all deserts) was in charge of all deserts. He is the one who gives the camel his hump as a punishment for refusing to work and saying "Humph!" repeatedly.

109. In William Blake's poem "The School Boy", the unhappy school boy compares himself to a caged bird that cannot sing happily and to a withered plant that has lost its joy and growth. These comparisons reflect his sorrow and loss of freedom caused by formal schooling.

110. In the sentence "She gave him a present," the word 'him' is the indirect object because it indicates the person who receives the direct object ("a present"). The structure is: Subject (She) + Verb (gave) + Indirect Object (him) + Direct Object (a present).

111. In the humorous poem "Dad and the Cat and the Tree" by Kit Wright, Dad tries several plans to rescue the cat stuck on the tree. Plan A and Plan B fail, but Plan C finally succeeds — though Dad himself ends up stuck on the tree while the cat jumps down safely. Thus, Plan C succeeds despite the final comic problem.

112. The Translation-cum-Grammar Method emphasizes learning through translation and grammar rules but gives little or no attention to oral communication or conversation practice. Hence, it lacks the ability to help students speak fluently in English.

113. In the story "Bringing Up Kari" by Dhan Gopal Mukerji, the narrator explains that teaching an elephant the master call — a special sound used only in emergencies — is the most difficult part of training. The elephant takes five years to learn it perfectly. This master call, a combination of hissing and howling, is used when the elephant's help is urgently needed, showing both the animal's intelligence and the trainer's patience.

114. The correct phrasal verb to replace "extinguished" is "put out". The sentence thus becomes: "The firemen put out the fire," meaning they successfully stopped it from burning.

115. In the story "Fair Play" by Munshi Premchand, Algu sells his bullock to Samjhu Sahu, a cart driver. Later, when the bullock dies and a dispute arises over payment, Jumman acts as the head panch and gives a fair judgment in Algu's favor.

116. A gerund is the -ing form of a verb used as a noun. In this sentence, "riding" is the object of the preposition "of" and functions as a noun, showing the activity the person is fond of. Hence, it is a gerund.

117. A noun clause functions as a noun within a sentence — it can act as a subject, object, or complement. Here, "Where he lives" acts as the subject of the verb "is," making it a noun clause.

118. In the sentence "We had a lovely time with them," the word 'lovely' describes the noun "time," telling us the kind or quality of time. Therefore, it is an adjective.

119. In the story "The Shepherd's Treasure", the shepherd hadn't been to school because there were very few schools in those days. Yet, he was wise, humble, and just, earning the king's admiration.

120. The sentence pattern here is Subject + Verb + Subject Complement. "This" is the subject, "is" is the linking verb, and "a pen" is the subject complement because it renames or defines the subject.

121. The correct sentence is "When she heard the little orphan crying, the mother in her was roused." Here, the article 'the' is used because the phrase "the mother in her" refers to a specific quality or emotion — the maternal instinct — that already exists within her. The definite article identifies that particular aspect of her personality being awakened, not just any general sense of motherhood.

122. In the story "Jody's Fawn" by Marjorie Kinnan Rawlings, Jody's father was bitten by a rattlesnake while protecting their family. To draw out the poison and save his life, he killed a doe and used its liver as a poultice. This incident leads Jody to feel responsible for the orphaned fawn.

123. In the story "A Pact with the Sun" by Zakir Hussain, the Sun is described as the father of rays, who helps bring light and warmth to the world, aiding in healing and life. The story metaphorically shows the power of sunlight in restoring health.

124. The correct phonetic transcription of the word **"record"** as a **noun** is **/'rekɔ:d/**. The stress falls on the first syllable (indicated by the mark ' before *rek*), making it pronounced as *RE-kord*. This distinguishes it from the verb form, which places the stress on the second syllable — re-CORD (**/rɪ'kɔ:d/** in British English or **/rɪ'kɔ:rd/** in American English). Hence, the noun form's pronunciation is **/'rekɔ:d/**.

125. The correct correlative conjunction is "No sooner... than", not "No sooner... when" or "scarcely... than." Hence, this sentence is grammatically correct and properly structured in past tense.

126. The modal 'would' is used to express a past habitual action—something done regularly in the past but not necessarily continued in the present. Therefore, the correct sentence is "She would sit for hours in the garden and knit," indicating her past habit of spending long hours knitting.

127. The given sentence "The mason is building the wall" is in the present continuous tense. Its passive form uses is *being + past participle*, hence it becomes "The wall is being built by the mason."

128. The sentence "There was hardly any food in the house" can be rephrased as "There was little food in the house." The word 'little' here conveys a negative quantity, meaning almost none, matching the sense of "hardly any."

129. The poem "The Rebel" is written by D.J. Enright. It humorously describes a person who always behaves contrary to what others do, highlighting individuality and nonconformity in society.

130. The modal verb 'may' expresses possibility. Therefore, the correct sentence is "It may rain tomorrow," indicating that rain is possible but not certain.

131. This statement is false. In fact, form words (also known as function or structural words) include prepositions, conjunctions, articles, pronouns, and auxiliary verbs — all of which help give grammatical structure to sentences. Hence, saying they are "not structural or functional words" is incorrect.

132. In Michael Morpurgo's story "The Best Christmas Present in the World", Jim Macpherson, the English officer from Dorset, was a school teacher in peacetime, while Hans Wolf, the German officer from Düsseldorf, was a cello player in an orchestra. During the Christmas truce of 1914, they discovered their shared humanity despite being enemies in war. Their conversation revealed that before the war, both were men of peace, art, and learning—Macpherson teaching in a classroom and Wolf creating music on his cello.

133.
- A. Communicative approach → (*iv*) Less stress on grammar – focuses on communication over grammar accuracy.
- B. Structural approach → (*i*) Gradation of structure – language taught through graded patterns and sentence structures.
- C. Situational approach → (*ii*) Language item and real situation – teaches language through real-life contexts.
- D. Bilingual method → (*iii*) C.J. Dodson – introduced by C.J. Dodson combining native and target language use.

134. The given lines—"They give it its body and swing / And everyone today is longing to hear / Some fresh and beautiful thing"—are from the poem "The Wonderful Words" by Mary O'Neill, which celebrates the beauty and power of words as tools for creative expression.

135. The given interrogative sentence "Shall I ever forget those happy days?" expresses a strong emotion of remembrance. Its assertive form is "I shall never forget those happy days." This changes the question into a firm statement of certainty.

136. The Substitution Table Method was developed by Harold E. Palmer, a British linguist and educationist. This method helps learners construct correct sentences by substituting words or phrases within a fixed structure. It emphasizes pattern practice, enabling students to internalize grammatical structures through repetition and controlled variation.

137. In the story "How the Dog Found Himself a New Master", the dog first served a wolf, then a bear, followed by a lion, and finally chose man as his master. The dog admired man's strength and intelligence and has remained his loyal companion ever since.

138. "The Ant and the Cricket" is a fable, a short story that teaches a moral lesson, usually through talking animals. It tells how the lazy cricket suffers in winter because he wasted his summer singing instead of storing food like the hardworking ant.

139. This statement is false. In the story "Children at Work" by Gita Wolf and Anushka Ravishankar, Jam Bazaar Jaggi is the junk dealer who regularly buys items from ragpickers like Jaya and Velu. Hence, the claim that he "never bought anything" is incorrect.

140. In John Keats's poem "On the Grasshopper and the Cricket", both the grasshopper (symbolizing summer) and the cricket (symbolizing winter) sing songs representing the poetry of the earth, which never ceases throughout the changing seasons.

141. In the poem, it is Love who comes to Flora, the goddess of flowers, asking her to choose a flower that would be the undisputed queen among all flowers.

142. The poem states that the lily and the rose had long been rivals for the title of queen of flowers, as poets (bards) had sung in praise of both.

143. The line "Like the pale lily with her Juno mien" compares the stately beauty of the lily to Juno, the Roman goddess known for her majestic and queenly appearance.

144. The line "But of what colour?" is spoken by Flora to Love, when she asks which colour the flower should have, after Love describes the qualities he wants.

145. Love desired a flower that was red like the rose and white like the lily, combining the beauty and stateliness of both flowers.

146. The word "Bards" in the poem means poets, those who wrote verses praising the lily and the rose as rivals.

147. The repetition of the consonant sound "l" in "lily" and "long, long had been" makes this line an example of alliteration.

148. The word "strife" (found in the line "Flower factions rang the strife in Psyche's bower") means conflict or struggle, referring to the rivalry between the flowers.

149. The comparison "delicious as the rose / And stately as the lily" uses 'as', which makes it a simile, comparing the desired flower's qualities to those of the rose and lily.

150. The lines "Rose-red," "No, lily-white," and "Or, both provide" are all spoken by Love, who expresses his wish for a flower that combines both colours and qualities, leading Flora to create the lotus.

YOUR SPACE

Previous Years' Paper

Haryana Teacher Eligibility Test (HTET)

TGT English (Level-2), Exam 2023

(Exam held on 03-12-2023)

PART-I : CHILD DEVELOPMENT AND PEDAGOGY

1. According to which psychologist, the role of social and cultural factors are important in the cognitive development of children?
A. Vygotsky B. Piaget
C. Bruner D. Hull

2. Which teaching support material is **not** useful for visually impaired students?
A. Braille materials B. Talking books
C. Film strips D. Embossed map

3. The education which promotes 'learning by doing' and ensures the student's interaction with their environment to learn, that is known as:
A. Special education B. Progressive education
C. Integrated education D. Inclusive education

4. Inclusive Education means:
A. Education for socially deprived children
B. Education for disabled children
C. Education for normal and disabled children
D. Education for all children

5. Which teaching learning strategy is most useful for students in context of social learning?
A. Field trip B. Lecture
C. Experiment D. Brain storming

6. Which of the following is **not** an objective type question?
A. Matching questions
B. Analytical questions
C. Multiple choice questions
D. Blank space questions

7. Which educational intervention is **not** suitable for slow learners?
A. Acceleration
B. Remedial teaching
C. Drill work
D. Cooperative teaching method

8. When the lesson to be learned by a child is long and difficult and requires a lot of understanding, then which method of learning will be appropriate?
A. Spaced method B. Whole method
C. Massed method D. Incidental method

9. Choose the **correct** code for the approved social behaviour pattern in adolescene:
(*a*) Leadership skills (*b*) Empathy
(*c*) Ego-centrism (*d*) Stereotyping

Codes:
A. (*a*) & (*b*) B. (*b*) & (*d*)
C. (*a*), (*b*) & (*c*) D. (*a*), (*c*) & (*d*)

10. Which of the following pair is **not** correct regarding motivational theories and their proponents?

	Motivational Theories	Proponent
A.	Instinct theory	Atkinson
B.	Need Hierarchical theory	Maslow
C.	Drive theory	Woodworth
D.	Achievement Motivation theory	Mc'Clelland

11. Which of the following is **not** a performance test of intelligence?
A. Koh's Block Design Test
B. Alexander's Pass Along Test
C. Saguine Form Board Test
D. Stanford-Binet Test

12. Which of the following is **not** a principle of development?
A. Development is the product of heredity and environment.
B. Developmental pattern is predictable.
C. Development follows linear path.
D. Development proceeds from general to specific.

1. A **2.** C **3.** B **4.** D **5.** A **6.** B **7.** A **8.** A **9.** A **10.** A
11. D **12.** C

13. According to Gagne, to what highest level of learning should a teacher strive to take students?
A. Concept learning
B. Problem solving learning
C. Rule learning
D. Discrimination learning

14. Choose the **correct** code of the following factors, which affects learning:
(*a*) Motivation
(*b*) Aptitude
(*c*) Interest
(*d*) Attention

Code:
A. (*c*) & (*d*) B. (*a*), (*b*) & (*d*)
C. (*a*) & (*c*) D. (*a*), (*b*), (*c*) & (*d*)

15. Which of the following is **not** a common characteristic of social development in adolescence?
A. Harmonious relationship with parents
B. New social grouping
C. Search for identity
D. Hero-worship

16. Which of the following factor does **not** influence the development of child under environmental factors?
A. Nutrition
B. Mental stress of the mother during pregnancy
C. Accidents
D. Endocrine glands

17. 'Law of use' and 'Law of disuse' is related with which law of learning according to Thorndike's learning theory?
A. Law of readiness
B. Law of exercise
C. Law of effect
D. Law of multiple response

18. Which of the following characteristics is **not** related to the concrete operational stage of the Cognitive Development theory propounded by Piaget?
A. Reversibility B. Serialization
C. Animism D. Conservation

19. Which teaching maxim is **not** beneficial for the learning disabled children?
A. Simple to complex
B. Abstract to concrete
C. Direct to indirect
D. Known to unknown

20. Which stages of Kohlberg's moral development theory are **not** related to level of conventional morality?
(*a*) Individualism and exchange
(*b*) Good interpersonal relations
(*c*) Maintaining the social order
(*d*) Social contracts and individual rights

Choose the **correct** code:

Code:
A. (*a*) & (*b*) B. (*b*) & (*c*)
C. (*a*) & (*d*) D. (*c*) & (*d*)

21. Which of the following laws is **not** related to heredity?
A. Law of Similarity
B. Law of Variation
C. Law of Regression
D. Law of Progression

22. Which of the following factors does **not** affect the teaching learning process?
A. Physical appearance of teacher
B. Mental health of teacher
C. Content knowledge of teacher
D. Communication skills of teacher

23. According to Moral Development theory of Piaget, adolescent period is:
A. Stage of moral realism
B. Stage of morality constraint
C. Stage of heteronomous morality
D. Stage of autonomous morality

24. Which statement is **not** correct in context of individual differences?
A. Two persons are not exactly same.
B. Individual differences are deviation in regards to characteristics.
C. Individual differences distinguish individuals in their totality.
D. Individual differences are the sole result of heredity.

25. Learning through mental processes like attention and reflection is called:
A. Imitative learning B. Motor learning
C. Cognitive learning D. Affective learning

26. Which of the following is **not** a principle of effective learning?
A. Motivation B. Individual approach
C. Passive attendance D. Feedback

13. B **14.** D **15.** A **16.** D **17.** B **18.** C **19.** B **20.** C **21.** D **22.** A
23. D **24.** D **25.** C **26.** C

27. The **true** meaning of continuous and comprehensive evaluation is:
(*a*) Taking frequent tests
(*b*) Taking continuous tests at appropriate intervals
(*c*) To evaluate scholastic and co-scholastic both aspects
(*d*) Measuring only educational achievements

Choose the **correct** code:

Code:
A. (*b*) & (*d*) B. (*b*) & (*c*)
C. (*a*), (*b*) & (*c*) D. (*b*), (*c*) & (*d*)

28. A learning difficulty that create problem for a child to distinguish letters and words is:
A. Dysplasticia B. Dyslexia
C. Dysgraphia D. Dyscalculia

29. Which three aspects of intelligence are emphasized in the triarchic theory of Sternberg?
(*a*) Componential (*b*) Experiential
(*c*) Operational (*d*) Contextual

Choose the **correct** code:

Code:
A. (*a*), (*b*) & (*c*) B. (*b*), (*c*) & (*d*)
C. (*a*), (*b*) & (*d*) D. (*a*), (*c*) & (*d*)

30. In Pavlov's conditioning theory, which factor does **not** positively affect the conditioning between natural and artificial stimuli?
A. Appropriate timing of stimuli presentation
B. Repetition of stimuli
C. Controlled environment
D. Lack of motive

PART-II : भाषा – हिन्दी

31. निम्न में से कौन-सा संधि शब्द अपने युग्म से सुमेलित **नहीं** है?
A. अजंत - व्यंजन संधि
B. वयोवृद्ध - विसर्ग संधि
C. महौदार्य - वृद्धि स्वर संधि
D. तेजोपुंज - गुण स्वर संधि

32. किस विकल्प के शब्दों में वार्तनिक अशुद्धि **नहीं** है?
A. सुधीजन, शताब्दी B. साधूवाद, सुरसरी
C. शूभेषी, भार्यापति D. चन्द्रमोलि, पुत्रेषणा

33. वाक्यांश के लिए एकल शब्द के संबंध में कौन-सा युग्म **असंगत** है?
A. जिसे वहन करना कठिन हो – दुर्विभाव्य
B. जिसे किसी ने न सूँघा हो – अनाघ्रात
C. कोई काम करने की इच्छा – चिकीर्षा
D. विजय प्राप्ति की तीव्र इच्छा – विजीगिषा

34. निम्न में से कौन-सा शब्द 'धनुष' का पर्यायवाची **नहीं** है?
A. चाप B. कार्मुक
C. शरासन D. कासार

35. 'नीम हकीम खतरे जान' उक्त लोकोक्ति का **सही** अर्थ है :
A. पहले स्वार्थ बाद में परमार्थ करना।
B. अल्पज्ञान खतरनाक होता है।
C. दोषी के साथ निर्दोष को सजा मिलना।
D. अत्यन्त धीरे काम चलना।

36. किस क्रमांक में 'कादंबरी-कादंबिनी' शब्द-युग्म का क्रमशः **सही** अर्थ है?
A. शराब, घटा B. कुशल, सेवक
C. विनीत, बुराई D. कुशल, पवित्र

37. संज्ञा के संबंध में कौन-सा कथन संगत **नहीं** है?
A. व्यक्तिवाचक संज्ञाओं का प्रयोग सदैव (आदरार्थक के अतिरिक्त) एकवचन में होता है।
B. देश, त्योहार, नदी उक्त व्यक्तिवाचक संज्ञा के उदाहरण हैं।
C. 'द्रव्यवाचक' तथा 'समूहवाचक', जातिवाचक संज्ञा के ही भेद माने जाते हैं।
D. 'विद्वत्ता', 'पांडित्य' उक्त यौगिक भाववाचक संज्ञा के उदाहरण हैं।

38. विलोम शब्द के संबंध में कौन-सा युग्म **असंगत** है?
A. घमण्डी - विनीत
B. चिरायु - दीर्घायु
C. तारुण्य - वार्धक्य
D. तेजस्वी - निस्तेज

39. उपसर्ग की दृष्टि से किस विकल्प का शब्द-युग्म **असंगत** है?
A. निर् - निराकरण, निरपराध
B. अनु - अनूदित, अन्वीक्षण
C. परा - परार्थ, पराश्रित
D. सु - सुदूर, सुकृत

27. B **28.** B **29.** C **30.** D **31.** D **32.** A **33.** A, D **34.** D **35.** B **36.** A
37. B **38.** B **39.** C

40. सर्वनाम के संबंध में कौन-सा युग्म संगत **नहीं** है?
A. मैंने आज व्याकरण पढ़ा - पुरुषवाचक सर्वनाम
B. कमरे में कोई हँस रहा है - अनिश्चयवाचक सर्वनाम
C. इसी ने मेरी जिंदगी बचाई थी - प्रश्नवाचक सर्वनाम
D. वह स्वयं को सुधार रहा है - निजवाचक सर्वनाम

41. तत्पुरुष समास का कौन-सा समस्तपद अपने युग्म से सही सुमेलित **नहीं** है?
A. गुरुदक्षिणा - संबंध तत्पुरुष
B. देशाटन - अधिकरण तत्पुरुष
C. रेखांकित - करण तत्पुरुष
D. देशनिर्वासित - अपादान तत्पुरुष

42. विशेषण के संबंध में कौन-सा कथन **असंगत** है?
A. जिस विकारी शब्द से संज्ञा की व्याप्ति मर्यादित होती है, उसे विशेषण कहते हैं।
B. 'भला, दानी, दुष्ट' उक्त शब्द, गुणवाचक विशेषण के उदाहरण हैं।
C. 'कक्षा में साठ छात्र पढ़ते हैं' संख्यावाचक विशेषण का उदाहरण है।
D. संकेतवाचक विशेषण में किसी वस्तु की नाप या तौल का बोध होता है।

43. निम्न में से कौन-सा शब्द 'अपत्यवाचक तद्धित प्रत्यय' से निर्मित **नहीं** है?

A. वैनतेय	B. कौरव
C. वासुदेव	D. वैधव्य

44. 'ग', 'ल' तथा 'ब' उक्त वर्णों का क्रमशः उच्चारण स्थान है:

A. तालु, कण्ठ, ओष्ठ	B. दन्त, कण्ठ, तालु
C. कण्ठ, दन्त, ओष्ठ	D. ओष्ठ, कण्ठ, तालु

45. किस विकल्प का वाक्य पूर्वकालिक क्रिया का उदाहरण **नहीं** है?
A. राम खेलकर चला गया।
B. तुम्हें ऐसा करना शोभा नहीं देता है।
C. सीता खाना बनाकर जयपुर जाएगी।
D. अध्यापक उदाहरण देकर छात्रों को पढ़ाते हैं।

PART-II : LANGUAGE – ENGLISH

46. Choose the option that gives the **correct** meaning of the given phrasal verb:

Give in

A. distribute	B. deposit
C. donate	D. surrender

47. Fill in the blank with the most appropriate modal auxiliary:

Your mother is seriously ill. You ______ leave for home at once. (obligation)

A. needs	B. might
C. could	D. must

48. Choose the **correct** preposition to fill in the blank.

He told all _______ the incident.

A. between	B. among
C. beside	D. about

49. Choose the most appropriate preposition to fill in the blank:

I am going home the day _______ tomorrow.

A. in	B. on
C. after	D. at

50. Choose the most appropriate preposition to fill in the blank:

Mohan gazed _____ the sky in the hope of rain.

A. at	B. unto
C. besides	D. into

51. Choose the **correct** option that gives the correct passive voice of the given sentence:

Have they done the work?
A. Have the work been done?
B. Has the work been done?
C. Had the work been done?
D. Will the work be done?

52. Choose the **correct** tense form to fill in the blank.

The Headmaster __________ to meet you.

A. want	B. wants
C. is wanting	D. was wanting

53. Choose the part of sentence which is **incorrect**:

(*a*) Has Sachin / (*b*) not breaked/ (*c*) the record held/ (*d*) by Bradman who/ made 10,000 runs in his career?

A. (*a*)	B. (*b*)
C. (*c*)	D. (*d*)

40. C **41.** A **42.** D **43.** D **44.** C **45.** B **46.** D **47.** D **48.** D **49.** C
50. A **51.** B **52.** B **53.** B

54. Choose the **correct** option to fill in the blank:

______ had the police reached than the thieves fled.

A. As soon as
B. No sooner
C. Scarcely
D. As well

55. Choose the **correct** tense form to fill in the blank:

She jumped off the train while it _______ .

A. moved
B. had moved
C. has moved
D. was moving

56. Change the narration to Reported speech and choose the **right** option:

I said to him, "Do you know when she will go home?"

A. I told him if he knew when she will go home?
B. I said to him that did he knew when she would go home.
C. I asked him if he knew when she would go home.
D. I said to him that did he know when will she go home?

57. Choose the **correct** option for the given one word:

Sinecure

A. one who lives by himself
B. an office with no work but high pay
C. surgery without anesthesia
D. cure by naturopathy

58. Choose the option that gives the **correct** meaning of the given phrasal verb:

Send for

A. start on a journey
B. reach to a decision
C. call someone in
D. improve

59. Choose the option that gives the **correct** meaning of the phrasal verb:

Turn out

A. to evict someone
B. to kill someone
C. to ridicule someone
D. to give legal notice to someone

60. Fill in the blank with the most appropriate meaning of the underlined idiom:

Rakesh had to deal with all his problems by himself, because he didn't want to depend on his fair weather friends.

A. Friends who come from rich family.
B. Friends who are loyal only during a time of success.
C. Friends with whom one lived in one's college time.
D. Friends who no longer live with you.

PART-III : GENERAL STUDIES

Quantitative Aptitude, Reasoning Ability and GK & Awareness

61. In a family, A is the father of X, B is the mother of Y. The sister of X and Z is Y. Which of the following statement is definitely **not** true?

A. B is the wife of A
B. B has a daughter
C. X is the son of A
D. Y is the sister of Z

62. If A walks 8 km South then turn right and walks 6 km and again turns North-East and walks 10 km. How far is A from the starting point?

A. 0 km
B. 8 km
C. 10 km
D. 12 km

63. If 10 persons can complete (2/5)th of a work in 8 days, then how many persons are required to complete the remaining work in 12 days?

A. 6
B. 8
C. 10
D. 12

64. The base of a right prism is a triangle whose perimeter is 32 cm and the inradius of the triangle is 6 cm. If the volume of the prism is 576 cc, then its height is:

A. 4 cm
B. 5 cm
C. 6 cm
D. 8 cm

65. If the number of diagonals of a regular polygon is 27, then the number of sides is:

A. 6
B. 9
C. 10
D. 12

54. B **55.** D **56.** C **57.** B **58.** C **59.** A **60.** B **61.** C **62.** A **63.** C
64. C **65.** B

66. In two alloys A and B, the ratio of copper and zinc is 5 : 2 and 3 : 4 respectively. 7 kg of alloy A and 21 kg of the alloy B are mixed together to form a new alloy. What will be the ratio of copper and zinc in the new alloy?
A. 1 : 2 B. 2 : 1
C. 2 : 3 D. 1 : 1

67. If 7 cosec θ – 3 cot θ = 7 where θ is in first quadrant, then the value of 7 cot θ – 3 cosec θ is equal to:
A. 3 B. 5
C. 3/7 D. 5/7

68. If an equilateral triangle ABC be inscribed in a circle, then the tangents at their vertices will form another triangle is:
A. Scalene triangle B. Isosceles triangle
C. Equilateral triangle D. Right angled triangle

69. A shopkeeper sells an article at 15% gain. Had he sold it for ₹ 18 more; he would have gained 18%. The cost price (in ₹) of the article is:
A. 600 B. 540
C. 350 D. 380

70. Find the **wrong** number in the given series:

0, 3, 9, 12, 36, 39, 42, 120, 360
A. 12 B. 39
C. 42 D. 360

71. The difference between two positive numbers is 3. If the sum of their squares is 369, then sum of the numbers is:
A. 25 B. 27
C. 31 D. 33

72. In a division sum, the divisor is 12 times the quotient and 5 times the remainder. If the remainder is 36, then the dividend is:
A. 2706 B. 2736
C. 2796 D. 2766

73. If A denotes 'divided by', B denotes 'added to', C denotes 'subtracted from' and D denotes 'multiplied by', then 20 C 12 B 8 A 2 D 6 is equal to:
A. 16 B. 18
C. 32 D. 36

74. A person covers 12 km at 3 km/hr, 18 km at 9 km/hr and 24 km at 4 km/hr. The average speed in covering the whole distance is:
A. 4 km/hr B. 4.2 km/hr
C. 4.4 km/hr D. 4.5 km/hr

75. Find the odd word from the given alternatives:
A. Violin B. Harp
C. Guitar D. Flute

76. If 16 – 4 = 2, 9 – 3 = 2, 81 – 3 = 4, then the value of 64 – 4 is:
A. 3 B. 2
C. 4 D. 6

77. The missing term of the following series is:

DBC, KIJ, QOP, __?__, ZXY
A. VUW B. USV
C. UTV D. VTU

78. If 'PROJECT' is coded as 'CEOPRT' and 'PLANE' is coded as 'ELNP' then the 'ORGANISED' will be coded as:
A. ADEGIOSR B. ADEGIROS
C. ADEGOIRS D. ADEGIORS

79. In a row of boys, A is 7th from the left and B is 12th from the right. If they interchange their positions A becomes 22nd from the left. How many total boys are there in a row?
A. 27 B. 31
C. 33 D. 34

80. A travels 8 km from East to West and turns right and travel 2 km. Now again he turn right and travel 5 km. In which direction is he now positioned with reference to starting point?
A. South-West
B. North-West
C. North-East
D. South-East

81. Who is the Chief Information Officer of Haryana?
A. Smt. Jyoti Arora
B. Dr. Jagbir Singh
C. Shri Vijay Vardhan
D. Smt. Kamaldeep Bhandari

82. In Haryana, where the Vulture Conservation Centre is located?
A. Jind B. Pinjore
C. Mahendragarh D. Ambala

83. The UPSC Chairman, who subsequently became the Governor of Haryana:
A. Dr. A.R. Kidwai
B. Shri Muzaffar Husain Berney
C. Shri B.N. Chakravarti
D. Shri Mahabir Prasad

66. D	**67.** A	**68.** C	**69.** A	**70.** C	**71.** B	**72.** B	**73.** C	**74.** D	**75.** D
76. A	**77.** D	**78.** D	**79.** C	**80.** B	**81.** C	**82.** B	**83.** A		

84. In which district of Haryana, the Khelo India Women's Archery ranking competition was organised?
A. Sonipat
B. Panipat
C. Karnal
D. Yamunanagar

85. How many Tehsils are there in Haryana?
A. 95 B. 49
C. 143 D. 74

86. The Scheme, which is being run by the Haryana government to replace paddy crop with more tradition crops is:
A. Meri Fasal Mera Byora
B. Meri Virasat
C. Mera Pani Meri Virasat
D. Hamara Dhan

87. Where in the Haryana, the National Institute of Fashion Technology is located?
A. Panipat B. Ambala
C. Panchkula D. Kurukshetra

88. Who among the following Sages of Haryana was popularly known as Puran Bhagat?
A. Baba Mast Nath B. Baba Gorakh Nath
C. Baba Chaurangi Nath D. Baba Puran Nath

89. The Morni hills of Haryana belongs to:
A. Aravalli range
B. Hindukush range
C. Outer range of Himalayas
D. Inner range of Himalayas

90. During the revolt of 1857, who among the following attacked British establishments in Rohtak?
A. Tafzal Husain B. Imam Ali
C. Mohar Singh D. Harsukh Rai

PART-IV : SUBJECT KNOWLEDGE—ENGLISH

Directions (Qs. No. 91-95): *Read the following passage and answer the questions that follow.*

It was morning, and the new sun sparkled gold across the ripples of a gentle sea.

A mile from shore a fishing boat chummed the water and the word for Breakfast Flock flashed through the air, till a crowd of a thousand seagulls came to dodge and fight for bits of food. It was another busy day beginning.

But way off alone, out by himself beyond boat and shore, Jonathan Livingston seagull was practising. A hundred feet in the sky he lowered his webbed feet, lifted his beak, and strained to hold a painful hard twisting curve through his wings. The curve meant that he would fly slowly, and now he slowed until the wind was a whisper in his face, until the ocean stood still beneath him. He narrowed his eyes in fierce concentration, held his breath, forced one _____ single _____ more _____ inch _____ of _____ curve _____ Then his feathers ruffled, he stalled and fell.

Seagulls, as you know, never falter, never stall. To stall in the air is for them disgrace and it is dishonour.

But Jonathan Livingston Seagull, unashamed, stretching his wings again in that trembling hard curve – slowing, slowing, and stalling once more - was no ordinary bird.

Most gulls don't bother to learn more than the simplest facts of flight - how to get from shore to food and back again. For most gulls, it is not flying that matters, but eating. For this gull, though, it was not eating that mattered, but flight. More than anything else, Jonathan Livingston seagull loved to fly.

This kind of thinking, he found, is not the way to make one's self popular with other birds. Even his parents were dismayed as Jonathan spent whole day alone, making hundreds of low-level glides, experimenting.

91. For Jonathan Livingston flying was:
A. life itself
B. a matter of shame and disgrace
C. means of finding food
D. way to make one-self popular

92. Choose **appropriate** antonym for 'gentle' from the passage:
A. Falter → To loose strength & momentum.
B. Fierce →
C. Twisting
D. Concentration

93. Choose the word that means "avoid by sudden quick movement":
A. Ruffled B. Webbed
C. Dodge D. Chummed

84. A **85.** A **86.** C **87.** C **88.** C **89.** C **90.** A **91.** A **92.** B **93.** C

94. The line "But Jonathan Livingston Seagull unashamed, stretching his wings again", shows about Jonathan's:

A. Shamelessness B. Menace
C. Exhaustion D. Perseverance

95. "Even his parents were dismayed as Jonathan spent whole day alone making hundreds of low-level glides, experimenting."

The word 'dismayed' in the line means:

A. felt proud B. felt giddy
C. felt disappointed D. felt detached

96. In the poem 'Macavity : The Mystery cat', the ginger cat Macavity is an embodiment of:

A. Professor Conan Doyle
B. Professor Moriarty
C. Professor Alexei
D. Professor Louis Brus

97. Choose the word that means "lying on the ground face downwards":

A. Palanquin B. Prostrate
C. Procastinate D. Prevaricate

98. "Two Roads diverged in a wood, and I – I took the one less travelled by, And that has made all the difference."

The above lines are extracted from which of the following poem?

A. Songs of the Open Road
B. The Road Not Taken
C. The Rolling English Road
D. Roads

99. What is the part of the sentence which denotes the person or thing about which something is said?

A. Predicate B. Subject
C. Phrase D. Clause

100. The number of vowel and consonant sounds in English is indicated respectively:

A. 20, 26 B. 22, 22
C. 20, 24 D. 6, 26

Directions (Qs. No. 101-105): *Read the following poem and answer the questions that follow.*

Now, joy is born of parents poor,
And pleasure of our richer kind;
Though pleasure's free, she cannot sing
As sweet a song as joy confined.

Pleasure's a Moth, that sleeps by day
And dances by false glare at night
But Joy's a Butterfly, that loves
To spread it wings in Nature's light.

Joy's Like a Bee that gently sucks
Away on blossoms its sweet hour;
But pleasure's like a greedy wasp,
That plums and cherries would devour.

Joy's like a Lark that lives alone,
Whose ties are very strong, though few;
But Pleasure like a Cuckoo roams,
Makes much acquaintance, no friends true.

Joy from her heart doth sing at home,
With little care if others hear;
But pleasure then is cold and dumb,
And sings and laughs with strangers near.

101. "Joy is like a Lark that lives alone", which figure of speech is employed in the line quoted above?

A. Alliteration B. Onomatopoeia
C. Oxymoron D. Refrain

102. What is the central idea of the poem?

A. It focuses on the beauty of nature.
B. It lays stress on joy than pleasure.
C. It establishes superiority of pleasure over joy.
D. Considers both joy and pleasure as fleeting emotions.

103. "Pleasure is like a greedy wasp, That plums and cherries would devour."

In the above lines the word 'devour' means:

A. To enjoy greatly
B. To dance beautifully
C. To sing melodiously
D. To eat something eagerly

104. In the poem 'Joy' is compared with a bird that sings:

A. for one's own self B. for strangers
C. for Cuckoo D. for poor parents

105. "Pleasure's a Moth that sleep by day"

Choose the literary device used in the line quoted above:

A. Metaphor B. Assonance
C. Hyperbole D. Anti-thesis

94. D	**95.** C	**96.** B	**97.** B	**98.** B	**99.** B	**100.** C	**101.** A	**102.** B	**103.** D
104. A	**105.** A								

106. Identify the **appropriate** example of Anti-thesis from the sentences given below:
A. He was gathered to his fore-fathers.
B. I came, I saw, I conquered.
C. O what a fall was there, my countrymen!
D. To err is human, to forgive divine.

107. Which of the following is an abstract noun?
A. Crowd B. Gang
C. Student D. Experience

108. Michael West's 'New Method' of teaching English lays stress on:
A. Listening B. Speaking
C. Reading D. Writing

109. "Never, never and never again shall it be that this beautiful land will again experience the oppression of one by another."
The above line is a statement by ______.
A. Jawaharlal Nehru
B. Nelson Mandela
C. Mahatma Gandhi
D. Abdul Kalam Azad

110. Identify the author of the story 'Princess September':
A. Hector Hugh Munro
B. William Somerset Maugham
C. Ahmad Nadeem Qasmi
D. Stephanie Parker

111. The poem 'A Legend of the Northland' by Phoeby Cary is a:
A. Sonnet B. Ballad
C. Lyric D. Elegy

112. Which of the following idiom means "A cause of dispute"?
A. A big fish in the little pond
B. A bone of contention
C. A bloody fool
D. A feast for the eye

113. What is a scientist who studies the rings that appear each year in the tree trunk is called?
A. Archaeologist B. Dendrochronologist
C. Anthropologist D. Ethologist

114. Fill in the blank with the **most suitable** phrasal verb:
The meeting was ______ due to pandemic.
A. called off B. called into
C. called back D. called down

115. Identify the **correct** sequence of language skills:
A. Listening, Reading, Writing, Speaking
B. Listening, Speaking, Reading, Writing
C. Speaking, Writing, Listening, Reading
D. Speaking, Listening, Reading, Writing

116. Find the word which is spelt **correctly** from the given words:
A. Amatuer B. Ameteur
C. Amateur D. Amature

117. Identify the phonetic symbol of the underlined sound:
Book
A. ʌ B. ʊ
C. ∂ : D. ɛ

118. Whose fable is the poem 'The Ant and the Cricket' adapted from?
A. Homer B. Rudyard Kipling
C. Vishnu Sharma D. Aesop

119. Identify the part of speech of the underlined word in the sentence given below:
He is asleep.
A. Object B. Verb
C. Adverb D. Adjective

120. Study of meaning in a language is known as ______.
A. Syntax B. Semantics
C. Morphology D. Linguistics

121. Which of the following words **correctly** define 'the ability to deal with any kind of hardship and recover from its effects?
A. Resilience
B. Retrogression
C. Recurrence
D. Repugnance

122. A lyric poem of moderate length, with a serious subject, an elevated style and an elaborate stanza pattern is called:
A. Ballad B. Ode
C. Haiku D. Limerick

123. Select the most **appropriate meaning** of the given idiom:
"To bury the hatchet."
A. To hide something
B. To talk about unimportant thing
C. Come to peaceful terms
D. To understand more than actual

106. D	**107.** D	**108.** C	**109.** B	**110.** B	**111.** B	**112.** B	**113.** B	**114.** A	**115.** B
116. C	**117.** B	**118.** D	**119.** D	**120.** B	**121.** A	**122.** B	**123.** C		

124. Select the option that expresses the given sentence in passive voice:

They made me laugh.

A. I was made to laugh.
B. I am made to laugh.
C. I was made to be laughed.
D. I am made to be laughed.

125. Fill in the blank with the **correct** conjunction.

______ doing the cooking I look after the garden.

A. Besides B. Still
C. Though D. If

126. From which collection the story 'The Three Questions' by Leo Tolstoy is taken?

A. The Paper Menagerie
B. What Men Live By, and Other Tales.
C. A Flight of Pigeons
D. Angry River

127. What is 'Lingua Franca'?

A. Language used by people who live in France.
B. The shared language of communication used by people belonging to different languages.
C. Language of Western Science and Arts.
D. Language of Science and Technology.

128. What name did Anne Frank give to her diary?

A. Kitty B. Memories
C. Reminiscence D. Salima

129. Select the option that expresses the given sentence in reported speech:

Rita said, "I wish I were a princess."

A. Rita said that she wished she were a princess.
B. Rita said that she wished I were a princess.
C. Rita said that I wished she were a princess.
D. Rita said that she wished she is a princess.

130. Fill in the blanks with **correct** preposition given below:

The house is ______ fire! We had better get ______!

A. on, into B. on, out
C. in, on D. above, out

131. People <u>who have poor diets</u> are likely to catch colds.

The underlined part in the above sentence is:

A. Adverb Clause B. Noun Clause
C. Adjective Clause D. Adverb Phrase

132. Who among the following is the Irish National poet?

A. William Butler Yeats
B. Robert Frost
C. Walt Whitman
D. Rudyard Kipling

133. "Death in an open field is better than life in a small hut".

Who said the above statement to whom?

A. Abu Kaka to Chandni
B. Chandni to herself
C. Old Goat to Abu Kaka
D. Wolf to Chandni

134. The Bilingual method of English language Teaching was first developed by:

A. C.J. Dodson B. A.C. Wards
C. F.G. French D. Sydney Walce

135. Identify the literary term used in the following sentence:

"Let not Ambition mock their useful toil".

A. Irony B. Metonymy
C. Personification D. Litotes

136. What is the poem 'Chivvy' about?

A. The journey of an old man
B. Paradoxical attitude of parents and elders
C. Power of love
D. Mortality of mankind

137. What is the moral of the poem 'Dad and the Cat and the Tree'?

A. Be kind to everyone
B. Don't be over-confident
C. Save Trees
D. Respect Elders

138. 'A Period Plan' is also known as ______.

A. Unit Plan B. Year Plan
C. Lesson Plan D. Daily Plan

139. Who wrote the Lucy Poems?

A. William Shakespeare B. William Wordsworth
C. Douglas James D. Gieve Patel

140. What did Major Ahluwalia and Phu Dorjee leave on the Mt. Everest respectively?

A. A picture of Guru Nanak, relic of Lord Buddha
B. A picture of Goddess Durga, A Cross
C. A picture of Guru Nanak, A Cross
D. A Cross, a picture of Goddess Durga

124. A	**125.** A	**126.** B	**127.** B	**128.** A	**129.** A	**130.** B	**131.** C	**132.** A	**133.** B
134. A	**135.** C	**136.** B	**137.** B	**138.** C	**139.** B	**140.** A			

141. The poem 'A House, A Home' is penned by:
A. Lorraine M. Halli
B. Harry Behn
C. E-Yeh-Shure
D. Peter Dixon

142. Which of the following sentence is framed according to the pattern given below?

Sub + V + noun/pronoun + adjective
A. Israel attacked Gaza with missilery.
B. She gave me a good shawl.
C. We saw him by the sea-side.
D. He painted the ceiling white.

143. Choose the pen-name by which William Sydney Porter is better known:
A. Saki
B. O. Henry
C. O. Neil
D. Robert Galbraith

144. Fill in the blank with **correct** modal auxiliary:

All men ______ die. (certainty)
A. can B. must
C. should D. used to

145. What is Intonation in Phonetics?
A. The alteration of voice, pitch or tone in speech.
B. Use of language with fewer errors.
C. Form of a spoken language peculiar to a region.
D. A term expressing an action or a state of being.

146. Fill in the blank with **correct** article:

Sita Devi has become ______ M.L.A.
A. an B. a
C. the D. zero article

147. Which of the following is **not** included in non-fiction writing?
A. Autobiographies B. Diary
C. Bio-graphies D. Short-stories

148. Choose the **correct** form of verb for the blank space in the given sentence:

Here ______ the Indigo! (come)
A. come B. comes
C. has come D. is come

149. What was the unusual thing about Hafeez in the story 'The Treasure Within'?
A. Making Predictions
B. Having a photo-graphic memory
C. Coining stories
D. Foresightedness

150. What is the general aim of teaching English?
A. To enable the learners to know the cultural groups of the world.
B. To open the treasure of rich English literature for all.
C. To inculcate the integrative quality of English language.
D. To make the learner an effective user of English language.

EXPLANATORY ANSWERS

1. (A): Lev Vygotsky emphasized the crucial role of social and cultural factors in a child's cognitive development, distinguishing his perspective from others like Piaget who focused more on individual cognitive stages. Vygotsky's sociocultural theory proposes that children learn actively and through hands-on experiences, and their learning is deeply influenced by the cultural contexts in which they grow up.

2. (C): Film strips are not suitable for visually impaired students because they rely heavily on visual content which cannot be perceived by students with visual impairments. In contrast, Braille materials, talking books, and embossed maps are specifically designed to be accessible for the visually impaired, utilizing tactile or auditory information.

3. (B): Progressive education is an educational movement emphasizing real-world experiences, problem-solving, and critical thinking. This approach encourages 'learning by doing,' where students actively engage with their environment to foster learning, reflecting the principles set out by educational reformers like John Dewey.

4. (D): Inclusive education refers to the educational model that seeks to include all children within the mainstream educational system, regardless of their physical, intellectual, social, emotional, linguistic, or other conditions.

This approach aims to provide equal opportunities for all students, not just those who are disabled or socially deprived.

141. A **142.** D **143.** B **144.** B **145.** A **146.** A **147.** D **148.** B **149.** B **150.** D

5. (A): A field trip is an effective teaching-learning strategy in the context of social learning because it allows students to interact directly with the environment and engage socially with peers and guides. This hands-on experience not only enhances learning but also supports social development by fostering communication and observational skills in a real-world context. This method aligns closely with social learning theory, which emphasizes learning through observation and interaction within social settings.

6. (B): Analytical questions require detailed analysis and are typically answered in an essay or short-answer format, making them not objective. Objective type questions, like matching, multiple choice, and blank space questions, require students to select or write a specific answer without requiring extended reasoning or explanation.

7. (A): Acceleration is not suitable for slow learners as it involves progressing through education at a faster rate than typical, which can be overwhelming for these students. Remedial teaching, drill work, and cooperative teaching methods are more beneficial as they provide additional support, practice, and collaborative learning opportunities, respectively.

8. (A): The spaced method is appropriate for learning long and difficult lessons as it involves breaking the learning into shorter sessions over a longer period. This method allows for better understanding and retention by providing time for reflection and assimilation of the material, as opposed to the massed method which involves cramming the information in a short time.

9. (A): Approved social behaviour patterns in adolescence include leadership skills and empathy. Leadership skills involve guiding others and making decisions responsibly, while empathy entails understanding and sharing the feelings of others. Ego-centrism, focusing on oneself, and stereotyping, applying generalized beliefs to individuals, are generally not seen as positive behaviours.

10. (A): The instinct theory is associated with William McDougall, not John Atkinson, making option A incorrect. Atkinson is known for his work on the Expectancy-Value Theory, not the Instinct Theory. Maslow's Need Hierarchical Theory, Woodworth's Drive Theory, and McClelland's Achievement Motivation Theory are correctly paired with their respective proponents.

11. (D): The Stanford-Binet Test is not a performance test of intelligence but a standardized IQ test that measures cognitive abilities through verbal, quantitative, and non-verbal reasoning. Performance tests of intelligence, like Koh's Block Design Test, Alexander's Pass Along Test, and Saguine Form Board Test, typically involve manipulating materials and require minimal verbal instruction, focusing instead on tasks that demonstrate practical problem-solving and spatial reasoning.

12. (C): Development does not necessarily follow a linear path, as this implies a fixed sequence of stages or progress that is the same for everyone. In reality, developmental patterns can vary greatly between individuals and can be influenced by numerous factors, making development multi-directional rather than strictly linear. Other listed principles, such as development being a product of heredity and environment, and developmental patterns being predictable, are generally accepted in developmental psychology.

13. (B): According to Robert Gagne, the highest level of learning a teacher should strive to take students to is problem-solving learning. This level involves applying rules to solve problems in new situations, which represents a higher-order cognitive skill encompassing understanding and application, beyond simple concept or rule learning.

14. (D): All the factors listed—motivation, aptitude, interest, and attention—affect learning. These elements are crucial as they determine how effectively an individual engages with educational content. Motivation drives effort, aptitude influences ability to understand, interest enhances engagement, and attention is necessary for effective information processing.

15. (A): A harmonious relationship with parents is not a common characteristic of social development in adolescence. Typically, adolescence is marked by a quest for greater independence, which can often lead to conflicts with parents as the individual seeks to establish a separate identity. Other options, such as new social groupings, a search for identity, and hero-worship, are more typically associated with adolescent social development.

16. (D): Endocrine glands are not an environmental but a biological factor influencing child development. These glands play a critical role in physical and hormonal development through the secretion of hormones. Environmental factors typically include elements like nutrition, the mental state of the mother during pregnancy, and accidents, which have external impacts on a child's growth and development.

17. (B): The 'Law of Use' and 'Law of Disuse' relate to Thorndike's Law of Exercise. According to this law, connections between stimuli and responses are strengthened through use and weakened through disuse, implying that practicing a skill improves it, whereas failing to practice leads to its decay.

18. (C): Animism is not a characteristic related to Piaget's concrete operational stage of cognitive development. Animism, the belief that inanimate objects have life and feelings, is more typical of the earlier preoperational stage. The concrete operational stage, however, is marked by abilities such as reversibility, serialization, and conservation, where children begin to understand logical operations and are less egocentric.

19. (B): The teaching maxim "abstract to concrete" is not typically beneficial for learning-disabled children who generally benefit more from concrete to abstract approaches. Learning-disabled students often find it easier to understand and retain information when taught from simple to complex, direct to indirect, and known to unknown, as these methods build a foundation of understanding by starting with tangible, familiar concepts.

20. (C): The stages of "Individualism and exchange" and "Social contracts and individual rights" in Kohlberg's moral development theory are not part of the conventional level of morality. These stages belong to the pre-conventional and post-conventional levels, respectively. The conventional level involves maintaining social order and good interpersonal relations, focusing on complying with laws and the expectations of others to uphold societal norms.

21. (D): The "Law of Progression" is not typically associated with heredity. Heredity laws such as the Law of Similarity, Law of Variation, and Law of Regression deal with how genetic traits are passed down and vary among individuals. The Law of Progression suggests a forward movement or development which is more general and not specifically tied to genetic inheritance.

22. (A): The physical appearance of a teacher does not fundamentally affect the teaching-learning process. While factors like the mental health of the teacher, content knowledge, and communication skills directly influence the effectiveness of teaching and the learning environment, physical appearance is not directly related to educational outcomes.

23. (D): According to Jean Piaget's theory of moral development, the adolescent period is characterized as the "Stage of Autonomous Morality". At this stage, individuals begin to see morality as based on mutual respect and cooperation, moving beyond the earlier stages where rules are seen as unchangeable and imposed by authority.

24. (D): The statement that individual differences are solely the result of heredity is incorrect. While heredity plays a significant role, environmental factors, experiences, and personal choices also contribute substantially to individual differences. Other statements recognize the complexity and uniqueness of individual differences.

25. (C): Cognitive learning involves the use of mental processes such as attention, memory, and reflection. This type of learning is concerned with the acquisition of problem-solving abilities and understanding, rather than just the mechanical repetition of actions, distinguishing it from imitative, motor, and affective learning.

26. (C): Passive attendance is not a principle of effective learning. Effective learning principles emphasize active engagement, motivation, individualized approaches, and feedback, which are crucial for enhancing the learning experience and ensuring better educational outcomes.

27. (B): Continuous and comprehensive evaluation means evaluating both scholastic and co-scholastic aspects of a student's performance, not just through continuous tests, but also at appropriate intervals to monitor progress comprehensively. It encompasses a broader understanding of student abilities and development, beyond mere academic achievements.

28. (B): Dyslexia is a learning difficulty characterized by problems with accurate and/or fluent word recognition, poor spelling, and decoding abilities. It specifically affects the ability to distinguish letters and words, which is different from other learning difficulties like dysgraphia (writing disorders) or dyscalculia (math difficulties).

29. (C): According to Sternberg's Triarchic Theory of Intelligence, the three aspects of intelligence are Componential (analytical), Experiential (creative), and Contextual (practical). These elements encompass the ability to analyze information, use creativity to solve problems, and adapt to different environments, respectively.

30. (D): In Pavlov's conditioning theory, a lack of motive does not positively affect the conditioning between natural and artificial stimuli. Effective conditioning generally requires appropriate timing, repetition of stimuli, and a controlled environment to establish a strong association. Motivation or a relevant stimulus is often necessary to create a meaningful connection for the conditioned response.

31. (D): 'तेजोपुंज' शब्द गुण स्वर संधि का उदाहरण नहीं है। यह शब्द 'तेजस्' और 'पुंज' का समास है, न कि संधि। संधि में दो शब्दों के मिलने से उनके बीच के ध्वनियों में परिवर्तन होता है। यहाँ पर गुण स्वर संधि नहीं हुई है।

32. (A): 'सुधीजन' और 'शताब्दी' शब्दों में वर्तनी सही है। ये दोनों शब्द उचित रूप से लिखे गए हैं और इनमें किसी प्रकार की अशुद्धि नहीं है, जबकि अन्य विकल्पों में वर्तनी संबंधी गलतियाँ पाई गई हैं।

34. (D): 'कासार' शब्द 'धनुष' का पर्यायवाची नहीं है। 'धनुष' के पर्यायवाची शब्द होते हैं 'चाप', 'कार्मुक', और 'शरासन'। 'कासार' का अर्थ एक छोटा तालाब या पोखर होता है। अतः यह 'धनुष' से संबंधित नहीं है।

35. (B): 'नीम हकीम खतरे जान' लोकोक्ति का अर्थ है कि अल्पज्ञान खतरनाक होता है। यह उक्ति उन लोगों के बारे में है जिन्हें थोड़ा ज्ञान होता है और वे उसे अधिक समझते हैं, जिससे कि अक्सर गलतियां हो जाती हैं और यह खतरनाक साबित हो सकता है।

36. (A): 'कादंबरी' का अर्थ है शराब और 'कादंबिनी' का अर्थ है घटा। इस युग्म का क्रमशः सही अर्थ दिया गया है जो संस्कृत साहित्य में प्रयोग होता है। 'कादंबरी' बाणभट्ट की प्रसिद्ध कृति का नाम भी है और इसका संदर्भ शराब से है, जबकि 'कादंबिनी' बादलों की शृंखला या घटा को दर्शाता है।

37. (B): देश, त्योहार, नदी ये व्यक्तिवाचक संज्ञाओं के उदाहरण नहीं हैं, बल्कि ये जातिवाचक संज्ञा के उदाहरण हो सकते हैं। व्यक्तिवाचक संज्ञा विशेष व्यक्ति, स्थान, या वस्तु के नाम होते हैं जैसे कि राम, दिल्ली, गंगा आदि। इसलिए यह कथन संगत नहीं है।

38. (B): 'चिरायु' और 'दीर्घायु' दोनों का अर्थ है दीर्घ जीवन या लंबी आयु होना। इसलिए यह विलोम शब्द का युग्म नहीं है क्योंकि दोनों शब्दों के अर्थ समान हैं। विलोम शब्द का अर्थ होता है विपरीत अर्थ वाले शब्द।

39. (C): 'परा' उपसर्ग का प्रयोग 'परार्थ' और 'पराश्रित' जैसे शब्दों में गलत है जबकि अन्य उपसर्गों के शब्द-युग्म सही हैं।

40. (C): 'इसी ने मेरी जिंदगी बचाई थी' में 'इसी' एक निश्चयवाचक सर्वनाम है, न कि प्रश्नवाचक सर्वनाम। प्रश्नवाचक सर्वनाम वे होते हैं जो प्रश्न पूछने के लिए प्रयुक्त होते हैं जैसे कि कौन, क्या, कहाँ, आदि। इसलिए यह युग्म संगत नहीं है।

41. (A): 'गुरुदक्षिणा' वास्तव में कर्मधारय समास है, जहाँ 'गुरु' और 'दक्षिणा' दोनों शब्द स्वतंत्र अर्थ रखते हैं लेकिन संयुक्त रूप से एक विशेष प्रकार की दक्षिणा का बोध कराते हैं, जो गुरु को दी जाती है। यह संबंध तत्पुरुष समास नहीं है क्योंकि वहाँ उत्तरपद प्रधान होता है और पूर्वपद उसकी विशेषता बताता है।

42. (D): संकेतवाचक विशेषण में वस्तु की नाप, तौल, मात्रा का बोध नहीं होता है। यह परिभाषा वास्तव में परिमाणवाचक विशेषण के लिए उपयुक्त है। संकेतवाचक विशेषण उन शब्दों को कहते हैं जो किसी वस्तु की स्थिति, स्थान, या समय का बोध कराते हैं, जैसे कि 'यह', 'वह', 'यहाँ', 'वहाँ'।

43. (D): 'वैधव्य' अपत्यवाचक तद्धित प्रत्यय से निर्मित नहीं है। यह शब्द 'विधवा' से बना है, जो किसी व्यक्ति की स्थिति या अवस्था का बोध कराता है। अन्य शब्द जैसे 'वैनतेय', 'कौरव', और 'वासुदेव' व्यक्तियों के नामों से जुड़े हुए हैं और उनके पिता या पूर्वजों का संकेत देते हैं।

44. (C): 'ग', 'ल', और 'ब' का उच्चारण स्थान क्रमशः कण्ठ, दन्त, ओष्ठ है। 'ग' वर्ण का उच्चारण कण्ठ से होता है, 'ल' का दन्त से, और 'ब' का ओष्ठ से होता है। ये उच्चारण स्थान इन वर्णों के उत्पादन की स्थिति को सही ढंग से दर्शाते हैं।

45. (B): "तुम्हें ऐसा करना शोभा नहीं देता है।" यह वाक्य पूर्वकालिक क्रिया का उदाहरण नहीं है। पूर्वकालिक क्रियाएं वे होती हैं जहां एक क्रिया के पूरा होने के बाद दूसरी क्रिया होती है, जैसे कि अन्य विकल्पों में दिखाया गया है। यह वाक्य एक सामान्य निषेधात्मक वाक्य है जो किसी क्रिया के अनुचित होने का संकेत देता है।

46. (D): "Give in" as a phrasal verb means to yield or surrender under pressure, not to distribute, deposit, or donate. This expression is typically used when someone reluctantly agrees to something after a period of resistance. Thus, the correct answer that conveys this meaning is "surrender."

47. (D): The modal auxiliary "must" is used to express obligation or necessity. In the sentence provided, "Your mother is seriously ill. You must leave for home at once," it indicates that it is necessary or obligatory for the person to go home immediately due to the serious illness of their mother.

48. (D): The correct preposition to use when someone is conveying information about a topic is "about." The sentence "He told all about the incident" means that he provided information concerning the incident to everyone involved or present.

49. (C): The phrase "the day after tomorrow" is used to refer to the day that follows the next day. Therefore, the most appropriate preposition to use in the sentence "I am going home the day after tomorrow" is "after," which properly links the timing of the action to the day being referred to.

50. (A): When discussing the act of looking with focus or attention at something, "at" is the correct preposition. In the sentence "Mohan gazed at the sky in the hope of rain," "at" correctly describes Mohan's action of looking intently towards the sky.

51. (B): The passive voice of the sentence "Have they done the work?" is "Has the work been done?" This transformation from active to passive voice correctly maintains the present perfect tense and agrees in number with the singular noun "work."

52. (B): The correct form of the verb to fit the sentence "The Headmaster wants to meet you" is "wants." This form agrees with the singular subject "The Headmaster" and is in the simple present tense, which is used for stating general facts or habitual actions.

53. (B): The incorrect part of the sentence is "not breaked." The correct past participle of "break" is "broken." Thus, the sentence should read, "Has Sachin not broken the record held by Bradman who made 10,000 runs in his career?"

54. (B): The expression "No sooner had the police reached than the thieves fled" is correct for describing events that occurred almost simultaneously. "No sooner" is followed by "than" to indicate that soon after one event happens, another follows immediately.

55. (D): The correct tense form for the sentence "She jumped off the train while it was moving" is "was moving." This form indicates that the action of the train (moving) was ongoing at the time she jumped off, which is best expressed using the past continuous tense.

56. (C): The original sentence is in direct speech and asks a question. When changing to reported speech, the structure needs to reflect that it's a question being relayed indirectly. The correct transformation would be, "I asked him if he knew when she would go home." This maintains the interrogative nature inside the indirect structure and properly shifts the tense from "will go" to "would go."

57. (B): "Sinecure" refers to a position that requires little to no responsibility, effort, or actual work but still offers financial compensation. This term typically applies to jobs that are given more for patronage or reward than for the purpose of actually performing duties. This option correctly describes a job with high pay and minimal responsibilities.

58. (C): "Send for" means to request someone to come to you, typically by sending a message or calling them. It's often used in contexts where assistance or presence is needed. The correct meaning in this context is "call someone in," which implies requesting someone's arrival at a location for consultation or help.

59. (A): The phrasal verb "turn out" has several meanings depending on the context, but a common one, especially when used with "someone," is to expel or evict them from a place, which fits with the general idea of forcing someone out. Therefore, "to evict someone" is the correct interpretation in this context.

60. (B): "Fair weather friends" are those who are supportive or friendly only when it is easy or beneficial to be so, particularly during good times. When challenges arise, these friends typically disappear or are not dependable. This idiom accurately describes friends who are loyal only during a time of success.

61. (C):

A —Wife→ B
Father: X → A
X → Z —Sister→ Y

Here, option (C) 'X is the son of A' Definitely not true, because it is not sure, whether X is daughter or son.

62. (A): Here, P = Starting point,

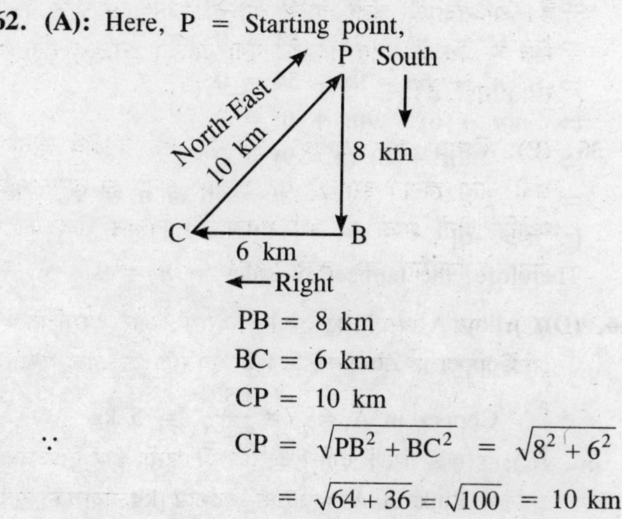

PB = 8 km

BC = 6 km

CP = 10 km

$\because$ CP $= \sqrt{PB^2 + BC^2} = \sqrt{8^2 + 6^2}$

$= \sqrt{64 + 36} = \sqrt{100} = 10$ km

A starts walking from P and finally reaches at P Therefore, A is 0 km away from starting point (P).

63. (C): $\because \quad \dfrac{m_1d_1h_1}{w_1} = \dfrac{m_2d_2h_2}{w_2}$

$\therefore \quad \dfrac{10 \times 8 \times h}{\frac{2}{5}} = \dfrac{m_2 \times 12 \times h}{\left(1-\frac{2}{5}\right)}$

$\Rightarrow \quad \dfrac{10 \times 8}{\frac{2}{5}} = \dfrac{m_2 \times 12}{\frac{3}{5}}$

$\Rightarrow \quad \dfrac{10 \times 8}{2} = \dfrac{m_2 \times 12}{3}$

$\Rightarrow \quad 40 = 4m_2$

$\Rightarrow \quad m_2 = 10$

Therefore, required number of persons = 10.

64. (C): Perimeter of a right prism triangle = 32 cm

Semi-perimeter, S = $\dfrac{32}{2}$ = 16 cm

Inradius of the triangle, r = 6 cm

$\therefore$ Area of the right prism triangle,

A = Sr = 16 × 6 = 96 cm^2

$\therefore$ Volume of the prism = A × h

(Where, h = height of the prism)

$\Rightarrow \quad 576 \text{ cm}^3 = 96 \text{ cm}^2 \times h$

$\therefore \quad h = \dfrac{576}{96} = 6$ cm

Hence, height of the prism = 6 cm.

65. (B): Given, the number of diagonals of a regular polygon = 27

$\Rightarrow \quad \dfrac{n(n-3)}{2} = 27$

$\Rightarrow \quad n^2 - 3n = 54$

$\Rightarrow \quad n^2 - 3n - 54 = 0$

$\Rightarrow \quad n^2 + 6n - 9n - 54 = 0$

$\Rightarrow \quad n(n + 6) - 9(n + 6) = 0$

$\Rightarrow \quad (n + 6)(n - 9) = 0$

$\Rightarrow \quad n = -6$ or $n = 9$

$[\because n \neq -6]$

Therefore, the number of sides = n = 9.

66. (D): Alloy A = 7 kg

Copper : Zinc = 5 : 2

$\therefore$ Copper in A = $7 \times \dfrac{5}{5+2}$ = 5 kg

Zink in A = $7 \times \dfrac{2}{7}$ = 2 kg

and Alloy B = 21 kg

Copper : Zinc = 3 : 4

$\therefore$ Copper in B = $21 \times \dfrac{3}{3+4}$

$= 21 \times \dfrac{3}{7}$ = 9 kg

Zinc in B = $21 \times \dfrac{4}{7}$ = 12 kg

$\because$ Alloy A and Alloy B are mixed together to form a new alloy

$\therefore$ Total copper in new alloy = 5 + 9 = 14 kg

and total zinc in new alloy = 2 + 12 = 14 kg

Hence, the ratio of copper and zinc in the new alloy = 14 : 14 = 1 : 1.

67. (A): 7 cosec θ – 3 cot θ = 7

or $\quad \cot\theta = \dfrac{7}{3}(\text{cosec}\,\theta - 1)$

$\Rightarrow \quad 7\,\text{cosec}\,\theta - 7 = 3\cot\theta$

$\Rightarrow \quad 7(\text{cosec}\,\theta - 1) = 3\cot\theta$

Squaring both sides

$49(\text{cosec}\,\theta - 1)^2 = 9\cot^2\theta$

$\Rightarrow 49(\text{cosec}\,\theta - 1)^2 - 9(\text{cosec}^2\,\theta - 1) = 0$

$\Rightarrow (\text{cosec}\,\theta - 1)[49(\text{cosec}\,\theta - 1) - 9(\text{cosec}\,\theta + 1)] = 0$

$\therefore \quad \text{cosec}\,\theta = 1$

or, $\quad 40\,\text{cosec}\,\theta - 58 = 0$

$\Rightarrow \quad \text{cosec}\,\theta = \dfrac{58}{40} = \dfrac{29}{20}$

$\therefore \quad \cot\theta = 0$ or $\dfrac{21}{20}$

$\left[\cot\theta = \dfrac{7}{3}(\text{cosec}\,\theta - 1)\right]$

Here, 7 cot θ – 3 cosec θ = 0 – 3 × 1 = –3

or, $\quad 7\cot\theta - 3\,\text{cosec}\,\theta = 7 \times \dfrac{21}{20} - 3 \times \dfrac{29}{20}$

$= \dfrac{3}{20}(49 - 29)$

$= \dfrac{3}{20} \times 20 = 3$

Hence, 7 cot θ – 3 cosec θ = 3

$\therefore$ Option (A) is correct.

68. (C): In a circle, if an equilateral triangle is inscribed, the tangents at the vertices will also form an equilateral triangle. This follows because the symmetry and equal angles of the inscribed equilateral triangle ensure that the angles between the tangents at each vertex are also equal, making the triangle formed by these tangents equilateral.

69. (A): Let the cost price of an article = ₹ x

Then, S.P. of an article = $\frac{115}{100}x$

According to question,

$$\frac{115}{100}x + 18 = \frac{118}{100}x$$

$$\Rightarrow \frac{118}{100}x - \frac{115}{100}x = 18$$

$$\Rightarrow \frac{3}{100}x = 18$$

$$\Rightarrow x = 600$$

Hence, the cost price of the article = x = ₹ 600.

70. (C): 0 3 9 12 36 39 117 120 360

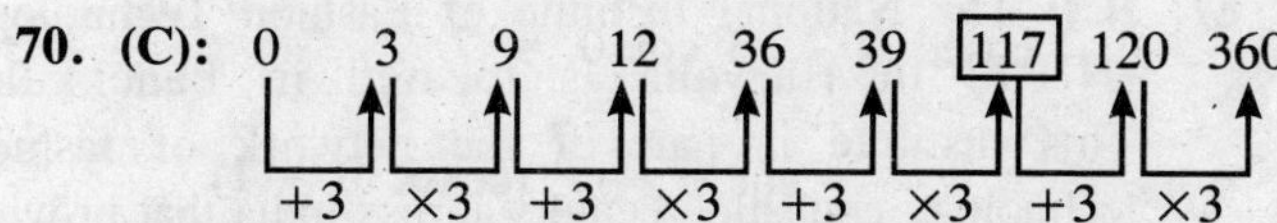

In place of 42, it should be 117.

Therefore, the wrong number in the given series = 42.

71. (B): Let two positive numbers be x and y

Then, $x - y = 3$

and $x^2 + y^2 = 369$

$\because (x - y)^2 = x^2 + y^2 - 2xy$

$\therefore 3^2 = 369 - 2xy$

$\Rightarrow 2xy = 369 - 9$

$\Rightarrow 2xy = 360$

Now, $(x + y)^2 = x^2 + y^2 + 2xy$

$= 369 + 360$

$\Rightarrow (x + y)^2 = 729 = (27)^2$

$\therefore x + y = 27$

Hence, sum of the numbers is 27.

72. (B): Given, remainder = 36

$\therefore$ Divisor = 5 × 36 = 180

and quotient = $\frac{180}{12} = 5$

Now, Divident = Divisor × Quotient + Remainder

= 180 × 15 + 36

$\Rightarrow$ Dividend = 2700 + 36 = 2736

Hence, the dividend is 2736.

73. (C): Given, A = ÷, B = +, C = –, D = ×

$\therefore$ 20 C 12 B 8 A 2 D 6

= 20 – 12 + 8 ÷ 2 × 6

= 20 – 12 + 4 × 6

= 20 – 12 + 24

= 44 – 12 = 32.

74. (D): The average speed = $\frac{\text{Total distance}}{\text{Total time}}$

$$= \frac{12 + 18 + 24}{\frac{12}{3} + \frac{18}{9} + \frac{24}{4}}$$

$$= \frac{54}{4 + 2 + 6}$$

$$= \frac{54}{12} = \frac{9}{2}$$

= 4.5 km/hr.

75. (D): Violin, Harp, and Guitar are string instruments where the sound is produced by the vibration of strings. Flute, however, is a woodwind instrument where sound is produced by the flow of air across an opening. Therefore, Flute is the odd one out.

76. (A): Given, 16 – 4 = 2

$\Rightarrow 16 = 4^2$

9 – 3 = 2

$\Rightarrow 9 = 3^2$

81 – 3 = 4

$\Rightarrow 81 = 3^4$

$\therefore$ 64 – 4 = 3

$\Rightarrow 64 = 4^3$

77. (D): Given,

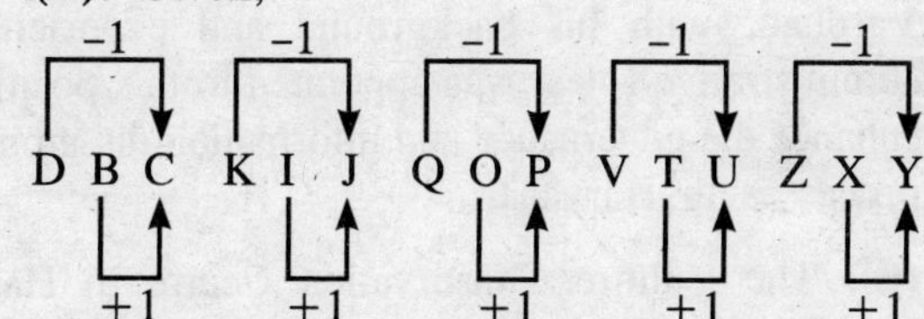

$\therefore$? = The missing term in the series = VTU.

78. (D): Given,

'P	R	O	J	E	C	T'	=	'C	E	O	P	R	T'
16	18	15	10	5	3	20		3	5	15	16	18	20

P	L	A	N	E	=	E	L	N	P
16	12	1	14	5		5	12	14	16

In both cases, Middle letter is removed and remaining letters are arranged in alphabetic order.

Similarly,

O	R	G	A	N	I	S	E	D
15	18	7	1	14	9	19	5	4

=	A	D	E	G	I	O	R	S
	1	4	5	7	9	15	18	19

Therefore, 'ORGANISED' will be coded as 'ADEGIORS'.

79. (C):

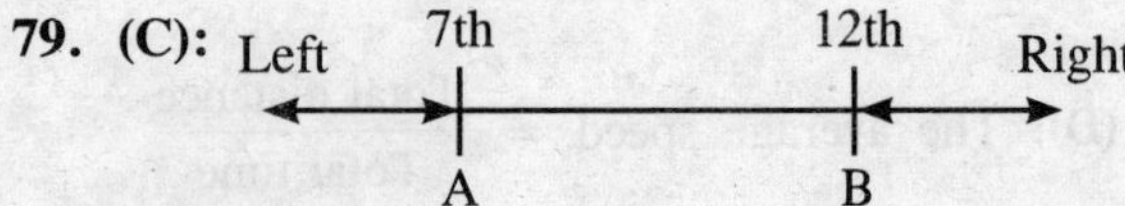

After interchanging their position

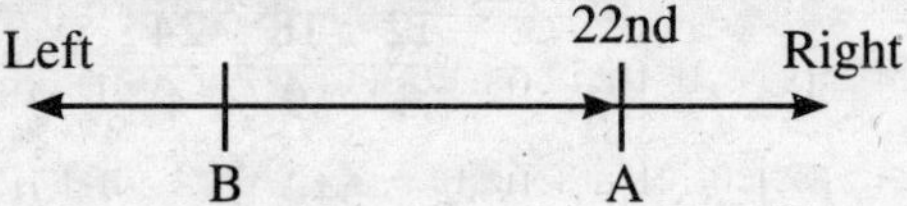

∴ Total boys in a row = 22 + 11 = 33.

80. (B):

Right→
C 5 km D
↑ Right 2 km
B 8 km A
←West

Here, Starting point = A

AB = 8 km; BC = 2 km

CD = 5 km

Therefore, He is now in North-west positione with refrence to starting point.

81. (C): Shri Vijay Vardhan is the current Chief Information Officer of Haryana, also known as the Chief Information Commissioner. This role involves overseeing the application of the Right to Information Act within the state, ensuring transparency and accessibility of information to the public. Vijay Vardhan, with his background and experience in administrative roles, was appointed to this position to enhance the governance and information dissemination processes in Haryana.

82. (B): The Vulture Conservation Centre in Haryana is located in Pinjore. This center plays a significant role in the conservation and rehabilitation of vultures, which are critically endangered species. The efforts here are part of a broader initiative to protect these birds from extinction, addressing environmental concerns and promoting biodiversity.

83. (A): Dr. A.R. Kidwai, who served as the UPSC Chairman, later became the Governor of Haryana. His tenure in both roles highlighted his significant contributions to public administration and governance, reflecting his commitment to civil service and administrative reforms.

84. (A): The Khelo India Women's Archery ranking competition was organized in the district of Sonipat, Haryana. This event is part of the Khelo India initiative, aimed at fostering sports development and encouraging participation in sports across various levels, particularly among women in archery.

85. (A): Haryana has a total of 95 Tehsils. This administrative division is crucial for local governance and facilitates the management of resources and developmental programs at a more localized level, ensuring that administrative services are accessible to the residents of the state.

86. (C): The Haryana government runs the scheme "Mera Pani Meri Virasat" to encourage farmers to shift from water-intensive paddy crops to more traditional and less water-consuming crops. This initiative is aimed at sustainable agriculture practices, addressing water scarcity, and promoting the cultivation of crops better suited to the regional climate and soil health.

87. (C): The National Institute of Fashion Technology (NIFT) in Haryana is located in Panchkula. This institute is part of the network of fashion technology education centers across India that provide professional training and education in the field of design, technology, and management, tailored to the evolving needs of the fashion industry.

88. (C): The sage known as Puran Bhagat in Haryana was Baba Chaurangi Nath. He is revered in local folklore and religious traditions, embodying the spiritual and cultural heritage of the region. His life and teachings continue to be celebrated and have a lasting influence on the local communities.

89. (C): The Morni Hills in Haryana are part of the outer range of the Himalayas. This geographical feature is significant for its natural beauty and biodiversity, making it a popular destination for eco-tourism and nature enthusiasts. The hills provide a serene environment and are home to a variety of flora and fauna.

90. (A): During the revolt of 1857, Tafzal Husain led attacks on British establishments in Rohtak, Haryana. This participation was part of the wider Indian uprising against British colonial rule, with local leaders like Tafzal Husain playing crucial roles in mobilizing resistance and fighting for independence.

91. (A): Jonathan Livingston Seagull's passion for flying is evident throughout the passage, where it is described as more than just a means to an end; it is his joy and primary motivation in life. Unlike other seagulls, who view flying merely as a way to travel from the shore to food, Jonathan sees it as a crucial part of his existence. This love of flying transcends the basic survival instinct seen in his peers, emphasizing it as a profound part of his life.

92. (B): The word "gentle" describes something mild or not harsh. In the context of the sea, it suggests calm and smoothness. The antonym, therefore, needs to suggest the opposite quality. "Fierce" fits this as it conveys intensity and aggressiveness, which is a stark contrast to gentleness. The other options, such as "Falter," "Twisting," and "Concentration," do not directly oppose the meaning of "gentle."

93. (C): The word "dodge" specifically means to avoid something by making a sudden quick movement, which fits the context of the seagulls quickly maneuvering to catch bits of food. The other options—'Ruffled', 'Webbed', and 'Chummed'—do not convey the meaning of sudden movement to avoid something, making "Dodge" the correct choice.

94. (D): Jonathan Livingston Seagull's actions described by "unashamed, stretching his wings again" clearly illustrate his perseverance. Despite experiencing setbacks like stalling in the air, which is considered a disgrace among seagulls, he continues to try and perfect his flight. This persistence in the face of failure and dishonor highlights his determined character.

95. (C): The word "dismayed" means to feel consternation and distress. In the context of the passage, Jonathan's parents are dismayed not because they are proud or detached, but because they are disappointed by his unconventional actions. This disappointment stems from their concern over him spending time alone and focusing on what they likely see as unproductive or risky behaviours.

96. (B): Macavity from the poem "Macavity: The Mystery Cat" by T.S. Eliot is often compared to Professor Moriarty, a character from the Sherlock Holmes stories. Both are master criminals, known for their cunning and elusiveness, which makes Moriarty a fitting metaphorical comparison for Macavity. This embodiment captures Macavity's character as a clever and elusive criminal, mirroring the attributes of Professor Moriarty.

97. (B): The word "prostrate" literally means lying stretched out on the ground, typically face downwards, which is often done in submission or adoration. This definition directly matches the context needed, distinguishing it from the other options—'Palanquin' (a type of litter used for transportation), 'Procrastinate' (to delay or postpone action), and 'Prevaricate' (to speak or act in an evasive way).

98. (B): The lines are from Robert Frost's poem "The Road Not Taken." This poem famously concludes with the narrator reflecting on his life choices, symbolized by his decision to take the less traveled road in a wood, which he says has made all the difference in his life. The poem explores themes of individuality and the consequences of our choices.

99. (B): The subject of a sentence is the part that denotes the person or thing about which something is said, acting as the focus of the sentence. In grammatical terms, the subject typically performs the action of the verb or is described by the predicate. It's essential for forming complete thoughts and sentences.

100. (C): In phonetics, English is recognized to have approximately 20 vowel sounds and 24 consonant sounds. This varies slightly depending on dialects and accents, but the general count allows for a broad representation of the sounds used in spoken English. This distinction is crucial for phonetic studies and teaching English pronunciation.

102. (B): The central idea of the poem revolves around contrasting joy and pleasure, highlighting the deeper, more intrinsic value of joy compared to the fleeting, superficial nature of pleasure. Through various natural metaphors, the poet illustrates how joy, although born of simpler circumstances, brings a more genuine and fulfilling happiness than pleasure.

103. (D): The word 'devour' in the context of the poem means to eat something eagerly or greedily. This vividly conveys the consuming and somewhat aggressive nature of pleasure, as opposed to the gentle, enriching experience of joy.

104. (A): In the poem, joy is compared to a bird, specifically a lark, that sings for its own satisfaction and not for the entertainment of others. This metaphor emphasizes joy's inherent and self-contained nature, suggesting that true joy is personal and internally fulfilling.

105. (A): The line "Pleasure's a Moth that sleeps by day" uses a metaphor, a literary device that directly compares two unrelated subjects without using "like" or "as." Here, pleasure is metaphorically described as a moth, suggesting it is something that is inactive or hidden during times of light and only comes alive under deceptive circumstances.

106. (D): The sentence "To err is human, to forgive divine" is an example of antithesis because it juxtaposes two contrasting ideas—human fallibility and divine forgiveness—in a manner that highlights the contrast between common human behaviour and the idealized qualities of divinity.

107. (D): 'Experience' is an abstract noun because it refers to an idea, experience, or state of being that cannot be directly perceived by the senses. Unlike 'Crowd,' 'Gang,' and 'Student,' which are concrete nouns referring to tangible entities, 'Experience' encapsulates an intangible concept.

108. (C): Michael West's 'New Method' of teaching English lays stress on reading. This educational approach is designed to improve language acquisition through structured and intensive reading exercises, promoting a deep understanding of language mechanics and vocabulary.

109. (B): The line is a statement by Nelson Mandela. This powerful quote reflects his dedication to ensuring that apartheid's oppression would never recur in South Africa, emphasizing a vision of equality and unity for the country's future.

Nelson Rolihlahla Mandela was a South African anti-apartheid activist, politician, and statesman who served as the first president of South Africa from 1994 to 1999. He was the country's first black head of state and the first elected in a fully representative democratic election. His government focused on dismantling the legacy of apartheid by fostering racial reconciliation. Ideologically an African nationalist and socialist, he served as the president of the African National Congress (ANC) party from 1991 to 1997. The Nobel Peace Prize 1993 was awarded jointly to Nelson Mandela and Frederik Willem de Klerk "for their work for the peaceful termination of the apartheid regime, and for laying the foundations for a new democratic South Africa".

110. (B): The auther of the story 'Princess September' is William Somerset Maugham. He was an English writer, known for his plays, novels and short stories. Born in Paris, where he spent his first ten years, Maugham was schooled in England and went to a German university. His first novel, Liza of Lambeth (1897), a study of life in the slums, attracted attention, but it was as a playwright that he first achieved national celebrity. Maugham's novels after Liza of Lambeth include Of Human Bondage (1915), The Moon and Sixpence (1919), The Painted Veil (1925), Cakes and Ale (1930) and The Razor's Edge (1944). His short stories were published in collections such as The Casuarina Tree (1926) and The Mixture as Before (1940); many of them have been adapted for radio, cinema and television.

111. (B): "A Legend of the Northland" by Phoeby Cary is a ballad, a type of poem that typically narrates a story in short stanzas. This form is often used to tell legendary or folk tales, making it ideal for Cary's subject matter which involves storytelling about legendary or mythical events, often set in the distant past.

112. (B): "A bone of contention" is an idiom that means a subject or issue over which there is ongoing argument or disagreement. This phrase is often used to describe the main point of contention in disputes, reflecting its metaphorical meaning of something that two parties might figuratively fight over, much like dogs might fight over an actual bone.

113. (B): Archaeology or archaeology is the study of human activity through the recovery and analysis of material culture. The archaeological record consists of artifacts, architecture, biofacts or ecofacts, sites, and cultural landscapes. Archaeology can be considered both a social science and a branch of the humanities. Archaeologists study human prehistory and history, from the development of the first stone tools at Lomekwi in East Africa 3.3 million years ago up until recent decades.

Dendrochronology (dendron= tree, khronos= time, logia= the study of) is the science that deals with dating and the study of annual growth increments in trees and shrubs. It was founded by Andrew E. Douglas in the 1920s. It is also known as Tree-ring dating. It is useful in Radiocarbon dating, Archaeology, and Paleontology.

Anthropology is the scientific study of humanity, concerned with human behaviour, human biology, cultures, societies, and linguistics, in both the present and past, including archaic humans. Social anthropology studies patterns of behaviour, while cultural anthropology studies cultural meaning, including norms and values. The term sociocultural anthropology is commonly used today. Linguistic anthropology studies how language influences social life. Biological or physical anthropology studies the biological development of humans.

Ethology, the study of animal behaviour. Although many naturalists have studied aspects of animal behaviour through the centuries, the modern science of ethology is usually considered to have arisen as a discrete discipline with the work in the 1920s of biologists Nikolaas Tinbergen of the Netherlands and Konrad Lorenz of Austria. The ethologist is interested in the behavioural process rather than in a particular animal group and often studies one type of behaviour (e.g., aggression) in a number of unrelated animals.

114. (A): The phrasal verb "called off" means to cancel something that has been planned. In the context of the sentence, it suggests that the meeting was cancelled due to concerns or restrictions related to the pandemic. Other phrasal verbs like "called into," "called back," and "called down" do not convey the meaning of cancellation.

115. (B): The best sequence for learning English language is Listening, Speaking, Reading, Writing as:

- **Listening** is the primary learning skill. It is known as a responsive ability, or a latent skill, as it expects us to utilize our ears and our minds to understand. It is the first learning skills.
- **Speaking** is the communication medium of learning orally. Speaking is the second of the four learning skills.
- **Reading** is a process of looking at a series of written words/symbols and getting meaning from them. It is the third learning skills.
- **Writing** is the fourth language expertise we may gain in our learning. Writing abilities might be improved by giving activities on a piece and exploratory writing.

Hence, it could be concluded that 'Listening, Speaking, Reading and Writing' is correct sequence of basic skills of language.

116. (C): The correct spelling of the word is "Amateur," which refers to a person who engages in a particular activity or field of study non-professionally. The other options provided contain common misspellings of the word.

117. (B): The phonetic symbol 'ʊ' (as in option B) represents the vowel sound in the word "book." This symbol is used in the International Phonetic Alphabet to denote a near-close, near-back rounded vowel, commonly found in English words like "foot" and "could."

118. (D): The fable "The Ant and the Cricket" is adapted from Aesop's fables. Aesop, a storyteller believed to have lived in ancient Greece, is famous for his fables, moral stories that typically feature animals conveying human-like qualities and moral lessons.

119. (D): In the sentence "He is asleep," the word "asleep" functions as an adjective. It describes the state of the subject 'He.' This usage is part of a category of adjectives known as predicative adjectives, which come after a linking verb and describe the subject.

120. (B): Semantics is the study of meaning in language. It encompasses the meanings of words, phrases, sentences, and texts, and how these meanings are interpreted by speakers. This field addresses how context influences the interpretation of meaning and how language users understand and construct meanings in communication.

121. (A): Resilience refers to the capacity of an individual to withstand or recover quickly from difficult conditions. This includes bouncing back from adversities such as trauma, tragedy, health-related issues, or stress, which makes it a suitable choice for describing the ability to deal with hardships and their effects. The other options do not correctly represent this concept.

122. (B): An ode is a type of lyric poem, usually of significant length, that is dedicated to a specific subject and is often elevated in style and tone. It typically follows an elaborate stanza structure and is marked by its solemn and serious nature, making it fitting for expressing profound sentiments.

123. (C): The idiom "To bury the hatchet" means to make peace or resolve a conflict. It originates from the practice where Native Americans would literally bury their weapons as a sign of peace. This expression metaphorically implies putting away past disputes to come to a peaceful understanding.

124. (A): The passive voice of "They made me laugh" is correctly expressed as "I was made to laugh." This transformation adheres to the rules of changing active sentences to passive, where the object of the active sentence becomes the subject in the passive form, and the main verb is adjusted accordingly.

125. (A): "Besides" is the correct conjunction to use in the sentence "______ doing the cooking I look after the garden." It implies that in addition to the activity of cooking, another activity, looking after the garden, is also being performed. It connects two tasks being done concurrently by the speaker.

126. (B): "The Three Questions" by Leo Tolstoy is taken from his collection "What Men Live By, and Other Tales." This collection includes several of Tolstoy's short stories that explore deep moral and spiritual questions through simple yet profound narratives.

Leo Tolstoy, was a Russian writer. He is regarded as one of the greatest and most influential authors of all time. He received nominations for the Nobel Prize in Literature every year from 1902 to 1906 and for the Nobel Peace Prize in 1901, 1902, and 1909. He was already known as a brilliant writer for the short stories in Sevastopol Sketches (1855–56) and the novel The Cossacks (1863) when War and Peace (1865–69) established him as Russia's preeminent novelist.

127. (B): 'Lingua Franca' refers to a language systematically used to make communication possible between people not sharing a mother tongue, particularly when it is a third language distinct from both speakers' native languages. A lingua franca also known as a bridge language, common language, trade language, auxiliary language, vehicular language, or link language, is a language systematically used to make communication possible between groups of people who do not share a native language or dialect, particularly when it is a third language that is distinct from both of the speakers' native languages.

Linguae francae have developed around the world throughout human history, sometimes for commercial reasons (so-called "trade languages" facilitated trade), but also for cultural, religious, diplomatic and administrative convenience, and as a means of exchanging information between scientists and other scholars of different nationalities. The term is taken from the medieval Mediterranean Lingua Franca, a Romance-based pidgin language used especially by traders in the Mediterranean Basin from the 11th to the 19th centuries. A world language—a language spoken internationally and by many people—is a language that may function as a global lingua franca.

128. (A): Anne Frank famously named her diary "Kitty." She addressed many of her diary entries to Kitty as if writing letters to a friend. The Diary of a Young Girl, commonly referred to as The Diary of Anne Frank, is a book of the writings from the Dutch-language diary kept by Anne Frank while she was in hiding for two years with her family during the Nazi occupation of the Netherlands. The family was apprehended in 1944, and Anne Frank died of typhus in the Bergen-Belsen concentration camp in 1945. Anne's diaries were retrieved by Miep Gies and Bep Voskuijl. Miep gave them to Anne's father, Otto Frank, the family's only survivor, just after the Second World War was over.

The diary has since been published in more than 70 languages. It was first published under the title Het Achterhuis.

The diary is not written in the classic forms of "Dear Diary" or as letters to oneself; Anne calls her diary "Kitty", so almost all of the letters are written to Kitty. Anne used the above-mentioned names for her annex-mates in the first volume, from 25 September 1942 until 13 November 1942, when the first notebook ends. It is believed that these names were taken from characters found in a series of popular Dutch books written by Cissy van Marxveldt.

129. (A): Rita's direct speech, "I wish I were a princess," when converted into reported speech becomes "Rita said that she wished she were a princess." This maintains the original's subjunctive mood (were) and shifts the pronoun appropriately from first person to third person to fit the reported speech format.

130. (B): The correct prepositions in the sentence "The house is _______ fire! We had better get _______!" are "on" and "out." This combination correctly conveys that the house is experiencing a fire (on fire) and that it is urgent to exit the building (get out), matching common English usage for these scenarios.

131. (C): The bracketed part in the sentence "People (who have poor diets) are likely to catch colds" functions as an adjective clause. This clause provides additional information about "people," specifying which people are being referred to, thereby modifying the noun "people" like an adjective would.

132. (A): William Butler Yeats is considered the Irish National poet. His works are celebrated for their complex symbolism and deep national and historical themes, and he played a significant role in the Irish Literary Revival. Yeats' poetry and dramatic works have had a lasting impact on Irish culture and literature.

William Butler Yeats was an Irish poet, dramatist and writer, and one of the foremost figures of 20th century literature. He was a driving force behind the Irish Literary Revival, and along with Lady Gregory founded the Abbey Theatre, serving as its chief during its early years. He was awarded the 1923 Nobel Prize in Literature, and later served two terms as a Senator of the Irish Free State.

A Protestant of Anglo-Irish descent, Yeats was born in Sandymount, Ireland. His father practised law and was a successful portrait painter. He was educated in Dublin and London and spent his childhood holidays in County Sligo. He studied poetry from an early age, when he became fascinated by Irish legends and the occult. While in London he became part of the Irish literary revival. His early poetry was influenced by John Keats, William Wordsworth, William Blake and many more. These topics feature in the first phase of his work, lasting roughly from his student days at the Metropolitan School of Art in Dublin until the turn of the century. His earliest volume of verse was published in 1889, and its slow-paced, modernist and lyrical poems display debts to Edmund Spenser, Percy Bysshe Shelley and the poets of the Pre-Raphaelite Brotherhood.

133. (B): The statement "Death in an open field is better than life in a small hut" was said by Chandni to herself. This line reflects Chandni's feelings and thoughts about her own freedom and existence, representing a profound moment of self-reflection in the narrative.

134. (A): The Bilingual method of English language teaching was first developed by C.J. Dodson. This method emphasizes the use of both the native language and the target language in the classroom to aid in teaching and understanding, providing a bridge between familiar and new language structures.

Objectives of the method:

- to make the learners of a second/foreign language fluent and accurate in the spoken word.
- to make the learners accurate in the written word.
- to prepare the learners in such a manner that he may be able to achieve through bilingualism.

Principles of the Bilingual Method:

- The understanding of words and sentences in foreign languages can be made easier by the use of mother tongue.
- There is no need to create artificial situations for explaining the meaning of words and sentences of the target language.
- The Bilingual Method is a combination of the Direct Method and the Grammar Translation Method.

135. (C): The literary term used in the sentence "Let not Ambition mock their useful toil" is personification. Personification involves giving human traits, ambitions, or feelings to non-human entities. In this sentence, "Ambition" is personified as capable of mocking someone, which is a human action.

136. (B): The poem 'Chivvy' discusses the paradoxical attitude of parents and elders towards children, where they often give contradictory advice or commands. This poem highlights the confusing array of dos and don'ts faced by children and critiques the way adults often handle young people's autonomy.

137. (B): The moral of the poem 'Dad and the Cat and the Tree' is not to be over-confident. The narrative humorously illustrates the father's misguided confidence in his ability to rescue a cat from a tree, leading to a series of misadventures that underscore the theme of humility and recognizing one's limitations.

138. (C): 'A Period Plan' is also known as a Lesson Plan. This term is used in educational contexts to describe a detailed outline prepared by the teacher to guide a classroom session or period. The plan typically includes the objectives, teaching materials needed, and a step-by-step guide on how to conduct the lesson.

139. (B): William Wordsworth wrote the Lucy Poems, a series of five poems that are focused on the elusive character of Lucy, who is a mysterious and abstract figure in Wordsworth's works. These poems are noted for their emotional depth and the depiction of nature intertwined with human life.

140. (A): Major Ahluwalia and Phu Dorjee left a picture of Guru Nanak and a relic of Lord Buddha on Mt. Everest, respectively. These items were left as symbols of their faith and cultural heritage, representing significant gestures of reverence and personal accomplishment.

Phu Dorjee Sherpa was the first Nepali man and 23rd person in the world to climb Mount Everest. He was a member of the third Indian Everest Expedition 1965, led by Captain M S Kohli, which was the first successful Indian Everest Expedition. The group consisted of 21 major expedition members and 50 Sherpas. The initial attempt was at the end of April, when they returned to base camp due to bad weather and waited 2 weeks for better weather. On 29 May 1965, on the fourth and final attempt on the 12th anniversary of the first conquest of Mount Everest, together with H. P. S. Ahluwalia and Harish Chandra Singh Rawat, Phu Dorjee summited Mount Everest. This was the first time that these three climbers climbed the mountain together. He died in a fall on Mount Everest on 18 October 1969.

141. (A): The poem 'A House, A Home' is written by Lorraine M. Walli. This poem beautifully contrasts the physical structure of a house with the emotional warmth and inclusiveness of a home, emphasizing the aspects that turn a mere building into a place filled with love and care.

142. (D): The sentence "He painted the ceiling white" fits the pattern Sub + V + noun/pronoun + adjective. Here, 'He' is the subject, 'painted' is the verb, 'the ceiling' is the noun, and 'white' is the adjective describing the noun. This structure effectively demonstrates the action and its result on the object.

143. (B): William Sydney Porter is better known by his pen name, O. Henry. He is renowned for his witty, playful, and often ironic style of storytelling. O. Henry's work frequently features surprise endings and a sharp observation of the peculiarities of human nature.

O. Henry was an American short-story writer whose tales romanticized the commonplace—in particular the life of ordinary people in New York City. His stories expressed the effect of coincidence on character through humour, grim or ironic, and often had surprise endings, a device that became identified with his name and cost him critical favour when its vogue had passed. His works include "The Gift of the Magi", "The Duplicity of Hargraves", and "The Ransom of Red Chief", as well as the novel Cabbages and Kings. Porter's stories are known for their naturalist observations, witty narration, and surprise endings.

144. (B): The modal auxiliary "must" is used to express certainty or necessity, fitting the context of the sentence "All men must die." It emphasizes the inevitability of death, which is a fact of life that cannot be avoided or altered.

145. (A): Intonation in phonetics refers to the variation of pitch while speaking, which can alter the meaning of words and sentences. It involves changes in voice pitch across different parts of a sentence and is used to convey different meanings or to add emotional subtlety to speech.

146. (A): The correct article to use in the sentence "Sita Devi has become an M.L.A." is 'an'. This usage is due to the phonetic rule that applies to acronyms or initialisms starting with a vowel sound, despite their first letter. 'M.L.A.' begins with the sound of 'em,' which starts with a vowel sound, thus 'an' is the appropriate article to use before it.

147. (D): In non-fiction writing, short-stories are not included as they are a form of fictional literature. Non-fiction writing is based on factual events or realities, and includes genres like autobiographies, diaries, and biographies, where the content is based on real events and real people.

148. (B): The correct form of the verb for the sentence "Here comes the Indigo!" is 'comes'. This is because the subject 'the Indigo' is singular, and the verb must agree in number, making 'comes' the appropriate choice.

149. (B): In the story 'The Treasure Within', Hafeez is notable for having a photographic memory. This unique ability allows him to remember information in great detail, which is central to the narrative and his character's development throughout the story.

150. (D): The general aim of teaching English is to make the learner an effective user of English language. This encompasses developing the ability to communicate clearly and effectively in English, both in spoken and written forms, and understanding and using various forms of the language contextually.

Previous Paper (Solved)

Haryana Teacher Eligibility Test (HTET)

TGT English (Level-2), Exam 2022

(Exam held on 04 December, 2022)

PART-I

Child Development and Pedagogy

Directions: *Answer the following questions by selecting the **most appropriate** option.*

1. Thematic Apperception Test is used to measure the ______ of students.

A. Intelligence B. Aptitude
C. Attitude D. Personality

2. Which of the following statement is ***correct*** about the development of children?

A. Development is a product of only hereditary.
B. Development follows a random pattern.
C. Development is a cumulative process.
D. Different aspects of development are not inter-related.

3. 'Acceleration' is an important plan for education of which type of special children?

A. Gifted B. Slow learner
C. Learning disabled D. Mentally retarded

4. Which of the following factors does ***not*** affect the teaching-learning process?

A. Teaching skill of teacher
B. Mental health of teacher
C. Subject knowledge of teacher
D. Physical appearance of teacher

5. Which of the following is ***not*** a characteristic of creativity?

A. Originality B. Flexibility
C. Rigidity D. Fluency

6. Which of the following is ***not*** a subjective method of personality assessment?

A. Interview
B. Observation
C. Autobiography
D. Word Association

7. Who propounded the Triarchic theory of Intelligence?

A. Gardner B. Guilford
C. Sternberg D. Vernan

8. 'Family and School' are the examples of which environmental system in Bronfenbrenner's Bio-ecological Model theory?

A. Macro system B. Micro system
C. Exosystem D. Chromosystem

9. Which of the following pair is ***not*** correct?

Theory Propounder	Theory
A. Piaget	– Cognitive Development Theory
B. Bandura	– Social Learning Theory
C. Erikson	– Psycho-socio Development Theory
D. Vygotsky	– Moral Development Theory

10. What is the mechanism called, through which a child tries to change his own ego to that of someone else?

A. Identification B. Rationalization
C. Sublimation D. Projection

11. Who developed the Socio-cultural theory of development?

A. Vygotsky B. Erikson
C. Kohlberg D. Bronfenbrenner

12. Which of the following is ***not*** an extrinsic motive?

A. Competing in sport for trophy
B. Doing job for salary
C. Doing social service for self-satisfaction
D. Buy one get one free

13. "Mental health is the full and harmonious functioning of the whole personality". This definition of mental health is given by whom?

A. Menninger B. Hadfield
C. Drever D. Waltin

14. 'Development proceeds in the direction of longitudinal axis (head to foot)', called:

A. Cephalic-Caudal
B. Proximodistal
C. Spiral
D. Circular

15. What type of reinforcement schedule is to reinforce each correct response of the learner, in operant conditioning?
A. Fixed interval
B. Variable interval
C. Fixed ratio
D. Continuous

16. Who propounded the 'Need of Hierarchy Theory' of Motivation?
A. Hull
B. Maslow
C. Atkinson
D. Thomson

17. Meenal is average in intelligence and low in creativity and high level in adjustment. This is an example of:
A. Inter Individual Differences
B. Intra Individual Differences
C. Observable Differences
D. Expected Differences

18. Which of the following elements is ***not*** related to Skinner's operant conditioning theory?
A. Extinction
B. Discrimination
C. Spontaneous recovery
D. Reinforcement

19. Which of the following is ***not*** the characteristic of a well-adjusted person?
A. Awareness of his own potentials and limitations
B. Respecting himself and others
C. Balanced aspirations
D. Rigidity in behaviour

20. According to Piaget's cognitive development theory, the 'ability of reversibility' develops during which developmental stage?
A. Sensory motor
B. Pre-operational
C. Concrete-operational
D. Formal-operational

21. Out of the following Psychologists, who is ***not*** related with Gestaltism?
A. Kohler B. Koffka
C. Kretschmer D. Wertheimer

22. Which of the following statement is ***not*** correct with reference to adjustment?
A. It creates imbalance.
B. It motivates to change the life as per the demand of the situation.
C. It gives ability to bring desirable changes in the conditions of environment.
D. In the absence of adjustment one is surrounded by tension an anxiety.

23. Which type of curriculum did Bruner suggest to follow for the cognitive development of children?
A. Inclusive curriculum
B. Special curriculum
C. Spiral curriculum
D. Integrated curriculum

24. Cattell's culture free test of intelligence is a type of:
A. Individual Verbal Test
B. Group Verbal Test
C. Non-Verbal Test
D. Verbal and Non-Verbal Test

25. A type of intelligence test in which the questions are similar in difficulty level but more importance is given to the time element:
A. Speed Test
B. Power Test
C. Verbal Test
D. Performance Test

26. What kind of changes does growth bring about in children?
A. Structural
B. Functional
C. Structural and functional both
D. None of these

27. Which of the following component is ***not*** the part of Guilford structure of Intellect model?
A. Operation
B. Cognition
C. Content
D. Product

28. Which of the following statement is ***not*** correct with reference to Attitude?
A. Attitude has motivational affective characteristics.
B. Attitude can range strongly positive to strongly negative.
C. Attitude have a subject-object relationship.
D. Attitude is innate and acquired both.

29. Which of the following match is ***not*** correct?

	Erikson's Stages of Psycho-social Development	Serial Number of Stages
A.	Initiative Vs Guilt	– Stage 3
B.	Identity Vs Role Confusion	– Stage 5
C.	Autonomy Vs Shame and Doubt	– Stage 1
D.	Industry Vs Inferiority	– Stage 4

30. Which of the following is ***not*** a projective technique of personality assessment?
A. Word-association
B. Sentence completion
C. Expressive movement
D. Sociometry

PART-II

भाषा : हिन्दी

निर्देश: *निम्नलिखित प्रश्नों के उत्तर देने के लिए **सबसे उचित** विकल्प चुनिए।*

31. उच्चारण की दृष्टि से 'ग' व्यंजन की ध्वनिगत विशेषताएँ हैं :
A. कंठ्य, अघोष, महाप्राण B. कंठ्य, सघोष, महाप्राण
C. कंठ्य, सघोष, अल्पप्राण D. कंठ्य, अघोष, अल्पप्राण

32. वचन की दृष्टि से कौन-सा युग्म **सही** है?
A. दर्शन — दर्शनों
B. प्राण — प्राणों
C. नारी — नारियों
D. हस्ताक्षर — हस्ताक्षरों

33. 'गिरीश' शब्द में कौन-सी संधि है?
A. दीर्घ स्वर संधि B. गुण स्वर संधि
C. यण् स्वर संधि D. व्यंजन संधि

34. 'जाह्नवी' शब्द का पर्याय है :
A. मंदाकिनी B. कुमुदनी
C. पथगामिनी D. नलनी

35. 'सरसिज' शब्द में कौन-सा समास है?
A. कर्मधारय समास B. द्वन्द्व समास
C. अव्ययीभाव समास D. अलुक् तत्पुरुष समास

36. विलोम की दृष्टि से असंगत विकल्प चुनिए :
A. ग्रस्त — मुक्त
B. व्यष्टि — समष्टि
C. आविर्भाव — तिरोभूत
D. अर्वाचीन — प्राचीन

37. किस विकल्प में परिमाणवाचक विशेषण का प्रयोग हुआ है?
A. प्रणव पाँच किलो दूध पी गया।
B. प्रणव पाँच केले खा गया।
C. प्रणव पाँचवीं कक्षा में पढ़ता है।
D. प्रणव के साथ कुछ बच्चे खेल रहे हैं।

38. 'जिज्ञासा' का सटीक समानार्थी है :
A. उत्कंठा B. ज्ञानेप्सा
C. वांछा D. इच्छा

39. ''यह आपका माहात्म्य है।'' वाक्य में प्रयुक्त 'माहात्म्य' शब्द में कौन-सी संज्ञा है?
A. जातिवाचक B. भाववाचक
C. समूहवाचक D. व्यक्तिवाचक

40. ''सामने जो बड़ा-सा घर दिखाई दे रहा है, वह मेरा है।'' वाक्य में किस सर्वनाम का प्रयोग हुआ है?
A. पुरुषवाचक B. निजवाचक
C. निश्चयवाचक D. अनिश्चयवाचक

41. किस विकल्प में भाववाचक तद्धित प्रत्यय का प्रयोग हुआ है?
A. बुलावा B. चचेरा
C. सौजन्य D. लखेरा

42. किस शब्द में 'अन्' उपसर्ग का प्रयोग **नहीं** हुआ है?
A. अनुत्तर B. अनुपम
C. अनुद्धार D. अनुगमन

43. क्रिया की दृष्टि से असंगत विकल्प चुनिए :
A. रमेश पत्र लिखवाता है–प्रेरणार्थक क्रिया
B. बालक छत पर खड़ा है–अकर्मक क्रिया
C. अध्यापक बालक को हिंदी पढ़ा रहा है–द्विकर्मक क्रिया
D. प्रणीता जोर-जोर से हँस रही है–सकर्मक क्रिया

44. विसर्ग ध्वनि का प्रयोग किन शब्दों में होता है?
A. तत्सम शब्दों में B. देशज शब्दों में
C. तद्भव शब्दों में D. उपर्युक्त सभी शब्दों में

45. 'साध्वाचरण' शब्द का सही संधि-विच्छेद है :
A. साध्व + आचरण B. साध + आचरण
C. साधू + आचरण D. साधु + आचरण

Language : English

Directions: *Answer the following questions by selecting the **most appropriate** option.*

46. Choose the option that brings out the meaning of the underline idiom:
A lion's share of India's annual budget is for defence.
A. major share
B. minor amount
C. small
D. very little

47. Select the appropriate one word substitution for the following:
Former students of a school or college
A. Emblem B. Alumni
C. Expert D. Incharge

48. Select the ***correct*** preposition for the blank:
I shall do it ________ pleasure.
A. in B. with
C. about D. over

49. Change the Narration:

"I'm taking the children to the zoo tomorrow." She said.

A. She told that she would be taking the children to the zoo the day after
B. She said that she will take the children to the zoo the next day
C. She told that she will be taking the children to the zoo
D. She will take the children to the zoo, she said

50. Select the *correct* meaning of the underlined phrasal verb:

Who can say what will <u>turn up</u> next?

A. remember B. divide
C. end D. happen

51. Select the appropriate preposition for the blank:

He has not yet recovered _______ his illness.

A. over B. in
C. at D. from

52. Select the *correct* antonym of:

Gloomy

A. Praise B. Coarse
C. Cheerful D. Dismal

53. Choose the *correct* synonym of:

Genius

A. Happy B. Cheerful
C. Talented D. Comfort

54. Change the narration in Reported Speech. Choose the *right* option:

'Who has been using my typewriter?' Said Mother.

A. Mother asked who has been using her typewriter
B. Mother said who was using her typewriter
C. Mother asked who had been using her typewriter
D. Mother asked her typewriter was being used by who

55. Choose the appropriate conjunction for the blank:

I shall not go _______ I am invited.

A. and B. unless
C. but D. there

56. Choose the part of sentence that has error:

she does not (A)/ resemble to (B)/ either of (C)/ her parents (D).

A. A B. B
C. C D. D

57. Change the voice and select the *correct* option:

Somebody has put out the light.

A. The light has put out by somebody
B. The light has been put out by somebody
C. Somebody has been out to put light
D. The light is being put out by somebody

58. Select the *correct* tense form from the options given:

Peter (try) to come in quietly but his mother (hear) him

A. tried, heard
B. trying, hears
C. was trying, was hearing
D. is trying, hears

59. Select the *correct* tense form from the options given:

When I first (come) to this house, it (be) a very quiet area.

A. comes, is B. came, was
C. coming, is D. come, are

60. Change the voice from Active to Passive and select the *correct* options:

Bees make honey

A. Honey is make by bees
B. Bees are making honey
C. Honey are made by bees
D. Honey is made by bees

PART-III

General Studies : Quantitative Aptitude, Reasoning Ability and GK & Awareness

Directions: *Answer the following questions by selecting the* ***most appropriate*** *option.*

61. Find the value of:

$$\sqrt{8+2\sqrt{8+2\sqrt{8+....}}}$$

A. 8 B. 10
C. 11 D. 4

62. If each side of the square be increased by 50%, then find the percentage increase in the area:

A. 50% B. 100%
C. 125% D. 150%

63. If × stands for –, ÷ stands for +, + stands for ÷, – stands for ×, then what is the value of 15 – 5 ÷ 5 × 20 + 10?

A. 70 B. 78
C. 75 D. 73

64. By selling a commodity for ₹ 72,000, a person made a profit of 20%. What was the cost price of that commodity?
A. ₹ 60,000 B. ₹ 50,000
C. ₹ 40,000 D. ₹ 65,000

65. Which term is wrong in following series?
8, 13, 21, 32, 47, 63, 83
A. 13 B. 32
C. 47 D. 63

66. A solid cube is coloured red on a faces. It is cut into 64 smaller cube of equal size. How many small cube have no face coloured?
A. 24 B. 16
C. 8 D. 4

67. Find the next term in the following number series:
2, 7, 24, 77, 238, ...
A. 721 B. 722
C. 723 D. 733

68. Anil introduces Prashant, "He is the husband of the grand daughter of the father of my father". How is Prashant related to Anil?
A. Brother B. Brother-in-law
C. Nephew D. Son

69. Four groups of letters are given below, three of them are alike in certain way while one is different, choose the ***odd*** one:
A. STUA B. RQPA
C. MLKA D. HGFA

70. Earth is related to Axis in the same way as wheel is related to:
A. Tyre B. Car
C. Road D. Hub

71. Find the next term in the following letter series:
LXF, MTJ, NPN, OLR, ...
A. PHV B. PIU
C. PJW D. PKX

72. If A is 40 meter South-West of B, C is 40 meter South-East of B, then C is in which direction fo A?
A. East B. West
C. North-East D. South

73. The average marks obtained by 150 students was 35. If the average marks of passed students was 39 and that of the failed students was 15, find the number of students, who passed the examination:
A. 120 B. 125
C. 135 D. 140

74. If $a^x = b$, $b^y = c$ and $c^z = a$, then what is the value of xyz?
A. abc B. 1
C. $\frac{1}{abc}$ D. ab

75. Find the smallest perfect square number which is exactly divisible by 4, 5, 6, 15 and 18:
A. 800 B. 225
C. 900 D. 361

76. What is the value of $\left(\sqrt{5}\right)^{-5/2} \times \left(\sqrt{5}\right)^{-3/2}$?
A. $\frac{1}{25}$ B. $\frac{1}{125}$
C. $\frac{1}{325}$ D. $\frac{1}{625}$

77. A sum of money doubles itself in 15 years at compound interest. In how many years it will become 8 times at the same compound interest rate?
A. 30 years B. 40 years
C. 60 years D. 45 years

78. If 25 men can reap a crop in 60 days, then in how many days will 10 men reap the crop?
A. 125 days B. 92 days
C. 100 days D. 150 days

79. If $x + \frac{1}{x} = 5$, then what is the value of $x^3 + \frac{1}{x^3}$?
A. 125 B. 110
C. 115 D. 105

80. In a certain code '786' means 'Study very hard', '958' means 'Hard work pays', '645' means 'Study and work', which is the code for 'very'?
A. 8 B. 6
C. 7 D. 5

81. Percentage of posts which have been reserved for women in Panchayati Raj Institutions of Haryana:
A. 25% B. 33%
C. 66% D. 50%

82. The district, where first time in Haryana E-challan has been introduced:
A. Gurugram B. Panchkula
C. Hisar D. Rohtak

83. 'Global City Project' is being developed by:
A. HSIIDC, Govt. of Haryana
B. GMDA, Govt. of Haryana
C. HUDA, Govt. of Haryana
D. Ministry of Urban Development, Govt. of India

84. The district, where Dolomite is found:
A. Mahendragarh B. Gurugram
C. Faridabad D. Panipat

85. The award, which is given to a sport coach for excellence in coaching by the Haryana State:
A. Dronacharya award
B. Guru Vashistha award

C. Maharana Pratap award
D. Arjuna award

86. The Position of Haryana in India in respect of area is:
A. 11th B. 21st
C. 15th D. 18th

87. The place, which was visited and mentioned by Chinese traveller Yuan Chwang:
A. Agroha B. Sugh
C. Kurukshetra D. Panipat

88. The de jure head of the State Administration in Haryana is:
A. Chief Minister of the State
B. Divisional Commissioner
C. Advocate General of the State
D. Governor of the State

89. Under which scheme of Haryana Government the socio-economic data of all the families of Haryana is being created?
A. Antyoday Parivar Utthan Yojna
B. Parivar Pehchan Patra-Yojana
C. Mukhyamantri Parivar Samriddhi Yojna
D. Jan Aadhar Yojna

90. The smallest (in term of area) wild life sanctuary is:
A. Bhindawas B. Nahar
C. Saraswati D. Chhilchhila

PART-IV

Subject Knowledge—English

Directions: *Answer the following questions by selecting the most **appropriate** option.*

91. Which of the two words given below are synonymous?
(*a*) shun
(*b*) grant
(*c*) reverse
(*d*) avoid
(*e*) avail
A. (*b*) and (*e*) B. (*c*) and (*d*)
C. (*a*) and (*d*) D. (*d*) and (*e*)

92. A 'misogynist' is a person who:
A. hates women
B. believes in self-advancement
C. is interested in the welfare of others
D. talks about accomplishments

93. In which of the following sentences the '–ing' word is used as an adjective?
A. The long speech was boring the pupils.
B. She was standing on the platform whistling.
C. He showed us some exciting photographs.
D. The magician was entertaining the audience.

94. In Rabindranath Tagore's poem 'Where the Mind is Without Fear', 'dead habit' refers to:
A. meaningless conventions
B. old habits
C. petty quarrels
D. reason

95. Fill in the blanks with the suitable determiners.

______ are the old classrooms.

______ are the new ones.
A. These, Those B. This, Those
C. These, This D. These, Either

96. Which of the following sentences has an *adjective clause*?
A. The book with the red sleeve fell to the ground.
B. The elephant which is chained belongs to the temple.
C. The artist's painting of the sea and the hills was sold for a vast sum.
D. Those hills in the distance form the border between the two countries.

97. Which of the following groups of words is ***opposite*** to each other?
A. loquacious – talkative
B. gullible – shrewd
C. pompous – conceited
D. erudite – scholarly

98. Which of the following words mean 'to put things off until later'?
A. Prevaricate B. Procrastinate
C. Precipitate D. Perpetrate

99. When a word's vocalization imitates a natural sound, as can be heard in the words 'murmur', 'buzz' and 'pop', what do we call that device?
A. Anaphora B. Synecdoche
C. Personification D. Onomatopoeia

100. Who received the Nobel Prize for Literature in 2019?
A. Peter Handke B. Kazuo Ishiguro
C. Harold Pinter D. Toni Morrison

101. Which of the following words fits in best to the description given below?

Frugal? To the last ditch! People have even accused me of being tight-fisted and stingy, and I am afraid that if they are referring to my attitude toward spending money, they are correct. I am ______.

A. stoic B. dilettante
C. philistine D. parsimonious

102. Identify the part of speech of the underlined word in the given sentence:

They while away their evenings with books and games.

A. verb B. adjective
C. adverb D. preposition

103. The story 'Coachman Ali' is originally written in:

A. Assamese B. Hindi
C. Gujarati D. Urdu

104. Fill in the blank in the given sentence with one of the words that fits best:

He disliked his job heartily, and therefore it was no surprise that he discharged his duties so ______.

A. perfunctorily
B. dogmatically
C. sardonically
D. wantonly

105. Which of the following stories is ***not*** written by Oscar Wilde?

A. The Selfish Giant
B. The Happy Prince
C. The Canterville Ghost
D. The Man Who Would Be King

106. In which of the following sentences is the word 'after' used as a preposition?

(*a*) They arrived after us.
(*b*) They arrived after we had left.
(*c*) I went for a short walk after dinner.
(*d*) After he finished his studies, he went to America.

A. only (*a*) B. (*a*) and (*b*)
C. (*a*) and (*c*) D. (*b*) and (*d*)

107. Arrange the adjectives given below in their proper order to fill in the blanks in the given sentence:

Hamid bought a ______, ______, ______ jacket at the ______, ______, ______ bazaar.

A. disgusting, illfitting, plastic, busy, local, Sunday
B. illfitting, disgusting, plastic, Sunday, local, busy
C. plastic, illfitting, disgusting, busy, Sunday, local
D. local, plastic, illfitting, busy, disgusting, Sunday

108. In the poem 'Everyone Sang' what comparison does the poet Siegfried Sassoon, make in the first stanza?

A. The poet compares everyone singing to the cackling of the geese.
B. The poet compares the feeling of delight experienced by the people to the joy of freedom felt by the birds who are released from the prison.
C. The poet compares the delight to the beauty of the setting sun.
D. The poet compares the people to singing birds returning home to their chicks.

109. Which of the following is the ***correct*** indirect speech of the following?

'I am a doctor', explained the young lady on her arrival at the house 'and I have come here in answer to a call I received this morning. Is this the right house?'

A. On her arrival at the house the young lady explained that she was a doctor, and had gone there in answer to a call she had received that morning. She asked if that was the right house.
B. The young lady, on her arrival at the house, explained that she was a doctor and had come here in answer to a call she received that morning she asked if she was at the right house.
C. On her arrival at the house the young lady said that she is a doctor and that she had received a call from here and asked if it was the right house.
D. After having arrived at the house, the young lady explained that she was a doctor and she had come there in answer to a call she received that morning. She inquired if this was the right house.

110. Which of the following words mean 'easily deceived' too 'ready to accept whatever people say'?

A. Credible B. Creditable
C. Credulous D. Consequential

111. In which of the following sentences a gerund or a gerundial phrase is ***not*** used?

A. Finding a good job is becoming more and more difficult nowadays.
B. Spreading rumours is an anti-social activity.
C. The slamming of the doors had aroused mother.
D. Loudly knocking at the gate, he demanded admission.

Directions (Qs. No. 112-115): *Identify the* ***incorrect*** *sentence/s in the following.*

112. (*a*) Each of these boys plays games.
(*b*) Whoever does best he will get a prize.
(*c*) He is wiser than I.
(*d*) None of us has seen him.

A. only (*a*) B. only (*b*)
C. (*a*) and (*c*) D. (*c*) and (*d*)

113. (*a*) She played so long that she is very tired.
(*b*) He guessed what I am thinking.
(*c*) He looked as if he was going to faint.
(*d*) They were hoping that she will come.

A. (*a*) and (*b*) B. (*b*) and (*c*)
C. (*a*), (*b*) and (*d*) D. (*b*), (*c*) and (*d*)

114. (*a*) He found hundred rupees.
(*b*) He is best player.
(*c*) The Ganges is a river.
(*d*) Shakespeare is greater than any other poets.

A. only (*a*) B. (*b*) and (*c*)
C. only (*c*) D. (*a*), (*b*) and (*d*)

115. (*a*) The manager was angry on the worker's behaviour.
(*b*) The manager was angry with the workers.
(*c*) She is not accustomed to eating Indian Food as she is from England.
(*d*) The student was absorbed through an exciting novel.
A. (*a*) and (*b*) B. (*b*) and (*c*)
C. (*a*) and (*c*) D. (*a*) and (*d*)

116. Which of the following word/s belong to the feminine gender?
(*a*) Parent (*b*) Wizard
(*c*) Duck (*d*) Drake
A. (*a*) and (*b*) B. only (*b*)
C. only (*c*) D. (*a*), (*b*) and (*d*)

117. In the poem titled 'Manners' by Elizabeth Bishop, which of the following tips is ***not*** given by the old man to his grandchild?
A. Be sure to remember to always speak to everyone you meet.
B. Don't always offer everyone a side; don't forget that when you get older.
C. ______ answer nicely when ______ spoken to.
D. ______ to treat all with kindness man or beast.

118. Which of the following sentences has an *adverb clause*?
A. The policemen arrested the men who broke into the shop.
B. They saw the man who stole the umbrella.
C. The children went to the park after they had their lunch.
D. The judges declared that he was the winner.

119. Who is the author of the poem titled 'My Shadow'?
A. William Blake
B. Robert Frost
C. Robert Louis Stevenson
D. Emily Dickinson

120. The writer Gaurishankar Govardhanram Joshi is better know by his pen name ______.
A. Jwala B. Krashanu
C. Shuchi D. Dhumaketu

Directions (Qs. No. 121-130): *Read the following poem titled 'Last Lesson of the Afternoon' by D.H. Lawrence and answer the questions given below.*

When will the bell ring, and end this weariness?
How long have they tugged the leash, and strained apart,
My pack of unruly hounds! I cannot start
Them again on a quarry of knowledge they hate to hunt,
I can haul them and urge them no more.
No longer can I endure the brunt
Of the books that lie out on the desks; a full threescore
Of several insults of blotted pages, and scrawl
Of slovenly work that they have offered me.
I am sick, and what on earth is the good of it all?
What good to them or me, I cannot see!
So, shall I take
My last dear fuel of life to heap on my soul
And kindle my will to a flame that shall consume
Their dross of indifference; and take the toll of their insults in punishment? – I will not! –
I will not waste my soul and my strength for this.
What do I care for all that they do amiss!
What is the point of this teaching of mine, and of this
Learning of theirs? It all goes down in the same abyss.
What does it matter to me, if they can write
A description of a dog, or if they can't?
What is the point? To us both, it is all my aunt!
And yet I'm supposed to care, with all my might.
I do not, and will not; they won't and they don't; and that's all!
I shall keep my strength for myself; they can keep theirs as well.
Why should be beat our heads against the wall
Of each other? I shall sit and wait for the bell.

121. The poet shows his feelings in the poem. Which of the following words best describe them?
(*a*) harrowed
(*b*) exasperated
(*c*) deplores
(*d*) delighted
(*e*) disenchanted
(*f*) gratified
A. (*a*), (*b*) and (*d*) B. (*c*) and (*d*)
C. (*e*) and (*f*) D. (*a*), (*b*), (*c*) and (*e*)

122. The poet uses a metaphor in the first stanza. With which words is the metaphor sustained?
A. When will the bell ring, and end this weariness.
B. How long have they tugged the leash, and strained apart
My pack of unruly hounds.
C. I cannot start
Them again on a quarry of knowledge they hate to hunt.
D. I can haul and urge them no more.

123. How many students are there in the poet's class?
A. 20 B. 40
C. 60 D. 45

124. Which of the following is an antonym of 'endure'?
A. undergo B. withstand
C. sustain D. resist

125. The poet is baffled as all his attempts at teaching them have been futile. Which line from the poem suggests this?

A. What do I care for all that they do amiss!
B. What is the point of this teaching of mine, and of this learning of theirs?
C. It all goes down the same abyss.
D. And yet I'm supposed to care, with all my might.

126. Which of the following lines suggest that the poet is disillusioned with his work?

(*a*) When will the bell ring, and end this weariness.
(*b*) How long have they tugged the leash and strained apart.
(*c*) I can haul them and urge them no more.
(*d*) My last dear fuel of life to heap on my soul.
(*e*) I will not waste my soul and my strength for this.

A. only (*a*) B. (*b*) and (*d*)
C. (*a*), (*b*) and (*d*) D. (*a*), (*c*) and (*e*)

127. Which line in the poem means 'to waste one's time trying hard to accomplish something that is completely hopeless'?

A. To us both, it is all my aunt!
B. I shall keep my strength for myself.
C. Why should we beat our heads against the wall.
D. I shall sit and wait for the bell.

128. In the 2nd stanza, it is the ______ of the students that angers the poet.

A. sloppiness B. consideration
C. caution D. heedfulness

129. Which of the following is ***not*** a synonym of 'indifference'?

A. apathy B. recklessness
C. zeal D. callousness

130. What is an 'abyss'?

A. a deep or seemingly bottomless chasm of an immeasurable depth.
B. a part of a surface that is lower than the parts around it.
C. a weather condition in which the pressure of the air becomes lower, often causing rain.
D. a part of a surface that curves inward.

131. Which of the following is spelt ***correctly***?

A. irresistible B. irresistable
C. irrisistible D. irrisisteble

132. Which of the following are in the passive voice?

(*a*) Rioting workers were identified and persecuted.
(*b*) The living room is swept and dusted everyday.
(*c*) The class photograph will be taken tomorrow.
(*d*) The case was investigated rather clumsily.

A. (*a*) and (*b*) B. (*b*) and (*c*)
C. (*a*), (*c*) and (*d*) D. (*a*), (*b*), (*c*) and (*d*)

133. Choose the ***correct*** meaning of the underlined word.

A gregarious person is:

A. outwardly calm
B. very sociable
C. completely untrustworthy
D. self-effacing and timid

134. Which of these novels was ***not*** written in the 19th Century?

A. Moby Dick
B. The Old Curiosity Shop
C. Robinson Crusoe
D. Little Women

135. Which of the following words is ***misspelt***?

A. magnanimous B. unanimous
C. magnifiecence D. magniloquent

136. In which of the following sentence/s 'ought to' indicates 'advisability or desirability'?

(*a*) You ought to buy new tyres for your car; you may have an accident.
(*b*) We ought to help those people who are old and sick.
(*c*) There ought to be more goods available in this shop; it is supposed to be a supermarket.
(*d*) He left Delhi yesterday, so he ought to be here tomorrow.

A. only (*b*) B. (*a*) and (*c*)
C. (*b*) and (*c*) D. (*a*), (*b*) and (*d*)

137. Choose the ***correct*** meaning of the underlined word.

An audacious attempt means:

A. useless B. bold
C. foolish D. crazy

138. How many novels did Emily Bronte write?

A. 3 B. 7
C. 1 D. 19

139. Which of the following sentence/s is/are grammatically ***correct***?

(*a*) Mukesh was among the top five per cent of students in his class.
(*b*) There are a few naughty children among the students in our class.
(*c*) The mother shared the cake among her son and her daughter.
(*d*) Oranges were shared among the whole class.

A. only (*b*) B. (*b*) and (*d*)
C. (*a*) and (*c*) D. (*a*), (*b*) and (*d*)

140. If you have a skin disease, you will visit a ______ .

A. dermatologist B. ophthalmologist
C. internist D. obstetrician

141. Which of the following is/are ***not*** in the active voice?

(*a*) What cannot be cured must be endured.
(*b*) We hope that we shall finish the work in time.

(*c*) This arrangement is to be made by you.
(*d*) We went to see the launching of the ship.
A. only (*a*) B. (*a*) and (*c*)
C. only (*c*) D. (*b*) and (*d*)

142. Which of the following idioms fits this description?

A person who selfishly prevents others from using, enjoying or profiting from something even though he/she cannot use or enjoy it himself.
A. A Guinea Pig B. A Dog in the Manger
C. A Home Bird D. A Lame Duck

143. Which of the following sentence is ***correct***?
A. His day was long and his hobbies many.
B. I am going to the market but Meera not.
C. The boy was drinking milk, the mother tea.
D. You are working hard but not your friend.

144. Match the following with their writer:

(*a*) Vikram Seth	(*i*) The Ministry of Utmost Happiness
(*b*) V.S. Naipaul	(*ii*) The Golden Gate
(*c*) Amartya Sen	(*iii*) A House For Mr. Biswas
(*d*) Arundhati Roy	(*iv*) The Argumentative Indian

Codes:

	(*a*)	(*b*)	(*c*)	(*d*)
A.	(*ii*)	(*iii*)	(*iv*)	(*i*)
B.	(*iii*)	(*i*)	(*iv*)	(*ii*)
C.	(*iv*)	(*iii*)	(*ii*)	(*i*)
D.	(*ii*)	(*iv*)	(*i*)	(*iii*)

145. Portia is the protagonist of William Shakespeare's play ______.
A. Hamlet
B. The Merchant of Venice
C. As You Like It
D. Twelfth Night

146. Which of the following is ***not*** an abstract noun?
A. Laughter B. Judgement
C. Childhood D. Human

147. Which of these writers often deal with the experience of Indian immigrants in the United States?
A. Salman Rushdie B. Rabindranath Tagore
C. Zadie Smith D. Jhumpa Lahiri

148. Which of the following is/are verb/s?
(*a*) vain (*b*) agent
(*c*) serve (*d*) seize
A. only (*a*) B. (*a*) and (*b*)
C. (*b*) and (*c*) D. (*c*) and (*d*)

149. Identify the verbs/verb phrase in the following sentence:

He was searching furiously and ineffectually for some elusive or non-existent object; from time to time he dug a six penny coin out of a waistcoat pocket and stared at it ruefully, then recommenced the futile searching operations.
A. was searching; dug; stared; recommenced
B. furiously; ineffectually; ruefully; searching
C. elusive; non-existent; recommenced; searching
D. was searching; furiously; ineffectually; searching

150. Which of the following is ***not*** written by Chetan Bhagat?
A. The Immortals of Meluha
B. The 3 Mistakes of My Life
C. Revolution 2020
D. Five Point Someone

Answers

1. (D) **2.** (C) **3.** (A)
4. (D) **5.** (C) **6.** (D)
7. (C) **8.** (B) **9.** (D)
10. (A) **11.** (A) **12.** (C)
13. (B) **14.** (A) **15.** (D)
16. (B) **17.** (B) **18.** (*)
19. (D) **20.** (C) **21.** (C)
22. (A) **23.** (C) **24.** (C)
25. (A) **26.** (A) **27.** (B)
28. (D) **29.** (C) **30.** (D)
31. (C) **32.** (C) **33.** (A)
34. (A) **35.** (D) **36.** (C)
37. (A) **38.** (B) **39.** (B)
40. (C) **41.** (C) **42.** (D)
43. (D) **44.** (A) **45.** (D)
46. (A) **47.** (B) **48.** (B)
49. (*) **50.** (D) **51.** (D)
52. (C) **53.** (C) **54.** (C)
55. (B) **56.** (B) **57.** (B)
58. (A) **59.** (B) **60.** (D)

61. (D): Let $x = \sqrt{8+2\sqrt{8+2\sqrt{8}}}\ldots\ldots$

$$x^2 = 8 + 2x$$

$$\Rightarrow \quad x^2 - 2x - 8 = 0$$

$$\Rightarrow \quad (x-4)(x+2) = 0$$

$$\Rightarrow \quad x = 4 \text{ or } x = -2$$

$$\therefore \quad x = 4 \; (\because x > 0)$$

62. (C): Let each side of square = x

Area of the square = x^2

$$\text{Side increased} = x + \frac{50x}{100}$$

$$= x + \frac{x}{2} = \frac{3x}{2}$$

$$\text{Area} = \left(\frac{3x}{2}\right)^2 = \frac{9x^2}{4}$$

$$\text{Area increased} = \frac{9x^2}{4} - x^2 = \frac{5x^2}{4}$$

$$\%\ \text{area increased} = \frac{5x^2}{4 \times x^2} \times 100 = 125\%.$$

63. (B): $15 \times 5 + 5 - 20 \div 10$

$= 75 + 5 - 2$

$= 80 - 2$

$= 78.$

64. (A): 100 + 20 = ₹ 120

When SP ₹ 120 then C.P. = ₹ 100

When SP ₹ 72000 then C.P. = $\frac{100}{120} \times 72000$

= ₹ 60000

Hence, C.P. of the commodity = ₹ 60000.

65. (C):

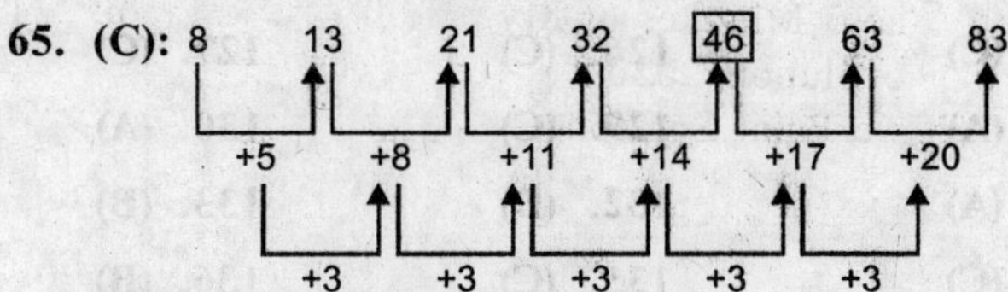

46 will come at the place of 47.

Hence, wrong number = 47.

66. (C)

67. (C): 2 7 24 77 238 723

× 3 + 1 × 3 + 3 × 3 + 5 × 3 + 7 × 3 + 9

Hence, 723 will come at the next term.

68. (B)

69. (A): First three letter of 'STUA' are in increasing order while first three letters in remaining three letter-clusters, i.e., 'RQPA', 'MLKA' and 'HGFA' are in decreasing order.

So, letter-cluster 'STUA' is odd.

70. (D): Earth is related to Axis in the same way as wheel is related to Hub.

71. (A):

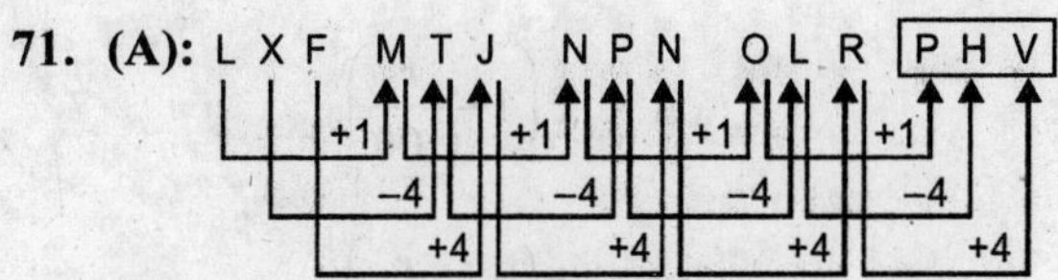

Hence, next term will be PHV.

72. (A):

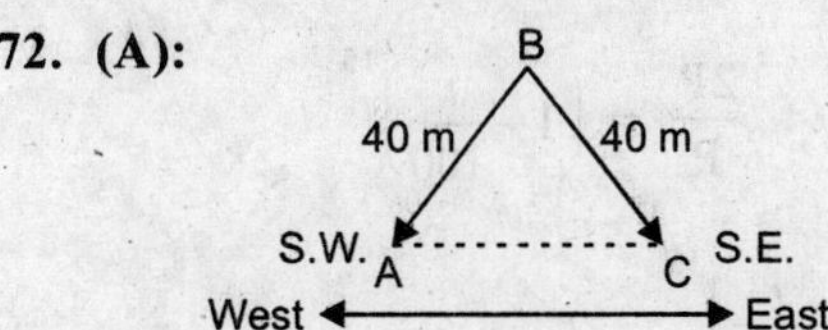

Clearly, C is in East direction of A.

73. (B): Total marks obtained by 150 students

$= 150 \times 35$

$= 5250$

Let number of passed students = y

∴ Number of failed students = $150 - y$

According to the question,

Total marks of passed students = $39y$

Total marks of failed students = $(150 - y) \times 15$

$$39y + (150 - y) \times 15 = 5250$$

$$\Rightarrow 39y + 2250 - 15y = 5250$$

$$\Rightarrow 24y = 3000$$

$$\Rightarrow y = 125$$

Hence, number of passed students = 125.

74. (B): ∵ $a^x = b$

$b^y = c$

and $c^z = a$

$\therefore \quad a^x \times b^y \times c^z = b \times c \times a$

$\Rightarrow \quad (abc)^{xyz} = (abc)^1$

$\Rightarrow \quad xyz = 1$

Hence, the value of $xyz = 1$.

75. (C): LCM of 4, 5, 6, 15 and 18 = 180

800 is not divided by 180

225 is not divided by 180

900 is divided by 180

Hence, 900 is the smallest perfect square number which is exactly divisible by 4, 5, 6, 15 and 18.

76. (A): The Value of $\left(\sqrt{5}\right)^{\frac{-5}{2}} \times \left(\sqrt{5}\right)^{\frac{-3}{2}}$

$$= \left(\sqrt{5}\right)^{\frac{-8}{2}} = \left(\sqrt{5}\right)^{-4}$$

$$= (5)^{\frac{1}{2} \times -4} = (5)^{-2}$$

$$= \frac{1}{5^2} = \frac{1}{25}.$$

77. (D): $A = P\left(1+\frac{r}{100}\right)^t$

$\Rightarrow \quad 2P = P\left(1+\frac{r}{100}\right)^{15}$

$\frac{2P}{P} = \left(1+\frac{r}{100}\right)^{15}$

$\Rightarrow \quad \left(1+\frac{r}{100}\right)^{15} = 2 \quad ...(i)$

Now, $A = P\left(1+\frac{r}{100}\right)^t$

$8P = P\left(1+\frac{r}{100}\right)^t$

$\frac{8P}{P} = \left(1+\frac{r}{100}\right)^t$

$8 = \left(1+\frac{r}{100}\right)^t$

$\Rightarrow \quad \left(1+\frac{r}{100}\right)^t = 8 = 2^3$

$= \left[\left(1+\frac{r}{100}\right)^{15}\right]^3$

$\Rightarrow \quad \left(1+\frac{r}{100}\right)^t = \left(1+\frac{r}{100}\right)^{45}$

Hence, t = 45 years.

78. (D): ∵ 25 men can reap a crop in 60 days

∴ 1 man can reap the crop in 60 × 25 days

∴ 10 men can reap the same crop in

$\frac{60 \times 25}{10} = 150$ days

Hence, 10 men can reap the crop in 150 days.

79. (B): ∵ $x+\frac{1}{x} = 5$

∴ $x^3+\frac{1}{x^3} = \left(x+\frac{1}{x}\right)^3 - 3x.\frac{1}{x}\left(x+\frac{1}{x}\right)$

$= (5)^3 - 3 \times (5)$

$= 125 - 15 = 110$

Hence, the value of $x^3+\frac{1}{x^3} = 110$.

80. (C)	**81. (D)**	**82. (A)**
83. (A)	**84. (A)**	**85. (B)**
86. (B)	**87. (B)**	**88. (D)**
89. (B)	**90. (D)**	**91. (C)**
92. (A)	**93. (C)**	**94. (A)**
95. (A)	**96. (B)**	**97. (B)**
98. (B)	**99. (D)**	**100. (A)**
101. (D)	**102. (A)**	**103. (*)**
104. (A)	**105. (D)**	**106. (C)**
107. (A)	**108. (B)**	**109. (A)**
110. (C)	**111. (D)**	**112. (B)**
113. (C)	**114. (D)**	**115. (D)**
116. (C)	**117. (B)**	**118. (C)**
119. (C)	**120. (D)**	**121. (D)**
122. (D)	**123. (C)**	**124. (D)**
125. (C)	**126. (C)**	**127. (C)**
128. (A)	**129. (C)**	**130. (A)**
131. (A)	**132. (D)**	**133. (B)**
134. (C)	**135. (C)**	**136. (B)**
137. (B)	**138. (C)**	**139. (D)**
140. (A)	**141. (B)**	**142. (B)**
143. (*)	**144. (A)**	**145. (B)**
146. (D)	**147. (D)**	**148. (D)**
149. (A)	**150. (A)**	

Previous Paper (Solved)

Haryana Teacher Eligibility Test (HTET)

TGT English (Level-2), Exam 2021

(Exam held on 19 December, 2021)

PART-I

Child Development and Pedagogy

Directions: *Answer the following questions by selecting the **most appropriate** option.*

1. What is the process of releasing the hidden emotional suffocation and powers inside the children called?

A. Emotional stability
B. Emotional sensitivity
C. Emotional catharsis
D. Emotional competency

2. When a person tried to make his/her thoughts and action according to other whom he like to follow, then this kind of activity called which type of defence mechanism?

A. Identification B. Projection
C. Rationalisation D. Displacement

3. According to Jean Piaget between which age the child develops abstract reasoning?

A. 6 to 8 years B. 8 to 10 years
C. 7 to 9 years D. 11 to 14 years

4. Which one of the following is ***not*** the common speech disorder of childhood?

A. Depletion of Energy
B. Lisping
C. Slurring
D. Stuttering

5. How many cards prescribed in Rorschach Ink Block Test?

A. 12 B. 10
C. 30 D. 31

6. What is the age range of puberty stage?

A. 10 to 12 years
B. 6 to 12 years
C. 11 to 16 years
D. 8 to 10 years

7. According to 'Ross', which stage of development is known as 'Pseudo Maturity' stage?

A. Infancy B. Childhood
C. Adolescence D. Adhulthood

8. Out of the following which one is ***not*** the type of performance test of intelligence?

A. Army alpha test
B. Koh's block design test
C. The cube construction test
D. The pass along test

9. Out of the following which one characteristic ***not*** suits to gifted children?

A. Learn rapidly and easily.
B. Perform difficult mental task.
C. Knows about many things of which most of the students are unaware.
D. Much drill is required to retain what he/she has heard or read.

10. Which one of the following is the ***correct*** logical order of observational learning process according Learning Theory of Bandura?

A. Attentional → Retentional → Motivational → Production
B. Attentional → Motivational → Retentional → Production
C. Motivational → Attentional → Retentional → Production
D. Attentional → Retentional → Production → Motivational

11. Who invented sociometric technique?

A. J.E. Anderson B. J.L. Moreno
C. E.B. Hurlock D. G.S. Marmor

12. Who stated that "An individual is intelligent in proportion as he is able to carry on abstract thinking?

A. Terman B. Dearborn
C. Buckingham D. Calvin

13. Girls surpass boys physically in:

A. Infancy B. Later childhood
C. Early childhood D. Adolescence

14. Who is known as father of Educational Psychology?

A. E.L. Thorndike B. Pestalozzi
C. Herbart D. Froebel

15. Out of the following which one is the subject matter for study of Gestalt Psychologist?
A. Cognitive processes
B. Consciousness
C. Mental and behavioural processes a wholes
D. Modes and problems of existence

16. Who stated that "Personality is the sum total of innate and acquired dispositions"?
A. Mortin Prince
B. Allport
C. Valentine
D. Cattell

17. Out of the following which one is ***wrong*** characteristic of Delinquents?
A. Damaging school property
B. Bullying and mockery
C. Torturing
D. Aesthanic in constitution

18. Which of the following is the characteristic of introverted thinking type personality?
A. Realistic and Practical
B. Absorbed in his own intellectual pursuit
C. Supports theory with facts
D. Propagates his views with insistence and vehemence

19. Out of the following which one activity is ***not*** suitable for satisfying the instincts curiosity?
A. Awarding positions in the class or school
B. Answering the questions of the students
C. Problem solving
D. Discussion in class

20. Out of the following which one is ***not*** the stage of creativity prescribed by Gordon in his Synectics Technique?
A. Detachment involvement
B. Finding something similar
C. Deferment
D. Concept formation

21. Out of the following which one of the statement is ***wrong*** in context of characteristics of sentiments?
A. Emotions are the basis of sentiments.
B. Sentiments are innate.
C. Sentiments get older with the passage of time and they may even change their state.
D. Most of the animals do not have sentiments because of they do not have intellectual comprehension.

22. A type of thinking in which one's interpret sensation with experience is known as what?
A. Reflective thinking
B. Perceptual thinking
C. Creative thinking
D. Critical thinking

23. Out of the following which is ***correct*** sequence given by James Lange's "Theory of Emotions"?
A. Situation → Bodily disturbance → Mental state
B. Situation → Mental state → Bodily expressions
C. Situation → Bodily expressions → Mental state
D. Situation → Mental state → Bodily disturbance

24. Sometimes the children of gifted parents are born with less intelligence than their parents or vice versa, which Law of Heredity is called?
A. Law of Regression
B. Law of Selective Traits
C. Law of Maternal and Paternal Lines
D. Law of Chance

25. Which is the fourth stage of psycho-social development of an individual according to Erikson?
A. Intimacy v/s isolation
B. Identity v/s role confusion
C. Industry v/s inferiority
D. Generativity v/s stagnation

26. Which one of the following is ***false*** statement in context of Development?
A. Development involves change
B. The development pattern is unpredicatble
C. Early development is more critical than later development
D. Development is the product of maturation and learning

27. Out of the following which one is the ***wrong*** statement in context of characteristics and nature of guidance?
A. Guidance is assisting the individual to adjust himself.
B. Guidance of promotion of the growth of the individual in self-Guidance.
C. Guidance is helping the individual himself through others efforts only.
D. Guidance is assisting an individual to find his place.

28. What did Freud consider the paternal love of girls?
A. Oedipus complex
B. Electra complex
C. Narcissism
D. Feeling of dependence

29. Which is the oldest method for the study of behaviour?
A. Experimental method
B. Clinical method
C. Psycho-physical method
D. Introspection method

30. Out of the following which one is ***not*** the characteristic of insight?
A. Incidental
B. Response in novel situation
C. Habit strength
D. Response spontaneity

PART-II

भाषा : हिन्दी

निर्देशः *निम्नलिखित प्रश्नों के उत्तर देने के लिए* **सबसे उचित** *विकल्प चुनिए।*

31. किस विकल्प के सभी शब्द विदेशज हैं?

A. लाजवाब, मशीन, पवन

B. कारीगर, अतिशयोक्ति, कहानी

C. मुमकिन, अमूमन, पक्षवार

D. किस्सा, स्कूल, हमला

32. प्रत्यय की दृष्टि से किस शब्द की रचना **अनुचित** है?

A. मुरेला – एला

B. कँटीला – ईला

C. विलीन – ईन

D. ससुराल – आल

33. किस वाक्य में सर्वनाम संबंधी **अशुद्धि** है?

A. तुम्हारी पुस्तक यह नहीं वह है।

B. मैं अपना कार्य कर रहा हूँ।

C. जिसने भी खाया है, सराहा है।

D. मेरे को कुछ भी याद नहीं आ रहा।

34. किस वाक्य में परिमाणवाचक विशेषण का प्रयोग हुआ है?

A. मैं नीली कमीज नहीं पहनता।

B. इस बार बारिश में बहुत ओले गिरे।

C. खेल का मैदान लम्बा है।

D. दिनेश अच्छा गायक है।

35. विलोम शब्द की दृष्टि से **अनुचित** युग्म पहचानिए :

A. बद – नेक

B. दुश्चरित्र – निश्चरित्र

C. विस्तृत – संक्षिप्त

D. मधुर – कटु

36. किस विकल्प में 'संकेतार्थक' वाक्य है?

A. प्रियतम मेरा मित्र है।

B. यदि तुम आओ तो मैं चलूँ।

C. हो सकता है कल मौसम ठीक हो जाए।

D. राजेश अपना कमरा साफ करो।

37. निम्न में से कौन-सा शब्द 'अनु' उपसर्ग से निर्मित **नहीं** है?

A. आनुपातिक   B. अनुदात्त

C. अनूदित   D. अनुरंजक

38. 'विपत्ति के समय थोड़ी सहायता भी बड़ी होती है' उक्त भाव की व्यंजक लोकोक्ति चुनिए :

A. डूबते को तिनके का सहारा

B. चुपड़ी और दो-दो

C. चार दिन की चाँदनी फिर अँधेरी रात

D. आम के आम गुठलियों के दाम

39. किस भाववाचक संज्ञा का निर्माण व्यक्तिवाचक संज्ञा से हुआ है?

A. बचपन

B. कैशोर्य

C. ऐश्वर्य

D. मातृत्व

40. क्रिया के संबंध में कौन-सा युग्म **अनुचित** है?

A. भिखारी सड़क पर चिल्ला रहे थे। –अकर्मक क्रिया

B. राधा श्याम को पत्र लिखती है। –द्विकर्मक क्रिया

C. बगीचे में मोर नाच रहा है। –सकर्मक क्रिया

D. वह विद्यालय से आकर खाना खाएगा। –पूर्वकालिक क्रिया

41. पर्यायवाची शब्दों के संदर्भ में **असंगत** विकल्प चुनिए :

A. जीभ – वाचा, रसना, वाणी

B. अहंकार – दंभ, दर्प, मद

C. किरण – रश्मि, मयूख, प्रभा

D. कौआ – प्रियक, मधुदूत, अतिसौरभ

42. समास-विग्रह की दृष्टि से कौन-सा विकल्प **उचित** है?

A. हथकरघा – हाथों से चलने वाला करघा

B. भुजग – भूमि में जन्म लेने वाला

C. देशभक्ति – देश के द्वारा भक्ति

D. पशुबलि – पशु के लिए बलि

43. किस विकल्प में संधि-विच्छेद **अनुचित** है?

A. बहिरेकता = बहिः + एकता

B. आशीर्वचन = आशीः + वचन

C. रतिरंश = रतिः + रंश

D. तपश्चर्या = तपः + चर्या

44. निम्न में से किस मुहावरे का अर्थ संगत **नहीं** है?

A. नहले पर दहला मारना – करारा जवाब देना

B. बत्तीसी बंद होना – चुप हो जाना

C. सिर का पसीना पाँव तक आना – कठिन परिश्रम करना

D. थाली का बैंगन होना – सर्व सुलभ होना

45. निम्न में से किस विकल्प का कथन **गलत** है?

A. 'ऋ' का उच्चारण स्थान 'मूर्धा' है।

B. विसर्ग ध्वनि की गणना नासिक्य वर्णों में की जाती है।

C. 'य' और 'व' को अर्ध स्वर भी कहा जाता है।

D. 'ड़' और 'ढ़' उत्क्षिप्त वर्ण कहलाते हैं।

Language : English

Directions: *Answer the following questions by selecting the **most appropriate** option.*

46. Select the ***appropriate*** modal for the expression given:

Harish has annoyed his boss today. He ______ be fired soon. (probability)

A. may B. can
C. ought to D. would

47. Choose the ***correct*** tense form to fill in the blank:

Municipality has decided to ______ the overhead wires.

A. did away with
B. do away with
C. had done away with
D. had done away wtih

48. Select the ***appropriate*** modal to fill in the blank:

Trespassers _______ be punished. (legal notice)

A. shall
B. may
C. should
D. ought to

49. Select the ***appropriate*** preposition to fill in the blank:

His hut is _______ hotel Taj.

A. above
B. out
C. besides
D. beside

50. Choose the ***correct*** meaning of the underlined words:

The law and order situation will only become worse in the state due to the riots, if the government does not do something right now to <u>nip it in the bud</u>.

A. To plan in detail to stop a threat
B. To destroy the problem in the initial stage only
C. To arrest the culprits
D. To stop something harmful in the initial stage

51. Select the ***correct*** option (Phrasal Verb) for the underlined word:

She <u>rejected</u> his request to take her home.

A. turned up
B. turned down
C. turned out
D. turned off

52. Choose the ***correct*** option to fill in the blank:

This pen is both good _______ cheap.

A. as well as B. as well
C. but only D. and

53. Choose the ***correct*** option for the following:

One who wastes a lot of money is:

A. frugal B. recluse
C. prodigal D. reticent

54. Choose the part of the sentence which is ***incorrect***:

The party president made *(a)*/ Rakesh *(b)*/ a M.P. candidate *(c)*/ for the coming election. *(d)*

A. *(a)* B. *(b)*
C. *(c)* D. *(d)*

55. Select the ***correct*** option (Phrasal Verb) for the blank left in the sentence:

Cholera has ______ in this village.

A. broken out
B. broken down
C. broken up
D. broken off

56. Choose the ***correct*** meaning of the underlined words:

The hostess <u>broke the ice</u> by introducing the strangers to each other.

A. To make people relax with each other
B. To make people perplexed with each other
C. To serve welcome drink to the guests
D. To start a game of puzzle

57. Choose the ***correct*** tense form to fill in the following:

I had consulted my lawyer before I ______ the complaint.

A. did lodged
B. had lodged
C. lodge
D. lodged

58. Choose the ***appropriate*** modal to fill in the blank:

He ______ listen to the stories of his Grand Ma before he slept. (Past habit)

A. could B. shall
C. would D. might

59. Choose the part of the sentence which is ***incorrect***:

He did not *(a)*/ keep his words *(b)*/ to pick him up *(c)*/ from WTP. *(d)*

A. *(b)* B. *(c)*
C. *(d)* D. *(a)*

60. Choose the ***appropriate*** preposition to fill in the blank:

What is the time ______ your watch?

A. in B. from
C. by D. on

PART-III

General Studies : Quantitative Aptitude, Reasoning Ability and GK & Awareness

Directions: *Answer the following questions by selecting the **most appropriate** option.*

61. The sum of length, breadth and depth of a cuboid is 19 cm and its principal diagonal is $5\sqrt{5}$ cm, then its surface area is:

A. 361 cm^2 B. 286 cm^2
C. 236 cm^2 D. 340 cm^2

62. In a row of boys, A is 15th from the left and B is fourth from the right. There are three boys between A and B, C is first left of A. What is the position of C from the right?

A. 9th B. 10th
C. 12th D. 13th

63. Among five persons A, B, C, D and E, A is shorter than B but taller than E. C is the tallest. D is shorter than B but taller than A. Who among them is shortest?

A. B B. A
C. D D. E

64. A train 140 metre long is running at 60 km/hour. How much time will it take to pass a platform 260 metre long?

A. 18 sec B. 24 sec
C. 30 sec D. 32 sec

65. Two alloys are both made up of copper and tin. The ratio of copper and tin in the first alloy is 1 : 3 and in second alloy is 2 : 5. In what ratio should two alloys be mixed, to obtain a new alloy such that the ratio of copper and tin be 3 : 8?

A. 3 : 5 B. 4 : 9
C. 4 : 7 D. 3 : 8

66. If 4 men or 6 women can do a piece of work in 12 days working 7 hours a day. How many days will it take to complete a work twice as large with 10 men and 3 women working together 8 hours a day?

A. 6 B. 7
C. 8 D. 9

67. If $x = \dfrac{1}{1+\sqrt{2}}$, then the value of $x^2 + 2x + 3$ is:

A. 0 B. 1
C. 4 D. 2

68. The next term of the following letter series will be:
CAE, HFJ, MKO, RPT, ____

A. UTY B. WUY
C. VUZ D. WUZ

69. The length of a wire is 66 metre, then the number of circles of circumference 1.32 cm that can be made from the wire is:

A. 1000 B. 50
C. 500 D. 5000

70. The sum of two numbrs is 520. If the bigger number is decreased by 4% and the smaller number is increased by 12%, then the obtained numbers are equal, then smaller number is:

A. 210 B. 240
C. 270 D. 300

71. A cloth merchant on selling 33 metre of cloth obtains a profit equal to the selling price of 11 metre of cloth. The profit percentage is:

A. 11% B. 22%
C. 50% D. 40%

72. A said, "that boy is the grandson of my mother's husband. I have no brother or sister." How is the boy related to A?

A. Uncle B. Son
C. Nephew D. Cousin

73. Find the ***wrong*** number in the following series?
135, 226, 353, 552, 739

A. 353 B. 226
C. 552 D. 739

74. The difference between simple interest and the compound interest compounded annually at the rate of 12% per annum on ₹ 5000 for two years will be:

A. ₹ 72 B. ₹ 84
C. ₹ 96 D. ₹ 36

75. The perimeter of a rhombus is 100 cm and one of its diagonal is 40 cm. Then its area is:

A. 300 cm^2 B. 600 cm^2
C. 780 cm^2 D. 900 cm^2

76. Find the ***wrong*** term of the following series:
G4T, J9R, M20P, P41N, S90L

A. J9R B. M20P
C. P41N D. S90L

77. If W = 23, STRONG = 93, then WEAK is equal to:

A. 40 B. 41
C. 43 D. 44

78. If a person walks 8 km towards South then turns right and walks 8 km, again turns left and walks 10 km. In which direction is he from starting point?

A. East-South B. North-East
C. North-South D. South-West

79. If $5a+\frac{1}{3a}=5$, then the value of $9a^2+\frac{1}{25a^2}$ is:

A. $\frac{51}{5}$ B. $\frac{29}{5}$

C. $\frac{52}{5}$ D. $\frac{39}{5}$

80. A person walks 2 km towards East and then he turns to South and walk 1 km. Again he turns to East and walks 2 km after that he turns to North and walk 4 km. Now how far is he from his starting point?

A. 5 km B. 6 km
C. 3 km D. 4 km

81. Read the following statements about Haryana Sahitya Academy:

(*i*) The Chief Minister serves as the President of the academy.

(*ii*) 'Harigandha' is the Magazine of the academy.

Choose the ***correct*** code:

A. Only statement (*i*) is correct
B. Only statement (*ii*) is correct
C. Neither (*i*) nor (*ii*) is correct
D. Both the statements are correct

82. Where the 'Panchwati' pilgrimage site is located in Haryana?

A. In Palwal B. In Ambala
C. In Hathin D. In Ballabhgarh

83. In which district the 'Chinkara' Breeding Centre' is situated?

A. Kaithal B. Panchkula
C. Hisar D. Bhiwani

84. Match the following

Name	Place
(*a*) Birbal's Rang Mahal	(*i*) Narnaul
(*b*) Spiritual Museum	(*ii*) Gurugram
(*c*) Chor Gumbad	(*iii*) Yamunanagar
(*d*) Sohna Fort	(*iv*) Panipat

Code:

	(*a*)	(*b*)	(*c*)	(*d*)
A.	(*ii*)	(*iii*)	(*iv*)	(*i*)
B.	(*iii*)	(*iv*)	(*i*)	(*ii*)
C.	(*iv*)	(*ii*)	(*iii*)	(*i*)
D.	(*iii*)	(*ii*)	(*i*)	(*iv*)

85. How many gold medals were won by Haryana state in the '36th National Junior Athletics Championship', which was held in February, 2021?

A. 13 B. 18
C. 21 D. 24

86. Who among the following was the longest serving Governor of Haryana?

A. B.N. Chakraborty B. A.R. Kidwai
C. Jagannath Pahadia D. Kaptan Singh Solanki

87. Which of the following pair/pairs is/are ***true***?

(*i*) State Animal – Black buck
(*ii*) Saraswati Wild Life Sanctuary – Kaithal
(*iii*) Nahar Wild Life Sanctuary – Jhajjar

Choose the ***correct*** code:

A. Only (*i*) B. (*i*) and (*iii*)
C. (*i*) and (*ii*) D. Only (*iii*)

88. The hero of 1857 Revolution Abdurrahman Khan was related to:

A. Bahadurgarh B. Farrukhnagar
C. Jhajjar D. Yamunanagar

89. The amount which is given to the sports woman on the occasion of marriage under 'Mukhyamantri Vivah Shagun Yojana'?

A. ₹ 11,000 B. ₹ 21,000
C. ₹ 31,000 D. ₹ 51,000

90. The minimum number of members in the Council of Minister of Haryana can be:

A. 10 B. 12
C. 14 D. 06

PART-IV

Subject Knowledge—English

Directions: *Answer the following questions by selecting the* ***most appropriate*** *option.*

91. Choose the ***correct*** antonym of the word 'Benign'?

A. Malign B. Gentle
C. Kind D. Mild

92. Match the phrases in Column A with their meaning in Column B:

A	B
(*i*) Broke out	(*a*) was not able to tolerate
(*ii*) In accordance with	(*b*) began suddenly in a violent way
(*iii*) A Helping hand	(*c*) assistance
(*vi*) Could not Stomach	(*d*) acc. to a particular rule, principle or system

	(*i*)	(*ii*)	(*iii*)	(*iv*)
A.	(*b*)	(*d*)	(*c*)	(*a*)
B.	(*a*)	(*b*)	(*c*)	(*d*)
C.	(*d*)	(*c*)	(*b*)	(*a*)
D.	(*b*)	(*c*)	(*d*)	(*a*)

93. The story, 'A Different Kind of School' talks about:
A. Below Average Kids B. Differently Abled
C. Meritorious Kids D. None of the above

94. Convert the following positive sentence into comparative sentence:

This knife is not as sharp as that one.
A. This knife is sharper than that one.
B. This knife is sharper.
C. That knife is sharpest of all.
D. This knife is more sharper than that one.

95. Identify the figure of speech in the following lines:
"The Moan of doves in immemorial elms and murmuring of innumerable bees."
A. Alliteration B. Assonance
C. Onomatopoeia D. Simile

96. Fill in the blank with the ***correct*** article:

I went to ______ Church to see the Golden statue of Jesus Christ.
A. The B. A
C. An D. Zero article

97. Who's the author of the story, "Three questions"?
A. Leo Tolstoy B. Ruskin Bond
C. H.G. Wells D. Graham Greene

98. Fill in the blank with the ***correct*** phrasal verb:

The car ____ when we were driving through the desert.
A. Broke down B. Break out
C. Broke off D. Break in

99. Identify the underlined part of speech in the following sentence:

The moral law is above the civil.
A. Adverb B. Preposition
C. Noun D. Adjective

100. Identify the ***correct*** sentence pattern of the given sentence:

They elected him chairman.
A. S + V + O + C B. S + V + O + O
C. S + V + C + C D. S + O + O + C

Directions (Qs. No. 101-106): *Read the following poem and answer the questions given below:*

A silly young cricket, accustomed to sing through the warm, sunny months of gay summer and spring,
Begain to complain when he found that, at home,
His cupboard was empty, and winter was come.
Not a crumb to be found
on the snow-covered ground:
Not a flower could he see,
Not a leaf on a tree.
"Oh! what will become, "Says the cricket.
"Of me?"
At last by starvation and famine made bold.
All dripping with wet, and all trembling with cold
Away he set off to a miserly ant.
To see if, to keep him alive, he would grant
Him shelter from rain
And a mouthful of grain
He wished only to borrow;
He'd repay it tomorrow;
If not, he must die of starvation and sorrow,

101. For what did the cricket go to ant?
A. To give him food
B. To give flowers and leaf on tree
C. To protect himself from sun
D. Shelter from rain and mouthful of grain

102. What does the word "crumb" mean in the poem?
A. A small piece of bread
B. A little stick
C. A protected area
D. Something inedible

103. What did the cricket complain of?
A. The warm sunny days
B. The empty cupboards
C. The boring surroundings
D. Not able to sing

104. A story with animal is characters, that conveys a moral is called:
A. A Lyric B. A Fable
C. An Anecdote D. A Novel

105. The coming of 'which weather' made the cricket 'complain'?
A. Winter B. Spring
C. Summer D. Autumn

106. Pick out the word which means, "Severe suffering due to a lack of Nutrition".
A. Trembling B. Miserly
C. Starvation D. Complain

107. "Every year on the occasion of Eid, there was a fair in our village."

These lines occur in which story?
A. A Game of Chess B. Eid Celebrations
C. Village Fair D. A Game of Chance

108. Choose the ***correct*** option for the underlined modal:

We should go on a holiday.
A. Suggestion B. Permission
C. Ability D. Necessity

109. Fill in the blank, with the ***correct*** option:

India is a noble, generous land, teeming _____ natural wealth.
A. On B. With
C. For D. At

110. Which of the following is spelt ***correclty***?
A. Enterttainment B. Environonment
C. Juxtaposition D. Numerologgy

111. Identify the phonetic symbol of the underlined sound:
gun come luck
A. ^ B. ∂ :
C. μ : D. ⊃

112. Identify the poet of the poem 'Vocation' from the choices given below:
A. Rabindranath Tagore B. William Wordsworth
C. Sarojini Naidu D. John Keats

113. Which of the word is ***incorrectly*** formed in plural?
A. Scarves B. Dwarves
C. Handkerchiefs D. Loavfs

114. Identify the phonetic symbol of the underlined sounds:
Thin, Method, Author
A. θ B. t ʃ
C. F D. ^

115. Fill in the blank with the correct modal:
He _______ not enter my house again. (command)
A. Shall B. May
C. Might D. Should

116. Where was Kalpana Chawla born?
A. Karnal B. Sonipat
C. Ambala D. Gurugram

117. Fill in the blank with the correct conjunction:
It is _______ useful _______ ornamental.
A. Whether, or B. Both, or
C. Neither, nor D. Either, but also

118. The word "Weird" in the story "A Gift of Chappals" mean:
A. Sweet B. Malicious
C. Orthodox D. Strange

119. The Magistrate was a man with a kindly nature.
Identify the underlined phrase.
A. Noun phrase B. Adverb phrase
C. Adjective phrase D. Participle phrase

120. How old was Evelyn when she went to the Royal Academy of Music?
A. Seventeen B. Twenty Two
C. Nineteen D. Thirteen

121. Identify the underlined word in the sentence:
We met a girl carrying a basket of flowers.
A. Noun B. Participle
C. Gerund D. Infinitive

122. Fill in the blank with the ***correct*** preposition:
There was a beautiful lake _______ us in the valley.
A. Below B. Into
C. Over D. With

123. "My Childhood" is an extract from:
A. My family B. The solar system
C. My Ambition D. Wings of fire

124. Write the Synonym of the word "Benevolent":
A. Malevolent B. Harsh
C. Altruistic D. Traitor

125. Fill in the blank with the ***correct*** option:
The report must be read _______ so that the performance can be improved.
A. Sorrowfully B. Awfully
C. Mischievously D. Carefully

126. Name the writer of the story, "The Banyan Tree":
A. William James B. Anna Hathway
C. E.V. Lucas D. Ruskin Bond

127. Early man was frightened of what in the chapter, "Fire, Friends and Foe"?
A. Lightining and Volcanoes
B. Fire
C. Rain and Thunderstorm
D. Animals

128. Which of the following is ***not*** a Collective Noun?
A. Fleet B. Crowd
C. Army D. Childhood

129. Choose the sentence which is grammatically ***correct***?
A. Between you and me, Mr. Sharma is not to be trusted.
B. Between you and I, Mr. Sharma is not to be trusted.
C. Between I and me, Mr. Sharma is not to trusted.
D. Between you and you, Mr. Sharma is not to be trusted.

130. Taro in the story,"Taro's Reward" is a:
A. Woodcutter B. Painter
C. Magician D. Gatekeeper

131. The story, 'A visit to Cambridge in a meeting' between:
A. Firdaus Kanga and Issac Newton
B. Stephen Hawking and Marie Curie
C. Stephen Hawking and Firdaus Kanga
D. Henry James and William Chang

132. Which of the following is spelt ***correctly***?
A. Conoiseur B. Conooiseur
C. Connoisseur D. Conoisseur

133. Who is the poet of the poem, "The School Boy"?
A. William Blake B. William Wordsworth
C. William Henry D. William James

134. What did the writer find in the secret drawer in the story, "The Best Christmas Present in the World"?
A. A Necklace B. Jim's Last Letter
C. Jim's autobiography D. A Pen

135. Identify the grammatically ***correct*** sentence:
A. All the passengers, with the driver, is killed in the accident.
B. All the passengers, with the driver, be killed in the accident.
C. All the passengers, with the driver, were killed in the accident.
D. All the passengers, with the driver, was killed in the accident.

136. A poem of 14 lines is called:
A. An Elegy B. An Epic
C. An Allegory D. A Sonnet

137. Why does Jody want to bring the fawn home?
A. To beat it
B. To raise it
C. To gift it to his friend
D. To show his father his bravery

138. Fill in the blank with ***correct*** determiner:
I have quite ______ books on art.
A. Little B. A few
C. The D. This

139. Put the verb in the ***correct*** form.
It ________ since early morning.
A. has been raining B. have been raining
C. had rained D. is been raining

140. Fill in the blank with ***correct*** preposition:
Most people work ______ nine to five.
A. Since B. At
C. For D. From

141. Match the words and phrases in Column A & B:

A	B
(*i*) Homesick	(*a*) Terrible
(*ii*) Ghastly	(*b*) In pain
(*iii*) Gradually	(*c*) Wanting to be home
(*vi*) Painfully	(*d*) Slowly

	(*i*)	(*ii*)	(*iii*)	(*iv*)
A.	(*d*)	(*c*)	(*b*)	(*a*)
B.	(*c*)	(*a*)	(*d*)	(*b*)
C.	(*a*)	(*b*)	(*c*)	(*d*)
D.	(*b*)	(*a*)	(*c*)	(*d*)

142. Complete the blank phrase with a suitable word:
A _______ of ships.
A. Fleet B. Bundle
C. Pack D. Herd

143. Name the poem that talks about making choices and the choices that shape us:
A. The Road not taken
B. Wind
C. The Lake isle of Innisfree
D. Rain on the Roof

144. Fill in the blank with ***appropriate*** modal:
When I was young I ______ climb any treen in the forest. (Past ability)
A. Could B. Can
C. Might D. May

145. Fill in the blank with the ***correct*** option:
Thieves broke ______ my house.
A. Into B. At
C. Onto D. Under

146. What does the phrase, "Hue and cry" mean?
A. To be kind B. To Hit someone
C. Angry protest D. Welcome gesture

147. The antonym of the word 'Triumph' is:
A. Success B. Conquest
C. Win D. Defeat

148. Transform the following into a negative sentence:
Only a fool could have done it.
A. Nobody other than a fool will do it.
B. None but a fool could have done it.
C. Not a fool is going to do it.
D. None, not only a fool could do it.

149. "The bicycle goes easily enough in the morning and a little stuffy after lunch." The remark is:
A. Humiliating B. Humorous
C. Sarcastic D. Pinching

150. The ***correct*** synonym of the word 'Innocuous' is:
A. Nocuous B. Harmless
C. Toxic D. Harmful

Answers

1	2	3	4	5	6	7	8	9	10
C	A	D	A	B	C	B	A	D	D
11	**12**	**13**	**14**	**15**	**16**	**17**	**18**	**19**	**20**
B	A	D	A	C	C	D	B	A	B
21	**22**	**23**	**24**	**25**	**26**	**27**	**28**	**29**	**30**
B	B	A	A	C	B	C	B	D	C
31	**32**	**33**	**34**	**35**	**36**	**37**	**38**	**39**	**40**
D	C	D	B	B	B	B	A	C	C

41	42	43	44	45	46	47	48	49	50
D	A	C	D	B	B	B	A	D	D
51	**52**	**53**	**54**	**55**	**56**	**57**	**58**	**59**	**60**
B	D	C	C	A	A	D	C	A	C
61	**62**	**63**	**64**	**65**	**66**	**67**	**68**	**69**	**70**
C	A	D	B	C	B	C	B	D	B
71	**72**	**73**	**74**	**75**	**76**	**77**	**78**	**79**	**80**
C	B	C	A	B	C	A	D	D	A
81	**82**	**83**	**84**	**85**	**86**	**87**	**88**	**89**	**90**
D	A	D	B	C	A	C	C	C	A
91	**92**	**93**	**94**	**95**	**96**	**97**	**98**	**99**	**100**
A	A	B	A	C	A	A	A	B	A
101	**102**	**103**	**104**	**105**	**106**	**107**	**108**	**109**	**110**
D	A	B	B	A	C	D	A	B	C
111	**112**	**113**	**114**	**115**	**116**	**117**	**118**	**119**	**120**
A	A	D	A	A	A	C	D	C	A
121	**122**	**123**	**124**	**125**	**126**	**127**	**128**	**129**	**130**
B	A	D	C	D	D	B	D	A	A
131	**132**	**133**	**134**	**135**	**136**	**137**	**138**	**139**	**140**
C	C	A	B	C	D	B	B	A	D
141	**142**	**143**	**144**	**145**	**146**	**147**	**148**	**149**	**150**
B	A	A	A	A	C	D	B	B	B

Explanatory Answers

61. Given, $l + b + h = 19$ cm

$\Rightarrow (l + b + h)^2 = (19)^2$

$\Rightarrow l^2 + b^2 + h^2 + 2(lb + bh + lh) = 361 \text{ cm}^2$ ...(*i*)

and given, principal diagonal $= 5\sqrt{5}$ cm

$\Rightarrow \sqrt{l^2 + b^2 + h^2} = 5\sqrt{5}$ cm

$\Rightarrow l^2 + b^2 + h^2 = 125 \text{ cm}^2$ ...(*ii*)

From (*i*) and (*ii*)

$125 + 2(lb + bh + lh) = 361$

$\Rightarrow 2(lb + bh + lh) = 361 - 125$

$\Rightarrow 2(lb + bh + lh) = 236 \text{ cm}^2$

Hence, the surface area $= 236 \text{ cm}^2$.

62. Given, in a row of boys

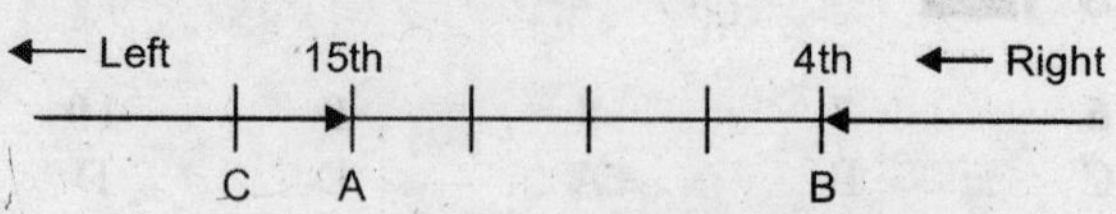

A = 15th from the left

B = 4th from the right

C = first left of A

and 3 boys between A and B

Hence, the position of C from the right

$= 4 + 3 + 2 = 9$th

63. Among five persons

C > B > D > A > E

Hence, E is the shortest among them.

64. A train to cover distance $= 140 + 260 = 400$ m

and speed of the train $= 60$ km/hr

$= 60 \times \frac{5}{18}$ m/s

$= 10 \times \frac{5}{3} = \frac{50}{3}$ m/s

$\therefore$ Train will take time to pass a platform

$= \frac{400}{\frac{50}{3}} = \frac{400 \times 3}{50} = 24$ seconds.

65. Let x units and y units of alloy were taken out from each alloy.

Then copper and tin in the first alloy will be $\frac{1}{4}x$ and $\frac{3}{4}x$ while in the second alloy, copper and tin will be $\frac{2}{7}y$ and $\frac{5}{7}y$ respectively.

From the question,

$$\frac{\frac{1}{4}x+\frac{2}{7}y}{\frac{3}{4}x+\frac{5}{7}y} = \frac{3}{8} \text{ or } \frac{7x+8y}{21x+20y} = \frac{3}{8}$$

or, $56x + 64y = 63x + 60y$

or, $7x = 4y$

or, $\frac{x}{y} = \frac{4}{7}$

Hence, $x : y = 4 : 7$.

66. Here, $M_1 = 6$ women, $d_1 = 12$ days, $h_1 = 7$ hours, $w_1 = 1$ and $M_2 = 3+10\times\frac{6}{4} - 3 + 15 = 18$ women, $d_2 = ?$, $h_2 = 8$ hours, $w_2 = 2$

[4 men = 6 women ⇒ 1 men = $\frac{6}{4}$ women]

$\because \quad \frac{M_1 d_1 h_1}{w_1} = \frac{M_2 d_2 h_2}{w_2}$

$\Rightarrow \quad \frac{6\times12\times7}{1} = \frac{18\times d_2\times8}{2}$

$\Rightarrow \quad d_2 = \frac{6\times12\times7}{9\times8} = 7$ days.

67. Given, $x = \frac{1}{1+\sqrt{2}}$

$= \frac{1}{1+\sqrt{2}}\times\frac{\sqrt{2}-1}{\sqrt{2}-1} = \frac{\sqrt{2}-1}{2-1} = \left(\sqrt{2}-1\right)$

$\therefore \quad x^2 = \left(\sqrt{2}-1\right)^2 = 2+1-2\sqrt{2} = 3-2\sqrt{2}$

$x^2 + 2x + 3 = 3-2\sqrt{2}+2\left(\sqrt{2}-1\right)+3$

$= 3-2\sqrt{2}+2\sqrt{2}-2+3$

$= 6 - 2 = 4.$

68.

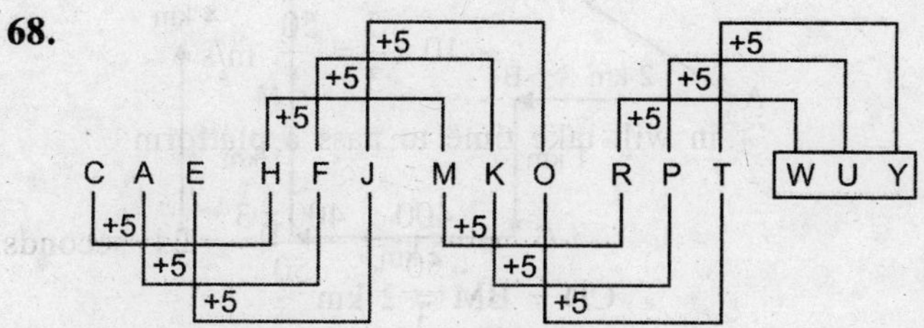

Hence, the next term = WUY.

69. Given, the length of a wire = 66 m

$= 66 \times 100$ cm $= 6600$ cm

$\therefore$ Circumference = 6600 cm

and circumference of small circle = 1.32 cm

$\therefore$ The required number of circumferene

$= \frac{6600}{1.32} = 5000.$

70. Let the two numbers are x and $(520 - x)$

The smaller number = x, bigger number = $(520 - x)$

Then, $(520-x)\times\frac{100-4}{100} = x\times\frac{100+12}{100}$

$\Rightarrow \quad 96(520 - x) = 112x$

$\Rightarrow \quad 96 \times 520 - 96x = 112x$

$\Rightarrow \quad 208x = 96 \times 520$

$\Rightarrow \quad x = \frac{96\times520}{208}$

$\Rightarrow \quad x = \frac{40\times96}{16} = 40 \times 6 = 240$

Hence, the smaller number, $x = 240$.

71. Let the selling price of 1 m cloth = ₹ 1

Then, the selling price of 33 m cloth = ₹ 33

$\therefore$ Profit = Selling price of 11 m cloth = ₹ 11

$\therefore$ The cost price of 33 m cloth

= 33 − 11 = ₹ 22

Hence, the profit percentage = $\frac{\text{Profit}\times100}{\text{C.P.}}$

$= \frac{11\times100}{22} = 50\%.$

72.

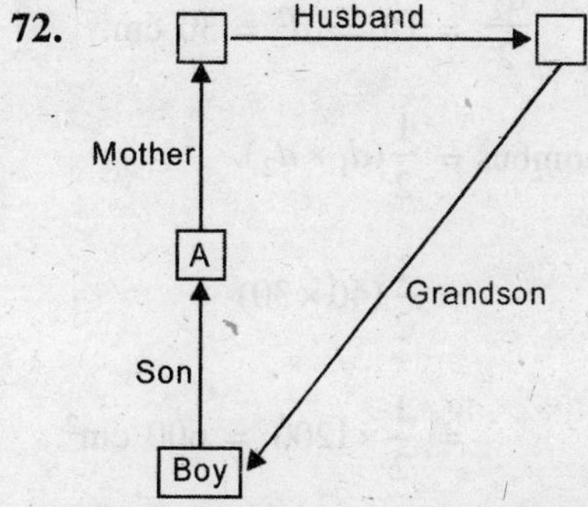

Here, The Boy is the son of A.

74. Given, P = ₹ 5000, $r = 12\%$ p.a., $t = 2$ years

$\therefore$ Compound interest

$= P\left(1+\frac{r}{100}\right)^n - P = P\left[\left(1+\frac{r}{100}\right)^n - 1\right]$

$= 5000\left[\left(1+\frac{12}{100}\right)^2 - 1\right] = 5000\left[\left(\frac{28}{25}\right)^2 - 1\right]$

$= 5000\left[\frac{784}{625} - 1\right] = 5000\left[\frac{159}{625}\right]$

$= 8 \times 159 =$ ₹ 1272

and Simple interest $= \frac{Prt}{100} = \frac{5000\times12\times2}{100}$

$= 50 \times 24 =$ ₹ 1200

Hence, the required difference = C.I. = S.I.

= ₹ 1272 − ₹ 1200 = ₹ 72.

75. Given, the perimeter of a rhombus = 100 cm

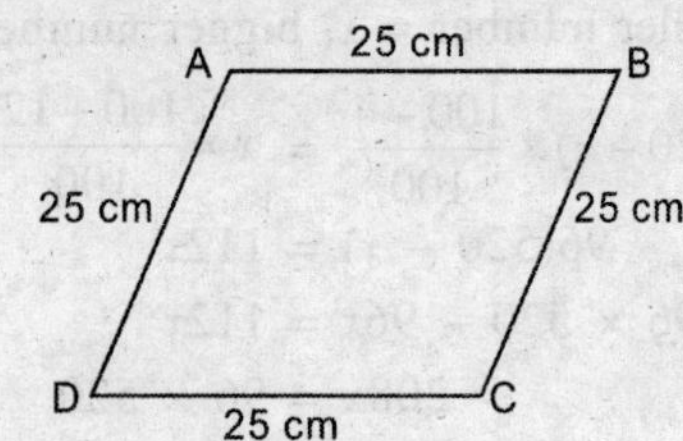

One diagonal (d_1) = 40 cm

$$\left(\frac{d_1}{2}\right)^2 + \left(\frac{d_2}{2}\right)^2 = (25)^2$$

$$\Rightarrow \quad (20)^2 + \left(\frac{d_2}{2}\right)^2 = 625$$

$$\Rightarrow \quad \left(\frac{d_2}{2}\right)^2 = 625 - 400$$

$$\Rightarrow \quad \left(\frac{d_2}{2}\right)^2 = 225$$

$$\Rightarrow \quad \left(\frac{d_2}{2}\right)^2 = (15)^2$$

$$\Rightarrow \quad \frac{d_2}{2} = 15 \Rightarrow d^2 = 30 \text{ cm.}$$

$$\therefore \text{ Area of the rhombus } = \frac{1}{2}(d_1 \times d_2)$$

$$= \frac{1}{2}(40 \times 30)$$

$$= \frac{1}{2} \times 1200 = 600 \text{ cm}^2.$$

76.

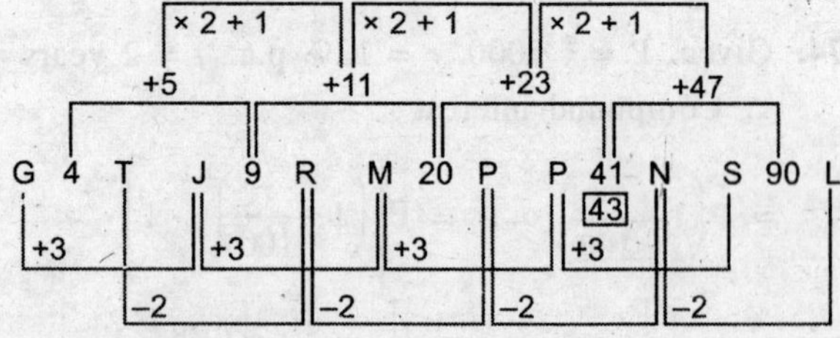

For middle number, in term P4IN
Place of 41 should be 43
Hence, the wrong term P4IN.

77. Given, W = 23

STRONG = 93

$\Rightarrow$ 19 + 20 + 18 + 15 + 14 + 7 = 93

Similarly, WEAK = 23 + 5 + 1 + 11

$\Rightarrow$ WEAK = 40.

78. Here, starting point = A

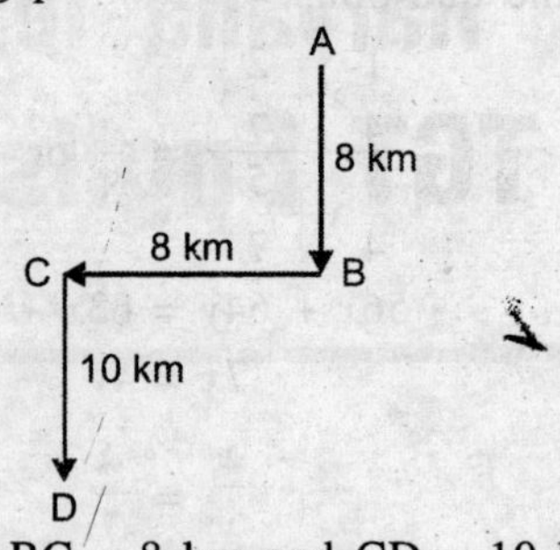

AB = 8 km, BC = 8 km and CD = 10 km

Hence, He (D) is in the South-west direction from starting point (A).

79. Given, $5a + \frac{1}{3a} = 5$

Multiplying both by $\frac{3}{5}$

$$\therefore \quad \frac{3}{5}\left(5a + \frac{1}{3a}\right) = 5 \times \frac{3}{5}$$

$$\Rightarrow \quad 3a + \frac{1}{5a} = 3$$

Squaring both sides,

$$9a^2 + \frac{1}{25a^2} + 2.3a.\frac{1}{5a} = 9$$

$$\Rightarrow \quad 9a^2 + \frac{1}{25a^2} = 9 - \frac{6}{5}$$

$$\Rightarrow \quad 9a^2 + \frac{1}{25a^2} = \frac{39}{5}.$$

80. Here, Starting point = A

AB = 2 km, BC = 1 km, CD = 2 km, DE = 4 km

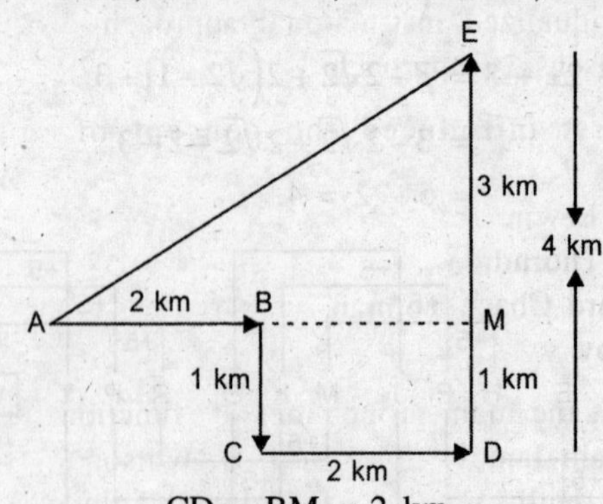

CD = BM = 2 km

BC = DM = 1 km

ME = DE – DM = 4 – 1 = 3 km

and AM = AB + BM = 2 + 2 = 4 km

$\because$ $EA^2 = ME^2 + AM^2$

$\therefore$ $EA^2 = 3^2 + 4^2 = 9 + 16 = 25 = 5^2$

$\Rightarrow$ $EA^2 = 5^2 \Rightarrow EA = 5$ km

Hence, He is 5 km far from his starting point (A).

Previous Paper (Solved)

Haryana Teacher Eligibility Test (HTET)

TGT English (Level-2), Exam 2020

(Exam held on 3 January, 2021)

PART-I

Child Development and Pedagogy

Directions: *Answer the following questions by selecting the* ***most appropriate*** *option.*

1. Which of the following is ***not*** the main law of learning as prescribed by Thorndike?
A. Law of Exercise
B. Law of Effect
C. Law of Readiness
D. Law of Generalization

2. Who first introduced the word 'Emotional Intelligence'?
A. Fredrick and Kirk
B. Henry and Peter
C. John and Cronback
D. Mayer and Salovey

3. Which of the following approach is based on analysing the behaviour of disabled child and find out the root cause of his/her learning deficiency?
A. Psychoanalytic approach
B. Behavioural approach
C. Individualized instructional approach
D. Multisensory approach

4. Who first introduced the concept of "Latent Learning"?
A. Kurt Lewin
B. E.L. Thorndike
C. Edward Chace Tolman
D. Pavlov

5. Who was the main propounder of 'functionalism'?
A. William James B. J. B. Watson
C. Clark Hull D. Edward Tolman

6. Which of the following is example of Innate Motive?
A. Award B. Hunger
C. Punishment D. Incentives

7. In which stage of development, the sexual changes that occur in the child's body starts to appear?
A. Early childhood B. Later Adolescence
C. Adulthood D. Puberty

8. What is the other name of classical conditioning?
A. Type S conditioning
B. Type R conditioning
C. Type S-R conditioning
D. Type U conditioning

9. What is age group given by Erikson for the stage "industry vs inferiority"?
A. 6 to 11 years
B. 12 to 20 years
C. 3 to 6 years
D. 18 months to 3 years

10. Out of the following which is ***not*** correct principle of 'Development'?
A. Principle of continuity
B. Principle of individual difference
C. Principle of uniformity of pattern
D. Principle of proceeding from specific to general responses

11. Which of the 'thoughts of school' in Psychology is also called as 'Black box theory'?
A. Behaviourism B. Structuralism
C. Functionalism D. Gestaltism

12. Which of the following is ***not*** the characteristic of Good Mental Health?
A. Ability to adjust B. Emotional Maturity
C. Self-confidence D. Intolerance

13. Scale I in Cattell Culture Free Intelligence Test was prepared for whom?
A. For 8 to 12 years mental deficient person
B. For 4 to 8 years mental deficient person
C. For 12 to 15 years mental deficient person
D. For 2 to 4 years mental deficient person

14. Which of the following is the ***correct*** logical order for 'process of creativity'?
A. Insight → Preparation → Incubation → Verification
B. Preparation → Insight → Incubation → Verification
C. Preparation → Incubation → Insight → Verification
D. Preparation → Insight → Verification → Incubation

15. Which of the following terms is ***not*** related with the operant conditioning?
A. Insight
B. Reinforcement
C. Spontaneous Recovery
D. Extinction

16. Who introduces 'Learning Disable' word very first for the children suffered from various learning problems?
A. Heward B. Samuel Kirk
C. Van Riper D. Birch

17. Which of the following Psychologist is ***not*** supporter of views about "Psychology as a Science of Soul"?
A. Plato B. Aristotle
C. Descartes D. Wundt

18. In which branch of Psychology there is a scope of study of Telepathy, Rebirth etc.?
A. Physiological Psychology
B. Clinical Psychology
C. Parapsychology
D. Developmental Psychology

19. According to Jean Piaget in which stage child is able to understand Hypothesis and getting thinking ability on the basis of logical statement?
A. 0 to 2 years B. 2 to 6 years
C. 6 to 11 years D. 11 to 15 years

20. Which of the following Psychology studies about man's thinking, memory, language, perception etc.?
A. Humanist Psychology
B. Cognitive Psychology
C. Abnormal Psychology
D. Clinical Psychology

21. Which of the following is ***not*** the type of personality given by Kretschmer?
A. Athletic B. Aesthetic
C. Asthenic D. Pyknic

22. What is the age group for the moral development stage "Heteronomy Reciprocity" given by Jean Piaget?
A. 0 to 5 years B. 13 to 18 years
C. 5 to 8 years D. 11 to 13 years

23. Which of the following is ***not*** the characteristic of Learning Disabled Children?
A. Perceptual effectiveness
B. Emotional instability
C. Disorder of attention
D. Impulsivity

24. What is the I.Q. Range of severe mental retarded child?
A. 50 to 60 B. 36 to 51
C. 20 to 35 D. below 20

25. In which stage of development, interest/friendship develops towards same sexual groups?
A. 12 to 14 years B. 15 to 18 years
C. 10 to 12 years D. 19 to 21 years

26. Which of the following is ***not*** the type of Realistic thinking?
A. Convergent thinking B. Creative thinking
C. Evaluative thinking D. Autistic thinking

27. Out of the following which psychologist was ***not*** supporter of 'Humanist Psychology'?
A. Freud B. Maslow
C. Rogers D. Arthur Combs

28. Who was the propounder of 'structuralism'?
A. William James B. William West
C. Wilhelm Wundt D. Wilhelm Hunt

29. Which of the following component is ***not*** related with the 'Motivation Cycle'?
A. Need B. Drive
C. Emotion D. Incentive

30. The 'emotion of fear' associated with which basic instinct?
A. Repulsion B. Pugnacity
C. Appeal D. Escape

PART-II

भाषा : हिन्दी

निर्देशः *निम्नलिखित प्रश्नों के उत्तर देने के लिए **सबसे उचित** विकल्प चुनिए।*

31. किस वाक्य में संबंधसूचक अव्यय का प्रयोग हुआ है?
A. राधा ऊपर नाचती है।
B. अनिता राधा से मधुर गाती है।
C. राम बहुत तेज चल रहा था।
D. मोहन आजकल ज्यादा बोलता है।

32. 'अक' प्रत्यय युक्त पद ***नहीं*** है :
A. विधायक B. प्रेरक
C. निंदक D. लड़ाक

33. किस विकल्प में नित्य पुल्लिंग संज्ञा है?
A. खरगोश B. गिलहरी
C. बटेर D. कोयल

34. समास विग्रह की दृष्टि से ***अनुचित*** विकल्प चुनिए :
A. मातृभक्ति = माता के लिए भक्ति
B. वाग्वीर = वाक् (वाणी) में वीर
C. इन्द्रियजय = इन्द्रियों के लिए जय
D. जीवदया = जीवों पर दया

35. ***गलत*** समास विग्रह चुनिए :

A. दूर के लिए दर्शन = दूरदर्शन

B. दूर से आगत = दूरागत

C. पाठ के लिए शाला = पाठशाला

D. सभा के लिए मण्डप = सभामण्डप

36. नामधातु क्रिया ***नहीं*** है :

A. लतियाना B. सजाना

C. झुठलाना D. गलियाना

37. वर्णोच्चारण की दृष्टि से ***बेमेल*** चुनिए :

A. ओ, औ - कंठोष्ठ B. व, फ - दन्तोष्ठ

C. द, ध - तालु D. ठ, ड - मूर्धा

38. किस विकल्प में 'अनु' उपसर्ग का प्रयोग ***नहीं*** हुआ है?

A. अनुस्वार B. अनुषंग

C. अनुदार D. अनुशास्ति

39. वार्तनिक दृष्टि से ***अशुद्ध*** शब्द चुनिए :

A. तिरपन B. अजमाइश

C. अन्त्याक्षरी D. छिपकली

40. अनिश्चयवाचक सर्वनाम वाला वाक्य चुनिए :

A. मैं कुछ पुस्तकें लाया हूँ, इन्हें तुम रख लो।

B. दाल में कुछ काला है।

C. केवल वही तुम्हारी प्रशंसा कर सकता है।

D. वह चाहता है कि तुम सदैव आगे बढ़ो।

41. 'सु' उपसर्ग-रहित पद चुनिए :

A. सुषुप्ति B. स्वस्थ

C. स्वल्प D. सौष्ठव

42. किस शब्द में व्यंजन सन्धि का प्रयोग हुआ है?

A. वागीश्वर B. धातूष्मा

C. अधमर्ण D. पूर्णोपमा

43. संधि विच्छेद की दृष्टि से ***असंगत*** चुनिए :

A. फणि + इन्द्र = फणीन्द्र B. सुधी + इन्द्र = सुधीन्द्र

C. अभि + इष्ट = अभीष्ट D. रजनी + ईश = रजनीश

44. ''टहलना स्वास्थ्य के लिए लाभकारी है।'' वाक्य में प्रयुक्त क्रिया है :

A. प्रेरणार्थक क्रिया B. संयुक्त क्रिया

C. रंजक क्रिया D. क्रियार्थक संज्ञा

45. प्रत्यय की दृष्टि से ***असंगत*** विकल्प चुनिए :

A. हथ + औड़ी = हथौड़ी B. अणु + इक = आणविक

C. साँप + ओला = सँपोला D. भाँग + एड़ी = भँगेड़ी

Language : English

Directions: *Answer the following questions by selecting the **most appropriate** option.*

46. Choose the part of the sentence which is ***incorrect***:

(*a*) His/(*b*) new film/(*c*) is really worth/(*d*) to be seen.

A. (*a*) B. (*b*)

C. (*c*) D. (*d*)

47. Select the ***appropriate*** modal for the expression given:

When .... we expect you? (possibility)

A. may B. will

C. have to D. dare

48. Select the ***correct*** option (phrasal verb) for the underlined word:

Most of the patients respect Dr. John for his kindness.

A. pay back B. zest for

C. make over D. look up to

49. Choose the ***correct*** meaning of the underlined words:

The baby monkeys ran every which way.

A. up B. straight

C. in different directions D. down

50. Choose the ***correct*** tense form:

Nanny died last week. She .... from cancer for some time. (suffer)

A. suffering B. is suffering

C. had been suffering D. suffers

51. Select the ***appropriate*** modal for the expression given:

If you do that again you .... be punished. (threat)

A. may B. shall

C. can D. ought

52. Choose the ***correct*** option for the following:

An instrument for detecting earthquakes is:

A. A Fathometer B. Lithoscope

C. A Seismograph D. Cardiograph

53. Choose the ***correct*** meaning of the underlined words:

It's a pity you don't like football. But each to their own.

A. everyone has different opinions

B. everyone has similar opinions

C. each and all are same

D. each one likes football

54. Choose the ***correct*** option to fill the blank :

Immediately after the operation he could see nothing .... vague shadows.

A. as long as B. however

C. but D. notwithstanding

55. Select the ***correct*** option (phrasal verb) for the underlined word:

I don't know how we are going to cope with the cold during winters.

A. make up for B. put up with
C. put down D. set up

56. Select ***appropriate*** preposition to fill in the blank:

They walked .... the footpath until they came to a bridge.

A. into B. since
C. along D. in

57. Choose the ***correct*** tense form :

My car .... for the third time since I got it. (break down)

A. break down
B. has broken down
C. was broke down
D. has broken

58. Choose the part of the sentence which is ***incorrect*** :

(*a*) James/(*b*) is busy/(*c*) to prepare/(*d*) tonight's dinner.

A. (*a*) B. (*b*)
C. (*c*) D. (*d*)

59. Choose the ***correct*** option to fill the blank :

The room was empty ...... for a chair in the corner.

A. except B. and
C. between D. behind

60. Select ***appropriate*** preposition to fill in the blank :

The programme was broadcasted ...... the world.

A. in B. off
C. onto D. across

PART-III

General Studies : Quantitative Aptitude, Reasoning Ability and GK & Awareness

Directions: *Answer the following questions by selecting the* ***most appropriate*** *option.*

61. Among five persons P, Q, R, S and T, T is shorter than R and S. Q is not as tall as T but taller than one person. R is shorter than one person.

Who among them is the tallest?

A. R B. Q
C. S D. P

62. Three numbers are in the ratio 2 : 3 : 4. The sum of their cubes is 33957, then the numbers are :

A. 14, 21, 28
B. 12, 18, 24
C. 8, 12, 16
D. 4, 6, 8

63. A is father of X; B is mother of Y. The sister of X and Z is Y. Which of the following statement is necessarily not true?

A. B is the mother of Z.
B. X is the sister of Z.
C. B is the wife of A.
D. Y is the son of A.

64. A person walks 1 km towards East and then he turns to South and walks 5 km. Again he turns to East and walks 2 km, after this he turns to North and walks 9 km. Now, how far is he from his starting point?

A. 4 km B. 5 km
C. 7 km D. 9 km

65. Find the next term of the following letter series :

DHL, PTX, BFJ, ...

A. CGK B. KOS
C. NRV D. OVZ

66. 12 men take 18 days to complete a job whereas 12 women in 18 days can complete $\frac{3}{4}$ part of the same job. How many days will 10 men and 8 women together take to complete the same job?

A. 6 B. $7\frac{1}{2}$
C. $13\frac{1}{2}$ D. 14

67. The radius of a sphere is doubled. What per cent of its volume is increased?

A. 200% B. 450%
C. 550% D. 700%

68. A dealer sells an article for ₹ 24 and gains as much per cent as the price of the article, then the cost price of the article is:

A. ₹ 15 B. ₹ 17
C. ₹ 18 D. ₹ 20

69. In a group of 15 people, 7 read Hindi, 8 read English and 3 read none of these language. How many people read Hindi and English both?

A. 0 B. 3
C. 4 D. 5

70. If p and q are rational numbers and $\frac{3+\sqrt{5}}{3-\sqrt{5}} = p + q\sqrt{5}$, then value of p and q are:

A. $p = \frac{2}{7}; q = \frac{3}{2}$ B. $p = \frac{7}{2}; q = \frac{2}{7}$

C. $p = \frac{7}{2}; q = \frac{3}{2}$ D. $p = \frac{7}{2}; q = \frac{7}{2}$

71. If the compound interest on a certain sum for two years at 3% p.a. be ₹ 101.50, then what would be the simple interest on the same sum for same period?

A. ₹ 50 B. ₹ 100

C. ₹ 125 D. ₹ 147

72. Find the ***missing*** term of the following letter series :

A, CD, GHI, ? , UVWXY

A. LMNO B. MNO

C. MNOP D. NOPQ

73. One angle of a quadrilateral is 108° and the remaining three angles are equal. Find each of the three equal angles :

A. 63° B. 74°

C. 84° D. 96°

74. Amit is West to Prakash and North to Sumit. Tarun is in East of Sumit. Tarun is in which direction with reference to Amit ?

A. North-West B. South

C. South-East D. North

75. If DRIVER = 12, PEDESTRIAN = 20, ACCIDENT = 16, then CAR = ?

A. 3 B. 6

C. 8 D. 16

76. Find the ***wrong*** number in the following series :

69, 55, 26, 13, 5

A. 5 B. 13

C. 26 D. 55

77. If $2^x = 4^y = 8^z$ and $\frac{1}{2x} + \frac{1}{4y} + \frac{1}{4z} = 4$, then the value of x is:

A. $\frac{7}{16}$ B. $\frac{7}{17}$

C. $\frac{7}{19}$ D. $\frac{7}{23}$

78. In a journey of 80 kms a train covers the first 60 kms at 40 km/hr. and the remaining distance at 20 km/hr. The average speed for the whole journey is:

A. 24 km/hr. B. 30 km/hr.

C. 32 km/hr. D. 36 km/hr.

79. A swimming pool, 30 m long has a depth of water 0.80 m at one end and 2.4 m at the other end. The area of the vertical cross-section of the pool along the length is:

A. 48 m^2 B. 72 m^2

C. 156 m^2 D. 192 m^2

80. Anil is standing at 16th position from the left end in a row. Vikas is at 18th position from the right end. Gopal is 11th from Anil towards the right and 3rd from Vikas towards the right end. How many persons are standing in this row?

A. 41 B. 42

C. 48 D. 49

81. Which of the following are ***true*** about the functions of HAFED?

(*i*) It procures agriculture products.

(*ii*) It markets agriculture products.

(*iii*) It supplies agriculture inputs.

Choose the ***correct*** code :

A. (*i*) and (*ii*) B. only (*i*)

C. (*i*) and (*iii*) D. (*i*), (*ii*) and (*iii*)

82. Where in Haryana 'City-forest' is being developed?

A. Murthal B. Sohna

C. Yamunanagar D. Hansi

83. 'Air Shuttle Service' has been started from which city of Haryana?

A. Hisar B. Karnal

C. Rohtak D. Ambala

84. The President of 'Haryana Sahitya Academy' is:

A. Dr. Kumud Bansal B. Sh. Manohar Lal

C. Dr. Ashok Batra D. Sh. Rana Oberoi

85. Consider the following statements about Minty Agarwal:

(*a*) Minty Agarwal, a native of Haryana, is a Squadron Leader in Indian Air Force.

(*b*) She is the first woman, who received Yudha Seva Medal.

Choose the ***correct*** answer :

A. Statement (*a*) is true

B. Statement (*b*) is true

C. Both (*a*) and (*b*) are false

D. Both (*a*) and (*b*) are true

86. Ancient Bhawani Amba Mata temple is situated in:

A. Jind B. Ambala

C. Sonipat D. Kurukshetra

87. In January 2020, which of the following Nagar Palika was raised to the status of Nagar Parishad (Municipal Council)?

A. Rania B. Jhajjar

C. Beri D. Sirsi

88. Who was the Nawab of Jhajjar during the uprising of 1857?

A. Abd-ur Rahman Khan
B. Nawab Shamsuddin
C. Sadruddin
D. Bisarat Ali

89. The original founding place of Topara Inscription of Ashoka is located in:
A. Ambala district
B. Yamunanagar district
C. Kurukshetra district
D. Kaithal district

90. Identify the rivers, which flows from Mahendragarh district:

(*i*) Ambumati (*ii*) Dohan
(*iii*) Kasavati (*iv*) Indori

Choose the ***correct*** code :
A. (*i*) and (*iii*)
B. (*ii*) and (*iii*)
C. (*i*), (*iii*) and (*iv*)
D. (*i*), (*ii*), (*iii*) and (*iv*)

PART-IV

English

Directions: *Answer the following questions by selecting the* ***most appropriate*** *option.*

91. Fill in the blank with the ***correct*** option:
I applied for the job in Japan, but they .... my application because I did'nt know Japanese.
A. turned down B. turned out
C. turned in D. turned on

92. Fill in the blank with the ***correct*** modal:
Children .... obey their parents. (Duty / Obligation)
A. should B. can
C. shall D. will

93. Fill in the blank with the ***correct*** preposition:
Thieves broke .... my house.
A. into B. under
C. at D. over

94. Fill in the blank with the ***correct*** present perfect tense:
I .... the instructions, but I don't understand them.
A. had reading B. have read
C. have been read D. read

95. Fill in the blank with ***appropriate*** modal:
He .... not enter my house again. (Command)
A. should B. might
C. can D. shall

96. Identify the ***correct*** dipthong in the underlined words: boy, coy
A. |a|| B. |e||
C. |⊃|| D. |∂||

97. Identify the phonetic symbol of the underlined sounds:
Sheep, Shine, Trash
A. |ʃ| B. (ʒ|
C. |Z| D. |tʃ|

98. Identify the grammatically ***correct*** sentence:
A. John is resembling his older sister.
B. John resembles his older sister.
C. John resembles his senior sister.
D. John has resembling his sister.

99. Who is the author of, "A Different Kind of School"?
A. Carol Moore B. E.V. Lucas
C. Hary Behn D. A Japanese Story

100. Fill in the blank with the ***correct*** option:
It rained .... three days without stopping.
A. during B. for
C. at D. while

Directions (Qs. No. 101-106): *Read the following poem and answer the questions given below.*

The poetry of earth is never dead:
When all the birds are faint with the hot sun,
And hide in cooling trees, a voice will run
From hedge to hedge about the new-mown mead,
That is the grasshopper's – he takes the lead
In summer luxury – he has never done
With his delights, for when tired out with fun
He rests at ease beneath some pleasant weed.
The poetry of earth is ceasing never:
On a lone winter evening when the frost
Has wrought a silence, from the stove there shrills
The Cricket's song, in warmth increasing ever,
And seems to one in drowsiness half lost;
The Grasshopper's among some grassy hills.

101. What kind of sonnet is the above mentioned poem?
A. Shakespearean B. Petrarchan
C. Horatian D. Pindaric

102. Who provides the music in the "Winter Evening"?
A. The Grassy Hills B. The Trees
C. The Cricket D. The Grasshopper

103. Which season does the Grasshopper symbolise in the poem?
A. Summer B. Winter
C. Autumn D. Spring

104. The birds in the poem 'take rest', because of:
A. Hunger B. The music
C. The cool breeze D. The hot sun

105. The word, "Faint" in the poem means:
A. Lacking strength B. Having vigour
C. Beauty D. Refreshed

106. "A voice will run from hedge to hedge ...." whose voice is this?
A. The Grasshopper B. The Cricket
C. The Gnats D. The Poet

107. Which of the following is ***not*** a synonym of the word 'Lethargic'?
A. Sluggish B. Lazy
C. Agile D. Torpid

108. Identify the phonetic symbol of the underlined sounds:
Cheers, March, Chair
A. |tʃ| B. |J|
C. |j| D. |ch|

109. Which of the following is ***not*** a Collective Noun?
A. Fleet B. Crowd
C. Family D. Judgement

110. Identify the ***correct*** sentence pattern of the given sentence:
They painted the door green.
A. S + V + O + O B. S + V + O + C
C. S + O + V + C D. S + V + C + O

111. What did Patrick think his cat was 'playing with'?
A. A Doll B. A Horse
C. A Card D. A Trumpet

112. Put the verb in the ***correct*** form:
Ryaan is very good at languages. He .... four languages very well.
A. speaking B. speaks
C. speak D. spoken

113. Fill in the blank with the correct preposition:
.... doing the cleaning, I help my mother in cooking.
A. Beside B. For
C. Besides D. By

114. Which of the following is spelt ***incorrectly***?
A. Environment B. Psychology
C. Curriculum D. Education

115. Transform the following into a negative sentence:
He is greater than me.
A. I am not so great as him.
B. I am not great.
C. He is more great than me.
D. He is not great.

116. Identify the figure of speech in the following lines:
"The fair breeze blew, the white foam flew
The furrow followed free"
A. Alliteration B. Simile
C. Metaphor D. Pun

117. Fill in the blank with the ***correct*** option:
I have .... a little money for rainy days.
A. put back B. put down
C. put aside D. put off

118. Which of the following is spelt ***correctly***?
A. Succeession B. Sucession
C. Succession D. Succeesion

119. Messengers were sent everywhere in the kingdom by the king in the story.
"Three Questions":
A. To find answers to the questions
B. To fetch wise men
C. To look for the wise hermit
D. To announce a reward for those who could answer the questions

120. Identify the part of speech of the underlined word:
He takes after his grandmother.
A. Preposition B. Verb
C. Adverb D. Adjective

121. Identify the underlined phrase in the sentence below:
He answered in a very rude manner.
A. Noun phrase B. Adverb phrase
C. Adjective phrase D. Prepositional phrase

122. How does camel survive in a desert without drinking water?
A. By the hump on its back
B. From desert plants
C. By eating other animals
D. Because of their long shaggy coats

123. Who is a Rebel?
A. A person who resists an established authority
B. A person who is obedient
C. A person who agrees to do what others say
D. A person widely popular

124. Fill in the blank with the ***correct*** conjunction:
The girls danced .... the boys played.
A. only B. without
C. while D. lest

125. Which of the following word is ***incorrectly*** formed in plural?

A. Thieves B. Cargoes

C. Matches D. Calfes

126. Who is the poet of the poem titled, "Trees"?

A. Shirley Bauer

B. John Keats

C. William Shakespeare

D. Arun Kolatkar

127. 'I took out a small black tin box.'

The underlined phrase is:

A. Adverb phrase B. Adjective phrase

C. Noun phrase D. Gerundial phrase

128. The poem, "The School Boy" is written by:

A. Boris Johnson

B. William Dalrymple

C. William Wordsworth

D. William Blake

129. A fictitious narrative, intended to enforce some useful truth, usually with animals as characters is called:

A. A Fable B. A Sonnet

C. A Lyric D. A Story

130. Who is Bijju calling in the mist in the story "A Short Monsoon Diary"?

A. His sister B. His uncle

C. The author D. His brother

131. With whom did the man, strike the bargain in the end, in the poem, "The Last Bargain"?

A. A child B. An old man

C. A king D. Fair maid

132. "I got up early, for me I made an effort."

For what did the writer say this?

A. For catching a train

B. For a long bicycle ride

C. For a trip to Bahamas

D. For morning exercises

133. Identify the underlined word in the sentence:

The old man was tired of walking.

A. Gerund B. Participle

C. Infinitive D. Noun

134. Fill in the blank with the ***correct*** word:

Why didn't you turn up at the party?

We were all .... waiting for you.

A. densely B. perfectly

C. nearly D. eagerly

135. The antonym of the word 'Popular' is:

A. Anonymous B. Famous

C. Well-known D. Widely Admired

136. Which of the following is ***not*** an Abstract Noun?

A. Goodness B. Youth

C. Poverty D. Parliament

137. 'Miss Beam' is a character of which story?

A. A House, a Home

B. A Game of Chance

C. A Different Kind of School

D. The Banyan Tree

138. Who is the speaker in the poem, "The Shed"?

A. The Poet B. A Wise man

C. The Brother D. The Spider

139. Choose the sentence which is grammatically ***correct***:

A. What you would like to drink?

B. What would you like to drink?

C. Would you what like to drink?

D. Would you drink like to?

140. Fill in the blank with the ***correct*** article:

.... tallest boy in the class has grey hair.

A. A B. An

C. The D. Zero article

141. Convert the following positive sentence into comparative sentence:

Few historians write as interestingly as Habib.

A. Habib writes more interestingly than most historians

B. Habib writes very interestingly than more historians

C. Habib writes the most interestingly than more historians

D. Habib writes interestingly than most historians

142. The ***correct*** antonym of the word "Grow" is ....

A. Long B. Cut

C. Sober D. Disturbance

143. Match the words in Column A with their meaning in Column B and select the correct answer using codes given below:

A	B
(*i*) Fierce	(*a*) Moved suddenly
(*ii*) Darted	(*b*) Brave enough to do something
(*iii*) Dared	(*c*) A steep, high rock
(*iv*) Cliff	(*d*) Violent

Codes:

	(*i*)	(*ii*)	(*iii*)	(*iv*)
A.	(*d*)	(*a*)	(*b*)	(*c*)
B.	(*b*)	(*a*)	(*d*)	(*c*)
C.	(*a*)	(*b*)	(*c*)	(*d*)
D.	(*c*)	(*b*)	(*a*)	(*d*)

144. Fill in the blank with the ***correct*** phrasal verb :

A fund has been .... for the soldier's families.

A. set up B. set aside

C. set out D. set in

145. Fill in the blank with the ***correct*** option:

I had .... biscuits for my breakfast.

A. a few B. fourth
C. each D. an

146. The word 'Morsels' in the story "The Banyan Tree" means:

A. Small pieces of food
B. Watch secretly
C. Going deep into
D. Dislike

147. Identify the underlined part of speech in the following sentence:

He came before the appointed time.

A. Adverb
B. Conjunction
C. Noun
D. Preposition

148. Match the words in Column A with their meaning in Column B and select the correct answer using codes given below:

A	B
(i) Scrawny	(*a*) Strange
(*ii*) Weird	(*b*) Moved along smoothly
(*iii*) Glided	(*c*) Short sleep
(*iv*) Snooze	(*d*) Thin

Codes:

	(*i*)	(*ii*)	(*iii*)	(*iv*)
A.	(*d*)	(*a*)	(*b*)	(*c*)
B.	(*a*)	(*b*)	(*c*)	(*d*)
C.	(*b*)	(*c*)	(*a*)	(*d*)
D.	(*d*)	(*c*)	(*b*)	(*a*)

149. Fill in the blank with the ***correct*** determiner:

Who is .... girl sitting there?

A. a B. an
C. those D. the

150. Where do the snakes and rodents take shelter in the story, "A Short Monsoon Diary"?

A. In Roofs and Attics
B. In Holes and Burrows
C. On Roads and Pavements
D. In Sea and Grass

Answers

1	2	3	4	5	6	7	8	9	10
D	D	C	C	A	B	D	A	A	D
11	**12**	**13**	**14**	**15**	**16**	**17**	**18**	**19**	**20**
A	D	*	C	A	B	D	C	D	B
21	**22**	**23**	**24**	**25**	**26**	**27**	**28**	**29**	**30**
B	C	A	C	C	D	A	C	C	D
31	**32**	**33**	**34**	**35**	**36**	**37**	**38**	**39**	**40**
B	D	A	C	A	B	C	C	B	B
41	**42**	**43**	**44**	**45**	**46**	**47**	**48**	**49**	**50**
B	A	A	D	A	D	A	D	C	C
51	**52**	**53**	**54**	**55**	**56**	**57**	**58**	**59**	**60**
B	C	A	C	B	C	B	C	A	D
61	**62**	**63**	**64**	**65**	**66**	**67**	**68**	**69**	**70**
C	A	D	B	C	C	D	D	B	C
71	**72**	**73**	**74**	**75**	**76**	**77**	**78**	**79**	**80**
B	C	C	C	B	A	A	C	A	A
81	**82**	**83**	**84**	**85**	**86**	**87**	**88**	**89**	**90**
D	A	A	B	D	B	B	A	B	B
91	**92**	**93**	**94**	**95**	**96**	**97**	**98**	**99**	**100**
A	A	A	B	D	C	A	B	B	B
101	**102**	**103**	**104**	**105**	**106**	**107**	**108**	**109**	**110**
B	C	A	D	A	A	C	A	D	B

111	112	113	114	115	116	117	118	119	120
A	B	C	C	A	A	C	C	D	A
121	**122**	**123**	**124**	**125**	**126**	**127**	**128**	**129**	**130**
B	B	A	C	D	A	C	D	A	A
131	**132**	**133**	**134**	**135**	**136**	**137**	**138**	**139**	**140**
A	B	A	D	A	D	C	A	B	C
141	**142**	**143**	**144**	**145**	**146**	**147**	**148**	**149**	**150**
A	B	A	A, B	A	A	D	A	D	A

Explanatory Answers

62. Let, numbers are $2x$, $3x$ and $4x$

Then, $(2x)^3 + (3x)^3 + (4x)^3 = 33957$

$\therefore\ 8x^3 + 27x^3 + 64x^3 = 33957$

$\Rightarrow\quad 99x^3 = 33957$

$x^3 = \dfrac{33957}{99}$

$= 343$

$= (7)^3$

$\therefore\quad x = 7$

Hence, numbers $= 2x,\ 3x,\ 4x = 14,\ 21,\ 28.$

64.

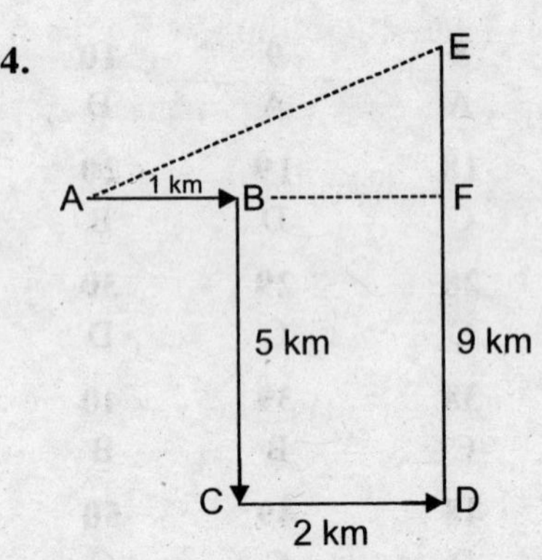

Here, starting point = A

AB = 1 km,

BC = 5 km,

CD = 2 km,

DE = 9 km

$\because$ BC = DF = 5 km

and CD = BF = 2 km

$\therefore$ FE = DE − DF

= DE − BC

= 9 − 5

= 4 km

AF = AB + BF

= 1 + 2 = 3 km

$\because\quad AE^2 = (EF)^2 + (FA)^2$

$\Rightarrow\quad = 4^2 + 3^2$

$\Rightarrow\quad = 16 + 9$

$\Rightarrow\quad = 25$

$\Rightarrow\quad = 5^2$

$\therefore\quad AE = 5$ km

Hence, he is 5 km far from his starting point.

65.

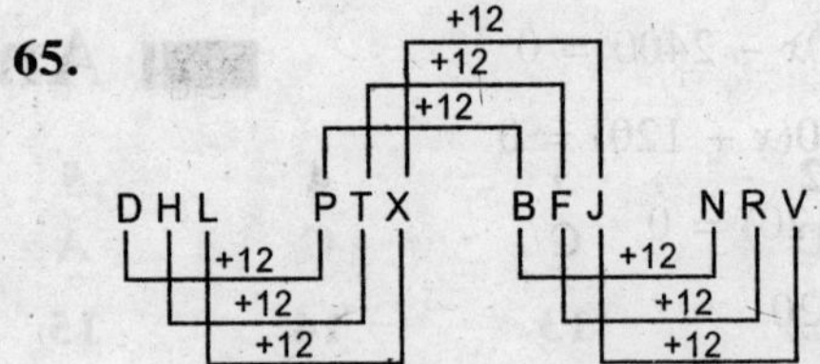

Hence, the next term of the letter series is NRV.

66. $\because$ 12 men take 18 days to complete a job.

$\therefore$ 1 man's 1 day's job is $\dfrac{1}{18 \times 12}$

and 12 women complete $\dfrac{3}{4}$ part of work in 18 days.

$\therefore$ 1 women's 1 day's job is $\dfrac{1}{24 \times 12}$

$\therefore$ 10 men and 8 women 1 day work

$= \dfrac{10}{18 \times 12} + \dfrac{8}{24 \times 12}$

$= \dfrac{1}{24}\left[\dfrac{10}{9} + \dfrac{8}{12}\right]$

$= \dfrac{1}{24}\left[\dfrac{40 + 24}{36}\right]$

$= \dfrac{1}{24}\left[\dfrac{64}{36}\right]$

$$= \frac{8}{3 \times 36}$$

$$= \frac{2}{3 \times 9}$$

$$= \frac{2}{27}$$

Hence, required time $= \frac{27}{2}$ days

$= 13\frac{1}{2}$ days.

68. Let the cost price of the article = ₹ x

Then, Profit = Selling Price – Cost Price

∴ Profit = ₹ $24 - x$

∴ $$\text{Profit \%} = \frac{\text{Profit} \times 100}{\text{Cost Price}}$$

According to the question,

$$x = \frac{(24 - x) \times 100}{x}$$

∴ $x^2 = 2400x - 100x$

$\Rightarrow x^2 + 100x - 2400 = 0$

$\Rightarrow x^2 + 120x - 20x - 2400 = 0$

$\Rightarrow x(x + 120) - 20(x + 120) = 0$

$\Rightarrow (x - 20)(x + 120) = 0$

$\Rightarrow x = 20, x = -120$

Hence, cost price of the article = ₹ 20

69. Let, Hindi = H, and English = E

Then, $n(\text{H}) = 7$, $n(\text{E}) = 8$

$n(\text{H} \cup \text{E}) = 15 - 3 = 12$

$\because n(\text{H} \cup \text{E}) = n(\text{H}) + n(\text{E}) - n(\text{H} \cap \text{E})$

$\therefore 12 = 7 + 8 - n(\text{H} \cap \text{E})$

$\Rightarrow n(\text{H} \cap \text{E}) = 15 - 12 = 3$

Hence, number of people read both Hindi and English

$= n(\text{H} \cap \text{E}) = 3$.

71. Let the principal = ₹ P,
Given, $r = 3\%$, Compound interest = ₹ 101.50
and $n = 2$ years

$\because$ Compound interest $= \text{P}\left(1 + \frac{r}{100}\right)^n - \text{P}$

$\Rightarrow \quad 101.50 = \text{P}\left(1 + \frac{3}{100}\right)^2 - \text{P}$

$\Rightarrow \quad 101.50 = \text{P}\left[\left(\frac{103}{100}\right)^2 - 1\right]$

$\Rightarrow \quad 101.50 = \text{P}[(1.03)^2 - 1]$

$\Rightarrow \quad 101.50 = \text{P}[1.0609 - 1]$

$\Rightarrow \quad 101.50 = \text{P}[0.0609]$

$$\text{P} = \frac{101.50}{0.0609}$$

$$= \frac{101.5000}{0.0609}$$

$$= ₹\frac{1015000}{609}$$

Then, Simple interest $= \frac{p \times r \times t}{100}$

$$= \frac{\frac{1015000}{609} \times 2 \times 3}{100}$$

$$= \frac{10150 \times 2}{203}$$

$$= \frac{20300}{203}$$

$= 100$

Hence, required simple interest = ₹ 100.

73. Let the value of each of the three equal angles $= x°$

Then, sum of four angles of quadrilateral = 360°

∴ $108° + 3x = 360°$

$3x = 360 - 108$

$3x = 252$

$$x = \frac{252}{3}$$

$= 84°$

74. According to question,

Amit ← West — Prakash

North (Sumit ↑ Amit)

Sumit — East → Tarun

Tarun is in South-East of Amit.

75. Given,

DRIVER = 12,

PEDESTRIAN = 20

ACCIDENT = 16

$\because$ Number of alphabet in DRIVER = 6

Here, number of letters is multiplied by 2

$\therefore \quad 6 \times 2 = 12$

Similarly,

Number of alphabet in PEDESTRIAN = 10

$\therefore \quad 10 \times 2 = 20$

Number of alphabet in ACCIDENT = 8

$\therefore \quad 8 \times 2 = 16$

Similarly,

Number of alphabet in CAR = 3

$\therefore \quad 3 \times 2 = 6$

Hence, CAR = 6.

77. Given, $2^x = 4^y = 8^z$

$\Rightarrow 2^x = 4^y = 2^{3z}$

$\Rightarrow 2^x = 4^{2y} = 2^{3z}$

$\Rightarrow x = 2y = 3z$

$\therefore$ $4y = 2x$ and $3z = x$

$\Rightarrow \quad 4z = \frac{4}{3}x$

$\therefore \quad \frac{1}{2x}+\frac{1}{4y}+\frac{1}{4z} = 4$

$\Rightarrow \quad \frac{1}{2x}+\frac{1}{2x}+\frac{1}{\frac{4}{3}x} = 4$

$\Rightarrow \quad \frac{1}{2x}+\frac{1}{2x}+\frac{3}{4x} = 4$

$\Rightarrow \quad \frac{1}{x}+\frac{3}{4x} = 4$

$\Rightarrow \quad \frac{4+3}{4x} = 4$

$\Rightarrow \quad \frac{7}{4x} = 4$

$\Rightarrow \quad 7 = 16x$

$\Rightarrow \quad x = \frac{7}{16}$

78. Average speed for the whole journey

$$= \frac{80}{\frac{60}{40}+\frac{20}{20}} \text{ km/hr.}$$

$$= \frac{80}{\frac{3}{2}+1}$$

$$= \frac{80}{\frac{5}{2}}$$

$$= 80 \times \frac{2}{5}$$

$$= 16 \times 2$$

$$= 32 \text{ km/hr.}$$

Previous Paper (Solved)

Haryana Teacher Eligibility Test (HTET)

TGT English (Level-2), Exam 2019

(Exam held on 17 November, 2019)

PART-I

Child Development and Pedagogy

Directions: *Answer the following questions by selecting the **most appropriate** option.*

1. Out of the following which activity/area may ***not*** be considered as co-scholastic aspect of learner?
A. Social skill B. Attitude and values
C. Creative skill D. Curricular subjects

2. Out of the following which is ***not*** related with 'Cognition'?
A. Perception B. Thinking
C. Walking D. Concept formation

3. A student learns new concepts such as 'Carnivorous animal' on the basis of words known by him such as tiger, dog, lion, leopard etc. This type of learning is known as what?
A. Combinational learning
B. Subordinate learning
C. Correlative learning
D. Superordinate learning

4. "Children's understanding that their gender will not change even if they adopt the behaviour, dress, or hairstyles of the other gender". This type of children's understanding is known as what?
A. Gender identity B. Gender stability
C. Gender consistency D. Gender stereotypes

5. What is the age group of late childhood stage?
A. 2 to 6 years B. 6 to 12 years
C. 4 to 7 years D. 11 to 15 years

6. Assessment of all-round development of the child's personality is known as which type of evaluation?
A. Continuous evaluation
B. Comprehensive evaluation
C. Above (A) and (B) both
D. Neither (A) nor (B) above

7. According to Bronfrenbrener, law and customs are examples of which of the following ecological system of child?
A. Micro system B. Macro system
C. Meso system D. Exo system

8. Who was the propounder of N.D.I. motivation formula?
A. McDougall B. Hilgard
C. Blair and Jones D. Maslow

9. Out of the following which alternative shows characteristics of "Concrete Operational Stage" given by Jean Piaget?
A. Development of idea of 'cause-effect relationship' and 'object permanence' in children.
B. The child gains understanding of principles such as conservation logical thought emerges.
C. The child begins to represent the world symbolically.
D. Becomes capable of creating several forms of logical thought.

10. Out of the following which is ***not*** the other name of childhood?
A. Elementary school age
B. Smart age
C. Pre-gang age
D. Gang age

11. Who proposed "Sociocultural Theory" of cognitive development?
A. Jean Piaget B. Lev Vygotsky
C. J.S. Bruner D. Kohlberg

12. Which word was used by Thurstone for 'intelligence'?
A. Primary Mental Abilities
B. Universal Mental Abilities
C. Neutral Mental Abilities
D. Higher Mental Abilities

13. Which of the following is ***not*** a defence mechanism?
A. Identification B. Compensation
C. Rationalisation D. Association

14. Which of the following is ***not*** an element of emotional intelligence?
A. Entrepreneurial competence
B. Self-motivation
C. Empathy
D. Handling relationships

15. Characteristic of good adjustment is:
A. Tolerance
B. Lack of confidence
C. Emotional unstability
D. Irregular life habit

16. The first psychological laboratory was established by whom?
A. Galton B. Cattell
C. Pestalozzi D. Wundt

17. "Incorporation of new information into existing mental frame works" is known as what?
A. Assimilation
B. Accommodation
C. Equilibration
D. Organisation

18. For the emotional development of his pupil the teacher should:
A. Try to usurp the place of pupil's parents.
B. Develop love and affection for his pupil.
C. Take a loveable attitude towards the mischief of the pupil.
D. Show favours to few selected pupils.

19. Which is *not* the cause of delinquency?
A. Physical defect
B. Poverty
C. Failure
D. Proper home environment

20. A type of intelligence which is mostly visible in dancers, athletes, surgeons etc., is known as what?
A. Bodily-kinesthetic intelligence
B. Spatial intelligence
C. Logical-mathematical intelligence
D. Musical intelligence

21. 'Out of sight out of mind' is characteristic of which of the following developmental stage?
A. Sensory-motor stage
B. Pre operational stage
C. Concrete operational stage
D. Formal operational stage

22. Which is *not* the component of motivation?
A. Needs B. Rote Memory
C. Drives D. Incentives

23. Out of the following which is *not* the other name of Adolescence?
A. Transitional period of childhood and adulthood
B. Problem age
C. Stage of stress, strain and storm
D. Smart age

24. Out of the following which is *not* the type of group non-verbal intelligence test?
A. Army Beta test
B. Army Alpha test
C. Chicago test
D. Revence progressive matrices

25. According to Kohlberg "a stage of moral development during which individuals judge morality largely in terms of existing social norms or rules" is known as which level of morality?
A. preconventional level of morality
B. conventional level of morality
C. postconventional level of morality
D. unconventional level of morality

26. A type of learning in which students try to learn by emerging new rule through given learning material, is known as what?
A. Rote learning B. Meaningful learning
C. Reception learning D. Discovery learning

27. Out of the follwoing alternative which does *not* come under processes in socialization?
A. learning to behave in socially approved ways
B. playing approved social roles
C. development of social attitudes
D. egocentric behaviour

28. What is the approximate I.Q. range of 'Mangolism' meantally retarded children?
A. 20 to 25 B. below 20
C. 25 to 36 D. 36 to 51

29. Direct method of personality adjustment is:
A. Sublimation B. Projection
C. Regression D. Removing of hurdles

30. Out of the following which is fourth level of Taylor's level theory of creativity?
A. Expressive creativity B. Productive creativity
C. Innovative creativity D. Inventive creativity

PART-II

भाषा : हिन्दी

निर्देशः *निम्नलिखित प्रश्नों के उत्तर देने के लिए* ***सबसे उचित*** *विकल्प चुनिए।*

31. किस विकल्प में विसर्ग संधि का प्रयोग ***नहीं*** हुआ है?
A. तिरोधान B. शिरोधार्य
C. दीपोत्सव D. रजोभव

32. 'हेमन्त को खीर अच्छी लगती है'— वाक्य किस कारक का उदाहरण है?
A. कर्मकारक B. सबंध कारक
C. संप्रदान कारक D. अधिकरण कारक

33. एकवचन से बहुवचन बने विकल्पों में असंगत चुनिए :

A. डाकू–डाकुओं B. वधू–वधुएँ
C. तरबूजा–तरबुजाओं D. भालू–भालुओं

34. वार्तनिक दृष्टि से अशुद्ध विकल्प चुनिए :

A. दवाइयाँ B. प्राणिविज्ञान
C. वृत्यानुप्रास D. मृत्यूपरान्त

35. किस वाक्य में 'आज्ञार्थ' (विध्यर्थ) वृत्ति का प्रयोग हुआ है?

A. तुम अगर कहते तो मैं ऐसा जरूर करती।
B. सभी को अपरिग्रह की भावना रखनी चाहिए।
C. नेता को चाहिए कि वह समूह के प्रत्येक व्यक्ति का सम्मान करे।
D. मैं चाहता हूँ कि तुम भले इंसान बनो।

36. प्रत्यय की दृष्टि से असंगत विकल्प बताइए :

A. विचार + ईय = विचारणीय
B. दृश् + तव्य = द्रष्टव्य
C. वृष्णि + एय = वार्ष्णेय
D. वल्मीक + इ = वाल्मीकि

37. किस विकल्प में द्वन्द्व समास का उदाहरण ***नहीं*** है?

A. भक्ष्याभक्ष्य B. कृष्णार्जुन
C. रुद्रप्रिया D. उचितानुचित

38. स्त्रीलिंग-पुल्लिंग की दृष्टि से अनुचित विकल्प छाँटिए :

A. कुँजड़ा–कुँजड़िन B. तीतर–तीतरिन
C. धोबी–धोबिन D. पापी–पापिन

39. किस विकल्प में 'आ' उपसर्ग का प्रयोग हुआ है?

A. आत्यन्तिक B. आतिथ्य
C. आख्यायिका D. आधिपत्य

40. विलोम की दृष्टि से बेमेल को छाँटिए :

A. आर्य–अनार्य B. उर्वर–अनुर्वर
C. ऐच्छिक–अनिवार्य D. खल–दुर्जन

41. पर्यायवाची की दृष्टि से असंगत विकल्प चुनिए :

A. पक्षी– शकुंत, द्विज, नभचर
B. बैल– ऋषभ, वृषभ, अक्षधर
C. वेद– आम्नाय, आगम, आकर
D. हरिण– कुरंग, प्लवंग, सारंग

42. 'भाववाच्य' वाला विकल्प चुनिए :

A. नानी द्वारा कहानी सुनाई गई।
B. गर्मियों में रोज नहाया जाता है।
C. भारत द्वारा नया उपग्रह छोड़ा गया।
D. कोहली ने शतक लगाया।

43. निम्न में से किस विकल्प में 'कम' शब्द का विशेषणीय प्रयोग किया गया है?

A. गर्मी में 'कम' खाना चाहिए। B. आज उसने 'कम' खाना खाया।
C. 'कम' ही पढ़ पाते हैं। D. 'कम' बोलना ही श्रेयस्कर है।

44. किस वाक्य में 'निपात' का प्रयोग हुआ है?

A. राम और श्याम दिनभर से खेल रहे हैं।
B. कविता आज दिल्ली जा रही है।
C. तुम आज दिनभर सोते ही रहोगे।
D. मेरी भारी भूल थी जो उसके बहकावे में आ गया।

45. 'दुर्घटना क्या और कैसे हुई' – वाक्य में प्रयुक्त क्रिया-विशेषण का भेद इंगित कीजिए :

A. परिमाणवाचक B. कालवाचक
C. रीतिवाचक D. स्थानवाचक

Language : English

Directions: *Answer the following questions by selecting the* ***most appropriate*** *option.*

46. Choose the correct presposition.

I had not slept or eaten anything properly .... two days.

A. since B. from
C. in D. for

47. Fill in the blank with the correct option :

.... doing the cooking, I look after the garden.

A. Beside B. However
C. Besides D. Therefore

48. Choose the correct synonym for the word given below :

Gallant

A. Valiant B. Impolite
C. Rude D. Fearful

49. Choose the correct option for the underlined word.

Our parents have <u>raised</u> us to be a good citizen.

A. Brought up B. Brought by
C. Brought out D. Brought down

50. Choose the correct determiner.

.... knowledge is a dangerous thing.

A. The little B. Little
C. A little D. The few

51. Choose the correct form of verb.

Did you not .... about the world Atlas.

A. knew B. known
C. know D. knows

52. Choose the correct passive construction for the sentence given.

We visited the zoo of Jaipur on last Sunday.

A. Zoo of Jaipur were visited by us on last Sunday.
B. On last Sunday the zoȯ of Jaipur was visited by us.
C. We were visited the zoo of Jaipur on last Sunday.
D. Zoo of Jaipur was being visited on Sunday last by us.

53. Cooking is his hobby.

The underlined word is used as a :

A. Verb B. Gerund
C. Participle D. Infinitive

54. Choose the word which is spelt correctly.

A. Commited B. Committed
C. Comitteed D. Committeed

55. Fill in the blank by choosing the correct option.

The Headmaster and the Secreatry .... present in the meeting.

A. was B. were
C. was being D. were being

56. Choose the most appropriate form of Indirect speech for the given sentence.

The teacher said to Hari, "Why did you not do your homework yesterday"?

A. The teacher asked Hari why had he not done his homework the previous day?
B. The teacher asked Hari why he had not done his homework the previous day?
C. The teacher said to Hari why had he not done their homework the previous day?
D. The teacher said Hari that he had not done his homework the previous day.

57. Choose the correct antonym for the word given below:

Bankrupt

A. Penniless B. Insolvent
C. Ruined D. Solvent

58. Fill in the blank with appropriate preposition.

I paid the bill .... cash.

A. in B. at
C. for D. with

59. Choose the correct modal.

Some people .... ski better than others.

A. must B. can
C. could D. should

60. Choose the correct word for the sentence.

A man who is womanish in his habits.

A. Arsonist B. Epicure
C. Effeminate D. Fealty

PART-III

General Studies : Quantitative Aptitude, Reasoning Ability and GK & Awareness

Directions: *Answer the following questions by selecting the **most appropriate** option.*

61. Which is the correct conclusion based on given statements?

Statement:

I. All leaves are roots.
II. Some roots are branches.

Conclusion:

A. Some leaves are branches.
B. Some branches are not roots.
C. No branch is leaf.
D. Some roots are leaves.

62. Two persons depart from their office towards their houses. First person goes 8 km in north direction and second person goes 6 km in east direction and reach their houses, find out the direct distance of their Houses?

A. 10 km
B. 12 km
C. 14 km
D. 15 km

63. What will be the angle between minute end and hour end in a Clock at 7 : 20?

A. 160° B. 100°
C. 260° D. 120°

64. Complete the following Series:
WE, SG, PJ, LN, IS, ?

A. FZ B. FX
C. EY D. EX

65. In a code language GRANT is written as UOBSH, TIME is written as FNJU how is PRIDE written in that language?

A. QSJEF B. OQHCD
C. FEJSQ D. TPMED

66. Find the next term of the following letter series :
DHL, PTX, BFJ, ...

A. CGK B. KOS
C. NRV D. OVZ

67. The population of a town is 8,500. In first year it was increased by 20% and in second year again increased by 25%, then what is the total population after two years?

A. 10,950 B. 12,750
C. 11,950 D. 12,550

68. What is the difference between compound interest and simple interest on the amount of ₹ 18,000 in 2 years with the rate of 10% per year?
A. ₹ 150 B. ₹ 180
C. ₹ 210 D. ₹ 316

69. The total amount of ₹ 14,500 with simple interest in 6 years is ₹ 21,460, find out the Rate of interest per annum?
A. 4% B. 10%
C. 6% D. 8%

70. The sides of a triangular farm are 20 m, 21 m and 29 m respectively. How much will be total expenses for cutting the crop at the rate of ₹ 15 per square meter?
A. ₹ 21,00 B. ₹ 1,890
C. ₹ 3,150 D. ₹ 2,500

71. Average runs of 6 players in cricket match was 36. If one player made 16 runs, then what is the average run of remaining players?
A. 24 B. 30
C. 36 D. 40

72. Complete the following series:

24, 60, 120, 210, ?
A. 336 B. 270
C. 512 D. 500

73. The ratio of speeds, of a Bus and Car is 6 : 7. If car covers 364 km distance in 4 hours, what is the speed of Bus?
A. 60 km/h B. 72 km/h
C. 78 km/h D. 84 km/h

74. In a certain code language "go home" is written as "ta na", "sweet home" is written as "na ja", "Sweet and Sour" is written as "pa sa ja", then how "Sour" is coded as?
A. pa B. sa
C. pa or sa D. na

75. The ratio of two numbers are 3 : 5 and the addition of those numbers is 240, what is the difference of those numbers?
A. 60 B. 100
C. 120 D. 90

76. If 3/5 of 60% of a Number is 36, then the value of the number is:
A. 60 B. 100
C. 120 D. 150

77. If DRIVER = 12, PEDESTRIAN = 20, ACCIDENT = 16, then CAR = ?
A. 3 B. 6
C. 8 D. 16

78. A and B together can do a work in 15 days, if B alone can do that work in 20 days. Then how many days will A take to do same work alone?
A. 60 B. 45
C. 40 D. 30

79. Anil is standing at 16th position from the left end in a row of boys. Vikas is at 18th position from the right end. Gopal is 11th from Anil towards the right and 3rd from Vikas towards the right end. How many boys are standing in this row?
A. 41 B. 42
C. 48 D. 49

80. Which of the following is a leap year?
A. 1800 B. 1900
C. 1700 D. 2000

81. How many Administrative divisions are there in Haryana?
A. Four B. Five
C. Six D. Seven

82. The city of Haryana, which is ***not*** part of National Capital Region :
A. Gurugram B. Sonipat
C. Faridabad D. Hisar

83. Gurugram is related to which ancient Guru?
A. Ved Vyas B. Dronacharya
C. Parashuram D. Kripacharya

84. Who is the brand ambassador of 'Beti Bachao-Beti Padhao Campaign' in Haryana?
A. Anu Kumari B. Sakshi Malik
C. Kalpna Chawala D. Saina Nehwal

85. The district which does ***not*** share boundary with other states is:
A. Panipat B. Rohtak
C. Rewari D. Palwal

86. The river, which makes border between Haryana and Uttar Pradesh:
A. Yamuna B. Ganga
C. Sahibi D. Markanda

87. Where Pratap Singh revolted against the British?
A. Rohtak B. Jind
C. Ambala D. Sirsa

88. Where is the National Cancer Institute situated?
A. Sampla B. Meham
C. Badsa D. Kalanaur

89. Sohna town is famours for:
A. Historical Lake B. Historical Palace
C. Hot water Springs D. Gardens

90. State animal of Haryana is :
A. Black buck B. Asiatic Lion
C. Chinkara D. Tiger

PART-IV

English

Directions: *Answer the following questions by selecting the* ***most appropriate*** *option.*

91. Identify the initial consonant in the following words : Chin, Chat, Chest.

A. tʃ B. dz
C. k D. c

92. Fill in the blank with the correct phrasal verb:

I was very tired this morning, I could not ....

A. get on in B. get by
C. get up D. get round

93. Choose the correct alternative for the following sentence:

He must stop smoking.

A. Smoking must be stopped by him
B. Smoking stopped by him.
C. Smoking was stopped by order.
D. Smoking should be stopped by him.

94. Fill in the blank with suitable determiners:

Could I have .... cup of coffee?

A. other B. another
C. many D. few

95. "Everything Suddenly looked black". Who said these words?

A. Ron Forbes B. Evelyn Glennie
C. Anne Richlin D. Sarah Cowley

96. What is stored in the hump of camel?

A. Water B. Fat
C. Oil D. Salt

97. A person who loves books is called a ....

A. Philatelist B. Numismatist
C. Bibliophile D. Antiquarian

98. Who's the writer of the book 'A Brief History of Time'?

A. M.K. Gandhi B. Firdaus Kanga
C. Abdul Kalam D. Stephen Hawking

99. Match the following phrasal verbs in Column-A with the blanks in Column-B:

Column-A	Column-B
(*i*) Break in	(*a*) He ..... the box
(*ii*) Took off	(*b*) A plane ....
(*iii*) Clear away	(*c*) If the door is locked, I will try to ..... .
(*iv*) Handed over	(*d*) I'll help you .... the dishes.

	(*i*)	(*ii*)	(*iii*)	(*iv*)
A.	(*c*)	(*b*)	(*d*)	(*a*)
B.	(*d*)	(*a*)	(*b*)	(*c*)
C.	(*a*)	(*b*)	(*c*)	(*d*)
D.	(*a*)	(*b*)	(*d*)	(*c*)

100. Insert the appropriate modal in blank:

You .... not ask for more money now. (Prohibition)

A. must B. might
C. would D. need not

101. In poetry and prose, the repetition of consonants is called ....

A. Pun B. Irony
C. Alliteration D. Accent

102. The poem 'The Last Bargain' is written by ....

A. William Wordsworth B. Keats
C. Rabindranath Tagore D. Sarojini Naidu

103. Which one of the following is not a nasal consonant?

A. m B. n
C. ŋ D. k

104. Identify the underlined word in the given sentence:

Children love <u>making</u> mud castles.

A. Participle B. Noun
C. Gerund D. Adjective

105. Put the verb in brackets in the correct tense:

I (lose) my pen, please help me find it.

A. have lost B. did lost
C. will lose D. loose

106. Where was Kalpana Chawla born?

A. Noida, New Delhi B. Karnal, Haryana
C. Sikar, Rajasthan D. Madurai, Tamil Nadu

107. Which of the following word does not take 'ies' to form a plural?

A. family B. valley
C. responsibility D. beauty

108. Fill in the blank with the correct adjective:

There is .... hope of his recovery.

A. any B. every
C. a little D. few

109. Choose the correct spelling:

A. Dissiertation B. Dessertation
C. Dissertation D. Disertation

110. Which of the following sentences has a gerund phrase:

A. She enjoys playing tennis

B. The children come running to meet us
C. We soon got talking
D. She sat smiling at me

Directions (Qs. No. 111-113): *Read the passage and answer the questions.*

Those responsible for teaching young people have resorted in different periods of history, to a variety of means for making their pupils learn. The earliest of these was the threat of punishment, which meant that the pupil who was slow, careless or inattentive risked either physical chastisement or the loss of some expected privilege or treat. Learning was thus, to some extent, associated with fear, particularly in the minds of those who found certain subjects hard to master.

At a later period, pupils were encouraged to learn in the hope of some kind of reward. This after took the form of marks awarded daily or weekly for work done, and sometimes of prizes given at the end of each year to best scholars. Such a system appealed to the competitive spirit, but it often had just as depressing an effect as the older system of punishment on the slow but willing pupil.

The two systems suggest that teachers felt that their pupil had to be either compelled or bribed to learn. In the nineteenth century, however, there sprang up a different type of teacher, passionately convinced that learning was worthwhile for its own sake, and that the young learner's principal stimulus should be neither anxiety to avoid a penalty nor ambition to win a reward, but sheer desire to learn. These teachers used their best endeavours to render the process of learning pleasant and where this was not possible, to show that hard plodding would yield results of practical value to the learner. Interest, direct or indirect became the keyword of instruction, and so it has remained.

The earlier methods, however, though now practised less frequently, have not been completely abandoned. If you walk into a modern classroom that contains all the most up-to-date equipment, you may observe a highly trained teacher inspiring boys and girls with his own enthusiasm for his subject yet you will probably find that he awards marks for the work done by his pupils, and you will certainly find that the careless or inattentive pupil is liable to be punished.

111. The earliest method of making pupils learn was through:
A. Love B. Threat of punishment
C. Repetition D. Rote

112. In which century, did the 'type of teacher generate' that said learning was worthwhile for its own sake?
A. 20th century B. 19th century
C. 5th century D. 18th century

113. What does the word 'Encourage' mean?
A. To motivate; to mentally support
B. To kill
C. To snub
D. To ask favour

114. Choose the right alternative to fill in the blank:
.... the book, I returned it to the library.
A. Reading B. Having Read
C. Will Read D. Read

115. Choose the correct phonetic transcription of the word 'School':
A. Sku:l B. Skɔ:l
C. Ckɔl D. S^eiul

116. Choose the correct passive of the sentence:
He looked after the children well.
A. The children were looked well.
B. The children were well looked after
C. The children were treated well.
D. Well looked after the children were.

117. Choose the correct plural of the noun 'dwarf':
A. Dwarves B. Dwarfes
C. Dwaffers D. Dwarfees

118. The poem 'The Road Not Taken' was written by ....
A. Robert Frost B. John Milton
C. P.B. Shelley D. W.B. Yeats

119. "This made Taro sadder than ever" 'This' refers to:
A. A strong wind that began to blow
B. Taro's father's old age
C. Taro's inability to buy expensive sake for his father
D. To purchase a new house

120. Choose the correct spelling:
A. Icconoclastic B. Icoonoclaastic
C. Icconoclastic D. Iconoclastic

121. Identify the figure of speech in the following sentence:
Curses are like chickens; they come home to roost.
A. Simile B. Anticlimax
C. Assonance D. Allegory

122. Which hill station does the author describe in the story 'A Short Monsoon Diary'?
A. Nainital B. Shimla
C. Leh D. Mussoorie

123. Identify the figure of speech in the following lines:
Then soars like a ship with only a sail.
A. Metaphor B. Simile
C. Assonance D. Paradox

124. We can .... cat now .... after the show – it's up to you.
A. neither – nor B. either – or
C. alway – or D. either – not

125. In which year the atomic bomb was dropped on Hiroshima and Nagasaki?
A. 1935 B. 1945
C. 1960 D. 1947

126. Choose the correct option to fill in the blank in the given sentence:

When I reflect on the pleasant memories of my childhood, I am overcome by a wave of ....
A. nostalgia B. frustration
C. enernation D. benevolence

127. Identify the function of the underlined word in the sentence:

They arrived soon after.
A. Noun B. Adverb
C. Adjective D. Gerund

128. What is the one thing that the child does not wish to become in the poem 'Vocation'?
A. Hawker B. Gardener
C. Watchman D. Tailor

129. Identify the underlined clause in the given sentence:

He says that he won't go.
A. Adverb clause B. Adjective clause
C. Prepositional clause D. Noun clause

130. Choose the correct option of the following sentence:

'Bring me a glass of milk,' said the Swami to the villagers.
A. The Swami asked the villagers to bring him a glass of milk.
B. The Swami wanted a glass of milk.
C. The villagers offered milk to the Swami.
D. The Swami told the villagers to get him a glass of milk.

131. Fill in the blanks with the correct option:

My friend lost his chemistry book. Now he doesn't know .... to do and .... to look for it.
A. what, where B. where, what
C. which, how D. how, when

132. Choose the correct active voice of the sentence given below:

My pocket has been picked.
A. Someone has picked my pocket.
B. Picked was my pocket.
C. Do you know who picked my pocket?
D. My pocket was picked.

133. Name the poet of the poem 'Trees' from the options given below:
A. Jerome K. Jerome B. Muriel L. Stone
C. Frank Flynn D. Shirley Bauer

134. Choose the antonym of the word 'Careless':
A. Careful B. Slow
C. Timid D. Introvert

135. Choose the correct option for the underlined words:
They tried to find fault with us.
A. Gerund B. Participle
C. The Infinitive D. Verb

136. If the rebel in the poem 'The Rebel' has a dog for a pet, what is everyone else likely to have?
A. An Elephant B. A Cat
C. A Tortoise D. A Bird

137. Who's the poet of the poem 'where do all the teachers go'?
A. Mary O'Neill B. Robert Lowell
C. T.S. Eliot D. Peter Dixon

138. Choose the correct past form of the verb 'Choose':
A. Chosen B. Chose
C. Choosed D. Choose

139. A story often with animals as characters, that conveys a moral is called ....
A. Fable B. Epic
C. Ballad D. Novel

140. Choose the incorrect use of the prefix — Post:
A. Postscript B. Postdate
C. Postpone D. Posting

141. Choose the word with the correct accent:
A. a'bility B. abili'ty
C. 'ability D. ability'

142. Who's the only woman in the world who has scaled Mt. Everest twice?
A. Deborah Cowley B. Mithila
C. Santosh Yadav D. Maria Sharapova

143. "He Sat up straight to cat a nut
He liked to tease and play"

What does "He" refer to in the above lines?
A. A Cat B. A Squirrel
C. A Bird D. A Bee

144. Match the phrases in Column-A with their meaning in Column-B:

Column-A	**Column-B**
(i) Set aside	*(a)* begin & seem likely to continue
(ii) Set down	*(b)* save or keep for a particular purpose
(iii) Set out	*(c)* write or record
(iv) Set in	*(d)* start on a journey

	(i)	*(ii)*	*(iii)*	*(iv)*
A.	*(b)*	*(c)*	*(d)*	*(a)*
B.	*(a)*	*(b)*	*(c)*	*(d)*
C.	*(c)*	*(d)*	*(a)*	*(b)*
D.	*(d)*	*(c)*	*(a)*	*(b)*

145. Match the phrasal verbs in Column-A with their meaning in Column-B:

Column-A	Column-B
(*i*) Look into	(*a*) Admire; respect
(*ii*) Look upto	(*b*) Be careful; beware
(*iii*) Look out	(*c*) Despise
(*iv*) Look down on	(*d*) Investigate

	(*i*)	(*ii*)	(*iii*)	(*iv*)
A.	(*d*)	(*a*)	(*b*)	(*c*)
B.	(*a*)	(*b*)	(*c*)	(*d*)
C.	(*c*)	(*a*)	(*d*)	(*b*)
D.	(*b*)	(*a*)	(*c*)	(*d*)

146. What did Patrick think his cat was playing with?
A. A little doll B. A mouse
C. A piece of cloth D. A stick

147. Fill in the blank with the correct option:
'Would you like milk in your coffee?' Yes, please ....
A. a few B. few
C. little D. a little

148. Where does the snake disappear in the poem. 'The Snake Trying'?
A. Among the woods B. In the garden
C. In the ripples D. In the house

149. A very large and powerful wave caused by earthquake under the sea is called ....
A. Wave B. A tsunami
C. Tremor D. Avalanche

150. The emotion that gripped Mr. Ahluwalia while standing on the summit of Everest was one of:
A. Humility and a sense of smallness
B. Victory over hurdles
C. Joy of discovery
D. Greatness and self importance

Answers

1	2	3	4	5	6	7	8	9	10
D	C	D	C	B	B	B	B	C	C
11	**12**	**13**	**14**	**15**	**16**	**17**	**18**	**19**	**20**
B	A	D	A	A	D	A	B	D	A
21	**22**	**23**	**24**	**25**	**26**	**27**	**28**	**29**	**30**
A	B	D	A	B	D	D	A	D	C
31	**32**	**33**	**34**	**35**	**36**	**37**	**38**	**39**	**40**
C	C	C	C	B	A	C	B	C	D
41	**42**	**43**	**44**	**45**	**46**	**47**	**48**	**49**	**50**
C	B	B	C	C	D	C	A	A	C
51	**52**	**53**	**54**	**55**	**56**	**57**	**58**	**59**	**60**
C	B	B	B	B	B	D	A	B	C
61	**62**	**63**	**64**	**65**	**66**	**67**	**68**	**69**	**70**
D	A	B	C	C	C	B	B	D	C
71	**72**	**73**	**74**	**75**	**76**	**77**	**78**	**79**	**80**
D	A	C	C	A	B	B	A	A	D
81	**82**	**83**	**84**	**85**	**86**	**87**	**88**	**89**	**90**
C	D	B	B	B	A	B	C	C	A
91	**92**	**93**	**94**	**95**	**96**	**97**	**98**	**99**	**100**
A	C	A	B	B	B	C	D	A	A
101	**102**	**103**	**104**	**105**	**106**	**107**	**108**	**109**	**110**
C	C	D	C	A	B	B	C	C	A
111	**112**	**113**	**114**	**115**	**116**	**117**	**118**	**119**	**120**
B	B	A	B	A	B	A	A	C	D
121	**122**	**123**	**124**	**125**	**126**	**127**	**128**	**129**	**130**
A	D	B	B	B	A	B	D	D	A
131	**132**	**133**	**134**	**135**	**136**	**137**	**138**	**139**	**140**
A	A	D	A	C	B	D	B	A	D
141	**142**	**143**	**144**	**145**	**146**	**147**	**148**	**149**	**150**
A	C	B	A	A	A	D	C	B	A

Explanatory Answers

61. Statement:

I. All leaves are roots.

II. Some roots are branches.

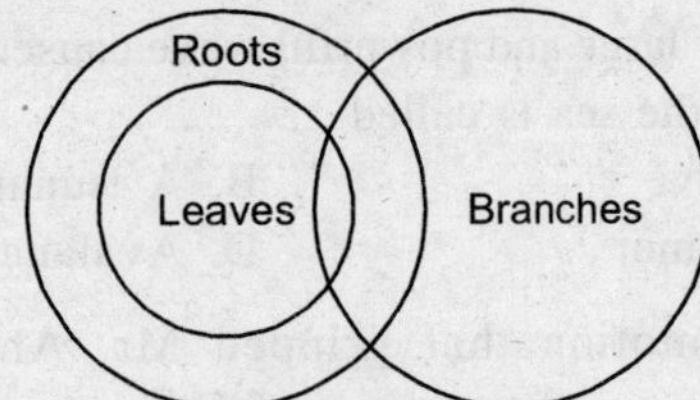

Conclusion: Some roots are leaves.

62.

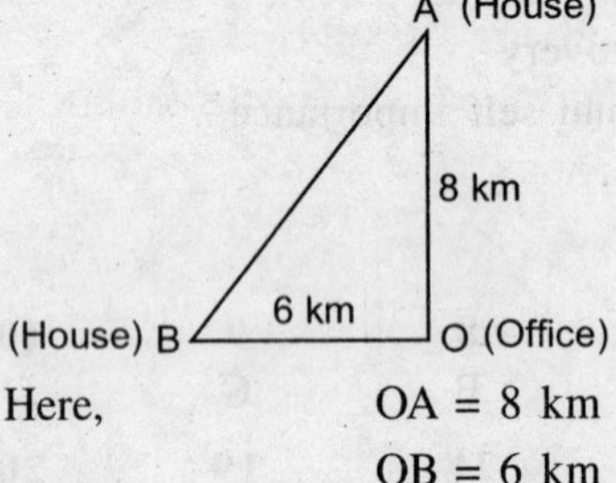

Here, OA = 8 km

OB = 6 km

Distance of their house

$$AB = \sqrt{OA^2 + OB^2}$$

$$= \sqrt{8^2 + 6^2}$$

$$= \sqrt{64 + 36}$$

$$= \sqrt{100}$$

= 10 km.

63. $\because$ 60 minutes = 360°

$\therefore$ 1 minute = 6°

The angle between minute hand and hour hand in a clock at 7 : 20.

= 16.7 minutes

= 16.7 × 6° = 100.2°

= 100° (Approx.)

64.

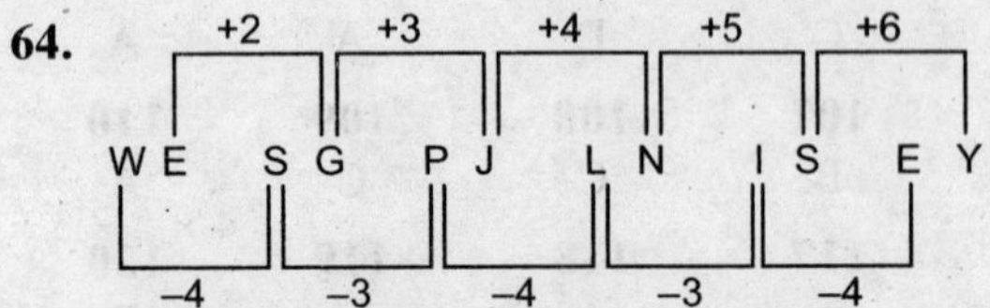

Here, next term in the series = EY.

65. As,

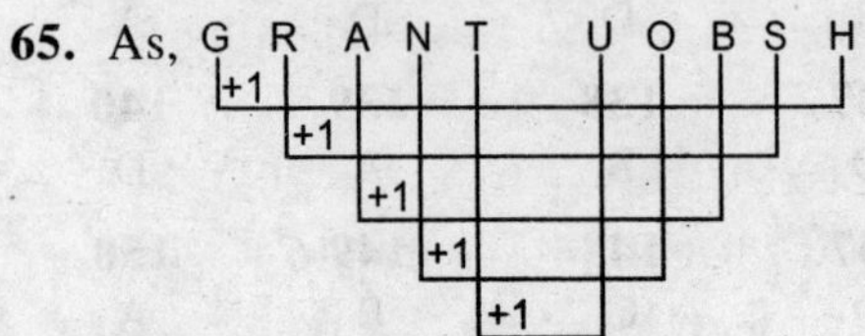

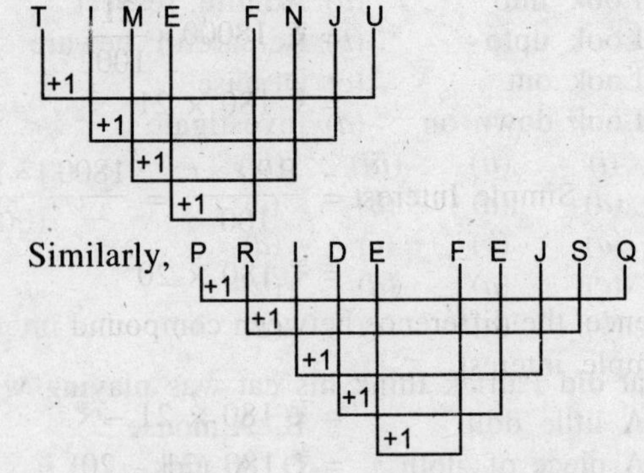

Similarly, P R I D E F E J S Q

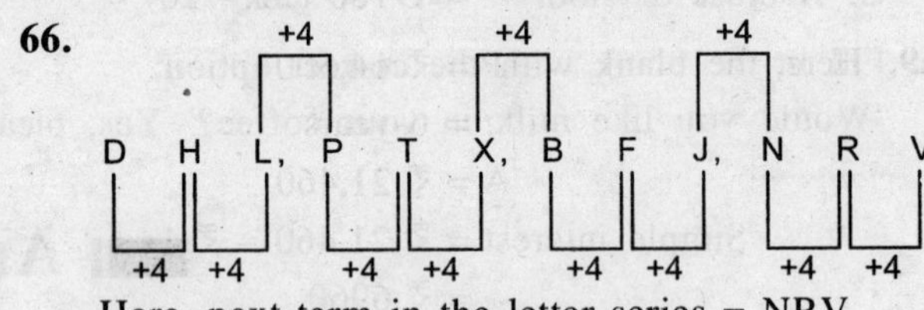

66.

+4		+4		+4	
D H L,		P T X,		B F J,	N R V
+4 +4		+4 +4		+4 +4	+4 +4

Here, next term in the letter series = NRV

67. Here, P = 8500, r_1 = 20%, r_2 = 25%

$\therefore$ The total population after two years

$$= P\left(1 + \frac{r_1}{100}\right)\left(1 + \frac{r_2}{100}\right)$$

$$= 8500\left(1 + \frac{20}{100}\right)\left(1 + \frac{25}{100}\right)$$

$$= 8500\left(1 + \frac{1}{5}\right)\left(1 + \frac{1}{4}\right)$$

$$= 8500\left(\frac{6}{5}\right)\left(\frac{5}{4}\right)$$

$$= 8500 \times \frac{3}{2} = 12{,}750.$$

68. Here, P = ₹ 18000,

t = 2 years,

r = 10%

$$\therefore \text{Compound Interest} = P\left(1 + \frac{r}{100}\right)^n - P$$

$$= ₹\ 18000\left(1 + \frac{10}{100}\right)^2 - 18000$$

$$= ₹\ 18000\left[\left(1 + \frac{1}{10}\right)^2 - 1\right]$$

$$= ₹\ 18000\left[\left(\frac{11}{10}\right)^2 - 1\right]$$

$$= ₹\ 18000\left[\frac{121}{100}-1\right]$$

$$= ₹\ 18000 \times \frac{21}{100}$$

$$= ₹\ 180 \times 21$$

$$\text{Simple Interest} = \frac{P \times r \times t}{100} = \frac{18000 \times 10 \times 2}{100}$$

$$= ₹\ 180 \times 20$$

Hence, the difference between compound interest and simple interest

$$= ₹\ 180 \times 21 - ₹\ 180 \times 20$$

$$= ₹\ 180\ (21 - 20) = ₹\ 180.$$

69. Here, P = ₹ 14,500

$t = 6$ years

A = ₹ 21,460

Simple interest = ₹ 21,460 − ₹ 14,500

= ₹ 6960

$$\text{Rate} = \frac{\text{S.I.} \times 100}{P \times t}$$

$$\therefore \quad r = \frac{6960 \times 100}{14500 \times 6}$$

$$= \frac{6960}{145 \times 6} = \frac{6960}{870} = 8\%.$$

70. Let the sides of a triangular farm are

$a = 20$ m, $b = 21$ m and $c = 29$ m

$$\text{Then,} \quad s = \frac{a+b+c}{2}$$

$$= \frac{20+21+29}{2} = \frac{70}{2} = 35 \text{ m}$$

Area of a triangular farm

$$= \sqrt{s(s-a)(s-b)(s-c)}$$

$$= \sqrt{35(35-20)(35-21)(35-29)} \text{ m}^2$$

$$= \sqrt{35 \times 15 \times 14 \times 6}$$

$$= \sqrt{7 \times 5 \times 5 \times 3 \times 7 \times 2 \times 3 \times 2}$$

$$= 7 \times 5 \times 3 \times 2 \text{ m}^2$$

Hence, the total expenses for cutting at the rate of ₹ 15 per m^2

$$= ₹\ 15 \times 7 \times 5 \times 3 \times 2 = ₹\ 3150.$$

71. The total run of 6 players in a cricket match

$$= 6 \times 36 = 216$$

The total run of remaining 5 players

$$= 216 - 16 = 200$$

∴ The average run of remaining players

$$= \frac{200}{5} = 40.$$

72. 24, 60, 120, 210, ?

Dividing each term by 6

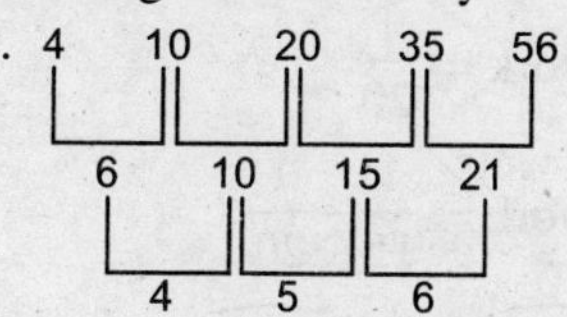

Here, next term in the given series = 56 × 6 = 336.

73. Let the speed of a Bus and Car is $6x$ km/h and $7x$ km/h

Then, $7x \times 4 = 364$ (Speed × Time = Distance)

$$\Rightarrow \quad 28x = 364$$

$$\Rightarrow \quad x = \frac{364}{28} = \frac{52}{4} = 13$$

∴ Speed of Bus = $6x$ km/h

$$= 6 \times 13 = 78 \text{ km/h}.$$

74. Given, code language

"go home" → "ta na"

"sweet home" → "na ja"

"sweet and sour" → "pa sa ja"

Here, "home" → "na"

"sweet" → ja

go → ta

"and sour" → "pa sa"

∴ "sour" is coded as "pa" or "sa".

75. Let the two numbers are $3x$ and $5x$

$$\text{Then,} \quad 3x + 5x = 240$$

$$\Rightarrow \quad 8x = 240$$

$$\Rightarrow \quad x = 30$$

∴ The difference of these numbers

$$= 5x - 3x$$

$$= 2x = 2 \times 30 = 60.$$

76. Let the number is x

Then, $\frac{3}{5}$ of 60% of $x = 36$

$$\Rightarrow \quad x \times \frac{60}{100} \times \frac{3}{5} = 36$$

$$\Rightarrow \quad x \times \frac{3}{5} \times \frac{3}{5} = 36$$

$$\Rightarrow \quad x = \frac{36 \times 5 \times 5}{3 \times 3} = 4 \times 5 \times 5 = 100$$

Hence, the value of the number x is 100.

77. Given, DRIVER = 12

Here, number of letters is multiplied by 2

∴ 6 × 2 = 12

PEDESTRIAN = 10 × 2 = 20

ACCIDENT = 8 × 2 = 16

∴ CAR = 3 × 2 = 6.

78. (A + B)'s 1 day's work = $\frac{1}{15}$

B's 1 day's work = $\frac{1}{20}$

$\therefore$ A's 1 day's work = $\frac{1}{15} - \frac{1}{20}$

$= \frac{4-3}{60} = \frac{1}{60}$

$\therefore$ A's time = 60 days.

79. ← Left Right →

16 18 11

Anil Vikas Gopal

Anil is 16th from the left.

Vikas is 18th from the right.

Gopal is 11th from Anil towards the right and 3rd from Vikas towards the right end.

$\therefore$ The Number of boys between Anil and Vikas

$= 11 - 4 = 7$

$\therefore$ The number of boys standing in this row

$= 16 + 7 + 18$

$= 16 + 25 = 41.$

81. Haryana is one of the 28 states in India, located in the northern part of the country. It was carved out of the former state of East Punjab on 1 November 1966 on a linguistic basis. Chandigarh is the state capital, Faridabad in National Capital Region is the most populous city of the state, and Gurugram is a leading financial hub of the NCR, with major Fortune 500 companies located in it. Haryana has 6 administrative divisions.

83. Gurgaon was historically inhabited by the Hindu people, and in early times it formed a part of an extensive kingdom ruled over by Ahir clan. In Earlier History it is told that it was the Village of guru Dronacharya who was the Teacher of Kauravas and Pandvas. During Akbar's reign, Gurugram fell within the governing regions of Delhi and Agra. As the Mughal empire started to decline, the place was torn between contending powers. By 1803 most of it came under the British rule through the treaty of Surji Arjungaon with Sindhia. The town was first occupied by the cavalry unit posted to watch the army of Begum Samru of Sirdhana. It become a Part of the district, which was divided into units called parganas. These units were given to petty chiefs for the military service rendered by them. Eventually these units came under direct control of the British, with the last major administrative change in 1836. After the revolt of 1857, it was transferred from the North-Western provinces to Punjab province. In 1861, the district, which Gurugram was a part of was rearranged into five tehsils: Gurgaon, Ferozepur Jhirka, Nuh, Palwal and Rewari (10) and the modern-day city came under the control of Gurgaon tehsil. In 1947, Gurgaon became a part of independent India and fell under the Indian state of Punjab. In 1966, the city came under the administration of Haryana with the creation of the new state.

84. The Beti Bachao, Beti Padhao (BBBP) scheme was launched on 22 January 2015 by PM Narendra Modi. It aims to address the issue of the declining child sex ratio image (CSR) and is a national initiative jointly run by the Ministry of Women and Child Development, the Ministry of Health and Family Welfare and the Ministry of Education. It initially focused multi-sector action in 100 districts throughout the country where there was a low CSR. On 26 August 2016, Olympics 2016 bronze medallist Sakshi Malik was made brand ambassador for BBBP.

86. The Yamuna is the second-largest tributary river of the Ganga and the longest tributary in India. Originating from the Yamunotri Glacier at a height of 6,387 metres on the southwestern slopes of Banderpooch peaks of the Lower Himalaya in Uttarakhand, it travels a total length of 1,376 kilometres and has a drainage system of 366,223 square kilometres, 40.2% of the entire Ganga Basin. It merges with the Ganga at Triveni Sangam, Prayagraj, which is a site of the Kumbh Mela, a Hindu festival held every 12 years. It crosses several states: Haryana and Uttar Pradesh, passing by Uttarakhand and later Delhi, and meeting its tributaries on the way, including Tons, Chambal, its longest tributary which has its own large basin, followed by Sindh, the Betwa, and Ken.

89. Sohna is a town and a municipal committee in the Gurgaon district of Haryana, India. A popular tourist weekend and conference retreat, it is on the highway from Gurgaon to Alwar near a vertical rock. Sohna is known for its hot springs and Shiva temple. Sohna tehsil is part of Ahirwal Region.

90. Black Buck, common name for an antelope, mainly is a resident of India but with other small populations in Pakistan and Nepal. The Black Buck has ringed horns that have a moderate spiral twist of three to four turns and are up to 70 cm (28 inch) long. The name Black Buck has also been applied to the sable antelope of Africa. The adult male stands about 80 cm (about 32 inch) at the shoulder and weighs 32 to 43 kg (71 to 95 lb). The body's upper parts are black; the underparts and a ring around the eyes are white. The light-brown female is usually hornless. Males are dark brown.

Previous Paper (Solved)

Haryana Teacher Eligibility Test (HTET)

TGT English (Level-2), Exam 2018*

PART-I

Child Development and Pedagogy

Directions: *Answer the following questions by selecting* ***the most appropriate*** *option.*

1. Which of the following is ***not*** true about dramatic play?
A. It is a form of active play.
B. It is known as make believe play.
C. It involve overt behaviour.
D. It is always reproductive.

2. 'Dyscalculia' is a type of:
A. Locomotor Disability
B. Learning Disability
C. Intellectual Disability
D. Visual Impairment

3. Which of the following is ***not*** true about the Broca's area of brain?
A. It is located in the left frontal lobe.
B. It supports grammatical processing.
C. It is responsible for language production.
D. It is responsible for comprehending word meaning.

4. Which of the following theory assumes that Child Development is ***not*** a continuous process?
A. Cognitive Development theory of Piaget
B. Behaviourism
C. Social learning theory
D. Ecological system theory

5. The statement 'Personality is nothing but a set of learned responses', best describe which of the following view about personality?
A. Behaviouristic view
B. Structuralist view
C. Functionalist view
D. Cognitivist view

6. Which of the following is ***not*** an example of newborn 'reflexes'?
A. Eye blink B. Sucking
C. Swimming D. Driving Car

7. Which of the following is ***not*** true about children's play?
A. The number of play activities decrease with increasing age.
B. Play becomes increasingly social with increasing age.
C. The number of playmates increases with increasing age.
D. Play become increasingly sex-appropriate with increasing age.

8. The 'Three Stratum Theory' of Intelligence was given by:
A. Piaget B. Binnet
C. Carrol D. Cattle

9. Four year old Binny started wetting her bed after her parents brings home a new baby. Which of the following type 'defense mechanism' it is?
A. Regression B. Suppression
C. Rationalization D. Displacement

10. Which of the following statement is ***not*** true?
A. Classical conditioning deals with voluntary behaviours.
B. Operant conditioning deals with voluntary behaviours.
C. Classical conditioning deals with involuntary behaviours.
D. In operant conditioning, 'consequences' are important in framing an association.

11. Knowing 'how to ride a bicycle' is an example of:
A. Procedural knowledge
B. Declarative knowledge
C. Explicit knowledge
D. No option is correct

12. If a child is sharing with you what he did after he got up in the morning, he is using his:
A. Semantic Memory B. Sensory Register
C. Procedural Memory D. Episodic Memory

***Exam held on 6 January, 2019.**

13. Which of the following type is ***not*** a type of Intelligence, as given in Sternberg's Triarchial Theory of successful intelligence?
A. Analytical Intelligence B. Creative Intelligence
C. Musical Intelligence D. Practical Intelligence

14. The seat belt buzzer of a car, stops as soon as the driver put on the seat belt. It is an example of:
A. Positive Reinforcement
B. Negative Reinforcement
C. Positive Punishment
D. Negative Punishment

15. The example 'you scratch my back and I will scratch yours', indicates which type of morality as given by Piaget?
A. Beginning of Morality of Cooperation
B. Pre-conventional morality
C. Realism
D. Not related to moral concern

16. Meeta has overcome her fear of toy-snakes. However on one occasion her fear returned when she found toy-snake on her bed. Such return of fear can be termed as:
A. Stimulus Generalization
B. Stimulus Discrimination
C. Spontaneous Recovery
D. Extinction

17. Which of the following is ***not*** true about 'Zone of Proximal Development'?
A. It is related to Vygotsky's theory.
B. It sets the upper limit on what the child is capable to learn.
C. It is a range of tasks that a learner cannot perform without help of others but yet cannot perform independently.
D. It is the upper limit of a task that a learner can successfully perform independently.

18. Out of the following alternative which one is ***not*** comes under processes in socialization?
A. Learning to behave in socially approved way
B. Playing approved social roles
C. Development of social attitude
D. Approval of egocentric behaviour

19. Presentation of an unpleasant stimulus to decrease the occurrence of a response is known as:
A. Positive Reinforcement
B. Negative Reinforcement
C. Punishment
D. Motivator

20. According to Kohlberg, Good Boy/Good Girl orientation indicates:
A. Pre conventional Morality
B. Post conventional Morality
C. Conventional Morality
D. Relative Morality

21. Which of the following system contains 'Parents Work Place' as per the Bronfenbrenner's Ecological Theory of Development?
A. Micro System B. Macro System
C. Meso System D. Exo System

22. Which of the following statement is ***not*** correct?
A. Intellectual Disability and Learning Disability are not same.
B. A child with learning disability essentially has an IQ score less than 70.
C. Intellectual Disability occurs before age 18.
D. Intellectual Disability and learning Disability both are Developmental Disability.

23. The Assessment done during or before instruction is known as:
A. Summative Assessment B. Formative Assessment
C. Formal Assessment D. Diagnostic Assessment

24. 'Autism' was first described by:
A. Samuel Kirk B. Leo Kanner
C. B.F. Skinner D. J.B. Watson

25. During the developmental period of foetus, head is well developed before his legs. This best describes which of the following tendency of development?
A. Proximo-distal B. Cephalo-caudal
C. Uniformity D. Integration

26. Which of the following is ***not*** a process of Cognitive Development as given by Piaget?
A. Assimilation B. Accommodation
C. Adaptation D. Shaping

27. Which of the following is ***not*** a type of intelligence as proposed by Gardener?
A. Musical Intelligence
B. Linguistic Intelligence
C. Logico-Mathematical Intelligence
D. Creative Intelligence

28. Which of the following is ***not*** related to the classical conditioning experiment?
A. Extinction B. Spontaneous Recovery
C. Shaping D. Stimulus Discrimination

29. A mother gently strokes her infant's forehead each time immediate before breast feeding. Soon, she noticed that each time the baby's forehead is stroked, he makes active sucking movement. The baby's behaviour best describes:
A. Trial and Error learning B. Classical Conditioning
C. Operant Conditioning D. Social Learning

30. In which of the following stage of Cognitive Development, as described by Jean Piaget, a child become capable of understanding 'Conservation'?
A. Sensory Motor Stage
B. Pre-operational Stage
C. Concrete Operational Stage
D. Formal Operational Stage

PART-II

भाषा-I: हिन्दी

निर्देशः *निम्नलिखित प्रश्नों के उत्तर देने के लिए* **सबसे उचित** *विकल्प चुनिए।*

31. असंगत कथन छाँटिए :
A. नापाक इरादे से की जाने वाली मंत्रणा–दित्सा
B. दोपहर से पहले का समय–पूर्वाह्न
C. जिसे देखकर रोंगटे खड़े हो जाएँ–लोमहर्षक
D. बालुका युक्त तट/भूमि–सिकता

32. किस वाक्य में सर्वनाम पदबंध का प्रयोग हुआ है?
A. मेरे रिश्तेदारों में से कोई समय पर नहीं पहुँचा।
B. रिश्तों में स्वार्थ देखने वाले युवा सान्निध्य की ऊष्मा पहचानें।
C. राम ने लंका के अत्याचारी, राक्षस-राज रावण को मार डाला।
D. पाँचवीं मंजिल से गिरा, मरेगा नहीं तो क्या जिंदा रहेगा।

33. ***अशुद्ध*** संधि वाला विकल्प चुनिए :
A. मद + उन्मत्त = मदोन्मत्त
B. विद्वत् + मुख = विद्वन्मुख
C. तत् + उपरान्त = तदोपरान्त
D. षट् + आयतन = षडायतन

34. किस विकल्प में तत्पुरुष समास ***नहीं*** है?
A. वाक्चातुर्य
B. तीर्थाटन
C. अरण्यरोदन
D. मीनकेतु

35. तत्सम-तद्भव की दृष्टि से ***असंगत*** विकल्प चुनिए :
A. वार्ताक – बैंगन
B. लोहमशा – लोमड़ी
C. मस्तक – माथा
D. शण्ठिका – सोंठ

36. वार्तनिक दृष्टि से ***अशुद्ध*** विकल्प चुनिए :
A. विद्वता
B. गीतांजली
C. पक्षिगण
D. स्वामिभक्त

37. किस वाक्य में सार्वनामिक विशेषण का प्रयोग हुआ है?
A. तुम सब आ गए; अच्छे कहाँ रह गए।
B. जो बाहर खड़ा है उसे अन्दर बुलाओ।
C. तुम छात्रों के लिए कुछ किताबें ले आओ।
D. कुछ तुम करो; कुछ मैं करूँगा।

38. निम्न में से किस विकल्प में 'गरुड़' का पर्याय ***नहीं*** है?
A. अहिभोजी B. वैनतेय
C. हेरम्ब D. खगनाथ

39. 'वयोवृद्ध' शब्द में संधि है :
A. स्वर संधि
B. वर्णागम संधि
C. विसर्ग संधि
D. व्यंजन संधि

40. किस विकल्प में दो उपसर्गों का प्रयोग ***नहीं*** हुआ है?
A. सारोपा
B. सहगामिनी
C. पुनरुद्धार
D. समाधि

41. ***अशुद्ध*** वाक्य चुनिए :
A. आपसे मिलकर मुझे आनन्द का आभास हुआ।
B. मेरठ में कई दर्शनीय स्थल हैं।
C. यह छात्रवृत्ति केवल छात्राओं के लिए है।
D. मैं अपना मत स्पष्ट करना चाहता हूँ।

42. किस वाक्य में 'इच्छार्थ वृत्ति' का प्रयोग हुआ है?
A. ईश्वर तुम्हारा भला करे।
B. कृपया यह प्रकरण जाँच दीजिए।
C. लगता है इस वर्ष खूब वर्षा होगी।
D. यदि वह पढ़ता तो आज सफल हो जाता।

43. निम्न में से भाववाच्य चुनिए :
A. गर्मियों में रोज नहाया जाता है।
B. नानी द्वारा कहानी सुनाई गई।
C. कुत्ता सारी रात भौंकता है।
D. किसानों द्वारा फसल काट ली गई है।

44. निम्न में 'संकर शब्द' किस विकल्प में ***नहीं*** है?
A. विज्ञापनदाता
B. डबलरोटी
C. आमचुनाव
D. हिन्दीकरण

45. 'वह दिनभर लिखता रहा।' वाक्य में प्रयुक्त क्रिया विशेषण का भेद इंगित कीजिए :
A. कालवाचक क्रिया विशेषण
B. रीतिवाचक क्रिया विशेषण
C. स्थानवाचक क्रिया विशेषण
D. परिमाणवाचक क्रिया विशेषण

PART-II

Language-II : English

Directions: *Answer the following questions by selecting the **most appropriate** option.*

46. Choose the word which is spelt ***correctly***:
A. Disentigration
B. Disintegration
C. Dissintegration
D. Desintegration

47. Choose the ***correct*** word for the following expression:
One who makes maps or charts.
A. Cartoonist
B. Cartographer
C. Choreographer
D. Choirmaster

48. Fill in the blank with appropriate conjunction:
Grievances cannot be redressed .... they are known.
A. unless B. and
C. but D. before

49. "He wore a turban made of silk."
The underlined words are:
A. Adverb
B. Adverb Phrase
C. Adjective Phrase
D. Noun Phrase

50. "There is a mystery about his death and the police are looking into it."
The underlined phrasal verb means:
A. To investigate
B. To take care of
C. To look behind
D. To revise quickly

51. Fill in the blank with appropriate preposition:
We stayed .... Mumbai for five days.
A. in B. at
C. into D. by

52. *Hearing* the noise, the boy woke up:
A. Pronoun
B. Noun
C. Verb
D. Participle

53. Fill in the blank with the correct option:
I have not heard the .... news.
A. latest B. late
C. latter D. later

54. Choose the most appropriate modal for the blank:
When I was young, I .... climb any tree in the forest.
A. can
B. must
C. may
D. could

55. Fill in the blank with appropriate preposition:
We're going for a drive .... the country.
A. on
B. at
C. in
D. for

56. Fill in the blank by choosing the ***correct*** option:
He is .... his glasses.
A. look for
B. look
C. looking for
D. will look

57. Choose the ***correct*** answer from the options below:
"I took it home with me", She said.
A. She just took it home.
B. She said she had taken it home with her.
C. She said she would take it home.
D. She said she will take it home with her.

58. Choose the ***correct*** passive construction for the given sentence.
They were carrying the injured player off the field.
A. The injured player was being carried off the field.
B. The injured player will be carried off the field.
C. The injured player must be taken off the field.
D. Carry the injured player off the field.

59. Choose the ***correct*** verb for the blank from the options below:
The earth .... round the sun.
A. move
B. moved
C. moves
D. shall move

60. "They arrived soon-after."
The word 'after' is used as:
A. Preposition
B. Adverb
C. Adjective
D. Conjunction

PART-III

General Studies : Quantitative Aptitude, Reasoning Ability and GK & Awareness

Directions: *Answer the following questions by selecting the **most appropriate** option.*

61. Arjun travels half of his journey by train at the speed of 120 km/hr and rest half by car at 80 km/hr. What is his average speed?

A. 88 km/hr B. 92 km/hr
C. 96 km/hr D. 100 km/hr

62. If 11 oranges are bought for ₹ 10 and sold 10 oranges for ₹ 11. What is the gain in percentage?

A. 11% B. 21%
C. 25% D. 28%

63. Amulya does a piece of work in 2 days and Bindu does it in 6 days. In how many days will the two do it together?

A. 2/3 days B. 3/2 days
C. 5/3 days D. 3 days

64. A total of 324 coins of 20 paise and 25 paise make a sum of ₹ 71, then number of 20 paise coins is:

A. 124 B. 140
C. 200 D. 210

65. How many 6's are there in the following number series, each of which is immediately preceded by 1 or 5 and immediately followed by 3 or 9?

263756429613416391569231654321967

A. One B. Two
C. Three D. Four

66. If "BORN" is coded as "APQO" and "LACK" is coded as "KBBL", then "GRID" will be coded as:

A. FSEH B. SFHE
C. FSHE D. FHSE

67. There are deer and peacocks in a zoo. By counting heads they are 80. The number of their legs is 200. How many peacocks are there?

A. 20 B. 40
C. 52 D. 60

68. Which set of numbers is like the given set?

2, 14, 16

A. 2, 7, 8
B. 2, 9, 16
C. 3, 21, 24
D. 4, 16, 18

69. Statements:

I. All players are doctors.
II. Some doctors are musicians.

Conclusions:

I. Some doctors are players as well as musicians.
II. All musicians are doctors.

Then which of the following is ***correct***?

A. Only conclusion I follows.
B. Only conclusion II follows.
C. Both conclusion I and II follow.
D. Neither conclusion I nor II follows.

70. If '+' mean '÷', '×' mean '–', '÷' mean '+' and '–' mean '×', then

16 ÷ 8 × 6 – 2 + 12 = ?

A. 22 B. 24
C. 23 D. 120

71. A is B's sister, C is B's mother, D is C's father, E is D's mother, then how is A related to D?

A. Daughter B. Mother
C. Grand Mother D. Grand Father

72. Find the next term of the following series:

0, 5, 22, 57, 116, ?

A. 205 B. 216
C. 192 D. 207

73. A tank is $\frac{2}{5}$ part full. If 16 litres of water is added to the tank, it becomes $\frac{6}{7}$ part full, then total capacity of tank is:

A. 24 litres B. 35 litres
C. 38 litres D. 42 litres

74. What is the number of odd days in a leap year?

A. 0 B. 1
C. 2 D. 3

75. Find the least number, when divided by 12, 15, 20 and 54, leaves in each case a remainder of 8:

A. 504 B. 540
C. 546 D. 548

76. If A's income is 40% less than that of B. How much per cent B's income is more than that of A?

A. 25% B. 40%
C. $33\frac{1}{3}\%$ D. $66\frac{2}{3}\%$

77. Find the least number by which 294 must be multiplied to make it a perfect square.

A. 3 B. 4
C. 6 D. 12

78. If the fractions $\frac{2}{5}, \frac{3}{8}, \frac{4}{9}, \frac{5}{13}$ and $\frac{6}{11}$ are arranged in ascending order, which one will be fourth place?

A. $\frac{3}{8}$ B. $\frac{4}{9}$

C. $\frac{5}{13}$ D. $\frac{6}{11}$

79. Find the average of first seven prime numbers.

A. 8 B. 9

C. $8\frac{1}{7}$ D. $8\frac{2}{7}$

80. Find out the odd-one:

A. EJNO B. HMQR

C. KPSU D. NSWX

81. The Wahabi leader, who was arrested in charge of Sedition during 19th century:

A. Muhammad Zafar B. Ghazzan Khan

C. Mubarak Ali D. Salman Khan

82. Match the following:

Education Institute	**District**
(*a*) I. I. I. T.	(*i*) Rohtak
(*b*) I. I. M.	(*ii*) Sonipat
(*c*) N.I.D.	(*iii*) Punchkula
(*d*) N. I. F. T.	(*iv*) Kurukshetra

Choose the ***correct*** code:

	(*a*)	(*b*)	(*c*)	(*d*)
A.	(*ii*)	(*i*)	(*iii*)	(*iv*)
B.	(*ii*)	(*i*)	(*iv*)	(*iii*)
C.	(*iv*)	(*i*)	(*iii*)	(*ii*)
D.	(*i*)	(*ii*)	(*iii*)	(*iv*)

83. How many Wildlife Sanctuaries are there in Jhajjar district?

A. Two B. Three

C. One D. Four

84. How many Tahsils are there in Haryana?

A. 71 B. 93

C. 76 D. 68

85. The area of Haryana, which was considered under the sphere of influence of Bhadanakas during the Pre-medieval period:

A. Rewari B. Ambala

C. Panipat D. Kurukshetra

86. Consider the following statements about Lala Murlidhar:

(*a*) He practiced Law at Ambala.

(*b*) He attended the first session of Congress held at Bombay.

Which of the above statement/statements is/are true?

A. Only (*a*) is true.

B. Only (*b*) is true.

C. Neither (*a*) nor (*b*) is true.

D. Both (*a*) and (*b*) are true.

87. Consider the following statements about KMP Expressway:

(*a*) It is also known as Western Peripheral Expressway.

(*b*) Five new cities will be developed along with the KMP Expressway.

Which of the above statement/s is/are true?

A. Only (*a*) is true.

B. Only (*b*) is true.

C. Neither (*a*) nor (*b*) is true.

D. Both (*a*) and (*b*) are true.

88. Who among the following athletes won the Gold in Men's 800 m. race at Asian Games—2018?

A. Jinson Johnson B. Manjit Singh

C. Arpinder Singh D. Rakesh Kumar

89. Where the Vulture Conservation and Breeding Center situated?

A. Kairu B. Morni

C. Zhabua D. Pinjore

90. Which of the following districts has the lowest urban population?

A. Mewat B. Mahendragarh

C. Jind D. Sirsa

PART-IV

English

Directions: *Answer the following questions by selecting the* ***most appropriate*** *option.*

91. Who read popular Tamil thrillers and could weave endless stories and anecdotes on varied subjects in R.K. Laxman's story in the textbook 'Moments'?

A. Mahendra B. Tenali

C. Umashankar D. Iswaran

92. Which of the following is ***not*** a collective noun?

A. Audience B. Choir

C. Jury D. Country

93. Choose the ***correct*** negative transformation of the sentence:

'How can I ever repay your debt?'

A. I cannot ever repay your debt.

B. I can never repay your debt.
C. How can I not ever repay your debt?
D. I cannot never repay your debt.

94. In which of the following sentences the word 'bank' is ***not*** used as a 'noun'?
A. We bank with the ICICI.
B. The bank was within reach.
C. His bank account was rarely over five hundred.
D. How could a man with two million in the bank be in financial danger?

95. Choose the ***correct*** word to complete the sentence below:
It is often difficult to ________ a yawn when you listen to a long speech on the value of time.
A. cause B. smother
C. fire D. allow

96. In K.A. Abbas's story titled *'Bholi'*, who helped Bholi overcome social barriers by encouraging and motivating her?
A. Bholi's teacher B. Bholi's mother
C. Bholi's grandfather D. Bholi's sisters

97. Which of the following nouns is singular?
A. lice B. geese
C. acquarium D. bacteria

98. *'The Road Not Taken'* is a poem by:
A. Lord Alfred Tennyson B. William Wordsworth
C. William Blake D. Robert Frost

99. Which of the following sentences is grammatically ***correct***?
A. If you will run, you will catch the bus.
B. He is more intelligent than either of his four brothers.
C. You should settle the dispute in amicable way.
D. He is making a determined effort to succeed in the examination.

100. What disease does Johnsy have in O. Henry's story 'The Last Leaf'?
A. Autism B. Cancer
C. Schizophrenia D. Pneumonia

Directions (Qs. No. 101-108): *Read the following poem and answer the questions given below.*

I wandered lonely as a cloud
That floats on high o'er vales and hills,
When all at once I saw a crowd.
A host, of golden daffodils;
Beside the lake, beneath the trees,
Fluttering and dancing in the breeze.

Continuous as the stars that shine
And twinkle on the milky way,
They stretched in never ending line
Along the margin of a bay:
Ten thousand saw I at a glance,
Tossing their heads in sprightly dance.

The waves beside them danced; but they
Out–did the sparkling waves in glee:
A poet could not but be gay,
In such a jocund company:
I gazed–and gazed–but little thought
What wealth the show to me had brought:

For oft, when on my couch I lie
In vacant or in pensive mood,
They flash upon that inward eye
Which is the bliss of solitude;
And then my heart with pleasure fills,
And dances with the daffodils.

101. The poet was _____ to see a host of golden daffodils.
A. thrilled B. alarmed
C. amused D. dejected

102. The poet compares the daffodils with ______ .
A. clouds
B. sparkling waves
C. countless twinkling stars in a milky way
D. sprightly dance

103. What is ***not*** stated in the poem?
A. The sight of daffodils fills the poet's mind with delightful wonder and pleasure.
B. The recollection of that scene brings the same joy later too.
C. Nature has the power to bring joy in sadness.
D. The poet experiences loneliness and sadness at the sight of daffodils.

104. The first line 'I wondered lonely as a cloud' is an example of:
A. Alliteration B. Hyperbole
C. Metaphor D. Simile

105. Identify the figure of speech in 'Fluttering and dancing in the breeze', and 'Tossing their heads in sprightly dance':
A. Simile B. Metaphor
C. Personification D. Alliteration

106. *'Ten thousand saw I at a glance,*
Tossing their heads in sprightly dance'.
Here 'sprightly dance' means:
A. a slow dance B. lively dance
C. dance of the spirits D. a listless dance

107. *'A poet could not but be gay,*
In such a jocund company':
Here 'jocund company' refers to:
A. high spirited, merry friends of the poet.

B. A host of golden daffodils.
C. stars twinkling in the milky way.
D. waves dancing in glee.

108. Which of the following is ***not*** a synonym of 'pensive'?
A. reflective B. thoughtless
C. philosophical D. wistful

109. 'Spreading rumours is an anti-social activity.'

The underlined is a/an:
A. Participle B. Infinitive
C. Gerund D. None of these

110. ______ is a political system that separates people according to their race.
A. Immigrent B. Handicapped
C. Apartheid D. Marginalised

111. What are the precious things mentioned in Oscar Wilde's story *'The Happy Prince'*?
A. The statue of the happy prince
B. A large red ruby
C. The leaden heart and the dead bird
D. The happy prince and the swallow

112. Which of the following words does ***not*** take the vowel sound /i : /?
A. deep B. complete
C. dream D. this

113. Who is the writer of *'How I Taught My Grandmother to Read'*?
A. Sudha Murty B. R.K. Narayan
C. Ruskin Bond D. Chetan Bhagat

114. Transform the following into assertive sentence.

'How wise of her to anticipate these problems?'
A. It is wise of her to anticipate these problems.
B. She is very wise and anticipates the problems.
C. It was indeed very wise of her to anticipate their problems.
D. She anticipated the problems in advance.

115. Which of the following is ***not*** an abstract noun?
A. death B. fear
C. darkness D. dirt

116. Rearrange the following words and phrases to form a meaningful sentence:

Other species/human species/the/of/many/the/very existence/is threatening.
A. Many of the other species very existence is threatening human species.
B. Human species very existence is threatening the many of other species.
C. The human species is threatening the very existence of many other species.
D. The very existence of other species is threatening the human species.

117. 'The Hundred Dresses' by El. Bsor Ester is:
A. a story about an eight year old girl's first bus journey into the world outside her village.
B. a story about a selfish teenage girl who was obsessed with clothes.
C. a sensitive account of how a poor young girl is judged by her classmates.
D. None of these

118. Complete the word 'Consci ______' using the appropriate suffix:
A. ance B. ence
C. ense D. enscie

119. In H.G. Wells's story *'Footprints Without Feet'*. Griffin the scientist had carried out experiment after experiment to prove that:
A. There is life after death
B. We can travel in future time
C. The human body could become invisible
D. Man can live in space

120. Which of the following words will take only 's' to form a plural?
A. hero B. radio
C. box D. fly

121. Which of the following sentences has a Noun Clause?
A. You said that he was busy.
B. This is the house that Arjun built.
C. She has not called me since she went to Delhi.
D. If the weather is fine, we will go for a picnic.

122. Which of the following words does ***not*** take a dipthong?
A. here B. boy
C. my D. cat

123. What sort of proposal is Anton Chekhov's play *'The Proposal'* about?
A. A suggestion, plan or scheme for doing something
B. An offer for a possible plan or action
C. The act of asking someone's hand in marriage
D. The ownership of the Oxen Meadows

124. What is the meaning of the underlined idiomatic expression in the following sentence?

'He is afraid of his own shadow'.
A. Constant attendant or companion
B. Very timid and suspicious
C. Unwilling to do anything
D. Lives with a painful memory of something

125. Choose the ***correct*** phrase in place of the underlined word in the given sentence:

'Sunil, there's a letter for you in today's post. There's one for me also.'
A. as a matter of fact B. as well as
C. as well D. alright

126. Transform the following into an *exclamatory* sentence:

'It is a lovely place.'

A. How lovely place!
B. A lovely place, wow it is!
C. Oh, it was a lovely place!
D. What a lovely place!

127. Identify the underlined subordinate clause in the sentence:

'The boy who stole the watch was caught.'

A. Noun clause B. Adjective clause
C. Adverb clause D. None of these

128. Which of the following is ***not*** a complex sentence?

A. As he was sick, he could not work.
B. He is very learned, yet humble.
C. Whoever is learned is respected.
D. He liked what I suggested.

129. Choose the ***correct*** one word for the underlined in the sentence given:

'In India, in the field of industry, there is more than the needed amount of labour, so the workmen cannot stick out for higher wages.'

A. Superfluous
B. Superstitious
C. Superspecialist
D. Superstructured

130. Which of the following sentence is ***not*** in the passive voice?

A. My parents were regarded as an ideal couple.
B. I was asked to go and sit on the back bench.
C. Such problems have to be confronted.
D. They buy and sell second-hand books on the pavent every Saturday.

Directions (Qs. No. 131-134): *Fill in the blanks in the following sentences.*

131. He strained his ears _________ the sound of the train.

A. to look for B. to catch
C. to hold D. to fetch

132. If I _______ that you were coming today, I would have met you at the station.

A. knew B. know
C. had known D. had knowed

133. It has been two years _______ I last saw her.

A. since B. for
C. before D. when

134. My father doesn't allow anybody _______ in our house.

A. to have smoke B. to smoke
C. smoking D. for smoke

135. Which of the following has a different verb pattern?

A. The children kept quiet.
B. The boy lost his pen.
C. Rajni opened the door.
D. My father helped the poor.

136. Which of the following is misspelt?

A. auspicious B. austere
C. authentic D. avalanchae

137. Who has illustrated the story *'Madam Rides the Bus'* by Vallikkannen?

A. K.S. Sundaram B. R.K. Laxman
C. R.K. Narayan D. M.F. Husain

138. Which of the following sentences is grammatically ***incorrect***?

A. Eistein was the greatest scientist of our century.
B. You are a mechanic, isn't it?
C. Trespassers will be prosecuted.
D. Das Kapital is one of the most important books ever written.

139. Choose the ***correct*** meaning of the word 'uncanny' from the options given below:

A. a quarrel or an argument
B. strange, mysterious, difficult to explain
C. complete confusion and disorder
D. something unremarkable

140. The underlined word in the given sentence is a/an:

'Her selection as Principal of the local school was celebrated by the village community.'

A. Noun B. Pronoun
C. Verb D. Adjective

141. In Ruskin Bond's story *'The Adventures of Toto'*, Toto is a:

A. Monkey B. Squirrel
C. Tortoise D. Parrot

142. Adrienne Rich in her poem *'The Trees'* compares the branches (boughs shuffling under the roof _____) to:

A. newly discharged patients heading for the clinic doors
B. the moon shining in a sky still open
C. prisoners escaping the prison
D. a bird released from a cage

143. Which of the following words is used to denote the skin of some animals?

A. hide B. blanket
C. cloak D. camouflage

144. Which of the following sentence has a 'be' form of verb?

A. I am a teacher.
B. My sister wrote a letter.
C. He can swim.
D. They have a lot of money.

145. Which of the following words will be used to describe a negative quality?

A. diligent B. sagacious
C. tiresome D. tireless

146. Who gobbles up the pirate in Ogden Nash's poem *'The Tale of Custard the Dragon'*?

A. A barrel full of bears
B. Ink, the little black kitten
C. Mustard, the little yellow dog
D. Custard, the cowardly dragon

147. Identify the underlined part of speech in the following sentence:

'I ate some rice.'

A. Adverb B. Pronoun
C. Adjective D. Preposition

148. Rudyard Kipling's poem beginning *'The Camel's Hump'* is an ugly lump ______ is:

A. a cautionary tale about what happens 'if we haven't enough to do'
B. is a tale of how the camel got his hump
C. how to sit still with a book by the fire
D. about shivering, scowling, grunting and growling

149. To whom does Mme Loisel go to borrow jewellery in Guy De Maupassant's story *'The Necklace'*?

A. M. Loisel
B. Mme Forestier
C. Mme George Ramponneau
D. Mme Pompadour

150. Which of the following is spelt ***correctly***?

A. Perempotory B. Paedagogy
C. Parliamenterian D. Pathetic

Answers

1	2	3	4	5	6	7	8	9	10
D	B	D	A	A	D	C	C	A	A
11	**12**	**13**	**14**	**15**	**16**	**17**	**18**	**19**	**20**
A	D	C	B	A	C	D	D	C	C
21	**22**	**23**	**24**	**25**	**26**	**27**	**28**	**29**	**30**
D	B	B	B	B	D	D	C	B	C
31	**32**	**33**	**34**	**35**	**36**	**37**	**38**	**39**	**40**
A	A	C	D	B	A,B	C	C	C	B
41	**42**	**43**	**44**	**45**	**46**	**47**	**48**	**49**	**50**
A	A	A	A	A	B	B	A	C	A
51	**52**	**53**	**54**	**55**	**56**	**57**	**58**	**59**	**60**
A	D	A	D	C	C	B	A	C	B
61	**62**	**63**	**64**	**65**	**66**	**67**	**68**	**69**	**70**
C	B	B	C	B	C	D	C,D	D	C
71	**72**	**73**	**74**	**75**	**76**	**77**	**78**	**79**	**80**
*	A	B	C	D	D	C	B	D	C
81	**82**	**83**	**84**	**85**	**86**	**87**	**88**	**89**	**90**
A	B	A	B	A	D	D	B	D	A
91	**92**	**93**	**94**	**95**	**96**	**97**	**98**	**99**	**100**
D	D	B	A	B	A	C	D	D	D
101	**102**	**103**	**104**	**105**	**106**	**107**	**108**	**109**	**110**
A	C	D	D	C	B	B	B	C	C
111	**112**	**113**	**114**	**115**	**116**	**117**	**118**	**119**	**120**
C	D	A	A	D	C	C	B	C	C
121	**122**	**123**	**124**	**125**	**126**	**127**	**128**	**129**	**130**
A	D	C	B	C	D	B	B	A	D
131	**132**	**133**	**134**	**135**	**136**	**137**	**138**	**139**	**140**
B	C	A	B	A	D	B	B	B	A
141	**142**	**143**	**144**	**145**	**146**	**147**	**148**	**149**	**150**
A	A	A	A	C	D	C	A	B	D

Explanatory Answers

61. Let total distance = x km

$\therefore$ Average speed = $\dfrac{\text{Total distance}}{\text{Total time taken to travel distance}}$

$$= \frac{x}{\left(\frac{\frac{x}{2}}{120}\right)+\left(\frac{\frac{x}{2}}{80}\right)}$$

$$= \frac{1}{\frac{1}{240}+\frac{1}{160}} = \frac{480}{2+3}$$

$$= \frac{480}{5} = 96 \text{ km/hr.}$$

62. Cost price of one orange = ₹ $\dfrac{10}{11}$

Selling price of one orange = ₹ $\dfrac{11}{10}$

Gain percentage = $\dfrac{\text{SP}-\text{CP}}{\text{CP}}\times 100$

$$= \frac{\frac{11}{10}-\frac{10}{11}}{\frac{10}{11}}\times 100$$

$$= \frac{\frac{121-100}{100}}{\left(\frac{10}{11}\right)}\times 100$$

$$= \frac{21\times 11}{110\times 10}\times 100$$

= 21%.

63. Amulya one day work = $\dfrac{1}{2}$

Bindu one day work = $\dfrac{1}{6}$

Amulya and Bindu one day work = $\dfrac{1}{2}+\dfrac{1}{6}$

$$= \frac{3+1}{6} = \frac{4}{6} = \frac{2}{3}$$

$\therefore$ Required time = $\dfrac{3}{2}$ days.

64. Let 20 paise coins = x

$\therefore$ 25 paise coins = $324 - x$

Then, $20x + 25(324 - x) = 71 \times 100$

$20x + 8100 - 25x = 7100$

$-5x = -1000$

$x = 200$

Hence, 20 paise coins are 200.

66. As, B O R N → (−1, +1, −1, +1) → A P Q O; L A C K → (−1, +1, −1, +1) → K B B L

Similarly, G R I D → (−1, +1, −1, +1) → **F S H E**

67. Let the number of peacocks = x and the number of deer = y

Then, $x + y = 80$ ...(*i*)

$2x + 4y = 200$ ...(*ii*)

equation (*i*) × 4 − equation (*ii*)

$2x = 120$

$x = 60$

Hence, number of peacocks be 60.

70. $16 + 8 - 6 \times 2 \div 12$

According to BODMAS Rule,

$= 16+8-6\times\dfrac{2}{12}$

$= 16 + 8 - 1$

$= 24 - 1$

$= 23.$

72. 0, 5, 22, 57, 116, **205**

$1^3 - 1$, $2^3 - 3$, $3^3 - 5$, $4^3 - 7$, $5^3 - 9$, $6^3 - 11$

73. Let total capacity of tank = x litres

Then, $\dfrac{2}{5}x+16 = \dfrac{6}{7}x$

$\dfrac{6}{7}x-\dfrac{2}{5}x = 16$

$\dfrac{30x-14x}{35} = 16$

$16x = 16 \times 35$

$x = 35$

Hence, total capacity of tank is 35 litres.

74. Total days in a leap year = 366

$\therefore$ 366 days = 52 week + 2 day (odd days)

Hence, 2 odd days in a leap year.

75. Required least number

2	12,	15,	20,	54
2	6,	15,	10,	27
3	3,	15,	5,	27
3	1,	5,	5,	9
3	1,	5,	5,	3
5	1,	5,	5,	1
	1,	1,	1,	1

= LCM (12, 15, 20, 54) + 8

= (2 × 2 × 3 × 3 × 3 × 5) + 8

= 540 + 8 = 548.

76. Let B's income = ₹ 100

Then, A's income = ₹ 60 (40% less than B's income)

Then B's income more than A's income

= 100 − 60 = ₹ 40

$$\text{Required percentage} = \frac{40}{60} \times 100$$

$$= \frac{200}{3} = 66\frac{2}{3}\%.$$

77.

2	294
3	147
7	49
7	7
	1

$\therefore$ 294 = 2 × 3 × 7 × 7

$= 6 \times (7)^2$

Required number = 6.

78. $\because \frac{2}{5} = 0.4$

$\frac{3}{8} = 0.375$

$\frac{4}{9} = 0.444$

$\frac{5}{13} = 0.385$

$\frac{6}{11} = 0.545$

$\because 0.375 < 0.385 < 0.4 < 0.444 < 0.545$

$$\frac{3}{8} < \frac{5}{13} < \frac{2}{5} < \frac{4}{9} < \frac{6}{11}$$

Hence, the fraction which comes at fourth place be $\frac{4}{9}$.

79. First seven prime numbers are

2, 3, 5, 7, 11, 13, 17

$$\text{Required Average} = \frac{2+3+5+7+11+13+17}{7}$$

$$= \frac{58}{7}$$

$$= 8\frac{2}{7}.$$

80. A. E →(+5) J →(+4) N →(+1) O

B. K →(+5) P →(+3) S →(+2) U

C. H →(+5) M →(+4) Q →(+1) R

D. N →(+5) S →(+4) W →(+1) X

Hence, option (C) KPSU is odd-one.

Previous Paper (Solved)

Haryana Teacher Eligibility Test (HTET)

TGT English (Level-2), Exam 2017*

PART-I

Child Development and Pedagogy

Directions: *Answer the following questions by selecting the* ***most appropriate*** *option.*

1. Which of the following is ***not*** a subordinate law given in 'trial and error'?
A. Law of Multiple response
B. Law of Attitude
C. Law of Exercise
D. Law of Response by analogy

2. According to Piaget, the age range of the substage 'mental representation', of the sensory motor stage is:
A. Birth to 1 month
B. 4 to 8 months
C. 8 to 12 months
D. 18 months to 2 years

3. The psychologist who tried to develop a learning theory using principles of topology (A branch of Mathematics) is:
A. Kurt Lewin B. Sigmund Freud
C. William James D. Skinner

4. Which of the following is ***not*** an example of children with special needs as per RPWD Act, 2016?
A. Acid attack victims
B. Cerebral palsy
C. Children with visual impairment
D. None of these

5. Testing used during instruction to aid in planning and diagnosis is known as:
A. Formative Assessment
B. Summative Assessment
C. Normative Assessment
D. None of these

6. The teacher said Rekha that she is not allowed to participate in Game period as she has not completed her home work. It is an example of:
A. Negative reinforcement
B. Punishment
C. Positive reinforcement
D. Tangible reward

7. The ability of classification develops at:
A. Sensory motor stage
B. Preoperational stage
C. Concrete operational stage
D. None of the above

8. Which type of teaching material is most effective for a child with visual impairment?
A. Video based B. Visual material
C. Tactile based D. None of these

9. Modelling is the concept given by:
A. Albert Bandura B. J.B. Watson
C. Freud D. Vygotsky

10. Which of the following has viewed the child as 'Tabula-Rasa' (Blank-Slate)?
A. Freud B. Piaget
C. Skinner D. John Locke

11. Which of the following theory viewed cognitive development as a socially mediated process?
A. Socio Cultural Theory
B. Social Learning Theory
C. Psycho Sexual Theory
D. Sign Learning Theory

12. A three year old boy says, "The sun is angry'. It is an example of:
A. Animism B. Egocentrism
C. Criticism D. Intuition

13. Which of the following is ***not*** a type of Intelligence as given by Gardner?
A. Musical intelligence
B. Spatial intelligence
C. Interpersonal intelligence
D. Analytical intelligence

14. "TEACCH" programme is mostly used to teach children with:
A. Hearing impairment
B. Gifted students
C. Intellectual disability
D. Autism

***Exam held on 24-12-2017.**

15. Which of the following studied moral development in children?
A. Kohlberg B. Piaget
C. Both A and B D. None of the above

16. Providing salary to the teacher at the end of every month, which schedule of reinforcement it reflects?
A. Fixed ratio B. Variable ratio
C. Fixed interval D. Variable interval

17. Who proposed that all children have language acquisition device?
A. Piaget B. Chomsky
C. Vygotsky D. Dan Slobin

18. Who proposed Advanced Organizer Model of teaching?
A. Bruner B. Pavlov
C. Ausubel D. Piaget

19. Multiple Intelligence theory was proposed by:
A. Alfred Binet B. Jean Piaget
C. Harward Gardner D. Jensen

20. According to Freud the age range of 'Oral stage' of psycho-sexual development is:
A. Birth to one year
B. Birth to two years
C. Birth to three years
D. None of these

21. The long-term memory for 'how to do things' is known as:
A. Procedural memory B. Episodic memory
C. Immediate memory D. Sensory memory

22. The triarchic theory of successful intelligence was given by:
A. Spearman B. Binet
C. Thorndike D. Sternberg

23. The law which is ***not*** a part of Gestalt views of learning is:
A. Law of similarity B. Law of proximity
C. Law of closure D. Law of use

24. After occurrence of a desirable behaviour, the teacher says 'very good' to the child. She has used:
A. Primary reinforcer
B. Secondary reinforcer
C. Negative reinforcement
D. None of the above

25. According to Ecological system theory, which system includes 'values'?
A. Micro system B. Macro system
C. Meso system D. Exo system

26. Using our current 'schemes' to interpret the external world is known as:
A. Assimilation B. Accommodation
C. Organization D. None of these

27. Which of the following is ***not*** an example of acquired motive?
A. Attitude B. Interest
C. Curiosity D. Hunger

28. Which of the following is an example of Developmental Disorder?
A. Blindness B. Hearing impairment
C. Intellectual disability D. Leprosy

29. Which part of the brain supports grammatical processing and language production?
A. Broca's area B. Frontal lobe
C. Perietal lobe D. Occipital lobe

30. Programmed learning is based on the work of:
A. Skinner B. Piaget
C. Pavlov D. Bandura

PART-II

भाषा-I: हिन्दी

निर्देश: *निम्नलिखित प्रश्नों के उत्तर देने के लिए* **सबसे उचित** *विकल्प चुनिए।*

31. कौन-सा शब्द उर्दू उपसर्ग से निर्मित है?
A. खुशबू B. स्वयंसिद्ध
C. अधकच्चा D. निहत्था

32. ***अशुद्ध*** विलोम युग्म को पहचानिए :
A. आध्यात्मिक-आधिदैविक B. स्मरण-विस्मरण
C. हेय-स्तुत्य D. वृद्धि-क्षय

33. किस विकल्प में वर्तनी की दृष्टि से ***अशुद्ध*** शब्द है?
A. दवाईयाँ B. पौलस्त्य
C. आभिजात्य D. आपराधिक

34. किस विकल्प में संधि नियम का उल्लंघन होने के कारण ***अशुद्ध*** शब्द बना है?
A. अभिषेक B. निषेध
C. अनुशंगी D. सुषुप्ति

35. किस विकल्प में ऊनतावाचक तद्धित प्रत्यय है?
A. बहूटी B. बहिनापा
C. दूधैल D. चुड़िहारा

36. *''कोमल गात, मृदुल बसंत, हरे-हरे ये पात''*
—उक्त पंक्ति में प्रयुक्त पदों में से कौन-सा पद विशेषण **नहीं** है?
A. मृदुल B. गात
C. हरे-हरे D. कोमल

37. निम्न में से किस विकल्प में कर्मधारय का उदाहरण है?
A. सूरकृत B. नीलगगन
C. आजीवन D. रामोपासक

38. कौन-सा विकल्प लिंग सम्बन्धिनी ***अशुद्धि*** से युक्त है?
A. पापिनी स्त्री B. बुद्धिमती भार्या
C. गुणवान कन्या D. प्रभावशालिनी भाषा

39. निम्न में से कौन-सा शब्द 'योगरूढ़' है?
A. अहिंसा B. पाशविक
C. मुख्यमंत्री D. चक्षुःश्रवा

40. किस शब्द में विसर्ग संधि का प्रयोग ***नहीं*** हुआ है?
A. यशोदा B. पयोद
C. तमोगुण D. महोदधि

41. किस विकल्प में 'नामधातु' क्रिया है?
A. धड़धड़ाहट B. खिलवाना
C. उठना D. गरमाना

42. 'परुष' का समानार्थक (पर्याय) शब्द है :
A. कठोर B. पुरुष
C. परख D. प्रणाली

43. 'आप भला तो जग भला' वाक्य किस सर्वनाम का उदाहरण बनेगा?
A. संबंधवाचक सर्वनाम B. निजवाचक सर्वनाम
C. निश्चयवाचक सर्वनाम D. पुरुषवाचक सर्वनाम

44. कौन-सा शब्द स्त्रीलिंग बोधक ***नहीं*** है?
A. मृत्यु B. ऋतु
C. रेणु D. तालु

45. निम्न कथनों में से कौन-सा कथन ***असत्य*** है?
A. 'ङ्' उत्क्षिप्त व्यंजन है।
B. 'स्' संघर्षी व्यंजन है।
C. 'द्' स्पर्शी व्यंजन है।
D. 'र्' पार्श्विक वर्ण है।

PART-II

Language-II : English

Directions: *Answer the following questions by selecting the* ***most appropriate*** *option.*

46. 'Dancing is her hobby.'
The underlined word is used as a:
A. verb B. gerund
C. participle D adjective

47. Choose the most appropriate modal for the blank:
She .... swim for hours at the age of eight.
A. can B. may
C. might D. could

48. "The girl who is wearing a red ribbon is my sister."
The underlined words are a:
A. Noun Clause B. Adjective Clause
C. Adverb Clause D. None of the above

49. Choose the most appropriate form of indirect speech for the given sentence:
He said to her, "you are a very reasonable person."
A. He said to her she is a very reasonable person.
B. He told her that she was a very reasonable person.
C. He told to her that he is a very reasonable person.
D. He said to her that she is a very reasonable person.

50. Fill in the blank with the appropriate preposition.
He lost all his property because of his addiction .... drinking and gambling.
A. with B. in
C. to D. of

51. "Business falls off during summer months."
The underlined phrasal verb means:
A. to decline B. to grow
C. to increase D. to disappear

52. Fill in the blank with the appropriate option:
"I paid the bill but the cashier did not give the ...."
A. receipt B. receive
C. receiving D. received

53. 'She could not figure out the theme of the play clearly.'
The underlined phrasal verb means:
A. comprehend B. examine
C. enjoy D. draw

54. Fill in the blank by choosing the correct option.
"Asha and I .... on M.G. Road when we saw an old man walking slowly."
A. were shopping B. have been shopping
C. had been shopping D. shopping

55. Choose the correct Passive Construction for the sentence given:
"Mrs. Sharma knows me."
A. I am known by Mrs. Sharma.
B. I was known by Mrs. Sharma.
C. I am known to Mrs. Sharma.
D. I have known to Mrs. Sharma.

56. Choose the correct word for the following expression:

One who is present everywhere

A. Omnipotent
B. Omniscient
C. Omnipresent
D. Omnission

57. Choose a suitable connector for the blank from the options given:

"My father burnt his hand .... he was lighting a candle."

A. but B. while
C. because D. since

58. "Maharana Pratap fought bravely and won the war." The underlined word in the sentence has been used as a:

A. Noun B. Verb
C. Adverb D. Adjective

59. 'Agreement' is a noun with 'ment' as a suffix. Which of the following options will become a noun if we add the suffix 'ment' to it?

A. amuse B. extort
C. correct D. colour

60. Choose the word which is spelt correctly:

A. comittee B. committe
C. committee D. commitee

PART-III

General Studies : Quantitative Aptitude, Reasoning Ability and GK & Awareness

Directions: *Answer the following questions by selecting the **most appropriate** option.*

61. If income of A is 20% less than income of B. How much percentage is B's income more than income of A?

A. 20% B. 25%
C. $16\frac{2}{3}\%$ D. $33\frac{1}{3}\%$

62. How many 9's are there which are followed by 9 in given series?

98799029990319927965697819678992 90

A. 2 B. 4
C. 5 D. 6

63. $\frac{3}{7}$th part of a bucket can be filled in one minute. Rest part of the bucket can be filled in:

A. $\frac{7}{3}$ minutes B. 21 minutes
C. $\frac{4}{7}$ minute D. $\frac{4}{3}$ minutes

64. A number, when divided by 8, 12 and 15, gives always remainder 5. Then number is:

A. 9505 B. 9605
C. 9705 D. 9805

65. Find the smallest number such that if it is added to sum of squares of 9 and 10, then complete square is obtained:

A. 0 B. 3
C. 8 D. 15

66. $13\frac{1}{2}-\left[4\frac{1}{2}-\left\{3-\left(2-\frac{1}{2}\right)\right\}\right]$ is equal to:

A. $9\frac{1}{2}$ B. $10\frac{1}{2}$
C. $10\frac{3}{4}$ D. $13\frac{1}{2}$

67. Average of eight numbers is 12. If each number is increased by 2, then average of new numbers is:

A. 13 B. 12
C. 15 D. 14

68. How many numbers are there from 1 to 100 which are completely divisible by 7?

A. 9 B. 11
C. 17 D. 14

69. Which of the following fraction is greater than 1/3?

A. $\frac{27}{82}$ B. $\frac{20}{61}$
C. $\frac{16}{45}$ D. $\frac{51}{154}$

70. Find the smallest number such that by multiplying it with 24, a complete square number is obtained:

A. 2 B. 3
C. 4 D. 6

71. Find the odd-one:

A. Oxygen
B. Ice
C. Water
D. Steam

72. The number of triangles shown in the figure is:

A. 6 B. 8
C. 10 D. 12

73. If GRASP is coded as INOPQ, BROWN is coded as RNSTU, then SPARROW will be coded as:
A. PQONNST B. PQONNOT
C. POQNNSU D. PQONNSU

74. Statements : I. A triangle has 3 angles.
II. A square has 4 angles.
Conclusion : A polygon has many angles.
Then which of the following is ***correct***?
A. Conclusion is correct.
B. Conclusion is wrong.
C. Conclusion is not logical.
D. None of these

75. In given figure, circle represents rich people, rectangle represents hardworking and triangle represents rural people. Then rural people who are hardworking but poor, are indicated by:

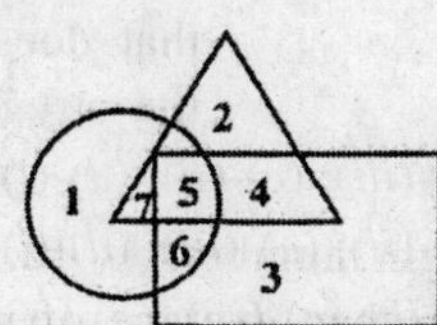

A. 5 B. 7
C. 4 D. 6

76. The maximum possible number of Sundays in 3 consecutive calendar months is:
A. 14 B. 15
C. 13 D. 12

77. A is brother of B, B is wife of C, C is son of D and D is wife of E. What is E to B?
A. Son-in-law B. Father-in-law
C. Brother-in-law D. Mother-in-law

78. There are seven numbers. Average of first four numbers is 4. Average of last four numbers is also 4. Average of all seven numbers is 3. Find the fourth number:
A. 4 B. 3
C. 11 D. 7

79. Find the missing number in given square:

5	25	18
15	10	12
20	5	?

A. 15 B. 10
C. 20 D. 25

80. Find the missing term of the series:
2, 7, 17, 32, ?, 77
A. 47 B. 52
C. 57 D. 62

81. The Deputy Speaker of 13th Legislative Assembly of Haryana is:
A. Kuldeep Sharma
B. Kanwar Pal
C. R.K. Nandal
D. Santosh Yadav

82. The river of Haryana, which originates from Rajasthan, is:
A. Markanda B. Sahibi
C. Ghaggar D. Saraswati

83. 'The Technological Institute of Textile and Science' is situated at:
A. Gurugram B. Bhiwani
C. Rohtak D. Panchkula

84. As per the Census-2011, the population density of Haryana is (in per square k.m.):
A. 478 B. 573
C. 385 D. 325

85. The first Nuclear Power Project of Haryana is being set-up at:
A. Gorakhpur B. Kakroi
C. Sampla D. Yamunanagar

86. Where has the Haryana government organised Pravasi Haryana Divas in 2017?
A. Ashoka University, Sonipat
B. Kingdom of Dream, Gurugram
C. Pinjore Garden, Panchkula
D. Vigyan Bhawan, New Delhi

87. The Math (Monastery), which was rejuvenated and chosen as main center by Baba Mastnath, was:
A. Kansrati
B. Asthal Bohar
C. Pehwa
D. Jalandhar

88. The tomb of Bu Ali Shah is situated at:
A. Hissar B. Yamunanagar
C. Panipat D. Jind

89. In which of the following locations, a National Park is situated?
A. Sultanpur
B. Bhindawas
C. Nahan
D. Abubshahar

90. The partner Nation in 31st Surajkund International Crafts Mela was:
A. Egypt B. China
C. Thailand D. Japan

PART-IV

English

Directions: *Answer the following questions by selecting the* ***most appropriate*** *option.*

91. An adverb:
A. Describes action
B. Modifies verbs
C. Modifies adjectives
D. All options are right

92. A system of racial domination against the dark-skinned people practised by the seat of white supremacy is called:
A. Colonialism B. Apartheid
C. Atheism D. Autocracy

93. Read the following sentence and select the ***correct*** option in reported/indirect speech of the same:

Sentence : Sheela asked the children, "Are you ready to do the work?"
A. Sheela asked the children if/whether they were ready to do the work.
B. Sheela asked the children that if you are ready to do the work.
C. Sheela asked the children if/whether they are ready to do the work.
D. Sheela asked the children to be ready to do the work.

94. Learning can be made more reliable, easy and natural if teachers work on the following principles except one:
A. The only disability in life is bad attitude.
B. Giftedness and learning disabilities go hand in hand.
C. Class toppers may end up doing very ordinary jobs in their lives.
D. One learns only by what academics would teach.

95. To what/whom does "a cruel eye outworn" refer in William Blake's poem "The School Boy"?
A. The Bird
B. The Teacher
C. The Father and the Mother
D. The Tender Plants

96. To fill the gaps in the following sentence select the appropriate set of co-ordinating conjunctions from the given options:

Sentence : The dog, being afraid of the cruel pair, would .... eat .... move.
A. neither, nor B. either, or
C. not only, but also D. although, yet

97. What prompted Anne Frank to keep a diary in the first place?
A. She was feeling a little depressed
B. She was completely alone in the world
C. She wanted a true and real friend
D. She loved writing

98. Match the following by filling up the gaps in the appropriate sentence:

Phrasal Verb	***Sentence with gap***
(*a*) Give up	(*i*) A communal war .... when the place of worship was set ablaze by some riotous people.
(*b*) Carry on	(*ii*) If you want to go out, I will .... the children.
(*c*) Look after	(*iii*) He realized that he could not .... working with this company.
(*d*) Broke out	(*iv*) There is something in you that does not let you .... the struggle.

A. (*a*)-(*iv*); (*b*)-(*iii*); (*c*)-(*ii*); (*d*)-(*i*)
B. (*a*)-(*iv*); (*b*)-(*ii*); (*c*)-(*iii*); (*d*)-(*i*)
C. (*a*)-(*i*); (*b*)-(*ii*); (*c*)-(*iii*); (*d*)-(*iv*)
D. (*a*)-(*i*); (*b*)-(*iii*); (*c*)-(*ii*); (*d*)-(*iv*)

99. The following expression best illustrates:

Expression: "So it was always winter there, and the North Wind and the Hail, and the Frost, and the snow danced about through the trees."
A. Symbol B. Metaphor
C. Personification D. None of these

100. "Steet smart" means:
A. One who has nightmares about learning.
B. One who is smart at learning course material.
C. One who is smart at learning languages.
D. One who becomes smart by doing things independently or by choice rather than force.

101. Choose the correct passive verb form (simple present tense form) against the verb form given in the bracket in the following sentence:

Sentence : Second-hand books (buy and sell) on the pavement every Sunday on this road.
A. are bought and sold
B. were bought and sold
C. had been bought and sold
D. will be bought and sold

102. Choose the ***correct*** verb/tense form to complete the blank space in the following sentence from the given options:

Sentence: When the oxygen in the air .... with carbon and hydrogen in a fuel, a chemical reaction .... place.

A. Combined; has taken
B. Combines; takes
C. Combined; takes
D. Combined; is taking

103. The 'schools of the future' may not allow the children 'the fun' of having:

A. A real classroom in the schoolyard with real classmates and a human teacher.
B. A virtual classroom with a virtual reality created by computer software.
C. A Robotic teacher showing lessons and asking questions.
D. A virtual classroom where learning is through books on computer or television screen.

104. A green patch with fresh water and green trees in the middle of a vast desert is called:

A. an oasis B. an island
C. a sand-dune D. a mound

105. John Milton was born in the year:

A. 1602 B. 1596
C. 1578 D. 1608

106. Match the following:

(A)	(B)
(*a*) Oxymoron	(*i*) Crying smiles
(*b*) A fable	(*ii*) Words are the food and dress of thought
(*c*) Metaphor	(*iii*) Site; cite
(*d*) Homophones	(*iv*) A story with animals as characters conveying a moral.

A. (*a*)-(*i*); (*b*)-(*iv*); (*c*)-(*ii*); (*d*)-(*iii*)
B. (*a*)-(*i*); (*b*)-(*ii*); (*c*)-(*iii*); (*d*)-(*iv*)
C. (*a*)-(*iv*); (*b*)-(*ii*); (*c*)-(*i*); (*d*)-(*iii*)
D. (*a*)-(*iv*); (*b*)-(*iii*); (*c*)-(*ii*); (*d*)-(*i*)

107. Which one of the following words ***cannot*** be used both as a noun and as a verb?

A. Hope B. Surprise
C. Demand D. Devote

108. "Death in an open field is for better than life in a small hut" : This sentence suggests the idea of:

A. Courage B. Safety
C. Freedom D. Happiness

109. The poem 'The Rime of the Ancient Mariner' was written by:

A. John Milton B. William Wordsworth
C. S.T. Coleridge D. Lord Byron

110. In Robert Frost's poem "The Road not Taken" roads stand for:

A. Having experiences in life that guide us.
B. Making choices in life that shape us.
C. Roads diverged in a yellow wood.
D. Roads less travelled.

111. "How beautiful those hills are!"
It is an example of:

A. Imperative sentence
B. Exclamatory sentence
C. Interrogative sentence
D. Rhetorical question

112. "Today Tommy found a real book!" What does "a real book" stand for?

A. A very old book
B. A book printed on paper
C. A book on computer screen
D. A book on television screen

113. Which one of the following is ***not*** an example of adjectival phrase?

A. Frightened voices B. Excited snakes
C. Clever lizards D. Their houses

114. Which one of the following statements is ***not*** true about Albert Einstein?

A. He published his general theory of relativity in 1915.
B. He received the Nobel Prize in literature in 1921.
C. He warned American President about the adverse effects of the atomic bomb.
D. He proposed the formation of a world government.

115. "Hyenas come with merry smiles;
But if they weep they're Crocodiles."
What does the above lines tell us about hyenas?

A. Hyenas are friendly
B. Hyenas are crocodiles
C. Hyenas are happy
D. Hyenas are deceptive

116. "Cambridge was my metaphor for England" : Who said these words?

A. Stephen Hawking B. Firdaus Kanga
C. Issac Newton D. None of these

117. Who out of the following is known as the 'Bard of Avon'?

A. William Wordsworth B. W.B. Yeats
C. Robert Browning D. William Shakespeare

118. What makes a differently-abled person feel stronger?

A. Seeing somebody like himself achieving something huge.
B. People asking him to be brave.
C. Living with the reality of one's body.
D. Accepting the disability and often laughing inside.

119. Which *one* of the following options has a ***correct order*** so as to form a meaningful sentence?
A. Stop/and tell me/beating about/what you want/the bush?
B. Stop/beating about/the bush/and tell me/what you want?
C. What you want/the bush/and tell me/stop/beating about?
D. Stop/and tell me/what you want/beating about/the bush?

120. Choose the correct article for the blank spaces in the following sentence:
(all the four blank spaces will require the same article here)
Sentence : History is not only .... story of .... Alexanders, ... Napoleons and .... Hitlers, but of ordinary people as well.
A. the B. an
C. a D. all options are wrong

121. Match the following:

Books/Titles	**Type of Writing**
(*a*) Heaven Lake	(*i*) Ballad
(*b*) Wings of Fire	(*ii*) Travelogue
(*c*) The Proposal	(*iii*) Autobiography
(*d*) A Legend of Northland	(*iv*) Play

A. (*a*)-(*i*); (*b*)-(*ii*); (*c*)-(*iii*); (*d*)-(*iv*)
B. (*a*)-(*ii*); (*b*)-(*iii*); (*c*)-(*iv*); (*d*)-(*i*)
C. (*a*)-(*iv*); (*b*)-(*iii*); (*c*)-(*ii*); (*d*)-(*i*)
D. (*a*)-(*iv*); (*b*)-(*ii*); (*c*)-(*i*); (*d*)-(*iii*)

122. Which one of the following conditional sentences is ***incorrect***?
A. If a king knew three things, he would never fail.
B. If I see Tom, I had tell him the news.
C. If she knows we have a cat, she will leave the house.
D. If you spit on the road, you will be fined.

123. Who received the Nobel Prize for literature in the year 2016?
A. Bob Dylan B. Alice Munro
C. Patrick Modiana D. Svetlana Alexievich

124. "The man who has been to the mountains is never the same again" because:
A. There would be nothing higher to climb.
B. The climber attains communion with God.
C. Mountains are attractive.
D. He becomes conscious in a special manner of his own smallness in this large universe.

125. "The summit of the mind" refers to:
A. a sense of victory and happiness
B. an inspiration to face life's obstacles resolutely
C. a battle fought and won
D. a sense of conquering the highest and the mightiest

126. "A Truly Beautiful Mind" tells the story of the mind of:
A. Albert Einstein B. Nelson Mandela
C. A.P.J. Abdul Kalam D. None of these

127. Which one of the following compound words can function both as a noun and a verb?
A. Daylight B. Daydream
C. Daybreak D. Daytime

128. Who out of the following authors received the booker prize?
A. Arundhati Roy B. Amitav Ghosh
C. Rama Mehta D. Jhumpa Lahiri

129. The underlined words in the following lines are an appropriate example of:
Lines : "No prophet <u>durst</u> declare;
Nor did the <u>wisest wizard</u> guess"
A. Rhyme B. Alliteration
C. Rhythm D. Onomatopoeia

130. "And I shall have some peace there, for peace comes dropping slow"—Where shall the speaker have peace in this context?
A. At Innisfree B. By the shore
C. On the roadway D. On the pavements

131. Choose the most suitable adverb to complete the following sentence:
Sentence: We should ...... get down from a moving train.
A. never B. often
C. sometimes D. ever

132. Which figure of speech has been used in the following expression?
Expression : "A first glimpse of him is shocking because he is like a still photograph."
A. Oxymoron B. Alliteration
C. Simile D. Metaphor

133. A song narrating a story in short stanzas depicting folk/popular culture and passed on orally from one generation to the next is:
A. a sonnet B. a ballad
C. an elegy D. an ode

134. Match the following:

Idiom	**Meaning**
(*a*) At the finger tips	(*i*) to destroy or stop something at an early stage of its development.
(*b*) Took the world by storm	(*ii*) a sudden and wonderful change.
(*c*) To nip something in the bud	(*iii*) to know thoroughly
(*d*) To turn over a new leaf	(*iv*) to have a great and rapid success

A. (*a*)-(*iii*); (*b*)-(*iv*); (*c*)-(*i*); (*d*)-(*ii*)
B. (*a*)-(*i*); (*b*)-(*ii*); (*c*)-(*iii*); (*d*)-(*iv*)
C. (*a*)-(*ii*); (*b*)-(*i*); (*c*)-(*iv*); (*d*)-(*iii*)
D. (*a*)-(*iv*); (*b*)-(*iii*); (*c*)-(*ii*); (*d*)-(*i*)

135. Certain words 'go together'; such 'Word friends' are called:
A. Compound words B. Collocations
C. Idioms D. Phrasal Verbs

136. Select the correct verb/tense form to complete the following sentence:
Sentence: I reached the market when most of the shops ....
A. has closed B. closed
C. had closed D. has been closed

137. Select the option with a different Consonant sound (underlined) in the words given below:
A. shine B. ashes
C. fish D. pitcher

138. Match the following as to make the expression meaningful:

(A)	(B)
(*a*) Save	(*i*) over spilt milk
(*b*) Don't cry	(*ii*) while the sun shines
(*c*) Make hay	(*iii*) before the horse
(*d*) Don't put the cart	(*iv*) for a rainy day

A. (*a*)-(*i*); (*b*)-(*ii*); (*c*)-(*iii*); (*d*)-(*iv*)
B. (*a*)-(*iv*); (*b*)-(*iii*); (*c*)-(*ii*); (*d*)-(*i*)
C. (*a*)-(*iv*); (*b*)-(*i*); (*c*)-(*ii*); (*d*)-(*iii*)
D. (*a*)-(*i*); (*b*)-(*iii*); (*c*)-(*ii*); (*d*)-(*iv*)

139. Match the following and complete the sentences in **column 'B'**:

(A) Adjectives	(B) Sentences
(*a*) the biggest	(*i*) Reading stories is .... than watching television.
(*b*) fewer	(*ii*) Australia is .... island in the world.
(*c*) the eldest	(*iii*) She makes .... mistakes than any other student in the class.
(*d*) more interesting	(*iv*) Of his three sons, Ramesh is ....

A. (*a*)-(*ii*); (*b*)-(*iii*); (*c*)-(*iv*); (*d*)-(*i*)
B. (*a*)-(*i*); (*b*)-(*ii*); (*c*)-(*iii*); (*d*)-(*iv*)
C. (*a*)-(*iv*); (*b*)-(*iii*); (*c*)-(*ii*); (*d*)-(*i*)
D. (*a*)-(*iii*); (*b*)-(*ii*); (*c*)-(*iv*); (*d*)-(*i*)

140. What is the most difficult thing to teach an elephant?
A. The signal to walk
B. The signal to sit down
C. The master call
D. The signal to make him quiet

141. Match the following:

Clauses	Sentences
(*a*) Adjectival clause	(*i*) He speaks much better than he writes.
(*b*) Adverbial clause of time	(*ii*) That is the man who taught me lessons in science.
(*c*) Adverbial clause of reason	(*iii*) Wait here till I come back
(*d*) Adverbial clause of comparison	(*iv*) He will win the election because he is very popular.

A. (*a*)-(*i*); (*b*)-(*ii*); (*c*)-(*iii*); (*d*)-(*iv*)
B. (*a*)-(*ii*); (*b*)-(*iii*); (*c*)-(*iv*); (*d*)-(*i*)
C. (*a*)-(*iv*); (*b*)-(*iii*); (*c*)-(*ii*); (*d*)-(*i*)
D. (*a*)-(*iii*); (*b*)-(*ii*); (*c*)-(*i*); (*d*)-(*iv*)

142. Choose the word with a different Vowel sound from the given options:
A. Good B. Food
C. Wood D. Cook

143. The underlined words in the following extract suitably exemplify:
Extract : He came to the door of a cottage,
In travelling round the earth,
Where a little woman was making cakes,
And baking them on the hearth;
A. Rhyme B. Rhythm
C. Alliteration D. Assonance

144. The romantic revival is associated with:
A. French Revolution B. Spanish Civil War
C. World War I D. World War II

145. "Every tinkle on the shingles"
Has an echo in the heart,
The underlined words in the above lines best illustrate the use of:
A. Onomatopoeia B. Alliteration
C. Consonance D. Assonance

146. Pick out the word from the following options without a prefix:
A. Encourage B. Energy
C. Enclose D. Endanger

147. "The Hundred Dresses" is a sensitive account of:
A. How a Polish immigrant young girl judges her classmates?
B. How a Polish immigrant young girl judges her teachers?
C. How a Polish immigrant young girl is judged by her parents?
D. How a Polish immigrant young girl is judged by her classmates and teachers?

148. Choose the word with a different sound from the given options (in the underlined letter):
A. Rough B. Enough
C. Dough D. Tough

149. A situation in which what happens is the opposite of what one expects or what is said is ***not*** what is exactly meant is:
A. Irony B. Fate
C. Chance D. None of these

150. "Then the bird opened its wings and flew right away into the blue."
To what does "the blue" refer here?
A. Flight B. Bird
C. Colour D. Sky

Answers

1	2	3	4	5	6	7	8	9	10
C	D	A	D	A	B	C	C	A	D
11	**12**	**13**	**14**	**15**	**16**	**17**	**18**	**19**	**20**
A	A	D	D	C	C	B	C	C	A
21	**22**	**23**	**24**	**25**	**26**	**27**	**28**	**29**	**30**
A	D	D	B	B	A	D	C	A	A
31	**32**	**33**	**34**	**35**	**36**	**37**	**38**	**39**	**40**
A	A	A	C	A	B	B	C	D	D
41	**42**	**43**	**44**	**45**	**46**	**47**	**48**	**49**	**50**
D	A	B	D	D	B	D	B	B	C
51	**52**	**53**	**54**	**55**	**56**	**57**	**58**	**59**	**60**
A	A	A	A	C	C	B	C	A	C
61	**62**	**63**	**64**	**65**	**66**	**67**	**68**	**69**	**70**
B	C	D	B	D	B	D	D	C	D
71	**72**	**73**	**74**	**75**	**76**	**77**	**78**	**79**	**80**
A	C	A	A	C	A	B	C	B	B
81	**82**	**83**	**84**	**85**	**86**	**87**	**88**	**89**	**90**
D	B	B	B	A	B	B	C	A	A
91	**92**	**93**	**94**	**95**	**96**	**97**	**98**	**99**	**100**
D	B	A	D	B	A	C	A	C	D
101	**102**	**103**	**104**	**105**	**106**	**107**	**108**	**109**	**110**
A	B	A	A	D	A	D	C	C	B
111	**112**	**113**	**114**	**115**	**116**	**117**	**118**	**119**	**120**
B	B	D	B	D	B	D	A	B	A
121	**122**	**123**	**124**	**125**	**126**	**127**	**128**	**129**	**130**
B	B	A	D	B	A	B	A	B	A
131	**132**	**133**	**134**	**135**	**136**	**137**	**138**	**139**	**140**
A	C	B	A	B	C	D	C	A	C
141	**142**	**143**	**144**	**145**	**146**	**147**	**148**	**149**	**150**
B	B	A	A	A	B	D	C	B	D

Explanatory Answers

61. Let B's income = ₹ 100

Then, A's income = ₹ 80

B's income more than A's income

$$= \frac{100-80}{80} \times 100 = \frac{20}{80} \times 100 = 25\%.$$

63. $\frac{3}{7}$ part filled in 1 minute

1 part filled in $\frac{7}{3}$ minutes

Rest part $\left(1-\frac{3}{7}\right) = \frac{4}{7}$

$\frac{4}{7}$ th part filled $= \frac{1}{\left(\frac{3}{7}\right)} \times \frac{4}{7}$

$= \frac{7}{3} \times \frac{4}{7} = \frac{4}{3}$ minutes.

64. LCM (8, 12, 15) = 120

Check the option,

(*a*) 9505 ÷ 120

Remainder = 25

(*b*) 9605 ÷ 120

Remainder = 5

∴ 9605 is the number which gives remainder 5 after dividing 8, 12 and 15.

65. Let the number = x

According to question,

$$= (9)^2 + (10)^2 + x$$
$$= 81 + 100 + x$$
$$= 181 + x$$

Nearest square number of 181 is 196

$\therefore \quad x = 196 - 181 = 15.$

67. We know that,

If each number is increased by x, then their average will also increase by x.

$\therefore$ Average of new number = 12 + 2 = 14.

66. $13\frac{1}{2}-\left[4\frac{1}{2}-\left\{3-\left(2-\frac{1}{2}\right)\right\}\right]$

$$= \frac{27}{2}-\left[\frac{9}{2}-\left\{3-\frac{3}{2}\right\}\right]$$

$$= \frac{27}{2}-\left[\frac{9}{2}-\frac{3}{2}\right] = \frac{27}{2}-3 = 10\frac{1}{2}.$$

68. 1 to 100, Numbers which are divisible by 7

7, 14, 21, 28, 35, 42, 49, 56, 63, 70, 77, 84, 91, 98

$\therefore$ Total number = 14.

69. $\because \quad \frac{1}{3} = 0.333$

(*a*) $\frac{27}{82} = 0.329$

(*b*) $\frac{20}{61} = 0.327$

(*c*) $\frac{16}{45} = 0.355$

(*d*) $\frac{51}{154} = 0.331$

$\therefore \quad \frac{16}{45}$ is greater than $\frac{1}{3}$.

70. 24 × 6 = 144

which is a square number of 12

$\therefore$ 6 is the smallest number such that by multiplying it with 24, we obtain a square number.

71. Except (A), all others are the three stage of water while oxygen is a gas.

72.

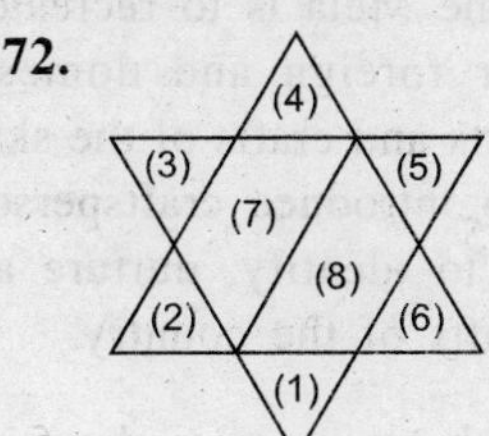

Total triangles = 8 + 2 = 10.

73. As, G R A S P → I N O P Q (↓ each letter); B R O W N → R N S T U (↓ each letter)

	G	R	A	S	P		B	R	O	W	N
	↓	↓	↓	↓	↓		↓	↓	↓	↓	↓
	I	N	O	P	Q		R	N	S	T	U

Similarly,

S	P	A	R	R	O	W
↓	↓	↓	↓	↓	↓	↓
P	Q	O	N	N	S	T

76. In Calendar year 2017

October Month's total days = 31

Sundays in October = 5 (1, 8, 15, 22, 29)

November Month's total days = 30

Sundays in November = 4 (5, 12, 19, 26)

December Month's total days = 31

Sundays in December = 5 (3, 10, 17, 24, 31)

Total Sundays in 3 months = 5 + 4 + 5

= 14.

This happens first sunday falls on the 1st of any of three month.

77.

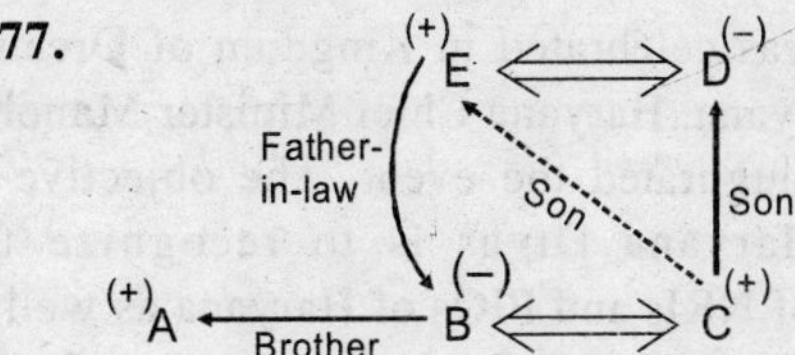

78. Fourth Number = (4 × 4 + 4 × 4) – 7 × 3

= (16 + 16) – 21

= 32 – 21 = 11.

79. Column I ⇒ 5 + 15 + 20 = 40

Column II ⇒ 25 + 10 + 5 = 40

Column III ⇒ 18 + 12 + ? = 40

30 + ? = 40

? = 10

80. 2   7   17   32   [52]   77

+ 5   + 10   + 15   + 20   + 25

82. The **Sahibi river,** also called the **Sabi River,** is an ephemeral, rain-fed river flowing through Rajasthan, Haryana and Delhi states in India. It drains into Yamuna at Delhi, where its channelled course is also called the Najafgarh drain, which also serves as Najafgarh drain bird sanctuary. Sahibi is a seasonal river which is 120 km long and flows from Aravalli hills in Rajasthan to Haryana, of which 100 km is in Haryana.

83. The Technological Institute of Textile and Sciences (TIT&S), founded in 1943, offers engineering programs and postgraduate programs. The institute is located in Birla Colony, opposite Bhiwani railway station. It is one of the oldest colleges in India. The Technical College established in 1943 was initially affiliated to the Department of Industrial Training, Punjab for

3-year Diploma course in Spinning Technology and Weaving Technology. TITS remained a part of the Birla Education Trust up to 31 March, 1985. From 1 April, 1985 it was separated from the Trust and an independent Society known as "The Technological Institute of Textiles" was formed to manage it which was registered under the West Bengal Societies Registration Act 1961. To reflect the expanded instructional facilities and new courses the Society was rechristened as "The Technological Institute of Textile & Sciences".

85. Nuclear Power Corp of India Ltd (NPCIL) has selected Gorakhpur village (around 175 km from Delhi) in Fatehabad district of Haryana to set up the states first 4 × 700 mw nuclear power plant. The foundation stone of the 2800 Megawatt nuclear power plant was laid on 13 January, 2014. The first phase of the project will have an installed capacity of 1400 MW and is expected to be completed by 2021.

86. On 10-11 January 2017; the first-ever Pravasi Haryana Divas—2017 was celebrated in Kingdom of Dreams, Gurugram, Haryana. Haryana Chief Minister Manohar Lal Khattar inaugurated the event. The objective of the Pravasi Haryana Divas is to recognize the achievements of NRIs and PIOs of Haryana as well as those persons from Haryana who are now settled in other States of India and to harness their energies in the future development of Haryana.

87. Shri Baba Mast Nath Math, Asthal Bohar is the oldest and most popular place of Nath Sect belonging to kanphada Yogis. This is the main Tapasthali (Place of Worship) of Nath Yogi and is situated 5 kms away from Rohtak city and 1 km away from M.D. University Campus on Delhi-Rohtak National Highway No. 10. The Math has been the centre and live-wire of ancient civilization and has been doing Yeo-man services for the benefit of mankind. Shri Baba Mast Nath Ji rejuvenated the Math Ashtal Bohar in 18th Century. His able pupils have been rightfully performing the duties and responsibilities of a Mahent. Late Mahent Shreo Nath Yogi (Ex-Health Minister for Haryana Govt.) the most able and active in series of pupils had raised many institutions in the sweet memory of his Guru Baba Mast Nath Ji, so has done his immediate follower and present incumbent to the Gaddi, Mahent Chand Nath Yogi.

88. Shaikh Sharafuddeen Bu Ali Qalandar Panipati also called Bu Ali Qalandar (1209-1324 CE probably born at Panipat, Haryana) in India was a Sufi saint of the Chisti order. His dargah (mausoleum) in the town of Panipat is a place of pilgrimage.

The dargah (mausoleum or shrine), mosque and enclosure at the Qalandar Chowk in Panipat were constructed by Mahabat Khan, a general in the service of the Mughal Emperor Jahangir. Mahabat Khan's own tomb in red sandstone is adjacent to the saint's mausoleum. The tombs of Hakim Mukaram Khan and the Urdu poet Maulana Altaf Hussain Hali are also located within the enclosure. A nearby structure is the tomb of the last Lodi dynasty ruler of Delhi, Ibrahim Lodi, killed in the First Battle of Panipat (1526).

89. Sultanpur Bird Sanctuary is a very popular national park located in Gurgaon district in Haryana State. Sultanpur is located 40 kilometres (25 mi) from Dhaula Kuan in Delhi and 15 kilometres (9.3 mi) from Gurgaon on the Gurgaon-Farrukhnagar Road. This Bird Sanctuary, ideal for birding and bird watchers, is best visited in winters when a large number of migratory birds come here.

Among approximately 1,800 migratory bird species out of total 10,000 species of birds in the world, nearly 370 species migrate to India due to seasonal changes, including 175 long-distance migration species that use the Central Asian Flyway route which also include Amur falcons, Egyptian vultures, plovers, ducks, storks, ibises, flamingoes, jacanas, pochards and sociable lapwing. Among these approximately 250 species of Birds are found at Sultanpur Bird Sanctuary. Some of them are resident, while others come from distant regions like Siberia, Europe and Afghanistan.

90. Egypt was the Partner Nation during the Surajkund International Crafts Mela. Hosted jointly by the Haryana government and the Surajkund Mela Authority, in collaboration with the union ministries of Tourism, Textiles, Culture and External Affairs, the Surajkund Mela showcased some of the most exquisite handloom, handicraft and culture diversity of India and other countries. "For the first time, Egypt had the honour of becoming the Partner Nation during the much-admired festival... Egypt had always been keen to interconnect with India on a cultural, people-to-people level, especially when it come to preserving and disseminating cultural heritage across the globe.

The Mela showcased the richness and diversity of the handicrafts, handlooms and the cultural heritage of India. The idea of hosting the Mela is to recreate a pristine rural ambience for foreign and domestic tourists, tell the patrons of arts and crafts of the skills involved in creative arts, to introduce craftspersons directly to the buyers, and to identify, nurture and preserve the languishing crafts of the country.

Child Development & Pedagogy

CHILD DEVELOPMENT

CONCEPT OF DEVELOPMENT AND ITS RELATIONSHIP WITH LEARNING

The discipline of Child Development is concerned with the changes in the behaviour of children over time and explains why and how they occur. It aims to describe and explain development in the areas of physical, social, emotional, language and cognitive functioning.

Development and Growth

The term 'development' is used for changes in a person's physical and behavioural traits that emerge in orderly ways and last for a reasonable period of time. The three main characteristics of these changes are progressive, orderly and long lasting. Development refers to both quantitative as well as qualitative changes. It includes changes not only in structure but also in function.

'Growth' refers to physical increase in the size of the body. Increase in weight, height and internal organs is growth. Growth refers to a quantitative change, that is, a change that can be measured.

Growth is only one aspect of the larger process of development. Development continues even when physical changes are not visible. Physical growth slows down considerably after adolescence but development does not.

Stages of Development

The human life span has been divided into the stages of infancy, childhood, adolescence and adulthood.

The period from birth to two years of age is referred to as the period of infancy. In this period the child is totally dependent on the caregiver for the fulfilment of his needs. After birth, this is the period of most rapid growth and development. The child's skills and abilities increase. By the end of infancy he is able to walk, run, communicate his needs verbally, feed himself, identify family members, recognise himself and venture confidently in familiar surroundings.

The period of childhood is from two to twelve years of age. Development at this stage is not as rapid as during infancy. During this period the child refines the skills he has acquired during infancy and learns new skill as well. During childhood he also learns the ways of behaviour that are considered appropriate by the society. The child meets many people outside the family and forms attachments with more people. As the child grows and his thinking capacities mature, he realises that he can do many things. This gives him a feeling of confidence. During this period he becomes more independent though adult guidance is constantly needed. The period of childhood is divided into two stages : the period of early childhood (2–6 years) and middle childhood (6–12 years). The period of early childhood is also referred to as the preschool age because at this age the child is learning skills that will help him to do tasks associated with schooling. The preschooler has mastered the words to ask questions about things and people. He learns about numbers, colours, shapes and the reasons for everyday events. All these concepts develop from actually seeing things and doing various activities. The child in the age group 6–12 years has matured a great deal and is expected to behave more responsibly than the preschooler.

The next stage is referred to as the period of adolescence (12–18 years). The beginning of this period is marked by puberty. Puberty refers to the stage around 11–14 years of the age, when there is a spurt in physical growth. This results in a rapid increase in height and weight and the emergence of secondary sexual characteristics. These rapid physical changes lead to a need for emotional readjustment.

At this age the peer group becomes very important and the adolescent follows the rules and the codes of her group. Feelings of loyalty and pride for the group are very strong. At times the values of the peer group may become more important than those of the family. During adolescence thinking develops further and becomes more complex. The individual can understand and deal with varied situations. He can think of abstract problems and work out their solutions. All this helps him to prepare for the roles and responsibilities, which he will be expected to carry out as an adult.

After the age of 18 years the person is referred to as an adult. Physical changes are completed in this stage and person becomes mature.

Areas of Development

The various developments that take place during the life span of an individual can be classified thus: physical and motor development, social development, emotional development, cognitive and language development.

Physical development refers to the physical changes in the size, structure and proportion of the parts of the body that take place from the moment of conception.

Motor development means the development of control over body movements. This results in increasing coordination between various parts of the body. As a result of physical and motor development the child acquires many abilities. These developments will bring about the change from an infant who at the time of birth is capable of only lying on his back to one who learns to roll over, hold his head, sit, walk, run and climb stairs. The improving coordination between the eye and the hand movements will help him to eat food without smearing it on his face. Gradually he will learn to clothe himself, draw, skip, paint, ride a bicycle and type. As he grows he will refine the skills already acquired as well as develop new ones.

Language development refers to those changes that make it possible for an infant, who in the early months uses crying for communication, to learn words and then sentences to converse fluently. How the child learns to speak grammatically correct sentences is amazing! At first the child indicates his need for water through crying. Then he learns to say ''water''. A little later he says, ''Mummy water'' and finally he speaks a complete sentence, ''Mummy, I want to drink water''. He will be about three years by this time.

Cognitive development concerns the emergence of thinking capabilities in the individual. We can see how the child's thinking develops and changes from one age to the next. The infant is not born with the reasoning and thinking, abilities of adults. In fact, the infant acts as if an object that is removed from his sight has ceased to exist. Gradually he learns that objects and people are permanent and they exist even if he cannot see them. Around five years of age he can understand concepts such as heavy and light, fast and slow, colours and sizes which he did not comprehend earlier. Exploration of the surroundings and the questions regarding the 'why' and 'how' of things result in an increasing store of information. His thought develops but he is still unable to see a situation from another person's point of view. For example, he is unable to understand why another child cannot climb the tree when he can do so. He thinks that everybody else should be able to do what he can and feel the way he does. He believes that all things have life and feelings like him including the sun, stone, pencil and table. A ten year old has learnt to reason and analyze but this ability is limited to real life concrete situations. He cannot usually think in abstract terms or predict future event. The capacity for abstruct thinking develops fully during the period of adolescence. He can now handle complex situations. Thus at each stage of a person's life, the ability to think is qualitatively different and more developed compared to the earlier stage.

Cognitive development is the process of mental development from infancy to adulthood. Cognition refers to the process of 'coming to know', which is accomplished through the gathering and processing of information. It includes perceiving, learning, remembering, problem solving, and thinking about the world. Intelligence is a term difficult to define. Nevertheless, according to a well known definition, it refers to the individual's ability to ''act purposefully, think rationally and deal effectively with the environment''.

Social development refers to the development of those abilities that enable the individual to behave in accordance with the expectations of the society. It is concerned with the child's relationships with people and his ways of interaction with them. The infant instinctively reaches out to the person who approaches him with love and affection. Gradually he learns to recognize his mother and other caregivers and forms attachment to them.

Emotional development refers to the emergence of emotions like anger, joy, delight, happiness, fear, anxiety and sorrow and the socially acceptable ways of expressing them. As the child grows up and becomes aware of acceptable ways of behaviour, a variety of emotions also emerge. As an infant he expresses only discomfort and delight. As he grows older, expressions of joy, happiness, fear, anger and disappointment appear. He learns to express these emotions in a healthy manner. For example, initially the child hits out when angry. Gradually he learns to control this and expresses anger in other ways.

Theories of Child Development and Learning

Maturationist Theory

The maturationist theory was advanced by the work of Arnold Gessell. Maturationists believe that development is a biological process that occurs automatically in predictable, sequential stages over time. This perspective leads many educators and families to assume that young children will acquire knowledge naturally and automatically as they grow physically and become older, provided that they are healthy.

School readiness, according to maturationists, is a state at which all healthy young children arrive when they can perform tasks such as reciting the alphabet and counting; these tasks are required for learning more complex tasks such as reading and arithmetic. Because development and school readiness occur naturally and automatically, maturationists believe the best practices are for parents to teach young children to recite the alphabet and count while being patient and waiting for children to become ready for kindergarten. If a child is developmentally unready for school, maturationists might suggest referrals to transitional kindergartens, retention, or holding children out of school for an additional year. These practices are sometimes used by schools, educators, and parents when a young child developmentally lags behind his or her peers. The young child's underperformance is interpreted as the child needing more time to acquire the knowledge and skills needed to perform at the level of his or her peers.

Environmentalist Theory

Theorists such as John Watson, B.F. Skinner, and Albert Bandura contributed greatly to the environmentalist perspective of development. Environmentalists believe the child's environment shapes learning and behaviour in fact, human behaviour, development, and learning are thought of as reactions to the environment. This perspective leads many families, schools, and educators to assume that young children develop and acquire new knowledge by reacting to their surroundings.

Kindergarten readiness, according to the environmentalists, is the age or stage when young children can respond appropriately to the environment of the school and the classroom (*e.g.*, rules and regulations, curriculum activities, positive behaviour in group settings, and directions and instructions from teachers and other adults in the school). The ability to respond appropriately to this environment is necessary for young children to participate in teacher-initiated learning activities. Success is dependent on the child following instructions from the teacher or the adult in the classroom. Many environmentalist-influenced educators and parents believe that young children learn best by rote activities, such as reciting the alphabet over and over, copying letters, and tracing numbers. This viewpoint is evident in kindergarten classrooms where young children are expected to sit at desks arranged in rows and listen attentively to their teachers. At home, parents may provide their young children with workbooks containing such activities as colouring or tracing letters and numbers—activities that require little interaction between parent and child. When young children are unable to respond appropriately to the classroom and school environment, they often are labelled as having some form of learning disabilities and are tracked in classrooms with curriculum designed to control their behaviours and responses.

Constructivist Theory

The constructivist perspective of readiness and development was advanced by theorists such as Jean Piaget, Maria Montessori, and Lev Vygotsky. Although their work varies greatly, each articulates a similar context of learning and development. They are consistent in their belief that learning and development occur when young children interact with the environment and people around them. Constructivists view young children as active participants in the learning process. In addition, constructivists believe young children initiate most of the activities required for learning and development. Because active interaction with the environment and people are necessary for learning and development, constructivists believe that children are ready for school when they can initiate many of the interactions they have with the environment and people around them.

Constructivist-influenced schools and educators pay a lot of attention to the physical environment and the curriculum of the early childhood classroom. Kindergarten classrooms often are divided into different **learning centers** and are equipped with developmentally appropriate materials for young children to play with and manipulate. Teachers and adults have direct conversations with children, children move actively from one center to another, and daily activities are made meaningful through the incorporation of children's experiences into the curriculum. At home, parents engage their young children in reading and storytelling activities and encourage children's participation in daily household activities in a way that introduces such concepts as counting and language use. In addition, parents may provide young children with picture books containing very large print, and toys that stimulate interaction (such as building blocks and large puzzles). When a young child encounters difficulties in the learning process, the constructivist approach is neither to lable the child nor to retain him or her; instead, constructivists give the child some individualized attention and customize the classroom curriculum to help the child address his or her difficulties.

Today, most researchers have come to understand child development and the learning process as articulated by the constructivists. However, this view has not been widely translated into practice. Many kindergarten teachers and parents still believe that young children are not ready for school unless they can recite the alphabet, count, and have the ability to follow instructions from adults.

PRINCIPLES AND THEORIES OF CHILD DEVELOPMENT

Studying and understanding child growth and development are important parts of teaching young children. No two children are alike. Children differ in physical, cognitive, social and emotional growth patterns. Even identical twins, who have the same genetic makeup, are not exactly alike. They may differ in the way they respond to play, affection, objects and people in their environment.

Knowledge of the areas of child development is basic to guiding young children. Linked to this is the understanding of healthy brain development. These stimuli begin at birth. Therefore, it is vital for children to have loving caregivers. Young children need dependable, trusting relationships. They thrive in environments that are predictable and nurturing. Understanding theories about how people develop helps form your knowledge base in caring for young children.

Child Development

Development refers to change or growth that occurs in children. It starts with infancy and continues to adulthood. By studying child development, you will form a profile of what children can do at various ages.

Different names are used to describe young children at different ages. From birth through the first year, children are called **infants. Toddlers** are children from age one up to the third birthday (Because of an awkward style of walking, the name toddler describes this age group). The term **preschooler** is often used to describe children ages three to six years of age.

Areas of Development

The study of child development is often divided into three main areas. These include physical, cognitive and social-emotional development. Dividing development into these areas makes it easier to study.

Physical development refers to physical body changes. It occurs in a relatively stable, predictable sequence. It is orderly, not random. Changes in size and weight are also part of physical development.

Physical skills, such as crawling, walking and writing, are the result of physical development. These skills fall into two main categories:

1. **Grossmotor development :** It involves improvement of skills using the large muscles in the legs and arms. Such activities as running, skipping and bike riding fall into this category.
2. **Fine-motor development :** It involves the small muscles of the hands and fingers. Grasping, holding, cutting and drawing are some activities that require fine-motor development.

Environmental factors also affect what children can do physically. These factors include proper nutrition and appropriate toys and activities.

Cognitive development, sometimes called **intellectual development,** refers to processes people use to gain knowledge. Language, thought, reasoning and imagination are all included. Identifying colours and knowing the difference between one and many are examples of cognitive tasks.

Language and thought are a result of cognitive development. These two skills are closely related. Both are needed for planning, remembering and problem solving. As children mature and gain experience with their world, these skills develop.

The third area of development is called social-emotional development. These two areas are grouped together because they are so interrelated. Learning to relate to others is social development. Emotional development, on the other hand, involves feelings and expression of feelings. Trust, fear, confidence, pride, friendship and humor are all part of social-emotional development. Other emotional traits include timidity, interest and pleasure.

Learning to express emotions in appropriate ways begins early. Caregivers promote this learning when they positively model these skills. A person's self-concept and self-esteem are also part of this area. As children have success with all skills confidence flourishes. This leads to a healthy self-concept and sense of worth.

The physical, cognitive and social-emotional areas of development are linked to one another. Development in one area can strongly influence another area. For instance, writing words requires fine-motor skills. It also requires cognitive development. Language, a part of cognitive development, is needed to communicate with others. It is also necessary for growing socially and emotionally.

Principles of Development

Although each child is unique, the basic patterns or principles of growth and development are universal, predictable and orderly. Through careful observation and interaction with children, researchers and those who work with children understand the characteristics of the principles that follow:

1. Development tends to proceed from the head downward. This is called the **cephalocaudal principle.** According to this principle, the child first gains control of the head, then the arms, then the legs. Infants gain control of head and face movements within the first two months after birth. In the next few months, they are able to lift themselves up using their arms. By 6 to 12 months of age, infant start to gain leg control and may be able to crawl, stand or walk.
2. Development also proceeds from the center of the body outward according to the **proximodistal principle**. Accordingly, the spinal cord develops before other parts of the body. The child's arms develop before the hands and the hands and feet develop before the fingers and toes. Fingers and toes are the last to develop.
3. Development also depends on maturation. **Maturation** refers to the sequence of biological changes in children. These orderly changes give children new abilities. Much of the maturation depends on changes in the brain and the nervous system. These changes assist children to improve their thinking abilities and motor skills. A rich learning environment helps children develop to their potential.

Children must mature to a certain point before they can gain some skills. For instance, the brain of a four-month-old has not matured enough to allow the child to use words. A four-month-old will babble and coo. However, by two years of age, with the help of others, the child will be able to say and understand many words. This is an example of how cognitive development occurs from simple tasks to more complex tasks. Likewise, physical skills develop from general to specific movements. For example, think about the way an infant waves its arms and legs. In a young infant, these movements are random. In several months, the infant will likely be able to grab a block with his or her whole hand. In a little more time, the same infant will grasp a block with the thumb and fore finger.

INFLUENCE OF HEREDITY AND ENVIRONMENT

Heredity and environment greatly influence the growth, development and behaviour of a child. Each child inherits certain capacities for growth. The way in which these capacities develop is influenced by the opportunities afforded by the environment, for example, the height to which the individual is capable of growing is determined by heredity. The environment cannot change the limits imposed by heredity. Whereas a poor environment *i.e.*, lack of exposure will slow down a child who is genetically clever, a rich environment which provides and exposes a child to a lot of educational facilities will not change a child who is genetically born not clever to become clever. A good environment will enable the individual to reach these limits. The environment influences the speed with which the child develops. The environment shapes the individual's development in the sense that it promotes the growth of certain capacities and neglects the growth of others. For instance, if the child experiences more emphasis on academic and no attachment to physical education, the child's capacity to develop certain skills will be neglected.

Effects of Heredity and Environment on Development of Personality

Before discussing the contribution of hereditary factors let us see what is meant by heredity when we talk of heredity we usually have biological heredity in mind. The term 'heredity' may also be used in another sense, for example, if a child is brought up in a particular social environment say of a tribe, the value of that tribe and the norms of that tribe are inculcated in him through other members of that social group and we call it **social heredity.** In the same way, a student in a classroom situation brings with him a specific cultural heredity also. Here our discussion will be focused on the influence of only biological heredity on individual differences. Each individual has a specific set of potentials which are developed through the environment. These potentialities and characteristics possessed by the individual are the result of his biological heredity. The influence of heredity is so strong that twins brought up in drastically different environment show very much similarity in terms of their mental abilities and other traits. This shows that even drastically different environments are not capable of overcoming hereditary influences.

Hereditary, or the genetic transmission of characteristics from parents to offspring, determine personality to a certain extent. Hereditary characteristics manifest at birth such as hair and eye colour, skin colour and body type. Hereditary also includes aptitude or the capacity to learn a skill or inclination for a particular body of knowledge. It establishes the limits of one's personality traits that can be developed. This aptitude creates the desire for a person to learn something. For instance, the son of a sports hero like a boxer superstar is expected to inherit the genes of his father. His capacity for growth in the boxing arena is immense because he is born with the ability.

Behavioural geneticists, Dr. David Reiss and colleagues from George Washington University, conducted a thorough and long-term study on the effects of genetics to a person's personality. The result of their study revealed that 'it seems that genetic influences are largely responsible for how 'adjusted' kids are : how well they do in school, how they get along with their peers, whether they engage in dangerous or delinquent behaviour'.

Effect of Environment on Personality Development

Apart from heredity, environment also effects the child development. The concept of environment needs little clarification when we say the environment of the child is not good, sometimes we mean that he is living in a locality which does not have desirable people or we mean that he is living in the rural area where he does not have access to many things which an urban environment may provide. As has rightly been said, the psychological environment consists of the sum total of the stimulation the individual receives from conception till death. This is an active concept of environment *i.e.*, the physical presence of objects does not in itself constitute environment unless the objects serve as stimuli for the individual.

The role of the prenatal environment on the development of the child is well known and has been demonstrated through various experiments. The diet a mother takes at the time of pregnancy, her mental status, glandular secretions and even the thinking process influence the development of the child. Environmentalists firmly believe that, under favourable circumstances, every individual is almost infinitely improvable.

Newman, Freeman and Holzinger conducted thorough research on nineteen pairs of identical twins reared in different environments. Initially they found that the pairs reared apart show mere differences in I.Q. But Woodworth (1941) in his analysis of the results pointed out a factor called error of measurement that is always involved in intelligence testing. When this factor was taken into account and results interpreted, Woodworth concluded that environmental differences do operate to produce I.Q. differences in persons with exactly the same hereditary potentialities. But the magnitude of these differences is not as large as those found among children whose heredity is not alike.

Environment and its Interaction with Hereditary Factors

Nature refers to what a child has inherited genetically, from the parents (*e.g.* eye colour, appearance, etc). The influence of environment on the development of the child (*e.g.* liking for a type of music) is referred to as nurture. The earlier view of child development focused either entirely on nature or nurture. Many favoured heredity, and believed that we are born with certain talents and personalities. These determine who we are and what we become.

In the other view, the focus was on the role of environment. We learn to do things for which we get rewards (or praises) and do not do things for which we are punished (including disapproval from elders). Both views contained some truth but neither is complete. To understand the development of a person, we have to study the complex interaction between nature and nurture (or heredity and environment).

Let us consider an example. A child is born with a talent for music. In the child's family, this talent for music is expressed by the child at an early age, through his activities of singing and listening to music. The parents notice the child's interest in music and expose the child to more music and give him a toy musical instrument (*e.g.* ek tara or flute). The child's interest in music grows further and his talent develops and this make the parents offer even more musical experiences (*e.g.* playing music on stage, attending music concerts etc.). This has a further positive effect on the child's talent and his desire to play music.

It is thus clear that both the child's inherited talent and environment shaped his/her development. The child had the talent for music, but this led to a change in the environment by making her parents provide more musical experiences at home. Now these experiences in the environment further developed the child's talent and motivation and made the parents introduce more musical experiences to the child. The process goes on and on like this in a form of transaction. This approach to understanding development is called a transactional model (TA).

The TA model is able to explain why brothers and sisters, though physically in the same environment, always grow up in 'different' ways. This simply means that the environment of family life is always changing in the process of adjusting to the personalities of its members. A first born child grows up with very different experiences than a middle born or youngest child. A child who displays temper tantrums (getting angry easily, without sufficient cause) has a very different experience with her parents as compared to her easy going brother.

Let us take another example to make the point more clear. Suppose you as a parent (if not today, then in the future) are facing difficulty with your argumentative 12-year-old. The TA model reminds you that you must first think about the factor which has brought your child to this point. Is it a personality trait that is troubling you? Is she stubborn (does not listen to others) all the time and is thus part of her nature? Does she resist any change in her usual routine? Does she lack the ability to talk to you about what's troubling her, and could that be upsetting her? The child represents one part of the puzzle or problem which has to be solved.

The next questions you have to ask are : What is my role in all this? Am I somehow rewarding the very behaviours? Am I trying to stop by paying too much attention to them? Am I having too much expectation from a 12-year old? Am I reminded of my younger sister with whom I had faced a similar problem, and could be causing irritation in me now? The environment which includes you forms the other-part of the picture.

Finally, you need to put the two together to obtain a full picture of what is going on and how to bring about a positive change. In which way my behaviour is affecting my child? And most importantly, what do I need to change to break this pattern of behaviour (argumentation in the child) located in its transactions with nurture? How can I better understand the forces behind my child's behaviour so as to improve my response to it?

This may sound very theoretical to some of you but it's exactly the questions which many parents are always asking themselves, even if they are not aware of it. By understanding the TA-model you will be in a better position to understand the interaction between nature and nurture which is responsible for your child's behaviour and development. This will help you in deciding which role you can play for effective development and improve the child's behaviour.

In summary according to the transactional model of development, the child changes the environment which in turn changes the child. The child's development is like a complex dance in which nature and nurture both lead, and are led.

SOCIALISATION PROCESS

As a child grows up, there is a deliberate and conscious effort made through active training to make the child learn the values and expectations of the society he or she lives in. The child has to learn to adjust and accommodate her behaviour according to the rules for appropriate behaviour in the society. Parents, teachers, elders as well as the peers (same age group children) all influence and control the behaviour of a child.

According to the Indian view, a child comes to this world with certain behavioural tendencies which carry over from previous birth. The role of the family is to bring up the child in such a way that her positive capacities are developed fully and negative tendencies are controlled. Apart from the family, there are also other influences on the child from the outside environment. The important agents of socialisation include media, day-care centers, peer group, school and religion.

Parents have the most direct effect on the socialisation of the child. They are role models for children. Their responses to child behaviour, giving approval or disapproval etc. mould the personality of child and plays a very important role in acquiring rules. In addition, parents arrange the environment of a children in different ways. They take the child outside in specific settings like museum, church, temple, mosque, hill station, sea beach. The grand parents and aunts and uncles of the child also contribute in the socialisation process. Children learn manners and skills by observing parents. During the life span of a person, at different ages, specific rituals are performed. These rituals represent the changes in the child from one stage to another. They contribute in forming the identity of the child.

The influence of the **peer group** of the child, particularly during middle childhood is very important. In the interactions with the children of the same age group, a child learns the importance of team work, sharing and trust. One of the significant effects of this is that the child learns to adjust and accommodate to the view point of the others.

The school which the child attends is another very important socializing agent. The child learns different types of social, intellectual and physical skills in school. The school provides the child with a miniature society where he or she has to learnt the right values and rules and follow them. Values such as honesty, democracy and fairness etc. are learnt in the school setting.

Now-a-days, children search and know the world through TV, magazines, books, comics, radio and films. This media influences the socialisation of the child in significant ways. A positive influence can be learning the importance of family values by watching good and informative programmes. Watching aggressive programmes and programmes based on violence can influence the child negatively.

In the present way of life, when both parents are doing jobs, very young children have to be left at day-care centers. These centers, therefore, play an important role in the socialisation of the child because the child will learn many things about appropriate behaviour in the society. For children from poor background the Aganwadis under the programme of Integrated Child Developments (ICDs) help children to learn about appropriate social behaviour and the importance of community life.

Theories of Development

Psychologists continue to study human development. They are learning more about what people are like and how they develop. Over the past century, many psychologists have provided theories that are considered practical guides. A theory is a principle or idea that is proposed, researched and generally accepted as an explanation. Developmental theories provide insights into how children grow and learn. Theories are helpful for understanding and guiding developmental processes.

Theories can be useful decision-making tools. Since a variety of theories exists, teachers need to understand these different approaches for working with children. Theories will help you understand strategies for promoting children's development. Four major theories about how children learn are important. These include theories of mid-twentieth century psychologists Erik Erikson, Jean Piaget and Lev Vygotsky. The final theorist, Howard Gardner, is a twenty first century developmental psychologist. These theories are based on observation and experiences with children.

Erikson's Psychosocial Theory

Erik Erikson proposed a theory of psychosocial development. He believed development occurs throughout the life span. His theory provided new insights into the formation of a healthy personality. It emphasizes the social and emotional aspects of growth. Children's personalities develop in response to their social environment. The same is true of their skills for social interaction.

Erikson's theory includes eight stages. At each stage, a social conflict or crisis occurs. These are not generally tragic situations; however, they require solutions that are satisfying both personally and socially. Erikson believed that each stage must be resolved before children can ascend to the next stage.

Maturity and social forces help in the resolution of the crisis or conflict. Therefore, teachers and parents play a powerful role in recognizing each stage. By providing social opportunity and support, teachers and parents can help children overcome each crisis. Following table contains the first four stages of Erikson's theory. These stages occur during the early childhood years. The paragraphs that follow give a brief overview of these early stages.

Erikson's Stages of Development During Early Childhood

Stage	Approximate Age	Psychosocial Crisis
I	Birth–18 months	Trust versus mistrust
II	18 months–3 years	Autonomy versus shame and doubt
III	3–5 years	Initiative versus guilt
IV	6–12 years	Industry versus inferiority

Note : *The first four stages of Erikson's theory concern children from birth to twelve years.*

Stage 1 : Trust Versus Mistrust

During the first eighteen months of life, children learn to trust or mistrust their environment. To develop trust, they need to have warm, consistent, predictable, and attentive care. They need caregivers who will accurately read and respond to their signals. When infants are distressed, they need to be comforted. They also need loving physical contact, nourishment, cleanliness, and warmth. Then they will develop a sense of confidence and trust that the world is safe and dependable. Mistrust will occur if an infant experiences an unpredictable world and is handled harshly.

Stage 2 : Autonomy Versus Shame and Doubt

This second stage occurs between eighteen months and three years of age. During this stage, toddlers use their new motor and mental skills. They want to be independent and do things for themselves. They are in the process of discovering their own bodies and practicing their developing locomotor (physical movement) and language skills.

The objective of this stage is to gain self-control without a loss of self-esteem. Fostering independence in children is important. At this age, toddlers start to become self-sufficient. They need to learn to choose and decide for themselves. To do this, toddlers need a loving, supportive environment. Positive opportunities for self-feeding, toileting, dressing and exploration will result in *autonomy,* or independence. On the other hand, overprotection or lack of adequate activities results in self-doubt, poor achievement, and shame.

Stage 3 : Initiative Versus Guilt

Between three and five years of age, the third stage occurs. According to Erikson, it emerges as a result of the many skills children have developed. Now children have the capacity and are ready to learn constructive ways of dealing with people and things. They are learning how to take initiative without being hurtful to others. They are also busy discovering how the world works. Children begin to realize that what they do can have an effect on the world, too. Challenged by the environment, children are constantly attempting and mastering new tasks. Aided by strong initiative, they are able to move ahead energetically and quickly forget failures. This gives them a sense of accomplishment.

Children at this stage need to develop a sense of purpose. This happens when adults direct children's urges toward acceptable social practices. If children are discouraged by criticism, feelings of incompetence are likely to emerge. This can also occur if parents demand too much control.

Stage 4 : Industry Versus Inferiority

The major crisis of this stage occurs between six and twelve years of age. At this time, children enjoy planning and carrying out projects. This helps them learn society's rules and expectations. During this stage, children gain approval by developing intellectual skills such as reading, writing, and math.

The way family, neighbours, teachers, and friends respond to children affects their future development. Realistic goals and expectations enrich children's sense of self. Children can become frustrated by criticism or discouragement, or if parents demand too much control. Feelings of incompetence and insecurity will emerge.

PIAGET'S COGNITIVE DEVELOPMENT THEORY

Jean Piaget's thinking has challenged teachers to focus on the *ways* children come to know as opposed to *what* they know. His theory of cognitive development focuses on predictable cognitive (thinking) stages. Piaget believed that thinking was different during each stage of development. His theory explained mental operations. This includes how children perceive, think, understand and learn about their world.

Piaget believed that children naturally attempt to understand what they do not know. Knowledge is gathered gradually during active involvement in real-life experience. By physically handling objects, young children discover that relationships exist between them. Terms Piaget used to describe these processes were *schemata, adaptation, assimilation* and *accommodation.* These processes occur during each stage of development.

Schemata are mental representations or concepts. As children receive new information, they are constantly creating, modifying, organizing and reorganizing schemata.

Adaptation is a term Piaget used for children mentally organizing what they preceive in their environment. When new information or experiences occur, children must adapt to include this information in their thinking. If this new information does not fit with what children already know, a state of imbalance occurs. To return to balance, adaptation occurs through either assimilation or accommodation.

Assimilation is the process of taking in new information and adding it to what the child already knows.

Accommodation is adjusting what is already known to fit the new information. This process is how people organize their thoughts and develop intellectual structures.

Piaget's stages of cognitive development are the same for all children. Most children proceed through the stages in order. Each stage builds on a previous stage. However, the age at which a child progresses through these stages is variable due to differences in maturation.

Although Piaget did not apply his theory directly to education, he did strongly influence children's early education. Many teaching strategies have evolved from his work. Caregivers and teachers now know that learning is an active process. Providing children with stimulating, hands-on activities helps them build knowledge. Piaget's theory includes four stages: sensorimotor, preoperational concrete, and formal operations. The first three stages occur during early childhood and the early school-age years. The following paragraphs describe these stages.

Piaget's Stages of Development

The **sensorimotor stage** takes place between birth and two years of age. Infants use all their senses to explore and learn. In this way, sensory experiences and motor development promote cognitive development. Babies' physical actions, such as sucking, grasping and hitting, help them learn about their surroundings. Movements are random at first. Gradually they become intentional as behaviours are repeated. Children begin to learn that objects still exist even when they are out of sight. This is known as *object permanence.* Through exploration and exposure to new experiences, new concepts are learned.

The **preoperational stage** takes place between ages two and seven. Children during this stage are very *egocentric.* This means that they assume others see the world the same way they do. Children do not yet have the ability to see others' points of view. During this time, representation skills are learned. These skills include language, symbolic play, and drawing. Children learn to use symbols and internal images, but their thinking is illogical. It is very different from that of adults. Children begin to understand that changing the physical appearance of something does not change the amount of it. They are able to recognize the difference between size and volume. For example, a ball of clay can be stretched into a long rope. Even if the physical appearance changes, the amount of the object does not change. This skill is called *conservation.* At this stage, children can also classify groups of objects and put objects in a series in order.

During the ages of seven to eleven years, **concrete operations** begin. Children develop the capacity to think systematically, but only when they can refer to actual objects and use hands-on activities. Then they begin to internalize some tasks. This means they no longer need to depend on what is seen. They become capable of reversing operations. For example, they understand that 3 + 1 is the same as 1 + 3. When real situations are presented, they are beginning to understand others' points of view.

The fourth stage, *formal operations,* takes place from eleven years of age to adulthood (the age range you are in right now). According to Piaget, young people develop the capacity to think in purely abstract ways. They no longer need concrete examples. Problem solving and reasoning are key skills developed during this stage.

VYGOTSKY'S SOCIOCULTURAL THEORY

Both Jean Piaget and Lev Vygotsky believed that children build knowledge through experiences. Piaget believed this happened through exploration with hands-on activities. Vygotsky, on the other hand, believed that children learn through social and cultural experiences. Interactions with peers and adults help children in this process. While interacting with others, children learn the customs, values, beliefs, and language of their culture. For this reason, families and teachers should provide plently of social interaction for young children.

Vygotsky believed language is an important tool for thought and plays a key role in cognitive development. He introduced the term ***private speech***, or self-talk. This refers to when children "think out loud". After learning language, children engage in this self-talk to help guide their activity and develop their thinking. Generally, self-talk continues until children reach school age.

One of Vygotsky's most important contributions was the *zone of* ***proximal development*** (ZPD). This concept presents learning as a scale. One end of the scale or "zone" includes the tasks that are within the child's current development level. The other end of the scale includes tasks too difficult for children to accomplish, even with help. In the middle are the tasks children cannot accomplish alone. These are achieved with help from another knowledgeable peer or adult. The term used for this assistance is ***scaffolding***. Just as a painter needs a structure on which to stand and point a building, scaffolding provides the structure for learning to occur. For example, a teacher could scaffold a child's learning while constructing a puzzle. The teacher might demonstrate how a piece fits or provide clues regarding colour, shape or size. The "zone" is constantly changing. In contrast to Piaget, Vygotsky believed that learning was not limited by stage or maturation. Children move forward in their cognitive development with the right social interaction and guided learning.

KOHLBERG'S THEORY OF DEVELOPMENT

According to him moral development of the child proceeds in sequential but distinctive stages. These stages are given below:

(a) **Stage-I :** In the early years of a child's life (from zero-four years) the physical consequences of an action determines its goodness or badness. If fire burns the child, he does not touch it. The child is ego-centric and standards of morality are external here.

(b) **Stage-II :** The child gives importance to his own point of view, (his self) and is able to take account of other's roles insofar as he can use them in his own way. This is a period of make belief. Right action is what which satisfies the needs of the child. The role of others is also important in the sense that a child does only what can bring approval of others. Thus, only that behaviour is moral which can satisfy not only self needs of the child but it must please others also.

(c) **Stage-III :** At this stage the child adopts the view pints of others on the basis of their consequences. He does not question the views of others. The child considers only that thing as right which are considered as right by others. Thus, the child is totally conformist to the standard of the society.

(d) **Stage-IV:** At this stage, the child is able to make any moral decision on his own without caring for the thinking of others. Though he considers laws and regulations set by the society as the essence of morality, yet he develops his own principles of morality on various occasions. Thus, he is a non-conformist to the norms of the society to a great extent.

(e) **Stage-V :** Standards and norms are more internalized here. The adolescents examine various view points prepared by different societies and recognize them. They think that the laws prepared by their own society are correct. Other societies may have good moral principles that must be adopted after careful appraisal.

(f) **Stage-VI :** This is the last stage of moral development according to Kohlberg. Here the universality of the view points of the individual is seen. He formulates his own universal moral principles which he thinks that all societies should adhere to it. True understanding of right and wrong is developed at this stage.

Gardner's Multiple Intelligences Theory

Howard Gardner has helped teachers rethink how they work with young children. Traditional intelligence tests mainly focus on language and math/logic skills. In contrast, Gardner's theory of **multiple intelligences** emphasizes that there are different kinds of intelligences used by the human brain. Gardner believes intelligence is the result of complex interactions between children's heredity and experiences. This theory focuses on how cultures shape human potential.

Gardner claims that children learn and express themselves in many different ways. In the process, they are using several types of intelligence. Each intelligence functions separately, but all are closely linked. According to Gardner, a potential intelligence will not develop unless it is nurtured. Learning can best be achieved by using a child's strongest intelligence. Gardner claims, however, that all children need opportunities to develop all areas of intelligence.

The multiple intelligence theory allows teachers to see the positive attributes of all children. Teachers also view Gardner's theory as a meaningful guide for making curriculum decisions. It gives them a chance to assess children's learning strengths. From this data, teachers can plan a wide variety of learning experiences. Following chart lists Gardner's eight intelligences. The paragraphs that follow explain these intelligences in detail.

(i) Bodily-Kinesthetic Intelligence

Bodily-kinesthetic intelligence involves the ability to control body movements. This includes using parts of the body to solve problems, handle objects, and express emotions. People with this type of intelligence typically enjoy sports, dance or creative drama. They are able to express themselves with their entire bodies. Children will benefit from creative-movement experiences and role-playing.

Children with this type of intelligence process knowledge through sensation. They enjoy touch and creating with their hands. Therefore, daily opportunities should be provided for hands-on activities. Clay, sand, dough, feely boxes and other sensory activities help them develop fine-motor skills. Movement is also needed for gross-motor skills and coordination. It is important for caregivers and teachers to provide activities involving physical challenges. These may include playing kickball, jumping rope, and moving to music.

(ii) Musical-Rhythmic Intelligence

Musical-rhythmic intelligence involve the ability to recognize musical patterns. It also includes the ability to produce and appreciate music. Since music evokes emotion, this is one of the earliest intelligences to emerge. Composers and musicians are examples of people with this type of intelligence.

Children with this type of intelligence love listening to music. They are drawn to the art of sound and appreciate all forms of musical expression. They have a well-developed auditory sense and can discriminate tone, pitch and rhythmic patterns. As a result, they often cannot get songs out of their minds. You will hear them repeatedly singing or humming. This helps them understand concepts and remember information.

Activities to support musical intelligence can be included throughout the day. Offer opportunities for sound exploration through listening and singing. Use songs for directions and moving children from one activity to another. Play background music during self-selected play. Include songs during large and small group activities. Record the children creating their own music while singing or chanting. Explore rhythm by moving to recorded music. Use different instruments and instruments from other cultures to add variety.

(iii) Logical-Mathematical Intelligence

Logical-mathematical intelligence is more than just the ability to use math. It is the ability to use logic and reason to solve problems. Math experts have this form of intelligence. Scientists and composers may also have it. This intelligence involves the ability to explore categories, patterns and other relationships. It includes applying the principle of cause and effect. It also involves the skill to make predictions about patterns.

Children with this type of intelligence take pleasure in finding patterns and relationships. They enjoy discovering similarities and differences. Manipulatives for matching, measuring, and counting should be provided. Blocks can encourage the children's problem-solving and reasoning skills. Storybooks that show a sequence of events hold appeal for this type of intelligence. Water and sand activities with different-size containers help teach the concept of volume.

(iv) Verbal-Linguistic Intelligence

Verbal-linguistic intelligence involves the ability to use language for expression. People with this type of intelligence have well-developed language skills. They demonstrate sensitivity to the meaning, sound and rhythm of words. Lawyers, poets, public speakers and language translators have this type of intelligence.

Young children with this intelligence learn best by talking, listening, reading and writing. These children quickly learn the words to new stories, songs and finger plays. They enjoy talking to other people and are able to speak in an interesting and engaging manner. They are also able to learn a second language with ease.

This intelligence can be nurtured by environments rich with language opportunities. Children learn language in setting where it is used. Teachers need to follow the children's interests. They can then use these interests to engage children in meaningful conversations. Children's storybooks, songs, poetry, chants, and rhymes can serve as means for learning new vocabulary words. Listening to and telling stories can also promote language development.

(v) Interpersonal Intelligence

People with *interpersonal intelligence* display excellent communication and social skills. These people have a gift for understanding the feelings, behaviours, moods and motives of others. They make friends easily. They use language to develop trust and bonds with others. They are also skilled in supporting others and empathizing with them. These skills are important for teachers, politicians, salespeople and people working in the service industry.

These skills are nurtured in young children when caring behaviours are modeled for them. Teachers should keep this in mind. They can share experiences and provide the children with chances for verbal interaction. Books focusing on emotions can be acted out.

(vi) Intrapersonal Intelligence

Intrapersonal intelligence is the ability to understand the inner self. This is also known as *self-awareness.* It involves knowing your skills, limits, and feelings. It includes understanding your desires and motives. The ability to organize groups of people is part of this strength. Communicating needs clearly is another aspect. Psychologists, social workers, religious leaders, and counsellors are examples of people with this type of intelligence.

How can you foster this type of intelligence? In the classroom, share emotions that all children experience. These include joy, sadness, regret and disappointment. Classroom examples should be shared as well as storybooks that contain emotional concepts.

(vii) Visual-Spatial Intelligence

Visual-spatial intelligence allows people to use their vision to develop mental images. People who have this type of intelligence show a preference for pictures and images. Photographers and artists are some examples. Architects, engineers, and surgeons also need this ability. They use it to see the relationship of objects in space.

Teachers can foster this intelligence by providing children with unstructured materials. Building blocks and puzzles strengthen this type of intelligence, 4-18. Make and use visual aids wherever possible. For example, classroom schedules, recipes, and stories can all be displayed on charts. Shelving units can be labelled with pictures cut from equipment catalogs.

(viii) Naturalistic Intelligence

Naturalistic intelligence is developed from the need to survive. This is the ability to classify objects in nature such as animals and plants. It depends on a type of pattern recognition. This strength also includes the ability to distinguish among types and brands of objects. Sailors, gardeners, chefs, and farmers are people who have this intelligence.

To build on this intelligence, provide cooking activities and nature walks. These help develop use of the senses to gather information. Planting and growing a garden helps the children observe cycles. Rocks, seashells, flowers, leaves, seeds, and coins can also be collected. In the classroom, they can be sorted and classified. Post picture collections and share books about natural events.

CONCEPTS OF CHILD-CENTERED AND PROGRESSIVE EDUCATION

Child-Centered Education

Child-centered education is the idea that the needs and desires of the child should take precedence in structuring the learning day. The whole idea is that learning should be fun and engaging for the child, and is most likely to be that way if the child is incharge of the learning experience, rather than the adult parent or teacher.

Child-centered education is most characterised by learning 'centers' in a classroom that promote hands-on, active participation by the child. There may be magnifying glasses and bug slides in the science center, books and puppets that could be used to re-tell the stories in the language arts center, and wood blocks and shapes in the math center. The children are free to manipulate the objects in these centers. It is the process, the activity, the experience, that is valuable, not the facts, ideas, concepts or skills.

It is a relatively new approach to education. For centuries past, adults defined what education should be and children were the ones who did the adjusting. Education was considered work, not play.

Then came the softening influences of child psychologist Jean-Jacques Rousseau, as well as Dr. Marria Montessori, John Dewey, Jean Piaget and Lev Vygotsky, who all contended that a child's self-esteem and self-concept should be built up in order to create a better learner. Soon, the colleges of education were promoting child-centered education instead of instructionally centered education.

Role of Learner in Child-Centered Education

Learners are active as opposed to passive recipients of knowledge. Learners may assume a decision-making role in the classroom. Learners often decide what is to be learned, through which activities and at what pace. Learners can also produce materials and provide activities for the classroom.

Role of Teacher in Child-Centered Education

To put this approach into practice, teachers need to help students set achievable goals; they encourage students to assess themselves and their peers; help them to work co-operatively in groups and ensure that they know how to make use of all the available resources for learning.

Progressive Education

During most of the twentieth century, the term 'progressive education' has been used to describe ideas and practices that aim to make schools more effective agencies of a democratic society. Although there are numerous differences of style and emphasis among progressive educators, they share the conviction that democracy means active participation by all citizens in social, political and economic decisions that will affect their lives. The education of engaged citizens, according to this perspective, involves two essential elements: (1) respect for diversity, meaning that each individual should be recognised for his or her own abilities, interests, ideas, needs, and cultural identity, and (2) the development of critical, socially engaged intelligence, which enables individuais to understand and participate effectively in the affairs of their community in a collaborative effort to achieve a common good. These elements of progressive education have been termed 'child-centered' and 'social reconstruction' approaches, and while in extreme forms they have sometimes been separated, in the thought of John Dewey and other major theorists they are seen as being necessarily related to each other.

The term 'progressive' arose from a period (roughly 1890–1920) during which many Americans took a more careful look at the political and social effects of vast concentrations of corporate power and private wealth. Dewey, in particular, saw that with the decline of local community life and small scale enterprise, young people were losing valuable opportunities to learn the arts of democratic participation, and he concluded that education would need to make up for this loss. In his Laboratory School at the University of Chicago, where he worked between 1896 and 1904, Dewey tested ideas he shared with leading school reformers such as Francis W. Parker and Ella Flagg Young. Between 1899 and 1916 he circulated his ideas in works such as The School and Society, The Child and the Curriculum, Schools of Tomorrow, and Democracy and Education, and through numerous lectures and articles. During these years other experimental schools were established around the country, and in 1919 the Progressive Education Association was founded, aiming at "reforming the entire school system of America".

Therefore, progressive education is a reaction against the traditional style of teaching which teaches facts largely at the expense of understanding what is being taught. According to **John French,** "The progressive school teaches the child to think for himself instead of passively accepting stereotyped ideas. It keeps always in mind that each child is different from every other, and that what makes an educated person useful in his particular walk of life, what makes him interesting, what makes him an individual, is not his resemblance to other people, but his differences".

Philosophies and Practices of Progressive Education

1. Curriculum is strongly influenced by what the children are interested in, and is child-centered rather than adult driven.
2. Learning is 'hands-on', experiential and the emphasis is on process rather than product children are 'learning to learn'.
3. Children learn through integrated, theme-based units or inquiry projects and the 'theme' often emerges from the children.
4. Assessment is authentic and holistic. Children are well known by their teachers and peers.

There are no tests or letter grades. Instead, narrative reports are written about children that cover all aspects of their development: social, emotional, personal, physical and intellectual level.

5. Classes are usually of mixed ages and no ability grouping is used. Children are able to work at their own pace and cross-age friendships are encouraged.
6. Progressive education practices a developmental approach which holds that each child is a unique being unfolding and developing at their own pace according to a specific pattern. At each stage of development there are things that can be learned and things that should not be learned. Respecting a child's development is central to progressive education.

Types of Progressive Education

1. **Humanistic :** The humanistic form of progressive education focuses on the humanities, arts and social sciences. Its emphasis is on the individual child and not the curriculum. This type of progressivism aims to build a well-rounded individual with highly developed critical thinking and reasoning skills. The children learn think for themselves instead of accepting everything teachers tell them. Social development and interaction among the students are seen as valuable learning techniques.
2. **Constructivism :** Constructivism is a type of child-centered progressivism. It focuses on the child's creativity and learning abilities. Teachers should build the curriculum around the requirements and interests of the child. It maintains that education should consider children's developmental stages. Swiss psychologist **Jean Piaget** influenced the theories of constructivist education. Experiential learning, or learning by doing, allows students to construct their own knowledge.
3. **Montessori :** Italian doctor Marria Montessori started the Montessori progressive educational system. She developed her teaching theories by clinical observation and analysis of how children learn. Her method of education focused on how children naturally learn, all by themselves, without the help of adults. Maria Montessori concluded that children teach themselves, and it's the job of teachers to facilitate this process, not dominate it. Montessori teachers provide a sensory-rich environment and hands-on activities.

CRITICAL PERSPECTIVE OF THE CONSTRUCT OF INTELLIGENCE

Introduction

The most important variable that affects schooling or performance on a job is intelligence. Psychologists have interpreted the term intelligence in different ways and there is no consensus among them on the term even so far. In psychology this term is treated as a construct whose structure is different in different individuals.

The vagueness of the term arises due to the fact that intelligence is not a concrete material. It is rather abstraction from the behaviour of the individual which is indirectly inferred and elaborated as an adjective.

The dictionary meaning of term "intelligence" is the capacity to acquire and apply knowledge. **Boring** defines intelligence as intelligence is what an intelligence test measures.

Definitions of Intelligence

Several psychologists have classified and defined intelligence in several ways. Some of them are given below:

1. Vernon's Classification of Intelligence

(a) *Biological Approach:* Man is an organism among millions living on earth. Environment works as a foe for him. Intelligence is the capacity to adapt to the environment or new situations of life at every moment.

This definition of intelligence can be criticized on the ground that there have been many intelligent and renowned persons who were ill adapted to their social and physical environment. Besides, if we want to study individual differences in a society, this definition serves no practical purpose.

(b) *Psychological Approach :* According to psychologists intelligence is the relative effects of heredity and environment both. An English psychologist, **C. Burt** defined intelligence as the innate general cognitive ability.

In support of psychological definitions of intelligence **Hebb** and **R.B. Catell** distinguished two kinds of intelligence. The first is intelligence "A" which is Fluid intelligence and which is related to genetic potentialities or innate qualities of the individual's nervous system. Second is intelligence "B" which is crystalised "intelligence" and which is related to experiences, learning and environmental factors. These two types of intelligence in normal circumstances so much overlap on each other that they are practically indistinguishable.

(c) *Operational Approach :* These definitions help us to understand the concept of intelligence in clear and definite terms. In this approach scientific terms are first of all defined operationally and then observations are conducted with reference to these terms. For example, in order to determine a child's IQ, we first administer a test of a specific kind. Then we observe his performance on the test and finally draw certain conclusions in the context of the pre-determined objectives.

2. Freeman's Classification

(a) *Ability of adjustment :* An individual is intelligent to the extent to which he is able to adjust to new situations and problems of life. The more a person is intelligent, the more he is able to adapt to his environment in antagonistic conditions. The person who is low in intelligence has less capacity to adjust to the new situations of life.

(b) *Ability of learning :* Learning ability is also an index of intelligence. The more a person is intelligent, the more he will be able to learn new things.

(c) *Ability to carry on abstract thinking :* This category of definitions of intelligence is related to the effective use of concepts and symbols in dealing with situations and solving the problems through the use of verbal and numerical symbols. According to **Terman**, an individual is intelligent to the extent he is able to carry on abstract thinking.

3. E.L. Thorndike's Classification

(a) *Concrete intelligence :* The intellectual ability in relation to concrete materials is called concrete intelligence. It is the ability of a person to comprehend the actual situations and react to them adequately. This kind of intelligence is measured by using performance tests or picture tests in which the subject manipulates the concrete materials.

(b) *Abstract intelligence :* It is the ability to respond to words, letters, numbers or symbols. This type of intelligence is required in all academic activities in schools or outside the schools. The highest level of abstract intelligence is manifested in the thoughts of philosophers or in the inventions of scientists and mathematicians.

(c) *Social intelligence :* It is the ability of an individual to react to social situations of life. It is the ability to understand others and to react to them in such a manner that they may not feel unjust attitude regarding them.

4. Intelligence as a Global Capacity

A comprehensive definitions of intelligence : **Stoddard** (1943) and **Wechsler** (1944) have defined intelligence in the following words :

"Intelligence is the aggregate or the global capacity of the individual to act purposefully, to think rationally and to deal with the environment effectively".

Stoddard further elaborated that intelligence is the capacity of a person to undertake such activities which are: (*i*) difficult (*ii*) complex (*iii*) abstract (*iv*) economical (*v*) goal directed (*vi*) valuable from social view points (*vii*) original. These activities demand concentration of energy and a resistance to emotional forces.

Characteristics of Intelligence

From the above definitions of intelligence, we can draw the following characteristics of intelligence:

(*i*) Intelligence is the composite of several intellectual skills, such as thinking, doing, reasoning, dealing, learning etc.

(*ii*) Intelligence is displayed by the behaviour of the individual as a whole and intelligent behaviour is always goal directed.

(*iii*) Intelligence is the ability to adjust to abnormal and challenging situations of life.

(*iv*) Intelligence is not related to ordinary tasks of life. It is always related to extra ordinary manipulation.

(*v*) Wechsler has included the concepts of drive and incentive which are implied in his statement. "To act purposefully" and "to deal effectively". But many psychologists are of the view that drive and incentive are non-intellectual traits of personality and if they are included in a test of mental ability, more confusions will be created thereof.

(*vi*) There are seven fundamental elements of intelligence according to **Stoddard.** Intelligent person can undertake difficult and abstract tasks with ease. He can manipulate and deal the abstract ideas and concepts efficiently. Similarly, economy refers to the rate at which a mental task is done or a problem is solved. If "A" solves a problem sooner than 'B' then 'A' will be considered more intelligent than 'B'. The term social value indicates whether a mental task performed by a person is in accordance with the socially desirable and acceptable norms or not. The last term original refers to a person's, ability to discover something new and different, *i.e.*, this term is directly related to creative potential of a person. Discovery of some new facts and principles and inventions of new concrete materials by the scientists are few examples of originality.

Stoddard's definition of intelligence has been criticized on two grounds :

(a) It includes social values in intelligence, *i.e.*, intelligent task must be socially desirable. Psychologists criticize this point by saying that social value is a subjective phenomenon, *i.e.*, what is desirable for me, may not be necessarily desirable for others. So, there is no scope of subjectivity in an objective intelligence test.

(b) He has included two conditions of intelligent behaviour in his definition. First is concentration of energy and second is resistance to emotional forces. Psychologists say that these elements are non-intellectual traits and hence they should not be included in mental abilities at any cost.

Theories of Intelligence

1. Faculty theory of intelligence:

This is the oldest theory of intelligence given during the period of pre-experimental psychology. According to this theory mind is made up of different faculties like reasoning, logic, memory, imagination and discrimination. These faculties are independent of each other and can be developed by rigorous mental exercises of the difficult subject-matter.

This theory does not take the hereditary factors of intelligence into account and thus this theory was discarded by the later psychologists who believed that we can never improve the intellectual capacity of a person if he is mentally slow by birth.

2. Unifactor theory:

According to Alfred Binet (1916) intelligence is a general intellectual ability which is made up of several discrete abilities. These abilities include

(i) to reason well with abstract material

(ii) to comprehend well

(iii) to have a clear direction of thoughts

(iv) to relate thinking with the attainment of a desirable end and

(v) to be self-critical.

All these abilities combined together is called general mental ability. Thus, intelligence is a single but complex mental process which can be measured by different kinds of materials designed for the purpose.

3. Two factors theory:

This theory was developed by an English psychologist, **Charles Spearman** in 1904. According to him, intellectual abilities consist of two factors, general ability known as 'G' factors and specific abilities known as 'S' factors.

Characteristics of G factors

(i) It is universal inborn ability.

(ii) It is general mental energy.

(iii) It is constant, *i.e.*, it remains the same in all the individuals and does not change with time.

(iv) The amount of G differs from person to person depending on his genes.

(v) It is used in every life activity.

(vi) Greater the amount of G in an individual, larger is the chance of his success in life.

Characteristics of 'S' factors

(i) It is learnt and hence acquired in the environment.

(ii) It varies from activity to activity in the same individual.

(iii) The amount of S also differs from person to person due to his accessibility to learning situations.

(iv) 'S' factors are related to the specific activity. A low correlation between two or more functions or activities indicates the presence of 'S' factor involved in the activity. A person can be expert only in one or few activities because of the specific factors involved in the activity.

According to Spearman, out of these two factors 'G' factor is more important and thus it is an important measure of intelligence. So, any intelligence test should measure only 'G' factor because it provides most important basis of predicting a person's behaviour in different situations. Raven's Progressive Matrices and Catell's Culture Fair Test both measure 'G' factor.

Spearman has explained his theory with the help of a tetrad equation which is given below :

$$rap \times rbq - raq \times rbp = 0$$

Here,

a = opposites
b = discrimination
p = completion
q = cancellation

Thus, rap means correlation between opposites and completions, rbq means correlation between cancellation and discrimination, raq means correlation between opposite and cancellation and rbp means correlation between discrimination and completion. This theory can also be explained with the help of a diagram given below :

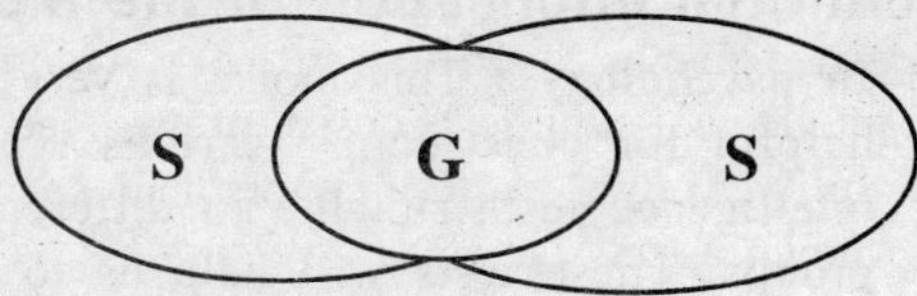

4. Multi-factors theory :

This theory was developed by an American psychologist, **E.L. Thorndike.** He opposed the theory of general intelligence by saying that there are specific stimuli and specific mental responses. Intelligence is nothing more than a potential specific connections between these stimuli and responses. Differences of intelligence among people are due to the different number of such connections in the neurological system. This theory is also called **atomistic theory** of intelligence. There are **four attributes of intelligence** according to him:

(a) *Level :* It refers to the difficulty of a task that can be removed by using intelligence. If different tasks are arranged in increasing difficulty order, then the height that a person can attain determines his level of intelligence. It is a kind of power test.

(b) *Range :* It refers to the number of tasks of the same difficulty value that a person can do in a certain period of time. Theoretically, an individual possessing a certain level of intelligence should be able to solve the whole range of tasks at a given level. It is a kind of speed test.

Range and level can not be completely isolated from each other. We can not measure range without altitude (level) and vice versa.

(c) *Area :* It refers to the total numbers of situations at each level to which the individual is able to respond. Area is the summation of all ranges at each level of intelligence. Area = Level × Range.

(d) *Speed :* It refers to the rapidity with which an individual can respond to a test items. Speed and level are positively correlated. It is different from range in the sense that no specific time is given here to complete a task.

Every intelligence test should consist of these four attributes.

5. Group factor structure of intelligence (PMA Test) :

This theory was developed by **L.L. Thurstone.** According to him, intelligence is not an expression of general factor but a combination of group of traits. They are intermediate factors, *i.e.*, they are not so universal as 'G' factor and they are not so specific as 'S' factor. This primary group of factors give the common mental abilities, a functional cohesiveness and then constitute a group. Another group of common mental abilities is said to have another primary factor and so on. In this way, there are a number of groups of mental abilities each of which has its own primary factors. On the basis of factor analysis of these groups, Thurstone identified the following seven group factors which are termed as primary mental abilities (PMA).

1. Number factor (N) : It is the ability to do numerical calculations rapidly and accurately.
2. Verbal factor (V) : They are related to the operations involving verbal comprehension.
3. Space factor (S) : It is related to the tasks in which subject manipulates an object imaginary in space.
4. Word fluency factor (W) : It is involved to the situation when the subject is asked to think of isolated words at a fast rate.
5. Reasoning factors (R) : It is used in those tasks that require the subject to discover a rule or principles involved in series or groups of letters.
6. Rote memory (M) : It is the ability to memorize a fact quickly.
7. Perceptual speed (P) : It is the ability to note perceptual (visual) details rapidly.

The point to be noted here is that these seven abilities are significantly correlated with each other.

6. Structure of intelligence (SI) model :

This model was given by **J.P. Guilford** in 1966 in the University of California on the basis of factor analysis of many tests. According to him human mind is composed of at least three dimensions—operations, contents and products, and each dimension of intellect is sufficiently distinct which can be detected by factor analysis. These three dimensions of mind are given below:

(A) **Operations :** Operations can be divided into five major groups of intellectual abilities.

- **Cognition :** It includes discovery, recognition of informations and new understanding of the facts.
- **Memory :** It is the ability to recognize or recall previously learnt material.
- **Divergent thinking :** This operation is closely associated with creative potential.

It refers to the ability to search out and think in a novel out of track way.

- **Convergent thinking :** It refers to the generation of information from given information and drawing conclusion from the given facts.
- **Evaluation :** It is the ability to make judgement on the basis of merits and demerits of a phenomenon. Here, value judgement on knowledge and thoughts is placed after critically examining them.

(B) Contents : Five kinds of contents are involved here. Operations are performed on these contents.

- **Figural content :** It is the concrete material perceived through the senses. Visual materials have three properties, size, form and colour.
- **Auditory content :** It includes nature and characteristics of sound perceived.
- **Symbolic content :** It includes letters, digits and other conventional signs usually organised in general pattern.
- **Semantic content :** It refers to those verbal meanings, ideas and concepts for which no examples are necessary.
- **Behavioural content :** It includes knowledge regarding other persons.

(C) Products : When five operations are applied to five types of contents, six kinds of products are made.

- **Units :** It refers to the production of a single word, definition or isolated bits of informations.
- **Classes :** It refers to the production of a concept.
- **Relations :** It refers to the production of any form of relationship, such as, analogy, opposite or similar ones.
- **System :** It refers to the production of internally consistent set of classification of various forms.
- **Transformation :** It refers to the production of changes in meaning, organisation or some other arrangement.
- **Implication :** It refers to the production of such information which is beyond the data given.

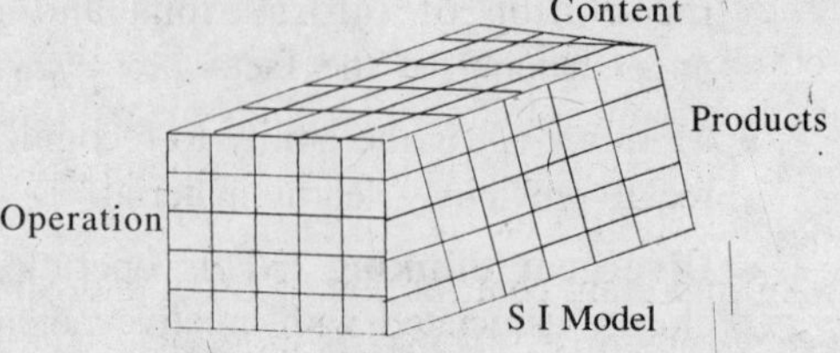

S I Model

On the basis of the model given above it can be stated that there are $5 \times 5 \times 6 = 150$ factors involved in intelligent acts.

Educational Implication of the Model

(a) In psychology : This model is very much helpful for constructing various types of intelligence tests suitable to different age groups. These tests will help us to study individual differences in the society. This model is taxonomic in nature and has discovered many abilities which were not known before. If test maker has included items representing contents and operations, he can see whether products are same or different. Conversely, if products are shown by the subject through the test, the test maker can find out the content and operation and match them with the items given in the test.

(b) In vocational testing : This model shows that there are 150 intellectual abilities. This model predicts five kinds of mental abilities classified as content. This means that different kinds of test items are needed in vocational testing. Six types of products are also tested on the basis of items representing the products. For example, if a person is able to deal with items of figural contents, he can deal with machines, operators, engineers etc. and any or all of the six types of products can be made by him, such as, he can define a machine or any operator. He can give clear concept about how a machine is operated and so on.

(c) In the field of education : Conventionally, learner was considered to be a kind of stimulus response device. Once the stimulus is given to him, he will respond but the new conception of the learner in the light of SI model is that of electronic computer which not only stores information but uses that information to generate new information either by divergent or convergent thinking.

Thus, this model gives the idea that learning is not merely the association of informations but it is the discovery of information as well. Model suggests that in order to understand human learning and higher mental processes of thinking, some drastic modifications are to be made in our theory of curriculum construction and pedagogy of instruction.

Similarly, education is no longer considered to be the training of mind. Now, main emphasis on education is given to the learning of specific skills and modification of behaviour and all these materials are not taught merely for the purpose of training the mind of humans.

7. Two Level Process Theory of Intelligence :

This theory was developed by **Jensen** in 1968. According to him intelligence is a combination of two levels of processes. One is associative intelligence and the other is abstract intelligence. Associative intelligence includes those kinds of tests that depend upon memory and simple verbal association. Abstract intelligence includes those factors as concept learning, thinking, problem solving skills, multiple discrimination, principle learning etc.

8. Burt and Vernon's hierarchy theory :

Burt (1940) separated four factors of intelligence by using statistical techniques :

- General factors (common to all traits)
- Group factors (common to some of the traits)
- Specific factors (limited to few traits)
- Error factors (limited to a particular trait when it is measured)

When human mind is put at the top, there will be 5 level hierarchical model of intelligence where general factors will come next to intelligence and error factors will come in the last.

Vernon, on the other hand, suggested that intelligence tests measure an overall factor G as well as two other mental abilities. First are related to verbal, numerical and educational. Second are related to practical, mechanical, spatial and physical. These two major factors can be divided into minor group factors. These minor factors can further be divided into various specific factors and so on.

MEASUREMENT OF INTELLIGENCE

Historical development of mental testing can be divided into three periods for the purpose of convenience.

(A) Pre-Binet Period :

In the 19th century, there was a good deal of interest in the field of psychophysics in which attempts were made to develop general rule of sensory judgement. The functioning of sensory reactions of the typical individuals is actually studied in psycho-physics. Method of limits procedure was used here to measure the extent to which people were able to differentiate between stimuli. But the limitation of these experiments was that accurate generalization of the result was not possible.

Francis Galton was the first psychologist who took interest in studying whether individual characteristics are acquired or inherited. For this purpose, he studied the lives of prominent English men and in his book "Hereditary Genius" he demonstrated that personal characteristics, (mental and physical) of men are inherited. He developed a series of tests to measure these characteristics. It was the starting point of mental measurement.

The first laboratory of experimental psychology was established by **Wundt** in 1879 in Leiping. He employed two methods to test vision, hearing, reaction time and psychosomatic problems—*(i)* psycho-physical method *(ii)* Introspection method. He also developed mental tests which could measure the keenness of vision and hearing, muscular strength, reaction time and other sensory motor functions of body.

Many of **Galton's** ideas were brought to USA by an American psychologist **J.M. Catell.** Like **Galton** he also believed that intellectual functions can best be measured by the reaction time and sensory discrimination tests.

In the last quarter of the 19th century, many psychological laboratories came into existence and studies of individual differences in mental abilities started.

The word "**Mental Test**" was first used by Catell in 1890 but his tests were actually tests of sensory discrimination, speed of motor responses and the like.

Thus, upto this period mental ability was identified as sensory acuity of an individual. The correlation between mental abilities and academic achievements was not known at the time.

Drawbacks of this period:

- Psychologists were unable to identify and define the nature of intelligence. Keenness of sensory motor reactions were related to intelligence.
- They were unable to measure the complex functions of the body.
- Intelligence tests developed during this period were measuring other than intelligence.

(B) Binet Period :

An important incident led the people to think about mental measurement during this period. In the beginning of the 20th century in France, a large number of students failed in the examination. For this teachers and students blamed each other. Seeing this, superintendent of public instruction appointed a committee to device some techniques to screen out slow learners in the schools. Binet and Simon were among members of the committee. They developed a variety of paper pencil tests in their psychological laboratory established in 1889, to administer them on children of different ages. Through these tests Binet tried to measure more complex mental functions such as power of judgement and reasoning, memory, arithmetic ability, etc.

An important contribution of Binet and Simon is that they categorised their tests in terms of age levels by administering their test items to children of different ages. In this way, an age scale of intelligence was also developed. For example, if an item was correctly answered by majority of seven years old children but only few six years old children could respond it correctly, then this item was reserved for seven years old children. In this way, Binet and Simon developed separate tests for different ages.

Similarly, if an item suited to eight years old child was correctly answered by a child of 6 years and if the same trend was shown by the six years old child in most of the cases of a test, then the mental age of the child was considered to be eight years not six years, though his chronological age is six years only. Thus, the concept of mental age was also introduced by Binet and Simon for the first time in the history of mental testing and with the help of this concept we could assess the intellectual ability of a person. Some of the tests developed during this period are given below:

Binet-Simon Scale

The first scale of Binet-Simon was published in 1905. This scale consisted of 30 items arranged in increasing order of difficulty. This scale was a crude measure of intelligence of school going children.

In order to remove some of its defects they revised their scale in 1908. It was the first age based scale and it created a lot of interest among the psychologists across the world. The items in the tests were grouped according to the appropriate age levels from 3 to 13 years.

Some items for three years age

- Point to your nose, eyes and mouth.
- Repeat two digits 3, 5.
- Repeat sentences of six syllables.
- Enumerate objects in a picture.
- Give family names.

Some items of eight years age

- Read a passage and remember two lines.
- Add up the value of five coins.
- Name four colours.
- Count reverse from 20 to zero.
- Give differences between two objects.

1908 revision of Binet-Simon Scale was adopted by many psychologists of America, Switzerland and Germany and many suggestions were given by them for the improvement of the scale. Binet-Simon accepted their suggestions and revised their scale again in 1911.

Some sample items of 1911 scale are given below:

(A) Age = 8 years

- Gives difference between two objects.
- Counts reverse from 20 to zero.
- Points out omissions from unfinished pictures.
- Tells the dates correctly.
- Repeats the digits.

(B) Age = 10 years

- Arranges five blocks in order of increasing weights.
- Reproduces two geometric designs by using memory.
- Criticizes absurd statements.
- Comprehends and answers difficult questions.
- Uses three given words in two sentences.

Main Features of Binet-Simon Scale

(i) They are really scales, *i.e.*, items of the tests are arranged in the increasing difficulty order. Easiest items are put in the beginning and the most difficult item is put in the last. Thus, these scales measure the level or aptitude of an examinee and not their speed.

(ii) These tests measure the general abilities of intelligence instead of specific abilities.

(iii) They can also measure the mental growth of the subject because they are arranged according to different ages from 3 to 14 years.

(iv) They are administered on subjects individually.

(v) Their system of scoring is tied to age norms. A child's performance on the scale will be compared to that of children of his own age.

L.M. Terman's revision of Binet–Simon Scale: L.M. Terman of **Stanford** University revised this scale in 1916 to adapt to American situations. He introduced one new concept which was intelligence Quotient (IQ) in his revision. His scale consisted of 90 items ranging from 3 to 14 years of age. Some items of this scale are given below:

Age = 7 years

- Knows number of fingers on both hands.
- Describes pictures.
- Repeats five digits.
- Gives differences between paired objects.
- Ties a bowknot.

1937 Revision of Binet-Simon Scale : Terman along with his associate Merill revised 1916 scale again in 1937. This revision had two equivalent forms L and M. The number of items in the test was raised to 129 in each L M. forms. A new change was also introduced in the test which was the calculation of chronological age. Upto 13 years CA was taken to be as original but after 13 years CA was computed in the following manner.

At 14 years = 13 yrs+2/3 of 14th year = 13 2/3 years.

At 15 years = 13+2/3 of 2 years = 14 1/3 years.

At 16 years = 13+2/3 of 3 years = 15 years.

Besides, 16 years was taken to be the last age for calculation of IQ. After that, CA was taken to be constant.

LM form revision of 1960 : Binet-Simon scale was last revised in 1960 in which items of both L and M forms were included in the scale. This revision has a range of 2 years of mental age scores to 22 years and 11 months of mental age score. This form of the test measures abilities from 7 categories namely, language, memory, reasoning, social intelligence, conceptual phenomenon, numerical, reasoning and visual motor. Test items are in the form of words, objects and pictures and the responses given by the examinees are in the form of drawing, calculating, writing and speaking. Administration of the test requires one full hour. In this revision intelligence is expressed in terms of standard scores of the deviation IQ.

Wechsler Scale : This scale may be considered an improvement over Binet-Simon scale as it can measure the intelligence of adults very effectively. David Wechsler developed this scale in 1939. This scale was developed in two equivalent forms, each form consisted of ten subtests of which five tests were verbal and five were non-verbal or performance type. This scale was revised in 1955 and was renamed as Wechsler Adult Intelligence Scale (WAIS). It comprised of 11 sub tests of which six were verbal and five were non-verbal. This scale is used on persons above 16 years of age upto 64 and administration time of the scale is one hour. The detail of these 11 subtests are given below:

(a) Verbal subtests :

1. *Information* : 29 questions are given here to test the recall of knowledge concerning wide varieties of information.
2. *Comprehension* : 14 questions are given here to test understanding of knowledge concerning a particular subject or event.
3. *Arithmetic* : 14 questions are given here to test numerical ability. These questions are solved orally without using paper and pencil at all.
4. *Similarity* : 13 questions are given here to measure abstract verbal reasoning. Examinees are required here to compare two objects and find out the relationship between them.
5. *Digit span* : Memory for digits are measured here. In the first half, the examinee is asked to repeat in the same order, three to nine digits presented in the forward directions and in the second half, the digits are repeated in a backward direction.
6. *Vocabulary* : 40 words of increasing difficulty value are presented before the examinees here and they are asked to tell the meaning of these words.

(b) Non-verbal or performance subtests:

1. *Digit symbol* : Nine digits each with different digit symbols are given to the examinees here and they are asked to give the right code for each digits or symbols.
2. *Picture completion* : This subtest measures the ability of the examinees to analyse the parts from the whole. Examinees are given 21 cards containing incomplete pictures and they are asked to fill the missing part of each picture.
3. *Block design* : Its purpose is to measure the ability to analyse the complex whole. There are only 7 designs in these blocks which have red, white and red-white sides. Examinees are asked to produce a given design with the help of these blocks.
4. *Picture arrangement* : Its purpose is to measure the ability to identify the whole from the parts. Here six set of pictures are given to the examinees and they are asked to arrange them in an order which tells a meaningful story.
5. *Object assembly* : Its purpose is to measure the ability to synthesise the whole with the help of parts. Here examinees are given some puzzle pictures each representing some parts of the human body and they are asked to assemble them in the form of a complete man.

Speed and accuracy factors are also scored in Arithmetic, digit symbol, block design, picture arrangement and object assembly. Raw scores of each subject are converted into normalized standard scores with a mean of 10 and SD of 3. This makes the scores of each sub tests comparable. Separate IQ for verbal and non-verbal subtest forms is calculated by adding up the respective subtests of the two forms and if we add up scores on all the 11 subtests, we obtain total scale score. These standard scores are expressed in the form of deviation IQ with a mean of 100 and SD of 15.

Wechsler developed another scale known as Wechsler intelligence Scale for Children in 1949 to test the intelligence of children from 5 to 15 years of age. It also takes one hour to administer, though there are 12 subtests in this scale. Maze test is the only test which is extra in WISC. Maze subtest has eight mazes to be traced by the examinee with a pencil. These mazes are given in increasing order of difficulty.

The scoring system of both the tests WAIS and WISC are the same. Here also the total scores are converted into deviation IQ with a mean of 100 and SD of 15.

Advantages of Wechsler Scales

(i) Though Binet's scale and Wechsler's scale both are individual scales, yet the later can be administered on small groups of children and adults.

(ii) Wechsler's scale is easier to administer than Binet's Scale and its scoring is also less complex than the former.

(iii) Wechsler has prepared separate scales for children and adults Binet's scale does not possess this advantage.

Other differences of Wechsler Scales and Stanford Binet Scale

(i) In Wechsler scale, items are not grouped in terms of mental age as is the case of Stanford-Binet scale. Points are given here for all correct responses. Thus, WAIS or WISC is a point scale.

(ii) In Stanford-Binet scale items are interpreted in terms of different age levels of the examinees but in WAIS or WISC similar types of items are grouped together to form subtests.

(iii) WAIS has separate age norms for adults but in SB Scale all the individuals above 18 are treated in a similar manner as far as computation of IQ is concerned. Thus, people of all age levels are treated as 18 years of age after 18.

(iv) In SB tests items are varied, unrelated and upgraded but in WAIS and WISC tests, items are graded according to various range of ages.

(v) SB scale is internally standardized and rigid but WAIS is externally standardized and flexible.

(vi) SB scale refers to qualitative evaluation while WAIS refers to quantitative evaluation.

(vii) Slight chance of statistical treatment is possible in SB scale but WAIS is fully subject to all statistical analysis.

(c) Post Binet period :

This period is particularly known for testing intelligence in groups and thus group test of intelligence became popular during this periods.

A group test is one that can be given to a number of subjects at a time by a single examiner. This type of test came into being during first World War for the purpose of classifying soldiers for various jobs in accordance with their mental abilities. Army Alpha and Army Beta, two tests were developed during this period. Army Alpha is a verbal group test of intelligence meant for literate people. Army beta is a non-verbal group test of intelligence meant for illiterate persons.

We will discuss here some more group test of intelligence :

1. **Catell's Culture Fair Test :** This test was developed by RB Catell and was published by IPAT (Institute for Personality and Ability Testing) in 1961. The test has three scales and can be administered on children and adults both.

   Scale I meant for 4-8 years

   Scale II meant for 8-15 years

   Scale III meant for 15 years and above

   This test measures the general intelligence factor and takes 30-60 minutes to administer. The test has been prepared in such a manner that previously learnt skill or knowledge does not help the examinee to score more on this test. That is why, it is said to be independent of school achievement, social advantages and environmental influences.

2. **Large Thorndike's Intelligence Test :** This test is meant for primary and secondary school children graded into five different levels. The purpose of the test is to measure verbal comprehension, numerical skill and reasoning abilities. Test has verbal as well as non-verbal items. Only non-verbals items are, however, included at the lower levels. The administration of the test takes 30 minutes in all.

3. **Raven Progressive Matrices Test :** This test was developed in England. It consists of geometric figures and designs. The subjects find out the relationship between figures and select appropriate parts for completion of each pattern of relations.

Classification of Intelligence Test

(A) Classification from the point of view of administration

1. **Individual intelligence test :** An individual intelligence test is one which is administered to only one person at a time. Binet-Simon is an example.

2. **Group intelligence test :** A group intelligence test is one which can be administered to more than one persons at a time. Army Alpha and Army Beta are two examples of such tests.

Some general characteristics of group intelligence tests are as follows :

(i) They have been developed on the assumption that intelligence is a general capacity and can be measured by sampling a variety of mental activities.

(ii) In group tests the similar types of items are pooled together in different subtests.

(iii) Every group test is standardized for a special range of ages or school grades.

(iv) Construction of individual test is also very difficult and costly as compared to group tests. Their scoring and standardization is also time consuming process.

(v) It is very difficult to establish rapport between the examiner and the examinees and hence examinees can not be motivated properly in group tests of intelligence. These two limitations are not seen in individual tests.

(vi) Group tests are superior to individual tests in the sense that norms established here are more dependable than that of individual tests. It is because these norms are calculated on the basis of a very large sample.

(vii) Individual test provides qualitative performance of the individual while group tests are mostly point scale and express the performance in quantities.

(B) Classification from the point of view of nature of items of the test

1. **Verbal test :** Verbal test of intelligence is one in which instructions and items are produced before the examinees through the written language. So, examinees must be literate to take these tests. Mohsin's General intelligence Test, Joshi's General Mental Ability test and Jalota's Group General Mental Ability Test are some examples of verbal tests of intelligence of Indian origin.
2. **Non-verbal test :** A non-verbal test is one which requires the use of language only to impart instructions. The examinees are asked to manipulate the test materials in their own way. Since language is not needed to respond to items here, it can be administered to illiterate persons as well. They are also culturally free and hence they can be applied to any situation representing any culture. Test items are usually of figured relation type. Army Beta is a good example of non-language test.
3. **Performance test :** A performance test is one in which a subject has to perform some thing or to manipulate some concrete materials without much use of the language ability. Non-verbal and performance tests are useful for the following groups of people:

   (a) Deaf and Dumb : Those children who cannot hear or speak can be tested with the help of performance test.

   (b) Illiterates : Verbal test of intelligence is useless for those who cannot read or write. Performance test is useful for them.

   (c) Shy children : Many withdrawn children are hesitant to express before others. Performance and non-verbal test of intelligence will suit them very much.

   (d) Educationally deficient children : Verbal test of intelligence generally measure learning along with intelligence. If children are educationally poor, they will perform poorly on intelligence test too and thus they will be wrongly declared as children of below average intelligence. Such a problem can be overcome by using performance test or non-verbal intelligence test.

   (e) Useful for children of other culture : A particular culture dominates in every verbal intelligence test and thus the test can not be adopted by other cultures. Due to free from culture, performance test is suitable for these foreign students.

Some performance tests of intelligence are given below :

(a) Pintner Paterson Scale : This is the first systematic performance test. This scale was standardized in 1917. It consists of 15 subtests.

(b) Goodenough Drawing Test : This scale was developed by Florence Goodenough in 1926. Here child is asked to draw the picture of a man as best as possible without any time limit. This is especially useful for those children who are suspected to be mentally retarted.

Weaknesses of performance test :

- Here the subject can score high due to practice effect and chance success is more frequent than verbal tests. Because of this reason, reliability coefficient is very low.
- They fail to distinguish between gifted and average children due to limited scope of these tests.
- These scales fail to test fine mental abilities such as, ability to make abstraction or concept formation or evaluation abilities of mind.

Interpretation of Intelligence Test Scores : Intelligence test scores can be interpreted in the following three ways:

1. **Mental age :** This concept was first introduced by **Afred Binet** of France in 1908. It refers to a score that is determined by comparing a child's score with the scores obtained by younger or older children in the norming group. Here a child's score is compared with the average score of his own age. For example, if a 9-year-old child scores 60 on an

intelligence test and suppose mental age norms for that scale are as follows:

Mental age of 8 years = 60

Mental age of 9 years = 70

Mental age of 10 years = 80

Then, in that case, mental age of the child will be considered as 8 years instead of 9 though his chronological age is 9 years.

Similarly, if another child of 8 years obtains a score of 80, then his mental age will be 10 years, though his chronological age is 8 years only.

Thus, we can say that the mean performance of each age level becomes the mental age for that age level.

2. **Intelligent Quotient (IQ) :** IQ is also based on the concept of mental age. It is the ratio of mental age to the chronological age multiplied by 100.

$$IQ = \frac{MA}{CA} \times 100.$$

Suppose, the mental age of a 10-year-old child is 12 years on the basis of his scores on an intelligence test, his IQ will be

$$\frac{12}{10} \times 100 = 120.$$

Similarly, if mental age of a person is nine years two months and his age is 12 years 6 months, then his IQ will be

$$\frac{110}{150} \times 100 = 73.3.$$

General classification of persons in terms of IQ

IQ	Classification
140 and above	Genius
130-140	Very superior
120-130	Superior
110-120	Bright
90-110	Average
80-90	Dull
70-80	Borderline
Below 70	Mentally retarded.

Shortcomings of IQ: Some of the main short comings of IQ are as follows:

(*i*) It is a well-known fact that after 18 years, the mental age of a person tends to stabilize. Thus, if IQ is calculated after this age, the result will be misleading, *i.e.*, a person will be less intelligent if he grows in age.

(*ii*) Variability of IQ scores from one test to another is not the same. As a result IQ scores for different tests would not be directly comparable.

(*iii*) It has also been found that variability in IQ scores for the different age levels on the same test is not the same. In that case IQ scores would be a misleading index because it would indicate that a person's IQ may increase or decrease as he grows in age. An example will illustrate this point.

Age	IQ	SD
9 years old child	120	12
7 years old child	120	9

Here IQ of 120 of both the children is not the same due to difference in SD.

3. **Deviation IQ :** Now-a-days IQ ratio is converted into a normalized standard score with a fixed mean of 100 and SD of 15. This is known as DIQ. This fixed mean and SD remain constant through all the age levels. It means that if a child's score is 1 SD above the mean his DIQ will be 100 + 15 = 115. Similarly, if his score is 1 SD below the mean his DIQ will be 100 – 15 = 85 and so on. Thus, with the help of these **DIQ** scores inter age comparison is also possible.

Uses of Intelligence Test

Intelligence tests can be applied in the following situations.

1. **Measurement of general learning abilities:** Intelligence and achievement in schools are highly correlated. If a person is high on an intelligence test, he is expected to score high on school achievements also. Conversely if a person scores high on an intelligence test and still his school achievement is very poor, we can find out other reasons for his educational backwardness.
2. **Assessment of individual differences and categorization :** With the help of intelligence tests we can categories a particular class into several convenient groups and plan our instructional strategies accordingly. Thus, intelligence testing is very useful for educational guidance.
3. **Exact definition of mental retardation is possible :** It is said that those who are below 70 in IQ are retarded but to what extent they are mentally retarded can further be studied with the help of higher screening. We may define the three groups of mentally retarted in the following ways.

Category	IQ level
Morons	45-69
Imbeciles	25-45
Idiots	Below 25

4. **Identification of gifted children :** Gifted children are the treasure of the society. They must be identified in the earlier stages of their lives so that they can be fully guided and helped for their better advancement which is directly related to the advancement of the society as well. Intelligence testing will help the concerned organisations to chalk out plans in the desired manner.
5. **Vocational guidance :** Some children are very forward in verbal abilities and some are superior in non-verbal abilities. This identification is possible only with the help of intelligence tests. Since academic subjects need verbal intelligence and technical subjects need non-verbal or performing abilities, hence children may be guided accordingly.
6. **Screening :** In today's age of competition and rush, screening has become a necessity. Every school has limited seats of admission and it has to select only those students who can raise the academic level of the school high and get name for it. Same is the case with appointments in jobs. For all these purposes, intelligence testing is a must.
7. **Study of mental growth :** Mental abilities develop in a sequential order onward. We can use intelligence tests for studying the trends of mental development of individuals. Intelligence tests have made it clear that mental development of children is a steady consistent process from year-to-year till the age of 25. Intelligence tests show that mind does not develop rapidly in the period of adolescence like the physical and emotional development, but in childhood, it develops rapidly.

Limitations of Intelligence Tests

1. Generally intelligence test shows what a person can do at a certain point of time. These abilities are tested on the basis of certain items included in the test. In order to make the results dependable, a proper size of the sample must be selected for standardization of the test.
2. Some people may be fatigued earlier than others when take a test. This extent of fatigue may reduce their scores and hence intelligence testing will not be accurate. So scores should be taken with caution.
3. No intelligence test is fully free from cultural influences. So, home or school background may affect the intelligence test scores of subjects.
4. Administration of the test also affects the scores of subjects. If proper rapport is there between the examiner and the examinee. IQ scores may be high. On the other hand, if children are frightened with the testing situation as is case of slow learners they will perform poorly on the test.
5. Taking intelligence scores in absolute form is misleading. Intelligence tests do not reveal all the mental abilities in most of the cases. So, intelligence test must be supplemented with clinical setting and case history method to collect detailed information about a subject as is done in clinics by physician who does not entirely believe in physical investigations. He rather takes the help of clinical diagnosis before giving remedial treatment to the patients.

THOUGHT AND LANGUAGE

In this section we examines the relationship between language and thought: that language determines thought, that thought determines language, and that thought and language have different origins. Let us examine these three viewpoints in some detail.

Language as Determinant of Thought

In Hindi and other Indian languages we use a number of different words for various kinship relationships. We have different terms for mother's brother, father's elder brother, father's younger brother, mother's sister's husband, father's sister's husband and so on. An English person uses just one word *uncle* to describe all these kinship relationships. In the English language there are dozens of words for colours whereas some tribal languages have only two to four colour terms. Do such differences matter for how we think? Does an Indian child find it easier to think about and differentiate between various kinship relationships compared to her English-speaking counterpart? Does our thinking process depend on how we describe it in our language?

Benjamin Lee Whorf was of the view that language determines the contents of thought. This view is known as **linguistic relativity hypothesis**. In its strong version, this hypothesis holds what and how individuals can possibly think is determined by the language and linguistic categories they use **(linguistic determinism).** Experimental evidence, however, maintains that it is possible to have the same level or quality of thoughts in all languages depending upon the availability of linguistic categories and structures. Some thoughts may be easier in one language compared to another.

Thought as Determinant of Language

The noted Swiss psychologist, Jean Piaget believed that thought not only determines language, but also precedes it. Piaget argued that children form an internal representation of the world through thinking. For example, when children see something and later copy it (a process called imitation), thinking does take place, which does not involve language. A child's observation of other's behaviour and imitation of the same behaviour, no doubt involves thinking but not language. Language is just one of the vehicles of thinking. As actions become internalised, language may affect children's range of symbolic thinking but is not necessary for the origins of thought. Piaget believed that though language can be taught to children, understanding of the words require knowledge of the underlying concepts (*i.e.* thinking). Thus, thought is basic, and necessary if language is to be understood.

Different Origins of Language and Thought

The Russian psychologist, Lev Vyogotsky, argued that thoughts and language develop in a child separately until about two years of age, when they merge. Before two years thought is preverbal and is experienced more in action (Piaget's sensory motor stage). The child's utterances are more automotic reflexes—crying when uncomfortable—than thought-based. Around two years of age, the child expresses thought verbally and her/his speech reflects rationality. Now children are able to manipulate thoughts using soundless speech. He believed that during this period the development of language and thinking become interdependent; the development of conceptual thinking depends upon the quality of inner speech and vice versa. Thought is used without language when the vehicle of thinking is non-verbal such as visual or movement-related. Language is used without thought when expressing feelings or exchanging pleasantries, for example ''Good morning! How are you?'' ''Very well, I am fine''. When the two functions overlap, they can be used together to produce verbal thought and rational speech.

Development of Language

Language is a complex system and unique to human beings. Psychologists have tried to teach sign language, use of symbols to chimpanzees, dolphins, parrots, etc. But it is observed that, human language is more complex, creative, and spontaneous than the system of communication other animals can learn. There is also a great deal of **regularity** with which children all over the world seem to be learning the language or languages to which they are exposed. When we compare individual children, we find that they differ a great deal in the rate of their language development as well as in how they go about it. But when we take a general view of children's acquisition of language all over the world we find some *predictable pattern* in which children proceed from almost no use of language to the point of becoming competent language users. Language develops through some of the stages discussed below.

Newborn babies and young infants make a variety of sounds, which gradually get modified to resemble words. The first sound produced by babies is crying. Initial crying is undifferentiated and similar across various situations. Gradually, the pattern of crying varies in its pitch and intensity to signify different states such as hunger, pain, and sleepiness, etc. These differentiated crying sounds gradually become more meaningful *cooing sounds* (like 'aaa', 'uuu', etc). usually to express happiness.

At around six months of age children enter the *babbling* stage. Babbling involves prolonged repetition of a variety of consonants and vowel sounds (for example, da—, aa—, ba—). By about nine months of age these sounds get elaborated to strings of some sound combinations, such as 'dadadadadada' into repetitive patterns called *echolalia.* While the early babblings are random or accidental in nature, the later babblings seem to be imitative of adult voices. Children show some understanding of a few words by the time they are six months old. Around the first birthday (the exact age varies from child-to-child) most children enter the *one-word-stage.* Their first word usually contains one syllable—*ma or da*, for instance. Gradually they move to one or more words which are combined to form whole sentences or phrases. So they are called *holophrases*. When they are 18 to 20 months of age, children enter a *two-word stage* and begin to use two words together. The two-word stage exemplifies *telegraphic speech.* Like telegrams (got admission, send money) it contains mostly nouns and verbs. Close to their third birthday, *i.e.* beyond two-and-a-half years, children's language development gets focused on rules of the language they hear.

How is language acquired? You must be wondering: ''How do we learn to speak?'' As with many other topics in psychology, the questions of whether a behaviour develops as a result of inherited characteristics (nature) or from the effects of learning (nurture) has been raised with regard to language. Most psychologists accept that both nature and nurture are important in language acquisition.

Behaviourist B.F. Skinner believed we learn language the same way as animals learn to pick keys or press bars. Language development, for the behaviourists follow the learning principles, such as association (the sight of bottle with the word 'bottle'), imitation (adults use of word ''bottle''), and reinforcement (smiles and hugs when the child says something right). There is also evidence that children produce sounds that are appropriate to a language of the parent or care-giver and are reinforced for having done so. The principle of shaping leads to successive approximation of the desired responses so that the child eventually speaks as well as the adult. Regional differences in pronunciation and phrasing illustrate how different patterns are reinforced in different areas.

Linguist Noam Chomsky put forth the innate proposition of development of language. For him the *rate at which children acquire words and grammar* without being taught can not be explained only by learning principles. Children also *create all sorts of sentences* they have never heard and, therefore, could not be imitating. Children throughout the world seem to have a *critical period*—a period when learning must occur if it is to occur successfully—for learning language. Children across the world also go through the same stages of language development. Chomsky believes language development is just like physical maturation given adequate care, it ''just happens to the child''. Children are born with ''universal grammar''. They readily learn the grammar of whatever language they hear.

Skinner's emphasis on learning explains why infants acquire the language they hear and how they add new words to their vocabularies. Chomsky's emphasis on our built-in readiness to learn grammar helps explain why children acquire language so readily without direct teaching.

GENDER AS A SOCIAL CONSTRUCT; GENDER ROLES, GENDER-BIAS AND EDUCATIONAL PRACTICE

Gender refers to the social distinctions between boys and girls and men and women that are socially constructed rather than biologically determined. These distinctions are reflected in the roles that boys and girls play in society and the status that they occupy within it. Gender roles tend to be dynamic. They vary from one culture and time period to another and are characterized by unequal power relationships.

Ending gender bias and discrimination is crucial to the empowerment of women and girls and to the achievement of gender equality in education. Applying a gender perspective helps to make differences in power relations visible. It also helps us to see more clearly the needs and rights of girls and boys in particular geographical, cultural and economic contexts.

The ultimate goal is to eliminate gender biases and discriminatory practices and policies, both overt and covert. This is at the heart of gender analysis. Gender analysis should therefore be a prerequisite for identifying and understanding problems as they relate to education, and especially to the continued exclusion of girls from quality schooling. Gender analysis guides the process of finding viable and sustainable solutions to the problems of access, quality and learning achievement.

Gender analysis of what learners bring to education (including early childhood socialization, feeding and health access, cultural heritage and language), the content of education, teaching and learning processes, learning environments and learning outcomes help to highlight bad (and good) educational practices and policies. This analysis, in turn, should form the basis for educational interventions that are sensitive to both gender and human rights.

Gender Bias in Teaching

A common response from teachers when asked about gender inequity in classrooms is that they treat all their students the same. There are two problems with this statement. First, students are diverse and have different learning issues, thus treating all students in the same way means that some students will have a better learning experience than their peers. Second, teachers may be ignoring their unconscious gender biases towards their students, their schools and themselves. If ignored, these gender biases, which may have developed from cultural norms, may lead to bias in the classroom.

Gender bias occurs when people make assumptions regarding behaviours, abilities or preferences of others based upon their gender. Because there are strong gender role stereotypes for masculinity and femininity, students who do not match them can encounter problems with teachers and with their peers. For example, the expectation is that boys naturally exhibit boisterous, unruly behaviour, are academically able, rational, and socially uncommunicative, whereas girls are quiet, polite, and studious. Girls are also expected to possess better social skills than boys and to excel at reading and the language arts. So girls who present discipline problems for teachers, or quiet, studious boys, may encounter a lack of understanding from peers and teachers. Within the classroom, these biases unfold in students' practices and teachers' acceptance of certain behaviours from one student or another based upon the students' gender. Also, bias due to a person's gender is not mutually exclusive of other social categories such as race, ethnicity, class, religion, and language. For example, some teachers may perceive African American or other Black girls as loud and uncontrollable because the girls do not exhibit the feminine behaviours associated with White women, such as quiet, self-effacing and malleable.

Gender bias can occur within subject areas and school activities. For example, in subjects such as mathematics and the sciences, there are different participation patterns for girls and boys. Gender bias promulgates a myth that boys are naturally better at mathematics and science than girls. The implications are that if girls succeed in these subjects it is due to their hard work, not their intelligence, whereas boys' success is credited to their natural talent. There are some signs that gender bias in schools may be decreasing in some areas. The percentage of girls participating in science has increased and achieved parity with boys in biology, chemistry and algebra. However, subjects that are prerequisites for college majors such as engineering or physics remain dominated by men. Only 25% of high school students enrolled in physics are female. Moreover, there has been little increase in the percentage of women in engineering programs.

Males are also more likely than females to be in remedial programs and students' race also impacts these patterns. For example, African American males are more likely than White or female peers to enroll in remedial reading and mathematics courses. And non-White students have a higher representation in vocational and noncollege preparatory courses than their White peers. Teachers are critical components in challenging gender bias in schooling, but they also can be major contributors to it as well, through their pedagogical practices, curriculum choices, and assessment strategies.

Gender Bias in Teachers

Teachers' unconscious gender biases can produce stereo-typic expectations for students' success and participation in the classroom. Teachers view male students' domination of the classroom and their time as typical masculine behaviour. However, these biases have consequences for the students and the classroom climate. More than two decades ago, researchers identified and named groups of students who dominated the teacher's time and the classroom resources as ''target students'' (Tobin & Gallagher, 1987). Target students were typically white and male. They answered most of the teacher's questions and also asked most of the questions. This behaviour pattern was particularly insidious in mathematics and science classrooms because teachers did not expect girls to have competent knowledge in these subject areas. Classroom observations documented that target students typically called out answers to the teacher's questions, thus denying other students the opportunity to engage in dialogue with the teacher or get to grips with the subject matter. Furthermore, because boys are perceived as having natural talent in science, teachers asked boys harder and more complicated questions than girls. If girls attempted to answer more difficult questions than boys and faltered, teachers often repeated the question and asked that another student, typically a boy, provide the answer. However, if a boy failed to answer correctly, teachers reframed the question or broke it into a series of simpler questions that could help the student find the answer. Teachers' unconscious stereotyped gender bias that boys are smarter than girls, especially in mathematics and the sciences, meant they were willing to work with boys to reach the answer because they perceived boys were capable of achieving that goal but girls were not. Conversely, teachers of subjects perceived as feminine will spend more time engaged with girls.

Teachers' gendered perceptions of students' ability is also reflected in the type of praise and expectations they have of their students. Teachers often give girls less meaningful and less critical praise than boys. Boys' work is described as unique or brilliant, while girls' work is often undervalued, critically ignored and praised for its appearance. This aspect of teachers' behaviour is particularly detrimental to girls because it means they do not receive feedback on their work that could help them develop deeper understandings of concepts (Liu, 2006).

Teachers also use target students to maintain the tempo and pace of classroom instruction. For example, in a lecture or whole class discussion when a teacher is posing questions to the class, he or she may encourage target students to call out answers in order to keep the lesson moving, rather than wait for the other students to process the question and provide an answer. This short ''wait time'' may be detrimental to learning. More than three decades ago, researchers found that if teachers waited three to five seconds before accepting a student's answer, more students became engaged in the classroom and also improved their understanding of the content. Moreover, the longer wait time meant that teachers began to ask more cognitively challenging questions. However, the existence of target students in classes who often call out answers without direction from teachers meant that fewer students, especially girls, engaged in the lessons. In the absence of proactive teacher intervention, these patterns in which males dominate classroom interactions also occur in mixed-gender, small groups.

Target students dominate classroom interactions and exchanges at all education levels. In the early

2000s, researchers identified these same patterns of engagement in a professional development program for science teachers. When alerted to the invasive behaviours of the male teachers in the cohort, faculty began using overt breaching strategies to stop the target students calling out answers, dominating the human and materials resources of the classroom, and showing disrespect to their peers (Martin Milne & Scantlebury, 2006).

Teachers' gender bias towards students can also extend to their response to students who challenge their authority. Such risk-taking behaviour in boys is expected and at times praised, but assertiveness in girls is viewed negatively and labelled unfeminine. Similarly, boys who do not exhibit stereotypic masculine behaviours may be ridiculed (Renold, 2006).

Teachers use gender expectations as a means of maintaining classroom control. For example, teachers will seat undisciplined boys next to girls as a classroom management strategy. Further, teachers use the gendered expectation that girls' nurturing characteristics will lead them to place others' needs before their own. In other words, teachers often ask girls to assume mothering roles towards students who have fallen behind with learning because of inattentiveness, absenteeism through truancy, or in-school disciplinary procedures, and often those students are male.

Effects of Gender Bias

Gender bias can impact students' attitudes towards learning and their engagement with the subject. If affected by gender bias, girls will tend to believe that any success they have is due to hard work rather than any innate talent or intelligence. Boys may be encouraged to believe that success in science and mathematics should come easily to them because of their gender. Some males report dropping out of college science and mathematics programs because they no longer perceive these subjects as easy. Overall, teachers have lower expectations for girls' academic success compared to boys, and their attitudes are shown through the type and quality of the student-teacher interaction. The type and quality of critique teachers give their students can also have an impact. Teachers' comments on girls' work focuses on its appearance but with boys' work teachers focus on the content. Girls often do not receive substantive comments or criticism from teachers from which they could improve their ability to learn. During the many hours spent in classrooms, girls receive less time and attention from teachers than their male peers. Teachers usually ask girls easier questions than they ask boys. Typically, girls receive fewer opportunities to engage in classroom discourse, use equipment and assert their knowledge in classrooms.

Reducing Gender Bias

Gender bias in education is a series of microinequities whose impact is cumulative and often ignored. Girls are rewarded and praised for compliant behaviour. Teachers do not challenge girls with questions and rarely offer criticisms of their works. Teachers can reduce and challenge gender bias through an examination of their pedagogical practices and by posing simple questions about their practices. For example, which students do they frequently interact with? Are target students evident in their classroom? If so, how does the teacher deal with those students? What questioning techniques does the teacher use to engage students? Does the teacher ask complicated questions to girls as well as boys? Does the teacher use a variety of pedagogical and assessment practices? Which students are engaged with the curriculum?

Another way of reducing gender bias would be for teachers to videotape their classes and review their interactions with the students. Or they could invite a colleague to watch their teaching and record which students are being asked questions and what type of questions. However, teachers must also prepare for the consequences of changing their practices. Girls are conditioned to receiving less of the teacher's attention, and they do not usually cause discipline problems if they are not receiving their fair share, but boys can react negatively to losing the teacher's attention, causing disruption to lessons and becoming discipline problems. Moreover, research has also shown that boys avoid written work and often have poor communication skills when asked to work in singlesex groups.

However, the gains in reducing gender bias in education may disappear with the requirements of high-stakes testing required by No Child Left Behind (NCLB). NCLB requires that states report academic achievement data in most social categories, except gender (Kahle, 2004). This may result in less attention being placed on gender bias and less data that might reveal it. Continued monitoring of gender bias is necessary to minimize its impact on students' opportunities for learning and achievement.

INDIVIDUAL DIFFERENCES AMONG LEARNERS

It is not unusual to find a wide range of differences among students in a class or a group. These differences are invariably identified in terms of student's characteristics such as physical (appearance, height, size, sex, colour, etc.), demographic (age, caste, socio-economic status, etc.) and cognitive behaviour (thinking, remembering, problem solving, creating idea, etc.). The differences that exist among students due to physical, demographic, affective behaviour and cognitive behaviour characteristics are referred to as individual differences.

Differences due to physical and demographic characteristics are conspicuous and easy to identify. However, the differences that exist in the way they solve problem in Mathematics or in their ability to interpret and explain ideas are not easily visible but are identified through their performance. Let us examine, for instance, the answers given by Bitto and Neha, two students of the same class to the following proverb.

Interpret the saying, "Pen is mighter than the sword".

Bitto's Interpretation

It means that writing had always been able to influence mankind more than any amount of sheer physical strength; writing undoubtedly makes a more lasting impact in the minds of the people than any form of physical demonstration. In the case of the latter the impact might be forceful though less lasting. Great thinkers, writers and philosophers have from time immemovial been able to hold sway over the minds of the people by means of their profound knowledge through their writings. For example, Socrates won the wrath of a powerful state, because of his great ability to hold spellbound the young through his discourses. Similarly, the writing of Voltaire and Rousseau inspired the French to rise up in revolt.

Neha's Interpretation

It is a common proverb which simply means that through writing it is possible to win more victories than by using physical force and weapons. When any good book is read it is possible to retain in our memory the message it contains. On the other hand, success achieved through physical might is not for mankind.

The above illustration reflects the differences between Bitto and Neha in their interpretation of the proverb. While Bitto delves deep in her interpretation, Neha states only the meaning.

According to Skinner, individual differences in learner behaviours are the result of the organism's genetic endowment and reinforcement. Thus, Skinner believed that defective genetic endowment and/or defective reinforcement contingencies in an individual's experience result in a failure to acquire a variety of learned behaviours.

The process of an individual's mental activities such as remembering, analysing, interpreting, reasoning, problem solving and thinking are cognitive domain behaviours and are essential for learning and achievement. How we think, what and how we remember, how we solve problem and how we create ideas are cognitive domain behaviours and individuals differ by these behaviours. Such differences are often identified by psychologists in terms of intelligence, aptitude, creating and academic achievement.

Individual differences are crucial for teachers who are responsible for guiding all forms of learning. In fact, many educators would suggest that the primary role of teachers is to provide education to meet the individual differences and to develop student cognitive process.

Do Individuals Differ in Intelligence?

Well, they do differ. But how? Differences are due to the differences in the level of general intellectual ability and the underlying cognitive process among individuals.

How do we identify differences in intelligence?

Using suitable intelligence tests we can measure and identify the difference. An intelligence test may contain sub-tests (sub-sections) and each sub-test represents a different set of ability. The scores obtained in all sub-tests are added up to obtain a single score to represent the general ability of the student. Thus, the single score obtained for each individual in a test is expressed in terms of **intelligence quotient** (IQ). IQ is a measure of intelligence and is defined as the ratio of mental age (average age of children who give correct responses/ answers in an intelligence test) to the chronological age (actual age) multiplied by 100 (to avoid fraction). Thus mental age is:

$$IQ = \frac{\text{Mental age}}{\text{Chronological age}} \times 100$$

IQ scores help us estimate individual differences by categorising individuals on the basis of their IQs. These differences have important consequences for learning and performance. Let us examine the different categories of students based on their intelligence level.

Gifted : Those students who possess IQs of 130 or above are called gifted students. They are superior in intelligence and have high ability to reason. As compared to other children, they can perform academic activities grasping concepts, memorising, perceiving, seeing relationships, generalising, dealing with abstract ideas, critical thinking and solving problems more effectively and quickly. They have a broad attention span that permits concentration and the ability for a high level of academic performance. They take initiative in intellectual work and follow complex directions. Such individuals are small in number as compared to normal or average children. Normal groups have those children whose IQs range from 90 to 110 and they are able to profit from regular school programmes with varying degrees of effort.

Disabled : There are children with **disability** due to low level to intellectual functioning or specific learning deficits. Children with low level or below-average intellectual functioning are called mentally retarded. The children with inadequate level of intelligence are impaired in their ability to learn and to adapt to the demands of society. Mentally retarded children are of different categories. They can be:

- **Border line** (IQ ranges 90-70) and **educable mentally retarded** (IQ ranges 70-50) children can perform academic activities but are slow in their learning. Special instructional strategies can help them to profit from learning activities. They can take care of themselves and live independently as adults.
- **Trainable mentally retarded** (IQ ranges 50-35) are capable of learning only certain rudimentary literacy materials and simple occupational skills. They possess some ability to take care of their personal needs and can be trained in daily living skills. Such children require special classes or schools to study in.
- **Severely retarded** (IQ below 35) have quite limited adaptive behaviour and are never found in school. They are dependent on their families for their personal needs.

Children with specific learning defects are called learning disabled group. They are normal to above-average on intelligence but have difficulties in one or more psychological processes involved in understanding or in using language or numbers (written or spoken). The difficulties manifest in their ability to listen, think, speak, read, write, spell or do mathematical calculations. These difficulties are identified as **aphasia** (difficulty in grasping spoken language), **dylesia** (difficulty in reading), **hyperlexia** (little or no comprehension), **dyscalculia** (difficulty in doing arithmetic) and **dysgraphia** (difficulty in writing). Some are hyperactive in the sense that they are excessively active inattentive and behave impulsively. They follow instructions poorly and do not often complete the assigned tasks.

Instructional Strategies for Handling Individual Differences

- Organise instruction for the development of cognitive process.
- Use existing cognitive level as base.
- Strengthen memory.
- Formulate level specific instructional strategy.
- Use individual meeting.
- Provide instructions to overcome learning disability.

Do Individuals Differ in Aptitude?

Yes, they do differ. An individual may have a mechanical aptitude, another may have an aptitude for mathematics or yet another may have an aptitude for language, music or athletics. Such differences are due to the differences in the combination of abilities related to the cognitive processes, and the sensory and psychomotor components. For instance, when we talk of mechanical aptitude, we may deal with ability for spatial relations, ability to acquire information on mechanical matters and ability to comprehend mechanical relations, besides sensory and psychomotor abilities. Similarly, when we discuss aptitude in music, we may identify ability for musical memory, pitch discrimination, loudness discrimination, time discrimination and judgement of rhythm. Likewise, abilities required for science or mathematics are different and each requires a separate set of abilities.

The differences in aptitude can be identified using aptitude tests. Aptitude tests for areas such as mechanical skills, mathematics, science, language, music and graphic art can be used to identify the aptitude of students in each area of performance. You might have heard of the use of aptitude tests in medicine, engineering, business management, law or teacher training for selection of students for studies in the respective fields. The aptitude test, in fact, provides a measure of the candidates promise or teachability in a field of study, say, medicine. In other words, the test would tell whether the candidate possesses the required aptitude or readiness to profit from studies in the concerned field of study.

Instructional Strategy for Handling Individual Differences

The suggested approach for handling individual differences is **adaptive instructional system**. In this approach at least two alternative instructional treatments are needed to ensure academic success. Which is the most appropriate instructional treatment for the student depends upon his or her existing level of aptitude (learning readiness). Students with high aptitude may choose unstructured instructional strategy. With minimum guidance from teacher, they may be encouraged to learn through the discovery oriented approach. You may use the inductive process but instructional treatment is essentially learner-centered.

In contrast, highly structured instructional treatment for low aptitude learners is designed in small units through sequential steps and feedback. Frequent summary and review with simplified illustration, analogy and precise explanation of concepts and principles to be learned will facilitate progressive learning. Periodic achievement and aptitude assessments and comparison of these scores with the aptitude scores obtained at the start of instruction would tell the degree to which each learner in the specific treatment group has achieved.

However, for those who are unable to profit from either of the alternative treatments presented above, **compensatory aptitude training** is suggested. This consists of directed reading skill, study habits, self-learning skills, note taking and related activities. The main aim of compensatory aptitude training is to develop readiness for entry into structured treatment. Periodic monitoring should be formulated to identify the students who reach the required level for entry into alternative treatment.

Do Learners Differ in their Academic Achievements?

They do differ, but how? We have seen that those who possess appropriate pre-requisite knowledge learn more effectively than those who lack such knowledge. Differences in pre-requisite knowledge possessed by students create differences in the attainment of knowledge. Further, knowledge is attained progressively. Progressive differences in knowledge attainment leads to cumulative differences in knowledge attainment and this form of differences is often called **Mathew Effect.** It means that academically rich get richer and those who are poor continue to be poor. Thus, differences in pre-requisites and cumulative knowledge lead to differences in the knowledge possessed by the students likewise, they also differ in their capabilities to manipulate the knowledge in a given situation and the differences are identified in terms of the abilities to apply, analyse, synthesise and evaluate knowledge. In fact, ability is an essential condition for learning and the abilities related to intelligence, aptitude and creativity are important for academic achievement. We have seen the instructional strategies for meeting the differences in intelligence, aptitude and creativity through classroom situations. It means that differences in intelligence, aptitude and creativity do create differences in academic achievement.

The differences in academic achievement can be identified using an achievement test in the concerned subject. However, if the achievement test contains only knowledge level items (questions), it tells only knowledge level differences. On the other hand, if it contains items (questions) on knowledge and capabilities—comprehension, application, analysis, synthesis and evaluation—the various levels of differences can be identified. Besides, the total marks, each level-wise total is needed to identify the strengths and weaknesses of every student as well as the differences among students. As a teacher, if you know the strengths and weaknesses of your students in a subject, you may be able to adopt appropriate instructional strategies to suit their strenghts and weaknesses in that subject.

Apart from these achievement differences are quite often identified in terms of categories of achievers by classifying students as high, average and low achievers. Though there is no strict cut-off points, these categories can be created using marks. High achievers are those who possess higher level of knowledge and capabilities (say, with marks 66% and above) than the rest and those who possess average level of knowledge and capabilities (say, with marks 36% to 65%) are called average achievers. On the other extreme, you may find learners with low level knowledge and capabilities (with 35% and below marks). They are called low achievers. If you are interested in identifying the high, average and low achievers in a subject, say Science or language, the categories are created using the marks obtained in the concerned subject. However, categories can also be created based on the overall achievement in a class.

As a teacher, you may be curious to know the strategies for meeting the achievement differences in your classroom or the challenges posed by the strengths and weaknesses of the students in teaching-learning situations. Let us discuss important instructional strategies.

What are Instructional Strategies?

Let us discuss the major strategies to cope up with the differences in academic achievement.

- Provide appropriate pre-requisites to organise and learn new information.
- Use visual aids.
- Use analogy, example and illustration.
- Ensure learner's active involvement in learning.
- Periodic assessment.

EVALUATION AND ASSESSMENT

Evaluation

Evaluation, particularly educational evaluation is a series of activities designed to measure the effectiveness of the teaching-learning systems as a whole. According to Mary Thorpe (1980), "Evaluation is the collection, analysis and interpretation of information about any aspect of a programme of education." Teaching-learning process is a continuous activity. It needs to be evaluated from beginning to end. Evaluation during the learning process (continuous assessment), often termed as "formative evaluation", is important for learners and teachers alike.

The bases of evaluation are learning objectives, performance standards and achievement tests on the one hand, and learners' and experts' opinions on the other. Evaluation helps to build an educational programme, assess its achievement and improve upon its effectiveness. It also provides valuable feedback on the design, development and implementation of the programme. It is, of course, an important component of the teaching-learning process. It helps in making the value judgement, determining educational status, or measuring achievement of learners.

The scope of evaluation in schools extents to almost all the areas of learner's personality development. It includes both scholastic and non-scholastic areas. It reveals the strengths and weaknesses of the learners, so that the learners have better opportunity to understand and improve themselves.

Evaluation is helpful to teachers also. It provides feedback to them to reshape their teaching strategies according to the needs of the learners. Evaluation in education in general and in distance education in particular becomes imperative to know as to what extent the goals of education have been achieved.

Thus, evaluation is not merely assigning grades to learners. It is a continuous process of acquiring and processing information in order to improve one's learning and to assess decisions made in designing an instructional system. If we analyse the above statement we easily notice that it has three important implications for the entire teaching-learning system. They are as follows:

1. Evaluation is a continuous process and not a one time performance measurement, effected at the end of a course/programme. It starts at the stage of curriculum development and continues until the instruction ends.
2. Evaluation process is goal-directed. It is aimed at finding ways and means to improve learning and thereby to achieve learning objectives more effectively and more efficiently.
3. Evaluation requires the use of accurate and appropriate measuring instructions to collect information for taking decisions about the quality and operation of education.

It is clear that in designing an effective learning system, one of the earliest steps we need to take is to prepare a comprehensive evaluation plan, which should be developed soon after the learning objectives have been formulated. This practice will help us to:

- determine whether the objectives are attainable or need revisions before we start designing the instructional system;
- collect data/information in a form that suits our purposes adequately and at a time when it is available, otherwise the opportunity to collect specific information may be lost; and
- have sufficient time to test the effectiveness of a design.

Continuous and Comprehensive Evaluation (CCE)

Continuous and Comprehensive Evaluation (CCE) refers to a system of school based evaluation of a student that covers all aspects of a student development. It is a developmental process of student which emphasizes on two fold objectives. These objectives are continuity in evaluation and assessment of broad based learning and behaviourial outcomes on the other.

The term **'continuous'** is meant to emphasise that evaluation of identified aspects of students **'growth and development'** is a continuous process rather than an event, built into the total teaching-learning process and spread over the entire span of academic session. It means regularity of assessment, frequency of unit testing, diagnosis of learning gaps, use of corrective measures, retesting and feedback of evidence to teachers and students for their self evaluation.

The second term **'comprehensive'** means that the scheme attempts to cover both the scholastic and the co-scholastic aspects of the students' growth and development. Since abilities, attitudes and aptitudes can manifest themselves in forms other than the written word, the term refers to application of variety of tools and techniques (both testing and non-testing) and aims at assessing a learner's development in areas of learning, like:

- Knowledge
- Understanding
- Applying
- Analyzing
- Evaluating
- Creating

Objectives of CCE

- To help develop cognitive, psychomotor and affective skills.
- To lay emphasis on thought process and de-emphasise memorization.
- To make evaluation an integral part of teaching-learning process.
- To use evaluation for improvement of students achievement and teaching-learning strategies

on the basis of regular diagnosis followed by remedial instructions.

- To use evaluation as a quality control device to maintain desired standard of performance.
- To determine social utility, desirability or effectiveness of a programme and take appropriate decisions about the learner, the process of learning and the learning environment.
- To make the process of teaching and learning a learner-centered activity.

Features of CCE

- The **'continuous'** aspect of CCE takes care of **'continual'** and **'periodicity'** aspect of evaluation.
- Continual means assessment of students in the beginning of instructions (placement evaluation) and assessment during the instructional process (**formative evaluation**) done informally using multiple techniques of evaluation.
- Periodicity means assessment of performance done frequently at the end of unit/term (**summative evaluation**).
- The **'comprehensive'** component of CCE takes care of assessment of all round development of the child's personality. It includes assessment in **Scholastic as well as Co-Scholastic** aspects of the pupil's growth.
- Scholastic aspects include curricular areas or subject specific areas, whereas Co-Scholastic aspects include Life Skills, Co-Curricular Activities, Attitudes and Values.
- Assessment in Scholastic areas is done informally and formally using multiple techniques of evaluation continually and periodically. The diagnostic evaluation takes place at the end of unit/term test. The causes of poor performance in some units are diagnosed using diagnostic tests. These are followed with appropriate interventions followed by retesting.
- Assessment in Co-Scholastic areas is done using multiple techniques on the basis of identified criteria, while assessment in Life Skills is done on the basis of Indicators of Assessment and Checklists.

Functions of CCE

- It helps the teacher to organize effective teaching strategies.
- Continuous evaluation helps in regular assessment to the extent and degree of Learner's progress (ability and achievement with reference to specific Scholastic and Co-Scholastic areas).
- Continuous evaluation serves to diagnose weaknesses and permits the teacher to ascertain an individual learner's strengths and weaknesses and her needs. It provides immediate feedback to the teacher, who can then decide whether a particular unit or concept needs a discussion again in the whole class or whether a few individuals are in need of remedial instruction.
- By continuous evaluation, children can know their strengths and weaknesses. It provides the child a realistic self assessment of how he/she studies. It can motivate children to develop good study habits, to correct errors, and to direct their activities towards the achievement of desired goals. It helps a learner to determine the areas of instruction in where more emphasis is required.
- Continuous and comprehensive evaluation identifies areas of aptitude and interest. It helps in identifying changes in attitudes and value systems.
- It helps in making decisions for the future, regarding choice of subjects, courses and careers.
- It provides information/reports on the progress of students in Scholastic and Co-Scholastic areas and thus helps in predicting the future success of the learner.

Continuous evaluation helps in bringing awareness of the achievement to the child, teachers and parents from time-to-time. They can look into the probable cause of the fall in performance if any, and may take remedial measures of instruction in which more emphasis is required. Many times, because of some personal reasons, family problems or adjustment problems, the children start neglecting their studies, resulting in sudden drop in their performance. If the teacher, child and parents do not notice the sudden drop in the performance of the child in academics, it could result in a permanent deficiency in the childs' learning.

The major emphasis of CCE is on the continuous growth of students ensuring their intellectual, emotional, physical, cultural and social development and therefore, it will not be merely limited to assessment of learner's scholastic attainments. CCE uses assessment as a means of motivating learners to provide feedback and follow up work to improve upon the learning in the classroom and to present a comprehensive picture of a learner's profile. It is this that has led to the emergence of the concept of **School Based Continuous and Comprehensive Evaluation.**

Scholastic and Co-Scholastic Assessment

In order to have Continuous and Comprehensive Evaluation, both Scholastic and Co-Scholastic aspects need to be given due recognition. Such a holistic assessment requires maintaining an ongoing and comprehensive profile for each learner that is honest, encouraging and discreet. While teachers frequently reflect, plan and implement remedial strategies, the child's ability to retain and articulate what has been learned over a period of time also requires periodic assessment. These assessments can take many forms but all of them should be as comprehensive and discreet as possible. **Weekly**, **fortnightly**, or **quarterly** reviews (depending on the learning area), that do not openly compare one learner with another are generally recommended. The objective is to promote and enhance not just learning and retention among children, but their soft skills as well.

Scholastic Assessment

The objectives of the Scholastic domain are:-

- Desirable behaviour related to the learner's knowledge, understanding, application, evaluation, analysis and the ability to apply it in an unfamiliar situation.
- To improve the teaching learning process.
- Assessment should be both **Formative** and **Summative**.

Summative and Formative Assessment

Assessment is often divided into formative and summative categories for the purpose of considering different objectives for assessment practices.

Summative Assessment

Summative assessment is intended to measure learning outcomes and report those outcomes to students, parents and administrators. In an educational setting, it generally occurs at the conclusion of a class, course, semester or academic year. In the context of a course summative assessments are typically used to assign students a course grade. It is also referred to in a learning context as **"assessment of learning"**. **Performance-based assessment** is similar to summative assessment, as it focuses on achievement. A well-defined task is identified and students are asked to create, produce, or do something, often in settings that involve real-world application of knowledge and skills. Proficiency is demonstrated by providing an extended response. Performance formats are further differentiated into products and performances. The performance may result in a product, such as a painting, portfolio, paper, or exhibition, or it may consist of a performance, such as a speech, athletic skill, musical recital, or reading.

Definitions of Summative Assessment

- "Good summative assessments—tests and other graded evaluations—must be demonstrably reliable, valid, and free of bias" (Angelo and Cross, 1993).
- '...assessment (that) has increasingly been used to sum up learning' (Black and William, 1999).
- '...looks at past achievements ... adds procedures or tests to existing work ... involves only marking and feedback grades to student ... is separated from teaching ... is carried out at intervals when achievement has to be summarized and reported.' (Harlen, 1998).

Features of Summative Assessment

- Assessment of learning.
- Generally taken by students at the end of a unit or semester to demonstrate the **"sum"** of what they have or have not learned.
- Summative assessment methods are the most traditional way of evaluating student work.

Formative Assessment

Formative assessment is generally carried out throughout a course or project. In an educational setting, formative assessment is used by teachers to consider approaches to teaching and next steps for individual learners and the class, and would not necessarily be used for grading purposes. Formative assessment, also referred to as **"educative assessment"** or **"assessment for learning"**, is used to aid learning. Assessment for learning is defined as "all those activities undertaken by teachers and/or students, which provide information to be used as feedback to modify the teaching and learning activities in which they are engaged" (Black and William 2004).

Definitions of Formative Assessment

- '... often means no more than that the assessment is carried out frequently and is planned at the same time as teaching'. (Black and William, 1999)
- '... provides feedback which leads to students recognizing the (learning) gap and closing it ... it is forward looking ...' (Harlen, 1998).
- '... includes both feedback and self-monitoring'. (Sadler, 1989)
- '... is used essentially to get a feedback into the teaching and learning process.' (Tunstall and Gipps, 1996)

Features of Formative Assessment

- Is diagnostic and remedial.
- Makes provision for effective feedback.

- Provides a platform for the active involvement of students in their own learning.
- Enables teachers to adjust teaching to take account of the results of assessment.
- Recognizes the profound influence assessment has on the motivation and self-esteem of students, both of which are crucial influences on learning.
- Recognizes the need for students to be able to assess themselves and understand how to improve.
- Builds on students' prior knowledge and experience in designing what is taught.
- Incorporates varied learning styles to decide how and what to teach.
- Encourages students to understand the criteria that will be used to judge their work.
- Offers an opportunity to students to improve their work after they get the feedback.
- Helps student to support their peer group and vice-versa.

A common form of formative assessment is **"diagnostic assessment"**. Diagnostic assessment measures a student's current knowledge and skills for the purpose of identifying a suitable program of learning. **"Self-assessment"** is a form of diagnostic assessment which involves students assessing themselves. **"Forward-looking assessment"** asks those being assessed to consider themselves in hypothetical future situations.

Co-Scholastic Assessment

The desirable behaviour related to learner's life skills, attitudes, interests, values, co-curricular activities and physical health are described as skills to be acquired in co-scholastic domain.

The process of assessing the students' progress in achieving objectives related to scholastic and co-scholastic domain is called comprehensive evaluation. It has been observed that usually under the scholastic domain such as knowledge and understanding of the facts, concepts, principles etc. of a subject are assessed. The Co-Scholastic elements are either altogether excluded from the evaluation process or they are not given adequate attention. For making the evaluation comprehensive, both Scholastic and Co-Scholastic aspects should be given importance. Simple and manageable means of assessment of Co-Scholastic aspects of growth must be included in the comprehensive evaluation scheme.

Comprehensive evaluation would necessitate the use of a variety of tools and techniques. This will be so because both different and specific areas of learner's growth can be evaluated through certain special techniques.

School Based CCE

School based Evaluation is held at school level unlike external examination conducted by the Boards of School Education. This is done by the teachers according to the schedule developed by the school and guidelines given by the Board. Though this evaluation has been done at school level all along, certain shortcomings have crept into this system. These shortcomings can be attributed to various factors. The basic factor is the misconception of teachers regarding the place of evaluation and its importance in the educational process. The other factor has been the imitation of the practice of external examination which is generally held at the end of the session.

In the School Based System of evaluation, the focus on the purpose of assessment has changed. Now, it includes readiness testing, screening of development, evaluation of performance in cognitive, affective and psychomotor domains more frequently, systematically and effectively.

In other words, School Based Evaluation is child-centred, school-centred and multidimensional evaluation. Hence, in its true spirit, it triggers an all round development of the learner. It encourages all kinds of learning in life both inside the school as well as outside it. It is child-centered as it attempts to consider the learner as a unique entity for its individual pattern of development. It builds on individual child's abilities, progress and development in achieving already set goals and objectives of education as an individual and not just his/her position in relation to other learners.

Further, this evaluation helps a learner to use his/her potential in a better manner and also provides insight to the teachers to discover the methods which may be helpful to the individual learner in resolving his/her problems and difficulties.

Besides being ***child-centred,*** this evaluation is ***school-centred*** as well. It means that no outside agency interferes in this evaluation process. It is entirely school based and done by the teacher. The teacher is trusted and given full responsibility of evaluating students with the brief that the teacher knows best about his/her students.

School Based Evaluation is ***multidimensional.*** Its multidimensional nature is reflected in recognizing and taking care of learners' social, emotional, physical, intellectual and other areas of development which are interrelated and cannot be considered in isolation. It also calls for the use of multiple techniques and tools of evaluation.

Aim of School Based CCE

- Elimination of chance element and subjectivity (as far as possible), de-emphasis on memorization, encouraging comprehensive evaluation incorporating both Scholastic and Co-Scholastic aspects of learners development.
- Continuous evaluation spread over the total span of the instructional time as an integral built-in aspect of the total teaching-learning process.
- Functional and meaningful declaration of results for effective use by teachers, students, parents and the society.
- Wider uses of test results for purposes not merely of the assessment of levels of pupils' achievements and proficiencies, but mainly for their improvement, thorough diagnosis and remedial/enrichment programmes.
- Improvement in the mechanics of conducting examinations for realizing a number of other allied purposes.
- Introduction of concomitant changes in instructional materials and methodology.
- Introduction of the semester system.
- The use of grades in place of marks in determining and declaring the level of pupil performance and proficiency.

Its Characteristics

School Based Evaluation has the following characteristics:

- Is broader, more comprehensive and continuous than traditional system.
- Aims primarily to help learners for systematic learning and development.
- Takes care of the needs of the learner as responsible citizens of the future.
- Is more transparent, futuristic and provides more scope for association among learners, teachers and parents.

School based evaluation provides opportunities to teachers to **know the following about their learners:**

- What they learn?
- How they learn?
- What type of difficulties/limitations they face in working in tandem?
- What do the children think?
- What do the children feel?
- What are their interests and dispositions?

The focus has shifted to developing a deep learning environment. There is a paradigm shift in the pedagogy and competencies from 'controlling' to 'enriching' to 'empowering' schools.

Traditional Schooling	**Enriching Schooling**	**Empowering Schooling**
• Teacher centred • Subjects and classes-teacher directed • Sorting and ranking individuals	• Student centred • Self directed • Continuous assessment	• Experience centred • Virtual authenticity • Multi literacies
Competency: • Memory • Competitive	**Competency:** • Critical thinking • Collaborative • Creative	**Competency:** • Risk taking • Ethical • Interactive

Implementing School Based Assessment would mean:

- Elimination of chance element and subjectivity (as far as possible), de-emphasis of memorization, encouraging Comprehensive evaluation incorporating both scholastic and co-scholastic aspects of learners development.
- Continuous evaluation spread over the total span of the instructional time as an integral built-in aspect of the total teaching-learning process.
- Functional and meaningful declaration of results for effective use by teachers, students, parents and the society.
- Wider uses of test results for purposes not merely of the assessment of levels of pupils' achievements and proficiencies, but mainly for its improvement, through diagnosis and remedial/enrichment programmes.
- Improvements in the mechanics of conducting examinations for realizing a number of other allied purposes.
- Introduction of concomitant changes in instructional materials and methodology.

- Introduction of the semester system from the secondary stage onwards.
- The use of grades in place of marks in determining and declaring the level of pupil performance and proficiency.

The above goals are relevant for both external examination and evaluation in schools.

Shortcoming of Traditional External Examination

- It is a one shot examination at the end of a year at the terminal stage of schooling.
- It mainly evaluates only the scholastic aspects of learning of the students.
- It does not evaluate all the abilities of the children. On the basis of marks obtained in written examination the students are declared pass or fail and further classified into predetermined divisions.
- Pass and fail system causes frustration and is inhumane because the failed candidates come to feel that they are good for nothing.
- Co-scholastic areas are almost totally ignored and have no place in the currently prevalent scheme of education and evaluation.
- The practice of testing of untaught content also reflects poor learning achievement.
- Only limited techniques of evaluation without potential for judging a student are being used.
- The aim of evaluation is to improve learner's quality which is not served by external examination.
- The current practice of awarding marks suffers from many discrepancies due to variety of errors.
- The varied ranges of obtained scores of students in different subjects create the problem in declaring reliable results.
- Analysis and interpretation of test results is not done in a scientific way.

School Based Continuous and Comprehensive Evaluation System should be Established to:

- reduce stress on children.
- make evaluation comprehensive and regular.
- provide space for the teacher for creative teaching.
- provide a tool of diagnosis and remediation.
- produce learners with greater skills.

Four Assessment Paradigms

Assessment *of* Learning

The 'assessment **of** learning' is defined as a process whereby someone attempts to describe and quantify the knowledge, attitudes or skills possessed by another. Teacher direction is paramount and the student has little involvement in the design or implementation of the assessment process in these circumstances.

- Teacher designs learning
- Teacher collects evidence
- Teacher judges what has been learnt (and what has not been learnt)

Assessment *for* Learning

The 'assessment **for** learning' involves increased level of student autonomy, but not without teacher guidance and collaboration. The assessment **for** learning is sometimes seen as being akin to 'formative assessment'. There is more emphasis towards giving useful advice to the student and less emphasis on the giving of marks and the grading function.

- Teacher designs learning
- Teacher designs assessment with feedback to student
- Teacher judges what has been learnt (student develops insight into what has not)

Assessment *as* Learning

The 'assessment **as** learning' is perhaps more connected with diagnostic assessment and can be constructed with more of an emphasis on peer learning. Assessment **as** learning generates opportunities for self assessment and peer assessment. Students take on increased responsibility to generate quality information about their learning and that of others.

- Teacher and student co-construct learning
- Teacher and student co-construct assessment
- Teacher and student co-construct learning progress map

Assessment **for** learning and assessment **as** learning activities should be deeply embedded in teaching and learning and be the source of interactive feedback, allowing students to adjust, re-think and re-learn.

Assessment *in* Learning

The 'assessment **in** learning' places the question at the centre of teaching and learning. It deflects the teaching from its focus on a 'correct answer' to a focus on 'a fertile question'. Through enquiry students engage in processes that generates feedback about their learning, which come from multiple sources and activities. It contributes to the construction of other learning activities, line of enquiry and the generation of other questions.

- Student as the centre of learning

- Student monitors, assesses and reflects on learning
- Student initiates demonstration of learning (to self and others)
- Teacher as coach and mentor.

Teachers and students need to understand the purpose of each assessment strategy. The overall assessment 'package' being used by learners and teachers should accurately capture, generate and use meaningful learning information to generate deep learning and understanding.

ASSESSING LEARNERS

Any meaningful report on the quality and extent of a child's learning needs to be comprehensive. We need a curriculum whose creativity, innovativeness, and development of the whole being, the hallmark of a good education makes uniform tests that assess memorised facts and textbook-based learning obsolete. We need to redefine and seek new parameters for and ways of evaluation and feedback. In addition to the learner's achievements in specific subject areas that lend themselves to testing easily, assessment would need to encompass attitudes to learning, interest, and the ability to learn independently.

ASSESSMENT IN THE COURSE OF TEACHING

Preparing report cards is a way for the teacher to think about each individual child and review what she/he has learnt during the term, and what she/he needs to work on and improve. To be able to write such report cards, teachers would need to think about each individual child, and hence pay attention to them during their everyday teaching and interaction. One does not need special tests for this; learning activities themselves provide the basis for such ongoing observational and qualitative assessments of children. Maintaining a daily diary based on observation helps in continuous and comprehensive evaluation. An extract from the diary of a teacher for a week notes the following: ''Kiran enjoyed his work. He took an instant liking to the books that were informative and brief. He says that he likes simple and clear language. In noting down facts, he goes for short answers. He says that it helps him understand things easily. He favours a practical approach.'' Similarly, keeping samples and notes of the child's work at different stages provides both the teacher and the learner herself or himself with a systematic record of his/her learning progress.

The belief that assessment must lead to finding learning difficulties to then be remediated is often very impractical and not founded on a sound understanding of pedagogic practice. Problems regarding conceptual development cannot and do not wait for formal tests in order to be detected. A teacher can, in the course of teaching itself, come to know of such problems by asking questions that make children think or by giving them small assignments. She can then attend to them in the process of teaching—by ensuring that her planning is flexible and responsive to the learners and their learning.

CURRICULAR AREAS THAT CANNOT BE 'TESTED FOR MARKS'

Each area of the curriculum may not lend itself to being 'tested'; it may even be antithetical to the nature of learning in the curricular area. This includes areas such as work, health, yoga, physical education, music and art. While the skill-based component of physical education and yoga could be tested, the health aspect needs continuous and qualitative assessments. Currently, this has the effect of making these subjects and activities 'less important' in the curriculum; these areas are inadequately provided for in terms of material resources and curricular planning, and marked by a lack of seriousness. Further, the time allocated for them is also frequently sacrificed to accommodate special classes. This is a serious compromise with parts of the curriculum that have deep educational significance and potential.

Even if 'marks' cannot be given, children can be assessed for their development in these areas. Participation, interest, and level of involvement, and the extent to which abilities and skills have been honed, are some markers that can help teachers to gauge the benefits of what children learn and gain through such activities. Asking children to self-report on their learning can also provide teachers with insight into children's educational progress and give them feedback on improving curriculum or pedagogy.

DESIGN AND CONDUCT OF ASSESSMENT

Assessments and examinations must be credible, and based on valid ways of gauging learning.

As long as examinations and tests assess children's ability to remember and recall textbook knowledge, all attempts to redirect the curriculum towards learning will be thwarted. First, tests in knowledge-based subject areas must be able to gauge what children have learnt, and their ability to use this knowledge for problem solving and application in the real world. In addition, they must also be able to test the processes of thinking to gauge if the learner has also learnt where to find information, how to use new information, and to analyse and evaluate the same.

The types of questions that are set for assessment need to go beyond what is given in the book. Often children's learning is restricted as teachers do not accept their answers if they are different from what is presented in the guidebooks.

Questions that are open-ended and challenging could also be used. Designing good test items and questions is an art, and teachers should spend time thinking about and devising such questions. The interest and ability of teachers to design good questions can be promoted through district—or state-level competitions. All question papers must be designed graded for difficulty in order to permit all children to experience a level of success, and to gain confidence in their ability to answer and solve problems.

Trying to devise a good and effective open-book examination can be a challenge that we must try to take up in our curricular efforts at all levels of school. This would require teachers and examination setters to emphasise the interpretation and application of learning over the arguments and facts that can be located in the book. There have been successful demonstrations that such examinations can be carried out on a large scale, and that teachers can themselves be trusted with moderating the results of such examinations. In this way, the assessment of projects and lab work can also be made credible and sound.

It is important that after receiving their corrected papers, children rewrite the answers and that these are again reviewed by teachers to ensure that children have learnt and gained something out of the ordeal.

Competition is motivating, but it is an extrinsic rather than intrinsic form of motivation. It is, of course, much easier to establish and to manipulate, and therefore frequently resorted to by teachers and school systems as a way creating and nurturing the drive for excellence. Schools begin 'ranking' children as early as their pre-primary years as a way of inculcating in them a competitive spirit. Such a competitive drive has several negative side effects on learning, often superficial learning is sufficient to create and maintain impressions, and over time students lose their ability to take initiative or do things for the fulfilment of one's own interest; hence, areas that cannot be 'marked' are neglected. This has unhealthy consequences for classroom culture, making children individualistic and unsuited to team work. There is an absurd and unnecessary importance given to term examinations, often accompanied by extreme arrangements of invigilation and secrecy. While the physical and psychological effects of this may not be readily visible until middle school, they frequently lead to high levels of stress in children, and cause early burnout. Schools and teachers need to ask themselves whether there is really much to be gained out of such practices and to what extent learning requires such systems of marking and ranking.

SELF-ASSESSMENT AND FEEDBACK

The role of assessment is to gauge the progress that both learner and teacher have made towards achieving the aims that have been set and appraising how this could be done better. Opportunity for feedback, leading to revision and improvement of performance, should constantly be available, without exams and evaluations being used as a threat to study.

Grading and correction carried out in the presence of students and providing feedback on the answers they get right and wrong, and why. Asking children about why they answered what they did assists teachers in going beyond the written answer to engage with children's thinking. Such processes also take away the frightening judgemental quality of marks obtained in a test, and enable children to understand and focus on their mistakes and learn through these mistakes. Sometimes head teachers object, claiming that correction in the presence of the child reduces 'objectivity'. This is a misplaced concern for 'objectivity', stemming from a competitive system that believes in judging children. Such a concern for 'objectivity' is misplaced in evaluation, which is consistent with educational goals.

Not only learning outcomes but also learning experiences themselves must be evaluated. Learners happily comment on the totality of their experience. Exercises, both individual and collective, can be designed to enable them to reflect on and assess their learning experiences. Such experiences also provide them with self-regulatory capabilities essential for 'learning to learn'. Such information is also valuable feedback to the teacher, and can be used to modify the learning system as a whole.

Every classroom interaction with children requires their evaluation of their own work, and a discussion with them about what should be tested and the ways of finding out whether the competencies are being developed or not. Even very young children are able to give correct assessments of what they can or cannot do well. The role of teaching is to provide an opportunity to each child to learn to the best of his or her ability and provide learning experiences that develop cognitive qualities, physical well-being and athletic qualities, as also affective and aesthetic qualities.

Report cards need to present to children and parents a comprehensive and holistic view of the child's development in many fields. Teachers must be able to say things about each child/student, that conveys to them a sense of individualised attention, reaffirms a positive self-image, and communicates personal goals for them to work towards. Whether it is marks or grades that are reported, a qualitative statement by the teacher is necessary to support the assessment. Only through such a relationship with each child can any teacher succeed in influencing him/her, and contributing to his/her learning. Along with the teacher assessing each child, each student could also assess himself or herself and include this self-assessment in the report card.

Currently, many report cards carry information on subject areas and have nothing to say about other aspects of the child's development, including health, physical fitness and abilities in games, social skills, and abilities in art and craft. Qualitative statements about these aspects of children's education and development would provide a more holistic assessment of educational concerns.

AREAS THAT REQUIRE FRESH THINKING

There are many areas of the curriculum that can be assessed but for which we still do not have reliable and efficient instruments. This includes assessing learning that is carried out in groups, and learning in areas such as theatre, work and craft where skills and competencies develop over longer time scales and require careful observation.

Continuous and comprehensive evaluation has frequently been cited as the only meaningful kind of evaluation. This also requires much more careful thinking through about when it is to be employed in a system effectively. Such evaluation places a lot of demand on teachers' time and ability to maintain meticulous records if it is to be meaningfully executed and if it is to have any reliability as an assessment. If this simply increases stress on children by reducing all their activities into items for assessment, or making them experience the teacher's 'power', then it defeats the purpose of education. Unless a system is adequately geared for such assessment, it is better for teachers to engage in more limited forms of evaluation, but incorporating into them more features that will make the assessment a meaningful record of learning.

Finally, there is a need to evolve and maintain credibility in assessment so that they perform their function of providing feedback in a meaningful way.

ASSESSMENT AT DIFFERENT STAGES

ECCE and Classes I and II of the Elementary Stage: At this stage, assessment must be purely qualitative judgements of children's activities in various domains and an assessment of the status of their health and physical development, based on observations through everyday interactions. On no account should they be made to take any form of test, oral or written.

Class III to Class VIII of the Elementary Stage: A variety of methods may be used, including oral and written tests and observations. Children should be aware that they are being assessed, but this must be seen by them as a part of the teaching process and not as a fearful constant threat. Grades or marks along with qualitative judgements of achievement and areas requiring attention are essential at this stage. Children's own self-evaluation can also be a part of the report card from Class V onwards. Rather than examinations, there could be short tests from time-to-time, which are criterion based. Term-wise examinations could be commenced from Class VII onwards when children are more psychologically ready to study large chunks of material and, to spend a few hours in an examination room, working at answering questions. Again, the progress card must indicate general observations on health and nutrition, specific observations on the overall progress of the learner, and information and advice for the parents.

Class IX to Class XII of the Secondary and Higher Secondary Stages: Assessment may be based more on tests, examinations and project reports for the knowledge-based areas of the curriculum, along with self-assessment. Other areas would be assessed through observation and also through self-evaluation.

Reports could include much more analysis about the students, various skill/knowledge areas and percentiles, etc. This would assist them by pointing out the areas of study that they need to focus on, and also help them by providing a basis for further choices that they make regarding what to study thereafter.

CONCEPT OF INCLUSIVE EDUCATION & UNDERSTANDING CHILDREN WITH SPECIAL NEEDS

INCLUSIVE EDUCATION: DEFINITION AND CONCEPT

Inclusive Education denotes that all children irrespective of their strengths and weaknesses will be part of the mainstream education. Thus, inclusive education means, "the act of ensuring that all children despite their differences, receive the opportunity of being part of the same classroom as other children of their age, and in the process get the opportunity to being exposed to the curriculum to their optimal potential."

Every child is special for his/her parent and, every child has a special need for love, acceptance and a feeling of belongingness. Here, we call **children with special needs** to those who are "different" from their cohorts. They are born equal with some limitations and with the help of inclusion be able to actively participate as equal citizens in all aspects of society and community life. Thus, children with special needs refer to "all those children who require adaptations to the normal process of education due to problems of vision, hearing, movement, learning and intellect." In other words, these children have some kind of **disability**.

Disability: Definitions

Disability refers to any limitations experienced by the disabled in comparisons to able persons of similar age, sex and culture. The UN Declaration on the Rights of Disabled Persons has defined disabled person as "any person unable to ensure by himself or herself, wholly or partly, the necessities of a normal individual and/or social life, as a result of a deficiency, either congenital or not, in his or her physical or mental capabilities".

DISTINCTIONS AMONG IMPAIRMENT, DISABILITY AND HANDICAP

The World Health Organisation (WHO) has made distinctions between the definitions of impairment, disability and handicap as follows:

- Impairment is any loss or abnormality of psychological, physiological or anatomical structure or function generally taken to be at organ level. Impairment is a damage to tissue due to disease or trauma.
- A disability is any restriction or lack of ability (resulting from an impairment) to perform an activity in the manner or within the range considered normal for a human being.
- A handicap is a disadvantage for an individual, resulting from impairment or disability that limits or prevents fulfilment of a role that is normal (depending on age, sex and social cultural factors) for that individual. Handicap is a condition or burden, which is imposed on the person confronted with the disability.

Types of Disability According to PWD Act, 1995

The PWD Act, 1995 has given the following seven types of disability as:

1. Blindness
2. Low Vision
3. Leprosy-cured
4. Hearing impairment
5. Locomotor disabilities
6. Mental retardation
7. Mental illness

EDUCATIONAL PROVISIONS FOR CHILDREN WITH SPECIAL NEEDS

The last two decades of the 19th century has witnessed the knowledge and processes of educating the disabled children through Christian Missionaries. The first school for the deaf was established in Mumbai in 1883 and the first school for the blind in Amritsar in 1887. At that time, it was believed that children with disabilities could not be educated alongwith normal children. Therefore, education to disabled children was offered through special school. This trend continued early sixties of the last century with the help of some international agencies who developed programme of integrated education. Here, children disabilities were placed in regular school so that they could study alongwith their non-disabled 'peers". The integrated education adopts various models for service deliver. Presently the emphasis is on the need to provide education for all in appropriate environment with inclusive philosophy through inclusive education.

Integrated Education for the Disabled Children (IEDC)

With the development of science and technology and improvement in Medical Services and Aggressive neo-natal intervention has ensured that a large number of babies who would earlier have not survived but often with different abilities. The number of differently abled children is on the increasing trend but it is not possible to create the required number of special schools throughout the country to meet this challenge due to the high cost and also due to the fact that the population is so scattered. The best alternative under these situations is to make use of the infrastructural facilities already present in terms of regular schools and integrate children into the mainstream of education.

Consequent on the success of international institutions in introducing differently abled children in regular schools, the planning commission, Govt. of India, in 1971 includes in its plan a programme for integrated education. In 1974, the Union Government introduced a scheme called "Integrated Schools" to do just this. This scheme was later revised and a plan of action formulated. The important aims of IEDC includes:

- Provide educational opportunity to differently abled children in regular schools.
- Facilitate retention of differently abled in the school system.
- Integrate children from special school to common schools.

The scope of the scheme of IEDC includes pre-school training, counselling for the parents, and special training in skills for all kinds of differently abled children. It provides facilities in the form of books, stationary, uniforms and allowances for transport, reader and escort etc.

Project Integrated Education for the Disabled (PIED)

This scheme was launched by MHRD Govt. of India in collaboration with UNICEF in 1987 to strengthen the integration of differently abled into regular schools. Under this scheme, a cluster instead of individual school is given importance. This scheme is an improvement over the special schools in one or many ways and provides a way towards universalisation of elementary education and Education for All including for differently abled children.

ASSUMPTION ABOUT INTEGRATED EDUCATION

Integrated education assumes a process of bringing disabled children into mainstream schools, where the system remains the same. As per the system, the child is the problem. So, it is essential to change the child where the resources are focused on the individual child. The failure is due to the child's problem; he is not able, not ready, not good enough to cope up with the system.

In integrated education; it is the children with disabilities who are seen as the problem, who must be "fixed", "changed" & "adapted" to suit the existing regular, mainstream school. It is the disabled child who is seen as a square peg in a round table. The system remains the same. The onus for successful integration therefore, is on the disabled child.

ASSUMPTION ABOUT INCLUSIVE EDUCATION

Assumptions of inclusive education is opposite to integrated education. Inclusive education assumes that changes the system to fit the child. It is essential to addresses all types of individual needs, not just disability. Teachers and schools are held responsible for children's learning. It focuses on flexibility of curriculum, teacher training and change in environmental. Failure is the problem with the system not with the child. It is quite essential to assumes that all children can learn and that all children need their learning to be supported in diverse ways.

In this model of inclusive education, it is not the child, but the education system, which is seen as a problem. Therefore, it is the system (with all its components) with should be changed, modified & made flexible enough to accommodate the diverse needs of all learners, including children with disabilities. The onus for success is therefore on the flexibility of the system. It focuses on the environment, as the "disabling" cause because it fails to provide appropriate access to equal opportunities for all persons to participate fully in social life.

Though integrated education of differently abled children has gained momentum all over the country since 1974, there are some other possibilities too for these children to get education. For example, the NIOS (National Institute of Open Schooling) offers education which have the advantage of being specially adopted to the needs of every child as well as aimed at giving the child every opportunity to progress at his/her pace. Another example is alternative schooling and community-based rehabilitation programmes.

EDUCATION FOR A COHESIVE SOCIETY

Despite more than half a century of independence, India is struggling for freedom from various kinds of biases and imbalances such as rural/urban, rich/poor, and differences on the basis of caste, religion, ideology, gender etc. Education can play a very significant role in minimising and finally eliminating these differences by providing equality of access to quality education and opportunity.

Equality of opportunity means ensuring that every individual receives suitable education at a pace and through methods suited to his/her being. Children of the disadvantaged, and socially discriminated groups and also those suffering from specific challenges must be paid special attention.

Provision for equal opportunity to all not only in access, but also in the conditions for success is a precondition for the promotion of equality. The curriculum must create an awareness of the inherent equality of all with a view to removing prejudices and complexes transmitted through the social environment and the factor of birth.

EDUCATION OF GIRLS

Equality among sexes is a fundamental right under the constitution of India. The state, however, also has the right to exercise positive protective discrimination in favour of the disadvantaged population groups including women. Emphasis in education has moved from 'Equality of Educational Opportunity' (NPE, 1968) to 'Education for Women's Equality and Empowerment' (1986). As a result, the curricular and training strategies for the education of girls now demand more attention. Besides, making education accessible to more and more girls, especially rural girls, removing all gender discrimination and gender bias in school curriculum, textbooks and the process of transaction is absolutely necessary. There is a need to develop and implement gender inclusive and gender sensitive curricular strategies to nurture a generation of girls and boys who are equally competent and are sensitive to one another, and grow up in a caring and sharing mode as equals, and not as adversaries.

EDUCATION OF LEARNERS FROM DISADVANTAGED GROUPS

For achieving a cohesive society it would be essential to respond to specific educational needs of learners from different sections of the society with special emphasis on the Scheduled Castes, the Scheduled Tribes and the other socially and economically disadvantaged groups. In order to do so, there is a need for integrating the socio-cultural perspectives partly by showing concern for their linguistic specificities and pedagogic requirements. Implications of the multilingual and multicultural environment shall have to be taken care of through specifically devised methodology. Contextualisation of curriculum shall have to be effected through curricular materials. The fundamental rights of the disadvantaged groups have to be consciously incorporated in the curriculum. Even the problem of educating the migrating population shall have to be handled through specific condensed educational programmes based on the main ingredients of the national curriculum.

EDUCATION OF THE GIFTED AND TALENTED

An educational system has the dual role of promoting equality as well as excellence. Education is increasingly called upon to liberate all the creative potentialities of human consciousness. Man essentially fulfils himself in and through creation. It is in the context of this, that education of gifted and talented children assumes great importance. A curricular programme while on the one hand should identify such children, on the other it should also nurture their diverse creative abilities by paying them special attention. It is also important that the identification and nurturance begins right from the earliest stage of education. Moreover, the task of identifying the gifted and talented must be accomplished on the basis of a broad conceptualisation of the process from multiple perspectives rather than as a search for a unitary human attribute. Not only their IQ (Intelligence Quotient) but also their EQ (Emotional Quotient) and SQ (Spiritual Quotient) ought to be assessed.

NATIONAL LEVEL POLICY AND LEGISLATION

Kothari Commission (1964-66)

The Kothari Commission first suggested that the education of handicapped children has to be organised not merely on humanitarian grounds, but also an aspects of utility. The commission emphasised that the education of children with disability should be "an inseparable part of the general education system. The commission also specifically emphasised that the education of children with disability should be "an inseparable part of the general education system. The commission also specifically emphasised. the importance of integrated education in meeting this target as it is cost effective and useful in developing mutual understanding between children with and without disabilities.

National Policy on Education (1986)

The National Policy on Education was adopted by Indian Parliament in 1986. The policy emphasized the removal of disparities, and ensuring equalisation of educational opportunity under its para education of the disabled.

National Policies for Persons with Disabilities (2006)

This recognises that persons with disabilities are valuable human resources for the country and seek to create an environment that provides them equal opportunities, protection of their rights and full participation in society.

Persons with Disabilities (Equal Opportunities, Protection of Rights & Full Participation) Act, 1995

Landmark legislation in the history of special education in India is the persons with Disabilities Act, 1995. This comprehensive Act covers seven disabilities, namely blindness, low vision, hearing impaired, loco-motor impaired, mental retardation, leprosy cured and mental illness.

The Rehabilitation Council of India (RCI) Act, 1992

This Act was passed in 1992 for the purpose of constituting the Rehabilitation Professionals and for maintenance of a Central Rehabilitation Register. It was amended by Rehabilitation Council of India (Amendment) Act, 2000 to provide for monitoring the training of rehabilitation professionals and personal, promoting research in rehabilitation and special education as additional objectives of the council.

LEARNING AND PEDAGOGY

HOW CHILDREN THINK AND LEARN

Children learn from anything and everything they see and act upon. They have learnt a lot before they join school, and they continue to learn outside the school hours. If we believe that children learn only in school, it is because of what we wrongly regard as learning. When a child spends hours on trying to solve a Jigsaw puzzle (say), he/she is often reprimanded by adults for wasting study time. Little do the grown-ups realise that it is through such interesting games that this child may be increasing his/her understanding of shapes and size. And, this learning is taking place outside the school hours, without formal instruction. A curriculum built upon assumptions about children's learning, that ignore this aspect, is also responsible for children losing interest in mathematics or in any formal learning.

From the time a child is born, his/her interaction with the world around his/her starts. He/she perceives things around his/her, and gradually makes sense of them. He/she slowly begins to recognise people and objects, relate more and more to the environment, and observe things through the senses of touch, sight, taste, smell and sound. There are **four different stages** of learning or development that each child goes through.

Sensorimotor

This is from the ages of birth to about two years old. During this time the child's primary mode of learning occurs through the five senses. He/she learns to experience environment. The child touches things, holds, looks, listens, tastes, feels, bangs, and shakes everything in sight. When the child adds motor skills such as creeping, crawling and walking, his/her environment expands by leaps and bounds. The child is now exploring their environment with both senses and the ability to get around.

Preoperational

This is the stages between ages two and seven. During this stage the child is busy gathering information or learning, and then trying to figure out ways that they can used what they have learned to begin solving problems.

During this stage of his/her life child will be thinking in specifics and will find it very difficult to get generalise anything. This is the time when a child learns by asking questions. The child generally will not want a real answer to his question at this point. When he asks why do we have grass .... He simply wants to know that it is for him to play in. No technical answers for know. The child in this age group judges everything on the 'me' basis—How does it affect me? Do I like it?

Concrete Operations Period

This is the period of time when child is between the ages of seven to ten. This is a wonderful age as this is when children begin to manipulate data mentally. They take the information at hand and begin to define, compare and contrast it. They, however, still think concretely.

The concrete operational child is capable of logical thought. This child still learns through their senses, but no longer relies on only them to teach him. He now thinks as well. A good teacher for this age group would start each lesson at a concrete level and then more toward a generalised level. The child, during this period, is very literal in their thinking.

Formal Operations Period

The period begins at about age eleven. At this time the child will break through the barrier of literalism and more on to thinking in more abstract terms. He no longer restricts thinking to time and space. This child now starts to reflect, hypothesize and theorize.

In the formal operation period, children need to develop cognitive abilities. The following is a list of six simple categories of cognitive abilities. The following is a list of six simple categories of cognitive abilities:

1. **Knowledge of facts and principals:** This is the direct recall of facts and principals. **Examples:** memorisation of dates, name, definition, vocabulary words.
2. **Comprehension:** Understanding of facts and ideas.
3. **Application:** Needs to know, rules, principles, and procedures and how to use them.
4. **Analysis:** Breaking down concepts into parts.
5. **Synthesis:** Putting together information or ideas.
6. **Evaluation:** Judging the value of information.

BASIC PROCESSES OF TEACHING AND LEARNING

Teaching-learning process is the heart of education. On it depends the fulfilment of the aims & objectives of education. It is the most powerful instrument of education to bring about desired changes in the students. Teaching learning are related terms. In teaching-learning process, the teacher, the learner, the curriculum & other variables are organised in a systematic way to attain some pre-determined goal.

Essential Aspects of the Teaching-learning Process

According to Diana Laurillard, there are four aspects of the teaching-learning process:

1. **Discussion**—between the teacher and learner.
2. **Interaction**—between the learner and some aspect of the world defined by the teacher.
3. **Adaptation**—of the world by the teacher and action by the learner.
4. **Reflection**—on the learner's performance by both teacher and learner.

According to **Burton** in the figure above

1. Teaching can become effective only by relating it to process of learning.
2. Teaching objective cannot be realised without being related to learning situation.
3. We may create and use teaching aids to create some appropriate learning situation.
4. The strategies and devices of teaching may be selected in such a manner that the optimal objectives of learning area achieved.
5. To understand principles, goals, objectives of education in right perspective.
6. Appropriate learning situation condition may be created for congenial and effective teaching.

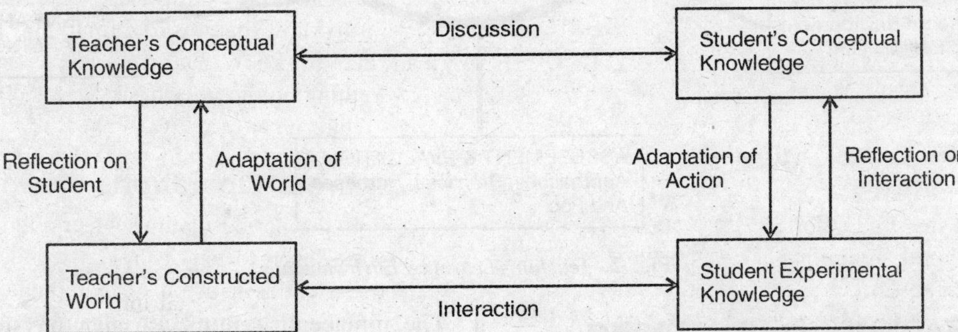

Fig. 1: *Essential aspects of the ideal teaching-learning process*

Approaches to Learning Theories

Aspect	Behaviourist	Cognitivist	Humanist
Learning theorists	Thorndike, Pavlov, Watson, Guthrie, Hull, Tolman, Skinner	Koffka, Kohler, Lewin, Piaget, Ausubel, Bruner, Gagne	Maslow, Rogers
View of the learning process	Change in behaviour	Internal mental process (including insight, information processing, memory, perception)	A personal act to fulfil potential
Locus of learning	Stimuli in external environment	Internal cognitive structuring	Affective and cognitive needs

Aspect	Behaviourist	Cognitivist	Humanist
Purpose in education	Produce behavioural change in desired direction	Develop capacity and skills to learn better	Become self-actualized autonomous
Educator's role	Arranges environment to elicit desired response	Structures content of learning activity	Facilitates development of the whole person
Manifestations in adult learning	Behavioural objectives	Cognitive development	Andragogy
	Competency-based education	Intelligence, learning and memory as function of age	Self-directed learning
	Skill development and training	Learning how to learn	

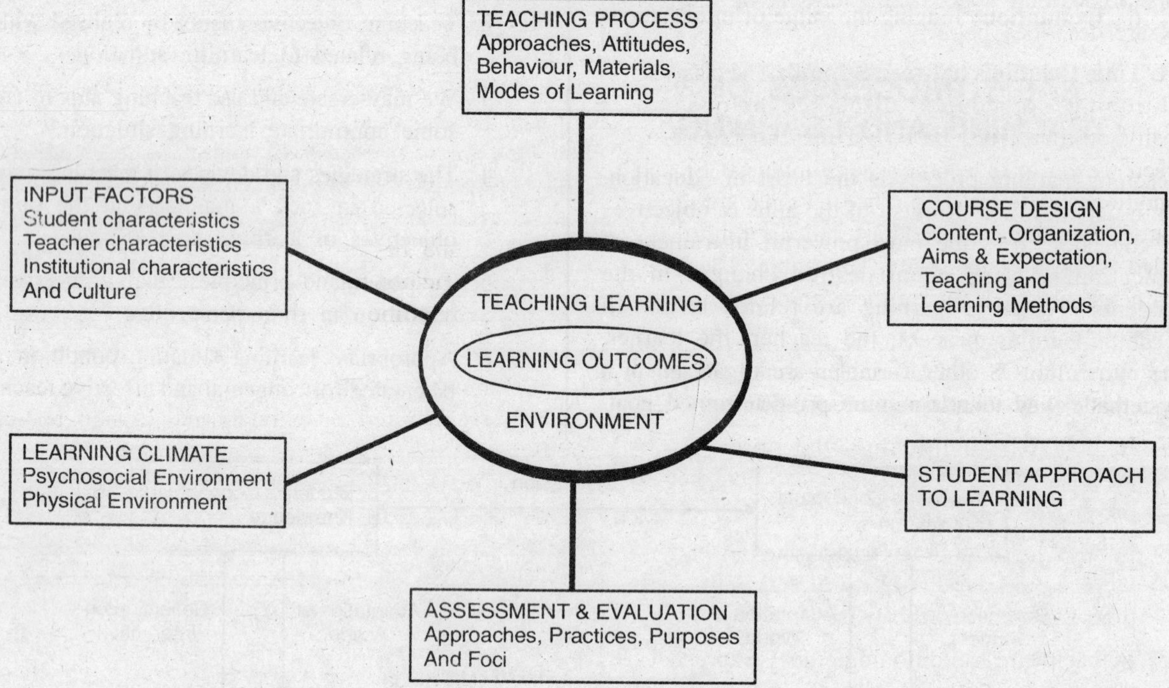

Fig. 2: *Teaching-Learning Environment*

PARADIGMS OF LEARNING

Learning takes place in many ways. There are some methods that are used in acquisition of simple responses while other methods are used in the acquisition of complex responses. The simplest kind of learning is called conditioning. Two types of conditioning have been identified. The first one is called classical conditioning and the second instrumental/operant conditioning. In addition, we have observational learning, cognitive learning, verbal learning, concept learning and skill learning.

Classical Conditioning

This type of learning was first investigated by Ivan P. Pavlov. Like many great scientific advances, classical conditioning was discovered accidentally. The nineteenth-century Russian physiologist Ivan Pavlov was looking at salivation in dogs in response to being fed, when he noticed that his dogs would begin to salivate whenever he entered the room, even when he was not bringing them food. However, when Pavlov discovered that any object or event which the dogs learnt to associate with food (such as the food bowl) would trigger the same response, he realised that he had made an important scientific discovery, and he devoted the rest of his career to studying this type of learning.

Classical conditioning is 'classical' in that it is the first systematic study of basic laws of learning. Classical conditioning involves learning to associate an unconditioned stimulus that already brings about a particular response (*i.e.* a reflex) with a new (conditioned) stimulus, so that the new stimulus brings about the same response. The unconditioned stimulus (or UCS) is the object or event that originally produces the reflexive/natural response.

Once the neutral stimulus has become associated with the unconditioned stimulus, it becomes a conditioned stimulus (CS). The conditioned response (CR) is the response to the conditioned stimulus. Thus, learning situation in classical conditioning is one of S-S learning in which one stimulus becomes a signal of another stimulus.

Determinants of Classical Conditioning

How quickly and strongly acquisition of a response occurs in classical conditioning depends on several factors. Some of the major factors influencing learning a CR are described below:

1. Time Relations between Stimuli: The classical conditioning procedures, discussed below, are basically of four types based on the time relations between the onset of conditioned stimulus (CS) and unconditioned stimulus (US). The first three are called forward conditioning procedures, and the fourth one is called backward conditioning procedure. The basic experimental arrangements of these procedures are as follows:

(*a*) When the CS and US are presented together, it is called simultaneous conditioning.

(*b*) In delayed conditioning, the onset of CS precedes the onset of US. The CS ends before the end of the US.

(*c*) In trace conditioning, the onset and end of the CS precedes the onset of US with some time gap between the two.

(*d*) In backward conditioning, the US precedes the onset of CS.

It is now well established that delayed conditioning procedure is the most effective way of acquiring a CR. Simultaneous and trace conditioning procedures do lead to acquisition of a CR, but they require greater number of acquisition trials in comparison to the delayed conditioning procedure. It may be noted that the acquisition of response under backward conditioning procedure is very rare.

2. Type of Unconditioned Stimuli: The unconditioned stimuli used in studies of classical conditioning are basically of two types, *i.e.* appetitive and aversive. Appetitive unconditioned stimuli automatically elicits approach responses, such as eating, drinking, caressing, etc. These responses give satisfaction and pleasure. On the other hand, aversive US, such as noise, bitter taste, electric shock, painful injections, etc. are painful, harmful, and elicit avoidance and escape responses. It has been found that appetitive classical conditioning is slower and requires greater number of acquisition trials, but aversive classical conditioning is established in one, two or three trials depending on the intensity of the aversive US.

3. Intensity of Conditioned Stimuli: This influences the course of both appetitive and aversive classical conditioning. More intense conditioned stimuli are more effective in accelerating the acquisition of conditioned responses. It means that the more intense the conditioned stimulus, the fewer are the number of acquisition trials needed for conditioning.

Operant/Instrumental Conditioning

B.F. Skinner is regarded as the father of operant conditioning, but his work was based on **Thorndike's law of effect.** In the late nineteenth century, psychologist Edward Thorndike proposed the law of effect. The law of effect states that any behaviour that has good consequences will tend to be repeated, and any behaviour that has bad consequences will tend to be avoided. In the 1930s, B.F. Skinner, extended this idea and began to study operant conditioning. Operant conditioning is a type of learning in which responses come to be controlled by their consequences.

Operants are those behaviours or responses, which are emitted by animals and human beings voluntarily and are under their control. The term operant is used because the organism operates on the environment. Conditioning of operant behaviour is called operant conditioning. Skinner conducted his studies on rats and pigeons in specially made boxes, called the Skinner Box.

Determinants of Operant Conditioning

The operant or instrumental conditioning is a form of learning in which behaviour is learned, maintained or changed through its consequences. Such consequences are called **reinforcers**. A reinforcer is defined as any stimulus or event, which increases the probability of the occurrence of a (desired) response. A reinforcer has numerous features, which affect the course and strength of a response. They include its type—positive or negative, number or frequency, quality—superior or inferior, and schedule—continuous or intermittent (partial).

Reinforcement may be positive or negative. Positive reinforcement involves stimuli that have pleasant consequences. They strengthen and maintain the responses that have caused them to occur. Positive reinforcers satisfy needs, which include food, water, medals, praise, money, status, information, etc. Negative reinforcers involve unpleasant and painful stimuli. Responses that lead organisms to get rid of painful stimuli or avoid and escape from them provide negative reinforcement. Thus, negative reinforcement leads to learning of avoidance and escape responses. For instance, one learns to put on woollen clothes, burn firewood or use electric heaters to avoid the unpleasant cold weather. One learns to move away from dangerous stimuli because they provide negative reinforcement. It may be noted that negative reinforcement is not punishment. Use of punishment reduces or suppresses the response while a negative reinforcer increases the probability of avoidance or escape response. For instance, drivers and co-drivers wear their seat belts to avoid getting injured in case of an accident or to avoid being fined by the traffic police.

Classical and Operant Conditioning : Differences

1. In classical conditioning, the responses are under the control of some stimulus because they are reflexes, automatically elicited by the appropriate stimuli. Such stimuli are selected as US and responses elicited by them as UR. Thus Pavlovian conditioning, in which US elicits responses, is often called respondent conditioning.

   In instrumental conditioning, responses are under the control of the organism and are voluntary responses or 'operants'. Thus, in the two forms of conditioning different types of responses are conditioned.
2. In classical conditioning, the CS and US are well-defined, but in operant conditioning CS is not defined. It can be inferred but is not directly known.
3. In classical conditioning, the experimenter controls the occurrence of US, while in operant conditioning the occurrence of the reinforcer is under the control of the organism that is learning. Thus, for US in classical conditioning the organism remains passive, while in operant conditioning the subject has to be active in order to be reinforced.
4. In the two forms of conditioning, the technical terms used to characterise the experimental proceedings are different. Moreover what is called reinforcer in operant conditioning is called US in classical conditioning. An US has two functions. In the beginning, it elicits the response and also reinforces the response to be associated and elicited later on by the CS.

OBSERVATIONAL LEARNING

The other form of learning takes place by observing others. Earlier this form of learning was called **imitation**. Bandura and his colleagues in a series of experimental studies investigated observational learning in detail. In this kind of learning, human beings learn social behaviours, therefore, it is sometimes called **social learning**. In many situations individuals do not know how to behave. They observe others and emulate their behaviour. This form of learning is called **modelling**.

Examples of observational learning abound in our social life. Fashion designers employ tall, pretty, and gracious young girls and tall, smart, and well-built young boys for popularising clothes of different designs and fabrics. People observe them on televised fashion shows and advertisements in magazines and newspapers. They imitate these models. Observing superiors and likeable persons and then emulating their behaviour in a novel social situation is a common experience.

The children observe adults' behaviours, at home and during social ceremonies and functions. They enact adults in their plays and games. For instance, young children play games of marriage ceremonies, birthday parties, thief and policeman, house keeping, etc. Actually they enact in their games what they observe in society, on television, and read in books.

Children learn most of the social behaviours by observing and emulating adults. The way to put on clothes, dress one's hair, and conduct oneself in society are learned through observing others. It has also been shown that children learn and develop various personality characteristics through observational learning. Aggressiveness, prosocial behaviour, courtesy, politeness, diligence, and indolence are acquired by this method of learning.

COGNITIVE LEARNING

Some psychologists view learning in terms of cognitive processes that underlie it. They have developed approaches that focus on such processes that occur during learning rather than concentrating solely on S-R and S-S connections. Thus, in cognitive learning, there is a change in what the learner knows rather than what he/she does. This form of learning shows up in insight learning and latent learning.

Insight Learning

Kohler demonstrated a model of learning which could not be readily explained by conditioning. He performed a series of experiments with chimpanzees that involved solving complex problems. Kohler placed chimpanzees in an enclosed play area where food was kept out of their reach. Tools such as poles and boxes were placed in the enclosure. The chimpanzees rapidly learned how to use a box to stand on or a pole to move the food in their direction. In this experiment, learning did not occur as a result of trial and error and reinforcement, but came about in sudden flashes of insight. The chimpanzees would roam about the enclosure for some time and then suddenly would stand on a box, grab a pole and strike a banana, which was out of normal reach above the enclosure. The chimpanzee exhibited what Kohler called insight learning—the process by which the solution to a problem suddenly becomes clear.

In a normal experiment on insight learning, a problem is presented, followed by a period of time when no apparent progress is made and finally a solution suddenly emerges. In insight learning, sudden solution is the rule. Once the solution has appeared, it can be repeated immediately the next time the problem is confronted. Thus, it is clear that what is learned is not a specific set of conditioned associations between stimuli and responses but a cognitive relationship between a means and an end. As a result, insight learning can be generalised to other similar problem situations.

Latent Learning

Another type of cognitive learning is known as latent learning. In latent learning, a new behaviour is learned but not demonstrated until reinforcement is provided for displaying it. Tolman made an early contribution to the concept of latent learning. To have an idea of latent learning, we may briefly understand his experiment. Tolman put two groups of rats in a maze and gave them an opportunity to explore. In one group, rats found food at the end of the maze and soon learned to make their way rapidly through the maze. On the other hand, rats in the second group were not rewarded and showed no apparent signs of learning. But later, when these rats were reinforced, they ran through the maze as efficiently as the rewarded group.

Tolman contended that the unrewarded rats had learned the layout of the maze early in their explorations. They just never displayed their latent learning until the reinforcement was provided. Instead, the rats developed a cognitive map of the maze, *i.e.* a mental representation of the spatial locations and directions, which they needed to reach their goal.

LEARNING AS A SOCIAL ACTIVITY

Learning is a social activity. Our learning is intimately associated with our connection with other human beings, our teachers, our peers, our family as well as casual acquaintances, including the people before us or next to us. We are more likely to be successful in our efforts to educate, if we recognise this principle rather than try to avoid it. Much of traditional education, as Dewey pointed out, is directed towards isolating the learner from all social interaction, and towards seeing education as a one-on-one relationship between the learner and the objective material to be learned. In contrast, progressive education (to continue to use Dewey's formulation) recognizes the social aspect of learning and uses conversations interaction with others, and the application of knowledge as an integral aspect of learning.

SOCIAL CONTEXT OF LEARNING

Social Learning theory

Social learning theory focuses on the learning that occurs within a social context. It considers that people learn from one another, including such concepts as observational learning, imitation, and modelling. Among others **Albert Bandura** is considered the leading proponent of this theory.

General Principles of Social Learning Theory Follows:

1. People can learn by observing the behaviour is of others and the outcomes of those behaviours.
2. Learning can occur without a change in behaviour. Behaviourists say that learning has to be represented by a permanent change in behaviour, in contrast social learning theorists say that because people can learn through observation alone, their learning may not necessarily be shown in their performance. Learning may or may not result in a behaviour change.
3. Cognition plays a role in learning. Over the last 40 years social learning theory has become increasingly cognitive in its interpretation of human learning. Awareness and expectations of future reinforcements or punishments can have a major effect on the behaviours that people exhibit.
4. Social learning theory can be considered a bridge or a transition between behaviourist learning theories and cognitive learning theories.

How the Environment Reinforces and Punishes Modelling:

People are often reinforced for modelling the behaviour of others. Bandura suggested that the environment also reinforces modelling. This is in several possible ways:

1. The observer is reinforced by the model. For example, a student who changes dress to fit in with a certain group of students has a strong likelihood of being accepted and thus reinforced by that group.
2. The observer is reinforced by a third person. The observer might be modelling the actions of someone else, for example, an outstanding class leader or student. The teacher notices this and compliments and praises the observer for modelling such behaviour thus reinforcing that behaviour.
3. The imitated behaviour itself leads to reinforcing consequences. Many behaviours that we learn from others produce satisfying or reinforcing results. For example, a student in my multimedia class could observe how the extra work a classmate does is fun. This student in turn would do the same extra work and also receive enjoyment.
4. Consequences of the model's behaviour affect the observers behaviour vicariously. This is known as vicarious reinforcement. This is where in the model is reinforced for a response and then the observer shows an increase in that same response. Bandura illustrated this by having students watch a film of a model hitting a inflated clown doll. One group of children saw the model being praised for such action. Without being reinforced, the group of children began to also hit the doll.

Contemporary Social Learning Perspective of Reinforcement and Punishment

1. Contemporary theory proposes that both reinforcement and punishment have indirect effects on learning. They are not the sole or main cause.
2. Reinforcement and punishment influence the extent to which an individual exhibits a behaviour that has been learned.
3. The expectation of reinforcement influences cognitive processes that promote learning. Therefore, attention pays a critical role in learning. And attention is influenced by the expectation of reinforcement. An example would be, where the teacher tells a group of students that what they will study next is not on the test. Students will not pay attention, because they do not expect to know the information for a test.

Cognitive Factors in Social Learning

Social learning theory has cognitive factors as well as behaviourist factors (actually operant factors).

1. **Learning without performance:** Bandura makes a distinction between learning through observation and the actual imitation of what has been learned.
2. **Cognitive processing during learning:** Social learning theorists contend that attention is a critical factor in learning.
3. **Expectations:** As a result of being reinforced, people form expectations about the consequences that future behaviours are likely to bring. They expect certain behaviours to bring reinforcements and others to bring punishment. The learner needs to be aware however, of the response reinforcements and response punishment. Reinforcement increases a response only when the learner is aware of that connection.
4. **Reciprocal causation:** Bandura proposed that behaviour can influence both the environment and the person. In fact each of these three variables, the person, the behaviour, and the environment can have an influence on each other.
5. **Modelling:** There are different types of models. There is the live model, and actual person demonstrating the behaviour. There can also be a symbolic model, which can be a person or action portrayed in some other medium, such as television, videotape, computer programs.

Behaviours that can be learned through modelling:

Many behaviours can be learned, at least partly, through modelling. Examples that can be cited are, students can watch parents read, students can watch the demonstrations of mathematics problems, or seen someone acting bravely and a fearful situation. Aggression can be learned through models. Much research indicate that children become more aggressive when they observed aggressive or violent models. Moral thinking and moral behaviour are influenced by observation and modelling. This includes moral judgments regarding right and wrong which can in part, develop through modelling.

Conditions Necessary for Effective Modelling to Occur:

Bandura mentions four conditions that are necessary before an individual can successfully model the behaviour of someone else:

1. **Attention:** the person must first pay attention to the model.
2. **Retention:** the observer must be able to remember the behaviour that has been

observed. One way of increasing this is using the technique of rehearsal.

3. **Motor reproduction:** the third condition is the ability to replicate the behaviour that the model has just demonstrated. This means that the observer has to be able to replicate the action, which could be a problem with a learner who is not ready developmentally to replicate the action. For example, little children have difficulty doing complex physical motion.
4. **Motivation:** the final necessary ingredient for modelling to occur is motivation, learners must want to demonstrate what they have learned. Remember that since these four conditions vary among individuals, different people will reproduce the same behaviour differently.

Effects of Modelling on Behaviour:

Modelling teaches new behaviours.

Modelling influences the frequency of previously learned behaviours.

Modelling may encourage previously forbidden behaviours.

Modelling increases the frequency of similar behaviours. For example, a student might see a friend excel in basketball and he tries to excel in football because he is not tall enough for basketball.

Educational implications of social learning theory:

Social learning theory has numerous implications for classroom use.

1. Students often learn a great deal simply by observing other people.
2. Describing the consequences of behaviour is can effectively increase the appropriate behaviours and decrease inappropriate ones. This can involve discussing with learners about the rewards and consequences of various behaviours.
3. Modelling provides an alternative to shaping for teaching new behaviours. Instead of using shaping, which is operant conditioning, modelling can provide a faster, more efficient means for teaching new behaviour. To promote effective modelling a teacher must make sure that the four essential conditions exist; attention, retention, motor reproduction, and motivation.
4. Teachers and parents must model appropriate behaviours and take care that they do not model inappropriate behaviours.
5. Teachers should expose students to a variety of other models. This technique is especially important to break down traditional stereotypes.
6. Students must believe that they are capable of accomplishing school tasks. Thus, it is very important to develop a sense of self-efficacy for students. Teachers can promote such self-efficacy by having students receive confidence-building messages, watch others be successful, and experience success on their own.
7. Teachers should help students set realistic expectations for their academic accomplishments. In general in my class that means making sure that expectations are not set too low. I want to realistically challenge my students. However, sometimes the task is beyond a student's ability, example would be the cancer group.
8. Self-regulation techniques provide an effective method for improving student behaviour.

CHILD AS A PROBLEM SOLVER AND A SCIENTIFIC INVESTIGATOR

Problem solving is the foundation of a young child's learning. It must be valued, promoted, provided for and sustained in the early childhood classroom. Opportunities for problem solving occur in the everyday context of a child's life. By observing the child closely, teachers can use the child's social, cognitive, movement and emotional experiences to facilitate problem solving and promote strategies useful in the lifelong process of learning.

Problem solving is thinking that is goal-directed. Almost all our day-to-day activities are directed towards a goal. Here, it is important to know that problems are not always in the form of obstacles or hurdles that one faces. It could be any simple activity that you perform to reach a defined goal, for example, preparing a quick snack for your friend who has just arrived at your place. In problem solving there is an initial state (*i.e.* the problem) and there is an end state (the goal). These two anchors are connected by means of several steps or mental operations. Following table would clarify our understanding of various steps through which one solves a problem.

Table: Mental Operations Involved in Solving a Problem

Let us look at the problem of organising a play in school on the occasion of Teachers' Day. Problem solving would involve the following sequence.

Mental operation	Nature of problem
1. Identify the problem	A week is left for teachers' day and you are given the task of organising a play.
2. Represent the problem	Organising a play would involve identification of an appropriate theme, screening of actors, actresses, arranging money, etc.
3. Plan the solution: Set sub-goals	Search and survey various available themes for a play, and consult teachers and friends who have the expertise. The play to be decided, based on such considerations as cost, duration, suitability for the occasion, etc.
4. Evaluate all solutions (plays)	Collect all the information/stage rehearsal.
5. Select one solution and execute it	Compare and verify the various options to get the best solution (the play).
6. Evaluate the outcome	If the play (solution) is appreciated, think about the steps you have followed for future reference for yourself as well as for your friends.
7. Rethink and redefine problems and solutions	After this special occasion you can still think about ways to plan a better play in future.

Learning Through Problem Solving

By exploring social relationships, manipulating objects, and interacting with people, children are able to formulate ideas, try these ideas out, and accept or reject what they learn. Constructing knowledge by making mistakes is part of the natural process of problem solving. Through exploring, then experimenting, trying out a hypothesis, and finally, solving problems, children make learning personal and meaningful. Piaget states that children understand only what they discover or invent themselves. It is this discovery within the problem solving process that is the vehicle for children's learning. Children are encouraged to construct their own knowledge when the teacher plans for problem solving; bases the framework for learning in problem solving; and provides time, space, and materials.

Teacher's Role

Changing through problem solving is modelled by adults and facilitated by the teacher in the classroom environment. When teachers articulate the problems they face and discuss solutions with children, children become more aware of the significance of the problem-solving process. Being a problem solver is modelled by the teacher and emulated by the children. The teacher's role is two-fold: first, to value the process and be willing to trust the learner, and second, to establish and maintain a classroom environment that encourages problem solving. It is the attitude of the teacher that must change first in the problem-solving classroom. Values and goals must be clearly defined to include a child-centered curriculum, the development of communication skills, promotion of cooperative learning, and inclusion of diverse ideas.

The teacher must be willing to become a learner, too. By being curious, observing, listening, and questioning, the teacher shares and models the qualities that are valued and promoted by the problem-solving process.

Planning for Problem Solving

A curriculum that accommodates a variety of developmental levels as well as individual differences in young children sets the stage for problem solving. Choices, decision-making, and a curriculum framework that integrates learning, such as Katz and Chard's project method, are especially appropriate for young learners. The project approach facilitates cooperative learning and promotes diverse ideas. Donna Ogle's K-W-L (what you KNOW, what you WANT to know, and what you have LEARNED) is another method of organizing work that promotes problem solving. Themes, units, webbing, and the KWL method are all ways of organizing curriculum that can support problem solving. Beginning with the needs and interests of the children, problem solving develops from meaningful experiences important to the children. The teacher-designed curriculum provides the classroom basis for these experiences.

For example, a second grade investigation of waste materials from a classroom led one group of young children to explore the topic in an integrated way. Reading, writing, counting, measuring, interviews of community people, and science experiments were planned, initiated and reported. Solutions to many problems posed during the investigation were tried out and some were found to be successful. Through group work, individuals were able to participate and communicate as cognitive and social needs were met. Each child, at individual levels and in individual ways, was successful within the group experience. Problem solving empowers children.

Providing for Problem Solving

Problem solving is a skill that can be learned and must be practiced. It is facilitated by a classroom schedule that provides for integrated learning in large blocks of time, space for ongoing group projects, and many open-ended materials. The teacher provides the time, space, and materials necessary for in-depth learning.

1. Time: Teachers can provide for problem solving by enlarging blocks of learning time during the school day. Because making choices, discussing decisions, and evaluating mistakes takes time, large time blocks best suit the problem-solving process. It is important that children know they have time to identify and solve problems.

2. Space: Projects and group meetings may require an assessment of classroom space. Moving desks and tables together facilitates communication and cooperation in the classroom. Once the teacher has observed the patterns of traffic in the classroom, equipment can be moved or eliminated to promote problem solving.

3. Materials: The open-ended materials that are needed for the construction and concrete solving of problems should be safe, durable, and varied. Well-marked storage units should be easily accessible to children, and materials should be available for ongoing exploration and manipulation. Access to a variety of materials encourages children to use materials in new and diverse ways. This freedom promotes problem solving.

The Problem-Solving Model

Individuals or groups can solve problems. Group problem solving is important to young children because many diverse ideas are generated. Both individual and group processes should be included in the early childhood classroom. Becoming skillful at problem solving is based on the understanding and use of sequenced steps. These steps are:

1. Identifying the problem,
2. Brainstorming a variety of solutions,
3. Choosing one solution and trying it out, and
4. Evaluating what has happened.

Choosing Good Problems

Goffin provides teachers with guiding questions that will help them identify appropriate problems for young children. Some of these are:

1. Is the problem meaningful and interesting?
2. Can the problem be solved at a variety of levels?
3. Must a new decision be made?
4. Can the actions be evaluated?

Problem solving is a way to make sense of the environment and, in fact, control it. The process allows children in an increasingly diverse world to be active participants and to implement changes. By including problem solving in the early childhood classroom, we equip children with a life-long skill that is useful in all areas of learning.

Obstacles to Solving Problems

Two major obstacles to solving a problem are mental set and lack of motivation.

Mental Set

Mental set is a tendency of a person to solve problems by following already tried mental operations or steps. Prior success with a particular strategy would sometimes help in solving a new problem. However, this tendency also creates a mental rigidity that obstructs the problem solver to think of any new rules or strategies. Thus, while in some situations mental set can enhance the quality and speed of problem solving, in other situations it hinders problem solving. You might have experienced this while solving mathematical problems. After completing a couple of questions, you form an idea of the steps that are required to solve these questions and subsequently you go on following the same steps, until a point where you fail. At this point you may experience difficulty in avoiding the already used steps. Those steps would interfere in your thought for new strategies. However, in day-to-day activities we often rely on past experiences with similar or related problems.

Like mental set, **functional fixedness** in problem solving occurs when people fail to solve a problem because they are fixed on a thing's usual function. If you have ever used a hardbound book to hammer a nail, then you have overcome functional fixedness.

Lack of Motivation

People might be great at solving problems, but all their skills and talents are of no use if they are not motivated. Sometimes people give up easily when they encounter a problem or failure in implementing the first step. Therefore, there is a need to persist in their effort to find a solution.

ALTERNATIVE CONCEPTIONS OF LEARNING

When teachers provide instruction on concepts in various subjects, they are teaching students who already have some pre-instructional knowledge about the topic. Student knowledge, however, can be erroneous, illogical or misinformed. These erroneous understandings are termed alternative conceptions or misconceptions (or intuitive theories). Alternative conceptions (misconceptions) are not unusual. In fact, they are a normal part of the learning process. We quite naturally form ideas from our everyday experience, but obviously not all the ideas we develop are correct with respect to the most current evidence and scholarship in a given discipline. Moreover, some concepts in different content areas are simply very difficult to grasp. They may be very abstract, counterintuitive or quite complex. Hence, our understanding of them is flawed. In addition, things we have already learned are sometimes unhelpful in learning new concepts/theories. This occurs when the new concept or theory is inconsistent with previously learned material. Accordingly, as noted, it is very typical for students (and adults) to have misconceptions in different domains (content knowledge areas). Indeed, researchers have found that there is a common set of alternative conceptions (misconceptions) that most students typically exhibit. There is one class of alternative theories (or misconceptions) that is very deeply entrenched. These are "ontological misconceptions," which relate to ontological beliefs (*i.e.*, beliefs about the fundamental categories and properties of the world).

Alternative conceptions (misconceptions) can impede learning for several reasons. First, students generally are unaware that the knowledge they have is wrong. Moreover, misconceptions can be very entrenched in student thinking. In addition, new experiences are interpreted through these erroneous understandings, thereby interfering with being able to correctly grasp new information. Also, alternative conceptions (misconceptions) tend to be very resistant to instruction because learning entails replacing or radically reorganizing student knowledge. Hence, conceptual change has to occur for learning to happen. This puts teachers in the very challenging position of needing to bring about significant conceptual change in student knowledge. Generally, ordinary forms of instruction, such as lectures, labs, discovery learning, or simply reading texts, are not very successful at overcoming student misconceptions. For all these reasons, misconceptions can be hard nuts for teachers to crack. However, several instructional strategies have been found to be effective in achieving conceptual change and helping students leave their alternative conceptions behind and learn correct concepts or theories.

Instructional strategies that can lead to change in students' alternative conceptions (misconceptions) and to learning of new concepts and theories

1. Present new concepts or theories that you are teaching in such a way that students see as plausible, high-quality, intelligible and generative.
2. Use students' correct conceptions and build on those by creating a bridge of examples to the new concept or theory that students are having trouble learning due to misconceptions they hold.
3. Use model-ased reasoning, which helps students construct new representations that vary from their intuitive theories.
4. Use diverse instruction, wherein you present a few examples that challenge multiple assumptions, rather than a larger number of examples that challenge just one assumption.
5. Help students become aware of (raise student metacognition about) their own alternative conceptions (misconceptions).
6. Present students with experiences that cause cognitive conflict in students' minds. Experiences (as in strategy 3 above) that can cause cognitive conflict are ones that get students to consider their erroneous (misconception) knowledge side-by-side with, or at the same time as, the correct concept or theory.
7. Engage in Interactive Conceptual Instruction (ICI).
8. Develop students' epistemological thinking, which incorporates beliefs and theories about the nature of knowledge and the nature of learning, in ways that will facilitate conceptual change. The more naive students' beliefs are about knowledge and learning, the less likely they are to revise their misconceptions.
9. Help students "self-repair" their misconceptions.
10. Once students have overcome their alternative conceptions (misconceptions).

Presenting new concepts or theories

In presenting new concepts or theories, teachers should be sure to show these theories or concepts as:

1. Plausible: The new information should be shown to be consistent with other knowledge and able to explain the available data. Learners must see how the new conception (theory) is consistent with other knowledge and a good explanation of the data.

2. High quality: Of course, the theory/concept to be taught is of high quality from a scientific point of view, since it is a correct theory. However, the presented theory should take a better account of the data than what students currently have available to them. For example, the instructor should deal with the problem from the perspective of the students (*e.g.*, students for whom a "flat earth" theory provides a better account of the data available than does a "spherical earth" theory). Hence, the quality of the new theory must be considered along with the kind of data that students know about.

3. Intelligible: Teachers should do what they can to increase the intelligibility of the new theory. Learners must be able to grasp how the new conception works. To increase intelligibility, teachers can use methods such as use of:

(*a*) analogies,

(*b*) models, and

(*c*) direct exposition.

4. Generative/fruitful: Teachers should show that the new concept/theory can be extended to open up new areas of inquiry. Learners must be able to extend the new conception to new areas of inquiry. Teachers might accomplish this by illustrating the application of the new concept/theory to a range of problems. These problems can include familiar ones and new ones.

UNDERSTANDING CHILDREN'S 'ERRORS' AS SIGNIFICANT STEPS IN THE LEARNING PROCESS

The legacy of Jean Piaget to the world of early childhood education is that he fundamentally altered the view of how a child learns. And a teacher, he believed, was more than a transmitter of knowledge she was also an essential observer and guide to helping children build their own knowledge.

As a university graduate, Swiss-born Piaget got a routine job in Paris standardizing Binet-Simon IQ tests, where the emphasis was on children getting the right answers. Piaget observed that many children of the same ages gave the same kinds of incorrect answers. What could be learned from this?

Piaget interviewed many hundreds of children and concluded that children who are allowed to make mistakes often go on to discover their errors and correct them, or find new solutions. In this process, children build their own way of learning. From children's errors, teachers can obtain insights into the child's view of the world and can tell where guidance is needed. They can provide appropriate materials, ask encouraging questions, and allow the child to construct his own knowledge.

Piaget's continued interactions with young children became part of his life-long research. After reading about a child who thought that the sun and moon followed him wherever he went, Piaget wanted to find out if all young children had a similar belief. He found that many did indeed believe this. Piaget went on to explore children's countless "why" questions, such as, "Why is the sun round?" or "Why is grass green?" He concluded that children do not think like adults. Their thought processes have their own distinct order and special logic. Children are not "empty vessels to be filled with knowledge" (as traditional pedagogical theory had it). They are "active builders of knowledge-little scientists who construct their own theories of the world."

COGNITION & EMOTIONS

What is Cognition?

Cognition is the ability to preceive, memorise, reason and understand. These abilities change with age. As the child grows, her thinking becomes more mature and efficient. Therefore, cognition can simply be defined as the process of acquiring, processing, organising and using knowledge. The development of cognition means development of all these abilities. A child's thinking changes as result of both age (maturation) and increased experiences.

Major Cognitive Characteristics of Children

Infancy

It is interesting to see the number of changes that take place in the first two years. Children at this stage are very active learners. Even when it seems the child is only lying and looking at nothing (e.g. 2 month old) she is actually looking at and trying to understand the things around her.

The first two years children begin by exploring their own bodies and move to the outside objects. Children at 2/3 months discover their thumb or hand or occasionally their own foot. These fascinate them they try to play with them. For a two month old a toy is not as satisfying as her/his own thumb in her/his mouth. Gradually, by about six months, children begin to play with objects outside the body. This could be the toy, the sheet, the bottle, etc. Later, by two years they can even indulge in pretend play [example doctor-doctor, house-house, etc.].

What children also achieve by two years is the understanding of object permanance. **Object**

permanance is the understanding that things exist even if you can not see them. Let us take an example. If you show a five month old a toy she gets excited. If you hide the toy the child soon forgets that any toy even existed. This is because she thinks out of sight is out of mind. Do the same thing with a 1½ year old and you will find the child is either looking for it or asks you to find it. This is because she knows the toy exists even if she can not see it. This understanding, that things exist even if you can not see them, is called object permanance.

The other major development that happens by two years is that children begin to learn the symbols. What are symbols? A two year old can convey her thoughts and desires through language. All these are essential processes of cognition.

Early Childhood

This is a period when the childs mastery in use of symbols increases. We can observe this in the everyday behaviour and activities of the child, *i.e.* in what she plays, her language etc. Gradually her representations of objects become more flexible and less self centred. A one year old while playing does not need a toy phone to pretend speaking on the phone. She can use any object. This is indicative of flexibility in thinking. Gradually, children also start directing play between dolls, *e.g.,* one doll is the mother and the other doll the child. This is indicative of the child moving away from self to becoming less self centred.

Children at this stage also believe that all objects have feelings like human beings. That is why you will often see the child feeding her teddy bear.

Children at this stage can also focus on only one aspect of a situation and can not go back. Let us now take an example. You offer cola to a 4 yr old in a tall glass. You then change your mind and pour the coke from the tall glass to a short glass and give it to the child. You will find the child will say I want the big glass. This is because she can only focus on one aspect (height) at a time. Also, she is not able to go back mentally and realise that in the process of pouring from big to small glass, no cola was taken away.

Similarly, take two plates and put in one 6 pieces of chocolate spreadout and in the other make a tower of 6 pieces of chocolate. You will find the child thinking the spread out chocolate is more. This is because the child can only focus on one aspect at a time. This limitation seriously restricts the problem solving and logical thinking abilities of the child.

It also indicates the child's inability to understand that another point of view different from her own can exist, *e.g.,* you often find children responding to your question by nodding their heads, even if they are not in the same room as you. This is because they do not see another's point of view.

Middle Childhood

During this period, children begin to understand that another view point can exist. They are also able to focus on more than one aspect of a situation and go back and forth on their thinking. This makes their thinking more logical and efficient. However, children are only comfortable with concrete ideas/objects. It means, something that is real for them, *i.e.,* either something they have seen, *e.g.,* a house or something is in front of them, a plant or something linked to what they know, *e.g.,* blue like the sky. They are not able to think about abstract ideas, *e.g.,* what would happen if everyone could fly?

Emotion

Emotions, put simply, are feelings. In infants we can see these very clearly in the form of joy, anger and fear. These are similar to the emotions that adults have.

1. **The variety of emotions increases with age:** The basic emotions of joy, fear, anger are visible in infants. Gradually, as a sense of self develops; children begin to relate with people around them and value their opinions. Then we can see the emotion like pride, shame, sympathy, guilt also developing in them.
2. **The expression of emotion also changes with age:** Emotions are both innate and learnt. The instinctive response to a stimulus is innate but how to express that feeling is learnt, *e.g.* taking away of a toy makes the child angry (innate) but instead crying she is encouraged to ask for it back (learnt). Frustration tolerance increases with age. As children grow older, their responses change in both as well as instinctive method of expression, *e.g.,* when 2 year old falls downs she cries loudly and later forgets quickly. A 6 year old on the other hand, may not cry but forgets far less easily.
3. **The triggers or cause of emotions change with age:** The stimuli that elicit emotion also change with age, *e.g.,* an infant may cry on hearing the loud explosion of a cracker but a middle childhood child may laugh. Sucking a thumb may give great joy to an infant but provides no pleasure to a child is middle childhood.
4. **The coping techniques change with age:** Methods of coping with frustration and stress change with age. While a younger child may cry, or cling to the adult, an older child is likely to suppress the emotion.

Factors Affecting Emotional Development

If we look round in our environment, we will find that people differ in the emotions they experience and express. Some are happy, some are angry, some moody, some helpful. What then affects our emotional development?

1. **Parenting style:** Democratic parenting where induction is used as a method of disciplining allows for more mature emotional development and also for development of personal behaviour.
2. **Role model:** There are two factors which influence what a child ultimately learns:
   (i) How adults and others in the child's environment handle their emotions.
   (ii) How successful is the emotional expression in achieving their needs.
3. **Violence in the child's environment:** The kind of behaviour the child see in the community (*e.g.* during riots) or on TV will affect her expressions of emotions.
4. **Cultural norms:** Emotional expressions are learnt from the environment. It is the environment that tells us how to react in a situation (*e.g.* some people feel the emotion of fear when a black cat crosses their path). It is also the environment that tells us the acceptable way of expressing ones emotions (*e.g.* in many families it is unacceptable for boys to express their distress by crying). Therefore, our cultural beliefs and values also influence our emotional development.

MOTIVATION AND LEARNING

Motivation

Motivation is the heart of the learning process. It generates the will in an individual to do something. Adequate motivation not only engages the student in an activity which results in learning, but also sustains and directs learning. Two types of motivation are commonly recognised. These are: intrinsic and extrinsic motivation.

Intrinsic motivation arises when the resolution of tension is to be found in mastering the learning task itself; the material learned provides its own reward. For example, the student who studies the construction of model aeroplanes diligently so that he can make a model, is experiencing a kind of intrinsic motivation.

Extrinsic motivation occurs when a student pursues a learning task, but for reasons which are external. If a student engages in construction of model aeroplanes because he thinks it will please his father, who is an ex-pilot, rather than because of intrinsic motivation. We should remember that in most learning situations motivation can not be dichotomised so neatly. It is the function of the total learning situation and hinges on some blend of personal concern for the work itself and the concern for some extrinsic factors as well. As a working principle, motivation is probably a function of an interactive situation where reward to a particular action acts as an incentive. Some of the common forms of extrinsic motivation are:

- **Purposive striving, goals and ideals:** The goal and purposes of learning clearly perceived by the individual, provide strong motivation for better action and learning.
- **Knowledge of results:** Knowledge of results in terms of success and failure provides incentive for greater efforts on the part of the student. If a student practices a task without knowing the accuracy or inaccuracy of his performance, he may practise wrong task. In such a case, all learning will be futile. Therefore, if results of performance are known to the student, he learns better as compared to when he does not know about the results. Mere repetition of a task without knowledge of its results fails to bring about learning. Knowledge of results serves two purposes: (i) it enables the subject to evaluate his efficiency and to change his responses in the direction of greater accuracy, and (ii) it adds to the satisfaction in reaching a goal, one tends of repeat rewarded responses.
- **Punishment and rewards:** Punishment can be understood as an act of inflicting pain deliberately with the purpose of affecting the future conduct of an individual being punished. Punishment is based on fear of physical pain, embarrassment and loss of status. Thus, punishment of fear of being punished is one of the common and obvious methods of keeping under control and guiding the students. Punishment or fear is a very strong stimuli, a negative incentive to learning especially when errors occur. Thorndike showed that generally punishment speeds up learning and reduces the number of errors as it produces emotional excitement which tends to fix at punished response. But it does not mean that punishment under all the circumstances and with all the students is equally effective. For example, it may prove disastrous and destructive when task is very difficult.

  Contrary to punishment, rewards are certainly better and positive incentives to learning. They are responsible for initiative, energy, competition, self-expression and creative ability. According to law of effect, reward is satisfying and pleasant, thus reward strengthens learning. Rewards may in the form of gifts, prizes, money, badges, cups, certificates of merit, or other objects of some value. Motivation through such objects feeds the natural drive in all the human beings. But, when these rewards are too much strived for, they degenerate the whole learning.

- **Praise and blame:** These are also strong incentives for effective learning. Praise stimulates average and inferior children, but has less effect on those of superior intelligence. Reproof is felt most by superior children, but girls seem more susceptible to praise than do boys. Regardless of age sex, or initial ability, praise is the most effective of the incentives. Reproof seems to be less effective for all students. Chase (1932) reported praise to be less effective than blame with young children, but Hurlock (1920) generalised, still accepted by contemporary investigators, that praise is more effective stimulus in motivating both immediate and long-continued tasks.
- **Rivalry:** The rivalry between students which leads to resentment, jealousy, etc., or rivalry between groups of students which creates hatred, is the least desirable type of incentive to be encouraged in the schools. Self-rivalry or rivalry in the form of healthy competition is the most valuable type. This tendency should be developed in the student. Though experimental researchers have shown rivalry to be a powerful motivation influence, the emotional and social consequences of rivalry must be considered by the teacher.

Functions of Motivation

The major functions of motivation in learning are as follows:

- To energies the students in learning
- To direct behaviour
- To select behaviour
- To help capture the attention
- To help in acquiring knowledge
- To help in character formation
- To develop social qualities

Attention in Relation to Motivation

Attention is the basic pre-requisite of all learning in the classroom. Learning is possible only if students concentrate their attention on the object or stimuli to be learnt. Attention increases the amount and rate of learning, and also the efficiency of work.

Attention is closely related to motivation. Attention is motivated behaviour, in which the student makes a variety of efforts for achieving the goal. Thus motivation helps in capturing attention. You can help your students by motivating them to concentrate their attention on the tasks to be learnt by them.

Between the two types of motivation, intrinsic motivation should be preferred to extrinsic motivation. It produces better learning because it is related to interest. The learner pursues the activity in which he has interest without waiting for any external pressure. When the learner does not show any intrinsic motivation or interest in learning we have to resort to extrinsic motivation by the use of 'incentives'—whether financial or non-financial (monetary or non-monetary)—such as rewards, awards, prizes, competitions, praise, etc.

In-built Motivation

Another type of motivation is called in-built motivation. Whatever may be the type of motivation, it should be an in-built component of the whole programme of education/training. Right type of trainers, attractive and need-based reading materials, supportive training methodologies, constant awareness of the new dimensions of the programme will facilitate motivation in an in-built manner.

Theories of Motivation

The main theories of motivation are: (a) Psycho-analytic Theory, (b) Maslow's Theory of Self-actualisation, (c) Physiological Theory and (d) Achievement-Motivation Theory.

Psycho-Analytic Theory

According to this theory, motivation gives the vital life forces which are the prime mover of life and its activities. 'It is will power that motivates a person', *i.e.,* 'no will power—no activity'. All these versions agree on one point *i.e.,* 'building ego of man'.

Maslow's Theory of Self-Actualisation

This theory is based on human needs and their satisfaction. Maslow (1998) has arranged man's basic needs in a hierarchy, *i.e.,* some needs are strong or more important than others. According to him the five basic needs, progressing from physiological needs through safety needs, love, esteem needs and the need for self-actualisation. These basic needs are described here under:

- **Physiological needs:** Maslow states that physiological needs are undoubtedly the most powerful of all needs. Examples are the needs for food, sleep or rest. Until the biological needs are met, an individual may lack awareness of other needs. When a person is gratified he/she is released and higher needs can emerge. Some potential adult learners from low-economic background actually have unmet physiological needs, such as hunger, which prevent them from learning. An old person may not be able to see or hear well and he might not be open to satisfying other needs.

- **Safety Needs:** When physiological needs are satisfied, safety needs emerge, such as need for security, for physical safety, for stability in one's life. Safety needs are seen when a person prefers the familiar over the unfamiliar. An adult would rather go to a meeting in a building with which he is familiar than in a building new to him.
- **Love or Belongingness:** If both the physiological and safety needs are gratified, the needs for love, affection and belongingness emerge. Love needs involve both giving and receiving love. They involve the feeling of being wanted. The person who does not feel he belongs, no matter what the reason, probably will not continue with the group and discontinue his participation in adult education programme. The teacher should be affectionate towards adult learners and develop a group spirit among learners.
- **Esteem:** All people in our society have a need, a desire, for self-respect or self-esteem and for the esteem of others. There are two types: The desire for achievement and the desire for prestige or recognition from others. Satisfaction of the need for self-esteem leads to feelings of self-confidence and of being useful to the society. Thwarting of these needs produce feelings of inferiority or weakness. Fear or failure or lack of self-esteem might prevent an adult from participating in educational activities.
- **Self-Actualisation:** Even after the earlier needs are satisfied a person might still feel restless unless he becomes everything he is capable of becoming. This is called self-fulfilment or self-actualisation. The specific form of this needs varies from person-to-person. One person might desire to be an ideal mother or an ideal leader.
- **Implications for Adult Learning:** Before starting the adult education class, the basic needs of the learners should be studied. It may be possible that due to poverty and less per capita income, the basic biological needs of the learners may not be fulfilled. Then the main aim of adult education should be to provide regular income to the learners. This can be done by starting various income generating projects. The educators should also help by marketing of such products produced by the learners. The officials connected with adult education should take steps to start such programmes. This will make the classes more interesting to the learners. The teacher needs to strengthen the group spirit among learners and should identify himself/herself with the group. The learning experiences in the centres should promote the talents, attitudes capacities and potentialities of adults.

Physiological Theory of Motivation

This theory has been developed by Clifford Morgan and William James. According to this theory of the body determines attitudes and interests and explains activities and behaviour of people.

Implications for Adult Education: Participa-tion in physical activities decrease with age so also interests change as a person becomes older. Many physical limitations affect the amount of time an adult has for educational activities. After working all day at a job, some adults are too tired to participate in educational activity, such people can be motivated giving them work which gives them relaxation. Hearing and vision also decrease with age. The ages of the group members will determine the size of letters that a teacher writes on a black board, the colour of the chalk used, the size of the articles he holds for the adults to see, and how loudly and distinctly he speaks. The size, type and quality of handout material are also important.

Achievement-Motivation Theory

This theory has been developed by McClelland (1985). According to this theory all human behaviour is intended to reduce tension and reach a state of physiological and psychological equilibrium. It is a desire to do better, to achieve unique accomplishment, to compete with a standard of excellence and to involve oneself with long term achievement goals. It can be identified on the basic of individual expectation of success. It applies only when the individual knows that his/her performance will be evaluated by himself or by others in terms of excellence, and that the consequences of his action will either succeed or fail.

FACTORS CONTRIBUTING TO LEARNING

Introduction

Learning, can be considered as the process by which skills, attitudes, knowledge and concepts are acquired, understood, applied and extended. All human beings, whether grown ups or children engage in the process of learning, either consciously, sub-consciously or subliminally. It is through learning that their competence and ability to function in their environment get enhanced. It is important to understand that while we learn some ideas and concepts through instruction or teaching, we also learn through our feelings and experiences. Feelings and experiences are a tangible part of our lives and these greatly influence what we learn, how we learn and why we learn.

Learning has been considered partly a cognitive process and partly a social and affective one. It qualifies as a cognitive process because it involves the functions of attention, perception, reasoning, analysis, drawing of conclusions, making interpretations and giving meaning to the observed phenomena. All of these are mental processes which relate to the intellectual functions of the individual. Learning is a social and affective process, as the societal and cultural context in which we function and the feelings and experiences which we have, greatly influence our ideas, concepts, images and understanding of the world. These constitute inner subjective interpretations and represent our own unique, personalized constructions of the specific universe of functioning. Our knowledge, ideas, concepts, attitudes, beliefs and the skills which we acquire are a consequence of these combined processes.

CLASSIFICATION OF FACTORS: PERSONAL & ENVIRONMENT

To understand how we categorise the factors affecting learning, let us begin by considering the following examples:

- Ravi is sixteen year old and wants to please his mother by getting good results in his board examinations. He is so eager to please her, that he spends long hours of concentrated time and energy on his studies. He consciously tries to control other sources of distraction in his life and reduces the time spent on watching television, playing games and chatting with his friends.
- Rita Williams wants to be a famous tennis player. To achieve her goal, she practices tennis whenever she can, even though she gets no encouragement from her family. She makes it a point to watch tennis matches and maintain a good rapport with her sports teacher.
- Yuvraj is a good student, but lately he has been scoring very low marks at school. He is not able to concentrate or pay attention and his class work and home assignments reflect a very poor quality. Sources revealed that his parents fight a lot with each other and are about to get divorced.
- Arti and Kavita are two sisters. Arti is very good at art and craft and can sketch just about anything she sees. Kavita has a ear for music. She knows most songs and can sing them even if she has heard them only once. Both of them spend hours together pursuing their respective interest areas.
- Sayeeda is tall, attractive and has a very good figure. She wants to be a model or an air-hostess and nurtures this secretly as her dream. She is too scared to share her wishes with her family, since she belongs to an orthodox family, where girls at best can pursue teaching as a career. When she tries telling her mother what she wants, she is firmly told that she can only do her B.Ed and can go to the coaching classes for these.

The above cited examples illustrate that learning is a universal phenomenon mediated by a number of factors, both personal and environmental in nature. The dictum "everybody learns" is as true as its corollary, *i.e.*, everybody learns in accordance with his/her unique, individualized blend of personal and environmental factors. For example, in case of Ravi, the desire to please his mother, striving to do well in his board exams and managing his life situations appropriately constitute the key factors which influence him. For Rita Williams, it is her intrinsic desire to be a good tennis player which is paramount. She is not deterred by the lack of family support and continues to make efforts to promote her love for tennis on her own and fulfil her desire to be successful.

In case of Yuvraj, in spite of his innate capacity to study and perform well, his lack of achievement can be attributed to the emotional insecurity stemming from his parents' divorce. As far as Arti and Kavita are concerned, their special interests and talent in art and music respectively, seem to guide their activities.

For Sayeeda, the home environment and family culture and values determine her professional choice. Her own inner interests, desires and wishes are not to be taken into cognizance.

In all the examples cited, we can find evidence of both personal and environmental factors influencing the process of learning. Learning can thus be defined as a function of the interaction of personal and environmental factors.

$L = f(EF \times PF)$

L = learning; f = function; EF = environmental factors; PF = personal factors.

Personal factors are the intra individual factors like motivation, interests, abilities etc which predispose an individual towards learning as in the case of Rita Williams, Arti and Kavita. Environmental factors on the other hand, are those contextual factors which highlight the role of the environment in learning, such as the socio-emotional, societal and cultural factors as seen in the case of Yuvraj and Sayeeda. Although the two factors represent different categories, they operate in a common system. The environmental factors provide the context within which the personal factors, operate. The learner and the learning process can only be completely understood with reference to the interaction of both environmental and personal factors. This may be diagrammatically represented as follows:

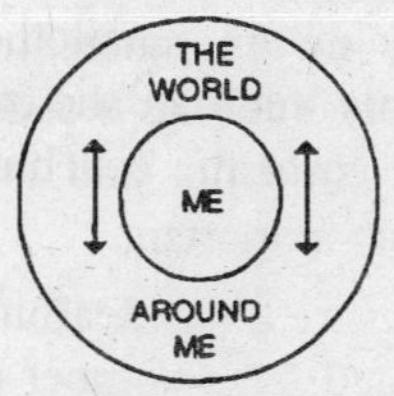

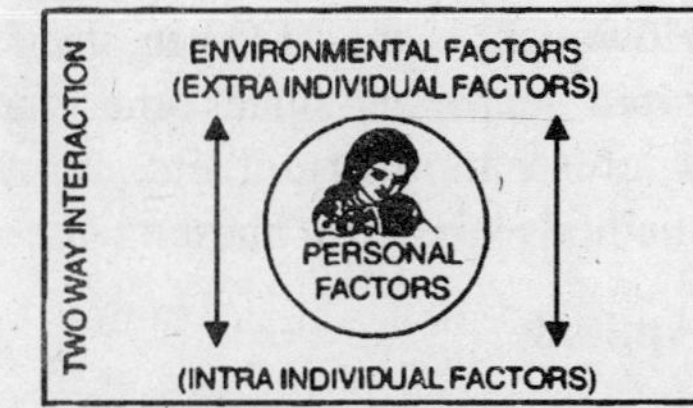

Fig: *Factors affecting learning*

Personal Factors Influencing Learning

The process of learning is influenced by a variety of personal factors. A thorough knowledge of these factors will prove very helpful for teachers and parents in understanding and guiding their children's learning. Some of the personal factors that influence the learning process may be classified as under : sensation and perception, fatigue and boredom, maturation, emotional condition, needs, interests, motivation, attention, intelligence, aptitude, attitude, etc. Let us discuss the important personal factors in the following sub-sections.

Sensation and Perception

Apart from the general health of the students, sensation and perception are the psychological factors which help in learning. Sensation is at the core of perception. There are five sense organs *i.e.*, skin, ears, tongue, eyes and nose. These sense organs are the gateways of knowledge and help in perception of various stimuli in the environment. Any defect in any of the sense organs will affect learning and hence acquisition of knowledge. For example, defects of vision such as myopia, hypermetropia, astigmatism, etc., cause headaches, nausia and general disinclination to study. A blind person depends upon the sense of touch or skin for learning and thus acquires knowledge and skills, as he can not visualise the objects. The stimuli are preceived and assimilated, and hence learnt through various sense organs. In this way we can say that sensation and perception is the bases of knowledge and learning.

Fatigue and Boredom

It is virtually boredom or lassitude rather than fatigue which bothers the students. The difference between the two is that fatigue is mental or physical tiredness which decreases in efficiency and competency to work. Boredom, on the other hand, is a lack of desire on an aversion to work. Such an aversion makes one feel fatigued without being actually fatigued. Studying seldom causes fatigue. It is mainly boredom which, besides causing the impression of fatigue, decreases student efficiency in learning.

Age and Maturation

Learning is directly dependent upon age and maturation. No learning can take place unless individual is matured enough to learn. Some children can learn better at earlier age while others take more time to learn the same content.

Mental age increases with the chronological age and ceases at about the age of sixteen years. Increase in age means intellectual maturation which helps in solving difficult problems. The principle of maturation warns us against enforcing learning on a child when he is not mature enough to learn the specific skills. Teachers should explain this principle to parents who are over ambitious or over enthusiastic in sending their children to school at the very early age.

Emotional Conditions

Desirable emotional conditions enhance the quality and speed of learning. Happiness, joy and satisfaction are always favourable for any type of learning. Adverse emotional conditons, on the other hand, hinder learning. Many studies have established the fact that emotional strain, stress, tensions, disturbances, etc., are extremely inimical to scholastic pursuits.

Needs

A need is the lack of something which, if provided, would facilitate child's usual behaviour. The lack of something is experienced by the child. The child then tries to perform that activity which culminates in the satisfaction of the need. Thus, the needs are associated with goals. Among human beings, the needs are realtively permanent tendencies which seek satisfaction in achieving certain specific goals. When these goals are achieved, the particular need is satisfied or met for the time being, but it recurs sooner or later and energises further activity. The needs in human beings can be physiological such as need for oxygen, food, water, etc. They may be social such as the need for affection, recognition, self-regard, etc. Social needs are however, quite different from physiological needs. Social needs might originate after physiological needs are satisfied. These needs have a complex structure and dominate the individual's behaviour.

There is not equal urgency in the satisfaction of all needs. Some have to be satisfied before others can manifest themselves.

In schools, children are not expected to do any intellectual thinking unless their physiological needs are satisfied. Poor, starved children may concentrate less on attainment of knowledge than on food. Similarly, very cold or hot classrooms or over-crowded seats will not be conducive to good learning. Likewise the need for safety, love and esteem, all act as powerful motives in the learning situations. If the child is afraid of the teacher or feels unsafe while in the school on account of too much beating or some other form of punishment, no learning can take place. Similarly, his needs for warmth and affection are very stimulating and hence results in effective learning.

Interests

Various types of interests of the students can be exploited to facilitate their learning. The interests during early infancy are mostly limited and short lived. As the child grows older his interests diversify and stabilize. You, a school teacher, should have thorough knowledge of children's interests. You can eliminate much drudgery, monotony and boredom from the school work if you make your instruction lively and stimulating and arouse student interest in it.

Once the students' interest is aroused in an activity you should expend more effort on it. No learning can be achieved without proper expenditure of effort on it. Students can even overcome distraction, fatigue and boredom if they feel interested in your instruction and class activities. It has often been found that, in most cases, fatigue in reality is loss of interest in the learning activity. Interest, should be exploited to yield results of greater quantity and quality learning in school.

Life is so exciting that many interesting things and activities often clamor to attract our attention. Children frequently face the dilemma of mutually conflicting interests. Immediate interests often seem to be clashing with the remoter ones. A student might be in a quandary at least for the time being when his interest in sports impels him towards the play-field and his interest in studies force him to concentrate on books.

In such cases of conflicting interests a lot of hesitancy, wastage, frustration and unhappiness is bound to follow. What is needed is education at home and school which helps/trains children to achieve a healthy balance in their interests. They should be trained to budget their time in such a manner as to pay a reasonable attention to various interests, scholastic, athletic, social etc., within the time at their disposal.

Motivation

Motivation is the heart of the learning process. It generates the will in an individual to do something. Adequate motivation not only engages the student in an activity which results in learning, but also sustains and directs learning. Two types of motivation are commonly recognised. These are: intrinsic and extrinsic motivation.

Intelligence

Intelligence as expressed by an I.Q. score on an intelligence test is positively related to learning. Generally, students with higher I.Q. learn rapidly. However, higher I.Q. in itself is no guarantee for rapid learning, since other factors such as needs, interest, motivation, etc., of the students and the methods used for learning are also important.

Aptitude

A student who possesses appropriate aptitude for a particular subject of study or skill, will learn better and retain it for a longer time. On the other hand, he will require relatively longer time to study a subject for which he lacks natural aptitude. He is liable to forget it soon besides feeling bored and unhappy all the time while learning it. Hence, it is extremely desirable to analyse the aptitude of students before prescribing courses of study for them.

Attitude

The learning process is also influenced considerably by the attitude of the student. If he is alert, attentive and interested in the material to be learnt, he is bound to have a favourable attitude towards it. Such an attitude will enable him to tackle the learning situation economically, pleasantly and effectively. Conversely, if he is inattentive and is uninterested in the material his attitude is bound to be unfavourable. This will hinder the smooth learning of the material in hand besides involving undue strain and tension in the learner.

Environmental Factors

Environmental influences begin since the time of the conception of the child in the womb of the mother. Mother's mental, physical and emotional conditions influence the development of foetus in the womb. The external environment starts from the time of birth of the child. It (external environment) refers to the surroundings which prevail in home, school and locality. At these places, the child interacts with members of the family, teachers, classmates or peers and neighbours and establishes relationship with them. The relationship with the members of the society, and the surroundings may affect the development of the child and also the way he learns. Some of the environmental factors are discussed as follows:

Surrounding : Natural, Social and Cultural

As the title of the sub-section indicates, we shall discuss here natural, social and cultural environment the child interacts with and get influenced.

Natural surrounding covers the climatic and atmospheric condition. These conditions affect learning directly. It has been found that high temperature and humidity reduces mental efficiency. For a limited time, humidity and high temperature can be tolerated but prolonged humidity and high temperature become unbearable and decrease mental efficiency. The intellectual productivity and creativeness of people living in hot regions are much low. Likewise, the morning time is always better for mastering difficult tasks. Mental efficiency decreases due to increased humidity and temperature. Studies on the academic progress of evening school students shows losses of efficiency varying from one to six per cent.

Social surrounding includes especially the environment of home, school and locality. Physical conditions at home such as large family, small family, (specific place of the study), insufficient ventilation, improper lighting, uncomfortable temperature, noisy home environment due to use of radio, TV, etc., noisy neighbourhood, constant visits by friends or relatives, etc., influence the intellectual learning of the student. The socio-emotional factors such as child rearing practices, reward and punishment, scope for freedom and independence in activities and decision making, play and study facilities, ambitions and aspirations of the parents, disorganisation and discord among birth positions such as eldest, youngest or single child have their definite influence on learning. For example, a student who comes from a very poor family and never had any intellectual stimulation at home remains dull and unresponsive in the class. In some societies there is a strong sex bias. Girls are directly or indirectly told that education is not meant for them. In the middle class families, on the other hand, parents are rather over-ambitious. They wish their children to make quick academic progress, grow-up and find a respectable vocation preferably a white collar job. Such children, therefore get sufficient incentive from their families. This, of course, is most favourable to scholastic learning, although an overdose of family emphasis on acquiring academic excellence might affect the child's mental and physical health adversely. Similarly, school activities, study facilities and teaching methods and behaviour of teachers, principals and non-teaching staff have an impact upon learning. If the school atmosphere is unconducive, it adversely affects the learning process. Locality also has an influence on a child. If the locality is bad, the learning will be ineffective to some extent.

Cultural demands and social expectations also influence learning. The spirit of culture is reflected in its social and educational institutions. Children's learning, therefore, is greatly determined by the demands and expectations of their culture. Thus, for instance, in an industrialized culture the emphasis mostly centres mechanical sciences and preparing children for highly mechanised vocations. In an agriculture based community, on the other hand, the educational process focusses on preparing its members for those skills which are suited to the needs of an agrarian community.

The philosophical elements of culture also influence the spirit of children's learning. Children in a democratic culture tend to acquire democrative and values and attitudes. A feudal, aristocratic or dictatorial culture, on the other hand, promotes autocratic modes of thought and behaviour.

Relationship with Teacher, Parents and Peers

The teacher is an important constituent in the instructional process. She/he plays an important role in shaping the behaviour of students. The way he teaches and manages the students has an affect on their learning. An authoritarian teacher will create an aggression and hostility among students while a democratic teacher will create a participatory climate for learning. The democratic environment leads students to constructive, thoughtful and cooperative behaviour. Generally, students learn better in a democratic set up because they like democratic procedures. The teacher is no more an instructor or the director of learning in a democratic set up. She/he helps his/her students in their learning. The teachers no more dominate the scene, they can get better results by decentralizing authority, increasing independence of students. They can attend to the comments and questions of the students. They can encourage students to participate in learning activities in and outside the class. There should be more emphasis on activity-centred classroom where student's active participation in the teaching-learning process is encouraged and the teacher acts as a guide to promote learning.

Relationship with parents plays a vital role in the learning process of the student. If the child-parents relationship is based on mutual respect and faith, it can provide the child a congenial atmosphere which in turn can facilitate his/her learning. A distorted and unhealthy environment, on the other hand, adversely affects the learning of the student. The upward mobility brings resistance on the part of the student to learn. Students in such families find themselves unable to cope up. A subtle but powerful influence on the growing child arises from his/her position among the children in the family. The parents of the first born expect the child to act like miniature adults and hence the first-born are found to encounter a variety of expectations and stresses. Whereas parents tend to be more relaxed in their do's and dont's with the last-born. Factors like traumatic events at home, separation or death can also precipitate learning problems in the normal child.

A healthy peer group relationship also plays an important role in learning. Student-student relationship in the classroom, school, society, etc., create a particular type of emotional climate. The climate solely depends upon their relationships. A sound relationships provides a tension free environment to the student to learn more and to compete in the class. If the relationship among peers is not good, it adversely affects their learning. Therefore, to improve the classroom learning climate, free discussion should be there. You should help your students understand each other in formal or informal meetings. They should be encouraged to meet each other and their teachers freely. If any mis-understanding is created or developed, it should be immediately clarified so as to maintain the healthy climate and cordial relationship among peers.

Media Influence on Learning

Media has been considered an important component of transmitting information. Media can be divided into two broad categories—print and non-print media. Print media refers to texts or printed materials. It is economical and has traditionally been used for pedagogical purposes.

But, it may not be the only or the perfect medium to impart education. Non-print media, also known as modern electronic media, have certain unique qualities which, in certain cases, facilitate learning much more faster than the print medium. These helps meet diverse learning objectives more efficiently than the printed matter.

Certain non-print media formats and delivery systems contribute well to student's learning actitivies, For example, audio tapes or computers can be used effectively to drill and practice in language and learning arithmatic. Electronic media can help promote the discovery approach to learning. For example, a film can be exploited for discovery teaching in the physical sciences. Students keep watching the various sections of the film until they perceive the relationships between the visuals. Then they are curious to find out the principles that explain those relationships. Likewise, in the social sciences various media can be used to present students with visual and auditory experiences that provide related inquiry. Films and stimulation are often used to present real-life or laboratory learning situations to students.

The role of the electronic media has proved effective for teaching students. These excite the student psychologically and prepare/motivate them to participate in teaching-learning activites. Non-print media perform following fuctions:

- direct attention,
- arouse motivation,
- increase student's concentration, and
- help them actively involve in the learning process.

PRACTICE PAPER

1. Mass media, cinema and library are passive agencies of education because
   (a) learner can not react to the feedback system of these agencies directly
   (b) they provide informal education
   (c) they can not come closer to the educant
   (d) all of these
2. Education of a child really begins
   (a) Once he takes birth
   (b) Once he attains the age of three
   (c) Once he is admitted to post nursery schools
   (d) Once he learns to speak
3. Family is the original social institution from which all other institutions emerged, who said this
   (a) Brown (b) Ballard
   (c) Machiver (d) None of them
4. Which of the following is not the primary function of schools
   (a) reorganization and reconstruction of Human experiences
   (b) all-round development of the child
   (c) to make the children self reliant
   (d) advancement of culture
5. In a democratic country, school should reflect
   (a) National aspirations
   (b) Community related local aspirations
   (c) Both of these
   (d) None of these
6. The best teacher in a village school is he who
   (a) carries community experiences to the class room
   (b) prepares instructional programmes in the interest of the community
   (c) carries classroom experiences to the community
   (d) all of these
7. Universalisation of education is the concept adopted by
   (a) modern state (b) democratic state
   (c) totalitarian state (d) religious state
8. Secular education in India means
   (a) an education opposed to religion
   (b) an education indifferent to religion
   (c) an education emphasizing equality of religions
   (d) none of these
9. School works as a social sub system for
   (a) transmission of culture
   (b) preservation of culture
   (c) advancement of culture
   (d) all of these
10. "Society is nothing but a process of interaction among people." Who said this?
    (a) Lapier (b) Cuber
    (c) Reuter (d) Payne
11. The best model of schooling is
    (a) Close interaction between education of society
    (b) Self reliant society by education
    (c) Reflection of openness by schools
    (d) All of these
12. Special provisions have been made for socially and educationally backward classes of the nation under article
    (a) 29 (b) 31
    (c) 15 (d) 19
13. Religious education is prohibited in government schools and colleges under Article
    (a) 29 (b) 28 (1)
    (c) 39 (2) (d) 15 (a)
14. Religious and linguistic minorities shall have the right to establish and administer their own educational institutions under Article
    (a) 30(1) (b) 31(2)
    (c) 40 (d) 41
15. Article 351 is about
    (a) education of tribals
    (b) promotion of Hindi
    (c) promotion of secularism
    (d) English as official language
16. Status of central university is given to any educational institution under union list of
    (a) Entry 65 (b) Entry 63
    (c) Entry 66 (d) None of these
17. Entry 25 of concurrent list states about
    (a) vocational and technical training of labour
    (b) the education of working class
    (c) the education of disabled
    (d) none of the above

18. Education in the mother tongue at primary stage to children belonging to linguistic minorities has been mentioned in Article
(*a*) 250 (*b*) 350
(*c*) 349 (*d*) 351

19. Educational and economic interests of SCs and STs have been safeguarded under Article
(*a*) 46 (*b*) 45(a)
(*c*) 351 (*d*) 52

20. Education of union territories is administered by the central government under Article
(*a*) 350 (*b*) 229
(*c*) 239 (*d*) 50

21. Education was transferred from state list of subjects to concurrent list in
(*a*) 1976 (*b*) 1972
(*c*) 1980 (*d*) 1950

22. Which of the following statements about growth and development is not correct?
(*a*) Growth generally refers to quantitative changes while development refers to qualitative changes
(*b*) Growth is a function of the environment
(*c*) Growth is not possible without development and vice versa
(*d*) Growth is determined by intrinsic and genetic factors of the organism

23. The limit of growth is fixed by
(*a*) internal factors of the organism
(*b*) nutrition and exercise
(*c*) both of these
(*d*) none of these

24. Development is
(*a*) Maturation
(*b*) Learning
(*c*) Synthesis of abilities
(*d*) All of these

25. Development takes place when
(*a*) environmental forces work on the organism
(*b*) environmental forces interact with the hereditary forces in an organism
(*c*) both of these
(*d*) none of these

26. Which of the following statements about development is correct?
(*a*) Process of development can be improved by exercise and nutrition
(*b*) Development may be positive and negative both
(*c*) Development proceeds from general to specific
(*d*) All of these

27. The son of a goldsmith becomes an expert goldsmith. It is an example of a
(*a*) biological heredity
(*b*) social heredity
(*c*) transfer of instinct
(*d*) none of these

28. All humans contain .... chromosomes.
(*a*) 26 (*b*) 36
(*c*) 46 (*d*) 42

29. DNA test helps us to know
(*a*) the genetic traits of a person
(*b*) nature of personality and its composition
(*c*) both of these
(*d*) none of these

30. The law of inheritance was discovered by Gregor Mendel in
(*a*) 1866 (*b*) 1911
(*c*) 1888 (*d*) 1920

31. Which of the following statements regarding personality traits is correct?
(*a*) Traits of personality can not be developed in isolation without taking the help of environment
(*b*) Subjective traits of the individual are determined by genetic factors
(*c*) Bad environment can surpass good inheritance but good environment is not a substitute for poor heredity
(*d*) All of these

32. Which of the following characteristics denote infancy period?
(*a*) Physical growth is curvilinear
(*b*) Physical growth is rapid
(*c*) Head grows at relatively slower rate as compared to other parts of the body
(*d*) All of these

33. Which of the following is not the characteristic of infancy period?
(*a*) From bilateral to unilateral trend in motor organs
(*b*) From general to specific trend in motor organs
(*c*) Emotional/social development is not associated with motor development
(*d*) Steady mental development

34. Which of the following illustrates conceptual development?
(*a*) Perception is the beginning of concept formation
(*b*) Concept changes with changes in experiences
(*c*) Concept changes with age
(*d*) All of these

35. There is one thing common in language and physical development what is that?
(*a*) Spurts of development at different ages
(*b*) Dependence on experience
(*c*) Dependence on training
(*d*) None of these

36. Which of the following characteristics is not associated with emotional development?
(a) Emotion is accompanied by physiological changes
(b) Emotions start immediately after birth
(c) Intense form of emotions are seen during early childhood period
(d) Emotions are unrelated to physical development

37. The child acquires about three fourth of the brain weight by the age of
(a) 2½ years (b) 2 years
(c) 6 years (d) 8 years

38. Social development of an infant depends on
(a) his chance of interaction with others
(b) love and affection shown to the child
(c) the extent to which he is able to attract the attention of others
(d) all of the above

39. In which of the following stages the child looks self centred?
(a) Infancy (b) Early childhood
(c) Adolescence (d) Adulthood

40. In the period of infancy, emotions are
(a) intense, frequent and unstable
(b) like an open book(overt)
(c) need based
(d) all of these

41. Which of the following organs of the body shows rapid growth in infancy?
(a) growth of hands (b) growth of head
(c) growth of legs (d) growth of fingers

42. In normal learning environment, forgetting is caused
(a) due to back of practice for a long time
(b) due to the interference of other learnt material
(c) due to lack of consolidation of memory traces
(d) all of these

43. Clear conception of size, weight, colour, time etc., is seen at the age of
(a) six (b) four
(c) four and half (d) five

44. Which of the following is not the characteristics of intellectual development of early childhood?
(a) increased span of attention
(b) exploration of the environment
(c) ability to verbalize all known concepts
(d) ability to distinguish past, present and future

45. Social development by the end of early childhood is marked by
(a) the feeling of autonomy
(b) the end of solitary plays
(c) the temperament of co-operation and friendliness
(d) all of these

46. Fictional world of the child starts at the age of
(a) 5-6 (b) 6-8
(c) 3-4 (d) 4-5

47. Girls are more dominating than boys in social situations in which of the following periods?
(a) pre-adolescent period
(b) early childhood period
(c) both of these
(d) none of these

48. In the period of early childhood, child is
(a) helpless to hide his emotions
(b) seen shifting his emotions very rapidly and frequently
(c) guided by his innate tendencies and instincts
(d) all of these

49. A nursery teacher should organize
(a) group games in the school
(b) those games which involve motor organs of the body
(c) those games which help the child to manipulate the environment
(d) all of these

50. Later childhood is called latency period because
(a) creative potentials are dormant
(b) sex remains dormant
(c) it is a period of inactivity
(d) all of these

51. Physical development of later childhood is marked by
(a) Auscification of bones
(b) Permanent teeth
(c) Excessive motor activity
(d) All of these

52. Girls surpass boys physically in
(a) infancy
(b) later childhood
(c) early childhood
(d) adolescence

53. The period of later childhood is marked by
(a) intellectual maturity
(b) high muscular energy
(c) hero worship
(d) all of these

54. Which of the following is not the characteristics of intellectual development of later childhood?
(a) High interest in science fiction
(b) Increased logical power
(c) Careful for future
(d) End of imaginary fears

55. Children are very much hateful or indifferent to opposite sex at the age of
(a) 11-12 (b) 13-14
(c) 10-11 (d) 15-16

56. Period of later childhood is marked by
(*a*) slow and steady physical growth
(*b*) stability in emotions
(*c*) anger against injustice
(*d*) all of these

57. At the end of later childhood period, the child
(*a*) feels himself superior to girls
(b) becomes independent of his family
(c) wants to become hero
(d) all of these

58. The best place of social development for a 12 years old child is
(*a*) neighbourhood
(*b*) family
(*c*) playground
(*d*) school

59. Group activities and group loyalties are at its peak at the age of
(*a*) 10-12 (*b*) 13-15
(*c*) 8-10 (*d*) 18-20

60. A teacher should not let a 12 years old child any time free because
(*a*) child is always interested to get involve in physical or mental activities
(*b*) spurts of creativity are seen at this age
(*c*) child is frustrated
(*d*) all of these

61. Elektra complex refers to
(*a*) daughter comes closer to the father
(*b*) son comes closer to the mother
(*c*) inferiority complex in the presence of girls
(*d*) none of these

62. According to Freud, super ego is properly developed during
(*a*) latency period (*b*) anal period
(*c*) phallic period (*d*) none of these

63. Development is a process of observable social interaction. This is the opinion of
(*a*) Erikson (*b*) Skinner
(*c*) Robert Sears (*d*) None of these

64. The secondary behaviour of the child according to Robert Sears starts with
(*a*) reinforcement (*b*) imitation
(*c*) modelling (*d*) none of these

65. The period of sensory motor adoptation of Piaget is
(*a*) 0-2 years (*b*) 1-3 years
(*c*) 3-5 years (*d*) 4-6 years

66. The child adopts the view points of others on the basis of consequences of these views in the
(*a*) third stage of Kohlberg's theory
(*b*) second stage of Kohlberg's theory
(*c*) fourth stage of Kohlberg's theory
(*d*) fifth stage of Kohlberg's theory

67. Which of the following is not the view point of cognitive theories of development?
(*a*) moral principles are acquired automatically with age
(*b*) super ego is formed during the period of adolescence
(*c*) Moral values are determined by culture
(*d*) Mural principles are universal

68. Organization of sensory experiences about a particular object is called
(*a*) percepts (*b*) reasoning
(*c*) concept (*d*) none of these

69. The concept building in a person depends on
(*a*) the age and maturity of the person
(*b*) past experiences of the learner
(*c*) intelligence of the learner
(*d*) all of these

70. Agreement on a concept is possible because
(*a*) concepts are subjective
(*b*) concepts are objective
(*c*) concepts are hierarchical
(*d*) b and c both

71. Which of the following statements about concepts is correct?
(*a*) Some concepts are more powerful than others
(*b*) All concepts are universal
(*c*) Concepts are differentiated on the basis of their attributes
(*d*) None of these

72. Which is the highest level of concept formation?
(*a*) formal level (*b*) sensory level
(*c*) concrete level (*d*) none of these

73. How many steps of problem solving has been given by Gates?
(*a*) Six (*b*) Seven
(*c*) Five (*d*) Ten

74. Freeman considers intelligence as an ability
(*a*) to adjust in an adverse situation
(*b*) to learn better and faster
(*c*) to manipulate abstract materials
(*d*) all of these

75. Single factor theory of intelligence was given by
(*a*) Alfred Binet (*b*) Thorndike
(*c*) Freeman (*d*) None of them

76. Which of the following is not the characteristics of 'S' factor according to Spearman ?
(*a*) It is the acquired capacity of the individual
(*b*) Specialization in only one trade is possible
(*c*) It varies from activity to activity in the same individual
(*d*) Individuals differ only in 'S' factor of intelligence

77. In multifactor theory, range is related to
(*a*) Number of tasks that a person can do in a limited period of time

(b) Difficulty level of items
(c) General intelligence of learners
(d) None of these

78. SI model of intelligence was given by J P Guilford in
(a) 1911 (b) 1904
(c) 1967 (d) 1975

79. Hierarchy theory of intelligence was given by
(a) Jenson
(b) Thorndike
(c) Burt and Vernon
(d) None of them

80. In the pre-Binet period, intelligence was considered as
(a) Sensory acuity of the individual
(b) Verbal ability of the individual
(c) Associative ability of the individual
(d) All of these

81. An age scale of intelligence was first developed by
(a) Spearman (b) Terman
(c) Binet-Simon (d) None of them

82. Binet-Simon scale of intelligence measures
(a) General mental abilities not specific ones.
(b) Mental growth of the individual over a period of time
(c) The aptitude or level of an examinee not their speed
(d) All of these

83. WAIS came into being in
(a) 1939 (b) 1955
(c) 1960 (d) 1964

84. Wechsler developed an intelligence test for children in
(a) 1939 (b) 1949
(c) 1955 (d) 1956

85. Catell's culture fair test of intelligence was developed in
(a) 1960 (b) 1961
(c) 1965 (d) 1955

86. Non-verbal test of intelligence is suitable for
(a) deaf and dumb
(b) illiterates
(c) backward children
(d) all of these

87. Intelligence testing is useful for knowing
(a) individual difference
(b) mental retardation
(c) educational backwardness
(d) all of these

88. Scores on intelligence tests can not be fully relied on because
(a) fatigue level can influence the performance
(b) cultural factors can influence the score
(c) they generally do not reveal all the mental abilities of a person
(d) all of these

89. Who among the following psychologists is of the view that a learner can be motivated by satisfying his needs?
(a) Henry Murray (b) Abraham Maslow
(c) Both of these (d) None of these

90. Permanent change in behaviour brought about by experience or training is called.
(a) Learning (b) Motivation
(c) Assimilation (d) None of these

91. The book "**A Theory of Motivation**" has been written by
(a) Maslow (b) K B Madson
(c) Murray (d) None of them

92. Motivated behaviour of a person is
(a) Well directed and well guided towards the goal
(b) Agitated until the goal is achieved
(c) Both of these
(d) None of these

93. Factors affecting motivations are
(a) Physiological factors only
(b) Psychological factors only
(c) Psycho-social factors
(d) All of these

94. Process of motivation is affected by all except
(a) Habits
(b) Mental sets and values
(c) Physical factors
(d) None of these

95. Which of the following does not come under the category of social motives?
(a) Prestige and Status
(b) Social approval
(c) Personal goal
(d) Money hoarding

96. Our action and behaviour is motivated by the desire for getting pleasure and avoiding pain. This is the opinion of
(a) Thomas Hobbes (b) Descartes
(c) Kant (d) John Locke

97. Fundamental instincts of humans are inherited rather than acquired. These instincts are the spring of human behaviour. The above opinion was held by
(a) Charles Darwin (b) Mc Dougall
(c) Both of these (d) None of these

98. Instinct theory of behaviour was rejected by psychologists on which of the following grounds?
(a) Adult behaviour is guided by experience and learning also. It is not always guided by instinct
(b) Human behaviour is affected by the cultural factors also

(c) Human being is a rational animal. He is not supposed to be directed by instincts only
(d) All of these

99. Central motive state was explained by
(a) Morgan
(b) Mc Dougall
(c) Murray
(d) None of them

100. Abraham Maslow was basically a
(a) Pragmatist (b) Humanist
(c) Realist (d) All of them

101. A self actualized person is one who
(a) Does not accept restrictions imposed by the society
(b) Always seeks perfection
(c) Is very good in inter personal relationship with others
(d) All of these

102. The theory of achievement motivation was developed by Mc Clelland of Harward University in
(a) 1949 (b) 1951
(c) 1965 (d) 1944

103. Achievement motive in a child can be developed by
(a) Proper guidance and high expectation from the child
(b) Telling the stories of great men to the child
(c) Setting a realistic goal for the child
(d) All of these

104. Which of the following is not a characteristic of learning?
(a) Learning is a relatively permanent change in behaviour
(b) Learning is a growth of the organism
(c) Learning is directly observed
(d) Learning is a goal directed process

105. In the beginning of life, the baby is guided by
(a) maturation
(b) instincts
(c) learning
(d) none of these

106. Accumulation of knowledge or facts becomes learning when
(a) It is applied in real life situation
(b) It is done by the learner himself
(c) It is provided by the teacher
(d) None of these

107. Dancing, driving, writing etc are the examples of
(a) Mechanical learning
(b) Perceptual motor learning
(c) Psychomotor learning
(d) both (b) and (c)

108. In Gagne's hierarchy, learning has been divided into
(a) eight parts (b) nine parts
(c) seven parts (d) none of the above

109. Match the following:

(A)	(B)
(i) Classical conditioning	1. Kohler
(ii) Drive reduction	2. Hull
(iii) Sign gestalt	3. Pavlov
(iv) Learning by insight	4. Tolman

	(i)	(ii)	(iii)	(iv)
(a)	1	2	3	4
(b)	3	2	4	1
(c)	2	1	3	4
(d)	4	3	2	1

110. Reflexes are of two types according to Pavlov. They are physiological and
(a) Psychic (b) Neural
(c) Mental (d) None of these

111. In classical conditioning, extinction will take place when
(a) Organism is poor in generalization
(b) CS is given without UCS for a long time
(c) CS > UCS
(d) None of these

112. Backward conditioning will take place when
(a) UCS is presented prior to CS
(b) CS is presented prior to UCS
(c) Reward is not given to the organism
(d) None of these

113. When connection is not established between a CS and CR, due to any factor, that is called
(a) Spontaneous recovery
(b) Extinction
(c) Inhibition
(d) None of these

114. When a child responds to all women who wear black suit because of the black suit of her mother, it is the example of
(a) internal inhibition
(b) generalization
(c) assimilation
(d) all of these

115. Which of the following is not a behaviourist?
(a) Watson
(b) Skinner
(c) Pavlov
(d) Lewin

116. Learning according to Watson is
(a) the shifting of old responses to the new stimuli
(b) the result of connection between S-R formed in the brain
(c) both of these
(d) none of these

117. Which of the following points differentiates the theories of Watson and Guthrie?
(a) law of contiguity
(b) law of recency
(c) generalization
(d) law of frequency

118. In operant conditioning reward works as motives but in Guthrie's theory motives are
(a) Stimuli given to the learner
(b) Actions done by the learner
(c) Both of these
(d) None of these

119. We forget something not by disuse but by other learning. This is the theory of
(a) contiguity
(b) trial and error
(c) learning by insight
(d) perception

120. Which of the following is not an essential requirement for trial and error learning?
(a) Drive
(b) Barrier
(c) Chance success
(d) Selective movement of the organism

121. According to the law of trial and error, learning occurs when
(a) it is satisfying for the learner
(b) bond between S-R is strengthened by the repeated use
(c) drive is there in the learner to act
(d) all of these

122. Which of the following facilitates learning according to Thorndike?
(a) Transfer of training
(b) Mental set of the learner
(c) Law of contiguity
(d) All of these

123. In Hull's theory, for learning to occur, the S-R connection must be associated with the
(a) cognitive field of the learner
(b) diminution of the need
(c) both of these
(d) none of these

124. Reinforcement in Skinner's theory is similar to drive reduction in which theory
(a) Hull's theory
(b) Guthrie's theory
(c) Lewin's theory
(d) None of these

125. Which of the following theories is most quantitatively measurable?
(a) Pavlov's
(b) Skinner's
(c) Hull's
(d) None of these

126. In drive reduction theory, the effective stimulus in learning is the trace. It is formed
(a) in the brain
(b) by the bond of S-R
(c) in the nervous system
(d) none of these

127. In drive reduction theory, habit formation is a function of
(a) stimulus potential
(b) stimulus generalization
(c) reaction potential
(d) all of these

128. Hull may be considered superior to other S-R Theorists in the sense that he was able to measure
(a) latency of response
(b) reinforcement potential
(c) both of these
(d) none of these

129. Which of the following points differentiates Skinner from other S-R theorists?
(a) His operant conditioning (type R learning)
(b) His schedule of reinforcement
(c) His way of shaping behaviour
(d) All of these

130. Skinner's theory is more objective in nature than the others because
(a) operant behaviour is external
(b) reflexes never have zero strength
(c) reinforcement is followed by responses
(d) all of these

131. Aversive stimuli in operant conditioning means
(a) individual will not do a particular act because of fear of such stimuli
(b) individual will not do a particular act because of the disapproval from others
(c) both of these
(d) none of these

132. In Skinner's theory, reinforcement is given to the learner when
(a) his response is 100% correct
(b) his response is closer to the correct behaviour
(c) both of these
(d) none of these

133. Which of the following statements regarding S-R theories is not correct?
(a) Man behaves like a machine
(b) Behaviour is overt and can be objectively measured
(c) Learning proceeds from simple to complex
(d) Things are perceived in the context of figure ground *i.e.*, in relation to other things

134. Which of the following statements regarding field theories are correct?
(a) Learning is not additive

(*b*) Molar approach of behaviour is followed here
(*c*) Interaction between organism and the environment is essential for learning
(*d*) All of these

135. Operant conditioning is different from respondent conditioning in which of the following points
(*a*) In OC reinforcement is given after the response is made
(*b*) In operant conditioning, behaviour is controlled by central nervous system
(*c*) A chain of responses is needed for shaping the behaviour (learning)
(*d*) All of these

136. Thorndike and Skinner do not differ at all in
(*a*) the law of effect
(*b*) law of readiness
(*c*) law of contiguity
(*d*) all of these

137. According to gestalt psychologists, behaviour can not be quantified because
(*a*) it is always changeable
(*b*) it is governed by the configuration produced in the mind
(*c*) it is rarely overt
(*d*) all of these

138. Law of pragnanz is the other name of the law of
(*a*) continuity
(*b*) closure
(*c*) contiguity
(*d*) none of these

139. How does the law of similarity work according to field theorists?
(*a*) Similar ideas and experiences get associated to form a whole
(*b*) Similar objects or experiences are easily learnt
(*c*) Both of these
(*d*) None of these

140. Learning by insight looks similar to some extent to which of the following theories?
(*a*) Need reduction theory
(*b*) R type of learning
(*c*) Trial and error theory
(*d*) None of the above

141. The other name of conditioned reflexes is
(*a*) psychic reflexes
(*b*) motor reflexes
(*c*) physiological reflexes
(*d*) none of the above

142. According to Renzuli, a gifted child is one
(*a*) Who possesses above average ability in almost every field
(*b*) Who is committed to task and highly motivated
(*c*) Who is definitely creative
(*d*) All of these

143. Gifted and talented children must be identified as early as possible because
(*a*) If their potentials are not developed by proper guidance of the teacher, it is a loss of the society
(*b*) They are likely to create problems for others, if they are not given work according to their ability
(*c*) Ordinary level of curriculum will not suit to these children
(*d*) All of these

144. Achievement test can be a good indicator of intellectual power if
(*a*) It is conducted immediately after the teaching is over
(*b*) A student shows good performance consistently on different achievement test
(*c*) Both of these
(*d*) None of these

145. Which of the following skills does not require high intellectual ability?
(*a*) Technical skills
(*b*) Mechanical skills
(*c*) Teaching skills
(*d*) Management skills

146. Cognitive abilities related to giftedness are all except
(*a*) High comprehensive and analytical abilities
(*b*) High level of verbal intelligence
(*c*) High retention power
(*d*) None of these

147. A superior child is advanced to a normal child by at least
(*a*) 2½ years
(*b*) Four years
(*c*) 1 years
(*d*) 1½ years

148. A gifted child is
(*a*) realistic in his approach
(*b*) highly interested in solving social problems
(*c*) more frequently chosen by his age mates and peers
(*d*) all of these

149. Which of the following enrichment programmes is suitable for gifted children in the school?
(*a*) Mathematics or Science Olympiad
(*b*) Challenging home assignments
(*c*) Map work during studies
(*d*) All of these

150. Which of the following does not come under the category of acceleration for gifted children?
(*a*) Skipping of classes

(*b*) Early admission
(*c*) Extra laboratory work
(*d*) Organizing summer camps

151. Under achievers are those who
(*a*) Score low on intelligence tests
(*b*) Achieve low in the class consistently despite their superior intelligence
(*c*) Are unable to correspond their achievement to the level of their innate abilities
(*d*) Both (*b*) and (*c*)

152. Which of the following conditions must be satisfied in order to designate a person mentally retarded?
(*a*) Sub-normal intellectual functioning
(*b*) Very poor adaptive ability
(*c*) Dependability on others
(*d*) All of these

153. The best measure of identifying mildly mentally retarded is
(*a*) Administration of standardized intelligence test
(*b*) Administration of behaviour test
(*c*) Administration of adjustment test
(*d*) A combination of all

154. Physical trauma during pregnancy may cause
(*a*) Mental retardation
(*b*) Blindness
(*c*) Deafness
(*d*) All of these

155. All of the following may cause mental retardation except
(*a*) Blood incompatibility
(*b*) Action of toxic agent
(*c*) Radio-activity
(*d*) None of these

156. Which of the following is an important postnatal cause of mental retardation?
(*a*) Brain injury
(*b*) Infection
(*c*) Severe malnutrition
(*d*) All of these

157. Dullers do not differ from normal children in
(*a*) Physical characteristics
(*b*) Level of social expectancy
(*c*) Both of these
(*d*) None of these

158. Which of the following things is not required for educating mildly mentally retarded children?
(*a*) Regular counseling
(*b*) Remedial teaching
(*c*) Modification in the curriculum
(*d*) Regular evaluation

159. Teaching of which of the following skills is not suitable to borderline cases?
(*a*) Electric fitting
(*b*) Repairing of electric or electronic equipments
(*c*) Oratory skills
(*d*) Activity based skills

160. IQ range of morons are in the range of
(*a*) 60-90 (*b*) 50-75
(*c*) 60-80 (*d*) 30-50

161. Morons are slow in
(*a*) Physical growth
(*b*) Thinking and planning
(*c*) Taking initiative
(*d*) All of these

162. Unsatisfactory relation of a mentally retarded child with the environment is technically called
(*a*) Autism
(*b*) Maladjustment
(*c*) Pseudo-dullness
(*d*) None of these

163. All of the following are characteristics of morons except
(*a*) They are restricted to unskilled or semi skilled occupations
(*b*) They are likely to be delinquent more easily
(*c*) They have stronger sex drives than the normals
(*d*) They are educable upto normal level but at a slower rate

164. Which of the following modifications in the curriculum is needed for morons?
(*a*) Activity based curriculum
(*b*) Skill dominated curriculum
(*c*) Emphasis on social training
(*d*) All of these

165. Which of the following things can not be taught to Imbeciles?
(*a*) Self help skills
(*b*) Unskilled job to be performed under supervision
(*c*) Writing skills
(*d*) Social skills

166. In which of the following cases divergent thinking is required?
(*a*) Attempting a multiple choice items
(*b*) Writing an essay
(*c*) Doing a research activity
(*d*) Both (*a*) and (*c*)

167. Which of the following tests is similar to Guilford's test of cognitive abilities?
(*a*) Word association test
(*b*) Things test
(*c*) Hidden shapes test
(*d*) None of these

168. In Hidden shapes test of creativity, which of the following things is used?
(*a*) Pictures

(*b*) Words
(*c*) Things
(*d*) None of them

169. A creative child in the class can not be satisfied unless
(*a*) He is given freedom to manipulate ideas or things
(*b*) He is allowed to ask questions in his own way
(*c*) Both of these
(*d*) None of these

170. A creative child is one who
(*a*) Is ideationally productive and unconventional
(*b*) Does not stick to social and religious norms in a hard manner
(*c*) Is all the time restless to do something uncommon and unique
(*d*) All of these

171. For the development of creative potential of a child, the teacher should
(*a*) Allow him to be critical to ideas and people
(*b*) Give them chance of problem solving
(*c*) Both of these
(*d*) None of these

172. New ideas (Eureka) suddenly comes in the minds of the creative children in the stage of
(*a*) Preparation
(*b*) Illumination
(*c*) Revision
(*d*) Incubation

173. The technique to foster creativity in children is
(*a*) Brain storming
(*b*) Problem solving
(*c*) Both of these
(*d*) None of these

174. A teacher can foster creativity in children by
(*a*) Developing confidence in them
(*b*) Giving them opportunity to express
(*c*) Both of these
(*d*) None of these

175. Learning disabled children are
(*a*) Deficient in using potentials
(*b*) Low in intelligence
(*c*) Slow in activity
(*d*) None of these

176. Learning disabled children perform very poorly in
(*a*) academic areas
(*b*) technical areas
(*c*) both of these
(*d*) none of these

177. Problem of learning disability is more complex than that of other disabilities because
(*a*) Its causes can not be easily ascertained by applying usual tests
(*b*) It is associated to behaviour problems
(*c*) Both of these
(*d*) None of these

178. Educationally, learning disabled look similar to
(*a*) dullers
(*b*) backward children
(*c*) both of these
(*d*) none of these

179. In which of the following physical characteristics learning disabled children differ from the normal ones?
(*a*) They are all the time clumsy and awkward
(*b*) Poor coordination of motor abilities
(*c*) Height, weight and health
(*d*) All of these

180. Which of the following methods is most suitable for learning disabled children?
(*a*) Behaviour guidance method
(*b*) Remedial teaching
(*c*) Brain storming
(*d*) None of them

181. In order to improve work habits of learning disabled what should be done?
(*a*) Unattending behaviour should be penalized
(*b*) Close monitoring of the behaviour is needed
(*c*) Cues and prompt should be given
(*d*) All of these

182. Those who are normal in intelligence but slow in academic achievement due to psycho-social reasons are called
(*a*) Backward children
(*b*) Gifted under achievers
(*c*) Both of these
(*d*) None of these

183. Consistent low achievement leads to low intelligence because
(*a*) 50% intellectual ability is expressed in verbal form
(*b*) Learning develops thinking and reasoning power
(*c*) Both of these
(*d*) None of these

184. Which of the following situations may lead to educational backwardness?
(*a*) Sensory impairment
(*b*) Motor disability
(*c*) Long diseases and health problems.
(*d*) All of these

185. Emotional disturbances may lead to educational backwardness because
(*a*) Proper emotional development is necessary for social interactions
(*b*) Emotions will develop intellectual power, *i.e.*, emotional intelligence

(c) Both of these
(d) None of these

186. Which of the following factors will not lead to educational backwardness?
(a) Poor socio economic status of the family
(b) Poor educational environment of the school
(c) Occupation of the family
(d) Poor emotional climate of the family

187. Which of the following is an important cause of educational backwardness at primary level of education in India?
(a) Poor school organisation
(b) Lack of accountability
(c) Attitude of the masses towards education
(d) All of these

188. Which of the following measures should be adopted by the teacher to check educational backwardness?
(a) Continuous evaluation and regular feedback
(b) Remedial teaching
(c) Adjustment and behaviour training
(d) All of these

189. Teaching by small steps and frequent short assignment techniques are useful for
(a) Slow learners
(b) Learning disabled
(c) Educationally backward children
(d) Children of all types of disabilities

190. Special schools are required for backward children when
(a) Backwardness is due to any serious physical handicap
(b) The size of population of backward children in the society is very large as is the case of Gujarat where the achievement of students in mathematics is always seen very low
(c) Both of these
(d) None of these

191. Which of the following should be considered the most important quality of a teacher at primary level?
(a) Patience and perseverance
(b) Competence in methods of teaching and knowledge of subjects
(c) Competence to teach in highly standardised language
(d) Eagerness to teach

192. A teacher, because of his/her democratic nature, allows students to sit all over the class. Some sit together and discuss or do group reading. Some sit quietly and read themselves. A parent does not like it. Which of the following may be the best way to handle the situation?
(a) Parents should request the principal to change the section of their ward
(b) Parents should show trust in the teacher and discuss the problem with the teacher
(c) Parents should take away the child from that school
(d) Parents should complain against the teacher to the principal

193. The stage in which a child begins to think logically about objects and events is known as
(a) Formal operational stage
(b) Pre-operational stage
(c) Concrete operational stage
(d) Sensori-motor stage

194. 'Mind mapping' refers to
(a) a plan of action for an adventure
(b) drawing the picture of a mind
(c) researching the functioning of the mind
(d) a technique to enhance comprehension

195. The best way, specially at primary level, to address the learning difficulties of students is to use
(a) expensive and glossy support material
(b) easy and interesting textbooks
(c) story-telling method
(d) a variety of teaching methods suited to the disability

196. Which of the following will foster creativity among learners?
(a) Providing opportunities to question and to nurture the innate talents of every learner
(b) Emphasizing achievement goals from the beginning of school life
(c) Coaching students for good marks in examination
(d) Teaching the students the practical value of good education

197. According to Piaget, at which of the following stages does a child begin to think logically about abstract propositions?
(a) Formal operational stage (11 years and up)
(b) Sensori-motor stage (Birth–02 years)
(c) Pre-operational stage (02–07 years)
(d) Concrete operational stage (07–11 years)

198. Learning can be enriched if
(a) more and more teaching aids are used in the class
(b) teachers use different types of lectures and explanation
(c) due attention is paid to periodic tests in the class
(d) situations from the real world are brought into the class in which students interact with each other and the teahcer facilitates

199. Which of the following statements ***cannot*** be considered as a feature of the process of learning?
(a) Learning is a comprehensive process
(b) Learning is goal-oriented
(c) Unlearning is also a learning process
(d) Educational institutions are the only place where learning takes place

200. A student of V-grade with 'visual deficiency' should be
(*a*) helped with his/her routine-work by parents and friends
(*b*) treated normally in the classroom and provided support through Audio CDs
(*c*) given special treatment in the classroom
(*d*) excused to do a lower level of work

201. Which of the following is ***not*** related to the socio-psychological needs of the child?
(*a*) Need for emotional security
(*b*) Regular elimination of waste products from the body
(*c*) Need for company
(*d*) Need for appreciation or social approval

202. Which is the place where the child's 'cognitive' development is defined in the best way?
(*a*) School and classroom environment
(*b*) Auditorium
(*c*) Home
(*d*) Playground

203. .... is considered a sign of motivated teaching.
(*a*) Remedial work given by the teacher
(*b*) Questioning by students
(*c*) Pin drop silence in the class
(*d*) Maximum attendance in the class

204. Which of the following is ***not*** a sign of an intelligent young child?
(*a*) One who has the ability to communicate fluently and appropriately
(*b*) One who carries on thinking in an abstract manner
(*c*) One who can adjust oneself in a new environment
(*d*) One who has the ability to cram long essays very quickly

205. "Children actively construct their understanding of the world" is a statement attributed to
(*a*) Pavlov (*b*) Kohlberg
(*c*) Skinner (*d*) Piaget

206. Kritika who does ***not*** talk much at home, talks a lot at school. It shows that
(*a*) teachers demand that children should talk a lot at school
(*b*) she does not like her home at all
(*c*) her thoughts get acknowledged at school
(*d*) the school provides opportunities to children to talk a lot

207. A teacher should make an attempt to understand the potentialities of her/his students. Which of the following fields is related to this objective?
(*a*) Social Philosophy
(*b*) Media – Psychology
(*c*) Educational Psychology
(*d*) Educational Sociology

208. Motivation, in the process of learning,
(*a*) differentiates new learning from old learning
(*b*) makes learners think unidirectionally
(*c*) creates interest for learning among young learners
(*d*) sharpens the memory of learners

209. The term 'curriculum' in the field of education refers to
(*a*) overall programme of the school which students experience on a day-to-day basis
(*b*) evaluation process
(*c*) text-material to be used in the class
(*d*) methods of teaching and the content to be taught

210. At lower classes, play-way method of teaching is based on
(*a*) principles of methods of teaching
(*b*) psychological principles of development and growth
(*c*) sociological principles of teaching
(*d*) theory of physical education programmes

211. "A young child responds to a new situation on the basis of the response made by him/her in a similar situation as in the past." This is related to
(*a*) 'Law of Effect' of learning
(*b*) 'Law of Attitude' of learning process
(*c*) 'Law of Readiness' of learning
(*d*) 'Law of Analogy' of learning

212. .... is ***not*** considered a sign of 'being gifted'.
(*a*) Fighting with others
(*b*) Novelty in expression
(*c*) Curiosity
(*d*) Creative ideas

213. Education of children with special needs should be provided
(*a*) by methods developed for special children in special schools
(*b*) in special schools
(*c*) by special teachers in special schools
(*d*) along with other normal children

214. To make assessment a 'useful and interesting' process, one should be careful about
(*a*) labelling students as intelligent or average learners
(*b*) using a variety of ways to collect information about the student's learning across the scholastic and co-scholastic boundaries
(*c*) using technical language to give feedback
(*d*) making comparisons between different students

215. 'Dyslexia' is associated with
(*a*) Mathematical disorder

(b) Reading disorder
(c) Behavioural disorder
(d) Mental disorder

216. Parents should play a .... role in the learning process of young children.
(a) proactive
(b) sympathetic
(c) neutral
(d) negative

217. "Development is a never ending process." This idea is associated with
(a) Principle of continuity
(b) Principle of integration
(c) Principle of interaction
(d) Principle of interrelation

218. The 'insight theory of learning' is promoted by
(a) Pavlov
(b) Jean Piaget
(c) Vygotsky
(d) 'Gestalt' theorists

219. In which of the following stages do children become active members of their peer group?
(a) Adulthood
(b) Early childhood
(c) Childhood
(d) Adolescence

220. Four distinct stages of children's intellectual development are identified by
(a) Erikson (b) Skinner
(c) Piaget (d) Kohlberg

ANSWERS

1	2	3	4	5	6	7	8	9	10
(a)	(a)	(b)	(d)	(c)	(d)	(a)	(c)	(d)	(c)
11	12	13	14	15	16	17	18	19	20
(a)	(c)	(b)	(a)	(b)	(b)	(a)	(b)	(a)	(c)
21	22	23	24	25	26	27	28	29	30
(a)	(b)	(a)	(d)	(c)	(d)	(b)	(c)	(c)	(a)
31	32	33	34	35	36	37	38	39	40
(d)	(d)	(c)	(d)	(a)	(d)	(b)	(d)	(a)	(d)
41	42	43	44	45	46	47	48	49	50
(c)	(d)	(a)	(c)	(d)	(a)	(c)	(d)	(d)	(b)
51	52	53	54	55	56	57	58	59	60
(d)	(b)	(d)	(c)	(a)	(d)	(d)	(c)	(a)	(a)
61	62	63	64	65	66	67	68	69	70
(a)	(a)	(c)	(b)	(a)	(a)	(c)	(a)	(d)	(d)
71	72	73	74	75	76	77	78	79	80
(b)	(a)	(c)	(d)	(a)	(d)	(a)	(c)	(c)	(a)
81	82	83	84	85	86	87	88	89	90
(c)	(d)	(b)	(b)	(b)	(d)	(d)	(d)	(c)	(a)
91	92	93	94	95	96	97	98	99	100
(a)	(c)	(d)	(d)	(c)	(a)	(c)	(d)	(a)	(b)
101	102	103	104	105	106	107	108	109	110
(d)	(b)	(d)	(c)	(b)	(a)	(d)	(a)	(b)	(a)
111	112	113	114	115	116	117	118	119	120
(b)	(a)	(c)	(b)	(d)	(c)	(d)	(a)	(a)	(d)
121	122	123	124	125	126	127	128	129	130
(d)	(d)	(b)	(a)	(c)	(c)	(a)	(a)	(d)	(a)
131	132	133	134	135	136	137	138	139	140
(a)	(c)	(d)	(d)	(d)	(a)	(b)	(b)	(a)	(c)
141	142	143	144	145	146	147	148	149	150
(a)	(d)	(d)	(c)	(a)	(d)	(a)	(d)	(d)	(c)
151	152	153	154	155	156	157	158	159	160
(d)	(d)	(d)	(d)	(d)	(d)	(c)	(c)	(c)	(b)

161	162	163	164	165	166	167	168	169	170
(*d*)	(*a*)	(*d*)	(*d*)	(*d*)	(*d*)	(*b*)	(*a*)	(*c*)	(*a*)
171	**172**	**173**	**174**	**175**	**176**	**177**	**178**	**179**	**180**
(*c*)	(*b*)	(*c*)	(*c*)	(*d*)	(*a*)	(*a*)	(*b*)	(*b*)	(*a*)
181	**182**	**183**	**184**	**185**	**186**	**187**	**188**	**189**	**190**
(*d*)	(*a*)	(*c*)	(*d*)	(*c*)	(*c*)	(*d*)	(*d*)	(*d*)	(*c*)
191	**192**	**193**	**194**	**195**	**196**	**197**	**198**	**199**	**200**
(*a*)	(*b*)	(*c*)	(*c*)	(*d*)	(*a*)	(*d*)	(*d*)	(*d*)	(*b*)
201	**202**	**203**	**204**	**205**	**206**	**207**	**208**	**209**	**210**
(*b*)	(*a*)	(*b*)	(*d*)	(*d*)	(*c*)	(*c*)	(*c*)	(*a*)	(*b*)
211	**212**	**213**	**214**	**215**	**216**	**217**	**218**	**219**	**220**
(*a*)	(*a*)	(*d*)	(*b*)	(*b*)	(*a*)	(*a*)	(*d*)	(*d*)	(*c*)

GLOSSARY

Accommodation : Piaget used this term for modification or reorganisation of existing cognitive structure (schemata) to deal with environmental demands. Accommodation is the adjustment the individual makes when incorporating external reality. Piaget uses this concept in conjunction with assimilation, which is the individual's response to the immediate and compelling environmental demands that have been and are being assimilated.

Advance organisers : Introductory information intended to facilitate a student's learning by providing a framework and organisation for the material to be learned.

Affective domain : One of the categories of educational objectives for students attitudes, values and emotional growth. The affective domain includes five basic categories: receiving, responding, valuing, organisation and characterisation by a value.

Assimilation : Assimilation is the process of taking within or internalising, one's environmental experience. The term is used by Piaget for the process of making sense of experiences and perceptions by fitting them into previously established cognitive structure (schemata). Assimilation is used by Piaget in conjunction with the concept of accommodation. Piaget believes that assimilation is a spontaneous process on the part of the child.

Attitudes : A learned predisposition to respond either positively or negatively to persons, situations, or things. Attitudes carry a strong emotional component and therefore can never be neutral.

Attribution theory : The term attribution refers to the explanation a person gives for his or her own or another person's actions or beliefs. An attribution based on internal factors is called a dispositional attribution, and one based on external factors is called a situational attribution.

Behaviourism : A school of thought in Psychology usually considered to have originated in the work and writings of John B. Watson in 1913. Watson argued against the use of introspection in gathering psychological data. He considered observable behaviour the only valid data in Psychology. According to Watson, any concepts, like mind or consciousness, that have mentalistic overtones must be purged from the field of psychology. The most famous current representative of this tradition is Harvard University's B.F. Skinner.

Classical conditioning : A procedure in which the conditioned stimulus after being paired with the unconditioned stimulus often enough, can then be substituted for it. It is often called ''stimulus substitution.''

Cognition : The process of faculties by which knowledge is acquired and manipulated (*e.g.*, thinking or remembering).

Cognitive domain : A part of Bloom's Taxonomy of educational objectives. Bloom divided the objectives in the cognitive domain into six categories: knowledge, comprehension, application, analysis, synthesis and evaluation.

Cognitive style : The consistent way in which an individual responds to a wide range of perceptual tasks.

Computer-assisted instruction (CAI) : The use of a computer as tutor to present information, give students opportunities to practice what they learn, evaluate student achievement, and provide additional instruction.

Concept learning : The acquisition of pattern-recognition knowledge involving the learning of a rule or rules for classifying a number of objects into mutually exclusive categories based on one or more salient characteristics of the objects.

Conditioned response : A response elicited by a conditioned stimulus. The response is similar but not identical to its associated unconditioned response.

Cognitive learning : The view that learning is based on a restructuring of perceptions and thoughts occurring within the organism is called cognitive learning. This restructuring allows the learner to perceive new relationships, solve new problems and gain understanding of a subject area. Cognitive learning theorists stress the reorganisation of one's perceptions in order to achieve understanding, as opposed to the behaviourist theorists, who stress the importance of associations formed between stimuli and responses.

Conditioned response : The term is used both in classical conditioning, and in operant conditioning. In classical conditioning, the conditioned response is the response being elicited by the conditioned stimulus. The stronger the conditioning, the greater the magnitude of the conditioned response and the shorter its latency. In Pavlov's experiment the conditioned response was the dog's salivation to the tone.

In operant conditioning, since the response must precede the reinforcer, the conditioned response is defined not in terms of magnitude or latency, but in terms of either the rate of response or its resistance to extinction. For example, a strongly conditioned operant will occur for more rapidly than one that has been only weakly conditioned. Also, a strongly conditioned operant will be far more difficult to extinguish.

Conditioned stimulus : In classical conditioning, the previously neutral stimulus takes on the power to elicit the response through association with an unconditioned stimulus. For this to occur, the conditioned stimulus must precede the unconditioned stimulus on enough occasions to cause the conditioned stimulus to serve as a signal that the unconditioned stimulus will follow. In Pavlov's experiment on conditioning the dog, the tone was used as the conditioned stimulus. The tone was consistently followed by the meat powder, until the dog began salivating to the tone alone.

Conditioning : Process of learning whereby stimuli and responses become associated through training. There are two general types of conditioning, classical and operant. In classical conditioning a conditioned stimulus is presented, followed by an unconditioned stimulus. Conditioning is exhibited when the organism learns to respond to the conditioned stimulus alone. In operant conditioning the operant is allowed to occur and then is followed by a reinforcing stimulus. Operant conditioning is exhibited when the rate of responding increases over the original, preconditioned rate.

Convergent thinking : A term used by Guilford to describe the type of thinking in which an individual produces a single response to a specific question or problem.

Creativity : The capacity of individuals to produce novel or original answers or products.

Culture : The ways in which a group of people think, feel, and react in order to solve problems of living in their environment.

Cumulative records : A file on a student that includes such information as family data, health, academic grades, standardized test scores, attendance and teacher comments.

Discovery learning : Term is used to describe a form of learning that results not from rote memorisation or conditioning but from the active exploration of alternatives on the part of the learner. This learning is largely a result of learner's own efforts. Learning attained through discovery is more meaningful and long-lasting than that from memorisation.

Divergent thinking : A term used by Guilford to describe the type of thinking wherein an individual produces multiple responses or solutions (often non-traditional) to a single question or problem. Divergent thinking is associated with creativity.

Egocentrism : Piaget's term for describing children in the preperational stage, who have difficulty in assuming the point of view of others.

Enactive : Bruner's first stage of cognitive development, in which children understand the environment through physical action on that environment.

Encoding : The short-term memory process of transforming incoming information into episodic or semantic form and associating it with old knowledge for storage in long-term memory.

Entry behaviour : The knowledge, skills, or attitudes that a learner brings into a new learning situation.

Formal-operations stage : This is a stage of cognitive development according to Jean Piaget, occurring during early adolescence. The period of formal operations (eleven to sixteen years) is the last of Piaget's stages and is characterised by the youth's ability to develop full, formal patterns of thinking based on abstract symbolism. The youth is able to reason things out logically at the abstract level, develop symbolic meanings, and generalize to other situations. This is the highest level of thinking and according to Piaget, must await the maturation of certain structures in the brain for its full development.

Equilibration : A motivation principle in Piaget's theory that identifies human beings as active and exploratory in attempting to impose order and meaningfulness on experiences. This order or balance occurs through the processes of assimilation and accommodation.

Evaluation : This is a process of obtaining information to form judgments so that educational decisions can be made.

External locus of control : A feeling that one has little control over one's and the failure to perceive a cause-and-effect relationship between actions and consequences.

Extrinsic motivation : Motivation influenced by external events such as grades, marks or money.

Gestalt psychology : A school of thought maintaining that the organised whole, configuration, or totality of psychological experience should be the proper object of study. Founded in Germany by Max Wertheimer in the early 1900s, gestalt psychology's first interest was in the field of perception. Later, under Wolfgang Kohler's direction, studies were done in the area of learning, and under Kurt Lewin's direction, in the area of motivation. Gestalt psychologists tend to emphasize cognitive processes in the study of learning. They stress that true understanding occurs only through the reorganisation of ideas and perceptions, not through memorisation or conditioning.

Information processing : Theory of learning and remembering that is based on the computer as a model. Information is seen as following into and within the organism. The sense organs respond to incoming information, and it is passed along and encoded in the memory and nervous system. The encoded information may then be stored and processed and finally retrieved and acted on. As with the computer, there is information input, storage and/or processing, and output.

Insight : A suddenly realised solution to a problem, sometimes called the ''a-ha! phenomenon''. Introduced by Wolfgang Kohler, the concept of insight is used to explain the apparently spontaneous appearance of a solution to a problem. Insight results from the reorganisation of ideas and perceptions rather than from simple trial-and-error behaviour. The concept of insight is used typically by gestalt psychologists.

Inquiry learning : A process that is similar to discovery learning. Students learn strategies to manipulate and process information, test hypothesis and apply their conclusions to new content or situations.

Intelligence : The capacity, or a set of capacities that allows an individual to learn, solve problems, and/or interact successfully with his or her environment. As hypothetical construct, intelligence has come to mean higher-level thought processes, or intellectual abilities. Statistical studies of intelligence utilise the concept of measured intelligence, which is the score received on a standardised intelligence test.

Intelligence Quotient (IQ) : Originally, a measure of intelligence calculated by dividing a student's mental age (MA) by the chronological age (CA) and multiplying by 100, that is, IQ = MA/CA × 100. This is called the ratio method of obtaining an IQ.

More recently, IQ has been computed by the deviation method. One's deviation IQ is defined by one's relative standing among peers. The deviation IQ is computed on the basis of how far one's score deviates from the mean score obtained for the entire group of individuals of the same chronological age. This technique is based on the standard, or z-score concept and assumes a normal distribution for each age group.

Law of effect : This is one of E.L. Thorndike's main laws of learning. It states that when an association between a stimulus and response is followed by a satisfying state of affairs, the association (or connection) is strengthened. When the association is followed by an annoying state of affairs, it is weakened. In brief, reward strengthens and punishment weakens any connection between stimuli and responses. In a later version of the law, Thorndike soft-pedaled the importance of punishment of a weakening agent. Thorndike's law of effect is considered by many psychologists to be the cornerstone on which B.F. Skinner built his system of operant conditioning.

Law of exercise : One of E.L. Thorndike's three main laws of learning. It states that the more frequently a stimulus response connection occurs, the stronger the resulting association and hence, the stronger the learning. The repetition of a learned response strengthens the bond between stimulus situation and the response. The law was later amended to incorporate the importance of the consequences of the action; thus, practice without knowledge of results is not nearly as effective as when the consequences become known to the learner.

Law of readiness : One of E.L. Thorndike's three main laws of learning. It states that learning occurs when the student is mentally ready to learn. The reference here is to momentary readiness rather than maturational readiness.

Learning : Learning is a very general term refering to a process that leads to a relatively permanent change in behaviour resulting from experience. Thus, such activities as acquiring physical skills, memorizing poems, acquiring attitudes, etc., are all examples of learning. Learning may be conscious or unconscious, adaptive or maladaptive, overt or covert. Although the learning process is typically measured on the basis of a change in performance, most psychologists agree that an accompanying change occurs within the nervous system. Though there are a great many theories and explanations concerning learning, there is general agreement regarding its definition.

Locus of control : The concept identifies the type of personal control used by an individual. When the locus of control is internal, individual views himself as personally in charge of his own destinies. When the locus of control is external, the person feels he is at the mercy of external circumstances.

Long-term memory (LTM) : In the information-processing system, LTM is the second of the two main storage systems. Information that is in short-term memory may, under certain conditions, be passed along for processing and consolidation into a more permanent storage site, long-term memory. Long-term memory has the potential for holding encoded information for long periods.

Mental age : Term first used by Alfred Binet as the unit for measuring intelligence. Binet defined mental age in terms of the age at which a given number of test items are passed by an average child. If, for example, the average six-year-old could correctly answer a certain number of items, then any other child correctly answering the same number of items would be assigned at least a mental age of six.

Motivation : A general psychological term used to explain behaviour initiated by needs and directed towards a goal. Motives may be biogenic (that is stemming from tissue needs within the organism) or acquired (that is, learned through interaction with the environment, especially the social environment).

Among learning theorists, Jerome Bruner makes much of the principle of motivation, assuming that almost all children have a built-in ''will to learn''.

Nature-nurture controversy : Debate over which component, nature (heredity) or nurture (environment), is more influential in determining behaviour. In Psychology the behaviourists consistently argued on behalf of nurture, and the intelligence testers favoured nature. Educational Psychology has long been the battleground on which this issue has been fought, since the psychologists primarily concerned with this issue were the learning theorists (largely behaviourists).

Need hierarchy : Theory proposed by Abraham Maslow that suggests that human beings place their needs on the following universal, order-of-importance scale: (*i*) physiological needs, (*ii*) safety needs, (*iii*) love needs, (*iv*) esteem needs, and (*v*) self-actualising needs.

Needs : The part of the motivational cycle seen as deficits that lie within the individual. These may be physiological (*e.g.*, the needs for food) or psychological (*e.g.*, the need for approval).

Non-verbal behaviour : Body language. Based largely on the theroy of Charles Galloway and some research by Robert Rosenthal, the teacher's non-verbal behaviour represents an important avenue for the transmission of teacher expectations. Galloway has shown how non-verbal behaviour can promote or reduce student learning. Rosenthal has shown how his test (Profile of Non-verbal Sensitivity) can identify the channels for communicating how teachers really feel about their students.

Operants : Responses, according to B.F. Skinner, for which the original stimuli are either unidentified or non-existent are called operants. The consequences of operant behaviour can be observed even though the stimulus is not known. For example, if a rat presses the lever in a Skinner box and this results in reinforcement, an increase in operant rate will be observed despite the fact that no stimulus could be identified as initiating the original stimulus could be identified as initiating the original lever pressing. In operant conditioning, reinforcement is contingent on the operant's first being emitted. The organism must in some way ''operate'' on the environment in order that the reinforcement will follow. Operant responding at one time was called instrumental responding by some psychologists.

Operant conditioning : A type of learning that involves an increase in the probability that a response will occur as a function of reinforcement. This is a forn of conditioning, described by B.F. Skinner, in which the free operant is allowed to occur and is followed by a reinforcing stimulus that is, in turn, followed by an increased likelihood of the operant's occurring again. For optimum conditioning the reinforcing stimulus should follow the operant immediately. The rate of responding for a conditioned operant may jump dramatically over the preconditioned rate (operant level).

Operant level : The original, or preconditioned, rate of operant responding before any reinforcing stimuli have been introduced. If a rat happens to press the lever in a Skinner box four times an hour (without being reinforced), the operant level for that response is established at four per hour. Thus, the operant level is the rate at which the free operant is typically emitted prior to conditioning.

Positive reinforcement : A procedure that maintains or increases the rate of a response by presenting a stimulus (a positive reinforcer) following the response.

Preoperational stage : The second stage in Piaget's theory of cognitive development, in which the lack of logical operations forces children to make decisions bases on their perceptions.

Primary reinforcement : The process of using a stimulus that is reinforcing in the absence of any learning. Such stimuli as food and water are primary reinforcers.

Programmed instruction (PI) : PI is an arrangement of instructional material in a step-by-step sequence designed to lead the student to a specified goal. The material being presented is broken down into small steps called frames. There are two general approaches to programming: (*i*) linear programmes, in which all students go through the entire programme and the frames gradually increase in difficulty, and (*ii*) branched programmes, in which the student skips forward or backward in the programme (the order of the frame presentation varies) as a result of the success or failure experienced in responding.

PI can be in book form, or it can be presented through the use of a teaching machine and/or computer. The concept of programmed instruction is credited to B.F. Skinner.

Psychoanalytic theory : This reveals the theory/ method of studying and treating mental illness presented by Sigmund Freud. The theory attempts to give a rational explanation for irrational thoughts and responses. Psychoanalytic theory states (*i*) that all behaviour is determined by specific motives; (*ii*) that most human motives lie at the unconscious level, and therefore people are unaware of the reasons for most of their own behaviour; (*iii*) that neurotic symptoms result from an individual's inner conflicts; and (*iv*) that inner conflicts are a product of childhood trauma and anxiety. The technique is based on the therapist's revealing to the patient the source of his or her anxiety and helping the patient achieve insight and emotional release.

Puberty : The biological changes that lead to reproductive maturity. Its onset is identified by such factors as the growth of body hair, voice changes in males, and menstruation and breast development in females.

Punishment : A method for controlling behaviour through the use of aversive stimulation. In other words, punishment is a procedure in which an aversive stimulus is presented immediately following a response, resulting in a reduction in the rate of response. Punishment, though not itself causing the extinction of a conditioned response, does severely reduce the rate of responding while the punishment is in force. Punishment should not be confused with negative reinforcement.

Reinforcement : Any stimulus that increases the likelihood of a response's recurring. Reinforcement, as a Skinnerian concept, should not be confused with reward, feelings of pleasure, or any other concept with subjective of mentalistic overtones. Reinforcement may be used in either classical (respondent) or operant conditioning. In respondent condition the unconditioned stimulus serves as the reinforcement. In operant conditioning the presentation of any stimulus following the emitted response can be considered a reinforcement if it results in a higher response rate.

Schemata : Cognitive structures created through the abstraction of previous experience. Schemata function in the comprehension and recall of data and can aid learning or be responsible for many types distortion in recall.

Secondary reinforcement : A process that uses a stimulus that is not originally reinforcing but that acquires reinforcing properties when paired with a primary reinforcer. Money is a secondary reinforcer.

Self-actualization : Maslow's term for the psychological need to develop one's capabilities and potential in order to enhance personal growth. It refer to a person's constant striving to realise the potential within and to develop inherent talents and capabilities.

Self-concept : The total organisation of the perceptions individuals have of themselves.

Self-esteem : The value, or judgement, individuals place on their behaviour. Self-esteem and self-concept are often used interchangeably in educational literature.

Self-reinforcement : A procedure in which individuals reinforce their own behaviour.

Sensitive period : This is a time period when an organism is susceptible to a change in behaviour due to certain kinds of environmental stimulation. The sensitive periods typically occur early in the organism's life and tend to produce behaviour changes that are relatively long-lasting. The process of mother-infant bounding is said to occur only during the baby's first three days of life.

Short-term memory (STM) : In the information processing system, STM is the first of two main storage systems. Sometimes it is called working or active memory. Estimates of how long information may be retained in short-term memory vary from about twenty seconds to over a minute.

Social facilitation : The concept from the field of social psychology is used to explain the fact that in some circumstances individuals perform more quickly when in a group situation than when alone. Social facilitation is most pronounced in the case of fairly simple mechanical tasks. The more difficult and the more intellectual the task, the less the effect of social facilitation.

Social learning theory : Theory, proposed by Albert Bandura, suggests that a large part of what a person learns occurs through imitation or modelling. Bandura's major concern is with learning that takes place in the context of a social situation in which individuals come to modify behaviour as a result of how others in the group respond. Social learning does not require primary reinforcement.

Stimulus-response : A theory that stresses the importance of the build up of stimulus response associations in defining learning. Most behaviourists adhere to stimulus response learning theories, the major exception being E.C. Tolman. The leading stimulus response theorists are E.L. Thorndike, Ivan Pavlov, J.B. Watson, Edwin Guthrie, C.L. Hull, and B.F. Skinner. Stimulus response theorists stress the importance of nurture in the nature-nurture debate. Most theories of learning during the first half of the twentieth century were stimulus response theories. The cognitive-gestalt position, however, was not based on a stimulus-response theory.

Stimulus variety : Variation, at all sensroy modes, of stimulus inputs. Stimulus variety was seen by many early-experience theorists as the crucial ingredient in intellectual development. The more the child hears, sees, and touches, the more he or she will want to hear, see, and touch and the more intellectual growth will occur.

Teaching machine : A device used to present an instructional programme one step (or frame) at a time. The student either writes in answers or presses a button corresponding to the correct alternative. The advantages of the teaching machine are that (*i*) the student can proceed at his or her own pace; (*ii*) the student receives immediate feedback; (*iii*) for many students the machines are intrinsically motivating.

Unconditioned response : An unconditioned response is any response that can be elicited automatically by the presentation of a certain stimulus, without any training or learning. The term is used in classical conditioning and in Ivan Pavlov's original experiment the unconditioned response was salivation to the stimulus of meat powder being placed in the dog's mouth.

Unconditioned stimulus : Any stimulus that will elicit a given response automatically, without any training or learning. The term is used in classical conditioning and in the case of Ivan Pavlov's own experiment, the unconditioned stimulus was meat powder placed in the dog's mouth.

English Literature & Grammar

SHAKESPEARE'S WORKS

WILLIAM SHAKESPEARE (16116)

Life

1. He was born on or about 23 April, 1564 at Stratford-on-Avon, Warwickshire.
2. His father was a prospersons tradesman.
3. He was sent to a Grammar school where he learnt "small Latin and less Greek."
4. Later misfortunes overtook the family.
5. In his 19th year, he married Anne Hathaway, who was eight years his seniors.
6. His marriage seems to have been an unhappy one.

7. *(i)* There are several anecdotes why he left for London, but we need not study them here.
(ii) It is almost certain that he went to London in or about 1587 to seek fortunes there.

8. It was the time when drama was being popularized by the University Wits.

9. *(i)* There are again several stories how he came on the stage, but what we are concerned here is that soon he gained popularity and appeared on the stage as an actor.
For example, he acted in Ben Jonson's "Everyman in His Humour."
(ii) Soon alongwith being an actor, he became a playwright also.

10. It is certain from the deathbed words of Greene who called him an "upstart" that by 1592, Shakespeare had quite established himself as a playwright.

11. Soon he became a shareholder in prestigious theatres such as the Globe and the Blackfriars.

12. *(i)* He also purchased property in London and Stratford.
(ii) It is clear that he had become sufficiently prosperous.

13. However, misfortunes were not late in visiting him:
(i) His only son died in 1596.
(ii) His father died in 1601.
(iii) His mother died in 1608.

14. Still, financially he was sound.

15. Between 1610 and 1612 he retired to his hometown, Stratford, where he bought the largest house in the town named the New Place.

16. As his health broke down, he died on 23rd April, 1616.

Works

In all, he wrote :

(i) 37 plays
(ii) Two narrative poems:
(a) Venus and Adonis
(b) Lucrece
(iii) 154 sonnets:
(a) 126 addressed to a man—a patron or friend.
(b) the rest 28 addressed to a dark lady.

His dramatic work is generally divided in four periods:

1. The First Period (1588-93) : It was the period of apprenticeship and experiment. It included:

(i) Revision of old plays such as:
(a) Henry VI
(b) Titus Andronicus,
(ii) the first comedies such as :
(a) Love's Labour's Lost
(b) Two Gentlemen of Verona
(c) The Comedy of Errors, and
(d) A Midsummer Night's Dream, and
(iii) the first attempt at writing a tragedy—Romeo and Juliet.

2. The Second Period (1594-1600) : It was the period of the great Comedies and Chronicle Plays, such as

(a) Richard II
(b) King John
(c) The Merchant of Venice
(d) Henry IV Part I
(e) Henry IV Part II
(f) Henry V
(g) The Taming of the Shrew
(h) The Merry Wives of Windsor
(i) Much Ado About Nothing
(j) As You Like It, and
(k) Twelfth Night

3. The Third Period (1601-08): This was the period of his great tragedies and sombre comedies, such as

(i) Julius Caesar
(ii) Hamlet
(iii) All's Well That Ends Well
(iv) Measure for Measure
(v) Troilus and Cressida
(vi) Othello
(vii) King Lear
(viii) Macbeth
(ix) Antony and Cleopatra
(x) Coriolanus
(xi) Timon of Athens

4. The Fourth Period (1608-12): This was the period of later comedies or what are known as "Dramatic Romances"—

(a) (i) Cymbeline
(ii) The Tempest
(iii) Winter's Tale

(b) There are two other plays of this period which are only partly written by Shakespeare
(i) Pericles
(ii) Henry VIII

(**Note :** Henry VIII was completed by his friend, Fletcher (1579-1625) after his death.)

Characteristics : Characteristics of Shakespeare's works can be studied from two angles:

(i) According the periods of their production.
(ii) As general characteristics of his overall work.

According to the Periods

1. The First Period (1588-93) : According to Hudson, "The work of this period as a whole is extremely slight in texture; the treatment of life in it is superficial; there is little depth of thought or characterisation; and the art is marked immature."

Hudson goes on : "The prominence of rime in the dialogue, the stiffness of the blank verse, and the constant use of puns, conceits and other affectations, are among its outstanding technical features."

2. The Second Period (1594-1600): Hudson observes: In this period, "The characterisation and humour have become deep and penetrative, and there is a great growth in the weight of thought. Shakespeare has also outgrown, or is fast outgrowing, the immaturities of his former style. The youthful crudeness, extravagance, and strain are disappearing, rime is largely abandoned for prose and black verse, and the black verse itself has lost it stiffness, and is free and flexible."

3. The Third Period (1601-08): As per Hudson, "In this period all Shakespeare's powers—his dramatic power, his intellectual power and his power of expression—are at their highest."

4. The Fourth Period (1608-12): To quote Hudson again, "They show very fully the decline of Shakespeare's dramatic powers. They are often careless in construction and unsatisfactory in characterisation, while in style and versification they will not bear comparison with the work of preceding ten years."

Shakespeare's Characteristics in General

1. No single writer has contributed to literature as much literary work as Shakespeare has done.
2. There is "infinite variety" in his work.
3. He was indisputably a versatile genius—a deft master both at prose and verse of all kinds:
(i) blank verse
(ii) rhyme
(iii) dramatic verse
(iv) narrative verse, etc.
4. He is the most often quoted among all the English writers.
5. He is one of the greatest poets and dramatists of the world, probably the greatest.
6. It is said that he is the only man in the history of mankind who has said all that is worth-saying.
7. He himself might not be a great thinker, but he could reproduce the borrowed matter in an original form such as none else perhaps could do.
8. No other writer, not even Dickens, has been able to produce so many living and throbbing characters as he has done.
9. It is estimated that he coined more than 15000 (some say, about 18000) words which he contributed to the English language.
10. He is the single writer who has given such a solid footing to the English language that its undying endurance over the centuries can hardly ever be doubted.
11. Needless to say his command over the language he uses is unrivalled.
12. Though a romantic writer, he is all the same the master of realism.
13. He steered the drama clear of stiff classical rules based on ancient masters, and made it a national movement.
14. With all the brutalities as shown by him like other dramatists, unlike them, he upheld the moral law such that truth triumphs in the long run, though poetic justice is not essentially done.
15. Thus his dramas are true to life and human nature.
16. There is a mixture of tragedy and comedy in his dramas as in life.
17. He is the master of true humour and has genuine sympathy with mankind.

Shakespeare's Faults : He is not without faults:

1. The feeling of hastiness is evident at places in his works.
2. At places, he uses claptrap methods and means to cater to the 'groundlings', thus sacrificing some of the essential elements of genuine drama, consistency of character and propriety.
3. As Hudson points out, "At places his psychology is hopelessly crude and unconvincing; his style vicious; his wit forced and poor; his tragic language bombastic."
4. At some places there are factual errors in his dramas such that the story, plot, scenes and characters start seeing unreal, *e.g.*
(i) The modern Switzerland in 'Winter's Tale' is shown as having a sea-coast.
(ii) There are trees of coconut and palm-dates side by side in 'As You Like It'.
(iii) Sometimes, the "mistaken identity" scenes as in 'The Merchant of Venice' and 'Twelfth Night' seem unreal.

(**Note:** Here are some extracts from some of his works for study :

Hamlet

(From Act I)

King: ....think of us
As of a father, for let the world take note
You are the most immediate to our throne,
And with no less nobility of love
Than that which dearest father bears his son
Do I impart toward you. For your intent
In going back to school in Wittenberg,.
It is most retrograde to our desire,
And we beseech you, bend you to remain
Here in the cheer and comfort of our eye,
Our chiefest courtier, cousin, and our son.
Queen: Let not thy mother lose her prayers, Hamlet.
I pray thee stay with us, go not to Wittenberg.
Hamlet. I shall in all my best obey you, madam.
King: why, 'tis a loving and a fair replay.
Be as ourself in Denmark. Madam, come.
This gentle and unforced accord of Hamlet
Sits smiling to my heart, in grace whereof
No jocund health that Denmark drink today,
But the great cannon to the clouds shall tell,
And the King's rouse the heaven shall bruit again,
Respeaking earthly thunder. Come away.
Flourish. Exeunt all but Hamlet
Hamlet: O that this too sullied flesh would melt
Thaw, and resolve itself into a dew,
Or that the Everlasting had not fixed,
His cannon 'gainst self-slaughter. O God, God,
How weary, stale, flat, and unprofitable
Seem to me all the uses of this world!
Fie on't, ah, fie, 'tis an unweeded garden
That grows to seed. Things rank and gross in nature
Possess it merely. That it should come to this:
But two months dead, nay, not so much, not two,
So excellent a king, that was to this
Hyperion to a satyr, so loving to my mother
That he might not beteem the winds of heaven
Visit her face too roughly. Heaven and earth,
Must I remember? Why, she would hang on him
As if increase of appetite had grown
By what if fed on; and yet within a month—
Let me not think on't: frailty, thy name is woman—
A little month, or ere those shoes were old
With which she followed my poor father's body
Like Niobe. all tears, why she, even she—
O God, a beast that wants discourse of reason
Would have mourned longer—married with my uncle,
My father's brother, but no more like my father
Than I to Hercules. Within a month,
Ere yet the salt of most unrighteous tears
Had left the flushing in her gallèd eyes,
She married O, most wicked speed, to post
With such dexterity to incestuous sheets!
It is not, nor it cannot come to good.
But break my heart, for I must hold my tongue.
Enter Horatio, Marcellus, and Barnardo.
Horatio: Hail to your lordship!
Hamlet: I am glad to see you well.
Horatio—or I do forget myself.
Horatio: The same, my lord, and your poor servant ever.
Hamlet: Sir, my good friend, I'll change that name with you.
And what make you from Wittenberg, Horatio?

Hamlet

(Act III)

Polonius: Ophelia, walk you here.—Gracious, so please you.
We will bestow ourselves. [*To Ophelia*] Read on this book,
That show of such an exercise may colour
Your loneliness. We are oft to blame in this,
'Tis too much proved, that with devotion's visage
And pious action we do sugar o'er
The devil himself
King: [*Aside*] O, 'tis too true.
How smart a lash that speech doth give my conscience!
The harlot's cheek, beautied with plast'ring art,
Is not more ugly to the thing that helps it
Than is my deed to my most painted word.
O heavy burden!
Polonius: I hear him coming. Let's withdraw, my lord.
[*Exeunt King and Polonius.*]
Enter Hamlet.
Hamlet: To be, or not to be: that is the question:
Whether 'tis nobler in the mind to suffer
The slings and arrows of outrageous fortune,
Or to take arms against a sea of troubles,
And by opposing end them. To die, to sleep—
No more—and by a sleep to say we end
The heartache, and the thousand natural shocks
That flesh is heir to! 'Tis a consummation
Devoutly to be wished. To die, to sleep—
To sleep—perchance to dream: ay, there's the rub,
For in that sleep of death what dreams may come
When we have shuffled off this mortal coil,
Must give us pause. There's the respect
That makes calamity of so long life:
For who would bear the whips and scorns of time,
Th' oppressor's wrong, the proud man's contumely,
The pangs of despised love, the law's delay,
The insolence of office, and the spurns

That patient merit of th' unworthy takes,
When he himself might his quietus make
With a bare bodkin? Who would fardels bear,
To grunt and sweat under a weary life,
But that the dread of something after death,
The undiscovered country, from whose bourn
No traveler returns, puzzles the will,
And makes us rather bear those ills we have,
Than fly to others that we know not of?
Thus conscience does make cowards of us all,
And thus the native hue of resolution
Is sickled o'er with the pale cast of thought,
And enterprises of great pitch and moment,
With this regard their currents turn awry,
And lose the name of action.—Soft you now,
The fair Ophelia!—Nymph, in thy orisons
Be all my sins remembered.
Ophelila: Good my lord,
How does your honor for this many a day?
Hamlet: I humbly thank you; well, well, well.
Ophelia: My lord, I have remembrances of yours
That I have longèd long to redeliver.
I pray you now, receive them.
Hamlet: No, not I,
I never gave you aught.
Ophelia: My honored lord, you know right well you did,
And with them words of so sweet breath composed
As made these things more rich. Their perfume lost,
Take these again, for to the noble mind

Hamlet

(Act IV)

[Scene IV. *A plain in Denmark.*]
Enter Fortinbras with his Army over the stage.
Fortinbras: Go, Captain, from me great the Danish king.
Tell him that by his license Fortinbras
Craves the conveyance of a promised march
Over his kingdom. You know the rendezvous.
If that his Majesty would aught with us,
We shall express our duty in his eye;
And let him know so.
Captain: I will don't, my lord.
Fortinbras: Go softly on.
[*Exeunt all but the Captain.*]
Enter Hamlet, Rosencrantz, & c.
Hamlet: Good sir, whose powers are these?
Captain: They are of Norway, sir.
Hamlet: How purposed, sir, I pray you?
Captain: Against some part of Poland.
Hamlet: Who commands them, sir?
Captain: The nephew to old Norway, Fortinbras.
Hamlet: Goes it against the main of Poland, sir,
Or for some frontier?
Captain: Truly to speak, and with no addition,
We go to gain a little patch of ground
That hath in it no profit but the name.
To pay five ducats, five, I would not farm it,
Nor will it yield to Norway or the Pole
A ranker rate, should it be sold in fee.
Hamlet: Why, then the Polack never will defend it.
Captain: Yes, it is already garrisoned.
Hamlet: Two thousand souls and twenty thousand ducats.
Will not debate the question of this straw.
This is th' imposthume much wealth and peace,
That inward breaks, and shows no cause without
Why the man dies. I humbly thank you, sir.
Captain: God by you, sir. [*Exit.*]
Rosencrantz: Will't please you go, my lord?
Hamlet: I'll be with you straight. Go a little before.
[*Exeunt all but Hamlet.*]
How all occasions do inform against me
And spur my dull revenge! What is a man,
If his chief good and market of his time
Be but to sleep and feed? A beast, no more.
Sure he that made us with such large discourse,
Looking before and after, gave us not
That capability and godlike reason
To fust in us unused. Now, whether it be
Bestial oblivion,° or some craven scruple
Of thinking too precisely on th' event—
A thought which, quartered, hath but on part wisdom
And ever three parts coward—I do not know
Why yet I live to say, "This thing's to do,"
Sith I have cause, and will, and strength, and means
To do't. Examples gross as earth exhort me.
Witness this army of such mass and charge,
Let by a delicate and tender prince,
Whose spirit, with divine ambition puffed,
Makes mouths at the invisible event,
Exposing what is mortal and unsure
To all that fortune, death, and danger dare....

Shakespeare writes highly quotable lines which are pithy and epigrammatic and full of wisdom. Here are examples from some of his plays:

From All's Well That Ends Well

1. A young man married is a man that's marred.
II, iii, 315
2. The web of one life is of a mingled yarn, good and ill together.
IV, iii, 83
3. There's place and means for every man alive.
iii, 379

From 'Antony and Cleopatra'

1. There's beggary in the love that can be reckoned.
—I, i, 5
2. In Nature's in finite book of secrecy A little I can read.
—I, ii, 11

3. Eternity was in our lips and eyes, Bliss in our brows. —I, iii, 135
4. Age cannot wither her, nor custom stale
Her infinite variety. —II, ii, 243
5. Music, moody food of us that trade in love. —II, v, 1
6. Though it be honest, it is never good
To bring bad news. —II, v, 85
7. We have kissed away kingdom and provinces. —III, viii, 17

As You Like It

1. Let us sit and mock the good housewife fortune from her wheel, that her gifts may henceforth be bestowed equally. —I, ii, 35
2. O, how full of briers is this working-day world! —I, iii, 12
3. Beauty provoketh fools sooner than gold. —I, iii, 113
4. Sweet are the uses of adversity,
Which like the toad, ugly and venomous,
Wears yet a precious jewel in his head;
And this our life, exempt from public haunt,
Finds tongues in trees, books in the running brooks,
Sermons in stones and good in everything. —II, i, 12
5. I can such melancholy out a song, as a weasel sucks eggs. —II, v, 12
6. Who doth ambition shun,
And loves to live i' the sun,
Seeking the food he eats,
And pleased with what he gets. —II, v, 38
7. Blow, blow, thou winter wind,
Thou art not so unkind
As man's ingratitude —II, vii, 74
8. Most friendship is feigning, most loving mere folly. —II, vii, 181

Cymbeline

1. "Fear no more the heat O' the sun,
Nor the furious winter's rages;
Thou thy wordly task hast done,
Home are gone and ta'en thy wages:

Hamlet

1. This sweaty haste
Doth make the night joint-labourer with the day. —I, i, 77
2. But, look, the morn in russet mantle clad,
Walks o'er the dew of you high eastern hill. —I, i, 166
3. With one auspicious and one dropping eye,
With mirth in funeral and with dirge in marriage,
In equal scale weighing delight and dole —I, ii, 11
4. The head is not more native to be heart —I, ii, 47
5. All that live must die,
Passing through nature to eternity. —I, ii, 72
6. Frailty, thy name is woman —I, ii, 146
7. Give it an understanding but no tongue. —I, ii, 249
8. Neither a borrower nor a lender be. —I, iii, 75
9. That one may smile, and smile, and be a villain. —I, v, 108
10. There are more things in heaven a earth, Horatio,
Than are dreamt of in your philosophy. —I, v, 166
11. The time is out of joint. —I, v, 188
12. Brevity is the soul of wit. —II, ii, 90
13. To be honest, as this world goes,
Is to be one man picked out of ten thousand. —II, ii, 179
14. Though this be madness, Yet there is method in't. —II, ii, 211
15. On Fortune's cap we are not the very button. —II, ii, 237
16. There is nothing either good or bad, but thinking makes it so. —II, ii, 259
17. To be or not to be: that is the question. —III, i, 56
18. For to the noble mind
Rich gifts wax poor when givers prove unkind. —III, i, 100
19. O! that this two solid flesh would melt,
Thaw, and resolve itself into a dew..... —I, ii, 129

King Lear

1. Nothing will come of nothing. —I, i, 92
2. How sharper them a serpent's tooth it is
To have a thankless child! —I, iv, 312
3. Striving to better, of we mar what's well. —I, iv, 370
4. I am a man
More sinned against than sinning. —III, ii, 59
5. As flies to wanton boys, are we to the gods;
They kill us for their sport. —IV, i, 36
6. Wisdom and goodness to the vile seem vile. —IV, ii, 38
7. It is the stars,
The stars alone us, govern our conditions —IV, iii, 34
8. How tearful
And dizzy 'tis to cast one's eyes so low!. —IV, vi, 12
9. Though tattered clothes small vices do appear;
Robes and furred gowns hide all. —IV, vi, 169
10. When we are born, we cry that we are come
To this great stage of fools. —IV, vi, 187

11. Men must endure
There going hence, evening as their coming hither:
Ripeness is all. —V, ii, 9
12. The gods are just, and of our pleasant vices
Make instruments that plague us. —V, iii, 172
13. The wheel is come full circle. —V, iii, 176
14. Her voice was ever soft,
Gentle and low, an excellent thing in woman.
—V, iii, 274

It is important to elaborate further on Shakespeare. Let us take typically his play "Antony and Cleopatra". Here is a part of Scene *(i)* from Act I :

Antony and Cleopatra

Act I

Scene I. Alexandria. A room in Cleopatra's palace.

Enter Demetrius and Philo.

Phi: Nay, but this dotage of our general's
O'erflows the measure: those his goodly eyes.
That o'er the files and musters of the war
Have glow'd like plated Mars, now bend, now turn,
The office and devotion of their view
Upon a tawny front: his captain's heart,
Which in the scuffles of great fights hath burst
The buckles on his breast, reneges all temper,
And is become the bellows and the fan
To cool a gipsy's lust.

Flourish. Enter Antony, Cleopatra, *her Ladies*, the Train with Eunuchs fanning her.

Look, where they come :
Take but good note, and you shall see in him
The tripple pillar of the world transform'd
Into a strumpet's fool: behold and see.
Cleo: If it be love indeed, tell me how much.
Ant: There's beggary in the love that can be reckon'd.
Cleo: I'll set a bourn how far to be beloved.
Ant: Then must thou needs find out new heaven, new earth.

Enter an Attendant.

Att: News, my good lord, from Rome.
Ant: Grates me: the sum.
Cleo: Nay, hear them, Antony:
Fulvia perchance is angry; or, who knows
If the scarce-bearded Caesar have not sent
His powerful mandate to you, 'Do this, or this;
Take in that kingdom, and enfranchise that;
Perform't or else we damn thee.'
Ant: How, my love!
Cleo: Perchance! nay, and most like:
You must not stay here longer, your dismission
Is come from Caesar; therefore hear it, Antony.
Where's Fulvia's process? Caesar's
I would say? both?
Call in the messengers. As I am Egypt's queen,
Thou blushest, Antony; and that blood of thine
Is Caesar's homager; else so thy cheek pays shame
When shrill-tongued Fulvia scolds. The messengers!
Ant: Let Rome in Tiber melt, and the wide arch
Of the ranged empire fall! Here is my space.
Kingdoms are clay: our dungy earth alike
Feeds beast as man: the nobleness of life
Is to do thus: when such a mutual pair
[*Embracing.*
And such a twain can do't, in which I bind,
On pain of punishment, the world to weed
We stand up peerless.
Cleo: Excellant falsehood!
Why did he marry Fulvia, and not love her?
I'll seem the fool I am not: Antony
Will be himself.
Ant: But stirr'd by Cleopatra.
Now, for the love of Love and her soft hours,
Let's not confound the time with conference harsh!
There's not a minute of our lives should stretch
Without some pleasure now. What sport tonight?

Act IV

In Act IV we learn how Antony feels on being "betrayed" by Cleopatra. Here are scene (xii) and part of scene (xiii) (Act IV):

Scene (XII). Another part of the same.

Enter Antony and Scarus.

Ant: Yet they are not join'd: where yond pine does stand, I shall discover all: I'll bring thee word
Straight, how 'tis like to go. [*Exit.*
Scar: Swallows have built
In Cleopatra's sails their nests; the augurers
Say they know not, they cannot tell; look grimly,
And dare not speak their knowledge. Antony
Is valiant, and dejected; and by starts,
His fretted fortunes give him hope, and fear,
Of what he has, and has not,
[*Alarum afar off, as at a sea fight.*
Re-enter Antony.
Ant: All is lost
This foul Egyptian hath betrayed me:
My fleet hath yielded to the foe; and yonder
They cast their caps up and carouse together
Like friends long lost. Triple-turn'd whore! 'tis thou
Hast sold me to this novice; and my heart
Makes only wars on thee. Bid them all fly;
For when I am revenged upon my charm,
I have done all. Bid them all fly; begone.
[*Exit Scarus.*
O sun, thy uprise shall I see no more:
Fortune and Antony part here; even here

Do we shake hands. All come to this?
The hearts
That spaniel'd me at heels, to whom I gave
Their wishes, do discandy, melt their sweets
On blossoming Caesar; and this pine is bark'd,
that overtopp'd them all. Betray'd I am:
O this false soul of Egypt! this gave charm,—
Whose eye beck'd forth my wars, and call'd them home;
Whose bosom was my crownet, my chief end,—
Like a right gipsy, hath, at fast and loose,
Beguiled me to the very heart of loss.
What, Eros, Eros!

Enter Cleopatra.

Ah, thou spell! Avaunt!
Cleo: Why is my lor enraged against his love?
Ant: Vanish, or I shall give thee thy deserving,
And blemish Caesar's triumph. Let him take thee,
And hoist thee up to the shouting plebeians:
Follow his chariot, like the greatest spot
Of all thy sex; most monster-like, be shown
For poor'st diminutives, for doits: and let
Patient Octavia plough thy visage up
With her prepared nails. [*Exit Cleopatra.*
'Tis well thou'rt gone,
If it be well to live; but better 'twere
Thou fell'st into my fury, for one death
Might have prevented many. Eros, ho!
The shirt of Nessus is upon me: teach me,
Alcides, thou mine ancestor, thy rage:
Let me lodge Lichas on the horns o' the moon;
And with those hands, that grasp'd the heaviest club,
Subdue my worthiest self. The witch shall die:
To thy young Roman boy she hath sold me, and I fall
Under this plot; she dies for't Eros, ho! [*Exit.*

Scene XIII. *Alexandria. Cleopatra's place.*

Enter Cleopatra, Charmian, Iras and Mardian.

Cleo: Help me, my woman! O, he is more made
Than Telamon for his shield; the boar of Thessaly
Was never so emboss'd.
Char: To the monument!
There lock yourself, and send him word you are dead.
The soul and body rise not more in parting
That greatness going off.

Note: One may find fault with the beloved when he/she is alive.

But on his/her death, one feels the pangs of remorse and the separation. This is how Antony feels on Cleopatra's death.

The extract is from Scene (XIV)

Act IV

Enter Mardian.

O, thy vile lady!
She has robb'd me of my sword.
Mar: No, Antony;
My mistress loved thee, and her fortunes mingled
With thine entirely.
Ant: Hence, saucy eunuch; peace!
She hath betray'd me and shall die the death.
Mar: Death of one person can be paid but once,
And that she has discharged: what thou wouldst do
Is done unto thy hand: the last she spake
Was 'Antony! most noble Antony!'
Then in the midst a tearing groan did break
The name of Antony; it is divided
Between her heart and lips: she render'd life,
Thy name so buried in her.
Ant: Dead, then?
Mar: Dead.
Ant: Unarm, Eros; the long day's task is done,
And we must sleep. [*To Mar.*] That thou depart'st hence safe,
Does pay thy labour richly; go [*Exit Mardian.*
Off. pluck off:
The seven-fold shield of Ajax cannot keep
The battery from my heart. O, cleave, my sides!
Heart, once be stronger than thy continent,
Crack thy frail case! Apace, Eros, apace.
No more a soldier: bruised pieces, go;
You have been nobly brone. From me awhile.
[*Exit Eros.*
I will o'ertake thee, Cleopatra, and
Weep for my pardon. So it must be, for now
All length is torture: since the torch is out,
Lie down, and stray no farther: now all labour
Mars what it does; yea, very force entangles
Itself with strength: seal them, and all is done
Eros! I come, my queen:—Eros!—Stay for me:
Where souls do couch on flowers, we'll hand in hand,
And with our sprightly port make the ghosts gaze:
Dido and her Aeneas shall want troops,
And all the haunt be ours. Come, Eros, Eros!

Re-enter Eros.

Eros: What would my lord?
Ant: Since Cleopatra died,
I have lived in such dishonour, that the gods
Detest my baseness. I, that with my sword
Quarter'd the world, and o'er green Neptune's back
With ships made cities, condemn myself to lack
The courage of women; less noble mind
Than she which by her death our Caesar tells
'I am conqueror of myself.' Thou art sworn, Eros,
That when the exigent should come, which now
Is come indeeed, when I should see behind me
The inevitable prosecution of
Disgrace and horror, that, on my command,
Thou then wouldst kill me: do 't; the time is come:
Thou strikest not me, 'tis Caesar thou defeat'st.

Put colour in thy cheek.
Eros: The gods withhold me!
Shall I do that which all the Parthian darts,
Though enemy, lost aim, and could not?
Ant: Eros,
Wouldst thou be window'd in great Rome andsee
Thy master thus with pleach'd arms, bending down
His corrigible neck, his face subdued
To penetrative shame, whilst the wheel'd seat
Of fortunate Caesar, drawn before him, branded
His baseness that ensued?
Eros: I would not see 't.

"Criticism on Antony and Cleopatra"

We have elaborate criticism on Antony and Cleopatra", some of which is given below :

(1)

F.S. Boas

"Certainly in consummate delineation of character, and in the superb rhythmical swell of many passages, the work is unsurpassed. But it has a grave share of the defects to which Romantic Drama had been liable from the first, especially when it was drawing upon historical material ....Shakespeare seems to have felt a conscientious obligation to introduce every incident, political, private, mentioned by Plutarch, and the result is a loss of dramatic unity and perspective. The multiplicity of details is bewildering, and no single event stands out boldly as the pivot on which the catastrophe turns. But this artistic defect is here in part the outcome of a significant peculiarity in Shakespeare's treatment of love as a dramatic theme. Sexual passion is the immediate obect of only three plays, *Romeo and Juliet, Troilus and Cressida and Antony and Cleopatra.* In each case of emotional interest is interwoven with elements of a political nature—the civil strife of Montagues and Capulets, the war between the Greeks and the Trojans, the struggle for the lordship of the Roman world. Thus, Shakespeare even when making an elaborate study of amorous passion, does not isolate it from the wider, more material, issues of surrounding civic or national life. He thus avoids the disastrous pitfall of treating love as the exclusive factor in existence—a method which, according to the nature of the love chosen for analysis, tends to produce an unwholesome sentimentality or a still more unwholesome experience. Shakespeare opens to our view hearts aflame with chaste affection or with sensous desire, but he never cheats himself or others into the belief that sexual relationship is the solitary, imperious concern of all mankind. From the Kaleidoscopic changes of Cleopatra's moods, he turns our gaze to the legions tramping in solid array through the uttermost parts of the earth, or to the council-chambers where the destinies of kingdoms are being decided by the stroke of a pen. We are shown in turn of the most materialistic age in the world's history, the age when Roman civic virtue was, in its death-throes, suffocated by the plethora of its golden spoils from the South and the East.

(2)

Hazlitt

Hazlitt's views are very pertinent in regard to Antony and Cleopatra :

"This is a very noble play. Though not in the first class of Shakespeare's productions, it stands next to them, and is, we think, the finest of his Historical plays, that is, of those in which he made poetry the organ of history, and assumed a certain tone of character and sentiment, in conformity to known facts, instead of trusting to his observations of general nature or to the unlimited indulgence of his own fancy. What he has added to the history, is upon a par with it. His genius was, as it were, a match for history as well as nature, and could grapple at will with either. This play is full of that pervading comprehensive power by which the poet could always make himself master of time and circumstances. It presents a fine picture of Roman pride and esteem magnificence: and in the struggle between the two, the empire of the world seems suspended, 'like the swan's down feather', 'That stands upon the swell at full of tide, And neither way inclines.' The characters breath, move and live. Shakespeare does not stand reasoning on what his characters would do or say, but at once *becomes* them, and speaks and acts for them. He does not present us with groups of stage-puppets on poetical machines making set speeches on human life, and acting from a calculation of ostensible motives, but he brings living men and women on the scene, who speak and act from real feelings, according to the ebbs and flows of passion, without the least tincture of the pedantary of logic or rhetoric. Nothing is made out of inference or analogy, by climax and antithesis, but everything takes place just as it would have done in reality, according to the occasion."

(3)

Paul Stepfer

Reflecting on the subject of Antony and Cleopatra, Stepfer says,

"The subject of Shakespeare's tragedy is the guilty love of Antony and Cleopatra, a subject that would have presented an almost insuperable difficulty to a poor little poet of a narrow and mediocre type; quite at a loss, and biting his pen the while, he would have said to himself, 'What is to be done? Cleopatra is a very wicked woman, *a monster*, as. Horace calls her,—a mixture of all we must hate and despise, she is a coquette, timid, cowardly, cringing perfidious, tyrannical, cruel and wanton. To interest decent people in such a creature is clearly impossible, except by making a selection from among the contradictory features of her character, and since Plutarch speaks of her as being occasionally geneous, tender and devoted, heroic and sublime, I must convert the conception into the rule, and put an expurgated Cleopatra on the stage.' But Shakespeare reasoned in a very different manner. He started with the notion of Cleopatra as an enhantress, and he trusted with quiet confidence to the power of his poetry, and to his sure knowledge of the human heart, to make the same fascination that she exercised over her lovers be felt by us : her faults, her vices, her crimes—what do they matter? Besides which, it betrays a good deal of simplicity to suppose that certain sins which are repulsive in a man are equally odious when met with in a woman. A man is ugly, and has hard work to atone for his natural ugliness, but, as a poet has said,—and it is no empty compliment, but an astute psychological truth,—women, do what they will, are always charming.

Shakespeare has not deemed it necessary to leave out any of the stains, big or little, in Cleopatra's character, as he was obliged to do in Antony's; and this, instead of depriving the lovely little monster of a single charm, only makes her the more irresistible."

(4)

A.C. Bradley

Bradley, who is an acknowledged authority on "Shakespearean Tragedy", says about Antony and Cleopatra,

"A comparison of Shakespearean tragedies seems to prove that the tragic emotions are stirred in the fullest possible measure only when such beauty or nobility of character is displayed or commands unreserved admiration or love; or when, in default of this, the forces which move the agents, and the conflict which results from these forces attain a terrifying and overwhelming power. The four most famous tragedies satisfy one or both these conditons; 'Antony and Cleopatra', though a great tragedy, satisfies neither of them completely. But to say this is not to criticize it. It does not attempt to satisfy these conditions, and then fail in the attempt. It attempts something different, and succeeds as triumphantly as 'Othello' itself. In doing so it gives us what no other tragedy can give and it leaves us, no less than any other, lot in astonishment at the powers which created it."

(5)

W.J. Courthope

Courthope has the following opinion on Antony and Cleopatra :

"Antony's character in its extraordinary versatility—orator, soldier and debauchee; a Henry V without his power of self-control—furnished one of those contradictory problems of human nature which Shakespeare was accustomed to study with the most sympathetic insight; and the meretricious fascination of Cleopatra, as recorded by Plutarch, joined (for she is no Cressida) to a certain greatness of soul and fidelity of passion, must have struck the poet's imagination by its likeness, as well as its contrast, to some woman whose character he painted in the *Sonnets*. The use of the word 'will' in this remarkable play is noticeable. When Antony has left the battle of Actium, to his own dishonour, in pursuit of the flying Cleopatra the queen asks the shrewd, worldly, and calculating Enobarbus, who is introduced into the play as a kind of chorus to comment on Antony and his fortunes: 'Is Antony or we in fault for this?' Enobarbus replies: Antony only, that would make his will Lord of his reason.' (III, XIII) Yet Antony throughout the play recognises that he is acting against his deliberate resolution, under the irresistible influence of passion: 'I followed that I blush to look upon: My very hairs do mutiny; for the white Reprove the brown for rashness, and they them for fear and doting,' (III, XI). So that his conduct is what Iago calls 'merely a lust of the blood and *permission* of the will' (1. III). This is the very helplessness spoken of in *Sonnet* CL: 'O from what power hast thou this powerful might with insufficiency my heart to sway? To make me give the lie to my true sight and swear that brightness doth not grace the day? Whence hast thou this becoming of things ill, that in the very refuse of thy deeds. There is such strength and warrantise of skill. That, in my mind, thy worst all best exceeds?

(6)

H.A. Taine

Taine's views on the play are expressed in an impassioned language :

"How much more visible is this impassioned and unfettered genius of Shakespeare in the great characters which sustain the whole weight of the drama! The startling imagination, the furious velocity of the manifold and exuberant ideas, the unruly passion, rushing upon death and crime, hallucinations, madness, all the ravages of delirium bursting through will and reason: such are the forces and ravings which engender them. Shall I speak of dazzling Cleopatra, who holds Antony in the whirwind of her devices and caprices, who fascinates and kills, who scatters to the winds the lives of men as a handful of desertdust, the fatal Eastern sorceress who sports with life of death, headstrong, irresistible, child of air and fire, whose life is but a tempest, whose thought, ever re-pointed and broken, is like the crackling of lighting."

(7)

Dowden

Dowden, the great critic, who is known for the proverbial division of Shakespeare's artistic periods, has the following words to say on Antony and Cleopatra :

"The spirit of the play, though superficially it appears voluptuous, is essentially severe. There is to say, Shakespeare is faithful to the fact. The fascination exercised by Cleopatra, is not so much that of the senses as of the sensuous imagination. A third of the world is theirs. They have left youth behind with is slight, melodious raptures and despairs. Their is the deeper intoxication of middle age, when death has become a reality, when the world is limited and positive when life is urged to yield up quickly its utmost treasures of delight. What may they not achieve of joy who have power and beauty, and pomp, and pleasure all their own? How shall they fill every minute of their time with the quintessence of enjoyment and of glory? 'Let Rome in Tiber melt! and the wide arch of the ran'd empire fall! here is my 'space'.' Only *one* thing they had not allowed for,—that over and above power, and beauty pleasure, and pomp, there is a certain inevitable fact, a law which cannot be evaded. Pleasure sits enthroned as queen; there is a revel, and the lords of the earth, crowned with roses, dance before her to the sound of lascivious flutes. But presently, the scene changes; the hall of revel is transformed to an arena; the dancers are armed gladiators; and as they advance to combat they pay the last homage to their Queen with the words *Morituri te salutant.*"

(8)

Objections by Gervinus

Gervinus has raised some important objections against the play :

"There arises, moreover, an ethical objection (to this play) which will prejudice the majority of readers against it, and against Coleridge's opinion of it. Among the *Dramatis Personae* there is no great and noble character, and in the actions of the drama no really elevating feature, either in its politics or in its love-affairs. This play seems to make us intuitively aware how much we should lose in Shakespeare, if, with his confessedly great knowledge of men and nature there did not go, hand in hand, aesthetic excellence (the ideal concentration of actors and actions), and ethical excellence (the ideal height of what is represented as human nature). The poet had to set forth a debased period in his *Antony and Cleopatra*; for the truth of history, he did adequately; but this did not exclude him from giving a glance at a better state of human nature, which, amid so much degradation, might comfort and elevate us. If we recall the *Historical Plays*, where Shakespeare had to depict generations, for the most part degenerate and ruined, we shall find that in Richard II there was, as a compensation, a Gaunt and a Carlisle; and even in Richard III, the few strokes that depicted the sons of Edward, are beneficent counterpoise to the widespread wickedness. Here, however, there is nothing of the kind, and we may even affirm that the opportunity for such a counterbalance has been conspicuously evaded : it would surely have been easy, in the characters of Octavia at least, to keep before us some views of what is more noble in human nature: even if it were only a few traits, which would have exhibited her to us in action, where now she is merely described to us in words."

Shakespearean Criticism (General)

There has been a lot of Shakespearean criticism over the centuries. It will be enough to give only a few examples :

(1)

T.S. Baynes

According to T.S. Baynes:

"Shakespeare's work alone can be said to possess the organic strength and infinite variety, the troubling fulness, vital complexity, and breathing truth of Nature herself. In points of artistic resource and technical ability—such as copious and expressive diction, freshness and pregnancy of verbal combination, richly modulated verse, and structural skill in the handling of incident and action—Shakespeare's supremacy is indeed sufficiently assured. But, after all, it is of course, in the spirit and substance of his work, his power of piercing to the hidden centres of character, of touching the deepest springs of impulse and passion, out of which emerge the issues of life, and of evolving those issues dramatically with a flawless strength, subtlety, and truth, which raises him so immensely above and beyond not only the best of the play, Wrights who went before him, but the whole line of illustrious dramatists that came after him. It is Shakespeare's unique distinction that he has an absolute command over all the complexities of thought and feeling that prompt action and bring out the dividing lines of character. He sweeps with the hand of a master the whole gamut of human experience from the lowest note to the very top of its compass, from the sportive childish treble of Mamilius, and the pleading boyish tone of Prince Arthur, up to the spectre-haunted terrors of Macbeth, the tropical passion of Othello, the agonised sense and torture spirit of Hamlet, the sustained elemental grandeur, the Titanic force, the utterly tragical pathos of King Lear."

(2)

George Lord Littleton

"No other author has ever so copious, so bold, so *creative* an imagination, with so perfect a knowledge of the passions, humours, and sentiments of mankind. He painted all characters. From kings down to peasants, with equal truth and equal force. If human nature were destroyed and no monument were left of it expect his works, other beings might know *what man was* from those writings."

(3)

Dr. Johnson

(i) Johnson says of Shakespeare, "In tragedy he often writes, with great appearance of toil and study, what is written at last with little felicity, but in his comic scenes, he seems to produce, without labour, what no labour can improve."

(ii) Shakespeare's "scenes are occupied only by men, who act and think."

(4)

T.S. Eliot

T.S. Eliot defends Johnson's views on Shakespeare. He says,

"This is an opinion which we cannot lightly dismiss. Johnson is quite aware that the alternation of 'tragic' and 'comic' is something more than an alternation; he perceives that something different and new is produced. The interchanges of mingled scenes seldom fail to produce the intended vicissitudes of passion."

(5)

Hazlitt

According to Hazlitt,

"His plays alone are properly expressions of the passions, not descriptions of them. His characters are real beings of flesh and blood; they speak like man, not like author."

(6)

Pope

(i) Commenting on Shakespeare's originality, Pope says,

"If ever any author deserved the name of an *original* it was Shakespeare. Homer himself drew not his art so immediately from the fountains of Nature; it proceeded through Egyptian strainers and channels, and came to him not without some tincture of the learning or some cast of the models, of those before him. The poetry of Shakespeare was inspiration indeed; he is not so much an imitator as an instrument of Nature : and it is not so just to say that he speaks from her, as that she speaks through him."

(ii) Pope expresses his opion about Shakespeare's characters in the following words :

"His *characters* are so much Nature herself, that it is a sort of injury to call them by so distant a name as copies of her. Those of other poets have a constant resemblance, which shows that they received them from one another and were but multipliers of the same image : each picture, like a mock rainbow, is but the reflection of a reflection. But every single character in Shakespeare is as much an individual as those in life itself; it is an impossible to find any two alike; as such as from their relation of affinity in any respect appear most to be twins, will upon comparison be found remarkably distinct. To this life and variety of character we must add the wonderful preservation of it, which is such throughout his plays, that, had all the speeches been printed without the very names of the persons, I believe one might have applied them with certainty to every speaker."

(7)

David Masson

Commenting on Shakespeare's power of imagination David Masson says,

"Shakespeare is as astonishing for the exuberance of his genius in abstract notions, and for the depth of his analytic and philosophic insight, as for the scope and minuteness of his poetic imagination. It is as if into a mind poetical in *form* there had been poured all the *matter* that existed in the mind of his contemporary Bacon. In Shakespeare's plays, we have thought, history, expedition, philosophy, all within the round of the poet."

(8)

W. Richardson

W. Richardson thus comments on Shakespeare's ability to blend the two essential powers of dramatic invention, which mentions in his statement :

"Many dramatic writers of different ages are capable, occasionally, of breaking out, with great fervour of genius, in the natural language of strong emotion. No writer of antiquity is more distinguished for abilities of this kind than Euripides. His whole heart and soul seem torn and agitated by the force of the passion he imitates. He ceases to be Euripides; he is Medis; he is Orestes. Shakespeare, however, is most eminently distinguished, not only by these occasional sallies, but by imitating the passion in all its aspects, by pursuing it through all its windings and labyrinths, by moderating or accelerating its importuosity according to the influence of other principles and of external events, and finally by combining it in a judicious manner with other passions and propensities, or by setting it aptly in opposition. He thus unites the two essential powers of dramatic invention, that of forming characters; and that of imitating in their natural expressions, the passions and affections of which they are composed."

(9)

Thomas Fuller

Expressing his views on Shakespeare's in born faculties, Fuller says,

"He was an eminent instance of the truth of that rule, *poeta non fit sed masciture*; one is *not made*, but *born* a poet. Indeed his learning was very little, so that, as Cornish diamonds are not polished by any lapidary, but are pointed and smoothed even as they are taken out of the earth, so nature itself was all the *art* which was used upon him.

Many were the wit-combats betwixt him and Ben Jonson; which two I behold like a Spanish great galleon and an English man of war; Master Jonson (like the former) was built far higher in learning; solid but slow in his performances. Shakespeare, with the English man of war, lesser in bulk, but lighter in sailing, could turn with all tides, tack about, and advantage of all winds, by the quickness of his wit and invention."

(10)

A.C. Swinburne

Expressing his views on Shakespeare's tragic art which owed a lot to Marlowe and on his broad and all empracing humanity, Swinburne says,

"Through all the forenoon of our triumphant day till the utter consummation and ultimate ascention of dramatic poetry incarnate and transfigured in the master-singer of the world, the quality of his tragedy was at that of Marlowe's broad, single and intense; large of hand, voluble of tongue, direct of purpose. With the dawn of its latter epoch a new power comes upon it, to find clothing and expression in new forms of speech and after a new style. The language has put off it foreign decoration of lyrics and elegiac ornament; it has found already its infinite gain in the loss of those sweet superfluous graces which encumbered the march and enchained the utterance of its childhood. The figures which it invests are now no more types of a single passion, the incarnations of a single thought. They now demand a scrutiny which tests the power of a mind and tries the value of a judgement; they appeal to something more than the instant apprehension which sufficed to respond to the immediate claim of those that went before them. Romeo and Juliet were simply lovers, and their name brings back to us no further thought than of their love and the lovely sorrow of its end; Antony and Cleopatra shall be before all things lovers, but the thought of their love and its triumphant tragedy shall recall other things beyond number—all the forces and fortunes of mankind, all the chance and all the consequence that waited on their imperial passion, all the infinite variety of qualities and power wrought together and welded into the frame and composition of that love which shook from end to end nations and kingdoms of the earth".

(11)

F.W. Robertson

Commenting on Shakespeare's genuine humanity and earthiness, Robertson says,

"What I admire in Shakespeare, however, is that his loves are all human—no earthliness hiding itself from itself in sentimental transcendentalism—no loves of the angels, which are the least angelic things, I believe, that float in the clouds, though they do look down upon mortal feelings with contempt just as the dark volumes of smoke which issue from the long chimney of a manufactory might brood very sublimely over the town which they blacken, and fancy themselves far more ethereal than those vapours which steam up from the earth by day and night. Yet these are pure water and those are destined to condense in black soot. So are the transcendentalisms of affection. Shakespeare is healthy, true to Humanity in this.........You always know that you are on an earth which has to be refined, instead of floating in the empyrean with wings of wax. Therein he is immeasurably greater than Shelley. Shelleyism is very sublime, sublimer a good deal than God, for God's world is all wrong and Shelley is all right—much purer than Christ, for Shelley can criticise Christ's heart and life—nevertheless, Shelleyism is only atmospheric profligacy at coin a Montgomeryism. I believe this to be one of Shakespeare's most wondrous qualities—the humanity of the nature and heart. There is a spirit of sunny endeavours about him, and an aquiescence in things as they are—not incompatible with a cheerful resolve to make them better."

(12)

Matthew Arnold

Expressing his views on Shakespeare's power of prosody and expression, Arnold says,

"Let me have the pleasure of quoting a sentence about Shakespeare, which I met my accident not long ago in the *Correspondent*, a French review which not a dozen English people, I suppose, look at. The writer is praising Shakespeare's prose. 'With Shakespare,' he says, 'prose come in whenever the subject, being more familiar is unsuited to the majestic English iambic.' And the goes on : 'Shakespeare is the king of poetic rhythm and style, as well as the king of the realm of thought along with his dazzling prose. Shakespeare has succeeded in giving us the most varied, the most harmonious verse which has ever sounded upon the human ear since the verse of the Greeks. M. Henry Cochin, the writer of this sentence, deserves our gratitude for it; it would not be easy to praise Shakespeare, in a single sentence, more justly."

(13)

Poetic Effusions

Some writers have gone wildly ecstatic in expressing themselves poetically on Shakespeare :

(i)

Milton

"The Sweetest Shakespeare, Fancy's Child!""

(ii)

W.W. Story

"And such was Shakespeare, whose strong soul
could climb
Steeps of sheer-terrors, sound the ocean grand
Of passions deep, or over Fancy's strand
Trip with his fairies, keeping step and time.
His too the power to laugh out full and clear,
With unembittered joyance, and to move
Along the silent, shadowy paths of love
As tenderly as Dante, whose austere
Stern spirit through the world below, above,
Unsmiling strode, to tell the tidings here."

(iii)

Garrick

"When Learning's Triumph o'er her barb'rous
Foes
First rear'd the stage, immortal Shakespeare rose;
Each change of many-coloured Life he drew,
Exhausted World, and then imagin'd new."

(iv)

M. Arnold

"Others abide our question :
Thou art free."

ROMANTIC PERIOD

PERCY BYSSHE, SHELLEY (1792-1822)

Life

1. He was born in Sussex in 1792.
2. His parents belonged to the class of nobility.
3. As a child, Shelley was highly fanciful like Blake.

Education

(i) After having got a brutal treatment in his Scotch public school, he joined Eton. But being a highly sensitive boy who held self-respect above anything else, he revolted against the tyrannical system in the new school.

(ii) Of course, he was ridiculed and called 'Mad Shelley' by other boys.

(iii) (a) While at Oxford, he published his pamphlet "The Necessity of Atheism."

(b) In writing this, he was influenced by the philosophy of Hume.

(c) He was expelled from the university for this.

Marriage

1. *(i)* First Shelley married Harriet Westbrook, a mere school girl whose parents never agreed to this marriage.
   (ii) Even Shelley's own parents disinherited him for this.
2. *(i)* Later, as Shelley came under the influence of Godwin—an anarchist philosopher—he eloped with his daughter, Mary, who later wrote "Frankenstein's Monster" which is so famous for its title if not much for its contents.
   (ii) Sadly, this elopement, however, led to Harriet's well-known suicide.

Exile

1. Just as Byron had earlier left England in 1816, never to return, Shelley did the same in 1818, though for reasons of health mainly and partly of hostility against his ideology of revolt, anarchism or cynicism (whatever we may call it), etc.
2. His shifting to Italy proved a boon, since—
   (i) here he wrote his best poetry
   (ii) here he was able to get the friendship of such personalities as: *(a)* Byron *(b)* Leigh Hunt *(c)* Trelawney, etc.

Death

Shelley met with a tragic death in 1822 while sailing in a boat off the Italian coast.

Works

1. *Alastor (or the Spirit of Solitude) (1816):*
   (i) It expresses Shelley's endless love for wandering in search of a dream girl who is the model of beauty.
   (ii) The poem is illusory in nature and lacks reality.
2. *Prometheus Unbound (1818-20):*
   (i) In this lyrical drama whilst Prometheus steals fire from heaven for mankind, Shelley, according to Long, "is the prophet of science and evolution."
   (ii) Studied in the proper prospective, the work suggests hope and promise for goodness to prevail at last.
   (iii) In his poem "The Cloud" Shelley takes recourse to exact geographical pheno-menon. Similar is the case in 'Ode to the West Wind'. Because of his correct use of geographical and scientific facts, he is sometimes called "the scientist poet."
3. *Other Revolutionary works:* Besides Promentheus, Shelley's other revolutionary works are:
   (i) Queen Mab (1813)
   (ii) The Revolt of Islam (1818)
   (iii) The Witch of Atlas (1820)
   (iv) Hellas (1821)
4. "Epipsychidion" (1821) is Shelley's work of Platonic love.
5. Perhaps Shelley's only work based on reality is his drama "The Cenci". Here below is an extract:

Beatrice's Last Words

Beatrice: Farewell, my tender brother. Think
Of our sad fate with gentleness, as now:
And let mild, pitying thoughts lighten for thee
Thy sorrow's load. Err not in harsh despair,
But tears and patience. One thing more, my child:
For thine own sake be constant to the love
Thou bearest us; and to the faith that I,
Though wrapped in a strange cloud of crime and shame,
Lived ever holy and unstained. And though
Ill tongues shall wound me, and our common name
Be as a mark stamped on thine innocent brow
For men to point at as they pass, do thou
Forbear, and never think a thought unkind
Of those, who perhaps love thee in their graves.
So mayest thou die as I do; fear and pain
Being subdued. Farewell! Farewell! Farewell!
Bernardo: I cannot say, farewell!
Camillo: Oh, Lady Beatrice!
Beatrice: Give yourself no unnecessary pain,
My dear Lord Cardinal. Here, Mother, tie
My girdle for me, and bind up this hair

In any simple knot; ay, that does well.
And yours I see is coming down. How often
Have we done this for one another! Now
We shall not do it any more. My Lord,
We are quite ready. Well, 'tis very well.

(End to *The Cenci*.)

6. *Adonais:* It is an elegy written on the death of Keats and is one of Shelley's most widely known poems.

Lyrics

(i) That Shelley is probably the greatest lyricist in English needs no emphasis.

(ii) Some of his famous lyrics are:

(a) The Cloud
(b) To A Skylark
(c) Ode to the West Wind
(d) To Night

Other works

Some of his other works are :

1. Hymn to Intellectual Beauty
2. Sensitive Plant
3. "Lament" with the first line—"O world, O life, O time"

Shelley and Wordsworth: Comparing Shelley with Wordsworth, Long says, "Wordsworth found and Shelley lost himself in nature."

Note: Here are some extracts from his works:

(i) **From Alastor**

Earth, ocean, air, belovèd brotherhood!
If our great Mother has imbued my soul
With aught of natural piety to feel
Your love, and recompense the boon with mine;
If dewy morn, and odorous noon, and even,
With sunset and its gorgeous ministers,
And solemn midnight's tingling silentness;
If autumn's hollow sighs in the sere wood,
And winter robing with pure snow and crowns
Of starry ice the grey grass and bare boughs;
If spring's voluptuous pantings when she breathes
Her first sweet kisses, have been dear to me;
If no bright bird, insect, or gentle beast
I consciously have injured, but still loved
And cherished these my kindred; then forgive
This boast, belovèd brethren, and withdraw
No portion of your wonted favour now!
Mother of this unfathomable world!
Favour my solemn song, for I have loved
Thee ever, and thee only; I have watched
Thy shadow, and the darkness of thy steps,

(ii) Passionless?—no, yet free from guilt or pain,
Which were, for his will made or suffered them,
Nor yet exempt, though ruling them like slaves,
From chance, and death, and mutability,
The clogs of that which else might oversoar
The loftiest stars of unascended heaven,
Pinnacled dim in the intense inane.

(*Prometheus*, end of Act iii.)

E. Blunden says of Shelley, "Shelley did not take up every subject for verse in the solemn, neutral way which we scholiasts are liable to ascribe to him. Much has been written on his address *To a Skylark*, and much without proper recognition of his actual occasion. Shelley, in that poems, was *talking*, at least at the point of departure. He was capable, there, of joking (for there is a free state of mind, which may not resemble the comic spirit of the *New Yorker*, or perhaps it may—but it is truly random); he did not start as an automatic machine delivering the weight and fortune for skylarks.

Hail to thee, blithe Spirit!

A skylark: but he refuses to believe the natural historians's limited definition. 'Bird thou never wert.' He also rejects the Shakespearean location of Heaven, or else is willing to play upon the neighbourhood ('Hark, hark, the lark at Heaven's gate sings') with his

That *from Heaven, or near it*,
Pourest thy full heart....

The numerous comparisons in the poem, which have been treated like realistic equations, are in fact so much talk, the gestures of a mind in play, the sportive balloon-flying of one who does not really wish to catch his lark.

There are several surviving protests against Shelley. He ought at all costs to have finished *The Boat on the Serchio*, a poem which, so far as it goes, seems to combine all his mystery and concept of our universe, and all his social grace and observation. When he set out on his last voyage, *mutatis mutandis* this is how he went; the biographers need not deplore the want of a log-book or a dictaphone; here is the voice, stir, and fascination of Shelley putting out to sea. Another complaint is that he set sail at such an inauspicious moment. He was, at the time, entering upon a new chapter of intellectual astuteness. In his last long poem, *The Triumph of Life*, though the confusion and agglomeration of his younger manner have not quite disappeared, there is a sinewy manner have not quite disappeared, there is a sinewy and ironic force which makes him jump almost a century. But apart from that, he was beginning, to live, and to cease to be 'at war with life'. Disturbance still embittered him, but exceptionally: a faultless ease was stealing upon his poetry,

The clearest echoes of the hills,
The softest notes of falling rills,
The melodies of birds and bees,
The murmurings of summer seas,
And pattering rain, and breathing dew,
And airs of evening; and it knew
That seldom-heard mysterious sound
Which, driven on its diurnal round,
As it floats through boundless day,
Our world enkindles on its way."

(**Note :** Please see more poems and extracts from Shelley to have a fair appraisal of his poetic art :

From Song to the Men of England

Men of England, wherefore plough
For the lords who lay ye low?
Wherefore weave with toil and care
The rich robes your tyrants wear?

Wherefore feed, and clothe, and save,
From the cradle to the grave,
Those ungrateful drones who would
Drain your sweat—nay, drink your blood?

Wherefore, Bees of England, forge
Many a weapon, chain, and scourge,
That these stingless drones may spoil
The forced produce of your toil?

Have ye leisure, comfort, calm,
Shelter, food, love's gentle balm?
Or what is it ye buy so dear
With your pain and with your fear?

The seed ye sow, another reaps;
The wealth ye find, another keeps;
The robes ye weave, another wears;
The arms ye forge, another bears.

Sow seed,—but let no tyrant reap;
Find wealth,—let no impostor heap;
Weave robes,—let not the idle wear;
Forge arms,—in your defence to bear.

Ozymandias

I Met a traveller from an antique land
Who said : Two vast and trunkless legs of stone
Stand in the desert.... Near them, on the sand,
Half sunk, shattered visage lies, whose frown,
And wrinkled lip, and sneer of cold command,
Tell that its sculptor well those passions read
Which yet survive, (stamped on these lifeless things,)
The hand that mocked them and the heart that fed :
And on the pedestal these words appear:
'My name is Ozymandias, king of kings:
Look on my works, ye Mighty, and despair!'
Nothing beside remains. Round the decay
Of that colossal wreck, boundless and bare
The lone and level sands stretch far away.

Stanzas Written in Dejection, Near Naples

The sun is warm, the sky is clear,
The waves are dancing fast and bright;
Blue isles and snowy mountains wear
The purple noon's transparent might;
The breath of the moist earth is light
Around its un-expanded buds;
Like many a voice of one delight,
The winds, the birds, the ocean floods,
The City's voice itself is soft Solitude's.

"I see the Deep's untrampled floor
With green and purple seaweeds strown;
I see the waves upon the shore,
Like light dissolved in star-showers, thrown:
I sit upon the sands alone,—
The lightning of the noontide ocean
Is flashing round me, and a tone
Arises from its measured motion,
How sweet! did any heart now share in my emotion.

Alas! I have nor hope nor health,
Nor peace within nor calm around,
Nor that content surpassing wealth
The sage in meditation found,
And walked with inward glory crowned—
Nor fame, nor power, nor love, nor leisure.
Others I see whom these surround—
Smiling they live, and call life pleasure;—
To me that cup has been dealt in another measure.

Yet now despair itself is mild,
Even as the winds and waters are;
I could lie down like a tired child,
And weep away the life of care
Which I have borne and yet must bear,
Till death like sleep might steal on me,
And I might feel in the warm air
My cheek grow cold, and hear the sea
Breathe o'er my dying brain its last monotony.

Some might lament that I were cold,
As I, when this sweet day is gone,
Which my lost heart, too soon grown old,
Insults with this untimely moan;
They might lament—for I am one
Whom men love not, and yet regret
Unlike this day, which when the sun
Shall on its stainless glory set,
Will linger, though enjoyed like joy in memory yet. "

The Cloud

I bring fresh showers
for the thirsting flowers,
From the seas and the streams,
I bear light shade
for the leaves when laid
In their noonday dreams.
From my wings are shaken the dews that waken
The sweet buds every one,
When rocked to rest on their mother's breast,
As she dances about the sun,
I wield the flail of the lashing hail,
And whiten the green plains under,
And then again I dissolve it in rain,
And laugh as I pass in thunder.

I sift the snow on the mountains below,
And their great pines groan aghast;
And all the night 'tis my pillow white,
While I sleep in the arms of the blast.
Sublime on the towers of my skiey bowers,
Lightning my pilot sits;
In a cavern under is fettered the thunder,
It struggles and howls at fits;
Over earth and ocean, with gentle motion,
This pilot is guiding me,
Lured by the love of the genii that move
In the depths of the purple sea;
Over the rills, and the crags, and the hills,
Over the lakes and the plains,
Wherever he dreams, under mountain or stream,
The Spirit he loves remains;
And I all the while bask in Heaven's blue smile,
Whilst he is dissolving in rains.

The sanguine Sunrise, with his meteor eyes,
And his burning plumes outspread,
Leaps on the back of my sailing rack,
When the morning star shines dead;
As on the jag of a mountain crag,
Which an earthquake rocks and swings,
An eagle alit one moment may sit
In the light of its golden wings.
And when Sunset may breathe, from the lit sea beneath,
Its ardours of rest and of love,
And the crimson pall of eve may fall
From the depth of Heaven above,
With wings folded I rest, on mine aery nest,
As still as brooding dove.

That orbed maiden with white fire laden,
Whom mortals call the Moon,
Glides glimmering o'er my fleece-like floor,
By the midnight breezes strewn;
And wherever the beat of her unseen feet,
Which only the angels hear,
May have broken the woof of my tent's thin roof,
The stars peep behind her and peer;
And I laugh to see them whirl and flee,
Like a swarm of golden bees,
When I widen the rent in my wind-built tent,
Till the calm rivers, lakes, and seas,
Like strips of the sky fallen through me on high,
Are each paved with the moon and these.

I bind the Sun's throne with a burning zone,
And the Moon's with a girdle a pearl;
The volcanoes are dim, and the stars reel and swim,
When the whirlwinds my banner unfurl.
From cape to cape, with a bridge-like shape,
Over a torrent sea,
Sunbeam-proof, I hang like a roof,—
The mountains its column be.

The triumphal arch through which I march
With hurricane, fire, and snow,
When the Powers of the air are chained to my chair,
Is the million-coloured bow;
The sphere-fire above its soft colours wove,
While the moist Earth was laughing below.

I am the daughter of Earth and Water,
And the nursling of the Sky;
I pass through the pores of the ocean and shores;
I change, but I cannot die.
For after the rain when with never a stain
The pavilion of Heaven is bare,
And the winds and sunbeams with their convex gleams
Built up the blue dome of air,
I silently laugh at my own cenotaph,
And out of the caverns of rain,
Like a child from the womb, like a ghost from the tomb,
I arise and unbuild it again.

To Night

Swiftly walk o'er the western wave,
Spirit of Night!
Out of the misty eastern cave,
Where, all the long and lone daylight,
Thou wovest dreams of joy and fear,
Which make thee terrible and dear,—
Swift be thy flight!

Wrap thy form in a mantle gray,
Star-inwrought!
Blind with thine hair the eyes of Day;
Kiss her until she be wearied out,
Then wander o'er city, and sea, and land,
Touching all with thine opiate wand—
Come, long-sought!

When I arose and saw the dawn,
I sighed for thee;
When light rode high, and the dew was gone,
And noon lay heavy on flower and tree,
And the weary Day turned to his rest,
Lingering like an unloved guest,
I sighed for thee.

Thy brother Death came, and cried,
Wouldst thou me?
Thy sweet child Sleep, the filmy-eyed,
Murmured like a noontide bee,
Shall I nestle near thy side?
Wouldst thou me?—And I replied,
No, not thee!

Death will come when thou are dead,
Soon, too soon—
Sleep will come when thou art fled;
Of neither would I ask the boon
I ask of thee, beloved Night—
Swift be thine approaching flight,
Come soon, soon!

To A Skylark

Hail to thee, blithe Spirit!
Bird thou never wert—
That from heaven or near it
Pourest thy full heart
In Profuse strains of unpremediated art.

Higher still and higher
From the earth thou springest,
Like a cloud of fire;
The blue deep thou wingest,
And singing still dost soar, and soaring ever singest.

In the golden light'ning
Of the sunken sun,
O'er which clouds are bright'ning,
Thou dost float and run,
Like an unbodied joy whose race is just begun.

The pale purple even
Melts around thy flight;
Like a star of heaven,
In the broad daylight
Thou art unseen, but yet I hear thy shrill delight—

Keen as are the arrows
Of that silver sphere
Whose intense lamp narrows
In the white dawn clear,
Until we hardly see, feel that it is there.

All the earth and air
With thy voice is loud,
As, when night is bare,
From one lonely cloud
The moon rains out her beams, and heaven is overflow'd.

What thou art we know not;
What is most like thee?
From rainbow clouds there flow not
Drops so bright to see,
As from thy presence showers a rain of melody—

Like a poet hidden
In the light of thought,
Singing hymns unbidden,
Till the world is wrought
To sympathy with hopes and fear it heeded not:

Like a high-born maiden
In a palace tower,
Soothing her love-laden
Soul in secret hour
With music sweet as love, which overflows her bower:

Like a glow-worm golden
In a dell of dew,
Scattering unbeholden
Its aerial hue
Among the flowers and grass which screen it from the view:

Like a rose embower'd
In its own green leaves,
By warm winds deflower'd,
Till the scent it gives
Makes faint with too much sweet these heavy wing'd thieves:

Sound of vernal showers
On the twinkling grass,
Rain-awaken'd flowers—
All that ever was
Joyous, and clear and fresh—thy music doth surpass.

Teach us, sprite or bird,
What sweet thoughts are thine:
I have never heard
Praise of love or wine
That panted forth a flood of rapture so divine.

Chorus hymeneal,
Or triumphal chaunt
Match'd with thine would be all
But an empty vaunt—
A thing wherein we feel there is some hidden want.

What objects are the fountains
Of thy happy strain?
What fields, or waves, or mountains?
What shapes of sky or plain?
What love of thine own kind? what ignorance of pain?

With thy clear keen joyance
Languor cannot be:
Shadow of annoyance
Never came near thee:
Thou lovest, but ne'er knew love's sad satiety.

Waking or asleep,
Thou of death must deem
Things more true and deep
Than we mortals dream,
Or how could thy notes flow in such a crystal stream?

We look before and after,
And pine for what is not:
Our sincerest laughter
With some pain is fraught;

Our sweetest songs are those that tell of saddest thought.
Yet, if we could scorn
Hate and pride and fear,
If we were things born
Not to shed a tear,
I know not how thy joy we ever should come near.
Better than all measures
Of delightful sound,
Better than all treasures
That in books are found,
Thy skill to poet were, thou scorner of the ground!
Teach me half the gladness
That thy brain must know;
Such harmonious madness
From my lips would flow,
The world should listen then, as I am listening now.

Ode to the West Wind

I

O wild West Wind, thou breath of Autumn's being,
Thou from whose unseen presence the leaves dead
Are driven like ghosts from an enchanter fleeing,

Yellow, and black, and pale, and hectic red,
Pestilence-stricken multitudes! O thou
Who chariotest to their dark wintry bed

The winged seeds, where they lie cold and low,
Each like a corpse within its grave, until
Thine azure sister of the Spring shall blow

Her clarion o'er the dreaming earth, and fill
(Driving sweet buds like flocks to feed in air)
With living hues and odours plain and hill;

Wild Spirit, which art moving everywhere;
Destroyer are preserver; hear, O, hear!

II

Thou on whose stream, 'mid the steep sky's commotion,
Loose clouds like earth's decaying leaves are shed,
Shook from the tangled boughs of Heaven and Ocean,

Angels of rain and lightning! there are spread
On the blue surface of thine aery surge,
Like the bright hair uplifted from the head

Of some fierce Maenad, even from the dim verge
Of the horizon to the zenith's height,
The locks of the approaching storm. Thou dirge

Of the dying year, to which this closing night
Will be the dome of a vast sepulchre,
Vaulted with all thy congregated might

Of vapours, from whose solid atmosphere
Black rain, and fire, and hail, will burst: O, hear!

III

Thou who didst waken from his summer dreams
The blue Mediterranean, where he lay,
Lulled by the coil of his crystalline streams,

Beside a pumice isle in Baiae's bay,
And saw in sleep old palaces and towers
Quivering within the wave's intenser day,

All overgrown with azure moss, and flowers
So sweet, the sense faints picturing them! Thou
For whose path the Atlantic's level powers

Cleave themselve into chasms, while far below
The sea-blooms and the oozy woods which wear
The sapless foliage of the ocean, know

Thy voice, and suddenly grow gray with fear,
And tremble and despoil themselves :O, hear!

IV

If I were a dead leaf thou mightest bear;
If I were a swift cloud to fly with thee;
A wave to pant beneath thy power, and share

The impulse of thy strength, only less free
Than thou, O uncontrollable! If even
I were as in my boyhood, and could be

The comrade of thy wanderings over Heaven,
As then, when to outstrip thy skiey speed
Scarce seemed a vision—I would ne'er have striven

As thus with thee in prayer in my sore need.
O! lift me as a wave, a leaf, a cloud!
I fall upon the thorns of life! I bleed!

A heavy weight of hours has chained and bowed
One too like thee—tameless, and swift, and proud.

V

Make me thy lyre, even as the forest is:
What if my leaves are falling like its own?
The tumult of thy mighty harmonies

Will take from both a deep autumnal tone,
Sweet though in sadness. Be thou, spirit fierce,
My spirit! Be thou me, impetuous one!

Drive my dead thoughts over the universe,
Like withered leaves, to quicken a new birth;
And, by the incantation of this verse,

Scatter, as from an unextinguished hearth
Ashes and sparks, my words among mankind!
Be through my lips to unawakened earth

The trumpet of a prophecy! O wind,
If Winter comes, can Spring be far behind?

Percy Bysshe Shelley

WILLIAM WORDSWORTH (1770-1850)

Life

1. He was born at Cockermouth, Cumberland. (A poet/critic has called him "the gander of Cockermouth").

2. He got education at Hawkeshead School, Lancashire, and Cambridge.

3. He paid two visits to France :

(i) The first time in 1790

(ii) The second time in 1791-92.

Long divides his life into four periods :

(i) 1770-87: It belongs to his childhood and youth-Cumberland.

(ii) 1787-97: This period covers :

(a) his life at Cambridge

(b) his travels abroad which enabled him to be influenced by the revolutionary ideas.

(**Note:** We know that his revolutionary enthusiasm died soon with :

(i) the excesses of the Revolution including what is called "The Reign of Terror,"

(ii) the rise of tyrannical Napoleon

(iii) 1797-99: This period was very significant as it enabled him to understand his own abilities and take full advantage of them.

(iv) 1799-1850: It was practically a period of retirement in the lake region of his birth and childhood and to remain in direct touch with nature.

Works

1. His "Lyrical Ballads"—a book which is often considered the start of the Revival of Romanticism in England appeared in 1798.

2. His Preface to the Lyrical Ballads is considered important in the history of Criticism of English literature.

3. *(i)* He intended to write a single great poem under the caption "The Recluse."

(ii) The poem was intended to give a comprehensive treatment of: *(a)* nature, *(b)* man and (c) society.

(iii) His intention was that his "The Prelude"—the Growth of a Poet's Mind—should introduce the Recluse.

(iv) *(a)* The first book of The Recluse "The Home at Grasmere" was published posthumously in 1888.

(b) The name of the second book was 'The Excursion.'

(c) The third was never completed by the poet.

His most famous poems are :

1. The Prelude
2. Tintern Abbey
3. Ode on Intimations of Immortality.
4. Ode to Duty or Education of Nature
5. The Rainbow
6. The Solitary Reaper
7. Michael
8. To a Skylark
9. Yarrow Revisited
10. Lucy Gray
11. She Dwelt Among the Untrodden Ways
12. Daffodils

He also wrote a large number of sonnets such as :

1. On Milton
2. On Westminster Bridge
3. The World is Too Much With Us, etc.

Important characteristics of his poetry and philosophy :

1. He was a great lover of nature.

2. He felt the presence of a spirit in nature, that is, the spirit of nature.

3. He believed in pantheism.

4. He believed that nature could bestow peace, sympathy, love, joy and other virtues on man.

5. He did not like to depict nature "red in tooth and claw."

6. He believed that nature gave purity to man and ennobled his heart.

7. He was a great lover of the common man and the rustic and rural life.

8. He loved the child and thought that because of its innocence, purity of thought and nearness to God, childhood was the golden period of human life.

9. He loved all creation and all kinds of creatures, including the smallest and most insignificant animals and insects.

10. He believed that "nature never did betray the heart that loved her."

11. He himself practised what he preached and spent most of his time in the company of nature.

12. His poetry is full of :

(i) vivid descriptions of scenes of nature.

(ii) simple human affections.

(iii) fervent adulations of childhood and love of animals.

(iv) depictions of country and village life.

(v) sweet and haunting music.

(vi) personal reminiscences and memories

(vii) autobiographical tones

(viii) adulation of simplicity and homeliness.

(ix) tones of true theism and fervent faith in greatness, goodness and benignity of nature.

13. Although much of his later poetry is dull and interesting, yet it contains flashes of imaginative lines and good poetry.

14. Here are some extracts from his poetry.

Lucy

A slumber did my spirit seal;
I had no human fears:
She seemed a thing that could not feel

The touch of earthly years.
No motion has she now, no force;
She neither hears nor sees;
Rolled round in earth's diurnal course,
With rocks, and stones, and trees.

(**Note:** It is still a matter of conjecture regarding the real child "Lucy" whose death the poet recalls in poem after poem belonging to this class).

The French Revolution

As it Appeared to Enthusiasts at its Commencement.
Oh! pleasant exercise of hope and joy!
For mighty were the auxiliars which then stood
Upon our side, we who were strong in love!
Bliss was it in that dawn to be alive,
But to be young was very heaven!—Oh! times,
In which the meagre, stale, forbidding ways
Of custom, law, and statute, took at once
The attraction of a country in romance!
When Reason seemed the most to assert her rights,
When most intent on making of herself
A prime Enchantress—to assist the work
Which then was going forward in her name!
Not favoured spots alone, but the whole earth,
The beauty wore of promise, that which sets
(As at some moment might not be unfelt
Among the bowers of paradise itself)
The budding rose above the rose full blown.
What temper at the prospect did not wake
To happiness unthought of? The inert
Were roused, and lively natures rapt away!
They who had fed their childhood upon dreams,
The playfellows of fancy, who had made
All powers of swiftness, subtility, and strength
Their ministers—who in lordly wise had stirred
Among the grandest objects of the sense,
And dealt with whatsoever they found there
As if they had within some lurking right
To wield it;—they, too, who, of gentle mood,
Had watched all gentle motions, and to these
Had fitted their own thoughts, schemers more mild,
And in the region of their peaceful selves;—
Now was it that both found, the meek and lofty
Did both find, helpers to their heart's desire,
And stuff at hand, plastic as they could wish;
Were called upon to exercise their skill,
Not in Utopia, subterranean fields,
Or some secreted island, Heaven knows where!
But in the very world, which is the world
Of all of us,—the place where in the end
We find our happiness, or not at all!

(**Note:** It is rightly said about Shakespeare that no historian could ever describe the situation and events as they prevailed or took place in Rome as described by Shakespeare in Julius Caesar. Likewise, it is perhaps true of Wordsworth that no historian could describe in so few words "The French Revolution" as described by Wordsworth in his poem of the same name).

In one of the most famous of his poems "Tintern Abbey" Wordsworth calls nature :

"The anchor of my purest thoughts, the nurse,
The guide, the guardian of my heart, and soul
Of all my moral being."

Here are the last lines of the celebrated poem :

Nor perchance,
If I were not thus taught, should I the more
Suffer my genial spirits to decay:
For thou art with me here upon the banks
Of this fair river; thou my dearest Friend,
My dear, dear Friend; and in thy voice I catch
The language of my former heart, and read
My former pleasures in the shooting lights
Of thy wild eyes. Oh! yet a little while
May I behold in thee what I was once,
My dear, dear Sister! and this prayer I make,
Knowing that Nature never did betray
The heart that loved her; 'tis her privilege,
Through all the years of this our life, to lead
From joy to joy: for she can so inform
The mind that is within us, so impress
With quietness and beauty, and so feed
With lofty thoughts, that neither evil tongues,
Rash judgements, nor the sneers of selfish men,
Nor greetings where no kindness is, nor all
The dreary intercourse of daily life,
Shall e'er prevail against us, or disturb
Our cheerful faith, that all which we behold
Is full of blessings. Therefore let the moon
Shine on thee in thy solitary walk;
And let the misty mountain-winds be free
To blow against thee: and, in after years,
When these wild ecstasies shall be matured
Into a sober pleasure, when thy mind
Shall be a mansion for all lovely forms,
Thy memory be as a dwelling-place
For all sweet sounds and harmonies; oh! then
If solitude, or fear, or pain, or grief,
Should be thy portion, with what healing thoughts
Of tender joy wilt thou remember me,
And these my exhortations! Nor, perchance—
If I should be where I no more can hear
Thy voice, nor catch from thy wild eyes these gleams
Of past existence—wilt thou then forget
That on the banks of this delightful stream
We stood together; and that I, so long
A worshipper of Nature, hither came
Unwearied in that service: rather say
With warmer love—oh! with far deeper zeal

Oh holier love. Nor wilt thou then forget
That after many wanderings, many years
Of absence, these steep woods and lofty cliffs,
And this green pastoral landscape, were to me
More dear, both for themselves and for thy sake!

Even if we do not find that level of loftiness and excellence in his "To The Cuckoo" as we find in his "Ode on Intimations of Immortality," yet the poem deserves appreciation : Here are the first five stanzas:

To The Cuckoo

O Blithe Newcomer! I have heard,
I hear thee and rejoice.
O Cuckoo! shall I call thee Bird,
Or but a wandering Voice?

While I am lying on the grass
Thy twofold shout I hear;
From hill to hill it seems to pass
At once far off and near.

Though babbling only to the Vale,
Of sunshine and of flowers,
Thou bringest unto me a tale
Of visionary hours.

Thrice welcome, darling of the Spring!
Even yet-thou art to me
No bird, but an invisible thing,
A voice, a mystery;

Wordsworth is also renowned for his sonnets, not only for their structural perfection, but also for introduction in them of the element of nature, humanity, concern for common man, simplicity, countryside, pantheism, love for God and his creatures, genuine description, high ethical sense, etc. Here is an example:

It is a Beauteous Evening

It is a beauteous evening, calm and free,
The holy time is quiet at a Nun
Breathless with adoration; the broad sun
Is sinking down in its tranquillity;
The gentleness of heaven broods o'er the Sea:
Listen! the mighty Being is awake,
And doth with his eternal motion make
A sound like thunder—everlastingly.
Dear Child! dear Girl! that walkest with me here,
If thou appear untouched by solemn thought,
Thy nature is not therefore less divine:
Thou liest in Abraham's bosom all the year;
And worshipp'st at the Temple's inner shrine,
God being with thee when we know it not.

Given below are the first eight lines (the octave) of one of his most famous sonnets :

The World is Too Much With us

The world is too much with us; late and soon,
Getting and spending, we lay waste our powers:
Little we see in Nature that is ours;
We have given our hearts away, a sordid boon!
This Sea that bares her bosom to the moon;
The winds that will be howling at all hours,
And are up-gathered now like sleeping flowers;
For this, for everything, we are out of tune;

Here are some extracts from his most powerful work "The Prelude" which has been so enthusiastically hailed by Hudson:

***(i)* One Summer Evening**

One summer evening (led by her)[1] I found
A little boat tied to a willow tree
Within a rocky cave, its usual home.
Straight I unloosed her chain, and stepping in
Pushed from the shore. It was an act of stealth
And troubled pleasure, nor without the voice
Of mountain-echoes did my boat move on;
Leaving behind her still, on either side,
Small circles glittering idly in the moon
Until they melted all into one track
Of sparkling light. But now, like one who rows,
Proud of his skill, to reach a chosen point
With an unswerving line, I fixed my view
Upon the summit of a craggy ridge,
The horizon's utmost boundary; for above
Was nothing but the stars and the grey sky.
She was an elfin pinnace; lustily
I dipped my oars into the silent lake,
And, as I rose upon the stroke, my boat
Went heaving through the water like a swan;
When, from behind that craggy steep, till then,
The horizon's bound, a huge peak, black and huge,
As if with voluntary power instinct.
Upreared its head. I struck and struck again,
And, growing still in stature, the grim shape
Towered up between me and the stars, and still,
For so it seemed with purpose of its own
And measured motion like a living thing,
Strode after me. With trembling oars I turned,
And through the silent water stole my way
Back to the covert of the willow tree;
There in her mooring-place I left my bark,—
And through the meadows homeward went, in grave
And serious mood; but after I had seen
That spectacle, for many days, my brain
Worked with a dim and undetermined sense
Of unknown modes of being; o'er my thoughts
There hung a darkness, call it solitude
Or blank desertion. No familiar shapes
Remained, no pleasant images of trees,
Of sea or sky, no colours of green fields;
But huge and mighty forms, that do not live
Like living men, moved slowly through the mind

By day, and were a trouble to my dreams.

(*Prelude*, i, II, 357-49)

1. her = Nature

Winander Lake

There was a Boy: ye knew him well, ye cliffs
And islands of Winander!—many a time
At evening, when the earliest stars began
To move along the edges of the hills,
Rising or setting, would he stand alone
Beneath the trees or by the glimmering lake,
And there, with fingers interwoven, both hands
Pressed closely palm to palm, and to his mouth
Uplifted, he, as through an instrument,
Blew mimic hootings to the silent owls,
That they might answer him; and they would shout
Across the watery vale, and shout again,
Responsive to his call, with quivering peals,
And long halloos and screams, and echoes loud,
Redoubled and redoubled, concourse wild
Of jocund din; and, when a lengthened pause
Of silence came and baffled his best skill,
Then sometimes, in that silence while he hung
Listening, a gentle shock of mild surprise
Has carried far into his heart the voice
Of mountain torrents; or the visible scene
Would enter unawares into his mind,
With all its solemn imagery, its rocks,
Its woods, and that uncertain heaven, received
Into the bosom of the steady lake.

(*Prelude*, v, II, 364-88)

(**Note :** Given below are three of his most famous poems :

(i) The Solitary Reaper
(ii) The Tintern Abbey
(iii) The Ode on Intimations of Immortality.)

The Solitary Reaper

Behold her, single in the field,
You solitary Highland Lass!
Reaping and singing by herself;
Stop here, or gently pass!
Alone she cuts and binds the grain,
And sings a melancholy strain;
O listen! for the Vale profound
Is overflowing with the sound.

No Nightingale did ever chaunt
More welcome notes to weary bands
Of travellers in some shady haunt,
Among Arabian sands:
A voice so thrilling ne'er was heard
In spring-time from the Cuckoo-bird,
Breaking the silence of the seas
Among the farthest Hebrides.

Will no one tell me what she sings?—
Perhaps the plaintive numbers flow
For old, unhappy, far-off things,
And battles long ago:
Or is it some more humble lay,
Familiar matter of to-day?
Some natural sorrow, loss, or pain,
That has been, and may be again?

Whate'er the theme, the Maiden sang
As if her song could have no ending;
I saw her singing at her work,
And o'er the sickle bending;—
I listened, motionless and still;
And, as I mounted up the hill,
The music in my heart I bore,
Long after it was heard no more.

Lines Composed A Few Miles Above Tintern Abbey

Five years have passed; five summers, with the length
Of five long winters! and again I hear
These waters, rolling from their mountain-springs
With a soft inland murmur.—Once again
Do I behold these steep and lofty cliffs,
That on a wild secluded scene impress—
Thoughts of more deep seclusion; and connect
The landscape with the quiet of the sky.
The day is come when I again repose
Here, under this dark sycamore, and view
These plots of cottage-ground, these orchard-tufts,
Which at this season, with their unripe fruits,
Are clad in one green hue, and lose themselves
'Mid groves and copses. Once again I see
These hedge-rows, hardly hedge-rows, little lines
Of sportive wood run wild; these pastoral farms,
Green to the very door; and wreaths of smoke
Sent up, in silence, from among the trees!
With some uncertain notice, as might seem
Of vagrant dwellers in the houseless woods,
Or of some Hermit's cave, where by his fire
The hermit sits alone.
These beauteous forms,
Through a long absence, have not been to me
As is a landscape to a blind man's eye:
But oft, in lonely rooms, and 'mid the din
Of towns and cities, I have owed to them,
In hours of weariness, sensations sweet,
Felt in the blood, and felt along the heart;
And passing even into my purer mind,
With tranquil restoration:—feelings too
Of unremembered pleasure: such, perhaps,
As have no slight or trivial influence
On that best portion of a good man's life,
His little, nameless, unremembered, acts
Of kindness and of love, Nor less, I trust,
To them I may have owed another gift,
Of aspect more sublime; that blessed mood

In which the burthen of the mystery,
In which the heavy and the weary weight
Of all this unintelligible world,
Is lightened:—that serene and blessed mood,
In which the affections gently lead us on,—
Until, the breath of this corporeal frame
And even the motion of our human blood
Almost suspended, we are laid asleep
In body, and become a living soul:
While with an eye made quiet by the power
Of harmony, and the deep power of joy,
We seen into the life of things.
If this
Be but a vain belief, yet, oh! how oft—
In darkness and amid the many shapes
Of joyless daylight; when the fretful stir
Unprofitable, and the fever of the world,
Have hung upon the beatings of my heart—
How oft, in spirit, have I turned to thee,
O sylvan Wye! thou wanderer thro' the woods,
How often has my spirit turned to thee!
And now, with gleams of half-extinguished thought,
With many recognitions dim and faint,
And somewhat of a sad perplexity,
The picture of the mind revives again:
While here I stand not only with the sense
Of present pleasure, but with pleasing thoughts
That in this moment there is life and food
For future years. And so I dare to hope,
Though changed, no doubt, from what I was when first
I came among these hills; when like a roe
I bounded o'er the mountains, by the sides
Of the deep rivers, and the lonely streams,
Wherever nature led : more like a man
Flying from something that he dreads than one
Who sought the thing he loved. For nature then
(The coarser pleasures of my boyish days,
And their glad animal movements all gone by)
To me was all in all.—I cannot paint
What then I was. The sounding cataract
Haunted me like a passion: the tall rock,
The mountain, and the deep and gloomy wood
Their colours and their forms, were then to me
An appetite; a feeling and a love,
That had no need of a remoter charm,
By thought supplied, nor any interest
Unborrowed from the eye.—That time is past
And all its aching joys are now no more,
And all its dizzy raptures. Not for this
Faint I, nor mourn nor murmur; other gifts
Have followed; for such loss, I would believe,
Abundant recompense. For I have learned
To look on nature, not as in the hour
Of thoughtless youth; but hearing oftentimes
The still, sad music of humanity,
Nor harsh nor grating, though of ample power
To chasten and subdue. And I have felt
A presence that disturbs me with the joy
Of elevated thoughts; a sense sublime
Of something far more deeply interfused,
Whose dwelling is the light of setting suns,
The dreary intercourse of daily life,
Shall e'er prevail aganst us, or disturb
Our cheerful faith, that all which we behold
Is full of blessings. Therefore let the moon
Shine on thee in thy solitary walk;
And let the misty mountain-winds be free
To blow against thee: and, in after years,
When these wild ecstasies shall be matured
Into a sober pleasure; when thy mind
Shall be a mansion for all lovely forms,
Thy memory be as a dwelling-place
For all sweet sounds and harmonies; oh! then,
If solitude, or fear, or pain, or grief,
Should be thy portion, with what healing thoughts
Of tender joy wilt thou remember me,
And these my exhortations! Nor, perchance—
If I should be where I no more can hear
Thy voice, nor catch from thy wild eyes these gleams
Of past existence—wilt thou then forget
That on the banks of this delightful stream
We stood together; and that I, so long
A worshipper of Nature, hither came
Unwearied in that service: rather say
With warmer love—oh! with far deeper zeal
Of holier love. Nor wilt thou then forget
That after many wanderings, many years
Of absence, these steep woods and lofty cliffs,
And this green pastoral landscape, were to me
More dear, both for themselves and for thy sake!

Intimations of Immortality from Recollections of Early Childhood

I

There was a time when meadow, grove, and stream,
The earth, and every common sight,
To me did seem
Apparell'd in celestial light,
The glory and the freshness of a dream.
It is not now as it hath been of yore;—
Turn wheresoe'er I may,
By night or day,
The things which I have seen I now can see no more.

II

The Rainbow comes and goes,
And lovely is the Rose;
The Moon doth with delight
Look round her when the heaven are bare,
Waters on a starry night
Are beautiful and fair;

The sunshine is a glorious birth;
But yet I know, where'er I go,
That there hath past away a glory from the earth.

III

Now, while the birds thus sing a joyous song,
And while the young lambs bound
As to the tabor's sound,
To me alone there came a thought of grief:
A timely utterance gave that thought relief,
And I again am strong:
The cataracts blow their trumpets from the steep;
No more shall grief of mine the season wrong;
I hear the Echoes through the mountains throng,
The Winds come to me from the fields of sleep,
And all the earth is gay;
Land and sea
Give themselves up to jollity,
And with the heart of May
Doth every beast keep holiday;—
Thou Child of Joy
Shout round me, let me hear thy shouts, thou happy
Shapherd-boy!

IV

Ye blessed Creatures, I have heard the call
Ye to each other make; I see
The heavens laugh with you in your jubilee;
My heart is at your festival,
My head hath its coronal,
The fullness of your bliss, I feel—I feel it all.
O evil day! if I were sullen
While Earth herself is adorning,
This sweet May-morning,
And the Children are culling
On every side,
In a thousand valleys far and wide,
Fresh flowers; while the sun shines warm,
And the Babe leaps up on his Mother's arm:—
I hear, I hear, with joy I hear!
—But there's a Tree, of many, one,
A single Field which I have look'd upon,
Both of them speak of something that is gone:
The Pansy at my feet
Doth the same tale repeat:
Whither is fled the visionary gleam?
Where is it now, the glory and the dream?

V

Our birth is but a sleep and a forgetting:
The Soul that rises with us, our life's Star,
Hath had elsewhere its setting,
And cometh from afar:
Not in entire forgetfulness,
And not in utter nakedness,
But trailing clouds of glory do we come
From God, who is our home:
Heaven lies about us in our infancy!
Shades of the prison-house begin to close
Upon the growing Boy
But He beholds the light, and whence it flows,
He sees it in his joy;
The Youth, who daily farther from the east
Must travel, still is Nature's Priest,
And by the vision splendid
Is on his way attended;
At length the Man perceives it die away,
And fade into the light of common day.

VI

Earth fills her lap with pleasures of her own;
Yearnings she hath in her own natural kind,
And, even with something of a Mother's mind,
And no unworthy aim,
The homely Nurse doth all she can
To make her Foster-child, her Inmate Man,
Forget the glories he hath known,
And that imperial palace whence he came.

VII

Behold the Child among his new-born blisses,
A six years' Darling of a pigmy size!
See, where 'mid work of his own hand he lies,
Fretted by sallies of his mother's kisses,
With light upon him from his father's eyes!
See, at his feet, some little plan or chart,
Some fragment from his dream of human life,
Shaped by himself with newly-learned art;
A wedding or a festival,
A mourning or a funeral;
And this hath now his heart,
And unto this he frames his song:
Then will he fit his tongue
To dialogues of business, love, or strife;
But it will not be long
Ere this be thrown aside,
And with new joy and pride
The little Actor cons another part;
Filling from time to time his 'humorous stage'
With all the Persons, down to palsied Age,
That Life brings with her in her equipage;
As if his whole vocation
Were endless imitation.

VIII

Thou, whose exterior semblance doth belie
Thy Soul's immensity;
Thou best Philosopher, who yet dost keep
Thy heritage, thou Eye among the blind,
That, deaf and silent, read'st the eternal deep,
Haunted for ever by the enternal mind,—
Mighty Prophet! Seer blest!

On whom those truths do rest,
Which we are toiling all our lives to find,
In darkness lost, the darkness of the grave;
Thou, over whom thy Immortality
Broods like the Day, a Master o'er a Slave,
A presence which is not to be put by;
Thou little Child, yet glorious in the might
Of heaven-born freedom on thy being's height,
Why with such earnest pains dost thou provoke
The years to bring the inevitable yoke,
Thus blindly with thy blessedness at strife?
Full soon thy Soul shall have her earthly freight,
And custom lie upon thee with a weight,
Heavy as frost, and deep almost as life!

IX

O joy! that in our embers
Is something that doth live,
That nature yet remembers
What was so fugitive!
The thought of our past years in me doth breed
Perpetual benediction: not indeed
For that which is most worthy to be blest;
Delight and liberty, the simple creed
Of Childhood, whether busy or at rest,
With new-fledged hope still fluttering in his breast:—
Not for these I raise
The song of thanks and praise;
But for those obstinate questionings
Of sense and outward things,
Fallings from us, vanishings;
Blank misgivings of a Creature
Moving about in worlds not realized,
High instincts before which our mortal Nature
Did tremble like a guilty Thing surprised:
But for those first affections,
Those shadowy recollections,
Which, be they what they may,
Are yet the fountain-light of all our day,
Are yet a master-light of all our seeing;
Uphold us, cherish, and have power to make
Our noisy years seem moments in the being
Of the eternal Silence: truths that wake,
To perish never:
Which neither listlessness, nor mad endeavour,
Nor Man nor Boy,
Nor all that is at enmity with joy,
Can utterly abolish or destroy!
Hence in a season of calm weather
Though inland far we be,
Our Souls have sight of that immortal sea
Which brought us hither,
Can in a moment travel thither,
And see the Children sport upon the shore,
And hear the mighty waters rolling evermore,

X

Then sing, ye Birds, sing, sing a joyous song!
And let the young Lambs bound
As to the tabor's sound!
We in thought will join your throng,
Ye that pipe and ye that play,
Ye that through your hearts to-day
Feel the gladness of the May!
What though the radiance which was once so bright
Be now for ever taken from my sight,
Though nothing can bring back the hour
Of splendour in the grass, of glory in the flower;
We will grieve not, rather find
Strength in what remains behind;
In the primal sympathy
Which having been must ever be;
In the soothing thoughts that spring
Out of human suffering;
In the faith that looks through death,
In years that bring the philosophic mind.

XI

And O, ye Fountains, Meadows, Hills, and Groves,
Forebode not any severing of our loves !
Yet in my heart of hearts I feel your might;
I only have relinquished one delight
To live beneath your more habitual sway.
I love the Brooks which down their channels fret,
Even more than when I tripped lightly as they;
The innocent brightness of a new-born Day
Is lovely yet;
The Clouds that gather round the setting sun
Do take a sober colouring from an eye
That hath kept watch o'er man's mortality;
Another race hath been, and other palms are won.
Thanks to the human heart by which we live,
Thanks to its tenderness, its joys, and fears,
To me the meanest flower that blows can give
Thoughts that do often lie too deep for tears.

—*William Wordsworth*

JOHN KEATS (1795-1821)

Life

1. He was born in London in 1795.
2. His father was a hostler and stable keeper.
3. Both his parents died before he was fifteen.
4. It is said that his guardians cheated him and his brothers and sisters.
5. At first, he started the profession of a surgeon but later abandoned it.
6. He was greatly impressed by Spenser, particularly his Faerie Queene which he read most fervently.

7. Byron and some other critics and literary men held, the view that savage criticism of Keats' "Endymion" in the Blackwood Magazine shortened the life of this young poet, but Matthew Arnold does not subscribe to this view.

8. Since he was suffering from tuberculosis and could not tolerate the severity and coldness of the British climate, he left for Italy, where in Rome, he settled with his friend Severn, but soon he breathed his last in February, 1821.

Works

1. His first work was 'Endymion' which although immature and imperfect, has flashes of beautiful and charming lines in it.

2. Odes : Keats is most famous for his odes, some of which are named below:

(i) Ode to a Nightingale
(ii) Ode on a Grecian Urn
(iii) Ode of Psyche
(iv) Ode to Autumn
(v) Ode of Indolence

(**Note :** He is undeniably the greatest ode writer in English literature.)

Last Work

1. His last volume which was composed in 1820, comprised the following poems :

(i) Lamia
(ii) Isabella
(iii) The Eve of St. Agnes, etc.

2. *(i)* Keats left his stupendously planned work: "Hyperion" a mere fragment.

(ii) The poem was to be a wonderful epic on a grand scale but were never completed.

(iii) It is in this work that the following celebrated line occurs :

"For it's the eternal law that the first in beauty shall be the first in might."

(**Note:** 1. Keats considered by many the greatest romanticist, had always been a lover of beauty. Thus, we have—

2. 'A thing of beauty is a joy for ever.'

—*Endymion*

3. 'Beauty is truth, truth beauty,
That is all ye know on earth
and all ye need to know."

—*Ode on a Grecian Urn*

4. One of his most famous poems is :
"La Belle Dame Sans Merci":
"O what can ail thee, knight -ate arms,
Alone and palely loitering?
The sedge is withered on the lake,
And no birds sing."

As a Sonneteer: Keats did not live to write many sonnets, but the few sonnets he wrote, are some of the best in English literature. Some of them are :

1. When I have fears that I may cease to be
2. Human Seasons
3. On Looking Into Chapman's Homer
4. Bright Star! .....

(1) The Eve of St. Agnes

I

St. Agnes' Eve—Ah, bitter chill it was!
The owl, for all his feathers, was a-cold;
The hare limp'd trembling through the frozen grass,
And silent was the flock in woolly fold:
Numb were the Beadsman's fingers, while he told
His rosary, and while his frosted breath,
Like pious incense from a censor old,
Seem'd taking flight for heaven, without a death,
Past the sweet Virgin's picture, while his prayer he saith.

II

His prayer he saith, this patient, holy man;
Then takes his lamp, and riseth from his knees,
And back returneth, meagre, barefoot, wan,
Along the chapel aisle by slow degrees:
The sculptur'd dead, on each side, seem to freeze,
Emprison'd in black, purgatorial rails:
Knights, ladies, praying in dumb orat'ries.
He passeth by; and his weak spirit fails
To think how they may ache in icy hoods and mails.

III

Northward the turneth through a little door,
And scarce three steps, ere Music's golden tongue
Flatter'd to tears this aged man and poor
But no—already had his deathbell rung:
The joys of all his life were said and sung:
His was harsh penance on St. Agnes' Eve:
Another way he went, and soon among
Rough ashes sat he for his soul's reprieve,
And all night kept awake, for sinner's sake to grieve.

Undoubtedly, the given lines corroborate a deft hand behind them: and a brain which is master of the arts of narration, plastic description and portrayal with all the delicacy and appropriateness of language. Had the terms impressionism, expressionism, imagism, Freudianism, surrealism, etc. existed in Keat's time, the critics would have surely included him into one or more of these folds. The real warmth of love, however, comes later in Madeline's room when we leave the coldness of the natural world and the Beadsman's Chapel.

(2) Ode on a Grecian Urn

I

Thou still unravish'd bride of quietness!
Thou foster-child of Silence and slow Time,
Sylvan historian, who canst thus express
A flowery tale more sweetly than our rhyme:
What leaf-fringed legend haunts about thy shape
Of deities of mortals, or of both,
In Tempe or the dales of Arcady?
What men or gods are these? What maidens loth?

What mad pursuit? What struggle to escape?
What pipes and timbrels? What wild ecstasy?

II

Heard melodies are sweet, but those unheard
Are sweeter; therefore, ye soft pipes, play on;
Not to the sensual ear, but, more endear'd
Pipe to the spirit ditties of no tone:
Fair youth, beneath the trees, thou canst not leave
Thy song, nor ever can those trees be bare;
Bold Lover, never, never canst thou kiss,
Though winning near the goal—yet, do not grieve;
She cannot fade, though thou hast not thy bliss,
For ever wilt thou love, and she be fair!

The poem is, undoubtedly, the triumph of art over the transcience of human life and is comparable to Yeats Lapis Lazily :

Every discoloration of the stone,
Every accidental crack of dent,
Seems a water-course or an avalanche,
Or lofty slope where it still snows
Though doubtless plum or cherry-branch
Sweetens the little half-way house
Those Chinamen climb towards, and I
Delight to imagine them seated there,
There, on the mountain and the sky,
On all the tragic scene they stare.
One asks for mournful melodies;
Accomplished fingers begin to play.
Their eyes mid many wrinkles, their eyes,
Their ancient, glittering eyes, are gay.

In both the poems, immortality of human life has been achieved through art, through same have found fault with the last two lines of Keat's poem:

"'Beauty is truth, truth beauty'—that is all
Ye know on earth, and all ye need to know,"

(3) Ode to Psyche

O brightest! though too late for antique vows,
Too, too late for the fond believing lyre,
When holy were the haunted forest boughs.
Holy the air, the water, and the fire;
Yet even in these days so far retired
From happy pieties, thy lucent fans,
Fluttering among the faint Olympians,
I see, and sing, by my own eyes inspired.
So let me be thy choir, and make a moan
Upon the midnight hours!

Keat's love of the Greek mythology which fits squarely in his Romantic moorings, is clearly brought home in these lines. His love of the mysterious, the haunted, the natural phenomenon, the religions (without being religious) is also brought out vividly.

(4) Ode to a Nightingale

VII

Thou wast not born for death, immortal Bird!
No hungry generations tread thee down;
The voice I hear this passing night was heard
In ancient days by emperor and clown :
Perhaps the self-same song that found a path
Through the sad heart of Ruth, when, sick for home,
She stood in tears amid the alien corn;
The same that oft-times hath
Charm'd magic casements, opening on the foam
Of perilious seas, in faery lands forlorn.

VIII

Foriorn! the very word is like a bell
To toll me back from thee to my sole self!
Adieu! the fancy cannot cheat so well
As she is fam'd to do, deceiving elf.
Adieu! adieu! thy plaintive anthem fades
Past the near meadows, over the still stream,
Up the hill-side; and now 'tis buried deep
In the next valley-glades:
Was it a vision, or a waking dream?
Fled is that music:—Do I wake or sleep?

We again find Keat's affinity with Yeats. After all, magic and dreams are unreal and short lived and both the poets had to go in for real life, as Keats went to Hyperion at last, in an epic way, though still in the form of a dream!

(5) Prologue to the Second Hyperion

Fanatics have their dreams, wherewith they weave
A paradise for a sect; the savage, too,
From forth the loftiest fashion of his sleep
Guesses at Heaven! Pity these have not
Traced upon vellum or wild Indian leaf
The shadows of melodious utterance.
But bare of laurel they live, dream and die;
For poesy alone can tell her dreams,—
With the fine spell of words alone can save
Imagination from the sable chain
And dumb enchantment.

(6) The Second Hyperion

Thou art a dreaming thing;
A fever of thyself: think of the earth:
What bliss, even in hope, is there for thee?
What haven? every creature hath its home,
Every sole man hath days of joy and pain,
Whether his labours be sublime of low—
The pain alone, the joy alone, distinct:
Only the dreamer venoms are his days,
Being more we than all his sins deserve."

Actually, Keats is interested in finding human life and realising its both beauty and misery through poetry which may even he dreaming.

But, he does want—
a nober life
Where I may find the agonies, the strife
Of human hearts.

(7) From : "Bards of Passion and Mirth." and full poems—

(i) Ode to Autumn, and

(ii) When I Have Fears That I May Cease To Be (Sonnet)

(iii) La Belle Dame Sans Merci.

Bards of Passion and Mirth

Bards of Passion and of Mirth,
Ye have left your souls on earth!
Have ye souls in heaven too,
Double lived in regions new?
Yes, and those of heaven commune
With the spheres of sun and moon;
With the noise of fountains wond'rous,
And the parle of voices thund'rous;
With the whisper of heaven's trees
And one another, in soft ease
Seated on Elysian lawns
Brows'd by none but Dian's fawns;
Underneath large blue-shells tented,
Where the daisies are rose-scented,
And the rose herself has got
Perfume which on earth is not;
Where the nightingale doth sing
Not a senseless, tranced thing,
But divine melodious truth;
Philosophic numbers smooth;
Tales and golden histories
Of heaven and its mysteries.

Thus ye live on high, and then
On the earth ye live again;
And the souls ye left behind you
Teach us, here, the way to find you,
Where your other souls are joying,
Never slumber'd, never cloying.
Here, your earth-born souls still speak
To mortals, of their little week;
Of their sorrows and delights;
Of their passions and their spites;
....

Ode To Autumn

Season of mists and mellow fruitfulness,
Close bosom-friend of the maturing sun;
Conspiring with him how to load and bless
With fruit the vines that round the thatch-eaves run;
To bend with apples the moss'd cottage-trees,
And fill all fruit with ripeness to the core;
To swell the gourd, and plump the hazel shells
With a sweet kernel; to set budding more,
And still more, later flowers for the bees,
Until they think warm days will never cease,
For Summer has o'er-brimm'd their clammy cells.

Who hath not seen Thee oft amid thy store?
Sometimes whoever seeks abroad may find
Thee sitting careless on a granary floor,
Thy hair soft-lifted by the winnowing wind;
Or on a half-reap'd furrow sound asleep,
Drows'd with the fume of poppies, while thy hook
Spares the next swath and all its twined flowers;
And sometimes like a gleaner thou dost keep
Steady thy laden head across a brook;
Or by a cider-press, with patient look,
Thou watchest the last oozings, hours by hours.

Where are the songs of Spring? Ay, where are they?
Think not of them, thou hast thy music too,
While barred clouds bloom the soft-dying day,
And touch the stubble-plains with rosy hue;
Then in a wailful choir the small gnats mourn
Among the river-sallows, borne aloft
Or sinking as the light wind lives or dies;
And full-grown lambs loud bleat from hilly bourn;
Hedge-crickets sing; and now with treble soft
The red-breast whistles from a garden-croft;
And gathering swallows twitter in the skies.

When I Have Fear That I May Cease To Be

When I have fears that I may cease to be
Before my pen has glean'd my teeming brain,
Before high-piled books, in charactery,
Hold like rich garners the full ripen'd grain;
When I behold, upon the night's starr'd face,
Huge cloudy symbols of a high romance,
And think that I may never live to trace
Their shadows, with the magic hand of chance;
And when I feel, fair creature of an hour,
That I shall never look upon thee more,
Never have relish in the faery power
Of unreflecting love;—then on the shore
Of the wide world I stand alone, and think
Till love and fame to nothingness do sink.

La Belle Dame Sans Merci

O, what can ail thee, knight-at-arms,
Alone and palely loitering?
The sedge is wither'd from the lake,
And no birds sing.
O, what can ail thee, knight-at-arms,
So haggard and so woe-begone?
The squirrel's granary is full,
And the harvest's done.

I see a lily on thy brow,
With anguish moist and fever-dew;
And on thy cheek a fading rose
Fast withereth too.

I met a lady in the meads,
Full beautiful—a faery's child,
Her hair was long, her foot was light,
And her eyes were wild.

I made a garland for her head,
And bracelets too, and fragrant zone;
She look'd at me as she did love,
And made sweet moan.

I set her on my pacing steed,
And nothing else saw all day long;
For sidelong would she bend, and sing
A faery's song.

She found me roots of relish sweet,
And honey wild, and manna dew,
And sure in language strange she said—
'I love thee true.'

She took me to her elfin grot,
And there she wept and sigh'd full sore,
And there I shut her wild eyes
With kisses four.

And there she lulled me asleep
And there I dream'd—Ah! woe betide!
The latest dream I ever dream'd
On the cold hill side.

I saw pale kings and princes too,
Pale warriors, death-pale were they all;
They cried—"La Belle Dame sans Merci
Hath thee in thrall!'

I saw their starved lips in the gloam,
With horrid warning gaped wide,
And I awoke and found me here,
On the cold hill's side.

And this is why I sojourn here
Along and palely loitering,
Though the sedge has wither'd from the lake,
And no birds sing.

John Keats

SAMUEL TAYLER COLERIDGE (1772-1834)

Life

1. Coleridge was born in Devonshire in 1772.

2. His father Rev. John Coleridge was a vicar and incharge of a primary school. He was an honest, sincere, religiously minded man who left the indelible mark of his personality on his children, including S.T. Coleridge.

3. Coleridge, was a precocious child who could read at three and recite from memory a great part of the Bible and the Arabian Nights.

4. It was at the Charity School of Christ's Hospital where he was sent when he was ten and where he made friendship with Lamb.

5. As a boy, he was largely poor and neglected but he was a great dreamer.

6. In 1791, he joined Cambridge as a charity student but left in 1794 without taking a degree.

7. Now, he met the youthful Southey with whom he planned to establish Pantisocracy (an ideal society), on the banks of the Susquehanna.

8. The plan regarding Pantisocracy failed and Coleridge went to Germany to study.

9. Thereafter, he went to Rome.

10. He started a paper "The Friend" which was devoted to truth and also started lectures on poetry and fine arts; he gained a good success, but since he was not regular in his engagements, his audiences ultimately dwindled.

Early works

Among his early poems, we have:

(i) A Day Dream
(ii) The Devil's Thoughts
(iii) The Suicide's Arguments
(iv) The Wanderings of Cain.

Later works

His later works which have made him immortal are:

1. Kubla Khan

It is just a fragment. It is commonly known that he composed the poem in a dream which he remembered and started writing as he woke up but was interrupted and forgot beyond what he had written (54 lines).

2. Christabel

(i) This poem is also a fragment.
(ii) Here, the heroine, Geraldine, is a German woman who, in fact, is a pure young girl who has fallen under the spell of a sorcerer.
(iii) The poem contains:
 (a) exquisitely poetic lines.
 (b) grotesque musical tones.
 (c) element of supernaturalism.
 (d) an atmosphere of awfulness.

3. The Rime of the Ancient Mariner

(i) It is Coleridge's most famous poem and as Long points out, "one of the world's masterpieces."
(ii) It was a part of the Lyrical Ballads which appeared in 1798.
(iii) The story is too well-known to be recounted.
(iv) Some of the important elements in the poem are:
 (a) supernaturalism
 (b) wonderful narration
 (c) triumph of story-telling art
 (d) exquisite poetry
 (e) sweet, luscious music
 (f) triumph of simplicity over complexity
 (g) wonderfully smooth sailing lines
 (h) a well-knit plot and anecdotes
 (i) an element of suspense
 (j) a true vindication of the moral purpose
 (k) a queer atmosphere
 (l) exact geographical positions
 (m) gorgeous scenery, as if painted.

(n) deep pathos
(o) value of repentance
(p) futility of boastful human endeavours.
(q) final predominance of fate and mysterious divine power ruling over mankind and all creatures.
(r) a true account of the life on the sea during Coleridge's days.
(s) freedom from obscurity of any sort despite the element of mystery and suspense.
(t) vindication of the "willing suspension of disbelief, etc. etc.

Coleridge's Shorter poems

Some of such poems are

1. Ode on Dejection
2. Frost at Midnight
3. Fears in Solitude
4. Love Poems
5. Hymn Before Sunrise in the Vale of Chamouni
6. Work without Hope
7. Religious Musing, etc.

Prose works

1. His most well-known prose-work is Biographia Literaria, or Sketches of My Literary Life and Opinions (1817).

2. His other prose works are :
   (i) Aids to Reflection (1815)
   (ii) Lectures on Shakespeare (1849)

As a Philosopher

As such, he was greatly influenced by the German idealistic philosophy which he introduced into England.

As a Music lover and critic

It is well-known that he loved music and was a keen, constructive critic of it.

Some extracts from his poems are given below :

(from the Rime of the Ancient Mariner)

(i) I took the oars: the Pilot's boy,
Who now doth crazy go,
Laughed loud and long, and all the while
His eyes went to and fro,
"Ha! ha!" quoth he, "full plain I see,
The Devil knows how to row."
And now, all in my own countree,
I stood on the firm land!
The Hermit stepped forth from the boat,
And scarcely he could stand.
"O shrieve me, shrieve me, holy man!"
The Hermit crossed his brow.
"Say quick," quoth he, "I bid thee say—
What manner of man art thou?"
Forthwith this frame of mine was wrenched
With a woful agony,
Which forced me to begin my tale;
And then it left me free.
Since then, at an uncertain hour,
That agony returns:
And till my ghastly tale is told,
This heart within me burns,
I pass, like night, from land to land;
I have strange power of speech;
That moment that his face I see,
I know the man that must hear me;
To him my tale I teach.
What loud uproar bursts from the door!
The wedding-guests are there:
But in the garden-bower the bride
And hark the little vesper bell,
Which biddeth me to prayer!
O Wedding-Guest! this sould hath been
Alone on a wide wide sea:
So lonely 'twas, that God himself
Scarce seemed there to be.

(ii) O sweeter than the marriage-feast,
'Tis sweeter far to me,
To walk together to the kirk
With a goodly company!—
To walk together to the kirk,
And all together pray,
While each to his great Father bends,
Old men, and babes, and loving friends
And youths and maidens gay!
Farewell, farewell! but this I tell
To thee, thou Wedding-Guest!
He prayeth well, who loveth well
Both man and bird and beast.
He prayeth best, who loveth best
All things both great and small;
For the dear God who loveth us,
He made and loveth all.'
The Mariner, whose eye is bright,
Whose beard with age is hoar,
Is gone: and now the Wedding-Guest
Turned from the bridegroom's door.
He went like one that hath been stunned,
And is of sense forlorn:
A sadder and a wiser man,
He rose the morrow morn.

(**Note :** Given below are :
(i) Kubla Khan a fragment (full poem)
(ii) Love (extract)
(iii) Reflections on Having Left A Place of Retirement:

From Kubla Khan

In Xanadu did Kubla Khan
A stately pleasure-dome decree:
Where Alph, the sacred river, ran
Through caverns measureless to man
Down to a sunless sea.
So twice five miles of fertile ground
With walls and towers were girdled round:

And there were gardens bright with sinuous rills,
Where blossomed many an incense-bearing tree;
And here were forests ancient as the hills,
Enfolding sunny spots of greenery.

But oh! that deep romantic chasm which slanted
Down the green hill athwart a cedarn cover!
A savage place! as holy and enchanted
As e'er beneath a waning moon was haunted
By woman wailing for her demon-lover!
And from this chasm, with ceaseless turmoil seething,
As if this earth in fast thick pants were breathing,
A mighty fountain momently was forced :
Amid whose swft half-intermitted burst
Huge fragments vaulted like rebounding hail,
Or chaffy grain beneath the thresher's flail;
And 'mid these dancing rocks at once and ever
It flung up momently the sacred river.
Five miles meandering with a mazy motion
Through wood and dale the sacred river ran,
Then reached the caverns measureless to man,
And sank in tumult to a lifeless ocean :
And 'mid this tumult Kubla heard from far
Ancestral voices prophesying war!
The shadow of the dome of pleasure
Floated midway on the waves;
Where was heard the mingled measure
From the fountain and the caves.
It was a miracle of rare device,
A sunny pleasure-dome with caves of ice!
A damsel with a dulcimer
In a vision once I saw:
It was an Abyssinian maid,
And on her dulcimer she played,
Singing of Mount Abora,
Could I revive within me
Her symphony and song,
To such a deep delight 'twould win me,
That with music loud and long,
I would build that dome in air,
That sunny dome! those caves of ice!
And all who heard should see them there,
And all should cry, Beware! Beware!
His flashing eyes, his floating hair!
Weave a circle round him thrice,
And close your eyes with holy dread,
For he on honey-dew hath fed,
And drunk the milk of Paradise.

Love

All thoughts, all passions, all delights,
Whatever stirs this mortal frame,
All are but ministers of Love,
And feed his sacred flame.
Oft in my waking dreams do I
Live o'er again that happy hour,
When midway on the mount I lay,
Beside the ruined tower.
The moonshine, stealing o'er the scene,
Had blended with the lights of eve;
And she was there, my hope, my joy,
My own dear Genevieve!

Reflections on Having Left a Place of Retirement

Low was our pretty Cot: our tallest Rose
Peeped at the chamber-window. We could hear
At silent noon, and eve, and early morn,
The sea's faint murmur. In the open air
Our Myrtles blossom'd; and across the porch
Thick Jasmines twined: the little landscape round
Was green and woody, and refreshed the eye,
It was a spot which you might aptly call
The Valley of Seclusion! Once I saw
(Hallowing his Sabbath-day by quietness)
A wealthy son of Commerce saunter by,
Bristowa's citizen : methought, it calmed
His thirst of idle gold, and made him muse
With wiser feelings; for the paused, and looked
With a pleased sadness, and gazed all around,
Then eyed our Cottage, and gazed round again,
And sighed, and said, it was Blessed Place.
And we *were* blessed. Oft with patient ear
Long-listening to the viewless skylark's note
(Viewless, or haply for a moment seen
Gleaming on sunny wings) in whispered tones
I've said to my beloved, "Such, sweet Girl!
The inobtrusive song of Happiness,
Unearthly minstrelsy! then only heard
When the Soul seeks to hear; when all is hush'd
And the Heart listens!"

(**Note :** It is clear that Coleridge is the master of :

(i) Creating supernatural atmosphere
(ii) Clear, simple, highly impressive musical lines
(iii) A certain philosophical tone pervading as backdrop.

NATHARIEL HAWTHORNE (1804-64)

1. He regarded himself as a romancer rather than a novelist.
2. He chiefly employed the device of symbolism in his novels.
3. He is a great novelist and allegorist.
4. He is constantly preoccupied with the themes of sin and evil, believing pride to be the principal sin.
5. Some of his works are :
(i) The Scarlet Letter (1850)
(ii) The House of Seven Gables (1851)
(iii) The Blithedale Romance (1852)
(iv) The Marble Faun (1860)

6. *(i)* He had already produced a juvenile novel; and a few short stories which were later on published "Twice Told Tales" in 1837.

(ii) Some of these stories had earlier appeared in the "The Token."

(iii) Some of the popular stories were :

(a) An Old Woman's Tale

(b) My Kinsman, Major Molinex (1832)

(c) The Gray Champion (1832)

(d) Young Goodman Brown (1835)

(e) Wakefield (1835), etc.

7. In 1846, his collection of 25 short stories, historical sketches and histories was published under the caption "Moses From an Old Mouse."

8. In 1884, he produced a history book for children under the caption: "Grandfather's Chair."

Certain Characteristics of Hawthorne

1. He is a great symbolist and allegorist.
2. He is fond of writing romances.
3. He is interested in the study of the Puritan conscience and the Calvinistic idea of the damnation of Man.
4. His chief theme is the impact of sin on the human soul.
5. He tries to introduce the supernatural element in his works, as, for instance, in The Scarlet Letter.
6. Henry James has complained of a lack of intricacy in the rendering of human reality in his novels.
7. Another complaint against him is the tightness of structure (as in the Scarlet Letter) which sometimes encroaches upon his otherwise imaginative and suggestive poetic style.
8. A deep psychoanalytic approach is writ large on almost every page of his novels.
9. The intention to destroy the human soul is something unpardonable in his view.
10. The social, economic, religious and political aspects emerge in one sweep in his novels.
11. His novels present suggestive comments on such themes as :

(i) Puritanism in general.

(ii) Human relations on all planes such as:

(a) sexual

(b) conjugal

(c) filial, etc.

(iii) mystery of life.

(iv) Characteristics of sin.

(v) value of repentance and redemption.

(vi) relationship with the past.

(vii) unexplored human psyche.

(viii) deviation of best intentions from their path.

(ix) Calvinistic Puritanism which enshrines chiefly:

(a) depravity of man

(b) Pre-destined nature of punishment for sinfulness.

(c) Not all are saved.

(d) God's grace has its own independent way of working.

(e) Those saved have to surrender their will to God.

12. Nature (as in the Forest Scene in The Scarlet Letter) as the representative of the Immanent Spirit.

13. The divine spark in man himself, (as in Pearl's elfin beauty).

Significance of intuition and imagination, as per transcendental doctrine, *vis-a-vis* the English eighteenth century stress correctness and refinement. (This may not be so marked in Hawthorne as in the main Transcendentalists like Emerson and Thoreau).

14. The intrinsic coherence of symbols despite their apparent incoherence, etc., etc.

ERNEST HEMINGWAY (1899-1961)

1. His novels and stories portray the real events honestly, where toughness and courage are the rule rather than the exception and emotion of often held in abeyance—a method reminiscent of Ezra Pound by whom he was influenced immensely.

2. Some of his works are :

(i) The Sun Also Rises (1926)

(ii) A Farewell To Arms (1929)

(iii) To Have and Have Not (1937)

(iv) For Whom the Bell Tolls (1940)

(v) The Old Man and The Sea (1952)
(This novelette won him the Nobel Prize in 1954)

3. He committed suicide in 1961.

4. He wrote several other books on :

(i) fiction

(ii) bull fighting

(iii) big game hunting in Africa, etc.

(iv) stories

5. Among his works which appeared posthumously, there are a number of poems also.

EMILY DICKINSON (1830-86)

1. She led a secluded life during the last 25 years of her life.

2. During this period, she cut herself up from all worldly contact except with some intimate friends.

3. *(i)* In her life she wrote more than one thousand lyrics, but she never cared to get them published during her lifetime.

(ii) During her life, only six of her poems were published.

4. Her poems often are about :

(i) life and death.

(ii) the mystery of death.

(iii) some mystic experiences.
(iv) visions.
(v) sound comments on various aspects of human life and destiny.
(vi) a sympathetic attitude to pathos of life.
(vii) expression of a poignant wit.

5. They contain :
(i) economy of expression.
(ii) novelty of expression.
(iii) new experiments even in simple old metres.
(iv) an aphoristic tone at places.
(v) mystic obscurity or ambiguity at other places.

6. After her death, her poems were published in a number of volumes.

Some of her well-known poems are mentioned below:

1. Success is counted Sweetest:
"Success is counted sweetest
By those who ne'er succeed.
To comprehend a nectar
Requires sorest need."
2. This is my Letter to The World.
3. I Never Saw a Moor
4. I Had Been Hungry
5. Hope is The Thing With Feathers
6. A Bird Came Down The Walk
7. The Sky is Low, the Clouds are Mean
8. A Light Exists in Spring
9. Before I God My Eye Put Out
10. The Heart Asks Pleasure First
11. The Brain Is Wider Than the Sky
12. I Taste A Liquor Never Brewed
13. A Narrow Fellow in the Grass
14. I Heard a Buzz when I Died
15. I Years Had Been from Home
16. A Bird Came Down the Walk
17. I Felt A Funeral in My Brain
18. Safe In Their Alabaster Chambers
19. Much Madness is Divinest Sense
20. The Soul Selects Her Own Society, etc.

Here are some extracts from her works :

1. Because I could not stop for Death,
He kindly stopped for me;
The carriage held but just ourselves
And Immortality. —*The Chariot*

2. How dreary to be somebody!
How public, like a frog
To tell your name the livelong day
To an admiring bog! —*Life*

3. I never saw a moor,
I never saw the sea;
Yet know I how the heather looks,
And what a wave must be.
—*Time and Eternity*

4. My life closed twice before its, close;
It yet remains to see
It Immortality unveil
A third event to me. —*Parting*

5. How much can come
And much can go,
And yet abide the world!
—*There Came a Wind*

6. Parting is all we know of heaven,
And all we need of hell.
—*Parting*

G.B. SHAW (1856-1950)

Life

1. He was born in Dublin, Ireland in a Protestant middle-class family.

2. His parents were, however, originally of English stock.

3. As Long points out, "Of music he knew a little, of art or drama nothing; but he had a naturally keen intellect, a vast conceit and what the Irish call a 'gift of gab'".

4. At first, he became a journalist living by his poem, a drama critic and only later a dramatist proper.

5. Before becoming a dramatist, he tried his hand at the novel, but all his novels flopped, *e.g.*
(i) The Irrational Knot
(ii) Love Among the Artists
(iii) An Unsocial Socialist, etc.

Works

1. (i) "Widowers' Houses" staged in 1893 was his first comedy.
(ii) It gave him some popularity and, surely, a new type of prose drama was on its way.

2. Then appeared his following dramas included in "Plays Pleasant and Unpleasant" (1898)
(i) The Philanderer
(ii) Mrs. Warren's Profession
(iii) Arms and the Man
(iv) Candida
(v) The Man of Destiny
(vi) You Never Can Tell

3. Thereafter appeared the following plays which were included in "Three Plays for Puritans, (1901):
(i) The Devil's Disciple
(ii) Caesar and Cleopatra
(iii) Captain Brassbound's Conversion

4. 'Man and Superman' appeared in 1903.

5. Thereafter appeared the following plays :
(i) John Bull's Other Island
(ii) Major Barbara
(iii) How he lied to her husband
(iv) The Doctor's Dilemma
(v) Getting Married
(vi) The Showing-up of Blanco Posnet

(vii) Misalliance
(viii) Fanny's First Play
(ix) Androcles and the Lion
(x) Pygmalion

6. Still later appeared in 1917:
(i) The Inca of Peruslam
(ii) Augustus does his Bit
(iii) Heartbreak House
(iv) Back to Methuselah (1920)
(v) Saint Joan (1923)
(For this, he received the Nobel Prize in 1925)
(vi) The Apple Cart (1929)
(vii) Too True to be Good (1932)
(viii) Geneva 1939
(ix) In Good King Charles's Golden Days (1939)

(**Note :** As stated above, Shaw received the Nobel Prize for literature on Saint Joan in 1925. Though Man and Superman is perhaps his most popular play, many regard Saint Joan as his best play. Given below are extracts from the Preface to the play and from the play itself :

Extracts from Preface to "Saint Joan" by G.B. Shaw

Joan and Socrates

If Joan had been malicious, selfish, cowardly, or stupid, she would have been one of the most odious persons known to history instead of one of the most attractive. If she had been old enough to know the effect she was producing on the men whom she humiliated by being right when they were wrong, and had learned to flatter and manage them, she might have lived as long as Queen Elizabeth. But she was too young and rustical and inexperienced to have any such arts. When she was thwarted by men whom she thought fools, she made no secret of her opinion of them or her impatience with their folly; and she was naive enough to expect them to be obliged to her for setting them right and keeping them out of mischief. Now it is always hard for superior wits to understand the fury roused by their exposures of the stupidities of comparative dollords. Even Socrates for all his age and experience, did not defend himself at his trial like a man who understood the long accumulated fury that had burst on him, and was clamouring for his death. His accuser, if born 2300 years later, might have been picked out of any first class carriage on a suburban railway during the evening or morning rush from or to the City; for he had really nothing to say except that he and his like could not endure being shewn up as idiots every time Socrates opened his mouth. Socrates, unconscious of this, was paralyzed by his sense that somehow he was missing the point of the attack. He petered out after he had established the fact that he was an old soldier and a man of honorable life, and that his accuser was a silly snob. He had no suspicion of the extent to which his mental superiority had roused fear and hatred against him in the hearts of men towards whom he was conscious of nothing but good will and good service.

Contrast with Napoleon

If Socrates was as innocent as this at the age of seventy, it may be imagined how innocent Joan was at the age of seventeen. Now Socrates was a man of argument, operating slowly and peacefully on men's minds, whereas Joan was a woman of action, operating with impetuous violence on thier bodies. That, no doubt, is why the contemporaries of Socrates endured him so long, and why Joan was destroyed before she was fully grown. But both of them combined terrifying ability with a frankness, personal modesty and benevolence which made the furious dislike to which they fell victims absolutely unreasonable, and therefore inapprehensible by themselves. Napoleon, also possessed of terrifying ability, but neither frank nor disinterested, had no illusions as to the nature of his popularity. When he was asked how the world would take his death he said it would give a gasp of relief. But it is not so easy for mental giants who neither hate nor intend to injure their fellows to realize that nevertheless their fellows hate mental giants and would like to destroy them, not only enviously because the juxtaposition of a superior wounds their vanity, but quite humbly and honestly because it frightens them. Fear will drive men to any extreme; and the fear inspired by a superior being is a mystery which cannot be reasoned away. Being immeasurable it is unbearable when there is no presumption or guarantee of its benevolence and moral responsibility: in other words, when it has no official status. The legal and conventional superiority of Herod and Pilate, and of Annas and Caiaphas, inspires fear; but the fear, being a reasonable fear of measurable and avoidable consequences which seem salutary and protective, is bearable; whilst the strange superiority of Christ and the fear it inspires elicit a shriek of Crucify Him from all who cannot divine its benevolence. Socrates has to drink the hemlock, Christ to hang on the cross, and Joan to burn at the stake, whilst Napoleon, though he ends in St. Helena, at least dies in his bed there; and many terrifying but quite comprehensible official scoundrels die natural deaths in all the glory of the kingdoms of this world, proving that it is far more dangerous to be a saint than to be a conqueror. Those who have been both, like Mahomet and Joan, have found that it is the conqueror who must save the saint, and that defeat and capture mean martyrdom. Joan was burnt without a hand lifted on her own side to save her. The comrades she had led to victory and the enemies she had disgraced and defeated, the French king she had crowned and the English king whose crown she had kicked into the Loire, were equally glad to be rid of her.

Was Joan Innocent or Guilty?

As this result could have been produced by a crapulous inferiority as well as by a sublime supriority, the question which of the two was operative in Joan's case has to be faced. It was decided against her by her contemporaries after a very careful and conscientious trial; and the reversal of the verdict twenty-five years later, in form a rehabilitation of Joan, was really only a confirmation of the validity of the coronation of Charles VII. It is the more impressive reversal by a unanimous Posterity, culminating in her canonization, that has quashed the original proceedings, and put her judges on their trial, which so far, has been much more unfair than their trial of her. Nevertheless the rehabilitation of 1456, corrupt job as it was, really did produce evidence enough to satisfy all reasonable critics that Joan was not a common termagant, not a harlot, not a with, not a blasphemer no more an idolater than the Pope himself...."

Joan's Voices and Visions

Joan's voices and visions have played many tricks with her reputation. They have been held to prove that she was mad, that she was a liar and impostor, that she was a sorceress (she was burned for this), and finally that she was a saint....... Socrates, Luther, Swedenborg, Blake saw visions and heard voices just as Saint Francis and Saint Joan did.... Gravitation, being a reasoned hypothesis which fitted remarkably well into the Copernicus version of the observed physical facts of the universe, established Newton's reputation for extraordinary intelligence, and would have done so no matter how fantastically he had arrived at it. Yet his theory of gravitation is not so impressive a mental feat as his astounding chronology, which establishes him as the king of mental conjurors, but a Bedlamite king whose authority no one now accepts. On the subject of the eleventh horn of the beast seen by the prophet Daniel he was more fantastic than Joan, because his imagination was not dramatic but mathematical and therefore extraordinarily susceptible to numbers: indeed if all his works were lost except his chronology we should say that he was as mad as a hatter. As it is, who dares diagnose Newton as a madman?

In the same way Joan must be judged a sane woman in spite of her voices because they never gave her any advice that might not have come to her from her mother wit exactly as gravitation came to Newton. We can all see now, especially since the late war threw so many of our women into military life, that Joan's compaigning could not have been carried on in petticoats. This was not only because she did a man's work, but because it was morally necessary that sex should be left out of the question as between her and her comrades-in-arms. She gave this reason herself when she was pressed on the subject; and the fact that this entirely reasonable necessity came to her imagination first as an order from God delivered through the mouth of Saint Catherine does not prove that she was mad. The soundness of the order proves that she was usually sane; but its form proves that her dramatic imagination played tricks with her senses. Her policy was also quite sound: nobody dipsutes that the relief of Orleans, followed up by the coronation at Rheims of the Dauphin as a counterblow to the suspicions then current of his legitimacy and consequently of his title, were military and political masterstrokes that saved France. They might have been planned by Napoleon or any other illusionproof genius. They came to Joan as an instruction from her Counsel, as she called her visionary saints; but she was none the less an able leader of men for imagining her ideas in this way.

The Evolutionary Appetite

What then is the modern view of Joan's voices and visions and messages from God? The nineteenth century said that they were delusions, but that as she was a pretty girl, and has been abominably ill-treated and finally done to death by a superstitious rabble of medieval priests hounded on by a corrupt political bishop, it must be assumed that she was the innocent dupe of these delusions. The twentieth century finds this explanation too vapidly common-place and demands something more mystic. I think the twentieth century is right, because an explanation which amounts to Joan being mentally defective instead of, as she obviously was, mentally excessive, will not wash. I cannot believe, nor, if I could, could I expect all my readers to believe, as Joan did, that three ocularly visible well dressed persons, named respectively Saint Catherine, Saint Margaret, and Saint Michael, came down from heaven and gave her certain instructions with which they were charged by God for her. Not that such a belief would be more improbable or fantastic than some modern beliefs which we all swallow; but there are fashions and family habits in belief, and it happens that, my fashion being Victorian and my family habit Protestant, I find myself unable to attach any such obective validity to the form of Joan's visions.

But that there are forces at work which use individuals for purposes far transcending the purpose of keeping these individuals alive and prosperous and respectable and safe and happy in the middle station in life, which is all any good bourgeois can reasonably require, is established by the fact that men will, in the pursuit of knowledge and of social readjustments for which they will not be penny the better, and are indeed often many pence the worse, face poverty, infamy, exile, imprisonment, dreadful hardship, and death. Even the selfish pursuit of personal power does not nerve men to efforts and sacrifies which are eagerly made in pursuit of extensions of our power over nature, though these extensions may not touch the personal life of the seeker at any point. There is no more mystery about this appetite for knowledge and power than about the appetite for food: both are known as facts and as facts only, the difference between them being that the appetite for food is necessary to the life of the hungry man and is therefore a personal appetite, whereas the other is an appetite for evolution; and therefore a superpersonal need.

The diverse manner in which our imaginations dramatize the approach of the superpersonal forces is a problem for the psychologist, not for the historian. Only, the historian must understand that visionaries are neither impostors nor lunatics. It is one thing to say that the figure

Joan recognized as St. Catherine was not really St. Catherine, but the dramatization by Joan's imagination of that pressure upon her of the driving force that is behind evolution which I have just called the evolutionary appetite. It is quite another to class her visions with the vision of two moons seen by a drunken person, or with Brocken spectres, echoes and the like. Saint Catherine's instructions were far too cogent for that; and the simplest French peasant who believes in apparitions of celestial personages to favored mortals is nearer to the scientific truth about Joan than the Rationalist and Materialist historians and essayists..... If Joan was mad, all Christendom was mad too...."

A Void in The Elizabethan Drama

I have, however, one advantage over the Elizabethans. I write in full view of the Middle Ages, which may be said to have been rediscovered in the middle of the nineteenth century after an eclipse of about four hundred and fifty years. The Renascence of antique literature and art in the sixteenth century, and the lusty growth of Capitalism, between them buried the Middle Ages; and the resurrection is a second Renascence. Now there is not a breath of medieval atmosphere in Shakespeare's histories. His John of Gaun is like a study of the old age of Drake. Although he was a Catholic by family tradition, his figures are all intensely Protestant, indvidualist, sceptical, self-centred in everything but their love affairs and completely personal and selfish even in them. His kings are not statesmen: his cardinals have no religion: a novice can read his plays from one end to the other without learning that the world finally governed by forces expressing themselves in religions and laws which make epochs rather than by vulgarly ambitious individuals who make rows. The divinity which shapes our ends, rough hew them how we will, is mentioned fatalistically only to be forgotten immediately like a passing vague apprehension. To Shakespeare as to Mark Twain, Cauchon would have been a tyrant and bully instead of a Catholic, and the Inquisitor Lemaitre would have been a Sadist instead of a lawyer. Warwick would have had not more feudal quality than his successor the King Maker has in the play of Henry VI. We should have seen them all completely satisfied that if they would only to their own selves be true they could not then be false to any man (a precept which represents the reaction against medievalism at its interest) as if they were being in the air, without public responsibilities of any kind. All Shakespare's characters are so: that is why they seem natural to our middle classes, who are comfortable and irresponsible at other people's expense, and are neither ashamed of the condition nor even conscious of it. Nature abhors this vacuum in Shakespeare; and I have taken care to let the medieval atmosphere blow through my play freely. Those who see it performed will not mistake the starting event it records for a mere personal accident. They will have before them not only the visible and human puppets, but the Church, the Inquisition, the Feudal System, with divine inspiration always beating against their too inelastic limits: all more terrible in their dramatic force than any of the little mortal figures clanking about in plate armor or moving silently in the frocks and hoods of the order of St Dominic.

Tragedy, not Melodrama

There are no villains in the piece. Crime, like disease, is not interesting: it is something to be done away with by general consent, and that is all about it. It is what men do at their best, with good intentions, and what normal men and women find that they must and will do in spite of their intentions, that really concern us. The rascally bishop and the cruel inquisitor of Mark Twain and Andrew Lang are as dull as pickpockets; and they reduce Joan to the level of the even less interesting person whose pocket is picked. I have represented both of them as capable and eloquent exponents of The Church Militant and The ChurchLitigant, because only by doing so can I maintain my drama on the level of high tragedy and save it from becoming a mere police court sensation. A villain in a play can never be anything more than *a diabolus ex machina*, possibly a more exciting expedient than *a deus ex machina*, but both equally mechanical, and therefore interesting only as mechanism. It is, I repeat, what normally innocent people do that concerns us; and if Joan had not been burnt by normally innocent people in the energy of their righteousness her death at their hands would have no more significance than Tokyo earthquake, which burnt a great many maidens. The tragedy of such murders is that they are not committed by murderers. They are judicial murders; pious murders; and this contradiction at once brings an element of comedy into the tragedy: the angels may weep at the murder, but the gods laugh at the murderers.

Extracts from Saint Joan

Here are some extracts from the play :

Joan [*trenchant and masterful*] Blethers! We are all like that to begin with. I shall put courage into thee.

Charles: But I don't want to have courage put into me. I want to sleep in a comfortable bed, and not live in continual terror of being killed or wounded. Put courage into the others, and let them have their bellyful of fighting; but let me alone.

Joan: It's no use, Charlie: thou must face what God puts on thee. If thou fail to make thyself king, thoult be a beggar: what else art fit for? Come! Let me see thee sitting on the throne. I have looked forward to that.

Charles: What is the good of sitting on the throne when the other fellows give all the orders? However! [*he sits enthroned, a piteous figure*] here is the king for you! Look your fill at the poor devil.

Joan: Thourt not king yet, lad: thourt but Dauphin. Be not led away by them around thee. Dressing up don't fill empty noddle. I know the people: the real people that make thy bread for thee; and I tell thee they count no man king of France until the holy oil has been poured on his hair, and himself consecrated and crowned in Rheims

Cathedral. And thou needs new clothes, Charlie. Why does not Queen look after thee properly?

Charles: We're too poor. She wants all the money we can spare to put on her own back. Besides, I like to see her beautifully dressed; and I don't care what I wear myself: I should look ugly anyhow.

Joan: There is some good in thee, Charlie; but it is not yet a king's good.

Charles: We shall see I am not such a fool as I look. I have my eyes open; and I can tell you that one good treaty is worth ten good fights. These fighting fellows lose all on the treaties that they gain on the fights. If we can only have a treaty, the english are sure to have the worst of it, because they are better at fighting than at thinking.

Joan: If the English win, it is they that will make the treaty: and then God help poor France! Thou must fight, Charlie, whether thou will or no. I will go first to hearten thee. We must take our courage in both hands : aye, and pray for it with both hands too.

Charles: [*descending from his throne and again crossing the room to escape from her dominating urgency*] Oh do stop talking about God and praying. I cant bear people who are always praying. Isnt it bad enough to have to do it at the proper times?

Joan: [*pitying him*] Thou poor child, thou hast never prayed in the life. I must teach thee from the beginning.

Charles: I am not a child: I am a grown man and a father; and I will not be taught any more.

Joan: Aye, you have a little son. He that will be Louis the Elventh when you die. Would you not fight for him?

Charles: No: a horrid boy. He hates me. He hates everybody, selfish little beast! I dont want to be bothered with children. I dont want to be a father; and I don't want to be a son: especially a son of St Louis. I don't want to be any of these fine things you all have your heads full of: I want to be Just what I am. Why cant you mind your own business. and let me mind mine?

Joan: [*again contemptuous*] Minding your own business is like minding your own body; it's the shortest way to make yourself sick. What is my business? Helping mother at home. What is thine? Petting lapdogs and sucking sugar-sticks. I call that muck. I tell thee it is God's business we are here to do: not our own. I have a message to thee from God; and though must listen to it, though thy heart break with the terror of it.

Charles: I don't want a message; but can you tell me any secrets? Can you do any cures? Can you turn lead into gold, or anything of that sort?

Joan: I can turn thee into a king, in Rheims Cathedral; and that is a miracle that will take some doing, it seems.

Charles: If we go to Rheims, and have a coronation, Anne will want new dresses. We can't afford them. I am all right as I am.

Joan: In God's name, then, let us cross the bridge, and fall on them.

Dunois: It seems simple; but it cannot be done.

Joan: Who says so?

Dunois: I say so; and older and wiser heads than mind are of the same opinion.

Joan: [*roundly*] Then your older and wiser heads are fatheads: they have made a fool of you; and now they want to make a fool of me too, bringing me to the wrong side of the river. Do you not know that I bring you better help than ever came to any general or any town?

Dunois: [*smiling patiently*] Your own?

Joan: No: the help and counsel of the King of Heaven. Which is the way to the bridge?

Dunois: You are impatient, Maid.

Joan: Is this a time for patience? Our enemy is at our gates; and here we stand doing nothing. Oh, why are you not fighting? Listen to me: I will deliver you from fear. I—

Dunois: [*laughing heartily, and waving her off*] No, no, my girl: if you delivered me from fear I should be a good knight for a story book, but a very bad commander of the army. Come! let me begin to make a soldier of you. [*He takes her to the water's edge*]. Do you see those two forts at this end of the bridge? the big ones?

Joan: Yes. Are they ours or the goddams'?

Dunois: Be quiet, and listen to me. If I were in either of those forts with only ten men I could hold it against an army. The English have more than ten times ten goddams in those forts to hold them against us.

Joan: They cannot hold them against God. God did not give them the land under those forts: they stole it from Him. He gave it to us. I will take those forts.

Dunois: Single-handed?

Joan: Our men will take them. I will lead them.

Dunois: Not a man will follow you.

Joan: I will not look back to see whether anyone is following me.

Dunois: [*recognizing her mettle, and clapping her heartily on the shoulder*] Good. You have the makings of a soldier in you. You are in love with war.

Joan: [*startled*] Oh! And the Archbishop said I was in love with religion.

Dunois: I, God forgive me, am a little in love with war myself, the ugly devil! I am like a man with two wives. Do you want to be like a woman with two husbands?

Joan: [*matter-of-fact*] I will never take a husband. A man in Toul took an action against me for a breach of promise; but I never promised him. I am soldier: I do not want to be thought of as a woman. I will not dress as a woman. I do not care for the things women care for. They dream of lovers, and of money. I dream of leading a charge, and of placing the big guns. You soldiers do not know how to use the big guns: you think you can win battles with a great noise and smoke.

Dunois: [*with a shrug*] True. Half the time artillery is more trouble than it is worth.

Joan: Aye, lad; but you cannot fight stone walls with horses: you must have guns, and much bigger guns too.

Dunois: [*grinning at her familiarity, and echoing it*] Aye, lass; but a good heart and a stout ladder will get over the stoniest wall.

Joan: I will be first up the ladder when we reach the fort, Bastard. I dare you to follow me.

Dunois: You must not dare a staff officer, Joan: only company officers are allowed to indulge in displays of personal courage. Besides, you must know that I welcome you as a saint, not as a soldier. I have daredevils enough at my calls, if they could help me.

Joan: I am not a daredevil: I am a servant of God. My sword is sacred: I found it behind the altar in the church of St. Catherine, where God hid it for me; and I may not strike a blow with it. My heart is full of courage, not of anger. I will lead; and your men will follow: that is all I can do. But I must do it: you shall not stop me.

ROBERT FROST (1874-1963)

1. He could not get good response from the American publishers in the beginning.

2. (*i*) His first volume of poems: "*A Boy's Will*" was published in 1913 by an English publisher.
   (*ii*) His second volume "*North of Boston*" was published by the same publisher in 1914.
   (*iii*) His first poem "The Butterfly" had already appeared in "The Independent" (New York) in 1894.

3. When he lived in Beaconsfield, England, most of his friends were Georgian poets.

4. Some of his other works which appeared later were:
   (*i*) Mountain Interval (1916)
   (*ii*) New Hampshire.... (1923)
   (*iii*) West-Running Brook (1928)
   (*iv*) A Further Range (1936)
   (*v*) A Witness Tree (1942)
   (*vi*) Steeple Bush (1947)

5. His "Complete Poems" appeared in 1949, at the end of which were placed two of his verse dramas:
   (*i*) A Masque of Reason (1945) and
   (*ii*) A Masque of Mercy (1947)

6. In his life, Frost received four Pulitzer Prizes, Poet Laureateship of New England and several other honours.

7. Before his death, he had become a national poet.

8. In his "The Figure a Poem Makes" (1949) which is a kind of Preface to his "Collected Poems," he gave his comments on a poem :
   (*i*) "(A poem) begins in delight and ends in wisdom.... it runs a course of lucky events, and ends in a clarification of life...."
   (*ii*) "The artist.... matches a thing from some previous order in time and space into a new order."

9. Some of the more famous poems of Frost are :
   (*i*) Neither Out Far Nor in Deep
   (*ii*) Birches
   (*iii*) The Onset
   (*iv*) The Pasture
   (*v*) Provide, Provide
   (*vi*) Mending Wall
   (*vii*) The Road Not Taken
   (*viii*) After Apple-Picking
   (*ix*) Two Tramps in Mud Time
   (*x*) Stopping By Woods on a Snowy Evening
   (*xi*) Directive
   (*xii*) Meetting and Passing
   (*xiii*) The Gift Outright
   (*xiv*) A Considerable Speck
   (*xv*) The Death of a Hired Man
   (*xvi*) West, Running Brook
   (*xvii*) Home Burial
   (*xviii*) Departmental
   (*xix*) Snow
   (*xx*) The Tuft of Flowers
   (*xxi*) Mowing
   (*xxii*) Acquainted with the Night
   (*xxiii*) The Need of Being Versed in County Things
   (*xxiv*) I Will Sing You One—O
   (*xxv*) Blueberries, etc.

10. Frost is studied on several levels:
   (*i*) As an American poet
   (*ii*) As a poet of nature
   (*iii*) As a poet of New England
   (*iv*) As a Rural poet
   (*v*) As a Modern poet
   (*vi*) As a poet of Truth
   (*vii*) As a poet of known for new type or techniques, etc.
   (*viii*) As a poet of New England/of New Hampshire, in particular.

10. He was invited by President John F. Kennedy to recite his patriotic poem "The Gift Outright" at the inaugural ceremony.

Given below are extracts from some of his poems :

1. *From After Apple-Picking*

"I feel the ladder sway as the boughs bend.
And I keep hearing from the cellar bin
The rumbling sound
Of load on load of apples coming in.
For I have had too much
Of apple-picking: I am overtired
Of the great harvest I myself desired."

The lines show, *inter alia*, the truth of life: man gets tired of the excess of a thing he previously so much longed for.

2. *From Design*

"Like the ingredients of a witches' broth—
A snow-drop spider, a flower like froth,
....

The wayside blue and the innocent heal-all?
What brought the kindred spider to that height,
Then steered the white moth thither in the night?
What but design of darkness to appall?
If design govern govern a thing so small."

Sometimes, Frost is censured for lack of depth. But the lines given here direct human attention to the great puzzle whether there is any design in objects of nature, big and small.

3. *From Fire and Ice*

Some say the world will end in fire,
Some say in ice,
From what I've tasted of desire
I hold with those who favour fire,
But if I had to perish twice,
I think I know enough of hate
To say that for destruction ice
Is also great
And would suffice.

The lines clearly show Frost's appeal to mankind to give up hatred and excessive desire and have a faith in mutual co-operation, goodwill and love. This is what seems implied in the poem.

4. *From Mending Wall*

In this famous poem, there is clear appeal for good neighbourliness, brotherhood and mutual cooperation.

"Something there is that doesn't love a wall,
....
There where it is we do not need the wall:
He is all pine and I am apple orchard
My apple trees will never get across
And eat the cones under his pines.
I tell him.
He only says, "Good fences make good neighbours.'
....

Frost's Later Poetry

A number of critics have condemned Frost's later poetry as being cold, unsympathetic, unemotional and the like. Rendall Jarrell is one of them. This is what he says about his later poetry:

"I never dared be radical when young for fear it would make me conservative when old" is truthful and his conservatism affected his poetry to a considerable extent. In the later poetry of Frost, one gets a self-made man's political editorial, full of cracker-box, philosophizing, almanac joke-cracking—of a snake oil statesman's mysticism, one gets sentimentality and whimsicality, an arch complacency, a complacent archness, and one gets Homely Wisdom till the cows come home. Often the later Frost makes demands on himself that are minimum; he uses a little wit and an observation and a little sentiment to stuff, not very tight—a little sonnet, and it's not bad, but not good enough to matter either. The extremely rare, extremely wonderful, dramatic and narrative element that is more important than anything else in his early poetry almost disappears from his later poetry; in his later work the best poems are usually special-case, rather than all out; full-scale affairs. The youngest Frost is surrounded by his characters, living being he has known or created; the older Frost is alone. But it is loneliness that is responsible for the cold finality of poems like "Neither Out Far Nor in Deep" or "Design". Frost's latest books deserve little more than a footnote, since they have had few of his virtues, most of vices, and all of his tricks, the heathen who would be converted to Frost by them is hard to construct...."

Frost's later poetry has also been condemned by Yuvor Winters:

....Frost, the rustic realist of North of Boston, appears in his old age as a standard exemplar of irresponsible Romantic irony, of the kind of irony that has degenerated steadily from the moderately low level of Laforgue, through Pound, Eliot, Cummings and their younger imitators."

Cowley also has said a lot about his later poems as compared to earlier poems which he greatly praises as under:

"It is a pleasure to name over the poems of youth and age that become more vivid in one's memory with each new reading: the dramatic dialogues like "The Death of the Hired Man" and "The Witch of Coos." Besides half a dozen others almost equally good, the descriptions or narrations that turn imperceptibly into Aesop's fables, like "The Grindstone" and "Cow in Apple Time," and best of all the short lyrics like "The Pasture," "Now Close the Windows," "The Sound of the Trees," "Fire and Ice," "Stopping by Woods on a Snowy Evening" (always a favourite with anthologists). "To Earthward," "Tree at My Window," "Acquainted with the Night," "Neither out Far Nor in Deep," "Beech," "Wilful Homing," "Come In "and I could easily add to the list."

Frost's Faults: Frost has been taken to account by several critics on several counts some of which are mentioned below :

1. Lack of profundity and Defective Style

Yuvor Winters says :

"The result in the didactic poems is the perversity and incoherence of thought, the result in the narrative poem is either slightness of subject or a flat and uninteresting apprehension of the subject, the result in the symbolic lyrics is a disturbing location between the descriptive surface, which is frequently lovely, and the ultimate meaning, which is usually sentimental and unacceptable. The result in nearly all the poems is a measure of carelessness in the style, sometimes small and sometimes great, but usually evident; the conversational manner will naturally suit a poet who takes all experience so casually, and it is only natural that the conversational manner should often become very conversational indeed."

2. Lack of Intensity of Language : According to Leonard Unqer and William Van O'Connor :

"There are marked limitations to the tonal range within which Frost works and his successes. One does not find intensity of language in Frost's poetry. Intensity is not characteristic of the Yankee manner. It is not produced by understatement, whimsey and casualness. But while Frost does not commit himself to intensity, he can achieve concentration of meaning."

3. Lack of Dramatic and narrative element :

Randall Jarrell opines, in his later poetry:

"The extremely rare, the extremely wonderful, dramatic and narrative element that is more important than anything else in his early poetry almost disappears from his later poetry."

4. Defective Social Philosophy :

See Short Essays

Given below are some important dates in the life of Frost :

1874	Born in San Francisco, California, March 26. Son of William Prescott Frost. Jr. and Isabelle Moodie Frost.
1874-85	Boyhood in San Francisco.
1885	Moves to Lawrence, Massachusetts, with his mother and sister, after the death of his father.
1885-95	School years and young manhood in Lawrence, Massachusetts.
1892	Graduates from Lawrence High School. Co-valedictorian with Elinor Miriam White. Attends Dartmouth College for few months.
1894	"My Butterfly" published in the *independent*, November.
1895	Marries Elinor Miriam White.
1895	Birth of first child, Eliot.
1897-99	Attends Harward as an undergraduate.
1899	Birth of daughter, Lesley.
1900-10	maintains Farms (near West Derry), writes poetry, and teaches school (Pinkerton Academy, Derry Village) in New Hampshire.
1900	Birth of son, Carol.
1903	Birth of daughter, Irma.
1905	Birth of daughter, Marjorie.
1907	Birth of daughter, Elinor Bettina, who dies in infancy.
1911-12	Teaches psychology at New Hampshire State Normal School, Plymouth, New Hampshire.
1912-15	Goes to England with wife and four children. Writes and maintains farms in Buckinghamshire and Herefordshire.
1913	*A Boy's Will.*
1914	*North of Boston.*
1915	Returns to America from England. Settles on a farm, Franconia, New Hampshire.
1916	*Mountain Interval.* Elected to National Institute of Arts and Letters.
1917-20	Professor of English Amherst College.
1919	Moves to new farm, South Shaftesbury, Vermont.
1920	Co-founder, Bread Loaf School of English, Middlebury College.
1921-23	Poet in Residence, University of Michigan.
1923	*Selected Poems. New Hampshire.*
1923-25	Professor of English, Amherst College.
1924	Pulitzer Prize for *New Hampshire.*
1925-26	Fellow in Letters, University of Michigan.
1926-38	Professor of English, Amherst College. John Woodruff Simpson Foundation.
1928	*West-Running Book.*
1930	A Way Out (One-act play, first printed in 1917; produced at Amherst College, Northampton Academy of Music, February 24, 1919). *Collected Poems.*
1931	Pulitzer Prize for *Collected Poems.*
1934	Death of Marjorie Frost Fraser.
1936	*A Further Range*, Charles Eliot Norton, Professor of Poetry, Harvard University.
1937	Pulitzer Prize for *A Further Range.*
1938	Death of Elinor White Frost.
1939	*Collected Poems.*
1939-42	Ralph Waldo Emerson Fellow in Poetry. Harvard University.
1940	Death of Card Frost.
1942	*A Witness Tree.*
1943	Pulitzer Prize for *A Witness Tree.*
1943-49	Ticknor Fellow in the Humanities, Dartmouth College.
1945	A Masque of Reason.
1947	*Steeple Bush. A Masque of Mercy.*
1949	*Complete Poems.*
1957	Litt. D.S. at Oxford and Cambridge Universities and National University of Ireland.
1958	Consultant in Poetry to Library of Congress.
1959	Eighty-fifth Birthday Anniversary.
1961	Reads "The Gift Outright" at Presidential Inauguration, January 20.
1962	*In the Clearing* appeared.
1963	Died on January 22.

ARTHUR MILLER (1915-)

1. Whereas O'Neill was the pioneer of American drama in the pre-First World War period, Miller and Tennessee Williams were the only two important American dramatists during the post war period.

2. *(i)* He got admission in the University of Michigan in 1934.

(ii) There he won the first Avery Hopwood Prize for the play: "The Grass Still Grows."

3. Some of his important works are :

(i) *Situation Normal (1944):* It is a volume of sketches pertaining to life in the army.

(ii) *The Man Who Had All the Luck:* It is his first novelistic play.

(iii) Focus (1945): It is his successful novel.

(iv) All My Sons (1947): It is his first highly successful play.

(v) Death of a Salesman (1949): It is generally considered his masterpiece.

(vi) The Crucible (1953): This play is a kind of modern parable.

(vii) *(a)* A Memory of Two Mondays (1955)

(b) A View From the Bridge (1955)

In these two plays, Miller's main focus is on the common man.

(viii) Misfits: In this play, the central theme is the effect of maladjustment in a matrimonial alliance.

(ix) After the Fall (1964): This emotional play is modelled on the stream of consciousness technique.

(x) Incident at Vichy (1964): It is a long one-act play based on the theme of individual gilt.

(xi) The Prince (1968): This play depicts a family feud between two brothers.

ANITA DESAI (1937-)

1. She is a renowned novelist and short story writer.
2. Some of her famous novels are :

(i) Cry, the Peacock (1963)

(ii) Voices in the City (1965)

(iii) Bye-Bye, Blackbird (1971)

(iv) Fire on the Mountain (1977)

(v) Clear Light of Day (1980)

3. Her collection of short stories is captioned "Games at Twilight" (1978)

NISSIN EZEKIEL (1924-)

(A) 1. He is a famous Bombayite who has written on all aspects of the mega-city.

2. He worked as an editor of the Quest and Poetry India and later became President of PEN (India).

3. He is also a poetry and an art critic. He is, however better known as a poet.

4. Some of his works are :

(i) A Time to Change (1952)

(ii) Sixty Poems (1953)

(iii) The Third (1959)

(iv) The Unfinished Man (1960)

(v) The Exact Name (1969)

(vi) The Sleepwalkers (1969)

(vii) Snakeskin and Other Poems (1974)

(viii) Hymns in Darkness (1976)

(ix) Latter Day Psalms (1982).

5. He won the Sahitya Akademi Award in 1983.

6. He had worked as a good samaritan collecting funds from Israel for the poor Bombay Jews children before he had to be hospitalised for Alzhmeir's Disease.

(B) Some of his most famous poems are :

1. Night of the Scorpion.
2. Poet, Lover, Birdwatcher.

In one of his interviews, he said, "A winter needs a national or cultural identity, without that you become a series of limitations, echoes, responses, but you do not develop because there is nothing at the core to develop."

(Interview with N.E. : Indian Literary Review Vol. 1, No 10, Feb. 1979, Bombay).

K. N. DARUWALLA (1937-)

1. He wrote short stories and his critical work has also often appeared in journals, but he is known more for his poetry.

2. He is one of the judges who decide the poetic works at competitions held by the All-India (English) Poetry Society and Sahitya Akademi, New Delhi.

3. He won the Sahitya Akademi Award for Poetry in 1984.

4. In his poetry, he is virtually a social protester, but he is known for his vivid imagery and accuracy of description.

5. He is one of the most famous living Indian English poets, who says about himself, "I am not an urban writer and my poems are rooted in the rural landscape. My poetry is earthy, and I like to consciously keep it that way..."

6. In all, he has published nine collections of poems so far (Dec. 2002).

Some of them are :

(i) Under Orion (1970)

(ii) Apparition in April (1971)

(iii) Crossing of Rivers (1976)

(iv) Winter Poems (1980)

(v) The Keeper of the Dead (1982)

(vi) Landscapes (1987)

(vii) The Map-Maker (Pub. by Ravi Dayal) (2002)

7. His poems have appeared in :

(i) Opinion

(ii) Poetry Australia, Sydney

(iii) Transatlantic Review, London

(iv) Triquarterly—Illinois

8. Some of his well-known poems are :

(i) The Epileptic

(ii) The Ghaghra in Spate

(iii) Rumination

(iv) Death of a Bird

(v) Fire-Hymn

(vi) Routine

(vii) Old Sailor (The opening poem of "The Map Maker")

(viii) The Birth of Maya } included in "The

(ix) Draupadi } Map Maker"

9. The famous collection of his short stories is entitled : "Sword and Abyss."

10. Some of the qualities of his poetry are :

(i) faithful depiction of north Indian landscape.
(ii) element of social protest.
(iii) a bitter, satiric tone.
(iv) concrete statuesque imagery.
(v) complete surrender of self to the poetic art.
(vi) crude earthiness.
(vii) mainly a rural atmosphere.
(viii) bringing into full poetic display of his experience in the police department :

"A crowd senses a mishap before it sees one."

11. Here are some extracts from his poems :

1. "The nights move on; you go by other signs:
it is not dreams I wish to talk about,
The body speaks of its premositions:
and you must always hear the body out..."
from "Old Sailor."

2. "The travails of Draupadi are never-ending.
It seems some people have it
in their bleeding stars.
First exploited by the Pandavas,
five to one,
then by the Kauravas,
hundred to one
and now by the feminists in million."

3. "There was nothing, neither air nor substance, "Draupadi"
Not energy, nor ether,
Not thought nor dream....."
—*"The Birth of Maya"*

R.K. NARAYAN (1906-2001)

1. Of the three great novelists, Narayan, Anand and Rao, it is Narayan who has won the maximum accolade both in India and abroad.

2. One of his great achievements is his creation of the famous town of Malgudi like Hardy's Wessex.

3. Narayan is the true master of humour, irony, realism, romance and artistry.

4. Most of his novels and stories depict the life of people of South India.

5. It is sometimes held that Narayan lacks true pathos, genuine depth of feeling, realistic description of poverty and misery, the elements which go in for making a novelist a great one.

6. However, he has earned much popularity as a novelist, and within the range of his own art, he cannot be taken except with due regard and attention.

Some of his famous novels are :

1. Swami and Friends (1935)
2. Bachelor of Arts
3. The English Teacher
4. The Financial Expert
5. Mr. Sampath (1949)
6. The Guide (1958)
7. The Man-eater of Malgudi
8. The Dark Room (1939)
9. Waiting for the Mahatma
10. The Vendor of Sweets
11. The Painter of Signs (1976)

(He won the Sahitya Akademi Award for 'Guide' in 1961)

R. K. Narayan as a short story writer

1. Some of his stories have appeared in the following collections:

(i) Malgudi Days
(ii) Dodu and Other Stories
(iii) Cyclone and Other Stories
(iv) Gods, Demons and Others

Narayan has written a few hundred stories, most of them quite interesting and highly readable:

Some of his famous short stories are :

1. The Golden
2. A Career
3. The Snake Song
4. Man Hunt
5. A Willing Slave
6. An Astrologer's Day
7. The Doctor's word
8. God of Troubles, etc.

MULK RAJ ANAND

1. He was greatly influenced by Premchand on the one hand and Tagore on the other.

2. According to Jack Lindsay, "And so there are in his work elements of nature poetry, breath of compassion, irony and serenity; a wealth of varying planes of perception, which Premchand could not encompass."

3. Anand is often known as the mouthpiece of the underdog.

4. According to Srinivas Iyengar, "...he is enough of an artist to save his excellent novels from the stigma of mere propaganda. And hence his characters.... at any rate, his Indian characters are almost as a rule recognizably human beings, not automats or formulae."

5. *(i)* His novels are surrealistic in structure.
(ii) Hence his plots lack the complexity which is the hallmark of more popular and artistic novels in the world.

6. Some of his novels lack organic unity, *e.g.* "Coolie" in spite of having won the Sahitya Akademi Award (in 1972) is at best a picaresque attempt, a loose tying up of detached episodes which may be called epical, but not quite artistic.

7. His women are not so lively and they are often subservient to the will of men.

Works

Some of his famous novels are :

1. The Village (1939)
2. Across the Black waters (1940)
3. The Sword and the sickle (1942)
4. Untouchable (1933) (his first novel)
5. Seven summers (1951)
6. Private Life of an Indian Prince (1953)
7. The Big Heart (1945)
8. Coolie (1936) (It was recast in seventies)
9. Two Leaves and a Bud (1937)
10. The Old Woman and the Cow (1960)
11. The Road (1961)
12. Death of a Hero (1963)
13. Confession of a Lover (1976)
14. Morning Face (1968)

Anand as a short story writer

1. Mr. Anand is also known as a great short story writer.

2. His stories appeared in a number of volumes.

(i) The Barber's Trade Union and Other Stories (1944).
(ii) The Tractor and The Corn Goddess (1947).
(iii) Reflections on the Golden Bed and Other Stories (1955-59).
(iv) Lajwanti and Other Stories (1966)
(v) The Lost child and Other Stories (1934)
(vi) Lament on the Death of a Master of Arts (1968)
(vii) Between Tears and Laughter (1973)
(viii) Power of Darkeness, and Other Stories (1959)

3. Mr. Anand has written realistic stories of all kinds which are often full of humour, pathos, irony and satire. According to V.S. Pritchett, "Mr Anand's picture is real, comprehensive and subtle, and his gifts in all moods from farce to comedy, from pathos to tragedy, from the realistic to the poetic, are remarkable."

Some of his well-known short stories are :

(i) A Pair of Mustachios
(ii) On the Border
(iii) The Cobbler and the Machine
(iv) A Promoter of Quarrels
(v) A Dark Night
(vi) A Rumour
(vii) Lullaby
(viii) Barber's Trade Union
(ix) The Parrot in the Cage
(x) The Liar
(xi) Mahadev and Parvati
(xii) The Lost Child

KHUSWANT SINGH

1. He is known for his novels :

(i) Train to Pakistan (his masterpiece)
(ii) I Shall Not Hear the Nightingale (1959). (It describes the social life of a Sikh family during the pre-Independence period).

2. "The Mark of Vishnu" is another of his well-known works.

3. Some of his known stories

(a) Karma
(b) When Sikh Meets Sikh
(c) The Rape, etc.

4. He is also known for his:

(i) A History of the Sikhs
(ii) Translation of Japji Sahib, etc.

5. His regular columns appear weekly in some dailies, *e.g.* :

(i) 'With Malice Towards One And All'—The Hindustan Times.
(ii) 'This Above All'—The Tribune.

6. Mulk Raj Anand is stated to have said that Khushwant Singh's "Train to Pakistan" is likely to last, while about his other creative literary work, one may have some doubts.

7. Among his latest work is "Truth, Love and Little Malice."

OBJECTIVE MULTIPLE CHOICE QUESTIONS

1. Who wrote Don Juan?
(a) Shakespeare *(b)* Tennyson
(c) Byron *(d)* T.S. Eliot

2. Who wrote The Life of Johnson?
(a) Boswell *(b)* Macaulay
(c) Churchill *(d)* Sir Walter Raleigh

3. Priest's Nun's Tale was written by
(a) Spenser *(b)* Charles Lamb
(c) Tennyson *(d)* Chaucer

4. Malvolio is a character in
(a) Macbeth
(b) Hamlet
(c) Twelfth Night
(d) Much Ado About Nothing

5. Pip is a character in
(a) Much Ado About Nothing
(b) Great Expectations
(c) Mrs. Dalloway
(d) A Passage to India

6. In which poem does the following line occur : "Our sweetest songs are those that tell of saddest thought"

(a) Ulysses (b) Faery Queene
(c) Ode to Skylark (d) The Wasteland

7. Who is said to have first used the term "Metaphysics"?
(a) Matthew Arnold (b) Sidney
(c) Donne (d) Dr. Johnson

8. The writer of Volpone is
(a) Johnson (b) Milton
(c) Jonson (d) Shelley

9. Which is the correct chronological sequence
(a) Spenser—Chaucer—Milton—Donne
(b) Spenser—Wordsworth—Tennyson—T.S. Eliot
(c) Milton—Shakespeare—Philip Larkin—Keats
(d) Auden—Eliot—Shelley—Keats

10. Pilgrim's Progress was written by
(a) Milton (b) Shelley
(c) Swinburne (d) John Bunyan

11. The writer of the line : "Stone walls do not a prison make" is
(a) Lovelace (b) Milton
(c) W.B. Yeats (d) T.S. Eliot

12. "Monkey's Paw" is a
(a) Poem (b) Drama
(c) Short story (d) Novel

13. Lyrical Ballads appeared in
(a) 1690 (b) 1798
(c) 1802 (d) 1800

14. The writer of 'A Pair of Blue Eyes' is
(a) Thackeray (b) Dickens
(c) George Eliot (d) Thomas Hardy

15. Hard Times was written by
(a) Thackeray (b) Dickens
(c) Trollope (d) Marquese

16. Elizabeth Bennet is a character in
(a) Emma (b) The Mill on the Floss
(c) Pride and Prejudice (d) Herzog

17. Ariel is a character in
(a) Tempest (b) Paradise Lost
(c) In Memoriam (d) Murder in the Cathedral

18. Which of the following poets was most impressed by the German philosophy?
(a) Chaucer (b) Wordsworth
(c) Coleridge (d) Southey

19. The two cities referred to in "A Tale of Two Cities" are
(a) London and Paris (b) London and Rome
(c) Rome and Paris (d) Moscow and Rome

20. The Peasant's Bread is a story by
(a) Maupassant (b) Tagore
(c) R.K. Narayan (d) Tolstoy

21. The Financial Express was written by
(a) Raja Rao (b) R.K. Narayan
(c) Tagore (d) Mulk Raj Anand

22. "Negative Capability" is a term associated with
(a) Tagore (b) Shelley
(c) Keats (d) Coleridge

23. The most impressive treatment of "imagination" has been given by
(a) Coleridge (b) Shelley
(c) Eliot (d) Yeats

24. Maggie is a character in
(a) The Middlemarch
(b) The Vanity Fair
(c) The Mill on the Floss
(d) None of these

25. Who said about poetry "Emotion recollected in tranquillity"
(a) Wordsworth (b) Eliot
(c) Shelley (d) Arnold

26. Lady Chatterley's Lover was banned because it was considered
(a) obscene (b) revolutionary
(c) obscurantist (d) None of these

27. For Whom The Bell Tolls was written by
(a) Marquese (b) Hemingway
(c) Hawthorne (d) None of these

28. Who said: "I awoke one morning and found myself famous"
(a) Byron (b) Tennyson
(c) Eliot (d) Keats

29. Paradise Lost comprises
(a) 10 books (b) 12 books
(c) 6 books (d) 8 books

30. Who used the expression "unaging monuments of intellect"?
(a) Yeats (b) Shakespeare
(c) Whitman (d) Auden

31. Which poet was invited by John F. Kennedy to his inauguration ceremony?
(a) Whitman (b) Frost
(c) Eliot (d) Masefield

32. The writer of : "A Pair of Mustachios" is
(a) Anand (b) Tagore
(c) Raja Rao (d) Anita Desai

33. Estella is a character in
(a) Joseph Andrews
(b) Great Expectations
(c) A Tale of Two Cities
(d) Old Man and the Sea

34. The writer of Scarlet Letter is
(a) Henry James (b) James Joyce
(c) Hawthorne (d) None of these

35. In which poem does the following line occur: "To strive, to seek, to find and not to yield"
(a) Morte de Arthur (b) Ulysses
(c) Maud (d) Ode to the West Wind

36. Rousseau is associated with
(a) French Revolution
(b) American War of Independence
(c) Russian (Bolshevik) Revolution
(d) None of these

37. Which of the following novelists got the Nobel Prize?
(*a*) Virginia Woolf (*b*) James Joyce
(*c*) Hemingway (*d*) Conrad

38. Which of the following statesmen got the Nobel Prize?
(*a*) M.K. Gandhi (*b*) Stalin
(*c*) Churchill (*d*) Saddam Hussein

39. Who wrote 'Train to Pakistan'
(*a*) Narayan (*b*) Manohar Malgaon
(*c*) Khushwant Singh (*d*) Anand

40. Henchard is the hero of
(*a*) Jude the Obscure
(*b*) The Return of the Native
(*c*) The Mayor of Casterbridge
(*d*) Far From the Madding Crowd

41. Who is the writer of Azadi?
(*a*) R.K. Narayan (*b*) Khushwant Singh
(*c*) Tagore (*d*) Chaman Nahal

42. "The God of Small Things" is written by
(*a*) R.K. Narayan (*b*) Hemingway
(*c*) Graham Greene (*d*) Arundhati Roy

43. Who wrote the poem "Listeners"?
(*a*) Tennyson (*b*) Thomas Hood
(*c*) Goldsmith (*d*) Walter de la Mare

44. In writing "Canterbury Tales" Chaucer was influenced by
(*a*) Decameron (*b*) The Divine Comedy
(*c*) The Holy Bible (*d*) None of these

45. Which poem starts with "Behold her single in the field...."
(*a*) Lucy Gray
(*b*) The Solitary Reaper
(*c*) Hymn to Intellectual Beauty
(*d*) Dover Beach

46. 'Animal Farm' was written by
(*a*) James Joyce (*b*) Virginia Woolf
(*c*) George Orwell (*d*) Hemingway

47. Shobha De is a
(*a*) poet (*b*) dramatist
(*c*) novelist (*d*) an actress

48. Dunciad was written by
(*a*) Dryden (*b*) Pope
(*c*) Tennyson (*d*) Shelley

49. King Magnus is a character in
(*a*) Apple Cart (*b*) Man and Superman
(*c*) Pygmalion (*d*) Saint Joan

50. Bernard Shaw got the Nobel Prize for
(*a*) Pygmalion (*b*) Man and Superman
(*c*) Saint Joan (*d*) None of these

51. The Victorian Period is marked by
(*a*) Great political upheavals
(*b*) Great social security
(*c*) Great wars
(*d*) Economic deprivation

52. In which play the hero demanded more food from the authorities
(*a*) Great Expectations (*b*) David Copperfield
(*c*) Pickwick Papers (*d*) Oliver Twist

53. Swift is known mainly as
(*a*) an essayist (*b*) a poet
(*c*) a satirist (*d*) a short story writer

54. Who wrote the line :
"Slow rises worth by poverty depressed"?
(*a*) Shakespeare (*b*) Wordsworth
(*c*) Dr. Johnson (*d*) Matthew Arnold

55. Who is the writer of the novel "The Village"
(*a*) Khushwant Singh (*b*) Anita Desai
(*c*) Mulk Raj Anand (*d*) R.K. Narayan

56. The most famous writer of the heroic couplet is
(*a*) Dryden (*b*) Chaucer
(*c*) Spenser (*d*) Pope

57. Who wrote: "Heard melodies are sweet but those unheard are sweeter"?
(*a*) Shelley (*b*) Keats
(*c*) Pope (*d*) Wordsworth

58. Who used the term "Egotistical sublime" for Wordsworth's poetry?
(*a*) Keats (*b*) Shelley
(*c*) Coleridge (*d*) Tennyson

59. Into how many acts did Marlowe originally divide his "Dr. Faustus"
(*a*) five (*b*) two
(*c*) four (*d*) one (no division)

60. Shakespeare died in
(*a*) 1620 (*b*) 1616
(*c*) 1606 (*d*) 1610

61. Macflecknoe is a poem written by
(*a*) Dryden (*b*) Pope
(*c*) Tennyson (*d*) Yeats

62. Who wrote 'Everyman in His Humour'
(*a*) Shakespeare (*b*) Jonson
(*c*) Milton (*d*) Keats

63. 'Indian Jugglers' is an essay by
(*a*) De Quincey (*b*) Gardiner
(*c*) Hazlitt (*d*) Lamb

64. In which poem did Tennyson say "Ring out the old, ring in the new"
(*a*) Mand (*b*) Ulysses
(*c*) In Memoriam (*d*) The Brook

65. Who wrote 'The Gropes of Wrath'
(*a*) Pearl Buck (*b*) Hemingway
(*c*) Virginia Woolf (*d*) John Steinbeck

66. Who rendered into English the ancient Greek tragedy "Atlanta in Calydon"
(*a*) Swinburne (*b*) Shelley
(*c*) Tennyson (*d*) Arthur Hugh Clough

67. The Deserted Village was written by
(*a*) Cowper (*b*) Goldsmith
(*c*) Keats (*d*) Johnson

68. 'Savitri' is an epic written by
(*a*) Tagore (*b*) Prem Chand
(*c*) Aurobindo (*d*) B.C. Chatterjee

69. The anthem "Vande Mataram" occurs in
(*a*) Godan (*b*) Anand Math
(*c*) Gora (*d*) Train to Pakistan

70. 'All Fool's Day' is an essay written by
(*a*) Charles Lamb (*b*) Hazlitt
(*c*) A.G. Gardiner (*d*) R.C. Stevenson

71. The drama Tamburlaine is written by
(*a*) Shakespeare (*b*) Marlowe
(*c*) Lyly (*d*) Green

72. The book "Appreciations" was written by
(*a*) Morris (*b*) Arnold
(*c*) Walter Pater (*d*) Christina Rossetti

73. "Strife" describes the strike by
(*a*) factory workers (*b*) office workers
(*c*) teachers (*d*) students

74. "The Admirable Crichton" was written by
(*a*) Steinbeck (*b*) T.S. Eliot
(*c*) Trollope (*d*) James Barrie

75. "The Death of a Salesman" was written by
(*a*) James Barrie (*b*) Eugene O'Neill
(*c*) Arthur Miller (*d*) None of these

76. Which king of England was beheaded
(*a*) James I (*b*) James II
(*c*) Charles I (*d*) Charles II

77. The Restoration period is said to have started from
(*a*) 1660 (*b*) 1676
(*c*) 1625 (*d*) 1645

78. Who gave up writing poetry for a long period for the sake of struggle for democracy
(*a*) Shakespeare (*b*) Donne
(*c*) Milton (*d*) Yeats

79. Who wrote "The Lady's Not for Burning"
(*a*) Barrie (*b*) Christopher Fry
(*c*) Robert Bridges (*d*) T.S. Eliot

80. Who wrote the poem "Brahma"
(*a*) T.S Eliot (*b*) Emerson
(*c*) Whitman (*d*) Frost

81. The writer of Walden is
(*a*) Tennyson (*b*) Whitman
(*c*) Thoreau (*d*) Frost

82. In 'Sons and Lovers' Lawrence has depicted the life of
(*a*) factory workers (*b*) miners
(*c*) farmers (*d*) animals

83. Who wrote Kim?
(*a*) Kipling (*b*) Tagore
(*c*) Lawrence (*d*) Narayan

84. 'The Hairy Ape' is a famous play by
(*a*) Barrie (*b*) Eugene O'Neill
(*c*) Christopher Fry (*d*) T.S. Eliot

85. Who at the time of his death asked a friend of his to pay his debt (a cock) after his death?
(*a*) Plato (*b*) Aristotle
(*c*) Socrates (*d*) Alexander

86. Who is the writer of Frankenstein
(*a*) George Eliot (*b*) Jane Austen
(*c*) Mary Shelley (*d*) Emile Bronte

87. Which poem was conceived in a dream?
(*a*) Ode to the West Wind
(*b*) Kubla Khan
(*c*) Ode to a Nightingale
(*d*) Lucy Gray

88. Lines from a poem by which poet were found written on the writing pad of Jawaharlal Nehru after his death?
(*a*) Whitman (*b*) Tagore
(*c*) Sarojini Naidu (*d*) Frost

89. Who wrote his own epitaph:
"Here lies the one whose name is writ in water?"
(*a*) Byron (*b*) Southey
(*c*) Keats (*d*) Yeats

90. Who wrote the 'Cries of Children'
(*a*) Robert Browning (*b*) Elizabeth Barrett
(*c*) Thomas Hood (*d*) Cowper

91. Which poet is known as poet's poet?
(*a*) Shakespeare (*b*) Milton
(*c*) Spenser (*d*) Shelley

92. Bohemia is a place in the drama
(*a*) Macbeth (*b*) Everyman in His Humour
(*c*) The Winter's Tale (*d*) Tempest

93. Caliban is a character in
(*a*) Hamlet
(*b*) Merchant of Venice
(*c*) The Admirable Crichton
(*d*) Tempest

94. Who wrote the maximum number of sonnets
(*a*) Shakespeare (*b*) Milton
(*c*) Sidney (*d*) Wordsworth

95. Which character in 'The Merchant of Venice' said, "The quality of mercy is not strained,"
(*a*) Bassanio (*b*) Portia
(*c*) Jessica (*d*) Antonio

96. Adonais is the eulogy written on the death of
(*a*) Coleridge (*b*) Byron
(*c*) Keats (*d*) Wordsworth

97. Oedipus Complex is expressed most strongly in
(*a*) David Copperfield (*b*) Great Expectations
(*c*) Pride and Prejudice (*d*) Sons and Lovers

98. Who was addicted to opium taking
(*a*) Keats (*b*) Wordsworth
(*c*) Coleridge (*d*) T.S. Eliot

99. Who wrote Mother
(*a*) Tolstoy (*b*) Maxim Gorky
(*c*) Chekhov (*d*) Hardy

100. Who is associated with Malgudi
(*a*) Narayan
(*b*) Anand
(*c*) Manohar Malgonkar
(*d*) Anita Desai

101. The author of Beowulf is
(*a*) Bede (*b*) Cynewulf
(*c*) Chaucer (*d*) Unknown

102. The Anglo-Saxon period is often said to be from 450 to ......
(*a*) 900 (*b*) 1000
(*c*) 1050 (*d*) 1100

103. The name of the monster in Beowulf is
(*a*) Gomanzo (*b*) Grendel
(*c*) Frankenstein (*d*) Mephistophilis

104. Who says "Life, life, eternal life"?
(*a*) Christian (*b*) Maggie
(*c*) Henchard (*d*) Chaucer's Parson

105. Beatrice was the woman whose love inspired a man to write an immortal poem. Who was that man?
(*a*) Shelley (*b*) Shakespeare
(*c*) Homer (*d*) Dante

106. Charles I was executed in
(*a*) 1648 (*b*) 1645
(*c*) 1649 (*d*) 1650

107. Alexander Pope died in
(*a*) 1740 (*b*) 1742
(*c*) 1744 (*d*) 1743

108. Burns was born in
(*a*) England (*b*) Ireland
(*c*) Scotland (*d*) France

109. "To a Mountain Daisy" is a poem by
(*a*) Wordsworth (*b*) Shelley
(*c*) Keats (*d*) Burns

110. Who wrote: "The Devil's Disciple"?
(*a*) Galsworthy (*b*) Barrie
(*c*) Shaw (*d*) Fry

111. George Eliot believed in
(*a*) A moral law (*b*) Promiscuity of sex
(*c*) Violent Revolution (*d*) Indiscriminate fate

112. "A foundling" is a part of the name of the novel
(*a*) Amelia (*b*) David Copperfield
(*c*) Oliver Twist (*d*) Tom Jones

113. Who wrote "The Decline and Fall of the Roman Empire"?
(*a*) Walter Raleigh (*b*) Trollope
(*c*) Smollett (*d*) Edward Gibbon

114. Richard Hooker was a prose writer of the
(*a*) Victorian period (*b*) Romantic period
(*c*) Elizabethan period (*d*) Chaucerian age

115. Sir Walter Raleigh died in
(*a*) 1622 (*b*) 1621
(*c*) 1618 (*d*) 1623

116. D' Artagnan is a character in
(*a*) The Three Musketeers
(*b*) Don Quixote
(*c*) Alice in Wonderland
(*d*) War and Peace

117. Alexander Dumas was
(*a*) an English writer (*b*) an American writer
(*c*) a French writer (*d*) a German writer

118. Who said about Wordsworth, "He uttered nothing base"
(*a*) Keats (*b*) Coleridge
(*c*) Byron (*d*) Tennyson

119. Which one was not one of the Lake poets?
(*a*) Shelley (*b*) Wordsworth
(*c*) Southey (*d*) Coleridge

120. Emma appeared in
(*a*) 1816 (*b*) 1815
(*c*) 1817 (*d*) 1820

121. Mrs. Browning's book "Sonnets from the Portuguese" is an inspiring book of
(*a*) nature poems
(*b*) metaphysical poems
(*c*) love poems
(*d*) didactic poems

122. D.G. Rossetti was the son of
(*a*) An Italian painter (*b*) A German poet
(*c*) French nobleman (*d*) An English peasant

123. The translation of Goethe's "Wilhelm Meister" appeared in
(*a*) 1822 (*b*) 1820
(*c*) 1832 (*d*) 1824

124. In 'The Doctor's Dilemma' Shaw makes fun of
(*a*) teachers (*b*) physicians
(*c*) painters (*d*) politicians

125. The Theory of Catharsis is associated with
(*a*) Plato (*b*) Dryden
(*c*) Aristotle (*d*) Sidney

126. Who wrote 'In Defence of Poetry'?
(*a*) T.S. Eliot (*b*) Yeats
(*c*) Keats (*d*) Shelley

127. 'The Playboy of the Western World' is a play by
(*a*) Barrie (*b*) Synge
(*c*) Fry (*d*) Eliot

128. For the best condensation of a novel Arnold Bennet won a prize of
(*a*) £ 100 (*b*) £ 50
(*c*) £ 25 (*d*) £ 20

129. Who wrote :
"The year's at the spring.
And day's at the morn."
(*a*) Tennyson (*b*) Robert Browning
(*c*) Keats (*d*) Swinburne

130. The Ring and the Book contains how many more lines than the Iliad?
(*a*) about three thousand
(*b*) about two thousand
(*c*) about four thousand
(*d*) about five thousand

131. In which poem do the following lines occur?
"...Do not all charms fly

At the mere touch of cold philosophy?"
(*a*) Ode To A Grecian Urn
(*b*) The Eve of St. Agnes
(*c*) Lamia
(*d*) Hyperion

132. Boswell was born in
(*a*) 1732 (*b*) 1740
(*c*) 1735 (*d*) 1742

133. 'Silent Woman' is a play by
(*a*) Marlowe (*b*) Shakespeare
(*c*) Ben Jonson (*d*) Lyly

134. The Duchess of Malfi was published in
(*a*) 1632 (*b*) 1635
(*c*) 1625 (*d*) 1623

135. The Scene of Beowulf is laid in
(*a*) England (*b*) France
(*c*) Spain (*d*) None of these

136. Pap is a character in
(*a*) Great Expectations (*b*) Hucklebery Finn
(*c*) Silas Mariner (*d*) The Mocking Bird

137. A Mad Tea-Party takes place in
(*a*) Don Quixote (*b*) The Three Musketeers
(*c*) Robinson Crusoe (*d*) Alice in Wonderland

138. What was the name of the girl whom Kalidas loved?
(*a*) Shakuntala (*b*) Nagini
(*c*) Kamini (*d*) Savitri

139. "Kidnapped" was written by
(*a*) Dickens (*b*) Thackeray
(*c*) Hardy (*d*) R.L. Stevenson

140. Mr. Collins is a character in
(*a*) Sense and Sensibility
(*b*) Pride and Prejudice
(*c*) Emma
(*d*) Hard Times

141. 'The Prisoner of Zenda' was written by
(*a*) Sterne (*b*) Trollope
(*c*) Anthony Hope (*d*) George Eliot

142. What was the full name of Cervantes
(*a*) Jim Cervantes
(*b*) John Cervantes
(*c*) Miguel de Cervantes
(*d*) Sir Roger Cervantes

143. The letter referred to in 'The Scarlet Letter' is
(*a*) A (*b*) B
(*c*) L (*d*) M

144. Robert Frost lived for sometime in
(*a*) France (*b*) Germany
(*c*) England (*d*) Italy

145. Besides being a poet, Chaucer was
(*a*) a trader (*b*) a manufacturer
(*c*) a teacher (*d*) a diplomat

146. Bacon's essays were influenced by
(*a*) Montesque (*b*) Montaigne
(*c*) Boccaccio (*d*) Pascal

147. Charles Lamb worked as a
(*a*) clerk (*b*) seaman
(*c*) teacher (*d*) mechanic

148. Who wrote: "Keep right on to the end of the road."
(*a*) Shakespeare (*b*) Milton
(*c*) Sir Harry Lauder (*d*) Chaucer

149. Who said: "Two men look out through the same bars: One sees the mud, and the one the stars."
(*a*) Chaucer (*b*) Keats
(*c*) Milton (*d*) Frederick Langbridge

150. In which book does the following line appear : "What a falling off was there."
(*a*) King Lear (*b*) Othello
(*c*) Hamlet (*d*) Antony and Cleopatra

151. The meaning of "widsith" in old English is
(*a*) width (*b*) widely
(*c*) wise (*d*) wanderer

152. The name of William Golding's first novel is
(*a*) The Inheritors (*b*) Lord of the Flies
(*c*) Pincher Martin (*d*) The Pyramid

153. In his "Progress and Poverty", Henry George is influenced by
(*a*) The American War of Independence
(*b*) The French Revolution
(*c*) The Marxian System
(*d*) None of these

154. The author of Erewhon is
(*a*) Hardy (*b*) Marquese
(*c*) Samuel Butler (*d*) Cervantes

155. Which of the following is a Comedy of Manners?
(*a*) The Way of the World
(*b*) The Duchess of Malfi
(*c*) The Lady's Not for Burning
(*d*) The Hairy Ape

156. Which one among the following is not a pessimist?
(*a*) Gissing (*b*) Browning
(*c*) Hardy (*d*) Thomson

157. Charles Reade's drama "Drink" was adapted from a work of
(*a*) Goethe (*b*) Zola
(*c*) Mallarwe (*d*) Tennyson

158. James Mill was born in
(*a*) France (*b*) Ireland
(*c*) Scotland (*d*) Italy

159. The classical theory of rent was advocated by
(*a*) Bentham (*b*) Ricardo
(*c*) James Mill (*d*) Marx

160. Which one among the following was not a utilitarian?
(*a*) Rousseau (*b*) James Mill
(*c*) Ricardo (*d*) Bentham

161. Kipling was born in
(*a*) 1872 (*b*) 1865
(*c*) 1870 (*d*) 1864

162. The monk Augustine came to England in
(*a*) 590 (*b*) 587
(*c*) 597 (*d*) 591

163. The Battle of Maldon was fought in
(*a*) 993 (*b*) 990
(*c*) 975 (*d*) 980

164. To whom are the following lines ascribed?
"When Adam delved and Eve span,
Who was then the gentleman?"
(*a*) Gower (*b*) John Ball
(*c*) Wat Tayler (*d*) Chaucer

165. 'The Praise of Folly' was written by
(*a*) Walter Raleigh (*b*) Thomas Moore
(*c*) Charles Lamb (*d*) Ruskin

166. Who wrote: "In Praise of Idleness"?
(*a*) Bertrand Russell (*b*) Thomas More
(*c*) Charles Lamb (*d*) Hazlitt

167. Which one of the following comprises one accented syllable followed by one unaccented syllable
(*a*) A Dactyl (*b*) An Anapaest
(*c*) A trochee (*d*) An iambus

168. In which work does the following line occur:
"That with no middle flight intends to soar."
(*a*) L'Allegro (*b*) Il Penseroso
(*c*) Paradise Lost (*d*) Lycidas

169. The trial scene in 'The Merchant of Venice' was presided over by
(*a*) Portia (*b*) Antonio
(*c*) Dr. Bellario (*d*) The Duke

170. The real name of Saki is
(*a*) H.H. Munro (*b*) Samuel Butler
(*c*) George Orwell (*d*) The Duke

171. Who started: "The Tatler"?
(*a*) Addison (*b*) Swift
(*c*) Steele (*d*) Stevenson

172. The poem 'The Song of the Shirt' was written by
(*a*) Mrs. Browning (*b*) Pope
(*c*) Shelley (*d*) Thomas Hood

173. Sir Roger was originally the creation of
(*a*) Addison (*b*) Dryden
(*c*) Steele (*d*) Milton

174. Who wrote: "Areopagitica"?
(*a*) Charles Lamb (*b*) Hazlitt
(*c*) De Quincey (*d*) Milton

175. Mary Lamb killed her
(*a*) mother (*b*) father
(*c*) sister (*d*) brother

176. 'The Selfish Giant' is a story written by
(*a*) Tagore (*b*) Oscar Wilde
(*c*) Maupassant (*d*) Tolstoy

177. Which one of the following is not a part of the proverbial "Three Unities"
(*a*) Unity of Purpose (*b*) Unity of Time
(*c*) Unity of Place (*d*) Unity of Action

178. Which one of the following letters is most often not pronounced before a consonant?
(*a*) p (*b*) r
(*c*) n (*d*) s

179. The setting of Walpole's novel "The Castle of Otranto" is
(*a*) ancient England (*b*) medieval France
(*c*) medieval Italy (*d*) ancient Ireland

180. Who wrote : "Four Quartets"?
(*a*) T.S. Eliot (*b*) W.B. Yeats
(*c*) W.H. Auden (*d*) Philip Larkins

181. Who wrote : "Look Back in Anger"?
(*a*) Steinbeck (*b*) Christopher Fry
(*c*) John Osborne (*d*) Barrie

182. Who wrote : "The Devils of Loundun"?
(*a*) Bertrand Russell (*b*) Aldous Huxley
(*c*) J.B. Priestley (*d*) Hazlitt

183. Iris Murdoch was born in
(*a*) 1921 (*b*) 1923
(*c*) 1930 (*d*) 1919

184. In the 'Heart of Darkness' Conrad has explored
(*a*) Ceylon (*b*) India
(*c*) Congo (*d*) Brazil

185. Virginia Woolf died in
(*a*) 1941 (*b*) 1940
(*c*) 1943 (*d*) 1935

186. In which one of the following words 'b' is not silent
(*a*) plumber (*b*) comb
(*c*) lumbago (*d*) lamb

187. Who wrote : "Principles of Human Knowledge"
(*a*) Milton (*b*) John Bunyan
(*c*) Nash (*d*) George Berkeley

188. Who wrote : "Liber Amoris"
(*a*) Lamb (*b*) Hazlitt
(*c*) Byron (*d*) Wordsworth

189. Fielding wrote Joseph Andrews in reaction against
(*a*) Pamela (*b*) Robinson Crusoe
(*c*) Jane Eyre (*d*) Roderick Random

190. Fielding was a
(*a*) Romanticist (*b*) Supernaturalist
(*c*) Realist (*d*) Science fiction writer

191. "A Railway Clerk" is a poem by
(*a*) Keki N. Daruwallah (*b*) Nissim Ezekiel
(*c*) Shiv K. Kumar (*d*) Jayanta Mahapatra

192. Raju is the hero of
(*a*) Guide (*b*) The Mark of Vishnu
(*c*) Azadi (*d*) The God of Small Things

193. The Indian novelist who won the Booker Prize in 1997 was
(*a*) Vikram Seth (*b*) Salman Rushdie
(*c*) R.K. Narayan (*d*) Arundhati Roy

194. Who won The Booker of Bookers
(*a*) Arundhati Roy (*b*) Khushwant Singh
(*c*) Mulk Raj Anand (*d*) Salman Rushdie

195. Who among the following is not a pre-Romantic poet
(*a*) William Mason (*b*) Beattie
(*c*) Bowles (*d*) Byron

196. Disraeli was influenced by
(*a*) Carlyle (*b*) Burke
(*c*) Benthem (*d*) Godwin

197. Dickens died in
(*a*) 1870 (*b*) 1865
(*c*) 1868 (*d*) 1872

198. Who is not a novelist besides being a poet
(*a*) Jayanta Mahapatra (*b*) Shiv K. Kumar
(*c*) Kamala Das (*d*) Tagore

199. The favourite poet of Jawaharlal Nehru was
(*a*) Whitman (*b*) Frost
(*c*) Eliot (*d*) Yeats

200. Who wrote: "The Battle of Books"
(*a*) Bacon (*b*) Hazlitt
(*c*) Swift (*d*) None of these

201. Which of the following sounds is not a guttural
(*a*) k (*b*) ng
(*c*) g (*d*) p

202. Which of the following consonants is not considered redundant
(*a*) c (*b*) q
(*c*) r (*d*) x

203. In which metre is Shelley's 'Ode to the West Wind' written
(*a*) Terza Rima (*b*) Ottava Rima
(*c*) Spenserian Stanza (*d*) Blank Verse

204. Who wrote the following lines:
"'Tis sweet to hear the watch dog's honest bark
Bay deep mouthed welcome as we near our home."
(*a*) Shakespeare (*b*) Byron
(*c*) Pope (*d*) Robert Bridges

205. Who wrote the following lines :
"The cock's shrill clarion, and the echoing horn,
No more shall rouse than from their lowly bed."
(*a*) Milton (*b*) Donne
(*c*) Gray (*d*) Cowper

206. In which class should we place Spenser's 'Shepherd's Calendar'?
(*a*) Pastoral (*b*) Romance
(*c*) Epic (*d*) Eulogy

207. In which book do the following lines occur :
"Here is thy footstool and there rest thy feet where live the poorest, and lowliest, and lost."
(*a*) Ramcharitmanas (*b*) The Rig Veda
(*c*) The Gitanjali (*d*) None of these

208. Who among the following was the contemporary of Tennyson
(*a*) Auden (*b*) Robert Browning
(*c*) Cowper (*d*) Day Lewis

209. Who wrote the following line:
"God made the country and man made the town".
(*a*) Blake (*b*) Cowper
(*c*) Wordsworth (*d*) Shelley

210. Which one among the following is the correct chronological order
(*a*) Faerie Queene—Paradise Lost—Lamia—Prospice
(*b*) Macbeth—Canterbury Tales—In Memoriam—Waste Land
(*c*) Faustus—The Duchess of Malfi—The Eve of St. Agnes—Ulysses
(*d*) Hamlet—Prelude—Hyperion—Comus

211. Who wrote: "Nectar in a Sieve"?
(*a*) Mulk Raj Anand
(*b*) Manohar Malgonkar
(*c*) Kamala Markandaya
(*d*) Pearl S. Buck

212. 'The Good Earth' was written by
(*a*) Raja Rao (*b*) R.K. Narayan
(*c*) Pearl S. Buck (*d*) Kamala Markandaya

213. The writer of 'The Dove Found No Rest' is
(*a*) Pearl S Buck (*b*) Hemingway
(*c*) Raja Rao (*d*) Dennis Stoll

214. Who wrote: "So Many Hungers"?
(*a*) Bhabani Bhattacharya
(*b*) Kamala Markandaya
(*c*) Manohar Malgonkar
(*d*) Chaman Nahal

215. The main theme of 'So Many Hungers' is
(*a*) necessity of a revolution
(*b*) degradation of humanity
(*c*) description of nature
(*d*) vision of India as a developed country

216. Who said about Shaw:
"He studied every known theory of socialism"
(*a*) Hudson (*b*) Hugh Walker
(*c*) Henderson (*d*) Legouis

217. Who is the writer of "The Middleman and Other Stories "?
(*a*) Mulk Raj Anand (*b*) Bharati Mukherjee
(*c*) Tagore (*d*) Prem Chand

218. Which one of the following is not an example of "fine writing" according to Prof. Terry Eagleton of St. Catherine College, University of Oxford
(*a*) Lamb (*b*) Macaulay
(*c*) Mill (*d*) Darwin

219. Which one among the following cannot be considered an early Indian English poet
(*a*) Henry Derozio (*b*) Toru Dutt
(*c*) Manmohan Ghosh (*d*) Kamala Das

220. Who declared that he would "sing the song" of his "experience."
(*a*) Shiv K. Kumar (*b*) Nissim Ezekiel
(*c*) Keki N. Daruwalla (*d*) Jayanta Mahapatra

221. Who said, "I only know how to work at one poem at a time, stitch by stitch"
(*a*) Nissim Ezekiel (*b*) A.K. Ramanujan
(*c*) Shiv K. Kumar (*d*) Arun Kolatkar

222. Cicero was a Roman
(*a*) philologist (*b*) physician
(*c*) orator (*d*) None of these

223. Who is the writer of "Gita Rahasya"?
(*a*) Tulsi Das (*b*) Vivekananda
(*c*) Shivananda (*d*) B.G. Tilak

224. In Arnold's 'The Scholar Gipsy,' the great modern melancholy is spiritualised into a symbol of
(a) the advent of a new age
(b) mystery and dreams
(c) a source of poetic inspiration
(d) an expectation of some divine dispensation.

225. 'The Rubaiyat of Omar Khayyam' was translated into English by
(a) Robert Browning (b) Tennyson
(c) Fitz Gerald (d) Hopkins

226. Mayakovsky was the famous poet of
(a) France (b) Italy
(c) Austria (d) Russia

227. Marquese originally wrote his "One Hundred Years of Solitude" in
(a) French (b) German
(c) Spanish (d) Italian

228. The word 'Dialogue' is derived from "dialogos" which is a
(a) German word (b) Latin word
(c) French word (d) Greek word

229. The word 'strength' is derived from 'strengthu' which is
(a) A French word
(b) A Latin word
(c) An Old English word
(d) An Italian word

230. Who said, "Poets are the unacknowledged legislators of the world"?
(a) Shelley (b) Keats
(c) Byron (d) Coleridge

231. In which of Shakespeare's plays does Lancelott Gobbo appear
(a) Tempest (b) The Merchant of Venice
(c) Winter's Tale (d) Cymbeline

232. In which year did Tagore receive the Nobel Prize?
(a) 1912 (b) 1913
(c) 1914 (d) 1915

233. In which year did the Bolshevik Revolution take place?
(a) 1918 (b) 1920
(c) 1921 (d) 1917

234. From the poem of which poet did E.M. Forster take the name of his novel "A Passage to India"?
(a) Frost (b) Sandburg
(c) Whitman (d) Yeats

235. Identify Emile Bronte's novel in the following
(a) Persuasion (b) Wuthering Heights
(c) Jane Eyre (d) Middlemarch

236. Which one is believed to be the first English tragedy
(a) Gorboduc
(b) The Spanish Tragedy
(c) Dr. Faustus
(d) The Jew of Malta

237. Which of the following works is not by Milton
(a) Paradise Lost (b) Il Penseroso
(c) Lycidas (d) Maud

238. 'Music At Night' is a book of essays by
(a) A.G. Gardiner (b) Bertrand Russell
(c) Aldous Huxley (d) Chesterton

239. The character of Sherlock Holmes was created by
(a) Arthur Conan Doyle
(b) Hazlitt
(c) I.A. Richards
(d) Agatha Christie

240. Who pruned the draft of the 'Waste Land' to about one third of its original length?
(a) I.A. Richards (b) W.B. Yeats
(c) Ezra Pound (d) Virginia Woolf

241. Who wrote the Preface to the Gitanjali
(a) W.B. Yeats (b) T.S. Eliot
(c) Auden (d) Philip Larkin

242. What can be said to be the tragic flaw in Hamlet?
(a) Revenge (b) Indecisiveness
(c) Hastiness (d) Suspicion

243. Who said the following words:
"There is Providence even in the fall of a sparrow"
(a) Tennyson (b) Shelley
(c) Keats (d) Eliot

244. Who wrote 'The Spanish Tragedy'
(a) Shakespeare (b) Thomas Kyd
(c) Marlowe (d) Lyly

245. Name the author of "1984"
(a) George Orwell (b) Graham Greene
(c) Naipaul (d) James Joyce

246. Who is the creator of Wessex
(a) Dickens (b) Smollett
(c) Meredith (d) Hardy

247. Columbus discovered America in
(a) 1490 (b) 1492
(c) 1482 (d) 1488

248. Who said of Keats that he was "snuffed out by an article"
(a) Shelley (b) Wordsworth
(c) Browning (d) Byron

249. Who said, "Poetry is the spontaneous overflow of powerful feelings".
(a) Herrick (b) Lovelace
(c) Wordsworth (d) Thomas Nash

250. Who said that democracy was like a balloon
(a) Galsworthy (b) Shaw
(c) Hardy (d) I.A. Richards

251. In which poem the following lines occur:
"Grow old along with me,
The best is yet to be."
(a) The Last Ride Together
(b) Rabbi Ben Ezra
(c) Prospice
(d) Sordello

252. Which of Browning's poems did Tennyson complain that it was unintelligible to him except for the first and the last lines both of which were wrong?
(a) The Grammarian's Funeral
(b) The Last Ride Together
(c) Sordello
(d) Prospice

253. Which of the following writers did not get the Nobel Prize?
(a) Octavio Paz *(b)* R.N. Tagore
(c) Aurobindo *(d)* W.B. Yeats

254. Who wrote the following lines :
"The wind disentangles itself from your frenzied body as hurricanes of dreams follow me."
(a) Nissim Ezekiel *(b)* R. Parthasarthy
(c) Jayanta Mahapatra *(d)* Pritish Nandy

255. Which one of the following is not Gurdial Singh's novel
(a) Addh Chanini Rat (Night of the Half-Moon)
(b) Parsa
(c) Godan
(d) Marhi Da Deeva (The Last Flicker)

256. Who made the sensational pronouncement of "end of ideology" in 1960
(a) David Bell *(b)* Graham Greene
(c) Mulk Raj Anand *(d)* Octavio Paz

257. Gurdial Singh was born in
(a) 1930 *(b)* 1931
(c) 1932 *(d)* 1933

258. Which novel of Sarat Chandra Chattopadhyaya has caught the imagination of the Indians the most, so much so that even another film bearing this name has been made?
(a) Ses Prasna *(b)* Grih Daha
(c) Devdas *(d)* Chritraheen

259. Whose rendering into English (as given below) are the following lines by Tagore:
"What voice is that I hear
From the land of dawn,
'Fear not! Fear not!
Who will give up his life
Retaining nothing
Will never end, never perish!'"
(a) Khushwant Singh
(b) Sir Jadunath Sircar
(c) Tagore himself
(d) Sister Nivedita

260. When was the famous Hindi poet Kumar Vikal born
(a) 1939 *(b)* 1930
(c) 1932 *(d)* 1935

261. Whose novel "The Foundation Pit?" was discovered only a few years ago?
(a) Andrey Platanov *(b)* Cherneshevysky
(c) Jane Austen *(d)* George Eliot

262. The novel "We" was written by
(a) Andrey Platanov *(b)* Tolstoy
(c) Maxim Gorky *(d)* Zamayatin

263. Name the writer of "What Is To Be Done"
(a) Zamayatin *(b)* Gorky
(c) Cherneshevysky *(d)* Chekhov

264. Who in 'Paradise Lost' tells Adam:
"Be lowly wise
Dream not of other worlds."
(a) Satan *(b)* Angel Gabriel
(c) Mammon *(d)* Mephistophilis

265. Name the writer of the novel "Les Miserables"
(a) Virginia Woolf *(b)* Mrs. Radcliffe
(c) Victor Hugo *(d)* James Joyce

266. Who wrote the following lines:
"Hurrah for revolution,
Let the cannon shoot."
(a) Eliot *(b)* Stephen Spender
(c) Auden *(d)* Yeats

267. Who was the renowned English novelist who became the first great foreign writer to show a keen interest in R.K. Narayan's fiction which finally made the latter so famous
(a) E.M. Forster *(b)* D.H. Lawrence
(c) Graham Greene *(d)* Virginia Woolf

268. R.K. Narayan was a
(a) Tamilian *(b)* Bengali
(c) Gujarati *(d)* Maharashtrian

269. Which of the following novels is not by Salman Rushdie?
(a) Midnight's Children
(b) Grimus
(c) The Moor's Last Sigh
(d) The Lighthouse

270. Which novel of Salman Rushdie was adjudged the best one to have won the Booker Prize in its first 25 years
(a) Grimus *(b)* Midnight's Children
(c) The Satanic Verses *(d)* Shame

271. When was Rushdie awarded the Austrian State Prize for European Literature
(a) 1993 *(b)* 1990
(c) 1991 *(d)* 1995

272. When was Ted Hughes made the poet laureate of England?
(a) 1980 *(b)* 1982
c) 1981 *(d)* 1984

273. In which year between 1921 and 1940 no Nobel Prize for Literature was awarded
(a) 1925 *(b)* 1930
(c) 1935 *(d)* 1939

274. In which year did Galsworthy receive the Nobel Prize
(a) 1930 *(b)* 1934
(c) 1931 *(d)* 1932

275. In which year did Dylan Thomas die?
(*a*) 1951 (*b*) 1950
(*c*) 1955 (*d*) 1953

276. Aurobindo's Savitri is
(*a*) en epic
(*b*) a long narrative poem
(*c*) a dramatic monologue
(*d*) a historical work

277. Lamb's essays are full of
(*a*) irony and satire (*b*) humour and pathos
(*c*) sarcasm (*d*) None of these

278. Shelley's genius was basically
(*a*) dramatic (*b*) narrative
(*c*) lyrical (*d*) descriptive

279. A sonnet comprises
(*a*) 16 lines (*b*) 14 lines
(*c*) 12 lines (*d*) 20 lines

270. Civil war in England was fought in .... century
(*a*) fifteenth (*b*) sixteenth
(*c*) seventeenth (*d*) fourteenth

281. The soldiers of Cromwell were known as
(*a*) Dark heads (*b*) Round heads
(*c*) Large heads (*d*) Brave heads

282. Who is renowned for his outstanding work "Holy Sonnets"
(*a*) Donne (*b*) Herrick
(*c*) Milton (*d*) Pope

283. When did Frederic Mistral of France and Jose Eizaguirre of Spain jointly win the Nobel Prize in Literature?
(*a*) 1910 (*b*) 1920
(*c*) 1902 (*d*) 1904

284. Name the Russian who won the Nobel Prize for literature in 1933
(*a*) Mayakovsky (*b*) Ivan Bunin
(*c*) Checkov (*d*) Stalin

285. In what field did Churchill win the Nobel Prize?
(*a*) Peace (*b*) Literature
(*c*) Economics (*d*) Medicine

286. From which book are the following lines taken :
"And Moses stretched out his hand over the sea; and the Lord caused the sea to go back by a strong east wind all that night, ..."
(*a*) The Holy Bible (*b*) Paradise Lost
(*c*) Pilgrim's Progress (*d*) None of these

287. In which book do the following lines occur:
"Heavens lights for ever shine,
Earth's shadows fly."
(*a*) The Holy Bible (*b*) Adonais
(*c*) Paradise Lost (*d*) Pilgrim's Progress

288. Who wrote the Latin "History of the Britons"
(*a*) Henry I (*b*) Geoffrey of Monmouth
(*c*) Wycliffe (*d*) Walter Giffart

289. When was the final result of slow transformation of Anglo-Saxon into modern English felt?
(*a*) In the fourteenth century
(*b*) In the fifteenth century
(*c*) In the sixteenth century
(*d*) In the seventeenth century

280. Normandy was lost by John Lackland in
(*a*) 1205 (*b*) 1204
(*c*) 1201 (*d*) 1203

291. Until about the middle of the 14th century English literature was mostly
(*a*) romantic (*b*) revolutionary
(*c*) metaphysical (*d*) religious and didactic

292. The book "Ormulum" comprised forty gospels translated and paraphrased by the monk named
(*a*) Augustine (*b*) Cynewulf
(*c*) Orm (*d*) John

293. Thomas Henry Huxley associates
(*a*) science with daily life
(*b*) God and man
(*c*) man and nature
(*d*) man and society

294. Brave New World was published in
(*a*) 1930 (*b*) 1928
(*c*) 1935 (*d*) 1932

295. Which of the following is not written by Hugo Charteris
(*a*) Pictures in the wall
(*b*) A Piece of String
(*c*) The Old Boys
(*d*) The Boarding House

296. Cecil Day Lewis's 'The Poetic Image' appeared in
(*a*) 1938 (*b*) 1945
(*c*) 1946 (*d*) 1947

297. Ann Jellicoe became famous in 1958
(*a*) with the production of a play
(*b*) by writing a novel
(*c*) by getting a poem published
(*d*) by getting a short story telecast over the T.V.

298. Which of the following statements is not true:
(*a*) Shelley was a cricketer
(*b*) Byron was a cricketer
(*c*) Keats had been a physician
(*d*) Lamb was a clerk

299. Which of the following statements is true :
(*a*) Shakespeare died by falling from a horse
(*b*) Dr. Johnson was a contemporary of Shakespeare
(*c*) Richardson's Pamela was written in the form of letters
(*d*) Shelley did not like revolutionary ideas.

300. Which of the following works is by H.G. Wells
(*a*) All in a Garden Fair
(*b*) The Invisible Man
(*c*) A Child of the Jago
(*d*) Point Counter Point

301. Who wrote : "The Ideal of a Christian Church"
(*a*) John Keble (*b*) Newman
(*c*) Nash (*d*) William George Ward

302. Which of the following is not the off-shoot of Romanticism
(a) Aesthetic Theory *(b)* Pre-Raphaelitism
(c) Classicism *(d)* Super-naturalism

303. The greatest worshipper of beauty among the Romantic poets was
(a) Keats *(b)* Shelley
(c) Byron *(d)* Wordsworth

304. Humanism is most pronounced in
(a) Romanticism *(b)* Renascence
(c) Classicism *(d)* Pre-Raphaelitism

305. When was Hazlitt born
(a) 1782 *(b)* 1780
(c) 1778 *(d)* 1785

306. Which of the following odes is not by Keats
(a) Ode on Intimations of Immortality
(b) Ode to a Nightingale
(c) Ode on a Grecian Urn
(d) Ode to Autumn

307. Which of the following is not a Romantic characteristic?
(a) An atmosphere of wonder
(b) An impression of strangeness
(c) A conscious adherence to set rules
(d) Spontaneousness

308. In which country was Romanticism associated with an innovatory aesthetic creed
(a) England *(b)* France
(c) Italy *(d)* Germany

309. English Romanticism from 1790 to 1830 being a native development, was partly influenced by
(a) Germany *(b)* France
(c) Spain *(d)* Italy

310. Crabbe was mainly a .... poet.
(a) Romantic *(b)* Realistic
(c) Metaphysical *(d)* None of these

311. Which characteristic among the following is not contained in "The Monk" by Lewis
(a) Lack of moral depth
(b) Highly religious atmosphere
(c) A sense of unreality
(d) Melodramaticism

312. Which of the following works is not that of David Hume
(a) Treatise of Human Nature
(b) The Rise and Fall of the Roman Empire
(c) Political Discourses
(d) History of Great Britain

313. In Tristram Shandy, the hero is born in
(a) the second book *(b)* the fourth book
(c) the third book *(d)* the fifth book

314. Don Quixote basically presents
(a) the romantic nature of man
(b) the contrasting glory and misery of mankind
(c) the greedy nature of man
(d) the foolish instincts inherent in man's nature

315. In writing Tristram Shandy, Sterne was mainly influenced by
(a) Shakespeare *(b)* Chaucer
(c) Cervantes *(d)* Lamb

316. Tristram Shandy is primarily a .... novel
(a) sentimental *(b)* romantic
(c) comical *(d)* intellectual

317. In the 'Vicar of Wakefield' Goldsmith mainly offers a .... figure
(a) romantic *(b)* moral
(c) carefree *(d)* extremely worried

318. What is A.C. Bradley mainly known for
(a) Shakespearean comedy
(b) Historical plays of Shakespeare
(c) Shakespearean tragedy
(d) Shakespeare's romances

319. Who is the writer of 'The School for Scandal'
(a) Ben Jonson *(b)* R.B. Sheridan
(c) Congreve *(d)* Webster

320. Raymond Williams is primarily a
(a) Dramatist *(b)* Novelist
(c) Essayist *(d)* Critic

321. Who is the writer of the poem "The Canonization"
(a) Milton *(b)* Dryden
(c) Donne *(d)* Chaucer

322. Name the writer of the poem "Wind Hour"
(a) Hopkins *(b)* Eliot
(c) Dryden *(d)* Yeats

323. Who is the writer of the poem "Adam's Course"
(a) Eliot *(b)* Tagore
(c) Yeats *(d)* Shelley

324. Who wrote the poem: "Lay Your Sleeping Head".
(a) Auden *(b)* Yeats
(c) Stephen Spender *(d)* Ted Hughes

325. The play "The Birthday Party" is written by
(a) G.B. Shaw *(b)* Galsworthy
(c) Harold Pinter *(d)* Osborne

326. Who is believed to be the writer of "On the Sublime"
(a) Aristotle *(b)* Longinus
(c) Plato *(d)* M. Arnold

327. Name the author of "An Essay on Dramatic Poesie"
(a) Dryden *(b)* Sidney
(c) Shelley *(d)* Arnold

328. Who is the writer of "Culture and Society"
(a) Cleanth Brooks
(b) Eliot
(c) Bertrand Russell
(d) Raymond Williams

329. The writer of the 'Mirror and the Lamp' is
(a) Hume *(b)* Lionel Trilling
(c) M.H. Abrams *(d)* Sean Lucy

330. The writer of "Provide Provide" is
(a) Whitman *(b)* Frost
(c) Yeats *(d)* Auden

331. In whose essays the idea of the "oversoul" pervades...........
(a) Thoreau *(b)* Emerson
(c) Whitman *(d)* Mark Twain

332. Who wrote "Desire Under the Elms"
(a) Arthur Miller *(b)* Osborne
(c) Eugene O'Neill *(d)* Shaw

333. Who is the writer of "A Severed Head"
(a) Iris Murdoch *(b)* Paul Scott
(c) Goldwing *(d)* Huxley

334. 'Das Kapital' is written by
(a) Engel *(b)* Freud
(c) Marx *(d)* Lawrence

335. "Waiting for Godot" is written by
(a) Samuel Beckett *(b)* Ibsen
(c) Brecht *(d)* Chekhov

336. Who is the writer of "A House for Mr. Biswas"?
(a) Salman Rushdie *(b)* V.S. Naipaul
(c) Vikram Seth *(d)* R.K. Narayan

337. Name which is not the work of Marlowe
(a) Richard I *(b)* Tambarlaine
(c) The Jew of Malta *(d)* Dr. Faustus

338. Name the writer of the poem "The Weary Blues"
(a) Longfellow *(b)* Whitman
(c) Frost *(d)* Langston Hughes

339. Which of the following poems is not written by Robert Lowell
(a) In the Cage *(b)* Dolphin
(c) Good Morning *(d)* The Old Flame

340. Which of the following poems is written by Wallace Stevens
(a) Red Sun Blues *(b)* Sunday Morning
(c) From Survivor *(d)* "Going"

341. Which of the following poems is not written by Philip Larkin
(a) Art Grass *(b)* Sad Steps
(c) Traveller *(d)* Church going

342. Oedipus Rex was written by
(a) Sophocles *(b)* Homer
(c) Seneca *(d)* Aeschylus

343. Flaubert's famous work is
(a) Odysseus *(b)* Madame Bovary
(c) The Trial *(d)* The Outsider

344. Northrop Fry is basically a
(a) Dramatist *(b)* Novelist
(c) Poet *(d)* Critic

345. The writer of "The Beauty in a State" is
(a) Raja Rao *(b)* Tagore
(c) Shelley *(d)* Ananda Coomaraswami

346. The most important work of K.R. Srinivas Iyengar is
(a) Indian Way of Writing
(b) Indians Under the Foreign Rule
(c) Indian Writing in English
(d) Indian Literary Scene

347. The writer of "The Swan and the Eagle" is
(a) M.K. Naik *(b)* C.D. Narasimhaiah
(c) Bruce King *(d)* V.K. Gokak

348. Name the writer of the book "Introducing Applied Linguistics" (Penguin)
(a) Allen *(b)* Mac Arthur
(c) G.A. Leech *(d)* S. Pittcorder

349. Danglars is a character in
(a) The Treasure Island *(b)* Monte Cristo
(c) Oliver Twist *(d)* Huckleberry Finn

350. "A sleepless hour or more has its strange value only in the middle."
Name the writer of the lines given above
(a) Kamala Das *(b)* Daruwalla
(c) Dilip Chitre *(d)* Nissim Ezekiel

351. Who said about Virginia Woolf "She had no taste for rough diamonds"
(a) A.D. Moody *(b)* E. Albert
(c) H.V. Routh *(d)* W. Allen

352. The name of Virginia Woolf's father was
(a) Stephen Woolf *(b)* John Woolf
(c) James Woolf *(d)* Robert Woolf

353. In which work does the following line appear : "Her sympathy seemed to fly back into her face, like a bramble spring."
(a) Mrs. Dalloway *(b)* Lord Jim
(c) To The Lighthouse *(d)* David Copperfield

354. Identify the last line of Whitman's "Passage to India"
(a) Passage to more than India
(b) O farther, farther, farther sail!
(c) O brave soul!
(d) Away O soul! Lost-instantly the anchor!

355. The generally accepted date of the death of Plato is
(a) 342 BC *(b)* 341 BC
(c) 348 BC *(d)* 340 BC

356. It is generally believed that Aristotle was born in
(a) 380 BC *(b)* 384 BC
(c) 390 BC *(d)* 391 BC

357. Aristotle was engaged as tutor to
(a) King Philip *(b)* King of Persia
(c) Alexander *(d)* Princess of Turkey

358. What was the most revolutionary deed done by Aristotle, regarding human rights and freedom, which he did before his death?
(a) He wrote Poetics
(b) He inverted most of Plato's theories
(c) He liberated all his slaves through his will
(d) He noted down everything that he studied at Plato's Academy

359. Which critic is most associated with the view that "Poetry is criticism of life."
(a) Dryden *(b)* Eliot
(c) Wordsworth *(d)* Matthew Arnold

360. What did Byron die of
(a) heart failure *(b)* fever
(c) dysentery *(d)* gouts

361. Which among the following critics did not believe in the authority of ancient classics
(*a*) Dryden (*b*) Jonson
(*c*) Wordsworth (*d*) Pope

362. Which of the following poets made a fortune by translating Homer
(*a*) Shelley (*b*) Dryden
(*c*) Spenser (*d*) Pope

363. Who is believed to have said :
"That which does not concern the common man, is of no significance."
(*a*) Voltaire (*b*) Rousseau
(*c*) Locke (*d*) Southey

364. Who is stated to have said
"Criticism is the art of interpreting art."
(*a*) Dryden (*b*) Arnold
(*c*) Walter Pater (*d*) Eliot

365. Who wrote the poem: "The Lake Isle of Innisfree"
(*a*) Yeats (*b*) Eliot
(*c*) Spender (*d*) Auden

366. Who is primarily associated with the term "Objective Correlative"
(*a*) Shelley (*b*) Sandburg
(*c*) Eliot (*d*) Hardy

367. Who is stated to have said, "What criticism undertakes is the profitable discussion of literature."
(*a*) Eliot (*b*) F.R. Leavis
(*c*) Middleton Murry (*d*) Chatterton

368. Who wrote : "The Lives of the Poets"
(*a*) Boswell (*b*) Hazlitt
(*c*) Macaulay (*d*) Dr. Johnson

369. Who is said to have used the term "high seriousness"
(*a*) Dryden (*b*) Sidney
(*c*) M. Arnold (*d*) Eliot

370. Who used the term "high disdain"
(*a*) Shakespeare (*b*) Milton
(*c*) Yeats (*d*) Darwin

371. Who wrote: "The Interpretation of Dreams"
(*a*) Marx (*b*) Jung
(*c*) Freud (*d*) Darwin

372. Who wrote : "Principles of Literary Criticism" (in 1924)
(*a*) T.R. Leavis (*b*) Kenneth Brooke
(*c*) I.A. Richards (*d*) A.G. Gardiner

373. Who said : "Poetry is not a turning loose of emotion, but an escape from emotion"
(*a*) Wordsworth (*b*) T.S. Eliot
(*c*) I.A. Richards (*d*) Wilson Knight

374. Who said : "Language may be defined as the expression of thought by means of speech sounds."
(*a*) Sapir (*b*) R.H. Robins
(*c*) Henry Sweet (*d*) A.H. Gardiner

375. In what respect among the following do the human beings and animals have at least partly identical station in the matter of language as a means of communication?
(*a*) acquired (*b*) instinctive
(*c*) grammaticality (*d*) behaviourial

376. Who said: "So, Here I am......
Twenty years largely wasted.....
Trying to use word......."
(*a*) Yeats (*b*) T.S. Eliot
(*c*) Wordsworth (*d*) Hardy

377. Who said: "Style is the skin and the mere coat."
(*a*) Shelley (*b*) Pater
(*c*) Carlyle (*d*) Quillar Couch

378. When did Trubetzkoy's "Principles of Phonology", appear
(*a*) 1942 (*b*) 1931
(*c*) 1930 (*d*) 1939

379. Whose book "Language" (1933) is considered "The Bible of American Linguistics"
(*a*) Robert A. Hall (*b*) Bloomfield
(*c*) Bernard Bloch (*d*) Edward Sapir

380. Who said: Language is "primarily an auditory system of symbols."
(*a*) Franz Boas (*b*) Bloch
(*c*) Sapir (*d*) Whitney

381. Which of the following poems is not by Frost.
(*a*) Design (*b*) Birches
(*c*) Reluctance (*d*) Michael

382. What does the term "Deus ex machina" mean?
(*a*) God out of the machine
(*b*) devil out of the machine
(*c*) man out of the machine
(*d*) beast out of the machine

383. The famous soliloquy "To be or not to be" occurs in
(*a*) Macbeth (*b*) King Lear
(*c*) Hamlet (*d*) Othello

384. Who wrote : "Flower in the crammied well
....
Little flower but if I could understand what you are
....
I should know what God and Man is."
(*a*) Wordsworth (*b*) Shelley
(*c*) Yeats (*d*) Tennyson

385. Which is the 'odd man out' in the following
(*a*) Paradise Lost (*b*) The Ramayana
(*c*) Essay on Man (*d*) Iliad

386. Which Italian poet is most famous for his sonnets
(*a*) Petrarch (*b*) Dante
(*c*) Ovid (*d*) None of these

387. Who wrote the following line :
"Blow, blow, thou winter wind"
(*a*) Milton (*b*) Tennyson
(*c*) Shakespeare (*d*) Browning

388. In which of the following word the adverb form is made by simply applying "ly" at the end
(*a*) Present (*b*) Incident
(*c*) Accident (*d*) Occasion

389. Tetra metre comprises a line with...........iambus
(a) Two *(b)* Three
(c) Four *(d)* Five

390. What figure of speech has been used in the following line:
"Milton! thou shouldnt be living with us at this hour."
—Wordsworth
(a) Hyperbole *(b)* Simile
(c) Metaphor *(d)* Apostrophe

391. Under which category should Dryden's Mac flecknoe be placed
(a) Satire *(b)* Epic
(c) Ode *(d)* Lyric

392. Which figure of speech has been used in the term : "immemorial elms"
(a) Allegory *(b)* Rhyme
(c) Alliteration *(d)* Oxymoron

393. Who is the writer of the following line :
"Busy old fool, unruly sun"
(a) Shelley *(b)* Milton
(c) Clough *(d)* Donne

394. What is the name of the central figure in Tagore's play "Muktadhara"
(a) King Vivajit *(b)* King Ranajit
(c) Prince Abhijit *(d)* Amba

395. Which play of Shaw is also sometimes called "The Chocolate Soldier"
(a) Arms and the Man *(b)* Candida
(c) Pygmalion *(d)* Saint Joan

396. In which episode of "The Merchant of Venice" did the Prince of Arragon make the choice of the silver casket
(a) The Bond Episode *(b)* The Casket Episode
(c) The Trial Scene *(d)* The Ring Episode

397. Which one among the following was not the demand of the Chartists in 19th century in England.
(a) annual parliaments
(b) pensions to all widows
(c) vote by ballot
(d) universal manhood suffrage

398. In which category among novelists should Mrs. Gaskell be placed
(a) humanitarian *(b)* determinist
(c) picaresque *(d)* revolutionary

399. Which one among the following cannot be deemed to be a writer of the "Problem Play"
(a) G.B. Shaw
(b) Galsworthy
(c) Harley Granville-Barker
(d) Eliot

400. In which decade of the twentieth century did the group of novelists commonly known as "Angry Young Men" appear?
(a) Thirties *(b)* Forties
(c) Fifties *(d)* Sixties

401. In which year was Magna Carta signed
(a) 1205 *(b)* 1212
(c) 1215 *(d)* 1220

402. To which King of England did Pope give the title 'Defender of the Faith'
(a) Henry VII *(b)* Henry VIII
(c) James I *(d)* Charles I

403. When did Mandeville's 'Travels' appear
(a) 1500 *(b)* 1501
(c) 1496 *(d)* 1490

404. Who is the writer of "Metamorphoses"
(a) Ovid *(b)* Dante
(c) Petrarch *(d)* Virgil

405. When is Wyclif believed to have died?
(a) 1380 *(b)* 1382
(c) 1383 *(d)* 1384

406. East India Company was set up in
(a) 1604 *(b)* 1603
(c) 1600 *(d)* 1605

407. G.M. Trevelyan was primarily a
(a) historian *(b)* dramatist
(c) poet *(d)* novelist

408. In which book does the following line appear:
"A god is not so glorious as a king." —Marlowe
(a) Dr. Faustus *(b)* The Jew of Malta
(c) Tamburlaine *(d)* Edward II

409. The book "Euphues" was written by
(a) Greene *(b)* Jonson
(c) Dryden *(d)* John Lyly

410. Bacon's essays are the finest example of
(a) wit and humour *(b)* practical wisdom
(c) pathos *(d)* irony

411. Tamberlaine is basically an expression of the spirit of .... in full measure
(a) Renaissance *(b)* Romanticism
(c) Imperialism *(d)* Materialism

412. In which poem do the following lines appear:
"Stone walls do not a prison make,
Nor iron bars a cage."
(a) "To Lucasta"
(b) 'To Althea, from Prison'
(c) Ballad Upon a Wedding
(d) None of these

413. Which one among the following was not a cavalier poet
(a) Herrick *(b)* Thomas Carew
(c) John Suckling *(d)* Robert Bridges

414. Which age in English literature is known as the Augustan Age
(a) That of Dryden
(b) That of Dr. Johnson
(c) That of Shakespeare
(d) That of Pope

415. Who wrote to Pope in 1706 :
"The best of the modern poets in all languages are those that have nearest copied the ancients."

(*a*) Addison (*b*) Steele
(*c*) Walsh (*d*) Dryden

416. The Age of Queen Anne in England was an era of
(*a*) political stability (*b*) political upheavals
(*c*) great social unrest (*d*) great natural calamities

417. When was Swift born?
(*a*) 1660 (*b*) 1661
(*c*) 1680 (*d*) 1667

418. Which is Swift's most powerful general satire
(*a*) Gulliver's Travels
(*b*) The Tale of a Tub
(*c*) The Battle of Books
(*d*) Nothing can be said in this connection

419. Who characterized D.G. Rossetti's poetry as belonging to "the fleshly school of poetry"
(*a*) Eliot (*b*) M. Arnold
(*c*) Robert Buchanan (*d*) Yeats

420. In which poem does the following line occur:
"The wild wine slips with the weight of its leaves."—Swinburne
(*a*) The Blessed Damozel
(*b*) Atalanta in Calydon
(*c*) The Hounds of Spring
(*d*) None of these

421. Which of the following should be regarded as the presiding deity of the Victorian period
(*a*) Mrs. Grundy (*b*) Mammon
(*c*) Cupid (*d*) Venus

422. Who is the heroine of 'Vanity Fair'
(*a*) Sophia (*b*) Estella
(*c*) Dora (*d*) Becky Sharp

423. The period of Edward VII's rule in England lasted from 1901 to ....
(*a*) 1912 (*b*) 1910
(*c*) 1909 (*d*) 1913

424. When was Old Age Pensions Act passed in England
(*a*) 1909 (*b*) 1907
(*c*) 1906 (*d*) 1908

425. In which decade in the nineteenth century did the Chartist Movement take a concrete shape in England?
(*a*) Thirties (*b*) Twenties
(*c*) Fifties (*d*) Sixties

426. Which one among the following was not the reason for the failure of the Chartist Movement?
(*a*) Peel's reforms and the growth of prosperity
(*b*) Lack of a powerful leader among the working classes
(*c*) Fake signatures of people presented to parliament
(*d*) Natural calamities

427. Which age is generally called the Age of Prose and Reason?
(*a*) Eighteenth century (*b*) Seventeenth century
(*c*) Nineteenth century (*d*) Sixteenth century

428. Who can be said to be the greatest writer of the Comedy of Humours?
(*a*) Dryden (*b*) Ben Jonson
(*c*) Congreve (*d*) Etherege

429. Which one among the following is not a play by Ben Johnson?
(*a*) Volpone
(*b*) Alchemist
(*c*) Every man out of His Honour
(*d*) The Way of the World

430. Who is the writer of the book "Prince"`
(*a*) Ovid (*b*) Boccaccio
(*c*) Machiavelli (*d*) Montaigne

431. Who is the writer of the essay "Simulation and Dissimulation"?
(*a*) Montaigne (*b*) Lamb
(*c*) De Quincey (*d*) Bacon

432. Name the figure of speech for which Lyly is chiefly remembered
(*a*) Malapropism (*b*) Euphuism
(*c*) Melodramaticism (*d*) None of these

433. Utopia was written by
(*a*) Walter Raleigh (*b*) Sir Thomas Moore
(*c*) Daniel Defoe (*d*) None of these

434. The other name for Euphues is
(*a*) The Anatomy of Melancholy
(*b*) The Anatomy of Joy
(*c*) The Anatomy of Wit
(*d*) None of these

435. Ferrex and Porrex is the other name for
(*a*) The Spanish Tragedy
(*b*) Dr. Faustus
(*c*) Goboduc
(*d*) None of these

436. In the 'Spanish Tragedy', there is the ghost of
(*a*) Andrea (*b*) Horatio
(*c*) Balthazar (*d*) Lorenzo

437. Which one among the following belongs to the group known as University Wits
(*a*) Shakespeare (*b*) Congreve
(*c*) Dryden (*d*) Marlowe

438. Astrophel and Stella is a
(*a*) play (*b*) novel
(*c*) sonnet sequence (*d*) short story

439. In the Duchess of Malfi, Ferdinand was the Duke of
(*a*) Milan (*b*) Calabria
(*c*) Rome (*d*) None of these

440. The Alchemist was published in
(*a*) 1610 (*b*) 1611
(*c*) 1612 (*d*) 1609

441. In the Duchess of Malfi, who spoke the following words "O horror, that not the fear of him which binds the devils can prescribe man obedicence."
(*a*) Ferdinand (*b*) Cardinal
(*c*) Bosola (*d*) Antonio

442. In 'Sons and Lovers', Paul Moral is the son of
(*a*) John Morel (*b*) Joseph Morel
(*c*) Walter Morel (*d*) James Morel

443. Which of the following is not one of the five movements in 'The Wasteland'
(*a*) The Burial of the Dead
(*b*) The Game of Chess
(*c*) The Fire Sermon
(*d*) The Joy of Riding

444. When was St. Thomas canonized : in
(*a*) 1170 (*b*) 1171
(*c*) 1173 (*d*) 1175

445. Who appointed St. Thomas Becket a Chancellor
(*a*) Henry III (*b*) Henry I
(*c*) Henry II (*d*) None of these

446. T.S. Eliot died in
(*a*) 1960 (*b*) 1962
(*c*) 1961 (*d*) 1965

447. When was Erewhon first published
(*a*) 1871 (*b*) 1872
(*c*) 1873 (*d*) 1874

448. What is the Greek meaning of 'Utopia'
(*a*) An ideal place
(*b*) A healthy place
(*c*) A lovely place
(*d*) Not a place (=ou=not; topos=a place)

449. What are the last words of Vanity Fair
(*a*) Shantih! Shantih! Shantih
(*b*) Vanitas Vanitatum!
(*c*) Amen!
(*d*) Let it be

450. 'Virtue Rewarded' is the other name for
(*a*) Pamela (*b*) Joseph Andrews
(*c*) Clarissa (*d*) Tom Jones

451. The word "Volksgeist" means
(*a*) The spirit of the age
(*b*) (As per) tradition, custom and consensus
(*c*) The essence of something
(*d*) None of these

452. When did the hundred years' war which started in 1337 come to an end?
(*a*) 1450 (*b*) 1451
(*c*) 1452 (*d*) 1453

453. The Age of chivalry was basically an age of
(*a*) war
(*b*) love
(*c*) love, war and religion
(*d*) religion

454. Cervantes practically rang the death-knell of
(*a*) war (*b*) love
(*c*) religion (*d*) chivalry

455. The "Black Death" in England as came in 1348 was known by this name because
(*a*) Black, knotty boils appeared on the bodies of the victims
(*b*) The country was attached by black vultures feeding on dead bodies
(*c*) The whole country became black with dead bodies
(*d*) It was a mournful event compelling people to wear black dress.

456. When did Peasants' Revolt take place in England?
(*a*) In 1380 (*b*) In 1384
(*c*) In 1381 (*d*) In 1390

457. Who was the king in England at the time of Peasants' Revolt?
(*a*) Richard II (*b*) Richard III
(*c*) Henry I (*d*) King John

458. Which one of the following was a contemporary of Chaucer
(*a*) Spenser (*b*) Herrick
(*c*) Robert Graves (*d*) John Gower

459. The famous work of Boccaccio is
(*a*) Decameron (*b*) Divine Comedy
(*c*) Essays (*d*) A collection of sonnets

460. When did Petrarch die?
(*a*) 1382 (*b*) 1389
(*c*) 1370 (*d*) 1374

461. Who has written the following line :
"Chaucer symbolises, as no other writer does, The Middle Ages."
(*a*) Legouis (*b*) Hugh Walker
(*c*) Compton-Rickett (*d*) Hudson

462. What is meant by "Grub Street"?
(*a*) The literary scene of hacks' crowds during Pope's period.
(*b*) Unhygienic streets of London
(*c*) Streets full of worms
(*d*) Plague-infested streets

463. Who wrote: "Idylls of the King"?
(*a*) Tennyson (*b*) Browning
(*c*) Spenser (*d*) Keats

464. Who started the Lollards' Movement?
(*a*) John Gower (*b*) Langland
(*c*) Wyclif (*d*) Wat Tylar

465. Who wrote the following lines :
"He loved gold in special,
For, gold in physic is a cordial."
(*a*) Langland (*b*) Wyclif
(*c*) John Ball (*d*) Chaucer

466. Sir Andrew Freeport is a member of
(*a*) The Royal Society of Science
(*b*) The Spectator Club
(*c*) The Royal Academy of Art
(*d*) The Royal Society of Physicians

467. What could be another name for Renaissance
(*a*) The New Learning
(*b*) The Reformation
(*c*) The Prostantism
(*d*) Humanism

468. Who wrote: 'Hudibras'
(*a*) Butler (*b*) Addison
(*c*) Steele (*d*) Goldsmith

469. When was the poet John Gay born?
(*a*) 1675 (*b*) 1681
(*c*) 1685 (*d*) 1687

470. "London" by Dr. Johnson is
(*a*) An epic (*b*) A verse satire
(*c*) A prose satire (*d*) A critical work

471. Cowper was born in
(*a*) 1730 (*b*) 1733
(*c*) 1731 (*d*) 1729

472. Who wrote Moll Flanders?
(*a*) Richardson (*b*) Fielding
(*c*) Smollett (*d*) Defoe

473. The Gothic novel was primarily a novel of
(*a*) Pity (*b*) Terror
(*c*) Love (*d*) Description of nature

474. When did Areopagitica appear?
(*a*) In 1641 (*b*) In 1642
(*c*) In 1643 (*d*) In 1644

475. The main plank of Areopagitica's argument was for the freedom of
(*a*) the press (*b*) worship
(*c*) movement (*d*) forming a political party

476. Philip Wakem is a character in
(*a*) The Middlemarch
(*b*) Great Expectations
(*c*) The Mill on the Floss
(*d*) Waiting for Godot

477. When was Walter Pater born?
(*a*) In 1836 (*b*) In 1837
(*c*) In 1839 (*d*) In 1841

478. Which one of the following writers is not dealt with in Pater's 'Appreciations'
(*a*) Southey (*b*) Lamb
(*c*) Coleridge (*d*) Rossetti

479. 'Unto This Last' is a work by
(*a*) Carlyle (*b*) Pater
(*c*) Oscar Wilde (*d*) John Ruskin

480. Thomas Gradgrind is a character that occurs in
(*a*) Hard Times (*b*) Candida
(*c*) Wasteland (*d*) Jude the Obscure

481. Which one among the following cannot strictly be called the writer of novels of purpose
(*a*) Dickens (*b*) Newman
(*c*) Jane Austen (*d*) Kingsley

482. Who among the following cannot be termed one of the Four Wheels of English Novel in the Eighteenth century?
(*a*) Jane Austen (*b*) Smollett
(*c*) Sterne (*d*) Fielding

483. Who is the writer of "The Blessed Damozel"?
(*a*) Christina Rossetti (*b*) Emile Bronte
(*c*) D.G. Rossetti (*d*) W.B. Yeats

484. Which is the correct chronological order?
(*a*) Utopia—Dr. Faustus—Areopagitica—Maud
(*b*) Henry V—The Faery Queene—Lyrical Ballads—The Compleat Angler
(*c*) Christabel—Canterbury Tales—Queen Mab—Corsair
(*d*) Kubla Khan—Othello—Paradise Lost—Michael

485. The word "compromise" is used with...age
(*a*) Elizabethan (*b*) Modern
(*c*) Victorian (*d*) Chaucerian

486. Which one of the following poets may to some extent be considered a continental poet
(*a*) Tennyson (*b*) Spenser
(*c*) Eliot (*d*) Byron

487. Which one among the following favoured most the imperialistic tendencies
(*a*) Shelley (*b*) Spenser
(*c*) Eliot (*d*) Kipling

488. Who among the following was not a critic?
(*a*) M. Arnold (*b*) Ruskin
(*c*) Dryden (*d*) Tennyson

489. "Liberty, Equality, Fraternity" was the slogan of
(*a*) French Revolution
(*b*) Bolshevik Revolution
(*c*) American Civil War
(*d*) Indian Freedom Movement

490. Francis Thompson the poet, died in
(*a*) 1910 (*b*) 1909
(*c*) 1907 (*d*) 1906

491. The most important aspect of Jane Austen's novels is
(*a*) Superb characterization
(*b*) Perfect Plot construction
(*c*) High moral sense
(*d*) Lively dialogues

492. The circle of Jane Austen's novels is
(*a*) The whole universe
(*b*) The whole word
(*c*) The whole of England
(*d*) A limited number of families

493. Which one among the following was not a contemporary or predecessor of Shakespeare?
(*a*) Marlowe (*b*) Kyd
(*c*) Fry (*d*) Greene

494. Who among the following was not a prose writer
(*a*) Ascham (*b*) Coleridge
(*c*) Hooker (*d*) Raleigh

495. Who among the following was not a character writer
(*a*) Wordsworth (*b*) Joseph Hall
(*c*) John Earle (*d*) Sir Thomas Overbury

496. Who among the following was not an essayist of the seventeenth century.
(*a*) Halifax (*b*) Sir Thomas Browne
(*c*) Hazlitt (*d*) Sir William Temple

497. About whom has it been said :
"He knew small Latin and less Greek"
(*a*) Ben Jonson (*b*) Shakespeare
(*c*) Milton (*d*) Aristotle

498. Who said about Shakespeare:
"He was not of age but of ages"

(*a*) Jonson (*b*) Johnson
(*c*) Dryden (*d*) Arnold

499. Pinpoint the correct chronological sequence
(*a*) Petrarch—Spenser—Wordsworth—Marlowe
(*b*) Wyclif—Lyly—Shelley—Tennyson
(*c*) Pope—Chaucer—Donne—Yeats
(*d*) M. Arnold—Dryden—Sidney—Yeats

500. Who wrote: 'Modern Painters.'
(*a*) Rossetti (*b*) Reynolds
(*c*) Hazlitt (*d*) Ruskin

501. When was Somerset Maugham born
(*a*) 1871 (*b*) 1872
(*c*) 1873 (*d*) 1874

502. In which book do the following lines occur :
"Around the ancient track marched, rank on rank,
The army of unalterable law."
(*a*) Sons and Lovers
(*b*) Michael
(*c*) 'Love in the Valley' by George Meredith
(*d*) Hyperion

503. Who is the writer of the following lines :
"Laugh and be merry, remember, better
the world with a song.
Better the world with a blow
in the teeth of a wrong."
(*a*) Wordsworth (*b*) Browning
(*c*) John Masefield (*d*) Yeats

504. When did Landon die?
(*a*) 1870 (*b*) 1874
(*c*) 1872 (*d*) 1873

505. Which one of the following is not the work of Lamb
(*a*) Of Style (*b*) All Fools' Day
(*c*) Dream Children (*d*) Grace Before Meat

506. Whose is the following line:
"A child's a plaything for an hour."
(*a*) Charles Lamb (*b*) Mary Lamb
(*c*) Shelley (*d*) Tagore

507. Who wrote the following line :
"The moon is nothing
But a circumambulatory aphrodisiac."
(*a*) Yeats (*b*) Shelley
(*c*) Keats (*d*) Fry

508. Who is stated to have said :
"veni, vidi, vici"
(*a*) Julius Caesar (*b*) Alexander
(*c*) Napoleon (*d*) Homer

509. The War of Troy was fought between
(*a*) The Greeks and the French
(*b*) The Greeks and the Trojans
(*c*) The Trojans and the Austrians
(*d*) The Trojans and the Turks

510. One of the heroes in the War of Troy bore the name of a city
(*a*) Paris (*b*) Prague
(*c*) Madrid (*d*) Rome

511. Who wrote : "The Advancement of Learning"
(*a*) Pope (*b*) Tennyson
(*c*) Bacon (*d*) Eliot

512. Who said : "My essays .... come home, to men's business, and bosoms."
(*a*) Lamb (*b*) Bacon
(*c*) Hazlitt (*d*) Stevenson

513. In which year did the 'Glorious Revolution' take place in England?
(*a*) 1685 (*b*) 1680
(*c*) 1681 (*d*) 1688

514. Who wrote: "We are hollow men."
(*a*) Eliot (*b*) Yeats
(*c*) Tagore (*d*) Ezekiel

515. Who used the term "The perpetual struggle for room and food."
(*a*) Amartya Sen (*b*) Laski
(*c*) Malthus (*d*) Marx

516. In which book do the following lines appear :
"O thou art fairer than the evening air, Clad in the beauty of a thousand stars."
(*a*) Dr. Faustus
(*b*) Tamburlaine
(*c*) The Spanish Tragedy
(*d*) Faerie Queene

517. Who wrote the following line :
"Our swords shall play the orators for us."
(*a*) Shakespeare (*b*) Marlowe
(*c*) Greene (*d*) Eliot

518. By which character is the following line in Shakespeare's Julius Caesar spoken?
"I'm well-armed in honesty."
(*a*) Caesar (*b*) Cassius
(*c*) Brutus (*d*) Cicero

519. Who said: "I teach you the superman.
Man is something that is to be surpassed."
(*a*) Mallarme (*b*) Zola
(*c*) Ibsen (*d*) Nietzsche

520. Who is stated to have called Turkey "a seriously sick man."
(*a*) Edward II (*b*) Nicholas I of Russia
(*c*) Napoleon (*d*) Churchill

521. Who gave the definition of a gentleman as "one who never inflicts pain."
(*a*) Nash (*b*) Wordsworth
(*c*) Newman (*d*) Yeats

522. To whom is the statement "Laws were made to be broken" originally ascribed
(*a*) Goldsmith, Oliver
(*b*) Christopher North (John Wilson)
(*c*) Bacon
(*d*) Hazlitt

523. Who wrote the following lines :
"My subject is war, and the pity of war. The poetry is in the pity."

(a) George Washington (b) Napoleon
(c) Tolstoy (d) Wilfred Owen

524. Who said: "He comes too near that comes to be denied."
(a) Milton (b) Overbury
(c) Addison (d) Stevenson

525. "Who wrote : "The dropping of rain hollows out of a stone."
(a) Milton (b) Shakespeare
(c) Virgil (d) Ovid

526. In which book do the following words appear :
"The mass of men lead dead lives of quiet desperation."
(a) Glimpses of World History
(b) Outline of World History
(c) Walden
(d) Emerson's Essays

527. In which book did Jawaharlal Nehru quote the following words of Goethe:
"If the Romans were great enough to invent things like that, we at least should be great enough to believe them."
(a) The Discovery of India
(b) Glimpses of World History
(c) An Autobiography
(d) None of these

528. Who said about Jawaharlal Nehru:
"...Thus there emerges the image of Jawaharlal Nehru as a humanist, full of the deepest tenderness for men everywhere, a polytheist who accepted all the gods of the world, a universalist."
(a) R.K. Narayan (b) Mulk Raj Anand
(c) Khushwant Singh (d) Indira Gandhi

529. Who said: "Nothing can harm a good man, either in life or after death."
(a) Newman (b) Chaucer
(c) Shakespeare (d) Socrates

530. Who said, "From forty to fifty a man is at heart either a stoic or a satyr."
(a) Sir Thomas Moore (b) Sir Arthur Pinero
(c) Horace Walpole (d) Yeats

531. 'The Way of All Flesh' was written by
(a) Swift (b) Congreve
(c) Butler (d) Addison

532. In which poem does the following line occur :
"Our birth is but a sleep and a forgetting."
(a) Tintern Abbey
(b) Hymn on Intellectual Beauty
(c) Ode on Intimations of Immortality
(d) Adam's Curse

533. In which play does the character "Maura" occur
(a) Riders to the Sea
(b) Lady's Not for Burning
(c) Murder in the Cathedral
(d) The Playboy of the Western World

534. When was 'The Wind Among The Reeds' written
(a) 1897 (b) 1899
(c) 1896 (d) 1900

535. Who was the chief co-founder of the (Irish) Abbey Theatre with W.B. Yeats
(a) Lady Gregory (b) Shaw
(c) Galsworthy (d) Maud Gonne

36. When did Housman die?
(a) 1933 (b) 1935
(c) 1936 (d) 1937

537. P.G. Wodehouse is generally known as a
(a) sad man
(b) 'Funny man' of contemporary literature
(c) man of romance
(d) None of these

538. Who said the following words :
"To be alone is the fate of all great minds."
(a) Plato
(b) Socrates
(c) The Buddha
(d) Arthur Schopenhauer

539. "There is no cure for birth and death save to enjoy the interval."
Who said the words mentioned above?
(a) Socrates (b) George Santayana
(c) M.K. Gandhi (d) Vivekananda

540. Who said, "I am the grass; I cover all."
(a) Whitman (b) Frost
(c) Sandburg (d) Emily Dickinson

541. Who is the writer of the line :
"Look back, and smile at perils past."
(a) Shakespeare (b) Scott
(c) Wordsworth (d) Yeats

542. Who wrote : "I must—I will—I can—I ought—I do."
(a) Congreve (b) Carlyle
(c) R.B. Sheridan (d) Etherege

543. Who is the writer of "The Good Companions"
(a) A.G. Gardiner (b) Chatterton
(c) Hazlitt (d) J.B. Priestley

544. Who among the following poets can be said to be a catalogue writer
(a) Lowell (b) Auden
(c) Eliot (d) Whitman

545. Which poet among the following can be said to be a poet of multitudes
(a) Auden (b) Yeats
(c) Whitman (d) Sandburg

546. Who is the writer of the poem 'Vagabond'?
(a) MacNeice (b) Masefield
(c) Sir Henry Newbolt (d) Rupert Brooke

547. Who said, "French is the only modern language fit for literature"
(a) Coleridge (b) Yeats
(c) Conrad (d) Synge

548. Which poem of Kipling was considered an offence to democracy

(*a*) 'Recessional'
(*b*) 'Rowers'
(*c*) 'Our Lady of the Snows'
(*d*) 'A Servant when He Reigneth'

549. Which one among the following was not one of the Decadents
(*a*) Oscar Wilde (*b*) Aubrey Beardsley
(*c*) Tennyson (*d*) Rupert Brooke

550. "If I should die, think only this of me." Who wrote the above line?
(*a*) Housman (*b*) Mare
(*c*) Yeats (*d*) Brooke

551. Which of the following statements is true :
(*a*) Browning's work is more original in content than that of Tennyson
(*b*) Wordsworth was the older brother of Coleridge
(*c*) Shelley was a pessimistic poet
(*d*) James Joyce received the Nobel Prize in 1933

552. Which of the following statements is true :
(*a*) Fanny Burney was a poetess of the first rank.
(*b*) Wordsworth and Coleridge were always at daggers' drawn with each other
(*c*) Keats died at the age of fifty
(*d*) Mrs. Virginia Woolf committed suicide

553. Which of the following statements is true :
(*a*) Goldsmith hated mankind
(*b*) Horace Walpole is an historian of the second order
(*c*) Crashaw was a Victorian novelist
(*d*) Donne was the grandson of Spenser

554. Which of the following statements is true :
(*a*) Mrs. Montagu is one of the queens of the Blue Stockings
(*b*) French Revolution had no effect on Shelley
(*c*) Southey fought in the battle of Blenheim
(*d*) Lamb had his hut in a forest

555. Dryden's comedy 'The Wild Gallant' belongs to the year
(*a*) 1661 (*b*) 1663
(*c*) 1665 (*d*) 1667

556. Sir Thomas Browne was overwhelmingly a
(*a*) poet of the first order
(*b*) a prose writer
(*c*) a dramatist
(*d*) a novelist

557. "Gallathea" in written by
(*a*) Spenser (*b*) Herbert
(*c*) Lyly (*d*) Shelley

558. In which category should Lyly's "Love's Metamorphosis" be counted:
(*a*) Tragedy (*b*) Historical Play
(*c*) Pastoral (*d*) None of these

559. When was James Thomson born
(*a*) 1701 (*b*) 1700
(*c*) 1702 (*d*) 1699

560. In which year was Jane Austen born
(*a*) 1775 (*b*) 1772
(*c*) 1780 (*d*) 1778

561. Blackwood's magazine was founded in
(*a*) 1815 (*b*) 1817
(*c*) 1816 (*d*) 1818

562. Which one among the following was a periodical
(*a*) The Spectator
(*b*) The Doll's House
(*c*) The Portrait of a Lady
(*d*) Shepherd's Calendar

563. The dramas of the nineteenth century England appeal to
(*a*) the eye (*b*) the imagination
(*c*) the reason (*d*) the conscience

564. Who wrote: "The Harp of India"
(*a*) Govind Chunder Dutt
(*b*) Michael Madhusudan Dutt
(*c*) Henry L.V. Derozio
(*d*) V.K. Gokak

565. "King Porus—A Legend of Old" is written by
(*a*) Henry Derozio (*b*) Toru Dutt
(*c*) Sarojini Naidu (*d*) Michael Madhusudan

566. Who is the writer of the poem "The Dance of the Eunuchs"
(*a*) Nissim Ezekiel (*b*) Kamala Das
(*c*) Daruwallah (*d*) A.K. Ramanujan

567. Which Indian poet wrote the poem "The Trojan War"
(*a*) Vikram Seth (*b*) Keki N. Daruwalla
(*c*) Sri Aurbindo (*d*) Tagore

568. Who wrote: "Jonathan Wild"
(*a*) Richardson (*b*) Smollett
(*c*) Defoe (*d*) Fielding

569. Which one among the following is not a Gothic novelist
(*a*) Mrs. Anne Radicliffe
(*b*) Virginia Woolf
(*c*) Horace Walpole
(*d*) Matthew Gregory Lewis

570. Horace Walpole was the .... of Mr. Walpole, the Prime Minister of England.
(*a*) son (*b*) brother
(*c*) cousin (*d*) father

571. Which one among the following cannot be regarded as a stream-of-consciousness novelist?
(*a*) Dorothy M. Richardson
(*b*) Thackeray
(*c*) Virginia Woolf
(*d*) James Joyce

572. What is it to which Stephen Dedalus finally gets inclined in "A Portrait of the Artist as A Young Man"?
(*a*) Religion (*b*) Art
(*c*) Nature (*d*) God

573. George Eliot's real name was
(*a*) Mary Evans (*b*) Maggie
(*c*) Sophia (*d*) Miss Crompton

574. Which one of the following novels created a lot of controversy even in America
(*a*) A Tale of Two Cities
(*b*) Ulysses
(*c*) The Mill on the Floss
(*d*) Pride and Prejudice

575. Which characters does Forster consider better in his Aspects of the Novel
(*a*) Flat (*b*) Oblong
(*c*) Rich (*d*) Round

576. Stephen Guest is a character in
(*a*) Adam Bede
(*b*) The Middlemarch
(*c*) The Mill on The Floss
(*d*) Silas Marner

577. "Of Revenge" is one of the essays of
(*a*) Lamb (*b*) Hazlitt
(*c*) Gardiner (*d*) Bacon

578. "Reading maketh a full man; conference a ready man; and writing an exact man."
In which of Bacon's essays does the sentence mentioned above appear?
(*a*) Of Studies
(*b*) Of King
(*c*) Of Simulation and Dissimulation
(*d*) Of Revenge

579. In which category should Samuel Pepys be placed
(*a*) A novelist (*b*) a poet
(*c*) a diarist (*d*) a dramatist

580. Addison wrote the autobiography of a coin. What was it?
(*a*) a pound (*b*) a shilling
(*c*) a pence (*d*) a half-crown

581. Which one among the following was the periodical to which Addison did not contribute his works?
(*a*) The Tafler (*b*) The Edinburg Review
(*c*) The Spectator (*d*) The Guardian

582. What secured Addison political patronage
(*a*) a poem (*b*) a drama
(*c*) an essay (*d*) a novel

583. 'Meditation on a Broomstick' by Swift is primarily a
(*a*) study in nature
(*b*) an anatomy of love
(*c*) a bitter criticism of human nature
(*d*) a dive into the spiritual world

584. Goldsmith died in
(*a*) 1772 (*b*) 1770
(*c*) 1774 (*d*) 1771

585. "Beau Tibbs" by Goldsmith is a satire on
(*a*) fops and beaus (*b*) politicians
(*c*) astrologers (*d*) social reformers

586. When did De Quincey die
(*a*) in 1860 (*b*) in 1862
(*c*) in 1861 (*d*) in 1859

587. About whom did Wordsworth write the following line?
"She was a phantom of delight."
(*a*) about Dorothy (*b*) his beloved
(*c*) his wife (*d*) Mrs. Coleridge

588. Who is one of the persons described in De Quincey's "Wordsworth's Household"
(*a*) Dorothy (*b*) Mary Shelley
(*c*) Jane Austen (*d*) Emile Bronte

589. Who accompanied Wordsworth when he was alone in the lap of nature?
(*a*) Mrs. Hutchinson (*b*) Dorothy
(*c*) His children (*d*) Coleridge

590. Who wrote: "The Confessions of An English Opium-Eater"?
(*a*) Coleridge (*b*) Shelley
(*c*) De Quincey (*d*) James Joyce

591. Charles Lamb was born in
(*a*) 1775 (*b*) 1776
(*c*) 1774 (*d*) 1778

592. Who among the following is called the Prince of Essayists?
(*a*) Bacon (*b*) Hazlitt
(*c*) De Quincey (*d*) Lamb

593. In which of his essays does Lamb use the oxymoron "busy-idle" diversions
(*a*) All Fools's Day
(*b*) Dream Children
(*c*) St. Valentine's Day
(*d*) Bachelors' Complaint Against the Behaviour of Married People.

594. What, according to Lamb, as in his essay " The Convalescent," comprise the mind of a sick man?
(*a*) humanism
(*b*) rationalism
(*c*) complete self-absorption
(*d*) philanthropy

595. Who focused attention on the metaphysical poets in the 20th century?
(*a*) Yeats (*b*) Joyce
(*c*) Virginia Woolf (*d*) T.S. Eliot

596. Mention the date of Eliot's Hollow Men
(*a*) 1922 (*b*) 1925
(*c*) 1927 (*d*) 1921

597. Who wrote the poem "Rhapsody on a Windy Day"?
(*a*) Yeats (*b*) Spenser
(*c*) Eliot (*d*) Housman

598. Who wrote the line :
"The weariness, the fever, and the fret"
(*a*) Shelley (*b*) Keats
(*c*) Southey (*d*) Swinburne

599. In which poem does the following poem by Keats occur?

"For ever wilt thou love
and she be fair."
(a) Ode to a Nightingale
(b) Hyperion
(c) Ode to a Grecian Urn
(d) Ode on Indolence

600. Who was Pericles?
(a) A great French poet
(b) A German philosopher
(c) An Italian sonnet-writer
(d) A great Athenian statesman

601. Who wrote : "The Parliament of Foules"
(a) Chaucer (b) Gower
(c) Langland (d) Dunbar

602. When did Chaucer die?
(a) 1401 (b) 1402
(c) 1400 (d) 1399

603. Of the following periods, which does not belong to Chaucer?
(a) The Period of French
(b) The Period of German
(c) The Period of Italian
(d) The English period or The Period of Maturity

604. Who wrote : "Epithalamion"?
(a) Chaucer (b) Milton
(c) Spenser (d) Lovelace

605. In which of Shakespeare's plays does the following line appear?
"Sigh no more, ladies, sigh no more."
(a) Midsummer Night's Dream
(b) Merchant of Venice
(c) As You Like It
(d) Much Ado About Nothing

606. In which of Dryden's poems does the following line occur :
"Love is that madness which all lovers have."
(a) Aureng-Zebe
(b) Absalom and Achitophel
(c) The Hind and the Panther
(d) The Conquest of Granada

607. Who said, "Pope's poetry exhibits always an equilibrium of many separate forces."
(a) Dryden (b) Johnson
(c) Tillotson (d) Hugh Walter

608. When did Spenser die?
(a) 1592 (b) 1599
(c) 1595 (d) 1600

609. When was Milton born?
(a) 1606 (b) 1602
(c) 1608 (d) 1605

610. When did Victoria ascend the throne?
(a) In 1835 (b) In 1837
(c) In 1838 (d) In 1839

611. Queen Victoria's period in literature is generally considered to start from
(a) 1829 (b) 1840
(c) 1845 (d) 1850

612. Who wrote :
"How fast has brother followed brother,
From sunshine to the sunless land!"
(a) Wordsworth (b) Coleridge
(c) Shelley (d) Yeats

613. Who is the writer of:
"Cast a cold eye
on life, on death,
Horseman, pass by!"
(a) Wordsworth (b) Keats
(c) Shelley (d) Yeats

614. Browning's Pauline was published in
(a) 1832 (b) 1833
(c) 1834 (d) 1835

615. 'Sartor Resartus' was written by
(a) Oscar Wilde (b) Ruskin
(c) Carlyle (d) Pafer

616. When did the French Revolution start?
(a) 1788 (b) 1785
(c) 1787 (d) 1789

617. When was slave trade abolished in England?
(a) 1805 (b) 1807
(c) 1806 (d) 1810

618. Which of the following writers did not belong to the 18th century?
(a) Cowper (b) Goldsmith
(c) Burke (d) Pafer

619. Which one of the following poets was not a Victorian poet?
(a) Keats (b) Swinburne
(c) Browning (d) Morris

620. Name of writer who "tried almost every kind of novel known to the 19th century."
(a) Charlotte Bronte (b) Emile Bronte
(c) G. Eliot (d) Bulwer Lytton

621. By writing "Truce of the Bear" which country did Kipling offend?
(a) Russia (b) Germany
(c) America (d) Canada

622. Which of Kipling's poems commemorate England's entrance into the First World War?
(a) Recessional
(b) For All We Have and Are
(c) The Ballad of Red Earl
(d) Ballad of East and West

623. When did Kipling receive the Nobel Prize?
(a) In 1905 (b) In 1902
(c) In 1907 (d) In 1904

624. Who was the Editor of the Cornhill Magazine?
(a) Thackeray (b) Coleridge
(c) Hazlitt (d) Goldsmith

625. Which of the following is not the work of Bunyan?
(a) The Holy War

(*b*) Grace Abounding....
(*c*) The Life and Death of Mr. Badman
(*d*) Samson Agonistes

626. Shakespeare's use of prose is usually limited to
(*a*) asides (*b*) plays within plays
(*c*) comic scenes (*d*) tragic scenes

627. Who said, "If Pope is not the poet, where is poetry to be found?"
(*a*) Dryden (*b*) Dr. Johnson
(*c*) Addison (*d*) Steele

628. "Fans" is a humorous essay by
(*a*) Addison (*b*) Sheridan
(*c*) Lamb (*d*) De Quincey

629. To commemorate whose death did M. Arnold write "Thyrsis"?
(*a*) Wordsworth (*b*) Dr. Johnson
(*c*) Tennyson (*d*) Arthur Hugh Clough

630. In which year was "The Princess" published
(*a*) 1850 (*b*) 1847
(*c*) 1849 (*d*) 1848

631. In which book of "The Task" by Cowper does the following line appear?
"God made the country, and men made the town".
(*a*) Bk I (*b*) Bk II
(*c*) Bk III (*d*) Bk IV

632. In which book of "The Task" does the following line appear?
"England, with all thy faults, I love thee still."
(*a*) Bk I (*b*) Bk II
(*c*) Bk III (*d*) Bk IV

633. In which drama of Shakespeare does the following line appear?
"Tu-whit, tu-who—a merry note."
(*a*) Midsummer Night's Dream
(*b*) Measure for Measure
(*c*) Love's Labours Lost
(*d*) As You Like It

634. Where is the scene of "The Devil's Disciple" located?
(*a*) London (*b*) Manchester
(*c*) Wessex (*d*) New Hampshire

635. Who wrote the following line :
"Much have I travelled in the realms of gold."
(*a*) Shelley (*b*) Wordsworth
(*c*) Morris (*d*) Keats

636. Burns' father was a
(*a*) poor peasant (*b*) rich business man
(*c*) collier (*d*) bank official

637. Who took Gray abroad?
(*a*) Blake (*b*) Gladstone
(*c*) Horace Walpole (*d*) Wilberforce

638. Wilberforce was mainly working for ....in the eighteenth century
(*a*) prison reforms
(*b*) the liberation of the slaves
(*c*) women's emancipation
(*d*) universal franchise

639. Who wrote the lines :
"There is not flesh in man's obdurate heart, It does not feel for man."
(*a*) Blake (*b*) Gray
(*c*) Cowper (*d*) Goldsmith

640. Which one of the following was not a part of the general nature of the Anglo-Saxons?
(*a*) love of personal freedom
(*b*) love of religion
(*c*) fondness for lewd way of living
(*d*) respect for women

641. The main aspect of the Anglo-Saxon language was
(*a*) Vigour (*b*) Sweetness
(*c*) Obscurity (*d*) Incoherence

642. The first important expression of melody is made in the works of
(*a*) Langland (*b*) Dunbar
(*c*) Spenser (*d*) Chaucer

643. Which one among the following could not be described as the 'matter' of early verse romances
(*a*) Matter of France (*b*) Spain
(*c*) Rome (*d*) Britain

644. In which year was Armada defeated?
(*a*) 1585 (*b*) 1587
(*c*) 1588 (*d*) 1590

645. When did Bacon die?
(*a*) 1622 (*b*) 1626
(*c*) 1630 (*d*) 1621

646. When was first the Divine Right of Kings proclaimed?
(*a*) 1605 (*b*) 1601
(*c*) 1604 (*d*) 1608

647. Who wrote the Ode, "Come Leave the Loathed Stage."?
(*a*) Milton (*b*) Massinger
(*c*) Fletcher (*d*) Ben Jonson

648. How many dramatists were with Ben Jonson in fighting against the romantic tendency?
(*a*) He was alone (*b*) 2
(*c*) 3 (*d*) So many

649. Which metre has Chaucer used in his Troilus and Criseyde
(*a*) Iambic pentametre
(*b*) Rime Royal
(*c*) Terza Rima
(*d*) None of these

650. Who is the writer of 'Piers Plowman'?
(*a*) Chaucer (*b*) Dunbar
(*c*) Langland (*d*) Wyclif

651. Who is the writer of the poem :
The Pied Piper of Hamelin?
(*a*) Tennyson (*b*) M. Arnold
(*c*) Wordsworth (*d*) Browning

652. The sculptures on the gateway of the Sanchi Stupa built by Emperor Ashoka in the 3rd century B.C., illustrate, *inter alia,*

(a) Jataka stories
(b) The stories of Aesop
(c) Stories from the Panchtantra
(d) Stories from the Punch

653. In which poem of Shelley does the following line occur :
"O antique verse and high romance."
(a) Ode to a Skylark
(b) Epipsychidion
(c) Hymn to Intellectual Beauty
(d) Hellas

654. Who is the writer of the following lines :
"Learn hence for ancient rules a just esteem
To copy Nature is to copy, them."
(a) Dryden (b) Ben Jonson
(c) M. Arnold (d) Pope

655. Who wrote about Vivekananda,
"If you want to know India, study Vivekananda. In him everything is positive, nothing negative."
(a) Gandhi (b) Jawaharlal Nehru
(c) Tagore (d) Sarojini Naidu

656. When did Swami Vivekananda die?
(a) July 2, 1902 (b) June 3, 1902
(c) July 14, 1902 (d) July 04, 1902

657. In which year did Vivekananda participate in the Parliament of Religions in Chicago, USA?
(a) 1891 (b) 1893
(c) 1895 (d) 1890

658. Who wrote : "Science and Life"?
(a) Newton (b) Einstein
(c) V.C. Ramana (d) J.B.S. Haldane

659. Who wrote the following line :
"History is largely a record of self-deception."
(a) A.G. Gardiner (b) Lynd
(c) J.B. Priestley (d) Lucas

660. Who spoke the following words in his defence in the court :
"I believe that only God is really wise, and ...... that man's wisdom is worth little or nothing."
(a) Gandhi (b) St. Joan
(c) Socrates (d) Oscar Wilde

561. In which work does the following sentence appear :
"Philosophy teaches us to feel uncertain about the things that seem to us self-evident."
(a) 'Skeptial Essays' by Russell
(b) 'An Autobiography' by Jawaharial Nehru
(c) 'My Experiments with Truth' by M.K. Gandhi
(d) 'Brave New World Revisited' by Aldous Huxley

562. What kind of book is
"Three Men In A Boat"?
(a) A funny or humorous book
(b) A melodramatic book
(c) A narrative book
(d) An extremely serious work

663. Which of the following is not concerned with fun or humour?
(a) Irony (b) Pathetic Fallacy
(c) Understatement (d) Exaggeration

664. In which book do the following words appear :
"...man is a brief episode in the life of a small plant in a little corner of the universe."
(a) Emerson's 'Essays'
(b) Huxley's 'Music At Night'
(c) Russell's 'Unpopular Essay'
(d) Gandhi's 'My Experiments with Truth.'

665. In which of Shakespeare's play does a character speak the following words:
"If your leisure serv'd,
I would speak with you."
(a) The Merchant of Venice
(b) Much Ado About Nothing
(c) Julius Caesar
(d) Cymbeline

666. Which kind of life can be best described as led by Dr. Jekyll in R.L. Stevenson's "The Strange case of Dr. Jekyll and Mr. Hyde."
(a) a double life (b) a single life
(c) a happy life (d) a sad life

667. Who was the founder of the system of philosophy known as "Positivism"
(a) Goethe (b) Victor Hugo
(c) Proust (d) Auguste Comte

668. What is meant by "sing-song tone"
(a) a happy tone
(b) a rash or flourishing tone
(c) a boring childish tone
(d) None of these

669. What is meant by 'jink and muck'?
(a) a new dress
(b) a colourful thing
(c) a dancing toy
(d) old thing of little or no value

670. Delphi was a place in ancient Greece which was known for the oracle of
(a) Apollo (b) Urania
(c) Venus (d) God Mercury

671. Who said the following words :
"I must set God's command above everything."
(a) Plato (b) Socrates
(c) Christ (d) Gandhi

672. What is meant by the expression "Homeric Fight"?
(a) a great fight (b) a foolish fight
(c) a cowardly fight (d) a stylish fight

673. Henry Dunant was associated with :
(a) Clearing of mines
(b) Red cross
(c) Anti-smuggling laws
(d) Demonstrations against the use and maintenance of nuclear weapons

674. The name of Shelley's wife who committed suicide was
(*a*) Mary (*b*) Sophia
(*c*) Hutchinson (*d*) Harriet

675. The philosopher who influenced Pope was
(*a*) Bolingbroke (*b*) Godwin
(*c*) Nietzsche (*d*) Kant

676. Who is the writer of the book "The Impact of Science on Society"?
(*a*) Huxley (*b*) Priestley
(*c*) B. Russell (*d*) Gardiner

677. Who wrote the following line :
"What, there's nothing in the moon noteworthy?" (in 'One Word More')
(*a*) Tennyson (*b*) Browning
(*c*) Keats (*d*) Wordsworth

678. Who was Michelangelo?
(*a*) A physician (*b*) A painter
(*c*) A musician (*d*) A statesman

679. Mention which of the following Tagore was not—
(*a*) school teacher (*b*) novelist
(*c*) dramatist (*d*) painter

680. Who is the writer of the following lines as quoted by M. Arnold at the start of his "Thyrsis".
"Thus yesterday, today, tomorrow come,
They hustle one another and they pass."
(*a*) Ovid (*b*) Lucretius
(*c*) Pericles (*d*) Chaucer

681. When did Arthur Hugh Clough die?
(*a*) 1861 (*b*) 1864
(*c*) 1863 (*d*) 1865

682. In which poem of M. Arnold does the following line appear?
"Where ignorant armies
clash by night."
(*a*) Sohrab and Rustam (*b*) Thyrsis
(*c*) Dover Beach (*d*) The Scholar Gipsy

683. Who is the writer of the play "The Miracle Merchant"
(*a*) Tagore (*b*) Synge
(*c*) Barrie (*d*) Saki

684. 'The Miracle Merchant" was based on the story
(*a*) 'The Hen' (*b*) Monkey's Paw
(*c*) Dusk (*d*) The Open Window

685. The essay "An Apology for Idlers" is written by
(*a*) Russell (*b*) Huxley
(*c*) R.L. Stevenson (*d*) Goldsmith

686. Who is the writer of the following line in his introduction to a book on social history :
"And Reality, if rightly interpreted is grander than Fiction."
(*a*) Macaulay (*b*) Trevelyan
(*c*) Legouis (*d*) Crompton

687. Who used the term "Dry as dust" for the antiquarian or historical researcher?
(*a*) Trevelyan (*b*) Macaulay
(*c*) Carlyle (*d*) Legouis

688. Who among Chaucer's characters spoke the following lines :
"Wold the see were kept for anything
Betwixt Middleburgh and Orewell
(*a*) Knight (*b*) Squire
(*c*) Nun (*d*) Merchant

689. Under what category, should Langland's 'The Piers Plowman' be placed
(*a*) Romance (*b*) Pastoral
(*c*) Religious allegory (*d*) Supernatural poetry

690. In which work do the following lines appear :
"Labourers that have no land to live on but their hands
Deigned not dine a day on worts a night old."
(*a*) Piers Plowman
(*b*) Prologue to the Canterbury Tales
(*c*) Faerie Queene
(*d*) Song to the Men of England

691. Wat Tyler was slain at......... in the presence of the mob be led
(*a*) London (*b*) Manchester
(*c*) Smithield (*d*) None of these

692. About which character does Chaucer say the following words :
"It snowed in his house of meat and drinke ofalle dainties that men could think."
(*a*) Merchant (*b*) Franklin
(*c*) Knight (*d*) Parson

693. By whom was Christ's Hospital founded?
(*a*) Edward II (*b*) Henry II
(*c*) Edward VI (*d*) Henry V

694. Kett's rising in Norfolk in 1549 was a
(*a*) Peasants' rising
(*b*) Factory workers' rebellion
(*c*) Barons' rebellion against the king
(*d*) Priests' uprising

695. Who is the writer of "Angler"
(*a*) Blake (*b*) Cowper
(*c*) Izaak Walton (*d*) Goldsmith

696. Name the writer of the book "Illusion and Reality"
(*a*) Christopher Caudwell
(*b*) Ruskin
(*c*) Carlyle
(*d*) Oscar Wilde

697. When did George II die?
(*a*) 1780 (*b*) 1760
(*c*) 1762 (*d*) 1765

698. George IV reigned from
(*a*) 1820-30 (*b*) 1820-25
(*c*) 1820-33 (*d*) 1820-35

699. Who wrote: 'Wealth of Nations'
(*a*) Malthus (*b*) Marx
(*c*) Engels (*d*) Adam Smith

700. Dr. Chalmers was associated with
(*a*) Evangelical revival

(*b*) Peasants' revolt
(*c*) Adult Franchise movement
(*d*) Restoration of monarchy

701. In which play of Shakespeare there exists "The Forest of Arden"
(*a*) Winter's Tale (*b*) Merry Wives of Windsor
(*c*) Tempest (*d*) As You Like It

702. What is the other name for Euphues
(*a*) The Anatomy of Melancholy
(*b*) The Anatomy of Wit
(*c*) The Anatomy of Wisdom
(*d*) The Anatomy of Joy

703. Heathcliff is the most important character in the novel
(*a*) Jane Eyre (*b*) Hard Times
(*c*) Wuthering Heights (*d*) Vanity Fair

704. 'Wuthering Heights' is the name of a farm owned by
(*a*) Earnshaws (*b*) Lintons
(*c*) Bennets (*d*) Georges

705. How many knights enter the cathedral to kill St. Thomas in 'Murder in the Cathedral.'
(*a*) Three (*b*) Four
(*c*) Five (*d*) Six

706. Which country could most probably stand for Samuel Butler's Erewhon which otherwise means nowhere?
(*a*) Australia (*b*) West Indies
(*c*) Bahamas (*d*) New Zealand

707. In which novel of Hardy does the character 'Arabella' exist?
(*a*) Jude the Obscure
(*b*) The Return of the Native
(*c*) Tess
(*d*) Far From the Madding Crowd

708. Most of Hardy's novels are
(*a*) Comedies (*b*) Histories
(*c*) Tragedies (*d*) Romances

709. What hastened Mr. Tulliver's death in "The Mill on the Floss".
(*a*) His terminal illness
(*b*) His uncordial relations with Tom
(*c*) His bankruptcy
(*d*) His fall from the horse

710. 'Rawdon Crawley' is a character in
(*a*) The Mayor of Casterbridge
(*b*) Vanity Fair
(*c*) Erewhon
(*d*) Don Quixote

711. In which poem do the following lines occur :
"Before the beginning of years
There came to the making of man
Time, with a gift of tears."
(*a*) Hellas (*b*) Ode to Melancholy
(*c*) Duncaid (*d*) Atlanta and Calydon

712. How many lines does each stanza of the "Scholar Gipsy" consist of
(*a*) Eight (*b*) Six
(*c*) Ten (*d*) Nine

713. Milton wrote 'Paradise Lost' mainly to
(*a*) justify ways of God to man
(*b*) justify ways of man to God
(*c*) get himself established as a great poet
(*d*) subtly reject the life in Charles II's court

714. The Rubaiyat of Omar Khayyam (English translation) is written in
(*a*) Six line stanzas (*b*) Quatrains
(*c*) Couplets (*d*) Three line stanzas

715. 'Maud' is a poem by
(*a*) Tennyson (*b*) Shelley
(*c*) Keats (*d*) Swinburne

716. In which poem does the following lyric in blank verse appear :
"Come down, O maid."
(*a*) Maud (*b*) The Princess
(*c*) In Memoriam (*d*) Sohrab and Rustam

717. What is the rhyme scheme of "In Memoriam"
(*a*) a b b a (*b*) a b a b
(*c*) a a b b (*d*) a b b b

718. Who satirised Wordsworth's poetic diction in the following lines :
"Who both by precept and example, shows
That prose is verse, and verse is merely prose."
(*a*) Tennyson (*b*) Arnold
(*c*) Byron (*d*) Eliot

719. Who is the writer of the following :
"Let me not to the marriage of true minds
Admit impediments..."
(*a*) Milton (*b*) Spenser
(*c*) Sidney (*d*) Shakespeare

720. Who wrote :
"Oh east is east and west is west,
And never the twain shall meet."
(*a*) Tennyson (*b*) Robert Bridges
(*c*) Kipling (*d*) Eliot

721. Who wrote : "English Bards and Scotch Reviewers"
(*a*) Burns (*b*) Byron
(*c*) Scott (*d*) Yeats

722. Who is the writer of the tragedy "Prometheus Bound."
(*a*) Shelley (*b*) Aeschylus
(*c*) Sophocles (*d*) Euripides

723. How many poems did Wordsworth contribute to Lyrical Ballads :
(*a*) 16 (*b*) 17
(*c*) 18 (*d*) 19

724. Samuel Gulliver in Gulliver's Travels is a
(*a*) merchant (*b*) sailor
(*c*) surgeon (*d*) carpenter

725. How many imaginary countries does Gulliver visit
(*a*) Three (*b*) Four
(*c*) Five (*d*) Six

726. Who is the writer of "Leviathan"
(*a*) Rousseau (*b*) Locke
(*c*) Adam Smith (*d*) Hobbes

727. Robinson Crusoe was published
(*a*) 1718 (*b*) 1717
(*c*) 1719 (*d*) 1720

728. In the Dunciad, Pope has satirised
(*a*) fallen literary standards
(*b*) the contemporary political scenario
(*c*) the ancient literary standards
(*d*) the miserable economic scene

729. "The Rape of the Lock" is a .... poem
(*a*) mock-heroic (*b*) tragedy
(*c*) comedy (*d*) dramatic monologue

730. The following lines occur in
"........ in Logic a great critic,
Profoundly skill'd in Analytic;
He could, distinguish and divide
A hair twixt south and south-west side."
(*a*) Macflecknoe (*b*) Deserted Village
(*c*) Hudibras (*d*) The Rape of the Lock

731. In which country was TS Eliot born :
(*a*) England (*b*) USA
(*c*) Germany (*d*) Scotland

732. The 'Forsyte Saga' was written by
(*a*) Shaw (*b*) H.G. Wells
(*c*) Galsworthy (*d*) Eliot

733. Arnold Bennet died in
(*a*) 1930 (*b*) 1931
(*c*) 1933 (*d*) 1932

734. Who is the writer of the comedy 'The Wild Gallant'
(*a*) Dryden (*b*) Pope
(*c*) Shakespeare (*d*) Lyly

735. When was Crashaw born
(*a*) 1610 (*b*) 1615
(*c*) 1617 (*d*) 1612

736. Who wrote the following line :
"Death, thou wast once an uncouth hideous thing."
(*a*) Donne (*b*) Herbert
(*c*) Crashaw (*d*) Lovelace

737. Robert Herrick died in
(*a*) 1670 (*b*) 1672
(*c*) 1674 (*d*) 1679

738. Thomas Carew died in
(*a*) 1636 (*b*) 1637
(*c*) 1638 (*d*) 1639

739. Hobbes can be regarded as a precursor and pioneer of modern
(*a*) poetry (*b*) prose
(*c*) drama (*d*) fiction

740. Which of the following is not a comic character
(*a*) Justice Shallow (*b*) Othello
(*c*) Juliet's nurse (*d*) Falstaff

741. To whom can "courtly wit" be ascribed :
(*a*) Lyly (*b*) Ford
(*c*) Heyword (*d*) Dekker

742. Who is the writer of the comedy "A New Way To Pay Old Debts."
(*a*) Webster (*b*) Massinger
(*c*) Lyly (*d*) Jonson

743. In one of whose works does the character 'Sir Epicure Mammon' exist
(*a*) Jonson (*b*) Massinger
(*c*) Ford (*d*) Fletcher

744. Who is now said to have collaborated with Fletcher in writing the following plays :
The False one, The Spanish Curate,
The Beggar's Bush, etc.
(*a*) Jonson (*b*) Field
(*c*) Massinger (*d*) Rowley

745. 'The Woman-Hater' is a mock-heroic comedy by
(*a*) Fletcher (*b*) Beaumont
(*c*) Ford (*d*) Massinger

746. 'Four Prentices of London' is written by
(*a*) Ford (*b*) Massinger
(*c*) Heywood (*d*) Fletcher

747. In Epicoene, Jonson's chief aim is
(*a*) to moralise
(*b*) to please the public
(*c*) to satirize old customs
(*d*) to catharsise the element of fear

748. In 'The Poetaster' Jonson presents one of the following as a bad poet
(*a*) Aristophanes (*b*) Fletcher
(*c*) Martson (*d*) Dryden

749. Who is the writer of the following lines :
"I'll strip the ragged follies of the time,
Naked as at their birth."
(*a*) Jonson (*b*) Fletcher
(*c*) Dryden (*d*) Shelley

750. Constantinople fell to the Turks in
(*a*) 1450 (*b*) 1453
(*c*) 1456 (*d*) 1459

751. In whose Ashram did Shakuntala live?
(*a*) Kanva (*b*) Vashisht
(*c*) Indra (*d*) Durvasa

752. The name of the king who came to the ashram where Shakuntala lived was
(*a*) Porus (*b*) Arjuna
(*c*) Dushyanta (*d*) Nala

753. Meghdoot was written by
(*a*) Bharitrihari (*b*) Valmiki
(*c*) Patanjali (*d*) Kalidas

754. Who is the writer of the following sentence:
"I think one of the reasons why I stopped writing novels is that the social aspect of the world changed so much."
(*a*) Tagore (*b*) Forster
(*c*) Joyce (*d*) Henry James

755. Who wrote the following:
"Agriculture is not one industry among many, but is a way of life."
(*a*) Macaulay (*b*) Jawaharlal Nehru
(*c*) Trevelyan (*d*) Birla

756. From which year is the modern period of English literature generally accepted to have started.
(*a*) 1897 (*b*) 1899
(*c*) 1901 (*d*) 1900

757. Who wrote the following sentence :
"It was in 1915 the old world ended."
(*a*) Forster (*b*) Huxley
(*c*) Lawrence (*d*) Russell

758. When did G.K. Chesterton die?
(*a*) 1932 (*b*) 1934
(*c*) 1936 (*d*) 1938

759. Who wrote 'The Second World War' (in six volumes)
(*a*) Stalin (*b*) Trevelyan
(*c*) Lenin (*d*) Winston Churchill

760. In which year was I.A. Richard's "The Meaning of Meaning" published
(*a*) 1930 (*b*) 1921
(*c*) 1923 (*d*) 1927

761. When did J.M. Barrie die?
(*a*) 1935 (*b*) 1939
(*c*) 1938 (*d*) 1937

762. When did Sean O'Casey die?
(*a*) 1961 (*b*) 1964
(*c*) 1971 (*d*) 1960

763. When did John Osborne die?
(*a*) 1981 (*b*) 1991
(*c*) 1994 (*d*) 1996

764. Who among the following may be described as a naturalist?
(*a*) Shaw (*b*) Aldous Huxley
(*c*) Noel Coward (*d*) None of these

765. Who among the following is a model more of Juvenalian rather than Horatian satire?
(*a*) Swift (*b*) Addison
(*c*) Steele (*d*) Goldsmith

766. Comedy of Manners flourished in the .... period
(*a*) Elizabethan (*b*) Restoration
(*c*) Victorian (*d*) Romantic

767. Which of the following is not a fictional satirist?
(*a*) Mark Twain (*b*) Rabelais
(*c*) Lamb (*d*) Cervantes

768. "Sestina" is
(*a*) the other name for a sonnet
(*b*) a complex French lyrical form
(*c*) the old English word 'seista'
(*d*) None of these

769. What is meant by "Envoy" in context with 'sestina'
(*a*) A message
(*b*) The first three lines
(*c*) The last three lines
(*d*) The first quatrain

770. What is the correct chronological sequence in the following :
(*a*) Alastor—Lycidas—Epithalamion—Lucy Gray
(*b*) Epithalamion—Alastor—Lucy Gray—Lycidas
(*c*) Lucy Gray—Epithalamion—Lycidas—Alastor
(*d*) Epithalamion—Lycidas—Lucy Gray—Alastor

771. Point out the correct chronological sequence
(*a*) Maud—Shakespeare—To Autumn—Christabel
(*b*) Christabel—To Autumn—Maud—Shakespeare
(*c*) To Autumn—Maud—Christabel—Shakespeare
(*d*) Shakespeare—Maud—Christabel—To Autumn

772. When did Coleridge die?
(*a*) 1836 (*b*) 1837
(*c*) 1834 (*d*) 1841

773. In which of the following poems of Chaucer do the following lines occur?
"O hateful harm! condicion of poverte!
With thrust, with cold, with hunger so confounded."
(*a*) The Prologe of the Mannes Tale of Lawe
(*b*) Prologue to the Canterbury Tales
(*c*) The Pardoner's Tale
(*d*) The Nonne Preeste's Tale

774. Spenser wooed Elizabeth Boyle (whom he later married) in his
(*a*) Faerie Queene (*b*) Amoretti
(*c*) Epithalamion (*d*) None of these

775. In his command of metaphor, Shakespeare
(*a*) has his peer in Milton
(*b*) has so many peers
(*c*) is alone
(*d*) cannot excel Yeats

776. In which book of Paradise Lost does Milton say—
"God is light"
(*a*) Bk I (*b*) Bk II
(*c*) Bk III (*d*) Bk VII

777. In which book of Paradise Lost does the following line occur :
"A Paradise within thee, happier far."
(*a*) Bk I (*b*) Bk II
(*c*) Bk VII (*d*) Bk XII

778. In which book of Milton does the following line occur :
"All is best, though we oft doubt."
(*a*) Paradise Lost (*b*) Samson Agonistes
(*c*) Comus (*d*) L'Allegro

779. Goldsmith's 'The Traveller' was published in
(*a*) 1761 (*b*) 1767
(*c*) 1763 (*d*) 1764

780. Who said the following words about Goldsmith:
"One of the first men we now have as an author."
(*a*) Jonson (*b*) Johnson
(*c*) Addison (*d*) Stevenson

781. Dr. Primrose is a character in
(*a*) Vanity Fair
(*b*) David Copperfield
(*c*) The Vicar of Wakefield
(*d*) The Mill on the Floss

782. Who is the writer of "Ode To Duty"
(*a*) Shelley (*b*) Plato
(*c*) Wordsworth (*d*) Byron

783. Who wrote: "The Retreat"
(a) Wordsworth (b) George Herbert
(c) Herrick (d) Vaughan

784. 'The Cloister and the Hearth" is a masterpiece by
(a) Trollope (b) Charles Reade
(c) Bulwer Lytton (d) Kingsley

785. Charlotte Bronte died in
(a) 1855 (b) 1857
(c) 1851 (d) 1853

786. Burton's Anatomy of Melancholy appeared in
(a) 1620 (b) 1621
(c) 1623 (d) 1622

787. The first regular newspaper "The Weekly News" appeared in
(a) 1621 (b) 1623
(c) 1622 (d) 1627

788. Bacon died in
(a) 1625 (b) 1626
(c) 1627 (d) 1628

789. About whom can it be most appropriately said, "a man of grief who makes the world glad"
(a) Wordsworth (b) Tennyson
(c) Shakespeare (d) Coleridge

790. What is the name of the hero in Shaw's 'The Devil's Disciple'
(a) Burgoyne (b) The Clergyman
(c) Dick (d) None of these

791. Who is the writer of "Waiting"
(a) Yeats (b) Katharine Tynan
(c) Synge (d) Barrie

792. Who is the writer of Novun Organum
(a) Bacon (b) Lamb
(c) Montaigne (d) Stevenson

793. Who said: "the world owes some of its greatest debts to man from whose memory the world recoils."
(a) Socrates (b) Stubb
(c) Pope (d) Shakespeare

794. Who is the writer of the lines :
"And as for me, though that my wit be lytë,
On bookës for to rede I am delytë."
(a) Chaucer (b) Langland
(c) Gower (d) Dunbar

795. In which play of Shakespeare do the following lines appear :
"On, on, you noblest English,
Follow your spirit."
(a) Henry IV (b) Julius Caesar
(c) Hamlet (d) Henry V

796. The complete cycle of early Miracle play of England was presented every year beginning on
(a) Corpus Christi day (b) Christmas day
(c) Good Friday (d) Easter day

797. Which of the following is not one of the known cycles of the Miracle play in England?
(a) Chester cycle (b) Manchester cycle
(c) York cycle (d) Wakefield

798. King Charles I ascended the throne in
(a) 1622 (b) 1625
(c) 1627 (d) 1621

799. Literary tastes of King James I were
(a) enlightened (b) average
(c) mean (d) uncertain

800. Who ruled over England from 1649-60
(a) James I (b) Charles I
(c) Olive Cromwell (d) James II

801. Which of the following was not the one who carried forward the tradition of Donne
(a) Vaughan (b) Marvell
(c) Crashaw (d) Swinburne

802. Which one among the following was not a Cavalier
(a) Herrick (b) Lovelace
(c) Donne (d) Suckling

803. Who wrote 'Cooper's Hill'
(a) Suckling (b) John Denham
(c) Marvell (d) Cowley

804. Name the writer of "Pindarique Odes"
(a) Cowley (b) Wordsworth
(c) Shelley (d) Keats

805. Who believed in the hedonist philosophy of 'eat, drink and be merry'
(a) Metaphysical poets (b) Puritans
(c) Cavaliers (d) Romantics

806. Name the writer of "Life of Cowley"
(a) Dr. Johnson (b) Boswell
(c) Dryden (d) Herbert

807. Marvell's love poem "To His Coy Mistress" is written in the .... tradition.
(a) metaphysical (b) romantic
(c) Elizabethan (d) Chaucerian

808. Who among the following formed prominently part of a Cambridge community of poets known as "the sons of Ben Jonson"
(a) Herrick (b) Herbert
(c) Vaughan (d) Dryden

809. Which one among the following should be considered a heroic play rather than a comedy
(a) Dryden's 'All for Love'
(b) Wycherley's 'The Country Wife'
(c) Farquhar's 'The Beaux Stratagem'
(d) Congreve's 'The Way of the World'

810. Which poet among the following may be said to be belonging to the Caroline period
(a) Dryden (b) Pope
(c) Donne (d) Tennyson

811. Which one among the following is prominently a satire
(a) Hudibras (b) Otway's Venice Preserv'd
(c) Pilgrim's Progress (d) The Country Wife

812. Who among the following cannot be said to treat poetry with fashionable irresponsibility?
(a) Earl of Rochester (b) Dryden
(c) Sir Charles Sedley (d) Earl of Dorset

813. Name the writer of "Humphry Clinker"
(*a*) Sterne (*b*) Smollet
(*c*) Richardson (*d*) Trollope

814. William Collins was born in
(*a*) 1722 (*b*) 1724
(*c*) 1721 (*d*) 1723

815. Boswell died in
(*a*) 1795 (*b*) 1791
(*c*) 1794 (*d*) 1793

816. Thomas Paine wrote "Rights of Man"
(*a*) in reply to Burke's Reflections on the French Revolution
(*b*) to express his personal views
(*c*) to elaborate the views of Rousseau
(*d*) as a reply to Godwin's 'Political Justice'

817. According to the French poet Baudelaire, romanticism was situated in
(*a*) mode of feelings (*b*) choice of subjects
(*c*) exact truth (*d*) None of these

818. Who said: "the essence of romantic art is that in it the spirit counts far more than the form"
(*a*) Hugh Walker (*b*) Grierson
(*c*) I.A. Richards (*d*) Abererombie

819. Which one of the following Lamb loved
(*a*) new books (*b*) new faces
(*c*) new years (*d*) old books

820. In which of Lamb's essay do the following sentences occur :
"Is the world all from up?
Is childhood dead?"
(*a*) Old Benchers of the Inner Temple
(*b*) New Years Eve
(*c*) Imperfect Sympathies
(*d*) All Fools' Day

821. Of which play of Shakespeare Desdemona is the heroine
(*a*) Othello (*b*) Macbeth
(*c*) King Lear (*d*) Antony and Cleopatra

822. Napoleon was defeated finally in the Battle of Waterloo in
(*a*) 1805 (*b*) 1815
(*c*) 1830 (*d*) 1810

823. Swift's Yahoos are creatures of
(*a*) reason (*b*) impulse
(*c*) high ideals (*d*) acute analytical minds

824. Who wrote the following lines :
"Bliss was it in that dawn to be alive,
But to be young was very heaven."
(*a*) Wordsworth (*b*) Shelley
(*c*) Byron (*d*) Coleridge

825. In which canto of Childe Harold's Pilgrimage does the following line occur :
"There is a pleasure in the pathless woods"
(*a*) I (*b*) II
(*c*) III (*d*) IV

826. In which poem does the following line occur:
"Thou wast not born for death, immortal bird"
(*a*) Ode To a Skylark
(*b*) To the Cuckoo
(*c*) Ode To a Nightingale
(*d*) None of these

827. In which year was "The Origin of Species" published?
(*a*) 1859 (*b*) 1861
(*c*) 1862 (*d*) 1857

828. Who was the most representative poet of the Victorian age
(*a*) Browning (*b*) Tennyson
(*c*) Arnold (*d*) Robert Bridges

829. In which work do two sisters Laura and Lizzy exist
(*a*) Goblin Market (*b*) David Copperfield
(*c*) Thyrsis (*d*) The Prince's Progress

830. Which of the following works is not by Mrs. Gaskell
(*a*) Cranford (*b*) Ruth
(*c*) Hypatia (*d*) North and South

831. Who wrote : "Westward Ho!"
(*a*) Kingsley (*b*) Mrs. Gaskell
(*c*) Thackeray (*d*) Hemingway

832. Which one among the following was Dickens' first work
(*a*) The Pickwick Papers
(*b*) Sketches by Boz
(*c*) Oliver Twist
(*d*) Nicholas Nickleby

833. Which is the correct chronological sequence
(*a*) The Happy Prince—The Newcomer—Michael—Adam Bede
(*b*) Adam Bede—The Newcomer—Michael—The Happy Prince
(*c*) Michael—The Newcomer—Adam Bede—The Happy Prince
(*d*) The Newcomer—Adam Bede—The Happy Prince—Michael

834. Who is the writer of "Vox Clamantis"
(*a*) Chaucer (*b*) Langland
(*c*) Wyclif (*d*) Gower

835. Gower was a contemporary of
(*a*) Chaucer (*b*) Spenser
(*c*) Donne (*d*) Dryden

836. Theophrastus was a .... writer
(*a*) Greek (*b*) Roman
(*c*) Latin (*d*) German

837. La Bruy'ere was a .... writer
(*a*) Greek (*b*) Latin
(*c*) French (*d*) Roman

838. Who wrote 'The Sound and the Fury"
(*a*) Saul Bellow (*b*) Hemingway
(*c*) Flaubert (*d*) Faulkner

839. Who wrote the character of 'Charles II'
(*a*) Halifax (*b*) Overbury
(*c*) Hall (*d*) None of these

840. In writing the characters of Virtues and Vices, Hall was influenced by
(*a*) Aristophanes (*b*) Theophrastus
(*c*) Euripides (*d*) Sophocles

841. A play which is usually written to be read rather than acted or performed is called a
(*a*) closet drama (*b*) melodrama
(*c*) comic play (*d*) an interlude

842. A pause in a line of verse necessary for the natural rhythm of the language is known as
(*a*) an acrostic (*b*) an allusion
(*c*) an assonance (*d*) a caesura

843. Copernicus brought about a revolution in the field of
(*a*) astronomy (*b*) astrology
(*c*) literature (*d*) science

844. Who among the following was not a university wit
(*a*) Marlowe (*b*) Lodge
(*c*) Shakespeare (*d*) Greene

845. In literature the term "Purism" *inter alia* means
(*a*) exclusion of dance from drama
(*b*) exclusion of music from drama
(*c*) maintenance of absolute standards of correctness in writing
(*d*) rejection of all kinds of immorality

846. In which play of Shakespeare, does the following line appear :
"Doomsday is near; die all, merrily"
(*a*) Henry V (*b*) Cymbeline
(*c*) Tempest (*d*) Henry IV, Part I

847. Who speaks the following words in Eliot's Murder in the Cathedral :
"We are not here to triumph by fighting....
...We have only to conquer
Now, by suffering."
(*a*) Thomas Becket (*b*) Ist Knight
(*c*) IInd Knight (*d*) 3rd Knight

848. Who is the writer of "Frogs"
(*a*) Aeschylus (*b*) Aristophanes
(*c*) Euripides (*d*) Plato

849. Which of the following is not the internal element of tragedy as enunciated by Aristotle
(*a*) Plot (*b*) Character
(*c*) Thought (*d*) Diction

850. Which is the only kind of poetry that Plato allows in his Republic
(*a*) that in the form of hymn to the gods and praises of famous men
(*b*) epic
(*c*) lyrical
(*d*) dramatic

ANSWERS

1	2	3	4	5	6	7	8	9	10
(*c*)	(*a*)	(*d*)	(*c*)	(*b*)	(*c*)	(*d*)	(*c*)	(*b*)	(*d*)
11	**12**	**13**	**14**	**15**	**16**	**17**	**18**	**19**	**20**
(*a*)	(*c*)	(*b*)	(*d*)	(*b*)	(*c*)	(*a*)	(*c*)	(*a*)	(*d*)
21	**22**	**23**	**24**	**25**	**26**	**27**	**28**	**29**	**30**
(*b*)	(*c*)	(*a*)	(*c*)	(*a*)	(*a*)	(*b*)	(*a*)	(*b*)	(*a*)
31	**32**	**33**	**34**	**35**	**36**	**37**	**38**	**39**	**40**
(*b*)	(*a*)	(*b*)	(*c*)	(*b*)	(*a*)	(*c*)	(*c*)	(*c*)	(*c*)
41	**42**	**43**	**44**	**45**	**46**	**47**	**48**	**49**	**50**
(*d*)	(*d*)	(*d*)	(*a*)	(*b*)	(*c*)	(*c*)	(*b*)	(*a*)	(*c*)
51	**52**	**53**	**54**	**55**	**56**	**57**	**58**	**59**	**60**
(*a*)	(*d*)	(*c*)	(*c*)	(*c*)	(*d*)	(*b*)	(*a*)	(*d*)	(*b*)
61	**62**	**63**	**64**	**65**	**66**	**67**	**68**	**69**	**70**
(*a*)	(*b*)	(*c*)	(*c*)	(*d*)	(*a*)	(*b*)	(*c*)	(*b*)	(*a*)
71	**72**	**73**	**74**	**75**	**76**	**77**	**78**	**79**	**80**
(*b*)	(*c*)	(*a*)	(*d*)	(*c*)	(*c*)	(*a*)	(*c*)	(*b*)	(*b*)
81	**82**	**83**	**84**	**85**	**86**	**87**	**88**	**89**	**90**
(*c*)	(*b*)	(*a*)	(*b*)	(*c*)	(*c*)	(*b*)	(*d*)	(*c*)	(*b*)
91	**92**	**93**	**94**	**95**	**96**	**97**	**98**	**99**	**100**
(*c*)	(*c*)	(*d*)	(*d*)	(*b*)	(*c*)	(*d*)	(*c*)	(*b*)	(*a*)
101	**102**	**103**	**104**	**105**	**106**	**107**	**108**	**109**	**110**
(*d*)	(*c*)	(*b*)	(*a*)	(*d*)	(*c*)	(*c*)	(*c*)	(*d*)	(*c*)
111	**112**	**113**	**114**	**115**	**116**	**117**	**118**	**119**	**120**
(*a*)	(*d*)	(*d*)	(*c*)	(*c*)	(*a*)	(*c*)	(*d*)	(*a*)	(*b*)
121	**122**	**123**	**124**	**125**	**126**	**127**	**128**	**129**	**130**
(*c*)	(*a*)	(*d*)	(*b*)	(*c*)	(*d*)	(*b*)	(*d*)	(*b*)	(*b*)

131	132	133	134	135	136	137	138	139	140
(c)	(c)	(c)	(d)	(d)	(b)	(d)	(c)	(d)	(b)
141	142	143	144	145	146	147	148	149	150
(c)	(c)	(a)	(c)	(d)	(b)	(a)	(c)	(d)	(c)
151	152	153	154	155	156	157	158	159	160
(d)	(b)	(c)	(c)	(a)	(b)	(b)	(c)	(b)	(a)
161	162	163	164	165	166	167	168	169	170
(b)	(c)	(a)	(b)	(b)	(a)	(c)	(c)	(d)	(a)
171	172	173	174	175	176	177	178	179	180
(c)	(d)	(c)	(d)	(a)	(b)	(a)	(b)	(c)	(a)
181	182	183	184	185	186	187	188	189	190
(c)	(b)	(d)	(c)	(a)	(c)	(d)	(b)	(a)	(c)
191	192	193	194	195	196	197	198	199	200
(b)	(a)	(d)	(d)	(d)	(b)	(a)	(a)	(b)	(c)
201	202	203	204	205	206	207	208	209	210
(d)	(c)	(a)	(b)	(c)	(a)	(c)	(b)	(b)	(a)
211	212	213	214	215	216	217	218	219	220
(c)	(c)	(d)	(a)	(b)	(c)	(b)	(d)	(d)	(b)
221	222	223	224	225	226	227	228	229	230
(b)	(c)	(d)	(b)	(c)	(d)	(c)	(d)	(c)	(a)
231	232	233	234	235	236	237	238	239	240
(b)	(b)	(d)	(c)	(b)	(a)	(d)	(c)	(a)	(c)
241	242	243	244	245	246	247	248	249	250
(a)	(b)	(c)	(b)	(a)	(d)	(b)	(d)	(c)	(b)
251	252	253	254	255	256	257	258	259	260
(b)	(c)	(c)	(d)	(c)	(a)	(d)	(c)	(b)	(d)
261	262	263	264	265	266	267	268	269	270
(a)	(d)	(c)	(b)	(c)	(d)	(c)	(a)	(d)	(b)
271	272	273	274	275	276	277	278	279	280
(a)	(d)	(c)	(d)	(d)	(a)	(b)	(c)	(b)	(c)
281	282	283	284	285	286	287	288	289	290
(b)	(a)	(d)	(b)	(b)	(a)	(b)	(b)	(c)	(b)
291	292	293	294	295	296	297	298	299	300
(d)	(c)	(a)	(d)	(b)	(d)	(a)	(a)	(c)	(b)
301	302	303	304	305	306	307	308	309	310
(d)	(c)	(a)	(b)	(c)	(a)	(c)	(b)	(a)	(b)
311	312	313	314	315	316	317	318	319	320
(b)	(b)	(c)	(b)	(c)	(a)	(b)	(c)	(b)	(d)
321	322	323	324	325	326	327	328	329	330
(c)	(a)	(c)	(a)	(c)	(b)	(a)	(d)	(c)	(b)
331	332	333	334	335	336	337	338	339	340
(b)	(c)	(a)	(c)	(a)	(b)	(a)	(d)	(c)	(b)
341	342	343	344	345	346	347	348	349	350
(c)	(a)	(b)	(d)	(d)	(c)	(b)	(d)	(b)	(d)
351	352	353	354	355	356	357	358	359	360
(c)	(a)	(c)	(b)	(c)	(b)	(c)	(c)	(d)	(b)
361	362	363	364	365	366	367	368	369	370
(c)	(d)	(b)	(c)	(a)	(c)	(b)	(d)	(c)	(b)
371	372	373	374	375	376	377	378	379	380
(c)	(c)	(b)	(c)	(d)	(b)	(b)	(d)	(b)	(c)
381	382	383	384	385	386	387	388	389	390
(d)	(a)	(c)	(d)	(c)	(a)	(c)	(a)	(c)	(d)
391	392	393	394	395	396	397	398	399	400
(a)	(c)	(d)	(c)	(a)	(b)	(b)	(a)	(d)	(c)

401	402	403	404	405	406	407	408	409	410
(c)	*(b)*	*(c)*	*(a)*	*(d)*	*(c)*	*(a)*	*(c)*	*(d)*	*(b)*
411	**412**	**413**	**414**	**415**	**416**	**417**	**418**	**419**	**420**
(a)	*(b)*	*(d)*	*(d)*	*(c)*	*(a)*	*(d)*	*(a)*	*(c)*	*(c)*
421	**422**	**423**	**424**	**425**	**426**	**427**	**428**	**429**	**430**
(a)	*(d)*	*(b)*	*(d)*	*(a)*	*(d)*	*(a)*	*(b)*	*(d)*	*(c)*
431	**432**	**433**	**434**	**435**	**436**	**437**	**438**	**439**	**440**
(d)	*(b)*	*(b)*	*(c)*	*(c)*	*(a)*	*(d)*	*(c)*	*(b)*	*(c)*
441	**442**	**443**	**444**	**445**	**446**	**447**	**448**	**449**	**450**
(a)	*(c)*	*(c)*	*(c)*	*(c)*	*(d)*	*(b)*	*(d)*	*(b)*	*(a)*
451	**452**	**453**	**454**	**455**	**456**	**457**	**458**	**459**	**460**
(b)	*(d)*	*(c)*	*(d)*	*(a)*	*(c)*	*(a)*	*(d)*	*(a)*	*(d)*
461	**462**	**463**	**464**	**465**	**466**	**467**	**468**	**469**	**470**
(c)	*(a)*	*(a)*	*(c)*	*(d)*	*(b)*	*(a)*	*(a)*	*(c)*	*(b)*
471	**472**	**473**	**474**	**475**	**476**	**477**	**478**	**479**	**480**
(c)	*(d)*	*(b)*	*(d)*	*(a)*	*(c)*	*(c)*	*(a)*	*(d)*	*(a)*
481	**482**	**483**	**484**	**485**	**486**	**487**	**488**	**489**	**490**
(c)	*(a)*	*(c)*	*(a)*	*(c)*	*(d)*	*(d)*	*(a)*	*(a)*	*(c)*
491	**492**	**493**	**494**	**495**	**496**	**497**	**498**	**499**	**500**
(b)	*(d)*	*(c)*	*(b)*	*(a)*	*(c)*	*(b)*	*(a)*	*(b)*	*(d)*
501	**502**	**503**	**504**	**505**	**506**	**507**	**508**	**509**	**510**
(d)	*(c)*	*(c)*	*(b)*	*(a)*	*(b)*	*(d)*	*(a)*	*(b)*	*(a)*
511	**512**	**513**	**514**	**515**	**516**	**517**	**518**	**519**	**520**
(c)	*(b)*	*(d)*	*(a)*	*(c)*	*(a)*	*(b)*	*(c)*	*(d)*	*(b)*
521	**522**	**523**	**524**	**525**	**526**	**527**	**528**	**529**	**530**
(c)	*(b)*	*(d)*	*(b)*	*(d)*	*(c)*	*(a)*	*(b)*	*(d)*	*(b)*
531	**532**	**533**	**534**	**535**	**536**	**537**	**538**	**539**	**540**
(c)	*(c)*	*(a)*	*(b)*	*(a)*	*(c)*	*(d)*	*(d)*	*(b)*	*(c)*
541	**542**	**543**	**544**	**545**	**546**	**547**	**548**	**549**	**550**
(b)	*(c)*	*(d)*	*(b)*	*(c)*	*(b)*	*(c)*	*(d)*	*(c)*	*(d)*
551	**552**	**553**	**554**	**555**	**556**	**557**	**558**	**559**	**560**
(a)	*(d)*	*(b)*	*(a)*	*(b)*	*(b)*	*(c)*	*(c)*	*(b)*	*(a)*
561	**562**	**563**	**564**	**565**	**566**	**567**	**568**	**569**	**570**
(b)	*(a)*	*(b)*	*(c)*	*(d)*	*(b)*	*(c)*	*(d)*	*(b)*	*(a)*
571	**572**	**573**	**574**	**575**	**576**	**577**	**578**	**579**	**580**
(b)	*(b)*	*(a)*	*(c)*	*(d)*	*(c)*	*(d)*	*(a)*	*(d)*	*(c)*
581	**582**	**583**	**584**	**585**	**586**	**587**	**588**	**589**	**590**
(b)	*(a)*	*(c)*	*(d)*	*(a)*	*(d)*	*(c)*	*(a)*	*(b)*	*(c)*
591	**592**	**593**	**594**	**595**	**596**	**597**	**598**	**599**	**600**
(a)	*(d)*	*(b)*	*(d)*	*(c)*	*(b)*	*(c)*	*(b)*	*(c)*	*(d)*
601	**602**	**603**	**604**	**605**	**606**	**607**	**608**	**609**	**610**
(a)	*(c)*	*(b)*	*(c)*	*(d)*	*(d)*	*(c)*	*(b)*	*(c)*	*(b)*
611	**612**	**613**	**614**	**615**	**616**	**617**	**618**	**619**	**620**
(d)	*(a)*	*(d)*	*(d)*	*(c)*	*(d)*	*(b)*	*(d)*	*(a)*	*(d)*
621	**622**	**623**	**624**	**625**	**626**	**627**	**628**	**629**	**630**
(a)	*(b)*	*(c)*	*(a)*	*(d)*	*(c)*	*(b)*	*(a)*	*(d)*	*(c)*
631	**632**	**633**	**634**	**635**	**636**	**637**	**638**	**639**	**640**
(a)	*(b)*	*(c)*	*(d)*	*(d)*	*(a)*	*(c)*	*(b)*	*(c)*	*(c)*
641	**642**	**643**	**644**	**645**	**646**	**647**	**648**	**649**	**650**
(a)	*(d)*	*(b)*	*(c)*	*(b)*	*(c)*	*(d)*	*(d)*	*(b)*	*(c)*
651	**652**	**653**	**654**	**655**	**656**	**657**	**658**	**659**	**660**
(d)	*(a)*	*(b)*	*(d)*	*(c)*	*(d)*	*(b)*	*(d)*	*(c)*	*(c)*
661	**662**	**663**	**664**	**665**	**666**	**667**	**668**	**669**	**670**
(d)	*(a)*	*(b)*	*(c)*	*(b)*	*(a)*	*(d)*	*(c)*	*(d)*	*(a)*

671	672	673	674	675	676	677	678	679	680
(b)	(a)	(b)	(d)	(a)	(c)	(b)	(b)	(a)	(b)
681	682	683	684	685	686	687	688	689	690
(a)	(c)	(d)	(a)	(c)	(b)	(c)	(d)	(c)	(a)
691	692	693	694	695	696	697	698	699	700
(c)	(b)	(c)	(a)	(c)	(a)	(b)	(a)	(d)	(a)
701	702	703	704	705	706	707	708	709	710
(d)	(b)	(c)	(a)	(b)	(d)	(a)	(c)	(c)	(b)
711	712	713	714	715	716	717	718	719	720
(d)	(c)	(a)	(b)	(a)	(b)	(a)	(c)	(d)	(c)
721	722	723	724	725	726	727	728	729	730
(b)	(b)	(d)	(c)	(b)	(d)	(c)	(a)	(a)	(c)
731	732	733	734	735	736	737	738	739	740
(b)	(c)	(b)	(a)	(d)	(b)	(c)	(d)	(b)	(b)
741	742	743	744	745	746	747	748	749	750
(a)	(b)	(a)	(c)	(b)	(c)	(b)	(c)	(a)	(b)
751	752	753	754	755	756	757	758	759	760
(a)	(c)	(d)	(b)	(c)	(c)	(c)	(c)	(d)	(c)
761	762	763	764	765	766	767	768	769	770
(d)	(b)	(c)	(d)	(a)	(b)	(c)	(b)	(c)	(d)
771	772	773	774	775	776	777	778	779	780
(b)	(c)	(a)	(b)	(c)	(c)	(c)	(b)	(d)	(b)
781	782	783	784	785	786	787	788	789	790
(c)	(c)	(d)	(b)	(a)	(b)	(c)	(b)	(d)	(c)
791	792	793	794	795	796	797	798	799	800
(b)	(a)	(b)	(a)	(d)	(a)	(b)	(b)	(c)	(c)
801	802	803	804	805	806	807	808	809	810
(d)	(c)	(b)	(a)	(c)	(a)	(a)	(a)	(a)	(c)
811	812	813	814	815	816	817	818	819	820
(a)	(b)	(b)	(c)	(a)	(a)	(a)	(b)	(d)	(a)
821	822	823	824	825	826	827	828	829	830
(a)	(b)	(b)	(a)	(d)	(c)	(a)	(b)	(a)	(c)
831	832	833	834	835	836	837	838	839	840
(a)	(b)	(c)	(d)	(a)	(a)	(c)	(c)	(a)	(b)
841	842	843	844	845	846	847	848	849	850
(a)	(d)	(a)	(c)	(c)	(d)	(a)	(b)	(d)	(a)

ENGLISH GRAMMAR

PARTS OF SPEECH

Part of speech	Definition or Function	Examples
Noun	Name of a person, place, animal, quality or thing	Ram, boy, dog pen, sun, Delhi, truth, honesty
Pronoun	Used in place of a noun	I, you, he she, they
Articles & Determiners	Points out indefinite and definite nouns	a, an, the, few, some
Adjective	Describes a noun or pronoun	big, honest, wooden valuable, quiet, deep, soft, narrow
Adverb	Describes a verb, an adjective or another adverb	silently, widely, softly, quietly, very, carefully
Verb	Tells about action or state of something or someone	is, am, was, have, do, like, walk, work, make, throw, tell
Conjuction	Joins words, clauses or sentences	and, but, when, yet, while, else
Preposition	Links a noun or pronoun to another word	at, to, after, on for, under, over, with
Interjection	Expresses sudden feelings or emotions	Ah!, Alas!, oh!, ouch!, hi!, well!, Hurrah!

NOUNS

A word which denotes a person, a thing, an animal or a place is said to be a noun.

There are two noun numbers in English — the *Singular* and the *Plural*.

Singular Numbers : A noun that denotes one person or one thing, is said to be in the Singular number. For example — book, pencil, bird, dog, hen etc. are in singular number.

Plural Number : A noun that denotes more than one person or one thing is said to be in plural number. For example — boys, pens, lions, girls, men etc. are in plural number.

REMEMBER

Singular	*Plural*	*Singular*	*Plural*
Cat	Cats	Book	Books
Pen	Pens	Room	Rooms
Tree	Trees	Bus	Buses
Bush	Bushes	Box	Boxes
Glass	Glasses	Dish	Dishes
Judge	Judges	Tax	Taxes
Watch	Watches	Calf	Calves
Thief	Thieves	Knife	Knives
Scarf	Scarves	Wife	Wives
Leaf	Leaves	Wolf	Wolves
Half	Halves	Monarch	Monarchs
Roof	Roofs	Hoof	Hoofs
Gulf	Gulfs	Staff	Staffs
Radio	Radios	Bamboo	Bamboos
Folio	Folios	Hero	Heroes
Volcano	Volcanoes	Mango	Mangoes
Potato	Potatoes	Photo	Photos
Piano	Pianos	Baby	Babies
Fly	Flies	Country	Countries
Lady	Ladies	Boy	Boys
Monkey	Monkeys	Ox	Oxen
Child	Children	Man	Men
Woman	Women	Tooth	Teeth
Axis	Axes	Basis	Bases
Foot	Feet	Goose	Geese
Englishman	Englishmen	Radius	Radii
Vertex	Vertices	Stimulus	Stimuli

1. Note the plurals of the following nouns:

Singular	*Plural*	*Singular*	*Plural*
copy	copies	cry	cries
baby	babies	duty	duties
body	bodies	country	countries
family	families	diary	diaries
fly	flies	fairy	fairies
city	cities	spy	spies
army	armies	storey	storeys
bay	bays	monkey	monkeys

2. The following nouns do not undergo any change in plural form, in general.

Singular	*Plural*	*Singular*	*Plural*
deer	deer	sheep	sheep
thousand	thousand	pair	pair
hundred	hundred	score	score
dozen	dozen	gross	gross

Note: We can write—

(*a*) thousands of men; (*b*) two pairs of shoes; (*c*) dozens of mangoes; (*d*) scores of people etc. But—(*a*) two thousand rupees; (*b*) three hundred men; (*c*) five dozen eggs, etc.

3. The following nouns are usually used in plural forms. They take a plural verb after them—

eatables	fetters	surroundings
riches	alms	spectacles
trousers	pants	scissors
premises	thanks	annals
congratulations	goods	shorts
tongs	pains	arms
breeches	(for troubles)	

4. The following are the nouns which are plural in appearance but are usually used in singular number. They are followed by a singular verb—

news	politics	physics
mathematics	economics	ethics
politics	classics	gallows
statistics	athletics	innings
mechanics	summons	mumps

5. Collective nouns often used as plurals—

public	police	cattle
audience	clergy	folk
people	poultry	nation
elite	gentry	glitterati

6. The nouns that are usually used in singular forms—

advice	hair	rice
fuel	alphabet	machinery
offspring	issue	furniture
mischief	stationery	luggage
bedding	information	abuse

7. Material nouns are always used in singular number—

gold	copper	milk
water	silk	wool

Note: They may be used in plural with a different meaning. copper coins (coppers), chains or fetters (irons), cans made of tin (tins).

GENDERS

The difference in sex is denoted by Gender in grammar. The various genders are as follows :

1. **Masculine Gender :** A noun that denotes a male is said to be of the masculine gender, as man, uncle, ox, boy etc.
2. **Feminine Gender :** A noun that denotes a female is said to be of feminine gender, as woman, aunt, princess, cow etc.
3. **Common Gender :** Nouns which denote both males and females are said to be of the common gender, as friend, cousin, person, parent, baby etc.
4. **Neuter Gender :** A noun that denotes the name of object without life is said to be of neuter gender, as **file, table, pencil.**

REMEMBER

Masculine	*Feminine*
Boy	Girl
Son	Daughter
Brother	Sister
Murderer	Murderess
Sorcerer	Sorceress
Son-in-law	Daughter-in-law
Father-in-law	Mother-in-law
Man-servant	Maid-servant
Land-lord	Land-lady
Bachelor	Maid
Gentleman	Lady
Monk	Nun
Earl	Countess
Lad	Lass
Sir	Madam
Duke	Dutchess
Emperor	Empress
Milk-man	Milk-maid
Pea-cock	Pea-hen
Step-father	Step-mother
Hero	Heroine
Viceroy	Vicerine
Mr.	Mrs.
Governor	Governess
Master	Mistress
Wizard	Witch
Heir	Heiress
Host	Hostess
Lion	Lioness
Mayor	Mayoress
Actor	Actress
Buck	Doe
Colt	Filly
Dog	Bitch
Horse	Mare
Count	Countess
Hunter	Huntress
Prince	Princess
Abbot	Abbess
God	Goddess
Author	Authoress
Ox	Cow
Widower	Widow
Grand-father	Grand-mother
He-goat	She-goat
Milk-man	Milk-woman
Bridegroom	Bride
Tiger	Tigress
Priest	Priestess
Poet	Poetess
Shepherd	Shepherdess
Nephew	Niece
Stag	Hind

PRONOUNS

The repetition of a noun in a sentence or a set of sentences is really boring. So, instead of repeating the noun, we can use a word (for that noun) called the pronoun.
"A pronoun is a word that we use instead of a noun".

Example:
This is *Sachin. He* plays cricket.
Note: *He* is the pronoun used in place of *Sachin.*

Kinds of Pronouns

1. **Personal pronouns :** A pronoun which is used instead of the name of a person is known as a 'Personal Pronoun'. A list of the 'Personal pronouns' is listed below :

   I, my, mine, me, we (First Person)
   Ycu, your, yours (Second Person)
   He, his, him, she, her, hers, it,
   its, they, their, theirs, them (Third Person)

2. **Demonstrative, Indefinite and Distributive Pronouns :**

   (a) Demonstrative Pronouns : Pronouns used to point out the objects to which they refer are called Demonstrative Pronouns.

   Examples :
   (i) *This* is a present from my uncle.
   (ii) *These* are merely excuses.
   (iii) Bembay mangoes are better than *those* of Bangaluru.

   (b) Indefinite Pronouns : All pronouns which refer to persons or things in a general way and do not refer to any particular person or thing are called Indefinite Pronouns.

   Examples :
   (i) *Somebody* has stolen my watch.
   (ii) *Few* escaped unhurt.
   (iii) Did you ask *anybody* to come?

   (c) Distributive Pronouns : Each, either, neither are called distributive pronouns because they refer to persons or things one at a time. For this reason they are always singular and followed by the verb in singular.

   Examples :
   (i) *Each* of the men received a reward.
   (ii) *These* men received *each* a reward.
   (iii) *Either* of you can go.

3. **Relative Pronouns :** A relative pronoun refers or relates to some noun going before, which is called its Antecedent.

   Examples :
   (i) I met Hari *who* used to live here.
   (ii) I have found the pen *which* I had lost.
   (iii) Here is the book *that* you lent me.

4. **Interrogative Pronouns :** These pronouns, are used for asking questions.

   Examples :
   (i) *Whose* book is this?
   (ii) *What* will all the neighbours say?
   (iii) *Which* do you prefer, tea or coffee?

Note : Interrogative pronouns can also be used in asking indirect questions. Consider the following examples :

(i) I asked *who* was speaking.
(ii) Tell me *what* you have done.
(iii) Say *which* you would like best.

Behaviour of the Pronouns

1. If three pronouns are used together in the same sentence they are arranged in the following order :

2	+	3	+	1
↓		↓		↓
Second Person		Third Person		First Person

   Examples :
   I, you and he must help *that* poor man. (Incorrect)
   You, he and I must help *that* poor man. (Correct)

2. When two or more singular nouns are joined by and, the pronoun used for them should be plural.

   Examples :
   Mohan and Sohan are friends. *They* play football. *They* live at Lajpat Nagar.

3. But if these nouns joined by and refer to the same person or thing, the pronoun used should be singular.

   Examples :
   (i) Delhi, the beautiful city and the capital of India, is famous for *its* historical monuments.
   (ii) The manager and owner of the firm expressed *his* views on the demands of the workers.

4. When two nouns are used with as well as, the pronoun agrees with the first subject.

   Examples :
   (a) Mohan as well as his friends is doing *his* work.
   (b) The students as well as their teachers are doing *their* work.

5. When two singular nouns joined by 'and' are preceded by *each* or *every,* the pronoun used must be singular and should agree in gender with the second noun.

   Examples :
   (a) Every man and every woman will do *her* best for the nation.
   (b) Each boy and each girl went to *her* house.

6. When two nouns are joined by using 'with', the pronoun agrees with the noun coming before 'with'.

   Examples :
   (a) The boy with *his* parents has gone to see a movie.

(b) The children with *their* parents have gone to picnic.

7. When two different nouns are joined by either......... or; neither .... nor, the pronoun is used according to the number and gender of the second noun.

Examples :

(a) Either your sister or you have done *your* work.

(b) Neither the students nor the teacher was in *his* class.

8. The pronoun coming after '*than*' must be in the same case as that coming before '*than*'.

Examples :

(a) She plays better than *me*. (Incorrect)
She plays better than *I*. (Correct)

(b) His elder brother is more intelligent than *him*. (Incorrect)
His elder brother is more intelligent than *he*. (Correct)

9. 'Many a' always takes a singular pronoun and singular verb.

Example :

Many a soldier has met *his* death in the battle field.

10. 'Who', 'Whose', 'Whom' are used only for persons.

Examples :

(a) *Who* is knocking at the door?

(b) *Whose* pen is this?

(c) *What* do you want?

11. 'Which' is used for things.

Example : *Which* game do you like?

MULTIPLE CHOICE QUESTIONS

Directions: *In the following questions choose the correct options to fill the blanks.*

1. The place was so dirty that ..... wished to run away from there.
A. everybody B. anybody
C. few D. some

2. ..... was there to help me.
A. Somebody B. Anything
C. Anybody D. Nobody

3. Is there .... to eat?
A. some B. something
C. any D. few

4. ..... of the students were making a great noise.
A. Anyone B. Somebody
C. Many D. Nobody

5. ..... of the students can solve this sum.
A. Someone B. Anybody
C. Somebody D. None

6. ...... of us should try our best to make India a heaven.
A. Any B. Somebody
C. Anybody D. All

7. ...... of us do not know the real meaning of our lives.
A. Any B. Something
C. Several D. Many

8. My .... black.
A. hairs are B. hair is
C. hairs shall D. hair will

9. She saw two .... on the last Sunday.
A. thiefs B. theifs
C. thieves D. theives

10. My sister is a ....
A. bacheloress B. bachelor
C. unmaried D. spinster

11. One is supposed to do ....
A. our duty B. their duty
C. one's duty D. his duty

12. Take anything .... you want.
A. that B. which
C. than D. then

13. I cannot tolerate ....
A. separated you
B. your separation
C. separation from you
D. you separated

14. He is .... faithful partner.
A. Yours B. You
C. Your D. Your's

15. Ajay is more smart than ....
A. her B. hers
C. herself D. she

16. Vivek works harder than ....
A. me B. I
C. her D. his

17. They should help ....
A. the poor people B. the poor
C. the poor persons D. the poor peoples

18. .... are mad.
A. All his sons B. His all sons
C. Sons all his D. All sons his

19. The poor fellow .... to fate.
A. resigned B. resigned himself
C. resigned itself D. resigned themselves

20. Nobody will help you but ....
A. I B. me
C. ours D. his

21. It is a good chance, You must avail .... this opportunity.
A. of B. yourself of
C. for D. from

22. The person who is elected .... my relative.
A. is B. he is
C. his D. him

23. He made ....
A. yours mention
B. mention of you
C. mention for you
D. mention about you

24. .... I know, he is quite faithful.
A. As far as B. So far as
C. So far this D. So far so

25. It is a duty of a person to take .... for his family.
A. pain B. pains
C. pain-killers D. pained

26. She does not love .... husband.
A. his B. her
C. its D. their

27. Let .... work together.
A. him and me B. he and I
C. he and him D. I and me

28. Copper, Silver and Gold ....
A. each will do B. either will do
C. any one will do D. any will do

29. Jessica and Roma are very irregular .... habits.
A. in her B. in their
C. in its D. in every

30. One likes to enjoy .... who was a great poet.
A. The sonnets of Shakespeare
B. Shakespeare's sonnets
C. Sonnets
D. Shakespeare

31. That is the boy .... everybody loves.
A. whom B. who
C. that D. whose

32. That is the girl .... won the first prize.
A. whom B. who
C. whose D. which

33. That is the man .... purse was lost.
A. who B. whom
C. whose D. their

ANSWERS

1	2	3	4	5	6	7	8	9	10
A	D	B	C	D	D	D	B	C	D
11	**12**	**13**	**14**	**15**	**16**	**17**	**18**	**19**	**20**
C	A	C	C	D	B	B	A	B	B
21	**22**	**23**	**24**	**25**	**26**	**27**	**28**	**29**	**30**
B	A	B	A	B	B	A	C	B	A
31	**32**	**33**							
A	B	C							

ARTICLES

The family of the articles has only three members. They are : A, An and The. However, they fall under two groups: *(a)* Definite Article *(b)* Indefinite Article

'The' is known as definite article whereas 'a' and 'an' are known as indefinite articles.

Use of the Definite Article 'The'

'The' is used before

1. The superlative degree :
   He is the ablest man of the town.
   (ablest is a superlative degree)
2. The name of states, countries etc. having a descriptive name :
   (i) The J & K is a small state. (J & K is a descriptive name)
   (ii) He lives in the U.S.A. (U.S.A. is a descriptive name)
   (But the Delhi and the America are wrong because neither Delhi nor America is a descriptive name)
3. The names of the scriptures :
   The Gita is a holy book. (Gita is a scripture)
4. Name of newspapers :
   The Tribune is published from Chandigarh.
5. Name of rivers, canals, seas, oceans, bays, gulfs, groups of islands etc. :
   (i) The Ganga is a holy river.
   (ii) The Indian Ocean is the deepest ocean.
   (iii) The Persian Gulf is a narrow gulf.
6. The name of famous buildings :
   The Taj is one of the best buildings in India.
7. The names of nationals, sects and communities:
   (i) The English defeated the Germans in the World War.
   (ii) The rich should help the poor.
   (iii) The Hindus believe in the caste system.
8. Proper nouns used as common nouns :
   (i) Kalidas is the Shakespeare of India.
   (ii) Delhi is the London of India.

9. Famous historical events :
   The Industrial Revolution changed the face of England.
10. The directions and the celestial bodies:
   The sun rises in the east.
11. Titles :
   Akbar, the Great was loved by his subjects.

Do not use 'the'

1. Before languages :
   The English is an international language. (Incorrect)
   English is an international language. (Correct)
2. Before the names of games :
   The hockey is a popular game. (Incorrect)
   Hockey is a popular game. (Correct)

Use of the Indefinite Articles 'A' and 'An'

'A' is used before :

1. All singular common nouns beginning with a consonant :
   (i) A boy sings a song.
   (ii) A black and a white cow were grazing in the field.
2. If a word begins with a vowel but gives the sound of a consonant, 'a' should be used before it :
   (i) He was helped in his work by a European.
   (ii) He is a one-eyed man.
   (iii) It is a useful work.

'An' is used as follows :

1. All singular common nouns beginning with a vowel (*i.e.*, a, e, i, o, u) :
   (i) He is an artist.
   (ii) He is an old man.
   (iii) I intend to buy an umbrella.
2. If a word starts with a consonant but gives the sound of a vowel, "an" should be used before it :
   (i) Brutus is an honourable man.
   (ii) He is an honour to his profession.
   (iii) He is an L.L.B.
   (iv) He is an M.A.
   (v) You will reach there in an hour.

Demonstratives, that, these and those

1. The demonstrative adjectives and pronouns are for objects nearby the speaker:
   this (singular) those (plural)
   and for objects far away from the speaker.
   That (singular) those (plural)
2. Demonstratives are the only adjectives that agree in number with their nouns.
   That hat is nice.
   Those hats are nice.
3. When there is the idea of selection, the pronoun "one" (or "ones") often follows the demonstrative.
   I want a book. I'll get this (one).
   If the demonstrative is followed by an adjective, "one"(or "ones") must be used.
   I want a book. I'll get this big one.

MULTIPLE CHOICE QUESTIONS

Directions: *In the following questions choose the correct options to fill the blanks.*

1. .... will have to be paid for this material.
A. Half rupee B. Half a rupee
C. A half rupee D. An half rupee

2. .... is taking keen interest in India.
A. The USA B. USA
C. An USA D. A USA

3. Only .... can save our country.
A. the Hitler B. a Hitler
C. Hitler D. an Hitler

4. I can run for ....
A. hundred miles B. the hundred miles
C. a hundred miles D. an hundred miles.

5. .... man-eater has been killed.
A. The B. A
C. An D. Either A or B

6. What .... fine idea!
A. the B. an
C. a D. No article

7. .... earth is moving around the sun.
A. An B. A
C. The D. No article

8. This is .... first example while I got.
A. the B. a
C. an D. No article

9. This is .... house which was built during earthquake.
A. a B. an
C. the D. No article

10. .... America is a rich country.
A. The B. An
C. A D. No article

11. .... U.S.A. is a developed country.
A. A B. An
C. The D. No article

12. .... Bible is a holy book.
A. A B. The
C. An D. No article

13. .... rich should help the poor.
A. The B. A
C. An D. No article

14. .... Gold is a costly metal.
A. The B. A
C. An D. No article

15. Kalidas is .... Shakespeare of India.
A. a B. an
C. the D. No article

16. I cannot do .... difficult work.
A. a such B. the such
C. such the D. such a

17. How foolish .... plan it is!
A. a B. an
C. the D. No article

18. An ink is .... useful article.
A. an B. a
C. the D. No article

19. There are .... husband and wife.
A. a B. an
C. the D. No article

20. He is learning .... French
A. the B. a
C. an D. No article

ANSWERS

1	2	3	4	5	6	7	8	9	10
B	A	B	C	D	C	C	A	C	D
11	**12**	**13**	**14**	**15**	**16**	**17**	**18**	**19**	**20**
C	B	A	D	C	D	A	B	D	D

ADJECTIVES & ADVERBS

An Adjective is a word which adds something to the meaning of a noun or a pronoun.

Mridula is an *intelligent* girl.

He has a *black* goat.

He is a *brilliant* student.

She is a *clever* girl.

It is a *beautiful* picture.

In the sentences given above, the words in italics are adjectives.

An Adverb is a word which qualifies the meaning of a Verb, an Adjective or another Adverb.

(*i*) He talks *slowly.*

(*ii*) He is a *very* good student.

(*iii*) He talks *very* slowly.

In sentence (*i*), *slowly* qualifies the verb *talks.*

In sentence (*ii*), *very* qualifies the adjective *good.*

In sentence (*iii*), *very* qualifies the adverb *slowly.*

Adjectives have three degrees of comparison :

1. **Positive Degree :** It expresses the common form of an adjective.

   Example :

   Ram is a *tall* boy.

   In the above sentence *tall* is an adjective and expresses the common form.

2. **Comparative Degree :** It expresses the more of the same form.

   Example :

   Ram is *taller* than Mahesh.

   In the above sentence *taller* is an adjective that expresses the more of the common form of the adjective *tall.*

"When and How to Use" Comparative Degree?

(a) Comparative Degree is used when two persons or two groups of persons or things are compared.

Examples :

(a) He is *wiser* than his younger brother.

(b) This glass is *cleaner* than the other.

(b) When two different qualities in the same person are compared, more is used instead of 'er' to form the comparative. The formula used in this case should be :

More + Positive Degree

She is *fairer* than polite. (Incorrect)

She is *more fair* than polite. (Correct)

(c) When selection of one out of two persons or things is meant, the degree of comparison is followed by of and *the* is used before it.

Example :

Zia is abler of *the* two sisters.

(d) If two comparatives are used in the same sentence to impress upon an idea, both should be preceded by the definite article.

Examples :

(i) The higher you go, the cooler it is.

(ii) The more we get, the more we desire.

(e) When one person or thing is compared with another of the same kind, other is used after the comparative degree. In such sentences other is normally preceded by any or all.

Examples :

(i) Kalidas is greater than any dramatist. (Incorrect)

Kalidas is greater than any other dramatist. (Correct)

(ii) Lead is heavier than all metals. (Incorrect)
Lead is heavier than all other metals. (Correct)

(f) Senior, junior, superior, inferior, prior, anterior (earlier than) and posterior (later than) are always followed by 'to'.

Examples :

(i) Ram is senior *to* Mohan by three years.
(ii) That pen is inferior *to* that.
(iii) He is junior *to* me in rank.
(iv) This event was posterior *to* that.

Note: Never use *than* after the above mentioned adjectives.

Important Information

(a) 'Preferable' is also used as an adjective of the comparative degree. As such, it is always followed by *to* and not *a*.
Death is preferable than dishonour. (Incorrect)
Death is preferable *to* dishonour. (Correct)

(b) To intensify the Degree of comparison, we use *far* or *much* before the comparative.

Examples :

(i) This book is *far* better than that.
(ii) His performance was *much* better than Mohan's.

Warning : Always avoid the use of double comparatives.

Don't say : Ram is more cleverer than his younger brother.

Say: Ram is cleverer than his younger brother.

3. **Superlative Degree :** It expresses the most of the common form of an adjective.

Example :

He is the ablest man of the town.

How and when to use the Superlative Degree?

(a) The Superlative Degree is used when more than two persons or things are compared.

(b) The Superlative Degree is generally preceded by 'the' and followed by 'of' in most of the cases or otherwise.

(c) When an adjective of the superlative degree is preceded by a Possessive Adjective or a Noun in the Possessive case, 'the' should not be used before it.

Example :

Which is Kalidas' best play?

It will be a blunder to use 'the' before the Superlative Degree in such cases.

Don't say : Which is Kalidas' the best play.

(d) To intensify the degree of comparison, *by far* is used before the superlative degree.

Example :

India is *by far* the most beautiful country of the world.

Note: Always avoid the use of double superlatives.

Don't say : He is the most strongest boy in the class.

Say : He is the strongest boy in the class.

Use of some Important Adjectives

1. (a) **'Some'** is used as follows :

(i) With countable nouns where it means— a little, a small quantity.
(ii) In a question which shows some request.

Examples :

(i) There is some water in the bottle.
(ii) Some of the students were absent yesterday.
(iii) Will you have some milk?
(iv) Will you buy some fruit for me?

(b) **'Any'** is used as follows :

(i) In negative sentences.
(ii) In interrogative sentences.
(iii) After 'Hardly', 'Scarcely' and 'Barely'.
(iv) After 'If'.

Examples :

(i) There is not any sugar in the pot.
(ii) We haven't any rice in the house.
(iii) I have hardly any money.
(iv) There are scarcely any plants in this field.
(v) If there is any danger, blow the whistle.

2. (a) **Older :** Older (and oldest) are used for persons animals and things. But 'Older' and 'Oldest' refer to the persons who do not belong to the same family.

Examples :

(i) Radha is older than Shyama.
(ii) John is the oldest member of the staff.
'Older' and 'Oldest' refer to the persons who do not belong to the same family.

(b) **Elder** (and **eldest**) are used in respect of the members of the same family like sons, daughters, brothers, sisters.

Examples :

(i) My elder sister is a lecturer.
(ii) Meenakshi is the eldest of the three sisters.

Note :

(i) 'Elder' is not followed by 'than'.
(ii) 'Elder' and 'Eldest' cannot be used for things.

3. (a) **'Few'** is negative and is the opposite of 'Many'. It means 'not many'.

(b) **'A few'** is positive and means 'some at least'. It is the opposite of 'None'.

(c) **'The few'** means 'minority' and suggests 'whether there is'.

Examples :

(i) We have few holidays in school.
(ii) Only a few boys will fail in the examination.
(iii) The few poems that he wrote are very popular.

4. (a) **Further** means 'something additional'.

(b) **Farther** means 'a greater distance'.

Examples :

(i) Further discussion will be held in the office of the principal.

(ii) Amritsar is farther from Delhi than Ambala.

5. (a) **Little** is negative. It means, 'not much', or 'hardly any'.

(b) **A little** is positive. It means 'some quantity'.

(c) **The little** denotes quantity. It means, 'not much but all that is, or whatever quantity there is'.

Examples :

(i) There is little hope of his success.

(ii) He knows a little of everything.

(iii) I have spent the little money I had.

(iv) The little knowledge of shoe-making proved very useful to me.

6. (a) **'Much'** expresses 'quantity'.

(b) **'Many'** expresses 'number'.

(c) **'Many a'**—'Singular noun' and 'Singular verb' are used with 'many a'.

Examples :

(i) There is not *much* water in the jug.

(ii) *Many* boys are absent today.

(iii) *Many* a battle has been fought on the soil of India.

7. (a) **'Less'** denotes 'in a small degree'.

(b) **'Fewer'** denotes 'number'.

Examples :

(i) He devotes less time to his studies.

(ii) There are no fewer than ten chairs in this room.

8. (a) **'Each'** is used for a single number of 'two persons' or 'things'.

(b) **'Every'** is used for a single number of 'many persons' or 'things'.

Examples :

(i) Each boy must take part in games.

(ii) There are only two poets. Each poet recited his poem.

(iii) Every man dies in this world.

(iv) Every man is expected to do his duty.

9. (a) **'Either'** means one of the two or both.

(b) **'Neither'** is negative of the either.

Examples :

(i) You may buy either of these two chairs.

(ii) Neither of them could speak on the stage.

10. (a) **'Later'** expresses 'late in time'.

(b) **'Latter'** means 'second in position or order'.

Examples :

(i) My father reached later than I expected.

(ii) The latter position was better than the former.

Use of some Important Adverbs

1. (a) Also, too, enough:

(i) He taught English. Also, he edited the school magazine

(ii) He is a writer and also he is a painter.

(iii) He is too obstinate to listen to any reason.

(iv) This is too difficult a piece for the junior students.

(v) Sarla was kind enough to help the poor.

(vi) He is brave enough to help the truth.

Note: 'Too' is used in a negative sense, but enough is used in a positive sense.

(b) Fairly and rather: Both suggest the meaning 'moderately'. But, mainly 'fairly' is used with the words that denote a positive meaning and rather is used with the words that denote a negative meaning:

(i) Rita did fairly well in that competition, but her performance was rather poor in sports.

(ii) Mona is fairly rich, but she is rather stingy.

Note: 'Rather' can also be used in a positive sense.

(i) This is a rather interesting job.

(ii) That boy is rather smart.

(c) Hardly, barely, scarcely: These words mostly convey the negative suggestions and are almost similar.

(i) I have hardly any strength now.

(ii) There was barely any supply to the township,

(iii) There were scarcely a hundred guests present.

Note: With slight variance in the meaning, the words given above convey the idea of 'very little', 'not enough', 'lack of quantity and number'.

(d) Yet, Still: These adverbs can often be used to connect the sentence units:

(i) He has been defeated many times in the contest; still he wants to be a competitor.

(ii) Mona was sick; yet she went on doing her work.

(e) Alone:

(i) He alone (none else) is capable of handling that fire,

(ii) He hunted all alone in the forest. (not in any company)

Special Note:

(a) Apart from their conventional positions the adverbs might be used in different positions with different meanings and angles.

(i) He had only four books.

(ii) John only contacted his friend in need.

(iii) He greeted me only.

(iv) Only he greeted me there.

(b) Inversion: Some adverbs can be inverted *i.e.* placed in the beginning of the sentence and then be followed by an interrogative form. The most common of these adverb are: so, seldom, never, nowhere, under no circumstances, hardly, scarcely etc.

(i) So big was the bus that it could not enter the narrow lane.

(ii) Hardly had he reached the station when he received the message.

MULTIPLE CHOICE QUESTIONS

Directions: *In the following questions choose the correct options to fill the blanks.*

1. The girl whom you met is the .... sister of Ravi.
A. eldest B. elder
C. older D. oldest

2. The historical place is ....
A. seeing worth B. worthy of seeing
C. worth seeing D. worthy seeing

3. These flowers smell ....
A. sweet B. sweetly
C. more sweetly D. sweetest

4. .... aspirant cannot pass the entrance examination.
A. Each B. Every
C. All D. No

5. Harivansh Rai .... second Shakespeare.
A. is a B. is
C. is the D. is an

6. .... student in the class got prizes.
A. Each and every B. Every and each
C. Every D. Never

7. It is .... picture than the one we saw last Monday.
A. interesting B. much interesting
C. more interesting D. most interesting

8. She is clever ....
A. that her mother is B. as her mother is
C. to her mother is D. than her mother is

9. They will get ....
A. Red, green and black paper
B. Red, green black paper
C. Red and green and black paper
D. Red green black paper

10. Health is .... wealth.
A. preferable to B. more preferable than
C. more preferable to D. most preferable then

11. .... water that was in the jug evaporated.
A. Little B. The little
C. Small D. A small

12. He has not sung .... songs.
A. much B. most
C. more D. many

13. Srishti has searched .... office.
A. whole the B. the whole
C. a whole D. some whole

14. Premchand was .... best and .... famous writer.
A. a, the most B. the, a most
C. the, more D. the, the most

15. William Shakespeare is famous as ....
A. a poet and a dramatist
B. a poet and dramatist
C. the poet and the dramatist
D. a poet and the dramatist

16. What does .... leader suggest?
A. other B. another
C. others D. anothers

17. He .... money.
A. has few B. have few
C. has little D. have little

18. The .... boys are rewarded.
A. first two B. two first
C. firsts two D. two's first

19. He is .... brave.
A. stronger than B. stronger then
C. more strong then D. more strong than

20. No sooner said ....
A. so done B. and done
C. then done D. but done

21. She returned .... than I had thought.
A. quickly B. more quicker
C. more quickly D. quicker

22. He is .... foolish person.
A. rather the B. a rather
C. rather a D. rather

23. This pen .... rupees.
A. costs twenty B. twenty costs only
C. costs only twenty D. only costs twenty

24. It is .... pride.
A. nothing else but B. nothing else than
C. else nothing than D. but

25. This tea is .... to drink.
A. too hot B. very hot
C. enough hot D. much hot

ANSWERS

1	2	3	4	5	6	7	8	9	10
A	C	A	B	A	C	C	C	A	A
11	**12**	**13**	**14**	**15**	**16**	**17**	**18**	**19**	**20**
B	D	B	D	B	B	C	A	D	C
21	**22**	**23**	**24**	**25**					
C	C	C	A	A					

DETERMINERS

Determiners are actually Adjectives. They are always followed by nouns.

Determiners are of the following kinds:

1. Demonstrative Determiners
this, that, these, those

2. Possessive Determiners
my, our, your, his, her, its, their

3. Quantitative Determiners
some, any, much, enough, sufficient, whole, a little, the little, little, all, both

4. Numerical Determiners
a few, some, few, the few, any, several, many, no, etc.

One, two, three ... (Cardinals)

First, second, third ... (Ordinals)

5. Distributive Determiners
either, neither

6. Articles

Indefinite: a, an

Definite: the

MULTIPLE CHOICE QUESTIONS

Directions: *In the following questions choose the correct options to fill the blanks.*

1. Give me .... rice.
A. some B. few
C. a few D. any

2. .... sheep grazing on the slope of the hill had gone away.
A. Any B. The few
C. This D. Much

3. Have you got .... magazines to read?
A. all B. much
C. some D. little

4. I have .... money that I want to spend on shares.
A. any B. much
C. less D. some

5. There is .... owl on the branch of the tree.
A. a B. the
C. an D. some

6. My brother is .... MBA.
A. a B. an
C. the D. any

7. Have you got .... cheese?
A. some B. many
C. a few D. few

8. No, I have not got .... cheese.
A. many B. few
C. any D. some

9. There is only .... milk left in the bottle.
A. enough B. few
C. much D. a little

10. There is .... hope of his recovery.
A. any B. little
C. many D. few

11. .... dogs were barking at the strangers.
A. Some B. Any
C. Much D. Less

12. The girl bought her father .... juice.
A. few B. some
C. any D. many

13. You should take .... honey everyday.
A. any B. many
C. a little D. a few

14. .... boy was punished by the teacher.
A. Either B. All
C. Any D. Many

15. .... girl was asked to join the army.
A. None B. Neither
C. All D. Any

16. .... water in the jug has been drunk by Mohan.
A. The little B. The few
C. A few D. Few

17. I shall play .... piano at the party.
A. some B. any
C. the D. few

18. .... labourers were found dead in the mine.
A. Any B. Fewer
C. Many D. Less

19. Could I borrow .... umbrella?
A. our B. your
C. yours D. my

20. My brother is standing in the .... row.
A. any B. many
C. some D. first

ANSWERS

1	2	3	4	5	6	7	8	9	10
A	B	C	D	C	B	A	C	D	B
11	**12**	**13**	**14**	**15**	**16**	**17**	**18**	**19**	**20**
A	B	C	A	B	A	C	C	B	D

THE VERB

A Verb is a word that tells something about the action or state of or happenning to a person or thing.

A Verb tells the following:

1. What a person or thing does.

Sachin goes to school daily.

The bell *rang* loudly.

Many birds fly in the sky.

She *sang* a song.

2. What a person or thing is.

India *is* the biggest democracy in the world.

Ram Mehar *is* very rich.

They *are* happy.

3. What is done to a person or thing.

You *are liked* by all.

Two thieves *were arrested.*

Four students *were punished* by the teacher.

4. What happens to a person or thing.

His maternal uncle *died* last week.

Two ships *sank* yesterday.

Leaves *turn* yellow in autumn.

5. What a person or thing has, had, and so on.

I *have* a new car.

He *had* a scooter last year.

He *has* several cows and goats.

It goes without saying that a verb is the most important part of a sentence. No sentence is complete without a Verb.

Important Information

1. If two or more singular nouns are joined by 'and' the verb used will be plural.

Example:

(i) He and I were going to the market.
(ii) Ram and Mohan are friends.

2. If two singular nouns joined by 'and' points out to the same thing or person, the verb used must be singular.

Example:

(i) Rice and curry is the favourite food of the Punjabis.
(ii) The Collector and District Magistrate is away.

3. In case two subjects are joined by 'as well as' the verb agrees with the first subject.

Example :

(i) Kanta as well as her children is playing.
(ii) Children as well as their mother are playing.

In the case of first sentence the verb (is) agrees with Kanta and in the case of second sentence the verb (are) agrees with the children.

4. 'Neither', 'Either', 'Every', 'Each', 'Everyone', and 'Many a' are followed by a singular verb.

Example :

(i) Either of the plans is to be adopted.
(ii) Neither of the two brothers is sure to pass.
(iii) Every student is expected to be obedient.
(iv) Everyone of them desires this.
(v) Many a person is drowned in the sea.

5. If two subjects are joined by 'Either .... or' / 'Neither .... nor', the verb agrees with the subject near to it.

Example :

(i) Either my brother or I am to do this work.
(ii) Neither he nor they are prepared to do this work.

6. 'A great many' is always followed by a 'plural noun' and a 'plural verb'. For example :
A great many students have been declared successful.

7. Similarly if two subjects are joined by 'with', 'together with', 'no less than', in addition to 'and not', etc. the verb agrees with the first subject.

Example :

(i) The boy with his parents has arrived.
(ii) He, no less than I, is to blame.

8. Nouns, plural in form, but singular in meaning, take a singular verb.

Example :

This news was broadcast from television yesterday.

MULTIPLE CHOICE QUESTIONS

Directions: *In the following questions choose the correct options to fill the blanks.*

1. The bus with all its passengers .... lost.

A. were B. was
C. are D. would

2. You as well as I .... responsible for this work.

A. am B. are
C. was D. is

3. Raghava like all his companions .... a spoiled child.

A. are B. were
C. is D. will be

4. Pen and ink .... required for me.

A. are B. were
C. is D. has required

5. Every girl and every boy .... attended the seminar.

A. have B. has
C. is D. are

6. Not only she but all her sisters ...... been married.
A. has B. have
C. is D. are

7. There .... nothing but miseries in life.
A. is B. are
C. were D. will be

8. Neither prose nor poem .... given.
A. were B. was
C. has D. have

9. Either he or I .... wrong.
A. is B. are
C. am D. were

10. Either Sulekha or Rekha .... coming here.
A. are B. is
C. were D. have

11. .... the child or his parents to blame?
A. Is B. Are
C. Were D. Has

12. You and I .... neighbours.
A. am B. are
C. was D. has

13. The house with all its belongings ..... sold away.
A. were B. are
C. was D. must

14. Either water or juice .... required.
A. is B. are
C. were D. has

15. There were not as many tables as .... required.
A. was B. were
C. is D. are

16. They each .... a book.
A. have B. are
C. has D. is

17. He and I .... class friends.
A. is B. am
C. was D. are

18. She as well as I .... guilty.
A. is B. are
C. am D. must be

19. Purushottam ...... not read more on this chapter.
A. needs B. has been need
C. need D. had been need

20. He came .... to his aunt.
A. run B. running
C. to run D. in run

21. She dislikes .... meat.
A. eat to B. to eat
C. eating D. to eating

22. He likes ....
A. sing to B. singing
C. to sing D. to singing

23. We are ready .... the match.
A. play to B. to playing
C. playing D. to play

24. .... is injurious to health.
A. Smoking B. To smoke
C. To smoking D. Smoke to

25. He loves .... raw vegetables.
A. eaten B. eating
C. to eating D. eat to

26. He seemed .... finished his homework.
A. have to B. to have
C. having D. to having

ANSWERS

1	2	3	4	5	6	7	8	9	10
B	B	C	C	B	B	A	B	C	B
11	**12**	**13**	**14**	**15**	**16**	**17**	**18**	**19**	**20**
A	B	C	A	B	A	D	A	C	B
21	**22**	**23**	**24**	**25**	**26**				
C	B	D	A	B	B				

CONJUNCTIONS

A conjunction is a word which connects words, clauses or sentences.

Look at the following sentences.

(i) He bought apples *and* mangoes.
(ii) God made the country *and* man made the town.
(iii) The door was open *but* there was no one in the house.
(iv) He knows that I am here *and* that I want to see him.

In the sentence (i), *and* connects two words—*apples* and *mangoes.*

In the sentence (ii), *and* connects two sentences—*God made the country* and *man made the town.*

In the sentence (iii), *but* connects two sentences— *The door was open* and *there was no one in the house.*

In the sentence (iv), *and* connects two clauses—*that I am here* and *that I want to see him.*

The main coordinating conjunctions are:

and, but, for, or, nor, also, either ..... or, neither ..... nor.

There are some conjunctions which are used in pairs. They are:

either .... or, ... neither .... nor, both .... and, though .... yet, whether .... or, not only .... but also.

Example: *Either* take it *or* leave it.

It is *neither* useful *nor* ornamental.

They *both* like *and* respect me.

Though he is suffering from high fever, *yet* he does not cry.

He does not care *whether* you go *or* stay.

He is *not only* doltish, *but also* obstinate.

The conjunctions which are used in pairs in this way, are called correlative conjunctions, or merely correlatives.

Use of Important Conjunctions

1. **As soon as :** As soon as denotes simultaneous time.
   Example : As soon as he saw his enemy, he took to his heels.
2. **No sooner .... than :**
   (a) 'No sooner' is always followed by 'than'.
   (b) Please remember that 'No sooner' is always followed by do/does/did. As such only first form of the verb should be used after the subject.
   Example :
   No sooner did he see his enemy than he took to his heels.
3. **Hardly :** Hardly is followed by when.
   Examples :
   (i) Hardly had I left the house when it started raining.
   (ii) We had hardly come into the room when his father began chastising him.
   Note :
   A. Hardly is never followed by than.
   B. 'Scarcely' can also be used in the sense and manner of 'Hardly'.
4. **Lest :** Lest is used in the sense of so that .... not. It is always followed by should. Lest is negative in sense. Hence 'not' should never be used with it.
   Example :
   Work hard lest you should fail.
   Note : 'Lest' is always followed by 'should' and not 'may'.
5. **Unless :** Unless expresses condition. It is also used in the negative sense. Use of 'not' is not allowed with unless because unless is already in the negative sense.
   Example :
   Unless you labour hard you will not pass.
6. **Until :** 'Until' expresses time. It means 'till not'.
   Example :
   Wait here until I return.
   Note : Until is in the negative sense. So 'not' should not be used with it. Example :
   Wait here until I do not return. (Incorrect)
   Wait here until I return. (Correct)
7. **As well as :** When two subjects are joined by 'as well as', the verb always agrees with the first subject.
   Examples :
   (i) The teacher as well as students is playing.
   (ii) Students as well as the teacher are playing.
   Note : 'Both' and 'as well as' cannot be used together in the same sentence.
   Examples :
   Both Sita as well as Kanta are beautiful. (Incorrect)
   Sita as well as Kanta is beautiful. (Correct)
   Both Sita and Kanta are beautiful. (Correct)
8. **As if :** 'As if' is used in the sense of pretension. While using 'as if' in a sentence, we should see that even the third person singular subject gets 'were'.
   Example :
   He talks as if he were mad.
9. **Till :** Till expresses time. Till is always used in the affirmative.
   Example :
   We did not come back till sunset.
10. **Rather than :** 'Rather than' is used in the sense of 'preference'. 'Rather' is always followed by 'than'.
    Example :
    I would rather die than submit.
11. **As long as/so long as :** Both express time during which an action or event takes place.
    Example :
    As long as there is life, there is hope.
12. **However :** It is both a subordinate and co-ordinate clause.
    Examples :
    (a) Mala worked hard, she however, failed.
    (b) However hard he may work, he cannot pass.
13. **Such as :** 'Such as' gives us the sense of 'like'. Such is always followed by 'as'.
    Example :
    Life is such a puzzle as cannot be solved.

MULTIPLE CHOICE QUESTIONS

Directions: *In the following questions choose the correct options to fill the blanks.*

1. Neither he .... his friend is good.
   A. or B. and
   C. but D. nor
2. The officer asked the peon .... why he was late.
   A. that B. if
   C. but D. No word needed

3. Both Ajay .... Vijay are intelligent.
A. or B. nor
C. and D. No word needed

4. No Sooner did the thief see the public .... he ran away.
A. then B. and
C. but D. than

5. Abhinav .... his brothers was going to Mumbai.
A. but B. yet
C. No word needed D. together with

6. He behaves .... he were the captain of the team.
A. as if B. as
C. No word needed D. that

7. Either Rupali .... Sonali is going to attend the meeting.
A. and B. but
C. nor D. or

8. Neither Nirmal .... Ashwinee is going to listen the speech.
A. and B. but
C. nor D. or

9. Ravi .... Prakash are going to Kolkata.
A. or B. nor
C. but D. and

10. Rice .... curry is my usual breakfast.
A. and B. but
C. then D. than

11. Hardly had he left .... his brother came.
A. then B. than
C. when D. that

12. I would rather have a copy .... a book.
A. then B. than
C. when D. that

13. He is no other .... my friend.
A. then B. than
C. when D. but

14. He saw a snake ....he awoke.
A. then B. when
C. than D. No word needed

15. Ten years have passed .... my grandmother died.
A. since B. when
C. then D. than

16. She is .... good .... bad.
A. either, not B. neither, or
C. neither, nor D. neither, than

17. The cellphone is both cheap .... best.
A. than B. and
C. then D. or

18. No sooner did the rogue see the police .... he disappeared.
A. then B. than
C. so D. because

19. Srishti will go .... Sanju goes.
A. if B. than
C. then D. although

20. She is wise .... timid.
A. and B. yet
C. but D. however

21. Make hay .... the sun shines.
A. though B. while
C. after D. before

22. He is so weak .... he cannot walk.
A. but B. that
C. then D. so

23. Although he is rich, ... he is unhappy.
A. but B. yet
C. so D. still

24. Wait here ...... I come back.
A. till B. until
C. before D. after

25. He is my friend .... I shall help him.
A. so B. hence
C. that is why D. therefore

26. He must go away .... he will be beaten.
A. otherwise B. and
C. or D. else

27. God loves good men .... good men love God.
A. and B. or
C. that D. those

28. He was late .... he was not punished.
A. but B. yet
C. still D. therefore

29. Walk slowly ...., you may fall.
A. and B. or
C. so D. otherwise

30. Work hard, ... you will fail.
A. and B. or
C. otherwise D. else

ANSWERS

1	2	3	4	5	6	7	8	9	10
D	D	C	D	D	A	D	C	D	A
11	**12**	**13**	**14**	**15**	**16**	**17**	**18**	**19**	**20**
C	B	B	B	A	C	B	B	A	C
21	**22**	**23**	**24**	**25**	**26**	**27**	**28**	**29**	**30**
B	B	B	A	B	C	A	C	D	D

PREPOSITIONS

A *Preposition* is a word which is placed before a noun or a pronoun to show its relation to some other word in the sentence.

1. I saw a goat *in* the field.
2. I am fond *of* hot coffee.

In sentence 1, the word *in* shows the relation between two things—*goat* and *field.*

In sentence 2, the word *of* shows the relation between the attribute expressed by the adjective *found* and *tea.*

The words *in* and *of* are here used as prepositions.

The noun or pronoun which is used with a preposition is called its object. The noun or pronoun is in the objective case. It is governed by the preposition. Now it is absolutely clear that in sentence 1, the noun *field* is in the objective case. The word *field* is governed by the preposition *in.*

A preposition may have two or more objects.

The road runs over *hill* and *plain.*

Here, the words *hill* and *plain* are used as objects.

Use of Important Prepositions

1. Among, Between

'**Among**' is used for more than two persons or things; '**Between**' is used only for two.

Examples :

(i) Distribute these sweets *among* the poor students of the class.

(ii) Distribute these books *between* Ram and Shyam.

2. Among, In

'**Among**' is used before collective plural nouns. '**In**' is used before collective singular nouns.

Examples :

(i) I found him standing *among* the crowd.

(ii) I saw him in the crowd.

3. Beside, Besides

'**Beside**' means 'by the side of'. '**Besides**' means 'in addition to'.

Examples :

(i) The daughter was sitting *beside* her mother.

(ii) *Besides* his relatives, he invited his friends also.

4. In, Within

'**In**' means at the expiry of a period of time in future, '**Within**' means before the expiry of a period of time in any tense.

Examples :

(i) She will return *in* a week.

(ii) I shall finish my work *within* a weak.

5. On, Upon

'**On**' is used for things at rest; '**Upon**' is used for things in motion.

Examples :

(i) He is sitting *on* the floor.

(ii) The dog sprang *upon* the table.

6. By, With

'**By**' denotes the agent or doer, '**With**' denotes the instrument with which anything is done.

Examples :

(i) The bird was killed *by* the hunter with an arrow.

(ii) He beat the dog *with* a stick.

(iii) I shall reach here *by* five o'clock.

7. After, In

'**After**' means at the end of a period of time in the past. '**In**' means at the end of a period of time in future.

Examples :

(i) I shall return your book *in* a week.

(ii) He returned the book *after* a week.

8. For, From, Since

'**For**' is used before a noun denoting a period of time with all the tenses. '**From**' is used before a noun or phrase denoting a point of time, it is used in all the tenses. '**Since**' is used before a noun or phrase denoting some point of time and is always produced by a verb in the perfect continuous tense or third form of a verb.

Examples :

(i) We have been playing cards *for* two hours.

(ii) She stayed with her uncle *from* the 15th of March to the 15th of May.

(iii) I have been reading this book *since* morning.

9. Above, Over

'**Above**' means 'higher from', **Over** is used in the following four senses :

(i) In the sense of 'above' :

At noon, the sun is *over* our heads.

(ii) In the sense of 'beyond' :

I cannot get *over* my disappointment.

(iii) In the sense of 'Superiority' :

God *over* all blesses for ever more.

(iv) In the sense of 'Conclusion' :

It is all *over* with me.

10. At, Towards

'**At**' denotes the idea of aim, '**Towards**' denotes the idea of destination.

Examples :

(i) He threw the stone *at* the cat.

(ii) He went *towards* the house.

11. At, In, On

'At' is used as follows :

(i) '**At**' is used with small towns and villages.

Examples:

(a) He was born *at* Sonepat.

(b) He lives *at* village Bangra. (Bangra is a village)

(ii) **'At'** is used before a noun denoting a definite point of time.

Example :

He called on me *at* 9 p.m. yesterday.

'In' is used as follows :

(iii) **'In'** is used with the names of big cities, provinces and countries.

Examples :

(a) His father lives *in* England.

(b) His younger brother lives *in* Calcutta.

(iv) **'In'** is used before the names of months and years.

Example :

His elder sister was born *in* 1972 *in* the month of May.

'On' is used with dates and names of days. **Examples :**

(a) I joined college *on* the 26th April.

(b) He will leave for Kolkata *on* Wednesday next.

Important Information

1. **'In'** is also used in the following phrases :
   In the morning; In the evening, In winter, In summer.
2. **'In'** also denotes a place inside anything.
   He travelled *in* a crowded bus.
3. **'At'** is used in the following phrases :
   At home, *At* the station, *At* work, *At* play.

12. Below, Beneath

Below means 'of lower level in position, dignity and expectation' etc. *Beneath* means 'under'.

Examples :

(i) It is *below* my dignity to talk to her.

(ii) They rested *beneath* the shade of a tree.

13. In, Into, To

'In' expresses Rest or Motion inside anything. **'Into'** expresses Motion towards the inside of anything or change from one medium to another. **'To'** denotes motion from one place to another.

Examples :

(i) The boys are *in* the room.

(ii) Translate this passage from English *into* Hindi.

(iii) Every morning he goes *to* the temple.

14. Till, By, Of, Off

- 'Till' means upto or not earlier than.
- 'By' means not later than.
- 'Of' shows cause, source, separation, quality, contents, possession, apposition, point of reference, space in time etc.
- 'Off' shows separation at a near distance, and detached condition.

Consider the following examples:

(i) I shall work *till* 5 a.m.

(ii) Madhu died *of* cancer.

(iii) The nib *of* the pen is made *of* gold.

(iv) He presented me a bottle *of* perfume.

(v) Our principal is a man *of* principle.

(vi) He lived in the house *of* his friend.

(vii) *By* this time tomorrow, I'll have finished my job.

(viii) My house is *off* the road.

(ix) The book fell *off* the table.

MULTIPLE CHOICE QUESTIONS

Directions: *Tick the correct preposition for the blank in each of the following sentences.*

1. He applied ...... the manager.
A. for B. to
C. with D. by

2. Trust ...... God and do the right.
A. in B. for
C. to D. with

3. She is worthy ...... a prize.
A. with B. for
C. to D. of

4. Mr. Gomes has no taste ...... music.
A. of B. for
C. with D. to

5. You are hard ...... hearing.
A. at B. of
C. with D. for

6. He is sure ...... his success
A. for B. with
C. on D. of

7. Preeti was warned ...... the danger ahead.
A. for B. at
C. of D. about

8. I am thankful ...... you for a good advice.
A. for B. with
C. to D. of

9. Deepak would not surrender ...... the police.
A. with B. to
C. for D. on

10. The small plant in your lawn is very sensitive ...... touch.
A. on B. with
C. to D. about

11. Divya was sure to succeed ..... the examination.
A. for B. in
C. to D. with

12. Geeta was jealous ...... Ravina's beauty.
A. to B. with
C. for D. of

13. He was ignorant ..... what was happening there.
A. for B. of
C. to D. with

14. Your pen is inferior ...... mine.
A. than B. with
C. from D. to

15. Reenu is no match ...... Meenu.
A. to B. for
C. with D. upon

16. It is necessary ...... you to apply for this job.
A. on B. with
C. for D. to

17. Be loyal ...... your country.
A. for B. to
C. on D. with

18. Mukesh is junior ...... me.
A. than B. to
C. from D. of

19. Deepika was innocent ...... the crime.
A. of B. with
C. from D. to

20. I am desirous.... joining the Indian cricket team.
A. for B. of
C. to D. on

ANSWERS

1	2	3	4	5	6	7	8	9	10
B	A	D	B	B	D	D	D	B	D
11	**12**	**13**	**14**	**15**	**16**	**17**	**18**	**19**	**20**
B	D	B	D	B	D	B	B	A	B

SYNONYMS

A synonym is a word which conveys a meaning similar to the given word.

REMEMBER

Words	*Synonyms*
Add	Increase
Adequate	Enough
Adjust	Adapt
All	Aggregate
Allow	Permit
Abode	Dwelling
Apt	Proper
Assess	Appraise
Accuse	Calumniate
Abashed	Timid
Annoy	Displease
Ample	Enough, Sufficient
Amplify	Increase
Apathetic	Unenthusiastic
Accost	Address
Authentic	True
Adjust	Fit
Approve	Assent, Allow, Accept
Adapt	Conform
Adversary	Opponent, Rival, Competitor
Beat	Whack
Benign	Kind
Breeze	Zephyr
Baffle	Puzzle
Booty	Spoil
Beauty	Charm
Beast	Animal
Bandit	Robber

Words	*Synonyms*
Blaze	Shine
Bond	Tie
Bend	Twist
Bate	Diminish
Beg	Plead
Barbaric	Wild, Savage
Bashful	Shy, Reserved
Begin	Start
Blend	Mix, Mingle
Bizarre	Funny
Below	Under
Bedevil	Confuse
Bemoan	Lament
Babble	Nonsense
Blame	Fault
Behaviour	Demeanour
Call	Accost
Copy	Imitate
Close	Shut
Caress	Love
Camp	Stay
Connect	Attach
Cut	Injure, Curtail
Cling	Stick
Conical	Funny
Convey	Carry
Conspicuous	Prominent
Cheerful	Happy, Pleasant
Curtail	Decrease
Cheerless	Sad, Dejected
Curious	Strange
Circumstance	Factor, Situation, Condition
Competent	Capable
Congruent	Overlapping

Words	*Synonyms*
Cope	Deal, Endure
Confident	Sure
Complex	Intricate
Cajole	Coax, Flatter
Cunning	Crafty
Delectable	Joyful, Delightful
Devilish	Diabolical
Delicate	Soft
Devil	Fiend
Delay	Postpone
Dislike	Repugnance
Destroy	Ruin
Dwell	Live, Dilate
Declare	Pronounce
Drunk	Flushed
Deficient	Lacking
Damn	Condemn, Curse
Decrease	Diminish
Destruction	Devastation
Efficient	Competent
Ethnic	Racial
Enthral	Enslave
Earnest	Serious
Envious	Jealous
Ending	Final
Egg	Incite
Extempore	At once
Extensive	Far-ranging
Extra	Surplus
Existence	Life
Exceed	Overstep
Enormous	Vast
Excessive	Superfluous
Free	Unhindered
Frigid	Cold
Feed	Cater
Fame	Reputation
Frame	Make
First	Initial
Frighten	Terrorise, Intimidate
Fervent	Fervid
Fall	Decline
Feeble	Frail
Fickle	Changeable
Finish	Conclude
Fraud	Deception
Forgiving	Placable
Grow	Develop
Greed	Avidity
Greet	Welcome
Grave	Serious
Group	Constellation
Given	Bestowed

Words	*Synonyms*
Gratitude	Thankfulness
Have	Possess
Hire	Rent
Hit	Strike
Handsome	Beautiful
Hinder	Prevent
Heap	Pile
Hope	Expect
Hard	Harsh
Help	Aid
Hymn	Song
Henpecked	Enslaved
Hoodwink	Mystify, Cheat
Humble	Polite, Urbane, Modest
Harass	Vex, Trouble
Impart	Instil
Intact	Untouched
Instal	Establish
Indict	Impeach
Imitate	Ape
Instigate	Incite
Initiate	Start, Introduce
Inimical	Unfriendly
Insufferable	Intolerable
Impartiality	Justice
Jolly	Merry
Joyful	Delectable
Join	Conjoin
Kind	Benign
Kill	Murder
Kindred	Similar
Kinship	Relationship
Keen	Sharp
Knowledge	Scholarship
Lazy	Slothful
Large	Substantial, Gargantuan
Listless	Careless, Lackadaisical
Lax	Loose
Little	Small
Lifelike	Realistic
Lofty	High
Lenient	Soft, Gentle
Lacking	Deficient, Wanting
Lessen	Decrease
Middleclass	Bourgeois
Mitigate	Lessen, Abate
Modesty	Humility, Lowliness
Mix	Mingle, Blend
Mixture	Mingling
Mixed	Assorted
Modify	Decrease
Mean	Imply
Multifarious	Varied

Words	Synonyms
Miscarry	Abort
Note	Notice
Noble	Stately
Native	Indigenous
Needful	Necessary
Notify	Declare
Nervous	Shaky, Tremulous, Timid
Natural	Spontaneous
Near	Close
Normal	Natural
Offend	Displease
Oppress	Persecute, Tyrannize
Opponent	Adversary
Obstruct	Hinder, Check
Offence	Fault
Offender	Villain
Overstep	Exceed
Overlapping	Congruent
Occult	Mystic
Profane	Unholy
Patience	Forbearance
Pornographic	Obscene
Plenitude	Abundance
Prominent	Important
Prodigal	Spender
Procrastinate	Postpone
Promote	Develop, Honour
Persecute	Tyrannise
Profess	Claim
Pliant	Flexible
Plebian	Common
Polished	Sophisticated
Quake	Shake
Quit	Leave
Queer	Eccentric
Quell	Suppress
Quantify	Allot
Reply	Answer
Relinquish	Retire
Read	Peruse
Relation	Reference
Render	Do
Remainder	Residuals
Repeat	Reiterate
Repentant	Contrite
Retaliative	Retaliatory
Rumour	Hearsay
Reveal	Divulge
Ritualistic	Ceremonious
Soft	Delicate
Sort	Kind, Choose, Select
Selfish	Egoistic
Sensual	Earthly

Words	Synonyms
Suppress	Quell, Check
Stimulate	Provoke
Tasteless	Insipid
Travel	Journey
True	Authentic, Faithful, Truthful
Turbulence	Turmoil
Tragedy	Calamity
Tasteful	Tasty, Delicious
Touching	Painful
Thankful	Grateful
Tremendous	Great, Huge
Tough	Strong
Terminate	Conclude, End
Theory	Doctrine
Tell	Relate
Tremble	Shake, Shiver
Urge	Spur
Unbeaten	Unsubdued
Use	Utilize, Practise
Underhand	Unfair, Undue
Unfair	Unjust
Unravel	Reveal, Divulge
Unimportant	Common
Unconcerned	Apathetic
Unimitated	Inimitable
Unfortunate	Unlucky
Understand	Perceive, Comprehend
Vain	Proud, Haughty, Conceited, Shameless
Vale	Valley, Dale, Dell
Vice	Fault
Virtue	Quality
Veracity	Reality
Value	Price, Prize
Vex	Tease
Vibrate	Quiver, Shake
Violent	Excessive
Vivid	Clear, Lucid
Victory	Triumph
Vulgar	Indecent
Virtuous	Honest
Variegated	Varied, Multifarious
Well	Good
Yell	Cry, Shout
Yonder	There
Yearn	Wish, Desire
Yoke	Slavery
Zest	Earnestness, Enthusiasm
Zealous	Earnest

ANTONYMS

A antonym is a word which conveys a meaning opposite to the given word.

REMEMBER

Words	*Antonyms*
Abhor	Love
Abnormal	Normal
Able	Unable
Acceptable	Unacceptable
Adequate	Inadequate
Amusing	Boring
Angry	Calm
Apex	Bottom
Attract	Repel
Bad	Good
Barren	Fertile
Beautiful	Ugly
Bitter	Sweet
Brave	Cowardly
Brief	Lengthy
Bright	Dull
Calm	Violent
Careful	Careless
Clear	Vague, Cloudy
Cold	Hot
Cruel	Kind
Dear	Cheap
Deep	Shallow
Difficult	Easy
Direct	Indirect
Dishonest	Honest
Disobey	Obey
Encourage	Discourage
Enormous	Tiny
Excellent	Bad
Expensive	Cheap
Eat	Fast
Fair	Unfair
Fake	Authentic
False	True
Famous	Notorious
Fool	Genius
Generous	Miserly
Genius	Fool
Genuine	Unauthentic
Gigantic	Tiny
Glad	Depressed
Good	Bad
Great	Little
Happy	Sad
Hard	Soft
Hate	Love
Honest	Dishonest

Words	*Antonyms*
Idle	Busy
Immoral	Moral
Include	Exclude
Incorrect	Correct
Intelligent	Unintelligent
Kind	Cruel
Like	Dislike
Long	Short
Lucid	Vague
Major	Minor
Naive	Experienced
Nadir	Apex
Neat	Clumsy
Obedient	Disobedient
Obscure	Clear
Oppose	Support
Optimistic	Pessimistic
Out	In
Patience	Impatience
Peaceful	Belligerent
Pious	Impious
Polite	Impolite
Potent	Impotent
Prominent	Unimportant
Proper	Improper
Pure	Impure
Quick	Slow
Quiet	Disturbance
Real	False, Unreal
Reject	Select, Choose
Reliable	Unreliable
Respect	Disrespect
Right	Wrong
Robust	Feeble, Weak
Sad	Happy
Secret	Open
Sensible	Insensible
Severe	Mild
Sharp	Blunt
Simple	Complex
Sociable	Unsociable
Tall	Short
Tidy	Untidy
Uncanny	Canny
Violent	Calm
Vivid	Vague
Strong	Weak
Big	Small
Easy	Difficult
Fast	Slow
High	Low
Catchy	Unattractive
Ugly	Handsome, Beautiful, Tidy
Tasty	Insipid
Sonorous	Harsh

MULTIPLE CHOICE QUESTIONS

Directions (Qs. 1 to 20): *In the following questions choose the word which best expresses the meaning of the given word.*

1. ABSURD
   A. Foolish B. Simple
   C. Courageous D. Silly
2. ABANDON
   A. Lose B. Profit
   C. Vacate D. Foil
3. CAJOLE
   A. Pause B. Lenient
   C. Blast D. Lure
4. COMBAT
   A. Fight B. Conflict
   C. Shoot D. Quarrel
5. LAMENT
   A. Condone B. Console
   C. Complain D. Contribution
6. DEBACLE
   A. Disgrace B. Defeat
   C. Collapse D. Decline
7. SHIVER
   A. Fear B. Tremble
   C. Shake D. Ache
8. TORTURE
   A. Terror B. Harassment
   C. Torment D. Tranquility
9. LAUDABLE
   A. Lovable B. Commendable
   C. Profitable D. Oblivious
10. FIXED
    A. Sterile B. Static
    C. Stubborn D. Parennial
11. QUEER
    A. Unfamiliar B. Cute
    C. Curious D. Strange
12. SUFFICIENT
    A. Fit B. Proper
    C. Adequate D. Vast
13. GLOSS
    A. Brightness B. Soothing
    C. Rubbing D. Miracle
14. LONGING
    A. Prune B. Apathy
    C. Curtail D. Craving
15. JEER
    A. Applaud B. Magnanimity
    C. Avoid D. Scoff
16. ZENITH
    A. Minimum B. Nadir
    C. Plant D. Peak
17. GARB
    A. Distort B. Dress
    C. Trivial D. Rage
18. ABHOR
    A. Rude B. Reconcile
    C. Crave D. Detest
19. YIELD
    A. Shum B. Incisive
    C. Retain D. Surrender
20. YOKE
    A. Twist B. Release
    C. Link D. Extra

Directions (Qs. 21 to 38): *In the following questions choose the word which best expresses the opposite of the given word.*

21. TRAGIC
    A. Dramatic B. Strong
    C. Gentle D. Comic
22. ORAL
    A. Verbal B. Sane
    C. Minor D. Written
23. ADMIRE
    A. Hate B. Unlike
    C. Dislike D. Enough
24. VIOLENT
    A. Gentle B. Savage
    C. Haughty D. Decline
25. ADVERSITY
    A. Windfall B. Inprosperity
    C. Prosperity D. Slave
26. GENUINE
    A. Spurious B. Obscure
    C. Countless D. Apathetic
27. GRUDGE
    A. Essence B. Guile
    C. Goodwill D. Ill-will
28. STIFF
    A. Soft B. Courteous
    C. Lively D. Flexible
29. VANITY
    A. Conceit B. Pride
    C. Ostentious D. Humility
30. FRONT
    A. Upper B. Unusual
    C. Back D. Rear

31. ATTRACT
A. Lured B. Longing
C. Repel D. Disguise

32. COMFORT
A. Discomfort B. Discontent
C. Uncomfort D. Miscomfort

33. WELCOME
A. Repel B. Accept
C. Resist D. Fight

34. TACTFUL
A. Naive B. Loose
C. Strict D. Uncivilized

35. DUTIFUL
A. Harmful B. Watchful
C. Forgetful D. Remiss

36. RIGID
A. Flux B. Adoptable
C. Yielding D. Adaptable

37. RARE
A. Petty B. Poor
C. Small D. Common

38. ZEAL
A. Despair B. Calmness
C. Passiveness D. Indifference

ANSWERS

1	2	3	4	5	6	7	8	9	10
D	C	D	A	C	C	B	C	B	B
11	**12**	**13**	**14**	**15**	**16**	**17**	**18**	**19**	**20**
D	C	A	D	D	D	B	D	D	C
21	**22**	**23**	**24**	**25**	**26**	**27**	**28**	**29**	**30**
D	D	C	A	C	A	C	D	D	D
31	**32**	**33**	**34**	**35**	**36**	**37**	**38**		
C	A	C	A	D	D	D	D		

SENTENCE COMPLETION

It is such an exercise which starts with the primary schools and continues in the highest level of competitive examinations. One must practise it regularly to score well.

Directions (Qs. 1 to 15): *Pick out the most effective word(s) from the given words to fill in the blanks to make the sentence meaningfully complete.*

1. The student ...... that book from the library to study at home.
A. issued B. borrowed
C. hired D. lent

2. I wish I ...... a king.
A. was B. am
C. should be D. were

3. He ...... to listen to my arguments and walked away.
A. denied B. disliked
C. objected D. refused

4. The flow of blood was so ...... that the patient died.
A. intense B. adequate
C. profuse D. extensive

5. When I met her yesterday, it was the first time I ...... her since Christmas.
A. saw B. have seen
C. had seen D. have been seing

6. Can you pay ...... all these articles?
A. for B. of
C. off D. out

7. I ...... you to be at the party this evening.
A. expect B. hope
C. look forward to D. desire

8. ...... being a handicapped person, he is very cooperative and self-reliant.
A. Because B. Although
C. Since D. Despite

9. The child broke ...... from his mother and ran towards the painting.
A. away B. after
C. down D. with

10. With his ...... income, he finds it difficult to live a comfortable life.
A. brief B. sufficient
C. meagre D. huge

11. He could ...... a lot of money in such a short time by using his intelligence and working hard.
A. spend B. spoil
C. exchange D. accumulate

12. Though the brothers are twins, they look ......
A. alike B. handsome
C. indifferent D. different

13. Unfavourable weather conditions can ..... illness.
A. cure B. detect
C. treat D. enhance

14. No sooner did the bell ring, ... the actor started singing.
A. when B. than
C. after D. before

15. If I ...... realised it, I would not have acted on his advice.

A. was B. had
C. were D. have

Directions (Qs. 16 to 25): *In each question, an incomplete statement (Stem) followed by four fillers is given. Pick out the best one which can complete the incomplete stem correctly and meaningfully.*

16. Unless you work harder you will fail, means .....
A. if you fail you will work harder.
B. you must at least plan well than you will not fail.
C. hardly you will fail if you do not desire so.
D. if you do not put more efforts, then you will fail.

17. Even if it rains I shall come, means .....
A. if I come it will not rain.
B. if it rains I shall not come.
C. I will certainly come whether it rains or not.
D. whenever there is rain I shall come.

18. Dinesh is as stupid as he is lazy means .....
A. Dinesh is stupid because he is lazy.
B. Dinesh is lazy because he is stupid.
C. Dinesh is either stupid or lazy.
D. Dinesh is equally stupid and lazy.

19. He is so lazy that he .....
A. cannot depend on others for getting his work done.
B. cannot delay the schedule of completing the work.
C. can seldom complete his work on time.
D. dislike to postpone the work that he undertakes to do.

20. He always stammers in public meetings, but his today's speech .....
A. was fairly audible to everyone present in the hall.
B. was not received satisfactorily.
C. could not be understood properly.
D. was free from that defect.

21. In order to raise the company's profit, the employees .....
A. demanded two additional increments.
B. decided to go on paid holidays.
C. requested the management to implement new welfare schemes.
D. offered to work overtime without any compensation.

22. Although, he is reputed for making very candid statements, ...
A. his today's speech was not fairly audible.
B. his promises had always been realistic.
C. his speech was very interesting.
D. his today's statements were very ambiguous.

23. I felt somewhat more relaxed .....
A. but tense as compared to earlier.
B. and tense as compared to earlier.
C. as there was already no tension at all.
D. and tension-free as compared to earlier.

24. With great efforts his son succeeded in convincing him not to donate his entire wealth to an orphanage .....
A. and lead the life of a wealthy merchant.
B. but to a home for the forsaken children.
C. and make an orphan of himself.
D. as the orphanage needed a lot of donations.

25. Even though it is a very large house, ...
A. there is a lot of space available in it for children.
B. there is hardly any space available for children.
C. there is no dearth of space for children.
D. the servants take a long time to clean it.

ANSWERS

1	2	3	4	5	6	7	8	9	10
B	D	D	C	C	A	A	D	A	C
11	**12**	**13**	**14**	**15**	**16**	**17**	**18**	**19**	**20**
D	D	D	B	B	D	C	D	C	D
21	**22**	**23**	**24**	**25**					
D	D	D	C	B					

SPOTTING ERRORS

The most common errors in English are of spellings, grammar and usage of words. By regular practice, the errors can be easily spotted and minimised.

MULTIPLE CHOICE QUESTIONS

Directions: *In the following questions some of the sentences have errors and some are correct. Find out which part of a sentence has an error, the number of that part is your answer. If a sentence is free from errors, then your answer is D i.e., No error.*

1. (A) Either Ram or/(B) you is responsible/(C) for this action./(D) No error.

2. (A) The student flatly denied/(B) that he had copied/(C) in the examination hall./(D) No error.

3. (A) By the time you arrive tomorrow/(B) I have finished/(C) my work./(D) No error.

4. (A) The captain with the members of his team/(B) are returning/(C) after a fortnight./(D) No error.

5. (A) After returning from/(B) an all-India tour/(C) I had to describe about it./(D) No error.

6. (A) The teacher asked his students/(B) if they had gone through/(C) either of the three chapters included in the prescribed text./(D) No error.

7. (A) Do you know/(B) how old were you/(C) when you came here?/(D) No error.

8. (A) Beware of/(B) a fair-weather friend/(C) who is neither a friend in need nor a friend indeed./(D) No error.

9. (A) Copernicus proved/(B) that Earth/(C) moves round the Sun./(D) No error.

10. (A) The property/(B) was divided/(C) among the two brothers./(D) No error.

11. (A) I am quite certain/(B) that the lady is not only greedy/(C) but miserly./(D) No error.

12. (A) The brilliant success in the examination/(B) as well as his record in sports/(C) deserves high praise./(D) No error.

13. (A) I cannot find/(B) where has he gone/(C) though I have tried may best./(D) No error.

14. (A) If I was/(B) the Prime Minister of India/(C) I would work wonders/(D) No error.

15. (A) If it weren't/(B) for you,/(C) I wouldn't be alive today./(D) No error.

16. (A) He looked like a lion/(B) baulked from/(C) its prey./(D) No error.

17. (A) Widespread flooding/(B) is affecting/(C) large areas of the villages./(D) No error.

18. (A) If we really set to/(B) we can get the whole house/(C) cleaned in an afternoon./(D) No error.

19. (A) It's arrogant for you/(B) to assume you'll/(C)win every time./(D) No error.

20. (A) The two books are the same/(B) except for the fact that this/(C) has an answer in the back./(D) No error.

21. (A) Your husband doesn't/(B) believe that you are older/(C) than I./(D) No error.

22. (A) I could not/(B) answer to/(C) the question./(D) No error.

23. (A) Two years passed/(B) since/(C) my cousin died./(D) No error.

24. (A) I am learning English/(B) for ten years/(C) without much effect./(D) No error.

25. (A) Ramesh has agreed/(B) to marry with the girl/(C) of his parent's choice./ (D) No error.

26. (A) When he was arriving./(B) the party was/(C) in full swing./(D) No error.

27. (A) The most studious boy/(B) in the class/(C) was made as the captain./(D) No error.

28. (A) I am participating/(B) in the two-miles race/(C) tomorrow morning./(D) No error.

29. (A) When the boy committed a mistake/(B) the teacher made him to do/(C) the sum again./(D) No error.

30. (A) Whenever a person lost anything/(B) the poor folk around/(C) are suspected./(D) No error.

ANSWERS

1	2	3	4	5	6	7	8	9	10
B	D	B	B	C	C	D	D	B	C
11	12	13	14	15	16	17	18	19	20
C	D	B	A	C	C	C	A	A	C
21	22	23	24	25	26	27	28	29	30
C	B	A	A	B	A	C	B	B	A

EXPLANATORY ANSWERS

1. Replace 'is' by 'are'.
2. No error.
3. Replace 'have' by 'would have'.
4. Replace 'are' by 'is'.
5. Replace 'had to describe' by 'described'.
6. Replace 'either' by 'any'.
7. No error.
8. No error.
9. Omit 'that'.
10. Replace 'among' by 'between'.
11. Add 'also'.
12. No error.
13. Replace 'has he' by 'he has'.
14. Replace 'was' by 'were'.
15. Replace 'wouldn't be' by 'would not have been'.
16. Replace 'its' by 'his'.

17. Replace 'areas' by 'area'.
18. Replace 'set to' by 'set on'.
19. Replace 'for' by 'of'.
20. Replace 'in' by 'on'.
21. Replace 'I' by 'me'.
22. Omit 'to'.
23. Replace 'passed' by 'have passed'.
24. Replace 'am' by 'have been'.
25. Omit 'with'.
26. Replace 'was arriving' by 'arrived'.
27. Omit 'as'.
28. Replace 'in' by 'at'.
29. Omit 'to'.
30. Replace 'lost' by 'loses'.

ONE WORD SUBSTITUTION

There are many single words in English language which can be perfectly used for a number of words. These words help in expressing ideas in a short and correct manner for the right occasion. Such words not only increase the vocabulary but also enable you to economise in the use of words to a great extent.

Multiple Word Expression	*Substitution*
One who always looks towards the bright side of things	**Optimist**
One who always looks towards the dark side of things	**Pessimist**
The time when one develops from a child into an adult	**Adolescence**
The process of growing more plants in order to form a forest.	**Afforestation**
The science which deals with farming	**Agriculture**
From some other country or place etc.	**Alien**
A term, etc. giving more than one meaning	**Ambiguous**
A vehicle which is used to carry sick persons	**Ambulance**
An animal which can live both in water and on land	**Amphibian**
A lawless situation when there is no government	**Anarchy**
Belonging to the history of thousands of years old	**Ancient**
Once a year	**Annual**
A very old object but still valuable	**Antique**
Words of opposite meanings	**Antonyms**
Words of similar meanings	**Synonyms**
Signatures of a famous person	**Autograph**
A government led by one person with absolute authority	**Autocracy**
A written work of one's own life history	**Autobiography**
A person who has never been married	**Bachelor**
A person usually having no hair on his head	**Bald**
A place where one can deposit money and get interest	**Bank**
A person who cuts our hair	**Barber**
A building/group of buildings where soldiers live	**Barracks**
A person who makes buns and biscuits	**Baker**
A person who lives by asking people for food and money without doing any useful job	**Beggar**
The crime of having married to two persons at the same time	**Bigamy**
The branch of science which deals with the study of plants	**Botany**
Able to speak two languages	**Bilingual**
Able to speak more than two languages	**Polyglot**
The branch of science which deals with the living organisms	**Biology**
A powerful snow storm	**Blizzard**
A great successful book or movie	**Blockbuster**
A short news on the radio or TV	**Bulletin**
A system in which the most important works are organised by the government officials	**Bureaucracy**

Multiple Word Expression	*Substitution*
A person who has no vision in his eyes	Blind
A page or a series of pages on which the information of days, weeks, months, etc. is given	Calendar
A person who eats human flesh	Cannibal
A complete list of items often arranged alphabetically	Catalogue
A sudden disaster	Catastrophe
A period of 100 years	Century
A branch of science which deals with chemicals	Chemistry
A printed leaf usually issued by banks that we sign to carry certain financial deal	Cheque
A person who makes or mends shoes	Cobbler
A group of people who has been chosen by others to make decisions on their own	Committee
A building in which nuns live	Convent
An animal which feeds on other animals	Carnivorous
A person who does criticism	Critic
A person who cannot hear	Deaf
A condition in which one loses a lot of water from one's body because of vomiting, etc.	Dehydration
A system of government in which the people cast their votes to elect their leaders	Democracy
The study of skin problems	Dermatology
A long piece of land covered with sand	Desert
The art of managing relationships between countries	Diplomacy
A piece of information about the words in a book form	Dictionary
A piece of information about the telephone numbers of the people in a book from	Directory
A person in charge of a newspapers, magazine etc.	Editor
A person who thinks he is better than the others	Egoist
To leave your country and settle in some other country	Emigrate
A book or series of books giving almost all knowledge about an area or some persons etc.	Encyclopaedia
Study of insects	Entomology
Time when day and night are of the same duration	Equinox
To sell things out of the country	Export
To purchase things from some other country	Import
A plant or animal no longer in existence	Extinct
A situation when there is a shortage of food for a long period of time	Famine
An amount of money that we pay for some action or services	Fee
Related to women	Feminine
An animal strong and aggressive	Ferocious
A piece of land where plants grow easily from the soil that is favourable to them	Fertile
A work of literature having some imaginary events	Fiction
A large amount of water covering certain area	Flood
A person who sells flowers	Florist
A religious ceremony for burying or cremating a dead person	Funeral
A substance which kills fungus	Fungicide
A person studying or having studied the diseases and the related things of female reproductory system	Gynaecologist
The murder of the person of the same group race or country	Genocide
A substance which kills germs	Germicide
A situation in which many people die because of fire during war	Holocaust
The act of killing a person deliberately	Homicide
A word having the pronunciation as the other one does but it differs in meaning	Homophone

Multiple Word Expression	*Substitution*
A word having the same spelling as the other one does but it is pronounced in some other way	Homonym
A person who is attracted towards the person of the same sex	Homosexual
Go across and parallel to the ground	Horizontal
A substance which kills the insects	Insecticide
That cannot be corrected	Incorrigible
That cannot be defeated	Invincible
That cannot be eaten	Inedible
That cannot be seen	Invisible
A place in a school or college where books are kept for the benefit of students, teachers etc.	Library
A place in a school or college where scientific experiments are performed	Laboratory
An official who is a judge in the lowest court	Magistrate
A piece of music or a book before it is printed	Manuscript
Related to men	Masculine
One who believes in the existence of God	A theist
One who does not believe in the existence of good	An atheist
That can be believed	Credible
That cannot be believed	Incredible
That which dissolves in a solvent	Soluble
That which does not dissolves in a solvent	Insoluble
Hard writing that can be read	Legible
Hard writing that cannot be read	Illegible
A person who does jobs beneficial to mankind	Philanthropist
A person who goes on foot	Pedestrian
A person who fights for his own country	Patriot
An act of killing oneself	Suicide
A woman whose husband is dead	Widow
A man whose wife is dead	Widower
A person who eats vegetarian and non-vegetarian diets	Omnivorous
Something which is everywhere at the same time	Omnipresent
One who knows everything	Omniscient
A child who does not have parents	Orphan
An award etc. given after the death of the person	Posthumous
The place where animals are kept for amusement and to increase the knowledge of the public	Zoo
The science which deals with the study of animals	Zoology

MULTIPLE CHOICE QUESTIONS

Directions: *In questions given below, out of the four alternatives, choose the one which can be substituted for the given words/sentences.*

1. Something that relates to everyone in the world
A. General B. Common
C. Usual D. Universal

2. An expression of mild disapproval
A. Warning B. Denigration
C. Impertinence D. Reproof

3. One who is not easily pleased by anything
A. Maiden B. Medieval
C. Precarious D. Fastidious

4. Murder of a king
A. Infanticide B. Matricide
C. Genocide D. Regicide

5. A remedy for all diseases
A. Stoic B. Marvel
C. Panacea D. Recompense

6. A dramatic performance
A. Mask B. Mosque
C. Masque D. Mascot

7. Study of birds
A. Orology B. Optology
C. Ophthalmology D. Ornithology

8. Ready to believe
A. Credulous B. Credible
C. Creditable D. Incredible

9. Incapable of being seen through
A. Ductile B. Opaque
C. Obsolete D. Potable

10. One who eats everything
A. Omnivorous B. Omniscient
C. Irresistible D. Insolvent

11. A place where bees are kept is called
A. An apiary B. A mole
C. A hive D. A sanctuary

12. One who cannot be corrected
A. Incurable B. Incorrigible
C. Hardened D. Invulnerable

13. One who is in charge of a museum
A. Curator B. Supervisor
C. Caretaker D. Warden

14. Continuing fight between parties, families, clans, etc.
A. Enmity B. Feud
C. Quarrel D. Skirmish

15. A voice loud enough to be heard
A. Audible B. Applaudable
C. Laudable D. Oral

16. A paper written by hand
A. Handicraft B. Manuscript
C. Handiwork D. Thesis

17. Habitually silent or talking little
A. Serville B. Unequivocal
C. Taciturn D. Synoptic

18. To slap with a flat object
A. Chop B. Hew
C. Gnaw D. Swat

19. A person who speaks many languages
A. Linguist B. Monolingual
C. Polyglot D. Bilingual

20. A light sailing-boat built specially for racing
A. Canoe B. Yacht
C. Frigate D. Dinghy

21. A fixed orbit in space in relation to earth
A. Geological B. Geo-synchronous
C. Geo-centric D. Geo-stationary

22. A style in which a writer makes a display of his knowledge
A. Pedantic B. Verbose
C. Pompous D. Ornate

23. A religious discourse
A. Preach B. Stanza
C. Sanctorum D. Sermon

24. A place that provides refuge
A. Asylum B. Sanatorium
C. Shelter D. Orphanage

25. Detailed plan of a journey
A. Travelogue B. Travelkit
C. Schedule D. Itinerary

26. A person who insists on something
A. Disciplinarian B. Stickler
C. Instantaneous D. Boaster

27. A drawing on transparent paper
A. Red print B. Blue print
C. Negative D. Transparency

28. One who believes that all things and events in life are predetermined is a
A. Fatalist B. Puritan
C. Egoist D. Tyrant

29. A school boy who cuts classes frequently is a
A. Defeatist B. Sycophant
C. Truant D. Martinet

30. The act of violating the sanctity of the church is
A. Blasphemy B. Heresy
C. Sacrilege D. Desecration

31. A place where monks live as a secluded community
A. Cathedral B. Diocese
C. Convent D. Monastery

32. One who is fond of fighting
A. Bellicose B. Aggressive
C. Belligerent D. Militant

33. Tending to move away from the centre or axis
A. Centrifugal B. Centripetal
C. Axiomatic D. Awry

34. Words inscribed on tomb
A. Epitome B. Epistle
C. Epilogue D. Epitaph

35. Leave or remove from a place considered dangerous
A. Evade B. Evacuate
C. Avoid D. Exterminate

36. Original inhabitants of a country
A. Abroge B. Aborger
C. Aborgory D. Aborigins

37. Government by the officials
A. Theocracy B. Plutocracy
C. Bureaucracy D. Democracy

38. Incapable of being exhausted
A. Inexhaustible B. Inaexhaustible
C. Exhaustable D. Non-tired

39. A person of good understanding, knowledge and reasoning power
A. Expert B. Intellectual
C. Snob D. Literate

40. One absorbed in his own thoughts and feelings rather than in things outside
A. Scholar B. Recluse
C. Introvert D. Intellectual

ANSWERS

1	2	3	4	5	6	7	8	9	10
D	D	D	D	C	C	D	A	B	A
11	**12**	**13**	**14**	**15**	**16**	**17**	**18**	**19**	**20**
A	B	A	B	A	B	C	D	A	B
21	**22**	**23**	**24**	**25**	**26**	**27**	**28**	**29**	**30**
D	A	D	A	D	B	D	A	C	C
31	**32**	**33**	**34**	**35**	**36**	**37**	**38**	**39**	**40**
D	A	A	D	B	B	C	A	B	C

SPELLING ERRORS

There are thousands of words in English language. It is difficult to remember the spellings and meanings of all at once. Try to learn as many as you can. Use a dictionary regularly.

Directions: *Find the correctly spelt words.*

1. A. Damage B. Dammage C. Damaige D. Dammege

2. A. Efficiant B. Effecient C. Efficient D. Eficient

3. A. Schedule B. Schdule C. Schedale D. Schedeule

4. A. Occurad B. Occurred C. Ocurred D. Occured

5. A. Grieff B. Grief C. Grieef D. Grrief

6. A. Guarantee B. Garuntee C. Guaruntee D. Gaurantee

7. A. Meddicine B. Medicine C. Medicene D. Medicinne

8. A. Benefeted B. Benefitted C. Benifited D. Benefited

9. A. Acommodation B. Acomodation C. Accomodation D. Accommodation

10. A. Querrelsome B. Quarrelsame C. Quarrelsome D. Querralsome

11. A. Sympathetic B. Smypathetic C. Sympothetic D. Sympethetic

12. A. Prograssive B. Progressive C. Progresive D. Prograsive

13. A. Uncivilized B. Uncevilized C. Uncivillized D. Uncevelized

14. A. Extravagant B. Extreragent C. Extreregant D. Extravegent

15. A. Missunderstood B. Miesunderstood C. Misunderstood D. Misunderstod

16. A. Belligirent B. Beligirent C. Belligarant D. Belligerrent

17. A. Astonished B. Astronished C. Astoneshed D. Asstonished

18. A. Sincerely B. Sencerely C. Sincerelly D. Sincerrely

19. A. Rigourous B. Rigerous C. Rigorous D. Regerous

20. A. Satellite B. Sattellite C. Satelite D. Sattelite

21. A. Pesanger B. Passenger C. Pessenger D. Pasanger

22. A. Humurous B. Humorous C. Humoreus D. Humorrous

23. A. Exeggerate B. Exaggerate C. Exadgerate D. Exagerate

24. A. Fariegn B. Forein C. Foriegn D. Foreign

25. A. Excesive B. Excessive C. Exccessive D. Excceive

26. A. Forcaust B. Forcast C. Forecast D. Forecaste

27. A. Paralleted B. Paralelled C. Parralleled D. Parallelled

28. A. Ocasion B. Occassion C. Occasion D. Ocassion

29. A. Boquet B. Bouquet C. Bouquete D. Bouquette

30. A. Chettering B. Chaterring C. Chattering D. Chatering

31. A. Discourage B. Disscourage C. Discourege D. Discaurage

32. A. Curageous B. Courageous
C. Courrageous D. Couregeous

33. A. Abandon B. Abanadon
C. Abendon D. Abbandon

34. A. Embarassment
B. Emberrassement
C. Embarrassment
D. Embbaresment

35. A. Eccintric B. Eccentrie
C. Eccentric D. Eccintrie

36. A. Occasional B. Occassional
C. Occesional D. Occessional

37. A. Querrel B. Querral
C. Quarrel D. Quarel

38. A. Contrebution B. Contribution
C. Contributtion D. Conterbution

39. A. Desgrace B. Disgrece
C. Disgrice D. Disgrace

40. A. Harassment B. Herassment
C. Harasment D. Harassmient

41. A. Imaginative B. Imeginative
C. Imagenative D. Imaginetive

42. A. Suficient B. Suficiant
C. Sufficient D. Sufficiant

43. A. Adequate B. Edequate
C. Adaquete D. Edaquete

44. A. Exparienced B. Experianced
C. Experienced D. Experrienced

45. A. Flatering B. Fletering
C. Flattering D. Fletaring

46. A. Cuttiveted B. Culltrivated
C. Cultivated D. Caltivated

47. A. Praiceworthy B. Peiseworthy
C. Praiseworthy D. Praisaworthy

48. A. Profesional B. Professionel
C. Professional D. Profissional

49. A. Ameteur B. Amateur
C. Amataur D. Amateor

50. A. Unfevourable B. Unfevaurable
C. Unfavourable D. Unfivourable

ANSWERS

1	2	3	4	5	6	7	8	9	10
A	C	A	B	B	A	B	B	D	C
11	**12**	**13**	**14**	**15**	**16**	**17**	**18**	**19**	**20**
A	B	A	A	C	A	A	A	C	A
21	**22**	**23**	**24**	**25**	**26**	**27**	**28**	**29**	**30**
B	B	B	D	B	C	A	C	B	C
31	**32**	**33**	**34**	**35**	**36**	**37**	**38**	**39**	**40**
A	B	A	C	C	A	C	B	D	A
41	**42**	**43**	**44**	**45**	**46**	**47**	**48**	**49**	**50**
A	C	A	C	A	C	C	C	B	C

FAMOUS AUTHORS IN DIFFERENT LANGUAGES

English	William Shakespeare, John Milton, Chaucer, Spenser, Lord Byron, P.B. Shelley, John Keats, Francis Bacon, T.S. Eliot, Cecil Dlay Lewis, Alduous Huxley, W.B. Yeats Bunyan, Dryden, Dr. Johnson, Alexander Pope, Robert Browning, Charles Lamb, Charles Dickens, Thomas Hardy, W.M. Thackeray, George Eliot, Alfred Tennyson, Robert Bridges, George Bernard Shaw, D.H. Lawrence, Oliver Goldsmith, Sheridan, Walter Scott, William Wordsworth, S.T. Coleridge, Henry Fielding, Somerset Maugham, J.K. Rowling.
French	Imile Zola, Gustave Flaubert, Moliere, Proudhon, Jean Paul Sartre, Le Sage, Victor Hugo, Alexander Dumas, Balzac.
German	Goethe, Hoffman, Lessing, Schelling, Schaupenhuer, Heinrich Heine, Guenter Grass
Russian	Tolstoy, Mikhail Solokhov, Turgenev, Dostoevsky, Maxim Gorky, Techov, Alexander Salzhenitsyn, Boris Pasternak
Greek	Homer, Aesop, Aristophanes, Euripedes, Herodotus, Hesoid, Theocritus, Xenophon, Aeschylus, Sophocles
Latin	Dante, Boccacio, Terence, Virgil, Ovid, Horace, Seneca
Norwegian	John Bojer, Ibsen
Persian	Ghalib, Umar Khyyam, Abul Fazal, Amir Khusro, Faiz, Firdausi, Mohd. Iqbal Saddi
Spanish	Juan Valera, Lope De Vega, Cervantes

FAMOUS CHARACTERS AND THEIR CREATORS

Character	Creator
Adam	Milton
Alice	Lewis Carroll
Ancient Mariner	Coleridge
Ariel	William Shakespeare
Antonio	William Shakespeare
Anna Karenina	Leo Tolstoy
Bassomio	William Shakespeare
Bertie Wooster	P.G. Wodehouse
Brutus	William Shakespeare
Beatrix	Thackery
Beatrice	William Shakespeare
Christian	John Bunyan
Cordelia	William Shakespeare
Cleopatra	William Shakespeare
Clare	Thomas Hardy
Claudius	William Shakespeare
David Copperfield	Charles Dickens
Dushyanta	Kalidas
Don Quixote	Cervantes
Eliza Doolittle	George Bernard Shaw
Estella	Charles Dickens
Faust	J.W. Von Goethe
Gora	Rabindranath Tagore
Hamlet	William Shakespeare
Harry Potter	J.K. Rowling
Hyde	R.L. Stevenson
Hercule Poirot	Agatha Christie
Hawkins	R.L. Stevenson
Hector	Homer
Ivanhoe	Sir Walter Scott
Iago	William Shakespeare

Character	Creator
James Bond	Ian Fleming
Juliet	William Shakespeare
Jessica	William Shakespeare
Jean Valjin	Victor Hugo
Jacques	William Shakespeare
Jeeves	P.G. Wodehouse
King Arthur	Tennyson
Kim	Rudyard Kipling
Long John Silver	R.L. Stevenson
Macbeth	William Shakespeare
Micawber	Charles Dickens
Miranda	William Shakespeare
Mephistopheles	J.W. Von Goethe
Mellors	D.H. Lawrence
Malaprop	Sheridian
Oliver Twist	Charles Dickens
Peggotty	Charles Dickens
Priyangbada	Kalidas
Portia	William Shakespeare
Pip	Charles Dickens
Perry Mason	Erle Stanley Gardner
Pickwick	Charles Dickens
Rip Van Winkle	Washington Irving
Sam Weller	Charles Dickens
Surpanakha	Valmiki
Shylock	William Shakespeare
Sherlock Halmes	Arthur Conan Doyle
Shakuntala	Kalidas
Sancho Panza	Cervantes Saavedra
Tess	Thomas Hardy
Watson	Arthur Conan Doyle
Zhivago	Boris Pasternak

GREAT POETS

Language	Poet
Hindi	Surdas, Tulsidas, Keshav
Sanskrit	Valmiki, Vedvyas, Kalidas
Bengali	Rabindra Nath Tagore
Urdu	Mirza Ghalib
Persian	Sheikh Saadi
Latin	Virgil

Language	Poet
Greek	Homer
English	Shakespeare
German	Goethe
Italian	Dante
French	Sully Proudhone
Punjabi	Waris Shah

GREAT INDIAN AUTHORS AND POETS IN ENGLISH

Kamala Das; Manohar Malgonkar; R.K. Narayan; Raja Rao; Mulk Raj Anand; Bhabani Bhatacharya; Sasthi Brata; Arun Joshi; Chaman Nahal; K.A. Abbas; Anita Desai; R. Prawer Jhabwala; Kamla Markandaya; Khushwant Singh; Manoj Dass.

WELL KNOWN QUOTATIONS

1. A thing of beauty is a joy for ever; Its loveliness increases; It will never pass into nothingness. — *Keats: Endymion*

2. A little knowledge is a dangerous thing — *Pope*

3. Beauty is truth, truth beauty that is all. Ye know on earth, all all ye need to know — *Keats: Ode on a Grecian urn*

4. All the world is a stage and all the man and women merely players — *Shakespeare: As you like it*

5. Some books are to be tested, others to be swallowed and some few to be chewed and digested — *Bacon*

6. Better to reign in hell than serve in heaven — *Milton: Paradise lost*

7. The child is father of the man — *Wordsworth: My heart leaps up*

8. A single step for man — a giant leap for mankind — *Neil Armstrong*

9. Dilli Chalo — *Netaji Subhash Chandra Bose*

10. To be or not to be — that is the question. — *Shakespeare: Hamlet*

11. Only free men negotiate. I shall never negotiate while I am still a prisoner — *Nelson Mandela*

12. Truth and non-violence are my God — *Mahatma Gandhi*

13. Let a hundred flowers bloom and let a thousand schools of thought contend — *Mao Tse-tung*

14. Jai Jawan, Jai Kisan — *Lal Bahadur Shastri*

15. Eureka! Eureka! — *Archimedes*

16. Some are born great, some achieve greatness and some have greatness thrust upon them — *Shakespeare*

17. Where wealth accumulates, men decay — *Goldsmith*

18. Power tends to corrupt and absolute power corrupts absolutely — *Lord Acton*

19. Man is by nature a political animal — *Aristotle*

20. I have nothing to offer but blood, toil, tears and sweat — *Winston Churchill*

21. I came, I saw, I conquered — *Julius Ceaser*

22. For fools rush in where angels fear to tread — *Pope*

23. Generations to come, it may, will scarce believe that such a one as this ever in flesh and blood walked upon this earth — *Einstein*

24. Government of the people, by the people, for the people — *Lincoln*

25. East is east and west is west and never the twain shall meet — *Kipling*

26. Swaraj is my birth right — *Bal Gangadhar Tilak*

27. Cowards die many times before their death: The valiant never taste of death but once — *Shakespeare: Julius Ceaser*

28. Where ignorance is bliss, It is folly to be wise — *Grey*

29. I know nothing except the fact of my ignorance — *Socrates*

30. We are such stuff as dreams are made of and our little life is rounded with a sleep — *Shakespeare: The Tempest*

31. What's in a name? That which we call a rose By any other name would smell as sweet — *Shakespeare: Merchant of Venice*

32. Patriotism is the best refuge of a scoundrel — *Samuel Johnson*

33. Reading maketh a full man; conference a ready man; and writing an exact man — *Francis Bacon*

34. It is excellent to love a giant's strength
but it is tyrannous to use it like a giant
— *Shakespeare: Measure to Measure*

35. Water, water everywhere
Not any drop to drink
— *S.T. Coleridge: The Ancient Mainer*

36. It is strange but true, for truth is always strange — *Byron: Don Juan*

37. Virtue is its own reward — *Cicero: De Fintibus*

38. Frailty, thy name is woman — *Shakespeare: Hamlet*

39. We don't fear to negotiate, but we do not negotiate out of fear — *J.F. Kennedy*

40. Give us good mothers and I shall give you good nation — *Napoleon*

41. The woods are lovely, dark and deep
But I have promises to keep
And miles to go before I sleep — *Robert Frost*

हिंदी

व्याकरण

व्याकरण वह शास्त्र है जिसके द्वारा किसी भी भाषा के शब्दों और वाक्यों के शुद्ध स्वरूपों एवं शुद्ध प्रयोगों का ज्ञान कराया जाता है।

व्याकरण के चार अंग हैं : (i) वर्ण विचार (ii) शब्द विचार (iii) पद विचार और (iv) वाक्य विचार

भाषा : भाषा अभिव्यक्ति का एक ऐसा साधन है जिसके द्वारा मनुष्य अपने विचारों को दूसरों पर प्रकट कर सकता है और दूसरों के विचार जान सकता है। भाषा के दो रूप हैं–(i) मौखिक और (ii) लिखित।

बोली : भाषा का क्षेत्रीय रूप बोली कहलाता है।

लिपि : किसी भी भाषा के लिखने की विधि को लिपि कहते हैं।

वर्ण : हिन्दी भाषा में प्रयुक्त सबसे छोटी ध्वनि वर्ण कहलाती है। जैसे–अ, आ, ई, क्, ख्, आदि

वर्णमाला : वर्णों के समुदाय को वर्णमाला कहते हैं। हिन्दी वर्णमाला में 44 वर्ण हैं। जिनमें 11 स्वर तथा 33 व्यंजन हैं।

स्वरवर्ण : उन वर्णों को कहते हैं, जिनका उच्चारण बिना किसी दूसरे वर्ण की सहायता से होता है। हिन्दी में 11 स्वर हैं–अ, आ, इ, ई, उ, ऊ, ए, ऐ, ओ, औ, ऋ।

व्यंजन वर्ण : उन वर्णों को कहते हैं, जिनका उच्चारण स्वर वर्णों की सहायता के बिना नहीं हो सकता है। इनकी संख्या 33 है–

क ख ग घ ड़ च छ ज झ ञ ट् ठ

ड ढ़ ण त थ द ध न प फ ब भ

म य र ल व श ष स ह।

वर्ण : एक या अधिक वर्णों से बनी हुई स्वतन्त्र सार्थक ध्वनि शब्द कहलाती है।

शब्दों को तत्सम, तद्भव, देशज और विदेशी भागों में बाँटा जाता है।

तत्सम : जो शब्द संस्कृत भाषा से हिन्दी में बिना किसी परिवर्तन के लिए जाते हैं वे तत्सम कहलाते हैं, जैसे– अग्नि, क्षेत्र, मित्र, नासिका आदि।

तद्भव : उन शब्दों को कहते हैं, जो संस्कृत से ही लिए गए हैं, परन्तु हिन्दी में आने पर जिनका रूप बदल गया है। जैसे–आग, खेत, रात आदि।

देशज : उन शब्दों को कहते हैं, जो बोलचाल तथा देश की अन्य भाषाओं से लिए गए हैं। जैसे–कटोरा, झंझत, डिबिया, लोटा आदि।

विदेशज या विदेशी : उन शब्दों को कहते हैं, जो किसी विदेशी भाषा से आए हैं। जैसे–स्कूल, कार, कमरा, खुदा, जोश, सरकार आदि।

शब्द सम्पदा

तत्सम शब्दों के तद्भव रूप

तत्सम	तद्भव	तत्सम	तद्भव
अग्नि	आग	अद्य	आज
अष्ट	आठ	अक्षि	आँख
अर्ध	आधा	अस्थि	हड्डी
अश्रु	आँसू	आम्र	आम
ग्राम	गाँव	गर्दभ	गधा
गृध्र	गीध	गौर	गोरा
गृह	घर	घट	घड़ा
धातु	धात	धृत	घी
लक्ष	लांख	सप्त	सात
त्वम्	तुम	दुग्ध	दूध
रत्न	रतन	वर्ष	बरस
भक्त	भगत	मर्कट	बन्दर
रात्रि	रात	उलूक	उल्लू
अन्धकार	अन्धेरा	क्षीर	खीर
निद्रा	नींद	पृष्ठ	पीठ
ज्येष्ठ	जेठ	स्वर्ण	सोना
श्वास	साँस	काक	काग
कार्य	काज	कर्ण	कान

तत्सम	तद्भव	तत्सम	तद्भव
पाद	पाँव	हस्त	हाथ
नासिका	नाक	कंटक	काँटा
दश	दस	दधि	दही
दीप	दीया	निद्रा	नींद
नव	नौ	पत्र	पत्ता
प्रस्तर	पत्थर	जिह्वा	जीभ
हस्ती	हाथी	दन्त	दाँत
क्षेत्र	खेत	नृत्य	नाच
सूचिका	सूई	स्वर्णकार	सुनार
लोक	लोग	पर्यड़्क	पलंग
स्वप्न	सपना	कातर	कायर
पुत्र	पूत	मानव	मनुष्य
शत	सौ	पुष्प	फूल
पक्व	पक्का	कृषक	किसान
कर्म	कार्य	आम्र	आम
कर्ण	कान	अष्ट	आठ
घंटिका	घंटी	चन्द्र	चन्द
यव	जौ	धूम्र	धुआँ

विराम चिह्न

विराम का अर्थ रुकना। अपने विचारों को ठीक ढंग से प्रकट करने के पढ़ते अथवा लिखते समय हमें कुछ रुकना पड़ता है। इस प्रकार के रुकने को विराम कहते हैं।

प्रत्येक-विराम के लिए अलग-अलग चिह्न हैं–

पूर्ण विराम	[।]
अल्प विराम	[,]
अर्ध विराम	[;]
प्रश्न बोधक	[?]
विस्मयादि बोधक	[!]
योजक	[–]
उद्धरण	[" "]

कारक

कारक शब्द उस रूप को कहते हैं, जिससे संज्ञा या सर्वनाम वाक्य के साथ सम्बन्ध जाना जाता है। जैसे–शीला कलम **से** लिखती है।

यह सीमा **की** पुस्तक है।

कारक के भेद विभक्ति चिह्नों सहित

कारक	**विभक्ति**
कर्त्ता	ने
कर्म	को
करण	से
सम्प्रदान	के लिए
अपादान	से
सम्बन्ध	का, के, की
अधिकरण	में, पर
सम्बोधन	हे, अरे!

पर्यायवाची शब्द

जिन शब्दों से एक समान अर्थ का बोध होता है, उन्हें पर्यायवाची या समानार्थी शब्द कहते हैं।

कुछ पर्यायवाची शब्दों के उदाहरण निम्नलिखित हैं–

आग – अग्नि, अनल, पावक, हुताशन, ज्वाला।
आकाश – नभ, आसमान, गगन, लोभ।
असुर – राक्षस, दानव, निशाचर, दैत्य।
अमृत – अभिय, पीयूष, सुधा, सोम।
अन्धकार – अन्धेरा, तिमिर, तम, तमिस्त्र।
आँख – नेत्र, नयन, लोचन, चक्षु, दृग।
कमल – जलंज, पंकज, नीरज, राजीव।
इन्द्र – सुरपति, देवेन्द्र, सुरेन्द्र, देवेश।
ईश्वर – प्रभु, भगवान, जगदीश, दीनबन्धु।
पक्षी – खग, विहग, चिड़िया, नभचर।
बादल – घन, जलधर, वारिद, नीरद।
गंगा – सुरसरि, जाह्नवी, त्रिपथगा, देवनदी, विष्णुपदी।
चन्द्रमा – शशि, मयंक, निशाकर, सुधाकर, सुधांशु, सोम हिमांशु, राकेश।
जल – पानी, नीर, लोभ, अम्बु, सलिल, क्षीर, वारि।
फूल – पुष्प, कुसुम, सुमन, प्रसून, सारंग।
पृथ्वी – भू, भूमि, धरा, वसुन्धरा, वसुधा, धरती क्षमा, लोक।
कपड़ा – पट, वस्त्र, चीर, अम्बर, दुकूल।
घर – गृह, गेह, निकेतन, आलय, निलय, भवन, शाला, धाम, सदन।
जंगल – वन, कानन, अरण्य, विपिन।
तालाब – सरोवर, ताल, जलाशय, तड़ाग।
दिन – दिवस, वासर, वार।
पहाड़ – गिरि, पर्वत, गूधर, नग, महीधर, मेरू।
पत्थर – पहाड़, प्रस्तर, पाहन।
पवन – वायु, समीर, हवा, मारुत, अनिल।
पुत्र – सुत, तनय, पूत, आत्मज।
बिजली – तड़ित, चपला, दामिनी।
वृक्ष – तरू, रूख, विटप, पेड़।
मनुष्य – नर, मानव, मनुज, आदमी।
हाथी – करि, हस्ती, गज।
मित्र – सखा, मीत, सहचर, दोस्त।
राजा – नरेश, नृप, महीप, भूप।
समुद्र – सागर, सिन्धु, जलधि, नीरधि।
सरस्वती – शारदा, वागेश्वरी, भारती, महाश्वेता।
साँप – पन्नग, सर्प, विषधर, अहि, व्याल।
सूर्य – दिनकर, दिवाकर, रवि, भानु, भास्कर।
स्त्री – नारी, महिला, दारा, वामा।
शरीर – देह, तन, काया, गात, बदन।
गणेश – गजानन, गणपति, विनायक, एकदन्त, गजवदन लम्बोदर, विघ्न नाशक।
घोड़ा – तुरंग, बाजि, हय, अश्व, घोटक।
युद्ध – समर, रण, संग्राम।
सिंह – केसरी, मृगराज, केहरी।
शत्रु – अरि, रिपु, बैरी।
विष्णु – हरि, कमलेश, रमापति, चक्रपाणि, केशव, माधव, पीताम्बर।
कोष – खजाना, भण्डार, निधि।
धन – दौलत, द्रव्य, मुद्रा।

तलवार – कृपाण, असि, खड्ग।
अंग – भाग, हिस्सा, अवयव।
चोर – तस्कर, दस्यु, रजनीचर।
पत्नी – भार्या, दारा, गृहिणी।
पुत्र – तनय, सुत, लड़का, बेटा।
पुत्री – तनया, सुता, लड़की, बेटी।
माता – जननी, अम्बा, अम्बिका, अम्मा, माँ, धात्री।
मोर – शिखी, नीलकण्ठ, मयूर।
मृत्यु – मौत, काल, देहान्त।
रक्त – रुधिर, शोणित, खून, लहू।
विष – जहर, हलाहल, गरल।
सोना – कंचन, स्वर्ण, कनक।
हृदय – उर, छाती, वक्ष, वक्षस्थल, हिय, हिया।
सभा – अधिवेशन, परिषद्, बैठक, महासभा, समागम, समिति, सम्मेलन।
यमुना – कालिन्दी, कृष्णा, जमुना, रविसुता तरणि-तनुजा।

विलोम-शब्द

शब्दों के अपने निश्चित अर्थ होते हैं। उन अर्थों के विपरीत अर्थ देने वाले शब्द को विलोम-शब्द कहते हैं।

शब्द	विलोम	शब्द	विलोम
अमृत	विष	उदार	संकीर्ण
अनुकूल	प्रतिकूल	अनुराग	विराग
आदि	अन्त	उत्थान	पतन
इच्छा	अनिच्छा	उचित	अनुचित
अल्पायु	दीर्घायु	अनुज	अग्रज
उन्नति	अवनति	आकाश	पाताल
अधिक	न्यून	आयात	निर्यात
एक	अनेक	अन्धकार	प्रकाश
अर्थ	अनर्थ	उदय	अस्त
परकीया	स्वकीया	जड़	चेतन
जय	पराजय	अनिवार्य	वैकल्पिक
नकद	उधार	अपेक्षा	उपेक्षा
उपस्थित	अनुपस्थित	आदर	अनादर
अन्धेरा	उजाला	अपना	पराया
उत्तम	अधम	आय	व्यय
सुपुत्र	कुपुत्र	स्वाधीन	पराधीन
आहार	निराहार	कठोर	कोमल
दाता	याचक	दोषी	निर्दोषि
खेद	प्रसन्नता	धनी	निर्धन
निकट	दूर	चर	अचर
देव	दानव	खरा	खोटा
गरीब	अमीर	प्रेम	घृणा
जीवन	मृत्यु	बुरा	भला
सजीव	निर्जीव	मित्र	शत्रु
सुगन्ध	दुर्गन्ध	मौखिक	लिखित
संक्षेप	विस्तार	कटु	मधुर
आरम्भ	अन्त	कड़वा	मीठा
कृतज्ञ	कृतघ्न	दिन	रात
साक्षर	निरक्षर	पवित्र	अपवित्र
पाप	पुण्य	जल	थल
धीर	अधीर	निर्मल	मलिन

शब्द	विलोम	शब्द	विलोम
गुण	अवगुण	नश्वर	अनश्वर
निन्दा	स्तुति	भारी	हल्का
मनुष्यता	पशुता	सरस	नीरस
मान	अपमान	क्रय	विक्रय
धर्म	अधर्म	गहरा	उथला
गुरु	शिष्य	पक्ष	विपक्ष
जन्म	मृत्यु	बन्धन	मुक्ति
यश	अपयश	ज्ञान	अज्ञान
आदर	अनादर	पूर्ण	अपूर्ण
सफल	असफल	शान्त	अशान्त
कीर्ति	अपकीर्ति	वादी	प्रतिवादी
आस्तिक	नास्तिक	स्वदेश	परदेश
सज्जन	दुर्जन	राग	द्वेष
ऊसर	उर्वर	उदार	कृपण
अगला	पिछला	अगम	सुगम
अग्नि	जल	अति	अल्प
अर्थ	अनर्थ	अतल	वितल
अत्यधिक	स्वल्प	अधः	उपरि
अधिकतम	न्यूनतम	अतिवृष्टि	अनावृष्टि
अनाथ	सनाथ	ईश्वर	जीव
अनुलोम	विलोम	अर्पण	ग्रहण
अवनि	अम्बर	अस्त	उदय
आकर्षण	विकर्षण	आगे	पीछे
आजाद	गुलाम	आदान	प्रदान
आधुनिक	प्राचीन	आना	जाना
आय	व्यय	आयात	निर्यात
आवश्यक	अनावश्यक	आशा	निराशा
आस्था	अनास्था	इहलोक	परलोक
उच्च	निम्न	उत्थान	पतन
उपकार	अपकार	उपयोग	दुरुपयोग
एकता	अनेकता	कल	आज
कृत्रिम	प्राकृत	कृष्ण	शुक्ल
कपूत	सपूत	कोमल	कठोर
गगन	धरा	ज्ञान	अज्ञान

लिंग

लिंग का अर्थ है 'चिह्न'। लिंग शब्द उस चिह्न को कहते हैं जिससे वस्तु के पुरुष या स्त्री होने की कल्पना हो। लिंग दो प्रकार के होते हैं— (1) पुल्लिंग (2) स्त्रीलिंग

पुल्लिंग–पुल्लिंग संज्ञा के उस रूप को कहते हैं जिससे उसके पुरुष होने का ज्ञान होता है। जैसे–राम, श्याम, घोड़ा, हाथी, कुत्ता आदि। **स्त्रीलिंग**–स्त्रीलिंग संज्ञा के उस रूप को कहते हैं जिससे उसके स्त्री होने का ज्ञान हो। जैसे–भैंस, गाय, बकरी, सीता, रमा इत्यादि।

पुल्लिंग	स्त्रीलिंग	पुल्लिंग	स्त्रीलिंग
इन्द्र	इन्द्राणी	मेहतर	मेहतरानी
नौकर	नौकरानी	जेठ	जेठानी
देवर	देवरानी	सेठ	सेठानी
पण्डित	पण्डिताइन	ओझा	ओझाइन
बनिया	बनियाइन	दुबे	दुबाइन
हलवाई	हलवाइन	चौबे	चौबाइन
गुरु	गुरुआइन	लड़का	लड़की
दास	दासी	कबूतर	कबूतरी
हिरण	हिरणी	क्षत्रिय	क्षत्राणी
मुगल	मुगलानी	हिन्दू	हिन्दुआनी
चौधरी	चौधरानी	भव	भवानी
लाला	ललाइन	पण्डा	पण्डाइन
ठाकुर	ठकुराइन	बाबू	बबुआइन
घोड़ा	घोड़ी	गूँगा	गूँगी
बच्चा	बच्ची	चाचा	चाची
बकरा	बकरी	मामा	मामी
मुर्गा	मुर्गी	साला	साली
चींटा	चींटी	रस्सा	रस्सी
देव	देवी	ब्राह्मण	ब्राह्मणी
बेटा	बेटी	बूढ़ा	बुढ़िया
चूहा	चुहिया	डिब्बा	डिबिया
गुड्डा	गुड़िया	कुम्हार	कुम्हारिन
सुनार	सुनारिन	नाती	नातिन
जुलाहा	जुलाहिन	दर्जी	दर्जिन
पापी	पापिन	हाथी	हथिनी

पुल्लिंग	स्त्रीलिंग	पुल्लिंग	स्त्रीलिंग
पिता	माता	बैल	गाय
कवि	कवयित्री	विधुर	विधवा
बाप	माँ	बादशाह	बेगम
नर	मादा	मर्द	औरत
युवक	युवती	वर	वधू
सम्राट्	सम्राज्ञी	साढ़ू	साली
फूफा	बुआ	पुत्र	पुत्री
पहाड़	पहाड़ी	गोप	गोपी
गधा	गधी	तरुण	तरुणी
नर्तक	नर्तकी	बेटा	बिटिया
बछड़ा	बछिया	चिड़ा	चिड़िया
बन्दर	बन्दरिया	कुत्ता	कुतिया
नाई	नाइन	धोबी	धोबिन
ग्वाला	ग्वालिन	भंगी	भंगिन
स्वामी	स्वामिनी	विद्वान्	विदुषी
साधु	साध्वी	पुरुष	स्त्री
पति	पत्नी	वीर	वीरांगना
साहब	मेम	सास	ससुर
मियाँ	बीबी	राजा	रानी
बिलाड़	बिल्ली	अनुज	अनुजा
छात्र	छात्रा	महोदय	महोदया
प्रिय	प्रिया	मामा	मामी
लोटा	लुटिया	मोर	मोरनी
शेर	शेरनी	जाट	जाटिन
डाक्टर	डाक्टरनी	मालिक	मालकिन
माली	मालिन	बाघ	बाघिन
हाथी	हथिनी	स्वामी	स्वामिनी
बालक	बालिका	धनवान	धनवती
धावक	धाविका	नेता	नेत्री
गुणवान	गुणवती	नर	मादा
अभिनेता	अभिनेत्री	प्राचार्य	प्राचार्या
प्रबन्धकर्ता	प्रबन्धकर्ती	दाता	दात्री
ननदोई	ननद	अध्यापक	अध्यापिका

वचन

शब्द के जिस रूप से उसके एक अथवा अनेक होने का बोध हो, उसे वचन कहते हैं।

हिन्दी में दो वचन होते हैं–

(1) एकवचन और (2) बहुवचन

एकवचन–शब्द के जिस रूप से एक ही वस्तु का बोध हो, उसे एकवचन कहते हैं। जैसे–लड़का, गाय, बकरी, घोड़ा, राम, सीता आदि।

बहुवचन–शब्द के जिस रूप से अनेकता का बोध हो उसे बहुवचन कहते हैं। जैसे–लड़के, कपड़े, गायें आदि।

एकवचन	बहुवचन	एकवचन	बहुवचन
लड़का	लड़के	कौवा	कौवे
बेटा	बेटे	कमरा	कमरे
कपड़ा	कपड़े	बहन	बहनें
चीज	चीजें	गधा	गधे
रुपया	रुपये	घोड़ा	घोड़े
नहर	नहरें	रात	रातें
बात	बातें	सड़क	सड़कें
दाना	दाने	लोटा	लोटे
पैसा	पैसे	पुस्तक	पुस्तकें
कन्या	कन्याएँ	वधू	वधुएँ
नारी	नारियाँ	लड़की	लड़कियाँ
मुर्गा	मुर्गे	घण्टा	घण्टे
गद्दा	गद्दे	हीरा	हीरे
बच्चा	बच्चे	प्याला	प्याले
छाता	छाते	गाय	गायें
कथा	कथाएँ	कविता	कविताएँ
बहू	बहुएँ	टोपी	टोपियाँ
नाली	नालियाँ	बेटा	बेटे
ताला	ताले	जूता	जूते

एकवचन	बहुवचन	एकवचन	बहुवचन
डिबिया	डिबियाँ	नाक	नाकें
पूँछ	पूँछें	मूँछ	मूँछें
चिड़िया	चिड़ियाँ	सरिता	सरिताएँ
बालिका	बालिकाएँ	चाभी	चाभियाँ
कहानी	कहानियाँ	दरवाजा	दरवाजे
कलम	कलमें	कुटिया	कुटियाँ
रानी	रानियाँ	नाई	नाइयों
माता	माताएँ	बाल	बालों
हाथ	हाथों	मुख	मुख
कोट	कोट	दाँत	दाँतों
नाखून	नाखूनों	पैर	पैरों
बैल	बैलों	माली	मालियों
राजा	राजाओं	पिता	पिता
चन्द्रमा	चन्द्रमा	कवि	कवियों
मुनि	मुनियों	कौआ	कौए
छात्रा	छात्राएँ	सेना	सेनाएँ
दिशा	दिशाएँ	गुड़िया	गुड़ियाँ
मेज	मेजें	भैंस	भैंसें
अंगूर	अंगूरों	समुद्र	समुद्र

अनेक शब्दों के लिए एक शब्द

जिसकी कोई उपमा न हो : **अनुपम**
तेज बुद्धि वाला : **कुशाग्रबुद्धि**
कल्पना से परे हो : **कल्पनातीत**
जो उपकार नहीं मानता है : **कृतघ्न**
जो उपकार मानता है : **कृतज्ञ**
किसी की हँसी उड़ाना : **उपहास**
ऊपर कहा हुआ : **उपर्युक्त**
ऊपर लिखा हुआ : **उपरलिखित**
जिस पर उपकार किया गया हो : **उपकृत**
इतिहास का ज्ञाता : **इतिहासज्ञ**
आलोचना करने वाला : **आलोचक**
ईश्वर में आस्था रखने वाला : **आस्तिक**
बिना वेतन का : **अवैतनिक**
जो कहा न जा सके : **अकथनीय**
जो गिना न जा सके : **अगणित**
जिसका कोई शत्रु ही न जन्मा हो : **अजातशत्रु**
जिसके समान कोई दूसरा न हो : **अद्वितीय**
जो परिचित न हो : **अपरिचित**
आकाश में उड़ने वाला : **नभचर**
जो टुकड़े-टुकड़े हो गया हो : **खण्डित**

मछली की तरह आँखों वाली : **मीनाक्षी**
मयूर की तरह आँखों वाली : **मयूराक्षी**
बच्चों के लिए काम की वस्तु : **बालोपयोगी**
जिसकी बहुत अधिक चर्चा हो : **बहुचर्चित**
जिस स्त्री को कभी सन्तान न हुई हो : **बन्ध्या (बाँझ)**
फेन से भरा हुआ : **फेनिल**
प्रिय बोलने वाली स्त्री : **प्रियम्वदा**
जिसकी उपमा न हो : **निरुपम**
जो थोड़ी देर पहले पैदा हुआ हो : **नवजात**
जिसका कोई आधार न हो : **निराधार**
नगर में वास करने वाला : **नागरिक**
रात में घूमने वाला : **निशाचर**
ईश्वर में विश्वास न रखने वाला : **नास्तिक**
माँस न खाने वाला : **निरामिष**
बिल्कुल बर्बाद हो गया : **ध्वस्त**
जिसकी धर्म में निष्ठा हो : **धर्मनिष्ठ**
देखने योग्य : **दर्शनीय**
बहुत तेज चलने वाला : **द्रुतगामी**
जो किसी पक्ष में न रहे : **तटस्थ**
तत्त्व को जानने वाला : **तत्त्वज्ञ**

तप करने वाला : **तपस्वी**
जिसे देखकर डर लगे : **डरावना**
जो जन्म से अन्ध हो : **जन्मान्ध**
जीने की प्रबल इच्छा : **जिजीविषा**
जिसने इन्द्रियों को जीत लिया हो : **जितेन्द्रिय**
चिन्ता में डूबा हुआ : **चिन्तित**
जो बहुत समय तक ठहरे : **चिरस्थायी**
जिसकी चार भुजाएँ हों : **चतुर्भुज**
जिसके हाथ में चक्र हों : **चक्रपाणि**
जिससे घृणा की जाए : **घृणित**
जिसे गुप्त रखा जाए : **गोपनीय**
गणित ज्ञाता : **गणितज्ञ**
आकाश को चूमने वाला : **गगनचुम्बी**
जिसका आदि न हो : **अनादि**
जो कुछ न जानता हो : **अज्ञ**
जो अनुकरण करने योग्य हो : **अनुकरणीय**
जिसका अन्त न हो : **अनन्त**
जो कभी न मरे : **अमर**
जो कम बोलता हो : **अल्पभाषी**
जिसका इलाज न हो : **लाइलाज**
जिसका कोई नाथ न हो : **अनाथ**
कम जानने वाला : **अल्पज्ञ**
जहाँ जाना सम्भव न हो : **अगम**
बड़ा भाई : **अग्रज**
कम खाने वाला : **अल्पाहारी**
जो बात पहले कभी न हुई हो : **अभूतपूर्व**
दूसरों के पीछे चलने वाला : **अनुचर**
जो पहले न पढ़ा हो : **अपठित**
जिसके आर-पार दिखाई देता हो : **पारदर्शी**
आज्ञा पालन करने वाला : **आज्ञाकारी**
काम से जी चुराने वाला : **कामचोर**
प्रतिदिन होने वाला : **दैनिक**
जिसका कोई अर्थ न हो : **निरर्थक**
हाथ से लिखा हुआ : **हस्तलिखित**
आँखों के सामने होने वाला : **प्रत्यक्ष**
जिसका आचरण अच्छा हो : **सदाचारी**
वह पुरुष जिसकी पत्नी मर गई हो : **विधुर**
वह स्त्री जिसका पति मर गया हो : **विधवा**
जिसका रूप अच्छा न हो : **कुरूप**
सदा सत्य बोलने वाला : **सत्यवादी**
बड़ी इमारत के टूटे-फूटे भाग : **खण्डहर**
प्रशंसा के योग्य : **प्रशंसनीय**

जहाँ अनाथ रहते हों : **अनाथालय**
प्रत्येक मास होने वाला : **मासिक**
जहाँ पानी के जहाज आकर रुकते हैं : **बन्दरगाह**
प्रत्येक सप्ताह होने वाला : **साप्ताहिक**
प्रत्येक वर्ष होने वाला : **वार्षिक**
जो कठिनाई से मिले : **दुर्लभ**
जिसका आकार हो : **साकार**
जिसका आकार न हो : **निराकार**
जो कभी बूढ़ा न हो : **अजर**
बहुत बोलने वाला : **वाचाल**
पृथ्वी पर रहने वाला : **थलचर**
जल में रहने वाला : **जलचर**
नभ में विचरण करने वाला : **नभचर**
जल-थल दोनों में रहने वाला : **उभयचर**
जिसमें रस न हो : **नीरस**
पढ़ने वाला : **पाठक**
जो भाषण देता हो : **वक्ता**
जो साथ में पढ़ता हो : **सहपाठी**
जिसके नीचे रेखा खींची हो : **रेखांकित**
जानने की इच्छा रखने वाला : **जिज्ञासु**
जिसकी कोई सन्तान न हो : **निःसन्तान**
जिसका कोई मूल्य न हो : **अमूल्य**
जो वन में घूमता हो : **वनचर**
जो इस लोक के बाहर की बात हो : **अलौकिक**
जो इस लोक की बात हो : **लौकिक**
जिसका सम्बन्ध पश्चिम से हो : **पाश्चात्य**
जो स्थिर रहे : **स्थावर**
दुःखान्त नाटक : **त्रासदी**
ज्ञान देने वाली : **ज्ञानदा**
भूत, वर्तमान भविष्य को देखने वाला : **त्रिकालदर्शी**
जो क्षमा के योग्य हो : **क्षम्य**
हिंसा करने वाला : **हिंसक**
हित चाहने वाला : **हितैषी**
सब कुछ जानने वाला : **सर्वज्ञ**
जो स्वयं पैदा हुआ हो : **स्वयंभू**
जो शरण में आया हो : **शरणागत**
जिसका वर्णन न किया जा सके : **वर्णनातीत**
व्याकरण जानने वाला : **वैयाकरण**
रचना करने वाला : **रचयिता**
खून से रंगा हुआ : **रक्तरंजित**
अत्यन्त सुन्दर स्त्री : **रूपसी**
कीर्तिमान पुरुष : **यशस्वी**

महत्त्वपूर्ण शब्दों की भाववाचक संज्ञा

शब्द	भाववाचक संज्ञा	शब्द	भाववाचक संज्ञा
दास	दासता	क्षत्रिय	क्षत्रियत्व
पशु	पशुता	बालक	बालकपन
बन्धु	बन्धुत्व	मित्र	मित्रता
बूढ़ा	बुढ़ापा	सती	सतीत्व
सेवक	सेवा	शिशु	शैशव
अपना	अपनत्व	पराया	परायापन
पण्डित	पाण्डित्य	पुरुष	पुरुषत्व
ब्राह्मण	ब्राह्मणत्व	बच्चा	बचपन
प्रभु	प्रभुता	नारी	नारीत्व
देव	देवत्व	लड़का	लड़कपन
मनुष्य	मनुष्यता	दानव	दानवता
निज	निजता	स्व	स्वत्व

शब्द	भाववाचक संज्ञा	शब्द	भाववाचक संज्ञा
अहं	अहंकार	अपना	अपनापन
व्यक्ति	व्यक्तित्व	मीठा	मिठास
गरीब	गरीबी	सफल	सफलता
बुरा	बुराई	स्वस्थ	स्वास्थ्य
सरल	सरलता	कंजुस	कंजुसी
कमजोर	कमजोरी	हरा	हरियाली
गर्म	गर्मी	मोटा	मोटाई
चालाक	चालाकी	गम्भीर	गम्भीरता
पढ़ना	पढ़ाई	लिखना	लिखाई
थकना	थकावट	लिखना	लिखावट
लूटना	लूट	लड़ना	लड़ाई
हँसना	हँसी	आप	अपनत्व

महत्त्वपूर्ण शब्दों के विशेषण

शब्द	विशेषण	शब्द	विशेषण
अंक	अंकित	अर्थ	आर्थिक
इतिहास	ऐतिहासिक	उदासी	उदास
कलंक	कलंकित	कुसुम	कुसुमित
जटा	जटिल	भार	भारी
बनारस	बनारसी	बाजार	बाजारू
प्यास	प्यासा	पुराण	पौराणिक
पंक	पंकित	पक्ष	पाक्षिक
धन	धनी	दो	दूसरा
तीन	तीसरा	झगड़ा	झगड़ालू
ठण्ड	ठण्डा	जाति	जातीय
काँटा	कँटीला	विदेश	विदेशी
रोज	रोजाना	भूगोल	भौगोलिक
पीड़ा	पीड़ित	पुत्र	पुत्रवान
आलस्य	आलसी	अंतर	आंतरिक
ईर्ष्या	ईर्ष्यालु	कर्म	कर्मठ
करुणा	कारुणिक	कृपा	कृपालु
गुण	गुणी	जल	जलमय
जीव	जैविक	तट	तटस्थ
तर्क	तार्किक	धर्म	धार्मिक
नमक	नमकीन	पत्थर	पथरीला
पल्लव	पल्लवित	पान	पनवाड़ी
मुख	मुखर	मिठास	मीठा
मास	मासिक	मद	मादक
रक्त	रक्तिम	रस	रसीला

शब्द	विशेषण	शब्द	विशेषण
वन	वन्य	विष्णु	वैष्णव
शहर	शहरी	तप	तपस्वी
जापान	जापानी	तेज	तेजस्वी
तत्त्व	तात्त्विक	दया	दयालु
देव	दैविक	निंदा	निंदक
नव	नवीन	पोषण	पोषक
पेट	पेटू	पाप	पापी
पूजा	पूज्य	भूख	भूखा
फेन	फेनिल	भारत	भारतीय
माया	मायावी	रंग	रंगीन
विष	विषैला	श्री	श्रीमान
सुर	सुरीला	विवाह	वैवाहिक
आदर	आदरणीय	ऋण	ऋणी
किताब	किताबी	क्रम	क्रमिक
ग्राम	ग्रामीण	घर	घरेलू
चतुर	चतुरता	जहर	जहरीला
सप्ताह	साप्ताहिक	अनुभव	अनुभवी
ओज	ओजस्वी	कल्पना	काल्पनिक
कुल	कुलीन	गाँव	गँवार
चमक	चमकीला	चाचा	चचेरा
दीन	दीनता	नगर	नागरिक
नागपुर	नागपुरी	परिवार	पारिवारिक
पुष्प	पुष्पित	पिता	पैतृक
फ्रांस	फ्रांसीसी	बाहर	बाहरी

शब्द	विशेषण	शब्द	विशेषण
भय	भयभीत	मधु	मधुर
मौन	मौनी	मन	मानसिक
मानव	मानवीय	रक्षा	रक्षक
रघु	राघव	रोग	रोगी
वर्ष	वार्षिक	शक्ति	शक्तिशाली
श्रम	श्रमिक	अंत	अंतिम
कागज	कागजी	मर्म	मार्मिक
शब्द	शाब्दिक	अज्ञान	अज्ञानी
गुलाब	गुलाबी	प्रकृति	प्राकृतिक
परिचय	परिचित	पूजा	पुजारी
रोग	रोगी	ग्राम	ग्रामीण
सुगंध	सुगंधित	मैं	मेरा
जो	जैसा	आप	आप-सा
तुम	तुम्हारा	कौन	कैसा
वह	वैसा	पढ़ना	पढ़ाकू

शब्द	विशेषण	शब्द	विशेषण
गाना	गायक	बेचना	बिकाऊ
भागना	भगोड़ा	वन्द	वन्दनीय
चलना	चलती	घूमना	घुमक्कड़
चलना	चालू	मरना	मरियल
भूलना	भुलक्कड़	पीछे	पिछला
भीतर	भीतरी	नीचे	निम्न
अणु	आणविक	अधिकार	आधिकारिक
अनुभव	अनुभवी	अन्याय	अन्यायी
अपमान	अपमानित	अभ्यास	अभ्यासी
अवश्य	आवश्यक	आदि	आदिम
आयु	आयुष्मान्	उदय	उदित
उपज	उपजाऊ	एकता	एक
अंत	अंतिम	कुल	कुलीन
खर्च	खर्चीला	खून	खूनी
गुण	गुणी		

श्रुतिसम भिन्नार्थक शब्द

शब्द	अर्थ	शब्द	अर्थ
आदि	आरम्भ	आदी	अभ्यस्त
कुल	वंश	कूल	किनारा
अरि	शत्रु	अरी	सम्बोधन
अगम	दुर्गम	आगम	शास्त्र
अयश	अपकीर्ति	अयस्क	लोहा
अपेक्षा	चाहना, तुलना में	उपेक्षा	निरादर
अनिल	हवा	अनल	आग
अवधि	काल, समय	अवधी	अवध की भाषा
आयात	बाहर से आना	आयत	एक आकृति
चिर	पुराना	चीर	कपड़ा
तनु	पतला	तनू	पुत्र, गाय
तरंग	लहर	तुरंग	घोड़ा
दारा	स्त्री	द्वार	दरवाजा
दूत	संदेशवाहक	द्यूत	जुआ
जलद	बादल	जलज	कमल
प्रदीप	दीपक	प्रतीप	उल्टा
प्रसाद	कृपा	प्रासाद	महल
पास	निकट	पाश	बन्धन
द्विप	हाथी	द्वीप	टापू
देव	देवता	दैव	भाग्य
नीर	जल	नीड़	घोंसला
पवन	वायु	पावन	पवित्र

शब्द	अर्थ	शब्द	अर्थ
बन्द	खुला नहीं	बद	बुरा
पथ	रास्ता	पथ्य	रोगी का भोजन
पुर	नगर	पूर	बाढ़
भवन	महल	भुवन	संसार
लक्ष्य	उद्देश्य	लक्ष	लाख
सर	तालाब	शर	बाण
सर्ग	अध्याय	स्वर्ग	एक लोक
कर्म	कार्य	क्रम	सिलसिला
चिता	शव जलाने के लिए लकड़ियों का ढेर	चीता	बाघ
शव	लाश	शब	रात
शस्त्र	हथियार	शास्त्र	ग्रन्थ
श्रवण	सुनना	श्रमण	बौद्ध संन्यासी
मत	विचार	मत्त	मस्त
शोक	दुःख	शौक	चाव
ग्रह	नक्षत्र	गृह	घर
कपट	धोखा	कपाट	दरवाजा
उपयुक्त	ठीक	उपर्युक्त	ऊपर कहा गया
सुत	बेटा	सूत	धागा
शूर	वीर	सूर	अंधा
श्याम	कृष्ण	शाम	संध्या
दिन	वार	दीन	गरीब
कटिबद्ध	तैयार रहना	करबद्ध	हाथ जोड़ना

अनेकार्थक शब्द

शब्द	विभिन्न अर्थ
अंक	संख्या, गोद
अक्षर	वर्ण, ईश्वर
पानी	जल, प्रतिष्ठा
अचल	पवर्त, स्थिर
आम	फल, सामान्य
अंबर	वस्त्र, आकाश
अवस्था	आयु, दशा
उत्तर	दिशा, जबाव
विधि	तरीका, भाग्य
कर	हाथ, टैक्स
कनक	सोना, धतुरा
गुरु	श्रेष्ठ, शिक्षक
हान	भारी हथौड़ा, बादल
जड़	मूर्ख, मूल
कल	मशीन, आनेवाला कल, चैन
सुर	देवता, स्वर

शब्द	विभिन्न अर्थ
द्विज	पक्षी, ब्राह्मण
तीर	किनारा, बाण
प्रकृति	स्वभाव, कुदरत
पत्र	चिट्ठी, पत्र
पद	पैर, उपाधि
फल	परिणाम, फल
तनु	पतला, कोमल
वर्ण	रंग, जाति
हल	समाधान, खेत जोतने का साधन
अशोक	राजा, वृक्ष
आभीर	अहीर, एक राग
एकाक्ष	काना, कौआ
खल	दुष्ट, खलिहान
घट	घड़ा, हृदय
जलज	कमल, मछली
हेम	सोना, जल

सामान्य अशुद्धियाँ

अशुद्ध	शुद्ध	अशुद्ध	शुद्ध
दुनियां	दुनिया	श्रीमति	श्रीमती
सामिग्री	सामग्री	वापिस	वापस
प्रदर्शिनी	प्रदर्शनी	द्वारिका	द्वारका
ऊत्थान	उत्थान	दुसरा	दूसरा
प्रशाद	प्रसाद	अमावश्या	अमावस्या
बसंत	वसंत	बर्ष	वर्ष
विना	बिना	बन	वन
दाइत्व	दायित्व	सम्वाद	संवाद
कुन्डली	कुण्डली	मॉसिक	मानसिक
कन्ठ	कण्ठ	अगामी	आगामी
सप्ताहिक	साप्ताहिक	संसारिक	सांसारिक
आधीन	अधीन	हस्ताक्षेप	हस्तक्षेप
बरात	बारात	क्षत्रीय	क्षत्रिय
तिथी	तिथि	कालीदास	कालिदास
पुर्ती	पूर्ति	अतिथी	अतिथि
नीती	नीति	ग्रहणी	गृहिणी
क्यूँ	क्यों	साधू	साधु
वधु	वधू	रेणू	रेणु
नुपुर	नूपुर	निर्वान	निर्वाण
जादु	जादू	द्रश्य	दृश्य

अशुद्ध	शुद्ध	अशुद्ध	शुद्ध
अनुग्रहीत	अनुगृहीत	बृज	ब्रज
बनस्पति	वनस्पति	श्राप	शाप
सैना	सेना	सेनिक	सैनिक
इतिहासिक	ऐतिहासिक	प्रथक	पृथक
सम्पति	सम्पत्ति	कृतघन	कृतघ्न
बिमारी	बीमारी	व्यक्तिक	वैयक्तिक
वितीत	व्यतीत	निस्वार्थ	निःस्वार्थ
परिस्थित	परिस्थिति	रचियता	रचयिता
मैथिलिशरण	मैथिलीशरण	आर्शिवाद	आशीर्वाद
निरिक्षण	निरीक्षण	पत्नि	पत्नी
शताब्दि	शताब्दी	लड़ायी	लड़ाई
स्थाई	स्थायी	लिखायी	लिखाई
अलोकिक	अलौकिक	कृप्या	कृपया
गंवार	गँवार	असोक	अशोक
दुस्कर	दुष्कर	मूल्यावान	मूल्यवान्
नवम्	नवम	क्षात्र	छात्र
छमा	क्षमा	प्रन्तु	परन्तु
प्रीक्षा	परीक्षा	मरयादा	मर्यादा
दुदर्शा	दुर्दशा	विषेश	विशेष
उज्वल	उज्ज्वल	आल्हाद	आहलाद्

अशुद्ध	शुद्ध	अशुद्ध	शुद्ध
महत्व	महत्त्व	उपलक्ष	उपलक्ष्य
लीये	लिये	पिओ	पियो
हुये	हुए	कवित्री	कवयित्री
प्रमात्मा	परमात्मा	घनिष्ट	घनिष्ठ
यथेष्ठ	यथेष्ट	पियास	प्यास
व्यस्क	वयस्क	त्यौहार	त्योहार
मुसलिम	मुस्लिम	ऐनक	ऐनक
नोकरी	नौकरी	कल्यान	कल्याण
पाणी	पानी	आसा	आशा
हृदय	हृदय	घ्रणा	घृणा
श्रंगार	शृंगार	हिन्दुस्थान	हिन्दुस्तान
प्रशन	प्रश्न	ग्यान	ज्ञान
अन्धेरा	अँधेरा	पेड	पेड़
महयान्ह्न	मध्यान्ह	मेंहदी	मेहंदी
शमशान	श्मशान	चिन्ह	चिह्न
कुंज	कुञ्ज	ग्रहस्थ	गृहस्थ
अजोध्या	अयोध्या	अनधिकार	अनाधिकार
अनिष्ठा	अनिष्ट	अनुकुल	अनुकूल
अनुसंगिक	आनुषंगिक	अनुशरण	अनुसरण
अभिसेक	अभिषेक	अरमाण	अरमान
अहिल्या	अहल्या	आदरनीय	आदरणीय
आविस्कार	आविष्कार	उँचाई	ऊँचाई
उत्तरदाई	उत्तरदायी	उपर	ऊपर
उपरोक्त	उपर्युक्त	उश्रृंखल	उच्छृंखल
कलस	कलश	कल्यान	कल्याण
गनित	गणित	जबाब	जवाब
तत्व	तत्त्व	तलाब	तालाब
तिरष्कार	तिरस्कार	त्रिवार्षिक	त्रैवार्षिक
दिपिका	दीपिका	देहिक	दैहिक
द्वन्द	द्वन्द्व	नरायन	नारायण
निरव	नीरव	निरोग	नीरोग
पुष्टी	पुष्टि	पुस्प	पुष्प
पेत्रिक	पैतृक	प्रनय	प्रणय

अशुद्ध	शुद्ध	अशुद्ध	शुद्ध
प्रनाम	प्रणाम	प्रयाप्त	पर्याप्त
प्रसंशा	प्रशंसा	प्रांगन	प्रांगण
प्रान	प्राण	पृष्ट	पृष्ठ
ब्रत	व्रत	भगीरथी	भागीरथी
भरथ	भरत	भष्म	भस्म
मंत्रीमंडल	मंत्रिमण्डल	रसायण	रसायन
राज्यमहल	राजमहल	रामायन	रामायण
वनोवास	वनवास	वानी	वाणी
वाल्मीकी	वाल्मीकि	वास्प	वाष्प
व्योहार	व्यवहार	सन्यासी	संन्यासी
सम्राज	साम्राज्य	सविनयपूर्वक	सविनय
सिंदुर	सिंदूर	स्त्रवण	श्रवण
हरीश्चन्द्र	हरिश्चन्द्र	हिन्दु	हिन्दू
हिन्दूस्तान	हिन्दुस्तान	बुद्धिवान	बुद्धिमान्
भाग्यमान	भाग्यवान	विद्वान	विद्वान्
श्रीमान	श्रीमान्	आंख	आँख
ऊंट	ऊँट	कंगना	कँगना
गँगा	गंगा	गांधी	गाँधी
जांच	जाँच	तांगा	ताँगा
दांत	दाँत	मंहगा	महँगा
मांस	माँस	मुंह	मुँह
सांप	साँप	सांस	साँस
हुँकार	हुंकार	निर्पेक्ष	निरपेक्ष
भाष्कर	भास्कर	सन्मुख	सम्मुख
माताहीन	मातृहीन	विद्यार्थि	विद्यार्थी
गुणि	गुणी	द्वैवाषिक	द्विवार्षिक
पूज्यनीय	पूजनीय	अकाश	आकाश
इद	ईद	इसलाम	इस्लाम
ऐसा	ऐसा	दोसरा	दूसरा
पुत्रि	पुत्री	प्रस्तूत	प्रस्तुत
हरयाली	हरियाली	दिवाली	दीवाली
राष्ट्रिय	राष्ट्रीय	एकहरा	इकहरा
एतबार	इतबार		

वाक्यगत अशुद्धियाँ

अशुद्ध	शुद्ध
हम अच्छी भाषण दिए थे।	हमने अच्छा भाषण दिया था।
आप खाए कि नहीं?	आपने खाया कि नहीं?
वह मुझे देखा तो घबरा गया।	उसने मुझे देखा तो घबरा गया।
मैं किताब पढ़ा हूँ।	मैंने किताब पढ़ी है।
मैं सारी पुस्तक पढ़ डाली।	मैंने सारी पुस्तक पढ़ डाली।
सीता भात खायी।	सीता ने भात खाया।
राम रोटी खाया।	राम ने रोटी खायी।
लड़की ने दही गिरा दी।	लड़की ने दही गिरा दिया।
शुद्ध गाय की घी दो।	गाय का शुद्ध घी दो।
तुम, मैं और वह चलेगा।	तुम, वह और मैं चलूँगा।
राम और सीता आयी थी।	राम और सीता आए थे।
भाई-बहन जा रही हैं।	भाई-बहन जा रहे हैं।

अशुद्ध	शुद्ध
वह लड़की को बुलाओ।	उस लड़की को बुलाओ।
मेरे लिए पढ़ता हूँ।	अपने लिए पढ़ता हूँ।
सीता राम की आज्ञाकारी पत्नी थी।	सीता राम की आज्ञाकारिणी पत्नी थीं।
देरी न करना।	देर न करना।
उसे मृत्युदण्ड की सजा मिली।	उसे मृत्युदण्ड मिला।
हमारे शिक्षक प्रश्न पूछते हैं।	हमारे शिक्षक प्रश्न करते हैं।
कै बजे? तीन बजा।	कितना बजा? तीन बजे।
उसका प्राण उड़ गया।	उसके प्राण उड़ गये।
मैंने आँख से देखा।	मैंने आँखों से देखा।
अपन को पढ़ना है।	मुझे पढ़ना है।
पुस्तक फट गया।	पुस्तक फट गई है।
घोड़ी तेज दौड़ता है।	घोड़ी तेज दौड़ती है।
मेरा प्रणम स्वीकार करो।	मेरा प्रणाम स्वीकार करो।
दो बालक खेलता है।	दो बालक खेलते हैं।

अशुद्ध	शुद्ध
ये सब मेरा पुस्तक है।	ये सब मेरी पुस्तकें हैं।
सूरज पूरब में उगते हैं।	सूरज पूर्व में उगता है।
वह लौट आए।	वे लौट आए।
वहाँ अनेकों लोग थे।	वहाँ अनेक लोग थे।
मेरे को मत मारो।	मुझे मत मारो।
मोहन ने पत्र को पढ़ा।	मोहन ने पत्र पढ़ा।
पुस्तक पर नहीं लिखो।	पुस्तक पर मत लिखो।
वह सज्जन पुरुष है।	वह सज्जन है।
आप हमारे घर आओ।	आप हमारे घर आइए।
हम आपसे कुछ कहे थे।	हमने आपसे कुछ कहा था।
मकान की दायीं ओर सड़क है।	मकान के दायीं ओर सड़क है।
पिताजी घर नहीं हैं।	पिताजी घर पर नहीं हैं।
घर पर सब कुशल हैं।	घर में सब कुशल हैं।
उसे भारी दुःख हुआ।	उसे बहुत दुःख हुआ।
सड़क में मत खेलो।	सड़क पर मत खेलो।

मुहावरे तथा लोकोक्तियाँ

- अँगूठी का नगीना–अत्यन्त महत्त्वपूर्ण।
- अंधा दरबार–न्यायहीन स्थान।
- अंधेर नगरी–न्याय का अभाव।
- अक्ल का दुश्मन–मूर्ख।
- अक्ल का दुम–मूर्ख।
- आँख का तारा–अतिप्रिय।
- ईद का चाँद–बहुत दिनों के बाद दिखाई देना।
- कछुआ चाल–धीमी गति।
- काला नाग–दुष्ट आदमी।
- किताबी कीड़ा–सदैव कुछ-न-कुछ पढ़ना।
- किस्मत का मारा–भाग्य का मन्द।
- कोल्हू का बैल–बहुत कठिन परिश्रम करनेवाला।
- कोड़ी का तीन–तुच्छ।
- खाली हाथ–पैसे का अभाव।
- गाजर-मूली–अशक्त।
- गुलर का फूल–दुर्लभ वस्तु।
- गोबर-गणेश–निरामूर्ख।
- घर का उजाला–कुल-दीपक।
- घड़ियाली आँसू–बनावटी शोक।
- चलता-पुरजा–चालाक।
- चाँद का टुकड़ा–परम सुन्दर वस्तु या व्यक्ति।
- चाँदी का जूता–रिश्वत।
- चार दिन की चाँदनी–थोड़े समय का सुख।
- जलती आँख–क्रोधाभिभूत।
- जीभ का पतला–लालची।
- टेढ़ी खीर–विकट काम।
- ठिकाने की बात–न्यायसंगत बात।
- अढ़ाई दिन की हुकूमत–थोड़े समय का ऐश्वर्य।
- तकदीर का सिकन्दर–भाग्य का बलवान्।
- थाली का बैंगन–मत बदलते रहना।
- दाँत कटी रोटी–घनिष्ठता।
- दाहिना हाथ–सहायक।
- दिल का बादशाह–बहुत बड़ा उदार।
- दूध का दूध और पानी का पानी–उचित न्याय।
- दूध का धोआ–निर्दोष।
- दो दिन का मेहमान–बहुत थोड़े समय ठहरने वाला।
- धरती का फूल–ऐसा व्यक्ति जो हाल में अमीर हुआ है।
- धोबी का कुत्ता–निकम्मा।
- नसीब का मारा–बुरे दिन देखनेवाला।
- निन्यानबे का फेरा–धन बढ़ाने की चिन्ता।
- पत्थर का कलेजा–हर दुःख सहने की शक्ति।
- पत्थर की लकीर–चिरस्थायी सदा सत्य।
- फूलों की सेज–आनन्ददायक कार्य।
- बगुला-भगत–कपटी व्यक्ति।

- बच्चों का खेल–साधारण काम।
- बलि का बकरा–निःसहाय व्यक्ति।
- बरसाती बादल–अस्थायी।
- बात का पक्का–सत्यवादी।
- बायें हाथ का खेल–सरल काम।
- बिन बादल बरसात–असमय लाभ।
- बे-पेंदी का लोटा–बे ठिकाने का आदमी।
- भागीरथ प्रयत्न–अत्यधिक परिश्रम।
- भीष्म प्रतिज्ञा–दृढ़ संकल्प।
- मक्खी चूस–कंजूस।
- मिट्टी के मोल–बहुत सस्ता।
- मोटा असामी–मूर्ख मालदार।
- राम कहानी–आत्मवृतान्त।
- लँगोटिया यार– बचपन का मित्र।
- हवाई महल–कोरी कल्पना।
- आँख लगना–नींद आना।
- आँख खुलना–होश में आना।
- आँखें दिखाना–क्रोध से घूरना।
- आँसू पोंछना–धैर्य बँधाना।
- अन्धे की लकड़ी–एकमात्र सहारा।
- कान भरना–चुगली करना।
- कान पर जूँ न रेंगना–कोई असर न होना।
- नाक कटना–प्रतिष्ठा खत्म होना।
- नाक रगड़ना–दीनता दिखाना।
- नाकों चने चबवाना–खूब सताना।
- मुँह की खाना–बुरी तरह हारना।
- आस्तीन का साँप–विश्वासघाती मित्र।
- कन्धे से कन्धा मिलाना–पूरा सहयोग करना।
- ईंट से ईंट बजाना–पूरी तरह नष्ट कर देना।
- नौ दो ग्यारह होना–भाग जाना।
- दाँत खट्टे करना–बुरी तरह हराना।
- हाथ मलना–पछताना।
- खून का प्यासा–जानी दुश्मन।
- घी के दिए जलाना–खुशी मनाना।
- चार चाँद लगाना–प्रतिष्ठा बढ़ाना।
- तीन तेरह होना–अलग-अलग होना।
- पानी फेर देना–नाश कर देना।
- गाल बजाना–डींगे मारना।
- जान से हाथ धो बैठना–मारा जाना।
- पानी-पानी होना–बहुत लज्जित होना।
- फूला न समाना–बहुत प्रसन्न होना।
- अपना उल्लू सीधा करना–अपना मतलब निकालना।
- आँखें चुरा लेना–अनदेखा कर देना।
- अन्धे की लाठी–एकमात्र सहारा।
- आसमान पर चढ़ना–बहुत अभिमान करना।
- आँखें खुलना–होश आना।
- चोरी और सीना जोरी–दोषी होकर धमकाना।
- आग में घी डालना–क्रोध को भड़काना।
- अँगुली पर नचाना– अच्छी तरह वश में करना।
- एक आँख से देखना–समान दृष्टि से देखना।
- एक ही थैले के चट्टे-बट्टे–एक जैसे।
- ओखली में सिर देना–जान-बूझकर आपत्ति मोल लेना।
- कलेजा मुँह को आना–बहुत दुःखी होना।
- कफन बाँधकर चलना–मौत से न घबराना।
- काँटे बिछाना–बाधा डालना।
- कलेजा ठण्डा होना–सन्तोष होना।
- कमर कसना–तैयार होना।
- खून खौलना–जोश में आना।
- खाक छानना–मारे-मारे फिरना।
- गागर में सागर भरना–थोड़े शब्दों में बहुत कुछ कह देना।
- घाव पर नमक छिड़कना–दुखी को अधिक दुखी करना।
- घी के दिए जलाना–खुशी मनाना।
- घोड़े बेचकर सोना–गहरी नींद में सोना।
- चल बसना–परलोक सिधारना।
- छठी का दूध याद आना–भारी संकट में पड़ना।
- छाती पर साँप लोटना–बहुत ईर्ष्या होना।
- जमीन पर पैर न रखना–अधिक घमण्ड होना।
- झक मारना–व्यर्थ समय खोना।
- टेढ़ी खीर–कठिन काम।
- डींग मारना–अपनी झूठी प्रशंसा करना।
- डूब मरना–बहुत लज्जित होना।
- तलवे चाटना–चापलूसी करना।
- ताक में रहना–मौका ढूँढ़ते रहना।
- दंग रह जाना–आश्चर्य में पड़ जाना।
- दाल न गलना–वश न चलना।
- दाल में काला होना–संदेह होना।
- पीठ दिखाना–हारकर भागना।
- मुँह तोड़ उत्तर देना–खरा उत्तर देना।

वस्तुनिष्ठ प्रश्न

अभ्यास-1

निर्देशः *नीचे प्रत्येक शुद्ध शब्द की वर्तनी के लिए चार विकल्प दिए गए हैं। आपको सही विकल्प का चयन करना है।*

1. A. ऋषि B. ऋषी
C. रिषी D. ऋसि

2. A. विषेसन B. विशेषण
C. विसेशन D. विशेशन

3. A. दुशासन B. दुसाशन
C. दूशाषण D. दुःशासन

4. A. संस्कृति B. संसकृति
C. संष्कृति D. संस्कृती

5. A. दूनियां B. दुनियां
C. दुनिया D. दूनिआ

6. A. टिपनी B. टिप्पणि
C. टिप्पणी D. टिप्पनी

7. A. शाषण B. साशन
C. शासन D. शाशन

8. A. किसमस B. किरसमस
C. क्रिसमूस D. कृसमस

9. A. अनुग्रहित B. अनुग्रहीत
C. अनुगृहीत D. अनुग्रहित

10. A. पराकम B. प्राक्रम
C. पराक्रम D. प्राकर्म

11. A. नायका B. नाइका
C. नाइक D. नायिका

12. A. समरिधी B. समद्धी
C. समृद्धि D. समरिद्धि

13. A. युधिष्ठर B. यूधिष्ठर
C. युधिष्ठिर D. युधिष्टर

14. A. वाल्मीकि B. बाल्मीकि
C. बालमीकि D. बाल्मिक

15. A. परलोकिक B. प्रलौकिक
C. पारलौकिक D. परलौकिक

16. A. त्रितीय B. तर्तीय
C. तृतीय D. तिरतीय

17. A. व्योहार B. व्यौहार
C. व्यवहार D. ब्यवहार

18. A. अहिल्यां B. अहल्या
C. अहिलया D. अहीलया

19. A. आदरनीय B. आदरणीय
C. आदरनीया D. आदरणीया

20. A. आर्द B. आद्र
C. आर्द्र D. आर्द्

21. A. आधीन B. अधिन
C. अधीन D. अधीम

22. A. आविस्कार B. आविष्कार
C. आवीस्कार D. आविश्कार

23. A. आसा B. आषा
C. आशा D. अशा

24. A. उज्वल B. उजज्ज्वल
C. उजज्वल D. उज्ज्वल

25. A. उन्नती B. उन्नित
C. उन्नति D. उन्नती

26. A. कलस B. कलष
C. कलश D. कलशा

27. A. गनीत B. गनित
C. गणीत D. गणित

28. A. तलाव B. तालाव
C. तलाब D. तालाब

29. A. दुष्ट B. दूष्ट
C. दुस्त D. दुश्त

30. A. निरोग B. निररोग
C. नीरोग D. नीरोगी

उत्तरमाला

1. A	2. B	3. D	4. A	5. C
6. C	7. C	8. C	9. C	10. C
11. D	12. C	13. C	14. A	15. C
16. C	17. C	18. B	19. B	20. C
21. C	22. B	23. C	24. D	25. C
26. C	27. D	28. D	29. A	30. C

अभ्यास-2

निर्देशः *नीचे कुछ शब्द दिए गए हैं। प्रत्येक के पर्यायवाची के चार विकल्प दिए गए हैं। इनमें से एक विकल्प सही पर्यायवाची है, उसका चयन कीजिए :*

1. अग्नि
A. अनिल B. अनल
C. गर्म D. ताप

2. अमृत
A. पीयूष B. गरल
C. सरस D. जीवनदायनी

3. आँख
A. लोचन B. आस्थि
C. वदन D. जलज

4. आकाश
A. अनन्त B. पाताल
C. वितल D. तल

5. कपड़ा
A. परिधान B. पटिका
C. पीताम्बर D. लँहगा

6. कमल
A. सरोज B. सरोवर
C. पंक D. पुष्प

7. गंगा
A. पाताल नदी B. हिमनदी
C. भागीरथ D. त्रिपथगा

8. चाँद
A. मयंक B. भानु
C. दिनकर D. रवि

9. नदी
A. सरिता B. प्रवाह
C. धारा D. जलधर

10. पर्वत
A. पत्थर B. चट्टान
C. शिखर D. मेरू

11. पवन
A. अनिल B. अनल
C. अग D. विहग

12. पति
A. साजन B. प्रिया
C. भार्या D. दारा

13. पानी
A. मही B. मेदिनी
C. अम्बु D. तरणी

14. पुत्र
A. आत्मज B. तनया
C. सुता D. आत्मजा

15. पुत्री
A. सुता B. सुत
C. आत्मज D. नन्दन

16. फूल
A. बहार B. मधु
C. माधव D. सुमन

17. वृक्ष
A. विटप B. अग्र
C. प्रसून D. रसा

18. बादल
A. अज B. व्यामोह
C. नीरद D. मधुप

19. बिजली
A. चंचला B. खटका
C. त्रास D. संत्रास

20. माता
A. धात्री B. धरणी
C. धरित्री D. श्यामा

21. घोषणा
A. आवाज B. पुकारना
C. ऐलान D. ललकारना

22. उत्कर्ष
A. आकर्षण B. विकर्षण
C. उन्नति D. निष्कर्ष

23. उदय
A. अन्त B. विकास
C. प्रगट D. व्यस्त

24. दक्ष
A. निपुण B. समर्थ
C. कर्मठ D. मेहनती

25. संवाद
A. विवाद B. झगड़ा
C. सम्बोधन D. वार्तालाप

उत्तरमाला

1. B	**2.** A	**3.** A	**4.** A	**5.** A
6. A	**7.** D	**8.** A	**9.** A	**10.** D
11. A	**12.** A	**13.** C	**14.** A	**15.** A
16. D	**17.** A	**18.** C	**19.** A	**20.** A
21. C	**22.** C	**23.** C	**24.** A	**25.** D

अभ्यास-3

निर्देशः *नीचे चार-चार शब्दों के समूह दिए गए हैं। प्रत्येक समूह में एक शब्द बेमेल है तथा शेष तीन शब्द पर्यायवाची हैं, आपको उस शब्द का चयन करना है, जो बेमेल है :*

1. A. तम B. अंधकार
C. तिमिर D. अंश

2. A. अनल B. आग
C. दहन D. तमिस्त्रा

3. A. अतुल B. अद्वितीय
C. अनुपम D. शुष्मा

4. A. अहं B. अहंकार
C. दर्प D. निराला

5. A. पता B. खोज
C. जाँच D. शोध

6. A. गरल B. पीयूष
C. सुधा D. सोम

7. A. कानन B. जंगल
C. पादप D. वन

8. A. अश्व B. गज
C. घोड़ा D. तुरंग

9. A. दानव B. मानव
C. दैत्य D. राक्षस

10. A. आँख B. चक्षु
C. नयन D. मुख

11. A. अन्तरिक्ष B. वसुन्धरा
C. आसमान D. गगन

12. A. इच्छा B. अभिलाषा
C. कामना D. प्रयोजन

13. A. कपड़ा B. चीर
C. वसन D. पोशाक

14. A. अब्ज B. कमल
C. राजीव D. आम्र

15. A. कोयल B. पिक
C. काग D. वनप्रिय

16. A. गंगा B. देवनदी
C. गोदावरी D. भागीरथी

17. A. गणेश B. एकदन्त
C. देवराज D. गणपति

18. A. घर B. निलय
C. निकेतन D. झोपड़ी

19. A. चाँद B. हिमांशु
C. विनायक D. सुधांशु

20. A. नदी B. तरणी
C. तटिनी D. सरिता

21. A. पक्षी B. चिड़िया
C. सुमन D. विहग

22. A. पवन B. अचला
C. वात D. वायु

23. A. समीर B. पृथ्वी
C. भू D. भूमि

24. A. पानी B. समीर
C. अम्बु D. जल

25. A. पुत्र B. तनया
C. तनय D. सुत

26. A. पुत्र B. तनया
C. सुता D. कन्या

27. A. गृहिणी B. आदमी
C. पुरुष D. नर

28. A. मधु B. फूल
C. पुष्प D. सुमन

29. A. माधव B. तरु
C. पेड़ D. वृक्ष

30. A. माता B. अम्बु
C. अम्मा D. जननी

उत्तरमाला

1. D	**2.** D	**3.** D	**4.** D	**5.** A
6. A	**7.** C	**8.** B	**9.** B	**10.** D
11. B	**12.** D	**13.** D	**14.** D	**15.** C
16. C	**17.** C	**18.** D	**19.** C	**20.** B
21. C	**22.** B	**23.** A	**24.** B	**25.** B
26. A	**27.** A	**28.** A	**29.** A	**30.** B

अभ्यास-4

निर्देशः *गहरे काले शब्द के विलोम शब्द का चयन कीजिए:*

1. उसे हर काम में **सफलता** मिल रही है।
A. असफलता B. सफल
C. कुशलता D. निपुणता

2. कभी किसी की **निन्दा** नहीं करनी चाहिए।
A. गुणगान B. स्तुति
C. प्रशंसा D. यशोगान

3. आलस्य व्यक्ति का सबसे बड़ा **दुश्मन** है।
A. शत्रु B. घातक
C. मित्र D. सहायक

4. वे बुढ़ापे से **दुखी** हैं।
A. अप्रसन्न B. सुखी
C. खुश D. नाराज

5. यहाँ उसकी **चतुराई** नहीं चली।
A. चालाकी B. बहादुरी
C. निपुणता D. मूर्खता

6. शहद की **मिठास** कम नहीं होती।
A. मीठा B. तीखा
C. कड़ुवा D. खट्टा

7. साहसी के **साहस** को देखकर मैं चकित रह गया।
A. हिम्मत B. बहादुरी
C. निडर D. भय

8. फिल्मोत्सव में सर्वश्रेष्ठ **अभिनेता** को पुरस्कार प्रदान किया गया।
A. हीरोइन B. नेत्री
C. मीनाक्षी D. अभिनेत्री

9. नाटक में नायक और **नायिका** की भूमिका महत्वपूर्ण होती हैः
A. हीरो B. नायक
C. नेत्र D. नेता

10. कवि-सम्मेलन में एक कवि और एक **कवयित्री** को आमंत्रित किया गया था।
A. लेखक B. सम्पादक
C. नेता D. कवि

11. विद्यालय के वार्षिकोत्सव के लिए नेता और एक **नेत्री** को आमंत्रित किया गया।
A. अभिनेता B. विद्वान्
C. विदुषी D. नेता

12. मोहन बहुत **चतुर** है।
A. निपुण B. तेज
C. सुस्त D. मूर्ख

13. सोहन अब पूर्ण **स्वस्थ** है।
A. प्रसन्न B. खुश
C. अस्वस्थ D. अप्रसन्न

14. पक्षी **आकाश** में उड़ते हैं :
A. गगन B. नभ
C. धरती D. पाताल

15. वह विद्यालय में देर से आया और **अनुपस्थित** हो गया।
A. पूर्व B. उपस्थित
C. प्रवेश D. समयपूर्व

16. **बालक** चाँद की ओर देख रहा है।
A. बालिका B. लड़का
C. बच्चा D. बच्ची

17. मैं उसके विचार से बिल्कुल **सहमत** नहीं हूँ।
A. समर्थन B. सहमति
C. असहमत D. प्रशंसक

18. उसकी हालत **अधिक** खराब है।
A. बहुत B. कम
C. ठीक D. कुशल

19. **धर्म** की सर्वत्र विजय होती हैः
A. अधर्म B. ज्ञान
C. भक्ति D. ईमानदारी

20. अच्छे चरित्र के बिना जीवन **निरर्थक** हैः
A. व्यर्थ B. अर्थपूर्ण
C. सार्थक D. कुशल

21. **ईमानदारी** बड़ी दुर्लभ वस्तु हैः
A. सच्चाई B. भलाई
C. बेइमानी D. परोपकारी

22. एवरेस्ट संसार का सबसे **ऊँचा** पर्वत हैः
A. नीचा B. वितल
C. पाताल D. मध्यम

23. वह विश्वास के **योग्य** नहीं हैः
A. काबिल B. विश्वासी
C. अयोग्य D. बेकार

24. क्या वह इतना **मूर्ख** है?
A. चालाक B. विद्वान्
C. बुद्धिमान D. धूर्त

25. कितना सुहावना **दृश्य** है!
A. अदृश्य B. दर्शनीय
C. सुन्दर D. व्यर्थ

उत्तरमाला

1. A	**2.** C	**3.** C	**4.** B	**5.** D
6. C	**7.** D	**8.** D	**9.** B	**10.** D
11. D	**12.** D	**13.** C	**14.** D	**15.** B
16. A	**17.** C	**18.** B	**19.** A	**20.** C
21. C	**22.** A	**23.** C	**24.** C	**25.** A

अभ्यास-5

निर्देशः नीचे प्रत्येक **काले गहरे शब्द** के चार विलोम दिए गए हैं। इनमें सही विलोम का चयन कीजिए :

1. अग्नि
A. आग B. अनल
C. दहन D. जल

2. अग्रज
A. अनुज B. भ्राता
C. भाई D. अम्बा

3. अच्छा
A. बुरा B. खराब
C. गंदा D. भ्रष्ट

4. अंत
A. प्रारम्भ B. समाप्त
C. शेष D. अल्प

5. अचल
A. विचल B. वितल
C. सजल D. चल

6. अति
A. अधिक B. बहुत
C. अल्प D. कम

7. अत्यधिक
A. अल्प B. अधिक
C. स्वल्प D. न्यूनतम

8. अंधकार
A. अंधेरा B. प्रकाश
C. रात्रि D. दिन

9. अतिवृष्टि
A. अनावृष्टि B. वृष्टि
C. वर्षा D. वर्षण

10. अनाथ
A. नाथ B. स्वामी
C. मासिक D. सनाथ

11. अनुकूल
A. मनोकूल B. प्रतिकूल
C. अनुकरण D. मनस्वी

12. अनुराग
A. राग B. विराग
C. विग्रह D. स्नेह

13. अन्त
A. श्री गणेश B. आदि
C. शुरुआत D. समाप्त

14. अपना
A. अपनत्व B. पराया
C. मित्र D. शत्रु

15. अपमान
A. मान B. सम्मान
C. वर्तमान D. स्वाभिमान

16. अपेक्षा
A. इच्छा B. स्वेच्छा
C. प्रविच्छा D. उपेक्षा

17. अमर
A. मर्त्य B. मृत्यु
C. सुधा D. गरल

18. अल्पायु
A. चिरायु B. उमरदराज
C. नश्वर D. सनातन

19. अस्त
A. उदय B. विकास
C. निर्माण D. सृष्टि

20. आकर्षण
A. प्रतिकर्षण B. विकर्षण
C. सम्मोहन D. विरत

21. आकाश
A. गगन B. नभ
C. वसुन्धरा D. पाताल

22. आगे
A. पीछे B. पूर्व
C. पृष्ट D. पृष्ठ

23. आजाद
A. स्वतंत्र B. स्वतंत्रतता
C. परतंत्र D. गुलाम

24. आदान
A. आयात B. निर्यात
C. प्रदान D. निदान

25. आधुनिक
A. अर्वाचीन B. नूतन
C. प्राचीन D. वर्तमान

उत्तरमाला

1. D	**2.** A	**3.** A	**4.** A	**5.** D
6. D	**7.** C	**8.** B	**9.** A	**10.** D
11. B	**12.** B	**13.** A	**14.** B	**15.** B
16. D	**17.** A	**18.** A	**19.** A	**20.** B
21. D	**22.** A	**23.** D	**24.** C	**25.** C

अभ्यास-6

निर्देशः नीचे कुछ शब्द दिए गए हैं प्रत्येक शब्द के चार वैकल्पिक अर्थ दिए गए हैं। सही अर्थ का चयन कीजिए :

1. सुरक्षित
A. कुशल B. घटना
C. दुर्घटना D. बचाव

2. प्रतिभाशाली
A. सज्जन B. कुशाग्र
C. विद्वान् D. वैभवशाली

3. आत्मसमर्पण
A. अपने आप को सौंपना B. समर्पण
C. अर्पण D. त्यागज

4. सिद्धहस्त
A. निपुण B. कर्मठ
C. मेहनती D. परिश्रमी

5. सुशोभित
A. मजेदार B. सुस्वागतम्
C. अच्छा D. शोभा पाना

6. स्वादिष्ट
A. मजेदार B. बेकार
C. मीठा D. तीखा

7. स्वावलम्बी
A. निर्भर B. परालंबी
C. आत्मनिर्भर D. अतिथि

8. उपकरण
A. साधन B. युक्ति
C. यंत्र D. मशीन

9. कीमत
A. क्रय B. विक्रय
C. मूल्य D. बिक्री

10. संगठन
A. एकता B. अनेकता
C. समूह D. संस्था

11. विपत्ति
A. दुख B. विपदा
C. मुसीबत D. सुख

12. तृण
A. तिनका B. धूल
C. धूप D. लकड़ी

13. आश्चर्य
A. निरीक्षण B. दृष्टिगोचर
C. हैरानी D. थकावट

14. हार्दिक
A. हृदय से B. शरीर से
C. मन से D. मस्तिष्क से

15. नियति
A. भाग्य B. किनारा
C. समय D. पवित्र

16. सुगन्धित
A. दुर्गन्ध B. खुशबू वाला
C. फूल D. कमल

17. उत्साह
A. होश B. हवास
C. जोश D. हिम्मत

18. सहयोग
A. मिलन सार B. मेहनती
C. परोपकारी D. आपसी सहायता

19. मुसीबत
A. विपत्ति B. सुशोभित
C. सहायता D. मदद

20. निरक्षर
A. साक्षर B. दर्शनीय
C. पठनीय D. अनपढ़

21. उपवन
A. वन B. तीर
C. जंगल D. बाग

22. मेघ
A. बादल B. पंकज
C. राजीव D. मेघनाद

23. आधुनिक
A. प्राचीन B. पुरातन
C. भूतकाल D. आज का

24. तीर
A. वाण B. धनुष
C. किनारा D. नदी

25. परीक्षण
A. जाँच B. पड़ताल
C. परीक्षा D. इम्तहान

26. अभिवादन
A. नमस्ते B. प्रणाम
C. बधाई D. शुभकामना

27. सर्वत्र
A. नश्वर B. सजीव
C. ईश्वर D. सभी जगह

28. हलवाहा
A. चरवाहा B. किसान
C. मजदूर D. हल चलाने वाला

29. शिखर
A. पर्वत B. पहाड़
C. टीला D. चोटी

30. भयानक
A. डरावना B. भयभीत
C. डरना D. खूँखार

उत्तरमाला

1. D	**2.** B	**3.** A	**4.** A	**5.** D
6. A	**7.** C	**8.** C	**9.** C	**10.** A
11. C	**12.** A	**13.** C	**14.** A	**15.** A
16. B	**17.** C	**18.** D	**19.** A	**20.** D
21. D	**22.** A	**23.** D	**24.** A	**25.** A
26. B	**27.** D	**28.** D	**29.** D	**30.** A

अभ्यास-7

निर्देशः *नीचे कुछ शब्द दिए जा रहे हैं। प्रत्येक शब्द के* **उपसर्ग** *के सन्दर्भ में चार विकल्प दिए गए हैं। आपको सही विकल्प का चयन करना है :*

1. अलबत्ता
A. अ B. अल
C. लब D. त्ता

2. अलगरज
A. अल B. लग
C. गर D. रज

3. कमसिन
A. क B. कम
C. सि D. सिन

4. अनमोल
A. अ B. अन
C. मो D. मोल

5. अनजान
A. अ B. अन
C. जा D. जान

6. अनपढ़
A. अ B. पढ़
C. प D. अन

7. अधखिला
A. अ B. अध
C. ला D. खिला

8. अधजला
A. अ B. ज
C. अध D. ला

9. अधपका
A. अ B. अध
C. पका D. का

10. अघखिला
A. अ B. अघ
C. खिला D. ला

11. उन्नीस
A. उन B. उन्
C. नीस D. स

12. उनसठ
A. उ B. उन
C. सठ D. ठ

13. दुकाल
A. द B. दुक
C. दु D. काल

14. दुबला
A. दब B. दुब
C. ला D. दु

15. निकम्मा
A. नि B. निक
C. कम्मा D. मा

16. निर्लज्ज
A. निर B. निल
C. नि D. लज्ज

17. बिनब्याहा
A. बि B. बिन
C. ब्याहा D. हा

18. भरपेट
A. भर B. पेट
C. पे D. ट

19. भरपाई
A. भ B. र
C. पा D. भर

20. कुपात्र
A. कु B. कुप
C. पा D. पात्र

21. सुजान
A. सु B. सुज
C. सुजा D. जान

22. गैर कानूनी
A. गै B. गैर
C. कानु D. नुनी

23. गैरसरकारी
A. गैर B. सर
C. का D. कारी

24. अपमान
A. अ B. अप
C. मा D. मान

25. अनुशासन
A. अ B. शासन
C. सन D. अनु

26. अविनीत
A. अवि B. अ
C. नी D. नीत

27. अभिमान
A. अभि B. अ
C. मा D. मान

28. अभियान
A. अ B. मान
C. यान D. अभि

29. अध्ययन
A. अध् B. अधि
C. यन D. न

30. निश्चल
A. नि B. निर
C. निस D. चल

उत्तरमाला

1. B	2. A	3. B	4. B	5. B
6. D	7. B	8. C	9. B	10. B
11. A	12. B	13. C	14. D	15. B
16. A	17. B	18. A	19. D	20. A
21. A	22. B	23. A	24. B	25. D
26. B	27. A	28. D	29. B	30. A

अभ्यास-8

निर्देश: *निम्नलिखित शब्दों में प्रयुक्त प्रत्यय सम्बन्धी चार विकल्प दिए गए हैं, सही विकल्प का चयन कीजिए :*

1. भलाई
A. ई B. लाई
C. आई D. भला

2. चतुराई
A. चतु B. रा
C. ई D. आई

3. भूखा
A. भू B. भूख
C. खा D. आ

4. भिड़न्त
A. भिड़् B. भि
C. न्त D. अन्त

5. प्यासा
A. आस B. सा
C. आसा D. सा

6. बिकाऊ
A. बिक B. काऊ
C. आऊ D. ऊ

7. तैराक
A. तै B. तैर
C. राक D. आक

8. सन्नाटा
A. सन् B. सन्ना
C. नाटा D. आटा

9. लोहार
A. लोह B. आरा
C. आरी D. आर

10. मिलान
A. आना B. आने
C. आनी D. आन

11. चढ़ाव
A. चढ़ B. चढ़ा
C. आव D. व

12. लगाव
A. लग B. अव
C. आव D. गाव

13. लिखावट
A. लिख B. लिखा
C. वट D. आवट

14. मिलावट
A. मिल B. वट
C. आवट D. ट

15. मिठास
A. मिठ B. ठास
C. आस D. स

16. चिकनाहट
A. चिक B. नाह्ट
C. हट D. आहट

17. सड़ियल
A. सड़ B. यल
C. ड़ियल D. इयल

18. मरियल
A. मर B. यल
C. मरि D. इयल

19. गड़रिया
A. गड़ B. इया
C. रिया D. या

20. सजीला
A. ईला B. इला
C. ला D. स

21. लुटेरा
A. लुट B. एरा
C. ऐरा D. रा

22. लठैत
A. ए B. ऐ
C. ऐत D. त

23. भगोड़ा
A. ओ B. ओड़ा
C. ड़ा D. भगो

24. खपत
A. ख B. प
C. त D. पत

25. जीवट
A. व B. अट
C. जीव D. जी

उत्तरमाला

1. C	**2.** D	**3.** D	**4.** D	**5.** D
6. C	**7.** D	**8.** D	**9.** D	**10.** D
11. C	**12.** C	**13.** D	**14.** C	**15.** C
16. D	**17.** D	**18.** D	**19.** B	**20.** A
21. B	**22.** C	**23.** B	**24.** C	**25.** B

अभ्यास-9

निर्देशः नीचे कुछ मुहावरे दिए गए हैं। प्रत्येक के अर्थ के लिए चार विकल्प दिए गए हैं। आपको सही विकल्प का चयन करना है :

1. अक्ल पर पत्थर पड़ना
A. बुद्धि काम न करना B. दुविधा होना
C. संकट में होना D. परेशान होना

2. अपना उल्लू सीधा करना
A. अवसर देखना B. काम निकालना
C. मतलब साधना D. मूर्ख बनाना

3. अपने मुँह मियाँ-मिट्ठू बनना
A. मिठाई खाना B. प्रशंसा करना
C. निंदा करना D. अपनी प्रशंसा स्वयं करना

4. अपने पाँव पर आप कुल्हाड़ी मारना
A. हानि पहुँचाना B. खेद होना
C. अपना पैर काटना D. अपनी हानि स्वयं करना

5. आँखें चुरा लेना
A. भाग जाना B. छिप जाना
C. अनदेखा करना D. मिल जाना

6. अक्ल का दुश्मन
A. मित्र होना B. शत्रु होना
C. महामूर्ख D. महाविद्वान्

7. अंधे की लाठी
A. एक मात्र सहारा B. मित्र होना
C. शत्रु होना D. दुख पहुँचाना

8. आकाश-पाताल एक करना
A. भाग-दौड़ करना B. परेशान होना
C. थक जाना D. कठिन परिश्रम करना

9. घड़ों पानी पड़ना
A. लज्जित होना B. तुच्छ समझना
C. लाभ होना D. थकावट

10. अगर-मगर करना
A. नुकसान करना B. बहाने बनाना
C. बदनाम करना D. कपट करना

11. मुँह की खाना
A. गिर जाना B. हार जाना
C. भाग जाना D. व्यर्थ होना

12. आस्तीन का साँप होना
A. शत्रु B. मित्र
C. कपटी मित्र D. दयालु

13. एक आँख से देखना
A. बुरा व्यवहार B. समान व्यवहार
C. कपट करना D. लज्जित होना

14. बाल-बाँका न होना
A. घायल होना B. साफ बच जाना
C. क्रोधित होना D. स्वस्थ होना

15. दाँतों तले उँगली दबाना
A. उँगली काटना B. चिंतित हो जाना
C. चकित रह जाना D. प्रसन्न हो जाना

16. जान के लाले पड़ना
A. मरने का खतरा होना B. भाग जाना
C. हार जाना D. मुश्किल में पड़ना

17. बोली मारना
A. ताना देना B. सताना
C. मजाक करना D. याद दिलाना

18. अंधों में काना राजा
A. मूर्खों में अल्पज्ञ को विद्वान् माना जाना
B. सबको मूर्ख समझना
C. अत्यधिक महत्त्वपूर्ण
D. काना राजा

19. अक्ल के घोड़े दौड़ाना
A. बुद्धि लड़ाना
B. कल्पना करना
C. तरह-तरह के उपाय सोचना
D. ज्ञान-प्राप्त करना

20. पानी उतर जाना
A. शर्म करना B. लज्जित न होना
C. भाग जाना D. इज्जत करना

21. तीन-पाँच करना
A. तितर-बितर करना
B. वचन देकर फिर जाना
C. घुमा-फिरा कर बातें करना
D. परेशान करना

22. हथियार डाल देना
A. हार जाना B. जीत जाना
C. धोखा देना D. विजय होना

23. आँख खुलना
A. होश में आना B. अत्यन्त प्यार होना
C. उल्टा काम करना D. क्रोध करना

24. कमर सीधी करना
A. थक जाना B. थकावट दूर करना
C. काम करना D. परिश्रम करना

25. पगड़ी रखना
A. चैन की सांस लेना B. अपमान करना
C. दया की भीख माँगना D. अपमान होना

26. लोहा मानना
A. संघर्ष करना B. विजय होना
C. श्रेष्ठता स्वीकार करना D. खुशामद करना

27. काठ मार जाना
A. दुःखी होना B. चुप होना
C. सफल होना D. मर जाना

28. चाँद पर थूकना

A. अपमान करना

B. बढ़कर बातें करना

C. महान पुरुष पर लांछन लगाना

D. महत्त्वाकांक्षी होना

29. उगल देना

A. अपराध स्वीकार कर लेना

B. सच बोलना

C. उल्टी करना

D. अनपच होना

30. हाथ मलना

A. पश्चाताप करना B. सर्दी मिटाना

C. दुख करना D. तैयार होना

उत्तरमाला

1. A	2. C	3. D	4. D	5. C
6. C	7. A	8. D	9. A	10. B
11. B	12. C	13. B	14. B	15. C
16. D	17. A	18. A	19. A	20. B
21. C	22. A	23. A	24. B	25. C
26. C	27. B	28. C	29. A	30. A

अभ्यास-10

निर्देशः *नीचे कुछ वाक्य खण्ड दिए गए हैं, पूरे वाक्य खण्ड के लिए एक शब्द का चयन कीजिए।*

1. जिसका आदि न हो

A. अनंत B. अमर

C. शाश्वत D. अनादि

2. जो कुछ न जानता हो

A. मूर्ख B. महामूर्ख

C. ज्ञानी D. अज्ञ

3. जो अनुकरण करने योग्य हो

A. अनुकरणीय B. अद्वितीय

C. आदरणीय D. अगम

4. जिसका अंत न हो

A. अनंत B. अनादि

C. आदि D. परलोक

5. जो कभी न मरे

A. मर्त्य B. मुर्त्त

C. अर्मुत्त D. अमर

6. जिसके समान दूसरा न हो

A. अनुकूल B. प्रतिकूल

C. कृतज्ञ D. अद्वितीय

7. जो कम बोलता हो

A. मृदुभाषी B. वाचाल

C. अल्पभाषी D. अल्पज्ञ

8. जिसका इलाज न हो

A. मरणशील B. अमरत्व

C. बिमारी D. लाइलाज

9. जिस का विश्वास न किया जा सके

A. विश्वसनीय B. अविश्वसनीय

C. विश्वासी D. धूर्त्त

10. जिसका कोई नाथ न हो

A. सनाथ B. स्वामी

C. नाथ D. अनाथ

11. कम जानने वाला

A. अल्पज्ञ B. अज्ञ

C. विद् D. विद्वान

12. जहाँ जाना संभव न हो

A. दुर्गम B. अगम

C. तल D. वितल

13. कम खाने वाला

A. बहुभोजी B. पेटु

C. कंजूस D. अल्पाहारी

14. जो बात पहले कभी न हुई हो

A. भूतपूर्व B. अभूतपूर्व

C. प्राचीन D. अर्वाचीन

15. जिस स्त्री के सन्तान न हों

A. बाँझ B. कुलटा

C. पतिता D. विधवा

16. जो कहा न जा सके

A. अकथनीय B. अकथ्य

C. करणीय D. सम्भव

17. एहसान न मानने वाला

A. कृतज्ञ B. कृतघ्न

C. आस्तिक D. विश्वासी

18. जिसने देश के साथ विश्वासघात किया हो

A. विश्वासघाती B. द्रोही

C. आतंकवादी D. देश द्रोही

19. जिसने राष्ट्र के हित में अपना जीवन बलिदान कर दिया हो

A. देशभक्त B. शहीद

C. राष्ट्रभूत D. भारतपुत्र

20. वह जमीन जिसमें कुछ भी पैदा न हो

A. ऊसर B. बंजर

C. उर्वर D. पथरीला

21. वह वस्तु जिसकी चाह हो

A. श्रेष्ठ B. आवश्यक

C. इच्छित D. अभीष्ट

22. दूसरों के पीछे चलने वाला
A. अनुयायी B. अनुज
C. अनुचर D. अनुकरणीय

23. जो पहले न पढ़ा हो
A. पठित B. अपठित
C. पठनीय D. अपठनीय

24. जिसके आर-पार दिखाई देता हो
A. अपारदर्शी B. गम्य
C. अगम्य D. पारदर्शी

25. आज्ञा पालन करने वाला
A. शिष्य B. शिष्या
C. अनुचर D. आज्ञाकारी

26. काम से जी चुराने वाला
A. कामचोर B. आलसी
C. कर्मठ D. परिश्रमी

27. प्रतिदिन होने वाला
A. दैनिक B. शाश्वत
C. सनातन D. अमर

28. जिसका कोई अर्थ न हो
A. सार्थक B. निरर्थक
C. आर्थिक D. अनार्थिक

29. उपकार मानने वाला
A. कृतज्ञ B. कृतघ्न
C. विश्वासी D. अनुयायी

30. हाथ से लिखा हुआ
A. पठनीय B. अपठनीय
C. स्पष्ट D. हस्तलिखित

उत्तरमाला

1. D	**2.** D	**3.** A	**4.** A	**5.** D
6. D	**7.** C	**8.** D	**9.** B	**10.** D
11. A	**12.** A	**13.** D	**14.** B	**15.** A
16. A	**17.** B	**18.** D	**19.** B	**20.** A
21. C	**22.** C	**23.** B	**24.** D	**25.** D
26. A	**27.** A	**28.** B	**29.** A	**30.** D

अभ्यास-11

निर्देशः *नीचे कुछ संज्ञा शब्द दिए जा रहे हैं। प्रत्येक के संज्ञा-भेद के लिए चार विकल्प दिए गये है। सही विकल्प का चयन कीजिए :*

1. तुलसीदास
A. जातिवाचक B. भाववाचक
C. व्यक्तिवाचक D. समूहवाचक

2. यमुना
A. व्यक्तिवाचक B. जातिवाचक
C. समूहवाचक D. भाववाचक

3. बच्चा
A. जातिवाचक B. समूहवाचक
C. भाववाचक D. व्यक्तिवाचक

4. मानवता
A. भाववाचक B. जातिवाचक
C. द्रव्यवाचक D. समूहवाचक

5. हिमालय
A. व्यक्तिवाचक B. जातिवाचक
C. भाववाचक D. समूहवाचक

6. भारत
A. जातिवाचक B. भाववाचक
C. व्यक्तिवाचक D. समूहवाचक

7. एशिया
A. व्यक्तिवाचक B. भाववाचक
C. द्रव्यवाचक D. समूहवाचक

8. महाराष्ट्र
A. जातिवाचक B. व्यक्तिवाचक
C. समूहवाचक D. द्रव्यवाचक

9. सूर सागर
A. व्यक्तिवाचक B. भाववाचक
C. द्रव्यवाचक D. समूहवाचक

10. सोमवार
A. जातिवाचक B. व्यक्तिवाचक
C. द्रव्यवाचक D. समूहवाचक

11. खटमल
A. जातिवाचक B. व्यक्तिवाचक
C. द्रव्यवाचक D. समूहवाचक

12. मैना
A. जातिवाचक B. व्यक्तिवाचक
C. द्रव्यवाचक D. समूहवाचक

13. चाँदी
A. द्रव्यवाचक B. समूहवाचक
C. भाववाचक D. व्यक्तिवाचक

14. अच्छाई
A. भाववाचक B. समूहवाचक
C. जातिवाचक D. व्यक्तिवाचक

15. पीतल
A. द्रव्यवाचक B. भाववाचक
C. व्यक्तिवाचक D. जातिवाचक

16. वीरता
A. भाववाचक B. जातिवाचक
C. द्रव्यवाचक D. समूहवाचक

17. रूस
A. जातिवाचक B. व्यक्तिवाचक
C. भाववाचक D. द्रव्यवाचक

18. लम्बाई
A. भाववाचक B. समूहवाचक
C. द्रव्यवाचक D. व्यक्तिवाचक

19. दल
A. जातिवाचक B. व्यक्तिवाचक
C. समूहवाचक D. द्रव्यवाचक

20. मार्च
A. समूहवाचक B. व्यक्तिवाचक
C. द्रव्यवाचक D. जातिवाचक

21. झुण्ड
A. समूहवाचक B. जातिवाचक
C. व्यक्तिवाचक D. द्रव्यवाचक

22. टोली
A. जातिवाचक B. व्यक्तिवाचक
C. समूहवाचक D. द्रव्यवाचक

23. सुभाष चौक
A. जातिवाचक B. समूहवाचक
C. व्यक्तिवाचक D. भाववाचक

24. संघ
A. जातिवाचक B. द्रव्यवाचक
C. समूहवाचक D. भाववाचक

25. गिरोह
A. समूहवाचक B. द्रव्यवाचक
C. जातिवाचक D. भाववाचक

उत्तरमाला

1. C	**2.** A	**3.** A	**4.** A	**5.** A
6. C	**7.** A	**8.** B	**9.** A	**10.** B
11. A	**12.** A	**13.** A	**14.** A	**15.** A
16. A	**17.** B	**18.** A	**19.** C	**20.** B
21. A	**22.** C	**23.** C	**24.** C	**25.** A

अभ्यास-12

निर्देश: *नीचे दिए गए वाक्य में रिक्त स्थान है। प्रत्येक वाक्य के नीचे कारक चिह्न दिए गए हैं। रिक्त स्थान की पूर्ति के लिए उपयुक्त कारक चिह्न का चयन कीजिए :*

1. निम्नलिखित शब्दों........अर्थ बताइए
A. का B. के
C. से D. पर

2. सरकार मुझे नौकरी........मत निकालिए
A. पर B. में
C. से D. को

3. इस कथन........पुष्टि कीजिए
A. को B. से
C. की D. ने

4. छात्र-छात्राएँ राष्ट्र........सम्पत्ति और उसके भावी कर्णधार होते हैं
A. के B. की
C. को D. में

5. प्रत्येक प्रश्न........चार सम्भावित उत्तर दिए गए हैं
A. के लिए B. में
C. के D. से

6. माता बच्चे........पढ़ाती है
A. को B. के
C. की D. से

7. गुरुजी........सबसे छोटे लड़के को एक नारंगी दी
A. ने B. को
C. से D. के लिए

8. मोहन सोहन से मिलने........गया है
A. से B. के
C. को D. के लिए

9. उसने कलम........लिखा
A. के B. में
C. पर D. से

10. मैं ड्राइवर........गाड़ी चलवाता हूँ
A. के B. पर
C. में D. से

11. शिक्षक छात्रों........पुस्तक पढ़वाते हैं
A. के लिए B. मैं
C. पर D. से

12. मैंने दाढ़ी........उसे मुसलमान समझ लिया
A. से B. के
C. को D. के लिए

13. श्याम अपने भाई हरि........आम लाया है
A. के B. के लिए
C. का D. पर

14. मोहन घर........आता है
A. में B. पर
C. से D. का

15. उसे पाँच दिनों........मूर्छा आया करती है
A. पर B. से
C. के D. को

16. मेधावी छात्र परीक्षा........चोरी नहीं करते
A. में B. पर
C. से D. के लिए

उत्तरमाला

1. A	**2.** C	**3.** C	**4.** B	**5.** C
6. A	**7.** A	**8.** D	**9.** D	**10.** D
11. D	**12.** A	**13.** B	**14.** C	**15.** B
16. D				

गद्यांश (अपठित-बोध)

गद्यांश 1

यदि हम निरन्तर प्रयत्न करेंगे तो निश्चय ही अपने सभी लक्ष्यों को प्राप्त कर लेंगे, किन्तु प्रायः देखा जाता है कि अधिक आशावादी लोग थोड़ा सा प्रयत्न करके अधिक फल की कामना करने लगते हैं और मनोवांछित फल प्राप्त न होने पर निराश हो जाते हैं। अतः जीवन में सफलता प्राप्त करने के लिए परिस्थितियों के समक्ष घुटने न टेकें, बल्कि दृढ़ता से उनका मुकाबला करें। याद रखें, जितना कठोर हमारा परिश्रम होगा उसका फल भी उतना ही मीठा होगा।

उपर्युक्त गद्यांश को ध्यानपूर्वक पढ़ें और निम्न प्रश्नों के उत्तर के लिए सही विकल्प को चुनें:

1. फल न मिलने पर कौन निराश हो जाते हैं?
   A. आशावादी लोग B. कम आशावादी लोग
   C. अधिक आशावादी लोग D. निराशावादी लोग
2. लक्ष्य प्राप्ति के लिए क्या किया जाना चाहिए?
   A. फल की कामना B. हिम्मत से मुकाबला
   C. निरन्तर प्रयत्न D. परिस्थितियों से मुकाबला
3. आशावादी शब्द का विलोम शब्द हैः
   A. निराश B. निराशावादी
   B. दुखी D. अप्रसन्न
4. मनोवांछित शब्द का क्या अर्थ है?
   A. इच्छित B. परीक्षित
   C. लाभदायक D. मन को खुश करने वाले
5. परिश्रम शब्द का अर्थ हैः
   A. साहस B. हिम्मत
   C. काम D. कठिन मेहनत

गद्यांश 2

पन्द्रह अगस्त 1947 को हमारा देश स्वतंत्र हुआ। स्वतन्त्रता प्राप्ति के बाद विश्व के दूसरे देशों के साथ भारत के राजनयिक एवं सांस्कृतिक सम्बन्ध जुड़े। पर्यटकों के साथ-साथ राजनीतिज्ञों और साहित्यकारों को भी विदेश यात्रा के पर्याप्त अवसर मिले। विभिन्न प्रकार की छात्रवृत्तियों के माध्यम से बहुत से लोग विदेशों में पढ़ने गए। बहुत से लोगों ने विदेशों में उपलब्ध आजीविका के अवसरों का लाभ उठाया। इन सबके परिणामस्वरूप प्रचुर मात्रा में यात्रावृत्तांत लिखे गए। विदेश-विषयक यात्रावृतांत्तों में रूस और स्वदेश-विषयक यात्रावृतांत्तों में लेखकों की दृष्टि कश्मीर से कन्याकुमारी तक व्याप्त हुई।

उपर्युक्त गद्यांश को ध्यानपूर्वक पढ़ें और निम्नलिखित प्रश्नों के उत्तर के लिए सही विकल्प को चुनें:

1. भारत कब स्वतंत्र हुआ?
   A. 15 अगस्त 1947 B. 15 अगस्त 1946
   C. 15 अगस्त 1948 D. 15 अगस्त 1949
2. स्वतंत्र भारत के अन्य देशों के साथ किस प्रकार के संबंध जुड़े?
   A. राजनीतिक
   B. राजनयिक
   C. धार्मिक
   D. राजनयिक एवं सांस्कृतिक
3. आजीविका का क्या अर्थ है?
   A. उपार्जन B. वेतन
   C. मेहनत D. रोजगार
4. यात्रा-वृत्तांत का क्या अर्थ है?
   A. भ्रमण B. पर्यटन
   C. सफरनामा D. विदेशभ्रमण
5. स्वतंत्र का विलोम शब्द हैः
   A. परतंत्र B. आजाद
   C. गुलामी D. मुक्ति

गद्यांश 3

युवा वर्ग का मस्तिष्क नई-नई बातों की ओर ज्यादा तेज दौड़ता है। उसमें अन्य वर्ग के व्यक्तियों से अधिक आवेश और शक्ति होती है। इस अवस्था में यदि सही शिक्षा और उचित मार्ग-दर्शन न मिले तो यही शक्ति प्रेरणा और निर्माण के स्थान पर विनाश की ओर ले जाती है। बिगड़ने और बनने की यही आयु होती है। दुर्भाग्य से हमारे देश में शिक्षा पद्धति केवल उपाधि बाँटने का काम ही करती है। एक सम्पूर्ण व्यक्तित्वपूर्ण मनुष्य बनाना आज की शिक्षा पद्धति के लिए मुश्किल है।

उपर्युक्त गद्यांश को ध्यानपूर्वक पढ़ें और निम्नलिखित प्रश्नों के उत्तर के लिए सही विकल्प को चुनें।

1. निर्माण का विलोम शब्द क्या हैं?
   A. रचना B. बनावट
   C. विनाश D. सृजन
2. मार्ग-दर्शन का क्या अर्थ है?
   A. उपाधि B. रास्ता
   C. उद्देश्य D. रास्ता दिखलाना
3. शक्ति विनाश की ओर कब अग्रसर होती है?
   A. अधिक आवेश और शक्ति के अभाव में
   B. सही शिक्षा और उचित मार्ग दर्शन के अभाव में
   C. दुर्भाग्यपूर्ण शिक्षा पद्धति के कारण
   D. इनमें से कोई नहीं
4. हमारे देश की शिक्षा पद्धति क्या कार्य करती है?
   A. मार्ग-दर्शन B. शक्ति प्रेरणा
   C. उपाधि देना D. उपर्युक्त सभी
5. दुर्भाग्य का विपरीत शब्द हैः
   A. भाग्य B. सौभाग्य
   C. भाग्यशाली D. भाग्यवान

गद्यांश 4

भिखारी की भाँति गिड़गिड़ाना प्रेम की भाषा नहीं है। यहाँ तक कि मुक्ति के लिए भगवान् की उपासना करना भी अधम उपासना में गिना जाता है। प्रेम कोई पुरस्कार नहीं चाहता। प्रेम सर्वथा प्रेम के लिए ही होता है। भक्त इसलिए प्रेम करता है कि बिना प्रेम किए वह रह ही नहीं सकता। जब तुम किसी मनोहर प्राकृतिक दृश्य को देखकर उस पर मोहित हो जाते हो तो तुम किसी फल की याचना नहीं करते और न वह दृश्य ही तुमसे कुछ माँगता है। फिर भी उस दृश्य का दर्शन तुम्हारे मन को आनंद से भर देता है।

उपर्युक्त गद्यांश को ध्यानपूर्वक पढ़ें और निम्नलिखित प्रश्नों के उत्तर के लिए सही विकल्प का चयन करें:

1. प्रेम का उद्देश्य क्या होता है?
   A. मुक्ति B. उपासना
   C. भक्ति D. प्रेम
2. मुक्ति का अर्थ है:
   A. आजादी B. स्वतंत्रता
   C. परतंत्र D. निर्वाण
3. कैसी उपासना अधम मानी गई है?
   A. प्रेम की उपासना B. भगवान की उपासना
   C. मुक्ति की उपासना D. भक्ति की उपासना
4. मनोहर शब्द हैं:
   A. विशेषण B. संज्ञा
   C. सर्वनाम D. अव्यय
5. प्राकृतिक शब्द का अर्थ है:
   A. ईश्वरीय B. मानव संबंधी
   C. प्रकृति संबंधी D. प्रेम संबंधी

गद्यांश 5

कुछ लोग भाग्यवादी होते हैं और सब-कुछ भाग्य के सहारे छोड़कर कर्म से विरत हो जाते हैं। ऐसे लोग समाज के लिए बोझ हैं। वे कभी कोई बड़ा काम नहीं कर पाते। बड़ी-बड़ी खोज, बड़े-बड़े आविष्कार और बड़े-बड़े निर्माण कार्य कर्मशील लोगों के द्वारा ही संभव हो सके हैं। हम अपनी बुद्धि और प्रतिभा तथा कार्य-क्षमता के बल पर सही मार्ग पर चल सकते हैं, किन्तु बिना कठिन श्रम के अपने लक्ष्य तक नहीं पहुँच सकते। कठिन परिश्रम करने के बाद पाई गई सफलता हमारे मन को अलौकिक आनंद से भर देती है। यदि हम अपने कार्य में अपेक्षित श्रम नहीं करते तो हमारा मन ग्लानि का अनुभव करता है।

उपर्युक्त गद्यांश को ध्यानपूर्वक पढ़ें और निम्नलिखित प्रश्नों के उत्तर के लिए सही विकल्प चुनें:

1. "आविष्कार" शब्द का अर्थ है :
   A. अनुसंधान B. खोज
   C. निर्माण D. विनाश
2. **अलौकिक** शब्द का क्या अर्थ है?
   A. संसारिक B. भौतिक
   C. अमानुषी D. प्राकृतिक
3. सफलता का विलोम क्या है?
   A. सफल B. असफल
   C. सफलतापूर्वक D. असफलता
4. परिश्रम करने और न करने से हमारे जीवन पर क्या प्रभाव पड़ता है?
   A. लोग भाग्यवादी बन जाते हैं
   B. कर्म से विरत हो जाते हैं
   C. मन में ग्लानि का अनुभव होता है
   D. इनमें से कोई नहीं
5. किस प्रकार के लोग समाज के लिए बोझ हैं?
   A. भाग्यवादी B. कर्मठ
   C. परिश्रमी D. प्रतिभाशाली

गद्यांश 6

वैदिक काल से हिमालय के पहाड़ बहुत पवित्र माने जाते हैं। इसमें कोई सन्देह नहीं कि हिमालय के पहाड़ों का दृश्य अति सुन्दर है। उसकी विशालता को देखकर मन में आनन्द और कृतज्ञता की लहर उठती है। ऐसा लगता है कि यह विशाल सृष्टि प्रभु की अनुपम देन है। सारी सृष्टि के प्रति समभाव जाग्रत होता है। वस्तुतः यह दृष्टि कोरी कल्पनात्मक या आध्यात्मिक नहीं है। देखा जाए तो सारे भारत की जलवायु का समतोल करने वाले यह हिमालय के पहाड़ हैं, विशेषकर उत्तरी भारत को वर्षा और पानी देने वाले ये ही हैं। गंगोत्री, यमुनोत्री, बद्री, केदार को तीर्थ माना जाता है, जो व्यर्थ कल्पना नहीं है। उन स्थानों से निकलने वाली पवित्र नदियाँ ही वास्तव में हमारी प्राणदात्री रही हैं।

उपर्युक्त गद्यांश को ध्यानपूर्वक पढ़ें और निम्नलिखित प्रश्नों के उत्तर के लिए सही विकल्प चुनें :

1. हिमालय के पर्वत बहुत पवित्र कब से माने जाते हैं?
   A. पाषाण काल से B. वैदिक काल से
   C. प्राचीन काल से D. आधुनिक काल से
2. विशालता शब्द है :
   A. जातिवाचक B. भाववाचक
   C. विशेषण D. सर्वनाम
3. भारत की जलवायु को समतोल कौन करता है?
   A. गंगोत्री B. यमुनोत्री
   C. केदार D. हिमालय
4. सृष्टि का समानार्थक शब्द है :
   A. सृजन B. रचना
   C. प्रकृति D. संसार
5. प्राणदात्री का क्या अर्थ है?
   A. गंगोत्री
   B. यमुनोत्री
   C. प्राणसंचार करने वाली
   D. समभाव जाग्रत करने वाली

गद्यांश 7

सच्चा मित्र एक शिक्षक की भाँति होता है। जिस प्रकार शिक्षक अपने छात्र को सन्मार्ग की ही ओर अग्रसर करता है, उसी प्रकार एक सच्चा मित्र अपने मित्र को पाप के गर्त में गिरने से बचाता है। मानव-जीवन अधिक रहस्यपूर्ण है। कभी-कभी जीवन में ऐसे अवसर उपस्थित हो जाते हैं, जब मनुष्य की धर्मबुद्धि नष्ट हो जाती है और उसका मन द्रुत गति से पाप की ओर दौड़ता है। ऐसे समय में मित्र का ही उपदेश अधिक कल्याणकारी सिद्ध होता है। मित्र के उपदेश का जितना प्रभाव हृदय पर पड़ता है, उतना और किसी का नहीं पड़ता है।

उपर्युक्त गद्यांश को ध्यानपूर्वक पढ़ें और निम्नलिखित प्रश्नों के उत्तर के लिए सही विकल्प चुनें :

1. सच्चा मित्र किस प्रकार का होता है?

A. विपत्ति में सहायता देने वाला
B. गलत मार्ग पर चलने से रोकने वाला
C. शिक्षक के भाँति
D. धार्मिक गुरु की तरह

2. सन्मार्ग शब्द का विपरीत शब्द है :

A. अग्रसर B. कुमार्ग
C. सुमार्ग D. मार्गदर्शक

3. व्यक्ति को पाप के गर्त्त में गिरने से कौन बचाता है?

A. शिक्षक B. भाई
C. पिता D. सच्चा मित्र

4. मानव पाप की ओर कब दौड़ता है?

A. जब स्वार्थी बन जाता है
B. जब धर्म-बुद्धि नष्ट हो जाती है
C. जब सच्चामित्र साथ छोड़ देता है
D. जब धनवान बन जाता है

5. उपदेश में कौन-सा उपसर्ग है?

A. उ B. उप
C. दे D. देश

गद्यांश 8

सब तरह के भावों को प्रकट करने की योग्यता रखने वाली और निर्दोष होने पर भी यदि कोई भाषा अपना निज का साहित्य नहीं रखती, तो वह रूपवती भिखारिन की तरह कदापि आदरणीय नहीं हो सकती। उनकी शोभा, उसकी बड़ी सम्पन्नता, उसकी मान-मर्यादा उसके साहित्य पर ही अवलम्बित रहती है। उसके विचारों और राजनैतिक स्थितियों का प्रतिबिम्ब देखने को यदि कहीं मिल सकता है, तो उसके ग्रन्थ साहित्य में मिल सकता है। सामाजिक शक्ति या सजीवता, सामाजिक अशक्ति या निर्जीवता और सामाजिक सभ्यता तथा असभ्यता का निर्णायक एकमात्र साहित्य है।

उपर्युक्त गद्यांश को ध्यानपूर्वक पढ़ें और निम्नलिखित प्रश्नों के उत्तर के लिए सही विकल्प चुनें :

1. साहित्य विहीन भाषा किस प्रकार की होती है?

A. आदरणीय B. भिखारिन
C. रूपवती D. रूपवती भिखारिन

2. रूपवती का पुल्लिंग रूप है:

A. रूपवान B. सुन्दर
C. सुन्दरी D. रूपवत

3. भाषा की मान मर्यादा किस पर निर्भर करती है?

A. लिपि पर B. साहित्यकार पर
C. भक्ति पर D. साहित्य पर

4. "सम्पन्नता" शब्द का विपरीत शब्द है:

A. गरीबी B. विपन्न
C. अमीर D. विपन्नता

5. राजनैतिक, सामाजिक शक्ति का दर्शन हमें किसमें मिलता है?

A. समाज B. राज्य
C. नेता D. साहित्य

गद्यांश 9

स्वतंत्र भारत का सम्पूर्ण दायित्व आज विद्यार्थियों के ही ऊपर है, क्योंकि आज जो विद्यार्थी हैं, वे ही कल स्वतंत्र भारत के नागरिक होंगे। भारत की उन्नति, उसका उत्थान उन्हीं की उन्नति और उत्थान पर निर्भर करता है। अतः विद्यार्थियों को चाहिए कि वे अपने भावी जीवन का निर्माण बड़ी सतर्कता और सावधानी के साथ करें। उन्हें प्रत्येक क्षण अपने राष्ट्र, अपने समाज, अपने धर्म, अपनी संस्कृति को अपनी आँखों के सामने रखना चाहिए, जिससे उनके जीवन से राष्ट्र को कुछ बल प्राप्त हो सके। जो विद्यार्थी राष्ट्रीय दृष्टिकोण से अपने जीवन का निर्माण नहीं करते, वे राष्ट्र और समाज के लिए भार-स्वरूप हैं।

उपर्युक्त गद्यांश को ध्यानपूर्वक पढ़ें और निम्नलिखित प्रश्नों के उत्तर के लिए सही विकल्प चुनें :

1. भारत की उन्नति किस पर निर्भर करती है?

A. युवाओं पर B. नेताओं पर
C. साहित्यकारों पर D. विद्यार्थियों पर

2. **उन्नति** का समानार्थक शब्द है :

A. पतन B. उत्थान
C. विकास D. उदय

3. **उत्थान** का विपरीत शब्द है :

A. उदय B. पतन
C. पराजय D. हार

4. किसे अपने जीवन का निर्माण सतर्कता और सावधानी से करना चाहिए?

A. युवाओं को B. नेताओं को
C. बच्चों को D. विद्यार्थियों को

5. धर्म, संस्कृति तथा समाज का रक्षक कौन है?

A. नागरिक B. ग्रामीण
C. विद्यार्थी D. युवा

गद्यांश 10

हास्य एक ऐसा माध्यम है, जो नीरस-जीवन को भी सुखद बना देता है। हास्य का जादू इतना प्रभावशाली होता है कि वह छूत के रोग की तरह चारों ओर फैल जाता है। जिसने कभी हँसना नहीं सीखा, सचमुच उसने जीना नहीं सीखा। सामान्यतः मनुष्य को जीवन में इतनी मुसीबतें झेलनी पड़ती हैं कि वह अपने जीवन को पहाड़ समझने लगता है। ऐसे दूभर जीवन को यदि जीने योग्य बनाना हो तो उसके लिए आवश्यक है कि जीवन में हँसने की गुंजाइश हो। हँसी के सहारे मनुष्य अपने कष्टों को भुलाने का प्रयत्न करता है। संघर्ष, तनाव, व्यस्तता, घुटन यदि आज के जीवन की सहज देन हैं, तो इनसे बचने के लिए यह आवश्यक है कि हम हँसना सीखें।

उपर्युक्त गद्यांश को ध्यानपूर्वक पढ़ें और निम्नलिखित प्रश्नों के उत्तर के लिए सही विकल्प चुनें :

1. नीरस जीवन को कौन सुखद बना देता है?
A. संगीत B. गीत
C. आमोद प्रमोद D. हास्य

2. नीरस का संधि विच्छेद है :
A. नी + रस B. नि + रस
C. निः + रस D. नीः + रस

3. किसका जीवन व्यर्थ है?
A. जिसने रोना नहीं सीखा
B. जिसने हँसना नहीं सीखा
C. जिसने गाना नहीं सीखा
D. इनमें से कोई नहीं

4. हँसना शब्द है :
A. संज्ञा B. विशेषण
C. क्रिया विशेषण D. क्रिया

5. तनाव और घुटन से बचने के लिए क्या करना चाहिए?
A. रोना चाहिए B. गाना चाहिए
C. हँसना चाहिए D. काम करना चाहिए

गद्यांश 11

किसी पुस्तक को पढ़ने में जल्दी नहीं करनी चाहिए, जो कुछ लेखक कहता है, उसे समझने की चेष्टा करनी चाहिए। प्रत्येक शब्द का अर्थ समझने की चेष्टा करनी चाहिए। यदि लेखक योग्य है, तो दूसरी बार वह पुस्तक और अधिक आनन्द देगी और तीसरी बार और अधिक। प्रत्येक बार अध्ययन करने पर आपको नवीन सुन्दर और नए विचार मिलेंगे और उसे आप जितना ही पढ़ेंगे, उतना ही स्नेह करने लगेंगे। सहस्रों व्यक्तियों ने गीता और रामायण तथा कुरान और बाइबिल को बार-बार पढ़ा है। उनका अनुभव है कि प्रत्येक बार उन्हें नई सूझ और नए विचार मिलते गए। कुछ लोग तो इस बात पर गर्व करते हैं कि उन्होंने अमुक पुस्तक को अनेक बार पढ़ा है, उन्हें कंठस्थ हो गई है।

उपर्युक्त गद्यांश को ध्यानपूर्वक पढ़ें और निम्नलिखित प्रश्नों के उत्तर के लिए सही विकल्प चुनें :

1. किसे समझने की चेष्टा करनी चाहिए?
A. पुस्तक B. रामायण
C. महाभारत D. गीता

2. पुस्तक की सजीवता किस पर निर्भर करती है?
A. लेखक B. प्रकाशक
C. पाठक D. चिन्तक

3. आनन्द का विपरीत शब्द है :
A. शोक B. दुख
C. संताप D. खुशी

4. नवीन, सुन्दर और नए विचार हमें कहाँ से प्राप्त होता हैं?
A. पुस्तक को बार-बार पढ़कर
B. सुनकर
C. भाषण से
D. अच्छे व्यक्तियों से मिलने पर

5. कंठस्थ शब्द का शब्दार्थ है :
A. कंठ में स्थित B. सुंदर कंठ
C. जबानी याद D. पंडित जी

गद्यांश 12

अहिंसा परम धर्म है और हिंसा आपद् धर्म। मनुष्य बराबर अहिंसा की ओर चलना चाहता है, किन्तु परिस्थितियाँ उससे हिंसा कराती है, अर्थात् परमधर्म की रक्षा के लिए आदमी बराबर आपद्धर्म से काम लेता रहा है। भारत अपनी सेनाओं को विघटित कर दे, तब भी उसका अपमान उससे अधिक होने वाला नहीं, जितना नेफा में हुआ। किन्तु परमधर्म पर टिकने की सामर्थ्य अगर भारत में नहीं है, तो आपद्धर्म पर उसे आना चाहिए। व्यवहारतः आपद्धर्म परमधर्म का विरोधी नहीं, उसका रक्षक है।

उपर्युक्त गद्यांश को ध्यानपूर्वक पढ़ें और निम्नलिखित प्रश्नों के उत्तर के लिए सही विकल्प चुनें :

1. परमधर्म का विपरीत शब्द है :
A. महान धर्म B. आपद्धर्म
C. सच्चाधर्म D. इनमें से कोई नहीं

2. आपद्धर्म किसे कहा जाता है?
A. अहिंसा B. सत्याग्रह
C. विपत्ति D. हिंसा

3. मानव से हिंसा कौन करवाती है?
A. लोभ B. स्वार्थ
C. द्वेष D. परिस्थितियाँ

4. सामर्थ्य का शब्दार्थ है :
A. संघर्ष B. परिश्रम
C. शक्ति D. पराक्रम

5. परमधर्म की रक्षा कौन करता है?
A. अहिंसा B. हिंसा
C. आपदधर्म D. युद्ध

गद्यांश 13

वर्तमान काल विज्ञापन का युग माना जाता है। समाचार-पत्रों के अतिरिक्त रेडियो और टेलीविजन भी विज्ञापन के सफल साधन हैं। विज्ञापन का मूल उद्देश्य उत्पादक और भोक्ता में सीधा सम्पर्क स्थापित करना होता है। जितना अधिक विज्ञापन किसी पदार्थ का होगा, उतनी ही उसकी लोकप्रियता बढ़ेगी। इन विज्ञापनों पर धन तो अधिक व्यय होता है, पर इनसे बिक्री बढ़ जाती है। ग्राहक जब इन आकर्षक विज्ञापनों को देखता है तो वह उस वस्तु-विशेष के प्रति आकृष्ट होकर उसे खरीदने को बाध्य हो जाता है।

उपर्युक्त गद्यांश को ध्यानपूर्वक पढ़ें और निम्नलिखित प्रश्नों के उत्तर के लिए सही विकल्प चुनें :

1. वर्तमान को किसका युग माना जाता है?
A. फैशन B. विज्ञापन
C. संगीत D. धन

2. उत्पादक तथा भोक्ता के बीच कौन संबंध स्थापित करता है?
A. टेलीविजन B. समाचार-पत्र
C. रेडियो D. विज्ञापन

3. **वर्तमान** शब्द का विपरीत शब्द है :
A. अर्वाचीन B. आधुनिक
C. आजकल D. प्राचीन

4. **आकर्षक** का शब्दार्थ है :
A. विकर्षक B. सुन्दर
C. मनमोहक D. आश्चर्यजनक

5. भोक्ता किस कारण वस्तुओं को खरीदने के लिए बाध्य हो जाता है?
A. विज्ञापन
B. आकर्षक विज्ञापन
C. लोकप्रियता के कारण
D. आसानी से उपलब्ध होना

गद्यांश 14

लगभग दो सौ वर्ष की गुलामी ने भारत के राष्ट्रीय स्वाभिमान को पैरों से रौंद डाला, हमारी संस्कृति को समाप्त कर दिया, हमारे विश्वासों को हिला दिया और हमारे आत्मविश्वास को चकनाचूर कर दिया, किन्तु अपने इस बूढ़े देश से प्यार करने वाले, इसके एक सामान्य संकेत पर प्राण न्यौछावर करने वाले दीवानों का अभाव न था। एक आवाज उठी और देखते ही देखते राष्ट्र का दबा हुआ आत्माभिमान उन्मत्त हो उठा। इतिहास साक्षी है जाने और अनजाने सहस्त्रों देशभक्त स्वतंत्रता की अनमोल निधि को पाने के लिए शहीद हो गए।

उपर्युक्त गद्यांश को ध्यानपूर्वक पढ़ें और निम्नलिखित प्रश्नों के उत्तर के लिए सही विकल्प चुनें :

1. **स्वाभिमान** का संधि विच्छेद है:
A. स्वा + भिमान B. स्वः + अभिमान
C. स्व + अभिमान D. स्वा + अभिमान

2. भारत का राष्ट्रीय स्वाभिमान किस कारण समाप्त हो गया था?
A. लम्बे गुलामी से B. निरंकुश शासक से
C. स्वार्थी मानव से D. धर्म के विनाश से

3. **आत्मविश्वास** का शब्दार्थ है
A. घमण्ड B. गर्व
C. अपने पर विश्वास D. अभिमान

4. भारत की अनमोल निधि को पाने के लिए कौन शहीद हो गए?
A. देशभक्त B. नेता
C. युवा D. युवती

5. **अनमोल निधि** का शब्दार्थ है:
A. अनन्त खजाना B. अमूल्य खजाना
C. बहुमूल्य D. स्वतंत्रता

गद्यांश 15

दुनिया के विभिन्न देशों के विकास पर विहंगम दृष्टि डालने से यह स्पष्ट हो जाता है कि आज जिस देश ने वैज्ञानिक उपलब्धियों के सहारे अपना औद्योगीकरण कर लिया, उसी को उन्नत देश कहा जाता है। जिस देश में औद्योगीकरण का स्तर नीचा है, वह पिछड़ा हुआ देश कहा जाता है। वैज्ञानिक आविष्कारों और औद्योगीकरण के आधार पर ही किसी देश की प्रगति को आँका जाता रहा है। विज्ञान ने मानव को पूरी तरह बदल दिया है।

उपर्युक्त गद्यांश को ध्यानपूर्वक पढ़ें और निम्नलिखित प्रश्नों के उत्तर के लिए सही विकल्प चुनें :

1. **विहंगम दृष्टि** का क्या अर्थ है?
A. एक झलक B. गहन दृष्टि
C. गहन चिन्तन D. इनमें से कोई नहीं

2. **विकास** का विपरीत शब्द है :
A. उत्थान B. उदय
C. पतन D. विनाश

3. **वैज्ञानिक** शब्द में कौन-सा प्रत्यय हैं?
A. निक B. वै
C. ईक D. इक

4. मानव जीवन को किसने बदल दिया है :
A. विकास B. वैज्ञानिक
C. विज्ञान D. उद्योग

5. किसी भी देश की स्तर को किससे नापा जाता है?
A. उपलब्धियों पर B. औद्योगीकरण से
C. वैज्ञानिकों से D. आविष्कारों से

गद्यांश 16

विश्व का वर्तमान उन्नत रूप मानव-श्रम की ही कहानी कह रहा है। गगन चुंबी अट्टालिकाएँ, लंबी-चौड़ी सड़कें, बड़े-बड़े विशाल नगर आकाश में उड़ते वायुयान तथा मानव-जीवन को सुखी और समृद्ध बनाने में योगदान करने वाले ज्ञान-विज्ञान के अनन्त रूप-ये सभी मनुष्य के श्रम का जयघोष करते हैं। स्पष्ट है कि मनुष्य और उसका शरीर विधाता की अनुपम रचना है जो निश्चय ही महान उद्देश्यों की संपूर्ति के

लिए दिया गया है। इस दुर्लभ तन को यदि हम आलस्य, प्रसाद अथवा घटिया कामों में गँवा देते हैं तो उस विधाता के प्रति अन्याय करते हैं।

उपर्युक्त गद्यांश को ध्यानपूर्वक पढ़ें और निम्नलिखित प्रश्नों के उत्तर के लिए सही विकल्प चुनें :

1. विश्व का वर्तमान रूप किसका उद्योतक है?
   A. चिन्तक का B. नेता का
   C. वैज्ञानिक का D. मानव श्रम
2. **गगन चुंबी अट्टालिकाएँ** का अर्थ है :
   A. आकाश में उड़ने वाला B. आकाश को छूने वाला
   C. बहुमंजिली इमारत D. इनमें से कोई नहीं
3. आकाश का समानार्थक शब्द है :
   A. वसुन्धरा B. धरा
   C. पयोद D. गगन
4. **सुखी** का विपरीत शब्द है :
   A. प्रसन्न B. अप्रसन्न
   C. दुखी D. उदासी
5. विधाता की अनुपम रचना क्या है?
   A. मानव शरीर B. समुद्र
   C. वन D. पृथ्वी

गद्यांश 17

हमारे देश में एक ऐसा भी युग था जब नैतिक और आध्यात्मिक विकास ही जीवन का वास्तविक लक्ष्य माना जाता था। अहिंसा की भावना सर्वोपरि थी। आज पूरा जीवन दर्शन ही बदल गया है। सर्वत्र पैसे की हाय-हाय तथा धन का उपार्जन ही मुख्य ध्येय हो गया है, भले ही धन-उपार्जन के तरीके गलत ही क्यों न हों? इन सबका असर मनुष्य के प्रतिदिन के जीवन पर पड़ रहा है। समाज का वातावरण दूषित हो गया है—

बाह्य वातावरण तो दूषित है ही, आज सब जानते हैं पर्यावरण की समस्याएँ कितनी चिन्तनीय हो उठी है। इन सबके कारण मानसिक और शारीरिक तनाव-खिंचाव और व्याधियाँ पैदा हो रही हैं।

उपर्युक्त गद्यांश को ध्यानपूर्वक पढ़ें और निम्नलिखित प्रश्नों के उत्तर के लिए सही विकल्प चुनें :

1. भारत का प्राचीन आदर्श था :
   A. सत्य और अहिंसा B. नैतिक और आध्यात्मिक विकास
   C. धन उपार्जन D. इनमें से कोई नहीं
2. **अहिंसा** का विपरीत शब्द है :
   A. हिंसा B. सत्याग्रह
   C. विनम्रता D. नैतिकता
3. जीवन दर्शन क्यों बदल गया है?
   A. हिंसा के कारण B. अहिंसा के कारण
   C. धन लिप्सा के कारण D. आध्यात्मिक विकास के कारण
4. समाज का वातावरण दूषित क्यों हो गया है?
   A. शारीरिक तनाव B. मानसिक व्याधियाँ
   C. पर्यावरण की समस्याएँ D. धन उपार्जन के गलत तरीके
5. **पर्यावरण** का शब्दार्थ है:
   A. जलमंडल B. स्थलमंडल
   C. वायुमंडल D. वातावरण

उत्तरमाला

गद्यांश 1
1. C 2. D 3. B 4. A 5. D

गद्यांश 2
1. A 2. D 3. D 4. C 5. A

गद्यांश 3
1. C 2. D 3. B 4. C 5. B

गद्यांश 4
1. D 2. D 3. C 4. A 5. C

गद्यांश 5
1. B 2. D 3. D 4. C 5. A

गद्यांश 6
1. B 2. B 3. D 4. A 5. C

गद्यांश 7
1. C 2. B 3. D 4. B 5. B

गद्यांश 8
1. D 2. A 3. D 4. D 5. D

गद्यांश 9
1. D 2. B 3. B 4. D 5. C

गद्यांश 10
1. D 2. C 3. B 4. D 5. C

गद्यांश 11
1. A 2. A 3. A 4. A 5. C

गद्यांश 12
1. B 2. D 3. D 4. C 5. C

गद्यांश 13
1. B 2. D 3. D 4. C 5. B

गद्यांश 14
1. C 2. A 3. C 4. A 5. B

गद्यांश 15
1. A 2. D 3. C 4. C 5. B

गद्यांश 16
1. D 2. C 3. D 4. C 5. A

गद्यांश 17
1. B 2. A 3. C 4. D 5. D

●●●

English Language

1

Comprehension Passages

ENGLISH LANGUAGE COMPREHENSION

The objective of language comprehension test is to ascertain the ability of the candidates to understand the passage properly.

Therefore candidates are required to take notice of the following points:

1. Read the full passage very attentively and intelligently.
2. Try to comprehend the gist of it.
3. Make a mental note of all the important details and points given in the passage.
4. Read the passage for the second time in case you have not been able to understand it satisfactorily.
5. Divide the time proportionately for all the passages.
6. Answer the questions on the basis of facts, as given in the paragraph.
7. Don't waste much time in answering the questions of any one passage.
8. Check all the answers once again, very carefully, to see whether any question is left unanswered by mistake.

MODEL QUESTIONS (FOR PRACTICE)

Directions: *Each of the following passages is followed by five questions. Read the passage carefully and then answer the questions that follow each. For each question, four probable answers A, B, C and D are given. Only one out of these is correct. Choose the correct answer.*

PASSAGE-1

The use of words like 'welcome', 'thank you', 'please', etc., at the right moment reflects a polite nature. The civic sense also lies within the scope of good manners. We should not shout or talk loudly in public places like hospitals and libraries and create disturbance. We should not cheat people or make fun of them. Cleanliness is also necessary. We must not throw the waste on roads and make use of dustbins. We should not harm the public property as it belongs to all of us. While in a queue, discipline should be maintained. We must give fair chance to others.

1. Expressions like 'welcome' 'thank you' and 'please' reflect
   A. happiness B. discipline
   C. civic sense D. polite nature
2. While in a library, we should
   A. respect others B. avoid arguments
   C. talk in low tone D. be courteous
3. A public property belongs to
   A. nobody B. all of us
   C. government D. one who maintains it
4. Discipline is
   A. the rule of proper conduct or action
   B. the rule of road sense
   C. making use of dustbins
   D. forming a queue
5. The most appropriate title for this passage would be
   A. Polite Nature B. Courtesy
   C. Good Manners D. Civic Sense

PASSAGE-2

There is an old proverb 'Early to bed and early to rise makes a man healthy and wise.' I am in the habit of getting up early in the morning and have formed the habit of taking long morning walks in the past two years. It is a light exercise and best for physical fitness. The morning air which is fresh and pure is beneficial for the lungs. The early rays of the rising sun are good for healthy skin. 'Health is wealth' and doctors also recommend morning walk to their patients for gaining sound health and freshness of energy.

1. What is good for lungs?
   A. Sunrays B. Fresh air
   C. Sound sleep D. Light exercise
2. What is a light exercise?
   A. Early to bed B. Early to rise
   C. Morning walk D. Gaining sound health
3. What is good for skin?
   A. Fresh air B. Morning air
   C. Morning walk D. Rising sun's rays
4. What is best for physical fitness?
   A. Light exercise B. Long morning walk
   C. Early to rise D. Fresh and pure air
5. Long morning walk
   A. bring sound sleep
   B. ensures physical fitness
   C. ensures healthy skin
   D. keeps healthy, wealthy and wise

PASSAGE-3

Mahatma Gandhi lived a splendid long life and has set great moral standards before us. He showed to the world the true way to peace. He wished to see India prosper but he became a martyr for the noble cause of Hindu-Muslim unity at the time of partition when a religious fanatic, Ṅathuram Godse, shot him dead on January 30, 1948. His last words were 'Hey Ram'. He lived and died for his country and countryman.

1. Mahatma Gandhi showed the world the true way to
A. prosperity B. love
C. truth D. peace

2. Mahatma Gandhi became a martyr for the noble cause of
A. truth B. non-violence
C. freedom of India D. Hindu-Muslim unity

3. Mahatma Gandhi was shot dead
A. before India achieved independence
B. by a mad man
C. by an intolerant religious person
D. by a non-religious person

4. Mahatma Gandhi set great moral standards. It means
A. he was a great religious teacher
B. he was a great moralist
C. he made India morally stronger
D. moral was everything to him

5. Gandhiji lived and died for his country and countryman. It means
A. he was born in India and died in India
B. he was a patriot
C. he was a great moralist
D. he sacrified his life for India and her people

PASSAGE-4

On one hot day a crow felt very thirsty. He flew from one place to another in search of water. After long hours of labour he found a pitcher. Eagerly, he perched on the mouth of the pitcher. He found that the water was at the bottom of the vessel. He tried his best to dip his beak but did not succeed. He did not know what to do. Suddenly some pebbles lying nearby gave him an idea. One by one he dropped the pebbles with his beak into the pitcher. The level of water slowly came up to the mouth of the pitcher. The crow then drank the water and quenched his thirst.

1. The crow found a pitcher
A. as it flew
B. after many hours of labour
C. full of water
D. which was empty

2. What is the moral of the passage?
A. No pains, no gains
B. God helps those who help themselves.
C. Necessity is the mother of invention
D. Try and try again, you will succeed at last

3. The crow flew from place to place
A. in search of pitcher B. in search of pebbles
C. in search of water D. in search of a vessel

4. The pitcher, the crow found
A. was full of water
B. was dry
C. had little water in the bottom
D. had water up to its mouth

5. As the crow dropped pebbles into the pitcher, what happend?
A. The pitcher broke down
B. The water leaked one of the pitcher
C. The level of water into the pitcher rose up slowly
D. Water level immediately rose to the mouth of the pitcher

PASSAGE-5

Once upon a time a crane and a fox lived in a forest. They were good friend. One day the fox invited the crane to a feast. He made a tasty food and served it before the crane on a plate. The crane could not eat anything because of the long beak. But the fox licked all his food. The crane felt insulted. He decided to teach the fox a lesson. Next day he invited the fox. He prepared the same tasty food and placed it in front of the fox inside a narrow glass. The crane ate easily while the fox looked on. Now, it was the fox's turn to remain hungry.

1. What is the moral of the passage?
A. Beware of the wicked
B. One good turn deserves another
C. Be contented with what you have
D. Tit for tat

2. The crane could not eat tasty food because the
A. food was served in a shallow plate
B. food was very hot
C. food was served in a long jar
D. crane was not hungry

3. The fox had to remain hungry because
A. the food served was not enough in quantity
B. the food was served inside a narrow glass
C. the food served was not tasty
D. the food was all liquid

4. Why did the crane feel insulted?
A. Because he was invited to feast but he could not eat anything
B. Because the food was served in a shallow plate and he could not eat
C. Because the food was too hot
D. Because the fox gulped all the food quickly

5. The crane successfully taught a lesson to the fox when he invited the fox to a feast and served the food
A. in a narrow glass B. in a large plate
C. in a broken plate D. in a long jar

PASSAGE-6

The family set down at the table and began to talk about the summer holidays. They had to decide a place to visit during the vacation. Should they go to their village or to a hill station? The parents preferred the village while the children wished to go the hill station. After few moments of discussion the elders decided to visit both the places. First they shall go to the village for a week and then stay at the hill station for the remaining days. For the first time the family shall be together during the holidays. The children were happy with the holiday plan.

1. The purpose for which the family set down at the table was
- A. to decide a place to visit during the vacation
- B. to educate the children how to carry articles during a visit to a hill station
- C. to decide the date when they should start their journey
- D. to tell the children that they will visit a hill station during this vacation

2. The final plan was to visit
- A. their village
- B. a hill station
- C. their village as well as a hill station
- D. their home town

3. The final decision was made by
- A. the boys B. the girls
- C. the women D. the elders

4. They decided first to go to their village and stay there for
- A. a day B. a week
- C. ten days D. a fortnight

5. Why were children happy?
- A. Because a hill station was included in their holiday plan
- B. Because a visit to their village was excluded from their holiday plan
- C. Because their choice prevailed
- D. Because they were going all alone to the hill station

PASSAGE-7

Once Govind intended to go on pilgrimage with his family. He asked Mirind to accompany. But for his trade's reason, he did not go with him. So Govind thought it safe to leave the box of his jewellery with him, as it was dangerous to leave it in a lone house or take it on the journey. So he went to him with the box. He took him to a lonely place under a tree and handed it over to him. He told Mirind, "Keep it safe with you. I shall return from the journey after six month then I shall take it back from you." Mirind said, "Don't worry, I shall keep it as safe as own."

1. Govind intended to go
- A. for a business trip
- B. to a hill station
- C. on a long journey to a sacred place
- D. to his home town for a long period

2. Why did Govind leave his box of jewellery with Mirind?
- A. Because it was not safe to take the box with him on a long journey
- B. Because Mirind was his fast friend
- C. Because the box was very heavy
- D. Because his house was unsafe

3. Why did Govind take Mirind to a lonely place?
- A. To tell him that the box contained valuable jewellery
- B. So that no third person could see box
- C. To show him what was within the box
- D. To tell him that the box will remain with him

4. Where did Govind hand over the box of jewellery to Mirind?
- A. At Mirind's house
- B. At his own house
- C. In a lonely place
- D. In a lonely place under a tree

5. It was not safe to leave the box in a lone house. Here the word 'lone house' means
- A. a house in a deserted place
- B. a house where none lives
- C. a house without door and lock
- D. a house near the forest

PASSAGE-8

Zahir-ud-din Babar was the first Mughal emperor of India. A descendent of Timur on father's side and Changez Khan on his mother's side, Babar was a brave warrior. After defeating Ibrahim Lodhi in the First Battle of Panipat in 1526 he entered Delhi and soon gained control over Agra. After many more battles with Rajputs he extended his empire over Punjab, Uttar Pradesh and north Bihar. He died at a young age of 48 years in 1530 at his capital Agra without getting much time to consolidate his victories.

1. Zahir-ud-din Babar was the first
- A. Muslim ruler of India B. Mughal ruler of India
- C. Afghan ruler of India D. Turk ruler of India

2. Babar was born in the years
- A. 1480 B. 1482
- C. 1492 D. 1962

3. Babar first occupied
- A. Punjab B. Agra
- C. Delhi D. Panipat

4. Babar was a brave warrior. Here brave warrior means
- A. courageous soldier B. a kind hearted soldier
- C. a clever fighter D. a victorious general

5. Babar extended his empire over Punjab and Uttar Pradesh after many more battles with the
- A. Afghans B. Rajputs
- C. Mughals D. Lodhies

PASSAGE-9

Our National Flag is tricolour. It has three equal horizontal strips. The strip at the top is saffron, in the middle is white and at the bottom is green. The ratio of width to length of the flag is 2 : 3. In the centre of the white strip is a wheel in navy blue. The wheel represents the *chakra.* Its design is similar to the wheel which appears on the abacus of the Sarnath Lion Capital of Ashoka. Its diameter approximates to the width of the white strip. The wheel has 24 spokes. It was adopted by Constituent Assembly on July 22, 1947. We love our national flag. We respect it. We are ready to sacrifice our life to protect its honour. It represents the nation. So it is a symbol of national honour.

1. In our national flag the wheel is located in the centre of
A. saffron strip B. white strip
C. green strip D. blue strip

2. In our national flag which of the strips is at the bottom in our national flag
A. blue C. saffron
B. white D. green

3. Why do we love our national flag?
A. Because it is tricolour
B. Because it has three strips
C. Because it has a wheel at the centre
D. Because it is a symbol of national honour

4. Our national flag was approved by
A. President
B. Lok Sabha
C. Parliament
D. Constituent Assembly

5. The diameter approximates to the width of the white strip. Here the word 'approximates' means
A. is more or less equal
B. is exactly equal
C. is not equal
D. is related

PASSAGE-10

Distance in large cities are long. All the people do not have their own means of transport. They have to depend upon the state or private buses. The number of bus users is very large. Every bus stop is, therefore, crowded. The number of buses is not adequate. Thus people suffer the torture of long wait at the bus stop. Some bus stops are quite orderly. People form queues and get into the buses turn by turn. However, often this order is forgotten and confusion spreads when the bus comes and the law of jungle prevails.

1. Why are the bus stops crowded?
A. Because they are small is size
B. Because the number of passengers is very large
C. Because they are situated at some busy centre
D. Because people do not form queues

2. Long wait at the bus stop is the result of
A. over-crowding in the buses
B. late running of buses
C. shortage of buses
D. slow speed of buses

3. Some bus stops are quite orderly where
A. there is no crowd
B. the number of buses is adequate
C. people do not have to wait for long
D. people form queues and enter the buses one by one

4. Most of the people who travel by buses are
A. non-working
B. do not have their own vehicles
C. have to go a long distance
D. live in large cities

5. What happens when people do not have their own transport?
A. They have to wait for a bus at a bus stop
B. They have to depend upon the state or private buses
C. They have to travel long distances
D. They form queues and get into buses one by one

ANSWERS

Passage	1	2	3	4	5
Passage 1.	D	C	B	A	C
Passage 2.	B	C	D	B	B
Passage 3.	D	D	C	B	D
Passage 4.	B	C	C	C	C
Passage 5.	D	A	B	B	A
Passage 6.	A	C	D	B	A
Passage 7.	C	A	B	D	B
Passage 8.	B	B	C	A	B
Passage 9.	B	D	D	D	A
Passage 10.	B	C	D	B	B

●●●

2

English Grammar

PARTS OF SPEECH

Part of speech	Definition or Function	Examples
Noun	Name of a person, place, animal, quality or thing	Ram, boy, dog pen, sun, Delhi, truth, honesty
Pronoun	Used in place of a noun	I, you, he she, they
Articles & Determiners	Points out indefinite and definite nouns	a, an, the, few, some
Adjective	Describes a noun or pronoun	big, honest, wooden valuable, quiet, deep, soft, narrow
Adverb	Describes a verb, an adjective or another adverb	silently, widely, softly, quietly, very, carefully
Verb	Tells about action or state of something or someone	is, am, was, have, do, like, walk, work, make, throw, tell
Conjuction	Joins words, clauses or sentences	and, but, when, yet, while, else
Preposition	Links a noun or pronoun to another word	at, to, after, on for, under, over, with
Interjection	Expresses sudden feelings or emotions	Ah!, Alas!, oh!, ouch!, hi!, well!, Hurrah!

NOUNS

A word which denotes a person, a thing, an animal or a place is said to be a noun.

There are two noun numbers in English — the *Singular* and the *Plural*.

Singular Numbers : A noun that denotes one person or one thing, is said to be in the Singular number. For example — book, pencil, bird, dog, hen etc. are in singular number.

Plural Number : A noun that denotes more than one person or one thing is said to be in plural number. For example — boys, pens, lions, girls, men etc. are in plural number.

REMEMBER

Singular	*Plural*	*Singular*	*Plural*
Cat	Cats	Book	Books
Pen	Pens	Room	Rooms
Tree	Trees	Bus	Buses
Bush	Bushes	Box	Boxes
Glass	Glasses	Dish	Dishes
Judge	Judges	Tax	Taxes
Watch	Watches	Calf	Calves
Thief	Thieves	Knife	Knives
Scarf	Scarves	Wife	Wives
Leaf	Leaves	Wolf	Wolves
Half	Halves	Monarch	Monarchs
Roof	Roofs	Hoof	Hoofs
Gulf	Gulfs	Staff	Staffs
Radio	Radios	Bamboo	Bamboos
Folio	Folios	Hero	Heroes
Volcano	Volcanoes	Mango	Mangoes
Potato	Potatoes	Photo	Photos
Piano	Pianos	Baby	Babies
Fly	Flies	Country	Countries
Lady	Ladies	Boy	Boys
Monkey	Monkeys	Ox	Oxen
Child	Children	Man	Men
Woman	Women	Tooth	Teeth
Axis	Axes	Basis	Bases
Foot	Feet	Goose	Geese
Englishman	Englishmen	Radius	Radii
Vertex	Vertices	Stimulus	Stimuli

1. Note the plurals of the following nouns:

Singular	*Plural*	*Singular*	*Plural*
copy	copies	cry	cries
baby	babies	duty	duties
body	bodies	country	countries
family	families	diary	diaries
fly	flies	fairy	fairies
city	cities	spy	spies
army	armies	storey	storeys
bay	bays	monkey	monkeys

2. The following nouns do not undergo any change in plural form, in general.

Singular	*Plural*	*Singular*	*Plural*
deer	deer	sheep	sheep
thousand	thousand	pair	pair
hundred	hundred	score	score
dozen	dozen	gross	gross

Note: We can write—

(*a*) thousands of men; (*b*) two pairs of shoes; (*c*) dozens of mangoes; (*d*) scores of people etc. But—

(*a*) two thousand rupees; (*b*) three hundred men; (*c*) five dozen eggs, etc.

3. The following nouns are usually used in plural forms. They take a plural verb after them—

eatables	fetters	surroundings
riches	alms	spectacles
trousers	pants	scissors
premises	thanks	annals
congratulations	goods	shorts
tongs	pains	arms
breeches	(for troubles)	

4. The following are the nouns which are plural in appearance but are usually used in singular number. They are followed by a singular verb—

news	politics	physics
mathematics	economics	ethics
politics	classics	gallows
statistics	athletics	innings
mechanics	summons	mumps

5. Collective nouns often used as plurals—

public	police	cattle
audience	clergy	folk
people	poultry	nation
elite	gentry	glitterati

6. The nouns that are usually used in singular forms—

advice	hair	rice
fuel	alphabet	machinery
offspring	issue	furniture
mischief	stationery	luggage
bedding	information	abuse

7. Material nouns are always used in singular number—

gold	copper	milk
water	silk	wool

Note: They may be used in plural with a different meaning. copper coins (coppers), chains or fetters (irons), cans made of tin (tins).

GENDERS

The difference in sex is denoted by Gender in grammar. The various genders are as follows :

1. **Masculine Gender :** A noun that denotes a male is said to be of the masculine gender, as man, uncle, ox, boy etc.
2. **Feminine Gender :** A noun that denotes a female is said to be of feminine gender, as woman, aunt, princess, cow etc.
3. **Common Gender :** Nouns which denote both males and females are said to be of the common gender, as friend, cousin, person, parent, baby etc.
4. **Neuter Gender :** A noun that denotes the name of object without life is said to be of neuter gender, as file, table, pencil.

REMEMBER

Masculine	*Feminine*
Boy	Girl
Son	Daughter
Brother	Sister
Murderer	Murderess
Sorcerer	Sorceress
Son-in-law	Daughter-in-law
Father-in-law	Mother-in-law
Man-servant	Maid-servant
Land-lord	Land-lady
Bachelor	Maid
Gentleman	Lady
Monk	Nun
Earl	Countess
Lad	Lass
Sir	Madam
Duke	Dutchess
Emperor	Empress
Milk-man	Milk-maid
Pea-cock	Pea-hen
Step-father	Step-mother
Hero	Heroine
Viceroy	Vicerine
Mr.	Mrs.
Governor	Governess
Master	Mistress
Wizard	Witch
Heir	Heiress
Host	Hostess
Lion	Lioness
Mayor	Mayoress
Actor	Actress
Buck	Doe
Colt	Filly
Dog	Bitch
Horse	Mare
Count	Countess
Hunter	Huntress
Prince	Princess
Abbot	Abbess
God	Goddess
Author	Authoress
Ox	Cow
Widower	Widow
Grand-father	Grand-mother
He-goat	She-goat
Milk-man	Milk-woman
Bridegroom	Bride
Tiger	Tigress
Priest	Priestess
Poet	Poetess
Shepherd	Shepherdess
Nephew	Niece
Stag	Hind

PRONOUNS

The repetition of a noun in a sentence or a set of sentences is really boring. So, instead of repeating the noun, we can use a word (for that noun) called the pronoun.
"A pronoun is a word that we use instead of a noun".

Example:
This is *Sachin. He* plays cricket.
Note: *He* is the pronoun used in place of *Sachin.*

Kinds of Pronouns

1. **Personal pronouns :** A pronoun which is used instead of the name of a person is known as a 'Personal Pronoun'. A list of the 'Personal pronouns' is listed below :
   I, my, mine, me, we (First Person)
   You, your, yours (Second Person)
   He, his, him, she, her, hers, it, its, they, their, theirs, them (Third Person)
2. **Demonstrative, Indefinite and Distributive Pronouns :**
   (a) Demonstrative Pronouns : Pronouns used to point out the objects to which they refer are called Demonstrative Pronouns.
   Examples :
   (i) *This* is a present from my uncle.
   (ii) *These* are merely excuses.
   (iii) Bembay mangoes are better than *those* of Bangaluru.
   (b) Indefinite Pronouns : All pronouns which refer to persons or things in a general way and do not refer to any particular person or thing are called Indefinite Pronouns.
   Examples :
   (i) *Somebody* has stolen my watch.
   (ii) *Few* escaped unhurt.
   (iii) Did you ask *anybody* to come?
   (c) Distributive Pronouns : Each, either, neither are called distributive pronouns because they refer to persons or things one at a time. For this reason they are always singular and followed by the verb in singular.
   Examples :
   (i) *Each* of the men received a reward.
   (ii) *These* men received *each* a reward.
   (iii) *Either* of you can go.
3. **Relative Pronouns :** A relative pronoun refers or relates to some noun going before, which is called its Antecedent.
   Examples :
   (i) I met Hari *who* used to live here.
   (ii) I have found the pen *which* I had lost.
   (iii) Here is the book *that* you lent me.
4. **Interrogative Pronouns :** These pronouns, are used for asking questions.
   Examples :
   (i) *Whose* book is this?
   (ii) *What* will all the neighbours say?
   (iii) *Which* do you prefer, tea or coffee?

Note : Interrogative pronouns can also be used in asking indirect questions. Consider the following examples :
(i) I asked *who* was speaking.
(ii) Tell me *what* you have done.
(iii) Say *which* you would like best.

Behaviour of the Pronouns

1. If three pronouns are used together in the same sentence they are arranged in the following order :

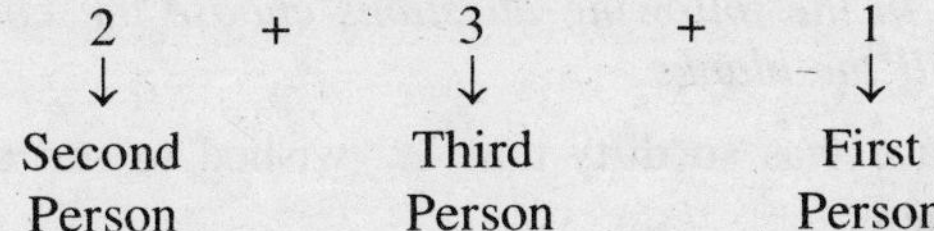

Examples :
I, you and he must help *that* poor man. (Incorrect)
You, he and I must help *that* poor man. Correct)

2. When two or more singular nouns are joined by and, the pronoun used for them should be plural.
   Examples :
   Mohan and Sohan are friends. *They* play football. *They* live at Lajpat Nagar.
3. But if these nouns joined by and refer to the same person or thing, the pronoun used should be singular.
   Examples :
   (i) Delhi, the beautiful city and the capital of India, is famous for *its* historical monuments.
   (ii) The manager and owner of the firm expressed *his* views on the demands of the workers.
4. When two nouns are used with as well as, the pronoun agrees with the first subject.
   Examples :
   (a) Mohan as well as his friends is doing *his* work.
   (b) The students as well as their teachers are doing *their* work.
5. When two singular nouns joined by 'and' are preceded by *each* or *every,* the pronoun used must be singular and should agree in gender with the second noun.
   Examples :
   (a) Every man and every woman will do *her* best for the nation.
   (b) Each boy and each girl went to *her* house.
6. When two nouns are joined by using 'with', the pronoun agrees with the noun coming before 'with'.
   Examples :
   (a) The boy with *his* parents has gone to see a movie.
   (b) The children with *their* parents have gone to picnic.
7. When two different nouns are joined by either......... or; neither .... nor, the pronoun is used according to the number and gender of the second noun.

Examples :

(a) Either your sister or you have done *your* work.

(b) Neither the students nor the teacher was in *his* class.

8. The pronoun coming after '*than*' must be in the same case as that coming before '*than*'.

Examples :

(a) She plays better than *me*. (Incorrect)
She plays better than *I*. (Correct)

(b) His elder brother is more intelligent than *him*. (Incorrect)
His elder brother is more intelligent than *he*. (Correct)

9. 'Many a' always takes a singular pronoun and singular verb.

Example :

Many a soldier has met *his* death in the battle field.

10. 'Who', 'Whose', 'Whom' are used only for persons.

Examples :

(a) *Who* is knocking at the door?

(b) *Whose* pen is this?

(c) *What* do you want?

11. 'Which' is used for things.

Example : *Which* game do you like?

MULTIPLE CHOICE QUESTIONS

Directions: *In the following questions choose the correct options to fill the blanks.*

1. The place was so dirty that ..... wished to run away from there.
A. everybody B. anybody
C. few D. some

2. ..... was there to help me.
A. Somebody B. Anything
C. Anybody D. Nobody

3. Is there ...... to eat?
A. some B. something
C. any D. few

4. ..... of the students were making a great noise.
A. Anyone B. Somebody
C. Many D. Nobody

5. ..... of the students can solve this sum.
A. Someone B. Anybody
C. Somebody D. None

6. ...... of us should try our best to make India a heaven.
A. Any B. Somebody
C. Anybody D. All

7. ...... of us do not know the real meaning of our lives.
A. Any B. Something
C. Several D. Many

8. My .... black.
A. hairs are B. hair is
C. hairs shall D. hair will

9. She saw two .... on the last Sunday.
A. thiefs B. theifs
C. thieves D. theives

10. My sister is a ....
A. bacheloress B. bachelor
C. unmaried D. spinster

11. One is supposed to do ....
A. our duty B. their duty
C. one's duty D. his duty

12. Take anything .... you want.
A. that B. which
C. than D. then

13. I cannot tolerate ....
A. separated you B. your separation
C. separation from you D. you separated

14. He is .... faithful partner.
A. Yours B. You
C. Your D. Your's

15. Ajay is more smart than ....
A. her B. hers
C. herself D. she

16. Vivek works harder than ....
A. me B. I
C. her D. his

17. They should help ....
A. the poor people B. the poor
C. the poor persons D. the poor peoples

18. .... are mad.
A. All his sons B. His all sons
C. Sons all his D. All sons his

19. The poor fellow .... to fate.
A. resigned B. resigned himself
C. resigned itself D. resigned themselves

20. Nobody will help you but ....
A. I B. me
C. ours D. his

21. It is a good chance, You must avail ...... this opportunity.
A. of B. yourself of
C. for D. from

22. The person who is elected .... my relative.
A. is B. he is
C. his D. him

23. He made ....
A. yours mention B. mention of you
C. mention for you D. mention about you

24. .... I know, he is quite faithful.
A. As far as B. So far as
C. So far this D. So far so

25. It is a duty of a person to take .... for his family.
A. pain B. pains
C. pain-killers D. pained

26. She does not love .... husband.
A. his B. her
C. its D. their

27. Let .... work together.
A. him and me B. he and I
C. he and him D. I and me

28. Copper, Silver and Gold ....
A. each will do B. either will do
C. any one will do D. any will do

29. Jessica and Roma are very irregular .... habits.
A. in her B. in their
C. in its D. in every

30. One likes to enjoy .... who was a great poet.
A. The sonnets of Shakespeare
B. Shakespeare's sonnets
C. Sonnets
D. Shakespeare

ANSWERS

1	2	3	4	5	6	7	8	9	10
A	D	B	C	D	D	D	B	C	D
11	12	13	14	15	16	17	18	19	20
C	A	C	C	D	B	B	A	B	B
21	22	23	24	25	26	27	28	29	30
B	A	B	A	B	B	A	C	B	A

ARTICLES

The family of the articles has only three members. They are : A, An and The. However, they fall under two groups :
(a) Definite Article *(b)* Indefinite Article
'The' is known as definite article whereas 'a' and 'an' are known as indefinite articles.

Use of the Definite Article 'The'

'The' is used before

1. The superlative degree :
He is the ablest man of the town.
(ablest is a superlative degree)
2. The name of states, countries etc. having a descriptive name :
(i) The J & K is a small state. (J & K is a descriptive name)
(ii) He lives in the U.S.A. (U.S.A. is a descriptive name)
(But the Delhi and the America are wrong because neither Delhi nor America is a descriptive name)
3. The names of the scriptures :
The Gita is a holy book. (Gita is a scripture)
4. Name of newspapers :
The Tribune is published from Chandigarh.
5. Name of rivers, canals, seas, oceans, bays, gulfs, groups of islands etc. :
(i) The Ganga is a holy river.
(ii) The Indian Ocean is the deepest ocean.
(iii) The Persian Gulf is a narrow gulf.
6. The name of famous buildings :
The Taj is one of the best buildings in India.
7. The names of nationals, sects and communities:
(i) The English defeated the Germans in the World War.
(ii) The rich should help the poor.
(iii) The Hindus believe in the caste system.
8. Proper nouns used as common nouns :
(i) Kalidas is the Shakespeare of India.
(ii) Delhi is the London of India.
9. Famous historical events :
The Industrial Revolution changed the face of England.
10. The directions and the celestial bodies:
The sun rises in the east.
11. Titles : Akbar, the Great was loved by his subjects.

Do not use 'the'

1. Before languages :
The English is an international language. (Incorrect)
English is an international language. (Correct)
2. Before the names of games :
The hockey is a popular game. (Incorrect)
Hockey is a popular game. (Correct)

Use of the Indefinite Articles 'A' and 'An'

'A' is used before :

1. All singular common nouns beginning with a consonant :
(i) A boy sings a song.
(ii) A black and a white cow were grazing in the field.
2. If a word begins with a vowel but gives the sound of a consonant, 'a' should be used before it :
(i) He was helped in his work by a European.
(ii) He is a one-eyed man.
(iii) It is a useful work.

'An' is used as follows :

1. All singular common nouns beginning with a vowel (*i.e.*, a, e, i, o, u) :
   (i) He is an artist. (ii) He is an old man. (iii) I intend to buy an umbrella.
2. If a word starts with a consonant but gives the sound of a vowel, "an" should be used before it :
   (i) Brutus is an honourable man.
   (ii) He is an honour to his profession.
   (iii) He is an L.L.B.

Demonstratives, that, these and those

1. The demonstrative adjectives and pronouns are for objects nearby the speaker:
   this (singular) those (plural)
   and for objects far away from the speaker.
   That (singular) those (plural)
2. Demonstratives are the only adjectives that agree in number with their nouns.
   That hat is nice.
   Those hats are nice.
3. When there is the idea of selection, the pronoun "one" (or "ones") often follows the demonstrative.
   I want a book. I'll get this (one).
   If the demonstrative is followed by an adjective, "one"(or "ones") must be used.
   I want a book. I'll get this big one.

MULTIPLE CHOICE QUESTIONS

Directions: *In the following questions choose the correct options to fill the blanks.*

1. .... will have to be paid for this material.
A. Half rupee B. Half a rupee
C. A half rupee D. An half rupee

2. .... is taking keen interest in India.
A. The USA B. USA
C. An USA D. A USA

3. Only .... can save our country.
A. the Hitler B. a Hitler
C. Hitler D. an Hitler

4. I can run for ....
A. hundred miles B. the hundred miles
C. a hundred miles D. an hundred miles.

5. .... man-eater has been killed.
A. The B. A
C. An D. Either A or B

6. What .... fine idea!
A. the B. an
C. a D. No article

7. .... earth is moving around the sun.
A. An B. A
C. The D. No article

8. This is .... first example while I got.
A. the B. a
C. an D. No article

9. This is .... house which was built during earthquake.
A. a B. an
C. the D. No article

10. .... America is a rich country.
A. The B. An
C. A D. No article

11. .... U.S.A. is a developed country.
A. A B. An
C. The D. No article

12. .... Bible is a holy book.
A. A B. The
C. An D. No article

13. .... rich should help the poor.
A. The B. A
C. An D. No article

14. .... Gold is a costly metal.
A. The B. A
C. An D. No article

15. Kalidas is .... Shakespeare of India.
A. a B. an
C. the D. No article

16. I cannot do .... difficult work.
A. a such B. the such
C. such the D. such a

17. How foolish .... plan it is!
A. a B. an
C. the D. No article

18. An ink is .... useful article.
A. an B. a
C. the D. No article

19. There are .... husband and wife.
A. a B. an
C. the D. No article

20. He is learning .... French
A. the B. a
C. an D. No article

ANSWERS

1	2	3	4	5	6	7	8	9	10
B	A	B	C	D	C	C	A	C	D
11	**12**	**13**	**14**	**15**	**16**	**17**	**18**	**19**	**20**
C	B	A	D	C	D	A	B	D	D

ADJECTIVES & ADVERBS

An Adjective is a word which adds something to the meaning of a noun or a pronoun.

Mridula is an *intelligent* girl. He has a *black* goat.
He is a *brilliant* student. She is a *clever* girl.
It is a *beautiful* picture.

In the sentences given above, the words in italics are adjectives.

An Adverb is a word which qualifies the meaning of a Verb, an Adjective or another Adverb.

(*i*) He talks *slowly*.
(*ii*) He is a *very* good student.
(*iii*) He talks *very* slowly.

In sentence (*i*), *slowly* qualifies the verb *talks*.
In sentence (*ii*), *very* qualifies the adjective *good*.
In sentence (*iii*), *very* qualifies the adverb *slowly*.

Adjectives have three degrees of comparison :

1. **Positive Degree :** It expresses the common form of an adjective.
   Example :
   Ram is a *tall* boy.
   In the above sentence *tall* is an adjective and expresses the common form.
2. **Comparative Degree :** It expresses the more of the same form.
   Example :
   Ram is *taller* than Mahesh.
   In the above sentence *taller* is an adjective that expresses the more of the common form of the adjective *tall*.

"When and How to Use" Comparative Degree?

(a) Comparative Degree is used when two persons or two groups of persons or things are compared.
Examples :
(a) He is *wiser* than his younger brother.
(b) This glass is *cleaner* than the other.

(b) When two different qualities in the same person are compared, more is used instead of 'er' to form the comparative. The formula used in this case should be :
More + Positive Degree
She is *fairer* than polite. (Incorrect)
She is *more fair* than polite. (Correct)

(c) When selection of one out of two persons or things is meant, the degree of comparison is followed by of and *the* is used before it.
Example :
Zia is abler of *the* two sisters.

(d) If two comparatives are used in the same sentence to impress upon an idea, both should be preceded by the definite article.
Examples :
(i) The higher you go, the cooler it is.
(ii) The more we get, the more we desire.

(e) When one person or thing is compared with another of the same kind, other is used after the comparative degree. In such sentences other is normally preceded by any or all.
Examples :
(i) Kalidas is greater than any dramatist. (Incorrect)
Kalidas is greater than any other dramatist. (Correct)
(ii) Lead is heavier than all metals. (Incorrect)
Lead is heavier than all other metals. (Correct)

(f) Senior, junior, superior, inferior, prior, anterior (earlier than) and posterior (later than) are always followed by 'to'.
Examples :
(i) Ram is senior *to* Mohan by three years.
(ii) That pen is inferior *to* that.
(iii) He is junior *to* me in rank.
(iv) This event was posterior *to* that.

Note: Never use *than* after the above mentioned adjectives.

Important Information

(a) 'Preferable' is also used as an adjective of the comparative degree. As such, it is always followed by *to* and not *a*.
Death is preferable than dishonour. (Incorrect)
Death is preferable *to* dishonour. (Correct)

(b) To intensify the Degree of comparison, we use *far* or *much* before the comparative.
Examples :
(i) This book is *far* better than that.
(ii) His performance was *much* better than Mohan's.
Warning : Always avoid the use of double comparatives.
Don't say : Ram is more cleverer than his younger brother.
Say: Ram is cleverer than his younger brother.

3. **Superlative Degree :** It expresses the most of the common form of an adjective.
   Example :
   He is the ablest man of the town.

How and when to use the Superlative Degree?

(a) The Superlative Degree is used when more than two persons or things are compared.

(b) The Superlative Degree is generally preceded by 'the' and followed by 'of' in most of the cases or otherwise.

(c) When an adjective of the superlative degree is preceded by a Possessive Adjective or a Noun in the Possessive case, 'the' should not be used before it.
Example :
Which is Kalidas' best play?

It will be a blunder to use 'the' before the Superlative Degree in such cases.

Don't say : Which is Kalidas' the best play.

(d) To intensify the degree of comparison, *by far* is used before the superlative degree.

Example :

India is *by far* the most beautiful country of the world.

Note: Always avoid the use of double superlatives.

Don't say : He is the most strongest boy in the class.

Say : He is the strongest boy in the class.

Use of some Important Adjectives

1. (a) '**Some**' is used as follows :
   (i) With countable nouns where it means— a little, a small quantity.
   (ii) In a question which shows some request.

   Examples :
   (i) There is some water in the bottle.
   (ii) Some of the students were absent yesterday.
   (iii) Will you have some milk?
   (iv) Will you buy some fruit for me?

   (b) **'Any'** is used as follows :
   (i) In negative sentences.
   (ii) In interrogative sentences.
   (iii) After 'Hardly', 'Scarcely' and 'Barely'.
   (iv) After 'If'.

   Examples :
   (i) There is not any sugar in the pot.
   (ii) We haven't any rice in the house.
   (iii) I have hardly any money.
   (iv) There are scarcely any plants in this field.
   (v) If there is any danger, blow the whistle.

2. (a) **Older :** Older (and oldest) are used for persons animals and things. But 'Older' and 'Oldest' refer to the persons who do not belong to the same family.

   Examples :
   (i) Radha is older than Shyama.
   (ii) John is the oldest member of the staff.
   'Older' and 'Oldest' refer to the persons who do not belong to the same family.

   (b) **Elder** (and **eldest**) are used in respect of the members of the same family like sons, daughters, brothers, sisters.

   Examples :
   (i) My elder sister is a lecturer.
   (ii) Meenakshi is the eldest of the three sisters.

   Note :
   (i) 'Elder' is not followed by 'than'.
   (ii) 'Elder' and 'Eldest' cannot be used for things.

3. (a) **'Few'** is negative and is the opposite of 'Many'. It means 'not many'.
   (b) **'A few'** is positive and means 'some at least'. It is the opposite of 'None'.
   (c) **'The few'** means 'minority' and suggests 'whether there is'.

   Examples :
   (i) We have few holidays in school.
   (ii) Only a few boys will fail in the examination.
   (iii) The few poems that he wrote are very popular.

4. (a) **Further** means 'something additional'.
   (b) **Farther** means 'a greater distance'.

   Examples :
   (i) Further discussion will be held in the office of the principal.
   (ii) Amritsar is farther from Delhi than Ambala.

5. (a) **Little** is negative. It means, 'not much', or 'hardly any'.
   (b) **A little** is positive. It means 'some quantity'.
   (c) **The little** denotes quantity. It means, 'not much but all that is, or whatever quantity there is'.

   Examples :
   (i) There is little hope of his success.
   (ii) He knows a little of everything.
   (iii) I have spent the little money I had.
   (iv) The little knowledge of shoe-making proved very useful to me.

6. (a) '**Much**' expresses 'quantity'.
   (b) '**Many**' expresses 'number'.
   (c) **'Many a'**—'Singular noun' and 'Singular verb' are used with 'many a'.

   Examples :
   (i) There is not *much* water in the jug.
   (ii) *Many* boys are absent today.
   (iii) *Many* a battle has been fought on the soil of India.

7. (a) '**Less**' denotes 'in a small degree'.
   (b) '**Fewer**' denotes 'number'.

   Examples :
   (i) He devotes less time to his studies.
   (ii) There are no fewer than ten chairs in this room.

8. (a) '**Each**' is used for a single number of 'two persons' or 'things'.
   (b) '**Every**' is used for a single number of 'many persons' or 'things'.

   Examples :
   (i) Each boy must take part in games.
   (ii) There are only two poets. Each poet recited his poem.
   (iii) Every man dies in this world.
   (iv) Every man is expected to do his duty.

9. (a) '**Either**' means one of the two or both.
   (b) '**Neither**' is negative of the either.

   Examples :
   (i) You may buy either of these two chairs.
   (ii) Neither of them could speak on the stage.

10. (a) '**Later**' expresses 'late in time'.
    (b) '**Latter**' means 'second in position or order'.

    Examples :
    (i) My father reached later than I expected.
    (ii) The latter position was better than the former.

Use of some Important Adverbs

1. (a) Also, too, enough:
   (i) He taught English. Also, he edited the school magazine
   (ii) He is a writer and also he is a painter.
   (iii) He is too obstinate to listen to any reason.
   (iv) This is too difficult a piece for the junior students.
   (v) Sarla was kind enough to help the poor.
   (vi) He is brave enough to help the truth.
   Note: 'Too' is used in a negative sense, but enough is used in a positive sense.

(b) Fairly and rather: Both suggest the meaning 'moderately'. But, mainly 'fairly' is used with the words that denote a positive meaning and rather is used with the words that denote a negative meaning:
   (i) Rita did fairly well in that competition, but her performance was rather poor in sports.
   (ii) Mona is fairly rich, but she is rather stingy.
   Note: 'Rather' can also be used in a positive sense.
   (i) This is a rather interesting job.
   (ii) That boy is rather smart.

(c) Hardly, barely, scarcely: These words mostly convey the negative suggestions and are almost similar.
   (i) I have hardly any strength now.
   (ii) There was barely any supply to the township,
   (iii) There were scarcely a hundred guests present.
   Note: With slight variance in the meaning, the words given above convey the idea of 'very little', 'not enough', 'lack of quantity and number'.

(d) Yet, Still: These adverbs can often be used to connect the sentence units:
   (i) He has been defeated many times in the contest; still he wants to be a competitor.
   (ii) Mona was sick; yet she went on doing her work.

(e) Alone:
   (i) He alone (none else) is capable of handling that fire,
   (ii) He hunted all alone in the forest. (not in any company)

Special Note:

(a) Apart from their conventional positions the adverbs might be used in different positions with different meanings and angles.
   (i) He had only four books.
   (ii) John only contacted his friend in need.
   (iii) He greeted me only.
   (iv) Only he greeted me there.

(b) Inversion: Some adverbs can be inverted *i.e.* placed in the beginning of the sentence and then be followed by an interrogative form. The most common of these adverb are: so, seldom, never, nowhere, under no circumstances, hardly, scarcely etc.
   (i) So big was the bus that it could not enter the narrow lane.
   (ii) Hardly had he reached the station when he received the message.

MULTIPLE CHOICE QUESTIONS

Directions: *In the following questions choose the correct options to fill the blanks.*

1. The girl whom you met is the .... sister of Ravi.
A. eldest B. elder
C. older D. oldest

2. The historical place is ....
A. seeing worth B. worthy of seeing
C. worth seeing D. worthy seeing

3. These flowers smell ....
A. sweet B. sweetly
C. more sweetly D. sweetest

4. .... aspirant cannot pass the entrance examination.
A. Each B. Every
C. All D. No

5. Harivansh Rai .... second Shakespeare.
A. is a B. is
C. is the D. is an

6. .... student in the class got prizes.
A. Each and every B. Every and each
C. Every D. Never

7. It is .... picture than the one we saw last Monday.
A. interesting B. much interesting
C. more interesting D. most interesting

8. She is clever ....
A. that her mother is B. as her mother is
C. to her mother is D. than her mother is

9. They will get ....
A. Red, green and black paper
B. Red, green black paper
C. Red and green and black paper
D. Red green black paper

10. Health is .... wealth.
A. preferable to B. more preferable than
C. more preferable to D. most preferable then

11. .... water that was in the jug evaporated.
A. Little B. The little
C. Small D. A small

12. He has not sung .... songs.
A. much B. most
C. more D. many

13. Srishti has searched .... office.
A. whole the B. the whole
C. a whole D. some whole

14. Premchand was ...... best and ...... famous writer.
A. a, the most B. the, a most
C. the, more D. the, the most

15. William Shakespeare is famous as ....
A. a poet and a dramatist
B. a poet and dramatist
C. the poet and the dramatist
D. a poet and the dramatist

16. What does .... leader suggest?
A. other B. another
C. others D. anothers

17. He .... money.
A. has few B. have few
C. has little D. have little

18. The .... boys are rewarded.
A. first two B. two first
C. firsts two D. two's first

19. He is .... brave.
A. stronger than
B. stronger then
C. more strong then
D. more strong than

20. No sooner said ....
A. so done B. and done
C. then done D. but done

21. She returned .... than I had thought.
A. quickly B. more quicker
C. more quickly D. quicker

22. He is .... foolish person.
A. rather the B. a rather
C. rather a D. rather

23. This pen .... rupees.
A. costs twenty B. twenty costs only
C. costs only twenty D. only costs twenty

24. It is .... pride.
A. nothing else but B. nothing else than
C. else nothing than D. but

25. This tea is .... to drink.
A. too hot B. very hot
C. enough hot D. much hot

ANSWERS

1	2	3	4	5	6	7	8	9	10
A	C	A	B	A	C	C	C	A	A
11	12	13	14	15	16	17	18	19	20
B	D	B	D	B	B	C	A	D	C
21	22	23	24	25					
C	C	C	A	A					

DETERMINERS

Determiners are actually Adjectives. They are always followed by nouns.

Determiners are of the following kinds:

1. **Demonstrative Determiners :** this, that, these, those
2. **Possessive Determiners :** my, our, your, his, her, its, their
3. **Quantitative Determiners :** some, any, much, enough, sufficient, whole, a little, the little, little, all, both
4. **Numerical Determiners:** a few, some, few, the few, any, several, many, no, etc.
   One, two, three ... (Cardinals)
   First, second, third ... (Ordinals)
5. **Distributive Determiners:** either, neither
6. **Articles: Indefinite:** a, an, **Definite:** the

MULTIPLE CHOICE QUESTIONS

Directions: *In the following questions choose the correct options to fill the blanks.*

1. Give me .... rice.
A. some B. few
C. a few D. any

2. ...... sheep grazing on the slope of the hill had gone away.
A. Any B. The few
C. This D. Much

3. Have you got .... magazines to read?
A. all B. much
C. some D. little

4. I have .... money that I want to spend on shares.
A. any B. much
C. less D. some

5. There is .... owl on the branch of the tree.
A. a B. the
C. an D. some

6. My brother is .... MBA.
A. a B. an
C. the D. any

7. Have you got .... cheese?
A. some B. many
C. a few D. few

8. No, I have not got .... cheese.
A. many B. few
C. any D. some

9. There is only .... milk left in the bottle.
A. enough B. few
C. much D. a little

10. There is .... hope of his recovery.
A. any B. little
C. many D. few

11. .... dogs were barking at the strangers.
A. Some B. Any
C. Much D. Less

12. The girl bought her father .... juice.
A. few B. some
C. any D. many

13. You should take .... honey everyday.
A. any B. many
C. a little D. a few

14. .... boy was punished by the teacher.
A. Either B. All
C. Any D. Many

15. .... girl was asked to join the army.
A. None B. Neither
C. All D. Any

16. .... water in the jug has been drunk by Mohan.
A. The little B. The few
C. A few D. Few

17. I shall play .... piano at the party.
A. some B. any
C. the D. few

18. .... labourers were found dead in the mine.
A. Any B. Fewer
C. Many D. Less

19. Could I borrow .... umbrella?
A. our B. your
C. yours D. my

20. My brother is standing in the .... row.
A. any B. many
C. some D. first

ANSWERS

1	2	3	4	5	6	7	8	9	10
A	B	C	D	C	B	A	C	D	B
11	**12**	**13**	**14**	**15**	**16**	**17**	**18**	**19**	**20**
A	B	C	A	B	A	C	C	B	D

THE VERB

A Verb is a word that tells something about the action or state of or happenning to a person or thing.

A Verb tells the following:

1. What a person or thing does.
Sachin goes to school daily.
The bell *rang* loudly.
Many birds fly in the sky.
She *sang* a song.

2. What a person or thing is.
India *is* the biggest democracy in the world.
Ram Mehar *is* very rich.
They *are* happy.

3. What is done to a person or thing.
You *are liked* by all.
Two thieves *were arrested.*
Four students *were punished* by the teacher.

4. What happens to a person or thing.
His maternal uncle *died* last week.
Two ships *sank* yesterday.
Leaves *turn* yellow in autumn.

5. What a person or thing has, had, and so on.
I *have* a new car.
He *had* a scooter last year.
He *has* several cows and goats.

It goes without saying that a verb is the most important part of a sentence. No sentence is complete without a Verb.

Important Information

1. If two or more singular nouns are joined by 'and' the verb used will be plural.
Example:
(i) He and I were going to the market.
(ii) Ram and Mohan are friends.

2. If two singular nouns joined by 'and' points out to the same thing or person, the verb used must be singular.
Example:
(i) Rice and curry is the favourite food of the Punjabis.
(ii) The Collector and District Magistrate is away.

3. In case two subjects are joined by 'as well as' the verb agrees with the first subject.
Example :
(i) Kanta as well as her children is playing.
(ii) Children as well as their mother are playing.
In the case of first sentence the verb (is) agrees with Kanta and in the case of second sentence the verb (are) agrees with the children.

4. 'Neither', 'Either', 'Every', 'Each', 'Everyone', and 'Many a' are followed by a singular verb.
Example :
(i) Either of the plans is to be adopted.
(ii) Neither of the two brothers is sure to pass.
(iii) Every student is expected to be obedient.
(iv) Everyone of them desires this.
(v) Many a person is drowned in the sea.

5. If two subjects are joined by 'Either .... or' / 'Neither .... nor', the verb agrees with the subject near to it.

Example :

(i) Either my brother or I am to do this work.

(ii) Neither he nor they are prepared to do this work.

6. 'A great many' is always followed by a 'plural noun' and a 'plural verb'. For example :

A great many students have been declared successful.

7. Similarly if two subjects are joined by 'with', 'together with'', 'no less than', in addition to 'and not', etc. the verb agrees with the first subject.

Example :

(i) The boy with his parents has arrived.

(ii) He, no less than I, is to blame.

8. Nouns, plural in form, but singular in meaning, take a singular verb.

Example :

This news was broadcast from television yesterday.

MULTIPLE CHOICE QUESTIONS

Directions: *In the following questions choose the correct options to fill the blanks.*

1. The bus with all its passengers .... lost.
A. were B. was
C. are D. would

2. You as well as I .... responsible for this work.
A. am B. are
C. was D. is

3. Raghava like all his companions .... a spoiled child.
A. are B. were
C. is D. will be

4. Pen and ink .... required for me.
A. are B. were
C. is D. has required

5. Every girl and every boy .... attended the seminar.
A. have B. has
C. is D. are

6. Not only she but all her sisters ...... been married.
A. has B. have
C. is D. are

7. There .... nothing but miseries in life.
A. is B. are
C. were D. will be

8. Neither prose nor poem .... given.
A. were B. was
C. has D. have

9. Either he or I .... wrong.
A. is B. are
C. am D. were

10. Either Sulekha or Rekha .... coming here.
A. are B. is
C. were D. have

11. .... the child or his parents to blame?
A. Is B. Are
C. Were D. Has

12. You and I .... neighbours.
A. am B. are
C. was D. has

13. The house with all its belongings ..... sold away.
A. were B. are
C. was D. must

14. Either water or juice .... required.
A. is B. are
C. were D. has

15. There were not as many tables as .... required.
A. was B. were
C. is D. are

16. They each .... a book.
A. have B. are
C. has D. is

17. He and I .... class friends.
A. is B. am
C. was D. are

18. She as well as I .... guilty.
A. is B. are
C. am D. must be

19. Purushottam .... not read more on this chapter.
A. needs
B. has been need
C. need
D. had been need

20. He came .... to his aunt.
A. run B. running
C. to run D. in run

ANSWERS

1	2	3	4	5	6	7	8	9	10
B	B	C	C	B	B	A	B	C	B
11	**12**	**13**	**14**	**15**	**16**	**17**	**18**	**19**	**20**
A	B	C	A	B	A	D	A	C	B

CONJUNCTIONS

A conjunction is a word which connects words, clauses or sentences.

Look at the following sentences.

(i) He bought apples *and* mangoes.

(ii) God made the country *and* man made the town.

(iii) The door was open *but* there was no one in the house.

(iv) He knows that I am here *and* that I want to see him.

In the sentence (i), *and* connects two words—*apples* and *mangoes.*

In the sentence (ii), *and* connects two sentences—*God made the country* and *man made the town.*

In the sentence (iii), *but* connects two sentences— *The door was open* and *there was no one in the house.*

In the sentence (iv), *and* connects two clauses—*that I am here* and *that I want to see him.*

The main coordinating conjunctions are:

and, but, for, or, nor, also, either ..... or, neither ..... nor.

There are some conjunctions which are used in pairs. They are:

either .... or, ... neither .... nor, both .... and, though .... yet, whether .... or, not only .... but also.

Example: *Either* take it *or* leave it.

It is *neither* useful *nor* ornamental.

They *both* like *and* respect me.

Though he is suffering from high fever, *yet* he does not cry.

He does not care *whether* you go *or* stay.

He is *not only* doltish, *but also* obstinate.

The conjunctions which are used in pairs in this way, are called correlative conjunctions, or merely correlatives.

Use of Important Conjunctions

1. **As soon as :** As soon as denotes simultaneous time.
   Example : As soon as he saw his enemy, he took to his heels.
2. **No sooner .... than :**
   (a) 'No sooner' is always followed by 'than'.
   (b) Please remember that 'No sooner' is always followed by do/does/did. As such only first form of the verb should be used after the subject.
   Example :
   No sooner did he see his enemy than he took to his heels.
3. **Hardly :** Hardly is followed by when.
   Examples :
   (i) Hardly had I left the house when it started raining.
   (ii) We had hardly come into the room when his father began chastising him.
   Note :
   A. Hardly is never followed by than.
   B. 'Scarcely' can also be used in the sense and manner of 'Hardly'.
4. **Lest :** Lest is used in the sense of so that .... not. It is always followed by should. Lest is negative in sense. Hence 'not' should never be used with it.
   Example :
   Work hard lest you should fail.
   Note : 'Lest' is always followed by 'should' and not 'may'.
5. **Unless :** Unless expresses condition. It is also used in the negative sense. Use of 'not' is not allowed with unless because unless is already in the negative sense.
   Example :
   Unless you labour hard you will not pass.
6. **Until :** 'Until' expresses time. It means 'till not'.
   Example : Wait here until I return.
   Note : Until is in the negative sense. So 'not' should not be used with it. Example :
   Wait here until I do not return. (Incorrect)
   Wait here until I return. (Correct)
7. **As well as :** When two subjects are joined by 'as well as', the verb always agrees with the first subject.
   Examples :
   (i) The teacher as well as students is playing.
   (ii) Students as well as the teacher are playing.
   Note : 'Both' and 'as well as' cannot be used together in the same sentence.
   Examples :
   Both Sita as well as Kanta are beautiful. (Incorrect)
   Sita as well as Kanta is beautiful. (Correct)
   Both Sita and Kanta are beautiful. (Correct)
8. **As if :** 'As if' is used in the sense of pretension. While using 'as if' in a sentence, we should see that even the third person singular subject gets 'were'.
   Example : He talks as if he were mad.
9. **Till :** Till expresses time. Till is always used in the affirmative.
   Example :
   We did not come back till sunset.
10. **Rather than :** 'Rather than' is used in the sense of 'preference'. 'Rather' is always followed by 'than'.
    Example :
    I would rather die than submit.
11. **As long as/so long as :** Both express time during which an action or event takes place.
    Example :
    As long as there is life, there is hope.
12. **However :** It is both a subordinate and co-ordinate clause.
    Examples :
    (a) Mala worked hard, she however, failed.
    (b) However hard he may work, he cannot pass.
13. **Such as :** 'Such as' gives us the sense of 'like'. Such is always followed by 'as'.
    Example :
    Life is such a puzzle as cannot be solved.

MULTIPLE CHOICE QUESTIONS

Directions: *In the following questions choose the correct options to fill the blanks.*

1. Neither he .... his friend is good.
A. or B. and
C. but D. nor

2. The officer asked the peon .... why he was late.
A. that B. if
C. but D. No word needed

3. Both Ajay .... Vijay are intelligent.
A. or B. nor
C. and D. No word needed

4. No Sooner did the thief see the public .... he ran away.
A. then B. and
C. but D. than

5. Abhinav .... his brothers was going to Mumbai.
A. but
B. yet
C. No word needed
D. together with

6. He behaves .... he were the captain of the team.
A. as if B. as
C. No word needed D. that

7. Either Rupali .... Sonali is going to attend the meeting.
A. and B. but
C. nor D. or

8. Neither Nirmal .... Ashwinee is going to listen the speech.
A. and B. but
C. nor D. or

9. Ravi .... Prakash are going to Kolkata.
A. or B. nor
C. but D. and

10. Rice .... curry is my usual breakfast.
A. and B. but
C. then D. than

11. Hardly had he left .... his brother came.
A. then B. than
C. when D. that

12. I would rather have a copy .... a book.
A. then B. than
C. when D. that

13. He is no other .... my friend.
A. then B. than
C. when D. but

14. He saw a snake ....he awoke.
A. then B. when
C. than D. No word needed

15. Ten years have passed .... my grandmother died.
A. since B. when
C. then D. than

16. She is .... good .... bad.
A. either, not B. neither, or
C. neither, nor D. neither, than

17. The cellphone is both cheap .... best.
A. than B. and
C. then D. or

18. No sooner did the rogue see the police .... he disappeared.
A. then B. than
C. so D. because

19. Srishti will go .... Sanju goes.
A. if B. than
C. then D. although

20. She is wise .... timid.
A. and B. yet
C. but D. however

21. Make hay .... the sun shines.
A. though B. while
C. after D. before

22. He is so weak .... he cannot walk.
A. but B. that
C. then D. so

23. Although he is rich, ... he is unhappy.
A. but B. yet
C. so D. still

24. Wait here .... I come back.
A. till B. until
C. before D. after

25. He is my friend .... I shall help him.
A. so B. hence
C. that is why D. therefore

26. He must go away .... he will be beaten.
A. otherwise B. and
C. or D. else

27. God loves good men .... good men love God.
A. and B. or
C. that D. those

28. He was late .... he was not punished.
A. but B. yet
C. still D. therefore

29. Walk slowly ...., you may fall.
A. and B. or
C. so D. otherwise

30. Work hard, ... you will fail.
A. and B. or
C. otherwise D. else

ANSWERS

1	2	3	4	5	6	7	8	9	10
D	D	C	D	D	A	D	C	D	A
11	**12**	**13**	**14**	**15**	**16**	**17**	**18**	**19**	**20**
C	B	B	B	A	C	B	B	A	C
21	**22**	**23**	**24**	**25**	**26**	**27**	**28**	**29**	**30**
B	B	B	A	B	C	A	C	D	D

PREPOSITIONS

A *Preposition* is a word which is placed before a noun or a pronoun to show its relation to some other word in the sentence.

1. I saw a goat *in* the field.
2. I am fond *of* hot coffee.

In sentence 1, the word *in* shows the relation between two things—*goat* and *field.*

In sentence 2, the word *of* shows the relation between the attribute expressed by the adjective *found* and *tea.*

The words *in* and *of* are here used as prepositions.

The noun or pronoun which is used with a preposition is called its object. The noun or pronoun is in the objective case. It is governed by the preposition. Now it is absolutely clear that in sentence 1, the noun *field* is in the objective case. The word *field* is governed by the preposition *in.*

A preposition may have two or more objects.

The road runs over *hill* and *plain.*

Here, the words *hill* and *plain* are used as objects.

Use of Important Prepositions

1. Among, Between

'**Among**' is used for more than two persons or things; '**Between**' is used only for two.

Examples :

(i) Distribute these sweets *among* the poor students of the class.

(ii) Distribute these books *between* Ram and Shyam.

2. Among, In

'**Among**' is used before collective plural nouns. '**In**' is used before collective singular nouns.

Examples :

(i) I found him standing *among* the crowd.

(ii) I saw him in the crowd.

3. Beside, Besides

'**Beside**' means 'by the side of'. '**Besides**' means 'in addition to'.

Examples :

(i) The daughter was sitting *beside* her mother.

(ii) *Besides* his relatives, he invited his friends also.

4. In, Within

'**In**' means at the expiry of a period of time in future, '**Within**' means before the expiry of a period of time in any tense.

Examples :

(i) She will return *in* a week.

(ii) I shall finish my work *within* a weak.

5. On, Upon

'**On**' is used for things at rest; '**Upon**' is used for things in motion.

Examples :

(i) He is sitting *on* the floor.

(ii) The dog sprang *upon* the table.

6. By, With

'**By**' denotes the agent or doer, '**With**' denotes the instrument with which anything is done.

Examples :

(i) The bird was killed *by* the hunter with an arrow.

(ii) He beat the dog *with* a stick.

(iii) I shall reach here *by* five o'clock.

7. After, In

'**After**' means at the end of a period of time in the past. '**In**' means at the end of a period of time in future.

Examples :

(i) I shall return your book *in* a week.

(ii) He returned the book *after* a week.

8. For, From, Since

'**For**' is used before a noun denoting a period of time with all the tenses. '**From**' is used before a noun or phrase denoting a point of time, it is used in all the tenses. '**Since**' is used before a noun or phrase denoting some point of time and is always produced by a verb in the perfect continuous tense or third form of a verb.

Examples :

(i) We have been playing cards *for* two hours.

(ii) She stayed with her uncle *from* the 15th of March to the 15th of May.

(iii) I have been reading this book *since* morning.

9. Above, Over

'**Above**' means 'higher from', **Over** is used in the following four senses :

(i) In the sense of 'above' :
At noon, the sun is *over* our heads.

(ii) In the sense of 'beyond' :
I cannot get *over* my disappointment.

(iii) In the sense of 'Superiority' :
God *over* all blesses for ever more.

(iv) In the sense of 'Conclusion' :
It is all *over* with me.

10. At, Towards

'**At**' denotes the idea of aim, '**Towards**' denotes the idea of destination.

Examples :

(i) He threw the stone *at* the cat.

(ii) He went *towards* the house.

11. At, In, On

'At' is used as follows :

(i) '**At**' is used with small towns and villages. **Examples:**

(a) He was born *at* Sonepat.

(b) He lives *at* village Bangra. (Bangra is a village)

(ii) '**At**' is used before a noun denoting a definite point of time.

Example :

He called on me *at* 9 p.m. yesterday.

'In' is used as follows :

(iii) '**In**' is used with the names of big cities, provinces and countries.

Examples :

(a) His father lives *in* England.

(b) His younger brother lives *in* Calcutta.

(iv) '**In**' is used before the names of months and years.

Example :

His elder sister was born *in* 1972 *in* the month of May.

'**On**' is used with dates and names of days. **Examples:**

(a) I joined college *on* the 26th April.

(b) He will leave for Kolkata *on* Wednesday next.

Important Information

1. '**In**' is also used in the following phrases :
   In the morning; In the evening, In winter, In summer.
2. '**In**' also denotes a place inside anything.
   He travelled *in* a crowded bus.
3. '**At**' is used in the following phrases :
   At home, *At* the station, *At* work, *At* play.

12. Below, Beneath

Below means 'of lower level in position, dignity and expectation' etc. *Beneath* means 'under'.

Examples :

(i) It is *below* my dignity to talk to her.

(ii) They rested *beneath* the shade of a tree.

13. In, Into, To

'**In**' expresses Rest or Motion inside anything. '**Into**' expresses Motion towards the inside of anything or change from one medium to another. '**To**' denotes motion from one place to another.

Examples :

(i) The boys are *in* the room.

(ii) Translate this passage from English *into* Hindi.

(iii) Every morning he goes *to* the temple.

14. Till, By, Of, Off

- 'Till' means upto or not earlier than.
- 'By' means not later than.
- 'Of' shows cause, source, separation, quality, contents, possession, apposition, point of reference, space in time etc.
- 'Off' shows separation at a near distance, and detached condition.

Consider the following examples:

(i) I shall work *till* 5 a.m.

(ii) Madhu died *of* cancer.

(iii) The nib *of* the pen is made *of* gold.

(iv) He presented me a bottle *of* perfume.

(v) Our principal is a man *of* principle.

(vi) He lived in the house *of* his friend.

(vii) *By* this time tomorrow, I'll have finished my job.

(viii) My house is *off* the road.

(ix) The book fell *off* the table.

MULTIPLE CHOICE QUESTIONS

Directions: *Tick the correct preposition for the blank in each of the following sentences.*

1. He applied ...... the manager.
A. for B. to
C. with D. by

2. Trust ...... God and do the right.
A. in B. for
C. to D. with

3. She is worthy ...... a prize.
A. with B. for
C. to D. of

4. Mr. Gomes has no taste ...... music.
A. of B. for
C. with D. to

5. You are hard ...... hearing.
A. at B. of
C. with D. for

6. He is sure ...... his success
A. for B. with
C. on D. of

7. Preeti was warned ...... the danger ahead.
A. for B. at
C. of D. about

8. I am thankful ...... you for a good advice.
A. for B. with
C. to D. of

9. Deepak would not surrender ...... the police.
A. with B. to
C. for D. on

10. The small plant in your lawn is very sensitive ...... touch.
A. on B. with
C. to D. about

11. Divya was sure to succeed ..... the examination.
A. for B. in
C. to D. with

12. Geeta was jealous ...... Ravina's beauty.
A. to B. with
C. for D. of

13. He was ignorant ..... what was happening there.
A. for B. of
C. to D. with

14. Your pen is inferior ...... mine.
A. than B. with
C. from D. to

15. Reenu is no match ...... Meenu.
A. to B. for
C. with D. upon

16. It is necessary ...... you to apply for this job.
A. on B. with
C. for D. to

17. Be loyal ...... your country.
A. for B. to
C. on D. with

18. Mukesh is junior ...... me.
A. than B. to
C. from D. of

19. Deepika was innocent ...... the crime.
A. of B. with
C. from D. to

20. I am desirous.... joining the Indian cricket team.
A. for B. of
C. to D. on

ANSWERS

1	2	3	4	5	6	7	8	9	10
B	A	D	B	B	D	D	D	B	D
11	**12**	**13**	**14**	**15**	**16**	**17**	**18**	**19**	**20**
B	D	B	D	B	D	B	B	A	B

SYNONYMS

A synonym is a word which conveys a meaning similar to the given word.

REMEMBER

Words	*Synonyms*
Add	Increase
Adequate	Enough
Adjust	Adapt
All	Aggregate
Allow	Permit
Abode	Dwelling
Apt	Proper
Assess	Appraise
Accuse	Calumniate
Abashed	Timid
Annoy	Displease
Ample	Enough, Sufficient
Amplify	Increase
Apathetic	Unenthusiastic
Accost	Address
Authentic	True
Adjust	Fit
Approve	Assent, Allow, Accept
Adapt	Conform
Adversary	Opponent, Rival, Competitor
Beat	Whack
Benign	Kind
Breeze	Zephyr
Baffle	Puzzle
Booty	Spoil

Words	*Synonyms*
Beauty	Charm
Beast	Animal
Bandit	Robber
Blaze	Shine
Bond	Tie
Bend	Twist
Bate	Diminish
Beg	Plead
Barbaric	Wild, Savage
Bashful	Shy, Reserved
Begin	Start
Blend	Mix, Mingle
Bizarre	Funny
Below	Under
Bedevil	Confuse
Bemoan	Lament
Babble	Nonsense
Blame	Fault
Behaviour	Demeanour
Call	Accost
Copy	Imitate
Close	Shut
Caress	Love
Camp	Stay
Connect	Attach
Cut	Injure, Curtail
Cling	Stick
Conical	Funny
Convey	Carry
Conspicuous	Prominent
Cheerful	Happy, Pleasant

Words	Synonyms	Words	Synonyms
Curtail	Decrease	Grow	Develop
Cheerless	Sad, Dejected	Greed	Avidity
Curious	Strange	Greet	Welcome
Circumstance	Factor, Situation, Condition	Grave	Serious
Competent	Capable	Group	Constellation
Congruent	Overlapping	Given	Bestowed
Cope	Deal, Endure	Gratitude	Thankfulness
Confident	Sure	Have	Possess
Complex	Intricate	Hire	Rent
Cajole	Coax, Flatter	Hit	Strike
Cunning	Crafty	Handsome	Beautiful
Delectable	Joyful, Delightful	Hinder	Prevent
Devilish	Diabolical	Heap	Pile
Delicate	Soft	Hope	Expect
Devil	Fiend	Hard	Harsh
Delay	Postpone	Help	Aid
Dislike	Repugnance	Hymn	Song
Destroy	Ruin	Henpecked	Enslaved
Dwell	Live, Dilate	Hoodwink	Mystify, Cheat
Declare	Pronounce	Humble	Polite, Urbane, Modest
Drunk	Flushed	Harass	Vex, Trouble
Deficient	Lacking	Impart	Instil
Damn	Condemn, Curse	Intact	Untouched
Decrease	Diminish	Instal	Establish
Destruction	Devastation	Indict	Impeach
Efficient	Competent	Imitate	Ape
Ethnic	Racial	Instigate	Incite
Enthral	Enslave	Initiate	Start, Introduce
Earnest	Serious	Inimical	Unfriendly
Envious	Jealous	Insufferable	Intolerable
Ending	Final	Impartiality	Justice
Egg	Incite	Jolly	Merry
Extempore	At once	Joyful	Delectable
Extensive	Far-ranging	Join	Conjoin
Extra	Surplus	Kind	Benign
Existence	Life	Kill	Murder
Exceed	Overstep	Kindred	Similar
Enormous	Vast	Kinship	Relationship
Excessive	Superfluous	Keen	Sharp
Free	Unhindered	Knowledge	Scholarship
Frigid	Cold	Lazy	Slothful
Feed	Cater	Large	Substantial, Gargantuan
Fame	Reputation	Listless	Careless, Lackadaisical
Frame	Make	Lax	Loose
First	Initial	Little	Small
Frighten	Terrorise, Intimidate	Lifelike	Realistic
Fervent	Fervid	Lofty	High
Fall	Decline	Lenient	Soft, Gentle
Feeble	Frail	Lacking	Deficient, Wanting
Fickle	Changeable	Lessen	Decrease
Finish	Conclude	Middleclass	Bourgeois
Fraud	Deception	Mitigate	Lessen, Abate
Forgiving	Placable	Modesty	Humility, Lowliness

Words	Synonyms
Mix	Mingle, Blend
Mixture	Mingling
Mixed	Assorted
Modify	Decrease
Mean	Imply
Multifarious	Varied
Miscarry	Abort
Note	Notice
Noble	Stately
Native	Indigenous
Needful	Necessary
Notify	Declare
Nervous	Shaky, Tremulous, Timid
Natural	Spontaneous
Near	Close
Normal	Natural
Offend	Displease
Oppress	Persecute, Tyrannize
Opponent	Adversary
Obstruct	Hinder, Check
Offence	Fault
Offender	Villain
Overstep	Exceed
Overlapping	Congruent
Occult	Mystic
Profane	Unholy
Patience	Forbearance
Pornographic	Obscene
Plenitude	Abundance
Prominent	Important
Prodigal	Spender
Procrastinate	Postpone
Promote	Develop, Honour
Persecute	Tyrannise
Profess	Claim
Pliant	Flexible
Plebian	Common
Polished	Sophisticated
Quake	Shake
Quit	Leave
Queer	Eccentric
Quell	Suppress
Quantify	Allot
Reply	Answer
Relinquish	Retire
Read	Peruse
Relation	Reference
Render	Do
Remainder	Residuals
Repeat	Reiterate
Repentant	Contrite
Retaliative	Retaliatory
Rumour	Hearsay
Reveal	Divulge

Words	Synonyms
Ritualistic	Ceremonious
Soft	Delicate
Sort	Kind, Choose, Select
Selfish	Egoistic
Sensual	Earthly
Suppress	Quell, Check
Stimulate	Provoke
Tasteless	Insipid
Travel	Journey
True	Authentic, Faithful, Truthful
Turbulence	Turmoil
Tragedy	Calamity
Tasteful	Tasty, Delicious
Touching	Painful
Thankful	Grateful
Tremendous	Great, Huge
Tough	Strong
Terminate	Conclude, End
Theory	Doctrine
Tell	Relate
Tremble	Shake, Shiver
Urge	Spur
Unbeaten	Unsubdued
Use	Utilize, Practise
Underhand	Unfair, Undue
Unfair	Unjust
Unravel	Reveal, Divulge
Unimportant	Common
Unconcerned	Apathetic
Unimitated	Inimitable
Unfortunate	Unlucky
Understand	Perceive, Comprehend
Vain	Proud, Haughty, Conceited, Shameless
Vale	Valley, Dale, Dell
Vice	Fault
Virtue	Quality
Veracity	Reality
Value	Price, Prize
Vex	Tease
Vibrate	Quiver, Shake
Violent	Excessive
Vivid	Clear, Lucid
Victory	Triumph
Vulgar	Indecent
Virtuous	Honest
Variegated	Varied, Multifarious
Well	Good
Yell	Cry, Shout
Yonder	There
Yearn	Wish, Desire
Yoke	Slavery
Zest	Earnestness, Enthusiasm
Zealous	Earnest

ANTONYMS

A antonym is a word which conveys a meaning opposite to the given word.

REMEMBER

Words	*Antonyms*
Abhor	Love
Abnormal	Normal
Able	Unable
Acceptable	Unacceptable
Adequate	Inadequate
Amusing	Boring
Angry	Calm
Apex	Bottom
Attract	Repel
Bad	Good
Barren	Fertile
Beautiful	Ugly
Bitter	Sweet
Brave	Cowardly
Brief	Lengthy
Bright	Dull
Calm	Violent
Careful	Careless
Clear	Vague, Cloudy
Cold	Hot
Cruel	Kind
Dear	Cheap
Deep	Shallow
Difficult	Easy
Direct	Indirect
Dishonest	Honest
Disobey	Obey
Encourage	Discourage
Enormous	Tiny
Excellent	Bad
Expensive	Cheap
Eat	Fast
Fair	Unfair
Fake	Authentic
False	True
Famous	Notorious
Fool	Genius
Generous	Miserly
Genius	Fool
Genuine	Unauthentic
Gigantic	Tiny
Glad	Depressed
Good	Bad
Great	Little
Happy	Sad
Hard	Soft
Hate	Love
Honest	Dishonest
Idle	Busy

Words	*Antonyms*
Immoral	Moral
Include	Exclude
Incorrect	Correct
Intelligent	Unintelligent
Kind	Cruel
Like	Dislike
Long	Short
Lucid	Vague
Major	Minor
Naive	Experienced
Nadir	Apex
Neat	Clumsy
Obedient	Disobedient
Obscure	Clear
Oppose	Support
Optimistic	Pessimistic
Out	In
Patience	Impatience
Peaceful	Belligerent
Pious	Impious
Polite	Impolite
Potent	Impotent
Prominent	Unimportant
Proper	Improper
Pure	Impure
Quick	Slow
Quiet	Disturbance
Real	False, Unreal
Reject	Select, Choose
Reliable	Unreliable
Respect	Disrespect
Right	Wrong
Robust	Feeble, Weak
Sad	Happy
Secret	Open
Sensible	Insensible
Severe	Mild
Sharp	Blunt
Simple	Complex
Sociable	Unsociable
Tall	Short
Tidy	Untidy
Uncanny	Canny
Violent	Calm
Vivid	Vague
Strong	Weak
Big	Small
Easy	Difficult
Fast	Slow
High	Low
Catchy	Unattractive
Ugly	Handsome, Beautiful, Tidy
Tasty	Insipid
Sonorous	Harsh

MULTIPLE CHOICE QUESTIONS

Directions (Qs. 1 to 20): *In the following questions choose the word which best expresses the meaning of the given word.*

1. ABSURD
A. Foolish B. Simple
C. Courageous D. Silly

2. ABANDON
A. Lose B. Profit
C. Vacate D. Foil

3. CAJOLE
A. Pause B. Lenient
C. Blast D. Lure

4. COMBAT
A. Fight B. Conflict
C. Shoot D. Quarrel

5. LAMENT
A. Condone B. Console
C. Complain D. Contribution

6. DEBACLE
A. Disgrace B. Defeat
C. Collapse D. Decline

7. SHIVER
A. Fear B. Tremble
C. Shake D. Ache

8. TORTURE
A. Terror B. Harassment
C. Torment D. Tranquility

9. LAUDABLE
A. Lovable B. Commendable
C. Profitable D. Oblivious

10. FIXED
A. Sterile B. Static
C. Stubborn D. Parennial

11. QUEER
A. Unfamiliar B. Cute
C. Curious D. Strange

12. SUFFICIENT
A. Fit B. Proper
C. Adequate D. Vast

13. GLOSS
A. Brightness B. Soothing
C. Rubbing D. Miracle

14. LONGING
A. Prune B. Apathy
C. Curtail D. Craving

15. JEER
A. Applaud B. Magnanimity
C. Avoid D. Scoff

16. ZENITH
A. Minimum B. Nadir
C. Plant D. Peak

17. GARB
A. Distort B. Dress
C. Trivial D. Rage

18. ABHOR
A. Rude B. Reconcile
C. Crave D. Detest

19. YIELD
A. Shum B. Incisive
C. Retain D. Surrender

20. YOKE
A. Twist B. Release
C. Link D. Extra

Directions (Qs. 21 to 26): *In the following questions choose the word which best expresses the opposite of the given word.*

21. TRAGIC
A. Dramatic B. Strong
C. Gentle D. Comic

22. ORAL
A. Verbal B. Sane
C. Minor D. Written

23. ADMIRE
A. Hate B. Unlike
C. Dislike D. Enough

24. VIOLENT
A. Gentle B. Savage
C. Haughty D. Decline

25. ADVERSITY
A. Windfall B. Inprosperity
C. Prosperity D. Slave

26. GENUINE
A. Spurious B. Obscure
C. Countless D. Apathetic

ANSWERS

1	2	3	4	5	6	7	8	9	10
D	C	D	A	C	C	B	C	B	B
11	**12**	**13**	**14**	**15**	**16**	**17**	**18**	**19**	**20**
D	C	A	D	D	D	B	D	D	C
21	**22**	**23**	**24**	**25**	**26**				
D	D	C	A	C	A				

●●●

3

Sentence Completion

It is such an exercise which starts with the primary schools and continues in the highest level of competitive examinations. One must practise it regularly to score well.

Directions (Qs. 1 to 15): *Pick out the most effective word(s) from the given words to fill in the blanks to make the sentence meaningfully complete.*

1. The student ...... that book from the library to study at home.
A. issued B. borrowed
C. hired D. lent

2. I wish I ...... a king.
A. was B. am
C. should be D. were

3. He ...... to listen to my arguments and walked away.
A. denied B. disliked
C. objected D. refused

4. The flow of blood was so ...... that the patient died.
A. intense B. adequate
C. profuse D. extensive

5. When I met her yesterday, it was the first time I ...... her since Christmas.
A. saw B. have seen
C. had seen D. have been seing

6. Can you pay ...... all these articles?
A. for B. of
C. off D. out

7. I ...... you to be at the party this evening.
A. expect B. hope
C. look forward to D. desire

8. ...... being a handicapped person, he is very cooperative and self-reliant.
A. Because B. Although
C. Since D. Despite

9. The child broke ...... from his mother and ran towards the painting.
A. away B. after
C. down D. with

10. With his ...... income, he finds it difficult to live a comfortable life.
A. brief
B. sufficient
C. meagre
D. huge

11. He could ...... a lot of money in such a short time by using his intelligence and working hard.
A. spend
B. spoil
C. exchange
D. accumulate

12. Though the brothers are twins, they look ......
A. alike B. handsome
C. indifferent D. different

13. Unfavourable weather conditions can ..... illness.
A. cure B. detect
C. treat D. enhance

14. No sooner did the bell ring, ... the actor started singing.
A. when B. than
C. after D. before

15. If I ...... realised it, I would not have acted on his advice.
A. was B. had
C. were D. have

Directions (Qs. 16 to 25): *In each question, an incomplete statement (Stem) followed by four fillers is given. Pick out the best one which can complete the incomplete stem correctly and meaningfully.*

16. Unless you work harder you will fail, means .....
A. if you fail you will work harder.
B. you must at least plan well than you will not fail.
C. hardly you will fail if you do not desire so.
D. if you do not put more efforts, then you will fail.

17. Even if it rains I shall come, means .....
A. if I come it will not rain.
B. if it rains I shall not come.
C. I will certainly come whether it rains or not.
D. whenever there is rain I shall come.

18. Dinesh is as stupid as he is lazy means .....
A. Dinesh is stupid because he is lazy.
B. Dinesh is lazy because he is stupid.
C. Dinesh is either stupid or lazy.
D. Dinesh is equally stupid and lazy.

19. He is so lazy that he .....
A. cannot depend on others for getting his work done.
B. cannot delay the schedule of completing the work.
C. can seldom complete his work on time.
D. dislike to postpone the work that he undertakes to do.

20. He always stammers in public meetings, but his today's speech .....
A. was fairly audible to everyone present in the hall.
B. was not received satisfactorily.
C. could not be understood properly.
D. was free from that defect.

21. In order to raise the company's profit, the employees.....
A. demanded two additional increments.
B. decided to go on paid holidays.
C. requested the management to implement new welfare schemes.
D. offered to work overtime without any compensation.

22. Although, he is reputed for making very candid statements, ...
A. his today's speech was not fairly audible.
B. his promises had always been realistic.
C. his speech was very interesting.
D. his today's statements were very ambiguous.

23. I felt somewhat more relaxed .....
A. but tense as compared to earlier.
B. and tense as compared to earlier.
C. as there was already no tension at all.
D. and tension-free as compared to earlier.

24. With great efforts his son succeeded in convincing him not to donate his entire wealth to an orphanage ....
A. and lead the life of a wealthy merchant.
B. but to a home for the forsaken children.
C. and make an orphan of himself.
D. as the orphanage needed a lot of donations.

25. Even though it is a very large house, ...
A. there is a lot of space available in it for children.
B. there is hardly any space available for children.
C. there is no dearth of space for children.
D. the servants take a long time to clean it.

ANSWERS

1	2	3	4	5	6	7	8	9	10
B	D	D	C	C	A	A	D	A	C
11	**12**	**13**	**14**	**15**	**16**	**17**	**18**	**19**	**20**
D	D	D	B	B	D	C	D	C	D
21	**22**	**23**	**24**	**25**					
D	D	D	C	B					

●●●

4

Spotting Errors

The most common errors in English are of spellings, grammar and usage of words. By regular practice, the errors can be easily spotted and minimised.

MULTIPLE CHOICE QUESTIONS

Directions: *In the following questions some of the sentences have errors and some are correct. Find out which part of a sentence has an error, the number of that part is your answer. If a sentence is free from errors, then your answer is D i.e., No error.*

1. (A) Either Ram or/(B) you is responsible/(C) for this action./(D) No error.

2. (A) The student flatly denied/(B) that he had copied/(C) in the examination hall./(D) No error.

3. (A) By the time you arrive tomorrow/(B) I have finished/(C) my work./(D) No error.

4. (A) The captain with the members of his team/(B) are returning/(C) after a fortnight./(D) No error.

5. (A) After returning from/(B) an all-India tour/(C) I had to describe about it./(D) No error.

6. (A) The teacher asked his students/(B) if they had gone through/(C) either of the three chapters included in the prescribed text./(D) No error.

7. (A) Do you know/(B) how old were you/(C) when you came here?/(D) No error.

8. (A) Beware of/(B) a fair-weather friend/(C) who is neither a friend in need nor a friend indeed./(D) No error.

9. (A) Copernicus proved/(B) that Earth/(C) moves round the Sun./(D) No error.

10. (A) The property/(B) was divided/(C) among the two brothers./(D) No error.

11. (A) I am quite certain/(B) that the lady is not only greedy/(C) but miserly./(D) No error.

12. (A) The brilliant success in the examination/(B) as well as his record in sports/(C) deserves high praise./(D) No error.

13. (A) I cannot find/(B) where has he gone/(C) though I have tried may best./(D) No error.

14. (A) If I was/(B) the Prime Minister of India/(C) I would work wonders/(D) No error.

15. (A) If it weren't/(B) for you,/(C) I wouldn't be alive today./(D) No error.

16. (A) He looked like a lion/(B) baulked from/(C) its prey./(D) No error.

17. (A) Widespread flooding/(B) is affecting/(C) large areas of the villages./(D) No error.

18. (A) If we really set to/(B) we can get the whole house/(C) cleaned in an afternoon./(D) No error.

ANSWERS

1	2	3	4	5	6	7	8	9	10
B	D	B	B	C	C	D	D	B	C
11	**12**	**13**	**14**	**15**	**16**	**17**	**18**	**19**	**20**
C	D	B	A	C	C	C	A	A	C

EXPLANATORY ANSWERS

1. Replace 'is' by 'are'.
2. No error.
3. Replace 'have' by 'would have'.
4. Replace 'are' by 'is'.
5. Replace 'had to describe' by 'described'.
6. Replace 'either' by 'any'.
7. No error.
8. No error.
9. Omit 'that'.
10. Replace 'among' by 'between'.
11. Add 'also'.
12. No error.
13. Replace 'has he' by 'he has'.
14. Replace 'was' by 'were'.
15. Replace 'wouldn't be' by 'would not have been'.
16. Replace 'its' by 'his'.
17. Replace 'areas' by 'area'.
18. Replace 'set to' by 'set on'.

●●●

5

One Word Substitution

There are many single words in English language which can be perfectly used for a number of words. These words help in expressing ideas in a short and correct manner for the right occasion. Such words not only increase the vocabulary but also enable you to economise in the use of words to a great extent.

Multiple Word Expression	*Substitution*
One who always looks towards the bright side of things	Optimist
One who always looks towards the dark side of things	Pessimist
The time when one develops from a child into an adult	Adolescence
The process of growing more plants in order to form a forest.	Afforestation
The science which deals with farming	Agriculture
From some other country or place etc.	Alien
A term, etc. giving more than one meaning	Ambiguous
A vehicle which is used to carry sick persons	Ambulance
An animal which can live both in water and on land	Amphibian
A lawless situation when there is no government	Anarchy
Belonging to the history of thousands of years old	Ancient
Once a year	Annual
A very old object but still valuable	Antique
Words of opposite meanings	Antonyms
Words of similar meanings	Synonyms
Signatures of a famous person	Autograph
A government led by one person with absolute authority	Autocracy
A written work of one's own life history	Autobiography
A person who has never been married	Bachelor
A person usually having no hair on his head	Bald
A place where one can deposit money and get interest	Bank
A person who cuts our hair	Barber
A building/group of buildings where soldiers live	Barracks
A person who makes buns and biscuits	Baker
A person who lives by asking people for food and money without doing any useful job	Beggar
The crime of having married to two persons at the same time	Bigamy
The branch of science which deals with the study of plants	Botany
Able to speak two languages	Bilingual
Able to speak more than two languages	Polyglot
The branch of science which deals with the living organisms	Biology
A powerful snow storm	Blizzard
A great successful book or movie	Blockbuster
A short news on the radio or TV	Bulletin
A system in which the most important works are organised by the government officials	Bureaucracy
A person who has no vision in his eyes	Blind
A page or a series of pages on which the information of days, weeks, months, etc. is given	Calendar
A person who eats human flesh	Cannibal
A complete list of items often arranged alphabetically	Catalogue
A sudden disaster	Catastrophe
A period of 100 years	Century

Multiple Word Expression	*Substitution*
A branch of science which deals with chemicals	Chemistry
A printed leaf usually issued by banks that we sign to carry certain financial deal	Cheque
A person who makes or mends shoes	Cobbler
A group of people who has been chosen by others to make decisions on their own	Committee
A building in which nuns live	Convent
An animal which feeds on other animals	Carnivorous
A person who does criticism	Critic
A person who cannot hear	Deaf
A condition in which one loses a lot of water from one's body because of vomiting, etc.	Dehydration
A system of government in which the people cast their votes to elect their leaders	Democracy
The study of skin problems	Dermatology
A long piece of land covered with sand	Desert
The art of managing relationships between countries	Diplomacy
A piece of information about the words in a book form	Dictionary
A piece of information about the telephone numbers of the people in a book from	Directory
A person in charge of a newspapers, magazine etc.	Editor
A person who thinks he is better than the others	Egoist
To leave your country and settle in some other country	Emigrate
A book or series of books giving almost all knowledge about an area or some persons etc.	Encyclopaedia
Study of insects	Entomology
Time when day and night are of the same duration	Equinox
To sell things out of the country	Export
To purchase things from some other country	Import
A plant or animal no longer in existence	Extinct
A situation when there is a shortage of food for a long period of time	Famine
An amount of money that we pay for some action or services	Fee
Related to women	Feminine
An animal strong and aggressive	Ferocious
A piece of land where plants grow easily from the soil that is favourable to them	Fertile
A work of literature having some imaginary events	Fiction
A large amount of water covering certain area	Flood
A person who sells flowers	Florist
A religious ceremony for burying or cremating a dead person	Funeral
A substance which kills fungus	Fungicide
A person studying or having studied the diseases and the related things of female reproductory system	Gynaecologist
The murder of the person of the same group race or country	Genocide
A substance which kills germs	Germicide
A situation in which many people die because of fire during war	Holocaust
The act of killing a person deliberately	Homicide
A word having the pronunciation as the other one does but it differs in meaning	Homophone
A word having the same spelling as the other one does but it is pronounced in some other way	Homonym
A person who is attracted towards the person of the same sex	Homosexual
Go across and parallel to the ground	Horizontal
A substance which kills the insects	Insecticide
That cannot be corrected	Incorrigible
That cannot be defeated	Invincible
That cannot be eaten	Inedible
That cannot be seen	Invisible
A place in a school or college where books are kept for the benefit of students, teachers etc.	Library
A place in a school or college where scientific experiments are performed	Laboratory

Multiple Word Expression	*Substitution*
An official who is a judge in the lowest court	Magistrate
A piece of music or a book before it is printed	Manuscript
Related to men	Masculine
One who believes in the existence of God	A theist
One who does not believe in the existence of good	An atheist
That can be believed	Credible
That cannot be believed	Incredible
That which dissolves in a solvent	Soluble
That which does not dissolves in a solvent	Insoluble
Hard writing that can be read	Legible
Hard writing that cannot be read	Illegible
A person who does jobs beneficial to mankind	Philanthropist
A person who goes on foot	Pedestrian
A person who fights for his own country	Patriot
An act of killing oneself	Suicide
A woman whose husband is dead	Widow
A man whose wife is dead	Widower
A person who eats vegetarian and non-vegetarian diets	Omnivorous
Something which is everywhere at the same time	Omnipresent
One who knows everything	Omniscient
A child who does not have parents	Orphan
An award etc. given after the death of the person	Posthumous
The place where animals are kept for amusement and to increase the knowledge of the public	Zoo
The science which deals with the study of animals	Zoology

MULTIPLE CHOICE QUESTIONS

Directions: *In questions given below, out of the four alternatives, choose the one which can be substituted for the given words/sentences.*

1. Something that relates to everyone in the world
A. General B. Common
C. Usual D. Universal

2. An expression of mild disapproval
A. Warning B. Denigration
C. Impertinence D. Reproof

3. One who is not easily pleased by anything
A. Maiden B. Medieval
C. Precarious D. Fastidious

4. Murder of a king
A. Infanticide B. Matricide
C. Genocide D. Regicide

5. A remedy for all diseases
A. Stoic B. Marvel
C. Panacea D. Recompense

6. A dramatic performance
A. Mask B. Mosque
C. Masque D. Mascot

7. Study of birds
A. Orology B. Optology
C. Ophthalmology D. Ornithology

8. Ready to believe
A. Credulous B. Credible
C. Creditable D. Incredible

9. Incapable of being seen through
A. Ductile B. Opaque
C. Obsolete D. Potable

10. One who eats everything
A. Omnivorous B. Omniscient
C. Irresistible D. Insolvent

11. A place where bees are kept is called
A. An apiary B. A mole
C. A hive D. A sanctuary

12. One who cannot be corrected
A. Incurable B. Incorrigible
C. Hardened D. Invulnerable

13. One who is in charge of a museum
A. Curator B. Supervisor
C. Caretaker D. Warden

14. Continuing fight between parties, families, clans, etc.
A. Enmity B. Feud
C. Quarrel D. Skirmish

15. A voice loud enough to be heard
A. Audible B. Applaudable
C. Laudable D. Oral

16. A paper written by hand
A. Handicraft B. Manuscript
C. Handiwork D. Thesis

17. Habitually silent or talking little
A. Serville B. Unequivocal
C. Taciturn D. Synoptic

18. To slap with a flat object
A. Chop B. Hew
C. Gnaw D. Swat

19. A person who speaks many languages
A. Linguist B. Monolingual
C. Polyglot D. Bilingual

20. A light sailing-boat built specially for racing
A. Canoe B. Yacht
C. Frigate D. Dinghy

21. A fixed orbit in space in relation to earth
A. Geological B. Geo-synchronous
C. Geo-centric D. Geo-stationary

22. A style in which a writer makes a display of his knowledge
A. Pedantic B. Verbose
C. Pompous D. Ornate

23. A religious discourse
A. Preach B. Stanza
C. Sanctorum D. Sermon

24. A place that provides refuge
A. Asylum B. Sanatorium
C. Shelter D. Orphanage

25. Detailed plan of a journey
A. Travelogue B. Travelkit
C. Schedule D. Itinerary

26. A person who insists on something
A. Disciplinarian B. Stickler
C. Instantaneous D. Boaster

27. A drawing on transparent paper
A. Red print B. Blue print
C. Negative D. Transparency

28. One who believes that all things and events in life are predetermined is a
A. Fatalist B. Puritan
C. Egoist D. Tyrant

29. A school boy who cuts classes frequently is a
A. Defeatist B. Sycophant
C. Truant D. Martinet

30. The act of violating the sanctity of the church is
A. Blasphemy B. Heresy
C. Sacrilege D. Desecration

31. A place where monks live as a secluded community
A. Cathedral B. Diocese
C. Convent D. Monastery

32. One who is fond of fighting
A. Bellicose B. Aggressive
C. Belligerent D. Militant

33. Tending to move away from the centre or axis
A. Centrifugal B. Centripetal
C. Axiomatic D. Awry

34. Words inscribed on tomb
A. Epitome B. Epistle
C. Epilogue D. Epitaph

35. Leave or remove from a place considered dangerous
A. Evade B. Evacuate
C. Avoid D. Exterminate

36. Original inhabitants of a country
A. Abroge B. Aborger
C. Aborgory D. Aborigins

37. Government by the officials
A. Theocracy B. Plutocracy
C. Bureaucracy D. Democracy

38. Incapable of being exhausted
A. Inexhaustible B. Inaexhaustible
C. Exhaustable D. Non-tired

39. A person of good understanding, knowledge and reasoning power
A. Expert B. Intellectual
C. Snob D. Literate

40. One absorbed in his own thoughts and feelings rather than in things outside
A. Scholar B. Recluse
C. Introvert D. Intellectual

ANSWERS

1	2	3	4	5	6	7	8	9	10
D	D	D	D	C	C	D	A	B	A
11	**12**	**13**	**14**	**15**	**16**	**17**	**18**	**19**	**20**
A	B	A	B	A	B	C	D	A	B
21	**22**	**23**	**24**	**25**	**26**	**27**	**28**	**29**	**30**
D	A	D	A	D	B	D	A	C	C
31	**32**	**33**	**34**	**35**	**36**	**37**	**38**	**39**	**40**
D	A	A	D	B	B	C	A	B	C

●●●

6

Spelling Errors

There are thousands of words in English language. It is difficult to remember the spellings and meanings of all at once. Try to learn as many as you can. Use a dictionary regularly.

Directions: *Find the correctly spelt words.*

1. A. Damage B. Dammage C. Damaige D. Dammege

2. A. Efficiant B. Effecient C. Efficient D. Eficient

3. A. Schedule B. Schdule C. Schedale D. Schedeule

4. A. Occurad B. Occurred C. Ocurred D. Occured

5. A. Grieff B. Grief C. Grieef D. Grrief

6. A. Guarantee B. Garuntee C. Guaruntee D. Gaurantee

7. A. Meddicine B. Medicine C. Medicene D. Medicinne

8. A. Benefeted B. Benefitted C. Benifited D. Benefited

9. A. Acommodation B. Acomodation C. Accomodation D. Accommodation

10. A. Querrelsome B. Quarrelsame C. Quarrelsome D. Querralsome

11. A. Sympathetic B. Smypathetic C. Sympothetic D. Sympethetic

12. A. Prograssive B. Progressive C. Progresive D. Prograsive

13. A. Uncivilized B. Uncevilized C. Uncivillized D. Uncevelized

14. A. Extravagant B. Extreragent C. Extreregant D. Extravegent

15. A. Missunderstood B. Miesunderstood C. Misunderstood D. Misunderstod

16. A. Belligerent B. Beligirent C. Belligarant D. Belligerrent

17. A. Astonished B. Astronished C. Astoneshed D. Asstonished

18. A. Sincerely B. Sencerely C. Sincerelly D. Sincerrely

19. A. Rigourous B. Rigerous C. Rigorous D. Regerous

20. A. Satellite B. Sattellite C. Satelite D. Sattelite

21. A. Pesanger B. Passenger C. Pessenger D. Pasanger

22. A. Humurous B. Humorous C. Humoreus D. Humorrous

23. A. Exeggerate B. Exaggerate C. Exadgerate D. Exagerate

24. A. Fariegn B. Forein C. Foriegn D. Foreign

25. A. Excesive B. Excessive C. Exccessive D. Exccesive

26. A. Forcaust B. Forcast C. Forecast D. Forecaste

27. A. Paralleted B. Paralelled C. Parralleled D. Parallelled

28. A. Ocasion B. Occassion C. Occasion D. Ocassion

29. A. Boquet B. Bouquet C. Bouquete D. Bouquette

30. A. Chettering B. Chaterring C. Chattering D. Chatering

31. A. Discourage B. Disscourage C. Discourege D. Discaurage

32. A. Curageous B. Courageous C. Courrageous D. Couregeous

33. A. Abandon B. Abanddon C. Abendon D. Abbandon

34. A. Embarassment B. Emberrassement C. Embarrassment D. Embbaresment

35. A. Eccintric B. Eccentrie C. Eccentric D. Eccintrie

36. A. Occasional B. Occassional C. Occesional D. Occessional

37. A. Querrel B. Querral C. Quarrel D. Quarel

38. A. Contrebution B. Contribution C. Contributtion D. Conterbution

39. A. Desgrace B. Disgrece
C. Disgrice D. Disgrace

40. A. Harassment B. Herassment
C. Harasment D. Harassmient

41. A. Imaginative B. Imeginative
C. Imagenative D. Imaginetive

42. A. Suficient B. Suficiant
C. Sufficient D. Sufficiant

43. A. Adequate B. Edequate
C. Adaquete D. Edaquete

44. A. Exparienced B. Experianced
C. Experienced D. Experrienced

45. A. Flatering B. Fletering
C. Flattering D. Fletaring

46. A. Cuttiveted B. Culltrivated
C. Cultivated D. Caltivated

47. A. Praiceworthy B. Peiseworthy
C. Praiseworthy D. Praisaworthy

48. A. Profesional B. Professionel
C. Professional D. Profissional

49. A. Ameteur B. Amateur
C. Amataur D. Amateor

50. A. Unfevourable B. Unfevaurable
C. Unfavourable D. Unfivourable

ANSWERS

1	2	3	4	5	6	7	8	9	10
A	C	A	B	B	A	B	B	D	C
11	12	13	14	15	16	17	18	19	20
A	B	A	A	C	A	A	A	C	A
21	22	23	24	25	26	27	28	29	30
B	B	B	D	B	C	A	C	B	C
31	32	33	34	35	36	37	38	39	40
A	B	A	C	C	A	C	B	D	A
41	42	43	44	45	46	47	48	49	50
A	C	A	C	A	C	C	C	B	C

●●●

REASONING ABILITY

SERIES

Directions : *In each of the following series determine the order of the letters. Then from the given options select the one which will complete the given series.*

1. BMK, DLM, FKO, HJQ, ?
A. JIR B. JIT
C. JHS D. JIS

2. A, CD, FGH, ?
A. IJKL B. KLMN
C. JKLM D. LMNO

3. BXJ, ETL, HPN, KLP, ?
A. PHR B. NIR
C. NHR D. MHR

4. PUF, QVG, RWH, ?
A. SXI B. SYZ
C. SXJ D. SVI

5. DEF, HIJ, MNO, ?
A. RTV B. STU
C. PTU D. SRU

Directions : *Which of the following groups of letters will complete the given series?*

6. ab---b-bbaa-
A. babba B. abaab
C. abbab D. baaab

7. aa-ab--aaa-a
A. baaa B. abab
C. aaab D. aabb

8. -baa-aab-a-a
A. baab B. abab
C. aaba D. aabb

9. -a cca-ccca-acccc-aaa
A. ccaa B. acca
C. caac D. caaa

10. c-bbb--abbbb-abbb-
A. abccb B. bacbb
C. aabcb D. abacb

Directions : *In the following questions, select the number(s) from the given options for completing the given series.*

11. 3, 9, 27, 81, 243, ?
A. 486 B. 729
C. 972 D. 359

12. 1, 6, 12, 19, 27, ?
A. 38 B. 35
C. 36 D. 54

13. 2, 6, 14, 30, 62, ?
A. 126 B. 128
C. 120 D. 130

14. 8, 48, 16, 96, 32, ?
A. 192 B. 150
C. 64 D. 288

15. 2, 8, 14, 24, 34, 48, ?
A. 66 B. 62
C. 58 D. 64

Directions : *In the given series find the number which is wrong.*

16. 5, 25, 120, 625, 3125, 15625
A. 15625 B. 625
C. 120 D. 5

17. 4, 8, 11, 22, 18, 36, 24, 50
A. 8 B. 22
C. 36 D. 24

18. 2, 4, 12, 24, 72, 142, 432
A. 432 B. 12
C. 142 D. 72

19. 2, 3, 4, 4, 6, 8, 9, 12, 16
A. 3 B. 9
C. 6 D. 12

20. 97, 91, 86, 83, 79, 77, 76, 76
A. 86 B. 76
C. 91 D. 83

ANSWERS

1	2	3	4	5	6	7	8	9	10
D	C	C	A	B	D	C	B	D	A
11	**12**	**13**	**14**	**15**	**16**	**17**	**18**	**19**	**20**
B	C	A	A	B	C	D	C	B	D

EXPLANATORY ANSWERS

1. The letters in one group correspond to the letters in the next group in the manner +2, –1, +2 respectively.

BMK DLM FKO HJQ JIS

+2 +2 +2 +2

–1 –1 –1 –1

+2 +2 +2 +2

2. The letters are in natural sequence and from one group to the next one letter is dropped. Also the number of letters in groups is increased by one.

A CD FGH JKLM

↓ ↓ ↓

B E I

3. The letters in one group correspond to the letters in the next group in the manner +3, – 4, +2 respectively, *i.e.*,

BXJ ETL HPN KLP NHR

+3 +3 +3 +3

–4 –4 –4 –4

+2 +2 +2 +2

4. The three letters in each group are moved one step forward.

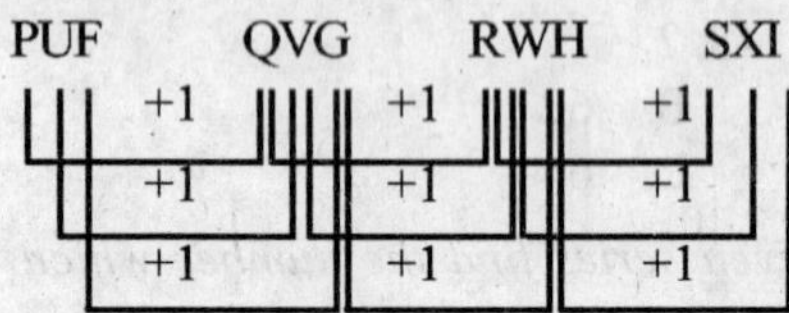

5. The letters are in natural order. The number of letters dropped in between the groups is increased by one at each step.

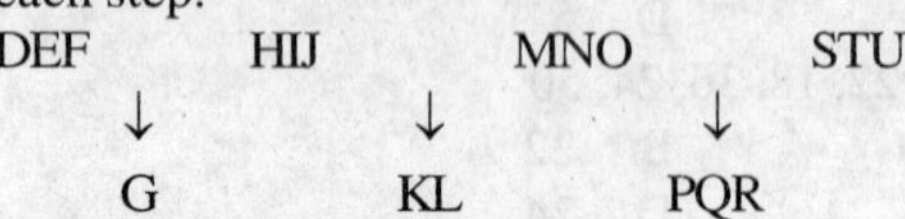

6. The series is abbaab, abbaab

7. The series is aaaaba, aaaaba

8. The series is aba, aba, aba, aba

9. The series is c,a,cc,aa, ccc, aaa, cccc, aaaa

10. The series is cabbbb, cabbbb, cabbbb

11. The numbers in the series are multiplied by 3 to get the next numbers.

12. The difference between the numbers in the series increases by 1, after beginning from 5, *i.e.*,

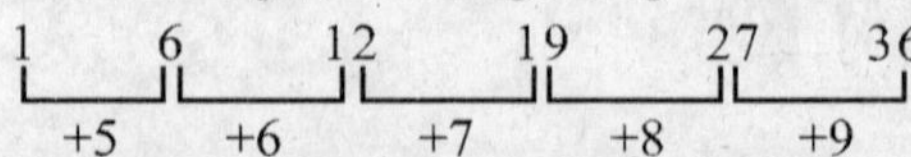

13. The difference between the numbers in the series doubles each time, after beginning from 4, *i.e.*,

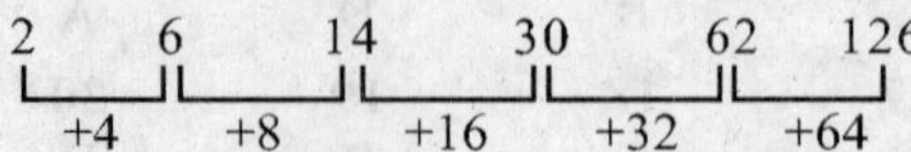

14. *Explanation I* : The sequence in the series is × 6, ÷ 3 which is repeated.

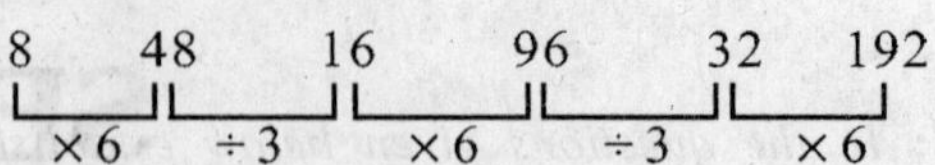

Explanation II : There are two alternate series and the numbers are multiplied by 2.

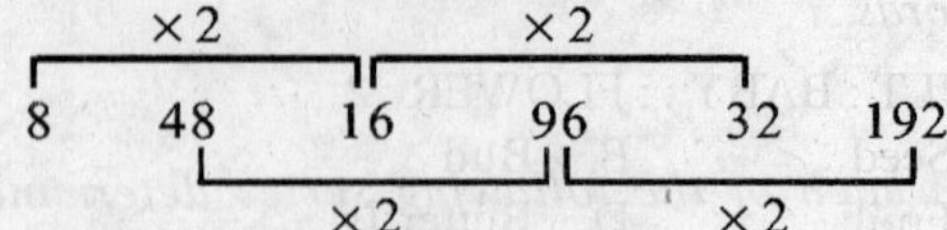

Series I : 8, 16, 32

Series II : 48, 96, 192

15. The sequence in the series is :

2 8 14 24 34 48 62

+6 +6 +10 +10 +14 +14

The difference increases by 4 at alternate step.

16. The numbers in the series are multiplied by 5 to get the next number.

∴ 125 should be in place of 120.

17. Two numbers form a pair. The first number increases by 7 for the next pair and the second number is the double of first number.

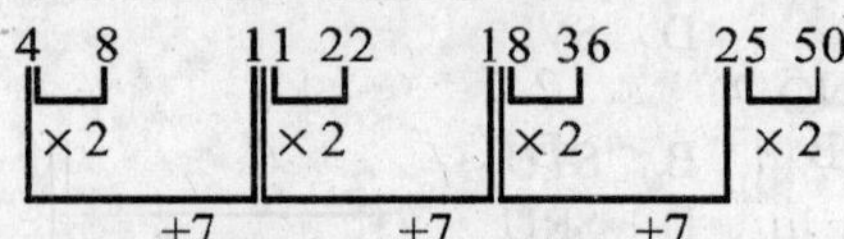

∴ 25 should be in place of 24.

18. There are two alternate series and in each series, the numbers are multiplied by 6 to get the next number.

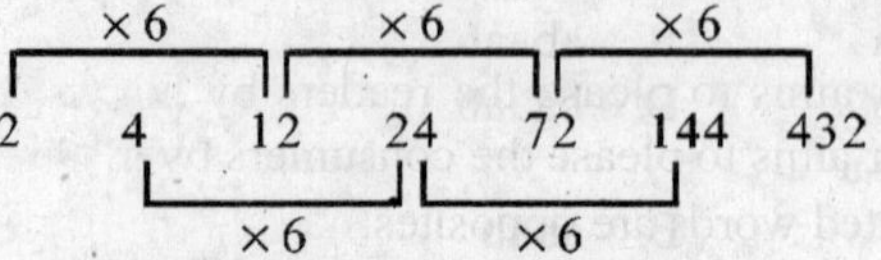

∴ 144 should be in place of 142.

19. There are three alternate series and in each series, the numbers are multiplied by 2 to get the next number.

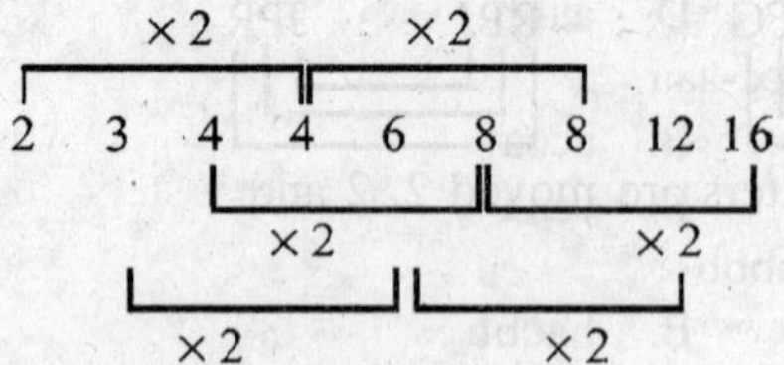

Series I : 2, 4, 8

Series II : 3, 6, 12

Series III : 4, 8, 16

∴ 8 should be in place of 9.

20. The difference between the consecutive numbers in the series decreases by 1 at each step.

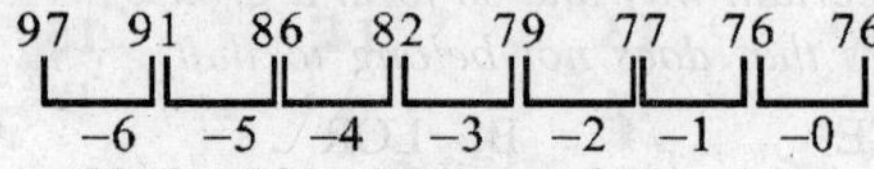

∴ 82 should be in place of 83.

ANALOGIES OR RELATIONSHIPS

Directions : *In the questions given below establish the relationship between the two words. Then from the given options select one which has the same relationship as of the given two words.*

1. ADULT : BABY : : FLOWER : ?
A. Seed B. Bud
C. Fruit D. Butterfly

2. WRITER : READER : : PRODUCER : ?
A. Creator B. Contractor
C. Creature D. Consumer

3. ENTRANCE : EXIT : : LOYALTY : ?
A. Treachery B. Patriotism
C. Fidelity D. Reward

4. MOTHER : MATERNAL : : FATHER : ?
A. Eternal B. Detrimental
C. Paternal D. Formidable

Directions : *In the questions given below one term is missing. Based on the relationship of the two given words find the missing term from the given options.*

5. GFC : CFG : : RPJ : ?
A. JRP B. JPR
C. PJR D. RJP

6. BCF : DEG : : MNQ : ?
A. OPR B. PQS
C. OPP D. QRT

7. NATION : ANITNO : : HUNGRY : ?
A. HNUGRY B. UNHGYR
C. YRNGUH D. UHGNYR

8. SSTU : MMNO : : AABC : ?
A. GGHH B. IJKK
C. XXYZ D. NOOP

ANSWERS

1	2	3	4	5	6	7	8
B	D	A	C	B	A	D	C

EXPLANATORY ANSWERS

1. The youngone of an adult is a baby and that of a flower is a bud.

2. A writer aims to please the readers by his writings, a producer aims to please the consumers by his products.

3. The related words are opposites.

4. Relations on the mother's side are maternal and on the father's side paternal.

5. The letters of the first group are reversed.

: :

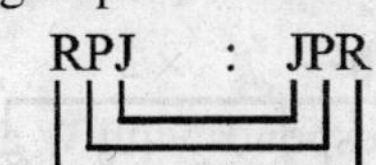

6. The three letters are moved 2, 2 and 1 steps forward respectively.

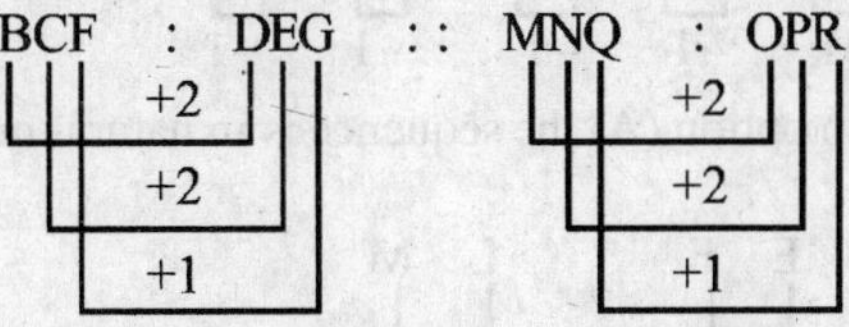

7. The word is divided in sections of two letters and the letters are reversed.

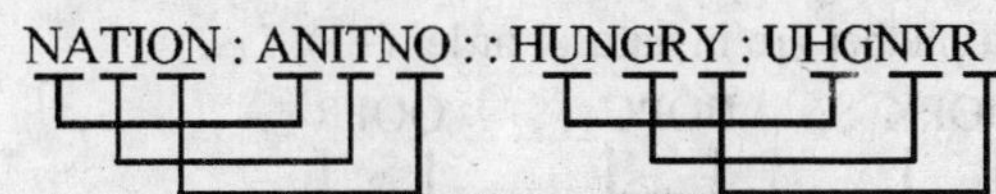

8. The first letter in each group is repeated and followed by two consecutive letters.

ODD ONE OUT

Directions : *Three of the following four in each question are alike in a certain way and so form a group. Select the group of letters that does not belong to that group.*

1. A. ACE B. LOR
C. GIK D. VXZ

2. A. TSR B. LKJ
C. PQO D. HGF

3. A. EF LM B. KJ SR
C. XW HG D. ED YX

4. A. JOPK B. BOPC
C. QOPR D. TOPS

5. A. DfH B. MoQ
C. UwY D. lnO

6. A. JKkL B. OPpQ
C. DEEf D. VWwX

7. A. BdfH B. FHJL
C. RTvX D. uVwX

8. A. DFHEG B. TWXUV
C. OQSPR D. JLNKM

9. A. FEUV B. DCXW
C. BAZY D. HGTS

10. A. UTSR B. XYZW
C. ONML D. IHGF

ANSWERS

1	2	3	4	5	6	7	8	9	10
B	C	A	D	D	C	D	B	A	B

EXPLANATORY ANSWERS

1. The sequence in each group is +2. Only option B has sequence in +3, *i.e.,*

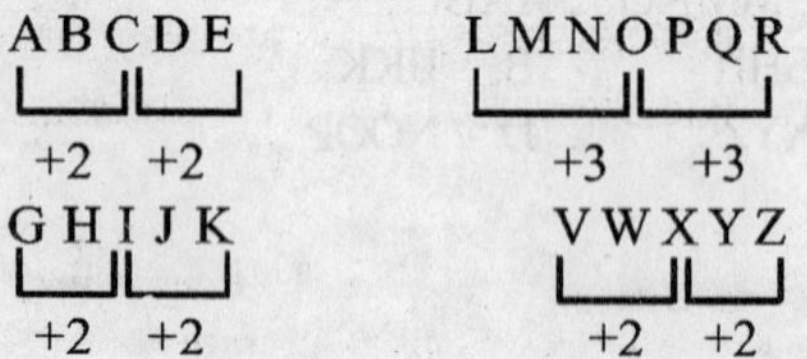

2. The sequence of alphabet in each group is in reverse order. Only option C has sequence in disturbed order.

3. Two consecutive alphabet in each group are in reverse sequence (–1), *i.e.,*

Only in option (A) the sequence is in natural order (+1), *i.e.,*

E F L M
+1 +1

4. In each group, letters 'OP' are common. The two corner alphabet are in natural order (+1); *i.e.,*

Only in option (D) they are in reverse order (–1); *i.e.,*

5. In other groups, only the alphabet in the centre is of lower case. In this option letter 'L' on the left is also in lower case.

6. In other groups, the third letter which is a repeat of the second alphabet is in lower case.

7. In each group, the sequence of the alphabet, irrespective of the case, is +2; *i.e.,*

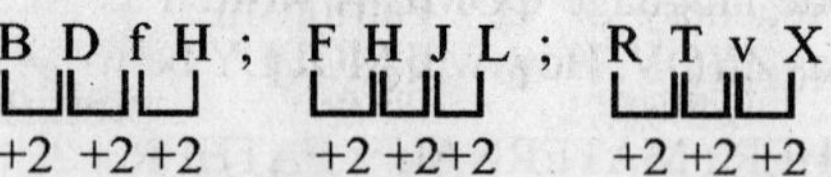

Only in option (D) the sequence is in natural order (+1), *i.e.,*

u V w X
+1 +1 +1

8. In each group; the alphabet at positions-first, fourth, second, fifth and third, form a natural sequence.

In option (B), the alphabet at positions first, fourth, fifth, second and third, form the natural sequence.

9. In each group, two alphabets in the corner and two alphabets in the centre correspond to their reverse order positioned alphabet. *i.e.,*

natural order → A B C D E F G H I J K L M
reverse order → Z Y X W V U T S R Q P O N
natural order → N O P Q R S T U V W X Y Z
reverse order → M L K J I H G F E D C B A

As such—

D corresponds with W and
C corresponds with X.
B corresponds with Y and
A corresponds with Z.
H corresponds with S and
G corresponds with T.

Similarly,

F should correspond with U and
E should correspond with V;
i.e. letters 'UV' should be written as 'VU'

10. In each group, the alphabet are in reverse order.

In option (B), the order is disturbed.

CODING AND DECODING

Directions : *In the following questions select the right option which indicates the correct code for the word or letter given in the question.*

1. If CHAIR is coded as FKDLU then RAID is coded as:

A. ULGD B. ULKG
C. ULDG D. UDLG

2. If CONDEMN is coded as CNODMEN, then TEACHER is coded as :

A. TEACHER B. TAEECHR
C. TCAEEHR D. TAECEHR

3. In a code language COME is written as XLNV and ABLE as ZYOV. How will MOLLY be written in that code?

A. NLOBO B. NLBOO
C. LNOOB D. NLOOB

4. In a certain code PROFESSION is written as EFORPNOISS. In the same code DICTIONARY will be written as :

A. YRANOITCID B. ITCIDYRANO
C. ITCIDYRNAO D. ITCDIYARNO

5. JUNE is coded as NXPF, how will STAY be coded in the same manner?

A. WWCZ B. WVCZ
C. WWDB D. VWZC

Directions : *In the following questions study the coded patterns and then select the right option from the given alternatives.*

6. In a certain language, (a) 'go ju mi' stands for 'plenty of money'; (b) pao ju go nei vu' for 'money creates lots of problems'; (c) 'kol vu nei' for 'problems create tension'; and (d) 'sol tun ju haw' for 'still money is needed'. Which of the following words stand for 'money'?

A. nei B. ju
C. haw D. go

7. In a certain language, (a) 'FOR' stands for 'old is gold'; (b) 'ROT' stands for 'gold is pure'; (c) 'ROM' stands for 'gold is costly'. How will 'pure old gold is costly' be written?

A. TFROM B. FOTRM
C. FTORM D. TOMRF

8. In a certain code '415' means 'milk is hot'; '18' means 'hot soup'; and '895' means 'soup is tasty'. What number will indicate the word 'tasty'?

A. 9 B. 8
C. 5 D. 4

9. In a certain code '643' means 'she is beautiful', '593' means 'he is handsome', and '567' means 'handsome meets beautiful'. What number will indicate the word 'meets'?

A. 5 B. 3
C. 7 D. 6

10. In a certain code language, (a) 'dugo hui mul zo' stands for 'work is very hard'; (b) 'hui dugo ba ki' for 'Bingo is very smart'; (c) 'nano mul dugo' for 'cake is hard', and (d) 'mul ki qu' for 'smart and hard'. Which of the following words stand for 'Bingo'?

A. jalu B. dugo
C. ki D. ba

ANSWERS

1	2	3	4	5	6	7	8	9	10
D	D	D	B	A	B	A	A	C	D

EXPLANATORY ANSWERS

2. In this word, the second and third letters interchange their places and the fifth and sixth letters do the same. Other letters retain their position.

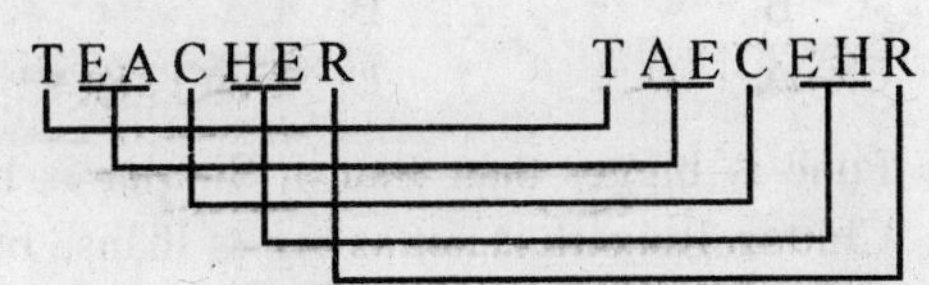

3. The letters of the word are coded by their represented letters in the reverse series.

C O M E → letters in natural series
X L N V → letters in reverse series
↓ ↓ ↓ ↓
3rd15th13th5th → position of letters
A B L E → letters in natural series
Z Y O V → letters in reverse series
↓ ↓ ↓ ↓
1st 2nd12th 5th → position of letters

Similarly,
M O L L Y → letters in natural series
N L O O B → letters in reverse series
↓ ↓ ↓ ↓ ↓
13th 15th 12th 12th 25th → position of letters

4. The word is divided into two equal parts and the letters of each part are written backwards.

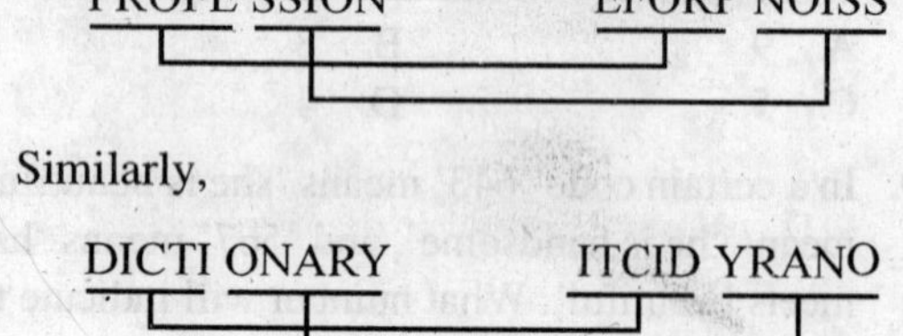

Similarly,

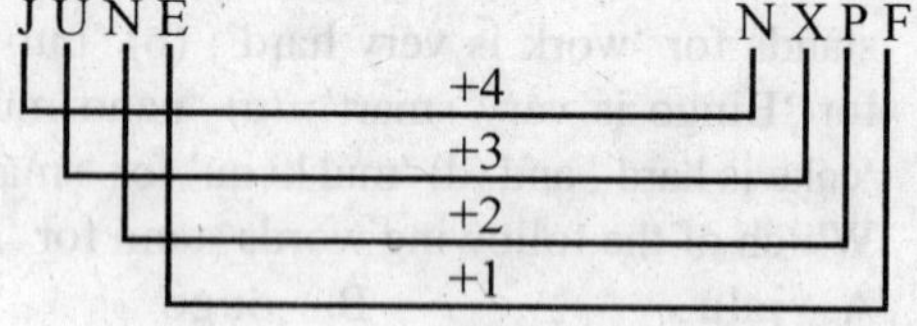

5. The word is coded by moving the letters +4, +3, +2, and +1 steps respectively.

JUNE → NXPF (+4, +3, +2, +1)

Similarly,

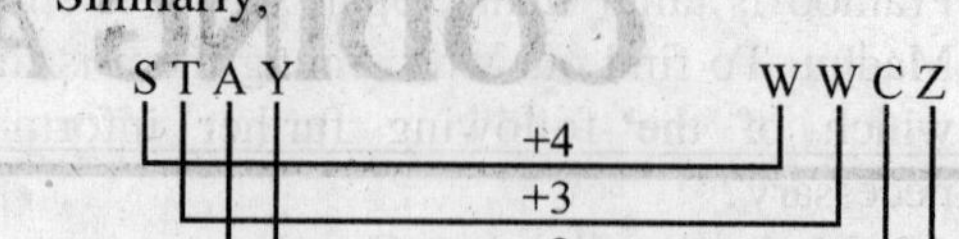

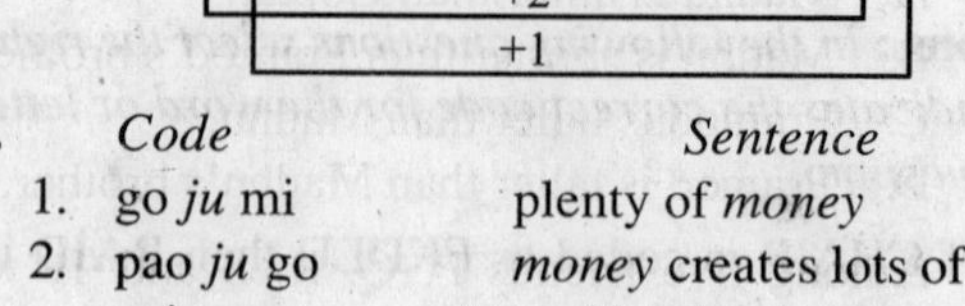

6.

	Code	Sentence
1.	go *ju* mi	plenty of *money*
2.	pao *ju* go nei vu	*money* creates lots of problems
3.	kol vu nei	problems create tension
4.	sol tun *ju* haw	still *money* is needed

In 1st, 2nd and 4th codes and their sentences the word 'ju' is repeated and so is 'money'.

8.

	Code	Sentence
1.	415	milk is hot
2.	18	hot soup
3.	895	soup is *tasty*

From 3rd code and its sentence neither number '9' is repeated nor the word 'tasty'.

9.

	Code	Sentence
1.	643	she is beautiful
2.	593	he is handsome
3.	567	handsome *meets* beautiful

From 3rd code and its sentence, neither number '7' nor the word 'meets' is repeated.

10.

	Code	Sentence
1.	*dugo hui* mul zo	work *is very* hard
2.	*hui dugo* **ba** *ki*	**Bingo** *is very smart*
3.	nano mul *dugo*	cake is *hard*
4.	mul *ki* qu	*smart* and hard

From 2nd code and its sentence, neither 'ba' nor 'Bingo' is repeated.
(Words repeated are in italics)

STATEMENT ANALYSIS

1. Among five friends, A is heavier than B; C is lighter than D; B is lighter than D but heavier than E. Who among them is the heaviest?

A. B
B. C
C. A
D. Can't say

2. Pune is bigger than Jhansi, Sitapur is bigger than Chittor. Raigarh is not as big as Jhansi, but is bigger than Sitapur. Chittor is not as big as Sitapur. Which is the smallest?

A. Jhansi
B. Pune
C. Chittor
D. Sitapur

3. Ajay works more than Ram. Alok works as much as Raju. Pankaj works less than Alok. Ram works more than Alok. Who works the most of all?

A. Ajay
B. Ram
C. Alok
D. Raju

4. Vipul is taller than Hans. Hans is taller than Anand. Alok is taller than Ashok. Ashok is taller than Hans. Who among them is the tallest?

A. Vipul
B. Alok
C. Ashok
D. Cannot be determined

5. Pramod is taller than Gopal. Gopal is shorter than Madhu. To find out who among them is the tallest, which of the following further informations is necessary?

A. Madhu is taller than Gopal.
B. Madhu is shorter than Pramod's brother
C. Pramod is taller than Madhu.
D. Pramod is taller than Madhu's brother.

6. Among five friends P, Q, R, S and T, who is the youngest? To arrive at the answer which of the following information given in the statements (*a*) and (*b*) is sufficient?

(*a*) R is younger than P and T.
(*b*) S is younger than Q.

A. Only (*a*) alone is sufficient
B. Either (*a*) or (*b*) is sufficient
C. Both (*a*) and (*b*) together are needed
D. Both (*a*) and (*b*) together are not sufficient

7. Sushma is richer than Rashmi whereas Anand is richer than Priya. Arun is as rich as Rashmi. Shoba is richer than Sushma.

Which of the following statements is correct according to the above propositions?

A. Rashmi is poorer than Priya.
B. Priya is richer than Arun
C. Arun is poorer than Sushma.
D. Anand is richer than Rashmi

8. A is elder to B while C and D are elder to E who lies between A and B. If C be elder to B, which one of the following statements is necessarily true?

A. E is elder to B
B. A is elder to C
C. C is elder to D
D. D is elder to C

9. Vikram is taller than Rajan but shorter than Annie. Jamal is taller than Annie. Sita is taller than Vikram. Rajan is shorter than Sita. Who is the shortest of all in the group?

A. Sita
B. Rajan
C. Vikram
D. Cannot be determined

10. Suresh is as much older than Kamal as he is younger than Prabodh. Navin is as old as Kamal. Which of the following statements is wrong?

A. Suresh is older than Navin
B. Kamal is younger than Suresh
C. Prabodh is not the oldest
D. Navin is younger than Prabodh

ANSWERS

1	2	3	4	5	6	7	8	9	10
D	C	A	D	C	D	C	A	B	C

EXPLANATORY ANSWERS

1. The five friends in descending order of weight are : A/D, B/C, E or A/D, B, C/E. Either A or D is the heaviest.

2. The order of cities in descending order of size is : Pune, Jhansi, Raigarh, Sitapur, Chittor.

3. On the basis of doing work, the descending order will be : Ajay, Ram, Alok/Raju, Pankaj.

4. On the basis of height, the descending order will be Vipul/Alok, Ashok, Hans, Anand. Either Vipul or Alok is the tallest.

5. According to the information both Pramod and Madhu are taller than Gopal. Option (c) decides who is the tallest.

6. Statements are not inter-related.

7. On the basis of wealth, the descending order will be :

1. Shobha, Sushma, Rashmi/Arun
2. Anand, *and* Priya

(The two statements are not inter-related.)

8. The order in descending seniority will be : A/C/D, E, B.

9. On the basis of height the descending order will be :

Jamal/Sita, Annie, Vikram, Rajan.

or

Jamal, Sita/Annie, Vikram, Rajan.

10. On the basis of age the descending order will be : Prabodh, Suresh, Kamal/Navin.

PLACE ARRANGEMENT

Directions: *In the following questions, understand the arrangement pattern and then select the right answer from the given options :*

1. Five boys are sitting in a row. Raghu is not adjacent to Shyam or Amit. Ajay is not adjacent to Shyam. Raghu is adjacent to Mayank. If Mayank is at the middle in the row, then Ajay is adjacent to whom out of the following?

A. Amit B. Raghu
C. Mayank D. Shyam

2. Mini is to the right of Rajni but to the left of Ananta. Saya is to the right of Mini but to the left of Jaya. Who is on the extreme left if all the girls are facing North?

A. Jaya B. Mini
C. Rajni D. Saya

3. Kittu is in-between Mohan and Sohan. Raju is to the left of Sohan and Shyam is to the right of Mohan. If all of the friends are sitting facing South, then who is on their extreme right?

A. Mohan B. Sohan
C. Kittu D. Shyam

4. A, B, C, D and E are running one behind the other. C is not near E and A is not near D. B is next to A and E is not near D. Who is in the middle?

A. B B. E
C. A D. Cannot be said

5. O, P, Q, R, S and T are standing on a bench according to their height. P is taller than O but shorter than S. Only S is taller than T. R is shorter than P but taller than Q. Who is the shortest?

A. O B. Q
C. P D. Cannot be said

ANSWERS

1	2	3	4	5
B	C	D	A	D

EXPLANATORY ANSWERS

1. The order of sitting is :

Amit, Shyam, Mayank, Ajay, Raghu

or

Ajay, Raghu, Mayank, Amit, Shyam

2. The order in which the girls are positioned is :

Rajni, Mini, Ananta, Saya, Jaya

or

Saya, Jaya, Ananta

or

Saya, Ananta, Jaya

3. The order of sitting while facing South is:

Shyam, Mohan, Kittu, Sohan, Raju.

4. The positions while running behind the other is :

E   E
A   A
B   *or*   B
C   D
D   C

5. In descending order of height, the standing positions are :

S   S
T   T
P   *or*   P
R   R
O   Q
Q   O

Either O or Q is the shortest. The information given is not enough to clarify the answer.

DIRECTION SENSE

Directions : *In the following questions, select the right answer from the given options to depict the correct direction/distance.*

1. Kittu walks towards East and then towards South. After walking some distance he turns towards West and then turns to his left. In which direction is he walking now?

A. North B. South
C. East D. West

2. A person is driving towards West. What sequence of directions should he follow so that he is driving towards South?
A. left, right, right
B. right, right, left
C. left, left, left
D. right, right, right

3. Richa drives 8 km to the South, turns left and drives 5 km. Again, she turns left and drives 8 km. How far is she from her starting point?
A. 3 km B. 5 km
C. 8 km D. 13 km

4. Dingi runs 40 km towards North then turns right and runs 50 km. He turns right and runs 30 km, and once again turns right and runs 50 km. How far is he from his starting point?
A. 90 km B. 50 km
C. 10 km D. 5 km

5. Debu walks towards East then towards North and turning 45° right walks for a while and lastly turns towards left. In which direction is he walking now?
A. North B. East
C. South-East D. North-West

ANSWERS

1	2	3	4	5
B	D	B	C	D

EXPLANATORY ANSWERS

1.
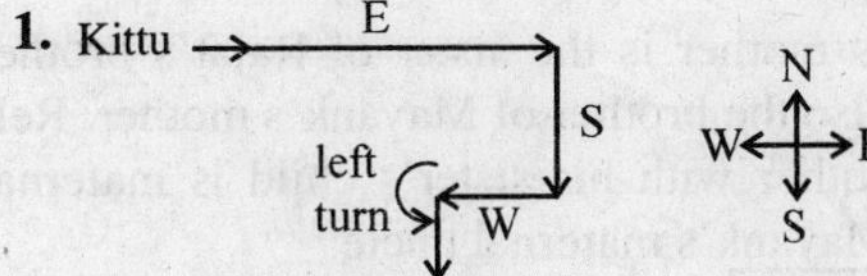

2.
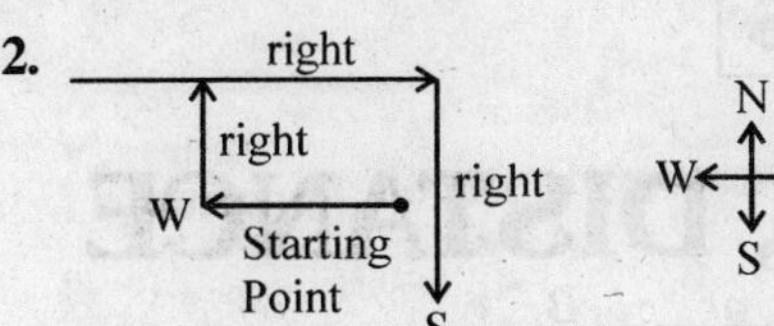

3.
Starting Point
Finishing Point
5 km
8 km
8 km
5 km
N
W
E
S

4.
50 km
N
W
E
S
40 km
Finishing Point
30 km
10 km
50 km
Starting Point

5.
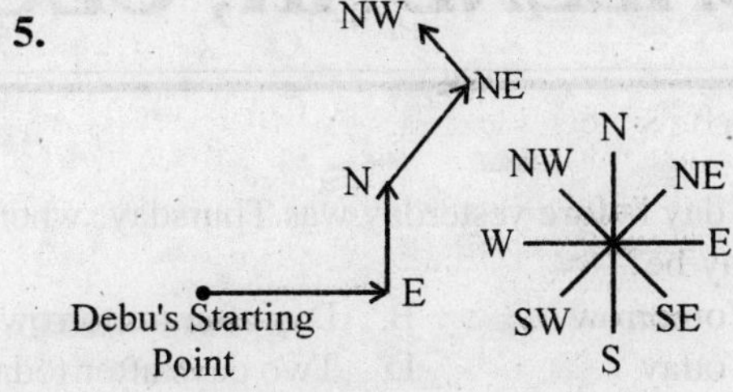

BLOOD RELATIONSHIPS

Directions : *In each of the following questions keenly study the relationship mentioned between the persons, and then from the given options select the right relationship as the answer.*

1. 'A' is the father of 'B' and 'C'. 'B' is the son of 'A' but 'C' is not the son of 'A'. What is 'C's' relation with 'A'?
A. Daughter B. Son
C. Niece D. Nephew

2. A lady said, "The person standing there is my grandfather's only son's daughter". How is the lady related to the standing person?
A. Sister B. Mother
C. Aunt D. Cousin

3. Ravi is the brother of Amit's son's son. What is Amit's relation to Ravi?
A. Cousin B. Father
C. Grandfather D. Son

4. Mayank said, "My mother is the sister of Rajat's brother." What is Rajat's relation with Mayank?

A. Cousin B. Maternal uncle
C. Uncle D. Brother-in-law

5. Introducing Lily, Raghav said, "Her father is my mother's only son". How is Lily related to Raghav?

A. Aunt B. Daughter
C. Mother D. Sister

ANSWERS

1	2	3	4	5
A	A	C	B	B

EXPLANATORY ANSWERS

1.

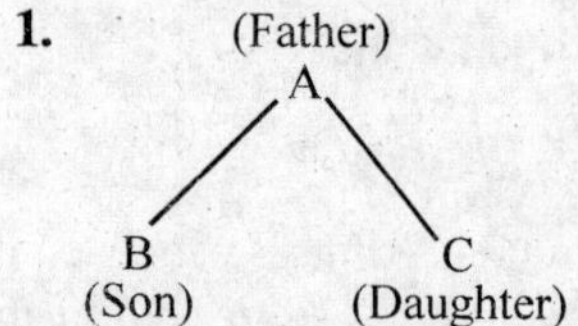

'C' is not the son of 'A', but 'A' is the father of 'C'. So, 'C' is the daughter of 'A'.

2.

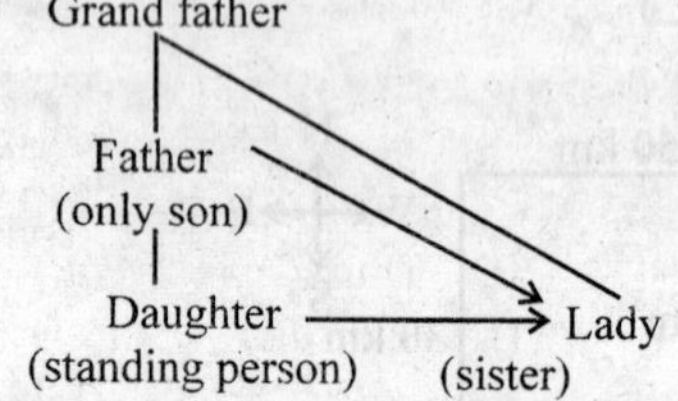

Lady's grandfather's son is lady's father and father's daughter will only be lady's sister.

4. Mother → (sister) Rajat's brother ← (brother) Rajat

Rajat → Maternal Uncle → Mayank

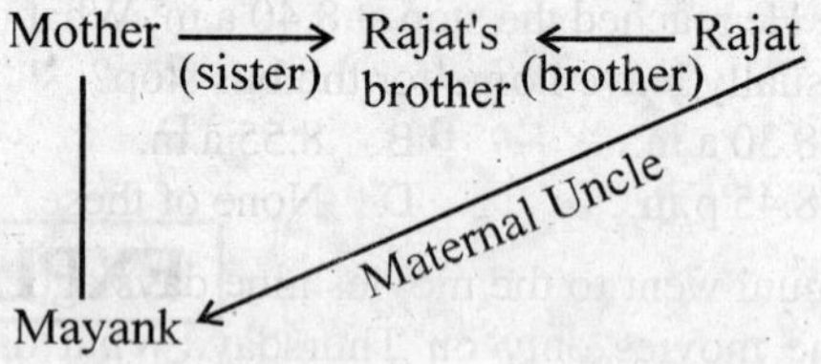

Mayank's mother is the sister of Rajat's brother. So Rajat is also the brother of Mayank's mother. Relation of the brother with his sister's child is maternal. So Rajat is Mayank's maternal uncle.

CALENDAR, CLOCK, TIME, DISTANCE

1. If the day before yesterday was Thursday, when will Sunday be?

A. Tomorrow B. Day after tomorrow
C. Today D. Two days after today

2. There are twenty people working in an office. The first group of five works between 8:00 A.M. and 2:00 PM. The second group of ten works between 10:00 AM to 4:00 PM. And the third group of five works between 12 noon to 6:00 PM. There are three computers in the office which all the employees frequently use. During which of the following hours the computers are likely to be used most?

A. 1:00 PM - 3:00 PM
B. 12 noon - 2:00 PM
C. 2:00 PM - 4:00 PM
D. 10:00 AM - 12 noon

3. If the seventh day of a month is three (3) days earlier than Friday, what day will it be on the nineteenth day of the month?

A. Sunday B. Monday
C. Wednesday D. Friday

4. Radha remembers that her father's birthday is after 16th but before 21st of March, while her brother Mangesh remembers that his father's birthday is before 22nd but after 19th of March. On which date is the birthday of their father?

A. 19th
B. 20th
C. 21st
D. Cannot be determined

5. A man is three (3) years older than his wife and four (4) times as old as his son. If the son attains an age of fifteen (15) years after three (3) years, what is the present age of the mother?

A. 45 years B. 51 years
C. 48 years D. 60 years

6. A clock is so placed that at 12 noon its minute hand points towards north-east. In which direction does its

hour hand point at 1.30 P.M.?
A. East B. West
C. North D. South

7. If in the above question clock is turned through an angle of 135° in an anticlockwise direction, in which direction will its minute hand point at 8.45 P.M.?
A. East B. West
C. North D. South

8. A couple married in 1980 had two children, one in 1982 and the other in 1984. Their combined ages will equal the years of the marriage in?
A. 1986 B. 1985
C. 1987 D. 1988

9. Manoj left home for the bus stop 15 minutes earlier than the usual time. It takes 10 minutes to reach the stop. He reached the stop at 8.40 a.m. What time does he usually leave home for the bus stop?
A. 8.30 a.m. B. 8.55 a.m.
C. 8.45 p.m. D. None of these

10. Mamuni went to the movies nine days ago. She goes to the movies only on Thursday. What day of the week is today?
A. Sunday B. Tuesday
C. Thursday D. Saturday

11. If Thursday was the day after the day before yesterday five days ago, what is the least number of days ago when Sunday was three days before the day after tomorrow?
A. Two days ago B. Three days ago
C. Four days ago D. Five days ago

12. 1.12.91 is the first Sunday. Which is the fourth Tuesday of December 91?
A. 31.12.91 B. 24.12.91
C. 17.12.91 D. 26.12.91

13. If the third day of a month is Monday, which of the following will be the fifth day from 21st of that month?
A. Tuesday B. Monday
C. Wednesday D. Thursday

14. Keshav runs a factory in three shifts of eight hours each with 210 employees. In each shift minimum of 80 employees are required to run the factory effectively. No employee can be allowed to work for more than 16 hours a day. At least how many employees will be required to work for 16 hours every day?
A. 30 B. 60
C. Data inadequate D. None of these

15. If 15 horses eat 15 bags of gram in 15 days, in how many days will one horse eat one bag of grain?
A. 15 days B. 1/15 days
C. 1 day D. 30 days

16. A century leap year is divisible by :
A. 4 B. 16
C. 40 D. 400

17. If the fifth day of a month is Friday, which of the following will be the Seventh day from 10th of that month?
A. Tuesday B. Monday
C. Wednesday D. Thursday

18. Day after tomorrow is my birthday. On the same day next week falls 'Holi'. Today is Monday. What will be the day after 'Holi'?
A. Wednesday B. Thursday
C. Friday D. Saturday

19. A clock shows the time as 3 : 30 p.m. If the minute hand gains 2 minutes every hour, how many minutes will the clock gain by 4 a.m.?
A. 23 Minutes B. 24 Minutes
C. 25 Minutes D. 26 Minutes

20. Two brothers were expected to return home on the same day. Rajat returned 3 days earlier but Rohit returned 4 days later. If Rajat returned on Thursday, what was the expected day when both the brothers were to return home and when did Rohit Return?
A. Wednesday, Sunday
B. Thursday, Monday
C. Sunday, Thursday
D. Monday, Friday

ANSWERS

1	2	3	4	5	6	7	8	9	10
A	B	A	B	A	A	D	A	D	D
11	**12**	**13**	**14**	**15**	**16**	**17**	**18**	**19**	**20**
A	B	C	D	A	D	C	B	C	C

EXPLANATORY ANSWERS

1. Thursday —Day-before-yesterday
Friday —Yesterday
Saturday —Today
Sunday — Tomorrow

2. 1. 5 people work between 8 a.m. to 2 p.m.

2. 10 people work between 10 a.m. to 4 p.m.

3. 5 people work between 12 noon to 6 p.m.

So, computers are used most between 12 noon to 2 p.m.

3. 7th day is 3 days earlier than Friday so, 10th day is Friday, so also is 17th.

∴ 19th day will be 2nd day ahead of Friday, *i.e.*, Sunday.

4. Father's birthday

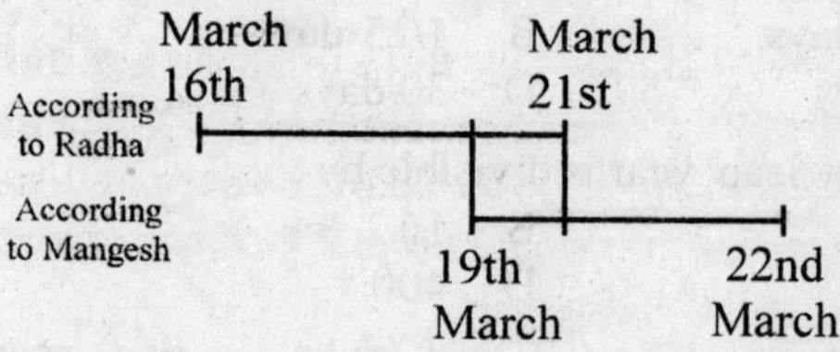

∴ Their father's birthday is on 20th March.

5. Present age of son is 15 – 3 = 12 years. Age of the man is 4 times the age of son, *i.e.*,

12 × 4 = 48 years

Man is 3 years elder to his wife/son's mother.

So Age of the mother is 48 – 3 = 45 years

6.

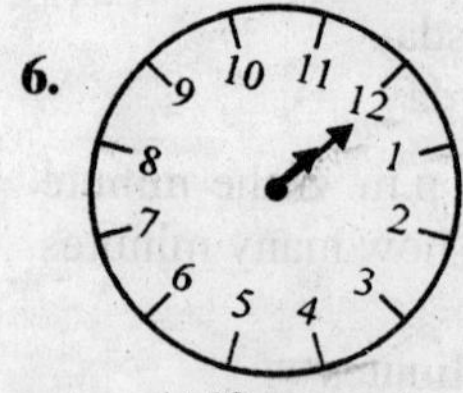

At 12 noon

At 1.30 p.m. the hour hand will point towards East.

7.

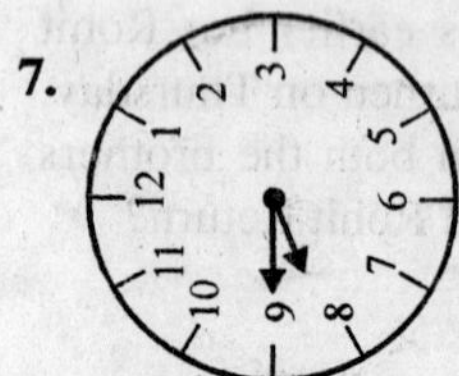

After rotating the clock in earlier question, its minute hand will point towards South at 8:45 p.m.

8. 1982 — 2 years later — 1st child

1984 — 4 years later — 2nd child

Total age of children — 2 years.

1985 — 5 years later — Total age of children: 4 years.

1986 — 6 years later — Total age of children : 6 years.

9. Manoj reached the bus stop at 8.40 a.m. He left his home at 8:40 – 10 minutes = 8:30 a.m. He left 15 minutes earlier than usual, so his actual time of leaving home is 8:30 am + 15 minutes = 8:45 a.m.

10. Mamuni goes to the movies on Thursday, so nine days ago was Thursday.

∴ Two days ago was also Thursday. So, today is Saturday.

11. Day after the day-before-yesterday five days ago is the 6th day which is Thursday. And so, the 3rd day will be Sunday. Three days before the day-after-tomorrow is Yesterday which is the 1st day of the five days. So, two days ago was Sunday.

12. First Sunday is on 1st December

First Tuesday is on 3rd December

3 weeks later, Fourth Tuesday will be on 3 + (7 × 3) = 24th December.

13. 3rd day of the month is Monday

5th day from 21st is 26th

26 – 3 = 23 days

23 days later, 23/7 leaves 2 days.

So, two days ahead of Monday will be Wednesday.

14. 80 employees are required for double shift.

15. 15 horses eat 15 bags of grain in 15 days

15 horses eat 1 bag of grain in 1 day

1 horse eats 1 bag of grain in 15 days

16. A leap year is divisible by 4 and a century leap year is divisible by 400.

17. Seventh day from 10th is 17th.

5th day is Friday. Next Friday is on 12th, 17 – 12 = 5, 5 days ahead of Friday will be Wednesday.

So, 17th is Wednesday.

18. Today is Monday

Day-after-tomorrow is Wednesday

Next week 'Holi' is also on Wednesday

So, Day after Holi is Thursday.

19. Hours between 3:30 p.m. and 4 a.m. are — 12½ hours.

Number of minutes gained will be 12½ × 2 = 25 minutes.

20. Rajat returned on Thursday. 3 days later was the day of expected return, *i.e.*, Sunday. Rohit returned 4 days after Sunday, *i.e.*, Thursday.

ROWS AND RANKS

1. In a row of trees, one tree is fifth from either end of the row. How many trees are in the row?

A. 11 B. 8
C. 10 D. 9

2. Jaya ranks 5th in a class of 53. What is her rank from the bottom in the class?

A. 49th B. 48th
C. 47th D. 50th

3. Mohan ranks twenty-first in a class of sixty-five students. What will be his (Mohan's) rank if the lowest candidate is assigned rank 1?

A. 44th B. 45th
C. 46th D. Data inadequate

4. If Rahul finds that he is 12th from the right in a line of boys and 4th from the left, how many boys should be added to the line such that there are 28 boys in the line?

A. 12 B. 14
C. 20 D. 13

5. In a row of boys, Rajan is tenth from the right and Suraj is tenth from the left. When Rajan and Suraj interchange their positions, Suraj will be twenty-seventh from the left. Which of the following will be Rajan's position from the right?

A. Tenth B. Twenty-sixth
C. Twenty-ninth D. None of these

6. Mahesh and Suresh are ranked 11th and 12th respectively from the top in a class of 41 students. What will be their respective ranks from the bottom?

A. 32nd and 33rd B. 29th and 30th
C. 30th and 31st D. 31st and 30th

7. Uma ranked 8th from the top and 37th from bottom in a class. How many students are there in the class?

A. 47 B. 46
C. 45 D. None of these

8. In a queue, Sadiq is 14th from the front and Joseph is 17th from the end, while Jane is in between Sadiq and Joseph. If Sadiq be ahead of Joseph and there be 48 persons in the queue, how many persons are there between Sadiq and Jane?

A. 5 B. 6
C. 7 D. 8

9. Rohan ranked eleventh from the top and twenty-seventh from the bottom among the students who passed the annual examination in a class. If the number of students who failed in the examination was 12, how many students appeared for the examination?

A. 48
B. 49
C. 50
D. Cannot be determined

10. Some boys are sitting in a row. P is sitting fourteenth from the left and Q is seventh from the right. If there are four boys between P and Q, how many boys are there in the row?

A. 19 B. 21
C. 25 D. 23

ANSWERS

1	2	3	4	5	6	7	8	9	10
D	A	B	D	D	D	D	C	B	C

EXPLANATORY ANSWERS

1.

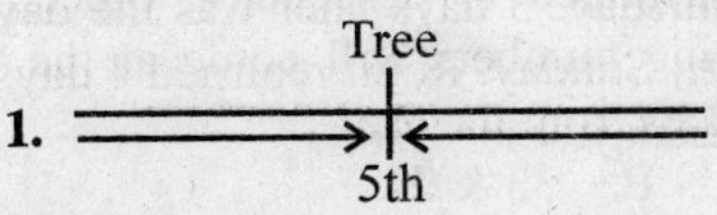

Total number of trees in the row are :
(5 + 5) –1 =9

2.

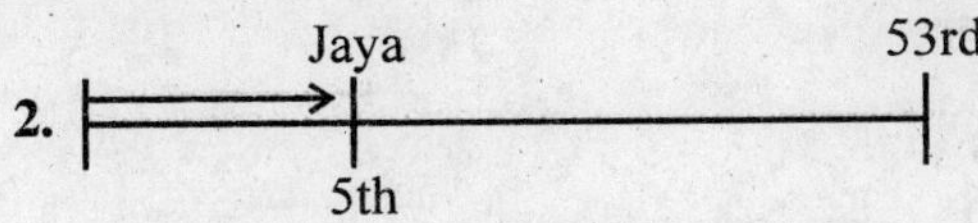

Jaya's rank from the bottom is :
(53 – 5) +1 = 49th.

3.

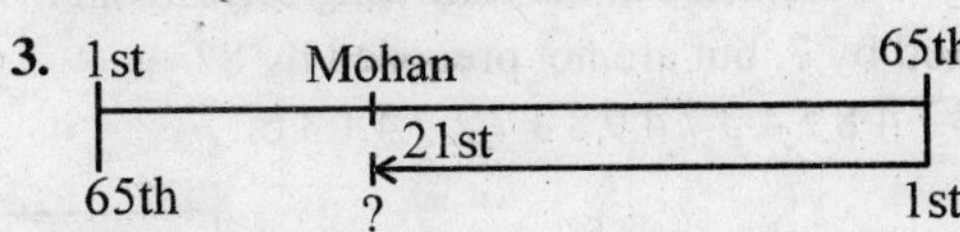

Note : Mohan's rank from the last or the question asked means the same.

Mohan's rank is (65 – 21) +1 = 45th

4. 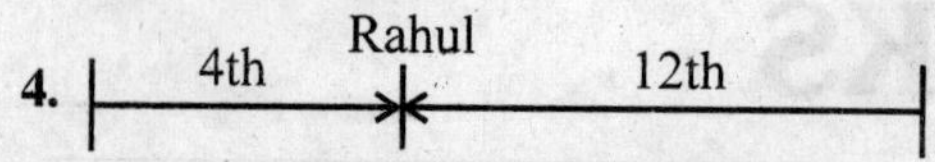

The number of boys in the line are :
(4 + 12) – 1 = 15
To make a line of 28 boys, (28 –15) *i.e.* 13 more boys are needed.

5. 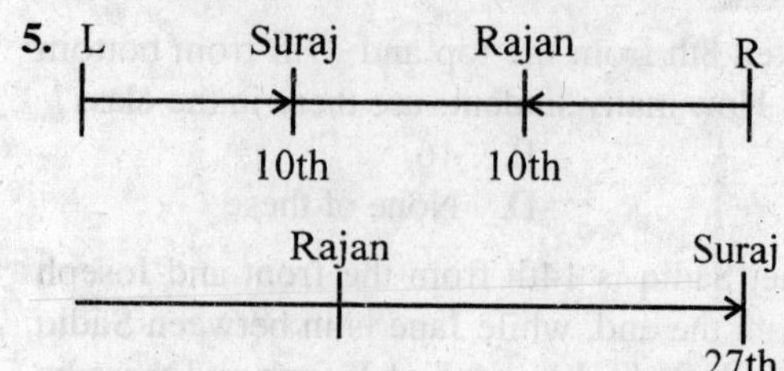

As the position of boys is equal from both ends, Rajan will also be 27th from the right after changing positions.

6. 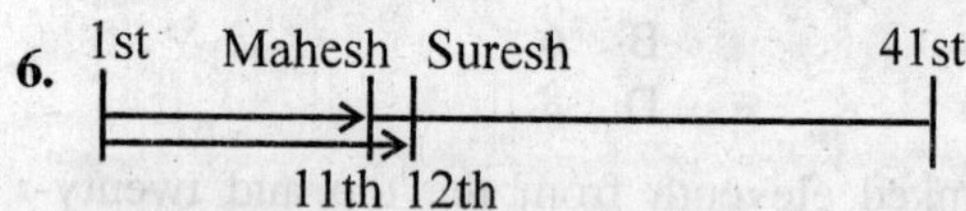

Mahesh's position from bottom is :
(41 – 11) + 1 = 31st
Suresh's position from bottom is :
(41 – 12) +1 = 30th

7. 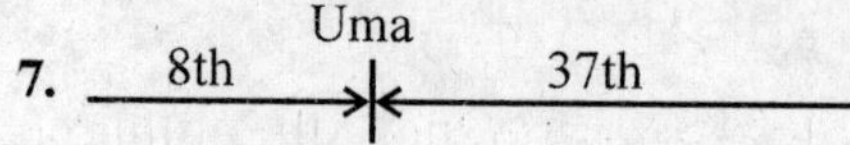

Total number of students in the class are :
(8 + 37) – 1 = 44

8. 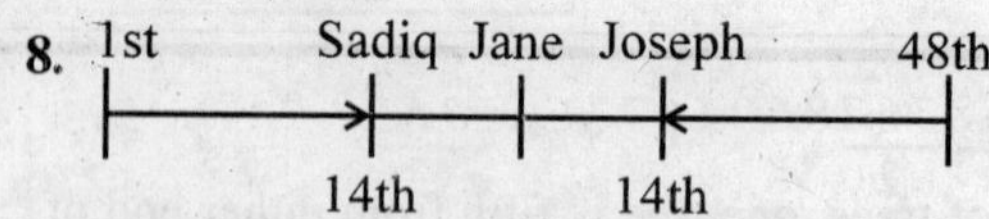

Sadiq's position from last is :
(48 – 14) + 1 = 35th
Number of persons between Sadiq and Joseph are (35 – 17) – 1 = 17
Jane is in-between Sadiq and Joseph *i.e.,* she's at 9th position from both the boys.
∴ there are 8 persons between Sadiq and Jane.
Note : (8 + 8) – 1 = 17

9. 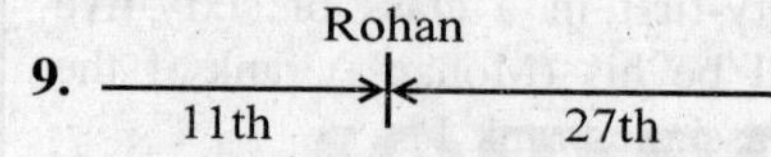

Number of students who passed the examination (11+ 27) – 1 = 37
Those who failed = 12
Total number of students who appeared in the examination = 37 + 12 = 49.

10. 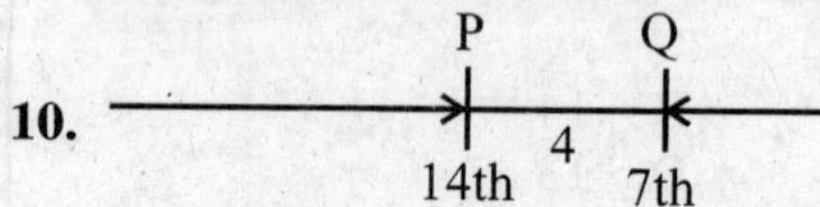

The number of boys in the row are :
(14 + 4 + 7) = 25

NUMBER PROBLEMS

1. How many 6's are there in the following series of numbers which are preceded by 7 but not immediately followed by 9?
6 7 9 5 6 9 7 6 8 7 6 7 8 6 9 4 6 7 7 6 9 5 7 6 3

A. One B. Two
C. Three D. Four

2. In a chess tournament each of six players will play every other player exactly once. How many matches will be played during the tournament?

A. 12 B. 15
C. 30 D. 36

3. How many 4's are there in the following series which are preceded by 7, but are not preceded by 8?
3 4 5 7 4 3 7 4 8 5 4 3 7 4 9 8 4 7 2 7 4 1 3 6

A. 1 B. 2
C. 3 D. 4

4. How many even numbers are there in the following series of numbers, each of which is immediately preceded by an odd number, but not immediately followed by an even number?
5 3 4 8 9 7 1 6 5 3 2 9 8 4 3 5

A. Nil B. 1
C. 2 D. 3

5. If all the numbers from 1 to 51 which are exactly divisible by 3 are arranged in descending order, which of the following numbers will come at the seventh and tenth places from the top?

A. 33 & 27 B. 33 & 21
C. 21 & 30 D. 33 & 24

ANSWERS

1	2	3	4	5
C	B	D	C	D

EXPLANATORY ANSWERS

1. $679569\underset{1}{\underline{768}}\underset{2}{\underline{767}}8694677695\underset{3}{\underline{763}}$

2. When all the players have to play with each other then the method of calculating the number of matches to be played is $\frac{n(n-1)}{2}$ where *'n'* is the number of players playing the match. So, the number of matches played will be :
$(6 \times 5) \div 2 = 30 \div 2 = 15$

3. $345\underset{1}{\underline{74}}3\underset{2}{\underline{74}}8543\underset{3}{\underline{74}}98472\underset{4}{\underline{74}}136$

4. $534897\underset{1}{\underline{165}}\underset{2}{\underline{329}}8435$

5. The numbers divisible by 3 in descending order are :
51, 48, 45, 42, 39, 36, 33, $\underset{7th}{\underline{30}}$, 27, $\underset{10th}{\underline{24}}$, 21, 18, 15, 12, 9, 6, 3.

SYMBOL SUBSTITUTION

1. If "+" means "–"; "–" means "×"; "×"means "÷" and "÷" means "+", then
$15 \times 5 \div 10 + 5 - 3 = ?$

A. 9.5 B. 0
C. – 2 D. 24

2. If "+" means "–"; "–" means "×"; "×"means "÷" and "÷" means "+", then
$15 \times 3 \div 15 + 5 - 2 = ?$

A. 0 B. 10
C. 20 D. 6

3. If "+" means "÷"; "×" means "–"; "÷"means "+" and "–" means "×", then
$16 \div 8 \times 6 - 2 + 12 = ?$

A. 22 B. 24
C. 23 D. 20

4. If "+" means "×"; "–" means "÷"; "÷"means "+" and "×" means "–", then what will be the value of $20 \div 40 - 4 \times 5 + 6 = ?$

A. 60 B. 1.67
C. 150 D. 0

5. If "+" means "×"; "–" means "÷"; "×"means "–" and "÷" means "+", then
$5 + 8 - 4 \times 2 \div 9 = ?$

A. 15 B. 13
C. 17 D. 11

ANSWERS

1	2	3	4	5
C	B	C	D	C

EXPLANATORY ANSWERS

1. $15 \div 5 + 10 - 5 \times 3$
$3 + 10 - 15 = -2$

2. $15 \div 3 + 15 - 5 \times 2$
$5 + 15 - 10 = 10$

3. $16 + 8 - 6 \times 2 \div 12$
$16 + 8 - 1 = 23$

4. $20 + 40 \div 4 - 5 \times 6$
$20 + 10 - 30 = 0$

5. $5 \times 8 \div 4 - 2 + 9$
$10 - 2 + 9 = 17$

MISSING NUMBERS

Directions: *In each question given below which one number can be placed at the sign of interrogation?*

1.

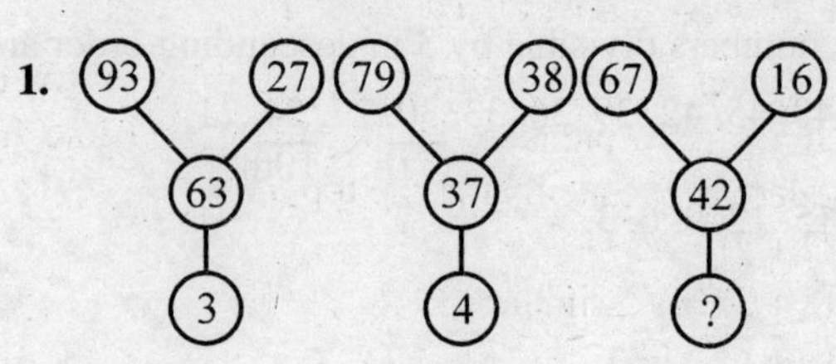

A. 5 B. 6
C. 8 D. 9

2.

4 8 5
6 14 6 14 6 ?
8 8 4
10 18 14 22 11 15

A. 8 B. 14
C. 10 D. 6

3.

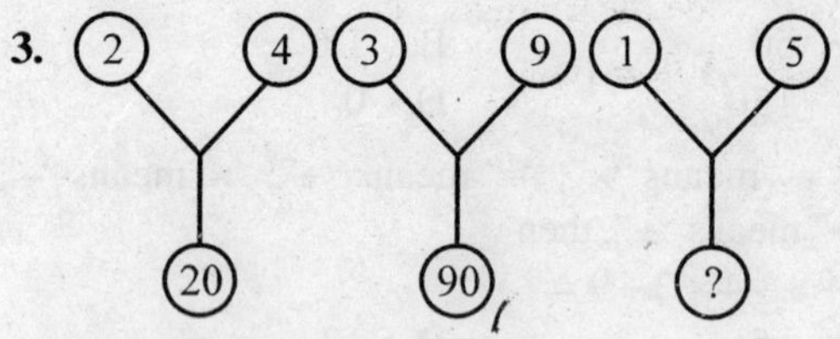

A. 20 B. 25
C. 26 D. 75

4. 27 22 50
13 12 26
9 2 ?

A. 12 B. 39
C. 18 D. 24

5.

5 3 7 5 6 4
19 ? 29
4 6 5

A. 25 B. 47
C. 37 D. 41

6.

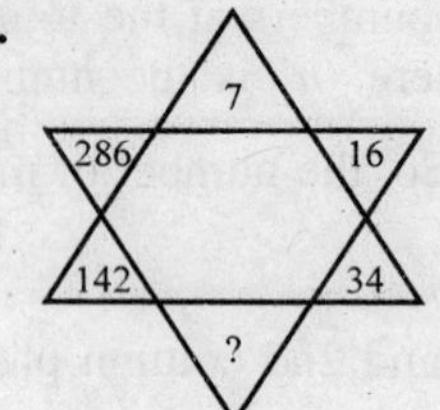

A. 70 B. 68
C. 56 D. 92

7.

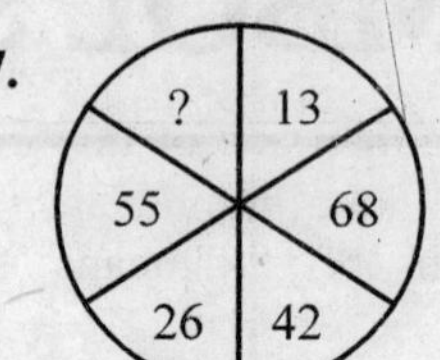

A. 41 B. 37
C. 29 D. 25

8.

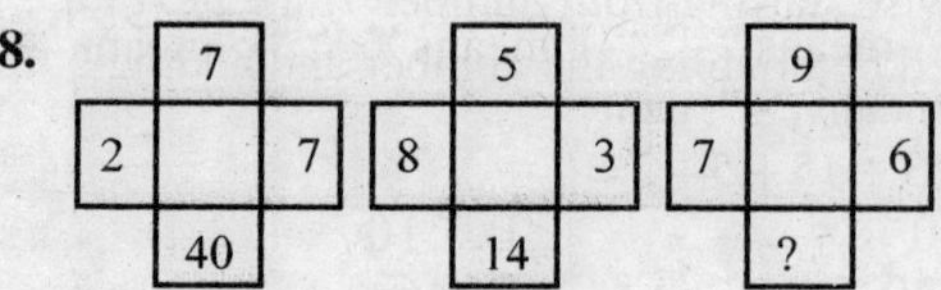

A. 72 B. 68
C. 82 D. 96

9. 42 (21) 22
78 (?) 84
162 (18) 99

A. 12 B. 13
C. 60 D. 72

10.

16 25 19
107 209 ?
7 10 20 4 2 17

A. 68 B. 93
C. 175 D. 217

ANSWERS

1	2	3	4	5	6	7	8	9	10
D	C	C	A	D	A	C	B	B	A

EXPLANATORY ANSWERS

1. The sum of numbers on right and centre subtracted from the number on the left gives the number at the bottom, *i.e.,*

$93 - (27 + 63) = 3$
$79 - (38 + 37) = 4$

Similarly,
$67-(16+42)=9$

2. The number inside each triangle is the difference of the numbers at its base *i.e.*
$10-4=6$, $18-4=14$ and $18-10=8$
$14-8=6$, $22-8=14$ and $22-14=8$, similarly
$11-5=6$, $15-5=10$ and $15-11=4$.

3. The sum of squares of two numbers at the top gives the third number below, *i.e.*,
$2^2+4^2=20$
$3^2+9^2=90$, similarly
$1^2+5^2=26$

4. The sum of numbers in 1st and 2nd column plus 1 is the number in the 3rd column, *i.e.*,
$27+22+1=50$
$13+12+1=26$, similarly
$9+2+1=12$

5. The product of numbers on either side of the triangle plus the number at the base is the number inside the triangle, *i.e.*,
$(5\times 3)+4=19$
$(6\times 4)+5=29$, similarly
$(7\times 5)+6=41$

6. Clockwise starting from number 7, the next number is obtained by doubling the number and adding 2, *i.e.*,
$(7\times 2)+2=16$
$(16\times 2)+2=34$ . . . , similarly
$(34\times 2)+2=70$
$(70\times 2)+2=142$
$(142\times 2)+2=286$

7. The difference between the numbers in opposite sectors is 13, *i.e.*,
$26-13=13$
$68-55=13$, similarly
The missing number is $42-13=29$
($42+13=55$ is not given as option)

8. The number at the bottom is obtained by subtracting the sum of two numbers in the centre grid line from the square of the number at the top, *i.e.*,
$7^2-(2+7)=40$
$5^2-(8+3)=14$, similarly
$9^2-(7+6)=68$

9. The number inside the brackets is obtained by multiplying the number on the left by 2 and then dividing the product by the sum of digits of number on the right, *i.e.*,
$(42\times 2)\div(2+2)=21$
$(162\times 2)\div(9+9)=18$, similarly
$(78\times 2)\div(8+4)=13$

10. Subtracting the sum of squares of two numbers at the base from the square of number at the apex gives the number inside the triangle, *i.e.*,
$16^2-(7^2+10^2)=107$
$25^2-(20^2+4^2)=209$, similarly
$19^2-(2^2+17^2)=68$

ALPHABET PROBLEMS

Directions : *The following questions are based on alphabet series in natural or reverse order and the combinations that can be made by changing the position of alphabet in given words.*

1. Which alphabet comes immediately before the sixth alphabet from the left extreme in alphabetical series?
A. U B. E
C. F D. V

2. Which letter is midway between G and S?
A. L B. N
C. M D. No letter

3. Which letter should be ninth letter to the left of ninth letter from the right if the first half of the alphabet is reversed?
A. I B. D
C. F D. E

4. If the alphabet is in reverse order, which letter will be eighth letter to the left of the seventh letter counting from the right end?
A. O B. P
C. N D. Q

5. What will be the fifth letter to the right of the thirteenth letter from the right?
A. R B. S
C. I D. O

ANSWERS

1	2	3	4	5
B	C	D	A	B

EXPLANATORY ANSWERS

1. 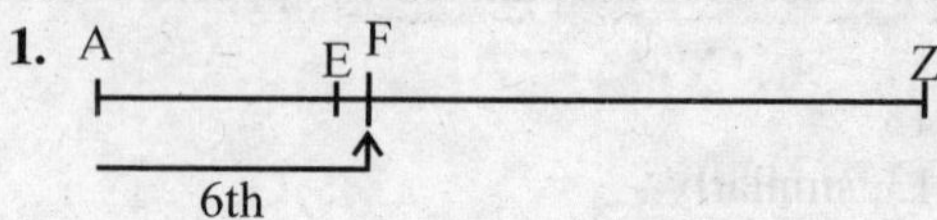

Sixth letter from left is 'F' and letter immediately before 'F' is 'E'.

2. 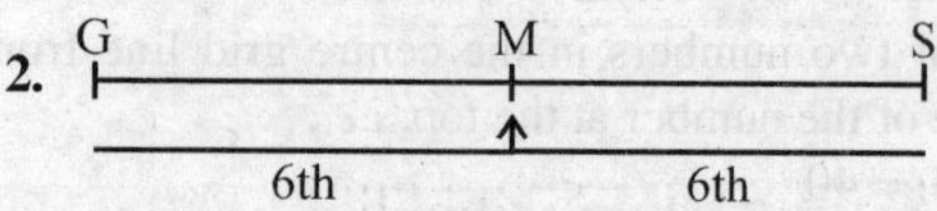

'M' is midway between G and S.

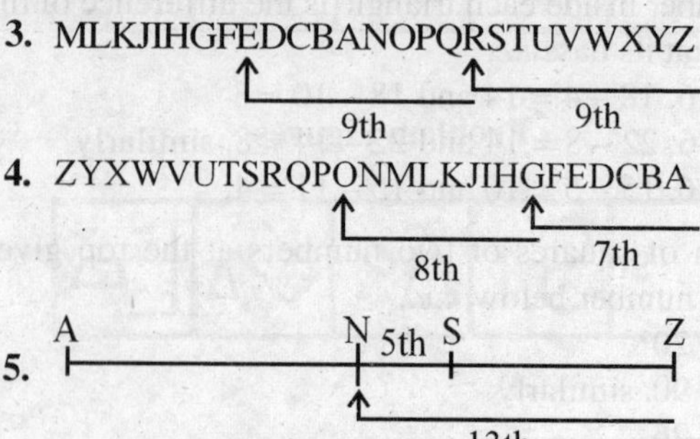

13th letter from right is 'N' and 5th letter to the right of 'N' is 'S'.

NON-VERBAL SERIES

Directions (Q. 1–10) : *In each of the following questions which one of the five answer figures given below should come after the problem figures if the sequence are continued?*

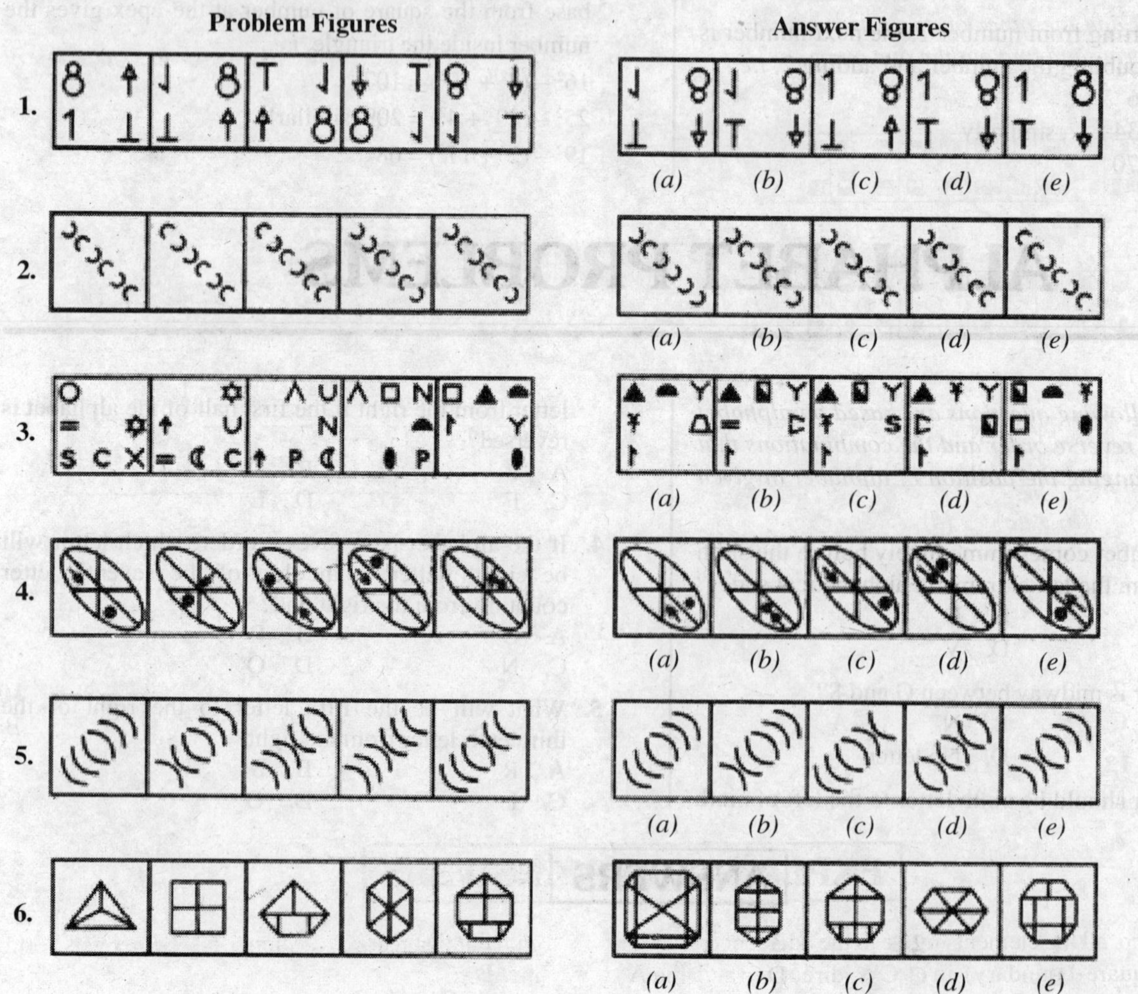

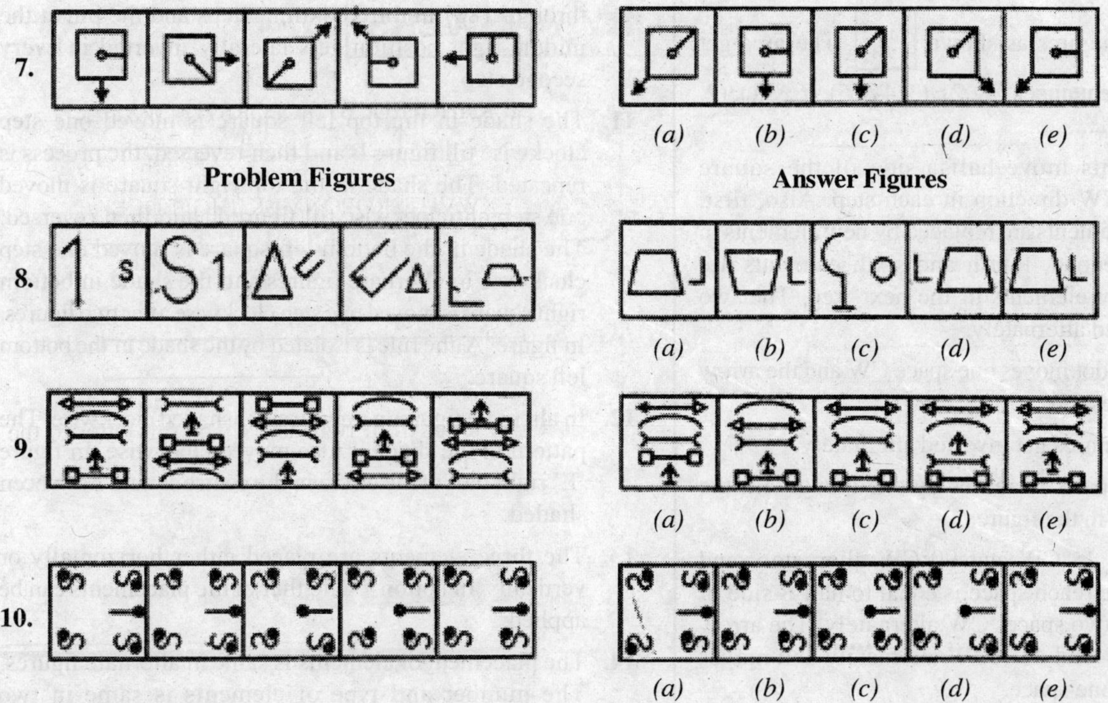

Directions (Q. 11-20) : *In each of these questions, a series begins with an unmarked figure on the extreme left in the row of figures. One and only one of the five lettered figures in the series does not fit into the series. The two unmarked figures, one on the extreme left and the other on the extreme right fit into the series. Take as many aspects into account as possible of the figures in the series and find out the one and only of the five marked figures which does not fit into the series. The letter of that figure is the answer.*

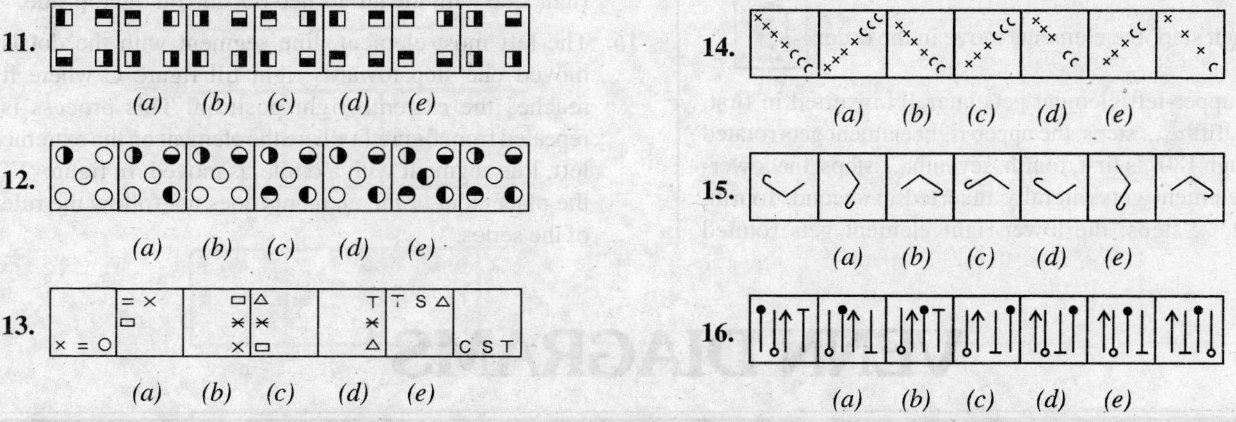

ANSWERS

1	2	3	4	5	6	7	8	9	10
D	C	D	A	C	E	C	E	C	B
11	**12**	**13**	**14**	**15**	**16**				
A	E	A	C	C	E				

EXPLANATORY ANSWERS

1. In each step, all the elements move to the adjacent corner (of the square boundary) in a CW direction and the element that reaches the upper-left corner gets vertically inverted.

2. We can label the arcs as shown . The arcs get inverted in the sequence (1 & 2), (3, 4 & 5), (6 & 1), (2, 3 & 4), (5 & 6), ...

3. All the elements move half-a-side of the square boundary in ACW direction in each step. Also, first, third and fifth elements are replaced by new elements in one step and second, fourth and sixth elements are replaced by new elements in the next step. The two steps are repeated alternately.

4. In each step, the dot moves one space CW and the arrow moves two spaces CW.

5. One arc and four arcs get inverted alternately.

6. The number of parts increases by one along with the number of sides in the figure.

7. The pin rotates 45°CW and 90°CW alternately and moves one space (each space is equal to half-a-side of the square) and two spaces CW alternately. The arrow rotates 90°ACW and 45°ACW alternately and moves two spaces and one space.

8. In one step, the two elements interchange positions and the smaller element gets enlarged while the larger element gets reduced in size. In the next step, the smaller element is replaced by a new small element and the larger element is replaced by a new large element.

9. In each step, the elements move in the order .

10. The upper-left element gets laterally inverted in first, third, fifth. .... steps; the upper-right element gets rotated through 180° is first, fourth, seventh,.... steps; the lower-left element gets laterally inverted in second, fourth, sixth, ... steps; the lower-right element gets rotated through 180° in third, sixth,... steps and the pin at the middle-right position gets laterally inverted in every second step.

11. The shade in the top left square is moved one step clockwise till figure B and then reversed, the process is repeated. The shade in the top right square is moved one step anticlockwise till figure D and then reversed. The shade in the bottom left square is moved one step clockwise in alternate figures and the shade in bottom right square is moved one step clockwise after two figures. In figure 'A' the rule is isolated by the shade in the bottom left square.

12. In alternate figures a new circle is shaded clockwise. The pattern of the shade is also moved clockwise. In figure 'E' right half of the circle in the centre should have been shaded.

13. The three elements are placed either horizontally or vertically. In option 'A' neither of the placements can be applied.

14. The placement of elements is same in alternate figures. The number and type of elements is same in two subsequent figures. In this manner, figure 'C' should have four crosses and two C shapes.

15. *(c)* **:** The element is moved one step anticlockwise and the arc at one end is turned outside and inside alternately. In figure 'C' the element should be on the right side with the arc turned outside on the top side.

16. The left most element, line segment with the dot is moved one step towards right till figure C where it reaches the extreme right position. This process is repeated from figure D where the element on the extreme left, line segment with a circle, is moved. In figure 'E' the placement of the elements does not follow the rule of the series.

VENN DIAGRAMS

1. What is the number which is common to only two geometrical figures?

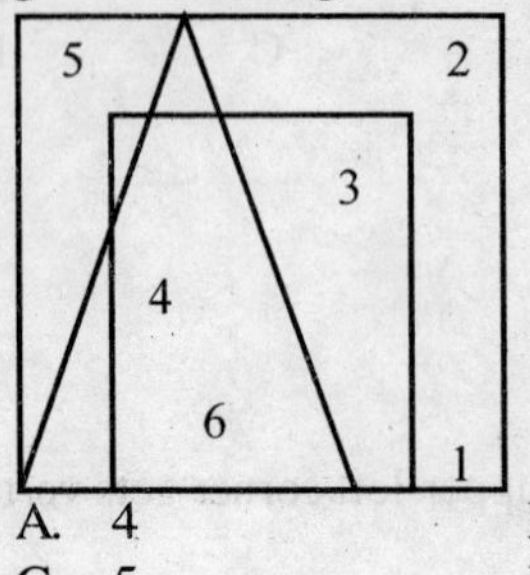

A. 4 B. 3
C. 5 D. 2

Directions (Qs. 2 and 3) : *In the following diagram, rectangle represents Hindi Announcers, circle represents English Announcers, square represents French Announcers, and triangle represents German Announcers.*

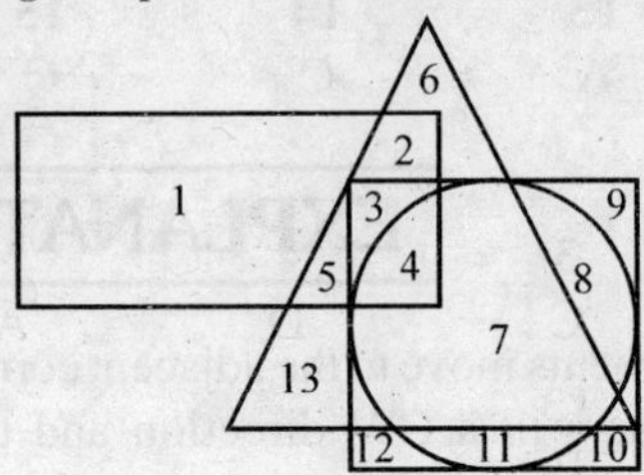

2. Which area represents those announcers who can present programmes in Hindi, French and German only?

A. 1 B. 2
C. 3 D. 4

3 Which area represents those announcers who can present programmes in French and English only?

A. 7 B. 9
C. 11 D. 13

Directions (Qs. 4 and 5) : *Study the diagram to answer these questions.*

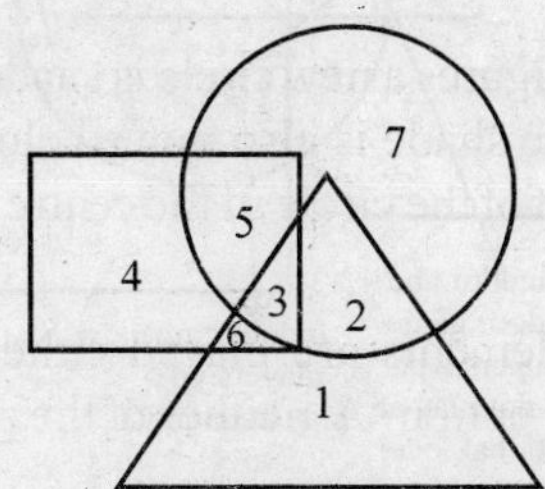

4. Which number is in all the geometrical figures?

A. 5 B. 6
C. 2 D. 3

5. Number 6 is in :

A. Rectangle and triangle
B. Circle and traingle
C. Rectangle and circle
D. Rectangle only

Directions (Qs. 6 to 9) : *In the following diagram*

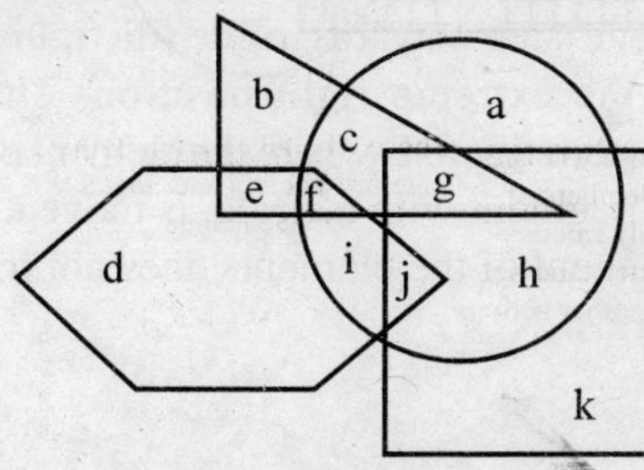

The Circle represents players
The Triangle represents outdoor games
The Hexagon represents indoor games and
The Square represents national level players
Study the diagram and answer the questions given below :

6. The letter in the section representing the players who play indoor games at national level is :

A. f B. i
C. j D. g

7. The letter representing the section of outdoor as well as indoor game players who do not play at the national level is :

A. c B. f
C. e D. i

8. The section representing national level players who do not play either outdoor or indoor games but still come under the category of players is :

A. k B. g
C. c D. h

9. Persons who play outdoor games but do not come under the category of players are represented in the section marked :

A. b B. c
C. a D. d

Directions (Qs. 10 to 13) : *Study the diagram given below.*

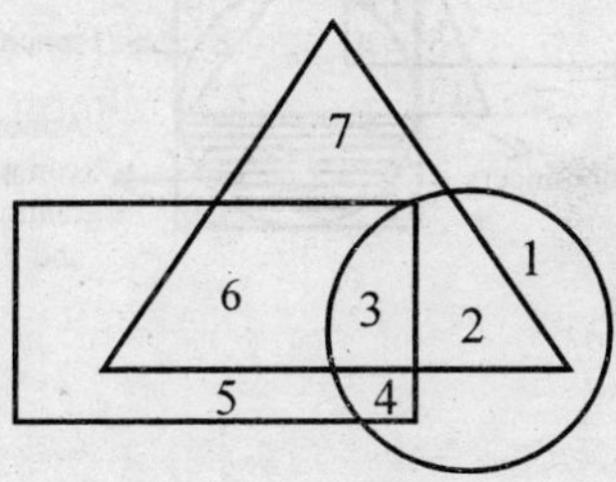

A college provides three different activities, students union represented by triangle, literary society represented by rectangle and social service league represented by circle.

10. Those who take part in both literary society and social service league but not in students union are represented by :

A. 3 & 4 B. 5 & 6
C. 5 & 1 D. 4

11. Those who take part in students union but not in social service league are represented by:

A. 2 & 7 B. 6 & 7
C. 6 D. 7

12. Those students who are members of literary society only and not of any other activity are represented by:

A. 2 B. 5
C. 3 & 4 D. 3

13. Those students who are members of all three groups are represented by :

A. 2 B. 3
C. 4 D. 6

ANSWERS

1	2	3	4	5	6	7	8	9	10
B	C	C	D	A	C	B	D	A	D
11	**12**	**13**							
B	B	B							

EXPLANATORY ANSWERS

1.

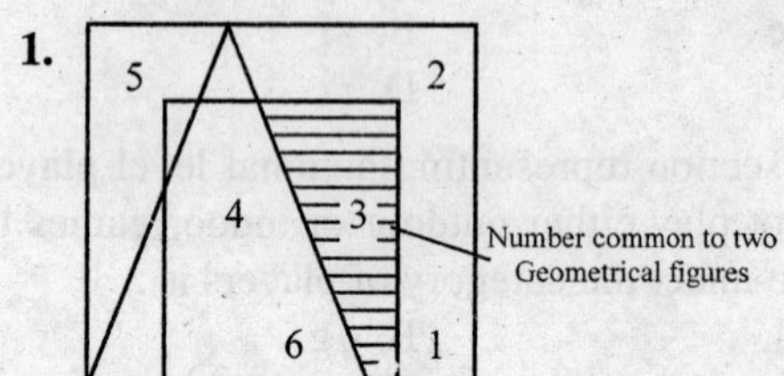

Note : Numbers 4 and 6 are common to all three geometrical figures.

Qs. 2 and 3.

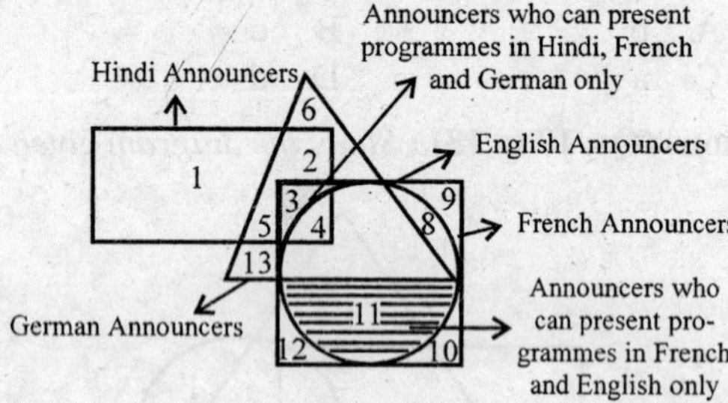

Qs. 4 and 5.

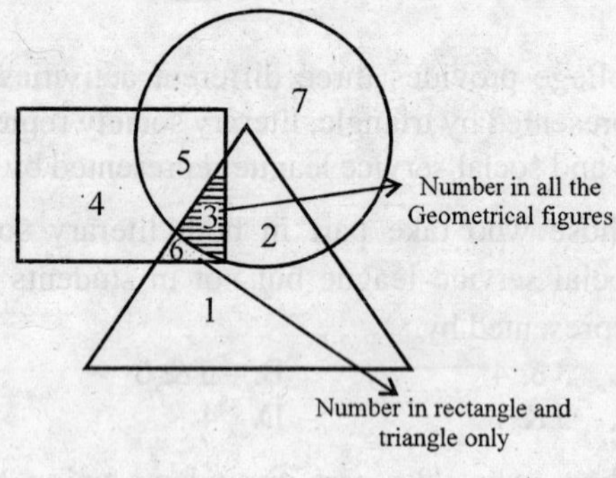

Qs. 6 to 9.

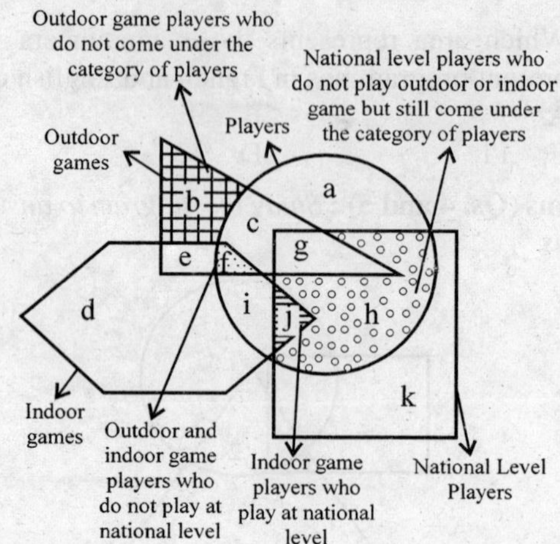

Qs. 10 to 13.

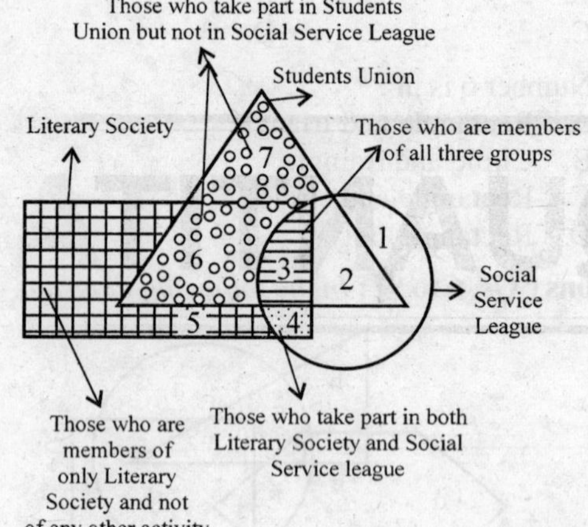

QUANTITATIVE APTITUDE

NUMBER SYSTEM

1. There are four numbers A, B, C and D. Average of the first three *i.e.*, A, B and C is 15 and that of B, C and D is 16. If the last number, *i.e.*, D is 19, then the first number is—
A. 15 B. 16
C. 17 D. 18

2. Of the three numbers, the first is twice the second and thrice the third. If the average of three is 22, the three numbers are—
A. 12, 18, 36
B. 18, 12, 36
C. 36, 12, 18
D. 36, 18, 12

3. If a person is standing on the sixth number in the queue from both the ends, the total persons in the queue are—
A. 9 B. 11
C. 12 D. 13

4. A number 'x' when multiplied by 5 and added to three times its own gives 64, the number is—
A. 8 B. 12
C. 14 D. 18

5. A number which when multiplied by 11 is as much above 180 as it was originally below it. The number is—
A. 25 B. 30
C. 40 D. 45

6. The sum of a number and its reciprocal is thrice the difference of the number and its reciprocal. Find the number.
A. $\sqrt{2}$ B. $\sqrt{3}$
C. $\sqrt{5}$ D. $\sqrt{7}$

7. A boy was asked to find $\frac{7}{9}$ of a fraction. He made a mistake of dividing the fraction by $\frac{7}{9}$ and so got an answer which exceeded the correct answer by $\frac{8}{21}$. Find the correct answer.
A. $\frac{2}{3}$ B. $\frac{5}{7}$
C. $\frac{7}{12}$ D. $\frac{7}{15}$

8. There are 408 boys and 312 girls in a school, which are to be divided into equal sections of either boys or girls alone. Find the maximum number of boys or girls that can be placed in a section. Also find the total number of sections thus formed.
A. 10, 20 B. 24, 30
C. 24, 40 D. 30, 30

9. The sum of all possible two-digit number formed from three different one-digit natural numbers, when divided by the sum of the original three numbers is equal to—
A. 11 B. 18
C. 22 D. 36

10. There are four prime numbers written in ascending order. The product of the first three is 385 and that of the last three is 1001. The last number is—
A. 19 B. 17
C. 13 D. 11

11. If the number 357 ★ 25 ★ is divisible by both 3 and 5, then the missing digits in the unit's place and thousandth place respectively are—
A. 0, 4 B. 5, 4
C. 5, 6 D. 0, 6

12. The difference between two numbers is 1365. When the larger number is divided by the smaller one, the quotient is 6 and the remainder is 15. The smaller number is:
A. 360 B. 295
C. 270 D. 240

13. When a number is divided by 31, the remainder is 29. When the same number is divided by 16, what will be the remainder?
A. 15 B. 13
C. 11 D. Data inadequate

14. In dividing a number by 585, a student applied the method of short division. He divided the number successively by 5, 9 and 13 (factor of 585) and got the remainders 4, 8 and 12. If he had divided the number by 585, the remainder would have been:
A. 584 B. 292
C. 144 D. 24

15. When a number divided by 6 leaves a remainder 3. When the square of the same number is divided by 6, the remainder is:
A. 3 B. 2
C. 1 D. zero

ANSWERS

1	2	3	4	5	6	7	8	9	10
B	D	B	A	B	A	C	B	C	C
11	**12**	**13**	**14**	**15**					
C	C	D	A	A					

EXPLANATORY ANSWERS

1. $\frac{A+B+C}{3} = 15,$

or, $A + B + C = 15 \times 3 = 45$ ... (*i*)

$\frac{B+C+D}{3} = 16,$

or $B + C + D = 48$ ... (*ii*)

$D = 19$

$\therefore\ B + C + 19 = 48$ or, $B + C = 48 - 19 = 29$

But, $A + B + C = 45$

Putting the value of $B + C = 29$ in the above equation (*i*), we get $A + 29 = 45$

$\therefore A = 45 - 29 = 16.$

2. Let the third number $= x$

$\therefore$ First number $= 3x$

Second number $= \frac{3x}{2}$

$\therefore \frac{1}{3}\left[x + 3x + \frac{3x}{2}\right] = 22 \Rightarrow \frac{11}{2}x = 66$

$\Rightarrow x = \frac{66 \times 2}{11} = 12 =$ Third number,

$12 \times 3 = 36 =$ First number,

$\frac{12 \times 3}{2} = 18 =$ Second number.

3. If the person is standing at sixth number in the queue from both sides, that means there are five persons ahead and five persons behind him. Hence, total number of persons in the queue is $5 + 1 + 5 = 11$.

4. $5 \times x + 3x = 64 \Rightarrow 8x = 64$

$\therefore\ x = \frac{64}{8} = 8.$

5. Let the number is x

$\therefore\ 180 - x = 11x - 180$

$\Rightarrow 180 + 180 = 11x + x$

$\Rightarrow 360 = 12x,$

$\Rightarrow x = \frac{360}{12} = 30.$

6. Let the no. $= x$ then its reciprocal $= \frac{1}{x}$

By the question, $\left(x + \frac{1}{x}\right) = 3\left(x - \frac{1}{x}\right)$

$\Rightarrow \frac{x^2+1}{x} = \frac{3(x^2-1)}{x}$

$\Rightarrow x^2 + 1 = 3x^2 - 3$

$\Rightarrow 3x^2 - x^2 = 3 + 1$

$\therefore\ x = \sqrt{2}.$

7. Let the required fraction $= x$

then, by the question $x \div \frac{7}{9} - x \times \frac{7}{9} = \frac{8}{21}$

$\Rightarrow x \times \frac{9}{7} - \frac{7x}{9} = \frac{8}{21}$

$\Rightarrow \frac{32x}{63} = \frac{8}{21}$

$\Rightarrow x = \frac{8}{21} \times \frac{63}{32} = \frac{3}{4}$

Hence, the correct answer $= \frac{3}{4} \times \frac{7}{9} = \frac{7}{12}.$

8.

```
312) 408(1
     312
     ---
      96) 312 (3
          288
          ---
           24) 96 (4
               96
               --
               ×
```

$\therefore$ Maximum number of girls or boys that can be placed in a section = 24 and total number of such section $= \frac{408}{24} + \frac{312}{24}$

$= 17 + 13 = 30$

9. Let three different one digit natural numbers be x, y and z.

Then, sum of all possible two digits numbers

$= (10x + y) + (10y + x) + (10x + z) + (10z + x) + (10y + z) + (10z + y)$

$= 22x + 22y + 22z = 22(x + y + z)$

Hence, required number = 22.

10. Let four prime numbers be a, b, c and d respectively.

Now, $\frac{abc}{bcd} = \frac{385}{1001}$

$\Rightarrow \frac{c}{d} = \frac{5}{13}$

Hence, $a = 5$ and $d = 13$

11. 357 ★ 25 ★

For divisible by 5, the last digit must be either 0 or 5.

If last digit is 0, then other required digit will be 2 or 5 or 8

Hence, the numbers are (0, 2) or (0, 5) or (0, 8)

If last digit is 5, then other required digit will be 0 or 3 or 6 or 9

Hence, the numbers are (5, 0) or (5, 3) or (5, 6) or (5, 9)

So, correct option is (c).

12. Here, $(x + 1365) = 6x + 15$

$\Rightarrow 5x = 1350$

$\therefore x = \frac{1350}{5} = 270$

Hence, the smaller number = 270.

13. The number = $31x + 29$.

Here, given data is inadequate.

14.

5	a
9	$b - 4$
13	$c - 8$
	$1 - 12$

Now, $c = 13 \times 1 + 12 = 25$

$b = 9c + 8 = 9 \times 25 + 8 = 233$

$a = 5b + 4 = 5 \times 233 + 4$

$= 1165 + 4 = 1169$

$1169 = 585 \times 1 + 584$

Hence, required remainder = 584.

15. The number = $6x + 3$

Now, $(6x + 3)^2 = 36x^2 + 36x + 9$

$= (36x^2 + 36x + 6) + 3$

$= 6(6x^2 + 6x + 1) + 3$

Hence, required remainder = 3.

LCM AND HCF

1. The L.C.M. and H.C.F. of two numbers are 4284 and 32 respectively. If one of the numbers is 204, the other is

A. 672 B. 576
C. 676 D. 572

2. Two numbers are in the ratio of 8 : 15. If their H.C.F. is 4, the numbers are

A. 32 and 60 B. 16 and 30
C. 80 and 150 D. 64 and 120

3. The greatest number that will divide 366, 513 and 324 leaving the same remainder in each case is

A. 21 B. 18
C. 27 D. 42

4. The L.C.M. of two numbers is 45 times their H.C.F. If the sum of the L.C.M. and the H.C.F. of these two numbers is 1150 and one of the numbers is 125, then the other number is

A. 256 B. 225
C. 250 D. 255

5. The H.C.F. and the L.C.M. of two numbers are 50 and 250 respectively. On dividing one of these numbers by 2, 50 is obtained as quotient. The numbrs are

A. 100, 125 B. 80, 100
C. 125, 100 D. 200, 250

6. Three bells ring respectively at an interval of 15 seconds, 20 seconds and 24 seconds. If they ring continuously for 12 minutes then how many times, during this period, will they ring together?

A. 2 times B. 6 times
C. 5 times D. 3 times

7. If the sum of two numbers is 55 and the H.C.F. and L.C.M. of these numbers are 5 and 120 respectively. Find the sum of their reciprocals.

A. $\frac{120}{11}$ B. $\frac{11}{120}$
C. $\frac{601}{55}$ D. $\frac{55}{601}$

8. The LCM of two numbers is 48. The numbers are in the ratio of 2 : 3. The sum of the numbers is

A. 64 B. 40
C. 32 D. 28

9. Find the greatest number that will divide 43, 91 and 183 so as to leave the same remainder in each case.

A. 13 B. 9
C. 7 D. 4

10. The greatest possible length which can be used to measure exactly the length 7m, 3m 85cm, 12m 95 cm is

A. 42 cm B. 35 cm
C. 25 cm D. 15 cm

11. A, B and C start at the same time in the same direction to run around a circular park. A completes a round in 252 seconds, B in 308 seconds and C in 198 seconds, all starting at the same point. After what time will they meet again at the starting point?

A. 46 minutes 12 seconds
B. 45 minutes
C. 42 minutes 36 seconds
D. 26 minutes 18 seconds

12. Which of the following has most numbers of divisors?

A. 182 B. 176
C. 101 D. 99

13. Which is of the following is a co-primes?

A. (23, 92) B. (21, 35)
C. (18, 25) D. (16, 62)

14. Let N be the greatest number that will divide 1305, 4665 and 6905, leaving the same remainder in each case. Then find the sum of the digits in N.

A. 8 B. 6
C. 5 D. 4

15. The greatest number which one dividing 1657 and 2037 leaves remainder 6 and 5 respectively, is:

A. 305 B. 235
C. 127 D. 123

ANSWERS

1	2	3	4	5	6	7	8	9	10
A	A	A	B	A	B	B	B	D	B
11	12	13	14	15					
A	B	C	D	C					

EXPLANATORY ANSWERS

1. 1st number × 2nd number = LCM × HCF

$\therefore$ 204 × 2nd number = 4284 × 32

$\therefore$ 2nd number $= \frac{4284 \times 32}{204} = 672$

$\therefore$ 2nd number = 672

2. Let the numbers be $8x$ and $15x$

$8x = 2 \times 2 \times 2 \times x$

$15x = 3 \times 5 \times x$

$\therefore$ LCM of $8x$ and $15x = 2 \times 2 \times 2 \times x \times 3 \times 5 = 120x$

Now, 1st number × 2nd number = HCF × LCM

$\Rightarrow 8x \times 15x = 4 \times 120x$

$\Rightarrow 120x^2 = 4 \times 120x$

$\Rightarrow x = 4$

$\therefore$ Numbers are 8 × 4 = 32 and 15 × 4 = 60

3. Difference between 366 and 513 = 513 – 366 = 147

and difference between 513 and 324 = 513 – 324 = 189

$\therefore$ HCF of 147 and 189

```
147) 189 (1
     147
   × 42) 147 (3
         126
       × 21) 42 (2
             42
              ×
```

$\therefore$ The required largest number is 21.

4. LCM of the two numbers = 45 × HCF

and LCM + HCF = 1150

$\Rightarrow$ 45 × HCF + HCF = 1150

$\Rightarrow$ HCF(45 + 1) = 1150

$\Rightarrow$ HCF $= \frac{1150}{46} = 25$

$\therefore$ LCM = 45 × 25 = 1125

$\because$ 1st number × 2nd number = LCM × HCF

$\therefore$ 125 × 2nd number = 1125 × 25

$\therefore$ 2nd number $= \frac{1125 \times 25}{125} = 225.$

5. According to the condition of the problem, 50 is obtained on dividing one of the numbers by 2

$\therefore$ One of the numbers = 50 × 2 = 100

Now, 1st number × 2nd number = LCM × HCF

$\therefore$ 100 × 2nd number = 250 × 50

$\therefore$ 2nd number $= \frac{250 \times 50}{100} = 125$

Hence, numbers are 100 and 125.

6. LCM of 15, 20 and 24

```
5 | 15, 20, 24
4 |  3,  4, 24
3 |  3,  1,  6
  |  1,  1,  2
```

LCM = 5 × 4 × 3 × 2 = 120

$\because$ 12 minutes = 12 × 60 = 720 seconds

$\therefore$ Number of times the bells will ring together during 12 minutes

$= \frac{720}{120} = 6$ times.

7. Let the number be x and y.
Then, $x + y = 55$;
$xy = \text{HCF} \times \text{LCM} = 5 \times 120$
$\therefore$ Sum of their reciprocals

$$= \frac{1}{x} + \frac{1}{y} = \frac{x+y}{xy} = \frac{55}{5 \times 120} = \frac{11}{120}.$$

8. Let the two numbers be $2x$ and $3x$;
their LCM = $6x$
Now, $6x = 48$ $\therefore$ $x = 8$
Hence, the numbers are 2×8, 3×8 = 16, 24
Their sum = 16 + 24 = 40.

9. 2240) 3360 (1 ... 2240 ... 1120) 2240 (2 ... 2240 ... × ; 1120) 5600 (5 ... 5600 ... ×

Hence, N = HCF of 3360, 2240 and 5600 = 1120
Sum of digits in N = 1 + 1 + 2 + 0 = 4.

10. 7m = 700 cm;
3m 85 = 385 cm;
12m 95cm = 1295 cm

385) 700 (1 ... 385 ... 315) 385 (1 ... 315 ... 70) 315 (4 ... 280 ... 35) 70 (2 ... 70 ... ×

35) 1295 (37 ... 105 ... 245 ... 245 ... ×

Hence, required length = HCF of 700 cm, 385 cm, 1295 cm = 35 cm.

11.

2	252, 308, 198
2	126, 154, 99
3	63, 77, 99
3	21, 77, 33
7	7, 77, 11
11	1, 11, 11
	1, 1, 1

Hence, LCM = 2 × 2 × 3 × 3 × 7 × 11 = 2772
Hence, A, B, C will meet again at the starting point after 2772 sec. = 46 min 12 sec.

12.

Numbers	***Their divisors***
182	→ 1, 2, 7, 13, 14, 26, 91 and 182
176	→ 1, 2, 4, 8, 16, 22, 44, 88 and 176
101	→ 1 and 101
99	→ 1, 3, 9, 11, 33 and 99

Therefore, 176 has the most number of divisors.

13. HCF of 23 and 92 = 23
HCF of 21 and 35 = 7
HCF of 18 and 25 = 1
HCF of 16 and 62 = 2
Hence, 18 and 25 are co-prime numbers.

14. N = HCF of (4665 – 1305), (6905 – 4665) and (6905 – 1305)
= HCF of 3360, 2240 and 5600 = 112
Sum of digit of 1 + 1 + 2 = 4.

15. Required number = HCF of (1657 – 6) and (2037 – 5)
= HCF of 1651 and 2032 = 127.

1651) 2032 (1 ... 1651 ... 381) 1651 (4 ... 1524 ... 127) 381 (3 ... 381 ... ×

AVERAGE

1. One-third of a certain journey was covered at the rate of 25 km per hour, one-fourth at the rate of 30 km per hour and the rest at the 50 km per hour. What is the average speed per hour for whole journey?

A. $33\frac{1}{3}$ kmph B. $44\frac{1}{4}$ kmph
C. $22\frac{1}{2}$ kmph D. 33 kmph

2. A batsman has a certain average of runs for 16 innings. In the 17th innings, he makes a score of 85 runs thereby increasing his average by 3. What is the average after the 17th inning?

A. 33 runs B. 34 runs
C. 37 runs D. 36 runs

3. The average of 6 observations is 12. A new seventh observation is included and the new average is decreased by 1. The seventh observation is

A. 1 B. 3
C. 5 D. 6

4. The average age of 30 students in a class is 12 years. The average age of a group of 5 of the students is 10 years and that of another group of 5 of them is 14 years. The average age of the remaining students is
A. 8 years B. 10 years
C. 12 years D. 14 years

5. Out of the three given numbers, the first number is twice the second and thrice the third. If the average of three numbers is 121, what is the difference between the first and third number?
A. 144 B. 77
C. 99 D. 132

6. If the average marks of three batches of 55, 60 and 45 students is 50, 55 and 60, then average marks of all the students is:
A. 55 B. 54
C. 54.68 D. 55.68

7. The average of 8 numbers is 20. The average of first two numbers is $15\frac{1}{2}$ and that of the next three is $21\frac{1}{3}$. If the sixth number is less than the seventh and eighth numbers by 4 and 7 respectively, then the eighth number is:
A. 27 B. 25
C. 22 D. 18

8. A pupil's marks were wrongly entered as 83 instead of 63. Due to that the average marks for the class got increased by half. What is the number of pupils in the class?
A. 73 B. 40
C. 40 D. 10

9. A cricketer whose bowling average is 12.4 runs per wicket takes 5 wickets for 26 runs and thereby decreases his average by 0.4. The number of wickets taken by him till the last match was:
A. 85 B. 80
C. 72 D. 64

10. The average weight of a class of 24 students is 35 kg. If the weight of the teacher is included, the average rises by 400 g. What is the weight of the teacher?
A. 55 kg B. 53 kg
C. 50 kg D. 45 kg

11. Nine men went to a hotel. Eight of them spent Rs. 3 for each over their meals and the ninth spent Rs. 2 more than the average expenditure of all the nine. What is the total money spent by them?
A. Rs. 29.25 B. Rs. 29.50
C. Rs. 29 D. Rs. 30

12. The average age of 24 students in a class is 10. If the teacher's age is included, the average increases by one. The age of the teacher is
A. 25 B. 30
C. 35 D. 40

13. The average of 5 consecutive even numbers A, B, C, D and E is 34. What is the product of B and D?
A. 1152 B. 1368
C. 1224 D. 1088

14. The average of 50 numbers is 30. If two numbers, 35 and 40 are discarded, then the average of the remaining numbers is nearly:
A. 29.68 B. 29.27
C. 28.78 D. 28.32

15. The average monthly salary of 20 employees of an organisation is Rs. 1500. If the manager's salary is added, then the average salary increases by Rs. 100. Find the manager's monthly salary?
A. Rs. 4800 B. Rs. 3600
C. Rs. 2400 D. Rs. 2000

ANSWERS

1	2	3	4	5	6	7	8	9	10
A	C	C	C	D	C	B	B	A	D
11	**12**	**13**	**14**	**15**					
A	C	A	A	B					

EXPLANATORY ANSWERS

1. Let the total distance covered during journey = 60 km

$\frac{1}{3}$ of the distance covered during journey

$= 60 \times \frac{1}{3} = 20$ km

$\frac{1}{4}$ of the distance covered during journey

$= \frac{1}{4} \times 60 = 15$ km

∴ The distance covered during the rest of journey = 60 − (20 + 15) = 25 km

Time taken to cover 20 km at 25 km/h

$$= \frac{20}{25} \text{ hours} = \frac{4}{5} \text{ hour}$$

Time taken to cover 15 km at 30 km/h

$$= \frac{15}{30} \text{ hours} = \frac{1}{2} \text{ hour}$$

Time taken to cover 25 km at 50 km/h

$$= \frac{25}{50} \text{ hours} = \frac{1}{2} \text{ hour}$$

$$\text{Total time taken} = \frac{4}{5} + \frac{1}{2} + \frac{1}{2}$$

$$= \frac{9}{5} \text{ hours}$$

$$\text{Hence average speed per hour} = 60 \div \frac{9}{5}$$

$$= \frac{60 \times 5}{9} = \frac{100}{3} \text{ km/h}$$

$$= 33\frac{1}{3} \text{ km/h}$$

2. Average increase in the score of 17 innings.

$= 3$ runs

Total increase in the score of 17 innings

$= 3 \times 17 = 51$ runs

$\therefore$ His average of 16 innings $= 85 - 51$

$= 34$ runs

Hence, average after the 17th innings

$= 34 + 3 = 37$ runs

3. Seventh observation $= (7 \times 11 - 6 \times 12) = 5$

4. Let, the required average age be x

Then, $5 \times 10 + 5 \times 14 + 20 \times x = 30 \times 12$

$\Rightarrow \quad 20x = 360 - 120$

$\Rightarrow \quad 20x = 240$

$\Rightarrow \quad x = 12$

5. Let the three numbers be x, $\frac{x}{2}$ and $\frac{x}{3}$ respectively,

$$\text{Now, } \frac{1}{3}\left(x + \frac{x}{2} + \frac{x}{3}\right) = 121$$

$$\Rightarrow \frac{11x}{6} = 121 \times 3$$

$$\therefore \ x = \frac{121 \times 3 \times 6}{11} = 198$$

$$\text{Hence, required difference} = x - \frac{x}{3} = \frac{2x}{3}$$

$$= \frac{2}{3} \times 198 = 132$$

6. Required average Marks

$$= \frac{55 \times 50 + 60 \times 55 + 45 \times 60}{55 + 60 + 45} = \frac{8750}{160} = 54.68$$

7. Let the sixth, seventh and eighth numbers are x, $x + 4$ and $x + 7$.

Sum of last three numbers

$$= 8 \times 20 - (2 \times \frac{31}{2} + 3 \times \frac{64}{3})$$

$\Rightarrow x + x + 4 + x + 7 = 160 - 95$

$\Rightarrow 3x + 11 = 65$

$\Rightarrow 3x = 54 \quad \therefore x = 18$

New eighth number $= x + 7 = 18 + 7 = 25$

8. Let the total number of pupils in the class be x; then,

$$\frac{83 - 63}{x} = \frac{1}{2} \quad \Rightarrow \frac{20}{x} = \frac{1}{2} \quad \therefore x = 40$$

9. Let the number of wickets taken by him be x till the last match.

$$\text{Then, } \frac{x \times 12.4 + 26}{x + 5} = 12$$

$\Rightarrow \quad 12.4x + 26 = 12x + 60$

$$\Rightarrow 0.4x = 34 \quad \therefore \quad x = \frac{340}{4} = 85$$

10. Let the weight of the teacher be x kgs, then

$$\frac{24 \times 35 + x}{25} = 35.4$$

$\Rightarrow \quad 840 + x = 885 \quad \therefore \quad x = 45$ kgs

12. Age of the teacher $= (25 \times 11 - 24 \times 10)$ years

$= 35$ years

13. Let 5 consecutive even numbers A, B, C, D and E be x, $x + 2$, $x + 4$, $x + 6$ and $x + 8$ respectively.

$$\text{Now, } \frac{x + x + 2 + x + 4 + x + 6 + x + 8}{5} = 34$$

$\Rightarrow 5x + 20 = 170$

$\Rightarrow 5x = 150 \quad \therefore x = 30$

Then, $B = x + 2 = 30 + 2 = 32$;

$D = x + 6 = 30 + 6 = 36$

Hence, their product $= 32 \times 36 = 1152$

14. The average of remaining 48 numbers

$$= \frac{50 \times 30 - (35 + 40)}{48} = \frac{1500 - 75}{48}$$

$$= \frac{1425}{48} = 29.68$$

15. Let manager's salary be Rs. x, then

$$\frac{20 \times 1500 + x}{21} = 1600$$

$\Rightarrow \quad 30{,}000 + x = 33600$

$\therefore \quad x =$ Rs. 3600

PROBLEMS BASED ON AGES

1. The ratio of ages of A and B is 3 : 11. After 3 years the ratio becomes 1 : 3. What are the ages of A and B?
A. 9 years, 33 years
B. 10 years, 40 years
C. 9 years, 27 years
D. None of these

2. Two years ago, the ratio of Ram's and Mohan's age was 3 : 2 and at present 7 : 5. What are their present ages?
A. 14 years, 10 years B. 15 years, 10 years
C. 13 years, 9 years D. None of these

3. The ages of Samir and Saurabh are in the ratio of 8 : 15 respectively. After 9 years the ratio of their ages will be 11 : 18. What is the difference between their ages in years?
A. 20 years B. 21 years
C. 22 years D. 24 years

4. The present age of father is 34 years more than that of his son. 12 years ago, father's age was 18 times the age of his son. The present age of son in years is:
A. 12 B. 14
C. 16 D. 18

5. A mother is 25 years older than her daughter. Five years ago, the age of the mother was 6 times the age of the daughter. What is the present age of mother?
A. 25 years B. 29 years
C. 32 years D. 35 years

6. The difference between the present ages of P and Q is 4 years. The ratio of their ages after 5 years will be 9 : 8. The present age of P is:
A. 24 years B. 30 years
C. 32 years D. None of these

7. Ten years ago, the age of Divya was half of the age of Namrata. If the ratio of present ages of both is 3 : 4, the sum of their present ages is:
A. 35 years B. 30 years
C. 25 years D. 18 years

8. The ratio between the present ages of A and B is 5 : 3 respectively. The ratio between A's age 4 years ago and B's age 4 years hence is 1 : 1. The ratio between A's age 4 years hence and B's age 4 years ago is:
A. 4 : 1 B. 3 : 1
C. 2 : 1 D. 1 : 3

9. Ram got married 8 years ago. His present age is $\frac{6}{5}$ times his age at the time of marriage. Ram's sister was 10 years younger to him at the time of his marriage. What is the present age of Ram's sister?
A. 40 years B. 38 years
C. 36 years D. 32 years

10. A father said to his son, "I was as old as you are at present at the time of your birth." If the father's age is 38 years now. Five years ago the age of son was:
A. 38 years B. 33 years
C. 19 years D. 14 years

ANSWERS

1	2	3	4	5	6	7	8	9	10
A	A	B	B	D	D	A	B	B	D

EXPLANATORY ANSWERS

1. Let the ages of A and B be $3x$ and $11x$ years; then

$$\frac{3x+3}{11x+3}=\frac{1}{3} \quad \Rightarrow \quad 9x+9=11x+3$$

$\Rightarrow 2x = 6 \quad \therefore \quad x = 3$

Hence, their present age, $3x = 3 \times 3 = 9$ years; $11x = 11 \times 3 = 33$ years

2. Let the present ages of Ram and Mohan are $7x$ and $5x$ years; then

$$\frac{7x-2}{5x-2}=\frac{3}{2} \quad \Rightarrow \quad 14x-4=15x-6 \quad \therefore x=2$$

Hence, their present ages : $7 \times 2 = 14$ years and $5 \times 2 = 10$ years

3. Let the present ages of Samir and Saurabh are $8x$ and $15x$ years respectively; then

$$\frac{8x+9}{15x+9}=\frac{11}{18} \quad \Rightarrow \quad 144x+162=165x+99$$

$\Rightarrow 21x = 63 \quad \therefore \quad x = 3$

Hence, difference of their ages $= 15x - 8x = 7x$ $= 7 \times 3 = 21$ years

4. Let the present ages of father and his son be $x + 34$ and x years respectively; then
$18(x - 12) = x + 34 - 12$
$\Rightarrow 18x - 216 = x + 22$
$\Rightarrow 17x = 238 \quad \therefore x = 14$
Hence, present age of his son = 14 years

5. Let the present ages of mother and her daughter are $(x + 25)$ and x years respectively; then
$6(x - 5) = x + 25 - 5$
$\Rightarrow 6x - 30 = x + 20$
$\Rightarrow 5x = 50 \quad \therefore x = 10$
Hence, the age of the mother = 10 + 25
= 35 years

6. Let the present ages of P and Q be $(x + 4)$ and x years;
then, $\frac{x+4+5}{x+5} = \frac{9}{8} \Rightarrow 8x + 72$
$= 9x + 45 \quad \therefore x = 27$
Hence, present age of P = 27 + 4 = 31 years

7. Let the present ages of Divya and Namrata are $3x$ and $4x$ years respectively; then
$\frac{3x-10}{4x-10} = \frac{1}{2}$
$\Rightarrow 6x - 20 = 4x - 10$
$\Rightarrow 2x = 10 \quad \therefore x = 5$
Hence, sum of their ages = $3x + 4x = 7x$
$= 7 \times 5 = 35$ years

8. Let the present ages of A and B are $5x$ and $3x$ years respectively; then,
$\frac{5x-4}{3x+4} = 1 \Rightarrow 5x - 4 = 3x + 4$
$\Rightarrow 2x = 8 \quad \therefore x = 4$
Hence, their present ages are 20 years and 12 years.
So, required ratio = (20 + 4) : (12 – 4)
= 24 : 8 = 3 : 1

9. Let the present age of Ram be x years; then
$\frac{x}{x-8} = \frac{6}{5} \Rightarrow 5x = 6x - 48$
$\therefore x = 48$
Hence, present age of Ram's sister
= 48 – 10 = 38 years.

10. Let the age of father was x years at the time of his son's birth, then present age of father and his son will be $2x$ and x years,
Now, $2x = 38 \quad \therefore x = 19$ years
Hence, 5 years ago the age of son was
19 – 5 = 14 years

CHAIN RULE

1. A fort has provision for 50 days. After 15 days a reinforcement of 150 men arrives and the provision now lasts 25 days. How many men were there in the fort?
A. 300 B. 225
C. 275 D. 200

2. In a fort there is provisions for 40 days for 275 persons. If after 16 days 125 persons leave the fort for how many more days the provisions will last?
A. 35 days B. 44 days
C. 45 days D. 53 days

3. 60 men could complete a work in 250 days. They worked together for 200 days. After that the work had to be stopped for 10 days due to bad weather. How many more men should be engaged to complete the work in time?
A. 20 B. 18
C. 15 D. 10

4. A contractor undertook to complete a project in 90 days and employed 60 men on it. After 60 days, he found that $\frac{3}{4}$ of the work has already been completed. How many men can he discharge so that the project may completed exactly on time?
A. 15 B. 20
C. 30 D. 40

5. A flagstaff 17.5 m high casts a shadow of length 40.25 m. The height of the building, which casts a shadow of length 28.75m under similar condition will be:
A. 21.25 m B. 17.5 m
C. 12.5 m D. 10 m

6. If 5 men or 9 women can do a piece of work in 19 days, then 3 men and 6 women will do the same work in how many days?
A. 21 B. 18
C. 15 D. 12

7. A certain number of men can finish a piece of work in 100 days. If there were 10 men less, it will take 10 days more for the work to be finished. How many men were there originally?
A. 110 B. 100
C. 82 D. 75

8. Some persons can do a piece of work in 12 days. Two times the number of such persons will do half of that work in:

A. 12 days B. 3 days
C. 6 days D. 4 days

9. 2 men and 7 boys can do a piece of work in 14 days; 3 men and 8 boys can do the same in 11 days. Then 8 men and 6 boys can do three times of this work in

A. 30 days B. 4 days
C. 21 days D. 18 days

10. If 3 men or 6 boys, working 7 hours a day can do a piece of work in 10 days; how many days will it take to complete a piece of work twice as large with 6 men and 2 boys working together for 8 hours a day?

A. 9 B. $8\frac{1}{2}$
C. $7\frac{1}{2}$ D. $6\frac{1}{2}$

11. If 15 men can do a certain amount of work in 20 days working 8 hours a day, in how many days will 10 men do three times the work working 6 hours a day?

A. 120 days B. 70 days
C. 100 days D. None of these

12. 40 men consume 60 kgs of rice in 15 days, then in how many days will 30 men consume 12 kgs of rice?

A. 9 days B. $6\frac{1}{4}$ days
C. 4 days D. $3\frac{1}{4}$ days

13. 56 men can complete a piece of work in 24 days. In how many days can 42 men complete the same piece of work?

A. 48 B. 32
C. 20 D. 16

14. Running at the same constant rate, 6 identical machines can produce a total of 270 bottles per minute. At this rate, how many bottles could 10 such machines produce in 4 minutes?

A. 1400 B. 1600
C. 1800 D. 2000

15. 400 persons, working 9 hours a day complete $\frac{1}{4}th$ of the work in 10 days. The number of additional persons, working 8 hours a day, required to complete the remaining work in 20 days, is:

A. 275 B. 250
C. 675 D. 200

ANSWERS

1	2	3	4	5	6	7	8	9	10
B	B	C	B	C	C	A	B	C	C
11	**12**	**13**	**14**	**15**					
A	C	B	C	C					

EXPLANATORY ANSWERS

1. Days Men
35↑ x
25 $x+150$↓

$$\Rightarrow \frac{x+150}{x} = \frac{35}{25} \Rightarrow 1 + \frac{150}{x} = \frac{35}{25}$$

$$\Rightarrow \frac{150}{x} = \frac{10}{25}$$

$$\therefore x = \frac{25}{10} \times 150 = 375$$

Required number of men = 375 – 150 = 225

2. Persons Days
275↑ 24
150 x↓

$$\Rightarrow \frac{x}{24} = \frac{275}{150} \quad \therefore \quad x = \frac{275}{150} \times 24 = 44 \text{ days}$$

3. Days Men
50↑ 60
40 x↓

$$\Rightarrow \frac{x}{60} = \frac{50}{40} \quad \therefore x = \frac{50}{40} \times 60 = 75 \text{ men}$$

Hence, number of additional men = 75 – 60 = 15

4. Work Days Men
$\frac{3}{4}$↓ 60 60
$\frac{1}{4}$ 30 x

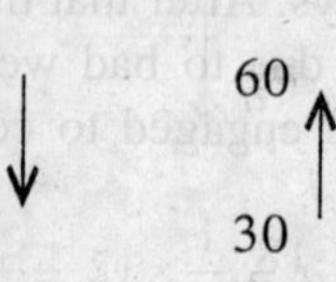
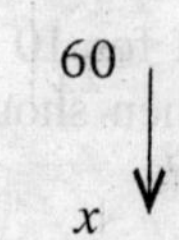

$$\Rightarrow \frac{x}{60} = \frac{60}{30} \times \frac{1/4}{3/4}$$

$$\therefore \quad x = \frac{60}{30} \times \frac{1}{3} \times 60 = 40 \text{ days}$$

Hence, number of men to be discharged

$= 60 - 40 = 20$

5.

Shadow (m)	Object (m)
40.25 ↓	17.5 ↓
28.75 ↓	x ↓

$$\Rightarrow \frac{x}{17.5} = \frac{28.75}{40.25}$$

$$\therefore\ x = \frac{28.75 \times 17.5}{40.25} = 12.5 \text{ m}$$

6. 5 men $\equiv$ 9 women

$$\therefore 3 \text{ men} = \frac{9}{5} \times 3 = \frac{27}{5} \text{ women}$$

Hence, 3 men and 6 women $= \dfrac{27}{5} + 6$

$$= \frac{57}{5} \text{ women}$$

Women	Days
9 ↑	19 ↓
$\frac{57}{5}$ ↑	x ↓

$$\Rightarrow \frac{x}{19} = \frac{9 \times 5}{57}$$

$$\therefore\ x = \frac{9 \times 5}{57} \times 19$$

$= 15$ days

7.

Days	Men
100 ↑	x ↓
110 ↑	$x - 10$ ↓

$$\Rightarrow \frac{x-10}{x} = \frac{100}{110}$$

$\Rightarrow 110x - 1100 = 100x$

$\Rightarrow 10x = 1100 \quad \therefore x = 110$

Hence, initially the number of men = 110

8.

Work	Persons	Days
1 ↓	x ↑	12 ↓
$\frac{1}{2}$ ↓	$2x$ ↑	a ↓

$$\Rightarrow \frac{a}{12} = \frac{x}{2x} \times \frac{1}{2} \quad \therefore\ a = \frac{1}{4} \times 12 = 3 \text{ days}$$

9. Here, 14×2 men $+ 14 \times 7$ boys $\equiv 11 \times 3$ men $+ 11 \times 8$ boys

$\Rightarrow$ 28 men + 98 boys $\equiv$ 33 men + 88 boys

$\Rightarrow$ 5 men = 10 boys

$\therefore$ 1 man = 2 boys

Then, 2 men and 7 boys $\equiv$ 4 boys + 7 boys

= 11 boys

& also, 8 men and 6 boys $\equiv$ 16 boys + 6 boys

= 22 boys

Work	Boys	Days
1 ↓	11 ↑	14 ↓
3 ↓	22 ↑	x ↓

$$\Rightarrow \frac{x}{14} = \frac{11}{22} \times \frac{3}{1}$$

$$\therefore\ x = \frac{1}{2} \times 3 \times 14$$

$= 21$ days

12.

Men	Rice (kgs)	Days
40 ↑	60 ↓	15 ↓
30 ↑	12 ↓	x ↓

$$\Rightarrow \frac{x}{15} = \frac{12}{60} \times \frac{40}{30}$$

$$= \frac{12}{60} \times \frac{40}{30} \times 15 = 4 \text{ days}$$

14.

Machines	Time (minutes)	Bottles
6 ↓	1 ↓	270 ↓
10 ↓	4 ↓	x ↓

$$\Rightarrow \frac{x}{270} = \frac{4}{1} \times \frac{10}{6}$$

$$\therefore\ x = \frac{4 \times 10}{6} \times 270$$

$= 1800$ bottles

15.

Work	Hours	Days	Persons
$\frac{1}{4}$ ↓	9 ↑	10 ↑	400 ↓
$\frac{3}{4}$ ↓	8 ↑	20 ↑	x ↓

$$\Rightarrow \frac{x}{400} = \frac{10}{20} \times \frac{9}{8} \times \frac{3/4}{1/4}$$

$$\therefore\ x = \frac{1}{2} \times \frac{9}{8} \times 3 \times 400 = 675$$

Hence, number of additional persons

$= 675 - 400 = 275$

TIME AND DISTANCE

1. Starting from a point at a speed of 4 km/hr a man reaches at a cerain place and returns back to the point from where he had started journey on bicycle at the speed of 16 km/hr. His average speed during the entire journey will be :

A. 6.4 km/h B. 8.4 km/h
C. 5.4 km/h D. 10 km/h

2. A motorist covers a certain distance at a average speed of 48 km/h in 45 minutes. What speed in km/h he must maintain to cover the same distance in 30 minutes?

A. 66 km/h B. 79 km/h
C. 80 km/h D. 72 km/h

3. A policeman saw a thief at a distance of 200 m. The policeman and the thief started running at the same time. If the policeman runs at a speed of $4\frac{1}{6}$ m per second and the thief at a speed of $3\frac{1}{3}$ m per second, after what time the policeman will catch the thief?

A. 12 min B. 10 min
C. 9 min D. 4 min

4. A monkey wants to climb up a glazed pole. He climbs 12 metres in 1 minute and then he slips back 3 metres in the next minute. If the pole is 63 metre high, how long does he take to climb at the top of the pole?

A. $11\frac{1}{4}$ min B. $12\frac{1}{2}$ min
C. $12\frac{3}{4}$ min D. $14\frac{3}{4}$ min

5. The distance between two stations A and B is 300 km. A train leaves the station A with a speed of 40 km/hr. At the same time another train departs from the station B with a speed of 50 km/hr. How much time will these two trains take to cross each other?

A. 3 hrs 40 min B. 3 hrs 20 min
C. 2 hrs 20 min D. 3 hrs 45 min

6. Nilesh goes to school from his village at the speed of 4 km/hr and returns from school to village at the speed of 2 km/hr. If he takes 6 hours in all, then what is the distance between the village and the school?

A. 8 km B. 6 km
C. 5 km D. 4 km

7. By increasing the speed of the bus by 10 km/hr the time of journey for 72 km is reduced by 36 minutes. What was the original speed of the bus?

A. 30 km/hr B. 35 km/hr
C. 40 km/hr D. 45 km/hr

8. A train covers a distance in 50 minutes, if it runs at a speed of 48 km/hr on an average. The speed at which the train must run to reduce the time of journey to 40 minutes will be:

A. 70 km/hr B. 60 km/hr
C. 55 km/hr D. 50 km/hr

9. A certain distance is covered by a vehicle at a certain speed. If half of this distance is covered by another vehicle in double the time, the ratio of the speeds of the two vehicles is:

A. 4 : 1 B. 1 : 4
C. 2 : 1 D. 1 : 2

10. A is faster than B. A and B each walk 24 km. The sum of their speeds is 7 km/hr and sum of times taken by them is 14 hours. What is the speed of A?

A. 7 km/hr B. 5 km/hr
C. 4 km/hr D. 3 km/hr

ANSWERS

1	2	3	4	5	6	7	8	9	10
A	D	D	C	B	A	A	B	A	C

EXPLANATORY ANSWERS

1. Average speed during the entire journey

$= \frac{2xy}{x+y} = \frac{2 \times 4 \times 16}{4+16} = \frac{8 \times 16}{20} = 6.4$ km/hr.

2. Let required speed be x km/hr; then

$x \times \frac{1}{2} = 48 \times \frac{3}{4} \quad \therefore \quad x = 48 \times \frac{3}{4} \times 2$

$= 72$ km/hr

3. Suppose the policeman will catch the thief after t seconds then, $\left(\frac{25}{6}-\frac{10}{3}\right)t = 200 \Rightarrow \frac{5}{6}t = 200$

$\therefore\ t = \frac{200\times 6}{5} = 240$ sec $= 4$ min.

4. The monkey climbs 12 metres in 1 minute and then he slips back 3 metres in the next minute

$\therefore$ The monkey climbs in the first 2 minutes $= 12 - 3 = 9$ metres

$\therefore$ In the first 12 minutes the monkey climbs $= 9 \times 6 = 54$ metres

Remaining height of the pole to be covered by the monkey $= 63 - 54 = 9$ metre

$\therefore$ The monkey will climb the height of 9 metres in the 13th minute

$\because$ The monkey climbs 12 metres in 1 minute

$\therefore$ The monkey will climb 9 metres in $\frac{1}{12}\times 9$

$= \frac{3}{4}$ minute

$\therefore$ Time spent in climbing at the top of the pole

$= \left(12+\frac{3}{4}\right)$ minutes $= 12\frac{3}{4}$ minutes

5. The two trains are moving in the opposite directions

$\therefore$ Relative speed $= 40 + 50 = 90$ km/hr.

$\therefore$ Time taken to cross each other $= \frac{300}{90} = 3\frac{1}{3}$ hours

or, 3 hours 20 minutes.

6. Let x km be the distance between village and the school; then

$\frac{x}{4}+\frac{x}{2}=6 \quad\Rightarrow \frac{3x}{4}=6$

$\therefore\ x = \frac{6\times 4}{3} = 8$ km

8. Let x km/hr be the required speed of the train; then

$x\times\frac{40}{60} = 48\times\frac{50}{60}$

$\therefore\ x = \frac{48\times 50}{40} = 60$ km/hr

9. Let x km/hr and t hr be the certain speed and certain time.

Then, ratio of their speeds $= \frac{x}{t}:\frac{x}{2\times 2t} = 1:\frac{1}{4} = 4:1$

10. Let speeds of A and B are x_1 and x_2 km/hr and times taken by them are t_1 and t_2 hrs, then

$x_1 + x_2 = 7$ km/hr ...(i)

$t_1 + t_2 = 14$ hrs ...(ii)

Now, $\frac{24}{x_1}+\frac{24}{x_2} = 14 \Rightarrow \frac{24(x_1+x_2)}{x_1x_2} = 14$

$\therefore\ x_1x_2 = \frac{24\times 7}{14} = 12$

Then, $x_1 - x_2 = \sqrt{(x_1+x_2)^2 - 4x_1x_2}$

$= \sqrt{(7)^2 - 4\times 12} = 1$ ...(iii)

Solving *(i)* and *(iii)* we get $x_1 = 4$ km/hr

TIME AND WORK

1. A and B working together complete a work in 35 days. If A takes 60 days to complete it, how long would B alone take to complete it?

A. 64 days B. 72 days
C. 81 days D. 84 days

2. A few children working together can do a piece of work in 18 days. If the number of children employed on the work is made double, how long would they take to complete half of the work?

A. $4\frac{1}{2}$ days B. $2\frac{1}{3}$ days
C. $8\frac{3}{4}$ days D. $6\frac{1}{2}$ days

3. 10 men or 18 boys can do a piece of work in 15 days. In how many days would 25 men and 15 boys complete the same work working together?

A. $5\frac{1}{2}$ days B. $4\frac{1}{2}$ days
C. $6\frac{2}{3}$ days D. $2\frac{1}{3}$ days

4. A cistern is filled by a tap in $3\frac{1}{2}$ hours. Due to a leak in the bottom of the cistern, it takes half an hour longer to fill the cistern. If the cistern is full, how long will it take the leak to empty it?

A. 28 hours B. 29 hours
C. $31\frac{1}{3}$ hours D. 38 hours

5. A is twice as good a workman as B and thrice as good a workman as C. If C alone can do a piece of work in 24 days, how long would the three persons take to finish the work working together?

A. $3\frac{3}{11}$ days B. $4\frac{4}{7}$ days

C. $4\frac{4}{11}$ days D. $3\frac{4}{11}$ days

6. If 3 men and 5 women can do a piece of work in 8 days and 2 men and 7 boys can do the same work in 12 days. Find the number of boys, the work done by whom can equate the work done by 10 women.

A. 19 boys B. 21 boys
C. 23 boys D. 15 boys

7. 8 men alone can complete a piece of work in 12 days. 4 women alone can complete the same piece of work in 48 days and 10 children alone can complete the piece of work in 24 days. In how many days can 10 men, 4 women and 10 children together complete the piece of work?

A. 6 B. 8
C. 10 D. 15

8. A works twice as fast as B. If B can complete a piece of work independently in 12 days. Find in how many days A and B together can complete the work?

A. 8 days B. 6 days
C. 4 days D. 18 days

9. A contractor undertook to complete a project in 90 days and employed 60 men on it. After 60 days, he found that $\frac{3}{4}$ of the work has already been completed. How many men can he discharge so that the project may be completed exactly on time?

A. 15 B. 20
C. 30 D. 40

10. A can do a piece of work in 25 days and B can do it in 20 days. They work together for 5 days and then A goes away. In how many days will B finish the remaining work?

A. 33 days B. 20 days
C. 11 days D. 10 days

ANSWERS

1	2	3	4	5	6	7	8	9	10
D	A	B	A	C	B	A	C	B	C

EXPLANATORY ANSWERS

1. (A + B)'s 1 day's work = $\frac{1}{35}$

and also, A's 1 day's work = $\frac{1}{60}$

Hence, B's 1 day's work = $\frac{1}{35} - \frac{1}{60} = \frac{5}{420} = \frac{1}{84}$

So, B will do the whole work in 84 days.

3. 10 men ≡ 18 boys

25 men ≡ $\frac{18}{10} \times 25 = 45$ boys

Hence, 25 men + 15 boys = 45 + 15 = 60 boys

Now, 18 boys can do a piece of work in 15 days.

Hence, 60 boys will do a piece of work in $\frac{15 \times 18}{60} = \frac{9}{2}$ days = $4\frac{1}{2}$ days.

4. In 1 hour $\frac{2}{7}$ cistern is filled by the tap.

Hence, in $\frac{1}{2}$ hour $\frac{2}{14} = \frac{1}{7}$ cistern is filled by the tap.

So, $\frac{1}{7}$ cistern is emptied by the leakage in 4 hours.

So, 1 cistern will be emptied by the leakage in 28 hours.

6. Here, (3 men + 5 women) × 8

≡ (2 men + 7 boys) × 12

⇒ 40 women ≡ 84 boys

∴ 10 women ≡ $\frac{84}{40} \times 10$ = 21 boys

Hence, work done by 10 women

= work done of 21 boys.

7. B's 1 day's work = $\frac{1}{4} - \frac{1}{12} = \frac{2}{12} = \frac{1}{6}$

Hence, B alone will complete the work in 6 days.

8. Ratio of efficiency of A and B = 2 : 1

Then, ratio of their time taking = 1 : 2

Hence, if B can complete the work in 12 days, then A in 6 days.

Now, (A + B)'s 1 day's work = $\frac{1}{6} + \frac{1}{12} = \frac{3}{12} = \frac{1}{4}$

So, A and B together can complete the work in 4 days.

9. After 60 days remaining work = $1-\frac{3}{4}=\frac{1}{4}$

In 60 days $\frac{3}{4}$ work has been done by 60 men

In 30 days $\frac{1}{4}$ work will be done by $60\times\frac{4}{3}\times\frac{1}{4}\times\frac{60}{30}$ = 40 men.

Hence, required number of men = 60 – 40 = 20 (which are to be discharged).

BOATS AND STREAMS

1. A boat goes 6 km upstream and back to the starting point in 2 hours. If the current of the stream runs at the rate of 4 km/hr, find the speed of the boat in still water.

A. 6 km/hr B. 8 km/hr
C. 10 km/hr D. 12 km/hr

2. A boat covers 24 km upstream and 36 km downstream in 6 hours, while it covers 36 km upstream and 24 km downstream in 6½ horus. Find the speed of the current.

A. 2 km/hr B. 4 km/hr
C. 6 km/hr D. 8 km/hr

3. A man can row 5 km/hr in still water and the speed of the stream is 1.5 km/hr. He takes an hour when he travels upstream to a place and back again to the starting point. How far is the place from the starting point?

A. 2.275 km B. 3.5 km
C. 1.5 km D. None of these

4. The speed of a boat in still water is 6 km/hr and the speed of the stream is 1.5 km/hr. A man rows to a place at a distance of 22.5 km and comes back to the starting point. Find the total time taken by him.

A. 8 hours B. 10 hours
C. 12 hours D. 4 hours

5. A boat covers 20 km downstream and 6 km upstream in 3 hours, while it covers 30 km downstream and 12 km upstream in 5 hours. What is the speed of boat in still water?

A. 6 km/hr B. 8 km/hr
C. 10 km/hr D. 12 km/hr.

6. Samir can travel 12 miles downstream in a certain river in 6 hours less than it takes him to travel the same distance upstream. But when he could double his rowing rate for his 24-mile round trip, the downstream 12 miles would then take only one hour less than the upstream 12 miles. Find the speed of the current in miles/hour.

A. $2\frac{2}{3}$ B. $2\frac{1}{3}$
C. $1\frac{2}{3}$ D. $1\frac{1}{3}$

7. A boat takes 6 hours to travel from place M to N downstream and back from N to M upstream. If the speed of the boat in still water is 4 km/hr; what is the distance between two places?

A. 6 kms B. 8 kms
C. 12 kms D. Data inadequate

8. A man can row upstream at 8 km/hr and downstream at 13 km/hr. The speed of the stream is:

A. 2.5 km/hr B. 4.2 km/hr
C. 5 km/hr D. 10.5 km/hr

9. A man's speed with the current is 15 km/hr and the speed of the current is 2.5 km/hr. The man's speed against the current is:

A. 12.5 km/hr B. 10 km/hr
C. 9 km/hr D. 8.5 km/hr

10. A motorboat, whose speed is 15 km/hr in still water goes 30 km downstream and comes back in a total of 4 hours 30 minutes. What is the speed of the stream (in km/hr)?

A. 10 B. 6
C. 5 D. 4

ANSWERS

1	2	3	4	5	6	7	8	9	10
B	A	A	A	B	B	D	A	B	C

EXPLANATORY ANSWERS

1. Let the speed of a boat in still water = x km/hr; then

$$\frac{6}{x-4}+\frac{6}{x+4}=2 \Rightarrow \frac{2x}{x^2-16}=\frac{1}{3}$$

$\Rightarrow x^2 - 6x - 16 = 0$

$\Rightarrow (x - 8)(x + 2) = 0$

Hence, the speed of the boat = 8 km/hr.

2. Let x km/hr and y km/hr be the speeds of the boat in still water and the speed of the current respectively, then

$$\frac{24}{x-y}+\frac{36}{x+y}=6 \Rightarrow \frac{4}{x-y}+\frac{6}{x+y}=1 \quad ...(i)$$

And, $$\frac{36}{x-y}+\frac{24}{x+y}=\frac{13}{2} \quad ...(ii)$$

Solving these two equations, we get

$x + y = 12; x - y = 8$

Hence, $y = \frac{1}{2}(12-8) = 2$ km/hr.

3. Let required distance be x km, then

$$\frac{x}{5-1.5}+\frac{x}{5+1.5}=1 \Rightarrow \frac{x\times 2}{7}+\frac{x\times 2}{13}=1$$

$\Rightarrow 40x = 91 \quad \therefore x = 91/40 = 2.275$ km

4. Required time period $= \frac{22.5}{6+1.5}+\frac{22.5}{6-1.5}$

$= \frac{45}{15}+\frac{45}{9} = 8$ hours.

5. Let x km/hr and y km/hr be the speed of boat in still water and speed of current respectively; then

$$\frac{20}{x+y}+\frac{6}{x-y}=3 \quad ...(i)$$

and also, $$\frac{30}{x+y}+\frac{12}{x-y}=5$$

$$\Rightarrow \frac{15}{x+y}+\frac{6}{x-y}=\frac{5}{2} \quad ...(ii)$$

Solving equations *(i)* & *(ii)*, we get $x + y = 10$ and $x - y = 6$

Since, $x = \frac{1}{2}(10 + 6) = 8$ km/hr.

6. Let x km/hr and y km/hr be the speed of rowing in still water and speed of the current respectively; then

$$\frac{12}{x-y}-\frac{12}{x+y}=6 \Rightarrow \frac{24y}{x^2-y^2}=6$$

$\Rightarrow x^2 = y^2 + 4y \quad ...(i)$

Again, $$\frac{12}{2x-y}-\frac{12}{2x+y}=1$$

$$\Rightarrow \frac{24y}{4x^2-y^2}=1 \Rightarrow x^2=\frac{y^2+24y}{4} \quad ...(ii)$$

From equations (i) and (ii), we get

$$y^2 + 4y = \frac{y^2+24y}{4} \Rightarrow 3y^2 = 8y$$

$\therefore y = \frac{8}{3} = 2\frac{1}{3}$ miles/hr.

8. The speed of the stream $= \frac{1}{2}(13 - 8) = \frac{5}{2}$

$= 2.5$ km/hr.

9. The man's speed in still water

$= 15 - 2.5 = 12.5$ km/hr

Hence, the men's speed against the current

$= 12.5 - 2.5 = 10$ km/hr

10. Let speed of the stream be x km/hr, then

$$\frac{30}{15+x}+\frac{30}{15-x}=4\frac{1}{2} \Rightarrow \frac{30\times 30}{225-x^2}=\frac{9}{2}$$

$$\Rightarrow \frac{200}{225-x^2}=1 \Rightarrow x^2 = 225 - 200$$

$\Rightarrow x^2 = 25 \quad \therefore x = 5$ km/hr.

ALLIGATION OR MIXTURE

1. A shopkeeper buys 26 kgs of milk @ Rs. 16 per kg. He also buys from another source an inferior quality of milk @ Rs. 10 per kg. How much quantity of the latter should he buy to mix it with the former so that he can sell the mixture @ Rs. 14 per kg without making any loss?

A. 13 kgs B. 12 kgs
C. 14 kgs D. 16 kgs

2. Two vessels A and B contain mixture of milk and water in the ratio 4 : 1 and 9 : 11 respectively. They are mixed in the ratio of 3 : 2. Find the ratio of milk : water in the resulting mixture.

A. 34 : 16 B. 33 : 17
C. 16 : 34 D. 17 : 33

3. A shopkeeper has 50 kgs of rice. He sells a part of it at 20% profit and the rest at 40% profit. If he gains 25% on the whole, find the quantity of each part.

A. 12.5 kgs and 37.5 kgs
B. 37.5 kgs and 12.5 kgs
C. 23.5 kgs and 21.5 kgs
D. 21.5 kgs and 23.5 kgs

4. A man bought a certain quantity of sugar for Rs. 8000. He sells one-fourth of it at 20% loss. At what per cent profit should he sell the remainder stock so as to make an overall profit of 20%?

A. 20% B. 30%
C. 35% D. 40%

5. Rs. 675 was divided among 75 boys and girls. Each boy gets Rs. 20 whereas a girl gets Rs. 5. Find the number of boys and girls.

A. 20, 55 B. 15, 60
C. 25, 50 D. 30, 45

6. A vessel contains mixture of liquids A and B in the ratio 3 : 2. When 20 litres of the mixture is taken out and replaced by 20 litres of liquid B, the ratio changes to 1 : 4. How many litres of liquid A was there initially present in the vessel?

A. 12 litres B. 18 litres
C. 24 litres D. 22 litres

7. A container is full of milk. One-third of milk is taken out of it and replaced by same quantity of water. Then again one-third of the mixture is taken out of it and replaced by the same quantity of water. The process is repeated 4 times. If 16 litres of milk is left in the container at the end of 4th operation, find the capacity of the container.

A. 76 litres B. 81 litres
C. 82 litres D. 85 litres

8. The cost of type-I rice is Rs. 15 per kg and type-II is Rs. 20 per kg. If both type I and type II are mixed in the ratio of 2 : 3, then find the price per kg of the mixed variety.

A. Rs. 19.50 B. Rs. 19
C. Rs. 18.50 D. Rs. 18

9. In what ratio must a grocer mix two varieties of tea worth Rs. 60 a kg and Rs. 65 a kg so that by selling the mixture at Rs. 68.20 a kg he may gain 10%?

A. 4 : 5 B. 3 : 5
C. 3 : 4 D. 3 : 2

10. A vessel contains 80 litres of milk. 16 litres of milk was taken out of the vessel and replaced by water. Then 16 litres of mixture was withdrawn and again replaced by water. The operation was repeated for third time. How much milk is now left in the vessel?

A. 96.40 litres
B. 50.36 litres
C. 40.96 litres
D. 32.76 litres

ANSWERS

1	2	3	4	5	6	7	8	9	10
A	B	B	B	A	B	B	D	D	C

EXPLANATORY ANSWERS

1.

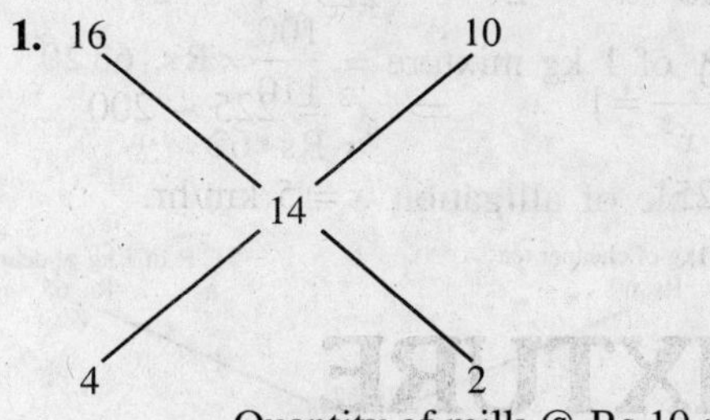

or 2 : 1 $\dfrac{\text{Quantity of milk @ Rs.10 per kg}}{\text{Quantity of milk @ Rs. 16 per kg}} = \dfrac{1}{2}$

So, quantity of milk @ Rs. 10 per kg. $= \dfrac{26}{2} = 13$ kgs.

2. Fraction is *Milk* *Water*

A : $\dfrac{4}{5}$ $\dfrac{1}{5}$

B : $\dfrac{9}{20}$ $\dfrac{11}{20}$

$(3A + 2B) = A \text{ and } B : \left(\dfrac{12}{5}+\dfrac{9}{10}\right)\left(\dfrac{3}{5}+\dfrac{11}{10}\right)$

$\dfrac{33}{10}$ $\dfrac{17}{10}$

So, Ratio of milk : water in the resulting mixture = 33 : 17.

3.

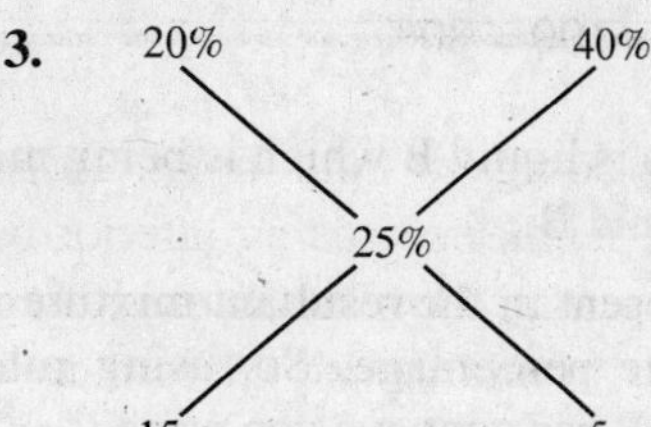

or 3 : 1

Quantity sold at 20% profit $= \frac{3}{3+1} \times 50$

$= 37.5$ kgs.

Quantity sold at 40% profit $= (50 - 37.5)$

$= 12.5$ kgs.

4. Let the remainder stock be sold at x% profit.

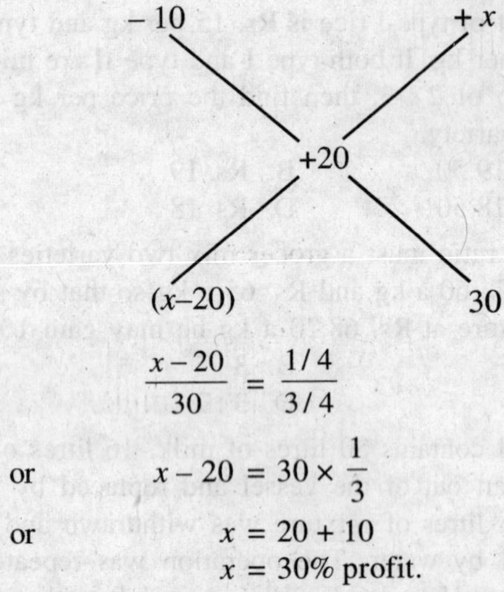

$$\frac{x-20}{30} = \frac{1/4}{3/4}$$

or $\quad x - 20 = 30 \times \frac{1}{3}$

or $\quad x = 20 + 10$

$x = 30\%$ profit.

5. Average money per head (boy or girl)

$= \text{Rs. } \frac{675}{75} = \text{Rs. } 9$

(Boys) Rs. 20   (Girls) Rs. 5

(Average) Rs. 9

4   11

Number of boys $= \frac{4}{4+11} \times 75 = 20$

Number of girls $= \frac{11}{4+11} \times 75 = 55.$.

6. % of liquid B initially present in the vessel

$= \frac{2}{3+2} \times 100 = 40\%$

% of liquid B finally present in the vessel

$= \frac{4}{1+4} \times 100 = 80\%$

The second solution is liquid B which is being mixed and it has 100% liquid B.

80% of liquid B present in the resultant mixture may be taken as average percentage. So, using rule of alligation on liquid B per cent, we can write,

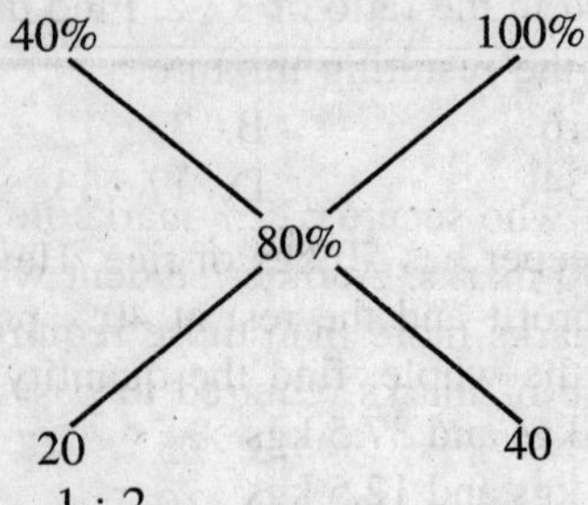

or $\quad 1 : 2$

The ratio of liquid left in the vessel to liquid B being mixed = 1 : 2

Since the quantity of liquid B being mixed is 20 litres, the quantity of liquid left in the vessel is 10 litres.

Therefore, the total quantity of liquid initially present in the vessel

$= 10 + 20 = 30$ litres

Quantity of liquid A $= \frac{3}{2+3} \times 30 = 18$ litres.

7. Let capacity of the container be x litre; then

$x(1 - 1/3)^4 = 16 \quad \Rightarrow \quad x\left(\frac{2}{3}\right)^4 = 16$

$\Rightarrow x \times \frac{16}{81} = 16 \quad \therefore \quad x = 81$ litres

8. Let the price per kg of mixed variety be Rs. x; then

By the rule of alligation,

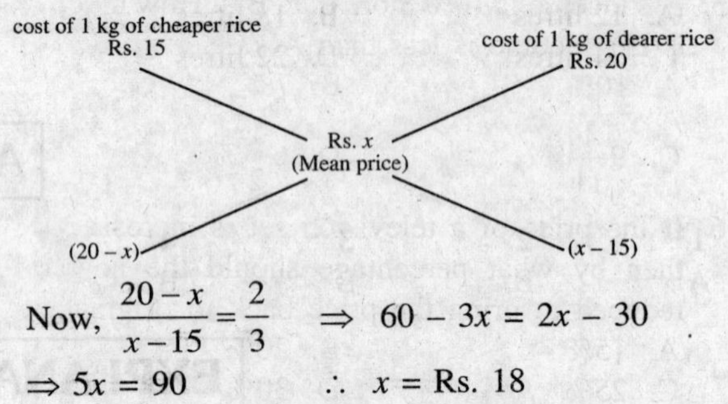

Now, $\frac{20-x}{x-15} = \frac{2}{3} \quad \Rightarrow \quad 60 - 3x = 2x - 30$

$\Rightarrow 5x = 90 \quad \therefore \quad x = \text{Rs. } 18$

9. S.P. of 1 kg mixture = Rs. 68.20, Gain % = 10%

Hence, C.P. of 1 kg mixture $= \frac{100}{110} \times \text{Rs. } 68.20$

$= \text{Rs. } 62$

By the rule of alligation

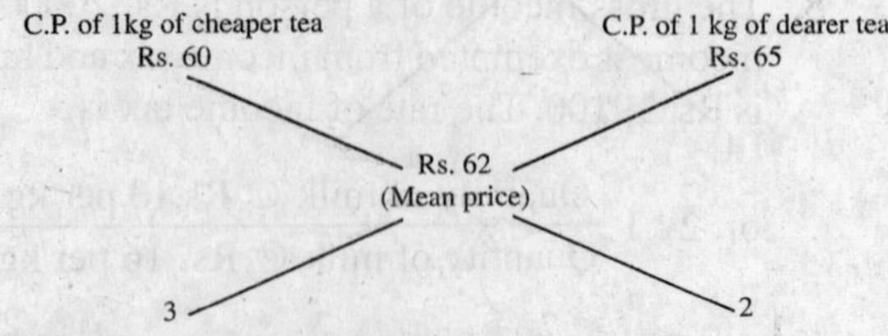

Hence, required ratio = 3 : 2

10. Amount of milk left $= 80\left(1 - \frac{16}{80}\right)^3 = 80\left(\frac{4}{5}\right)^3$

$80 \times \frac{64}{125} = 40.96$ litres.

PERCENTAGE

1. A student who secures 20% marks in an examination fails by 30 marks. Another student who secures 32% gets 42 marks more than those required to pass. The percentage of marks required to pass is:
A. 20 B. 25
C. 28 D. 30

2. In a college election, a candidate secured 62% of the votes and is elected by a majority of 144 votes. The total number of votes polled is:
A. 600 B. 800
C. 925 D. 1200

3. In an organisation, 40% of the employees are matriculates, 50% of the remaining are graduates and the remaining 180 are postgraduates. How many employees are graduates?
A. 360 B. 240
C. 300 D. 180

4. The population of a village is 4500. $\frac{5}{9}$th of them are males and rest females. If 40% of the males are married, then the percentage of married female is :
A. 35 B. 40
C. 50 D. 60

5. A's income is 10% more than B's. How much per cent is B's income is less than A's?
A. 10% B. 7%
C. $9\frac{1}{11}$% D. $6\frac{1}{2}$%

6. If the price of a television set is increased by 25%, then by what percentage should the new price be reduced to bring the price back to original level?
A. 15% B. 20%
C. 25% D. 30%

7. In an election one of the two candidates gets 40% votes and loses by 100 votes. Total number of votes is :
A. 500 B. 400
C. 600 D. 1000

8. The gross income of a person is Rs. 20000. 10% of his income is exempted from income tax and his net income is Rs. 19100. The rate of income tax is :
A. 3% B. 2%
C. 4% D. 5%

9. The owner of a cell phone shop charges his customer 32% more than the cost price. If a customer paid Rs. 6600 for the cell phone, then what was the cost price of the cell phone?
A. Rs. 5000 B. Rs. 5500
C. Rs. 5800 D. Rs. 6100

10. If the cost of pins reduced by Rs. 4 per dozen, 12 more pins can be purchased for Rs. 48. The cost of pins per dozen after reduction is:
A. Rs. 8 B. Rs. 12
C. Rs. 16 D. Rs. 20

11. In an examination 80% of the students passed in Mathematics and 70% passed in English, while 10% students failed in both the subjects. If 360 students passed in both the subjects, find the total number of students who appeared in the examination.
A. 400 B. 600
C. 630 D. 640

12. Electric tax is increased by 20% and its consumption is decreased by 20%. The change in the expenditure is:
A. 4% decrease B. 4% increase
C. 5% decrease D. 5% increase

13. The selling price of certain commodity was reduced by 25%. As a result of it, the sales increased by 30%. What was the effect of it on cash collected by daily sales?
A. 2.5% decrease B. 2.5% increase
C. 5% decrease. D. 5% increase

14. The wheat sold by a grocer contained 10% low quality wheat. What quantity of good quality wheat should be added to 150 kgs of wheat so that the percentage of low quality wheat becomes 5%?
A. 50 kgs B. 85 kgs
C. 135 kgs D. 150 kgs

15. Nilam spends 15% of her monthly income on household expenses. She spends 17% of the monthly income in travelling and 6% on medical expenses and saves the rest Rs. 15,500. What is her monthly income?
A. Rs. 20,000 B. Rs. 25,000
C. Rs. 30,000 D. Rs. 35,000

ANSWERS

1	2	3	4	5	6	7	8	9	10
B	A	D	C	C	B	A	D	A	B
11	**12**	**13**	**14**	**15**					
B	A	A	D	B					

EXPLANATORY ANSWERS

1. 20% of $x + 30 = 32\%$ of $x - 42$

$\Rightarrow$ 12% of $x = 72$

$$\Rightarrow \quad x = \frac{72 \times 100}{12} = 600$$

Pass Mark $= 20\%$ of $600 + 30 = 150$

$$\text{Pass percentage} = \left(\frac{150}{600} \times 100\right)\% = 25\%$$

2. $(62\%$ of $x - 38\%$ of $x) = 144$

$$\Rightarrow 24\% \text{ of } x = 144 \quad \Rightarrow x = \frac{144 \times 100}{24} = 600$$

3.
$$\text{Matriculates} = \frac{40}{100}x = \frac{2x}{5}$$

$$\text{Remaining} = \left(x - \frac{2x}{5}\right) = \frac{3x}{5}$$

$$\text{Graduates} = \frac{50}{100} \times \frac{3x}{5} = \frac{3x}{10}$$

$$\text{Remaining} = \frac{3x}{5} - \frac{3x}{10} = \frac{3x}{10}$$

$$\text{Now, } \frac{3x}{10} = 180 \quad \therefore x = \frac{10 \times 180}{3} = 600$$

$$\therefore \text{Graduates} = \frac{3 \times 600}{10} = 180.$$

4. $$\text{Males} = \left(\frac{5}{9} \times 4500\right) = 2500$$

Females $= 2000$

$$\therefore \text{Married males} = \frac{40}{100} \times 2500 = 1000$$

and married females $= 1000$

$\therefore$ Percentage of married females

$$= \left(\frac{1000}{2000} \times 100\right)\% = 50\%.$$

5. $$\text{Required percentage} = \left[\frac{10}{(100+10)} \times 100\right]\% = 9\frac{1}{11}\%.$$

6. $$\text{Required reduction} = \frac{25}{100+25} \times 100 = 20\%.$$

7. Out of 100, difference in votes $= (60 - 40) = 20$

20% of $x = 100$

$$\therefore x = \frac{100 \times 100}{20} = 500.$$

8. Gross income = Rs. 20000

Income exempted from income tax = 10% of gross income

$\therefore$ Income on which income tax is chargeable $= (100 - 10\%) = 90\%$ of gross income

$$= 20000 \times \frac{90}{100} = \text{Rs. } 18000$$

$\therefore$ Total income tax paid on

= Rs. 20000 – Rs. 19100 = Rs. 900

$$\therefore \text{Rate per cent of income tax} = \frac{900}{18000} \times 100 = 5\%$$

9. Let cost price of the cell phone be Rs. x; then

$$x + \frac{32}{100} \times x = 6600 \quad \Rightarrow \frac{132x}{100} = 6600$$

$$\therefore \quad x = \frac{100 \times 6600}{132} = \text{Rs. } 5000.$$

10. Let reduced price by Rs. x per dozen, then

$$\frac{48}{x} - \frac{48}{x+4} = 1 \quad \Rightarrow \frac{48 \times 4}{x^2 + 4x} = 1$$

$\Rightarrow$ $x^2 + 4x - 192 = 0$

$\Rightarrow$ $(x + 16)(x - 12) = 0$

$\therefore$ $x =$ Rs. 12.

11. Here, percentage of students failed in Mathematics and English be 30% and 20% respectively.

Percentage of students failed either one or both subjects $= 30 + 20 - 10 = 40\%$

Hence, percentage of pass students $= 100 - 40 = 60\%$

Now, $60\% = 360$

$$\therefore 100\% = \frac{360}{60} \times 100 = 600.$$

12. Let initially electric tax is Rs. 100 and consumption = 100 units

Decrease in consumption

$= 100 \times 100 - 120 \times 80 =$ Rs. 400

$$\text{Hence, decrease percentage} = \frac{400 \times 100}{100 \times 100} = 4\%.$$

13. Let the selling price of a commodity be Rs. 100 and number of sales = 100 units

Decrease in daily cash $= 100 \times 100 - 75 \times 130$

= Rs. 250

$$\text{Hence, decrease percentage} = \frac{250 \times 100}{100 \times 100} = 2.5\%.$$

14. Let x kg of good wheat be added; then

$$\frac{10}{100} \times 150 = \frac{5}{100}(150 + x)$$

$\Rightarrow 150 + x = 300 \quad \therefore \; x = 150$ kg.

15. Let her monthly income be Rs. x; then

$$x - \left(\frac{15}{100} \times x + \frac{17}{100} \times x + \frac{6}{100} \times x\right) = 15{,}500$$

$$\Rightarrow x - \frac{38x}{100} = 15500 \quad \Rightarrow \frac{62x}{100} = 15500$$

$$\therefore \quad x = \frac{15500 \times 100}{62} = \text{Rs. } 25000.$$

PROFIT AND LOSS

1. Ashok bought 25 kg of rice at the rate of Rs. 6 per kg and 35 kg of rice at the rate of Rs. 7 per kg. He mixed the two and sold the mixture at the rate of Rs. 6.75 per kg. What was his gain or loss in the transaction?

A. Rs. 16 gain B. Rs. 16 loss
C. Rs. 10 gain D. None of these

2. Profit after selling a commodity for Rs. 425 is same as loss after selling it for Rs. 355. The cost of the commodity is :

A. Rs. 285 B. Rs. 390
C. Rs. 295 D. Rs. 400

3. Ram bought 4 dozen apples at Rs. 12 per dozen and 2 dozen at Rs. 16 per dozen. He sold all of them to earn 20%. At what price per dozen did he sell the apples?

A. Rs. 14.40 B. Rs. 16.00
C. Rs. 16.80 D. Rs. 16.20

4. At what price must Kantilal sell a mixture of 80 kg sugar at Rs. 6.75 per kg with 120 kg at Rs. 8 per kg to gain 20%?

A. Rs. 7.50 per kg B. Rs. 8.20 per kg
C. Rs. 8.35 per kg D. Rs. 9 per kg

5. A person bought an article and sold it at a loss of 10%. If he had bought it for 20% less and sold it for Rs. 55 more, he would have had a profit of 40%. The C.P. of the article is :

A. Rs. 200 B. Rs. 225
C. Rs. 250 D. None of these

6. A dealer sold a machine to a shopkeeper at 20% profit. The shopkeeper sold the machine to a customer so as to get 25% profit for himself. The difference between the selling price of the dealer and that of the shopkeeper was found to be Rs. 129. What is the initial price of the machine?

A. Rs. 410 B. Rs. 420
C. Rs. 430 D. Rs. 440

7. A man bought a horse and cart. If he sold the horse at 10% loss and the cart at 20% gain he would not loss anything. If he sold the horse at 5% loss and the cart at 5% gain he would lose Rs. 10 in the bargain. What did he pay for each?

A. Rs. 400, Rs. 200 B. Rs. 300, Rs. 300
C. Rs. 250, Rs. 350 D. Rs. 350, Rs. 250

8. The marked price of a radio is 20% more than its cost price. If a discount of 10% is given on the marked price, the gain percentage is:

A. 8 B. 10
C. 12 D. 15

9. A dishonest dealer sells his goods at the cost price and still earns a profit of 60% by underweight. What weight does he use for a kg?

A. 625 gms B. 750 gms
C. 800 gms D. 850 gms

10. A man sells two horses for Rs. 990 each. On one he gains 10% and the other he loses 10%. What is his total percentage of gain or loss in the transaction?

A. 1% gain B. 1% loss
C. 2% gain D. 2% loss

ANSWERS

1	2	3	4	5	6	7	8	9	10
C	B	B	D	C	C	A	A	A	B

EXPLANATORY ANSWERS

1. C.P. of 60 kg mixture $=$ Rs. $(25 \times 6 + 35 \times 7)$
$=$ Rs. 395

S.P. of 60 kg mixtire $=$ Rs. (60×6.75)
$=$ Rs. 405

$\therefore$ Gain $=$ Rs. $(405 - 395)$
$=$ Rs. 10

2. Let C.P. $=$ Rs. x

Then, $425 - x = x - 355 \Rightarrow 2x = 780$

$\therefore$ $x =$ Rs. 390

3. C.P. of 6 dozen apples $=$ Rs. $(12 \times 4 + 16 \times 2)$
$=$ Rs. 80

$\therefore$ S.P. $=$ Rs. $\left(\frac{120}{100} \times 80\right)$
$=$ Rs. 96

$\therefore$ S.P. per dozen $=$ Rs. $\left(\frac{96}{6}\right) =$ Rs. 16

4. C.P. of 1 kg sugar $= \dfrac{80 \times 6.75 + 120 \times 8}{200}$

$= \text{Rs. } 7.50$

$\therefore$ S.P. of 1 kg $= \text{Rs.}\left(\dfrac{120}{100} \times 7.50\right)$

$= \text{Rs. } 9 \text{ per kg}$

5. Let, C.P. = Rs. x,

then, S.P. $= \dfrac{90}{100} \times x = \text{Rs. } \dfrac{9x}{10}$

Now, when C.P. $= \text{Rs. } \dfrac{80x}{100} = \text{Rs. } \dfrac{4x}{5}$;

then, S.P. $= \dfrac{140}{100} \times \dfrac{4x}{5} = \text{Rs. } \dfrac{28x}{25}$

But, $\dfrac{28x}{25} - \dfrac{9x}{10} = 55 \Rightarrow \dfrac{11x}{50} = 55$

$\therefore$ $x = \text{Rs. } 250$

6. Let the initial price = Rs. x; then C.P. for dealer

$= \dfrac{120}{100} \times x = \text{Rs. } \dfrac{6x}{5}$

Again, C.P. for shopkeeper $= \dfrac{125}{100} \times \dfrac{6x}{5}$

$= \text{Rs. } \dfrac{3x}{2}$

Now, $\dfrac{3x}{2} - \dfrac{6x}{5} = 129 \Rightarrow \dfrac{3x}{10} = 129$

$\therefore x = \dfrac{10 \times 129}{3} = \text{Rs. } 430$

7. Here, 10% C.P. of horse = 20% C.P. of cart; Hence, C.P. of horse = 2 × C.P. of cart;

Let C.P. of cart and horse be Rs. x and Rs. $2x$ respectively; then,

$\dfrac{5}{100} \times 2x - \dfrac{5}{100} \times x = 10 \Rightarrow \dfrac{1}{20} x = 10$

$\therefore x = 200$

Hence, C.P. of a cart = Rs. 200 and C.P. of a horse $= 2 \times 200 = \text{Rs. } 400$

8. Let C.P. be Rs. 100; then marked price = Rs. 120

Since, S.P. $= \dfrac{90}{100} \times 120 = \text{Rs. } 108$

$\therefore$ Profit = 108 – 100 = Rs. 8, Hence, **gain** = 8%.

9. Required weight $= \dfrac{100}{160} \times 1000 = 625$ gms.

10. Here, loss % $= \left(\dfrac{10}{10}\right)^2 = 1\%$.

SIMPLE INTEREST

1. A lent a sum of Rs. 1250 to B at a certain rate of interest for 3 years and a sum of Rs. 1500 to C at the same rate of interest for 2 years. If he was paid total Rs. 258.75 as interest in both cases, find the rate of interest at which money was lent by him.

A. $4\frac{1}{6}\%$ B. $6\frac{1}{4}\%$

C. $2\frac{1}{7}\%$ D. $3\frac{5}{6}\%$

2. A invested Rs. 5000 at a certain rate of simple interest and Rs. 4000 for the same period at 1% higher rate of interest. If the interest in both cases is same, the former rate of interest is :

A. 3% B. 4%

C. 6% D. 5%

3. If a certain sum of money at simple interest amounts to Rs. 1900 in 3 years and to Rs. 2050 in 5 years, the rate per cent per annum is :

A. 4½% B. 3½%

C. 2½% D. 5¼%

4. A certain sum of money lent out on simple interest amounts to Rs. 1760 in 2 years and to Rs. 2000 in 5 years. Find the sum.

A. Rs. 1650 B. Rs. 1500

C. Rs. 1580 D. Rs. 1600

5. Out of the sum of Rs. 1550, a part was lent out at 5% p.a. simple interest and the remaining at 8% p.a. simple interest. If the total interest in both cases after 3 years is Rs. 300, the sum of money lent out at 8% p.a. simple interest was:

A. Rs. 760 B. Rs. 775

C. Rs. 750 D. Rs. 780

6. If simple interest on a certain sum of money for 4 years at 5% p.a. is same as the simple interest on Rs. 840 for 10 years at the rate of 4% p.a., the sum of money is:

A. Rs. 1780 B. Rs. 1660

C. Rs. 1680 D. Rs. 1620

7. What equal instalment of annual payment will discharge a debt which is due as Rs. 848 at the end of 4 years at 4% per annum simple interest?

A. Rs. 200 B. Rs. 212
C. Rs. 225 D. Rs. 250

8. Madhavi lent Rs. 5000 to Kamla for 5 years and Rs. 3000 to Vimla for 4 years. Find the rate of interest, if Madhavi gets an interest of Rs. 600 in the end.

A. 1.62% B. 2.5%
C. 3% D. 4%

9. A sum of money doubles itself in 7 years at simple interest. In how many years it will become four fold?

A. 10 years B. 14 years
C. 21 years D. 35 years

10. An amount doubles itself at the end of 8 years with a certain rate of simple interest. What will be the total simple interest on Rs. 8000 at that rate at the end of 4 years?

A. Rs. 2000 B. Rs. 4000
C. Rs. 6000 D. None of these

ANSWERS

1	2	3	4	5	6	7	8	9	10
D	B	A	D	C	C	A	A	C	B

EXPLANATORY ANSWERS

1. $\frac{1250 \times R \times 3}{100} + \frac{1500 \times R \times 2}{100} = 258.75$

$\Rightarrow 6750\ R = 25875$

$\therefore \quad R = \frac{25875}{6750} = \frac{23}{6} = 3\frac{5}{6}\%$

2. Here, $\frac{5000 \times R \times T}{100} = \frac{4000 \times (R+1) \times T}{100}$

$\Rightarrow 5R = 4R + 4 \quad \therefore \quad R = 4\%$

3. Simple interest for 2 years

= Rs. 2050 – Rs. 1900 = Rs. 150

$\therefore$ Simple interest for 1 year = Rs. $\frac{150}{2}$ = Rs. 75

Since simple interest for 3 years = Rs. 75 × 3

= Rs. 225

$\therefore$ Principal = Rs. 1900 – Rs. 225 = Rs. 1675

Hence, Rate = $\frac{75 \times 100}{1675 \times 1} = 4\frac{1}{2}\%$

4. Interest for 3 years = Rs. 2000 – Rs. 1760

= Rs. 240

$\therefore$ Interest for 1 year = Rs. $\frac{240}{3}$ = Rs. 80

And interest for 2 years = Rs. 80 × 2 = Rs. 160

$\therefore$ Principal = Rs. 1760 – Rs. 160 = Rs. 1600

5. Let Rs. x and Rs $(1550 - x)$ were lent out at 8% and 5% respectively; then

$\frac{x \times 8 \times 3}{100} + \frac{(1550 - x) \times 5 \times 3}{100} = 300$

$\Rightarrow 24x + 23250 - 15x = 30000$

$\Rightarrow \quad 9x = 6750 \quad \therefore \quad x = \frac{6750}{9}$ = Rs. 750

6. Here, $\frac{P \times 5 \times 4}{100} = \frac{840 \times 4 \times 10}{100} \Rightarrow 5P = 8400$

$\therefore \quad P = \frac{8400}{5}$ = Rs. 1680

7. Let equal instalment be Rs. x; then

$x + \frac{x \times 4 \times 3}{100} + x + \frac{x \times 4 \times 2}{100} + x + \frac{x \times 4 \times 1}{100} + x = 848$

$\Rightarrow 4x + \frac{24x}{100} = 848 \quad \Rightarrow \quad \frac{106x}{25} = 848$

$\therefore x = \frac{848 \times 25}{106}$ = Rs. 200

8. $\frac{5000 \times R \times 5}{100} + \frac{3000 \times R \times 4}{100} = 600$

$\Rightarrow \quad 250\ R + 120\ R = 600$

$\Rightarrow \quad 370R = 600$

$\therefore \quad R = \frac{600}{370} = 1.62\%$

9. Let principal be Rs. x; then amount = Rs. $2x$, Hence, I = $2x - x$ = Rs. x.

$R = \frac{x \times 100}{x \times 7} = \frac{100}{7}\%$ p.a.

Now, amount = Rs. $4x$; then I = $4x - x$ = Rs. $3x$

Hence, $T = \frac{3x \times 100}{x \times \frac{100}{7}} = \frac{3 \times 100 \times 7}{100}$ = 21 years

10. Let principal = Rs. x; then amount = Rs. $2x$; I = $2x - x$ = Rs. x

$R = \frac{x \times 100}{x \times 8} = \frac{25}{2}\%$

Again, $I = \frac{8000 \times 25 \times 4}{100 \times 2}$ = Rs. 4000

COMPOUND INTEREST

1. The compound interest on a certain sum of money invested for 3 years at 5% per annum is Rs. 1891.50. What will be the simple interest on the same sum at the same rate for 2 years?

A. Rs. 1700 B. Rs. 1200
C. Rs. 1500 D. Rs. 2100

2. A sum of money lent out at a certain rate of simple interest amounts to Rs. 6600 in 2 years and to Rs. 6900 in 3 years. What will be the compound interest on the same sum of money if lent out at the same rate for 2 years?

A. Rs. 605 B. Rs. 715
C. Rs. 615 D. Rs. 595

3. A man deposits Rs. 1200 in a bank on the 1st day of each year. If the bank pays 5% per annum compound interest on deposited sum of money, what will be the amount to his credit on the 10th day of the second year?

A. Rs. 2560 B. Rs. 2460
C. Rs. 2370 D. Rs. 2860

4. If the difference between compound and simple interest on a certain sum of money for 3 years at 5% per annum is Rs. 244, the sum is :

A. Rs. 40000 B. Rs. 25000
C. Rs. 30000 D. Rs. 32000

5. A man purchased a sewing machine for Rs. 5000. If due to sustained use value of this sewing machine depreciates by 6% annually, find its value after 3 years.

A. Rs. 3775.67 B. Rs. 4152.92
C. Rs. 4250.25 D. Rs. 4356.25

6. Find the sum on which the difference between compound and simple interest for 3 years at 10% per annum will be Rs. 868.

A. Rs. 29500 B. Rs. 27625
C. Rs. 28500 D. Rs. 28000

7. Samir invested Rs. 15000 at the rate of interest 10% p.a. for 1 year. If the interest compound six months. What amount will Samir get at the end of the year?

A. Rs. 16,500 B. Rs. 16525.50
C. Rs. 16537.50 D. Rs. 18,150

8. The compound interest on a certain sum for 2 years at 10% per annum is Rs. 525. The simple interest on the same sum for double the time at half the rate per cent per annum is:

A. Rs. 800 B. Rs. 600
C. Rs. 500 D. Rs. 400

9. The least number of complete years in which a sum of money put at 20% compound interest will be more than doubled is:

A. 6 B. 5
C. 4 D. 3

10. On a sum of money, the simple interest for 2 years is Rs. 660, while the compound interest is Rs. 696.30, the rate of interest being the same in both cases. Find the rate of interest.

A. Rs. 12% B. 11%
C. 10% D. 9%

ANSWERS

1	2	3	4	5	6	7	8	9	10
B	C	B	D	B	D	C	C	C	B

EXPLANATORY ANSWERS

1. Here, $1891.50 = P\left[\left(1+\frac{5}{100}\right)^3 - 1\right]$

$\Rightarrow \quad 1891.50 = P\left[\left(\frac{21}{20}\right)^3 - 1\right]$

$\Rightarrow \quad 1891.50 = P\left(\frac{1261}{8000}\right)$

$\therefore \ P = \frac{1891.50 \times 8000}{1261} = \text{Rs. } 12000$

Now, $\text{S.I.} = \frac{12000 \times 5 \times 2}{100} = \text{Rs. } 1200$

2. Here, 1 year's S.I. = Rs. 6900 – Rs. 6600 = Rs. 300

$\therefore$ 2 year's S.I. = 300 × 2 = Rs. 600

$\therefore$ Principal = Rs. 6600 – Rs. 600 = Rs. 6000

Hence, $\text{Rate} = \frac{600 \times 100}{6000 \times 2} = 5\%$

$\therefore$ C.I. $= 6000\left[\left(1+\frac{5}{100}\right)^2-1\right]$

$= 6000\left[\left(\frac{21}{20}\right)^2-1\right] = \frac{6000\times 41}{400}$ = Rs. 615

3. Required amount $= 1200\left(1+\frac{5}{100}\right) + 1200$

$= 1200 \times \frac{21}{20} + 1200 = 1260 + 1200 =$ Rs. 2460

4. Here, $P\left[\left(1+\frac{5}{100}\right)^3-1\right] - \frac{P\times 5\times 3}{100} = 244$

$\Rightarrow P\times\frac{1261}{8000} - \frac{3P}{20} = 244 \Rightarrow P\times\frac{61}{8000} = 244$

$\therefore P = \frac{244\times 8000}{61}$ = Rs. 32000

5. Here, value of the machine after 3 years

$= 5000\left(1-\frac{6}{100}\right)^3 = 5000\times\frac{47}{50}\times\frac{47}{50}\times\frac{47}{50}$

= Rs. 4152.92.

6. Here, $P\left[\left(1+\frac{10}{100}\right)^3-1\right] - \frac{P\times 10\times 3}{100} = 868$

$\Rightarrow P\times\frac{331}{1000} - \frac{3P}{10} = 868$

$\Rightarrow P\times\frac{31}{1000} = 868 \;\therefore\; P = \frac{868\times 1000}{31}$

= Rs. 28000

7. $A = 15000\left(1+\frac{5}{100}\right)^2 = 15000\times\frac{441}{400}$

= Rs. 16537.50

8. Here, $P\left[\left(1+\frac{10}{100}\right)^2-1\right] = 525$

$\Rightarrow P\left[\frac{121}{100}-1\right] = 525 \Rightarrow P\times\frac{21}{100} = 525$

$\therefore P = \frac{525\times 100}{21}$ = Rs. 2500

Hence, required S.I. $= \frac{2500\times 5\times 4}{100}$ = Rs. 500

9. Here, $P\left(1+\frac{20}{100}\right)^n > 2P \Rightarrow \left(\frac{6}{5}\right)^n > 2$

Hence, if $n = 4$ then, $\left(\frac{6}{5}\right)^4 = \frac{1296}{625} > 2$

So, $n = 4$ years

10. Here, S.I. for 1 year = Rs. 330
Since, simple interest of Rs. 330 for 1 year
= 696.30 − 660 = Rs. 36.30

Hence, required rate $= \frac{36.30\times 100}{330\times 1} = \frac{3630}{330} = 11\%$

AREA AND PERIMETER

1. If side of a square is reduced by 50%, its area will be reduced by

A. 50% B. 75%
C. 80% D. 60%

2. If each side of a square is doubled, its area will become

A. double B. four times
C. three times D. eight times

3. Three sides of a triangle are in the ratio of 17 : 15 : 8. If the perimeter of this triangle is 40 m, find its area

A. 50 sq. m. B. 49 sq. m.
C. 60 sq. m. D. 69 sq. m.

4. If the length of a rectangle is increased by 20% and width is decreased by 15%, then its area

A. decreases by 4% B. increases by 2%
C. decreases by 2% D. increases by 3%

5. If the length of a rectangle is increased by 20%, then by how much per cent its breadth must be decreased so as to keep its area unaltered?

A. 25% B. $8\frac{1}{3}\%$
C. $16\frac{2}{3}\%$ D. 20%

6. The ratio of length and breadth of a rectangular plot is 71 : 61 respectively. The area of the plot is 17324 m^2. What is perimeter of the plot?

A. 264 m B. 284 m
C. 528 m D. 614 m

7. If the length and breadth of a rectangular field are increased, the area increases by 50%. If the increase in length was 20%, by what percentage was the breadth increased?

A. 20% B. 25%
C. 30% D. 40%

8. The length and breadth of a varandah is 40 m and 15 m respectively. How many stone slabs of size 6 decimetre × 5 decimetre each are needed in flooring it:

A. 1000 B. 2000
C. 3000 D. 4000

9. The circumference of a circular plot is 396 m. What is the area of the circular plot?

A. 9,446 m^2 B. 9,856 m^2
C. 12,474 m^2 D. 18,634 m^2

10. If the sides of an equilateral triangle are increased by 20%, 30% and 50% respectively to form a new triangle, the increase in the perimeter of the equilateral triangle is:

A. 25% B. $33\frac{1}{3}$%
C. 50% D. 100%

ANSWERS

1	2	3	4	5	6	7	8	9	10
B	B	C	B	C	C	B	B	C	B

EXPLANATORY ANSWERS

1. Area of the square = x^2 sq. m.

Side of the new square = $x - 50\%$ of $x = \frac{x}{2}$ m

$\therefore$ Area of the new square $= \left(\frac{x}{2}\right)^2 = \frac{x^2}{4}$ sq. m.

$\therefore$ Reduction in area of the square $= x^2 - \frac{x^2}{4}$

$= \frac{3x^2}{4}$ sq. m.

$\therefore$ Percentage reduction $= \frac{3x^2/4}{x^2} \times 100 = 75\%$

2. Area of the square = x^2 sq. m

Now, area of the new square = $(2x)^2 = 4x^2$ sq. m

Hence, it is clear that if side of a square is doubled, its area becomes four times.

3. Suppose sides of the triangle are $17x$ m, $15x$ m and $8x$ metres

$\therefore$ Perimeter $= 17x + 15x + 8x = 40x$

Now, $40x = 40$

$\Rightarrow$ $x = 1$ m

Therefore, the sides are $17 \times 1 = 17$ m, $15 \times 1 = 15$ m and $8 \times 1 = 8$ m

$\because$ $(17)^2 = (15)^2 + (8)^2$,

i.e., it is a right angled triangle

$\therefore$ Area of the right angled triangle

$= \frac{1}{2} \times 8 \times 15 = 60$ sq. m.

4. Area of the rectangle = xy sq. metre

Area of the new rectangle $= \frac{120}{100}x \times \frac{85}{100}y$

$= 1.020\, xy$ sq. metre

$\therefore$ Increase in the area $= 1.02\, xy - xy = .02\, xy$ sq. m.

$\therefore$ Percentage increase $= \frac{.02xy}{xy} \times 100 = 2\%$

5. Area of the rectangle = xy

On reducing the breadth by A% and increasing the length by 20%

Length of the new rectangle $= \frac{120x}{100} x = 1.2x$

Breadth of the new rectangle $= y - \text{A}\%$ of $y = y\left(1 - \frac{\text{A}}{100}\right)$

$\therefore$ Area of the new rectangle $= 1.2x \times y\left(1 - \frac{\text{A}}{100}\right)$

Now, $xy = 1.2\, xy\left(1 - \frac{\text{A}}{100}\right) \Rightarrow 1 = 1.2\frac{(100 - \text{A})}{100}$

$\Rightarrow$ $1.2\text{ A} = 120 - 100$

$\therefore$ $\text{A} = \frac{20}{1.2} = 16\frac{2}{3}\%$

6. Let length and breadth of a rectangle be $71x$ and $61x$ m; then

$71x \times 61x = 17324 \Rightarrow x^2 = \frac{17324}{71 \times 61} = 4$

$\therefore$ $x = 2$

Hence, length $= 71 \times 2 = 142$ m; breadth $= 61 \times 2 = 122$ m

Since, perimeter $= 2(142 + 122) = 2 \times 264 = 528$ m

7. Here, $20 + x + \frac{20 \times x}{100} = 50 \Rightarrow x + \frac{x}{5} = 30$

$\Rightarrow \frac{6x}{5} = 30$ $\therefore$ $x = \frac{5 \times 30}{6} = 25$

Hence, breadth was increased by 25%

8. Required number of stone slabs $= \frac{40 \times 15}{\frac{6}{10} \times \frac{5}{10}}$

$= \frac{40 \times 15 \times 100}{6 \times 5} = 2000$

VOLUME AND SURFACE AREA

1. If a solid sphere of 3 cm radius is melted and recast into a right circular cone whose base radius is same as that of the sphere, the height of the cone will be

A. 8 cm B. 12 cm
C. 6 cm D. 5 cm

2. Diameter of a roller is 2.4 m and it is 1.68 m long. If it takes 1000 complete revolutions once over to level a field, the area of the field is

A. 12672 sq. m B. 12671 sq. m
C. 12762 sq. m D. 11768 sq. m

3. If each edge of a cube is increased by 10%, then by how much per cent will the surface area of this cube be increased?

A. 21% B. 18%
C. 15% D. 20%

4. Height and base radius of a solid cylinder are 14 m and 4 m respectively. It is melted and recast into a solid cone of the same base radius as that of the cylinder, what will be the height of the cone?

A. 21 m B. 42 m
C. 48 m D. 54 m

5. A room is in the form of a cube of side 10 m. How many bales of cotton can be kept in it if each bale covers 5 cu m space?

A. 100 B. 175
C. 200 D. 225

6. Three cubes having side 2 cm, 3 cm and 4 cm respectively are melted together to form a new cube. The side of the new cube will be

A. 3.526 cm B. 4.628 cm
C. 4.626 cm D. 4.528 cm

7. If base diameter of a cylinder is increased by 50%, then by how much per cent its height must be decreased so as to keep its volume unaltered?

A. 45.56% B. 55.56%
C. 50.16% D. 62.33%

8. The surface area of a cube is 600 sq. m. Its diagonal is

A. $10\sqrt{3}$ cm B. $5\sqrt{3}$ cm
C. $4\sqrt{2}$ cm D. $10\sqrt{2}$ cm

9. The base diameter of a conical tomb is 28 m and its slant height is 50 m. Find the cost of white washing its curved surface at the rate of 80 paise per sq. m?

A. Rs. 1860 B. Rs. 1760
C. Rs. 1950 D. Rs. 1875

10. The volume of a cuboid is 1120 cu cm and its height is 5 cm while the length and the breadth of the cuboid are in the ratio 8 : 7. The length of this cylinder exceeds the breadth by

A. 4 cm B. 2 cm
C. 7 cm D. 5 cm

ANSWERS

1	2	3	4	5	6	7	8	9	10
B	A	A	B	C	C	B	A	B	B

EXPLANATORY ANSWERS

1. Volume of the cone = Volume of the sphere

$$\therefore \quad \frac{1}{3}\pi(3)^2 \times h = \frac{4}{3}\pi \times 3^3 \Rightarrow h = 12 \text{ cm}$$

Hence, height of the cone = 12 cm.

2. Surface area of the roller = $2\pi rh$

$$= 2\times\frac{22}{7}\times 1.2\times 1.68 = 12.672 \text{ sq. m}$$

In one complete revolution, the roller covers 12.672 sq. m.

∴ It will cover in 1000 revolutions

= 12.672 × 1000 = 12672 sq. m

Hence, area of the field = 12672 sq. m.

3. Percentage increase in the surface area of the cube

$$= \left(x+y+\frac{xy}{100}\right)\%$$

$$= \left(10+10+\frac{10\times 10}{100}\right)\% = 21\%.$$

4. Here,

volume of the cone = Volume of the cylinder

$$\Rightarrow \quad \frac{1}{3}\pi r^2 \times \text{height} = \pi r^2 \times 14$$

$$\therefore \quad \text{Height} = 14 \times 3 = 42 \text{ m}$$

Thus, height of the cone = 42 m.

5. Volume of the cubical room $= (10)^3$
$= 1000$ cu m

Number of cotton bales which can be placed in the room

$$= \frac{\text{Volume of the room}}{\text{Volume of each cotton bale}} = \frac{1000}{5} = 200.$$

6. Volume of the new cube $= 2^3 + 3^3 + 4^3$
$= 8 + 27 + 64 = 99$cu cm

$\therefore$ Side of the new cube $= \sqrt[3]{99} = 4.626$ cm.

7. Change in the volume of the cylinder

$$= \left(x+y+(-z)+\frac{xy+y(-z)+(-zx)}{100}+\frac{xy(-z)}{100^2}\right)\%$$

Since volume of the cylinder remains unchanged.
$\therefore$ Change = 0%

Now, $\left(50+50+(-z)+\frac{50\times50-50z-50z}{100}+\frac{50\times50\times(-z)}{100^2}\right)=0$

$\therefore\ 100 - z + 25 - z - .25z = 0$

$\Rightarrow 2.25z = 125 \Rightarrow z = \frac{125}{2.25} = 55.56$

$\therefore$ Height of the cylinder should be decreased by 55.56%.

8. Here, $6 \times (\text{side})^2 = 600$
$\Rightarrow \text{side}^2 = 100$
$\Rightarrow \text{side} = \sqrt{100} = 10$ cm

$\therefore$ Diagonal of the cube$= \sqrt{3}\times\text{side}$
$= \sqrt{3}\times10$
$= 10\sqrt{3}$ cm.

9. Area of the curved surface of the cone

$$= \frac{22}{7}\times\frac{28}{2}\times50 = 2200 \text{ sq. m.}$$

$\therefore$ Cost of white washing at 80 paise per sq. m

$$= 2200\times\frac{80}{100} = \text{Rs. } 1760.$$

10. Suppose the length and the breadth of the cuboid are $8x$ cm and $7x$ cm

$\therefore$ Here, $8x \times 7x \times 5 = 1120$

$\Rightarrow x^2 = \frac{1120}{280} = 4 = (2)^2 \quad \Rightarrow \quad x = 2$

$\therefore$ Length of the cuboid $= 8 \times 2 = 16$ cm
Breadth of the cuboid $= 7 \times 2 = 14$ cm

Hence, it is clear that length of the cuboid exceeds the breadth by 2 cm.

SERIES

Directions (Qs. 1 to 7) : *In the following number series, one of the numbers does not fit into the series. Find the wrong number.*

1. 2, 5, 10, 18, 26, 37, 50
A. 2 B. 5
C. 37 D. 18

2. 3 , 18, 38, 78, 123, 178, 243
A. 123 B. 178
C. 3 D. 38

3. 380, 188, 92, 48, 20, 8, 2
A. 188 B. 92
C. 48 D. 20

4. 5, 11, 23, 47, 96, 191, 383
A. 11 B. 23
C. 47 D. 96

5. 89, 78, 86, 80, 85, 82, 83
A. 78 B. 86
C. 80 D. 85

6. 58, 57, 54, 50, 42, 33, 32
A. 57 B. 54
C. 50 D. 32

7. 2, 20, 27, 44, 64
A. 27 B. 8
C. 20 D. 44

Directions (Qs. 8 to 10) : *Complete the following series.*

8. 1 4 9 16 25 36 49 ....
A. 54 B. 56
C. 64 D. 81

9. 11 13 17 19 23 29 31 37 41 ....
A. 43 B. 47
C. 53 D. 51

10. 3 7 6 5 9 3 12 1 15 ....
A. 18 B. 13
C. –1 D. 3

ANSWERS

1	2	3	4	5	6	7	8	9	10
D	C	C	D	A	C	C	C	A	C

EXPLANATORY ANSWERS

1. 2 5 10 18 26 37 50
   ↓ ↓ ↓ ↓ ↓ ↓ ↓
   1^2+1 2^2+1 3^2+1 4^2+1 5^2+1 6^2+1 7^2+1
   Wrong no. = 18, Correct no. = 17.
2. Only 3 is a prime number.
3. Wrong no. = 48, Correct no. = 44
   Each term will be four more than two times the next term.
4. 5 11 23 47 96 191 383

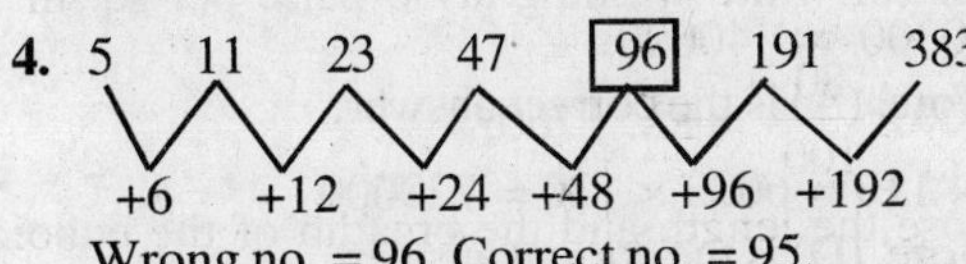

+6 +12 +24 +48 +96 +192
   Wrong no. = 96, Correct no. = 95.
5. If 87 is written in place of 78 then tens digit of each term will be 8.
6. 58 57 54 50 42 33 22
   –1 –3 –5 –7 –9 –11
   Wrong no. = 50, Correct no. = 49.
7. 2 20 27 44 64

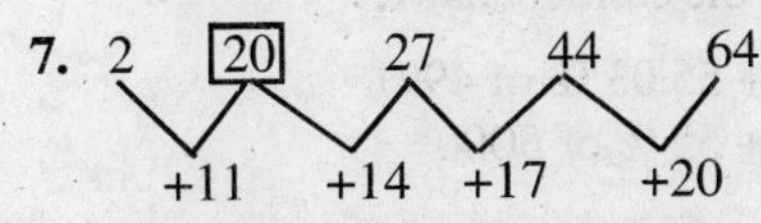

+11 +14 +17 +20
   Wrong no. = 20, Correct no. = 13.
8. Numbers are $1^2, 2^2, 3^2, 4^2, 5^2, 6^2, 7^2$.
   So, the next number is $8^2 = 64$.
9. Numbers are all primes. The next prime is 43.
10. There are two series, beginning respectively with 3 and 7. In one 3 is added and in another 2 is subtracted. The next number is $1 - 2 = -1$.

APPROXIMATE VALUES

1. $85432 \div 2106 + 59.5614 = ?$
   (*a*) 100 (*b*) 60
   (*c*) 80 (*d*) 140
2. $\sqrt{67621} = ?$
   (*a*) 320 (*b*) 260
   (*c*) 200 (*d*) 280
3. 9.7 % of 5011 + 55.03 % of 4991
   (*a*) 5500 (*b*) 7200
   (*c*) 6000 (*d*) 4200
4. $730 \times 199 = ?$
   (*a*) 350000 (*b*) 335000
   (*c*) 300000 (*d*) 34600
5. $.0144 \times 0.36 = ?$
   (*a*) 0.5 (*b*) 0.005
   (*c*) 0.05 (*d*) 0.005
6. 31% of 1508 + 26% of 2018
   (*a*) 1500 (*b*) 2000
   (*c*) 1000 (*d*) 1200
7. $3015 + 13594 + 3738 = ?$
   (*a*) 40000 (*b*) 36000
   (*c*) 42000 (*d*) 46000
8. $6012 \times 119 = ?$
   (*a*) 560000 (*b*) 448000
   (*c*) 900000 (*d*) 720000
9. $2712.1563 \div 1805.4018 + 3.4982 = ?$
   (*a*) 9 (*b*) 8
   (*c*) 4 (*d*) 5
10. $4182.365 \div 20.886 = ?$
    (*a*) 300 (*b*) 200
    (*c*) 150 (*d*) 250

ANSWERS

1	2	3	4	5	6	7	8	9	10
A	B	D	A	B	C	A	D	D	B

EXPLANATORY ANSWERS

1. $85432 \div 2106 + 60 = 40 + 60 = 100$
Therefore, (B) is the correct answer.

2. $\sqrt{67621} = \sqrt{67600} = 260$
Therefore, (B) is the correct answer.

3. 29.7 % of 5011 + 55.03 % of 4991
= 30 % of 5000 + 55 % of 5000
$= \frac{30}{100} \times 5000 + \frac{55}{100} \times 5000$
$= 1500 + 2750 = 4250 \Rightarrow 4200$
Therefore, (D) is the correct answer.

4. $1730 \times 199 = 1730 \times 200$
$= 346000 \Rightarrow 350000$
Therefore, (B) is the correct answer.

5. $0.0144 \times 0.36 = 0.0140 \times 0.36 = .005040$
$\Rightarrow .005$
Therefore, (B) is the correct answer.

6. 31% of 1508 + 26% of 2018
= 30% of 1500 + 25% × 2000
$= \frac{30}{100} \times 1500 + \frac{25}{100} \times 2000$
$= 450 + 500 = 950 \Rightarrow 1000$
Therefore, (C) is the correct answer.

7. $23015 + 13594 + 3738$
$= 23000 + 13600 + 3700$
$= 40300 \Rightarrow 40000$
Therefore, (A) is the correct answer.

8. $6012 \times 119 = 6000 \times 120 = 720000$
Therefore, (D) is the correct answer.

9. $2712.1563 \div 1805.4018 + 3.4982$
$= 2700 \div 1800 + 3.5 = 1.5 + 3.5 = 5$
Therefore, (D) is the correct answer.

10. $4182.365 \div 20.886 = 4200 \div 21 = 200$
Therefore, (B) is the correct answer.

HARYANA

General Knowledge & Awareness

Multiple Choice Questions

1. During the ancient age, modern Haryana state was known as:
(*a*) Brahmavarta (*b*) Brahmarshi region
(*c*) Uttravedi of Brahma (*d*) All of the above

2. Who of the following rulers of Bharata vamsha (descendants of Bharata, according to Rigveda, who were a group of people who lived in the north-west of India) started his campaign from Haryana for establishing his authority in various other Kingdoms of the time?
(*a*) Sudas (*b*) Arjuna
(*c*) Bharata (*d*) Bhishma

3. The famous war of Mahabharata was fought at which of the following places in Haryana?
(*a*) Panipat (*b*) Kurukshetra
(*c*) Jhajjhar (*d*) Ballabh Garh

4. During Mughals, Janapadas of this state were replaced by
(*a*) Gana Sangha (*b*) Gana System
(*c*) Khaps (*d*) Panchayata

5. The territory of modern Haryana was included in which of the following Mahajanapadas of Buddha period?
(*a*) Kuru and Panchala (*b*) Kosala and Vajji
(*c*) Sursena and Avanti (*d*) Asmaka and Vatsa

6. At which of the following places in the state, capital of the Agreyagana was situated?
(*a*) Rewari (*b*) Sirsa
(*c*) Hansi (*d*) Agroha

7. Mahamud Gaznavi attacked on Thanesar in:
(*a*) 1013 AD (*b*) 1014 AD
(*c*) 1016 AD (*d*) 1017 AD

8. Thanesar (now in Haryana) was the capital of which of the following famous rulers of ancient India?
(*a*) Harsha Vardhan
(*b*) Ashoka
(*c*) Chandragupta Vikramaditya
(*d*) Kanishka

9. During the 12th century A.D. who of the following rulers of Chauhan dynasty defeated Tomars of Haryana?
(*a*) Vigraha Raja VI (*b*) Vigrah Raja II
(*c*) Arno Raja (*d*) Prithvi Raj Chauhan

10. When did Sultan Balban of Ghulam dynasty attacked on Mevas of Haryana with a view to establish his authority on Mevas?
(*a*) 1260 AD (*b*) 1265 AD
(*c*) 1266 AD (*d*) 1267 AD

11. Feroz Tughlaq of Tughlaq dynasty built which of the following cities in Haryana?
(*a*) Tohana (*b*) Hansi
(*c*) Siwani (*d*) Fatehabad

12. Timur made an attack on which of the following cities of Haryana?
(*a*) Sirsa (*b*) Fatehabad
(*c*) Hissar (*d*) All of the above

13. The famous battle of 1526 between Babur and Ibrahim Lodi was fought at which of the following places of Haryana?
(*a*) Panipat (*b*) Kurukshetra
(*c*) Tawaru (*d*) Jind

14. Who was the King of Rewari during the reign of famous Mughal Emperor Akbar?
(*a*) Tularam (*b*) Karna Singh
(*c*) Hemachandra (Hemu) (*d*) Phool Singh

15. The famous second battle of Panipat between Akbar and Hemachandra (Hemu) was fought in:
(*a*) 1550 AD (*b*) 1552 AD
(*c*) 1554 AD (*d*) 1556 AD

16. Which of the following famous battle was fought in the state of Haryana between the Marathas and Ahmadshah Abdali?
(*a*) The third battle of Panipat
(*b*) The second battle of Panipat
(*c*) The first battle of Panipat
(*d*) None of these

17. George Thomas built his capital at which of the following places of the state?
(*a*) Raniya (*b*) Tohana
(*c*) The fort of Hansi (*d*) Behram Pur

18. In 1802 AD George Thomas died at which of the following places in Haryana?
(*a*) Mahendragarh (*b*) Behram Pur
(*c*) Narnaul (*d*) Bawal

19. During 1809-10 AD, entire territories of Haryana was under the control of:
(*a*) Marathas (*b*) Satnamies
(*c*) Mughals (*d*) Britishers

20. Modern Haryana state was built on:
(*a*) 1 November, 1966 (*b*) 5 January, 1967
(*c*) 1 November, 1958 (*d*) 15 August, 1947

21. Evidences of Early-Harappan, Mature Harappan and Late Harappan culture have been found at which of the following places in Haryana?
(*a*) Banawali (*b*) Sosawal
(*c*) Mirzapur (*d*) All of the above

22. The period of Aryans of Kuru Vamsha, centuries before the Mahabharata period was marked with the beginning of which of the following ages?
(*a*) Cultivation Age (*b*) Copper Age
(*c*) Iron Age (*d*) Metal Age

23. The essence of the philosophy of Bhagvad Gita preached by Lord Krishna to Arjuna, a noted Commander of the Mahabharata War in the form of a dialogue between the two was delivered at which of the following places of Haryana?
(*a*) Rewari (*b*) Pehwa
(*c*) Kurukshetra (*d*) Panipat

24. During Youdheya period, Haryana was known as:
(*a*) Youdheya confederacy (*b*) Bahudhanyaka region
(*c*) Matsya region (*d*) Gana region

25. The famous pilgrim Hiuen Tsang in his book Si-Yo-ki, has described the prosperity of which of the following cities of Haryana?
(*a*) Sthaneshwar (Thanesmar)
(*b*) Panipat
(*c*) Rohtak
(*d*) Ambala

26. Which of the following treatise provide valuable information about the advancement of trade, art and culture in Haryana during the reign of Tomar Kings?
(*a*) Tahkik-i-Hind (*b*) Harsh Charita
(*c*) Kadambari (*d*) Yashastilak Champu

27. Who was the ruler of the Tawaroo pargana during the invasion of Babur in 1526-27?
(*a*) Hasan Khan (*b*) Mohan Singh Mandhar
(*c*) Faizal Khan (*d*) Jalal Khan

28. During the period of Babur, the Rajput King Mohan Singh Mandhar had its kingdom in Haryana at:
(*a*) Mandhar Pargana of Kaithal
(*b*) Tawaroo
(*c*) Jind
(*d*) Panipat

29. During 1756-57, Haryana was under the control of:
(*a*) Mughals (*b*) Sikhs
(*c*) Marathas (*d*) Satnamies

30. While returning back to his homeland, Ahmad Shah Abdali put the northern part of Haryana (Ambala, Jind, Kurukshetra and Karnal Districts) under the charge of:
(*a*) Mughals
(*b*) Sikhs
(*c*) Jain Khan, the Governor of Sarhind
(*d*) Gen Khan the Governor of Durrani

31. In the sepoy mutiny that broke out in 1857 at Meerut, majority of soldiers who took part in the revolt hailed from which of the following districts of Haryana?
(*a*) Gurugram (*b*) Rohtak
(*c*) Hissar (*d*) All of these

32. Who of the following great warriors of Haryana was the Naib Kotwal of Meerut at the time of Sepoy mutiny:
(*a*) Abdus Samad Khan (*b*) Vikram Singh
(*c*) Rao Krishna Gopal (*d*) Rameshwar Dayal

33. In the battle (for the freedom of India) fought at the village Naseebpur situated near Narnaul, Britishers destroyed which of the following three powers?
(*a*) Rewari, Jhajjhar and Jodhpur
(*b*) Gurugram, Rewari and Jodhpur
(*c*) Jind, Jagadari and Pehwa
(*d*) Panipat, Jhajjhar and Tawaroo

34. In the first Freedom struggle, who of the following Kings of Ballabhgarh led the revolutionary army in Delhi?
(*a*) Raja Karn Singh (*b*) Raja Nahan Singh
(*c*) Raja Suraj Bhan (*d*) Raja Satyapal

35. Which of the following provinces of Haryana extended valuable cooperation to the British army in the revolt of 1857?
(*a*) Bahadurgarh (*b*) Tawaroo
(*c*) Jhajjhar (*d*) Jind

36. In the second Calcutta session of the Indian National Congress held in the year 1886, Haryana was represented by:
(*a*) Pandit Deen Dayal Sharma
(*b*) Lala Murlidhar
(*c*) Bal Mukund Gupta
(*d*) All of these

37. Lala Lajpat Rai had selected which of the following places situated in Haryana as his political and social work-field?
(*a*) Hissar (*b*) Sonipat
(*c*) Gurugram (*d*) Nooh

38. In the fourth session of the Indian National Congress held in 1888 at Allahabad who of the following national leaders represented Hissar?
(*a*) Lala Sultan Singh (*b*) Baldeo Singh
(*c*) Lala Lajpat Rai (*d*) Baini Singh

39. On 8 April, 1919, Gandhiji was arrested from which of the following places of Haryana?
(*a*) Kaithal (*b*) Palwal
(*c*) Gohana (*d*) Ambala

40. When was a conference held at Rohtak presided by Pt. Rambhaj Dutta in which a decision was taken to implement the Non-cooperation movement launched by Gandhiji?
(*a*) January, 1919 (*b*) November, 1919
(*c*) November, 1920 (*d*) September, 1921

41. In the annual session of Congress held at Nagpur, Haryana was represented by :
(*a*) Sardar Buta Singh (*b*) Lala Ugrasen
(*c*) Babu Shyam Lal (*d*) Pt. Neki Ram Sharma

42. On the appeal of Punjab Pradesh Congress, Independence Day was celebrated in entire Haryana on:
(*a*) 12 January, 1932 (*b*) 10 December, 1932
(*c*) 15 August, 1935 (*d*) 26 January, 1932

43. On which day was the Golden Jubilee of Congress celebrated in Haryana?
(*a*) 18 August, 1930 (*b*) 30 January, 1935
(*c*) 28 December, 1935 (*d*) 10 December, 1936

44. Who of the following was the great hero of Haryana who as a member of the INA hoisted the tricoloured flag for the first time on the land of Manipur?
(*a*) Major Pratap Singh (*b*) Major Suraj Mal
(*c*) Darbara Singh (*d*) Bhajan Lal

45. Chaudhary Chhotu Ram started a vigorous campaigns to popularize the Unionist Party in Haryana. In Haryana state this Party was called as:
(*a*) Zamindara League (*b*) Zamindari System
(*c*) Hindu-Muslim (*d*) None of these

46. Publication of which of the following weekly magazine was started by Chaudhary Chhotu Ram in 1916 from Rohtak?
(*a*) Hindu Gazette (*b*) Sikh Gazette
(*c*) Jat Gazette (*d*) None of the above

47. Chaudhary Chhotu Ram alongwith Shri Fazali Hussain set up the Unionist Party in Punjab in:
(*a*) 1919 (*b*) 1921
(*c*) 1922 (*d*) 1923

48. With a view to keep a control on the political activities in Patiala, Jind and Nabha states, a law was enforced in Samvat 1988 Vikrami. What was that law termed as:
(*a*) Hidayat Samvat (*b*) Hizri Samvat
(*c*) Vikram Samvat (*d*) Saka Samvat

49. In 1938, Jind Prajamandal was set up at Sangrur, the capital of Jind by:
(*a*) Rajendra Kumar Jain (*b*) Sadhu Ram
(*c*) Hansraj Rahbar (*d*) Nand Kishore

50. Gandhji was arrested from Palwal on:
(*a*) 5 January, 1919 (*b*) 8 May, 1920
(*c*) 8 April, 1919 (*d*) 17 April, 1921

51. Pt. Deen Dayal Sharma who made a very important contribution in popularizing Sanatan Dharma in whole of the Northern India, hailed from which of the following places of Haryana?
(*a*) Jhajjhar (*b*) Kaithal
(*c*) Hissar (*d*) Jind

52. In the Lahore Session of the Congress in 1892, Hissar was represented by:
(*a*) Balmukund Gupta (*b*) Lala Murlidhar
(*c*) Lala Lajpat Rai (*d*) Pt. Deen Dayal Sharma

53. When was Lala Lajpat Rai and Sardar Ajit Singh were arrested by the British Government and sent to Mandley Jail?
(*a*) In 1907 (*b*) In 1895
(*c*) In 1902 (*d*) In 1896

54. Mahatma Gandhi accompanied with Muhammad Ali and Shaukat Ali arrived Rohtak on:
(*a*) 10 January, 1919 (*b*) 8 October, 1920
(*c*) 1 October, 1920 (*d*) 18 March, 1920

55. The Divisional Political Conference of Ambala Division which was attended by Mahatma Gandhi alongwith Ali brothers, was held at Bhiwani in:
(*a*) March, 1918 (*b*) June, 1920
(*c*) October, 1919 (*d*) October, 1920

56. Even after India became free in 1947, Haryana remained a part of which of the following Indian Provinces?
(*a*) Delhi (*b*) Punjab
(*c*) Uttra Pradesh (*d*) Rajasthan

57. The state Restructuring Commission set up in 1955 by the Government of India had recommended to include which of the following two places in the state of Haryana?
(*a*) Mahendragarh and Jind (*b*) Patiala and Hissar
(*c*) Panipat and Kaithal (*d*) Rohtak and Gurugram

58. The tourist place called 'Tiliyar' is situated in which of the following districts of Haryana?
(*a*) Jind (*b*) Mahendragarh
(*c*) Rohtak (*d*) Kaithal

59. Who was the first Governor of Haryana?
(*a*) Shri Satyapal (*b*) Shri Dharmvir
(*c*) Shri Devilal (*d*) Shri Bansilal

60. Name of the first Non-Congress Chief Minister of Haryana who assumed this office on 24 March, 1967.
(*a*) Chaudhary Bhajan Lal (*b*) Devi Lal
(*c*) Bansi Lal (*d*) Rao Virendra Singh

61. Which of the following Rivers flow from the adjoining areas of Eastern Haryana and Uttar Pradesh?
(*a*) Ganga (*b*) Saraswati
(*c*) Ghaghghar (*d*) Yamuna

62. The main land of Haryana state stretches from 27° 39° N to 30° 55° N latitudes in the North-West of India. It stretches from .... E to .... E longitudes.
(*a*) 74° 28° E to 77° 36° E (*b*) 65° 33° E to 77° 28° E
(*c*) 50° 28° E to 64° 36° E (*d*) 84° 42° E to 89° 41° E

63. Which of the following states is located to the North of Haryana?
(*a*) Uttar Pradesh (*b*) Punjab
(*e*) Himachal Pradesh (*d*) Rajasthan

64. Which of the following states is located to the west of Haryana?
(*a*) Punjab (*b*) Rajasthan
(*c*) Uttar Pradesh (*d*) Himachal Pradesh

65. What is the area of the state of Haryana?
(*a*) 36,154 Sq. km. (*b*) 44,212 Sq. km.
(*c*) 49,105 Sq. km. (*d*) 51,206 Sq. km.

66. Which of the following state is not larger than Haryana by area?
(*a*) Meghalaya (*b*) Bihar
(*c*) Himachal Pradesh (*d*) Punjab

67. Dabwali is a subdivision of which district?
(*a*) Sirsa (*b*) Hissar
(*c*) Rohtak (*d*) Jhajjar

68. The mainland of Haryana is located at the height of .... from the sea level.
(*a*) 700 to 900 ft. (*b*) 750 to 880 ft.
(*c*) 800 to 1000 ft. (*d*) 900 to 1100 ft.

69. Shivalik range is located in which part of Haryana?
(*a*) North-West (*b*) North-East
(*c*) South-West (*d*) South-East

70. Which of the following rivers originate from Shivalik range to flow through the mainland of Haryana?
(*a*) Ghaghghar (*b*) Markanda
(*c*) Tangri (*d*) All of these

71. Which of the following natural parts of Haryana is the largest?
(*a*) the hilly region of the Shivalik
(*b*) the desert of Haryana
(*c*) the mainland of Haryana
(*d*) the dry plains of Aravali range

72. The famous Bibipur and Najafgarh lakes are located in which natural part of Haryana?
(*a*) The Plain
(*b*) The desert
(*c*) Hilly region of the Shivalik
(*d*) The dry plain of Aravali range

73. Which of the following cities of Haryana is not the part of National Capital Region?
(*a*) Sonipat (*b*) Faridabad
(*c*) Hisar (*d*) Gurugram

74. Which part of Haryana experiences maximum rainfall?
(*a*) South-Western Part (*b*) North-Eastern Part
(*c*) North-Western Part (*d*) South-Eastern Part

75. Which of the following parts of Haryana experiences minimum annual rainfall?
(*a*) North-Eastern Part (*b*) South-Eastern Part
(*c*) North-Western Part (*d*) South-Western Part

76. Which type of soil is found on Morney hills of the state?
(*a*) Sandy Soil (*b*) Brownish Soil
(*c*) Laterite Soil (*d*) Sandy Clayee Soil

77. Generally, which type of soil is found in the plains of Haryana?
(*a*) Fertile Soil of Yellow brownish colour
(*b*) Laterite Soil
(*c*) Sandy Soil
(*d*) Sandy Clayee Soil

78. In which of the following districts of Haryana, red
(*a*) Rohtak (*b*) Sirsa
(*c*) Yamuna Nagar (*d*) Bhivani

79. Which of the following rivers of the state of Haryana joins Markanda river near Mulana?
(*a*) Sahibi (*b*) Tangri
(*c*) Krishnawati (*d*) Dohan

80. Which of the following is the oldest and the most important canal of Haryana?
(*a*) Gurugram Canal (*b*) Bhiwani Canal
(*c*) Bhakra Canal (*d*) Western Yamuna Canal

81. Which of the following canals originates from the Yamuna river near Tazewala situated on the Jagadhari-Pona road?
(*a*) Bhakra Canal
(*b*) Western and Eastern Yamuna Canal
(*c*) Jawahar Lal Nehru Canal
(*d*) None of these

82. Jawahar Lal Nehru canal of Haryana originates from:
(*a*) Bhakra Canal (*b*) Bhiwani Canal
(*c*) Gurugram Canal (*d*) Yamuna Canal

83. Which of the following lakes is located in Haryana?
(*a*) Damdama Lake (*b*) Kotla Lake
(*c*) Khalilpur Lake (*d*) All of these

84. Which of the following lakes is situated in Farrukh Nagar block of the state?
(*a*) Sultanpur lake (*b*) Damdama lake
(*c*) Khalilpur lake (*d*) Kotla lake

85. The famous Badkal lake is situated in which of the following districts of Haryana?
(*a*) Gurugram (*b*) Bhivani
(*c*) Faridabad (*d*) Rohtak

86. Which of the following canals of Haryana originates from Yamuna river at Okhla in Delhi?
(*a*) Bhakra Canal (*b*) Gurugram Canal
(*c*) Eastern Yamuna Canal (*d*) None of these

87. Bhakra Canal provides water for irrigation in which of the following districts of Haryana?
(*a*) Sirsa (*b*) Hissar
(*c*) Rohtak (*d*) All of these

88. Which of the following districts of the state gets water for irrigation from Jawahar Lal Nehru Canal?
(*a*) Sirsa (*b*) Rohtak
(*c*) Mahendragarh (*d*) Jind

89. Bhiwani canal originates from which of the following canals?
(*a*) Bhakra Canal (*b*) Gurugram Canal
(*c*) Western Yamuna Canal (*d*) Eastern Yamuna Canal

90. When was the famous Badkal lake of Haryana built?
(*a*) In 1940 (*b*) In 1950
(*c*) In 1974 (*d*) In 1947

91. The famous tourist place 'Tajewala Headworks' is situated in which of the following districts of Haryana?
(*a*) Rohtak (*b*) Faridabad
(*c*) Gurugram (*d*) Yamuna Nagar

92. Haryana has been divided into:
(*a*) 6 Divisions (*b*) 5 Sub Divisions
(*c*) 4 Divisions (*d*) 8 Divisions

93. How many total sub-divisions exist in Haryana state till January, 2025?
(*a*) 60 Sub-Divisions (*b*) 65 Sub-Divisions
(*c*) 68 Sub-Divisions (*d*) 80 Sub-Divisions

94. How many total Tehsils exist in Haryana till January, 2025?
(*a*) 94 (*b*) 68
(*c*) 70 (*d*) 85

95. How many total sub-Tehsils exist in Haryana till January, 2025?
(*a*) 30 (*b*) 31
(*c*) 49 (*d*) 40

96. How many total Blocks exist in Haryana till January, 2025?
(*a*) 95 (*b*) 143
(*c*) 115 (*d*) 119

97. Total number of populated villages in Haryana is:
(*a*) 4,390 (*b*) 4,950
(*c*) 5,845 (*d*) 6,841

98. According to the Census of 2011, the total population of Haryana is:
(*a*) 2,53,51,462 (*b*) 2,40,55,400
(*c*) 2,25,83,912 (*d*) 2,20,45,657

99. Salarganj Gate is situated near which of the following town of Haryana?
(*a*) Rohtak (*b*) Hissar
(*c*) Panipat (*d*) Ambala

100. In terms of area the largest district of Haryana is:
(*a*) Rohtak (*b*) Sirsa
(*c*) Panipat (*d*) Ambala

101. Which of the following minerals is found in abundance in Mahendragarh district of Haryana?
(*a*) Lime stone (*b*) China clay
(*c*) Copper (*d*) All of these

102. At which of the following places in district Rewari, Slate-stone is found in abundance?
(*a*) Kund (*b*) Baval
(*c*) Kusal (*d*) Khol

103. Consider the following statements:
1. Nada Sahib Gurudwara is situated in Ambala.
2. Nada Sahib Gurudwara is situated on the bank of river Ghaggar.

Which of the above statements is/are correct?
(*a*) 2 only (*b*) Both 1 and 2
(*c*) Neither 1 nor 2 (*d*) 1 only

104. At which of the following places in district Bhiwani Granite stones are found?
(*a*) Village Nigana Kalan (*b*) Delheri
(*c*) Riwasa (*d*) All of these

105. When was Shri Krishna Museum established in Kurukshetra?
(*a*) 1987 (*b*) 1970
(*c*) 1989 (*d*) 1995

106. What is the area of the total forest land in Haryana?
(*a*) 1,428 Sq. km. (*b*) 1,614.26 Sq. km.
(*c*) 1,852 Sq. km. (*d*) 1,812 Sq. km.

107. During which of the following years, a comprehensive afforestation scheme 'Greening of Haryana' was started?
(*a*) 1982 - 83 (*b*) 1983 - 86
(*c*) 1989 - 90 (*d*) 1994 - 95

108. Haryana has announced its new Industrial Policy in ....
(*a*) 1995 (*b*) 2011
(*c*) 2005 (*d*) 2002

109. With the aid of the European Union "Haryana Community Development Scheme" (Haryana Samudayiki) was introduced in Haryana in:
(*a*) 1992 - 93 (*b*) 1994 - 95
(*c*) 1996 - 97 (*d*) 1998 - 99

110. Basai wetland is located in which district of Haryana?
(*a*) Gurugram (*b*) Jhajjar
(*c*) Faridabad (*d*) Kurukshetra

111. As per census 2011, literacy of Haryana is:
(*a*) 80.40% (*b*) 65.72%
(*c*) 75.6% (*d*) 68.85%

112. Which of the following tourist place is situated on Samauli Road Panipat?
(*a*) Jyotisar (*b*) Kala Amb
(*c*) Damdama Lake (*d*) King Fisher

113. Which of the following minerals is found in districts Hissar and Karnal?
(*a*) Pig Iron (*b*) Mica
(*c*) Nitre (*d*) Marble

114. Which of the following minerals is found in Rohtak district?
(*a*) Lime (*b*) Copper
(*c*) Manganese (*d*) Mica

115. Which of the following trees are found in abundance in Jind district of Haryana?
(*a*) Rosewood tree (Sesam) (*b*) Acacia tree (Kikar)
(*c*) Safeda (*d*) All of these

116. In the Agricultural University, Hissar 'research on Paddy' was started in:
(*a*) 1966 (*b*) 1970
(*c*) 1974 (*d*) 1989

117. Where is National Cancer Institute situated?
(*a*) Sampla (*b*) Meham
(*c*) Kalanaur (*d*) Badsa

118. Which of the following districts of Haryana is pre-eminent in the production of mushroom (Khumbhi) in India?
(*a*) Ambala (*b*) Sirsa
(*c*) Sonepat (*d*) Yamuna Nagar

119. Which of the following is a major crop produced in Rohtak district of Haryana?
(*a*) Pearl Millet (*b*) Great Millet
(*c*) Sugar cane (*d*) All of these

120. Sugar Mill is located at which of the following places in Kurukshetra?
(*a*) Pehwa (*b*) Shahabad Markanda
(*c*) Ladawa (*d*) Babain

121. Which of the following districts of Haryana is called "a big bowl of paddy" as it has gained world fame in the production of Basmati rice?
(*a*) Hissar (*b*) Kurukshetra
(*c*) Karnal (*d*) Jind

122. Navagrah temple in Haryana is located at ....
(*a*) Kurukshetra (*b*) Kaithal
(*c*) Gurugram (*d*) Faridabad

123. The total installed capacity of energy available to the state till 2023-24 is ....
(*a*) 8,575 MW (*b*) 8,200 MW
(*c*) 14,026.68 MW (*d*) 9,510 MW

124. What was the quantum of production of horticulture crops in Haryana during 2023-24?
(*a*) 41.20 Lakh M.T. (*b*) 85.63 Lakh M.T.
(*c*) 62.15 Lakh M.T. (*d*) 52.25 Lakh M.T.

125. In which of the following districts of Haryana, with a view to check the soil erosion in Shivalik areas, coordinated water flow Development Project is being implemented?
(*a*) Ambala (*b*) Panchkula
(*c*) Yamuna Nagar (*d*) All of these

126. Indira Gandhi Super Thermal Power Project is situated in which district of Haryana?
(*a*) Sirsa (*b*) Hisar
(*c*) Jind (*d*) Jhajjar

127. In the Ambala district of Haryana, canal irrigation system was made available after completion of which of the following irrigation project?
(*a*) Nangal Lift Irrigation Project
(*b*) Hathni Reservoir Barrage Project
(*c*) Jawahar Lal Nehru Irrigation Project
(*d*) Sewani Lift Irrigation Project

128. Which of the following system of irrigation is used in the sandy plains of Haryana?
(*a*) Canal
(*b*) Well
(*c*) With the help of Tubewell-Fountain irrigation
(*d*) Rain water

129. Water from western Yamuna Canal is used for irrigation in which of the following districts of Haryana?
(*a*) Karnal (*b*) Sonepat
(*c*) Rohtak (*d*) All of these

130. Besides Gurugram, in which of the following districts of Haryana water from Gurgaon canal is used for irrigation?
(*a*) Panipat (*b*) Faridabad
(*c*) Sonepat (*d*) Kaithal

131. Hathni Reservoir Barrage Project is related with which of the following districts of Haryana?
(*a*) Yamuna Nagar (*b*) Gurugram
(*c*) Rohtak (*d*) Faridabad

132. Which of the following irrigation projects was launched in Mahendragarh district of Haryana with a view to bring improvement in the field of agriculture?
(*a*) Loharu Lift Irrigation Project
(*b*) Western Yamuna Nagar Scheme
(*c*) J.L.N. Lift Irrigation Project
(*d*) Hathni Reservoir Barrage Project

133. When water was released for the first time from J.L.N. Lift Irrigation Project launched in Mahendragarh district of Haryana?
(*a*) In 1976 (*b*) In 1980
(*c*) In 1982 (*d*) In 1995

134. Which of the following irrigation projects provided irrigation facilities in Swarup Kalauda, Khurl Kalan, Bhikhewala, Kharadwala, Nehra, Fuliya kalan etc. villages of the state?
(*a*) Jhajjhar Lift Irrigation Project
(*b*) Nakhana Irrigation Project
(*c*) Nangal Lift Irrigation Project
(*d*) Jawahar Lal Nehru Lift Irrigation Project

135. Which of the following irrigation schemes was launched for providing irrigation facility in Ahriwal region of Haryana?
(*a*) Rewari Lift Irrigation Scheme
(*b*) Hathni Reservoir Barrage Irrigation Scheme
(*c*) Mewat Lift Irrigation Scheme
(*d*) Bhakra Canal Irrigation Scheme

136. The largest Animal Farm of Haryana is situated at which of the following places?
(*a*) Rohtak (*b*) Hissar
(*c*) Panch Kula (*d*) Jind

137. Which of the following breeds of the Buffalo of Haryana is famous in entire India?
(*a*) Murra (*b*) Tura
(*c*) Puspa (*d*) Chassa

138. At which of the following places of Haryana cooperative milk plant has been set up?
(*a*) Ambala (*b*) Bhivani
(*c*) Jind (*d*) All of the above

139. In the Thanesar town of district Kurukshetra, the building for Pouttry disease diagnosis Laboratory was built in:
(*a*) 1980 – 81 (*b*) 1984 – 85
(*c*) 1988 – 89 (*d*) 1995 – 96

140. Besides Nilokheri in Haryana, at which of the following places of the state, training in poultry is imparted?
(*a*) Ambala (*b*) Karnal
(*c*) Hissar (*d*) Kaithal

141. Consider the following statements:
1. Rohtak has a Police Commissionerate located there.
2. Sonipat has a Police Commissionerate located there.

Which of the above statements is/are correct?
(*a*) 2 only (*b*) Both 1 and 2
(*c*) Neither 1 nor 2 (*d*) 1 only

142. Intensive Animal Development project in district Bhivani was launched in:
(*a*) 1966 (*b*) 1970
(*c*) 1972 (*d*) 1978

143. At which place in district Mahendragarh a Semen Bank is located and a liquid Nitrogen Plant has been set-up?
(*a*) Ateli (*b*) Narnaul
(*c*) Nangal Chaudhary (*d*) Mahendragarh

144. In district Bhiwani of Haryana, for diagnosing the diseases in animals the District Village Development Body set up the "Animal Disease Diagnosis Laboratory" in:
(*a*) 1978 (*b*) 1980
(*c*) 1984 (*d*) 1990

145. Haryana gets an average rainfall of ....
(*a*) 100 cms. (*b*) 85 cms.
(*c*) 75 cms. (*d*) 45 cms.

146. The ancient town 'Bery' is situated in which of the following districts of Haryana?
(*a*) Jhajjar (*b*) Yamuna Nagar
(*c*) Karnal (*d*) Kurukshetra

147. Where in Haryana, the National Institute of Fashion Technology is located?
(*a*) Panipat (*b*) Ambala
(*c*) Panchkula (*d*) Kurukshetra

148. The products manufactured by the industrial units of district Yamuna Nagar are exported to which of the following countries?
(*a*) Dubai (*b*) Germany
(*c*) South Africa (*d*) All of the above

149. Saraswati Sugar Mill is located in which of the following districts of Haryana?
(*a*) Rohtak (*b*) Panipat
(*c*) Yamuna Nagar (*d*) Faridabad

150. In Yamuna Nagar, Yanuma Gases Limited was set up in:
(*a*) 1973 (*b*) 1975
(*c*) 1980 (*d*) 1981

51. Yamuna Gases Limited operating in Yamuna Nagar attained a leading position in the production of gases in the year:
(*a*) 1969 (*b*) 1973
(*c*) 1972 (*d*) 1975

52. Bharat Starch Chemical Ltd. was established in Yamuna Nagar in:
(*a*) 1929 (*b*) 1932
(*c*) 1938 (*d*) 1948

153. Before 1947, the Timber Market of Yamuna Nagar was known as:
(*a*) Abdullapur Mandi
(*b*) Sadapur Mandi
(*c*) Yamuna Nagar Mandi
(*d*) Yamuna Pur Mandi

154. Charkhi Dadri was carved out from which district?
(*a*) Bhiwani (*b*) Hissar
(*c*) Sirsa (*d*) Rewari

155. "Bhiwani Textile Mill" in Haryana was established in:
(*a*) 1930 (*b*) 1937
(*c*) 1942 (*d*) 1950

156. In Haryana, where the Vulture Conservation Centre is located?
(*a*) Pinjore (*b*) Jind
(*c*) Mahendragarh (*d*) Ambala

157. The Sahibi river does not flow in which of the following district?
(*a*) Rewari (*b*) Jhajjar
(*c*) Gurugram (*d*) Rohtak

158. Consider the following statements in respect of National Security Guards (NSG):
1. Operational Headquarter of NSG is in Manesar.
2. NSG comes under the control of Union Ministry of Home Affairs.

Which of the above statements is/are correct?
(*a*) 2 only (*b*) Both 1 and 2
(*c*) Neither 1 nor 2 (*d*) 1 only

159. Indian Cement Corporation, A Government of India undertaking, took possession of the factory located at Charkhi-Dadri of Haryana on:
(*a*) 5 April, 1980 (*b*) 23 June, 1981
(*c*) 10 June, 1984 (*d*) 23 June, 1988

160. National Beekeeping and Honey Mission (NBHM) Scheme was started in which year in Haryana?
(*a*) 2017 (*b*) 2018
(*c*) 2019 (*d*) 2020

161. Captive Electricity Plant has been set up in which of the following districts of Haryana?
(*a*) Panipat (*b*) Hissar
(*c*) Rohtak (*d*) Karnal

162. At Baholi of district Panipat which of the following factories has been set up?
(*a*) Cloth Factory
(*b*) Agricultural Implements Factory
(*c*) Oil Refinery
(*d*) Slippers Factory

163. 'Ammonia Plant' has been installed in which of the following districts of Haryana?
(*a*) Panipat (*b*) Kaithal
(*c*) Gurugram (*d*) Karnal

164. District Mahanderagarh ranks first in the state of Haryana in the production of:
(*a*) Rice (*b*) Utensils
(*c*) Mustard (*d*) Bicycle

165. According to the 2011 census sex ratio in the state is ....

(*a*) 787 (*b*) 879
(*c*) 987 (*d*) 973

166. Which of the following industries in Rewari district of Haryana is famous all over India?

(*a*) Shoe Sole Industry
(*b*) Brass Utensil Industry
(*c*) Hero Honda Motor Cycle Factory
(*d*) All of these

167. In addition to Bicycle Factory, which of the following other factories are located in Jind district of Haryana?

(*a*) Utensil Factory (*b*) Textile Factory
(*c*) Sugar Factory (*d*) Leather Shoe Factory

168. According to the 2011 census population density in the state is ....

(*a*) 573 (*b*) 752
(*c*) 482 (*d*) 531

169. Total covered area of the Shri Krishna Museum is:

(*a*) 8764 sq.m. (*b*) 8885 sq.m.
(*c*) 8129 sq.m. (*d*) 8649 sq.m.

170. Which of the following articles manufactured in Karnal district are exported to foreign countries also?

(*a*) Liberty Shoes (*b*) Paint
(*c*) Wooden Furnitures (*d*) Steel Furniture

171. Shahabad Cooperative Sugar Mill in district Kurukshetra was established in:

(*a*) 1976 – 77 (*b*) 1984 – 85
(*c*) 1991 – 92 (*d*) 1994 – 95

172. Which of the following factories have been set up in Faridabad District of Haryana?

(*a*) Tractor Factory (*b*) Refrigerator Factory
(*c*) Rubber Tyre Factory (*d*) All of these

173. In which year the strength of Haryana Assembly was raised to 90?

(*a*) 1977 (*b*) 1967
(*c*) 1971 (*d*) 1985

174. At which of the following places in Haryana Maruti Cars are manufactured?

(*a*) Gurugram (*b*) Ambala
(*c*) Faridabad (*d*) Hissar

175. Which among the following is the highly populated district, as per the 2011 census?

(*a*) Rohtak (*b*) Karnal
(*c*) Gurugram (*d*) Faridabad

176. During which of the following years Government of Haryana decided to confer honour on Freedom Fighters?

(*a*) 1980 (*b*) 1981
(*c*) 1985 (*d*) 1997

177. Which of the following districts of Haryana does not share its boundary with any other state of India?

(*a*) Charkhi Dadri (*b*) Palwal
(*c*) Gurugram (*d*) Jind

178. Skylark Tourist Complex is located at ....

(*a*) Faridabad (*b*) Panipat
(*c*) Karnal (*d*) Rohtak

179. Scheme of granting cash amount, amount payable annually and cash in lieu of land to the soldiers awarded with 'Yuddha Sewa Medal' was discontinued in 1988. This scheme was launched again by the Government of Bansi Lal in:

(*a*) April 1995 (*b*) April 1997
(*c*) April 1996 (*d*) April 1998

180. Chaudhary Devi Lal University in Haryana is located at:

(*a*) Hissar (*b*) Karnal
(*c*) Sirsa (*d*) Panipat

181. Who among the following was not the chief minister of Haryana?

(*a*) Babu Parmanand (*b*) B.D. Gupta
(*c*) Devi Lal (*d*) Hukum Singh

182. National Dairy Research Institute is located at ....

(*a*) Karnal (*b*) Hissar
(*c*) Sirsa (*d*) Rohtak

183. Who was the first governor of Haryana?

(*a*) R.S. Narula (*b*) G.D. Tapse
(*c*) Dharamvir (*d*) B.D. Sharma

184. Hostel for the boys of Scheduled Castes who are engaged in unclean occupation is located at:

(*a*) Karnal (*b*) Faridabad
(*c*) Ambala (*d*) All of these

185. Hostel for the boys of exempted castes is located at :

(*a*) Rohtak (*b*) Jind
(*c*) Faridabad (*d*) Gurugram

186. Legal provisions for ban on liquor were enforced in Haryana on:

(*a*) 1 December, 1991 (*b*) 1 June, 1993
(*c*) 1 July, 1996 (*d*) 1 May, 1997

187. Ban on the sale of liquor was lifted by the state government on:

(*a*) 1 May, 1996 (*b*) 1 May, 1997
(*c*) 1.February, 1996 (*d*) 1 April, 1998

188. Which of the following Child Development Projects is related with the State of Haryana?

(*a*) Coordinated Child Development Project
(*b*) Child Health Project
(*c*) Infant Nutrition Programme
(*d*) Helpless Child Development Project

189. Which of the following schemes are being run for the welfare of the girls belonging to poor families?

(*a*) Paraya Dhan Parayee Beti
(*b*) Apni Beti Paraya Dhan
(*c*) Apni Beti Apna Dhan
(*d*) None of these

190. The total length of National Highway in Haryana till November, 2024 is:
(*a*) 1900 kms. (*b*) 1503 kms.
(*c*) 1800 kms. (*d*) 3391 kms.

191. Each and every village of the State of Haryana became electrified on:
(*a*) 10 June, 1966 (*b*) 25 March, 1971
(*c*) 15 April, 1968 (*d*) 29 November, 1970

192. Aruna is the ancient name of which river?
(*a*) Markanda (*b*) Sahibi
(*c*) Ghaggar (*d*) Yamuna

193. Red Soil is found in ....
(*a*) Rohtak (*b*) Sirsa
(*c*) Karnal (*d*) Bihwani

194. With a view to bring improvement in the availability of electricity in Southern Haryana, a new 50 km long single circuit line has been laid from :
(*a*) Gurugram to Badshahpur
(*b*) Badshahpur to Rewari
(*c*) Faridabad to Rewari
(*d*) Jind to Kaithal

195. Which one of the following pairs is not correctly matched?
(*a*) Surajkund Lake – Kurukshetra
(*b*) Tilyaar Lake – Rohtak
(*c*) Damdama Lake – Gurugram
(*d*) Badkhal Lake – Faridabad

196. Sultanpur Lake is located in which district?
(*a*) Bhiwani (*b*) Mahendragarh
(*c*) Gurugram (*d*) Rewari

197. According to the demands made by farmers, which of the following systems for electricity on the basis of the depth of tubewells has been adopted in the entire state?
(*a*) Stove System
(*b*) Electricity Measurement System
(*c*) Test System
(*d*) None of these

198. Thermal Power Station is located at which of the following places in Haryana?
(*a*) Hissar (*b*) Kaithal
(*c*) Jind (*d*) Faridabad

199. At which of the following places, the Power Plant of 432 MW based on Gas has been installed by NTPC in Haryana?
(*a*) Gurugram (*b*) Faridabad
(*c*) Panipat (*d*) Karnal

200. What is the total length of road in Haryana till November, 2024?
(*a*) 33,453 km (*b*) 24,065 km
(*c*) 25,074 km (*d*) 40,760 km

201. The strength of Legislative Assembly of Haryana is ....
(*a*) 102 (*b*) 110
(*c*) 75 (*d*) 90

202. Where is Nahar Wildlife Sanctuary is situated?
(*a*) Ambala (*b*) Sonipat
(*c*) Rewari (*d*) Yamunanagar

203. When the Public Transport in Haryana was brought under the possession of the Government?
(*a*) In 1972 (*b*) In 1976
(*c*) In 1980 (*d*) In 1985

204. 'Rao Tej Singh Pond' is located in:
(*a*) Panipat (*b*) Sonipat
(*c*) Palwal (*d*) Rewari

205. The Magazine of Haryana Sahitya Academy is:
(*a*) Harigandha (*b*) Haryana Samvad
(*c*) Haryana Sandesh (*d*) Panchajanya

206. While travelling on the National Highway from Delhi to Ferozepur, which of the following important town of Haryana comes on the way:
(*a*) Rohtak (*b*) Sirsa
(*c*) Hissar (*d*) All of these

207. Manu Bhaker of Haryana is related with which sports?
(*a*) Badminton (*b*) Boxing
(*c*) Shooting (*d*) Wrestling

208. Which of the following tourist places is situated at Bahadurgarh in Haryana?
(*a*) Dairango Tourist Place (*b*) Gureya
(*c*) Jal Tarang (*d*) Tiliyar

209. In Haryana, in addition to Hissar, Karnal, Bhiwani, Narnaul and Jind, at which of the following airports metalled run-way has been built?
(*a*) Panipat (*b*) Pinjore
(*c*) Faridabad (*d*) Rewari

210. Where is Tilyar lake is situated?
(*a*) Rohtak (*b*) Gurugram
(*c*) Jind (*d*) Faridabad

211. At which of the following places in Haryana, Heavy Vehicle Driving Training Institute is located?
(*a*) Murthal (*b*) Charkhi-Dadri
(*c*) Ambala (*d*) Tawaroo

212. In Shivalik hills near Pinjore-Kalka in Haryana, utensils have been found which pertain to which of the following ages?
(*a*) Stone Age (*b*) Later Vedic Age
(*c*) Harappan Age (*d*) Early Vedic Age

213. In the treatise named "Avanti Sunderi Katha" Vaivast Manu who is known as the father of human beings is said to be the resident of which of the following places?
(*a*) Panipat (*b*) Rohtak
(*c*) Sthaneshwar (*d*) Panchkula

214. Evidences found from the excavations done at Banwali, Siswal, Kunal, Mirzapur, Daulatpur and Bhagawanpura in the state of Haryana revealed links dating back to:

(*a*) Early Harappan Culture
(*b*) Mature Harappan Culture
(*c*) Late Harappan Culture
(*d*) All of the above phases

215. Who of the following started archaeological survey in Haryana for the first time?
(*a*) Sir John (*b*) Alexander Kaningham
(*c*) Lord Munro (*d*) John Marshall

216. Archaeological Survey in Haryana started in:
(*a*) 1862 (*b*) 1892
(*c*) 1900 (*d*) 1905

217. Under the supervision of Dr. Suraj Bhan, excavations at which of the following places of Haryana brought out very valuable historical evidences?
(*a*) Mithathal (*b*) Dadri
(*c*) Ailanabad (*d*) Safidon

218. From which of the following sites of Haryana, evidences have been found for the first time regarding co-existence of the people of Late Harappan culture and Painted Grey Ware (PGW) culture?
(*a*) Narnaul (*b*) Bhagwanpura
(*c*) Sirsa (*d*) Mahendragarh

219. A great mound pertaining to Harappan culture is situated at which of the following places in district Jind of Haryana?
(*a*) Safidon (*b*) Uchana
(*c*) Narwana (*d*) Rakhigarhi

220. Remains of a Stupa have been found at Chaneti which is situated three kilometers east of Jagadhari. Height of this Stupa is 8 m. Its periphery is:
(*a*) 20 m (*b*) 30 m
(*c*) 45 m (*d*) 50 m

221. Consider the following statements:
1. Sonipat and Jhajjar share border with Delhi.
2. Rohtak does not share border with Delhi.
Which of the above statements is/are correct?
(*a*) 2 only (*b*) Both 1 and 2
(*c*) Neither 1 nor 2 (*d*) 1 only

222. A battle axe type Gold Coin which pertains to the age of Samudra Gupta has been found at which of the following places in Haryana?
(*a*) Kosali (*b*) Rohana
(*c*) Mithathal (*d*) Raniya

223. Which of the following areas of Haryana was under the control of Yudheyas during the 3rd century A.D.?
(*a*) Panipat (*b*) Rohtak
(*c*) Hissar (*d*) Ambala

224. The Gold Coin obtained from Jagadhari pertains to which of the following emperors of the ancient India?
(*a*) Kanishka (*b*) Kumar Gupta
(*c*) Pushyamitra Sunga (*d*) Samudragupta

225. From which of the following places in Haryana, copper coin of the age of Harsha Vardhan has been found which contains an account of Pushyabhuti dynasty of Thanesar?
(*a*) Sonepat (*b*) Sirsa
(*c*) Gurugram (*d*) Kaithal

226. At which of the following places located in district Hissar of Haryana excavations was done by Shri H.L. Srivastava of Archaeo-logical Survey of India?
(*a*) Uklana (*b*) Fatehabad
(*c*) Agroha (*d*) Adampur

227. What is the total number of Primary and Pre Primary Schools in Haryana till 2023-24?
(*a*) 9,872 (*b*) 9,399
(*c*) 11,582 (*d*) 8,780

228. What is the total number of Middle Schools in Haryana till 2023-24?
(*a*) 6,215 (*b*) 2,312
(*c*) 5,640 (*d*) 3,850

229. In Haryana 'Brahma Sarovar' is located in:
(*a*) Palwal (*b*) Kurukshetra
(*c*) Panipat (*d*) Sonipat

230. 'Uchana' is located in:
(*a*) Jind (*b*) Karnal
(*c*) Rohtak (*d*) Faridabad

231. The tenure of nagarpalika, municipality or municipal corporation in Haryana is ....
(*a*) 3 years (*b*) 1 year
(*c*) 4 years (*d*) 5 years

232. What is the area of Sirsa district?
(*a*) 4,277 sq.km (*b*) 5,780 sq.km
(*c*) 3,760 sq.km (*d*) 2,765 sq.km

233. What is the total number of literate people in Haryana?
(*a*) 1,66,25,728 (*b*) 1,65,98,988
(*c*) 1,78,10,882 (*d*) 1,32,58,652

234. The historical monument known as the corridor Chhatta of Rai Mukund Das (Birbal Ka Chhatta) is in:
(*a*) Panipat (*b*) Karnal
(*c*) Kaithal (*d*) Narnaul

235. Navodaya Vidyalaya is situated at which of the following places in the state?
(*a*) Titaram (Kurukshetra) (*b*) Odha (Sirsa)
(*c*) Deorala (Bhiwani) (*d*) All of these

236. During which of the following years Government of Haryana introduced 10+2+3 system of Education in Haryana?
(*a*) 1980 - 81 (*b*) 1976 - 77
(*c*) 1988 - 89 (*d*) 1985 - 86

237. M.D. University is located in which of the following towns of Haryana?
(*a*) Rohtak (*b*) Hissar
(*c*) Faridabad (*d*) Rewari

238. Chaudhary Charan Singh Agricultural University is located in which of the following towns of the state?
(*a*) Jind (*b*) Gurugram
(*c*) Hissar (*d*) Kurukshetra

239. In order to promote Punjabi language in Haryana it has been made the .... language of the state.
(*a*) First (*b*) Second
(*c*) Third (*d*) Fourth

240. Chaudhary Devilal University is located in which of the following towns of Haryana?
(*a*) Kurukshetra (*b*) Hissar
(*c*) Rohtak (*d*) Sirsa

241. In order to give promotion to sports in Haryana, the State Government has launched which of the following important schemes?
(*a*) Providing Grant in aid to the Sports Institutions
(*b*) Training Scheme
(*c*) Sports Stadium
(*d*) All of the above

242. In order to impart training to the players through modern and scientific methods, at which of the following places of Haryana a sports hostel has been set up?
(*a*) Gurugram (*b*) Rohtak
(*c*) Faridabad (*d*) Panipat

243. A sports school is situated at Rai in Sonepat district of Haryana. What is the name of this sports school?
(*a*) Jawahar Lal Nehru Sports School
(*b*) Indira Gandhi Sports School
(*c*) Moti Lal Nehru Sports School
(*d*) Rajiv Gandhi Sports School

244. Kamla Nehru School situated in the premises of Moti Lal Nehru Sports School at Rai in Sonepat district was established in
(*a*) 1970 (*b*) 1974
(*c*) 1982 (*d*) 1986

245. Haryana Shehari Vikas Pradhikaran (HSVP), formerly Haryana Urban Development Authority (HUDA) was constituted in ....
(*a*) 1977 (*b*) 1972
(*c*) 1970 (*d*) 1966

246. Who has variously been described as Plato of Jat Tribes?
(*a*) Suraj Mal (*b*) Churaman
(*c*) Raja Ram Bhajja (*d*) None of these

247. Khoria dance is famous in ....
(*a*) Eastern Haryana (*b*) Western Haryana
(*c*) Central Haryana (*d*) Northern Haryana

248. Which player of Haryana won gold medal in Tokyo Olympics 2020?
(*a*) Bajarang Punia (*b*) Neeraj Chopra
(*c*) Ravi Kumar (*d*) Vijendra Singh

249. The Haryana Shawl is known as ....
(*a*) Phulkari (*b*) Ghagra
(*c*) Iungis (*d*) Bagh

250. The famous story writer of Hindi Shri Vishvambhar Nath Kaushik was born in Haryana at
(*a*) Ambala Cantt (*b*) Sirsa
(*c*) Panchkula (*d*) Rohtak

251. Famous writer of Haryana Pt. Neki Ram Sharma had brought out which of the following papers from Bhiwani?
(*a*) Samvahak (*b*) Sandesh
(*c*) Nivaran (*d*) Vani

252. Who of the following players of Indian Cricket hails from Haryana?
(*a*) Kapil Dev (*b*) Sunil Gavaskar
(*c*) Ajay Jadeja (*d*) Azharuddin

253. The Cricket Test Match in which Kapil Dev of Haryana took 432nd wicket to make a record of taking maximum number of wickets was held on
(*a*) 10 January, 1992 (*b*) 8 December, 1996
(*c*) 8 February, 1994 (*d*) 12 August, 1997

254. Kapil Dev announced to abandon the international cricket on
(*a*) 6 November, 1993 (*b*) 2 November, 1994
(*c*) 18 November, 1997 (*d*) 15 November, 1998

255. Who of the following players of Haryana is not related with Gymnastic?
(*a*) Sunita Sharma (*b*) Sandhya
(*c*) Nirmala Guliya (*d*) Geeta Jutshi

256. Who of the following first ever poet is considered a native poet of Haryana?
(*a*) Goswami Tulsi Das (*b*) Kabir Das
(*c*) Kavi Chandbardai (*d*) Rahim Das

257. Who of the following Muslim Saints of Haryana had made significant contributions in the development of Hindi literature?
(*a*) Shekh-U-Alishaha Kalander
(*b*) Saint Sadullah
(*c*) Shekh Bahauddin Chishti
(*d*) All of these

258. Who of the following first ever poet is not related with Haryana?
(*a*) Virbhan (*b*) Mahatma Haridas
(*c*) Banarsi Das (*d*) Narottam Das

259. Haryana got the status of a full state on
(*a*) 1 November, 1964 (*b*) 10 December, 1965
(*c*) 1 November, 1966 (*d*) 15 June, 1968

260. The capital city of Haryana is
(*a*) Chandigarh (*b*) Rohtak
(*c*) Karnal (*d*) Yamuna Nagar

261. With a view to administrative convenience, Haryana has been divided into
(*a*) Three Divisions (*b*) 'Six Divisions
(*c*) Five Divisions (*d*) Four Divisions

262. The number of Districts in Haryana is
(*a*) 16 (*b*) 17
(*c*) 18 (*d*) 22

263. The tourist place called Oasis is situated at which of the following places in Haryana?
(*a*) Faridabad (*b*) Bhiwani
(*c*) Uchchhana (*d*) Rewari

264. Which of the following famous tourist place of Haryana is located at a distance of about 20 kms from Delhi?
(*a*) Suraj Kund (*b*) Red Robin
(*c*) Paracot (*d*) Damdama Lake

265. In vast rocky areas extended to the west of Faridabad by the Delhi-Mathura National Highway which of the following tourist place is situated?
(*a*) Damdama Lake (*b*) Badkhal Lake
(*c*) King Fisher (*d*) Dabchik

266. Between the hills of Arawali on Delhi-Alwar road which of the following famous tourist place of Haryana is located?
(*a*) Shama (*b*) Blue-ze
(*c*) Sohana (*d*) Dairangon

267. Who had discovered the Sultanpur Bird Sanctuary of Haryana situated on Gurugram Farrukh Nagar road?
(*a*) Peter Jackson (*b*) Thomar Roe
(*c*) Sir John Marshall (*d*) Robin Hood

268. On the Gurugram-Farrukhabad road which of the following tourist places of Haryana is situated?
(*a*) Dab-bich
(*b*) Sultanpur Bird Sanctuary
(*c*) Oasis
(*d*) Red Robin

269. The Turban worn by male in Haryana is called
(*a*) Khandwa (*b*) Paggada
(*c*) Toda (*d*) Pagari

270. The tourist centre called 'Shama' is situated at which of the following towns of Haryana?
(*a*) Faridabad (*b*) Kaithal
(*c*) Gurugram (*d*) Jind

271. In Haryana, the skirt worn by females from waist to ankle which is without any gusset and made of hand-spun coarse cloth knitted by using four blue and four red threads is called
(*a*) Dharna (*b*) Khara
(*c*) Thara (*d*) Kachara

272. Which of the following ornaments used in the state is not worn around neck?
(*a*) Hansla (*b*) Fool
(*c*) Galshree (*d*) Batan

273. Which of the following ornaments is worn on face and head on the ladies of the state?
(*a*) Singar Patti (*b*) Tagga
(*c*) Bessar (*d*) All of these

274. Which of the following ornaments used in the state is not worn on nose?
(*a*) Nath (*b*) Purli
(*c*) Dhede (*d*) Kokka

275. Which of the following ornaments used in the state is not worn on hands?
(*a*) Pauhchi (*b*) Kandulla
(*c*) Pachhelli (*d*) Bankri

276. According to the augury, which of the following is considered a good omen in the state of Haryana?
(*a*) A pitcher full of water
(*b*) To have a view of a deer
(*c*) A sweeper with a broom in hand
(*d*) All of the above

277. According to the augury, which of the following is considered a bad omen in the state of the Haryana?
(*a*) Empty pitcher
(*b*) To have a view of grass
(*c*) To experience an itching sensation in feet
(*d*) Meeting with a water carrier carrying water.

278. Which of the traditional ornaments is worn by males in Haryana?
(*a*) Goph (*b*) Tagari
(*c*) Nada (*d*) Kadi

279. At which of the following places of religious importance, lakhs of people from all over India go for a religious ritual on the occurrence of solar eclipse?
(*a*) Gurugram (*b*) Kurukshetra
(*c*) Jagadhari (*d*) None of these

280. At Islampur in the district Gurugram, which of the following festivals (Mela) is organised on the ninth day of Bhado (the sixth month of the year according to the Hindu calendar)?
(*a*) Guga Naumi (*b*) Nag Pooja
(*c*) Yamuna Snan (*d*) Shiv Mela

281. In the months of Chait and Aashadh (respectively the opening and the fourth month of the year according to the Hindu caldendar) in district Gurugram of Haryana on every Monday and Tuesday which of the following famous festivals (Melas) is organised?
(*a*) Buddho Mata Ka Mela
(*b*) Shivji Ka Mela
(*c*) Shitla Mata Ka Mela
(*d*) Baba Buddha Ka Mela

282. In which of the following districts of Haryana famous festivals of Ramsarai and Bhuteshwar are organised?
(*a*) Faridabad (*b*) Jind
(*c*) Rohtak (*d*) Jhajjhar

283. In the monastery at Asthal Bohar in Rohtak district of Haryana which of the following festivals (Melas) is organised during the months of February and March?
(*a*) Baba Mastnath Ka Mela
(*b*) Kapal Mochan Ka Mela
(*c*) Devi Mela
(*d*) Pathari Mata Ka Mela

284. Which of the following festivals (Melas) is organised on Kartik-Purnima at Bilaspur situated near Jagadhari?
(*a*) Aadi Badri Mela (*b*) Mela Kali Mai
(*c*) Kapal Mochan Mela (*d*) Panchmukhi Mela

285. At Lakhan Majra in Rohtak district "Gurudwara of Manji Sahib" is situated. Here which of the following festivals (Melas) is organised?
(*a*) Festival of Satya Teej
(*b*) Festival of Mohola Halla
(*c*) Bawan Dwadashi
(*d*) Maanu Mela

286. At Pathri in district Sonepat, on every Wednesday in the months of Chait and Aashadh, which of the following festivals (Melas) is organised?
(*a*) Mata Ka Mela (*b*) Shiva Mela
(*c*) Dehati Mela (*d*) Pathri Mata Ka Mela

287. At Kharak Ramji situated in district Jind, which of the following festivals (Melas) is organised on the day of Holi?
(*a*) Mata Ka Mela
(*b*) Nag Devata Ka Mela
(*c*) Baba Bhalu Nath Ka Mela
(*d*) Mela Sachcha Sauda

288. At Dubaldhan Majra in Rohtak district which of the following festivals (Melas) is organised in the months of February-March?
(*a*) Mela Mata (*b*) Mela Devi
(*c*) Mela Shyamji (*d*) Mela Baba Buddha

289. At Khori in the Gurugram district which of the following festivals (Melas) is organised during the months of April-May?
(*a*) Shah Chokha Khori Mela
(*b*) Shiva Ka Mela
(*c*) Nagpooja Ka Mela
(*d*) Baba Mast Nath Ka Mela

290. At which of the following places in district Sonepat, festival (Mela) of Dera Nagn Balaknath is organised during the months of February-March?
(*a*) Bega (Tehsil Sonepat)
(*b*) Mehripur (Tehsil Sonepat)
(*c*) Rabhara (Tehsil Gohana)
(*d*) Chulkana (Tehsil Sonepat)

291. Which of the following festivals (Melas) is oraganised at Khubadu situated in district Sonepat during the months of February-March?
(*a*) Satakumbha Mela (*b*) Mela Baba Shamakshah
(*c*) Mela Sanjhi (*d*) Devi Mela

292. Which amongst the following is the State Tree of Haryana?
(*a*) Sacred Fig (*b*) Mango Tree
(*c*) Sal Tree (*d*) Banyan Tree

293. At which of the following places in Haryana festival (Mela) of Baba Khedewala is organised on the day of Raksha Bandhan?
(*a*) Naurangabad (*b*) Kaharak Kalan
(*c*) Riwasa (*d*) Tosham

294. On which of the following occasions in the state of Haryana auspicious "Piliya" folk song is sung?
(*a*) In the months of July-August
(*b*) On the occasion of the birth of a male child in the family
(*c*) On the occasion of marriage ceremony
(*d*) In the months of February-March

295. On which of the following occasions, in the state of Haryana folk songs are sung?
(*a*) On the occasion of the birth of a male child in the family
(*b*) In the months of July-August
(*c*) On the occasion of a festival
(*d*) On all of the above occasions

296. In the state, males perform which of the following dances in open field at moon-lit night on flute, scooped gourd (Tumbi), etc.?
(*a*) Dhamal Dance (*b*) Manjeera Dance
(*c*) Loor Dance (*d*) Damru Dance

297. Which of the following dance performances is famous in Mewat area of Haryana which is accompanied with beating huge kettle drum, tambourine and cymbals?
(*a*) Ghora Dance (*b*) Dhamal Dance
(*c*) Manjeera Dance (*d*) Chhathi Dance

298. In Bagar area of Haryana which of the following dance performances is famous that is performed during the festival of Holi?
(*a*) Damru Dance (*b*) Manjeera Dance
(*c*) Ghora Dance (*d*) Loor Dance

299. The Ghora folk dance popular in Haryana is generally performed on which of the following occasions?
(*a*) On the occasion of marriage
(*b*) In the month of February-March
(*c*) On the occasion of birth of a male child in the family
(*d*) In the Month of July-August

300. In Haryana, which of the following dances is performed after the worship of Guggapir in the month of August-September?
(*a*) Dhamal Dance (*b*) Chchari Dance
(*c*) Loor Dance (*d*) Damru Dance

301. Which of the following folk dances is performed by women in the state?
(*a*) Teej Dance (*b*) Dhamal Dance
(*c*) Damru Dance (*d*) Khodiya Dance

302. Which dance is performed by males among the following folk dances practised in the state?
(*a*) Chhatthi dance (*b*) Teej dance
(*c*) Damru dance (*d*) Khodia dance

303. Which of the following folk dances is performed by men and women both in the state?
(*a*) Teej Dance (*b*) Loor Dance
(*c*) Khodiya Dance (*d*) Fag Dance

304. Which of the following Gurudwaras is situated near Pratap Gate in Kaithal town of Haryana?
(*a*) Gurudwara Neem Sahib
(*b*) Gurudwara Nauvi Patshahi
(*c*) Ragdhaar Gurudwara
(*d*) Gurudwara Chhathi Patshahi

305. Gurudwara Manji Sahib is situated in which of the following towns of Haryana?
(*a*) Karnal (*b*) Panipat
(*c*) Kaithal (*d*) Ambala

306. Which place in Haryana is called as "Chhoti Kashi" due to presence of "Navagraha Kunds"?
(*a*) Narnaul (*b*) Kaithal
(*c*) Gurugram (*d*) Kurukshetra

307. At a few distance from Kaithal in Haryana the grave of which of the following great men is situated where every year next dayof Dushera a large festival is organised?
(*a*) Baba Kali Kamli Wale
(*b*) Baba Haridas
(*c*) Baba Ladana
(*d*) Baba Ramdas

308. Which of the following famous places of pilgrimage is situated near Thanesar City Station in district Kurukshetra of Haryana?
(*a*) Brahma Sarovar (*b*) Hatakeshwar
(*c*) Dhosi (*d*) Pundarik Sarovar

309. Which of the following places of pilgrimage is situated on the Kurukshetra-Pehwa road near Kurukshetra Railway Station which is considered as the permanent abode of Lord Vishnu?
(*a*) Brahma Sarovar (*b*) Kaleshwar Tirth
(*c*) Sannihit Sarovar (*d*) Markanday Tirth

310. At which place of piligrimage in Kurukshetra district Shri Krishna had preached Arjuna?
(*a*) Brahm Sarovar (*b*) Kamal Nabh Tirth
(*c*) Prachi Tirth (*d*) Jyotishwar Sarovar

311. When did Maharaja Darbhanga build metalled platform around the Akshya Vat located near the Jyotishwar Sarovar situated in district Kurukshetra?
(*a*) In 1924 (*b*) In 1930
(*c*) In 1932 (*d*) In 1949

312. Who had built the Krishna-Arjuna Rath (Chariot) and the temple of Shankaracharya near the Jyotishwar Sarovar situated in district Kurukshetra?
(*a*) Maharaja Darbhanga
(*b*) Shankaracharya of Kam Koti Peeth
(*c*) King of Kashmir
(*d*) Swami Vishuddhananda Maharaj

313. What is the total length of Jyotishwar Sarovar situated in district Kurukshetra?
(*a*) 1000 ft. (*b*) 1500 ft.
(*c*) 2000 ft. (*d*) 2500 ft.

314. Who was the founder of "Baba Kali Kamli Wale Ka Dera" situated in district Kurukshetra?
(*a*) Swami Ram Tirth
(*b*) Shri Swami Vishuddhananda Maharaja
(*c*) Shankaracharya of Kamkoti Peeth
(*d*) Swami Parmananda Maharaj

315. Gaudiya Math (monastery) related with the period of Bhakti movement in India, is situated in which of the following districts of Haryana?
(*a*) Ambala (*b*) Jind
(*c*) Kurukshetra (*d*) Mahendragarh

316. At which of the following places in district Kurukshetra Baba Laxman Giri Maharaj went into eternal trance?
(*a*) Ban Ganga (*b*) Prachi Tirth
(*c*) Gaudiya Math (*d*) Balmiki Aashram

317. Raj Ghat Gurudwara is situated at which of the following places in Haryana?
(*a*) Kurukshetra (*b*) Yamuna Nagar
(*c*) Kaithal (*d*) Bhiwani

318. Which of the following places of pilgrimage is not situated in district Kurukshetra of Haryana?
(*a*) Kalkeshwar Tirth
(*b*) Prachi Tirth
(*c*) Dhosi Tirth
(*d*) Kuber Tirth

319. Which of the following places of pilgrimage is situated at a distance of 1 km. to the North-West of Kurukshetra University in district Kurukshetra of Haryana?
(*a*) Markandya Tirth
(*b*) Narakatari (Anrak Tirth)
(*c*) Prachi Tirth
(*d*) Kuber Tirth

320. Which of the following important places of pilgrimage is situated at a distance of 25 km to the west of Thanesar in Haryana that is given the same importance by the people of Haryana and adjoining areas as is given to Gaya by the people of Eastern region of India?
(*a*) Pehova (*b*) Panchavati
(*c*) Safeedon (*d*) Pandu-Pindara

321. In which district of Haryana the 'National Institute of Animal Genetics' is located?
(*a*) Hisar (*b*) Yamunanagar
(*c*) Karnal (*d*) Rohtak

322. A place of pilgrimage known as "Panchavati" is situated at which of the following districts of Haryana?
(*a*) Ambala (*b*) Jind
(*c*) Kurukshetra (*d*) Palwal

323. Which of the following is an ancient place of pilgrimage located by Jind-Gohana Road near Jind where a fair is organised every year on Somawati Amavasya?
(*a*) Pandu-Pindara
(*b*) Safeedon
(*c*) Hans Daihar
(*d*) None of the above

324. Temple of Sthaneshwar Mahadeva situated at a distance of a few kilometres from Thanesar was built by which of the following kings prior to Harshavardhan?
(*a*) Pushyabhuti (*b*) Adityavardhan
(*c*) Narvardhan (*d*) Prabhakarvardhan

325. Mahmud Ghaznavi during his return course to Ghazni took away with him from Haryana to Ghazni, statue of which of the ancient temple located in Haryana?
(*a*) Dukh Bhanjaneshwar Temple (Kuruk-shetra)
(*b*) Lord Shiva Temple (Narnaul)
(*c*) Sarveshwar Mahadeva Temple (Kuruk-shetra)
(*d*) Sthaneshwar Mahadeva Temple (Thanesar)

326. Sthaneshwar Temple of Haryana was reconstructed by
(*a*) Maratha Sadashiva Rao
(*b*) Chandra Gupta Vikramaditya
(*c*) Harshavardhan
(*d*) Narvardhan

327. Devikoop (Bhadra Kali Temple) is one of the 51 Shakti Peeths (Seats of goddess personifying divine power) of India. This temple is located at which of the following places in the state?
(*a*) Rohtak (*b*) Kurukshetra
(*c*) Panipat (*d*) Thanesar

328. Which of the following temples is situated near Sannihit Sarovar in Kurukshetra?
(*a*) Narayana Temple
(*b*) Laxmi Narayan Temple
(*c*) Dukh Bhanjaneshwar Temple
(*d*) Birla Mandir

329. Which of the following temples of Kurukshetra was built by the perfect Saint of Giri Sect Baba Shiv Giri Maharaj?
(*a*) Sarveshwar Mahadeva Temple
(*b*) Narayana Temple
(*c*) Laxmi Narayan Temple
(*d*) Dukh Bhanajaneshwar Temple

330. Who had built the famous 'Sarveshwar Mahadeva Temple' of Kurukshetra?
(*a*) Baba Shravan Nath (*b*) Baba Shiva Giri
(*c*) Baba Tarak Nath (*d*) Shri Jugal Kishore Birla

331. Birla Temple situated by the Kurukshetra-Pehova road was built by Shri Jugal Kishore Birla in
(*a*) 1950 (*b*) 1955
(*c*) 1965 (*d*) 1978

332. "Gyarah Rudri Shiva Temple" is situated in which of the following towns of Haryana?
(*a*) Jind (*b*) Panipat
(*c*) Hissar (*d*) Kaithal

333. Maratha General Mangal Raghu Nath Ji had built which of the following temples after the third battle of Panipat?
(*a*) Shiva Temple of Devi Pond
(*b*) Hanuman Temple
(*c*) Devi Temple
(*d*) Rudra Temple

334. In Amin village of Kurukshetra district which one of the following ancient temples is situated?
(*a*) Panchvati Temple
(*b*) Shiva Temple
(*c*) Temple of Aditi
(*d*) Temple of Dauji

335. In Vanchari village situated at a distance of 55 km. from Faridabad, which of the following ancient temples is situated?
(*a*) Temple of Dauji
(*b*) Temple of Aditi
(*c*) Panchvati Temple
(*d*) Temple of Chamunda Devi

336. The famous ancient temple of Mata Sheetala Devi is situated at which of the following places in Haryana?
(*a*) Rewari (*b*) Gurugram
(*c*) Narnaul (*d*) Jind

337. Temple of Mata Sheetala Devi situated at Gurugram was built by Maharaja of Bharatpur in
(*a*) 1620 (*b*) 1645
(*c*) 1648 (*d*) 1650

338. The ancient Shiva temple where the grave of Baba Thandipuri is also located, is situated at which of the following places?
(*a*) Pundrik Tirth (*b*) Gurugram
(*c*) Hissar (*d*) Rohtak

339. Which of the following ancient temples is situated at village Beri of district Jhajjar in Haryana?
(*a*) Old Shiva-Parvati Temple
(*b*) Temple of Mata Sheetala Devi
(*c*) Lal Rudhmal Temple
(*d*) Temple of Dauji

340. The height of the Shivalaya located in Rudhmal temple at village Beri in district Jhajjar of Haryana is
(*a*) 116 ft. (*b*) 122 ft.
(*c*) 132 ft. (*d*) 140 ft.

341. The Shivalaya located in Rudhmal temple at village Beri in district Jhajjar of Haryana was built in
(*a*) 1842 (*b*) 1850
(*c*) 1892 (*d*) 1899

342. The Shivalaya located in Rudhmal temple at village Beri in district Jhajjar was resurrected for the first time in
(*a*) 1943 (*b*) 1945
(*c*) 1950 (*d*) 1953

343. The temple of Chamunda Devi situated at Narnaul was built and resurrected by
(*a*) Raja Parikshit (*b*) Raja Dilip
(*c*) Raja Noorkaran (*d*) Pandavas

344. Chisti sect was established in Haryana by
(*a*) Boo Alishah Kalandar
(*b*) Shekh Farid (Farid-ud-din-Shakarganj)
(*c*) Altaf Hussain
(*d*) Ibrahim Abidullah

345. The eminent saint of Chisti sect Boo Alishah Kalandar made which of the following places the centre of his meditation?
(*a*) Panipat (*b*) Rohtak
(*c*) Sonepat (*d*) Gurugram

346. Dargah of Sufi Saint Altaf Hussain Hali is situated at which of the following places in Haryana?
(*a*) Jhajjhar (*b*) Rewari
(*c*) Panipat (*d*) Rohtak

347. Regarding which of the following Dargahs (tombs of saints which are pilgrimage spots and places of worship) situated at Panipat is believed that bowing heads by believers accomplishes their attending in celebration of Urs of Khwaza of Ajmer?
(*a*) Dargah of Khwaza Shamshuddin Makhdoom Zalaluddin
(*b*) Dargah of Shekh Usman Jindapeer
(*c*) Dargah of Gauss Alishah
(*d*) Dargah of Boo Alishah Kalandar

348. Dargah of which of the following famous saints is situated at village Dharsun which is at a distance of about 10 kms from Narnaul?
(*a*) Hazarat Shah Kalmuddin Hamzapeer Hussain
(*b*) Meer Shah (Baba Shah Khan)
(*c*) Sheikh Nijamuddin
(*d*) Sheikh Junaid

349. At Fatehabad in the courtyard of the tomb of which of the following Sufi saints inscription of Mughal emperor Humayun is engraved on a stone?
(*a*) Mir Taki Khan
(*b*) Mir Junaidi
(*c*) Sheikh Nizamuddin
(*d*) Mir Shah (Baba Shah Khan)

350. Which of the following tombs situated in Haryana has been declared a monument of National importance under the Archaeological Site and Remnant Act, 1958?
(*a*) Sheikh Chehli
(*b*) Boo Alishah Kalandar
(*c*) Sheikh Farid (Farid-ud-din-Shakarganj)
(*d*) Peer Jamal

351. Tomb of Baba Shah Kamal is situated at which of the following places in Haryana?
(*a*) Gohan (*b*) Fatehabad
(*c*) Kaithal (*d*) Rohtak

352. At which one of the following places in the state, tombs of four Sufi-saints (Kutub Sheikh Jamaluddin Ahmad, Kutub Maulana, Basohddin Sufi Qutubuddin Mannawar, Qutub Nuruddin) are located?
(*a*) Karnal (*b*) Hissar
(*c*) Palwal (*d*) Hansi

353. The tomb of who of the following Sufi-saints is situated between Shahabad and Ambala where watch is offered after a desire is fulfilled?
(*a*) Peer Nagauji (*b*) Hamja Peer
(*c*) Peer Naugaja (*d*) Ibrahim Abidullah

354. Which of the following mosques in Rohtak which was previously a temple was turned into a mosque during the reign of Aurangzeb?
(*a*) Qazi Ki Masjid (*b*) Dini Masjid
(*c*) Lal Masjid (*d*) None of these

355. The Lal Masjid situated in Rohtak was built by famous trader Haji Aashiq Ali in
(*a*) 1930 (*b*) 1931
(*c*) 1935 (*d*) 1939

356. Mosque at Sarai Alawardi village in district Gurugram was built during the reign of
(*a*) Babur (*b*) Jahangir
(*c*) Shahjahan (*d*) Alauddin Khilji

357. Which of the following ancient historical Mosques is situated at village Dujana, situated at a distance of 22 km by Jhajjhar road from Rohtak?
(*a*) Lal Masjid (*b*) Qaji Ki Masjid
(*c*) Karim Ji Ki Masjid (*d*) Jama Masjid

358. The famous historic Lal Masjid at Rewari was built during the reign of which of the following Mughal Emperors?
(*a*) Babur (*b*) Humayun
(*c*) Akbar (*d*) Jahangir

359. In addition to Narnaul, Panipat and Ambala, Sufi-saints made which of the following towns of Haryana as a centre of Sufi-sect?
(*a*) Kaithal (*b*) Thanesar
(*c*) Karnal (*d*) Sonepat

360. The majority of Sufi-saints who lived in Haryana for propagating sufi cult belonged to which of the following sects?
(*a*) Chisti (*b*) Nakshbandi
(*c*) Kadari (*d*) All of the above

361. Tomb of famous Sufi-saint Sheikh Chehli which is called as the Tajmahal of Haryana is situated at
(*a*) Hissar (*b*) Fatehabad
(*c*) Thanesar (*d*) Panipat

362. Tomb of which of the following saints is situated at Kalyana village of Charkhi Dadri district where fair is organised on every Wednesday?
(*a*) Peer Mubarak Shah
(*b*) Sheikh Usman Jindapeer
(*c*) Sheikh Nizamuddin
(*d*) Muhammad Afzal

363. Tomb of Meeran Sahib is situated in which of the following towns of Haryana?
(*a*) Ambala (*b*) Panipat
(*c*) Karnal (*d*) Kaithal

364. Where did Lord Krishna delivered his inspirational messages to Arjuna which have been described in "Gita" as a dialogue between the two?
(*a*) Panipat (*b*) Kurukshetra
(*c*) Hodal (*d*) Thanesar

—

365. Which of the following towns of Haryana was the capital of Shrikantha Janapada during ancient times?
(*a*) Thanesar (*b*) Chandigarh
(*c*) Rohtak (*d*) Gurugram

366. The detailed description of which of the following ancient cities of Haryana is given in the account presented by Chinese pilgrim Huen Tsang?
(*a*) Rohtak (*b*) Ambala
(*c*) Thaneshwar (*d*) Bhiwani

367. Thaneshwar City of this state was at the pinnacle of its glory during
(*a*) Vardhan period (*b*) Gupta period
(*c*) Sunga period (*d*) Maurya period

368. The famous battle between the armies of Babur and Ibrahim Lodi in 1526 was fought at which of the following places in Haryana?
(*a*) Jhajjhar (*b*) Kurukshetra
(*c*) Rohtak (*d*) Panipat

369. Panipat town was given the status of District on
(*a*) 1 January, 1988 (*b*) 1 November, 1989
(*c*) 1 December, 1990 (*d*) 17 June, 1980

370. Rewari district was formed on
(*a*) 10 June, 1977 (*b*) 5 February, 1979
(*c*) 1 November, 1989 (*d*) 17 June, 1980

371. Hissar is the birth place of which of the following famous kings?
(*a*) Shershah Suri (*b*) Akbar
(*c*) Muhammad Tughlaq (*d*) Feroz Tughlaq

372. In which of the following towns has the largest cattle farm of Haryana?
(*a*) Narnaul (*b*) Hissar
(*c*) Panipat (*d*) Karnal

373. In 1354, who of the following famous ruler of the medieval India built the town of Hissar as a fort?
(*a*) Muhammad Tughlaq (*b*) Balban
(*c*) Feroz Tughlaq (*d*) Alauddin Khilji

374. During ancient times, Mahendragarh town of this state was known as
(*a*) Janauva (*b*) Karnpur
(*c*) Mahipgarh (*d*) Kanaud

375. Name the last king of Ballabhgarh who died as a martyr during freedom struggle of 1857.
(*a*) Nahar Singh (*b*) Vijay Singh
(*c*) Pratap Singh (*d*) Mahar Singh

376. Ballabhgarh town is included in which of the following districts of Haryana?
(*a*) Rohtak (*b*) Faridabad
(*c*) Gurugram (*d*) Karnal

377. Narwana Tehsil is situated in which of the following Districts of the state?
(*a*) Sirsa (*b*) Bhiwani
(*c*) Jind (*d*) Fatehabad

378. Grave of the famous Sultana Raziya of Ghulam dynasty is located in which of the following districts of the state?
(*a*) Kaithal (*b*) Gurugram
(*c*) Ambala (*d*) Faridabad

379. Which of the following towns of Haryana is termed as 'a big bowl of paddy' and 'Paris of Haryana'?
(*a*) Rohtak (*b*) Sonepat
(*c*) Faridabad (*d*) Karnal

380. In 1607, Faridabad town was built by
(*a*) Feroz Shah (*b*) Mubarakshah
(*c*) Baba Farid (*d*) Mansub Ali

381. During the Mahabharata period Sirsa was known as
(*a*) Shishira (*b*) Shairishkam
(*c*) Saurish (*d*) Sirisa

382. During ancient times, Gohana town of the state was known as
(*a*) Gawabh Bhawana (*b*) Gadhana
(*c*) Gapat Zamana (*d*) None of these

383. During ancient times, Bahadurgarh town of the state was known as
(*a*) Bahawalgarh (*b*) Shafirabad
(*c*) Sharfabad (*d*) Balramgarh

384. Britishers confiscated Bahadurgarh from Scindia King and handed it as a Jaghir to the brother of Nawab of Jhajjhar in
(*a*) 1800 AD (*b*) 1801 AD
(*c*) 1805 AD (*d*) 1803 AD

385. Which of the following towns of the state was built by a Rajput named Amba in the 14th century?
(*a*) Jhajjhar (*b*) Rohtak
(*c*) Ambala (*d*) Bhiwani

386. Abdur Rahman Khan who sacrificed his life during freedom struggle, hailed from which of the following towns of Haryana?
(*a*) Kurukshetra (*b*) Jhajjhar
(*c*) Farrukh Nagar (*d*) Rewari

387. Farrukh Nagar was built by which of the following Biloch rulers?
(*a*) Dalel Khan (Faujdar Khan)
(*b*) Shaffuddin Khan
(*c*) Badar Khan
(*d*) Jamaluddin Khan

388. Biloch ruler Dalel Khan (Faujdar Khan) built the town of Farrukh Nagar in the name of which of the following Emperors?
(*a*) Fakhruddin Ahmad (*b*) Farukh Ali
(*c*) Ferozshah Tughlaq (*d*) Farrukh Siyar

389. Great epic Mahabharata was composed by Maharshi Ved Vyas in which of the following towns of Haryana?
(*a*) Panipat (*b*) Rewari
(*c*) Kurukshetra (*d*) Hissar

390. Rise of Vardhan dynasty took place in which of the following towns of Haryana?
(*a*) Thanesar (Sthaneshwar)
(*b*) Rohtak
(*c*) Panipat
(*d*) Kurukshetra

391. In 1556, the famous battle between the forces of Akbar and Hemchandra (Hemu) of Rewari was fought at which of the following places in Haryana?
(*a*) Rewari (*b*) Jind
(*c*) Kurukshetra (*d*) Panipat

392. In 1761 the third battle of Panipat was fought between the forces of
(*a*) Babur and Ibrahim Lodi
(*b*) Akbar and Hemchandra (Hemu)
(*c*) Afghans and Marathas
(*d*) Britishers and Sikhs

393. The town of Panipat was under which of the following districts of Haryana till 31 October, 1989?
(*a*) Rewari (*b*) Ambala
(*c*) Karnal (*d*) Hissar

394. Which of the following districts of the state was included under Gurugram and Mahendragarh districts before 1989?
(*a*) Mahendragarh (*b*) Faridabad
(*c*) Jind (*d*) Rewari

395. Jind was given the status of district in
(*a*) 1966 (*b*) 1972
(*c*) 1968 (*d*) 1975

396. Which of the following districts of Haryana has its headquarters at Narnaul?
(*a*) Hissar (*b*) Faridabad
(*c*) Mahendragarh (*d*) Karnal

397. Who amongst the following did not play for Haryana in Ranji Trophy?
(*a*) Kapil Dev (*b*) Rajinder Goel
(*c*) Sarkar Talwar (*d*) Maninder Singh

398. When Palwal came into existence as the 21st districts of Haryana?
(*a*) 2006 (*b*) 2005
(*c*) 2008 (*d*) 2007

399. During Mahabharat period, which of the following places was given by Raja Yudhishthir to his Guru Dronacharya as a gift?
(*a*) Gurugram village (*b*) Kaithal
(*c*) Hodal (*d*) Sirsa

400. Who was the Collector of Gurugram during the freedom struggle of 1857?
(*a*) Henry (*b*) Sir Helley
(*c*) John Marshall (*d*) Shri Ford

401. In 1858, which of the following districts of Haryana was included in Punjab?
(*a*) Faridabad (*b*) Gurugram
(*c*) Hissar (*d*) Mahendragarh

402. When Faridabad came into existence as the 12th district of Haryana?
(*a*) 15 August, 1970 (*b*) 02 August, 1979
(*c*) 26 January, 1979 (*d*) 8 March, 1982

403. Bahadurgarh town is included in which of the following districts of Haryana?
(*a*) Jhajjar (*b*) Karnal
(*c*) Yamun Nagar (*d*) Faridabad

404. The historical town Gohana is included in which of the following districts of Haryana?
(*a*) Panipat (*b*) Sirsa
(*c*) Sonepat (*d*) Rewari

405. In which year 'Sirsa' became a district?
(*a*) 1980 (*b*) 1975
(*c*) 1990 (*d*) 1995

406. Hodal Sub-division is located in which district of Haryana?
(*a*) Rohtak (*b*) Sonepat
(*c*) Palwal (*d*) Panipat

407. Tosham town of district. Bhiwani was given the status of Sub-Division on
(*a*) 27 April, 1993 (*b*) 10 June, 1995
(*c*) 5 March, 1997 (*d*) 27 April, 1998

408. Which of the following famous temples is situated at historical town "Sadhaura"of district Yamuna Nagar?
(*a*) Manokamna Temple (*b*) Gagarwala Temple
(*c*) Toranwala Temple (*d*) All of these

409. In which of the following historical towns of Yamuna Nagar district, the Gurudwara of Buddhushah is situated which had helped Guru Govind Singh in the battle of Bhagani?
(*a*) Sadhaura (*b*) Radaur
(*c*) Bilaspur (*d*) Chhachhrauli

410. In ancient times Bahadurgarh town of Haryana was called as
(*a*) Charkhabad (*b*) Hasinpur
(*c*) Sharfabad (*d*) Betawabad

411. The historical town of Maham is situated in which of the following districts of the state?
(*a*) Bhiwani (*b*) Rohtak
(*c*) Yamuna Nagar (*d*) Jhajjhar

412. Maham town situated in district Rohtak was rebuilt by a person called Peshora of Kayastha (Baniya) Community in
(*a*) 1266 (*b*) 1295
(*c*) 1298 (*d*) 1299

413. Ailanabad town situated in district Sirsa was earlier known as
(*a*) Ailisabad (*b*) Chavipur
(*c*) Kalisabad (*d*) Khariyal

414. What was the earlier name of the historical town 'Raniyan' situated in district Sirsa?
(*a*) Rajabpur (*b*) Sajupur
(*c*) Rajipur (*d*) Ratipur

415. Which of the following towns situated in district Ambala was built by the King of Sirmour (Himachal Pradesh) Raja Laxmi Narayan?
(*a*) Barara (*b*) Mulana
(*c*) Narayangarh (*d*) Raipur Rani

416. By excavations done in which of the following historical towns of Sonepat district, earthen utensils belonging to Mahabharata period have been found?
(*a*) Rai (*b*) Kheri Gujjar
(*c*) Gankaur (*d*) Gohana

417. Mythological village Aadi Badri is situated in which of the following districts of Haryana?
(*a*) Yamuna Nagar (*b*) Bhiwani
(*c*) Sirsa (*d*) Rewari

418. Which of the following historical villages situated in district Yamuna Nagar is associated with King Santanu of the Mahabharata period?
(*a*) Chhachhrauli (*b*) Aadi Badri
(*c*) Basantar (*d*) None of these

419. At which of the following places Mazaar of Altaf Hussain Hali is located?
(*a*) Sonepat (*b*) Gurugram
(*c*) Panipat (*d*) Jind

420. Which of the following places was made a powerful centre of Afghan chiefs by Ahmadshah Abdali before the third battle of Panipat?
(*a*) Gharauda (*b*) Nilpe Khedi
(*c*) Asangh (*d*) Kunjpura

ANSWERS

1	**2**	**3**	**4**	**5**	**6**	**7**	**8**	**9**	**10**
(*d*)	(*a*)	(*b*)	(*c*)	(*a*)	(*d*)	(*b*)	(*a*)	(*c*)	(*b*)
11	**12**	**13**	**14**	**15**	**16**	**17**	**18**	**19**	**20**
(*d*)	(*d*)	(*a*)	(*c*)	(*d*)	(*a*)	(*c*)	(*b*)	(*d*)	(*a*)
21	**22**	**23**	**24**	**25**	**26**	**27**	**28**	**29**	**30**
(*d*)	(*a*)	(*c*)	(*b*)	(*a*)	(*d*)	(*d*)	(*a*)	(*c*)	(*c*)
31	**32**	**33**	**34**	**35**	**36**	**37**	**38**	**39**	**40**
(*d*)	(*c*)	(*a*)	(*b*)	(*d*)	(*d*)	(*a*)	(*c*)	(*b*)	(*c*)
41	**42**	**43**	**44**	**45**	**46**	**47**	**48**	**49**	**50**
(*d*)	(*a*)	(*c*)	(*b*)	(*a*)	(*c*)	(*d*)	(*a*)	(*c*)	(*c*)
51	**52**	**53**	**54**	**55**	**56**	**57**	**58**	**59**	**60**
(*a*)	(*c*)	(*a*)	(*b*)	(*d*)	(*b*)	(*a*)	(*c*)	(*b*)	(*d*)
61	**62**	**63**	**64**	**65**	**66**	**67**	**68**	**69**	**70**
(*d*)	(*a*)	(*c*)	(*a*)	(*b*)	(*a*)	(*a*)	(*a*)	(*b*)	(*d*)
71	**72**	**73**	**74**	**75**	**76**	**77**	**78**	**79**	**80**
(*c*)	(*a*)	(*c*)	(*b*)	(*d*)	(*c*)	(*a*)	(*c*)	(*b*)	(*d*)
81	**82**	**83**	**84**	**85**	**86**	**87**	**88**	**89**	**90**
(*b*)	(*a*)	(*d*)	(*a*)	(*c*)	(*b*)	(*d*)	(*c*)	(*a*)	(*d*)
91	**92**	**93**	**94**	**95**	**96**	**97**	**98**	**99**	**100**
(*d*)	(*a*)	(*d*)	(*a*)	(*c*)	(*b*)	(*d*)	(*a*)	(*c*)	(*b*)
101	**102**	**103**	**104**	**105**	**106**	**107**	**108**	**109**	**110**
(*d*)	(*a*)	(*a*)	(*d*)	(*a*)	(*b*)	(*c*)	(*b*)	(*d*)	(*a*)
111	**112**	**113**	**114**	**115**	**116**	**117**	**118**	**119**	**120**
(*c*)	(*b*)	(*a*)	(*a*)	(*d*)	(*b*)	(*d*)	(*c*)	(*a*)	(*b*)
121	**122**	**123**	**124**	**125**	**126**	**127**	**128**	**129**	**130**
(*c*)	(*b*)	(*c*)	(*b*)	(*d*)	(*d*)	(*a*)	(*c*)	(*d*)	(*b*)
131	**132**	**133**	**134**	**135**	**136**	**137**	**138**	**139**	**140**
(*a*)	(*c*)	(*a*)	(*b*)	(*a*)	(*b*)	(*a*)	(*d*)	(*c*)	(*b*)
141	**142**	**143**	**144**	**145**	**146**	**147**	**148**	**149**	**150**
(*a*)	(*c*)	(*b*)	(*a*)	(*d*)	(*a*)	(*c*)	(*d*)	(*c*)	(*a*)
151	**152**	**153**	**154**	**155**	**156**	**157**	**158**	**159**	**160**
(*d*)	(*c*)	(*a*)	(*a*)	(*b*)	(*a*)	(*d*)	(*b*)	(*b*)	(*d*)
161	**162**	**163**	**164**	**165**	**166**	**167**	**168**	**169**	**170**
(*a*)	(*c*)	(*a*)	(*c*)	(*b*)	(*d*)	(*c*)	(*a*)	(*b*)	(*a*)

171 (*b*)	172 (*d*)	173 (*a*)	174 (*a*)	175 (*d*)	176 (*b*)	177 (*a*)	178 (*b*)	179 (*b*)	180 (*c*)
181 (*a*)	182 (*a*)	183 (*c*)	184 (*d*)	185 (*b*)	186 (*c*)	187 (*d*)	188 (*a*)	189 (*c*)	190 (*d*)
191 (*d*)	192 (*a*)	193 (*b*)	194 (*b*)	195 (*a*)	196 (*c*)	197 (*a*)	198 (*d*)	199 (*b*)	200 (*a*)
201 (*d*)	202 (*c*)	203 (*a*)	204 (*d*)	205 (*a*)	206 (*d*)	207 (*c*)	208 (*b*)	209 (*b*)	210 (*a*)
211 (*a*)	212 (*a*)	213 (*c*)	214 (*d*)	215 (*b*)	216 (*a*)	217 (*a*)	218 (*b*)	219 (*d*)	220 (*a*)
221 (*b*)	222 (*c*)	223 (*b*)	224 (*d*)	225 (*a*)	226 (*c*)	227 (*a*)	228 (*c*)	229 (*b*)	230 (*a*)
231 (*d*)	232 (*a*)	233 (*b*)	234 (*a*)	235 (*d*)	236 (*d*)	237 (*a*)	238 (*c*)	239 (*b*)	240 (*d*)
241 (*d*)	242 (*a*)	243 (*c*)	244 (*b*)	245 (*a*)	246 (*a*)	247 (*c*)	248 (*b*)	249 (*a*)	250 (*a*)
251 (*b*)	252 (*a*)	253 (*c*)	254 (*b*)	255 (*d*)	256 (*c*)	257 (*d*)	258 (*d*)	259 (*c*)	260 (*a*)
261 (*b*)	262 (*d*)	263 (*c*)	264 (*a*)	265 (*b*)	266 (*c*)	267 (*a*)	268 (*b*)	269 (*a*)	270 (*c*)
271 (*b*)	272 (*b*)	273 (*d*)	274 (*c*)	275 (*d*)	276 (*d*)	277 (*a*)	278 (*a*)	279 (*b*)	280 (*a*)
281 (*c*)	282 (*b*)	283 (*a*)	284 (*c*)	285 (*b*)	286 (*d*)	287 (*c*)	288 (*c*)	289 (*a*)	290 (*c*)
291 (*b*)	292 (*a*)	293 (*a*)	294 (*b*)	295 (*d*)	296 (*a*)	297 (*c*)	298 (*d*)	299 (*a*)	300 (*b*)
301 (*a*)	302 (*c*)	303 (*d*)	304 (*a*)	305 (*c*)	306 (*b*)	307 (*c*)	308 (*a*)	309 (*c*)	310 (*d*)
311 (*a*)	312 (*b*)	313 (*a*)	314 (*b*)	315 (*c*)	316 (*d*)	317 (*a*)	318 (*c*)	319 (*b*)	320 (*a*)
321 (*c*)	322 (*d*)	323 (*a*)	324 (*a*)	325 (*d*)	326 (*a*)	327 (*b*)	328 (*d*)	329 (*c*)	330 (*a*)
331 (*b*)	332 (*d*)	333 (*a*)	334 (*c*)	335 (*a*)	336 (*b*)	337 (*d*)	338 (*a*)	339 (*c*)	340 (*a*)
341 (*c*)	342 (*d*)	343 (*c*)	344 (*b*)	345 (*a*)	346 (*c*)	347 (*d*)	348 (*a*)	349 (*d*)	350 (*a*)
351 (*c*)	352 (*d*)	353 (*c*)	354 (*b*)	355 (*d*)	356 (*d*)	357 (*b*)	358 (*c*)	359 (*b*)	360 (*d*)
361 (*c*)	362 (*a*)	363 (*c*)	364 (*b*)	365 (*a*)	366 (*c*)	367 (*a*)	368 (*d*)	369 (*b*)	370 (*c*)
371 (*a*)	372 (*b*)	373 (*c*)	374 (*d*)	375 (*a*)	376 (*b*)	377 (*c*)	378 (*a*)	379 (*d*)	380 (*c*)
381 (*b*)	382 (*a*)	383 (*c*)	384 (*d*)	385 (*c*)	386 (*b*)	387 (*a*)	388 (*d*)	389 (*c*)	390 (*a*)
391 (*d*)	392 (*c*)	393 (*c*)	394 (*d*)	395 (*a*)	396 (*c*)	397 (*d*)	398 (*c*)	399 (*a*)	400 (*d*)
401 (*b*)	402 (*b*)	403 (*a*)	404 (*c*)	405 (*b*)	406 (*c*)	407 (*a*)	408 (*d*)	409 (*a*)	410 (*c*)
411 (*b*)	412 (*a*)	413 (*d*)	414 (*a*)	415 (*c*)	416 (*b*)	417 (*a*)	418 (*c*)	419 (*c*)	420 (*d*)

❑ ❑ ❑